NOTABLE
SPORTS
FIGURES

3

NOTABLE
SPORTS
FIGURES

Dana Barnes, Editor

VOLUME 3 • M-S

GALE®

THOMSON

GALE

Detroit • New York • San Diego • San Francisco • Cleveland • New Haven, Conn. • Waterville, Maine • London • Munich

Notable Sports Figures

Project Editor
Dana R. Barnes

Editorial
Laura Avery, Luann Brennan, Frank Castronova,
Leigh Ann DeRemer, Andrea Henderson,
Kathy Nemeh, Angela Pilchak, Tracie Ratiner,
Bridget Travers

Research
Gary J. Oudersluys, Cheryl L. Warnock,
Kelly Whittle

Editorial Support Services
Charlene Lewis, Sue Petrus

Editorial Standards
Lynne Maday

Permissions
Lori Hines

Imaging and Multimedia Content
Randy Basset, Dean Dauphinais, Leitha
Etheridge-Sims, Lezlie Light, Dan W. Newell,
Dave G. Oblender

Product Design
Jennifer Wahi

Manufacturing
Evi Seoud, Rhonda Williams

Library of Congress Cataloging-in-Publication Data

Notable sports figures / project editor, Dana R. Barnes.
        p. cm.
Includes bibliographical references and index.
ISBN 0-7876-6628-9 (Set Hardcover) -- ISBN 0-7876-6629-7 (Volume 1)
--ISBN 0-7876-6630-0 (Volume 2) -- ISBN 0-7876-6631-9 (Volume 3) --
ISBN 0-7876-7786-8 (Volume 4)
1. Sports--Biography. 2. Athletes--Biography. 3. Sports--History.
I. Barnes, Dana R.
GV697.A1N68 2004
796'.092'2--dc21
                                                    2003011288

Contents

Introduction

Notable Sports Figures provides narrative biographical profiles of more than 600 individuals who have made significant contributions to their sport and to society. It covers sports figures from the nineteenth, twentieth, and twenty-first centuries who represent a wide variety of sports and countries. Lesser-known sports such as cricket, equestrian, and snowboarding are featured alongside sports like baseball, basketball, and football. *Notable Sports Figures* includes not only athletes, but also coaches, team executives, and media figures such as sportscasters and writers.

Notable Sports Figures takes a close look at the people in sports who have captured attention because of success *on* the playing field or controversy *off* the playing field. It provides biographical coverage of people from around the world and throughout history who have had an impact not only on their sport, but also on the society and culture of their times. Each biography features information on the entrant's family life, early involvement in sports, career highlights, championships, and awards. *Notable Sports Figures* also examines the impact that the subject had and continues to have on his or her sport, and the reasons why the individual is "notable." This includes consideration of the successes and failures, on the field and off, that keep the person in the public eye.

The biographies in *Notable Sports Figures* profile a broad variety of individuals. Athletes such as **Babe Ruth, Michael Jordan,** and **Martina Navratilova** are featured for their record-breaking accomplishments. **Jackie Robinson** and **Janet Guthrie** remain in the public consciousness because of their determination to cross racial and gender boundaries. Other sports figures have captured our attention by their controversial activities. Skater **Tonya Harding** continues to hold public interest not because of any medals won, but because of the scandalous attack on **Nancy Kerrigan.** Baseball player **"Shoeless" Joe Jackson** was one of the greatest players of his era, but he is remembered more for his complicity in the **"Black Sox"** scandal of 1919 than for his accomplishments on the field. Their lives, accomplishments, and reasons for the public's ongoing fascination with them are examined in *Notable Sports Figures.*

SELECTION PROCESS AND CRITERIA

A preliminary list of athletes, team executives, sportswriters, broadcasters, and other sports figures was compiled from a wide variety of sources, including Hall of Fame lists, periodical articles, and other biographical collections. The list was reviewed by an advisory board, and final selection was made by the editor. An effort was made to include athletes of varying nationalities, ethnicities, and fields of sport as well as those who have contributed to the success of a sport or team in general. Selection criteria include:

- Notable "first" achievements, including those who broke racial or gender barriers and paved the way for others

- Impact made on the individual's sport and on society as a whole

- Records set and broken

- Involvement in controversial or newsworthy activities on and off the playing field

FEATURES OF THIS PRODUCT

For easy access, entries are arranged alphabetically according to the entrant's last name.

- **Timeline**—includes significant events in the world of sports, from historic times to the present.

- **Entry head**—lists basic information on each sports figure, including name, birth and death years, nationality, and occupation/sport played.

- **Biographical essay**—offers 1,000 to 2,500 words on the person's life, career highlights, and the impact that the individual had and continues to have on his or her sport and on society. Bold-faced names within entries indicate an entry on that person.

- **Photos**—provide a portrait for many of the individuals profiled. Several essays also include an action photo.

- **Sidebars**—present a chronology of key events in the entrant's life, a list of major awards and accomplishments, and, as applicable, career statistics, brief biographies of important individuals in the en-

trant's life, "where is s/he now" information on previously popular sports figures, and excerpts from
books and periodicals of significant events in the
entrant's life and career.

- **Contact Information**—offers addresses, phone
  numbers, and web sites for selected living entrants.

- **Selected Writings**—lists books and publications
  written or edited by the entrant.

- **Further Information**—provides a list of resources
  the reader may access to seek additional information on the sports figure.

- **Appendix**—offers a glossary of commonly used
  sports abbreviations.

- **Indices**—allow the reader to access the entrants by
  nationality or sport. A general subject index with
  cross-references offers additional access.

We Welcome Your Suggestions. Mail your comments
and suggestions for enhancing and improving *Notable
Sports Figures* to:

The Editors
Notable Sports Figures
Gale Group
27500 Drake Road
Farmington Hills, MI 48331-3535
Phone: (800) 347-4253

Advisory Board

Contributors

Don Amerman, Julia Bauder, Cynthia Becker, David Becker, Michael Belfiore, Kari Bethel, Michael Betzold, Tim Borden, Carol Brennan, Gerald Brennan, Paul Burton, Frank Caso, Gordon Churchwell, Gloria Cooksey, Andrew Cunningham, Lisa Frick, Jan Goldberg, Joyce Hart, Eve Hermann, Ian Hoffman, Syd Jones, Wendy Kagan, Aric Karpinski, Christine Kelley, Judson Knight, Eric Lagergren, Jeanne Lesinski, Carole Manny, Paulo Nunes-Ueno, Patricia Onorato, Tricia Owen, Kristin Palm, Mike Pare, Annette Petruso, Ryan Poquette, Susan Salter, Brenna Sanchez, Lorraine Savage, Paula Scott, Pam Shelton, Ken Shepherd, Ann Shurgin, Barbra Smerz, Roger Smith, Janet Stamatel, Jane Summer, Erick Trickey, Amy Unterburger, Sheila Velazquez, Bruce Walker, Dave Wilkins, Kelly Winters, Rob Winters, Ben Zackheim

Acknowledgments

Photographs and illustrations appearing in *Notable Sports Figures* have been used with the permission of the following sources:

AP/WIDE WORLD PHOTOS:
1980 U.S. Olympic hockey team, photograph. AP/Wide World Photos./ Aamodt, Kjetil Andre, photograph. AP/Wide World Photos./ Aaron, Hank, photograph. AP/Wide World Photos./ Abbott, Jim, photograph. AP/Wide World Photos./ Abdul-Jabbar, Kareem, photograph. AP/Wide World Photos./ Abdul-Jabbar, Kareem, photograph. AP/Wide World Photos./ Agassi, Andre, photograph. AP/Wide World Photos./ Aikman, Troy, photograph. AP/Wide World Photos./ Akers, Michelle, photograph. AP/Wide World Photos, Inc./ Albert, Marv, photograph by Ron Frehm. AP/Wide World Photos./ Albright, Tenley, photograph. AP/Wide World Photos./ Alexander, Grover Cleveland, photograph. AP/Wide World Photos./ Allison, Davey, photograph. AP/Wide World Photos./ Alamo, Roberto, photograph. AP/Wide World Photos./ Anderson, George "Sparky," photograph. AP/Wide World Photos./ Andretti, Mario, photograph. AP/Wide World Photos./ Anthony, Earl, photograph. AP/Wide World Photos./ Armstrong, Lance, photograph. AP/Wide World Photos./ Armstrong, Lance, photograph. AP/Wide World Photos./ Ashe, Arthur, photograph. AP/Wide World Photos./ Ashford, Evelyn, photograph. AP/Wide World Photos./ Auerbach, Red, photograph. AP/Wide World Photos./ Autissier, Isabelle, photograph. AP/Wide World Photos./ Bailey, Donovan, photograph. AP/Wide World Photos./ Banks, Ernie, photograph. AP/Wide World Photos./ Bannister, Roger, photograph. AP/Wide World Photos./ Barton, Donna, photograph. AP/Wide World Photos./ Baugh, Sammy, photograph. AP/Wide World Photos./ Baumgartner, Bruce, photograph. AP/Wide World Photos./ Baylor, Elgin, photograph. AP/Wide World Photos./ Beckenbauer, Franz, photograph. AP/Wide World Photos./ Becker, Boris, photograph. AP/Wide World Photos./ Bedard, Myriam, photograph by Roberto Borea. AP/Wide World Photos./ Bell, Bert, photograph. AP/Wide World Photos./Bell, James "Cool Papa," photograph by Leon Algee. AP/Wide World Photos./ Bench, Johnny, photograph. AP/Wide World Photos./ Berra, Yogi, photograph. AP/Wide World Photos./ Biondi, Matt, photograph. AP/Wide World Photos./ Bird, Larry, photograph. AP/Wide World Photos./Bjoerndalen, Ole Einar, photograph. AP/Wide World Photos./ Blair, Bonnie, photograph. AP Wide World Photos./ Blair, Bonnie, portrait. AP/Wide World Photos./ Blake, Sir Peter, photograph. AP/Wide World Photos./ Bogues, Tyrone, "Muggsy," photograph. AP/Wide World Photos./ Bonds, Barry, photograph. AP/Wide World Photos./ Bonds, Barry, photograph. AP/Wide World Photos./ Borders, Ila, photograph by Nick Ut. AP/Wide World Photos./ Borg, Bjorn, photograph. AP/Wide World Photos./ Bossy, Michael, photograph. AP/Wide World Photos./ Bradley, William Warren, photograph. AP/Wide World Photos./ Bradman, Don, photograph. AP/Wide World Photos./ Bradshaw, Terry, photograph. AP/Wide World Photos./ Brock, Lou, photograph. AP/Wide World Photos./ Brock, Lou, photograph. AP/Wide World Photos./ Brooks, Herb, photograph by Gene J. Puskar. AP/Wide World Photos./ Brown, Jim, photograph. AP/Wide World Photos./ Brown, Jim, photograph. AP/Wide World Photos./ Brown, Mordecai, "Three Finger," photograph. AP/Wide World Photos./ Brown, Tim, photograph. AP/Wide World Photos./ Bubka, Sergei, photograph. AP/Wide World Photos./ Budge, Don, photograph. AP/Wide World Photos./ Butcher, Susan, photograph. AP/Wide World Photos./ Button, Dick, photograph. AP/Wide World Photos./ Campanella, Roy, photograph. AP/Wide World Photos./ Campbell, Earl, photograph. AP/Wide

World Photos./ Canseco, Jose, photograph. AP/Wide World Photos./ Capriati, Jennifer, photograph. AP/Wide World Photos./ Capriati, Jennifer, photograph. AP/Wide World Photos./ Carter, Cris, photograph by Michael Conroy. AP/Wide World Photos./ Carter, Vince, photograph by Chuck Stoody. AP/Wide World Photos./ Carter, Vince, photograph. AP/Wide World Photos./ Cartwright, Alexander Joy, photograph. AP/Wide World Photos./ Caulkins, Tracy, photograph. AP/Wide World Photos./ Chamberlain, Wilt, photograph. AP/Wide World Photos./ Chelios, Chris, photograph. AP/Wide World Photos./ Chun, Lee-Kyung, photograph. AP/Wide World Photos./ Clark, Kelly, photograph. AP/Wide World Photos./ Clark, Kelly, photograph. AP/Wide World Photos./ Clemens, Roger, photograph. AP/Wide World Photos./ Clemens, Roger, photograph. AP/Wide World Photos./ Clemente, Roberto Walker, photograph. AP/Wide World Photos./ Coachman, Alice, photograph. AP/Wide World Photos./ Coleman, Derrick, photograph. AP/Wide World Photos./ Colorado Silver Bullets (Samonds, Shereen, and former major league pitcher Phil Niekro), photograph. AP/Wide World Photos./ Comaneci, Nadia, photograph. AP/Wide World Photos./ Connors, Jimmy, photograph. AP/Wide World Photos./ Conradt, Jody, photograph. AP/Wide World Photos./ Cooper, Cynthia, photograph by David J. Phillip. AP/Wide World Photos./ Cosell, Howard, photograph. AP/Wide World Photos./ Courier, Jim, photograph. AP/Wide World Photos./ Cousy, Bob, photograph. AP/Wide World Photos./ Daly, Chuck, photograph. AP/Wide World Photos./ Davis, Terrell, photograph by Ed Andrieski. AP/Wide World Photos./ Dawes, Dominique, photograph by John McConnico. AP/Wide World Photos./ Dean, Dizzy, photograph. AP/Wide World Photos./ Decker-Slaney, Mary, photograph. AP/Wide World Photos./ Deegan, Brian, photograph. AP/Wide World Photos./ DeFrantz, Anita, photograph by Douglas C. Pizac. AP/Wide World Photos./ De La Hoya, Oscar, photograph. AP/Wide World Photos./ Dickerson, Eric, photograph by Bill Janscha. AP/Wide World Photos./ Dimaggio, Joe, photograph. AP/Wide World Photos./Disl, Uschi, photograph. AP/Wide World Photos./ Ditka, Mike, photograph. AP/Wide World Photos./Doby, Larry, photograph. AP/Wide World Photos./ Dolan, Tom, photograph. AP/Wide World Photos./ Dorsett, Tony, photograph by Bruce Zake. AP/Wide World Photos./ Dravecky, Dave, photograph. AP/Wide World Photos./ Durocher, Leo, photograph. AP/Wide World Photos./ Dyroen, Becky, photograph. AP/Wide World Photos./ Earnhardt, Dale, photograph. AP/Wide World Photos./ Edwards, Teresa, photograph. AP/Wide World Photos./ Egerszegi, Krisztina, photograph. AP/Wide World Photos./ Elway, John, photograph. AP/Wide World Photos./ Erving, Julius, photograph. AP/Wide World Photos./ Esposito, Phil, photograph by Kevin Frayer. AP/Wide World./ Evans, Janet, photograph. AP/Wide World Photos./ Ewbank, Weeb, photograph. AP/Wide World./ Fangio, Juan Manuel, photograph by Eduardo DiBaia. AP/Wide World Photos./ Faulk, Marshall, photograph. AP/Wide World Photos./ Favre, Brett. AP/Wide World Photos./ Fernandez, Lisa, photograph. AP/Wide World Photos./ Figo, Luis, photograph. AP/Wide World Photos./ Fisk, Carlton, photograph. AP/Wide World Photos./ Fittipaldi, Emerson, photograph. AP/Wide World Photos./ Fleming, Peggy, photograph. AP/Wide World Photos./ Flowers, Vonetta, photograph by Darron Cummings. AP/Wide World Photos./ Foreman, George, photograph by Charles Rex Arbogast. AP/Wide World Photos./ Forsberg, Magdalena, photograph. AP/Wide World Photos./ Foyt, A.J., photograph. AP/Wide World Photos./ Foyt, A. J., photograph by Dave Parker. AP/Wide World Photos./ Freeman, Cathy, photograph. AP/Wide World Photos./ Gable, Dan, photograph. AP/Wide World Photos./ Galindo, Rudy, photograph by Craig Fujii. AP/Wide World Photos./ Garcia, Sergio, photograph by Beth A. Keiser. AP/Wide World Photos./ Garnett, Kevin, photograph. AP/Wide World Photos./ Gehrig, Lou, photograph. AP/Wide World Photos./ Gibson, Althea, photograph. AP/Wide World Photos./ Gibson, Josh, photograph. AP/Wide World Photos./ Gonzales, Richard "Pancho," photograph. AP/Wide World Photos./Goolagong, Evonne, photograph. AP/Wide World Photos./ Goosen, Retief, photograph. AP/Wide World Photos./ Gordeeva, Ekaterina, photograph. AP/Wide World Photos./ Graf, Steffi, photograph. AP/Wide World Photos./ Granato, Cammi, photograph. AP/Wide World Photos./ Grange, Harold "Red," photograph. AP/Wide World Photos./ Grange, Red, photograph. AP/Wide World Photos./ Graziano, Rocky, photograph. AP/Wide World Photos./ Greenberg, Hank, photograph. AP/Wide World Photos./ Greene, Joe, photograph. AP/Wide World Photos./ Griese, Bob, photograph. AP/Wide World Photos./ Griffey, Jr., Ken, photograph. AP/Wide World Photos./ Griffey, Ken, Jr., photograph by Jay Drowns. AP/Wide World Photos./ Griffin, Archie, photograph. AP/Wide World Photos./ Gwynn, Tony, portrait. AP/Wide World Photos./ Hackl, Georg, photograph. AP/Wide World Photos./ Halas, George, photograph. AP/Wide World Photos./ Hall, Glenn, photograph. AP/Wide World Photos./ Hamilton, Scott, photograph. AP/Wide World Photos./ Hamm, Mia, photograph. AP/Wide World Photos./ Hardaway, Afernee, photograph. AP/Wide World Photos./ Hardaway, Tim Duane, photograph by Lee Wilfredo. AP/Wide World Photos./ Harding, Tonya, photograph. AP/Wide World Photos./ Harkes, John, photograph. AP/Wide World Photos./ Harwell, Ernie, photograph. AP/Wide World Photos./ Heiden, Eric, photograph. AP/Wide World Photos./ Henderson, Rickey, photograph by Kevork Djansezian. AP/Wide World Photos./ Henie, Sonja, photograph. AP/Wide World Photos./ Henie, Sonja, photograph. AP/Wide World Photos./ Hernandez, Luis, photograph. AP/Wide World Photos./ Hill, Grant, photograph. AP/Wide World Photos./ Hirsch, Elroy Leon, photograph. AP/Wide World Photos./ Hogan, Ben, photograph. AP/Wide World Photos./ Holdsclaw, Chamique, photograph. AP/Wide World Photos./ Holmgren, Mike, photograph. AP/Wide World Photos./ Hornsby, Rogers, photograph. AP/Wide World Photos./ Hornung, Paul, photograph. AP/Wide World Photos./ Howe, Gordie, photograph. AP/Wide World Photos./ Howe, Gordie, photograph by Dawn Villella. AP/Wide World Photos./ Hughes, Sarah, photograph. AP/Wide World Photos./ Hull, Brett, photograph. AP/Wide World Photos./ Indurain, Miguel, photograph. AP/Wide World Photos./ Irvin, Michael, photograph AP/Wide World Photos./ Jackson, Bo (Vincent), photograph. AP/Wide World Photos./ Jackson, Joseph "Shoeless Joe," photograph. AP/Wide World Photos./ Jackson, Phil, photograph by Tim Boyle. (c) Tim Boyle of AP/Wide World Photos./ Jackson, Reginald Martinez, photograph by Ray Stubblebine. AP/Wide World Photos./ Jansen, Dan, photograph. AP/Wide World Photos./ Jenner, Bruce, photograph. AP/Wide World Photos./ Johnson, Earvin "Magic", photograph. AP/Wide World Photos./ Johnson, Junior, photograph. AP/Wide World Photos./ Johnson, Michael, photograph. AP/Wide World Photos./ Johnson, Randy, portrait. AP/Wide World Photos./ Jones, Kevin, photograph. AP/Wide World Photos./ Jones, Marion, photograph by Michael Probst. AP/Wide World Photos./ Jones, Robert Tyre, Jr., photograph. AP/Wide World Photos./ Joyce, Joan, photograph. AP/Wide World Photos./ Joyner, Florence Griffith, photograph. AP/Wide World Photos./ Joyner-Kersee, Jackie, photograph. AP/Wide World Photos./ Kaline, Al, photograph. AP/Wide World Photos./ Karelin, Alexander, photograph. AP/Wide World Photos./ Kariya, Paul, photograph. AP/Wide World Photos./ Karsten, Ekaterina, photograph. AP/Wide World Photos./ Kelly, Jim, photograph. AP/Wide World Photos./ Kemp, Shawn, photograph. AP/Wide World Photos./ Kidd, Jason, photograph. AP/Wide World Photos./ Killebrew, Harmon, photograph. AP/Wide World./ Killy, Jean-Claude, photograph. AP/Wide World Photos./ Killy, Jean-Claude, photograph. AP/Wide World Photos./ King, Billie Jean, photograph. AP/Wide World Photos./ King, Don, photograph. AP/Wide World./ Kiraly, Karch, photograph. AP/Wide World Photos./ Kirvesniemi, Harri, photograph. AP/Wide World Photos./ Klug, Chris, photograph. AP/Wide World Photos./ Klug, Chris, photograph. AP/Wide World Photos./ Knight, Bobby, photograph. AP/Wide World Photos./ Koch, Bill, photograph. AP/Wide World Photos./ Korbut, Olga, photograph. AP/Wide World Photos./ Kostelic, Janica, photograph. AP/Wide World Photos./ Kournikova, Anna, photograph by Bill Kostroun. AP/Wide World Photos./ Kronberger, Petra, photograph by Michel Lipchitz. AP/Wide World Photos./ Krone, Julie, photograph. AP/Wide World Photos./ Kuerten, Gustavo, photograph. AP/Wide World Photos./ Kummer, Clarence, photograph. AP/Wide World Photos./ Kwan, Michelle, photograph. AP/Wide World Photos./ Ladewig, Marion, photograph. AP/Wide World Photos./ Lalas, Alexi, photograph. AP/Wide World Photos./ Lambeau, "Curley," photograph. AP/Wide World Photos./ LaMotta, Jake, photograph. AP/Wide World Photos./ Largent, Steve, photograph. AP/Wide World Photos./ Lasorda, Tommy, photograph. AP/Wide World Photos./ Latynina, Larisa, photograph. AP/Wide World Photos./ Laver, Rod, photograph. AP/Wide World Photos./ Lemieux, Mario, photograph. AP/Wide World Photos./ Lemon, Meadowlark (George), photograph. AP/Wide World Photos./ Leonard, Sugar Ray, photograph by Eric Risberg. AP/Wide World Photos./ Leonard, Sugar Ray, photograph. AP/Wide World Photos./ Leslie, Lisa, photograph. AP/Wide World Photos./ Lewis, Carl, photograph. AP/Wide World Photos./ Lewis, Lennox, photograph by Adam Nadel. AP/Wide World Photos./

Lewis, Lennox, photograph. AP/Wide World Photos./ Lieberman-Cline, Nancy, photograph. AP/Wide World Photos./ Lipinski, Tara, photograph. AP/Wide World Photos./ Lloyd, Earl, photograph. AP/Wide World Photos./ Lobo, Rebecca, portrait. AP/Wide World Photos./ Lopez, Nancy, photograph by Pat J. Carter. AP/Wide World Photos./ Loroupe, Tegla, photograph. AP/Wide World Photos./ Louganis, Greg, photograph. AP/Wide World Photos./ Louis, Joe, photograph. AP/Wide World Photos./ Madden, John, photograph by Aaron Rapopart. AP/Wide World Photos./ Maddux, Greg, photograph. AP/Wide World Photos./ Mahre, Phil, photograph. AP/Wide World Photos./ Maier, Hermann, photograph. AP/Wide World Photos./ Malone, Karl, photograph. AP/Wide World Photos./ Malone, Moses, photograph. AP/Wide World Photos./ Mantle, Mickey, photograph. AP/Wide World Photos, Inc./ Mantle, Mickey, photograph. AP/Wide World Photos./ Marino, Dan, photograph. AP/Wide World Photos./ Martin, Billy, photograph. AP/Wide World Photos./ Martin, Casey, photograph by John Kicker. AP/Wide World Photos./ Martin, Christy, photograph. AP/Wide World Photos./ Masterkova, Svetlana, photograph. AP/Wide World Photos./ Maynard, Don, photograph. AP/Wide World Photos./ Mays, Willie, photograph. AP/Wide World Photos./ McCray, Nikki, photograph. AP/Wide World Photos./ McEnroe, John Patrick, Jr., photograph by Richard Drew. AP/Wide World Photos./ McGwire, Mark, photograph by Tom Gannam. AP/Wide World Photos./ McKinney, Tamara, photograph. AP/Wide World Photos./ Mears, Rick, photograph. AP/Wide World Photos./ Messier, Mark, photograph. AP/Wide World Photos./ Meyers, Ann, photograph. AP/Wide World Photos./ Mikita, Stan, photograph. AP/Wide World Photos./ Mingxia, Fu, photograph. AP/Wide World Photos./ Moceanu, Dominique, photograph. AP/Wide World Photos./ Montana, Joe, photograph. AP/Wide World Photos./ Monti, Eugenio, photograph. AP/Wide World Photos./ Moore, Archie, photograph. AP/Wide World Photos./ Morgan, Joe (Leonard), photograph. AP/Wide World Photos./ Morris, Jim, photograph. AP/Wide World Photos./ Moses, Edwin Corley, photograph by Lennox McLendon. AP/Wide World Photos./ Moss, Randy, photograph by Jim Mone. AP/Wide World Photos./ Muldowney, Shirley "Cha Cha," photograph. AP/Wide World Photos./ Murden, Tori, photograph by Bob Jordan. AP/Wide World Photos./ Musial, Stan, photograph. AP/Wide World Photos./ Musial, Stan, photograph. AP/Wide World Photos./ Mutombu, Dikembe, photograph. AP/Wide World Photos./ Naismith, James, photograph. AP/Wide World Photos./ Namath, Joe, photograph. AP/Wide World Photos./ Namath, Joe, photograph. AP/Wide World Photos./ Navratilova, Martina, photograph. AP/Wide World Photos./ Navratilova, Martina, photograph. AP/Wide World Photos./ Neely, Cam, portrait. AP/Wide World Photos./ Newby-Fraser, Paula, photograph. AP/Wide World Photos./ O'-Connor, David, photograph. AP/Wide World Photos./ Oerter, Al, photograph. AP/Wide World Photos./ Oh, Sadaharu, photograph. AP/Wide World Photos./ Ohno, Apolo Anton, photograph. AP/Wide World Photos./ Oldfield, Barney, photograph. AP/Wide World Photos./ Olsen, Merlin Jay, photograph. AP/Wide World Photos./ Olson, Lisa, photograph. AP/Wide World Photos./ O'Neal, Shaquille, photograph. AP/Wide World Photos./ O'Neil, Buck, photograph. AP/Wide World Photos./ O'Neill, Susan, photograph by Dennis Paquin. AP/Wide World Photos./ O'Sullivan, Sonia, photograph. AP/Wide World Photos./ Paige, Leroy Robert, "Satchel," photograph. AP/Wide World Photos./ Paige, Leroy Robert, photograph. AP/Wide World Photos./ Palmer, Shaun, photograph. AP/Wide World Photos./ Parcells, Bill, photograph by Bill Kostroun. AP/Wide World Photos./ Parra, Derek, photograph by Elaine Thompson. AP/Wide World Photos./ Paterno, Joe, photograph by Michael Conroy. AP/Wide World Photos./ Paterno, Joe, photograph. AP/Wide World Photos./ Patterson, Floyd, photograph. AP/Wide World Photos./ Payton, Gary, photograph. AP/Wide World Photos./ Payton, Walter, photograph by Fred Jewell. AP/Wide World Photos./ Pele, photograph. AP/Wide World Photos./ Perry, Gaylord, photograph. AP/Wide World Photos./ Pete Rose, photograph. AP/Wide World Photos./ Petty, Lee, photograph. AP/Wide World Photos./ Piniella, Lou, photograph. AP/Wide World Photos./ Pippen, Scottie, photograph by Tim Johnson. AP/Wide World Photos./ Podkopayeva, Lilia, photograph. AP/Wide World Photos./ Prost, Alain, photograph. AP/Wide World Photos./ Puckett, Kirby, photograph. AP/Wide World Photos./ Randle, John, photograph. AP/Wide World Photos./ Redgrave, Steve, photograph. AP/Wide World Photos./ Reece, Gabrielle, photograph. AP/Wide World Photos/Fashion Wire Daily./ Reese, Harold "Pee Wee," photograph. AP/Wide World Photos./ Retton, Mary Lou, photograph.

AP/Wide World Photos./ Rheaume, Manon, photograph. AP/Wide World Photos./ Rice, Jerry, photograph. AP/Wide World Photos./ Richard, Maurice, photograph. AP/Wide World Photos./ Richardson, Dot, photograph. AP/Wide World Photos./ Riddles, Libby, photograph. AP/Wide World Photos./ Rigby, Cathy, photograph. AP/Wide World Photos./ Riley, Pat, photograph by Mark Lennihan. AP/Wide World Photos./ Ripken, Calvin, photograph. AP/Wide World Photos./ Roba, Fatuma, photograph. AP/Wide World Photos./ Robertson, Oscar, photograph. AP/Wide World Photos./ Robinson, David, photograph. AP/Wide World Photos./ Robinson, Jackie, photograph. AP/Wide World Photos./ Rocker, John, photograph. AP/Wide World Photos./ Rodman, Dennis, photograph. AP/Wide World Photos./ Rodriguez, Alex, photograph. AP/Wide World Photos./ Roy, Patrick, portrait. AP/Wide World Photos./ Rubin, Barbara Joe, photograph. AP/Wide World Photos./ Ruud, Birger, photograph. AP/Wide World Photos./ Rudolph, Wilma, photograph. AP/Wide World Photos./ Russell, Bill, photograph. AP/Wide World Photos./ Ruth, Babe, photograph. AP/Wide World Photos./ Ryan, Lynn Nolan, photograph by Tim Sharp. AP/Wide World Photos./ Sabatini, Gabriela, photograph. AP/Wide World Photos./ St. James, Lyn, portrait. AP/Wide World Photos./ Sale, Jamie, and David Pelletier, photograph by Lionel Cironneau. AP/Wide World Photos./ Sampras, Pete, photograph. AP/Wide World Photos./ Sampras, Pete, photograph. AP/Wide World Photos./ Samuelson, Joan Benoit, photograph. AP/Wide World Photos./ Sanders, Barry, photograph by Rusty Kennedy. AP/Wide World Photos./ Sanders, Deion, photograph. AP/Wide World Photos./ Sanders, Deion, photograph by Rusty Kennedy. AP/Wide World Photos./ Sawchuk, Terry, photograph. AP/Wide World Photos./ Sayers, Gale, photograph. AP/Wide World Photos./ Schayes, Dolph, photograph. AP/Wide World Photos./ Schilling, Curtis Montague, photograph by Lenny Ignelzi. AP/Wide World Photos./ Schmeling, Max, photograph. AP/Wide World Photos./ Schmidt, Mike, photograph. AP/Wide World Photos./ Schmirler, Sandra, photograph. AP/Wide World Photos./ Schramm, Tex, photograph. AP/Wide World Photos./ Schumacher, Michael, photograph. AP/Wide World Photos./ Scott, Wendell Oliver, photograph. AP/Wide World Photos./ Scurry, Briana, photograph. AP/Wide World Photos./ Selanne, Teemu, photograph. AP/Wide World Photos./ Seau, Junior, photograph. AP/Wide World Photos./ Seaver, Tom, photograph. AP/Wide World Photos./ Secretariat, photograph. AP/Wide World Photos./ Secretariat, photograph. AP/Wide World Photos./ Seles, Monica, photograph. AP/Wide World Photos./ Selig, Bud, photograph. AP/Wide World Photos./ Sharp, Sterling, photograph. AP/Wide World Photos./ Shea, Jack, photograph. AP/Wide World Photos./ Sheffield, Gary, photograph. AP/Wide World Photos./ Shula, Don, photograph. AP/Wide World Photos./ Simpson, O. J., photograph. AP/Wide World Photos./ Smith, Tommie, photograph. AP/Wide World Photos./ Sosa, Sammy, photograph by Gary Dineen. AP/Wide World Photos./ Spinks, Michael, photograph. AP/Wide World Photos./ Spitz, Mark (Andrew), photograph. AP/Wide World Photos./ Sprewell, Latrell, photograph by John Dunn. AP/Wide World Photos./ Staley, Dawn, photograph by Rusty Kennedy. AP/Wide World Photos./ Starr, Bart, photograph. AP/Wide World Photos./ Staubach, Roger, photograph. AP/Wide World Photos./ Steinbrenner, George, photograph. AP/Wide World Photos./ Stengel, Casey, photograph. AP/Wide World Photos./ Stenmark, Ingemar, photograph. AP/Wide World Photos./ Stewart, Jackie, photograph. AP/Wide World Photos./ Stewart, Jackie, photograph. AP/Wide World Photos./ Stewart, Kordell, photograph. AP/Wide World Photos./ Stockton, John, photograph. AP/Wide World Photos./ Stojko, Elvis, photograph. AP/Wide World Photos./ Strawberry, Darryl, photograph. AP/Wide World Photos./ Strawberry, Darryl, photograph by Ron Frehm. AP/Wide World Photos./ Street, Picabo, photograph by David Longstreath. AP/Wide World Photos./ Street, Picabo, photograph. AP/Wide World Photos./ Strug, Kerri, photograph. AP/Wide World Photos./ Strug, Kerri, photograph. AP/Wide World Photos./ Suleymanoglu, Naim, photograph. AP/Wide World Photos./ Summitt, Pat, photograph. AP/Wide World Photos./ Suzuki, Ichiro, photograph by Eliane Thompson. AP/Wide World Photos./ Suzuki, Ichiro, photograph. AP/Wide World Photos./ Swoopes, Sheryl, photograph. AP/Wide World Photos./ Tarkanian, Jerry, photograph. AP/Wide World Photos./ Tarkanian, Jerry, photograph. AP/Wide World Photos./ Tarkenton, Fran, photograph. AP/Wide World Photos./ Taylor, Lawrence, photograph. AP/Wide World Photos./ Tendulkar, Sachin, photograph. AP/Wide World Photos./ Thomas, Frank, photograph. AP/Wide World Photos./ Thomas, Isiah, photograph by

Michael Conroy. AP/Wide World Photos./ Thomas, Isiah, photograph. AP/Wide World Photos./ Thomas, Thurman, photograph. AP/Wide World Photos./ Thompson, Jenny, photograph by Paul Sakuma. AP/Wide World Photos./ Thorpe, Ian, photograph by Russell McPhedran. AP/Wide World Photos./ Tomba, Alberto, photograph. AP/Wide World Photos./ Tomba, Alberto, photograph. AP/Wide World Photos, Inc./ Torrence, Gwen, photograph. AP/Wide World Photos./ Torvill, Jayne, and Christopher Dean, photograph. AP/Wide World Photos./ Trottier, Brian, photograph. AP/Wide World Photos./ Tunney, Gene, photograph. AP/Wide World./ Turner, Cathy, AP/Wide World Photos./ Tyson, Mike, photograph by Lennox McLendon. AP/Wide World Photos./ Tyus, Wyomia, photograph. AP/Wide World Photos./ Unitas, Johnny, photograph. AP/Wide World Photos./ Unitas, Johnny, photograph. AP/Wide World Photos./ Unser, Al, photograph. AP/Wide World Photos./ Vaughn, Mo, photograph. AP/Wide World Photos./ Ventura, Jesse, photograph. AP/Wide World Photos./ Vicario, Arantxa Sanchez, photograph. AP/Wide World Photos./ Vitale, Dick, photograph. AP/Wide World Photos./ Wagner, Honus, photograph. AP/Wide World Photos./ Waitz, Grete, photograph. AP/Wide World Photos./ Waitz, Grete, photograph. AP/Wide World Photos./ Walcott, Joe, photograph. AP/Wide World Photos./ Waldner, Jan Ove, photograph. AP/Wide World Photos./ Walton, Bill, photograph. AP/Wide World Photos./ Warne, Shane, photograph. AP/Wide World Photos./ Warner, Kurt, photograph by James A. Finley. AP/Wide World Photos./ Watters, Ricky, photograph. AP/Wide World Photos./ Webb, Anthony, "Spud," photograph. AP/Wide World Photos./ Webb, Karrie, photograph. AP/Wide World Photos./ Webber, Chris, photograph. AP/Wide World Photos./ Weber, Dick, photograph. AP/Wide World Photos./ Wehling, Ulrich, photograph. AP/Wide World Photos./ Weihenmayer, Erik, photograph. AP/Wide World Photos./ Weishoff, Paula, photograph. AP/Wide World Photos./ Weissmuller, Johnny, photograph. AP/Wide World Photos./ West, Jerry, photograph. AP/Wide World Photos./ West, Jerry, photograph. AP/Wide World Photos./ White, Reggie, photograph. AP/Wide World Photos./ Whitworth, Kathy, photograph. AP/Wide World Photos./ Wigger, Deena, photograph. AP/Wide World Photos./ Wilkens, Lenny, photograph. AP/Wide World Photos./ Wilkens, Lenny, photograph. AP/Wide World Photos./ Wilkins, Dominique, photograph. AP/Wide World Photos./ Wilkinson, Laura, photograph. AP/Wide World Photos./ Williams, Serena, photograph. AP/Wide World Photos./ Williams, Serena, photograph. AP/Wide World Photos./ Williams, Ted, photograph. AP/Wide World Photos./ Williams, Venus, photograph. AP/Wide World Photos./ Williams, Venus, photograph. AP/Wide World Photos./ Winfield, Dave, photograph. AP/Wide World Photos./ Witt, Katarina, photograph. AP/Wide World Photos./ Wooden, John, photograph. AP/Wide World Photos./ Wooden, John, photograph. AP/Wide World Photos./ Woods, Tiger, photograph by Dave Martin. AP/Wide World Photos./ Woods, Tiger, photograph by Diego Giudice. AP Wide World Photos./ Woodson, Charles, photograph. AP/Wide World Photos./ Woodson, Rod, photograph. AP/Wide World Photos./ Woodward, Lynette, photograph by Orlin Wagner. AP/Wide World Photos./ Wright, Mickey, photograph. AP/Wide World Photos./ Yamaguchi, Kristi, portrait. AP/Wide World Photos./ Young, Cy, photograph. AP/Wide World Photos./ Young, Sheila, photograph. AP/Wide World Photos./ Young, Steve, photograph. AP/Wide World Photos./ Zaharias, Babe (Mildred Ella) Didrikson, photograph. AP/Wide World Photos./ Zidane, Zinedine, photograph. AP/Wide World Photos./

ASSOCIATED FEATURES, INC.:
Dryden, Ken, photograph. Associated Features, Inc./ Esposito, Tony, photograph. Associated Features, Inc./ Hasek, Dominik, photograph. Associated Features./ Plante, Jacques, photograph. Associated Features./ Sakic, Joe, photograph. Associated Features.

BRUCE BENNETT STUDIOS, INC.:
Belfour, Ed, photograph. Courtesy of Bruce Bennett./ Bowman, Scotty, photograph. John Giamundo/B. Bennett./ Gretzky, Wayne, photograph. Courtesy of Bruce Bennett./ Gretzky, Wayne, photograph. Courtesy of Bruce Bennett./ Lefleur, Guy, photograph. Courtesy of Bruce Bennett./ Lemieux, Mario, photograph. Michael DiGirolamo/B. Bennett./ Lindros, Eric, photograph. Courtesy of B. Bennett./ Lindros, Eric, photograph. Courtesy of Bruce Bennett.

CORBIS:

Alexander, Grover Cleveland, photograph by George Rinhart. (c)Underwood & Underwood/Corbis./ Ali, Muhammad, photograph. UPI/Corbis-Bettmann./ Ali, Muhammad, photograph. (c) Bettmann/Corbis./ Allen, Marcus, photograph. (c)Bettmann/Corbis./ Ashe, Arthur, photograph. (c)Hulton-Deutsch Collection/Corbis./ Auerbach, Arnold, photograph. (c)Bettmann/Corbis./ Bench, Johnny Lee, photograph. (c)Bettmann/Corbis./ Benoit, Joan, photograph. Corbis-Bettmann./ Berra, Yogi, photograph. (c)Bettmann/Corbis./ Bird, Larry Joe, photograph. (c) Reuters New Media Inc./Corbis./ Blake, Hector "Toe", photograph. (c) Bettmann/Corbis./ Brisco-Hooks, Valerie, photograph. Corbis-Bettmann./ Brown, Paul, photograph. Corbis/ Bettmann./ Caray, Harry, photograph. UPI/CORBIS-Bettmann./ Carter, Don, photograph. (c) Bettmann/Corbis./ Chamberlain, Wilt, photograph. UPI/Corbis-Bettmann./ Chang, Michael, photograph. Reuters/Bettmann./ Clemente, Roberto, photograph. UPI/Bettmann./ Conner, Bart, photograph. (c)Bettmann/Corbis./ Connolly, Maureen, photograph. UPI/Corbis- Bettmann./ Corbett, James John, photograph. (c)Bettmann/Corbis./ Costas, Bob, photograph by Wally McNamee. Wally McNamee/Corbis./ Court, Margaret Smith, photograph. UPI/Corbis-Bettmann./ Court, Margaret Smith, photograph. UPI/Corbis-Bettmann./ Davis, Al, photograph. (c)AFP/Corbis./ De Varona, Donna, photograph. (c) Bettman/Corbis./ Devers, Gail, photograph. Reuters/Bettmann./ Faldo, Nick, photograph. Reuters/Bettmann./ Fleming, Peggy, photograph. Corbis./ Frazier, Joe, photograph. (c) Hulton-Deutsch Collection/Corbis./ Furtado, Julie, photograph. (c) Ales Fevzer/Corbis./ Gibson, Althea. Portrait. UPI/Bettmann./ Gifford, Frank, photograph. (c)Mitchell Gerber/Corbis./ Graf, Steffi, photograph. (c) Dimitri LundtCorbis./ Graham, Otto, photograph. Bettmann/Corbis./ Guthrie, Janet, photograph. Corbis-Bettmann./ Halas, George Stanley "Papa Bear," photograph. (c) Bettmann/Corbis./ Hamill, Dorothy, photograph. UPI/Bettmann./ Hamill, Dorothy, photograph. (c) Corbis./ Hawk, Tony, photograph by Jason Wise. (c) Duomo/Corbis./ Hayes, Robert, photograph. (c)Bettmann/Corbis./ Heisman, John, photograph. (c) Bettmann/Corbis./ Heisman, John, photograph. (c) Bettmann/Corbis./ Hill, Lynn, photograph. UPI/Corbis-Bettmann./ Hingis, Martina, photograph. (c) Torsten Blackwood/Corbis./ Hogan, Ben, photograph. (c) Bettmann/Corbis./ Holyfield, Evander, photograph. UPI/Corbis Bettmann./ Holyfield, Evander, photograph. Reuters/Bettmann./ Hornsby, Rogers, photograph. Bettmann/Corbis./ Hunter, Catfish, photograph. (c)Bettmann/Corbis./ Jagr, Jaromir, photograph. (c) Reuters NewMedia Inc./Corbis./ Jenner William Bruce, photograph Neal Preston. Corbis./ Johnson, Earvin "Magic," photograph. Bettmann Newsphotos./ Johnson, Jack, photograph. (c) Bettmann/Corbis./ Jordan, Michael, photograph. Reuters/Corbis-Bettmann./ Jordan, Michael, photograph. Reuters/Corbis-Bettmann./ Joyner-Kersee, Jackie, photograph. Reuters/Bettmann./ Kahanamoku, Duke, photograph. The Bettmann Archive./ King, Billie Jean, photograph. (c) Bettmann/Corbis./ Knight, Bobby, photograph by Gary Hershorn. NewMedia Inc./Corbis./ Korbut, Olga, photograph. Corbis./ Koufax, Sanford (Sandy), photograph. (c)Bettmann/Corbis./ Kwan, Michelle. Reuters/Corbis-Bettmann./ Landry, Thomas, photograph. (c)Bettmann/Corbis./ Laver, Rod, photograph. UPI/Corbis-Bettmann./ Lemon, Meadowlark, photograph. (c)Bettmann/Corbis./ Liston, Sonny, photograph. (c)Bettmann/Corbis./ Lombardi, Vince, photograph. Corbis/Bettmann./ Louis, Joe, photograph. Corbis-Bettmann./ Madden, John, photograph. (c) Bettmann/Corbis./ Maris, Roger (Eugene), photograph. (c)Bettmann/Corbis./ McEnroe, John, photograph. UPI/Corbis-Bettmann./ Mikan, George, photograph. (c)Bettmann/Corbis./ Miller, Shannon, photograph. (c)Mike King/Corbis./ Mirra, Dave, photograph. (c) Duomo/Corbis./ Moise, Patty, photograph. UPI/Corbis-Bettmann./ Montana, Joe, photograph. (c)Bettmann/Corbis./ Moody, Helen F., photograph by George Rinhart. (c)Underwood & Underwood/Corbis./ Moore, Archie Lee, photograph. (c)Bettmann/Corbis./ Olajuwon, Akeem, photograph. UPI/Corbis-Bettmann./ O'Neal, Shaquille, photograph. (c) Reuters NewMedia Inc./Corbis./ Orr, Bobby, photograph. (c) Bettmann/Corbis./ Owens, Jesse, photograph. UPI/Corbis-Bettmann./ Payton, Walter, photograph. (c)Bettmann/Corbis./ Piazza, Mike, photograph. (c)Reuters NewMedia Inc./Corbis./ Reeves, Dan, photograph. (c) Bettmann/Corbis./ Robinson, Brooks Calbert, Jr., photograph. (c)Bettmann/Corbis./ Robinson, Shawna, photograph. UPI/Corbis-Bettmann./ Robinson, Sugar Ray, photograph. (c) Bettmann/Corbis./ Rozelle, Pete, photograph by Sande. (c) Bettmann/Corbis./

Ryan, Nolan, photograph. UPI/Corbis-Bettmann./ Salming, Borje. (c) Bettmann/Corbis./ Sanders, Summer, photograph. UPI/Corbis-Bettmann./ Schott, Marge, photograph. (c) Bettmann/Corbis./ Seles, Monica, photograph. Reuters/Bettmann./ Shoemaker, Willie, photograph. (c) Bettmann/Corbis./ Simpson, O.J., photograph. (c) Bettmann/Corbis./ Smith, Emmitt, photograph. Rueters/Corbis-Bettmann./ Spitz, Mark, photograph. (c) Bettmann/Corbis./ Thorpe, Jim, photograph. Corbis./ Tilden, Bill, photograph. UPI/Corbis-Bettmann./ Tretiak, Vladislav, photograph. (c) Bettmann/Corbis./ Tyson, Michael, photograph. (c) Bettmann/Corbis./ Unser, Bobby, photograph. (c) Bettmann/Corbis./ Ventura, Jesse "The Body," photograph. (c) Corbis./ Williams, Esther, photograph. UPI/Bettmann./ Williams, Esther, photograph. (c) Bettmann/Corbis./ Williams, Ted, photograph. (c)Bettmann/Corbis./ Zaharias, Babe Didriksen. Portrait. UPI/Bettmann.

FISK UNIVERSITY LIBRARY:
Owens, Jesse, photograph. Fisk University Library./ Robinson, Sugar Ray, photograph. Fisk University Library.

THE GALE GROUP:
Earnhardt, Dale, photograph by Dennis Winn. The Gale Group.

GETTY IMAGES/ARCHIVE PHOTOS, INC.:
Aaron, Hank, photograph. Archive Photos, Inc./ Andretti, Mario, photograph. Archive Photos, Inc./ Aparicio, Luis, photograph. Archive Photos, Inc./ Bannister, Roger, photograph. Liaison Agency/Hilton Get./ Barclay, Charles, photograph by Sue Ogrocki. Archive Photos./ Beard, Amanda, photograph. Reuters/Gary Hershorn/Archive Photos./ Beckham, David, photograph. Anthony Harvey/Getty Images./ Belle, Albert, photograph by Scott Olson. Reuters/Archive Photos./ Bradshaw, Terry, photograph. Sporting News/Archive Photos, Inc./ Butkus, Dick, photograph. Sporting News/Archive Photos, Inc./ Campanella, Roy, photograph. Archive Photos./ Carter, Don, photograph. Archive Photos./ Casals, Rosemary, photograph. Archive Photos, Inc./ Cawley, Evonne, photograph. (c) Hulton Archive/Getty Images./ Chastain, Brandi, photograph. (c) Scott Harrison/Getty Images./ Cobb, Ty, photograph. Archive Photos, Inc./ Cobb, Ty, photograph. Archive Photos./ Connors, Jimmy, photograph. (c) Hulton Archive/Getty Images./ Cosell, Howard, photograph. Archive Photos, Inc./ Cousy, Bob, photograph. Archive Photos, Inc./ Dempsey, Jack, photograph. Archive Photos, Inc./American Stock./ DiMaggio, Joe, photograph. Archive Photos/Agip./ Duncan, Tim, photograph by Bob Padgett. Archive Photos./ Evert, Chris, photograph. Archive Photos, Inc./ Evert, Chris, photograph. Clive Brunskill/Allsport/Getty Images./ Federov, Sergei, photograph by Peter Jones. Reuter/Archive Photos./ Flutie, Doug, photograph by Brendan McDermid. Archive Photos, Inc./ Gehrig, Lou, photograph. Archive Photos, Inc./ Greenspan, Bud, photograph. (c) Matthew Stockman/Getty Images./ Hamm, Mia, photograph by Tony Quinn. ALLSPORT Photography USA Inc./ Havlicek, John, photograph. Archive Photos, Inc./ Hoffman, Mat, photograph. (c) J. Emilio Flores/Getty Images./ Iverson, Allen, photograph by Tom Mihalek. Hulton/Archive./ Johnson, Michael, photograph by Wolfgang Rattay. Reuter/Archive Photos./ Johnson, Rafer, portrait. (c) Getty Images./ Kirby, Karolyn, photograph. (c) Jonathan Ferrey/Getty Images./ Lipinski, Tara, photograph. Reuters/Str/Archive Photos./ Lombardi, Vince, photograph. Archive Photos, Inc./Sporting News./ Mack, Connie, photograph. APA/Archive Photos./ Maradona, Diego, photograph by S. Bruty. Allsport Photography (USA) Inc./ Marciano, Rocky, photograph. Archive Photos, Inc./ Martinez, Pedro, photograph. (c) Reuters/Colin Braley/Getty Images./ Mays, Willie, photograph. Archive Photos, Inc./ Meagher, Mary T., photograph. (c) Tony Duff/Getty Images./ Miller, Reggie, photograph by Ray Stubblebine. Reuter/Archive Photos./ Moon, Warren, photograph Susumu Takahashi. Archive Photos./ Nicklaus, Jack, photograph. Archive Photos, Inc./ Nomo, Hideo, portrait. Reuter/Archive Photos./ Palmer, Arnold, photograph. Archive Photos, Inc./ Pele, photograph. Archive Photos./ Petrenko, Viktor, photograph. (c) Pascal Rondeau/Getty Images./ Pierce, Mary, photograph by Jack Dabaghian. Reuter/Archive Photos./ Rickey, Branch, photograph. Archive Photos, Inc./Sporting News./ Ripken, Cal, Jr., photograph. Archive Photos, Inc./ Robinson, Frank, photograph. Archive Photos./ Robinson, Jackie, photograph. Archive Photos./

Rose, Pete, photograph. (c) Stephen Dunn/Getty Images./ Russell, Bill, portrait. (c) Sporting News/Getty Images./ Sayers, Gale, photograph. Sporting News/Archive Photos, Inc./ Shoemaker, Willie, photograph. APA/Archive Photos, Inc./ Shriver, Eunice, photograph. Archive Photos, Inc./ Skobilikova, Lydia, photograph. (c) Hulton Archive/Getty Images./ Sorenstam, Annika, photograph by Steve Marcus. Archive Photos./ Starr, Bart, photograph. Sporting News/Archive Photos, Inc./ Sullivan, John Lawrence, photograph. (c) Hulton Archive/Getty Images./ Swann, Lynn, photograph. Sporting News/Archive Photos./ Thomas, Derrick, photograph by Susumu Takahashi. Reuters/Archive Photos, Inc./ Torre, Joe, photograph. Reuters/Ray Stubblebine/Archive Photos./ Tretiak, Vladislav, photograph. (c) Getty Images./ Trinidad, Felix Tito, photograph. (c) Gary M. Williams/Liaison Agency/Getty Images/ El Neuvo Dia./ Turner, Ted, photograph. Archive Photo/Malafronte./ Van Dyken, Amy, photograph. Reuters/Eric Gailard/Archive Photos./ Wenzel, Hanni, photograph. (c) Tony Duffy/Getty Images./ Williamson, Alison, photograph. (c) Mark Dadswell, Getty Images./

HOCKEY HALL OF FAME:
Blake, Hector, photograph. Courtesy of Hockey Hall of Fame./ Vezina, Georges, photograph. Courtesy of Hockey Hall of Fame.

THE LIBRARY OF CONGRESS:
Dempsey, Jack, photograph. The Library of Congress./ Rockne, Knute, photograph. The Library of Congress. Rudolph, Wilma, photograph. The Library of Congress./ Ruth, Babe, photograph. The Library of Congress.

BILLY MILLS:
Mills, Billy, photograph. Courtesy of Billy Mills./ Mills, Billy, photograph. Courtesy of Billy Mills.

NATIONAL ARCHIVES AND RECORDS ADMINISTRATION:
Thorpe, Jim, photograph. National Archives and Records Administration.

NATIONAL BASEBALL LIBRARY & ARCHIVE:
Chicago White Sox team, photograph. National Baseball Library & Archive, Cooperstown, NY.

NEW YORK KNICKS
Ewing, Patrick, photograph by George Kalinsky. The New York Knicks.

THE NEW YORK PUBLIC LIBRARY:
Washington, Ora, photograph by D. H. Polk. Photographs and Prints Division, Schomburg Center for Research in Black Culture, The New York Public Library, Astor, Lenox and Tilden Foundations.

PENSKE MOTORSPORTS, INC.:
Jackson, Joe, photograph. From The Image of Their Greatness: An Illustrated History of Baseball from 1900 to the Present, revised edition, by Lawrence Ritter and Donald Honig. Crown Trade Paperbacks, 1992. Copyright (c) 1992 by Lawrence S. Ritter and Donald Honig./ Penske, Roger. Photo courtesy of Penske Motorsports, Inc.

POPPERFOTO:
Patterson, Floyd, photograph. Popperfoto/Archive Photos./ Retton, Mary Lou, photograph. Popperfoto.

MITCHELL B. REIBEL:
Borg, Bjorn, photograph. Mitchell Reibel.

SPORTSPICS:
Petty, Richard, photograph. SportsPics.

UNITED PRESS INTERNATIONAL:
U. S. Olympic Hockey team, 1980, photograph. Courtesy of United Press International.

WIREIMAGE.COM:
Bryant, Kobe, photograph. Steve Granitz/WireImage.com.

Entry List

VOLUME 3

M

VOLUME 4

T

Timeline

776 B.C.
Greece's first recorded Olympic Games. Only Greeks are allowed to compete, and the games are limited to foot races of approximately 200 yards.

490 B.C.
According to Greek satirist Lucian, a courier named Pheidippides runs from the plains of Marathon to Athens, a distance of about 22 miles, with news of a Greek victory over the Persians. This becomes the inspiration for modern-day "marathon" races.

1457
Scotland's Parliament forbids "futeball and golfe" as their popularity is distracting men from practicing archery which is required for military training.

1552
Scotland's Royal Golf Club of St. Andrews begins. Its official founding comes 200 years later in 1754.

1702
Queen Anne of England gives approval for horseracing and introduces the idea of sweepstakes.

1744
First recorded cricket match in England. Rules of the game are codified in 1788.

1842
Alexander Cartwright invents baseball. Although the game has been played for many years, Cartwright writes down rules of play.

1863
The official rules for soccer are established by the Football Association in England.

1869
Princeton and Rutgers play the first college football game. Rutgers wins 6-4.

1874
British sportsman Walter Clopton Wingfield codifies the rules for lawn tennis.

1875
First running of the Kentucky Derby, won by Aristides.

1876
The National League (NL) is formed. The NL becomes the first stable baseball major league.

1877
The first Wimbledon tennis championship is won by Spencer Gore.

1891
Basketball invented by **James Naismith,** a physical education instructor at Springfield Men's Christian Association Training School. Naismith wrote the first 13 rules for the sport.

1892
"Gentleman Jim" Corbett defeats **John L. Sullivan** to win the first boxing championship fought with padded gloves and under the Marquis of Queensberry Rules.

1896
First of the "modern" Olympics are held in Athens, Greece. Competing are 311 athletes from 13 countries.

1900
The American League (AL) is formed. It soon joins the National League as a baseball major league.

Britain's Charlotte Cooper wins the first women's Olympic gold medal in women's tennis. Margaret Abbott wins the nine-hole golf competition, becoming the first American woman to win Olympic gold.

1903
The National Agreement calls an end to the war between the American and National baseball leagues. The agree-

ment calls for each league to be considered major leagues, the same alignment as today.

The first World Series is played. It features the Pittsburgh Pirates of the National League and the Boston Pilgrims of the American League. Boston wins the series 5-3.

1908
Jack Johnson defeats Tommy Burns to become the first African American to hold the world heavyweight boxing championship.

1911
First Indianapolis 500 is run.

Cy Young retires with a career record 511 wins. The trophy given annually to the best pitcher in each league is named after Young.

1912
Jim Thorpe wins three Olympic medals, one of them a gold medal in the decathlon. The medals are stripped from him in 1913 when it is discovered that he accepted a token sum of money to play baseball. The medals are restored and returned to his family in 1982.

1917
The National Hockey League (NHL) is formed. The new league contains only four teams.

1919
The **Chicago "Black Sox"** throw the World Series against the Cincinnati Reds in the biggest sports gambling incident of all-time. Eight players, including the great **"Shoeless" Joe Jackson,** are banned from baseball by commissioner Kennesaw Mountain Landis.

1920
The New York Yankees purchase the contract of **Babe Ruth** from the Boston Red Sox. "The Curse of the Bambino" prevents the Red Sox from winning a World Series since.

The National Football League (NFL) forms in Canton, Ohio. The original league has 14 teams.

1926
Gertrude Ederle becomes the first woman to swim the English Channel. Her time is nearly five hours faster than the previous five men who made the crossing.

1927
Babe Ruth of the New York Yankees hits 60 home runs in one season, breaking his own single-season record.

His total is more than 12 *teams* hit during the season. Ruth retires with 714 career home runs, also a record at the time.

1928
Ty Cobb retires from baseball with a lifetime .366 average that still stands as a record today. Cobb also retired with the career record for hits (4,189) and runs (2,246).

1930
Uruguay hosts and wins the first soccer World Cup. The event has been held every four years since.

Bobby Jones wins "Grand Slam" of golf by capturing the U.S. and British Opens and Amateurs.

1931
Knute Rockne dies in a plane crash. He finishes with a 121-12-5 record, a winning percentage of .881. Rockne led Notre Dame to five unbeaten and untied seasons.

1932
The Negro National League is formed. This is the first "major" league set up for African-American players.

Babe Didrikson Zaharias wins three gold medals at the Summer Olympics in Los Angeles, California. She sets new world records in the javelin throw and 80-meter hurdles.

1936
Sonja Henie wins the Winter Olympics gold medal for women's figure skating for the third consecutive time.

Jesse Owens wins four gold medals in track and field at the Summer Olympics in Berlin, Germany. Owens' feat comes as a shock to German dictator Adolf Hitler.

1937
Don Budge wins tennis's "Grand Slam." He is the first player to win Wimbledon and the Australian, French, and U.S. championships in the same calendar year.

1938
Helen Wills wins the final of her 19 "Grand Slam" singles tennis titles. She wins eight Wimbledons, seven U.S. Opens, and four French Opens.

The great **Joe Louis** knocks out German fighter **Max Schmeling.** The victory carries extra meaning as it also marks a win against Nazi Germany.

1939
The first baseball game is televised. The game features Cincinnati and Brooklyn.

On July 4, **Lou Gehrig** gives his famous farewell speech. He dies soon after from Amyotrophic Lateral Sclerosis (ALS), now called Lou Gehrig's Disease.

1941

Ted Williams of the Boston Red Sox hits .406. He is the last player to hit over .400 for an entire season.

Joe DiMaggio of the New York Yankees hits safely in 56 consecutive games. He breaks the record of 44 set by Wee Willie Keeler.

1943

The All American Girls Professional Baseball League is formed. At its peak in 1948 the league boasts 10 teams.

1945

Brooklyn Dodgers' executive **Branch Rickey** signs **Jackie Robinson** to a minor league contract.

1946

The color line in football is broken. Woody Strode and Kenny Washington play for the Rams and Marion Motley and Bill Willis join the Browns.

The Basketball Association of America is founded. Within three years it becomes the National Basketball Association (NBA).

1947

Jackie Robinson breaks the color barrier in baseball. This heroic ballplayer is subjected to harsh treatment from fans, fellow ballplayers, and even teammates.

1949

The Ladies' Professional Golf Association (LPGA) forms. **Babe Didrikson Zaharias** is a co-founder.

1957

Althea Gibson becomes the first African American to win Wimbledon and U.S. tennis championships. She repeats her feat the next year.

1958

Baseball's Brooklyn Dodgers move to Los Angeles and New York Giants move to San Francisco. The moves devastate long-time fans of each team.

What is now called the "greatest game ever played" is won by the Baltimore Colts in sudden-death overtime over the New York Giants 23-17. The game is widely televised and has much to do with the growth in popularity of football.

1959

Daytona 500 is run for the first time. It now is one of the most watched sporting events in the United States.

The American Football League (AFL) is founded. The league brings professional football to many new markets.

1960

Sugar Ray Robinson retires from boxing. During his career he wins the welterweight title once and holds the middleweight title five times. His lifetime record is 182-19.

Cassius Clay wins a gold medal in the light-heavyweight class at the Summer Olympics in Rome, Italy. Later, Clay throws his medal into the Ohio River as a reaction against the racial prejudice with which he is forced to contend.

Wilma Rudolph becomes the first American woman to win three gold medals in one Summer Olympics in Rome, Italy. She wins the 100- and 200-meter dashes and is a part of the winning 4 x 100 relay team.

1961

Roger Maris of the New York Yankees hits a single-season record 61 home runs. His record is tarnished by some observers because Maris plays a 162 game schedule while **Babe Ruth,** whose record he broke, played only 154 games in 1927.

1962

Wilt Chamberlain of the Philadelphia Warriors scores 100 points in a single game. He accomplishes this feat on March 2 against the New York Knicks. Chamberlain goes on to set another record when he averages 50.4 points per game during the same season and also leads the NBA in rebounding with 25.7 boards per game.

Oscar Robertson averages a triple double for an entire NBA season. He averages 30.8 points, 12.5 rebounds, and 11.4 assists per game.

1964

Cassius Clay scores a technical knockout of **Sonny Liston** to win the heavyweight championship. The victory is seen as a gigantic upset at the time. The day after his victory over Liston, Clay announces that he is a member of the Nation of Islam. He also announces that he is changing his name to **Muhammad Ali.**

1965

Star running back of the Cleveland Browns, **Jim Brown,** retires to pursue an acting career. He leaves the game holding the record for most career rushing yards, 12,312, in only eight seasons.

1966

The Boston Celtics win their eighth consecutive championship. No other major sports franchise has won this many consecutive titles.

Texas Western beats Kentucky 72-65 for the NCAA basketball championship. The champions feature an all-African American starting five while Kentucky starts five white players.

1967

First Iditarod dog sledding race held. The race begins as a 56 mile race, but by 1973 it evolves into a 1,152 mile trek between Anchorage and Nome, Alaska.

Charlie Sifford becomes the first African American to win on the PGA golf tour when he captures the Greater Hartford Open.

The first Super Bowl is played between the Green Bay Packers and Kansas City Chiefs. It is originally called the AFL-NFL World Championship Game.

1968

Bill Russell becomes the first African-American coach in any major sport. He leads the Boston Celtics to two championships as player-coach.

Americans **Tommie Smith** and John Carlos protest racism in the U.S. by raising black glove-clad fists on the medal stand after finishing first and third in the 200-meters at the Mexico City Olympics. The two are suspended from competition.

Eunice Kennedy Shriver begins the Special Olympics. The program grows into an international showcase for mentally challenged athletes.

The "Heidi" game becomes a piece of sports history as fans in the East miss the Oakland Raiders's thrilling comeback against the New York Jets. NBC decides to leave the game with 50 seconds left to start the movie *Heidi* on time at 7:00 p.m. ET. The network is barraged with calls complaining about the decision.

The American Football League (AFL) and National Football League (NFL) merge. The league retains the NFL name and splits teams into American and National conferences.

1969

Rod Laver of Australia wins the tennis "Grand Slam" for the second time in his career. He also won the Slam in 1962 as an amateur.

1970

Pele plays in fourth World Cup for his home country of Brazil.

On September 21, ABC's Monday Night Football debuts. The game features a contest between the Cleveland Browns and New York Jets. **Howard Cosell** and Don Meredith are the commentators.

1971

Gordie Howe, "Mister Hockey," retires from the NHL. At the time he holds career records for goals (801), assists (1,049), and points (1,850). Howe goes on to play seven more seasons in the World Hockey Association (WHA).

1972

Congress passes the Education Amendment Act, which includes Title IX. Title IX bans sex discrimination in federally funded schools in academics and athletics. The new law changes the landscape of college athletics, as more playing opportunities and scholarships are open to women.

Secretariat wins horse racing's Triple Crown, setting records for every race. He is the only horse to run under two minutes in the Kentucky Derby and wins the Belmont Stakes by a record 31 lengths.

Mark Spitz wins seven Olympic swimming gold medals. He sets the record for most medals won at a single Olympic Games.

Black September, an Arab terrorist group, kills eleven Israeli athletes held captive in the Olympic Village. The Games are suspended the following morning for a memorial service, after which, with the approval of the Israelis, they reconvene.

Out of respect to the Native American population, Stanford University changes its nickname from Indians to Cardinals. Other schools do the same, but professional teams do not.

1973

UCLA wins its seventh consecutive NCAA basketball championship. Coached by the legendary **John Wooden,** the Bruins during one stretch win 88 games in a row. UCLA goes on to win three more titles under Wooden.

Billie Jean King defeats Bobby Riggs in a "Battle of the Sexes" tennis match. Riggs, a self-proclaimed "male chauvinist," is 25 years older than King.

Running back **O.J. Simpson** of the Buffalo Bills becomes the first NFL player to ever rush for over 2,000 yards in a season. Simpson is the only player to accomplish this feat in 14 games.

The Miami Dolphins finish the NFL season with a perfect 17-0 record. The Dolphins close out their season with a 14-7 victory over the Washington Redskins in

Super Bowl VII. No NFL team before or since has finished a season with a perfect record.

1974

Hank Aaron breaks **Babe Ruth**'s career home run record. Aaron has to overcome not only history but racist attacks as he hits number 715 in Atlanta.

Muhammad Ali stuns the world with his eighth round knockout of **George Foreman** in "The Rumble in the Jungle." Ali uses the "rope-a-dope" strategy to wear out the much more powerful Foreman.

1975

Muhammad Ali defeats **Joe Frazier** in the "Thrilla in Manila." The victory was Ali's second in three fights with Frazier.

Pitchers Dave McNally and Andy Messersmith win their challenge to baseball's "reserve clause." Arbitrator Peter Seitz rules that once a player completes one season without a contract he can become a free agent. This is a landmark decision that opens the door to free agency in professional sports.

1976

Romanian **Nadia Comaneci** scores perfect 10s seven times in gymnastics competition at the Summer Olympics in Montreal, Quebec, Canada. This marks the first time that a 10 has ever been awarded.

Kornelia Ender of East Germany wins four Olympic gold medals in swimming. Her time in every one of her races breaks a world record.

1977

Janet Guthrie qualifies on the final day for a starting spot in the Indianapolis 500. She becomes the first woman to compete in the Memorial Day classic.

A.J. Foyt wins the Indianapolis 500 for a record-setting fourth time.

1978

Nancy Lopez wins a record-breaking five LPGA tournaments in a row during her rookie season. She goes on to win nine tournaments for the year.

1979

ESPN launches the first all-sports television network. The network now carries all the major professional and college sports.

1980

The **U.S. men's Olympic ice hockey team** defeats the heavily favored team from the Soviet Union, 4-3, in what becomes known as the "Miracle on Ice." The Americans go on to win the gold medal.

Eric Heiden of the U.S. wins five individual gold medals in speed skating at the Winter Olympics in Lake Placid, New York. No one before or since has won five individual events in a single Olympic Games. No other skater has ever swept the men's speed skating events.

The U.S. and its allies boycott the Summer Olympics in Moscow, USSR. The Americans cite the Soviet invasion of Afghanistan as the reason for their action.

1981

Richard Petty wins the Daytona 500. His win is his record-setting seventh victory in the big race.

1982

Louisiana State defeats Cheney State for the title in the first NCAA women's basketball championship.

Wayne Gretzky, the "Great One," scores 92 goals in a season. He adds 120 assists to end the season with 212 points, the first time anyone has scored over 200 points in one season.

Shirley Muldowney wins last of three National Hot Rod Association (NHRA) top fuel championships. Muldowney won 17 NHRA titles during her career.

1983

Australia II defies the odds and wins the America's Cup after 132 years of domination by the U.S. defenders. The New York Yacht Club had won 24 straight competitions.

1984

The Soviet Union and its allies (except Romania) boycott the Summer Olympics held in Los Angeles, California. Many believe this is in response to the U.S. boycott of Moscow Games in 1980.

Carl Lewis repeats **Jesse Owens**'s feat of winning four gold medals in track and field at the Summer Olympics in Los Angeles, California. Lewis wins the same events as Owens: the 100- and 200-meters, the long jump, and the 4 x 100m relay.

Joan Benoit Samuelson wins the first ever Olympic marathon for women. Her winning time over the 26.2 mile course is 2:24.52.

Dan Marino of the Miami Dolphins throws for 5,084 yards and 48 touchdowns, both NFL single-season records.

1985

On September 11, **Pete Rose** breaks **Ty Cobb**'s record for career hits when he gets his 4,192nd hit. Rose finishes his career with 4,256 hits. Unfortunately, Rose is banned from baseball after allegations of his gambling on the sport come to light.

1986

Nancy Lieberman is the first woman to play in a men's professional league - the United States Basketball League.

Jack Nicklaus wins his record 18th and final major championship at the Masters. During his illustrious career he wins 6 Masters, 4 U.S. Opens, 3 British Opens, and 5 PGA Championships.

1988

Greg Louganis wins gold medals in both platform and springboard diving. He is the first person to win both diving medals in two consecutive Olympics. Louganis wins despite hitting his head on the board during the springboard competition.

Florence Griffith-Joyner sets world records in both the 100- and 200-meter dashes.

Steffi Graf of Germany wins the "Golden Slam" of tennis by winning each of the "Grand Slam" events in addition to the Olympic gold medal. Graf retires with a record 22 victories in "Grand Slam" events.

1992

Jackie Joyner-Kersee establishes herself as the most dominant athlete in the five-event heptathlon, winning her second consecutive Summer Olympics gold medal in the event. Joyner-Kersee had set the world record at 7,291 points and held the next five highest scores.

Cito Gaston becomes the first African-American manager to take his team to the World Series. He is also the first to manage the world champions as his Blue Jays win the title the same year.

1993

Michael Jordan retires from basketball after leading the Bulls to three consecutive NBA championships. He says he is retiring to try to play professional baseball.

Julie Krone becomes the first woman jockey to win a Triple Crown horse race. She rides Colonial Affair to victory in the Belmont Stakes.

The Miami Dolphins defeat the Philadelphia Eagles 19-14, giving Dolphins coach **Don Shula** his 325th win. The victory moved Shula into first place on the all-time list, beating the record held by **George Halas** of the Chicago Bears.

1994

The husband of figure skater **Tonya Harding** hires two men to attack Harding's rival, **Nancy Kerrigan.** The men strike at the U.S. Figure Skating Championships in Detroit, Michigan. Kerrigan is knocked out of the competition, but still qualifies for the Olympic team.

Speedskater **Bonnie Blair** wins her fifth Winter Olympic gold medal, the most by any American woman. She won the 500-meters in 1988 then won both the 500- and 1000-meters in 1992 and 1994. Blair won a total of seven Olympic medals.

Pole-vaulter **Sergei Bubka** of the Ukraine sets the world record in the pole vault with a jump of 6.14 meters. Bubka holds the top 14 jumps of all-time in the event.

A baseball player's strike wipes out the end of the regular season and, for the first time since 1904, the World Series. The strike hurts baseball's popularity for years to come.

1995

Michael Jordan returns to the Chicago Bulls. He leads Chicago to three consecutive championships then retires again in 1998. Jordan retires as a five-time winner of the NBA Most Valuable Player Award and six-time winner of the NBA Finals MVP.

Extreme Games (X Games) are held for first time in Rhode Island and Vermont. The X Games and Winter X Games have been held every year since.

1996

Sprinter **Michael Johnson** wins a rare double at the Summer Olympics in Atlanta, Georgia. He wins both the 200- and 400-meter races, the first man ever to accomplish this feat at the Olympics.

Carl Lewis wins the long jump gold medal at the Summer Olympics in Atlanta, Georgia. It is the athlete's ninth gold medal, tying him for the most all-time with Finnish track legend Paavo Nurmi and Soviet gymnast **Larisa Latynina.**

Jackie Joyner-Kersee wins a bronze medal in the long jump at the Summer Olympics in Atlanta, Georgia. This brings her medal total for three Olympic Games to six, making her the most decorated female track and field athlete in U.S. history.

U.S. women capture the first-ever women's soccer Olympic gold medal.

Dan Marino retires. He leaves the game holding the NFL career record for yards (51,636) and touchdown passes (369).

1997

The Women's National Basketball Association (WNBA) is formed.

Tiger Woods is only 21 when he wins the Masters by a record-shattering 12 strokes. He also sets a record by shooting 18 under par.

1998

Team USA captures the first women's ice hockey gold medal at the Winter Olympics in Nagano, Japan.

Cal Ripken, Jr. breaks **Lou Gehrig**'s iron man record when he plays in his 2,632nd game on September 19.

1999

Vote-buying scandal rips the International Olympic Committee (IOC). Several IOC members are forced to quit because they took bribes from cities hoping to host the Olympics.

Wayne Gretzky retires with NHL records that may never be broken. He holds or shares 61 single-season and career records including the career records for most goals (894), most assists (1,963) and points (2,857). Gretzky also holds the single-season records for goals (92), assists (163), and points (215).

2000

New York Yankees win their 26th World Series. The win makes the Yankees the winningest organization in sports history.

2001

Tiger Woods becomes the first golfer to hold the championship for all four professional "Grand Slam" events when he wins the Masters. His accomplishment is not called a "Grand Slam" because all his victories do not occur in the same calendar year.

Roman Sebrle of the Czech Republic earns the title of "world's greatest athlete" by setting a world record in the 10-event decathlon. His final score is 9,026 points, making him the first man to surpass the 9,000 barrier.

Barry Bonds of the San Francisco Giants hits 73 home runs, a new major league single-season record. The next season he becomes only the fourth major leaguer to hit over 600 career home runs.

Michael Jordan returns to the NBA, this time playing for the Washington Wizards, a team in which he holds partial ownership. His 30.4 career scoring average is the highest of all-time.

2002

Brazil wins record fifth World Cup championship.

Coach **Phil Jackson** of the Los Angeles Lakers sets a record by coaching his ninth NBA champion. He won six titles as coach of the Chicago Bulls and three with Los Angeles. Jackson also tied **Scotty Bowman** of the NHL for most professional titles won as coach.

Hockey coach **Scotty Bowman** retires. He holds career records for most regular season (1,244) and playoff (223) wins.

Lance Armstrong wins the Tour de France cycling race for the fourth straight year. His victory comes only six years after doctors gave him little chance of surviving testicular cancer that had spread to his lymph nodes and brain.

Pete Sampras breaks his own record by winning his 14th Grand Slam tournament, the U.S. Open. He defeats rival **Andre Agassi** in the final.

Emmitt Smith of the Dallas Cowboys sets a new NFL career rushing record with 17,162 yards. Smith passes the great **Walter Payton** of the Chicago Bears.

Jerry Rice scores the 200th NFL touchdown of his remarkable career, the only man to reach this plateau. He ends the 2002 season holding the records for receptions (1,456), yards receiving (21,597), and touchdowns (202).

2003

Serena Williams wins four "Grand Slam" tennis championships in a row. She defeats her sister, **Venus Williams,** in the final of every event.

Connie Mack
1862-1956

American baseball manager

Baseball was manager Connie Mack's lifelong career. He retired as manager of the Philadelphia Athletics in 1950 after fifty years on the job, spanning the first half of the twentieth century. Mack was known and loved for his gentlemanly conduct both in and out of the dugout. He represented a fatherly figure to his players and built teams through his superb ability as a baseball talent scout. From the dugout, he controlled every play with the wave of a scorecard and was far ahead of his time in tracking where batters hit the ball off particular pitches. He was also known as a shrewd businessman who sold off his best players to keep his team operating in the black and then later rebuilt the team when the economy improved. Mack's Athletics vacillated between long losing streaks and brilliant winning streaks, taking home five World Series championships and nine American League pennants.

From Player to Manager

Connie Mack was born Cornelius Alexander McGillicuddy on December 22, 1862, in East Brookfield, Massachusetts. He was the third of seven children of Irish immigrants Michael and Mary McKillop McGillicuddy. Cornelius's father died when the boy was a teen, and he went to work in a shoe factory to help support the family. He grew up so tall and thin that friends nicknamed him "Slats." Cornelius became the catcher on his town team, which won the Central Massachusetts championship. In 1884, at age twenty-one, he joined the Meriden, Connecticut team as catcher, making $90 a month. His mother disapproved, because at that time baseball was characterized by drinking, gambling, and fighting. Cornelius reassured her that he would not take part in these activities. True to his word, he never drank or swore, and he forbade his players from drinking alcohol during the baseball season. He later said, "There's room for gentlemen in every profession, and my profession is baseball."

Because Cornelius's name was too long to fit in a newspaper box score, it was shortened to "Connie

Connie Mack

Mack," and the name stuck for life. At 6'1" and 150 pounds, straight-backed and blue-eyed, Mack was popular with players and fans. Although he played every position except pitcher and third base, Mack was at his best as a catcher. He came to have great respect for pitchers and believed that pitching made up eighty percent of a game. His ability to analyze pitching became one of the skills that made him so successful as a manager.

After playing for Pittsburgh for four years, Mack was made manager as well as catcher. In 1897 his friend Ban Johnson offered him the managerial job with the minor league Milwaukee team; Mack held that position for four years. When Johnson founded the American League, he offered Mack the Philadelphia franchise. Mack kept

Chronology

1862	Born December 22 in East Brookfield, Massachusetts
1884	Joins professional Meriden team of Connecticut State League as catcher
1885	Plays for Hartford in Eastern League; traded to Washington of National League
1887	Marries Margaret Hogan on November 2; they will have three sons
1890	Joins Brotherhood of Professional Baseball Players in fighting for players' rights; revolt results in formation of Players' League
1890	Invests $500 savings in Buffalo team of Players' League; loses it all when league collapses
1892	Wife, Margaret, dies
1894	Becomes manager of Pittsburgh Pirates of the National League
1896	Is dismissed from Pittsburgh; accepts Ban Johnson's offer to manage the Milwaukee team in the Western League
1901	Buys minority interest in Milwaukee team and moves it to Philadelphia after Johnson renames league American League; team becomes the Philadelphia Athletics
1910	Athletics win first World Series and league pennant
1910	Marries Katherine Hallahan; they will have five children
1914	Facing financial difficulties, Mack sells or releases his star players, resulting in a seven-year losing streak for the Athletics
1926	Athletics play first Sunday game ever in Philadelphia, after Mack and Tom Shibe decide Sunday baseball is allowed and get court injunction to prevent police interference
1929	After Mack rebuilds the team, Athletics win league pennant and World Series; Mack is given the Edward W. Bok Prize
1930-31	Athletics win two more pennants and another World Series (1930)
1933	Great Depression forces Mack to again sell star players
1937	Becomes president and treasurer of Philadelphia Athletics, but team continues to lose
1937	Elected to Baseball Hall of Fame
1940	Acquires controlling interest in the Athletics from the Ben Shibe family for $42,000
1944	Voted favorite manager of sportswriters and players
1950	Mack retires from managing, at almost 88 years old; his sons take control of Athletics, although Mack remains president
1953	Shibe Park is renamed Connie Mack Stadium, in spite of Mack's objections
1954	Resigns as president of the Athletics, at age 92; sons persuade him to sign from his sickbed for the sale of the Athletics to Arnold M. Johnson of Chicago
1955	Johnson moves Athletics to Kansas City, Missouri
1956	Mack dies on February 8, at age 93, at daughter's home in Germantown, Pennsylvania

Awards and Accomplishments

1910-11, 1913, 1929-30	As manager of Philadelphia Athletics, wins World Series
1930	Edward W. Bok Prize for service to the city and its people after Athletics win World Series in 1929
1933	Chosen to manage first American League team in All-Star Game
1937	Inducted into Baseball Hall of Fame as one of fifteen Builders of Baseball
1938-39	May 17 designated Connie Mack Day in Pennsylvania; George M. Cohan writes song "Connie Mack Is the Grand Old Name"
1941	Shibe Park renamed Connie Mack Stadium
1944	Voted favorite manager of players and sportswriters; tribute is held before Athletics home game, featuring Mack's "dream team" in their old uniforms
1950	Named Honorary Manager of the All-Star Game by Major League baseball

blem and leading it to an American League pennant the following year.

The Athletics' first great winning streak came in 1910-1914, when they won four pennants and three World Series, with Mack's "$100,000 infield" and pitcher Chief Bender. However, with the coming of World War I and in competition with the wealthy Federal League, Mack was forced to sell some of his best players, and the team fell to eighth and last places over the next seven seasons.

In 1925, at age sixty-two and basking in the Golden Age of sports, Mack rebuilt a powerful team. It included catcher Mickey Cochrane, pitchers Lefty Grove and Rube Walberg, hitter Al Simmons, and outfielder Mule Haas. The Athletics won two more World Series (1929 and 1930) and three more pennants. Mack stunned everyone by using Howard Ehmke as his starting pitcher in the 1929 World Series game against the Chicago Cubs. Ehmke, age thirty-five and a second-line pitcher, set a World Series record by striking out thirteen for a 3-1 win. Mack knew that Ehmke could pitch to the Cubs' right-handed hitters.

After his second winning streak, the Great Depression forced Mack to again sell off his best players, and the team dropped to the bottom of the league for the next twelve years. By 1940, Mack had acquired a majority interest in the A's from the Shibe family, and Mack's sons were team executives and coaches.

Known as the Grand Old Man of Baseball and the Tall Tactician, Mack always appeared in the dugout wearing a crisp blue suit and a high, starched white collar and tie. In his seventies, Mack was expected to retire, but he held on until 1950, nearing 88. However, by this time the Phillies had become Philadelphia's favored team. After the 1954 season, Mack's sons sold the Athletics to Chicago businessman Arnold M. Johnson. Mack signed the papers from his bed during an illness, supposedly unaware that Johnson planned to move the

twenty-five percent and funded the rest through a partnership with Ben Shibe, the inventor of ball-winding machines. The Philadelphia Athletics played their first game under Mack's management in 1901.

Fifty Years of Ups and Downs

Over the next fifty years, the Athletics played in forty-three World Series games, winning five series, in 1910, 1911, 1913, 1929, and 1930. They brought home nine American League pennants. The A's were dubbed a "white elephant" by McGraw after Mack bought top hitter Napoleon Lajoie and the team only came in fourth place in their first year. Mack showed both humor and resiliency by making the white elephant his team's em-team to Kansas City, Missouri. Mack died fifteen months later, at age 93.

Connie Mack operated his baseball teams as a business, relying on their success for the support of his family. Thriving and surviving in an age when baseball lacked the facilities, transportation, financing, and media coverage of today, he is considered one of the great innovators of the game. Known for his kindness and his tact in dealing with players—he once paid off a pitcher's debts and got a shortstop paroled from prison—he endeared his team members into performing for him. Although sometimes viewed as a "pinchpenny" who broke apart championship teams, he operated one of the most highly paid teams in early baseball. Mack once wrote about entering baseball as a career: "Looking back at it, I can see every reason why I should not have taken the jump and only one reason why I did. Of course, I have made my living out of it, but more important than this, I love the game."

SELECTED WRITINGS BY MACK:

How To Play Base-Ball, Brewer, Barse & Co., 1908.
Connie Mack's Baseball Book, Knopf, 1950; rev. ed. published as *From Sandlot to Big League: Connie Mack's Baseball Book,* 1960.
My 66 Years in the Big Leagues: The Great Story of America's National Game, Winston, 1950.

FURTHER INFORMATION

Books

Encyclopedia of World Biography Supplement, Volume 19. "Connie Mack." Detroit: Gale Group, 1999.
Koppett, Leonard. *The Man in the Dugout: Baseball's Top Managers and How They Got That Way.* New York: Crown, 1993.
Voigt, David Quentin. "Connie Mack." *Dictionary of American Biography, Supplement* 6: 1956-1960. American Council of Learned Societies, 1980.

Periodicals

"Connie Mack, Mr. Baseball, Dies in Philadelphia at the Age of 93." *New York Times* (February 9, 1956): 1,31.
Stoddard, Maynard. "Baseball's Closest Calls." *Saturday Evening Post* (July-August 1989): 30.

Other

Baseball-Reference.com. http://www.baseball-reference.com/ (October 14, 2002), "Connie Mack."
Macht, Norman L. "Connie Mack." Baseball Library.com. http://www.pubdim.net/baseball library/ballplayers/ (October 14, 2002).

Sketch by Ann H. Shurgin

John Madden

John Madden
1936-

American football coach

Although John Madden became known as a great analyst and broadcaster for NFL (National Football League) games on the CBS (Columbia Broadcasting System), Fox, and ABC (American Broadcasting Companies), he began his career as a coach for the AFL (American Football League; later NFL) Oakland Raiders. Madden was a well-respected coach of the Raiders for ten years, winning the Super Bowl in 1977. He was the youngest NFL coach to win a Super Bowl. Madden capitalized on his celebrity by appearing in a number of commercials over the years. He was also known for his famous bus that he traveled in when he refused to fly in 1979.

Madden was born on April 10, 1936, in Austin, Minnesota, the son of Earl and Mary (O'Flaherty) Madden. Madden's father was an auto mechanic who wanted a better life for his family. To that end, he moved them to Daly City, California, in 1942 to get a better job.

Growing up in Daly City, Madden's father encouraged his son's interest in sports. Madden played football, as well as basketball and baseball at Jefferson High

School. However, much of his equipment was from castoffs. One job that Madden had in high school was as a golf caddy at the San Francisco Golf Club. It was there that he got the idea that successful people often went to college, and decided that he would be the first person in his family to attend.

Played College Football

Because of his prowess on the football field, Madden was given a football scholarship to the University of Oregon. He studied pre-law for a year, but was kept out of varsity competition because of a knee operation. After a year, he realized he did not like his pre-law studies and left the school and his scholarship behind.

Changing his educational path, Madden decided to pursue an education degree. To that end, he enrolled one semester at the College of San Mateo, then briefly attended Grays Harbor College. He resumed his football career when he transferred to California Polytechnic in San Luis Obispo, California. There he was a two-year starter as both an offensive and defensive tackle in football, as well as a catcher on the baseball team.

Drafted by the Eagles

In 1958, Madden was drafted by the Philadelphia Eagles in the 21st round. His one season as a professional player ended when he suffered a knee injury at training camp in 1959.

Began Coaching Career

Though Madden's professional playing career was over, he did not leave football. He returned to California Polytechnic to earn a master's degree in education. It was at California Polytechnic that Madden met his future wife, Virginia Fields, who was studying for her master's degree and teaching school. They later married and had two sons, Mike and Joe. Madden was also employed as a physical education teacher in Santa Maria, California, and had begun a coaching career on the college level, becoming assistant coach at Allan Hancock Junior College.

In 1962, Madden was promoted to head coach at Hancock, spending two years there. His team posted a record of 12-6 during his tenure as head coach. In 1964, Madden moved on to San Diego State University, working as a defensive coordinator. He spent two years there, and the team had a record of 26-4.

Became Professional Coach

Madden was offered a job with AFL's Oakland Raiders in 1967 as a linebacker coach. His first year with the team was effective. The Raiders made it to Super Bowl II, but lost to the Green Bay Packers. In 1969, Madden was promoted to head coach of the Raiders. The previous coach, John Rauch, had left the team because he believed the team's owner, **Al Davis** was interfering with the way he ran the team. When Madden took over as head coach, he was only 33 years old and the youngest coach in AFL history.

Madden was a successful head coach, spending ten years with the Raiders. The team won the Western Division title seven times, reached the playoffs eight times, and won at least ten games a season for seven seasons. In his rookie season as a coach, he posted a record of 12-1-1, and was named coach of the year. However, the Raiders lost in the AFL championship game to the Kansas City Chiefs, 17-7.

As a head coach, Madden had a flamboyant personality. He argued with officials over calls and was something of a spectacle on the sidelines during the games. But he also believed that communication was important, making it a point to talk to each of his players every day. It was Madden who kept the team together in the face of Davis and other pressures. Bill Toomay, a former player in Oakland told Ken Denlinger of *Washington Post* upon Madden's retirement, "He (Madden) is not a pretentious man. He has great insight into people, he's able to be successful with a broad spectrum of individuals. If the head coach wasn't able to do that, this team would have fallen apart years ago. … Madden was the cement that held it together."

Among Madden's best seasons as a coach was 1976-1977, when the Raiders posted a record of 13-1, won the AFC (American Football Conference) championship by defeating the Pittsburgh Steelers, and played in Super Bowl XI. Oakland won the Super Bowl, defeating the Minnesota Vikings 32-14. Madden was the youngest NFL coach to win a Super Bowl. He would later say that this was the highlight of his life in football. Madden told Walter Roessing of *Saturday Evening Post,* "The great thing about winning the Super Bowl was that it meant I had won every game in football there was to win—preseason, Pro Bowl, play-off, Super Bowl."

Retired as Coach

In 1979, after the 1978-179 season ended, Madden abruptly retired as coach of the Raiders. He was emotionally stressed and burned out. Madden had a bleeding ulcer and a strained relationship with his sons which he wanted to repair. Over the course of his coaching career with the Raiders, he posted a record of 103-32-7, with a .750 winning percentage. This marked the first time a head coach had spent ten years with the same team and had won more than 100 games. When he retired, Madden said he would never coach again.

Hired as Television Commentator

Madden spent some time at home, rather bored. He could not tolerate watching games in the stands. His agent soon convinced him to try television commentary on NFL games for CBS. Madden agreed to give it a try, though it was a big adjustment for someone who had spent two decades on the sidelines. Madden began as a fill-in, but his colorful personality worked well for television. He was very observant in his expert analysis, revealing his intelligence and humor. He also did his homework. To prepare for television, he asked others in the business for advice.

Despite his initial reluctance, Madden told Roessing, "When I did my first game, I immediately realized this was what I wanted to do. You see, I can't live without football. It's been part of my life since I was a little kid. I want to be involved in football and announcing the rest of my life."

Madden soon became better known for his commentary than for his outstanding coaching career. By the early 1980s, he was CBS's chief NFL analyst and teamed with Pat Summerall, with whom he would work until 2002. Madden and Summerall covered the big games of the week and the Super Bowl. Madden con-

John Madden, being carried off field

tributed a new approach to the way analysts approached game coverage. When he began in the late 1970s, little research was done. By the early 1980s, he used some techniques similar to coaches to break down the game or games he and Summerall would be analyzing for the week. Preparation was important to him and he took pride in doing it well.

Madden was successful because he could communicate his ideas about football in way his audience could understand. As Sarah Pileggi wrote in *Sports Illustrated,* "Talking is what Madden does best. He is a born communicator. His talent for putting thoughts into words that engage the attention of a particular audience and his special knack for infusing these words with his own personality have been the keys to his success not only as a broadcaster but also as a coach." This technique and Madden's approach came to define a new era of sports broadcasting.

Madden's work as analyst had several unexpected bonuses. He had an offer to have a recurring role on the television situation comedy *Cheers* but did not take it because it would have interfered with his football commitments. A popular video game was developed that bore his name, and he was a popular motivational speaker. His most visible bonus was in commercials. He took on many of the amazing number of commercial endorsement offers he received, representing Ace Hardware and Miller Lite beer for a number of years, as well as Tinactin, and many other products and services. Because of

---

Related Biography: Sports Announcer Pat Summerall

John Madden's play-by-play partner in the broadcast booth for over 20 years was Pat Summerall. The pair split after the 2002 Super Bowl (the eighth they called together), with Madden signing with ABC (American Broadcasting Companies) for *Monday Night Football* while Summerall remained with Fox handling regional broadcasts. Like Madden, Summerall had a playing career in professional football; he was drafted by the Detroit Lions in 1952 after an outstanding playing career at the University of Arkansas. Summerall, a place kicker and tight end, played with the Chicago Cardinals from 1952 through 1957, then the New York Giants from 195 until 1961. Summerall scored 567 points over the course of his career and played in the three NFL Championship games. After his playing career ended, Summerall worked in radio as the sports director and morning news host for WCBS Radio in New York City, and did work for the CBS Radio Network. In 1971, Summerall made the move to television, again with CBS, and was teamed with Madden in 1981. Summerall covered not only football, but also was the network's lead voice for golf coverage from 1968 to 1994, and covered tennis as well. Over the course of his career, Summerall garnered numerous broadcasting awards.

---

the sheer number of spots he appeared in, Madden eventually built a $1 million studio near his home so he would not have to travel to tape the commercials.

Travel was a big issue in Madden's life. He did not like to fly, and had been diagnosed as claustrophobic. His problems with claustrophobia began in 1960 when football players from his alma mater were killed in a plane crash that Madden should have been on. He suffered through flights while a coach, but refused to fly after November 1979. Early in his broadcasting career, Madden traveled to his CBS assignments by train, a mode of travel he enjoyed because it allowed him to interact with people. He later had an endorsement deal with Greyhound that gave him his own bus. After the deal ended, he kept the bus but attracted other sponsors to cover expenses. Though the bus was less people friendly, he got to see some of America on his travels and find his own favorite spots. Madden's bus became a signature part of his identity as a broadcaster.

Signed with Fox

In 1994, Madden (and Summerall) signed with Fox after the network bought the rights to football in 1993. He had considered going to ABC for *Monday Night Football* or NBC (National Broadcasting Company) which also had some football rights. (CBS lost their rights, though they regained some of them in a later deal.) Madden's deal was worth $8,000,000 a year over four years, a testament to his power and popularity as a broadcaster. With his new contract, Madden built his own customized bus, dubbed the Madden Cruiser. In 1998, when the contract expired, Madden signed a five-year deal with Fox, though he again thought about moving to ABC. Madden also continued to make millions per year for endorsements, remaining at the top of his game.

In 2002, after the Super Bowl, Madden and Summerall decided to call it quits as a duo. Summerall had decided

to retire from full-time work at Fox (though he did still do regional football broadcasts for the network). After considering his options, Madden finally decided to sign with ABC to do *Monday Night Football* broadcasts with Al Michaels. Madden was expected to raise the ratings of the show, which had been on the decline for several years.

Madden was well respected as a broadcaster, winning 13 of the 15 Emmy Awards he was nominated for over the course of his career, as well as a number of other awards. He planned to continue working as a broadcaster as long as he was physically capable of doing it. He told Michael Silver of *Sports Illustrated,* "It's fun, and it is my life and my passion and my recreation—it's everything. I was at a golf tournament, and I met a guy who was a year behind me in high school, and he's retiring. I said, 'Let me get this straight: You're retiring, and I just signed a four-year contract. One of us is going in the wrong direction.'"

CONTACT INFORMATION

Address: c/o 1 West 72nd St., New York, NY 10023.
Online: allmadden.com.

SELECTED WRITINGS BY MADDEN:

(With Dave Anderson) *Hey, Wait a Minute, I Wrote a Book,*New York: Villard Books, 1984.

(With Dave Anderson) *One Size Doesn't Fit All.* New York: Random House, 1985.

(With Dave Anderson) *One Knee Equals Two Feet: (And Everything Else You Need to Know About Football).*New York: Villard, 1986.

(With Dave Anderson) *First Book of Football.* New York: Crown Publishers, 1988.

(With Peter Kaminsky) *John Madden's Ultimate Tailgating.*New York: Viking, 1988.

(With Dave Anderson) *All Madden: Hey I'm Talking Football,* New York: HarperCollins, 1996.

FURTHER INFORMATION

Books

Athletes and Coaches of Winter. New York: Macmillan Reference USA, 2000.

Hickok, Ralph. *A Who's Who of Sports Champions: Their Stories and Records.* Boston: Houghton Mifflin Company, 1995.

Porter, David L., editor. *Biographical Dictionary of American Sports: Football.* New York: Greenwood Press, 1995.

Periodicals

Bonko, Larry. "Monday Night Football's New Strategy John Madden Partners with Al Michaels in the ABC Booth." *Virginia Pilot* (September 9, 2002): E1.

Brady, Dave. "Madden: Forever, for Now." *Washington Post* (January 7, 1979): D6.

Callahan, Gerry. "Hey, They Love This Guy!" *Sports Illustrated* (January 19, 1998): 20.

Callahan, Tom. "I'm Just a Guy." *Time* (January 11, 1988): 82.

Denlinger, Ken. "'Inner Turmoil' Part of Madden." *Washington Post* (January 5, 1979): C1.

Isaacs, Stan. "Madden a Success as Color Man By Taking Advice: 'Be Yourself'." *Washington Post* (December 9, 1980): D5.

King, Peter. "Busman's Holiday." *Sports Illustrated* (November 26, 1990): 80.

Leerhsen, Charles. "John Madden on a Roll." *Newsweek* (January 9, 1984): 66.

"Madden Signs Five-Year Deal to Stay at Fox." *Rocky Mountain News* (January 16, 1998): 5C.

Pileggi, Sarah. "Hey, Wait a Minute! I Want to Talk." *Sports Illustrated* (September 1, 1983): 39.

Reilly, Rick. "Split Personalities." *Sports Illustrated* (September 30, 2002): 102.

Roessing, Walter. "Talking Is Their Game." *Saturday Evening Post* (April 1987): 64.

Rushin, Steve. "America's Sweetheart: Whether Cruising or Schmoozing, John Madden Is the U.S.A.'s Ambassador to Itself." *Sports Illustrated* (January 28, 2002): 17.

Sandomir, Richard. "Madden at the Top of His Game." *New York Times* (August 20, 1991): B17.

Silver, Michael. "Monday Evening Quarterback." *Sports Illustrated* (July 29, 2002): 34.

Souhan, Jim. "In Austin, Madden May Be Bigger than Spam; Birthplace Warmly Greets Broadcaster." *Star Tribune* (January 17, 1999): 3S.

Other

"John Madden—Analyst." Monday Night Football. http://espn.go.com/abcsports/mnf/columns/madden_john/bio.html (January 13, 2003).

"Pat Summerall Steps Down as John Madden's Partner." Fox Sports. http://foxsports.lycos.com/content/view?contentID=300866 (January 20, 2003).

Sketch by A. Petruso

Greg Maddux

Greg Maddux
1966-

American baseball player

Greg Maddux's record speaks for itself: he is simply one of the best pitchers ever to play the position. The first player ever to win four consecutive Cy Young Awards, he also shines defensively, as evidenced by his 13 consecutive Golden Glove Awards since 1990. In 2002, Maddux posted 16 wins, becoming only the second player after **Cy Young** to record fifteen or more wins for fifteen consecutive years. After retiring, Maddux is almost assured a spot in the Hall of Fame. At 6 foot 180 pounds, Maddux is not a powerhouse pitcher; his fastballs rarely reach 90 miles per hour. Yet he is a craftsman in the art of changing pitches and speeds to confuse hitters. Maddux uses a wide variety of pitches such as his cut fastball, slider, and circle change up with pinpoint accuracy to stay ahead of the count. One of his strengths lies in forcing hitters to hit ground balls by pitching to the lower part of the strike zone. Like most of his fellow Braves pitchers, Maddux is a respectable hitter at the plate.

Born on April 14, 1966, Maddux spent most of his childhood in Madrid, Spain, where his father, Dave, was stationed with the Air Force. Dave Maddux taught his son to throw and encouraged him to play baseball. When Greg was ten his family moved back to the States. They had the good fortune to be stationed in Las Vegas where Ralph Medar, a retired major-league scout, was developing young baseball talent in the area. Greg's older brother Mike spent Sundays practicing under Medar's watchful eye. However, Dave Maddux was anxious to show Medar his younger son's arm. After a month of attending Sunday practices with Mike, Dave urged Mr. Medar to let Greg play. Watching Greg throw his first pitch Medar said, "I don't know where the boy got those

Career Statistics

Yr	Team	W	L	ERA	GS	CG	SHO	IP	H	R	BB	SO
1986	ChC	2	4	5.52	5	1	0	31.0	44	20	11	20
1987	ChC	6	14	5.61	27	1	0	155.2	181	111	74	101
1988	ChC	18	8	3.18	34	9	3	249.0	230	97	81	140
1989	ChC	19	12	2.95	35	7	1	238.1	222	90	82	135
1990	ChC	15	15	3.46	35	8	2	237.0	242	116	71	144
1991	ChC	15	11	3.35	37	7	2	263.0	232	113	66	198
1992	ChC	20	11	2.18	35	9	4	268.0	201	68	70	199
1993	ATL	20	10	2.36	36	8	1	267.0	228	85	52	197
1994	ATL	16	6	1.56	25	10	3	202.0	150	44	31	156
1995	ATL	19	2	1.63	28	10	3	209.2	147	39	23	181
1996	ATL	15	11	2.72	35	5	1	245.0	225	85	28	172
1997	ATL	19	4	2.21	33	5	2	232.2	200	58	20	177
1998	ATL	18	9	2.22	34	9	5	251.0	201	75	45	204
1999	ATL	19	9	3.57	33	4	0	219.1	258	103	37	136
2000	ATL	19	9	3.00	35	6	3	249.1	225	91	42	190
2001	ATL	17	11	3.05	34	3	3	233.0	220	86	27	173
2002	ATL	16	6	2.62	34	0	0	199.1	194	67	45	118
TOTAL		273	152	2.83	535	102	33	3750.1	3400	1348	805	2641

ATL: Atlanta Braves; ChC: Chicago Cubs.

mechanics, but let me tell you this: Don't let anybody change those mechanics. He is going to be something."

Medar's Influence

Medar was a careful and thoughtful coach who saw a pitching future for Maddux. Rather than teaching Greg to throw a curveball, which can seriously injure young arms, he showed him how to throw a changeup at the age of 13. *Sports Illustrated* quoted Medar counseling Maddux that, "The changeup is not going to be a good pitch against high school hitters - you could just throw your fastball and get most of them out - but down the line a good changeup is harder to hit than any other pitch." However, Maddux was doubtful that he would ever make it as a major league pitcher and told *Sports Illustrated* that at the age of 15 he preferred hitting.

Nevertheless, Medar was convinced that Maddux's true talent was pitching. He told the young player, "You're probably never going to throw hard enough to overpower people." Then he showed Maddux the pitch that would eventually bring him overwhelming success in the major leagues, a fastball with sidearm delivery created by gripping only two of the baseball's seams rather than the usual four. It is not the fastest fastball, reaching only an unremarkable 87 miles per hour, but tends to veer away from left-handed batters in an unpredictable way. Sadly, Medar died before Maddux graduated high school and never got to see him deliver the pitch against major league hitters.

Getting His Start

Although he was an all-state baseball player in both his junior and senior years of high school, there were not many offers on the table at graduation time. The agent Scott Boras who wanted to represent Maddux advised him to go to college. The Chicago Cubs had made him a second-round draft choice and offered him a signing bonus. Maddux took their offer and vowed not to touch the money until he made the major leagues.

Maddux started in the rookie league with Pikesville in 1984, where he won six games and lost three with an earned-run average of 2.63. He pitched two shutouts during the twelve starts he made that year. In 1985, Maddux pitched 13 wins in 27 starts and 186 innings for Peoria in the Midwest League and made the league All-Star Team.

The Youngest Cub

On September 1, 1986 Maddux was called up to the Cubs. On his first day in the dugout as a major league player he was mistaken for a batboy. Cubs manager Gene Michael recalled the scene for *Sports Illustrated*, "I was standing in the dugout with one of my coaches... and [he] says to me 'Aren't you going to say hello to your new pitcher?' ...And I say, 'That's a batboy.'" 20-year-old Maddux was the youngest Cub to play in 19 years on September 2, 1986 when he pitched against the Houston Astros. He won the first game he started, against the Cincinnati Reds 11-3. In the end of September, Greg pitched the first ever match up of rookie brothers in the major leagues when he faced his brother Mike. It the first time rookie brothers had faced each other as pitching counterparts. The Cubs won 8-3.

A Standout Player

Despite his obvious talent, Greg Maddux had a shaky start in the major league and didn't become a standout player until May of 1988. He pitched a consecutive 26

Chronology

1966	Born in San Angelo, Texas
1977	Moves to Las Vegas and plays in Ralph Medar's development camp
1983-84	Pitches on the Nevada All-State Team
1984	Drafted by the Chicago Cubs as a second round choice
1986	Promoted to Triple-A status, named to the Baseball America Triple-A All-Star Team
1990	Achieves his first 20 game season
1992	Becomes a free-agent and signs with the Atlanta Braves
1995	Becomes the first pitcher since Walter Johnson in 1918-19 to maintain an ERA below 1.80 for two consecutive seasons
1997	Signs a 5 year $57.5 million dollar contract to continue with the Braves
2002	Wins his 13th Golden Glove Award
2003	Asks for $16 million in arbitration with Atlanta Braves. Team offers 13.5 million

Related Biography: Pitching Coach Michael Maddux

Mike Maddux, Greg's older brother, was named pitching coach for the Milwaukee Brewers in 2002 after a 15-year major league career. Maddux spent three years playing college baseball at the University of Texas at El Paso, before cracking the major leagues. Both he and his brother began their major league careers in 1986. That same year, they made history as the first pair of rookie brothers to challenge each other on the pitcher's mound.

The year 1991 was Maddux's best season. He pitched relief for the San Diego Padres. Maddux co-led the pitching staff with 64 appearances and recorded seven victories, five saves and a 2.46 ERA. During his career Maddux played on nine different teams. In 2000 he signed with the Houston Astros. Before then he had donned the Phillies, Dodgers, Padres, Mets, Pirates, Red Sox, Mariners, and Expos uniforms.

and two-thirds scoreless innings. That season he enjoyed a nine game winning streak. In June, he was named Pitcher-of-the-Month for his 5-0 record and 2.22 ERA. He became the youngest player ever named to the All-Star Team at midseason and closed the year with an 18-8 record, 3.18 ERA and three shutouts.

1989 was another thrilling season for Maddux. His record of 19-12 was second in the National League for wins and his ERA was an exceptional 2.95. As a starter he pitched 35 games and led the Cubs to the National League East title. Continuing with the Cubs in 1990 and 1991 Maddux's statistics got progressively stronger. He was consistently a league leader in strikeouts, complete games, shutouts and wins.

The 1992 season was a watershed for Maddux, who had one of the best pitching seasons in the history of baseball. His record was 20-11 and for the first time in 15 years the Cubs had a 20-game winner. Maddux won the first of a record breaking four consecutive Cy Young Awards and his third consecutive Gold Glove Award as the best fielder in his position. At the end of the season, Maddux became a free agent and turned down a more lucrative offer from the Yankees to continue playing in the National League with the Atlanta Braves.

Wearing the Braves Jersey

The Braves were number one during the 1993 regular season. Atlanta sent three of their four pitchers to the All-Star Team and Maddux finished the season fourth in the National League with a 2.36 ERA, 267 innings pitched and eight complete games. He also won the Golden Glove Award and became one of the only players to take the honor in consecutive years playing for different teams. He told the *New York Times,* "You change teams and you want to make a good impression, I feel like I've done that. I didn't really change anything in the way that I pitched. I pretty much tried to do the same things that worked in the past."

During the 1994 and 1995 seasons Maddux remained dominant. He won Cy Young Awards both years and enjoyed the two lowest ERAs of his career, 1.56 and 1.63 respectively, substantially under the league average of 4.21. At the peak of his career Maddux declined a starting position on the 1995 All-Star Team and refused to do commercial endorsements. He told *Newsweek,* "Plugging products would just screw up a good day off."

The Best Pitcher in all of Baseball

In 1997, after leading the Braves for the third consecutive season to the National League Championship Series, Maddux signed a $57.5 million dollar contract to continue with the Braves for five years and has won the National League Golden Glove each year since then. In 2002, Maddux became the second pitcher, after Cy Young, in major league history to win at least 15 games a season for 15 consecutive seasons. Maddux currently ranks 2nd in the National League with an overall Earned Run Average of 2.62. Philadelphia Phillies manager Jim Fregosi is quoted in *Baseball Digest,* saying that, "He is the best pitcher in the National League. Maybe in all of baseball." Maddux takes his place among the legends of baseball with his usual nonchalance. He confessed to *Newsweek,* "I'll probably realize the meaning of all this after I'm gone, after I am history. But until then I'll just blow it off."

Giving Back

During the off season, Maddux and his wife, Kathy, and their two children live in Las Vegas. Greg and Kathy founded the Maddux Foundation. In addition to being involved with many charitable organizations, every year the foundation donates Braves tickets to non-profit organizations.

FURTHER INFORMATION

Periodicals

"Maddux Wins 13th Gold Glove." *New York Times* (November 15, 2002): 7.

Other

"Brewers Name Mike Maddux Pitching Coach, Wynegar Batting Coach." CBSSportsline.com. http://www.cbs.sportsline.com/ (December 10, 2002).

ESPN.com. http://www.espn.go.com/ (December 03, 2002).

Galenet.com. Biography Resource Center- Narrative Biography Display. http://galenet.galegroup.com/ (December 10, 2002).

"Mike Maddux Pitches In." Las Vegas Review Journal Online Edition. http://www.lvrj.com/lvrj_home/2001/Nov-28-Wed-2001/ (December 10, 2002).

Round Rock Express Baseball. http://www.roundrockexpress.com/ (December 10, 2002).

Sketch by Paulo Nunes-Ueno

Phil Mahre
1957-

American skier

Phil Mahre is the most successful ski racer in U.S. history; he has won more events and awards than anyone else, including a silver medal in the 1980 Olympics, three World Cup titles in 1981, 1982, and 1983, and a gold medal at the 1984 Olympics.

World Cup and Olympic Gold

Mahre, one of nine children, grew up skiing. His father Dave, a former apple grower, took a job as manager of a ski area in order to support his large family. Mahre and his siblings were often dressed in clothes from the lost-and-found at the White Pass Lodge in the Cascade Mountains of Washington, where their father worked. Their school was an hour and a half away but the ski slopes were right outside their door. Mahre did his homework during the long bus ride home, got off the bus, and hit the mountains, hiking in summer and skiing in winter. By the time Mahre and his twin brother Steve were nine, they were already winning local children's

Phil Mahre

races; Steve, who was born four minutes later than Mahre, was never quite as fast as Mahre, but he was still a top skier. Although the brothers competed with each other, they also celebrated each other's victories.

Mahre made the U.S. Ski Team at age fifteen. At the 1980 Olympics in Lake Placid, New York, Mahre won a silver medal in slalom. It was only the third Alpine medal won by an American male in ten Olympics over the past forty-four years; no American had ever won a gold medal in Alpine skiing. However, that would soon change.

Although Mahre was a top contender, he also emphasized enjoying his sport, and he was not motivated by medals and honors as much as other racers were. On the eve of the last race of the 1981 World Cup competition, when Mahre was under pressure to become America's first champion skier, Mahre played three hours of basketball despite friends' warnings not to waste energy. He told Tom Callahan in *Time,* "A lot of people say I'm crazy, but I think all these things are games, and games are for fun."

The fun paid off, because Mahre won the overall World Cup Championship that year, as well as in 1982 and 1983, an unprecedented feat for an American skier.

As a result of his win, Mahre became so well known in Europe that when he returned to the United States, where the public knows comparatively little about his sport, it was a relief for him to not be recognized on the street. "I don't think there are many Americans who un-

Chronology

1957	Born May 10, in White Pass, Washington
1972	Joins U.S. Ski Team
1980	Wins Olympic silver medal in slalom
1981-83	Wins three consecutive overall World Cup titles
1984	Wins Olympic gold medal in slalom
1984	Retires from World Cup racing, returns to Yakima, Washington
1984	With brother Steve, starts a ski apparel business
1987	With Steve, begins driving race cars
1988	Crashes car in 24 Hours of Daytona Race
1988	Returns to competitive skiing in order to finance car racing
1990	Wins eight-race American City series in Sports 2000 class
1991	Begins racing on GT-2 circuit for Trans Am cars
1991	Wins overall Plymouth Super Series Slalom; retires from ski competition
1992-present	Coaches young racers in U.S. ski program

Awards and Achievements

1980	Olympic silver medal, slalom
1981-83	Three consecutive overall World Cup titles
	Entire career Ranked 6th on all-time World Cup win list
1984	Olympic gold medal, slalom

derstand what I've done," he told Tom Callahan in *Time.* "That's unfortunate for skiing but nice for me. I'm not one for fame and fortune."

At the 1984 Olympics, held in Sarajevo, Yugoslavia, Mahre edged out brother Steve by .21 of a second, winning gold and leaving silver for Steve. Just after this win, Mahre found out that his wife Holly had just given birth to their youngest child, Alexander, in Scottsdale, Arizona. Mahre told Mark Beech in *Sports Illustrated,* "I couldn't tell you the date of any win I've ever had with the exception of that one. My son's birthday reminds me of the gold medal, not the other way around."

Mahre also told William Oscar Johnson in *Sports Illustrated,* "This, to me, is just another victory. It's wrong to say this is the best day of my life. If it were, what am I going to do with the rest of my life."

This modest assessment of Mahre's abilities, and those of his brother, was not shared by others in the ski world. Christin Cooper wrote in *Skiing* that the brothers "were a team unto themselves, riding their own comet that few ordinary mortals could seem to latch onto. The more momentum they gained, the farther behind the rest of our men seemed to fall."

Turns to Race Car Driving

At the end of the 1984 season, though, Mahre retired from World Cup racing. He returned to Yakima, Washington, with his family. However, he was not through with moving fast; he and his brother Steve started a ski instruction and apparel business, and in 1987 they became interested in driving race cars. In 1997, they raced a Pontiac Trans Am. Mahre told Robert Sullivan in *Sports Illustrated,* "It was a great year. We raced nine times, and I think we made progress." The brothers also learned about their new sport by attending the Skip Barber Racing School in Willow Springs, California.

The brothers focused on "endurance" motor racing, which involves events lasting longer than three hours, and for which they worked as a team. They discovered that on certain tracks, Phil was faster, and on others, Steve was. "Each time behind the wheel we learned something," Mahre told Sullivan. They noted that there were some similarities between skiing and racing: both require concentration, although the many hours required for racing were obviously much longer than the few minutes needed in ski racing. Both also require fast reflexes and reactions, as well as an analytical side: just as they studied the ski course before racing it, they look over a race track and discuss their strategy before getting in the car to race on it.

The brothers had a setback at the 24 Hours of Daytona Race in 1988, when Phil spun their car, and a third driver they had hired for the long race crashed it. In March, Mahre spun and crashed the car while on his eighth practice lap. He told Sullivan, "I was trying to go too fast on cold tires, which is something I learned not to do last year. . . . It was just as if I had hooked a tip [of a ski] and torn a ligament: I put us on the sidelines. I sure hope that's the low point of the season."

Some other drivers resented the Mahre brothers because they had arrived in racing with famous names and a reserve of funds from ski winnings. Racer Mark Hutchins told Sullivan, "A lot of drivers come from underprivileged backgrounds and have had to make serious personal sacrifices to be in racing. Yes, there's some resentment when others aren't required to work to get a ride." But he added, "Personally, I like having them out here."

Mahre told Sullivan, "I don't consider us a threat to anybody," and noted that he once told some of the famed drivers in the sport, "We'll just try to stay out of your way and try to be predictable. Just don't run us over." The drivers, he said, were "very friendly. They said, 'Good to have you here, it'll help the sport.'"

The brothers' car-racing hobby was expensive, though, so both twins went back to ski racing with the U.S. Pro Tour, hoping to win enough money to support their racing habit. Mahre won several races, but was not impressed with his competition. In 1991, he told Johnson, "I'm definitely a has-been, and they're all never-weres."

Mahre won the eight-race American City series in the Sports 2000 class in 1990, and in 1991 he and his brother began racing on the GT-2 circuit for Trans-Am cars.

Mahre bluntly told Johnson, "I expect to make only enough to pay the bills. But I've never lost sleep over winning or losing before, and I'm not going to start now."

In April of 1991, Mahre won the overall Plymouth Super Series Slalom at Steamboat Springs, Colorado, and again said he was retiring from ski competition, although he did not rule out the possibility of competing in occasional races to raise money for his cars.

Mahre's Influence

Of the Mahre brothers' influence on skiing, Christin Cooper wrote in *Skiing*, "The Mahres were both so uncommonly talented and so equally self-assured about their potential that they had little to do but reach it," and noted, "They were amazing on skis, and with their results destroyed the myth of European supremacy in World Cup racing."

Although Mahre no longer competes in skiing, he coaches young racers in the U.S. ski program. Mahre told Beech, "I still have a passion and love for the sport, so I stay in it. Most kids who are 13 or 14 are clueless as to who I am, which is kind of nice. I have a lot of fun with them."

CONTACT INFORMATION

Address: c/o SportsMark Management Group, 80 East Sir Francis Drake Blvd #2A, Larkspur, CA 94939. Fax: (415) 461-5804. Phone: (415) 461-5801. Email: Contact@smgnet.com. Online: www.smgnet.com.

FURTHER INFORMATION

Periodicals

Beech, Mark. "Tamara McKinney and Phil Mahre, Skiers" *Sports Illustrated* (March 18, 2002): 21.

Callahan, Tom. "For Purple Mountains' Majesty." *Time* (March 21, 1983): 67.

Callahan, Tom. "Their Success Is All in the Family." *Time* (January 30, 1984): 44.

Cooper, Christin. "Star Wars." *Skiing* (October, 1985): 51.

Johnson, William Oscar. "Happy Trails: Ski Racing Great Phil Mahre Calls It Quits." *Sports Illustrated* (April 8, 1991): 16.

Sullivan, Robert. "Two to Travel—Fast." *Sports Illustrated* (May 2, 1988): 94.

Other

Boyd, Tom. "Athlete Commission Distributes Winter Funds." *Vail Trail,* http://www.vailtrail.com/ (November 18, 2002).

"Phil Mahre." *Olympic-USA,* http://www.Olympic-use. org/ (November 12, 2002).

Sketch by Kelly Winters

Hermann Maier
1972-

Austrian skier

Austrian Alpine skier Hermann Maier burst from obscurity at the relatively old age of 25 to win three World Cup titles and two Olympic gold medals in 1998, despite a death-defying fall in an Olympic downhill race that season. He dominating the skiing world for the next three seasons, until a severe motorcycle accident in the summer of 2001 prevented him from competing during the 2001-02 season.

A Difficult Course

Maier, the older of his father Hermann Maier Sr.'s two children, first strapped on skis at age three. "Two days later he was off riding the lift by himself," the elder Maier, the owner of a skiing school, recalled to Tim Layden of *Sports Illustrated*. Skiing was a common passion in the Maiers' hometown of Flachau, Austria: The town had four other skiing schools, in addition to the Maiers', for a mere 2,500 inhabitants.

Maier was always recognized as a good skier, but Austria is full of good skiers. Although he was accepted to the Austrian national ski academy at the age of 15, after a year there he failed to stand out as a potentially great skier and he was asked to leave. Undeterred, he returned to Flachau, where he worked as a bricklayer in the summer. In the winters he taught skiing at his father's ski school for five hours a day and practiced his own skiing the rest of the time.

He soon established himself as the local champion in slalom and giant slalom, and in the spring of 1995 the president of his regional ski federation, Alex Reiner, helped to get him the opportunity to ski in the Austrian national championships. Maier finished eighteenth. Encouraged by this result, Maier quit his bricklaying job late in 1995 and started training full time again, hoping

Hermann Maier

Chronology

1972	Born December 7 in Altenmarkt, Austria, to Hermann and Gertraud Maier
1988	Begins attending Austrian national ski academy
1989	Leaves ski academy and begins studying to be a bricklayer
1993-95	Becomes Salzburg champion in super G, giant slalom, and slalom; Tyrolean champion in giant slalom; and Carinthian champion in slalom
1996	Earns his first World Cup points February 3
1997	Wins first World Cup race, in Garmisch, Germany, February 23
2001	Almost loses right leg in a motorcycle accident

to be able to qualify for the Europa Cup circuit, one step below the top World Cup circuit.

Reiner arranged another tremendous opportunity for Maier in January 1996. A World Cup giant slalom event was being held in Flachau. It is customary for a forerunner, a noncompeting skier, to ski the course before the competitors go down, and Reiner arranged for Maier to do this. Had Maier actually been a competitor, his time on the course would have placed him seventh after the first run-only a second behind then-champion **Alberto Tomba**-and eleventh after the second run. After those performances, he was offered a spot in the Austrian national program. He skied on the Europa Cup circuit for a few months and won the overall Europa Cup title. By the end of the season he had been promoted to the World Cup team.

Success at Last

Maier skied in only three World Cup races in the 1995-96 season, but he did manage to finish eleventh in one of them. The next season he broke his wrist and missed part of the season, but he still finished in the top five at four races. Along the way, many people took notice of Maier's style of skiing, which was considerably more aggressive than that of most top racers. Most skiers took wide, gliding lines on their curves, covering more distance but maintaining speed that would have been lost had they carved more and hewed closer to the

gates. Maier, on the other hand, had "the ability to glide while maintaining a tight line, which was always assumed to be impossible," his coach Werner Margreiter told Layden. "It's a very exciting thing to see."

In the 1997-98 season everything came together for Maier. He won three World Cup titles that season, the giant slalom and the super giant slalom (super G) as well as the overall. He also won two gold medals at the 1998 Olympics in Nagano, Japan, in the same two events. He might possibly have won another medal in the downhill, the first event he skied in in Nagano, as well, had he not had a spectacular crash during that event. On a particularly steep curve near the top of the course Maier lost control at around 65 miles per hour, went airborne, and cartwheeled through two snow fences. He landed in soft snow, walked away with only a dislocated shoulder and a sprained knee, and won the gold medal in the super G only three days later.

The video of Maier's crash was shown repeatedly around the world over the next few days, much to Maier's chagrin. "If you ask me," he told Hampton Sides of *Outside Online* magazine, "I would prefer to be famous for winning two gold medals in Nagano rather than for my screwup."

A Devastating Accident

Maier went on to win nine World Cup titles in the next three seasons. In 2000 he accomplished the rare feat of winning four World Cup titles-downhill, giant slalom, super G, and overall-in one year, and he repeated this accomplishment in 2001. That year he also tied famed Swedish skier **Ingemar Stenmark**'s record of 13 wins in World Cup races in a single season. He was "the Herminator," unstoppable. Then a horrible accident threatened to end his career, and possibly his life.

Maier was riding his motorcycle in Radstadt, Austria, on August 24, 2001, when he was hit by a car and thrown into a ditch. He suffered severe injuries in both legs, and doctors considered amputating his right leg. Ultimately the leg was saved, but Maier was in no shape to compete in the 2001-02 season. He first strapped on skis again that December. In the summer of 2002 Maier traveled to Chile to practice for his comeback, but he reinjured his leg. Finally, on January 14, 2003, Maier raced in his first World Cup event since the accident. He finished a disappointing thirty-first in the first run of this giant slalom event, missing the cutoff to compete in the second run by five-hundredths of a second, but he vowed to keep trying. "I have to admit I was expecting to do a bit better," Maier said after the race, Erica Bulman of the Associated Press reported. "But in reality, it's a victory for me just to be back racing."

CONTACT INFORMATION

Online: http://www.hm1.com.

FURTHER INFORMATION

Periodicals

Borzilleri, Meri-Jo. "Austrian Star Maier's Return This Season Up in the Air." *Gazette* (Colorado Springs, CO; December 9, 2002): SP6.

Coffey, Wayne. "King of the Hill Again." *Advertiser* (Adelaide, Australia; February 17, 1998): 75.

Ferguson, Julia, and Giselle Hutter. "Olympic Front-Runner Maier Pulls Out." *Scotsman* (Edinburgh, Scotland; January 17, 2002): 20.

Freestone, Nick. "Maier Ready for Return to Slopes." *Scotsman* (Edinburgh, Scotland; December 21, 2001): 19.

Layden, Tim. "He's the Mann." *Sports Illustrated* (February 2, 1998): 70-72.

———. "Street Fighting." *Sports Illustrated* (February 23, 1998): 40-45.

Masters, Sophie. "Maier Back in Training after Injury." *Independent* (London; January 8, 2003).

Other

Bulman, Erica. "Maier's Skiing Comeback Leaves Impression." Miami Herald: Herald.com. http://www.miami.com/mld/miamiherald/sports/4950088.htm (January 15, 2003).

"Hermann Maier: Overview." SKI-DB. http://www.ski-db.com/db/profiles/merhe.asp (January 8, 2003).

Sides, Hampton. "Thinking about Machine-Man." Outside Online. http://web.outsideonline.com/magazine/1198/9811machineman.html (January 8, 2003).

Sketch by Julia Bauder

Karl Malone
1963-

American basketball player

Karl Malone, a power forward who has been playing basketball with the Utah Jazz since 1985, earned the nickname "The Mailman" early in his career for his ability to deliver the ball to the hoop reliably, under any conditions. The long-time Jazz combination of Malone, the scorer, Malone's co-captain, point guard **John Stockton**, the passer, and Jerry Sloan, the head coach, is one of the most fearsome in the National Basketball Association (NBA), but despite making the playoffs every year that these men have been playing together, the Jazz has never won an NBA championship.

Hard Work

Malone, the eighth of nine children in a poor but fiercely independent family from a tiny town in northern Louisiana, has never been a stranger to hard work. His mother struggled to earn enough to raise her children, but she never applied for welfare even though the family was eligible. "It was my responsibility to take care of my own children. I believe every tub should sit on its own bottom," she later told *Sports Illustrated* reporter Craig Neff.

In the early 1980s Malone played college basketball for Louisiana Tech, only a short drive from his family's home in Summerfield. He was not eligible to play as a freshman because his high school grade point average (GPA) of 1.97 was below the 2.0 requirement, but by his junior year of college he saw this as a blessing. After leading his high school basketball team to three consecutive Class C state titles, "I was starting to think that I was better than other people, that I was special and things would just come to me," Malone told Neff. The shock of not being allowed to play forced him to put more effort into his studies, and by his junior year he had the third-highest GPA on the Louisiana Tech team.

Later in life, this willingness to work hard would do much for Malone's NBA career. A forty-eight percent foul shooter as a rookie, he concentrated on improving this aspect of his game and now makes three in four of

Karl Malone

Chronology

1963	Born July 24 to J. P. and Shirley Malone in Summerfield, Louisiana
1977	Father dies of cancer
1984	Cut from the U.S. Olympic basketball team in one of the last rounds
1985	Drafted by the Utah Jazz
1987	Future wife, Kay Kinsey, named Miss Idaho USA
1988	Jazz lose to the Los Angeles Lakers in the seventh game of the second round of the NBA playoffs
1991	Passes commercial driver's license test on the first try, buys a custom-painted trailer, and opens celebrity hauling business Malone Enterprises
1992	Plays on the "Dream Team," the U.S. men's Olympic basketball team
1994	Jazz owner Larry Miller orders coach Jerry Sloan, on national television, to pull Malone from a playoff game due to his poor play
1998	Suspended for one game and fined $5,000 for elbowing Dallas Spurs center David Robinson in the head during a game April 8, ending Malone's consecutive games played streak at 543

his free throws. He is legendary among NBA players for his rigorous training regimen, which includes cutting hay and branding cattle with his brother over the summer, on a ranch in Arkansas that he owns. Malone's teammates are invited to come along, but only one, former Jazz player Ike Austin, ever took him up on it. Austin, a protégé of Malone's who worked his way to a Most Improved Player award in 1997, told *Sport* magazine's Tom McEachin about one of their summer days together on Malone's ranch. The two got up at 5:00 a.m., spent forty-five minutes on the stair machine, another two-and-a-half hours lifting weights, and a few hours working in the fields—all before lunch. Then they lifted more weights after lunch. Austin recalled that when they were done "I couldn't lift my arms. When I got back from lifting, I just fell asleep, right there at the table. Everybody was laughing, and Karl was like, man, just go to your room." Malone's hard work has paid off. Since his rookie season he has more than halved his body fat percentage, from over ten percent to an even four.

The Great Team That Couldn't Go All the Way

Malone was drafted by the Utah Jazz in 1985. There he joined Stockton, who had been drafted a year before. The two were a powerful combination. Malone, a hard-driving power forward, was often in a position to score, and Stockton was usually poised to feed him the ball at just the right moment. Malone became the team's leading scorer during his sophomore season, and when

Stockton became the team's starting point guard in 1987 he wasted no time breaking the NBA's record for greatest number of assists in a single season. When assistant coach Jerry Sloan was promoted to the head coaching position in 1988, the final piece of this long-lived combination fell into place.

Despite the numerous records broken by Malone and Stockton, the Jazz have never been able to win an NBA championship, despite having made the playoffs every single year. After having been eliminated in the first or second round for many years, the Jazz made its first-ever trip to the Western Conference Finals in 1992. There they were eliminated by the Portland Trail Blazers in six games. The Jazz returned to the Western Conference Finals in 1995, only to be defeated by the Houston Rockets in five games. It took Seattle seven games to beat them in the Western Conference finals in 1996. The next year the Jazz finally made it the whole way to the NBA finals, where they played well but still lost to the Chicago Bulls. They returned to the NBA finals and faced the bulls again in 1998, but again they were defeated. Other notable post-seasons include 1988, when the Jazz forced the eventual NBA champions, the Los Angeles Lakers, to go a full seven games to eliminate them in the second round.

Malone the Inspiration

Malone has long been something of an elder statesman in the sport of basketball, serving as an inspiration not only for the younger members of the Jazz but for players across the league. In the summer of 1997 former Denver Nuggets player Bill Hanzlik, who was head coach of the Nuggets for the 1997-98 season, bumped into Malone while he was working out in a Salt Lake City gym. Hanzlik, who had come to town with several of his rookie players to participate in a summer league, thought that it

Career Statistics

Yr	Team	GP	PTS	FG%	3P%	FT%	RPG	APG	SPG	BPG	TO	PF
1985-86	UTA	81	1203	.496	.000	.481	8.9	2.9	1.30	.54	279	295
1986-87	UTA	82	1779	.512	.000	.598	10.4	1.9	1.27	.73	237	323
1987-88	UTA	82	2268	.520	.000	.700	12.0	2.4	1.43	.61	325	296
1988-89	UTA	80	2326	.519	.313	.766	10.7	2.7	1.80	.88	285	286
1989-90	UTA	82	2540	.562	.372	.762	11.1	2.8	1.48	.61	304	259
1990-91	UTA	82	2382	.527	.286	.770	11.8	3.3	1.09	.96	244	268
1991-92	UTA	81	2272	.526	.176	.778	11.2	3.0	1.33	.63	248	226
1992-93	UTA	82	2217	.552	.200	.740	11.2	3.8	1.51	1.04	240	261
1993-94	UTA	82	2063	.497	.250	.694	11.5	4.0	1.52	1.54	234	268
1994-95	UTA	82	2187	.536	.268	.742	10.6	3.5	1.57	1.04	236	269
1995-96	UTA	82	2106	.519	.400	.723	9.8	4.2	1.68	.68	199	245
1996-97	UTA	82	2249	.550	.000	.755	9.9	4.5	1.38	.59	233	217
1997-98	UTA	81	2190	.530	.333	.761	10.3	3.9	1.19	.86	247	237
1998-99	UTA	49	1164	.493	.000	.788	9.4	4.1	1.27	.57	162	134
1999-00	UTA	82	2095	.509	.250	.797	9.5	3.7	.96	.87	231	229
2000-01	UTA	81	1878	.498	.400	.793	8.3	4.5	1.15	.77	244	216
2001-02	UTA	80	1788	.454	.360	.797	8.6	4.3	1.90	.74	263	229

UTA: Utah Jazz.

would be an excellent lesson for these young men to see how hard Malone worked, even on a Sunday morning in the off season. Hanzlik woke four players up and brought them back to the health club, where Malone was in the middle of leading a spinning class. After the class was over, Malone spent fifteen minutes talking to these rookies about the devotion and hard work that it takes to be a success in basketball and about how getting caught up in a glamorous lifestyle would only distract them from that work. "That one meeting was worth more than the whole ten days we spent in summer camp," Hanzlik recalled to Tom McEachin of *Sport* magazine.

"Everybody asks me now: How many more years do you think you can keep up with the young guys?" Malone was quoted as saying by McEachin in 1998. "I ain't seen a young guy catch me yet. Why . . . do I need to start catching up to them?" With this attitude and continued hard work, Malone looks set to continue leading the NBA and inspiring young players well past his fortieth birthday.

CONTACT INFORMATION

Address: c/o Utah Jazz, 301 W. South Temple St., Salt Lake City, UT 84101.

FURTHER INFORMATION

Periodicals

Brody, Robert. "Karl Malone Takes it Personally." *Men's Health* (February, 1991): 72-75.

Jorgensen, Loren. "Candid Karl." *Sporting News* (April 20, 1998): 12-15.

"Karl Malone Scores for Kids." *Hunting* (March-April, 2002): 18.

"Karl Malone Wins Second MVP Award." *Jet* (June 21, 1999): 48.

Ladson, William. "Karl Malone: The Jazz Superstar Attempts to Get over the Hurt of Last Season." *Sport* (December, 1994): 86-91.

Lyons, Douglas C. "Karl Malone: The 'Mailman' Delivers." *Ebony* (February, 1991): 67-69.

"'The Mailman' Third NBA Player to Score 30,000 Points." *Jet* (February 21, 2000): 18.

McCallum, Jack. "Big Wheel." *Sports Illustrated* (April 27, 1992): 62-72.

McCallum, Jack. "Getting Straight: His Wife's Illness Forced Jazz Coach Jerry Sloan to Clean Up His Act. Now He's in No Rush to Leave the NBA." *Sports Illustrated* (February 11, 2002): 46.

McEachin, Tom. "Built from Scratch." *Sport* (February, 1998): 76-79.

McEachin, Tom. "The Mailman Still Delivers." *Basketball Digest* (January, 2001): 14.

Neff, Craig. "The Mailman Does Deliver." *Sports Illustrated* (January 14, 1985): 88-90.

"Utah's Karl Malone Makes NBA History as Member of All-NBA First Team for 11th Time." *Jet* (June 28, 1999): 46.

"Utah's Malone Sets NBA Free Throw Record." *Jet* (April 9, 2001): 52.

Vancil, Mark. "Banging and Running, a Routine Night's Work." *Sporting News* (November 8, 1993): S10-11.

Wiley, Ralph. "Does He Ever Deliver!" *Sports Illustrated* (November 7, 1988): 72-77.

Other

"Jazz History." NBA.com. http://www.nba.com/jazz/history/00400490.html (January 3, 2002).

Awards and Accomplishments

1986	Named to the NBA All-Rookie Team
1989	Named Most Valuable Player of the NBA All-Star game
1990	Scores a career-high sixty-one points in a game against the Milwaukee Bucks January 27
1992	Named to U.S. Olympic team
1993	Named co-Most Valuable Player (with John Stockton) of the NBA All-Star game
1996	Named to U.S. Olympic team
1996	Selected as one of the fifty greatest players in NBA history
1997	Named Most Valuable Player of the NBA
1997	Named Utahn of the Year by the *Salt Lake Tribune*
1998	IBM Award
1998	Henry B. Ida award for athletes who go out of their way to help others
1999	Most Valuable Player of the NBA
2000	Became only the third player in NBA history to score 30,000 points in his career

Named to the All-NBA First Team eleven times in a row, from 1988-89 through 1998-99, and to the All-Defensive First Team three times in a row, from 1996-97 through 1998-99.

Played in the NBA All-Star game twelve times, including ten consecutive appearances from 1991 to 2001.

Holds the NBA record for most consecutive seasons with over 2,000 points scored, with eleven from 1987-88 to 1997-98.

"Jerry Sloan." NBA.com. http://www.nba.com/coachfile/jerry_sloan (January 3, 2002).

"Karl Malone." NBA.com. http://www.nba.com/playerfile/karl_malone (November 28, 2002).

Sketch by Julia Bauder

Moses Malone

Moses Malone
1955-

American basketball player

In 1974, a 6-10 senior from Petersburg High school graduated from the courts of Virginia's public schools directly to the American Basketball Association (ABA), becoming the first professional player to skip college. During a career that spanned 21 years, seven teams and three most valuable player awards that youngster, Moses Malone, went on to become one of basketball's all-time great centers and 50 Greatest Players.

Wore Out Shoes Practicing

Born into a poor family in Petersburg, Virginia, Malone was raised by his mother Mary. Shy and awkward, the young Malone was already six-feet three-inches tall by the time he was 12 years old. From the very begin-

ning an unrelenting work ethic, the hallmark of Malone's success, was apparent.

In a *Playboy* interview Malone recounted, "I didn't pick up a basketball until I was 13 and a half, but I worked hard even then. Every day after school, I'd go over to the playground and play ball until about two in the morning. The only trouble I had was I kept wearing out my shoes. Back then, I didn't get no high-priced shoes; I had to get them old P.F. Flyers. I'd wear them for about five days and then it was time for a new pair."

Immediate Success

Malone sparked a bidding war among more than 300 colleges after he led Petersburg High School to 50 straight wins and two consecutive state championships. Always self-possessed, Malone told *Playboy* the feeding frenzy did not faze him. "Pressure? Pressure where? It was fun! I traveled every time I got a break. I visited at least 26 schools. I grew up thinking that Petersburg, Virginia was the best part of the world; but when I started visiting all those colleges, I realized Petersburg was the only part of the world I'd seen. It didn't change my feeling none about Petersburg, but things were a lot different on the West Coast, in the Southwest, in Hawaii, all over."

Finally choosing to enroll at the University Maryland in order to be near his mother, Malone attended classes for two and a half days before learning he had been drafted by the Utah Stars of the American Basketball

Association. He signed a $3 million, five year contract and proved to be an immediate success. Playing guard until he bulked up enough to withstand the hammering at center, Malone averaged an amazing 18 points and 14 rebounds as a rookie.

The Mark of a Champion

After two years in the ABA, Malone became a force to be reckoned with in the NBA for over ten years. He led the Houston Rockets to the NBA finals in 1981 and was key to the Philadelphia 76ers 1983 NBA Championship victory.

By the time he retired, following the 1994-95 season, Malone had produced an awe-inspiring NBA stat sheet, having scored 27,409 points and grabbed 16,212 rebounds. He ranks first in NBA history from the free throw line with 8,531 points and second behind **Wilt Chamberlain** in free throws attempts with 11,090. Malone's dominance in the paint is evidenced by his standing as one of the league's preeminent rebounders. He ranks as the all-time leader in offensive rebounds with 6,731 and second behind Robert Parish in defensive rebounds with 9,481.

When his two years in the ABA are added the picture is even more decisive. During his 21 years in professional basketball, Malone racked up 29,580 points, fourth in the all-time list after **Kareem Abdul-Jabbar**, Wilt Chamberlain and **Julius Erving**, and ranks as the third all-time greatest rebounder in history behind Chamberlain and **Bill Russell** at 17,834. He leads the all-time list in free throws made with 9,018 and free throws attempted with 11,864.

Not quite as big as the league's other renowned centers, Malone made the most of his quickness and strength. Besides dominating the boards, leading the league in rebounds six times in a seven year span, Malone drew upon a treasure trove of crafty moves to score or get to the free throw line, averaging more than 20 points per game for 11 years. What's more, he did all this with finesse, playing 1,207 consecutive games without fouling out, the NBA record.

Malone was not given to analyzing strategy for the media's sake. Quiet around reporters and cameras, he chose to use his deep understanding of the game for what mattered most: winning.

The NBA Years

After his two seasons in the ABA, Malone joined the NBA in 1974, playing for the Buffalo Bravos and later for the Houston Rockets. Malone earned his first Most Valuable Player Award. Just two years later, in the 1980-81 season, he led the underdog Rockets all the way to the NBA finals.

The following season Malone was awarded his second Most Valuable Player award after averaging an impressive 31.1 point and 14.7 rebounds per game. During the off season the Rockets traded him to the Philadelphia 76ers where Malone was to reach the peak of his career. The 76ers roster boasted some of the league's all-time best players including Julius Erving, after Bobby Jones and Andrew Toney. With the addition of Malone the 76ers became unstoppable, going 65-17 for the regular season and steamrolling the postseason 12-1 to win the 1983 NBA championship. Malone was named MVP of the regular season and the NBA finals that year.

The Later Years

During the 1985-86 season, in a game against Milwaukee, Malone suffered a broken eye orbit that cut his season short 8 games before the postseason. Without Malone, the 76ers did not fare well in the play-offs, los-

Career Statistics

Yr	Team	GP	PTS	FG%	3P%	FT%	RPG	APG	SPG	BPG	TO	P/G
1975	UTA	83	1557	.572	.000	.635	14.6	1.0	—	—	—	18.8
1976	StL	43	614	.514	.000	.612	9.6	1.3	—	—	—	14.3
1978	HOU	59	1144	.499	—	.718	15.0	0.5	.81	1.3	—	19.4
1979	HOU	82	2031	.540	—	.739	17.6	1.8	.96		—	24.8
1980	HOU	82	2119	.502	.000	.719	14.5	1.8	.97	1.3	1.5	25.8
1981	HOU	80	2222	.522	.333	.757	14.8	1.8	1.0	1.8	150	27.8
1982	HOU	81	2520	.519	.000	.762	14.7	1.8	.93	1.5	125	31.1
1983	PHIL	78	1908	.501	.000	.761	15.3	1.3	1.1	2	157	24.5
1984	PHIL	71	1609	.483	.000	.750	13.4	1.4	1	1.5	110	22.7
1985	PHIL	79	1941	.469	.000	.815	13.1	1.6	.84	1.6	123	24.6
1986	PHIL	74	1759	.458	.000	.787	11.8	1.2	.90	1.7	261	23.8
1987	WASH	73	1760	.454	.000	.824	11.3	1.6	.90	1.0	202	24.1
1988	WASH	79	1607	.487	.286	.788	11.2	1.4	.74	1.2	249	20.3
1989	ATL	81	1637	.491	.000	.789	11.8	1.4	1	1.2	245	20.2
1990	ATL	81	1528	.480	.111	.781	10.0	1.6	.6	1	232	18.9
1991	ATL	82	869	.468	.000	.831	8.1	0.8	.40	.90	137	10.6
1992	MILW	82	1279	.474	.375	.786	9.1	1.1	.90	.80	150	15.6
1993	MILW	11	50	.310	.000	.774	4.2	0.6	.01	.70	10	4.5
1994	PHIL	55	294	.440	.000	.769	4.1	0.6	.20	.30	59	5.3
1995	SA	17	49	.371	.500	.688	2.7	0.4	.11	.20	11	2.9
TOTAL		1329	27409	.491	.100	.769	12.2	1.4	.81	1.3	3804	20.6

ATL: Atlanta Hawks (NBA); HOU: Houston Rockets (NBA); MILW: Milwaukee Bucks (NBA); PHIL: Philadelphia 76ers (NBA); SA: San Antonio Spurs (NBA); StL: St. Louis Spirit (ABA); UTA: Utah Stars (ABA); WASH: Washington Bullets (NBA).

ing to the Bucks in the Eastern Conference Semifinals. After the end of the season the 76ers traded Malone to the Washington Bullets.

Malone continued to be among the league's top scorers and rebounders for the next four years, playing for the Washington Bullets and later for the Atlanta Hawks. Even late in his career Malone produced strong numbers. In the 1990-91 season, his 17th year as a professional, Malone averaged 10.6 points and 8.1 rebounds though he was now playing as a back-up for Jon Koncak. Playing for the Milwaukee Bucks in 1991-92 he averaged 15.6 points per game. After playing another season with the Bucks, Malone was signed as a free agent by Philadelphia for one more season primarily to mentor the 7 foot 6 inch rookie Shawn Bradley and finally finished his career as a backup player for San Antonio.

On October 4th, 2001 Malone was inducted in the Basketball Hall of Fame. When asked how he felt he replied, "When I first got the news, I really didn't give it much thought. Now I know it's one of the greatest honors you can get. Now you're at the top, the very top. There's nowhere else you can go in basketball once you get to the Hall of Fame. Everybody now recognizes you as one of the greatest players ever." In October 1996 the league named him one of the NBA's top 50 players of all-time.

Inspiring the Next Generations

Malone's jump from high school directly to the pro ranks and his ensuing success might have paved the way for other talented youngsters to do the same. Though there are a growing number of high school players naturally talented enough to make it onto an NBA court while in their teens, very few have the maturity, self possession and work ethic that it takes to remain a dominant player for nearly two decades.

After a 21 year career in basketball, Malone retired at the age of 40 in 1995. He has two sons, Moses Jr. and Michael with Alfreda Gill from whom he is now divorced. His ex-wife and Michael live in Friendswood, Texas while Malone now lives in Sugarland Texas. Moses Jr. is a leading college basketball player at South Carolina State University. Since retiring Malone aspires to be a coach. In the meantime he often speaks to young people about the value of education and the importance of getting a college degree.

FURTHER INFORMATION

Other

"Moses Malone." Galenet.com. Biography Resource Center. http:// galenet.galegroup.com/ (December 10, 2002).

NBA.com. NBA History: Moses Malone. http://www. nba.com/ (December 10, 2002).

Naismith Memorial Hall of Fame, Inc. Hoopfame.com. http://www.hoopfame.com (December 10, 2002).

Pilot Online. http://www.pilotonline.com/sports/sp0218 mol.html (December 03, 2002).

Sketch by Paulo Nunes-Ueno

Man o' War
1917-1947

American racehorse

In horse racing, there is one name which, after nearly a century, still represents "the greatest" in nearly every aspect of the sport: Man o' War. It may be argued that the 1970s icon **Secretariat** was the greatest equine athlete in American racing history. In fact, both horses made twenty-one professional starts in their lifetimes, but Secretariat suffered four defeats to Man o' War's one. The jazz-age stallion broke three world records, two American records, and three track records. What's more, Man o' War became the more influential sire, with offspring including Triple Crown champion War Admiral.

A Breed Apart

The thoroughbred who would become a legend was born March 29, 1917, at Nursery Farm in Lexington, Kentucky. His sire (father), Fair Play, came from a notable stallion named Hastings, a horse as feared for his relentless temper as he was admired for his blazing speed. The dam (mother) of the chestnut foal was named Mahubah, daughter of Rock Sand, 1903 winner of England's Epsom Derby. Man o' War's history extends even farther, however: his lineage can be traced back fifteen generations to the Godolphin Arabian, one of the three foundation sires that created the American Thoroughbred.

The name Man o' War was not given lightly. In 1917 America had just entered World War I, and patriotism was running high. The colt's breeder and owner was August Belmont II. His father was the founder of Belmont Park in Elmont, New York; the Belmont Stakes, the third jewel of racing's Triple Crown, was named in the senior's honor. It was Belmont Jr.'s wife who called the son of Fair Play "My Man o' War," after her soldiering husband, who was stationed in France, according to an ESPN biography. When the colt was later registered, "My" was dropped.

It was Belmont's military service that prompted the sale of all his 1917 foals. Samuel Riddle, owner of Glen Riddle Farm, consulted with his trainer, Louis Feustel,

and purchased the tall, thin yearling for $5,000 in the spring of 1918. They had a handful in the young horse. Inheriting the Hastings ill-will, Man o' War proved to be "a tiger," in the words of Riddle, quoted in the book *The Most Glorious Crown*. "He screamed with rage, and fought us so hard that it took several days before he could be handled with safety." The horse had sense, however, and "became docile enough when he finally understood that what these lowly humans wanted of him was to run, which is what he wanted too," as Kate Gilbert Phifer put it in her book *Track Talk*.

Post Time for "Big Red"

Once he became acquainted with the track, there was no stopping Man o' War. The colt entered—and won—his first race, at Belmont Park on June 6, 1919. Carrying the 115 pounds of jockey Johnny Loftus, the two-year-old streaked to a six-length maiden victory, running five furlongs in under one minute. In the next sixteen months Man o' War "rewrote the record books," according to Ron Hale in an article posted in about.com. The horse's stakes victories included the Keene Memorial, the Youthful, the Hopeful, the Hudson, Tremont, United States Hotel, and many others. "He was odds-on in all 21 of his races," noted Hale, "three times being quoted by bookmakers at 1-100."

As Man o' War's wins grew, so did the weight allowance that contributed to his handicap. Eventually, the chestnut was required to carry 130 pounds, more than his competitors. But it made no difference to the horse nicknamed "Big Red" after his bright chestnut coat. Only once in his storied career did Man o' War experience defeat. It was at the Sanford Memorial, August 13, 1919, at Saratoga. As Larry Schwartz explained in an espn.com article, "Starting gates were not yet used, and horses were led up to a tape barrier. A fill-in starter had difficulty getting the horses ready and they milled around. While Man o' War apparently was backing up, the tape was sprung." That bad start was compounded

Jockey Clarence Kummer riding Man o' War

when the chestnut was boxed in the pack. He broke free but not soon enough, finishing second. The one horse that bested Man o' War was appropriately named Upset.

During the horse's three-year-old campaign, under the hand of jockey Clarence Kummer, Man o' War continued to win. One notable contest of 1920 was spared of the Thoroughbred's presence: the Kentucky Derby. But "Big Red" did streak to the winner's circle in the two other races that make up the Triple Crown. He triumphed in the Preakness and the Belmont Stakes, winning the latter by twenty lengths in a new track record of 2:14 and 1/5. It would be more than fifty years before Secretariat would win the lengthy Belmont by such a commanding margin.

"Race of the Century"

Indeed, Man o' War didn't need the publicity of a Triple Crown to prove his mettle. In an age of tintype and telegraph, the horse's name and exploits were known around the world. The only problem was finding Thoroughbreds who could provide competition for the big colt. Only one horse challenged in the Belmont, two in the Tra-

vers Stakes, and one in the Lawrence Realization at Belmont Park. In the latter race, Man o' War outran a horse named Hoodwink by an astounding one-hundred lengths.

A contender finally arose. Canadian-bred Sir Barton had the previous year become the first winner of the Triple Crown. The horse-racing community of fans demanded a match race between the four-year-old Sir Barton and three-year-old Man o' War. The two were set to meet at Kenilworth Park in Windsor, Ontario, on October 12, 1920. Both horses had gone through their share of bad luck prior to the match: Sir Barton was said to be sore-footed; Man o' War had suffered a bowed tendon in the Potomac Handicap. But by race day both horses were pronounced fit to run, and bettors made Man o' War the overwhelming favorite at 5 to 100.

In preparing for the mile-and-quarter race, "the jockeys had been given identical instructions—get to the front and stay there," as Marvin Drager wrote in *The Most Glorious Crown.* "Man o' War was fractious at the barrier, which was located at the near turn of the track. Sir Barton, on the rail, was more docile and broke first with the flag." At the first turn Sir Barton led, but his ad-

Awards and Accomplishments	
1919	Winner of maiden race at Belmont in June
1919	Winner of next eight of nine starts, June-September
1920	Winner of the Preakness Stakes
1920	Winner of the Belmont Stakes by twenty lengths, setting a new track record
1920	Winner of all eleven starts
1920	Winner of match race against Triple Crown winner Sir Barton
1999	Named one of ESPN's one-hundred greatest athletes of the twentieth century

vantage was "short-lived," said Drager, "as Man o' War caught up quickly and went ahead to stay after they had traveled only sixty yards." When the shouting was over, "Big Red" had proven himself once again, beating the Triple Crown champion by a margin of seven lengths and at a time that clipped more than six seconds off the existing track record. "It was a ridiculously easy victory," noted Drager.

Man o' War's Kenilworth romp was big news: the first horse race "filmed in its entirety around a circular track," Drager reported. The race also marked the end of Man o' War's two-season career. After earning a record $249,465, he was retired to stud in 1921. The chestnut stallion became known as a prodigious producer of quality foals. In 1926, his offspring won more than $400,000; among his 366 registered foals were sixty-four stakes winners, Triple Crown champion War Admiral, Kentucky Derby winner Clyde Van Dusen, and Battleship, who took England's Grand National steeplechase in 1938. A grandson, Seabiscuit, became a popular money-winner in the 1930s.

A Legacy of Racing Talent

For decades, Man o' War continued to be the benchmark of racing quality. According to espn.com, by mid-century an Associated Press poll "overwhelmingly voted [him] the greatest thoroughbred of the first half of the twentieth century." The Man o' War Stakes is run in his name; a notable winner is Secretariat. Man o' War lived to a fine old age in equine terms; when he died at age thirty on November 1, 1947, thousands attended a memorial ceremony. In 1999 ESPN named the horse to its list of the one hundred greatest athletes of the twentieth century.

FURTHER INFORMATION

Books

Drager, Marvin. *The Most Glorious Crown*. Winchester Press, 1975.

Farley, Walter. *Man o' War*. Bullseye Books, 1962.

Phifer, Kate Gilbert. *Track Talk*. Robert B. Luce Co., 1978.

Other

"80 Years Ago." About.com. http://horseracing.about.com/ (October 4, 2002).

"Man o' War Came Close to Perfection." ESPN. http://espn.go.com/ (October 4, 2002).

"Man o' War." About.com. http://horseracing.about.com/ (October 4, 2002).

"Newport Notables." Newport Notables. http://www.redwood1747.org/ (October 25, 2002).

Sketch by Susan Salter

Mickey Mantle
1931-1995

American baseball player

Many argue that he was the greatest baseball player ever, and were it not for the almost constant menace of alcohol and health-related maladies during his long and successful career as a New York Yankee, chances are there would be no argument. Mickey Mantle played in twenty All-Star games, and he holds the record for most career World Series home runs, runs scored and runs batted in. He subscribed to the old adage that, "It is just as important to be lucky as it is to be good." But Mantle's luck would eventually run out. His body, hindered by alcoholism and physical afflictions, would eventually give up on him. Too weak to fight any longer, he would die of cancer in 1995 at the age of 63. In spite of his personal hardships, however, Mickey Mantle remains a hero in America.

Growing Up

Mickey Charles Mantle was born October 20, 1931, in Spavinaw, Oklahoma. His father, Elvin "Mutt" Mantle, worked in the Oklahoma zinc mines, and before his son could even walk, he was steering Mickey towards baseball (he named him after his favorite player, Philadelphia Athletics and then Detroit Tigers catcher Mickey Cochrane). When Mickey was four, Mutt went where there was work, and the family moved near Commerce, Oklahoma. Mantle's childhood was one marked by poverty, and as soon as he was old enough to help, he sought various odd jobs, as well as worked with his father in the mines to help make ends meet.

Mutt taught him to become a switch-hitter, knowing this would make Mickey even more of a threat at the plate. Mantle turned out to be a gifted athlete. He also played football in high school, but during a sophomore practice, he suffered the first of many physical afflic-

Mickey Mantle

Chronology	
1931	Born October 20 in Spavinaw, Oklahoma, to Elvin "Mutt" and Lowell Mantle
1935	Family moves near Commerce Oklahoma
1946	Develops osteomyelitis, a chronic bone disease, after getting kicked in the shin in high school football practice
1948	Begins minor league baseball career in Independence, Kansas, with a Class D team
1951	Joins New York Yankees and becomes part of legendary team that would dominate baseball in the 1950s and 1960s
1951	Trips on sprinkler head in outfield, tearing ligaments in his knee. Undergoes first of five knee operations
1951	Marries Merlyn Louise Johnson, his high school sweetheart and a teller in an Oklahoma bank
1952	Learns that his father, Mutt, has died of Hodgkin's disease at 39. Mantle takes death hard
1953	Hits fabled 565 foot home run at Griffith Stadium in Washington, D.C.
1956	Wins triple crown with 52 home runs, 130 runs batted in and a .353 batting average
1963	Comes to within a few feet of hitting the ball out of Yankee Stadium
1963	Breaks his ankle while playing in Baltimore. On disabled list for two months
1969	Announces his retirement at Yankees spring training
1974	Inducted unanimously into Baseball Hall of Fame
1988	Mantle and his wife separate
1989	Mantle's old teammate and drinking buddy Billy Martin dies in drunk driving accident
1994	Confronts his alcoholism and checks himself into Betty Ford clinic
1994	Mantle's own son Billy dies of heart failure
1995	Undergoes liver transplant but would die weeks later, on August 13, at age of 63

tions. After being kicked in the shin, he developed osteomyelitis—a chronic bone disease—a malady that would plague him for the rest of his life. At the time, his doctors felt it best to amputate the leg, but his father said no, and eventually, after many operations, the condition was arrested.

Semi-Pro During High School

In addition to playing football, Mantle played semi-pro baseball in high school. In a 1946 semi-pro game with his team, the Baxter Springs (Oklahoma) Whiz Kids, an umpire encouraged Mickey to try out for the pros. Mantle traveled to Joplin, Missouri, and tried out with the Yankees Farm club. A few years later, when Mickey Charles Mantle received his high school diploma, he also had a contract with the New York Yankees for $1000.

The Early Years

He began his professional baseball career in Independence, Kansas, playing on a Class D team. He was seventeen years old, shy, and insecure; in fact, Mickey was so in awe of the pros that, two years later, he found it impossible to speak to his teammate **Joe DiMaggio**.

When Mickey came up to the majors, Yankees Manager **Casey Stengel** created media interest by calling Mantle "my phenom." Stengel claimed he would be better than **Babe Ruth** or DiMaggio. Whether or not Stengel

was right, Mantle soon became part of the Yankee legend, remaining with the team from 1951 to 1968. Number 7, the former "Commerce Comet"—the kid from Oklahoma—would become a baseball hero.

His first few months in the majors he struck out too much—a common problem with many power hitters. Yet it was too much for Stengel, and he sent Mantle back to the minors. A short trip, however; less than two months later he was called back up to the squad, in time to join the Yankees as they played in the world series. Yet once more injury found its way to Mickey, and his season would be cut short when, trying to avoid an outfield collision with DiMaggio, he tripped on a sprinkler and tore the ligaments in his knee. He underwent four knee operations.

The Powerful Star is Born

In 1952 he became the Yankees starting center fielder, soon known around the league as a prodigious power hitter. In fact, the length of Mantle's home runs became the stuff of legend. In 1953 he hit a 565-foot home run at Griffith Stadium in Washington, D.C., one of the longest home runs ever hit in the major leagues. The ball sailed over 460 feet in the air, clearing the fifty-five foot wall and sixty foot sign, then landing in someone's

Awards and Accomplishments

1952-65, 1967-68	American League All-Star Team
1952, 1956-57	*Sporting News* Major League All-Star Team
1956	*Sporting News* Major League Player of the Year; Associated Press Male Athlete of the Year; Hickok Belt
1956-67, 1962	American League most valuable player
1956-62	*Sporting News* Outstanding American League Player
1961-62, 1964	*Sporting News* American League All-Star Team
1962	American League Gold Glove Award
1974	Inducted into National Baseball Hall of Fame
1999	MLB All-Century Team; Uniform number 7 retired by Yankees

backyard. Yankee pitcher Bob Kuzava said of the homer, "I never saw a ball hit so far. You could have cut it up into fifteen singles." The ball and bat are now in the Baseball Hall of Fame in Cooperstown, New York.

Tragic Hero?

Mantle's rise in popularity paralleled the rise in America's obsession with the television. When he started playing in 1951, baseball was at the peak of its popularity. After the war, the country flocked to ballparks and gathered around radios (and televisions, if they could find them). With Mantle's strong bat, his good looks and charm, the chance that when you tuned into a Yankee game you might see or hear Mickey hit one out of the park sparked excitement in fans of every age.

In addition to his individual appeal, Mantle played on the New York Yankees, a team that had, of course, the legend of The Babe. Yankee Stadium was "the House that Ruth built," and add to that **Willie Mays** concurrently playing center for the New York Giants, and Duke Snider in center for the Brooklyn Dodgers, and New York was a media frenzy. When the Yankees made it into their innumerable World Series games in the fifties, fans would remember Mickey Mantle as the hero of many of the games. At the conclusion of his career, Mantle had hit 536 home runs, batted in 1509 runs on 2415 hits and had ten out of eighteen seasons when he hit .300 or better. But he had also struck out a record 1710 times.

Perhaps what he's best remembered for was the 1961 season, when he and teammate **Roger Maris** attempted to break Babe Ruth's thirty-four year old mark of sixty home runs in a single season. Throughout the year, the two matched each other homer for homer. The contest—in actuality two friends playing the best baseball they could—became a media circus. Babe Ruth had also been a Yankee, which only added to the hype as the season wound down.

A few weeks before the season ended, Mantle developed a bad pain in his hip after a doctor had given him

Related Biography: Baseball Player Whitey Ford

Born on October 21, 1928, Eddie "Whitey" Ford earned his nickname as a towheaded boy playing baseball at the Astoria Boys Club. Yankees scout Paul Krichell saw him pitch his high school team, the Aviation Trades, to the New York Journal American Sandlot tournament championship. At the time, Ford was playing first base but had pitched in the game as a substitute.

In 1946, Ford signed a minor league Yankee contract. He would remain in the minors for several years, compiling a 51-20 record. When he finally made his way up into the majors, he was already pitching like a veteran player.

In his first season with the Yankees, Ford compiled a 9-1 record. He would leave for the next two seasons (1951 and 1952) to serve his country at Fort Monmouth.

When he returned, in 1953, Ford fell right back into the rotation. At 5'10" tall, Whitey was stocky, strong, and confident. It was his confidence that allowed him to make the high pressure pitches to get himself out of trouble.

In 1956 he led the league with a .760 winning percentage, winning nineteen games with a 2.47 ERA. In 1961, Whitey Ford won the Cy Young award with a record of 25-4.

After he retired, Ford spent two seasons coaching for the Yankees, later becoming a scout for the team. In his baseball career he amassed a won-loss record of 236-106, with a 2.75 ERA, forty-five shutouts and 1956 strikeouts.

One of Mantle's best friends during some of the most glorious years in Yankee history, Whitey Ford eventually joined Mantle in recalling the glory years in their 1978 book, *Whitey and Mickey: A Joint Autobiography of the Yankee Years.*

an injection. The wound never healed, and as the abscess grew worse and more painful, Mickey's performance faltered. He was eventually sidelined at fifty-four home runs, while Maris went on to reach the fabled "61" first.

An interesting side note to the battle between Mantle and Maris is that Mantle had been the fan favorite. By this point in his career, Mantle could talk to the media. Maris, on the other hand, who was shy and didn't give the reporters much camera time, soon found out that beating "The Mick" for the record was more of a burden than cause to celebrate.

After the 1963 season, a year which saw him come within only a few feet of hitting a baseball out of Yankee Stadium, Mantle's career began to fade. His knees were gone (so bad that many were amazed he could play at all). While playing in Baltimore, Mantle broke his ankle and didn't see any playing time for two months.

The injuries were beginning to pile up, and he found he was always in pain, had difficulty throwing, and had trouble batting from the left side. Over the final four years of his career he would never bat above .300, he hit fewer than thirty homers a season, and never again batted in sixty runs. He announced his retirement in 1969 at spring training.

He was unanimously voted into the Hall of Fame in 1974, his first year of eligibility. The Yankees retired the

Career Statistics

Yr	Team	AVG	GP	AB	R	H	HR	RBI	BB	SO	SB	E
1951	NYY	.267	96	341	61	91	13	65	43	74	8	6
1952	NYY	.311	142	549	94	171	23	87	75	111	4	14
1953	NYY	.295	127	461	105	136	21	92	79	90	8	6
1954	NYY	.300	146	543	129	163	27	102	102	107	5	9
1955	NYY	.306	147	517	121	158	37	99	113	97	8	2
1956	NYY	.353	150	533	132	188	52	130	112	99	10	4
1957	NYY	.365	144	474	121	173	34	94	146	75	16	7
1958	NYY	.304	150	519	127	158	42	97	129	120	18	8
1959	NYY	.285	144	541	104	154	31	75	93	126	21	2
1960	NYY	.275	153	527	110	145	40	94	111	125	14	3
1961	NYY	.317	153	514	132	163	54	128	126	112	12	6
1962	NYY	.321	123	377	96	121	30	89	122	78	9	5
1963	NYY	.314	65	172	40	54	15	35	40	32	2	1
1964	NYY	.303	143	465	92	141	35	111	99	102	6	5
1965	NYY	.255	122	361	44	92	19	46	73	76	4	6
1966	NYY	.288	108	333	40	96	23	56	57	76	1	0
1967	NYY	.245	144	440	63	108	22	55	107	113	1	8
1968	NYY	.237	144	435	57	103	18	54	106	97	6	15
TOTAL		.298	2401	8102	1677	2415	536	1509	1733	1710	153	107

NYY: New York Yankees.

famed "Number 7," the jersey of a man who played on twelve pennant-winning and seven World Series-winning teams. "Mantle" became synonymous with the New York Yankees and their mid-century dominance of baseball.

After the Game

Mantle was a heavy drinker during his baseball career. As with many celebrites, the success and glamour and the accompanying financial windfalls could become a burden, and for a star like Mantle, raised in poverty in the midwest, it was fame he had difficulty handling. During his years as a player, there was little public knowledge about his off-the-field exploits. He often teamed up with fellow Yankees **Billy Martin** and Whitey Ford, carrying on into the early hours of the morning. To many of his teammates and others who knew about the carousing, they often turned their heads. After all, he was still performing on the field, so wasn't this just harmless fun?

Reconciliation

Mantle later conceded that his drinking took years off his career. The bottle had deteriorated his health to the point that his body was unable to fight the diseases that afflicted him. Not sure of what to do once he retired, much of his time was spent drinking. He played in celebrity golf tournaments, took a shot at running a restaurant, and, like Willie Mays, did PR for an Atlantic City casino.

Mickey Mantle had married his wife, Merlyn, after the 1952 season, but after more than thirty years of dealing with his now infamous exploits, they separated in 1988. Merlyn, too, had problems with alcohol, but she sought help, something Mantle didn't do until it was too late.

In 1989 his old Yankee drinking buddy, Billy Martin, died in a drunk driving accident, but it would be almost five years before Mantle would seek help for his own problems. In early 1994, suffering from tremors and memory loss, he checked himself into the Betty Ford Clinic. But it was too late. Mantle would soon see his son Billy die of heart failure, in March of that same year. Afflicted by Hodgkin's disease (the same disease that killed Mantle's father when he was only 39, as well as his grandfather), Mantle's son had become addicted to drugs.

Too Little, Too Late

After he was released from the clinic, Mantle seemed ready to make amends for the wrongs in his life. He appeared before the press as an optimistic man, and he told *People* that "...all those years I lived the life of somebody I didn't know. A cartoon character. From now on Mickey Mantle is going to be a real person. I still can't remember much of the last ten years ... but I'm looking forward to the memories I'll have in the next ten."

Yet it was too late to make amends. On June 8, 1995, Mantle underwent a liver transplant to replace the one he had done so much damage to. Beset by cancer, hepatitis, and cirrhosis, the transplant was a success, but the cancer had spread beyond his liver to most of his internal organs. On August 13th, to the shock of much of the American public, Mantle died.

The contribution of Mickey Mantle to the game of baseball, and the memories he gave fans of the game, are without equal. Many would argue that he was one of the greatest baseball players ever, and undoubtedly, one of the best of his generation.

SELECTED WRITINGS BY MANTLE:

(With Ben Epstein) *The Mickey Mantle Story*, Holt, 1953.

(With Whitey Ford) *Whitey and Mickey: A Joint Autobiography of the Yankee Years*, New American Library, 1978.

(With Herb Gluck) *The Mick*, Doubleday, 1985.

(With Phil Pepe) *My Favorite Summer, 1956*, Doubleday, 1991.

(With Mickey Herskowitz) *All My Octobers*, Harper Collins, 1994.

FURTHER INFORMATION

Books

Berger, Phil. *Mickey Mantle*. New York: Park Lane, 1998.

Castro, Tony. *Mickey Mantle: America's Prodigal Son*. Washington, D.C.: Brassey's, Inc., 2002.

Creamer, Robert W, and *Sports Illustrated. Mantle Remembered. Sports Illustrated Presents*. New York: Warner, 1995.

Falkner, David. *The Last Hero: The Life of Mickey Mantle*. New York: Simon & Schuster, 1995.

Honig, Donald. *Mays, Mantle, Snider*. New York: Macmillan, 1987.

Mantle, Merlyn, Mickey Mantle Jr., David Mantle, and Dan Mantle. *A Hero All His Life*. New York: HarperCollins, 1996.

Mantle, Mickey and Ben Epstein. *The Mickey Mantle Story*. New York: Holt, 1953.

Mantle, Mickey and Whitey Ford. *Whitey and Mickey: A Joint Autobiography of the Yankee Years*. New York: New American Library, 1978.

Mantle, Mickey and Mickey Herskowitz. *All My Octobers*. New York: Doubleday, 1994.

Mantle, Mickey and Herb Gluck. *The Mick*. New York: Doubleday, 1985.

Mantle, Mickey and Phil Pepe. *My Favorite Summer, 1956*. New York: Doubleday, 1991.

Netley, John. *Mickey Mantle: The Unauthorized Biography*. Melville, NY: Personality Comics, 1992.

Shapiro, Herb. *Mickey Mantle and the Yankee's Greatest Decade, 1951-1961*. San Diego: Revolutionary Comics, 1992.

Schoor, Gene. *The Illustrated History of Mickey Mantle*. New York: Carroll and Graf, 1996.

St. James Encyclopedia of Popular Culture. Detroit: St. James Press, 2000.

Periodicals

Life (July 30, 1965): 47-53.

Look (February 23, 1965): 71-75.

Newsweek (June 25, 1956): 63-67.

Newsweek (August 14, 1961): 42-46.

New York Times (August 14, 1995): 1A.

People (August 28, 1995): 76.

Washington Post (August 14, 1995): 1A.

Other

"Mickey Mantle." http://www.baseball-reference.com/ (November 10, 2002).

"Mickey Mantle." http://www.pubdim.net/baseballlibrary/ (November 10, 2002).

FBI Documents Pertaining to Mickey Mantle. http://foia.fbi.gov/mantle/mantle.pdf/ (November 10, 2002).

Sketch by Eric Lagergren

Diego Maradona
1961-

Argentine soccer player

During the 1980s, Argentine midfielder Diego Maradona was one of soccer's greatest stars. Over the course of 483 games at the professional level, Maradona scored a record 255 goals, and was regularly hailed as the best living player in the world, second only to **Pelé** as the sport's most extraordinary talent. Yet Maradona often made unwise statements to the press, and began running into trouble with the law as his fame soured to infamy. His controversial goal in the 1986 World Cup contest earned him a permanent place in the annals of sports history: in a quarterfinals game against Britain, Maradona's hand touched the ball, but the resulting goal remained valid, and Argentina went on to beat West Germany for the World Cup that year. For that, Maradona was a beloved folk hero in his country, despite his highly publicized hijinks off the field. One pundit for the *Economist* remarked that Maradona "helped to liberate Argentine pride at a time when, under military rule, nationalism was a matter of some ambivalence."

Maradona was born in 1961 in the Villa Fiorito slum of Buenos Aires. The family was of Indio, or non-European heritage, and he was one of seven children in the poor household. His first soccer ball was a gift, and he allegedly became so attached to it that he began sleeping with it. A standout player even as a child, he led the city's Los Cebollitas youth team on a 140-game winning streak. At the age of 14 he joined the Argentinos Juniors franchise, and led them to the World Junior Championship. In 1977, he became the youngest player ever to win a spot on the Argentine national team; the following year, however, with the 1978 World Cup slated to begin in Argentina, he was denied a spot on the team. It was a slight he did not easily forget, and after playing with an-

Diego Maradona

other juniors team for a time in Buenos Aires, Maradona took his talents overseas.

A Star in Europe

Barcelona's professional soccer team spent $7.7 million to buy out Maradona's contract, a record at the time, and was rewarded richly for it; he quickly led the team to the Spanish League title. Maradona emerged as a speedy, slippery player, able to miraculously evade opposing players and hold the ball for yards as he ran down the field. Once near the goal, he possessed an uncanny ability to fake out the goaltender and land the ball in the net. He often scored nearly a dozen goals per season, and quickly became the object of much venom from other players. On the field, they kicked at his ankles or knees, hoping to injure him, and succeeded once in 1983 by dislocating his ankle.

Maradona's off-the-pitch antics around Barcelona began to capture press attention as well. He was known for leading his friends on long, carousing evenings, and the behavior continued when a failing Italian team, Napoli, signed him in 1984 to a $12 million, nine-year contract. Not surprisingly, the team emerged as a powerhouse in the Italian league, and won two championships with him as their star player. Yet Maradona's allegiance remained with Argentina for the World Cup contests, and in 1986, at the height of his career, he scored what would come to be known as the "hand of God" goal in

the annals of soccer. Argentina met England in the quarterfinals, and national tensions still ran high between the two countries over the Falklands, a group of islands off Argentina's eastern coast. In 1982, a military junta in power in Buenos Aires moved to retake the islands, but Britain sent a flotilla of ships and reasserted its claim to one of its last colonial outposts.

Claimed Divine Intervention

In Maradona's first goal of that game, the ball bounced off his fist, a violation of one of soccer's most stringent rules, but the referees did not see his hand touch the ball before it landed in the net. Maradona later said that it was not his hand, but rather the "hand of God" that had put the ball in the net. Later in the game, Maradona ran 55 yards down the field, deftly eluding England's defense, and again scored. England lost and was ejected from the quarterfinals, and Argentina went on to beat West Germany. In England, Maradona was excoriated in the press, derided for what was seen as a decidedly unsportsmanlike move; in Argentina, however, the win was heralded as yet another example of what Argentines prided themselves as possessing as a national character trait, *viveza,* or triumph through cunning.

Back in Naples, Maradona remained a major celebrity and inarguably the Italian League's biggest star. But stories of drug use and illegal gambling began to dog him, and he was rumored to have links to the Neapolitan *camorra,* or organized-crime syndicate. As he gained weight and grew sloppy in his training habits, Italian sportswriters enjoyed poking fun at him. At the time, he was soccer's highest earner. "For some veteran observers, Maradona is a symbol of all that has gone wrong with the sport of soccer," wrote *Sports Illustrated*'s Rick Telander. "He is aloof and mercenary, whereas most

---

Awards and Accomplishments

1978-80	Named top goal-scorer of the Metropolitan League with Argentinos Juniors
1979	Named South American Player of the Year
1979-80	Named "Olimpia de gold" as the best Argentine sportsman of the year (Círculo de Periodistad Deportivos)
1979-81	Won "The Golden Ball" as the best soccer player of the year by the Fédération Internationale de Football Association (FIFA)
1983	Won Spanish King's Cup with Barcelona
1986	Became World Champion with the Argentinian National Team
1986	Named "Olimpia de plata" as the best Argentine soccer player of the year (Círculo de Periodistad Deportivos)
1986	Won "The Golden Ball" as the best soccer player of the World Cup (FIFA)
1987, 1990	Won Italian League Crown with Naples team
1988	Was top goal-scorer of the Italian Major League with Naples team
1989	Won European Soccer Union Cup with Naples
1993	Named "Olimpia de plata" as the best Argentine soccer player of century (Círculo de Periodistad Deportivos)
1999	Named "Olimpia de plata" as the best Argentine sportsman of the century (Círculo de Periodistad Deportivos)
2000	Won FIFA Internet voting for best soccer player of the century

great former players were supposedly kind, grateful and dedicated beyond the limits of monetary reward."

Fewer Goals, More Acrimony

In early 1991, Maradona was arrested in Naples and charged with cocaine possession. A few months later, he tested positive for drugs and was suspended from international play for 15 months. He was then arrested in a raid on a Buenos Aires drug den, and Naples released him from the last year of his contract in 1992 so that he could play for Seville in the Spanish League. A year later, with that foray ending in more bitter words, Maradona returned to Argentina and played with Newell's Old Boys; again, he had further run-ins with the law, and tested positive for a stimulant once again during the 1994 World Cup championships, and was forced off the Argentine team. The drug, ephedrine, had been prescribed by his doctor for allergies, and some of Maradona's stauncher supporters suspected a set-up.

In 1995, Maradona played what would be his final pro season with the Boca Juniors in Argentina. His 1986 World Cup goal remains one of soccer's most memorable moments, replayed often for the way in which the announcer sobs in joy. In 2000, he was admitted to a hospital in Uruguay for a suspected cocaine overdose. He relocated to Cuba for a time, ostensibly to enter a rehabilitation program, and wrote his autobiography, *Yo Soy El Diego* ("I Am Diego"), that was an immediate bestseller in South America. That year, he also shared the Player of the Century award with Pelé in a contest held by the Fédération Internationale de Football Association (FIFA), and was the winner of the most FIFA Internet votes from around the world. In early 2002, he returned to Argentina from Cuba to take part in a farewell game and ceremony where the Argentine league officially retired his jersey. When he took a victory lap, around the pitch, fans sobbed in the stands.

CONTACT INFORMATION

Address: c/o FIFA House, P.O. Box 85, 8030 Zurich, Switzerland.

SELECTED WRITINGS BY MARADONA:

Yo Soy El Diego. Santiago: Planeta Publishing, 2000.

FURTHER INFORMATION

Books

"Diego Maradona." *Encyclopedia of World Biography Supplement,* Volume 20. Detroit: Gale, 2000.

Periodicals

"Argentines Ponder Maradona's Fall." *Economist* (January 15, 2000): 35.

"Cornered Kicker." *Sports Illustrated* (July 11, 1994): 10.

Gammon, Clive. "Pain and Glory for 'San Diego.'" *Sports Illustrated* (June 16, 1986): 54.

Gammon, Clive. "Tango Argentino!" *Sports Illustrated* (July 7, 1986): 14.

"Maradona's Autobiography Has Record Sale." Xinhua News Agency (October 4, 2000).

"Maradona Resurrected." *Sports Illustrated* (October 16, 1995): 20.

Telander, Rick. "Prima Dona." *Sports Illustrated* (May 14, 1990): 96.

Wahl, Grant. "Extreme Football." *Sports Illustrated* (February 26, 2002): 144.

Sketch by Carol Brennan

Rocky Marciano
1923-1969

American boxer

Rocky Marciano is the only heavyweight boxing champion ever to retire without being defeated. With a perfect 49-0 record—which included forty-three knockouts—he started his professional boxing career in 1947, and reigned as champion from 1952 until his re-

Rocky Marciano

tirement in 1956. He ranks among boxing's greats, along with such notables as **Muhammad Ali**, **Joe Louis** (whom he defeated the year before becoming world champion), and **Jack Dempsey**.

First a Baseball Player

Rocco Francis Marchegiano, the future Rocky Marciano, was born on September 1, 1923, in Brockton, Massachusetts, the son of working class parents. An immigrant from Italy, his father worked in a shoe factory. This factory made a big impression on the young Marciano. It was Marciano's job in the family to take lunch to his father at work each day, and there he saw first-hand the toll factory work took on the people who worked there. Marciano vowed that he would never make his living that way.

In high school, Marciano excelled in sports. He played on the Brockton High football team as a linebacker, once intercepting a pass and running sixty-seven yards for a touchdown. His dreams were of baseball, however, and he planned to become a professional player after he dropped out of school at the age of sixteen. He worked in blue-collar jobs, including a two month stint at the shoe factory, while he trained to become a professional baseball player. His fledgling baseball career was interrupted, however, when the United States entered World War II at the end of 1942.

Drafted into the army in 1943, Marciano discovered the sport that was to be his career when he took up boxing to avoid kitchen duty. After serving in Wales and at Ft. Lewis, Washington with the 150th Combat Engineers, Marciano was discharged following the close of the war. He worked at odd jobs to support himself while he pursued a career in baseball. His hard work paid off when he landed a tryout with the Chicago Cubs as a catcher and first baseman. But he failed to make he team after a throw from home plate to second base fell short.

Commits to Boxing

Returning to boxing, Marciano began to make a name for himself on the amateur circuit, quickly becoming known as a hard-hitting, if somewhat awkward fighter. He became a professional boxer in 1947. Managed first by a mechanic from his home town, he soon realized the need to place himself in the care of a well-known professional if he wanted to advanced his career. He switched to the management of Al Weill, a promoter from New York who was to remain his manager throughout his career. It was the right move. Weill introduced Marciano to famous trainer Charlie Goldman, who helped Marciano hone what was to become his signature fighting style, and made him into a true professional. At five feet, eleven inches, about 185 points, and with the shortest arms of any heavyweight champion in the modern era, Marciano also tended to slouch, and was not particularly agile. But he packed a powerful punch, and that's what Goldman trained him to focus on. He also taught him to emphasize his small stature, crouching low to avoid his opponents' own punches, and moving in with powerful right punches and left hooks. Marciano also developed the ability to absorb a tremendous amount of punishment, often coming back from blows that would have finished a lesser fighter, to knock his opponents out. Broken hands, back injuries, and countless facial cuts all were meted out to Marciano during the course of his career.

With Weill and Goldman's help, Marciano's career took off. He knocked out the first sixteen opponents he

<table>
<tr><td colspan="2">**Awards and Accomplishments**</td></tr>
</table>

1948	Golden Glove Champion
1951	Awarded Packy McFarland Memorial Trophy by an association of Chicago boxing writers
1952	World heavyweight boxing champion
1952	Awarded Edward Neil Memorial Plaque by an association of New York boxing writers
1952, 1954	Named Fighter of the Year by *Ring* magazine
1990	Inducted into the International Boxing Hall of Fame

In his nine years as a professional boxer, Marciano was never defeated, winning all of his forty-nine bouts, an astonishing forty-three of them in knockouts. He is the only heavyweight boxing champion to retire completely undefeated.

Rocky Marciano

Although no theatrical-release films have been yet been made about the life of Rocky Marciano, the Showtime cable TV network aired a dramatic interpretation of the famous fighter's life in 1999. Called *Rocky Marciano*, the 100-minute program featured Jon Favreau in the title role, and the great George C. Scott in one of his final roles, as Marciano's father.

Not praised for its brilliant acting or quality of writing, *Rocky Marciano* nevertheless distinguished itself by presenting a reasonably accurate portrayal of the boxer's beginnings, his rise to fame, and his post-boxing years. Of particular note was a lavish, stylized treatment of Marciano's fight with Joe Louis, mournfully underscored by the music of Samuel Barber. The program was directed by Charles Winkler, and written by Winkler with William Nack, Lary Golin, and Dick Beebe.

Rocky Marciano was later released on video.

faced in professional bouts, steadily moving up through the boxing ranks to face stronger and more skilled opponents. Maricano continued to prove his mettle through 1949, winning all of his fights, more than half of them by knockouts. Marciano knew that he had a chance to fight for the title of heavyweight champion of the world after he defeated Roland LaStarza on March 24, 1949. The fight lasted ten rounds, and was called Marciano's in a close decision. He received national attention after a fight with Carmine Vingo on December 20, 1949 in which Marciano seriously injured his opponent when he knocked him out.

At the Top of His Game

Marciano married his childhood sweetheart, Barbara M. Cousins on the last day of 1950. The couple eventually had one child of their own, Mary Anne, and adopted another, Rocky Kevin. Back in the ring soon after the wedding, Marciano continued his climb through the boxing ranks, fighting more and more powerful opponents, including Red Layne, whom he knocked out in six rounds on July 12, 1951.

Marciano faced his most powerful opponent yet when he squared off against former world champion Joe Louis on October 26, 1951. Louis was one of Marciano's idols, but at the end of his career, and Marciano, with thirty-seven wins to his credit so far, including thirty-two knockouts, was in his prime. The former champion went down under Marciano's onslaught in eight rounds. It happened after Marciano got Louis against the ropes, and managed to slip in a powerful left hook. Louis was stunned, dropping his guard, and Marciano immediately followed up with a right that knocked his hero out. "Imagine looking at Joe Louis lying there on the ropes," he was quoted as saying afterward by *Newsweek*. "And I did it. I don't know if I'm happy about it." So distraught was Marciano at felling his hero that he cried in the ex-champion's dressing room after the match.

The fight with Louis cleared the way for a championship bout with the heavyweight champion of the world, **'Jersey' Joe Walcott** in Philadelphia on September 23, 1952. Marciano got off to a bad start in the first round when he was knocked down. Off balance from then on, and behind on points, he got in one of his by-now-famous right hand punches to the jaw, flooring Walcott and knocking him out in the thirteenth round.

An Unbeatable Champion

With his defeat of Walcott, Marciano became the first white heavyweight boxing champion since 1937. He defended his title six times, winning each time. The first was in a rematch with Walcott on May 15, 1953, a bout he won handily with a knockout in the first round. He next faced his old adversary Roland LaStarza on September 24, 1953, and won in eleven rounds, putting LaStarza in the hospital for several days. LaStarza said afterwards that he wished Marciano had just knocked him out to end it instead of working him over for so long. A fifteen-round fight with former champion Ezzard Charles followed on June 17, 1954. Marciano won that match in a decision, and the two faced each other again later that year, on September 17, 1954. Charles got the better of Marciano in the sixth round, battering his nose so badly that Marciano's cornermen were unable to staunch the bleeding. The ring doctor very nearly called the fight, but Marciano rallied in the eighth round, knocking out his opponent.

Marciano's next title fight was against Don Cockell on May 16, 1955. In spite of pressure from organized crime elements to throw the fight, Marciano won it in a knockout in the ninth round, and moved on to what was to be his last title fight, on September 21, 1955. The bout took place at Yankee Stadium, and it was the third time he had defended his title there. His opponent was former light-heavyweight champion **Archie Moore**. Marciano knocked him out in nine rounds. The fight was witnessed by more than 400,000 people watching via the fairly new medium of television.

A Life Cut Short

The champion retired from boxing in 1956, when he was 31 years old. His record between 1947 and 1956 of forty-nine victories to zero losses included forty-three knockouts. Weary of training, and with tension rising between him and his manager, Al Weill (his arrangement with Weill required him to split all of his earnings 50-50), Marciano welcomed the opportunity to spend more time with his family. A careful manager of his own money, Marciano was set for life with a four million dollar fortune, and did not want to go out with a whimper as other champions had done, by continuing to fight past his prime. He did nearly succumb to temptation to stage a comeback in 1959, and spent a month training in secret before thinking better of it.

Now the only heavyweight boxing champion to retire completely undefeated, Marciano spent the next ten years making personal appearances. He died on the night of August 31, 1969 when the private plane in which he was a passenger crashed outside of Des Moines, Iowa. He died one day shy of his 46th birthday. He was survived by his wife Barbara—to whom he had been married for nineteen years—and his two children, Rocco Kevin, and Mary Anne. He was said to have had many close friends and to be a loving husband and father, but nevertheless to be extremely secretive about his post-boxing business dealings. He died without making a will, and without revealing where he had placed much of his fortune.

Somewhat awkward, not noted for his speed or agility, Marciano nevertheless overcame his opponents through sheer drive, determination, and the power of his punches. He remains today the only heavyweight champion boxer to retire completely undefeated.

FURTHER INFORMATION

Books

Dictionary of American Biography, Supplement 8: 1966-1970. New York: American Council of Learned Societies, 1988.

Encyclopedia of World Biography, 2nd ed. Detroit: Gale Group, 1998.

Periodicals

Anderson, Dave. "The Last Great White Hope." *New York Times* (September 15, 2002): section 7, p .21.

"Rocky Drops His Idol, Gender Politics on Center Court." *Newsweek* (October 25, 1999): 61.

Other

"Rocky Marciano." *American Decades CD-ROM*. Detroit: Gale Group, 1998.

"Rocky Marciano." Apollo Movie Guide. http://www.apolloguide.com/mov_fullrev.asp?CID=1 523=1531 (October 30, 2002).

"Rocky Marciano." Cyber Boxing Zone. http://www.cyberboxingzone.com/boxing/rocky.htm (October 15, 2002).

"Rocky Marciano." International Boxing Hall of Fame. http://www.ibhof.com/marciano.htm (October 15, 2002).

"Rocky Marciano." Internet Movie Database. http://us.imdb.com/Title?0183718 (October 30, 2002).

Sketch by Michael Belfiore

Dan Marino
1961-

American football player

He's considered the most prolific passer the National Football League (NFL) ever produced. During his seventeen seasons with the Miami Dolphins, Dan Marino generated one of the most remarkable quarterbacking careers in the history of football, averaging twenty-four touchdown passes per season offset by fewer than fourteen interceptions. Year after year, game after game, play after play, Marino's laser-sharp passes moved his team down the field and into scoring position. When Marino retired after the 1999 season, he held records for the most passing yards (61,361), completions (4,967), and touchdown passes (420) in NFL history. Over the years, this fiery competitor won not only games, but also the hearts of the South Florida people. His on-field heroics entertained them, while his off-field endeavors enhanced their lives. Without Marino, The Miami Children's Hospital Dan Marino Center wouldn't exist. Marino's charitable foundation helped build the 20,000-square-foot center, which serves children with chronic medical needs.

Learned Sports Fundamentals from Father

Daniel Constantine Marino, Jr., was born September 15, 1961, in Pittsburgh, Pennsylvania, to Veronica and Dan Marino, Sr. Marino grew up in a blue-collar section of Pittsburgh called Oakland, along with his two younger sisters. Marino's mother worked as a school crossing guard, and his father drove the midnight delivery truck for the *Pittsburgh Post-Gazette.*

Marino was young when his father, a sandlot football coach, taught him to toss a football. While waiting for dinner, the father and son pitched the ball back and forth in the living room. Early on, Marino developed a quick release as his father taught him to draw the ball back swiftly and release it with a flick of the wrist and a whip of the shoulders. By the time he entered the pros, Marino could take the ball from the center and get off a pass

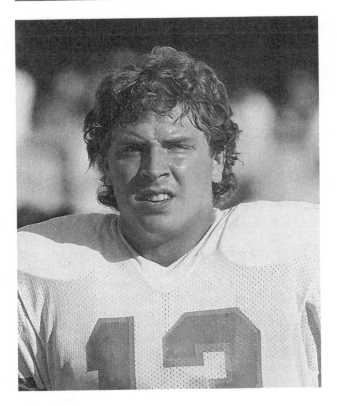

Dan Marino

Chronology

1961	Born September 15 in Pittsburgh, Pennsylvania
1971	Plays on the St. Regis grade school football team
1979	Graduates from Pittsburgh's Central Catholic High School
1979	Drafted on June 5 by Kansas City Royals to play baseball
1979	Begins football career at the University of Pittsburgh (Pitt)
1981	Plays in Sugar Bowl, coming away the game MVP
1983	Graduates from Pitt with a communications degree
1983	Taken by Miami Dolphins on April 26 as the 27th pick in the first round of the NFL draft
1983	Makes first pro start on October 9
1985	Plays in first (and only) Super Bowl on January 20, a loss to the San Francisco 49ers
1985	Marries Claire Veazey on January 30
1992	Establishes the Dan Marino Foundation
1993	Tears Achilles tendon on October 10; sits out remainder of season
1994	Plays self in movie *Ace Ventura: Pet Detective*
1999	Misses five starts due to pinched neck nerve
1999	Released by Miami Dolphins at end of season
2000	Announces retirement from football on March 13
2000	Joins HBO's "Inside the NFL" series as co-host
2002	Joins CBS' "The NFL Today" as co-host

in just 1.5 seconds, greatly decreasing the chances of getting sacked.

Besides teaching Marino basic sports fundamentals, Marino's father also taught him that hard work and determination were key to success. In his autobiography, Marino recalled that his father always told him, "'You don't deserve anything in life. You work for what you deserve.'"

Became High School Football, Baseball Star

At Central Catholic High School, Marino starred as a football quarterback and baseball pitcher. During both his junior and senior seasons, Marino passed for more than 1,000 yards, earning *Parade* magazine All-America honors in 1979, his senior year.

Marino could have played college football just about anywhere, but he chose to stay close to home and attend the University of Pittsburgh, or Pitt. After Marino signed with Pitt, the Kansas City Royals baseball team drafted him. Marino was thrilled. He planned to play baseball during the summers and attend college the rest of the year. However, Marino turned down the baseball contract when he found out that if he accepted it, he would lose his athletic scholarship and have to pay for college.

Became Hometown Hero at Pitt

In 1979, Marino entered Pitt, his hometown school. Part way through his freshman year, the 6-foot-4, 225-pound Marino took over for Pitt's injured star quarterback and never left the lineup. Marino led the Pittsburgh Panthers to an 11-1 record during each of his freshman, sophomore, and junior years. He also led his team to four post-season appearances, in the Fiesta, Gator, Sugar, and Cotton bowls.

Marino's junior year, 1981, proved the most prolific. That year, he rewrote the school's record books, setting single-season records for most completed passes (226), passing yard (2,876), and touchdown passes (37). He also led his team to a 24-20 Sugar Bowl victory over the University of Georgia with the go-ahead touchdown pass coming with 35 seconds left to play. For his efforts, Marino was named Sugar Bowl MVP and finished fourth in voting for the Heisman Trophy, given to the most outstanding college football player. By the time Marino finished his senior season at Pitt, he owned the school's all-time records for pass completions (693), yards gained (8,290), and career touchdown passes (79).

Drafted by Miami Dolphins

In the 1983 NFL draft, Marino was the 27th player drafted. It was a banner year for quarterback talent, and five other quarterbacks, including **John Elway** and **Jim Kelly**, were chosen before the Miami Dolphins picked Marino.

From the beginning, Marino and Miami Dolphins coach **Don Shula** hit it off. In his autobiography, Marino said he progressed rapidly because Shula forced him to call his own plays early on. Instead of relying on his coach, Marino had to learn to dissect the defense on his own. This forced Marino to study longer and play harder.

Career Statistics

Yr	Team	Passing									Rushing		
		ATT	COM	YDS	COM%	TD	INT	SK	RAT	ATT	YDS	TD
1983	Miami	296	173	2210	58.4	20	6	10	96.0	28	45	2
1984	Miami	564	362	5084	64.2	48	17	13	108.9	28	−7	0
1985	Miami	567	336	4137	59.3	30	21	18	84.1	26	−24	0
1986	Miami	623	378	4746	60.7	44	23	17	92.5	12	−3	0
1987	Miami	444	263	3245	59.2	26	13	9	89.2	12	−5	1
1988	Miami	606	354	4434	58.4	28	23	6	80.8	20	−17	0
1989	Miami	550	308	3997	56.0	24	22	10	76.9	14	−7	2
1990	Miami	531	306	3563	57.6	21	11	15	82.6	16	29	0
1991	Miami	549	318	3970	57.9	25	13	27	85.8	27	32	1
1992	Miami	554	330	4116	59.6	24	16	28	85.1	20	66	0
1993	Miami	150	91	1218	60.7	8	3	7	95.9	9	−4	1
1994	Miami	615	385	4453	62.6	30	17	18	89.2	22	−6	1
1995	Miami	482	309	3668	64.1	24	15	22	90.8	11	14	0
1996	Miami	373	221	2795	59.2	17	9	18	87.8	11	−3	0
1997	Miami	548	319	3780	58.2	16	11	20	80.7	18	−14	0
1998	Miami	537	310	3497	57.7	23	15	23	80.0	21	−3	1
1999	Miami	369	204	2448	55.3	12	17	9	67.4	6	−6	0
TOTAL		8358	4967	61361	59.4	420	252	270	86.4	301	87	9

Miami: Miami Dolphins.

On October 9, Marino got his first pro start and completed 19 of 29 passes, including three touchdowns, in a 38-35 overtime loss to Buffalo. He set many NFL records that year, including highest completion percentage for a rookie (58.4) and lowest percentage of interceptions for a rookie (2.0). As the leading passer for the American Football Conference (AFC), Marino became the first rookie chosen to start at the Pro Bowl and was named *The Sporting News* Rookie of the Year.

The following year, 1984, proved spectacular for Marino as he set NFL single-season records for touchdown passes (48), passing yards (5,084), and completions (362). With Marino's help, the Dolphins went 14-2 and won the AFC championship. They headed to Super Bowl XIX, where they faced **Joe Montana** and the San Francisco 49ers on January 20, 1985. Marino drove the ball 318 yards by completing 29 of 50 passes, but the Dolphins still lost 38-16.

Marino's strong arm and fierce competitive nature made his team a perennial contender.

"What I always admired about Dan Marino was the fire about him," NFL coach Marty Schottenheimer said, according to ESPN. "Everybody talks about his quick release . . . But I always saw the fire in his eyes. When you played against him, you knew he would probably have a good day. You just hoped it wasn't enough to beat you."

Racked up an 'Armful' of Records

Over the years, Marino's arm provided an amazing aerial show for spectators. With his phenomenal passes, Marino produced a crop of records. In 1986, Marino set an NFL record by throwing 100 career touchdowns in the fewest games-forty-four. **Johnny Unitas** held the old record, throwing his 100th touchdown at game fifty-three.

In 1991, Marino became the fourth player in NFL history to pass the 35,000-yard mark. In 1994, he tossed his 300th touchdown in his 157th game. **Fran Tarkenton** held the old record for fewest games to reach 300, though it took him 217 games. In 1998, he became the first quarterback to complete 400 touchdown passes.

As to be expected, there were setbacks along the way. In 1993, Marino tore his Achilles' tendon, ending a playing streak of 145 consecutive games—an NFL record for quarterbacks. By 1996, Marino had had five knee surgeries, or "oil changes" as he liked to call them.

Retired as Great Passer, Great Humanitarian

Though Marino never made it to a Super Bowl again after 1984, he continued to stack up the records. In 1999, Marino became the first quarterback to reach 60,000 yards. The year, however, was a tough one for Marino as a pinched neck nerve forced him to sit out five starts. The season ended with a devastating 62-7 playoff loss to the Jacksonville Jaguars on January 15, 2000. Following the playoffs, the Dolphins released Marino, and several NFL teams courted him. In the end, Marino decided to retire. Going somewhere else just didn't feel right.

Though Marino's records stand out, there is one hole in his resume: he never got to play on a Super Bowl-winning team, although he retired holding twenty-five NFL regular-season records. Marino, however, says that doesn't matter. As he told the *New York Post,* "I was extremely happy with my career.... I wouldn't trade 17

Where Is He Now?

Marino and his wife, Claire, whom he married in 1985, live in Weston, Florida. Their six children, including two who were adopted from China, keep them busy. Marino also serves as a co-host for HBO's "Inside the NFL" and CBS' "The NFL Today." A great deal of his time is spent on philanthropic gestures. Marino established the Dan Marino Foundation in 1992 shortly after his son, Michael, was diagnosed with autism. Over the years, the foundation has raised more than $3.6 million to help children with developmental disabilities. To stay active, Marino plays golf and hopes to some day qualify for the U.S. Open.

years with the Dolphins, my experiences and what I did as far as consistency and taking pride in my job for a Super Bowl and having the opportunity to play in one city and play as long as I did."

Marino will be remembered not only as a great passer but also as a great humanitarian. The Miami Children's Hospital Dan Marino Center was built with help from Marino. Each month, the center serves 2,000 children from Florida and across the world. More than seventy medical professionals, from speech pathologists to neurologists, work there. Marino helped found the center—a one-stop shop for children with medical needs—after his son, Michael, was diagnosed with autism. Marino was frustrated with having to travel all over the place to see specialists to get proper care. Marino has thus left a legacy on paper-the record books-and a legacy of brick and mortar-the center-that is daily changing lives.

CONTACT INFORMATION

Address: c/o Dan Marino Foundation, PO Box 267640, Weston, FL 33326. Fax: (954) 423-5355. Phone: (954) 888-1771. Email: dmfoundation@aol.com.

SELECTED WRITINGS BY MARINO:

(With Steve Delsohn) *Marino!*, McGraw-Hill, 1986.

(With Marc Serota and Mark Vancil) *Marino: On the Record*, Collins Publishers San Francisco, 1996.

FURTHER INFORMATION

Books

Marino, Dan. *Marino: On the Record*. San Francisco: Collins Publishers San Francisco, 1996.

Owens, Thomas S. *Dan Marino: Record-Setting Quarterback*. New York: The Rosen Publishing Group, Inc., 1997.

Periodicals

Attner, Paul. "A Jewel-Without the Jewelry." *Sporting News* (March 20, 2000): 58.

Bell, Jarrett. "Marino Enjoying Easy Street: Charitable Foundation, Golfing, Kids Take His Time." *USA Today* (August 23, 2000).

Fabrikant, Geraldine. "Playing It Cautious After the Game's Over." *New York Times* (November 17, 2002).

"5 Questions for Dan Marino." *New York Post* (September 20, 2002).

King, Peter. "Letting Go." *Sports Illustrated* (March 20, 2000): 64.

Rodriguez, Ken. "Dan Marino Still Sparkles in South Florida." Knight-Ridder/Tribune News Service (September 16, 2000).

Other

"Bristol University Discusses Dan the Man." ESPN. com. http://espn.go.com/nfl/marino/analysts.html (December 9, 2002).

"Dan Marino." ESPN.com. http://football.espn.go. com/nfl/players/stats?statsID=4 (December 9, 2002).

"Dan Marino Profile, Statistics and More." ESPN.com. http://espn.go.com/nfl/profiles/stats/primary/0004. html (December 5, 2002).

"The Complete Dan Marino." *(South Florida) Sun-Sentinel*. http://www.sun-sentinel.com/graphics/ marino/ (December 10, 2002).

"The Sporting News: Dan Marino." Sporting News.com. http://www.sportingnews.com/archives/marino/ career.html (December 10, 2002).

Sketch by Lisa Frick

Roger Maris
1934-1985

American baseball player

Sixty-one must have been Roger Maris' lucky number. In the last game of 1961, the New York Yankee hit his 61st home run of the season, entering Maris permanently into the baseball record books. With that 61st homer, Maris broke professional baseball's single-season home run record, previously set by **Babe Ruth** in 1927. Maris' record remained unbroken for twenty-seven years, until the St. Louis Cardinals' **Mark McGwire** bested it in 1998. Although qualified by the infamous, and invisible, asterisk—a verbal mark on the record added by then-Baseball Commissioner Ford Frick to note that Maris had played a longer season than Ruth—the feat instantly rendered Maris a baseball legend.

Just a Summer Sport

Baseball was not Maris' only sport. Growing up in North Dakota, it was never warm enough in spring to play baseball during the school year. At Fargo's Bishop Shanley High School Maris excelled in football, basketball and track. During his senior year he set a national high school record in football when he scored four touchdowns on returns in one game.

Maris was able to pick up a bat in the summer, though, when the American Legion ran a summer league. He was named league Most Valuable Player (MVP) in 1950. Upon graduation from high school in 1952 he considered playing football for the University of Oklahoma, but left the school during his entrance exam. He then opted to sign with a Cleveland Indians farm team.

Playing in the Class C Northern League in 1953, Maris was named the league's Rookie of the Year and the following season was promoted to the Class B Three-eye League. By 1956 he had been promoted to the Class AA farm team in Indianapolis and helped carry the team to the Little World Series Championship. During his time in the minors, Maris changed the spelling of his name from "Maras" to avoid the taunts of opposing fans.

Moves to Majors

In 1957 Maris was promoted to the major leagues, although he played only one season with the Indians. He was traded to the Kansas City Athletics during the 1958 season and, in 1960, he was traded to the Yankees. Maris made a mark on the team even before it appeared he would break Ruth's long-standing record. In his first year with the Yankees he hit thirty-nine home runs, was named the American League's Most Valuable Player and received a Gold Glove award.

Chronology	
1934	Born September 10 in Hibbing, Minnesota
1938	Family moves to Grand Forks, North Dakota
1944	Family moves to Fargo, North Dakota
1948	Enters Fargo High School
1949	Joins American Legion summer baseball team as outfielder and pitcher
1950	Named summer baseball league's MVP
1950	Transfers to Bishop Shanley High School and competes in football, basketball and track
1952	Graduates Shanley High
1953	Begins professional baseball career Cleveland Indians system in Class C Northern League and named Rookie of the Year
1954	Moves to Class B Three-Eye League
1955	Changes spelling of last name from "Maras" to "Maris"
1956	Helps carry Class AA Indianapolis farm team to Little World Series Championship
1956	Marries Pat Carvell
1957	Promoted to major leagues with Cleveland Indians
1957	Traded to Kansas City Athletics at end of season
1960	Traded to New York Yankees
1961	Baseball commissioner Ford Frick announces home run record will be qualified, due to increased number of games in season
1961	Hits 61 home runs, beating Babe Ruth's record
1966	Traded to St. Louis Cardinals
1968	Retires at end of season
1984	Yankees retire Maris' number
1985	Dies of lymphoma on December 14
1991	Baseball Commissioner Fay Vincent removes asterisk from Maris' home run record

For most of the 1961 season, Maris ran neck-and-neck with teammate and friend **Mickey Mantle** for the new home run record. While the media played up stories of a rivalry between the competing Yankees, the "M & Boys" laughed at the hoopla. "When they'd read the morning newspaper, one would say to the other, 'Hey, did you know we were fighting again?'" Maris' wife Pat told *People*.

61*

When Mantle suffered an injury after his 54th home-run it became clear that Maris would be the one to break Ruth's record. Maris did not receive the same unwavering adoration the Babe enjoyed thirty-four years earlier, however, in his race toward number sixty-one. His typically blunt responses to reporters led them to portray him as gruff and unlikable, whereas Mantle was a perennial favorite with fans and the press alike.

There was little support from above, either. In July of 1961 Baseball Commissioner Ford Frick had announced that the home run record would be qualified since the season had been expanded from 154 games in Ruth's day to 162. It has been alleged by some that Frick, as ghostwriter of Ruth's autobiography, issued the qualification more as a vendetta than as a statistical necessity. Indeed, both players had gone to bat nearly the same number of times. Maris believed Yankee management,

Career Statistics

Yr	Team	Avg	GP	AB	R	H	HR	RBI	BB	SO	SB	E
1957	CLE	.235	116	358	61	84	14	51	60	79	8	7
1958	CLE/KCA	240	150	583	87	140	28	80	45	85	4	9
1959	KCA	.273	122	433	69	118	16	72	58	53	2	6
1960	NYY	.283	136	499	98	141	39	112	70	65	2	4
1961	NYY	.269	161	590	132	159	61	142	94	67	0	9
1962	NYY	.256	157	590	92	151	33	100	87	78	1	3
1963	NYY	.269	90	312	53	84	23	53	35	40	1	2
1964	NYY	.281	141	513	86	144	26	71	62	78	3	1
1965	NYY	.239	46	155	22	37	8	27	29	29	0	2
1966	NYY	.233	119	348	37	81	13	43	36	60	0	1
1967	STL	.261	125	410	64	107	9	55	52	61	0	2
1968	STL	.255	100	310	25	79	5	45	24	38	0	3
TOTAL		.260	1463	5101	826	1325	275	851	652	733	21	49

CLE: Cleveland Indians; KCA: Kansas City Athletics; NYY: New York Yankees; STL: St. Louis Cardinals.

Awards and Accomplishments

1952	Set national high school record for scoring four touchdowns on returns in one game
1953	Class C Northern League Rookie of the Year
1960	Gold Glove Award
1960-61	American League MVP
1961	Hit 61 homeruns, beating Babe Ruth's record
1961	Awarded Hickok Belt
1961	Sultan of Swat Award
1984	Number retired by Yankees

like many fans, was rooting for Mantle. "Let's not kid anybody," he said. "They wanted Mantle, not me, to break the record. Some of them even tried to rig the line-up so he would get a better opportunity than me."

Still, the crowd cheered Maris on October 1, 1961 when, in the Yankees' last game of the season, he hit that 61st homer. Always modest and shy, Maris headed straight for the dugout after rounding the bases and only returned for a bow at his teammates' urging. The sizable number of Ruth devotees among the Yankees fans, however, only stepped up their taunting of Maris following his accomplishment. His subsequent, less stellar seasons with the Yankees (he never hit more than thirty-three home runs in one season again) became increasingly un-bearable and, in 1966, he asked to be traded.

Heads to St. Louis

Maris spent his last two seasons with the St. Louis Cardinals and, although he never came near his own record, he did help his new team reach the World Series for both seasons he was with them. Maris retired after the 1967 season, although his poor treatment at the hands of fans and baseball officials haunted him for many years after that. "My going after the record started off as such a dream," he recalled much later. "Too bad it ended so badly."

After retiring from baseball, Maris ran a beer distrib-utorship given to him by Anheuser-Busch, then-owners of the Cardinals. Although he had vowed never to step foot in Yankee Stadium after he left for St. Louis, he and Mantle both returned in 1978 to raise the 1977 pennant. He returned again for Old Timers' Day and once more in 1984 when the Yankees retired his number. By that time, Maris was enduring bouts of chemotherapy to treat lym-phatic cancer. He died from the disease on December 14, 1985 at the age of 51.

Overdue Honors

In 1991 Baseball Commissioner Fay Vincent an-nounced that the asterisk next to Maris' record would be removed. Maris' accomplishments were commemorated on a 1999 postage stamp, and his race to break Babe Ruth's record, and the accompanying controversy, was chronicled in the 2001 Billy Crystal film *61**.

Maris' record stood until September 8, 1998, when the Cardinals' Mark McGwire hit homerun number 62 with five of Maris' six children in attendance. After his ball cleared the fence, McGwire hugged all of the Marises and told them he had rubbed their father's bat for good luck that day.

Today, McGwire is not the only one remembering Maris in a much fonder light. Although Maris' record has been broken several times, most recently by the San Francisco Giants' **Barry Bonds**, the Yankee great's place in the annals of baseball history is both secure and, fi-nally, unqualified. Still, one honor remains to be be-stowed: induction into the Baseball Hall of Fame. Editor Steve Forbes has called for such an action in his influen-tial financial magazine *Forbes* and a Web site,

Roger Maris

61*

The race between Roger Maris and Mickey Mantle for Babe Ruth's home run record was chronicled in the 2001 HBO film *61**. The asterisk in the title refers to the qualification then-Baseball Commissioner Ford Frick, who also was the ghostwriter of Ruth's autobiography, attached to the record. Produced and directed by comedian and die-hard New York Yankees fan Billy Crystal and filmed at Tiger Stadium in Detroit, *61** is not so much a story of an athletic rivalry as it is an attempt to dispel the media-driven myth that Maris and Mantle were enemies, and to portray the intense public pressure placed on Maris by both the press and fans of Mantle and Ruth. "Why does everybody only have room in their hearts for one guy?" Maris, played by Barry Pepper, asks at one point in the film. Playing Maris took its toll on Pepper, who gained a deep appreciation of the stress the legendary Yankee suffered. "When I first read the script, I had nightmares," he told the *St. Petersburg Times*. "It was hard not to feel for all that Maris went through that year. He was just a farm boy . . . stuck in the middle of Babe Ruth and Mickey Mantle's legacy."

Billy Martin

www.ndrogermaris.com, has been dedicated to influencing the officials at Cooperstown. Two books, *Maris, Missing from the Hall of Fame* and *Roger Maris: Title to Fame* also make the case for induction.

FURTHER INFORMATION

Books

Edwards, C.W. *Maris, Missing from the Hall of Fame.* Fargo, ND: Prairie House Publishers, 1993.

Robinson, E. *Roger Maris: Title to Fame.* Fargo, ND: Prairie House Publishers, 1992

St. James Encyclopedia of Popular Culture, five volumes. Detroit: St. James Press, 2000

Periodicals

"Chasing History." *Sports Illustrated* (October 7, 1998): 12.

Forbes, Steve. "At Last, Justice." *Forbes* (September 30, 1991): 26.

Loizeaux, William. "Getting to Roger." *American Scholar* (autumn, 2001): 113.

"Spirit of '61." *People* (October 5, 1998): 130.

Other

Elect Roger Maris to the Hall of Fame. http://www.ndrogermaris.com/ (February 14, 2003).

Sketch by Kristin Palm

Billy Martin
1928-1989

American baseball player

Billy Martin was known as a "scrapper" for his tendency toward fist fights and arguments, but he was a spirited and brilliant baseball manager who brought his teams to the top of their league every time he took the helm. He was inclined to express his opinions, a trait that got him into trouble more than once. Martin began playing semiprofessional baseball in his teens, and by age twenty-two he was with the New York Yankees, where he was a protégé of manager **Casey Stengel** and was befriended by teammates **Joe DiMaggio**, Whitey Ford, and **Mickey Mantle**. His term with the Yankees ended, however, soon after his twenty-ninth birthday, when he was accused of instigating a brawl at a Manhattan nightclub. He was traded to six different ball clubs in five years following the incident. In 1965 he began coaching, and by 1968 he was offered his first managerial job. In 1975, he came full circle as manager of the New York Yankees. Over the next twelve years, Martin was fired and rehired five times by Yankee owner **George Steinbrenner**, with whom he had a "love-hate" relationship. Martin's successes with the Yankees, as well as his misbehavior on and off the field, became baseball legend.

"Belli," but Tough

Billy Martin was born Alfred Manuel Martin, the son of Joan Salvini Pesano Martin, an Italian-American woman whose mother had immigrated to California from near Foggia, Italy, and Alfred Manuel Martin, a Portuguese man from Hawaii. Billy never used "Jr." as

Chronology

1928	Born May 16 in Berkeley, California
1946	Graduates from Berkeley High School; begins playing baseball on an Oakland Oaks farm team
1947	Is hired to play for Phoenix in the Arizona-Texas league; leads league in hitting, at bats, hits, doubles, and runs batted in; as third baseman leads league in putouts, assists, and errors
1948	Plays professional baseball on Casey Stengel's Oakland Oaks team; team wins Pacific Coast League pennant
1950	Stengel, now with New York Yankees, brings Martin on board as a utility player; Martin marries Lois Elaine Berndt on October 4—they will have one daughter, Kelly Ann
1950-51	Serves in U.S. Army
1951	Meets Mickey Mantle at Yankees training camp and the two begin a lifelong friendship
1952	Steps in from second base to catch a pop-up ball, saving a seventh-game win for the Yankees over the Dodgers, making it the Yankees' fourth straight World Series win
1953	Plays second base in Yankees' fifth straight World Series-winning season, batting .500; is divorced from Berndt
1953-55	Serves in U.S. Army
1955-56	Plays with Yankees; team wins another World Series in 1956
1957	Martin is blamed for a headline-making brawl at Manhattan's Copacabana Club after his twenty-ninth birthday party; he is traded in June to the Kansas City Athletics and again at the end of the season, to Detroit
1958	Is traded to Cleveland; gets hit in the face by a pitch, breaking his jaw and ending his playing season; is traded to Cincinnati
1959	Marries Gretchen Winkler, an airline stewardess; they will have a son, Billy Joseph
1960	Jim Brewer and the Chicago Cubs file a $1 million lawsuit against Martin after a brawl with Brewer on the pitcher's mound; Martin is traded to the Milwaukee Braves
1961	Is traded to the Minnesota Twins
1962-64	Works as scout for the Minnesota Twins
1965-67	Works as third-base coach for Minnesota Twins
1968	Is hired as manager of Twins' Denver Bears farm club; team finishes fourth and makes playoffs
1969	Is hired as manager of Minnesota Twins; is fired at end of season
1971-73	Manages Detroit Tigers; is fired in September 1973
1973-75	Manages the Texas Rangers; is fired in July 1975
1975	Is hired to manage the New York Yankees; Yankees finish first in league in 1976 and 1977
1978	Martin resigns as Yankee manager after ongoing conflict with owner George Steinbrenner; Steinbrenner hires him back the next day for the 1979 season
1979	Steinbrenner fires Martin after Martin hits a marshmallow salesman in a barroom brawl in October
1980-82	Manages the Oakland Athletics, making "Billyball" famous; resigns after conflict with owner representative Roy Eisenhardt
1981	Is divorced from Gretchen Winkler
1983	Manages New York Yankees; is fired as manager after 1983 season but kept on payroll
1985	Is rehired as manager of Yankees but fired at end of season
1988	Marries Jill Guiver, a freelance photographer, with Mickey Mantle as best man; is hired for fifth time as manager of Yankees; is beaten up in a barroom brawl in Texas after losing a game in May; Steinbrenner fires him as manager in June but keeps him on as special adviser
1989	Dies of injuries sustained in a car accident on Christmas night, December 25, in Binghamton, New York, at age 61
1990	Martin's son, Billy Joe, throws out the ball to open the New York Yankees season; the Yankees win

part of his name, however. In fact, until he entered grade school he thought his given name was Billy, a corruption of the nickname his grandmother gave him at birth: "Bellissimos" (most beautiful), shortened to "Belli" and then transformed to Billy by his playmates. Billy's natural father left the family when Billy was eight months old. His mother later married Jack Downey, who was the only father Billy ever knew.

Growing up poor in a tough West Berkeley neighborhood during the 1930s and 1940s, Billy learned to fend off members of the massive street gangs. This "scrappiness" would follow him throughout his life. From childhood, his biggest dream was to be a major league baseball player. After graduation, he hoped to be signed by a Pacific Coast League team, but no one was interested because he was too small and thin. Finally, he got a call from an Oakland Oaks farm team, which sent him $300 to buy good clothes and a suitcase and hired him to play ball. Several weeks later he was playing in the Arizona-Texas League at Phoenix. He led the league in hitting (.392) and runs batted in (174) in 130 games, and at third base led the league in errors (55), putouts, and assists. This won him a spot with the Oaks, where he played for Casey Stengel, who immediately loved Martin for his outspoken toughness. He was a kid after Stengel's own heart.

New York Yankee

After Oakland won the Pacific Coast pennant, with Martin playing three infield positions, Stengel was hired to manage the New York Yankees. In 1950, Stengel signed Martin to play with the Yankees, although he spent much of his first year with the farm team. In 1951, Martin met the sensational new player Mickey Mantle, and the two young men—opposite in temperament—became lifelong friends.

When the Yankees played the Dodgers in the seventh game of the 1952 World Series, Martin made a name for himself by running up from second base to catch **Jackie Robinson**'s pop-up ball near the pitcher's mound, winning the game, and the World Series, for the Yankees, their fourth straight World Series victory. The following year, the Yankees made it five straight World Series titles. That season, Martin had twelve hits, batted .500, and played regular second base.

After returning from military service in 1955, Martin played in another World Series and then in 1956 played one more regular season with the Yankees. Then his world collapsed. For his twenty-ninth birthday party, on May 16, 1957, a group of players went to dinner with their wives, although Martin, being divorced, attended alone. Afterwards, they went to Manhattan's Copacabana Club, and player Hank Bauer supposedly got into a

Awards and Accomplishments

1952	Yankees won World Series
1953	Yankees won World Series; named Most Valuable Player in World Series
1956	Yankees won World Series; named to All-Star team
1974	Named Manager of the Year in the American League by the Associated Press
1976	As manager of New York Yankees, won American League pennant
1977-78	As manager of New York Yankees, won American League pennant and World Series

fight with men at the next table. The following day, the newspapers broadcast the story. Yankee owner George Weiss blamed Martin for the mess and called him a bad influence on Mantle. One month later, Weiss traded Martin to the Kansas City Athletics, ending his playing career with the Yankees and leaving him hurt and bitter for years to come.

The Hard Years

Martin remained a professional ball player over the next five years, but was traded to six different teams during the period: the Athletics, the Detroit Tigers, the Cleveland Indians, the Cincinnati Reds, the Milwaukee Braves, and the Minnesota Twins. In 1959 he was hit in the face with a pitch and suffered a broken jaw, which put him out of the game for the rest of the season. In 1960 he hit Chicago Cubs pitcher Jim Brewer on the mound after Brewer just missed Martin with a pitch. In the fight, Brewer suffered a broken bone near his eye socket. Although batters and pitchers routinely scuffled in such situations, Brewer and the Cubs sued Martin for $1 million, an unprecedented action. Martin eventually had to pay much of that amount.

Career Changes

Winding down as a player, Martin began scouting for the Twins in 1961 and held that position for three quiet years. He had remarried in 1959 and had a son, Billy Joseph. In 1965 he accepted a job as third-base coach for the Twins, where he remained until the beginning of the 1968 season. Then he was sent to manage the Denver Bears, the Twins' top farm club. After a successful season there, he was offered the job as manager of the Minnesota Twins.

Martin brought the team to first place, from seventh the previous year. However, Howard Fox, the Twins' road secretary and an old enemy of Martin's, wanted Martin out. The Twins fired him, but the Detroit Tigers hired him for the 1971 season. Martin came on board, bringing with him his right-hand man, pitching coach and friend, Art Fowler, whom he had met with the Bears in 1968. The two worked wonders with the Detroit team, bringing it up to second place from fourth.

Related Biography: Pitching Coach Art Fowler

John Arthur "Art" Fowler, born July 3, 1922, in Converse, South Carolina, was Billy Martin's pitching coach from the time Martin took over as manager of the Minnesota Twins in 1969 until George Steinbrenner, owner of the New York Yankees, fired Fowler in June 1983. He was rehired briefly during the mid-1980s but was fired again in June 1988, along with Martin.

Although some critics said Fowler was Martin's "drinking buddy," the two had great success with players. The tough and disagreeable Martin passed along his instructions to Fowler, who then, amicably and with a sense of humor, passed them along to the players. The three-way rapport worked well. The Twins came up from seventh to first place in the American League Western Division in 1969 under Martin and Fowler. In 1972 the pair helped to bring the Detroit Tigers in first, over the Baltimore Orioles, who had been on a winning streak. In 1974 the Texas Rangers improved by twenty-seven games and finished second to Oakland. Martin and Fowler went on to three American League pennants and two World Series wins with the New York Yankees from 1976 to 1978 and first- and second-place wins at Oakland in the early 1980s.

Fowler was mostly a relief pitcher during his playing days, with the Cincinnati Reds (1954-57), the Los Angeles Dodgers (1959), and the Los Angeles Angels (1961-64). His brother Jesse had played with the St. Louis Cardinals thirty years before Art began his career in the major leagues. Art finished his pitching career with a 54-51 record, 539 strikeouts and thirty-two saves.

Martin wrote in his autobiography *Billyball,* "My pitching coach, Art Fowler, has taught our pitchers how to throw the spitball." Fowler also encouraged them to throw strikes. Pitcher Matt Keough recalled, "Art was master of the psychological approach. If you weren't throwing strikes, you'd have to go to the bullpen and watch him . . . throw fifty pitches-and forty-five for strikes. It was embarrassing."

The next year, the Tigers came in first place, even though they lost the playoffs to Oakland. By 1973, however, Martin wanted to trade some aging Detroit players for new blood, but the general manager remained loyal to his longtime players. The team slipped to third place, and Martin, blamed for the downfall, was let go.

One week after Detroit fired him, the Texas Rangers hired Martin as manager. The team did poorly during the first season but in 1974 moved up to second place. By 1975, however, a new owner would not renew Martin's contract giving him control over hiring players. The owner then fired Martin when the team's ranking dropped.

Return to the Yankees

Just eleven days after the Rangers let him go, the New York Yankees asked Martin to be manager. In New York he began a tumultuous relationship with owner George Steinbrenner, who wanted control as much as Martin did. However, as Martin took the position once held by his mentor, Casey Stengel, he began to work miracles. With some new players, the team came in first place in 1976 but lost the World Series to the Cincinnati Reds. In 1977 they came in first again and this time won the World Series over the Los Angeles Dodgers. Martin managed for the first half of the 1978 season, but the tension with Steinbrenner, coupled with conflicts with player **Reggie Jackson**, pushed Martin to the breaking point. In late July he told sportswriters he was disgusted with both men.

"The two of them deserve each other," he said. "One's a born liar," (referring to Jackson) "and the other's convicted." (Steinbrenner had been convicted of perjury in 1972 in an elections law violation case.) He told the writers to print his statement and then resigned from the Yankees. The next day, Steinbrenner invited him back as manager for the 1979 season. He made the announcement at Yankee Old-Timers' Day, to the delight of 46,000 fans, who gave Martin a seven-minute standing ovation. Bob Lemon from Chicago took over for the rest of the 1978 season, and the Yankees won the World Series, so Steinbrenner kept him on until the middle of the 1979 season, when he fired Lemon and got Martin back.

Seasons of Billyball

The constant frustration drove Martin to heavier drinking and barroom brawls, which never failed to make headlines. In 1979 he punched a Minnesota marshmallow salesman in a bar, and Steinbrenner fired him again. This time Martin was hired to manage the Oakland Athletics. In 1980 the A's came in second in the league; the following year they were first and then second in a season split by a players' strike, but they were defeated by the Yankees in the World Series. In 1982 they fell to fifth place, even though **Rickey Henderson** stole a record-breaking 130 bases. Martin left, believing that the team owners had interfered with decision making and the pitchers had failed to stay in shape during the strike.

During Martin's seasons with Oakland, he built a playing strategy around Stengel's "run sheep run baseball" style. Columnist Ralph Wiley of the *Oakland Tribune* gave it a name: Billyball. Equipped with Henderson as a base stealer, Fowler as his pitching coach, and the freedom to hire players he thought could do the job, Martin developed Billyball as the envy of the baseball world. His plays included the hit-and-run, the double steal, and the suicide squeeze, adding up to a total of runs that led the league. Henderson said of Martin in 2001: "We did anything to get a run. He was a genius as a manager. He might not say anything until the sixth inning. He'd let you play until then. Then he would start managing."

Bouncing Back to the Yankees

When Martin left Oakland, his old antagonist Steinbrenner wanted him back again. The Yankees finished third in 1983, and Martin was suspended twice for abusing umpires—he kicked dirt on one and called another "a stone liar." In December, Steinbrenner fired Martin as manager but kept him on as adviser. In 1985, Steinbrenner fired manager **Yogi Berra** and rehired Martin, for the fourth time. The team finished second, and Martin was fired again but kept in the office. In 1988 Steinbrenner again put Martin in the manager's position, and the team was on a winning streak when Martin got injured in a brawl in a Texas nightclub. In June, Martin was let go again, and the Yankees finished fifth.

Billy Martin, catching ball

Martin was still employed by the Yankees as an adviser when, on Christmas night, 1989, he and longtime friend William Reedy, a Detroit bar owner, were driving on an icy road near Martin's home in Binghamton, New York. With Reedy at the wheel, the truck skidded off the road and Martin was thrown through the windshield, fracturing his neck and injuring his spinal column. He died soon afterward in a Binghamton hospital. Reedy was charged with driving while intoxicated.

Just eight days earlier, on December 17, Martin and Steinbrenner had read "The Night before Christmas" together at a charity concert. Rumors circulated that Steinbrenner was considering Martin for a sixth term as manager, but Steinbrenner told the *New York Times,* "No way. He was too happy doing what he was doing. He was coming upstairs. He was going to be there more than ever before."

Man and Manager

Billy Martin has been called a baseball genius, yet he seemed bent on self-destruction. Because of his many conflicts with umpires, Richie Phillips, general counsel of the Major League Umpires Association, called him "the quintessential recidivist in baseball." However, he had another side, one that the public rarely saw. Michael Goodwin wrote in the *New York Times* that away from the baseball stadium Martin was "generous, thoughtful, a loyal friend, wonderful with children, the elderly, and even strangers down on their luck." Matt Keough, a former Oakland pitcher now working as a scout, told journalist Ron Bergman in a 2001 interview, "It's a travesty that Billy's not in the Hall of Fame. He won with every kind of team he ever had."

Martin had firm convictions about his management style, and he adhered to them throughout his career, in spite of his seemingly brash personality. He told sportswriter and author Leonard Koppett, "For a team to win, a manager has to find ways to motivate different individuals. He has to judge correctly each man's abilities and weaknesses, and find the right ways and the right time to use them. He has to show them how something can be done better, and offer them loyalty and confidence. And he has to have authority, above all, because none of the other things can happen if the players don't have confidence in the manager's judgment." Martin established personal relationships with his players, and they loved him for it. He once said, "Out of 25 guys, there should be fifteen who would run through a wall for you, two or three who don't like you at all, five who are indifferent and maybe three undecided. My job is to keep the last two groups from going the wrong way."

SELECTED WRITINGS BY MARTIN:

(With Peter Golenbock) *Number One* (autobiography), Delacorte Press, 1980.
(With Phil Pepe) *Billyball*, Doubleday, 1987.

FURTHER INFORMATION

Books

Koppett, Leonard. *The Man in the Dugout: Baseball's Top Managers and How They Got That Way.* New York: Crown Publishers, 1993.

Periodicals

Bergman, Ron. "Ex-A's Look Back Fondly on the Summer of Billy Ball." *San Jose Mercury News* (July 3, 2001).
Creamer, Robert W. "Arrogance: Umpires Issue Resolution Censuring Billy Martin and Criticizing AL Pres. Bobby Brown's Light Sentence of Martin." *Sports Illustrated* (June 13, 1988): 13.
Creamer, Robert W. "Golden Friendships." *Sports Illustrated* (June 27, 1983): 18.
Harvin, Al. "An Outburst of Affection from Martin's Fans." *New York Times* (December 28, 1989): A27.
"Married, Billy Martin and Jill Guiver." *Time* (February 8, 1988): 71.
Neff, Craig. "A Pair of Battlers: Billy Martin and Doug Harvey Die." *Sports Illustrated* (January 8, 1990): 7.
"Road Accident Kills Billy Martin, Ex-Yankee Player and Manager." *New York Times* (December 28, 1989): A1.

Wickens, Barbara. "A Violent Death for Billy Martin." *Maclean's* (January 8, 1990): 35.

Other

Baseball Almanac. "Art Fowler." http://www.baseball-almanac.com/ (November 5, 2002).
Baseball-Reference.com. "Billy Martin." http://www.baseball-reference.com/managers/ (October 31, 2002).
Gallagher, Mark. "Billy Martin." BaseballLibrary.com. http://www.pubdim.net/baseballlibrary/ballplayers/ (November 4, 2002).
Historic Baseball: Art Fowler of South Carolina. http://www.historicbaseball.com/ (November 4, 2002).
Jozwik, Tom. "Art Fowler." BaseballLibrary.com. http://www.pubdim.net/baseballlibrary.com/ballplayers/ (November 4, 2002).
Newsmakers, Issue Cumulation. "Billy Martin." Gale Group, 1988. Reproduced in *Biography Resource Center.* http://www.galenet.com/servlet/BioRC (October 31, 2002).
Newsmakers 1990, Issue 2. "Billy Martin." Gale Group, 1990. Reproduced in *Biography Resource Center.* http://www.galenet.com/servlet/BioRC (October 31, 2002).

Sketch by Ann H. Shurgin

Casey Martin
1972-

American golfer

How physical is the game of golf? And do professional sports associations have the right to set their own rules? These questions were brought to new light by one golfer, Casey Martin, as he attempted to join the ranks of the Professional Golfers Association (PGA). Martin suffers from a rare birth defect called Klippel-Trenaunay-Weber Syndrome, which severely weakened his right leg. He cannot walk an eighteen-hole course; yet using a golf cart is in violation of PGA Tour rules. In order to play, Martin sued the PGA under the Americans with Disabilities Act (ADA). The three-year case ended in a controversial decision handed down by the U.S. Supreme Court.

A native of Eugene, Oregon, Martin was started in golf by his father, King Martin, at age six. But Casey confessed that his first love was for another sport. "I would have played basketball in a minute" if not for his leg, he told *Golf Digest* writer Tim Rosaforte. "I can't move, so I can't play." He recalled a lifetime of pain: "I can definitely remember one of the hardest parts about growing up

Casey Martin

was wanting to be active," Martin remarked. "I could never understand when I was done playing sports why I was in so much pain. I knew I had a problem."

A Gift for the Game

Nevertheless, the young man continued to excel on the links. "The first time [Stanford University] coach Wally Goodwin saw Casey Martin play golf in high school," noted Nick Charles in a *People* piece, "he noticed that the teenager kept his right leg bent just the way a good golfer should. Only later did he realize that Martin kept his right leg bent all the time." By the time Martin played on the same Stanford golf team as **Tiger Woods**, the disease had left the bones in his leg virtually eroded. When he played college golf, "even the opposition begged their coaches to lift the walking rule so that Martin could ride," noted *Golf Digest*'s Marcia Chambers. "They did, with the NCAA in full agreement." But when Martin, now a professional, approached the PGA with a cart request in 1997, "not only did the tour say no, but it refused even to look at the extensive and persuasive medical records Martin offered them," Chambers added.

In 1998 Martin was a member of the Nationwide Tour, earning his first win at the season-opening Lakeland Classic. He went on to make the cut in sixteen of twenty-two events, qualifying him to play in PGA Tours based on his low shooting scores. At the same time, the young professional became a spokesman for Nike athletic products; the shoe manufacturer created a commer-

cial celebrating Martin's unique abilities. In 1999 Martin performed even better, placing fourteenth on the money list with $122,742. But the PGA still balked at Martin's request to use a golf cart during its Tour events. According to the association's rules, players must walk the course. Martin decided to sue.

The news of the lawsuit broke in early 1998. "It's kind of tough," King Martin told Goodwin. "We've never been sued or sued anyone in our lifetime and never dreamt that we would." After winning a temporary court order, the Martins took their case to a federal judge in Eugene. The federal court ruled that the young man could take his cart on the course; the PGA appealed that ruling to the U.S. Supreme Court, which heard the case three years later.

Who Is Disadvantaged?

The PGA argued that by riding between the holes, Martin would gain an unfair advantage over the players who expended energy walking. But is walking intrinsic to the game? In May 2001, the Court handed down its 7-2 decision: Martin should be entitled to play on the Tour using a cart in accordance with the ADA's guidelines for employers and businesses to adopt "reasonable accommodation" for disabled employees or customers. Justice John Paul Stevens wrote for the majority: "From early on, the essence of the game has been shot-making" with walking a peripheral component of the sport. Speaking for the dissent was Justice Antonin Scalia, who said that PGA rules deemed walking as essential to the game. He also maintained that seven of his fellow justices "wrongly identified Martin and other pro golfers as PGA Tour 'customers' covered by ADA public accommodation rules," according to a Knight Ridder/Tribune News Service article by Michael Hisley.

Reaction to the ruling, noted *Sarasota Herald Tribune* columnist Rich Brooks, "has been predictable. One professional golfer said it's just a matter of time before someone with a sprained back or ankle seeks permission to ride in a cart." According to the article, links star **Jack Nicklaus** suggested that the justices try walking a tournament course to experience the effort for themselves. To Brooks, such arguments "deserve to be countered." First, he said, "for professional golfers to cite the fatigue

Awards and Accomplishments

1994	Member of NCAA championship golf team
1998	Won Nike Lakeland Classic
1998	Became a spokesman for Nike
1999	Finished fourteenth on the money list with $122,742
2000	Made the cut in fourteen out of twenty-nine starts, PGA Tour
2000	Finished sixth in tour driving distance, 288.3 yards
2000	Finished in top 25 Touchstone Energy Tucson Open
2001	Supreme Court ruled in Martin's favor
2002	Made the cut in five out of fourteen starts, Nationwide Tour

by walking eighteen holes is laughable. Such statements say more about the players' lack of physical conditioning than the kinetic requirements of the game." Paul Winston of *Business Insurance* held a similar view. The opinion of some, he said, is that "golf is a sport of athletic prowess and endurance, like the decathlon or pentathlon, rather than one of skill. I beg to differ. Some golfers . . . are in great shape, but it doesn't seem to help them win any more [tournaments]."

"What next?" asked a spokesperson for the Libertarian Party as quoted by Cybercast News Service: "Stilts for midgets who want to play professional basketball? How about rowboats for Olympic swimmers who suffer from aquaphobia? How about a 20-yard head start for slow people in the Olympic 100-yard dash?" *Sporting News* contributor Dave Kindred predicted, "Silly lawsuits will follow the Martin ruling just as silly lawsuits have followed other ADA precedents."

A Figure of Controversy

Absent in much of the debate, however, was the reality of daily life for Casey Martin. "It's not hard for Outsiders to overlook his pain, which is belied by his good looks and good nature," wrote Hisley. "He looks more like the impish Matthew Perry of the TV sitcom 'Friends' than a sad invalid." But Hisley saw a video made by Martin's attorneys of the golfer's affected limb. Within moments of being stripped of its protective wraps, "his right knee began swelling and became discolored." To Hisley, critics of the Supreme Court decision "who have not seen that swollen, discolored leg . . . do not understand that Martin suffers greater fatigue while using a cart than his competitors do while walking." Brian Ettkin in a *Sarasota Herald-Tribune* column maintained, "Golf is about ball striking and mental toughness.... TV analysts never compliment a player on his authoritative stride down the fairway."

In October, 2002, Martin spoke up for another category of golfers—women who wished to be admitted as members of the male-only Augusta National Golf Club. "I'm extremely conservative in most respects," he said to Steve Ellig in an article for Knight Ridder/Tribune News Service, "but on something like this, I think [Augusta National] should be forward-thinking instead of fighting it."

More than a golfer, Martin became a symbol embraced by both sides of the debate. "This goes against Martin's every intention," remarked Richard Hoffer in *Sports Illustrated*. "It's no fault of his that he has become more important for his news value than his swing. And it's too bad because, if he's not quite mythic, he's certainly decent beyond the requirements of his role." As for Martin, who faces the possibility of amputation, "you cannot devise a scenario where I would rather have my disability and a cart versus having two healthy legs," as he told Rosaforte. "You just can't." Asked what he would trade for two good legs, Martin replied, "All the fame and notoriety I've had. I'd give all that back in a heartbeat."

FURTHER INFORMATION

Books

Contemporary Heroes and Heroines, Book II. Detroit: Gale, 1992.

Periodicals

Brooks, Rich. "Objections to Disabled Golfer Just Aren't up to Par." *Sarasota Herald-Tribune* (June 2, 2001).

"Casey Martin Signs Long-Term Deal with Pro Tour Memorabilia." *Internet Wire* (April 9, 2002).

"Casey Martin: 'I Think This Opens the Door.'" *Business Week* (June 11, 2001).

Chambers, Marcia. "The Martin Decision." *Golf Digest* (August, 2001).

Charles, Nick. "Fairway or No Way." *People* (February 9, 1998).

Doherty, Brian. "PGA's Loss to Casey Martin Unfortunately Par for the Course in Law, in Which Everyone's Business is the Government's." Knight Ridder/Tribune News Service (February 13, 1998).

Elling, Steve. "Martin Says Augusta National Should Admit Female Members." Knight Ridder/Tribune News Service (October 2, 2002).

Ettkin, Brian. "Humanity is Winner in Ruling." *Sarasota Herald-Tribune* (May 31, 2001).

Hannigan, Frank. "Casey at the Bar." *Golf Digest* (March, 2001).

Hisley, Michael. "Martin Case Offers Some Ins and Outs." Knight Ridder/Tribune News Service (June 1, 2001).

Hoffer, Richard. "Ridin' That Train." *Sports Illustrated* (March 23, 1998).

Kindred, Dave. "Doomsday Is Not Nigh." *Sporting News* (June 11, 2001).

Leo, John. "Duffers in the Court." *U.S. News and World Report* (June 11, 2001).

Richman, Howard. "Golfer Casey Martin Tired of Nonstop Attention on Tour." Knight Ridder/Tribune News Service (July 17, 2001).

Rosaforte, Tim. "Casey's Last Stand." *Golf Digest* (May, 2001).

Sherman, Ed. "Casey Martin Left Searching for His Game." Knight Ridder/Tribune News Service (August 7, 2002).

Verdi, Bob. "Pedestrian Traffic Only." *Golf World* (July 20, 2001).

Winston, Paul. "Readers Teed off over Golf Column." *Business Insurance* (June 18, 2001).

Other

Burns, Jim. "Libertarians Criticize High Court Ruling in Casey Martin Case." Cybercast News Service. http://www.cnsnews.com/ (May 29, 2001).

Sketch by Susan Salter

Christy Martin
1969-

American boxer

Christy Martin

Christy Martin, named the best woman boxer in the world by the World Boxing Council in 1996, has, in the words of Bob Raissman, writing in the *Daily News* of New York, "put women's boxing on the map." Represented by the famous promoter Don King, Martin has worked to bring the sport of woman's boxing from the status of a fringe or novelty sport into wider acceptance, as legitimate as men's boxing. She made her mark fighting on the undercards of **Mike Tyson** fights, and at the close of 2002, was still one of he top woman boxers at the age of 33.

Christy Martin was born Christy Salters in 1969. She grew up in the small town of Bluefield, West Virginia, the daughter of a coal miner. Her younger brother, Randy, eventually became a coal miner as well. Both of Martin's grandfathers, too, were coal miners, and both died of black lung disease, an illness caused by inhaled particles of coal. In high school Martin was one of the best basketball players on her school team. After winning a basketball scholarship, Martin attended Concord College in Athens, West Virginia.

It was while she was a freshman at Concord in 1987 that Martin boxed for the first time. Friends encouraged her to box in an amateur contest, and she surprised herself by winning the match and taking home the $1,000 prize. Boxing excited Martin as no other sport she had played. Facing off against an opponent was an adrenaline rush, and so was the money. She fought in the same amateur contest the next two years running, winning the top prize of $1,000 each time.

Martin graduated from Concord with a degree in education. She worked as a substitute teacher in Mercer County in West Virginia for a time, but found the work less than satisfying. What Martin really wanted to do was box. After fighting in the occasional match for purses typically around $300, she decided to take her boxing to a new level in 1991 and begin formal training. Then 22 years old, Martin met trainer Jim Martin, an ex-fighter himself.

Reluctant at first to allow a woman to train in his gym, Jim Martin warmed to Martin after seeing what she could do in the ring. "I say it was love at first sight, after Jim got over being upset about me being in his gym," Martin later recalled to Evelyn Nieves in the *New York Times*. Martin and her new trainer fell in love and got married. They moved to Orlando, Florida, where they established a new gym, and Martin trained hard for professional bouts.

In 1993, Martin landed a contract with top fight promoter **Don King**, becoming the first female boxer on King's client roster, which included some of the best male fighters in the world. In February 1996, Martin fought in her first nationally televised match on the Showtime network, and the following month achieved acclaim in her second televised match, against Deirdre Gogart, which she won in six rounds. That second fight was more popular among fans than the Mike Tyson fight broadcast soon after as the main event.

It was after the Gogart fight that critics began to take Martin seriously. The fight was seen by more than a million viewers, and it, more than any fight before it, helped to move women's boxing from fringe status to widespread acceptance. It also landed Martin on the

<table>
<tr><td colspan="2">

Chronology

</td></tr>
<tr><td>1969</td><td>Born in Bluefield, West Virginia</td></tr>
<tr><td>1987</td><td>Earns her first paycheck as a boxer</td></tr>
<tr><td>1989</td><td>Becomes a professional boxer</td></tr>
<tr><td>1991</td><td>Mees trainer and future husband Jim Martin</td></tr>
<tr><td>1993</td><td>Signs with top boxing promoter Don King</td></tr>
<tr><td>1996</td><td>Fights in her first nationally televised match</td></tr>
<tr><td>1996</td><td>Appears on the cover of *Sports Illustrated*</td></tr>
<tr><td>1998</td><td>Loses top female boxing title to Sumya Amani</td></tr>
<tr><td>2000</td><td>Regains top female boxing title</td></tr>
</table>

Awards and Accomplishments

1987	Wins her first boxing match
1996	Becomes first woman boxer to be televised live on U.S. national television
1996	Named pound-for-pound best female boxer by the World Boxing Council
1996	Wins biggest purse in the history of women's boxing
2000	Regains top female boxing title

cover of *Sports Illustrated* and got her a spot on the Tonight Show with Jay Leno. By the end of 1996, Martin had earned the biggest purse ever awarded to a woman boxer, $75,000 for stopping Bethany Payne in a fight that lasted only two rounds.

In 1998, Martin's seven-year winning streak came to an end when she lost a bout with Sumya Amani by decision. Her defeat was devastating to Martin, and she stopped fighting for seven months. But Jim Martin talked her back into the ring. In 2000, she climbed back to the top of the women's boxing world by knocking out Sabrina Hall.

Both Don King, and Martin herself have acknowledged that their main goal is to make as much money as possible, and that elevating the sport of women's boxing is only a side effect. As Martin admitted to the *Denver Post,* "I know I have legitimized Christy Martin, that's as far as I can go. I can't put all the women on my shoulders and try to legitimize the whole sport."

Martin's fight to make the sport of women's boxing as lucrative as men's boxing has faced an uphill battle. Because woman's boxing still has yet to achieve the draw of the men's version of the sport, competent woman boxers have been in short supply. Many of the women enter the ring from other sports, often at ages at which male boxers typically retire. "Women's boxing as a whole, I don't see it moving (forward)," Martin acknowledged to Jeff Schultz in the *Atlanta Journal and Constitution.* "I'm moving. But, really, I don't see it moving with me. People think that's being arrogant and cocky. But that's the way I feel."

Martin was still going strong at the close of 2002, and still at the top of the world of women's boxing. As she told Bob Raissman of New York's *Daily News* in mid-2001, "Let's just say I'm closer to the middle of my career than I am to the beginning. As long as I'm feeling good and fulfill my expectations I will keep on fighting."

FURTHER INFORMATION

Periodicals

Berg, Aimee. "This Fighter Is Making Fans of Her Skeptics." *New York Times,* (March 17, 1996): Section 8, 2.

Borges, Ron. "Martin's Aim Straight and True in KO." *Boston Globe,* (September 8, 1996): C17.

Buffery, Steve. "Coal Miner's Daughter a Hit; Woman Boxer Bags Big Bucks." *Toronto Sun,* (June 29, 1997): SP3.

Cornwell, Tim. "Queen Bee." *Independent,* (November 11, 1996): Features, 6.

Goldman, Ivan. "It's Time to Run for Cover as Boxing's Long-Awaited Battle of the Cover Girls Finally Materializes." *Scotland on Sunday,* (December 1, 2002): 15.

"Martin Fights Own Battle." *Denver Post,* (July 11, 1996): 5D.

"Martin Has It Easy on Way to Record Purse." *St. Petersburg Times,* (November 10, 1996): 1C.

Nieves, Evelyn. "A Boxer in a Hurry." *New York Times,* (November 3, 1996): Magazine, 38.

Raissman, Bob. "Coal Miner's Daughter Is No Stranger to Big-City Pressure." *Daily News,* (May 13, 2001): Sports, 52.

Schultz, Jeff. "Boxing; Martin a Boxer, Not a Pioneer; Woman Fighter Says Her Career Must Come First." *Atlanta Journal and Constitution,* (June 23, 1997): 10D.

Stickney Jr., W.H. "Martin Regains Piece of Spotlight; Former Women's Champ Posts KO." *Houston Chronicle,* (December 3, 2000): Sports, 14.

Sketch by Michael Belfiore

Pedro Martinez
1971-

Dominican baseball player

Pedro Martinez is arguably the most dominant pitcher of his era. Hailing from the Dominican Republic, Martinez followed his brother Ramon to the United States and pitched with him for the Los Angeles Dodgers from 1992-93, and with the Boston Red Sox from 1999-2000. He quickly developed a reputation

Pedro Martinez

Chronology

1971	Born in Santa Domingo, Dominican Republic
1988	Signs with the Los Angeles Dodgers
1992	Makes first major league appearance
1993	Traded to the Montreal Expos
1995	Throws second perfect game into extra innings in history
1996	Makes first All-Star Game appearance
1997	Wins first Cy Young award
1998	Traded to the Boston Red Sox
1999	Wins second Cy Young award
2000	Wins third Cy Young award

that followed him from Los Angeles to Montreal and eventually to the Boston Red Sox. In Boston, he has revitalized World Series hopes in a city that has gone without since **Babe Ruth** left over 80 years ago. His numbers are reminiscent of a bygone era when pitchers dominated the game. Still in his prime, Martinez has debunked the myth of the juiced ball and overpowered the home run hitters that have hijacked headlines in recent years. He is among the most visible of the Latin players that have injected interest and mystique into a game that had lost some of its glory after the player's strike of 1994.

Born October 25, 1971 in Santa Domingo, he was the fifth of six children raised in Manoguyabo. His parents divorced when he was just nine years old, but Martinez remains very close to his family and especially his older brother Ramon. His father was an amateur pitcher who helped his sons develop their talent and passion for baseball. When Ramon was signed by the Los Angeles Dodgers, Pedro followed, carrying his brother's equipment bag to practice everyday. Their dream came true when the Dodgers signed the then sixteen-year-old Pedro to a contract. Although the brothers were developing at different times, they were teammates on the Dodgers from 1992-93.

The following year the Dodgers traded Martinez to the Montreal Expos. It was in Montreal that Pedro would develop into a dominating force. Martinez be-

came a starting pitcher in Montreal. Known more for a love of hockey than baseball, Montreal did nothing to increase Martinez's visibility on the national stage. His reputation within major league baseball, however, began to grow. An inside pitcher, Martinez was known for hitting batters and inciting fights. Far from intentional, his Dominican training and a lack of control were responsible for the trend. Martinez became the second pitcher in baseball history to pitch a perfect game into extra innings in 1995, but his bid was lost in the tenth inning when his perfect game was disrupted by a Bip Roberts double. Despite a reputation as an intimidator, Martinez continued to improve and in 1997 was the unanimous choice for the National League **Cy Young** Award. The Expos, however, was a team with a low payroll that could not afford to keep its superstars and the forever dismantling team was a frustration for Martinez. It soon became clear that Martinez's price would force him out of Montreal and after winning the Cy Young, he was in demand.

The Boston Red Sox would eventually win the bidding war that would make him the highest paid player in baseball. Although Martinez would have rather pitched in a warmer climate, Boston's rabid baseball fans convinced him that he would be at home in Fenway Park. In his first year with the Red Sox, Martinez led his team to the post-season and an 11-3 victory in game one of the their first round playoff. He continued his dominance in 1999 and 2000 when he led the American League in strikeouts.

After winning three Cy Young awards in four years, Martinez was sidelined with a shoulder injury in 2001. The injury, the result of years of overuse, threatened his ability to pitch as he always had. His brother Ramon's career was similarly affected by an injury that led to his early retirement. In 2002, Martinez and the Red Sox were determined to use him more judiciously. "If I go down tomorrow, I'll be happy," Martinez said in a *Sporting News* article. "I'll go home, send my cleats to my trophy room and leave them there. That will be it. I'm honestly really glad and really happy with God for putting me in this position. Remember, I was too skinny. I was too small. I wouldn't hold up for five innings,

Career Statistics

Yr	Team	W	L	ERA	IP	H	R	ER	BB	SO	SV
1992	LA	0	1	2.25	8.0	6	2	2	1	8	0
1993	LA	10	5	2.61	107.0	76	34	31	57	119	2
1994	MON	11	5	3.42	144.2	115	58	55	45	142	1
1995	MON	14	10	3.51	194.2	158	79	76	66	174	0
1996	MON	13	10	3.70	216.2	189	100	89	70	222	0
1997	MON	17	8	1.90	241.1	158	65	51	67	305	0
1998	BOS	19	7	2.89	233.2	188	82	75	67	251	0
1999	BOS	23	4	2.07	213.1	160	56	49	37	313	0
2000	BOS	18	6	1.74	217.0	128	44	42	32	284	0
2001	BOS	7	3	2.39	116.2	84	33	31	25	163	0
2002	BOS	20	4	2.26	199.1	144	62	50	40	239	0
TOTAL		152	63	2.62	1892.1	1406	615	551	507	2220	3

BOS: Boston Red Sox; LA: Los Angeles Dodgers; MON: Montreal Expos.

Awards and Accomplishments

1996	First All-Star Game Appearance
1997	Wins first Cy Young award
1999	Voted All-Star Most Valuable Player
1999	Wins second Cy Young award
2000	Wins third Cy Young award

I wouldn't stay in the big leagues. I wasn't a prospect. Then, all of a sudden, everything happened. I was a prospect. I proved I wasn't too small. I'm Pedro, three-time Cy Young Award winner. I'm making money. I'm secure. And I've been around for 10 years. That's a lot to ask."

Martinez still lives in Santo Domingo during the off season. He has built a church, gymnasium, two baseball diamonds and houses for his family. The immense pride he has in his Dominican heritage has inspired loyalty even among opposing fans. During a recent game against the Yankees when a fight broke out among Boston fans hanging strikeout signs from the bleachers, a group of Dominican Yankee fans came to the rescue. "It feels really good now to have some of my people come and bring flags and say 'Hey, we're Dominicans!'" he said.

Throughout his career Pedro Martinez has defied expectations and amazed his opposition. He has pitched in both leagues and dominated them both. Despite his small frame, he has proved both durable and effective. His visibility has opened the doors for other Latin players, including a younger brother who recently signed with the Los Angeles Dodgers. With the fame and fortune, Martinez has given back to his family and homeland. He has proven he has the ability and heart to continue to work and improve on a career that has already exceeded expectations.

FURTHER INFORMATION

Books

Sports Stars. Detroit: Gale Group, 1999.

Periodicals

"Ace in the Hole." *Sporting News* (June 12, 1995): 56.
"Inside Edition." *Sporting News* (July 18, 1994): 12.
"Passion in Every Pitch." *Newsweek* (April 6, 1998): 57.
"Pedro." *Time* (June 26, 2000): 52.
"Pedro in the Pantheon." *Baseball Research Journal* (annual, 2001): 71.
"Pitcher of the Year." *Baseball Digest* (January 2001).
"Real Funny." *Sporting News* (May 29, 2000): 16.
"Rocket Redux." *Sports Illustrated* (April 20, 1998): 38.
"The Case for Pedro Martinez." *Sports Illustrated* (September 15, 1997): 84.
"The Hits Stop Here." *Newsweek* (April 10,2000): 42.
"The Inside Story." *Sports Illustrated* (May 26, 1997): 82.
"The Latin All-Stars." *Time International* (October 4, 1999): 44.

Sketch by Aric Karpinski

Svetlana Masterkova
1968-

Russian track and field athlete

In 1996 internationally renowned Russian track and field athlete Svetlana Masterkova became the second women ever to win Olympic gold medals in both the

Svetlana Masterkova

Chronology

1968	Born in Adjinsk, USSR.
1991	Wins USSR national championships with an 800-meter time of 1:57:23.
1993	Sidelined from World outdoor Championships due to back injury.
1995	Gives birth to first child, Anastasiya, in March.
1996	Wins two gold medals at Summer Olympics.
1997	Finishes last in 1500-meter at World semifinals due to Achilles injury.
1999	Wins first and only World Track and Field Championship gold medal
1999	Has surgery on Achilles tendons.
2000	Injury during 1500-meter forces her withdrawal from Olympic Games
2000	Retires from international competition.

1500 and 800 meter runs. Previous to Masterkova, only Tatyana Kazankina had accomplished the same feat, earning her double gold at the Montreal Games 20 years before. Participating in two Olympic games during her career, Masterkova also won numerous world titles and remained well-known in the running world for her ability to overcome numerous setbacks and kick-start her professional career at an age when other runners were contemplating retirement. A strong sprinter, she used her competitive edge to set world records for both the mile and the 1000-meter during her career, both of which were still standing in 2001.

Running Career Determined Soviet-Style

Born in the USSR in 1968, Masterkova showed an early talent for track. Placed under the compulsory tutelage of a zealous and staunchly Soviet physical education teacher, she was competing by the time she was 12 and was clocked at an 800-meter time of 2:04:3 by age fifteen. She competed in middle-distance events, but only began to show the promise of her early talent in her late twenties, a period considered late in a professional runner's career. Her early races were uneven; a 1991 Soviet championship yielded her a first-place victory in the 800 meters, while the same distance at the World Track and Field Championships held in Tokyo, Japan a month later left her with a disappointing eighth. A virus sidelined her dreams of running at the 1992 Olympics in Barcelona, Spain, then back injuries forced her out of the Russian trials for the 1993 World Championships.

While such a run of bad luck may have discouraged some runners, the blonde-haired, energetic Masterkova held on to her dreams of running in the Olympics. In 1993 she raced and placed second in the 800 meters at the World Indoor Track and Field Championships in Toronto, Ontario, Canada.

Married to professional cyclist Assiat Saitov, Masterkova became pregnant in 1994 and took time off from competition to give birth to her daughter, Anastasia, in March of 1995. After nine months away from serious running, the five-foot-seven-inch runner quickly regained her racing weight of 130 pounds and threw herself back into a strenuous training regime designed by coach Svetlana Styrkina in order to regain her speed and stamina. By the time Anastasiya was two months old her mother was ready to return to competition. Once again in top form, she looked ahead to the July, 1996, Summer Olympics in Atlanta, Georgia.

Despite a winning performance at the Russian National Championships, Masterkova was considered a longshot for an Olympic victory, particularly against a strong 800-meter field that included world-class runners such as Mozambiquen Maria Mulota and Cuban Ana Quirot. Equally daunting was the 1,500-meter field, which included the talented Irish runner **Sonia O'Sullivan** alongside Romanian Gabriela Szabo, Hassiba Boulmerka, and Portugal's Carla Sacramento. But the Russian surprised everyone by taking the gold in both events, completing the 800 meter in 1:57:33 and the 1,500 meter five days later in just over four minutes.

Her wins in 1996 propelled Masterkova into the spotlight, and earned her more than just celebrity status. In addition to the Olympic prize money, the Russian government provided her with a new car, an upscale apartment, the equivalent of $250,000 in cash, and land on which she planned to build a vacation home. In December of 1996 she joined noted U.S. sprinter **Michael Johnson** as co-recipient of the Interna-

Awards and Accomplishments

1991	Wins Soviet title for 800 meters at Kiev National Championships.
1993	Second place, 800 meters, World Indoor Track and Field Championships.
1996	Wins gold medals for Women's 800 and 1500 meters at Olympic Games.
1996	First place, world record-setting time of 2:28.98 in Grand Prix 1000 meters.
1996	International Athletic Federation (IAF) Athletes' Legends prize.
1998	First place, 1500 meters, European Championships.
1998	First place, 1500 meters, World Cup.
1999	First place, 800 meters, with personal best of 1:55:87 at Moscow nationals.
1999	First place, 1500 meters, World Track and Field Championships.
1999	Third place, 800 meters, World Track and Field Championships.
2000	Qualifies for 2000 Olympics.

tional Athletic Federation's Athletes' Legends prize. She set two world records on the 1996 International Athletic Federation Grand Prix circuit. At Zurich, Switzerland she clocked a personal best of 4:12:56 seconds in her first-ever mile competition, then went on to win the 1,000-meter in the record-setting time of 2:28:98 in Brussels nine days later.

Competing in the 800-meter event requires immediate speed, while the longer 1,500-meter run draws on stamina and endurance as the runner must sustain race pace for a much longer period. Because she trained hard in running short intervals as well as incorporating longer tempo runs into her running schedule, Masterkova was able to excel in both speed and endurance. When racing, she often avoided taking the lead early on, preferring to "draft" off the front runner and then accelerate for her final "kick" past the front runner and across the finish line. Confident sometimes to the point of arrogance, she was known to disparage her opponents for not developing more aggressive racing strategies.

Unfortunately for Masterkova, the intensive training required for her to maintain peak physical performance began to take its toll. In addition to an abnormally high heart rate, in the wake of her 1996 Olympic victory her Achilles tendons began to hamper her performance, forcing her to cut back her training to one day in three. Although she was able to earn wins in the 800, her longer races suffered. Finally, following a last-place finish at the 1997 World semi-finals and a lackluster third-place finish in the 800 meter during 1999's World Track and Field Championships in Seville, Spain, Masterkova underwent surgery to correct the problem. It surprised no one when, as she had after giving birth to her daughter, the 30-year-old Masterkova quickly rebounded and resumed her rigorous training schedule. With one Olympic triumph under her belt, she looked ahead eagerly to the 2000 Games.

Believing herself to be fully recovered from her injury, Masterkova easily qualified for the upcoming games to be held in Sydney, Australia, beginning in mid-September of 2000. Unfortunately, the intensive training she undertook to prepare her for the 800 and 1,500 meter events rekindled her Achilles problems. Half way through her heat for the 1,500 meters, Masterkova collided with another runner and crumpled, the pain tearing up her calf bringing tears to her eyes. She limped off the track, her Olympic hopes dashed and her running career at an end.

Retiring from international competition shortly thereafter, the thirty-something Masterkova could look back on a career dotted by setbacks and yet successful in that she surprised the track world by attaining both Olympics and World Championship gold medals relatively late in her career.

CONTACT INFORMATION

Address: c/o International Olympic Committee, Chateau de Vidy, CH-1007, Lausanne, Switzerland.

FURTHER INFORMATION

Periodicals

New York Times, July 30, 1996; September 27, 1996; September 10, 2000.
Sunday Times, August 18, 1996: 14.

Sketch by Pamela L. Shelton

Helene Mayer
1910-1953

German fencer

Helene Mayer was Germany's only known Jewish member of its Olympic national team in the 1936 Summer Games in Berlin. The fencer competed in what derisively came to be called "Hitler's Games," for German chancellor Adolf Hitler and his Nazi Party commandeered this particular Olympiad and refashioned it into a blatant display of nationalist propaganda. Germany had recently stripped its large Jewish population of citizenship, and Mayer was initially one of several talented Jewish athletes ejected from official sporting organizations. International pressure forced Germany Olympic officials to allow Mayer, who had won a gold medal in her sport eight years earlier, to compete.

Mayer was born in 1910 in Offenbach, a town near Frankfurt am Main in central Germany. Only one par-

Chronology	
1910	Born in Offenbach, Germany
1914	Begins competing at the national level in women's fencing
1925	Wins first German women's title
1928	Wins gold medal at Amsterdam Games
1932	Places fifth in women's foil at Los Angeles Summer Games; settles in California
1933	Offenbach Fencing Club expels her
1936	Wins silver medal at Berlin Games
1952	Marries Baron von Sonnenburg and returns to Germany
1953	Dies of cancer in Frankfurt, Germany on October 16

Awards and Accomplishments	
1925-30	German women's foil champion
1928	Gold medalist in women's foil, Amsterdam Olympics
1929, 1931, 1937	World Fencing Championship title in women's foil
1934-35, 1937-39, 1941-42, 1946	U.S. Women's National Fencing Championship title
1936	Silver medalist in women's foil, Berlin Olympics

ent—her father, Dr. Ludwig Mayer—was Jewish, but this later classified Mayer as a "Mischling," or person of mixed blood, when Nazi Germany began enacting and enforcing anti-Semitic statutes in 1935. Mayer's father headed the sanitation department in Offenbach, where she grew up with two brothers. Her fencing career began at an early age and she soon proved to be a formidable opponent in this sport, which is known for its blend of athletic skill and nerve. She began competing in the women's foil class at the age of just 13 and proved a tremendous talent, winning the German national title in 1925. At 17, she took the gold medal at the 1928 Olympic Games in Amsterdam.

A celebrity in Germany, Mayer was regularly feted as one of the most impressive feminine competitors in the history of fencing. She continued to hold the women's national title in Germany, and in both 1929 and 1931 she took the women's world title in foil as well. She was deemed by the *Times* of London "admittedly the finest amateur swordswoman in the world." Mayer arrived in the United States in 1932 to compete in the Summer Olympic Games in Los Angeles, but fenced poorly and placed only fifth. Liking the area, however, she decided to stay. She enrolled in Scripps College in Claremont, California, and later entered the University of Southern California, where she took postgraduate courses in international law. By 1934, she had returned to top form and took the U.S. indoor women's title in foil.

During Mayer's absence, the fascist Nazi Party gained full political control of Germany, and the party's anti-Semitic political rhetoric quickly evolved into a series of repressive laws. The Nazis blamed Germany's Jewish population—many of whom were successful professionals, entrepreneurs, or artisans—for the economic woes that plagued the country after its defeat in World War I. In November of 1933 it was announced that Mayer had been expelled from her Offenbach Fencing Club. As its most famous member, the ejection was unusual, but even odder was the second official announcement that followed, which noted that Mayer would be allowed to keep her spot on the national federation.

In September of 1935, Germany enacted the Nuremberg Law, which revoked German citizenship for Jews and those with one Jewish parent, like Mayer. She remained in the United States, eventually finding a permanent job as a German instructor and fencing coach at an elite women's college, Mills College, in Oakland. As preparations were underway for Germany's first hosting of the Olympic Games in 1936, International Olympic Committee (IOC) members resisted Nazi-ordered attempts to turn the peacetime contest into a belligerent display of German superiority. At one point, Germany even tried to bar all Jewish athletes from competing; others protested so vehemently that there was a threat to remove the Games from Berlin altogether.

Pressured to allow Jewish athletes on their own national team, the Germans granted Mayer and a top women's track star, Gretel Bergmann, a place. Mayer was the sole Jewish athlete, however, to march in the opening ceremonies on August 1, 1936, at Berlin's new Olympic Stadium. Bergmann, who qualified for the high jump in trials, was told just days before the Games were to begin that Germany would use only two of its three allotted spots for the event and that she was being dropped from the team. The president of the Germany Olympic Committee, Captain Hans von Tschammer und Osten, claimed she Mayer was actually "Aryan," and with her blond hair, green eyes, and lithe height, she ironically exemplified a Nordic physique that the Nazis idealized.

In this era, women's Olympic fencing had just one event: the individual foil, and Mayer emerged as a frontrunner along with Ilona Schacherer-Elek of Hungary, who was also half-Jewish, and Austria's Ellen Preis, who had won the gold medal at the 1932 Games. The Berlin meets featured a new electronic-touch scoring apparatus, and in the trials Schacherer-Elek beat Mayer. Facing Preis in what Richard D. Mandell's *The Nazi Olympics* deemed "a contest that perhaps was the most dramatic fencing match of the age," Mayer parried and thrust into a three-draw score. Schacherer-Elek was awarded the gold medal, and Mayer's points earned her the silver. On the victory podium, she delivered the obligatory "Heil, Hitler" salute to the Fuehrer with her right arm, as the German athletes were compelled to do.

Mayer returned to California, joined the Los Angeles Fencing Club, and became a U.S. citizen. She won the U.S. women's national fencing title in 1937, and bested Schacherer-Elek that same year at the women's world championships in Paris. Mayer won the U.S. women's title five more times between 1939 and 1946. In 1952, she returned to Germany to become Baroness von Sonnenburg after her marriage to an engineer from Stuttgart. She died of cancer in October of 1953, and it was revealed that she had requested full German citizenship in exchange for competing for Germany in the 1936 Olympics.

Mayer endured some criticism for her participation in the "Nazi Olympics" from the American Jewish community, who felt that she served as Germany's token Jew. Her performance and silver medal—along with that of the first-place Schacherer-Elek, another "Mischling"—did serve to debunk Nazi claims of Aryan athletic superiority. Several other impressive feats during the Berlin Games also made a mockery of the racist atmosphere, most notably those of a black American, **Jesse Owens**, who set world records in the broad jump and 200-meter race. Other African Americans also had medal finishes, as did Jews and a slew of "non-Aryans" from around the globe. "The Olympics and sporting competitions," observed Mandell, "exist partly for this purpose."

FURTHER INFORMATION

Books

Hart-Davis, Dan. *Hitler's Games: The 1936 Olympics.* New York: Harper & Row, 1986.

Mandell, Richard D. *The Nazi Olympics.* Urbana: University of Illinois Press, 1987.

Periodicals

"Baroness von Sonnenburg." *Times* (London, England), (October 19, 1953): 10.

Berkow, Ira. "After 60 Years, Going for the Gold." *Daily News* (Los Angeles, CA), (June 23, 1996): N15.

"Foil Play for Women." *Times* (London, England), (December 3, 1930): 7.

"Helene Mayer, 43, Fencing Star, Dies." *New York Times* (October 16, 1953): 27.

Katz, Ian. "Leap of Faith Takes Athlete to the Games at 82." *Guardian* (London, England), (June 24, 1996): 9.

Sketch by Carol Brennan

Don Maynard
1935-

American football player

Don Maynard

Former New York Jets wide receiver Don Maynard is best known for playing a crucial role in winning the 1968 Super Bowl for the Jets. Maynard began his career with the New York Giants in 1958. He played only one season with that team before being let go. After a brief stint in the Canadian Football League, he joined the New York Titans in 1960. The Titans became the Jets in 1962, and Maynard stayed on the team until 1972. His shining moment came in the 1968 AFL Championship Game, in which the Jets defeated the Oakland Raiders 27-23. During the game, Maynard caught six passes, traveling 118 yards for two touchdowns. His first touchdown was off a 14-yard catch in the first period. Maynard won the game for the Jets in the fourth period with a 6-yard catch, allowing the team to go on to the Super Bowl. He ended his fifteen-year career with the St. Louis Cardinals in 1973, with a career total of 633 receptions for 11,834 yards, a 18.7-yard average. He made 88 touchdowns during his career, scoring 530 points.

Maynard's strength as a receiver came not from running complex, preplanned patterns, but in improvising in the heat of the moment. He was named to the American Football League's All-Time Team in 1969, played in three American Football League All-Star Games, and was inducted into the Pro Football Hall of Fame in 1987.

Donald Maynard was born in 1935 in Crosbyton, Texas. He grew up in the southwest of Texas in a succession of towns, including Denver City, Colorado City, and

Career Statistics

Yr	Team	Receiving				Rushing				
		REC	YDS	AVG	TD	ATT	YDS	AVG	TD	FUM
1958	NYG	5	84	16.8	0	12	45	3.8	0	3
1960	NYT	72	1265	17.6	6	0	0	0.0	0	0
1961	NYT	43	629	14.6	8	0	0	0.0	0	1
1962	NYT	56	1041	18.6	8	0	0	0.0	0	0
1963	NYJ	38	780	20.5	9	2	6	3.0	0	0
1964	NYJ	46	847	18.4	8	3	3	1.0	0	1
1965	NYJ	68	1218	17.9	14	1	2	2.0	0	1
1966	NYJ	48	840	17.5	5	0	0	0.0	0	0
1967	NYJ	71	1434	20.2	10	4	18	4.5	0	1
1968	NYJ	57	1297	22.8	10	0	0	0.0	0	0
1969	NYJ	47	938	20.0	6	1	-6	-6.0	0	0
1970	NYJ	31	525	16.9	0	0	0	0.0	0	1
1971	NYJ	21	408	19.4	2	1	2	2.0	0	0
1972	NYJ	29	510	17.6	2	0	0	0.0	0	0
1973	STL	1	18	18.0	0	0	0	0.0	0	0
TOTAL		633	11834	18.7	88	24	70	2.9	0	8

NYG: New York Giants; NYJ: New York Jets; NYT: New York Titans; STL: St. Louis Cardinals.

Chronology

1935	Born on January 25 in Crosbyton, Texas
1958	Signs with the New York Giants
1960	Signs with the New York Titans, which became the Jets in 1962
1968	Scores winning touchdown in playoff game against the Oakland Raiders, taking the Jets to the Super Bowl
1972	Is dismissed by the Jets
1973	Plays two games with the St. Louis Cardinals
1973	Retires from playing football

Awards and Accomplishments

1969	Named to the American Football League's All-Time Team
1987	Inducted into the Pro Football Hall of Fame

El Paso. His father worked in these towns as a cotton ginner, helping to process cotton for commercial use.

After starting out at Rice University, Maynard attended college at Texas Western University, where he was a star on the track team. He also played on the school football team as a halfback on offense and a safety on defense.

Maynard was drafted by the New York Giants in 1957, in time to take part in the Championship Game the Giants played against the Baltimore Colts in 1958. But 1958 was the only season Maynard played with the Giants; he was let go from the team after just one season. It was an event he had trouble understanding. As he later told Ira Berkow in the *New York Times,* "I couldn't understand some of the guys they kept. I could run faster backwards than they could run forwards." And as he told Mickey Herskowitz in the *Houston Chronicle,* "I kept a little bitterness in me. Who wouldn't? I knew I could play. And ten years later I had a chance to show them."

After a year in the Canadian Football League, Maynard became the first player signed to the new American Football League's New York Titans in 1960. The Titans

became the Jets in 1962, and Maynard remained with the team until 1972. In 1968, the best year of his career, Maynard averaged 22.8 yards per catch, the best in the American Football League.

During off seasons, Maynard returned to Texas to work regular jobs. He started as a plumber, and then moved on to become math and industrial arts teacher in high school. At times he had trouble believing his success in football. As he later told Berkow, "Sometimes I'd be in a huddle in Shea Statium, and I'd look up in the stands at 63,000 people screaming, and it was thrilling. I'd kinda think, 'What am I doing here? I oughta be gettin' autographs in the huddle.'"

Maynard's finest moment came during the 1968 American League Championship. The Jets were losing to the Oakland Raiders 23-20 in the final quarter when **Joe Namath** passed Maynard the ball. Maynard later described the play to Berkow in the *New York Times.* "The wind took the ball one way, and then another and I reached around about 180 degrees and caught it. My momentum took me to the six-yard line. It was a 52-yard pass play. On the next play, Joe hit me in the end zone for the winning touchdown." Looking back on it years later, Maynard recalled the play that set up the touchdown as the best of his career, a million dollar reception. The touchdown took the Jets to the Super bowl, which the team also won.

Maynard was 37 years old in 1972, and his yardages falling off, when he was let go by the Jets. It was the most painful moment of Maynard's career. "It was hard to deal with," Maynard admitted to the *San Antonio Express-News*'s Tom Orsborn many years later. "I wanted to quit as a Jet. I climbed the walls. I got to the point where I couldn't talk about it. I was emotional to the point of crying. . . . I was devastated."

But Maynard's career was not quite yet over. He immediately signed with the St. Louis Cardinals, for which he played two games in 1973 before retiring. In 1987, Maynard was inducted into the Pro Football Hall of Fame.

Don Maynard lives in El Paso, Texas. After retiring from playing football, he went to work in an insurance company as a financial planner. By the 1990s, he headed up his own financial services consulting firm, where he was still working into the 2000s. He has kept in touch with his former colleagues in the NFL. As he told Todd Hveem in the *Houston Chronicle* in September, 2002, "As time goes on, you keep up with players. You get closer and closer throughout the years." One way in which Maynard has kept up with other former football stars is by playing in celebrity golf tournaments whose proceeds are donated to charities and scholarship funds. "I play about once per month whether I need to or not," Maynard told Hveem. "I love playing in these things. We always have a great time."

FURTHER INFORMATION

Periodicals

Baker, Al. "25 Years Later, Football Legend Lives On." *Plain Dealer* (January 14, 1994): 2D.

Berkow, Ira. "He Came to Stay." *New York Times* (January 29, 1987): B11.

Herskowitz, Mickey. "Super Bowl XXXV Won't Be the First Time Baltimore and New York Have Squared off on the NFL's Biggest Stage." *Houston Chronicle* (January 21, 2001): Sports, 1.

Hveem, Todd. "Like Charities, Ex-NFL Players to Benefit from Tourney." *Houston Chronicle* (September 26, 2002): 15.

Orsborn, Tom. "Hard to Say Goodbye; As Father Time Grabs Hold of the Athlete, Many Grapple with the Decision of When Is the Right Time to Hang It Up." *San Antonio Express-News* (March 29, 2001): 1C.

Other

"Don Maynard Biography." Pro Football Hall of Fame. http://www.profootballhof.com/players/enshrinees/dmaynard.cfm (December 16, 2002).

"Don Maynard." JT-SW.com. http://www.jt-sw.com/football/pro/players.nsf/ID/03940005 (December 19, 2002).

"Don Maynard." Sport Classic Books. http://www.sportclassicbooks.com/bio-maynard.html (December 16, 2002).

Sketch by Michael Belfiore

Willie Mays
1931-

American baseball player

He hit more than 600 home runs. He could reach base almost at will. He had defensive skills that boggled the mind. Willie Mays was one of the finest baseball players to ever step on the baseball field. In a twenty-two-year professional career with the Giants of New York and San Francisco, Mays consistently appeared near or at the top of almost every major statistic. His fantastic play, year in and year out, makes Willie Mays one of the best players baseball has ever known.

Growing Up

Willie Mays was born on May 6, 1931, in Fairfield, Alabama. His father, William Howard, was a steelworker who mined in the all-black town of Fairfield, only thirteen miles from Birmingham. His parents, gifted athletes in their own right, were only sixteen at the time of his birth. Willie's father played center field for the Birmingham Industrial League Semi Pro team, while his mother Anna had been a high school track star. Willie stood to inherit quite a bit of athletic talent from his bloodlines. Even his grandfather pitched for a Negro League baseball team.

Willie's parents divorced when he was three, and he went to live with his father, who, to care for Willie while he was at work, brought in a homeless woman. Even at the age of three, his father had him playing catch, or placed him in the dugout at the Semi Pro games he played in. By the time Willie Mays was a young man, he'd already had more baseball education than most players receive in a lifetime. Since his high school had no baseball team, Willie was playing in the semi-pro leagues around Birmingham. Even if his school had a team, chances are he wouldn't have been challenged by the high school players.

A Way Out

As with many players who grew up poor, and especially black players in the rural South, Willie Mays knew baseball was his ticket out of poverty, a way out of the steelmill life his father knew. It was also a way out of the

Chronology

1931	Born May 6 in Fairfield, Alabama, the only child of William Howard and Anna Sattlewhite Mays
1934	Moves with his father after parents divorce; remains close to his mother
1937	Begins education in segregated school in Alabama
1944	Plays semiprofessional baseball at age 13 with the Gray Sox
1946	Enters Fairfield Industrial High School, takes courses in dry cleaning
1946	Plays center field for Birmingham Industrial League while his father plays left field
1947	Begins play for Birmingham Black Barons, playing baseball with men ten years his senior
1948	Makes professional Negro Leagues debut on July 4
1950	Graduates from Fairfield High School
1950	New York Giants buy out Mays' Black Barons Contract. He is youngest black man ever signed by the major leagues
1950	Racial bias in Sioux City prevents Mays from joining their minor league team
1950	Puts up impressive numbers with Class B Inter-State League in Trenton, New Jersey, hitting .477 and 8 home runs in 35 games
1951	Becomes #3 batter in Giants' starting lineup on May 25
1952	Drafted by U.S. Army in May. Continues to play baseball
1954	Receives honorable discharge and returns to Giants
1954	Makes spectacular over-the-shoulder no-look catch, known simply as "The Catch"

1954	Makes appearances on *Ed Sullivan Show* and *Colgate Comedy Hour*
1955	Bus boycott in Alabama, started by Rosa Parks, gains world's attention
1955	Moves to Englewood, New Jersey
1956	Marries Marguerite Wendell
1957	New York Giants move to San Francisco
1958	Adopts infant son Michael
1963	Divorces Marguerite Wendell
1964	Appointed captain of the Giants
1965	Becomes national spokeperson for the Job Corps
1965	Mays remains silent and uninvolved in Civil Rights struggles, says "I don't picket ... I'm not mad at the people who do. Maybe they shouldn't be mad at the people who don't"
1971	Marries Mae Louise Allen
1972	Traded to New York Mets
1973	Retires from Baseball
1973-79	Becomes coach and goodwill ambassador for New York Mets; would become public relations worker and make public appearances on behalf of many companies in 1980s and 1990s
1974	Inducted into the Black Hall of Fame
1979	Only player inducted into the Baseball Hall of Fame this year
2000	Honored with "Say Hey Day" at Pacific Bell Park in San Francisco
2002	Sees his godson, San Francisco Giants left fielder Barry Bonds, make it to the World Series

blatantly racist and segregated South. As a child, Mays would much rather have been playing ball than studying. Rather than books, he focused his intelligence on the only game that ever consumed him. Since he grew up in dugouts and watching his father play, he studied strategy and technique instead of reading and writing.

His time in the dugouts also taught him how to deal with the competition among men while he was just a boy. At only thirteen, Mays played on the Gray Sox, a semi-professional team. By he time he started high school at fifteen, he would make $250 a month on the Birmingham Black Barons. This seemed ideal for a person born into Mays' situation. The money coming in was more than any part time job would ever pay, and he made it doing what he loved. Mays finished high school, but he finished it as a professional baseball player.

Several Father Figures

A big influence on the young Mays was his Black Barons manager, Piper Davis. Davis, who had spent many years as a player and was now a player/manager, saw that Mays was no mere baseball player. Mays was someone with innate talent, and with tutoring and development, he believed Mays could become something even more special.

Tough Times in the North

By the time Willie Mays was nineteen, **Jackie Robinson** had already broken the color barrier in baseball. When a scout for New York Giants came to watch a Black Barons game, he didn't go to the field to watch Mays. Instead, it was one of his teammates who was supposed to get the looksee. But after a few minutes in the ballpark, the scout realized there was only one player there. Mays had caught his eye. He was signed for a $4000 bonus, plus $250 a month salary, to play in Sioux City, Iowa, on the Giants' Class A team.

Yet there were racial problems in Sioux City, and Mays wasn't allowed to join the team. Instead, the Giants moved him to Trenton, New Jersey, to play in a Class B Interstate League. Mays would become the first black to ever play in that league. But after only a season in Trenton, he went to the Minneapolis Millers to play Triple A ball. This was 1951, and Mays was but a short step from the majors after his first sixteen games of the season. He was batting .608, with a defense that was nothing short of spectacular. **Leo Durocher**, who would, like Piper Davis, take Mays under his wing, was the manager of the New York Giants. He called up Mays early in the '51 season. The Giants, rather mediocre that year, needed the help of Mays.

Willie Mays became the starting center fielder for the Giants on May 25, 1951. But whether it was nerves or something else, Mays could muster only one hit in his first twenty-five at bats. Durocher, however, saw the fire in Mays and knew that patience was necessary. He never lost faith. Though the Giants had a lackluster season, with the help of Mays—who eventually came out of his slump—they finished strong, tying their rivals the Brooklyn Dodgers in the last game of the season and forcing a playoff for the pennant.

Willie Mays

This put Mays in a game that would include one of the most famous hits in baseball history. Mays' teammate, Bobby Thompson, came to bat in the bottom of the ninth. The Giants were down, but Thompson hit a three run homer off of Brooklyn Dodger Ralph Branca. The "Shot Heard Round the World" clinched the pennant for the Giants, but they went on to lose to the Yankees in seven games.

In spite of his poor start that year, Mays garnered the National League Rookie of the Year honor for his twenty home runs and .274 batting average. At the conclusion of the season, however, he would be called into the army and serve his two years (primarily as a baseball instructor).

The First Full Season

Mays returned to the Giants in 1954 for his first full season and led his team to a world championship. That season he hit .345, blasted forty-one home runs, and won the league's Most Valuable Player (MVP) Award. He also led the league in batting average.

During the 1954 World Series, Mays made what is perhaps one of the most famous defensive plays in baseball. "The Catch," as it has come to be known, was a blind, over the shoulder basket pick Mays made while running down a ball heading toward the fence. When it dropped into his glove, the fans were amazed. Willie had robbed the Indians' Vic Wertz of what should have been

an extra base hit. Mays' catch held the Indians to only one run that inning, and the Giants re-tied the game, going on to win it in the tenth.

As recently as 2002 Mays would tell the *New York Daily News* that his famous catch, "Doesn't come close to the one I made in Ebbets Field off the Dodgers' Bobby Morgan the first week of the '52 season." That was a catch where, in the ninth with two outs and the bases loaded, Morgan's line drive over the shortstop found Mays diving, head first, to make the play. He hit the fence, knocked himself out, but still came up with the ball.

His accomplishments on the field could fill volumes. In 1955, Mays hit fifty-one homers, only the seventh person at the time to do so. He led the National League in triples and slugging percentage, and was second in stolen bases. In 1961 he became only the fifth player to hit four home runs in a single game. And then in 1962, led the Giants back into the World Series, the culmination of a stellar season, with 141 runs batted in—his career high.

Willie Mays made twenty-four straight All-Star appearances and had more than 3000 career base hits. His effortless play would be summed up in single word by writers and fans, who called him "graceful" and "elegant." Truly a joy to watch at every part of the game, Mays was perhaps most stunning on the basepaths. Starting in 1956, he led the league in stolen bases four years straight. In addition to this, he averaged forty-five home runs per season for the first half of the sixties. At the end of his career, he would walk away with 660 home runs and 1903 RBIs. Willie Mays was a Renaissance player, the guy who could do it all.

The Most Determined

Davis and Durocher were prophetic in their claims that there was something more to Mays than met the

Career Statistics

Yr	Team	AVG	GP	AB	R	H	HR	RBI	BB	SO	SB	E
1951	NYG	.274	121	464	59	127	20	68	57	60	7	9
1952	NYG	.236	34	127	17	30	4	23	16	17	4	1
1954	NYG	.345	151	565	119	195	41	110	66	57	8	7
1955	NYG	.319	152	580	123	185	51	127	79	60	24	8
1956	NYG	.296	152	578	101	171	36	84	68	65	40	9
1957	NYG	.333	152	585	112	195	35	97	76	62	38	9
1958	NYG	.347	152	600	121	208	29	96	78	56	31	9
1959	SFG	.313	151	575	125	180	34	104	65	58	27	6
1960	SFG	.319	153	595	107	190	29	103	61	70	25	6
1961	SFG	.308	154	572	129	176	40	123	81	77	18	8
1962	SFG	.304	162	621	130	189	49	141	78	85	18	4
1963	SFG	.314	157	596	115	187	38	103	66	83	8	8
1964	SFG	.296	157	578	121	171	47	111	82	72	19	6
1965	SFG	.317	157	558	118	177	52	112	76	71	9	6
1966	SFG	.288	152	552	99	159	37	103	70	81	5	7
1967	SFG	.263	141	486	83	128	22	70	51	92	6	7
1968	SFG	.289	148	498	84	144	23	79	67	81	12	7
1969	SFG	.283	117	403	64	114	13	58	49	71	6	5
1970	SFG	.291	139	478	94	139	28	83	79	90	5	7
1971	SFG	.271	136	417	82	113	18	61	112	123	23	6
1972	SFG	.184	19	49	8	9	0	3	17	5	3	0
	NYM	.267	69	195	27	52	8	19	43	43	1	4
1973	NYM	.211	66	209	24	44	6	25	27	47	1	4
TOTAL		.302	2992	10881	2062	3283	660	1903	1464	1526	338	156

NYG: New York Giants; NYM: New York Mets; SFG: San Francisco Giants.

eye. During his time with the Giants, depending on what the team needed and what Durocher asked of him, Mays was able increase the number of home runs if need be. Yet just as often, "Say Hey"—a nickname he earned because he often forgot his teammates' names—was satisfied reaching base. Once on base, he could drive pitchers nuts with his speed. Regardless of how he chose to hit the ball, he would average .300 for his career, with almost thirty home runs per season.

His greatness came with a small price, however. Though he was blessed with talent, his work ethic was above and beyond that of most ballplayers. Mays continually worked himself to the point of exhaustion—even once collapsing at the plate. Willie Mays simply wanted more than his body could physically give him.

Headed West

Mays married Marghuerite Wendell, in 1956. They had a baby boy, Michael, just two years later. In 1957 the Giants moved to San Francisco. Mays, however, wasn't on top of the world. He was a New York hero, and he loved it in The Big Apple. The move west would be difficult, and it sent bad blood flowing between Mays and the fans. The people in California didn't revere Mays like the folks did back in NYC. Additionally, he was having trouble at home, and his divorce to Marghuerite would become finalized in 1963.

Mays called it quits in 1973 while playing for the New York Mets. He has been called one of the—if not the—greatest baseball players of all time.

Though he came from the South and played baseball during the years when Civil Rights fighting was the toughest, Mays remained silent about his feelings throughout his career. He chose to take an apolitical stance, instead putting everything into baseball. Some critics say he should have given more back to the place he came from, but Mays chose to take his anger out on the little "white" ball that he could control, catching it effortlessly as well as hitting harder than most other players.

Asked years later why he never publicly supported the Civil Rights Movement, according to the *Encyclopedia of African-American Cuture and History*, he said: "I don't picket in the streets of Birmingham. I'm not mad at the people who do. Maybe they shouldn't be mad at the people who don't."

After his retirement Mays said that, "I've given every bit of energy to baseball." In 1979, along with **Mickey Mantle**, Mays was ordered to cut ties with baseball for doing PR work for an Atlantic City casino. This was the same year he was voted into the hall of fame, and he would be allowed fully and completely back into baseball in 1985, though not without some ill will towards the Commissioner of Baseball.

In his long career, Mays hit more than 600 home runs, tore up the basepaths with his speed, and robbed batters of sure hits with his phenomenal defense in the outfield. Willie Mays was one of the finest baseball players to ever step on the baseball field.

Awards and Accomplishments

1951	National League Rookie of the Year
1954	*Sporting News* Major League Player of the Year
1954	Associated Press Male Athlete of the Year
1954	Hickock Belt
1954, 1965	National League Most Valuable Player
1954-73	National League All-Star Team
1957-68	National League Gold Glove Award
1963, 1968	All-Star Game Most Valuable Player
1970	*Sporting News* Baseball Player of the Decade
1970	First Commissioner's Award
1973	Inducted into California Sports Hall of Fame
1975	Inducted into Black Athletes Hall of Fame
1979	Inducted into National Baseball Hall of Fame
1979	Inducted into Alabama Sports Hall of Fame
1999	MLB All-Century Team
1999	Uniform #24 retired by San Francisco Giants

CONTACT INFORMATION

Address: Say Hey Inc., 51 Mount Vernon Lane, Atherton, CA 94206.

SELECTED WRITINGS BY MAYS:

(With Jeff Harris) *Danger in Center Field,* Argonaut Books, 1963.

(With Howard Liss) *My Secrets of Playing Baseball* (illustrated by David Sutton), Viking, 1967.

(As told to Charles Einstein) *Willie Mays: My Life In and Out of Baseball,* Bookthrift Co., 1978.

(With Maxine Berger) *Play Ball,* Wanderer Books, 1980.

(With Lou Sahadi) *Say Hey: The Autobiography of Willie Mays,* Simon & Schuster, 1988.

(With Ron Smith) *The Sporting News Selects Baseball's Greatest Players: A Celebration of the 20th Century's Best (Sporting News Series),* McGraw Hill, 1998.

FURTHER INFORMATION

Books

Encyclopedia of World Biography. 2nd ed. 17 Volumes. Detroit: Gale, 1998.

Grabowski, John F. *Willie Mays.* New York: Chelsea House, 1990.

Mays, Willie, and Maxine Berger. *Play Ball.* Wanderer Books, 1980.

Mays, Willie (as told to Charles Einstein). *Willie Mays: My Life In and Out of Baseball.* Bookthrift Co., 1978.

Mays, Willie, and Jeff Harris. *Danger in Center Field.* Larchmont, NY: Argonaut Books, 1963.

Mays, Willie, and Howard Liss. *My Secrets of Playing Baseball* (illustrated by David Sutton). New York: Viking, 1967.

Willie Mays

Where Is He Now?

Mays continues to remain heavily involved in the world of baseball, and he remains in the spotlight. In the 2002 World Series, Mays received quite a bit of press. His godson, Giants slugger Barry Bonds—who is often compared to Mays—had a phenomenal Series, even though his team would eventually lose to the Angels.

Mays rarely gives interviews, but during the series the pride he felt for his godson was evident. Still, reporters could not get him to answer the question: "Who is the greatest, you or Barry?" Mays only answered, "We are not going to get into the greatest."

He has also served as a lecturer for the Federal Job Corps, done work for the Help Young America campaign, and makes appearances on behalf of several companies he's under contract with.

Mays, Willie, and Lou Sahadi. *Say Hey: The Autobiography of Willie Mays.* New York: Simon & Schuster, 1988.

Mays, Willie, with Ron Smith. *The Sporting News Selects Baseball's Greatest Players: A Celebration of the 20th Century's Best (Sporting News Series).* New York: McGraw Hill, 1998.

Periodicals

Adande, J.A. "One of Greatest Has a Special Bond With Barry." *Los Angeles Times* (October 21, 2002).

Atlanta Constitution (June 10, 1988).

Curry, Jack. "Even at 71, Mays Can Take Some Good Swings." *New York Times* (October 21, 2002).

Ebony (October 1966).

"Hall Induction Included Giant Letdown for Mays." *Los Angeles Times* (August 5, 1999).

Jet (March 27, 1980).

Jet (March 3, 1986).

Jet (April 10, 1989).

Los Angeles Times (March 13, 1989).

Madden, Bill. "Willie Mays says his best catch wasn't in 1954." Knight Ridder/Tribune News Service (July 9, 2002).

Martinez, Michael. "Willie Mays statue unveiled at Pac Bell." Knight Ridder/Tribune News Service (March 31, 2000).

New York Times (February 12, 1966).

New York Times (April 26, 1966).

New York Times Magazine (July 11, 1954).

Roderick, Joe. "Bonds swings for baseball Immortality." Knight Ridder/Tribune News Service (March 26, 2001).

Sporting News (September 1, 1986).

Sports Illustrated (October 6, 1986).

Time (July 26, 1954).

Time (November 12, 1979).

Time (April 1, 1985).

"Willie Mays says milestone HR was no big deal." Knight Ridder/Tribune News Service (July 4, 2002).

Other

"Willie Mays." http://www.baseball-reference.com/ (November 10, 2002).
"Willie Mays." http://www.pubdim.net/baseballlibrary/ (November 10, 2002).

Sketch by Eric Lagergren

Patricia McCormick
1930-

American diver

W omen divers gained popularity in the years before World War I, as much for their attractiveness as for their skill. Until Pat McCormick entered the scene in the late 1940s, displaying remarkable agility and toughness, no one dominated the sport. The first and only woman diver to win two gold medals in two consecutive Olympic Games (the double-double), McCormick earned the prestigious Sullivan Award in 1956 as the nation's top amateur athlete and became the first woman diver inducted into the International Swimming Hall of Fame. She belongs among the greatest names in Olympic history.

Raised Around Water

Pat McCormick was born Patricia Keller in Seal Beach, California, on May 12, 1930. Living above a grocery store and with little money in the family, she and her two older brothers were raised mostly by their mother, a nurse. Her alcoholic father was a sporadic presence in her life, although his belief in her was an important influence. In a 1999 interview with Dr. Margaret Costa for the Amateur Athletic Foundation of Los Angeles, McCormick described her early years: "I worked to help support the family from the time I was 10 years old. My brother was responsible for my involvement in athletics because I wanted to be just like him. We were good little urchins who had a lot of fun."

McCormick spent most of her spare hours swimming around the channels and the harbor and hanging out at Muscle Beach, where she enjoyed being tossed around by the brawny, acrobatic men. This pastime helped her develop strength and flexibility. Her love of competition prompted her to participate in small swim meets against anyone willing to race her. In her first meet, a two-mile pier-to-pier swim, she came in second. (There was only one other girl in the race.) But the trophy she received stoked her desire for more. At fourteen, she won the Long Beach city women's one-meter diving gold cup. A coach from the Los Angeles Athletic Club soon took notice and invited her to join the Club to begin rigorous training.

Pat McCormick

The training did little to interfere with her academics or social life at Wilson High School, but she was allowed to miss her last class period to take the trolley to Los Angeles. The 5'4", 125 pound diver trained for a year before entering local competitions. She went on to place second in the 1947 National Platform Championship. Her brother borrowed money so she could attend the 1948 Olympic tryouts, where she missed making the team by less than a point.

Determined to Succeed

Robert Condon, in his book *Great Women Athletes of the 20th Century,* quoted McCormick as saying, "That defeat was the greatest thing that ever happened to me because all of a sudden I knew I could win the Olympics . . . I realized that at Los Angeles I was working with world-class athletes every day."

She married Glenn McCormick in 1949 and started competing under her married name. Glenn, an airline pilot and aspiring Olympic diver, later became her coach. McCormick's training regimen consisted of 80 to 100 dives a day, six days a week. She persevered despite various injuries—a gash on her head requiring fifty stitches, chipped teeth, welts, a loose jaw, and a cracked rib.

The hard work quickly paid off. That same year, she won the National Platform Championship. She did it again in 1950, adding the one-meter and three-meter springboard titles. She won all five national titles in

Chronology

1930	Born May 12 in Seal Beach, California
1948	Misses qualifying for the Olympics by less than a point
1949	Marries Glenn McCormick
1950	Wins the first of 27 national diving titles
1956	Gives birth to son Timmy
1956	Becomes the first and only woman diver to win four gold medals in two consecutive Olympic Games
1960	Gives birth to daughter Kelly
1974	Ends marriage to Glenn McCormick
1984	One of nine athletes selected to carry the Olympic flag in the Opening Ceremonies of the 1984 Games
1984	Begins motivational speaking

Awards and Accomplishments

1950	Won the first of 27 national diving titles
1951	Gold medal at the Pan Am Games
1952	Two gold medals at the Summer Olympics in Helsinki, Finland
1955	Two gold medals at the Pan Am Games
1956	Two gold medals at the Summer Olympics in Melbourne, Australia
1956	Amateur Athletic Union's James E. Sullivan Memorial Trophy as amateur athlete of the year
1956	Babe Zaharias Trophy
1956	Helms Hall of Fame North American Athlete of the Year
1956	*Sports Illustrated* Athlete of the Year
1956	Associated Press Woman Athlete of the Year
1956	United Press International's Woman Athlete of the Year
1984	Inducted into the International Women's Sports Hall of Fame
1985	Inducted into the U.S. Olympic Hall of Fame
1987	Inducted into the Orange County (California) Sports Hall of Fame
1996	Inducted into the World Sports Humanitarian Hall of Fame

1951. In all, she won twenty-seven national titles. She also won three gold medals in two appearances at the Pan Am Games.

The Double-Double

McCormick's biggest splash came as an Olympian. At the 1952 Olympic Games in Helsinki, Finland, she swept both events, the platform and the springboard. She repeated those gold medal-winning performances at the 1956 Olympics in Melbourne, Australia, even though she was competing just months after giving birth to her son. It wasn't until 1988 that a man, **Greg Louganis**, was able to replicate McCormick's double-double.

Her Olympic success led to a long list of honors, including the Babe Zaharias Trophy, the Associated Press and the United Press International's Woman Athlete of the Year, *Sports Illustrated*'s Athlete of the Year, and the Helms Hall of Fame North American Athlete of the Year.

McCormick's daughter Kelly also became a diver. Kelly won a silver medal at the 1984 Olympics and a bronze in 1988, making the McCormicks the only mother-daughter duo in Olympic history to become medal winners.

Sharing the Olympic Spirit

McCormick's persistence paid off while combating another opponent: life after the Olympics. In a profile issued by the World Sports Humanitarian Hall of Fame in 1996, McCormick recalled the empty feeling that can hit athletes once Olympic glory fades: "You see, all our lives we have had someone to tell us what to do, how to do it. Then, your whole life dissolves into that one moment. When you step up on that victory stand, you're going to be deserted. All the support systems you had are going after their next project. They can't tell you how to handle success, they can only tell you how to achieve it. The trick is to stay on that victory stand."

Realizing the need for an education, McCormick enrolled at Long Beach City College in the 1960s, graduating thirteen years later. During an interview with Dr. Margaret Costa for the Amateur Athletic Association of Los Angeles, she explained the reason for her life-long motivation and self-discipline: "Not having the skills to do something I want to do has been the story of my life. Whether it was college or diving or being a parent, I have had to develop my own skills and knowledge on my own in order to be successful."

McCormick still enjoys an active sports life, especially horse riding, scuba diving, golfing, body surfing, and skiing. She has since focused her optimism and resolve on another arena—helping others realize their dream. This generosity of spirit, flowing from her extensive charity work and motivational speaking, is her way of remaining on the victory stand.

FURTHER INFORMATION

Books

Condon, Robert J. *Great Women Athletes of the 20th Century.* Jefferson, NC: McFarland & Company, Inc., 1991.

Periodicals

Day, Mary. "McCormick Did It Before Louganis." *Los Angeles Times [San Diego County Edition]* (October 22, 1988): 3.

Hicks, Jerry. "McCormick Has the Gold-Medal Touch as a Speaker Too." *Los Angeles Times [Orange County Edition]* (September 19, 1996): 1.

Stump, Al. "Fancy Diving Only Looks Like Fun." *Saturday Evening Post* (May 19, 1951): 27.

Weyler, John. "Orange County Sports Hall of Fame: The New Inductees; McCormick Took Plunge to Reach Dreams, Springboard to Success Starts With

Failures." *Los Angeles Times [Orange County Edition]* (February 14, 1987): 1.

Other

"Hall of Fame." Women's Sports Foundation. www. womenssportsfoundation.org/cg.../iowa/about/ awards/results.html?record=4 (December 4, 2002).

"ISHOF Honorees." International Swimming Hall of Fame. www.ishof.org/HonorM.html (January 7, 2003).

"An Olympian's Oral History: Pat McCormick." The Amateur Athletic Foundation of Los Angeles. www. aafla.org (January 3, 2002).

"Olympic Medal Winners." International Olympic Committee - Athletes. www.olympic.org/uk/athletes/ results/search_r_uk.asp (January 7, 2003).

"Pat McCormick." www.sportsstarsusa.com/olympians/ mccormick_pat.html (January 3, 2003).

"Pat McCormick." World Sports Humanitarian Hall of Fame. www.sportshumanitarian.com/induction/ pmccormick.htm (January 3, 2003).

"Pat McCormick, Olympic Diver." History's Women— An Online Magazine. www.historyswomen.com/ PatMcCormick.html (January 8, 2003).

"Patricia McCormick." International Olympic Committee—Athletes. www.olympic.org/uk/athletes/heroes/ bio_uk.asp?PAR_I_ID=503 (January 7, 2003).

"The Sullivan Award." www.hickoksports.com/history/ sulaward.shtml (January 7, 2003).

"U.S. Olympic Hall of Fame." www.hickoksports.com/ history/olymphof.shtml (January 7, 2003).

Sketch by Carole Manny

Nikki McCray
1971-

American basketball player

Power guard and forward Nikki McCray has played basketball with the WNBA's Washington Mystics and Indiana Fever, and the ABL's Columbus Quest. Earning multiple MVP awards, starter for the WNBA East All-Star team, and gold medals in two Olympics with the women's basketball team, "Nikki Mac" has been called a professional and a role model. With a desire to serve her community as well as her basketball teams, McCray has worked with the Boys & Girls Club and was named to the President's Council on Physical Fitness and Sports.

Just Want to Play Basketball

Nikki McCray began playing basketball at age 11 after her grandmother persuaded Nikki's male cousins to

Nikki McCray

let her play ball with them. She enjoyed the special attention, but she also proved her worth on the court. Although she also participated in track in high school, it was her performance on the school's basketball team that earned her the number ten spot on the National Federation of State High School Associations' list of all-time high school scorers. She worked hard to improve both her defensive and offensive skills.

McCray's high school performance attracted the attention of coach Pat Summitt of the Lady Volunteers women's basketball team at the University of Tennessee, who recruited the young hot-shot. McCray attended the university from 1991 to 1995, eventually earning a degree in sports marketing and education.

It was with the Lady Vols that the 5'11" McCray began a long string of accolades. During her four years at Tennessee, she compiled a 122-11 record. In her junior year alone, she led the team in scoring, averaging 16.3 points per game. Overall, she helped the team to win four consecutive SEC Championships and attend four NCAA Tournaments. McCray was named Best Defensive Player for Tennessee for the four years between 1992 and 1995, Lady Vols Scholar-Athlete for 1993, SEC Player of the Year for 1994 and 1995, collegiate All-American for those same years, MVP of the NCAA Mideast Regionals in 1995, and was a Coach's Award recipient. In addition, she was a nominee for the 1994 Honda-Broderick Award and a runner up for the Naismith Player of the Year for 1994 and 1995.

McCray signed a one-year contract with the American Basketball League in its 1996 inaugural season, joining the now-defunct Columbus Quest team for a reported salary of $150,000. During McCray's tenure, the team attended the 1997 ABL Championship, its first. She was named the ABL's Most Valuable Player for the 1996-97 season, and closed the season averaging 19.9 points per game, 5.0 rebounds per game, and 2.7 assists per game.

National and Olympic Teams

McCray joined the historic 1995-96 USA Basketball Women's National teams that compiled a combined 60-0 record and were named the 1996 US Olympic Committee and USA Basketball Team of the Year. She progressed to the US Olympic women's basketball team that won the gold medal in the 1996 Atlanta games, and repeated that success at the 2000 Olympic Games in Sydney. McCray listed her 1996 Olympic teammate **Teresa Edwards** as one of her role models.

In 1997, she decided to forego the current ABL season and transferred to the Women's National Basketball Association. She saw some of the world when she served on the 1997 and 1998 All-Star team that toured Brazil and Europe. During this time, she was named one of three finalists for the 1997 Women's Pro Basketball ESPY awards. She also played on the gold medal-winning US National Team at the 1998 FIBA international basketball association Women's World Championship in Germany.

Marvelous with the Washington Mystics

On January 27, 1998, McCray signed on with the WNBA and was the first player selected for the floundering Washington Mystics. The phenomenal forward and guard helped to turn the team around. In her first year, she led in scoring, 3-point percentage, and assists, and ranked second in 3-pointers made, and was third in

steals. The Mystics soon led the league in game attendance with an average of 16,000 fans per game and two sell-out crowds of 20,000, the largest number ever to watch US professional women's basketball.

McCray finished the 1999 WNBA season ranked fourth in the league for scoring, was named a starter for the 2000 WNBA All-Star Game, and was leading vote getter among all guards in the Eastern Conference.

In 2001, McCray was traded in the WNBA draft to Indiana Fever for the Fever's first round and third round picks. Her performance with the Mystics ranked her first with 13 consecutive games with a 3-point field goal, second in scoring average, and first in 3-point field goals attempted. In a game against Indiana in July 2001, she scored a season-high 25 points and hit 10 field goals. She has become the sixth leading scorer in WNBA history with 1,921 points and an average 15.8 points per game.

Committed to Community Service

A powerhouse off the court as well, McCray is noted as much for her community service and excellent singing voice as well as phenomenal basketball playing. She helps in her community by donating time to Boys and Girls Clubs where she talks to kids about sports and nutrition. She has even worked at the Abe's Table soup kitchen sponsored by Washington Wizards owner Abe Pollin. McCray is spokesperson for the Wizards and

Career Statistics

Yr	Team	GP	PTS	FG%	3P%	FT%	RPG	APG	SPG	BPG	TO	PF
1993	VOL	7	4.4	.519	0	.600	3.3	7	9	—	—	—
1995-96	VOL	49	6.2	.470	.260	.743	2.3	50	48	—	—	—
1996	CQ	8	9.4	.651	.333	.692	3.5	9	4	—	—	—
1997	AS	40	19.9	.452	.363	.781	5.0	106	69	—	—	—
1998	WAS	29	17.7	.418	.315	.748	2.90	3.1	1.48	.07	4.31	2.80
1999	WAS	32	17.5	.424	.301	.806	2.70	2.4	1.06	.03	3.34	2.70
2000	WAS	32	15.5	.434	.331	.769	1.80	2.7	1.41	.16	2.78	2.50
2001	WAS	32	11.0	.410	.232	.711	1.80	1.5	.81	.00	2.28	2.10
2002	IND	32	11.5	.415	.318	.816	3.00	2.2	.88	.09	2.56	2.30
TOTAL		157	14.6	.421	.301	.769	2.40	2.4	1.12	.07	3.03	2.50

AS: WNBA All Stars; CQ: Columbus Quest; IND: Indiana Fever; VOL: University of Tennessee Lady Volunteers; WAS: Washington Mystics.

Mystics Pick & Roll reading incentive program that enrolls 3,500 area students.

As captain of the WNBA Mystics, McCray delivered the 1999 Women's History Month keynote address at the Library of Congress. At the presentation, she was lauded as a "wonderful role model for young people" by the Federal Women's Program manager. In 2000, McCray was also named to the President's Council on Physical Fitness and Sports, which advises the President and Secretary of Health and Human Services on improving American's participation in sports and physical activity. The Tennessee Sports Hall of Fame named McCray Female Professional Athlete of the Year in 2001.

Possessing a fine singing voice, McCray sang the national anthem at an NBA game. Wowing them in her hometown of Collierville, Tennessee, as well, a park was recently named for her. McCray is married to Thomas Penson, who proposed to her in the middle of the basketball court after a game.

Ever since playing basketball with her cousins when she was in grade school, Nikki McCray has proven that girls can be as good as boys. Helping the Washington Mystics host a Girl Power! night on the Web, McCray said, "This is a great time to be a girl. Just look around at all the things that you can achieve—from playing in the WNBA to being an astronaut to being President. Find something that you like to do, whether it is a sport, school, music, or something else, give it your best effort, and you will succeed—that's Girl Power!"

FURTHER INFORMATION

Periodicals

"Nikki McCray: In Another League" *Sport* 88 (December 1997): 22.

"WNBA's Nikki McCray Named to President's Council on Fitness" *Jet* 97 (February 28, 2000): 50.

Other

African American Publications, http://www.africanpubs.com/Apps/bios/0424McCrayNikki.asp?pic=none (December 15, 2002).

All Sport, http://www.allsports.com/cgi-bin/showstory.cgi?story_id=18636 (December 15, 2002).

Girl Power!, http://www.girlpower.gov/girlarea/gpguests/mccray.htm (December 15, 2002).

Library of Congress, http://www.loc.gov/today/pr/1999/99-028.html (December 15, 2002).

USA Basketball, http://www.usabasketball.com/bioswomen/nikki_mccray_bio.html (December 15, 2002).

Women's National Basketball Association, http://www.wnba.com/playerfile/nikki_mccray (December 15, 2002).

Women's Sports Network, http://www.wsnsports.com/brochuresite/athletes_nikkimccray.html (December 15, 2002).

Sketch by Lorraine Savage

John McEnroe
1959-

American tennis player

One of most successful tennis players of all time, John McEnroe was a dominant force whose reputation was built just as much on his personality as it was on his fantastic play on the court. Known for his violent verbal abuse of ballboys, line judges, chair judges and himself, the McEnroe tirades became just as common as McEnroe victories—and he had plenty of those. During his career as a professional, John McEnroe won 17

John McEnroe

Chronology

1959	Born February 16 in Weisbaden, Germany
1959	Family returns to Queens, N.Y., when McEnroe is nine months old and settles in Douglaston
1970	Placed under instructorship of Tony Palafox and Harry Hopman at Port Washington Tennis Academy (at Long Island)
1975	Receives a six-month suspension from Tennis Academy for a prank. His parents switch him to Cove Racquet Club
1977	Graduates from Manhattan's Trinity School
1977	Qualifies for Wimbledon at age of 18 and becomes youngest player and first qualifier to reach semi-finals
1977	Enters Stanford University
1978	Wins NCAA Championship
1978	Turns professional
1979	Nicknamed "superbrat" by British Tabloids, later shortened to "McBrat"
1979	Starts playing guitar—rock and roll will become one of his passions
1979	Wins first U.S. Open, beating Vitas Gerulaitis in straight sets
1980	Lost Wimbledon to Bjorn Borg in what has been called the greatest match in sports history
1980	Wins U.S. Open
1981	Prevails this time and beat Bjorn Borg at Wimbledon; wins U.S. Open
1981	Important member of winning U.S. Davis Cup team
1982	Defeats Mats Wilander in a six hour 22-minute match at 1982 Davis Cup
1983	Wins Wimbledon
1984	Compiles an 82-3 record and wins a career high 13 tournaments, including his third Wimbledon and fourth U.S. Open
1986	Takes a sabbatical from Tennis; marries actress Tatum O'Neal—they have their first child, Kevin, three months prior (will later add another brother, Sean, and a sister, Emily)
1987	Fails to win a title for the first time since turning pro
1990	Disqualified at Australian Open for using abusive language at officials
1992	Divorces Tatum O'Neal
1992	Final year on ATP tour
1993	Meets Patty Smyth at a Christmas party
1995	Kicks off his broadcasting career at the French Open
1995	Opens the John McEnroe Gallery in SoHo
1997	Records album with his band, The Johnny Smyth Band. McEnroe wrote the lyrics and music
1997	Marries musician Patty Smyth
1999	Named captain of the U.S. Davis Cup team; performs poorly at it and quits after barely a year in the position
2001	Continues to lobby to become "Commissioner of Tennis" (a position that does not exist)
2002	Publishes autobiography, *You Cannot Be Serious*; has a bit part in Adam Sandlar movie *Mr. Deeds*
2002	Tries his hand at a game show, The Chair, on the BBC

Grand Slam titles, 77 career singles titles and 77 doubles titles. He has also been a mainstay of United States Davis Cup play, holding the American Davis Cup records for most wins, ties played, years played and singles wins (41). When he retired from the professional tour in 1992, he had an incredible singles record of 856 wins, 158 losses and 75 titles. Though he left professional tennis, John McEnroe remains a great presence in the sport as one of the mainstays on the Seniors Tour, as well as in the tennis broadcast booth.

Growing Up

John Patrick McEnroe, the eldest of three McEnroe boys, was born on February 16, 1959, in Wiesbaden, Germany. His father John Sr., served in the United States Air Force at the time and was stationed overseas, where McEnroe's mother, Kay, was a surgical nurse. But the family soon moved back to the United States, settling down in Douglaston, Queens, New York. The young McEnroe's athletic prowess showed up early. Whether it was on the basketball court or the tennis court, it was evident that this was a kid who played smart, but who also had superior hand-eye coordination and razor-sharp eyesight.

McEnroe's parents supported their son's tennis dreams. John Sr. earned enough money (he was a lawyer for a prestigious Manhattan law firm) to put his son into the well-known and expensive Trinity School in Manhattan (an Ivy League prep school). John fit in with the other students and was remembered for his sharp wit and the jokes he made. At the prep school he played soccer, tennis and basketball. But his interest in tennis—and perhaps the reason the Davis Cup would become so important to him—was spurred on in part by his association with coaches Tony Palafox and Harry "Hop" Hopman. Tennis soon rose to the top of the McEnroe list of

Awards and Accomplishments

1977	*Tennis* magazine's Rookie of the Year
1977	Wins French Open mixed doubles
1978	Wins NCAA Championship singles; Italian Indoor Championship doubles
1978	All-American; Association of Tennis Professionals Newcomer of the Year
1978-84, 1987-91	Member of United States Davis Cup Team
1979	Wins U.S. Open singles; Italian Indoor Championship doubles
1979-81, 1983-85	Ranked #1 in the world by Association of Tennis Professionals
1980	Wins U.S. Open singles; U.S. Indoor Championship singles; The Masters doubles; WCT Tournament of Champions doubles; U.S. Indoor Championship doubles; U.S. Clay Court Championship doubles; U.S. Pro Indoor doubles
1981	Wins U.S. Open singles; U.S. Open doubles; Wimbledon singles and Wimbledon doubles; WCT Tournament of Champions doubles; ATP Championship singles and ATP Championship Doubles
1981	Associated Press Male Athlete of the Year
1982	Wins ATP Championship doubles; U.S. Pro Indoor singles
1983	Wins U.S. Open doubles; Wimbledon singles and Wimbledon doubles; U.S. Indoor Championship singles; U.S. Pro Indoor singles
1983	Association of Tennis Professionals Player of the Year
1983-84	International Tennis Federation Player of the Year
1984	Wins U.S. Open singles; Wimbledon singles and Wimbledon doubles; Canadian Open singles and Canadian Open doubles; The Masters singles; U.S. Pro Indoor doubles; U.S. Pro Indoor singles
1985	Wins The Masters singles; U.S. Pro Indoor singles; Canadian Open singles
1989	Wins Hardcourt Championship singles
1999	Inducted into the International Tennis Hall of Fame

On winning Davis Cup team: (as player) 1978-79, 1981-82, 1992. In Davis Cup play he holds American Davis Cup records for wins, ties played, years played and singles wins (41). McEnroe retired with a singles record of 856 wins, 158 losses and 75 titles.

Whatever Happened to? John McEnroe

For some sportsmen there is no such thing as retirement, not really. Their game has usually chosen them, rather than the other way round, and they never lose respect for that fact.... McEnroe's forthcoming autobiography is not called Serious for nothing. Out on court at the Albert Hall he is giving a full house a perfect impression of the man and the player he always was: creating every angle, arguing every call, staring at every line, making every volley, torturing himself over every missed ball.

Source: *The Observer* (London, England) (February 3, 2002)

Who was this McEnroe? People were intrigued by this skinny young kid with pasty skin and wild curly hair. They were fascinated (some appalled, some entertained) by his mouth, which was just as quick—if not quicker—than Conners to holler at the judge or the audience. McEnroe, true to form, had given fans a taste of what was to come, and he did so as the youngest man ever to reach the Wimbledon semifinals.

Quickly from College to Pro

McEnroe did not collect any money for his participation in the 1977 Wimbledon tournament. He chose instead to retain his amateur status and returned to America to attend Stanford, remaining there only long enough to bring Stanford an NCAA Championship in tennis, in 1978. He turned pro after his freshman year, in 1978, going on to reach the semi-finals of the U.S. Open that first year, ascending in the world rankings to sixth and making his way onto the Davis Cup team. It was not often that such a young player handled the intense international competition of Davis Cup play so well. But young McEnroe did, helping his team beat England and securing the first U.S. Davis Cup victory in six years. By the end of the season McEnroe had received the Association of Tennis Professionals (ATP) Newcomer of the Year Award and finished ranked number four in the world.

McEnroe's fame seemed to rise in conjunction with his attendance at Wimbledon. Though he was eliminated in the first round in 1978—just one year after making it to the semi-finals as an amateur—he returned in 1979 and made it to the fourth round. His disappointment at not winning was relieved a few months later when he won the U.S. Open, the youngest player to do so since 1948. At the end of the season he again led the U.S. Davis Cup team to victory, keeping the cup in America for a second straight year (he also served on the winning cup team in '81 and '82, as well as in 1992).

McEnroe's return to Wimbledon in 1980 culminated in one of the more famous finals in the history of tennis. Many felt it was one of the best moments in sports history. In the forth set of the Wimbledon finals McEnroe launched an intense rivalry with Swedish tennis superstar **Bjorn Borg**. McEnroe and Borg entered a tiebreaker

sports. He seemed a natural talent on the court, and though often recognized as one of the top junior players in the country, he would never attain a ranking of number 1 on the National Junior circuit.

Palafox, a former Davis Cup player from Mexico, and Hopman, who had coached the Australian Davis Cup team, took McEnroe on as a student at the Port Washington Tennis Academy on Long Island. He remained at the academy until he was 16, at which time he was suspended for pulling a prank. His parents switched him to the Cove Racquet Club, where Palafox also went to continue working with the budding star.

McEnroe graduated from high school in 1977. At the time he was able to play in Europe, winning the French Juniors Tournament, and then qualifying for the men's competition at Wimbledon. In an amazing feat, McEnroe (who prior to qualifying for the men's tournament had been vying for the Wimbledon juniors) made it into the semi-finals. Though his inexperience prevented him from beating then-powerhouse **Jimmy Conners**, his performance caught the attention of the pros on tour.

in the fourth set. Neither man would break, and it finally took McEnroe 34 points (22 minutes—one of the longest tiebreakers in Grand Slam history) to win the set. It was not enough, however, as Borg came back to win the match (1-6, 7-5, 6-3, 6-7, 8-6), taking his fifth consecutive Wimbledon title. McEnroe recaptured his pride later that year when he took his second U.S. Open title, beating Borg 7-6, 6-1, 6-7, 5-7, 6-4.

Victory at Center Court

Johnny Mac—whom the British press preferred to call "Superbrat"—showed up at the 1981 Wimbledon championships ready to win. This time he beat Borg in only four sets (4-6, 7-6, 7-6, 6-4), then went on to defend his U.S. Open title against the Swedish superstar. McEnroe was the first person to win three consecutive U.S. Open titles since **Bill Tilden.**

In 1982 he was unable to secure victory in a Grand Slam event, but came back in 1983 to defeat Chris Lewis at Wimbledon in an easy final (6-2, 6-2, 6-2). The year led into one of McEnroe's best on tour. 1984 was a banner year for the champion, who won 82 of his 84 matches, including a fourth U.S. Open title. It was the last Grand Slam victory of his career.

Beginning to Descend

Though he would remain on tour for another eight years, finally retiring from professional tennis in 1992, McEnroe's meteoric rise to fame did not have the staying power that most had expected. Many fans had expected to see the skinny kid with the big mouth dominate the Grand Slam events throughout the eighties, but it was not to happen. In 1985 he won only eight singles titles, and his critics began attributing his decline to the McEnroe attitude.

McEnroe was notorious for a lifestyle not befitting that of a tennis star. At 20, McEnroe had developed a passion for rock music, and he often spent his free time (of which most tennis superstars do not have much) practicing and hanging out with rock stars. He was also sporadic in his training, relying on his natural talent to get by out on the court. This served him fine for when he was young, but in a world where the top players devote every minute to staying on top of their games, McEnroe's ways may have contributed to his early decline in the sport. In an article in *Sports Illustrated,* Sally Jenkins wrote that "McEnroe's seven Grand slam titles amount to about half of what he could have won had he bothered to train properly and gain control of his temper." It was about this time that he fell in love with the actress Tatum O'Neal, whom he married in 1986. Twice in the late eighties McEnroe would take sabbaticals from tennis, emerging after many months away, compiling some singles victories, then disappearing from the circuit yet again.

John McEnroe

Davis Cup Mistake

McEnroe played in the Davis Cup the year he retired from the game, but 1992 was his last time as a playing member of the team. Throughout the 1990s he pled his case for the head coaching spot, but he was repeatedly turned down. In typical McEnroe fashion, he blamed the U.S. Tennis Association, telling *Sports Illustrated* that, "If they want somebody who is going to suck up to the suits, they're never going to give it to me."

But they did give it to him in 2000, after years of pressure. It proved to be an unwise choice. According to Jon Wertheim of *Sports Illustrated,* "When he finally got the job, he alienated the top American players, trashed opposing athletes and coaches and blew off meetings and press conferences." At one point he even "showed up at a captains breakfast in a bathrobe." McEnroe quit as Davis Cup coach within a year.

Still an Impressive Player

These days McEnroe, when he is not commentating or involved in one of his many outside interests, is playing on the Seniors Tour, which serves players who no longer compete at the professional level but who still hunger for the competition of their peers. According to London's *The Observer,* "It is fair to say that without McEnroe, there would be no Seniors Tour." McEnroe is still the player out there who is most passionate about the game; his attitude is the same at 41 as it was at 21.

Where Is He Now?

Since retiring in 1992, McEnroe's been anything but absent from the game or from public scrutiny. In 1995 he started as a color commentator for Wimbledon, the French Open and the U.S. Open. Still contentious, McEnroe has been known to rub his co-commentors the wrong way, claiming at one point that women do not know how to comment on the men's game, as well as saying that someone who has never played a final on center court (referring to commentator Bud Collins) can ever know what is really going happening in a tennis match.

McEnroe remains an avid rock fan, playing in his own band—the Johnny Smyths—named in honor of his second wife, Patty Smyth, the rock star of "I Am the Warrior" fame, with whom he lives in New York City with their children. In the true Renaissance spirit, McEnroe tries to do a little bit of everything. He opened an art gallery in New York in the early nineties; he has hosted his own game show on the BBC (*The Chair,* which received poor reviews), and, in 2002 he penned his tell-all biography, *You Cannot Be Serious!* which brought him into the news once again because of its revelations of drug use by Tatum O'Neal when they first started going out in the mid-eighties.

Continuing Presence

One of most successful tennis players of all times, John McEnroe was a dominant force whose reputation was built just as much on his personality as it was on his fantastic finesse play on the court. Though he was not overpowering physically, his temper and attitude made up for any lack of physical strength. Often verbally abusive of ball boys, line judges, chair judges—and just about anyone else who came in his line of sight during a match—the McEnroe way of playing was something to see. His style brought more people to their television sets to watch tennis, and more often than not, in addition to watching the McEnroe outbursts, they witnessed a McEnroe victory.

During his professional career, McEnroe won 17 Grand Slam titles, 77 career singles titles and 77 doubles titles. He has also been a mainstay of United States Davis Cup play, holding the American Davis Cup records for most wins, ties played, years played and singles wins (41). He retired from the professional tour in 1992 with a singles record of 856 wins, 158 losses and 75 titles. John McEnroe is still visible as one of the mainstays on the Seniors Tour, as well as in the tennis broadcast booth.

CONTACT INFORMATION

Address: c/o International Management Group, 445 Wells, Suite 404, Chicago, IL, 60610.

SELECTED WRITINGS BY MCENROE:

(With Richard Evans) *The Davis Cup: Celebrating 100 Years of International Tennis.* Universe Books, 1999.

(With James Kaplan) *You Cannot Be Serious.* Putnam Publishers, 2002.

FURTHER INFORMATION

Books

Evans, Richard. *McEnroe: Taming the Talent,* 2nd ed. New York: Penguin Books, 1990.

"John McEnroe." *St. James Encyclopedia of Popular Culture.* 5 vols. St. James Press, 2000.

"John Patrick McEnroe, Jr." *Encyclopedia of World Biography,* 2nd ed. Farmington Hills, MI: Gale Research, 1998.

McEnroe, John and James Kaplan. *You Cannot Be Serious.* New York: Putman Publishers, 2002.

McEnroe, John and Richard Evans. *The Davis Cup: Celebrating 100 Years of International Tennis.* Universe Books, 1999.

Periodicals

Axthelm, Pete. "McEnroe: The Champ You Love to Hate." *Newsweek* (September 7, 1981).

Lidz, Franz. "An Invasion of Privacy." *Sports Illustrated* (September 9, 1996): 66.

McCann, Graham. "Be Still, My Pounding Heart." *The Financial Times* (September 4, 2002): 14.

Phillips, B. J. "Fire and Ice at Wimbledon." *Time* (July 13, 1981).

Price, S. L. "Captain Mac." *Sports Illustrated* (September 13, 1999): 82-83.

Sandomir, Richard. "You're Kidding, McEnroe is Blunt?" *The New York Times* (June 6, 1995).

Wertheim, L Jon. "Too-Big Mac." *Sports Illustrated* (September 17, 2001): 31.

"Whatever Happened to? John McEnroe." *The Observer* (London) (February 3, 2002): 40.

"You May Hate Him…" *Sports Illustrated* (December 21, 1992): 94.

Other

"Being John McEnroe." Sports Jones http://www.sportsjones.com/sj/323.shtml (January 20, 2003).

"John McEnroe: Player Profile." Tennis Corner http://www.tenniscorner.net/player.php?playerid=MCJ002=ATP (January 20, 2003).

Platt, Larry. "John McEnroe." salon.com http://www.salon.com (January 14, 2003).

Sketch by Eric Lagergren

Mark McGwire
1963-

American baseball player

Mark McGwire

F uture Hall of Famer Mark McGwire smashed once and for all one of baseball's most sacrosanct records: 60 home runs hit in one season by **Babe Ruth** in 1927. **Roger Maris** had hit 61 homers in 1961. But he had hit only one home run more than Ruth, and in a season that was about a week longer than in the Bambino's day. McGwire surpassed Ruth's mark decisively, hitting 70 home runs in 1998. And just to make sure everyone had noticed, he hit another 65 in 1999. McGwire is a storybook home-run hero for the turn-of-the-millennium. He hit a record number of homers as a rookie, 49. In six of his seventeen 17 seasons in the big leagues he hit more than 40 homers. He hit fifty home runs an unprecedented three seasons in a row, breaking another of Babe Ruth's records. Rounding out the picture, McGwire is apparently a genuinely nice person. He is devoted to his son and has donated millions of his own money to a foundation dedicated to helping abused children.

Early Life

Born in 1963 in Pomona, California, Mark McGwire was raised in a big, brawny, sports loving family. Mark and his four brothers, each of whom ended up over six feet tall and weighing over 200 pounds, grew up playing baseball, football, golf, soccer and other sports. Mark's brother Dan played football at the University of Iowa, and professionally with the Seattle Seahawks and Miami Dolphins. Their father, John, was a dentist who was also a well-liked Little League coach. Mark would later de-

Chronology

1963	Born to John and Ginger McGwire in Pomona California
1981	Accepts baseball scholarship from the University of Southern California (USC)
1982-84	Sets new USC home run record
1984	Plays on gold medal-winning U.S. Men's Baseball team in Summer Olympics in Los Angeles
1984	Signs with Oakland As
1990	Becomes first player to hit 30 or more homers in first four seasons
1996	Hits 52 homers, 113 RBIs, and a batting average of .312, hits his 300th home run
1996	Becomes 14th player in major league history to hit 50 or more home runs in one season
1997	Traded to St. Louis Cardinals
1998	Hits 70 home runs, a new major league single-season record
2001	Retires

scribe his childhood as typically middle class, and himself as a normal child who liked sports and had to work hard to be good at them.

Mark's first involvement with organized sports was Little League baseball. Despite his modesty, it was obvious from the start that Mark McGwire was an especially talented baseball player. In his first Little League at-bat, when he was just eight, he hit a home run off a pitcher who was four years older. Two years later he set his first home run record, 13 in one season in the Claremont Little League. He was also-like Babe Ruth sixty years earlier-a gifted pitcher, the best pitcher on his team, in fact. As a high school player, he could throw at nearly 90-miles-per hour, faster than many major league pitchers. His high school performance attracted the attention of major league scouts, and when he graduated in 1981, the Montreal Expos claimed him in the expansion draft. McGwire chose instead to accept a baseball scholarship from the University of Southern California (USC).

Potent College Player

As a freshman pitcher for the USC Trojans, McGwire compiled a 4-4 record with a 3.04 earned-run-average. Despite his growing prowess on the mound, his USC coaches regretted that as a pitcher McGwire's potent bat was only in the line-up every four days. When his freshman year ended, he played in Alaska with the Anchorage Glacier Pilots and began playing first base. His next year at USC, McGwire hit 19 home runs, a new school record. He led the school in earned runs and pitching victories as well. In his third and as it turned out last year at USC, he gave up pitching completely. Free to hit in every game, he compiled an average of .387, slammed 32 homers, a new record, and was named an All-American. In 1984 McGwire was selected for the U.S. baseball team that competed in the Los Angeles Olympics. It was the first time baseball was part of the Games and the United States took home the gold medal. The same year, McGwire married his girlfriend, Kathy Hughes, one of

Where Is He Now?

Mark McGwire lives in Orange County, California, close to his son, his ex-wife, and other family. He devotes his time to the Mark McGwire Foundation for Children, an organization dedicated to helping abused children. McGwire founded the foundation and has funded it with millions of dollars of his own money. In 2002 he began working with the National Kidney Foundation as well. Although he is still relatively young by baseball standards, he has said there is no chance he will ever come out of retirement and play the game again.

the Trojans ballgirls. They had one child, Matthew, before divorcing in the early 1990s.

After his team's Olympic success, McGwire was picked by the Oakland As in the first round of the college draft. McGwire hit with confidence and power in two years in the A's farm system, collecting 24 homers, 109 RBIs and an average of .298. He joined Oakland's big league club for some games at the end of the 1986 season, hitting his first home run on his second day in the majors. He got off to a slow start in 1987 but stuck with the A's until late April when he caught fire. Between April 20 and early July he went on a rampage hitting 33 homers. He was the first rookie ever to hit more than 30 before the All-Star game and richly deserved his spot on the American League All-Star team that year.

The Stuff of Legend

It was inevitable that reporters started comparing McGwire, the newest home run phenom, to the home run legends, Babe Ruth and Roger Maris. The unrelenting media attention irked McGwire, who valued his privacy. He felt added pressure to produce at the plate too and his home run production fell off in the second half of the season. Nonetheless at the start of the A's last game, he had hit 49 homers, the most-by far-ever hit by a rookie. It bespeaks McGwire's character that he chose to miss that last game and gave up the chance at 50 home runs to be present at the birth of his first child. He was the unanimous choice for 1987 American League Rookie of the Year, only the second in baseball history so voted. The next few years belonged to McGwire. Between 1988 and 1990, McGwire hit 104 home runs and 302 RBIs, leading the A's to three straight American League pennants, and a world championship in the earthquake-wracked 1989 Bay Bridge World Series with the San Francisco Giants.

The year 1991 saw a downturn in McGwire's batting fortunes. By then American League pitchers had adjusted to him but, as he later admitted, he had not readjusted to them in return. McGwire suddenly lost his stroke; his

average and home run production plummeted. A recurring back injury and the break-up of his marriage just made hitting more difficult. He hit a meager-for him-22 home runs with a .202 batting average that year. McGwire bounced back in 1992, however, hitting 42 homers and collecting 104 RBIs, earning him Comeback Player of the Year honors from United Press International. Although he continued to be plagued by injuries through the middle 1990s, the homers continued to jump off his bat: 39 in 1995 and 52 in 1996, the latter the most hit by an American Leaguer since Roger Maris hit 61 in 1961.

In 1997, the A's were but a shadow of the team that won four pennants at the beginning of the decade. McGwire was the last of the team's great players and his contract was coming up for renewal. Trade rumors abounded. Oakland was reluctant to pay the millions McGwire would demand as a free agent; moreover, McGwire was anxious to play for a contending ball club again. On July 31, 1997, he was dealt to the St. Louis Cardinals. Despite the switch to a new league, with different pitchers and ball parks, McGwire finished 1997 with 58 home runs. Still he left fans speculating if he would have broken Maris' home run record if he had stayed with Oakland.

Breaks Roger Maris's Record

In 1998 McGwire made it all happen. The second half of the season amounted to a daily countdown of home runs hit by McGwire and Sammy Sosa of the Chicago Cubs, both of whom were chasing Roger Maris' hallowed record of 61. They traded off the lead through the last months of the season. McGwire won the race on September 7, 1998, when he hit his 61st round tripper. A day later, ironically at Wrigley Field, Sammy Sosa's home field, McGwire became the first player in major league history to hit 62 homers in one season. Unlike Maris, there would be no asterisk next to McGwire's record. He needed nearly 100 fewer at-bats to hit his 62 than Ruth did to hit 60. Maris, by contrast, needed 50 at-bats more. McGwire ended 1998 with a total of 70, a new record. He broke another of Ruth's records at the same time, as the first player to hit 50 home runs or more three seasons in a row.

McGwire's last two years in baseball saw his home run numbers decline dramatically. Hobbled by a knee

Career Statistics

Yr	Team	AVG	GP	AB	R	H	HR	RBI	BB	SO	SB	E
1986	OAK	.189	18	53	10	10	3	9	4	18	0	6
1987	OAK	.289	151	557	97	161	49	118	71	131	1	13
1988	OAK	.260	155	550	87	143	32	99	76	117	0	9
1989	OAK	.231	143	490	74	113	33	95	83	94	1	6
1990	OAK	.235	156	523	87	123	39	108	110	116	2	5
1991	OAK	.201	154	483	62	97	22	75	93	116	2	4
1992	OAK	.268	139	467	87	125	42	104	90	105	0	6
1993	OAK	.333	27	84	16	28	9	24	21	19	0	0
1994	OAK	.252	47	135	26	34	9	25	37	40	0	4
1995	OAK	.274	104	317	75	87	39	90	88	77	1	12
1996	OAK	.312	130	423	104	132	52	113	116	112	0	10
1997	OAK	.284	105	366	48	104	34	81	58	98	1	6
1997	StL	.253	51	174	38	44	24	42	43	61	2	1
1998	StL	.299	155	509	130	152	70	147	162	155	1	12
1999	StL	.278	153	521	118	145	65	147	133	141	0	13
2000	StL	.305	89	236	60	72	32	73	76	78	1	1
2001	StL	.187	97	299	48	56	29	64	56	118	0	4
TOTAL		.263	1874	6187	1167	1626	583	1414	1317	1596	12	95

OAK: Oakland Athletics; StL: St. Louis Cardinals.

injury, he hit only 32 homers in 2000 and 29 in 2001. Such numbers only disappointed and frustrated McGwire. In November 2001, he announced his retirement from baseball. Not even an offer of $30 million to extend his contract with the Cardinals could make him change his mind. "After considerable discussion with those closest to me, I have decided not to sign the extension, as I am unable to perform at a level equal to the salary the organization would be paying me," he told the *Houston Chronicle*.

Mark McGwire is a virtual shoe-in for Baseball's Hall of Fame when he becomes eligible in 2007. His 583 homers were fifth on the all-time list when he left baseball. McGwire also boasted a career 1414 runs batted in and 1167 runs scored. More than merely a sports star, Mark McGwire proved himself an individual of the highest integrity as well, best exemplified by his outstanding efforts on behalf of abused children, work that led the *Sporting News* to name him their Sportsman of the Year in 1997. Hopefully such achievements will live in memory as long as McGwire's slugging pyrotechnics.

CONTACT INFORMATION

Address: Mark McGwire Foundation for Children, c/o Jim Milner, 6615 E. Pacific Coast Highway, Suite 260, Long Beach, CA 90803.

SELECTED WRITINGS BY MCGWIRE:

"Where Do I Go from Here?" *Sports Illustrated.* September 21, 1998.

FURTHER INFORMATION

Periodicals

Antonen, Mel. "Athletics' McGwire Powerless to Explain Sudden Turnaround." *USA Today,* April 27, 1992.

Boswell, Thomas. "The Mighty McGwire Is Marisesque." *Washington Post,* May 19, 1992.

Bush, David. "A Day With McGwire." *San Francisco Chronicle,* March 8, 1990.

Chass, Murray. "Chasing Records, Game by Game; Maris's Mark Remains Elusive." *The New York Times,* June 18, 1989.

Elderkin, Phil. "Mark My Words: McGwire Could be the Next Babe." *The Christian Science Monitor,* August 6, 1987.

Friend, Tom. "43 Booming Shots, And Still Swinging." *New York Times,* August 19, 1996.

Martinez, Michael. "After a Change of Seasons, McGwire's Fortunes Have Turned Golden." *New York Times,* May 15, 1992.

Maske, Mark. "The Bash is Back in McGwire." *Washington Post,* June 13, 1995.

"McGwire Says He's Outta Here—Cards Slugger Announces Retirement." *Houston Chronicle* November 12, 2001.

Perkins, Dave. "McGwire Truly Making His Mark Homer Pace Rivals Maris, Ruth Though 'I don't try to hit them'." *Toronto Star,* July 13, 1987.

Reilly, Rick. "The Good Father." *Sports Illustrated.* September 7, 1998.

Stein, Joel. "Long Live the King." *Time.* September 21, 1998.

Verducci, Tom. "The Greatest Season Ever." *Sports Illustrated.* October 5, 1998.

Sketch by Gerald E. Brennan

Tamara McKinney

Chronology

1962	Born October 16 to Rigan and Frances McKinney
1977	Joins the World Cup tour
1977	Older sister suffers major injuries during World Cup downhill race
1978	Finishes in top three in a World Cup event for the first time
1980	Competes in her first Olympics, falling in both events
1982	Fractures right hand
1984	Finishes fourth in the giant slalom at the Olympics
1987	Suffers a broken ankle that prevents her from competing for much of the early winter
1990	Retires from competitive skiing
1990	Brother, Steve, killed by drunk driver
1996	Becomes member of the FIS Women's Committee
1997	Daughter, Francesca, born

Tamara McKinney
1962-

American skier

Tamara McKinney was the best American woman on skis in the 1980s. She was only 16 when she first finished in the top three in a World Cup ski event in 1978, and her dominance in the sport continued through her victory in the combined event at the International Ski Federation (FIS) World Alpine Ski Championships in 1989. She is still the only American woman ever to have captured the World Cup overall title, and her 18 career first-place finishes (nine in slalom and nine in giant slalom) constitute an American record.

A Family Affair

Skiing runs in McKinney's family. Her mother, Frances, worked as a ski instructor in the Lake Tahoe area when McKinney was a child. McKinney, the youngest of Frances's seven children, was often left in the lift shack in the care of the lift operators and of her brothers and sisters while her mother taught. "I had skis on my feet before I could walk," McKinney told Deirdre Donahue of *People Weekly*. "My family strapped them on and toddled me around."

Three of McKinney's siblings skied on the U.S. ski team before she did, including her brothers Steve and McLane. Steve, who was killed by a drunk driver in 1990, was the first man to go faster than 200 kilometers per hour on skis, and he held the world speed-skiing record seven times. Sister Sheila McKinney first made the national team when she was 12 and skied in her first international race at 13. Her competitive skiing career ended at age 18, when she crashed into a pole during a World Cup downhill race at Heavenly Valley, Nevada, in 1977. She spent weeks in a coma, and although she did eventually recover, she did not return to skiing.

Skiing was not the only sport practiced by the family. McKinney's father, Rigan, owned and operated the Stony Point horse farm in Lexington, Kentucky, and was a championship-winning jockey in steeplechase before he died following a stroke in the mid-1980s. McKinney herself was an accomplished rider as a child. Her sister Laura now owns Stony Point, and McKinney and her daughter Francesca often return there for visits.

Skiing on the World Stage

McKinney joined the World Cup tour in 1977, the same year that her older sister Sheila was injured. By 1978 the tiny Tamara McKinney-she stands 5 foot, 3 inches "on tall days"-had already established herself as a contender, when she finished third in a World Cup slalom event in Piancavallo, Italy, shortly after turning 16. At 17 she competed in her first Olympics, in front of a friendly American crowd in Lake Placid, New York, but she fell in both the slalom and the giant slalom. "I was completely overwhelmed," she later recalled to Brian Bennett of the Louisville, Kentucky, *Courier-Journal*. "Once I got in the start [gate] and everybody started going crazy, I had like an out-of-body experience. I felt like I couldn't move my legs."

The next year McKinney proved her skill by winning the World Cup giant slalom title, and two years after that she stunned the world by winning the overall World Cup. No American woman had ever won the overall World

Cup before, and only one other non-European, Canadian Nancy Green, had ever managed the feat. McKinney was a favorite to win a medal in the 1984 Olympics, even appearing on the cover of *Sports Illustrated*'s Olympic preview issue, but the stress of having been a favorite for two years was beginning to show. She skied poorly in her first giant slalom run, and even though she had the fastest time on the second run, she still finished fourth, .43 of a second behind the bronze medal winner. She missed a gate and was disqualified in the slalom.

In 1989, after several weak years caused in part by family stress (both of McKinney's parents and her brother McLane died in the mid- to late 1980s), McKinney came back to reclaim her title as the best American woman on skis. Although she was unable to capture a World Cup title she did take the gold medal in the combined event at the FIS World Alpine Ski Championships in Vail, Colorado, finishing a mere .04 of a second ahead of Yugoslavian skier Mateja Svet. At a press conference after her win, McKinney revealed that her feet had been completely frozen when she raced-the slalom had been run when the air temperature was 24 degrees below zero-and that she was still suffering from frostbite on two toes on her left foot. McKinney retired in 1990, shortly after winning the World Championships.

A Different Kind of Education

McKinney, like most world-class skiers, was unable to go to college or to do many of the things that other normal teenagers and young adults do because she spent so much of her life training. But despite the fact that her formal education was interrupted, McKinney still tried to learn as much as she could anyway. As she told *Saturday Evening Post* contributor Walter Roessing: "There's no question that travel is educational. . . . I've been to some wonderful places that aren't usually seen by girls my age. I have enjoyed the chance to experience many different cultures, and I can speak German and a little French."

Life after Skiing

McKinney lives in Squaw Valley, California, with her daughter, Francesca, who was born in 1997. McKinney remains involved in skiing: She has served on the FIS Women's Committee since 1996, and she also coaches the Squaw Valley junior racing team, which included 2002 Olympic skiers Julia Mancuso and Marco Sullivan.

In the run-up to the 2002 Olympics McKinney carried the Olympic flame down a Squaw Valley ski slope in front of a crowd of more than 1,000 people who had gathered to cheer for her. She was accompanied by four-year-old Francesca, who is following in her mother's ski tracks: Francesca is already competing in skiing races. The large crowd that had gathered to watch McKinney ski and to get autographs at the bottom of the slope "kind of surprised me, because I had figured by now that everybody had forgotten me," McKinney told Bennett.

Awards and Accomplishments

1981	Scores first victory, in giant slalom in Switzerland
1983	World Cup champion, giant slalom
1983	World Cup champion, overall
1984	World Cup champion, slalom
1989	FIS World Championships, combined event

McKinney had 18 wins in World Cup races in her career, nine in slalom and nine in giant slalom.

As Bennett put it, "Not likely." As one of the most successful American skiers in history and the only American woman to have captured the overall World Cup title, McKinney is unlikely to be forgotten any time soon.

FURTHER INFORMATION

Periodicals

Beech, Mark. "Tamara McKinney and Phil Mahre, Skiers: February 6, 1984." *Sports Illustrated* (March 18, 2002): 21+.

Callahan, Tom. "Their Success Is All in the Family." *Time* (January 30, 1984): 44-47.

Donahue, Deirdre. "U.S. Alpine Racers Are Prospecting for Gold in the Snow." *People Weekly* (February 13, 1984): 39-42.

Johnson, William Oscar. "A Flight So Fancy." *Sports Illustrated* (February 13, 1989): 14-21.

———. "Mountain Melodrama." *Sports Illustrated* (February 20, 1989): 32-36.

Roessing, Walter. "High Hopes on the Slopes." *Saturday Evening Post* (December 1987): 64-67.

Other

Bennett, Brian. "McKinney's Flame Still Burns." *Courier-Journal* (Louisville, Kentucky). http://www.courier-journal.com/cjsports/news2002/02/03/sp020302s149449.htm (January 8, 2003).

"Tamara McKinney (USA)." Ski World Cup. http://www.skiworldcup.org/load/champions/women/mckinney/01.html (January 8, 2003).

Sketch by Julia Bauder

Mary T. Meagher
1964-

American swimmer

Olympic and championship swimmer Mary T. Meagher (pronounced MAW-her), known as

Mary T. Meagher

"Madame Butterfly," began setting world records in the 100-meter and 200-meter butterfly swim as a young teen. Thwarted in her prime by the United States' 1980 Olympics boycott, Meagher one year later set world records in the butterfly that stood for nearly two decades. After competing in the 1984 and 1988 Olympics, she retired from swimming with twenty-two U.S. championships, two world championships, and three Olympic gold medals. Her record in the 100-meter butterfly remained unbroken until 1999, when five-time Olympic gold medalist **Jenny Thompson** bested it with a swim of 57.88—.05 second ahead of Meagher's. Her world record in the 200-meter butterfly stood until 2000, when Australian champion swimmer **Susan O'Neill** broke it with a time of 2:05.81—.15 second ahead of Meagher's. O'Neill said she had tried for six years to break Meagher's record; she called doing so "one of the greatest moments of my life."

"The Butterfly Picked Me"

Mary Terstegge Meagher was born October 27, 1964, in Louisville, Kentucky, the daughter of Jim and Floy Terstegge Meagher. She grew up with nine sisters and one brother. One of her sisters was Mary Glen, so Mary was called Mary T.—or simply "T." She began swimming at age five, and by age twelve she had a world-class butterfly stroke. It came naturally, she said. She didn't pick the butterfly—it picked her.

Nicknamed Fishy by her school friends, at age fourteen, Mary began winning national and international titles. In 1979, as an eighth grader, she beat the world record of 2:09.77 in the 200-meter butterfly by .1 second at the Pan American Games in San Juan, Puerto Rico. The world could hardly believe that a fresh-faced teen with braces and a stuffed frog named Bubbles could swim so fast.

Madame Butterfly

About one month after the Pan Am Games, at the 1979 Long-Course Senior National Swimming Championships, Meagher broke her own world record in the morning preliminaries, swimming the 200-meter in

2:08.41. Coming back for the evening finals, she shattered that record with a time of 2:07.01. The fourteen-year-old girl swam a faster butterfly than nearly half of the men in the competition.

Setting her sights on the 1980 Olympic Games, Meagher broke another world record—in the 100-meter butterfly—at the 1980 Indoor National Swimming Championships, with a time of 59.26, .2 faster than German Olympic gold medalist Andrea Pollack's. By this time, Meagher had earned a new nickname: Madame Butterfly.

Olympics Only a Dream, but Meagher Sets Records

Meagher made the U.S. Olympic team for the 100-meter and 200-meter butterfly and for one freestyle race. At her peak, she was prepared for the 1980 Olympics, but her hopes were crushed along with those of many other American athletes when President Jimmy Carter issued a U.S. boycott of the Moscow Olympics to protest the Soviet invasion of Afghanistan. Later learning that she could have beaten the winners' time, Meagher was so downhearted she nearly gave up swimming. Instead, the following year she unleashed her Olympic energy at the Long-Course Senior National Swimming Championships in Brown Deer, Wisconsin, setting a world record in the 100-meter butterfly with a time of 57.93. She also won a gold medal in the 200-meter butterfly, setting a world record of 2:05.96 and finishing fifteen meters ahead of the second-place winner. The audience gave Madame Butterfly a standing ovation.

1984 Olympics and Beyond

Meagher entered the University of California, Berkeley, in 1982. She won a number of National Collegiate Athletic Association (NCAA) swimming championships. When the time came for the 1984 Olympics in Los Angeles—under a Communist boycott that included tough East German teams—Meagher had trained hard. She made the U.S. team in the 100-meter and 200-meter butterfly and the 4 x 100 medley relay. At the Olympics, she won a gold medal in each event. Afterward, she won gold in the Indoor Championships and in the Short- and Long-Course Championships. In 1986, she won a gold, a silver, and a bronze medal in the World Championships. In 1987 she was named Outstanding Female College Athlete of the Year and won the Honda Sports Award for the second time during her college career.

Olympics Bound Again

Meagher took five months off from swimming the year she graduated from college, to work as a teacher's aide and have a normal life. However, as the 1988 Olympics approached, she began training hard, at age twenty-three. This time, she would get to compete against the East German swimmers, and she also had hopes of breaking her own 200-meter record. To her dis-

Awards and Accomplishments	
1979	Gold medal, 200-meter butterfly, Pan American Games, with a time of 2:09.77, breaking world record by .09 second; broke this record in preliminaries at Long-Course Senior Swimming Championships, Fort Lauderdale, Florida, with a time of 2:08.41; at finals on the same day, broke this record with a time of 2:07.01
1980	First place, set world record in 100-meter butterfly at Indoor National Swimming Championships, with a time of 59.26; at mock Olympic Trials in Irvine, California, reduced her 200-meter record to 2:06.37
1981	Gold medal, 100-meter butterfly, at Long-Course Senior National Swimming Championships, Brown Deer, Wisconsin, setting a world record with a time of 57.93; gold medal, 200-meter butterfly at same event, setting world record of 2:05.96
1982	Gold medal in 100-meter butterfly and silver medal in 200-meter butterfly at World Championships
1983	Gold medal, 200-meter butterfly, National Collegiate Athletic Association (NCAA) Championships
1984	Gold medals in 100-meter butterfly, 200-meter butterfly, and 4 x 100 medley relay at Olympic Games in Los Angeles, California; gold medals, 100-meter and 200-meter butterfly, 200-meter freestyle, Indoor National Swimming Championships
1985	Gold medal, 100-meter and 200-meter butterfly, NCAA Championships; gold medals, 100-meter and 200-meter butterfly, Short-Course Senior National Championships; gold medals, 100-meter and 200-meter butterfly, Long-Course Senior National Championships; won Honda Sports Award for Swimming, for 1984-85 season
1986	Gold medal, 200-meter butterfly, NCAA Championships; gold medal in 200-meter butterfly, silver medal in 100-meter butterfly, bronze medal in 200-meter freestyle, World Championships
1987	Gold medal in 100-meter and 200-meter butterfly, NCAA Championships; won Honda Sports Award for Swimming, for 1986-87 season
1988	Gold medal, 200-meter butterfly, national championships; won 200-meter butterfly at Sundown Swim to Seoul in Boca Raton, Florida; won 100-meter and 200-meter butterfly at Pepsi Open in Charlotte, North Carolina; silver medal in 400-meter medley relay and bronze medal in 200-meter butterfly at Olympic Games in Seoul, South Korea
1993	Inducted into International Women's Sports Hall of Fame; inducted into International Swimming Hall of Fame
2002	Inducted into the Bay Area (California) Sports Hall of Fame

advantage, she would be competing against teenagers, ever reminded that she was just sixteen when she set her standing world records.

At the 1988 Olympics in Seoul, Korea, Meagher won the bronze medal in the 200-meter butterfly and a silver for her butterfly leg in the 400-meter medley relay. Disappointed that she did not set another world record, she was still ranked number one in the world for 1988 in the 200-meter butterfly.

Retirement

Meagher retired from competitive swimming soon after the 1988 Olympics with her world records intact. She worked at a bank in her native Louisville and then worked in private business through 1991. That year, she served as an athletes' representative for the U.S. Olympic Committee. When the Olympic Games were held in Atlanta, Georgia, in 1993, she was asked to be a flag bearer during the opening ceremonies. She lives in the Atlanta suburb of Peachtree City, Georgia, with her husband, sports executive Michael Plant—a former U.S. Olympic speed skater—and their two children, Andrew and Madeline, whom she has taught to swim.

In May 2000, on hearing that Susan O'Neill had finally broken her 200-meter butterfly record and earned the nickname "Madame Butterfly" in her place, Mary T. Meagher Plant said, "You couldn't ask for a nicer, more deserving person to break your record than Susie." However, Plant said she still believes she could have completed the 200-meter in 2 minutes, 4 seconds. "When I did 2:05, the last 25 meters felt real easy," she told the *Los Angeles Times*. "At the finish, I thought, 'I'm not tired, I could have kept going.'"

Mary T. Meagher was a gifted swimmer whose speed and strength in the butterfly were unparalleled during her career and for many years afterward. Dennis Pursley, one of her former coaches, said that Meagher had no weaknesses in her prime. He told *Sports Illustrated for Women,* "Motivation, technique, physical attributes—I don't know that I've ever seen an athlete who didn't have a weakness on that list—except Mary."

CONTACT INFORMATION

Address: Mary Plant, 404 Vanderwall, Peachtree City, GA 30269.

FURTHER INFORMATION

Periodicals

Neff, Craig. "The U.S. Will Rule the Pool." *Sports Illustrated* (July 18, 1984): 94.

"Olympic Hopefuls: Teens Who Dream of Gold." *Teen Magazine* (May, 1984): 22.

"Olympics Oldest Swim Mark Is Broken." *Seattle Times* (May 18, 2000): D4.

Penner, Mike. "Aussies Make Big Splash in Besting World Marks." *Los Angeles Times* (May 21, 2000): D-3.

Stathoplos, Demmi. "A Bid for the Last Hurrah." *Sports Illustrated* (July 18, 1988): 48.

Wade, S. Lamar. "The California Gold Rush of '84." *Saturday Evening Post* (July, 1983): 64.

Other

Biography Resource Center Online. "Mary T. Meagher." http://galenet.galegroup.com/. Detroit: Gale Group, 2000.

"Cal's Natalie Coughlin Wins Honda Sports Award for Swimming." University of California Golden Bears. http://calbears.ocsn.com/sports/ (January 24, 2003).

"Jenny Thompson Breaks World Record: Stanford Grad Bests 18-Year-Old Mark in 100 Fly." Stanford University Cardinal Athletics. http://gostanford.ocsn.com/sports/ (August 23, 1999).

J-Mac and Associates. "Mary T. Meagher—Swimming Olympic Gold Medalist." Golden Biography. http://home.earthlink.net/~athngold/golden_biography.htm (May 16, 1998).

"Sean Lampley Named Bay Area Male College Athlete of the Year: Former Cal Swimmer Mary T. Meagher Plant Also to Be Honored." University of California Golden Bears. http://calbears.ocsn.com/ (February 11, 2002).

Wertheim, L. Jon. "Mary T. Meagher." *Sports Illustrated for Women* http://www.cnnsi.com/ (January 24, 2003).

Sketch by Ann H. Shurgin

Rick Mears
1951-

American race car driver

Rick Mears dominated Indy car racing in the 1980s. He won a total of twenty-nine Indy car races for Team Penske, seven of which were on road courses instead of oval tracks. He won the coveted pole position forty times and he drove more miles during that decade than any other driver. Most impressively Mears won a record number of pole positions in 500-mile races, including six at the prestigious Indianapolis 500 race. Mears was also the Indianapolis 500 champion four times, tying two other drivers for the most wins at the Brickyard. Mears was named "Driver of the Decade" by the Associated Press for winning twenty races during the 1980s. After retiring in 1992 Mears continued to work for Roger Penske as a driving coach and adviser.

From Off-Road Champion to Indy Champion

Rick Ravon Mears was born on December 3, 1951 in Wichita, Kansas, to Bill Ravon and Mae Louise Simpson Mears. When he was five years old Mears and his family moved to Bakersfield, California. Bill Mears drove stock cars as a hobby and both he and his wife enjoyed riding motorcycles. As young children, Rick and his brother Roger would join their parents for motorcycle rides. Both boys took an early interest in racing. They would race motorcycles in the desert, as well as buggies and pickup trucks. While most Indy car drivers start their careers with sprint cars, Rick and Roger Mears earned their experience and their reputations as off-road drivers.

Rick Mears

Mears married at a young age and fathered two sons—Clint Ravon was born in 1973 and Cole Ray was born in 1975. Mears began driving professionally in the early 1970s for car owner and safety equipment manager Bill Simpson. He finished in the top ten of his first three races. In 1976 he drove an old, pink Eagle Indy car at the Ontario Speedway and he met racing legend **Roger Penske**. "Somebody told me to keep an eye on Rick," Penske said when recalling his first meeting with Mears to Sam Moses of *Sports Illustrated* in May of 1986. "He didn't know me; I didn't know him—and later on he came around our garage and just sort of hung around in the background and watched." Within a few years, everybody would know Mears. In 1976 he won the United States Auto Club (USAC) Rookie of the Year award.

Penske did keep an eye on Mears. In 1978 when Penske's main driver, **Mario Andretti**, took a break from Indy car racing to pursue the World Driving Championship, Penske called on Mears to substitute for Andretti on the Indy car circuit. Mears won his first Indy car championship for Penske at the Indy Lights race in Milwaukee that same year. Mears also participated in his first Indianapolis 500 in 1978. His qualifying run was fast enough to earn his the number three spot on the first row. He finished the race twenty-third because of engine trouble, but he did receive the Indianapolis 500 Rookie of the Year award.

Dominated Racing in the 1980s

The Indianapolis 500 is the most popular auto race among the general public and one of the most coveted championships among drivers. The track is called "The Brickyard" because it was paved with bricks when it was first built. Only a year after his debut, Mears returned to the Indianapolis 500 in 1979 to win both the coveted pole position and the championship. By this time Mears had competed in twenty-two Indy car races and he had never spun out in an Indy car either during a race or a practice session. Mears finished the year by clinching the Championship Auto Racing Teams (CART) national championship.

Mears continued to be successful on the CART circuit. In addition to mastering the oval tracks, Mears was the only Indy car driver to win every road course event in one season. Once again he earned the most points of the year to become CART national champion. He held the title for 1982 as well. In 1982 Mears won the pole position at the Indianapolis 500 for the second time. This was quite an accomplishment considering that Mears had suffered burns on his face from a pit fire earlier in the week. Mears came close to winning his second Indianapolis 500 title, but he was beaten by Gordon Johncock by only sixteen hundredths of a second. Mears was vindicated two years later when he won his second title at the Brickyard in 1984. He was racing against the

Awards and Accomplishments

1973	Firecracker 250 Champion
1973-74	Japan Grand Prix Off-Road Champion
1974	Nor-Cal 100 Champion
1976	United States Auto Championship Rookie of the Year
1978	Indianapolis 500 Rookie of the Year
1978	First Indy car win at Milwaukee
1979	First Championship Auto Racing Team National Championship
1979	Named Auto Racing All American by Auto Racing Writers and Broadcasters Association
1979, 1982, 1986, 1988-89, 1991	Indianapolis 500 pole position
1979, 1984, 1988, 1991	Indianapolis 500 Championship
1980-81	Mexico City Race Champion
1981	Watkins Glen Race Champion
1981	Second Championship Auto Racing Team National Championship
1981	Received United States Driver of the Year Jerry Titus Memorial Trophy
1982	Third Championship Auto Racing Team National Championship
1985, 1987	Pocono 500 Champion
1988-89	Milwaukee Indy Car Race Champion
1989	Laguna Seca Race Champion
1989	Named Driver of the Year by Auto Racing Analysis
1989	Named Driver of the Decade by the Associated Press
1990	Phoenix Race Champion
1992	Named One of Ten Champions for Life by Driver of the Year Awards

Where Is He Now?

Rick Mears retired from auto racing in 1992, but he remained a member of the Penske team. For the past decade Mears has served as an adviser and driving coach for younger drivers. He and his brother, Roger, also formed an Indy Lights team to promote their sons' racing careers. Rick's older son Clint, and Roger's son, Casey, both began racing careers in the mid-1990s. In 2002 Mears' personal problems became public when he divorced his second wife, Christyn Bowen. He also admitted to a drinking problem and checked himself into a treatment program. Mears still experiences pain in both of his feet from his dangerous crash in 1984.

Mears did not let his injuries deter his desire to drive and to win. In 1985 he won the Pocono 500 race, and he repeated this victory in 1987. In 1986 he not only captured the pole position at the Indianapolis 500 for the third time, but he also set a closed course Indy car speed record of 233.934 miles per hour at the Michigan International Speedway. In 1988 Mears managed to win both the pole position and the race at the Indianapolis 500, which was his third victory at the Brickyard. It was also the seventh victory for Penske, making him the car owner with the most victories.

Respected by His Peers

Despite all of his success, Mears did not garner as much public attention as other drivers of his time, such as the Unsers, the Andrettis, **A.J. Foyt**, or **Emerson Fittipaldi**. While other drivers were known for their aggressiveness, Mears was a calm and patient driver. "If my car is not working well, I try to let everybody else dictate the pace and work on not going a lap down," Mears explained his racing strategy to David Phillips of *Auto Week* in June of 1991. "If the car is good, I'll run at about 80 percent and just try to keep the leaders in sight." This laid-back attitude led the media to call him boring. "Rick Mears has fans, but not passionate followers. He has style, but not charisma," wrote Bruce Lowitt of the *St. Petersburg Times* in May of 1989. However, it was his skills that have earned Mears respect as a driver. "What makes Rick so great is his credibility with his peers," Penske told Sam Moses of *Sports Illustrated* in June of 1988. "Walking down pit row, you can't find a guy who doesn't have high praise for him, both as a driver and a man."

Mears won the most Indy car victories of any driver in the 1980s and was named Driver of the Decade by the Associated Press. However, Mears was not finished setting records yet. In 1991 he won the pole position at the Indianapolis 500 for a record-setting sixth time and he won the race for the fourth time. He tied A.J. Foyt and **Al Unser, Sr.** for the most wins at the Brickyard. He is also the only driver to win the Indianapolis 500 from the pole position three times.

In 1992 Mears set out for his 15th run at the Indianapolis 500. He was looking for his fifth win so that he could become the single driver with the most wins at the

pole winner, Tom Sneva, in the final laps of the competition when Sneva experienced car trouble. "When I won in 1979, I didn't know what it meant to win the Indy 500," Mears told Sam Moses of *Sports Illustrated* in June of 1984. "I didn't soak it in until a week later. This year I tried to soak it in before the race was over."

Mears earned a reputation as a safe driver who was always in control of his car. "He's a natural who rarely makes a wrong move," wrote Sam Moses of *Sports Illustrated* in June of 1984. However, Mears' luck ran out in 1984. During a practice session at the Sanair Super Speedway near Montreal, Canada in September of 1984, the two-time Indianapolis champion clipped another car and spun into a guardrail. The accident crushed both of his feet. His feet were so badly damaged that doctors were afraid they might have to amputate. Fortunately Penske was able to bring in Dr. Terry Trammell, an orthopedic surgeon from Indianapolis, who was able to save Mears' feet. It was still uncertain as to whether Mears would be able to walk again, let alone drive. However, Mears was convinced that as long as his feet were still there, he would return to driving. Mears divorced his first wife in 1983 and during his recovery in 1984 he became acquainted with Christyn Bowen, whom he had met the previous year at a Penske party. She became his second wife in 1986.

In 1985 Mears returned to racing with a vengeance. Although his weak ankles made shifting gears difficult,

Brickyard. Unfortunately, Mears crashed during a practice session. His car slid on water from a broken line and Mears hit the wall. Mears was lucky to escape with only a fractured foot and a sprained wrist. "This is a racetrack where you must be very precise," Mears described the Brickyard to the *Toronto Star* in May of 1986. "And at the speeds we're running at there, one mistake is all you get." He was able to compete on race day, but he finished only twenty-sixth because of another crash.

While Mears was recovering from his injuries he decided that 1992 would be his last year of racing, much to the surprise of his fellow drivers. "I truly admire the man," Mario Andretti told David Phillips and Larry Edsall of *Autoweek* in December of 1992. "He was a great racer, a real competitor, and it was truly fun to race against him." Although Mears did not win the record-setting fifth Indianapolis 500, he still made his mark on the racing world. Mears had a total of twenty-nine Indy car victories, including four at the Brickyard. He won the pole position a total of forty times and he won the most pole positions in 500-mile races with fifteen. Mears is also tied in second place for the most career victories in 500-mile races. He was inducted into the International Motosports Hall of Fame in 1997.

CONTACT INFORMATION

Address: 204 Spyglass Lane, Jupiter, FL, 33477-4091.

FURTHER INFORMATION

Periodicals

Brady, James. "In Step With: Rick Mears." *Houston Chronicle* (May 17, 1992): 10.

Clores, Cynthia, and Larry Edsall. "It's Better Late Than Never If You're a Rick Mears Fan." *Auto Week* (April 16, 1990): 63.

Davidson, Donald. "Indy Takes." *Auto Week* (June 3, 1991).

Hinton, Ed. "… And Lived to Tell About It." *Sports Illustrated* (May 18, 1992): 18-23.

"Indy Lights: Mears Following His Famous Father's Path." *Milwaukee Journal Sentinel* (June 1, 1997).

Jones, Graham. "Rick Mears Roars to Checkered Flag." *Toronto Star* (April 9, 1990): D6.

Kallmann, Dave. "Mears Brothers Watch Sons Grown on the Track." *Milwaukee Journal Sentinel* (May 28, 1997).

Kirby, Gordon. "72nd Indianapolis 500, Speedway, Ind.; Color Indy Yellow." *Auto Week* (June 6, 1988): 77.

Kirby, Gordon. "CART Champion Spark Plug 300, Monterey, Calif." *Auto Week* (October 23, 1989): 57.

Lowitt, Bruce. "'I Guess I'm Just Boring …' What Rick Mears Lacks in Charisma, He Makes Up for with Indy Wins." *St. Petersburg Times* (May 27, 1989): 1C.

Moses, Sam. "500 Miles To Go." *Sports Illustrated* (June 6, 1988): 24-29.

Moses, Sam. "Have No Fear - Mears Is Here." *Sports Illustrated* (May 26, 1986): 40-43.

Moses, Sam. "Making Waves at Indy." *Sports Illustrated* (June 4, 1984): 18-23.

Moses, Sam. "Mears to the Four; Rick Mears Won His Fourth Indy 500 by Making a Daring Pass and Then Dropping the Hammer." *Sports Illustrated* (June 3, 1991): 20-25.

"Penske." *Auto Week* (May 17, 1993): 34.

Phillips, David. "Mears Still Team Player, But From Other Side of Pit Wall." *Auto Week* (January 24, 1994): 44.

Phillips, David. "USAC Indianapolis 500, Speedway, Ind." *Auto Week* (June 3, 1991): 71.

Phillips, David, and Larry Edsall. "The Link Will Be Missing; Rick Mears' Retirement Signals End of an Era in Indycar Competition." *Auto Week* (December 21, 1992): 76.

"Rick Mears." *Toronto Star* (July 18, 1989): K15.

"Rick Mears Favored to Top Fastest Field Ever at Indy." *Toronto Star* (May 25, 1986): E4.

"Rick Mears Racks Up Miles." *USA Today* (September 14, 1989): 1C.

Siano, Joseph. "A Day at the Races; Rick Mears's Roar and Peace." *New York Times* (May 24, 1992).

Vettraino, J.P. "Don't Mess With the System; CART's Medical Team Is the Best in the Business." *Auto Week* (October 1, 2001): 63.

Other

CART World - Drivers - Rick Mears. http://www.cartworld.free-online.co.uk/drivers/rmears/index.html (January 20, 2003).

Harris, Mike. "Former Indy 500 Winner Rick Mears Sought Treatment for Alcohol Problem." Yahoo! Sports Canada. http://ca.sports.yahoo.com/020825/6/oj7t.html (January 20, 2003).

International Motorsports Hall of Fame. http://www.motorsportshalloffame.com (January 23, 2003).

Official Web site of the Indianapolis 500. http://www.indy500.com (January 20, 2003).

Sketch by Janet P. Stamatel

Mark Messier
1961-

Canadian hockey player

Mark Messier is considered by many to be one of the greatest leaders in sports. He served as the

Chronology

1961	Born January 18 in Edmonton, Alberta, Canada
1978-79	Begins professional career playing with the Cincinnati Stingers of the World Hockey Association
1979	Drafted by the Edmonton Oilers; begins playing for the team
1982	Plays in All-Star game
1984-85, 1987-88, 1990	Wins Stanley Cup with the Oilers
1991	In October, traded to the New York Rangers
1993	Founds the Mark Messier Point Club (a fundraising group for children's charity)
1994	Wins Stanley Cup with the New York Rangers
1997	Signs with the Vancouver Canucks in the off-season
1998	Plays in the All-Star game
2000	Signs with the New York Rangers

Mark Messier

captain of three National Hockey League (NHL) teams: the Edmonton Oilers, New York Rangers, and Vancouver Canucks. Messier won Stanley Cups with both Edmonton and New York. The centerman had a long-lived career, playing into his forties.

Messier was born on January 18, 1961, in Edmonton, Alberta, Canada, the son of Douglas and Mary-Jean Messier. His father was a minor league hockey player who later was a coach. Messier had an older brother Paul who was also a hockey player who played professionally with the Colorado Rockies.

Messier began playing hockey when he was five years old, and served as stick boy for his father's junior tier II team as a kid. Messier himself began playing junior hockey when he was fifteen, and became serious about hockey soon after. He quit high school in 12th grade to concentrate on the sport.

Began Professional Career

In 1978, Messier began his professional career with a five-game tryout with the Indianapolis Racers in the World Hockey Association, the upstart league that was competing with the NHL. The Racers folded, so Messier joined the WHA's Cincinnati Stingers in the 1978-79 season. He played in forty-seven games, garnering more penalty minutes (58) than points (11—only one was a goal).

Drafted by Edmonton

Messier's career began to take off when he joined the Edmonton Oilers in the NHL in 1979. The team, primarily because of coach and general manager Glen Sather, drafted him in the 1979 entry draft in the second round with the 48th pick. Messier's numbers improved immediately from the previous season, scoring twelve goals and twenty-one assists in seventy-five games.

Soon, Messier had a reputation as a goal scorer, though this was often overshadowed by his more famous goal scoring teammate **Wayne Gretzky**. In the 1981-82 season, Messier scored 50 goals and 38 assists, and the

team made playoffs. In 1983, team went all the way to the Stanley Cup Finals with Messier contributing fifteen playoff goals. Until the 1983-84 season he was primarily a left wing, then shifted to center. In 1984, Edmonton won the Stanley Cup, and Messier was named the playoff MVP. His reputation as a clutch player and leader in the locker room was cemented in this time period.

The Oilers won the Stanley Cup three more times in this decade, in 1985, 1987, and 1988. Gretzky played with Oilers until 1988 when he was traded to the Los Angeles Kings. When Gretzky was traded, Messier was named captain and became team's official leader. In the 1980s, Messier was recognized as one of the best players in hockey. Then teammate Kevin Lowe told Austin Murphy of *Sports Illustrated*, "You have to go back to **Gordie Howe** to find someone who can dominate every aspect of the game—puckhandling, checking, skating—the way Mark can, although I'm not sure Howe was as fast as Mark."

Messier and the Oilers won another Cup in 1990. This was the same year that he won Hart Trophy as league's most valuable player and the Lester B. Pearson Award (most valuable player as voted on by the players). He followed up this triumphant year with a relatively bad season in 1990-91 because a knee injury limited him to fifty-three games.

Traded to New York

After the 1991 season ended, Messier's contract had expired and he held out for more money at the begin-

Career Statistics

Yr	Team	GP	G	A	PTS	+/−	PIM	SOG	SPCT	PPG	SHG
1979-80	Edmonton	75	12	21	33	−10	120	113	10.6	1	1
1980-81	Edmonton	72	23	40	63	−12	102	179	12.8	4	0
1981-82	Edmonton	78	50	38	88	21	119	235	21.3	10	0
1982-83	Edmonton	77	48	58	106	19	72	237	20.3	12	1
1983-84	Edmonton	73	37	64	101	40	165	219	16.9	7	4
1984-85	Edmonton	55	23	31	54	8	57	136	16.9	4	5
1985-86	Edmonton	63	35	49	84	36	68	201	17.4	10	5
1986-87	Edmonton	77	37	70	107	21	73	208	17.8	7	4
1987-88	Edmonton	77	37	74	111	21	103	182	20.3	12	3
1988-89	Edmonton	72	33	61	94	−5	130	164	20.1	6	6
1989-90	Edmonton	79	45	84	129	19	79	211	21.3	13	6
1990-91	Edmonton	53	12	52	64	15	34	109	11.0	3	1
1991-92	New York	79	35	72	107	31	76	212	16.5	12	4
1992-93	New York	75	25	66	91	−6	72	215	11.6	7	2
1993-94	New York	76	26	58	84	25	76	216	12.0	6	2
1994-95	New York	46	14	39	53	8	40	126	11.1	3	3
1995-96	New York	74	47	52	99	29	122	241	19.5	14	1
1996-97	New York	71	36	48	84	12	88	227	15.9	7	5
1997-98	Vancouver	82	22	38	60	−10	58	139	15.8	8	2
1998-99	Vancouver	59	13	35	48	−12	33	97	13.4	4	2
1999-2000	Vancouver	66	17	37	54	−15	30	131	13.0	6	0
2000-01	New York	82	24	43	67	−25	89	131	18.3	12	3
2001-02	New York	41	7	16	23	−1	32	69	10.1	2	0
TOTAL		1602	658	1146	1814	203	1838	3998	15.8	170	60

Edmonton: Edmonton Oilers (NHL); New York: New York Rangers (NHL); Vancouver: Vancouver Canucks (NHL).

ning of the 1991-92 season. He asked to be traded, and wanted to go to New York, a city that fit his flamboyant personality. Messier was traded to New York Rangers in October 1991. He was named team captain as soon as the trade was complete.

Messier became a star in New York, the media capital of the world. He played well in 1991-92, scoring thirty-five goals and seventy-two assists. He won another Hart Trophy and Pearson Award in 1992. Messier then signed a five-year deal worth $13 million. While he made his teammates better, Messier did clash with management. He had conflicts with Roger Neilson, who was the coach of the Rangers at the time. This led to Neilson being fired in 1993.

Won Cup in New York

The Rangers had not won the Stanley Cup since 1940, and put together many mediocre teams. With Messier as captain, the team won the Cup in 1994. In the finals, Messier scored the Cup-winning goal in game seven after guaranteeing a victory in game six by scoring a hat trick. With this victory, Messier became the first to be captain for two Stanley Cup winning teams.

For the 1996-97 season, Messier got to play with Gretzky again when the latter signed with the Rangers in the off-season. However Messier's contract was up at the end of the 1996-97 season, but Rangers did not resign him, in part, it was speculated, because he was power hungry. He was offered a one-year deal, but Messier declined to take it.

Signed with Vancouver

In the 1997, Messier instead signed a three-year deal worth $20 million with the Vancouver Canucks. In Vancouver, he was again the team's captain and continued to play at high level, reaching many career milestones, including scoring his 600th goal. But the team struggled, never making the playoffs during his tenure.

When his contract was up in Vancouver, Messier returned to the Rangers, who now had former Edmonton general manager Sather as their general manager. The captaincy was returned to him. Though New York still struggled and did not make the playoffs, Messier was a leader on a problematic team. He continued to play past his 41st birthday, though he had injury problems that limited the number of games he played in. He planned on playing until he was 43, if his body held out.

In describing Messier as a leader, Charles McGrath wrote in the *New York Times Magazine,* "Messier is an authentically commanding figure who by force of his smoldering, dominating personality inspires—or scares— others into surpassing themselves. He leads by example, but also, when necessary, by hectoring, cajoling and preaching, and at times by stony, unforgiving silence. ..."

CONTACT INFORMATION

Address: c/o New York Rangers, 2 Pennsylvania Plaza, New York, NY 10121.

Podell, Ira. "Messier, Rangers agree to terms." Associated Press (September 11, 2002).

Reel, Ursula. "Messier to miss the rest of regular season." Associated Press (March 1, 2002).

Sell, Dave. "In New York Bonfire, Messier a Self-Starter." *Washington Post* (May 27, 1994): B1.

Swift, E.M. "The good old days." *Sports Illustrated* (October 7, 1996): 54.

Wise, Mike. "Messier Is Now Part of the City." *New York Times* (October 11, 2002): D1.

Other

"Glen Sather." New York Rangers Official Web Site. http://www.newyorkrangers.com/team/coach.asp?coachid=101 (December 16, 2002).

"Mark Messier." ESPN.com. http://sports.espn.go.com/nhl/players/statistics?statsId=10 (December 14, 2002).

Sketch by A. Petruso

Awards and Accomplishments	
1982	All-Star (first team); played in All-Star game
1983	All-Star (first team)
1984-85	Won Stanley Cup with the Oilers;
1984, 1987-88, 1990	Conn Smythe Trophy as playoff MVP
1990	All-Star (first team)
1990, 1992	Hart Trophy as league MVP
1990, 1992	Lester B. Pearson Award as league MVP as voted on by the players
1994	Won Stanley Cup with the New York Rangers

FURTHER INFORMATION

Books

Athletes and Coaches of Winter. New York: Macmillian Reference USA, 2000.

Fischler, Stan. *The All-New Hockey's 100.* Toronto: McGraw-Hill Ryerson, Ltd.

Hickok, Ralph. *A Who's Who of Sports Champions: Their Stories and Records.* Boston: Houghton Mifflin Company, 1995.

Periodicals

Bloom, Barry M. "An absolute mess." *Sport* (July 1998): 76.

Bondy, Filip. "Rangers Roll the Dice and Trade for Messier." *New York Times* (October 5, 1991): section 1, p. 27.

Bondy, Filip. "Why Wait? Messier for Mayor, and Anything Else He Wants to Be." *New York Times* (October 11, 1991): B11.

Farber, Michael. "Chain of Command." *Sports Illustrated* (October 16, 2000): 79.

Farber, Michael. "The look." *Sports Illustrated* (February 12, 1996): 66.

Gildea, William. "With Messier, the Rangers Are Reborn." *Washington Post* (February 27, 1992): B1.

Gulitti, Tom. "Messier back for more." *Record* (Bergen County, NJ)(September 12, 2002): S02.

Kennedy, Kostya. "The big mess." *Sports Illustrated* (April 13, 1998): 94.

Lapointe, Joe. "The Man Who Makes the Rangers Won." *New York Times* (November 5, 1995): section 8, p. 10.

Lapointe, Joe. "Messier Hurts Himself, But the Rangers Play On." *New York Times* (November 26, 2002): D3.

Lipsyte, Robert. "Captain Dad? Just Call Him the Captain." *New York Times* (February 9, 1995): B11.

McGrath, Charles. "Elders on Ice." *New York Times* (March 23, 1997): section 6, p. 34.

Murphy, Austin. "The look of a winner." *Sports Illustrated* (May 9, 1988): 52.

Murphy, Austin. "Still going great." *Sports Illustrated* (May 5, 1997): 48.

Ann Meyers
1955-

American basketball player

Basketball trailblazer Ann Meyers takes her hall-of-fame distinction to new limits, with eight enshrinements—including the Naismith Memorial Basketball Hall of Fame, California Youth Organization High School Hall of Fame, Orange County Hall of Fame, California High School Hall of Fame, National High School Hall of Fame, University of California at Los Angeles (UCLA) Hall of Fame, Women's Sports Hall of Fame, and Women's Basketball Hall of Fame. A three-time recipient of the most valuable player (MVP) award in high school, she lettered in seven sports. As a college player Meyers made the Kodak All-American team for each of the four years of her career. She is both a Broderick Cup athlete and an Olympic medallist, and she left twelve all-time women's basketball records at UCLA.

As the first pick in the inaugural draft of the Women's Basketball League (WBL), Meyers made a career of first-time athletic accomplishments: most notably as the first high school student to earn a spot on the U.S. national basketball team, first woman to receive a full basketball scholarship to UCLA, the first woman to sign as a free agent with the National Basketball Association (NBA), and the first woman to be nominated for induction into the Basketball Hall of Fame. An unforgettable role model of modern women's sports history, Meyers set the standard for women's athletics in the final quarter of the twentieth century.

Ann Meyers

Athletic as an Adolescent

Born Ann Elizabeth Meyers on March 26, 1955, in San Diego, she was the middle child in an athletic brood of eleven siblings. Their father, Robert Eugene (Bob) Meyers, played for the Milwaukee Shooting Stars with the American Basketball Association, following a varsity career at Marquette University. Meyers's mother, Patricia Anne (Burke) was a homemaker.

In fifth and sixth grade Meyers played basketball on an all-boys team after her parents argued for the inherent right of their daughter to play with the boys in the absence of an all-girls team. By freshman year at Sonora High School in La Habra, California, she was an impressive player and earned the Most Valuable Player (MVP) award from her school. She repeated the season MVP honor at a new school, Connelly High in Anaheim, as a sophomore and was named an All-Star. In addition to her competition in the El Dorado and Loara High School tournaments that year, she participated in the St. Anthony's high school tournament and earned the tournament MVP honor. In the eleventh grade she won season MVP honors for a third time, having returned to her former Sonora High that year. In addition to lettering in basketball, Meyers graduated from Sonora in 1974 with letters in field hockey, softball, tennis, track and field, volleyball—even badminton—for a total participation in seven sports. She was named an All-American for each of her four years of high school and played

Chronology

1955	Born March 26 in San Diego, California
1974	First high school player ever to join the U.S. national team; becomes first woman to receive a basketball scholarship to UCLA
1978	Leads University of California at Los Angeles to the national championship; is drafted by Houston as the first-ever WBL draftee
1979	Graduates with B.A. in sociology; signs as a free agent with the Indiana Pacers but fails to make the cut; signs for $145,000 for three seasons with the New Jersey Gems
1980-82	Takes first place in the ABC superstars competition; meets future husband, Don Drysdale; enrolls at broadcasting school and embarks on a new career
1986	Marries Drysdale in November
1994	First woman to play in Celebrity Golf Association Championship

with the Amateur Athletic Union (AAU) from 1970-74. As a senior in 1974 she was named the School Athlete of the Year and became the first high school student ever named to the U.S. national team.

Broke Gender Barriers

After touring the former Soviet Union with the national team, Meyers entered college at UCLA on an athletic scholarship the fall of 1974. In the context of the times the scholarship award by UCLA was unprecedented because Meyers received a full scholarship specifically to play women's basketball. Women's intercollegiate sports in the 1970s were administered by the Association of Intercollegiate Athletics for Women (AIAW), an organization that later went into competition with the National College Athletic Association (NCAA) for control of women's sports programs. It was not until the implementation of Title IX, a women's sports initiative, that colleges were compelled to fund sports programs for women on an equal basis with those for men. Formed in 1972, the AIAW was defunct by 1983, in part because Title IX forced a re-assessment of the profitability of women's sports. The year 1982 was the crossover year when the AIAW merged into the NCAA. The final AIAW tourney and the first NCAA women's tournament were held that year.

For Meyers, caught in the limbo of the AIAW just prior to the dawn of Title IX in 1979, the opportunity to play basketball on full scholarship for the UCLA Bruins stands as a significant commentary on her ability. She took up the challenge, achieving much more than anyone might have anticipated. With an average of 17.4 points per game, she led the school in scoring during her freshman season. She led also in field goal percentage, rebounding average, free throw percentage, assists, steals, and blocked shots, and was the first player—male or female—to be named a Kodak all-American for each of her four years of play. That honor was punctuated by a spot on the silver-medal U.S. Olympic team in 1976, which marked the inaugural appearance of women's

Awards and Accomplishments

1971-73	Named high school MVP three years in succession
1974	Leads college team in scoring, rebounds, and assists; only freshman named to Kodak College All-American team
1975	Gold medal at the Pan American Games
1975-78	Becomes first player named to All-American Team for four years in succession
1976	Silver medal at the summer Olympics; gold medal at the Jones Cup
1976-78	Named college All-American
1977	Silver medal in the World University Games
1977-78	Named most valuable player by the Amateur Athletic Union
1977-79	Amateur Athletic Union All-American
1978	Won Broderick Cup; has college jersey, Number 15, retired at the Naismith Memorial Hall of Fame
1979	Gold medal at the World Championship games; silver medal at the Pan American games; named most valuable player of the Women's Basketball League
1980-82	Takes the first place ($50,000 prize) in the American Broadcasting Company's Superstars competition
1993	Is enshrined as a player at the Naismith Memorial Hall of Fame on May 10
1999	Is enshrined with the inaugural class at the Women's Basketball Hall of Fame

Meyers left twelve college records when she graduated from University of California at Los Angeles, including third all-time career scorer, with 1,685 points. She led the school in career assists with 544 (5.6 average per game) and in steals with 403 (4.2 average per game). She was the only player at the school to post a quadruple double.

Related Biography: Baseball Player Don Drysdale

Right-handed Hall-of-Fame pitcher Donald Scott Drysdale was born in Van Nuys, California, on July 23, 1936.

A Cy Young Award winner in 1962, Drysdale played for the Dodgers in Brooklyn and later in Los Angeles. Together with Sandy Koufax in the 1960s Drysdale earned a reputation for his aggressive pitching style and sidearm fastballs. In 1968 he pitched a record fifty-eight scoreless innings. He retired having pitched six seasons with 200 or more strikeouts, which was a National League record at that time. As a right-handed batter Drysdale likewise left his mark as the only .300 hitter with the Dodgers in 1965.

After meeting on the set of ABC's sports Superstars, Drysdale and Meyers married in November 1986. Drysdale was fifty-one years old to the day when their eldest son, Don Jr., was born. They would have two more children together: Darren, and Drew, before his untimely death on July 3, 1993, at age 56. He died in Montréal, Quebec, Canada, of a heart attack.

Olympic basketball. A three-time All-American in college, from 1976-78, Meyers helped lead the Lady Bruins to the AIAW championship during her final season of competition in 1978. She graduated third in all-time scoring with 1,685 points, and led the school in career assists with 544 (5.6 average per game) and steals with 403 (4.2 average per game). Also among her 12 college records, she left UCLA as the only player to post a quadruple double, which she accomplished against Stephen F. Austin State University in 1978—with 20 points, 14 rebounds, 10 assists, and 10 steals.

With four seasons of college competition behind her, Meyers was the number one draft pick in the inaugural draft of the Women's Basketball League (WBL) in 1978. She refused an offer to play with the Houston Angels, however, in order to qualify for the U.S. Olympic team in 1980—In those days the Olympic regulations required athletes to maintain amateur status as a prerequisite for participation. While continuing with adult AAU competition, Meyers spent some time in 1979 completing the academic requirements for a bachelor's degree in sociology. She was named AAU All-American from 1977-79 and AAU MVP for the 1977-78 season.

1979 was a landmark year for women's amateur sports, with the passage of Title IX. Although Meyers was no longer a student athlete, the historic implications of the year were equally significant for her. Believing that she would not make the Olympic team, Meyers ac-

cepted an offer to sign as a free agent with the Indiana Pacers of the National Basketball Association (NBA). Some observers criticized the move very harshly, and it was seen as a publicity stunt in conjunction with the implementation of Title IX. However controversial, Meyers's free agency with the NBA was a dramatic milestone toward the advancement of social equality for women.

Although she had proven her talent as a powerhouse on the college hoop circuit, the 5-foot-9-inch, 135-pound athlete failed to make the NBA cut. Pacers coach Bob Leonard suggested that she was at least 6 inches and 40 pounds shy of the physical frame necessary to compete in the men's game, indicating that a man of her stature was at an equally severe disadvantage in the competition. According to the terms of her contract, Meyers was guaranteed work with the Pacers at an annual salary of $50,000, for broadcasting and public relations services. She accepted the alternative conditions, however briefly, but still wanted to play professional ball. She turned instead to the WBL, which was entering its second season of play.

Sports Career Played to Conclusion

In the women's league it was the New Jersey Gems that offered Meyers $145,000 to play for three years. She signed with the team on November 14, 1979. That season she was named to the All-Pro team and played for the East in the second-ever league All-Star game, held in Chicago on January 30, 1980. The West prevailed in the game, although the final score of 115-112 hinged on a controversial call over a play by Meyers.

Playing guard, and wearing jersey number 14 for the Gems, she culminated her first WBL season with an average of 22.2 points per game, to finish fifth in the league. She finished first in steals, with 4.9 per game, and third in assists with an average 5.9 per game. Additionally she was sixth in rebounds with 10.3 per game. In April 1980 she shared season MVP honors with Molly "Machine Gun" Bolin of the Iowa Comets.

As luck would have it the league was in dire straits, and teams began to fold even prior to the interim between the third and final season. Two of the 1979-80 expansion teams—the Philadelphia Fox and the Washington Metros—failed to complete their inaugural season. The Angels, the team that won the inaugural WBL championship in 1979, collapsed before the start of the 1980 season. Along with it went the 1979-80 champions, the New York Stars. Likewise the Iowa Comets and the Milwaukee Does suspended operations at that point.

When on January 20, 1980, President Jimmy Carter announced a U.S. boycott of that year's summer Olympics, the move devastated the WBL, which looked to the Olympic basketball competition to generate more interest in the women's sport. The boycott was confirmed by the U.S. Olympic Committee (USOC) on April 21, 1980. Although the decision by the USOC brought some of the finest U.S. amateur players, such as **Nancy Lieberman-Cline**, into the league, it was too little and too late.

Many of the WBL players received only partial salary payments as the season concluded in the spring of 1980. Meyers lost thousands of dollars of her pay and countered by failing to return to the team training camp in New Jersey in October 1980. She sat out the 1980-81 season. Other WBL stars—including co-MVP Bolin—had signed with the newly formed Ladies Professional Basketball Association for the 1980-81 season, causing further distress to the WBL. By 1981 both leagues had folded altogether, leaving Meyers unabated in her need for athletic competition.

A Career in Broadcasting

In 1979 Meyers entered the competition for the American Broadcasting Company's (ABC) *Superstars* title, an annually televised, all-around competition between prominent athletes. After a fourth-place finish in her first appearance, Meyers went into intensive training and followed up with first place finishes for three years in succession, from 1980-82. The event, which paid $50,000 for first place, brought Meyers a much greater reward in meeting her future husband, Don Drysdale, at the event. Drysdale, a hall-of-fame baseball pitcher, was working in retirement as a broadcaster. With Drysdale's encouragement, Meyers enrolled in broadcasting school and embarked on a new career as a sportscaster.

As a sportscaster and color analyst for two decades, Meyers reported on some of the most prominent and popular sporting events on record, having worked for many major networks and for several college athletic departments in addition to her arrangement with the Pacers of Indiana in 1979-80. In 1981-82 she announced games for the University of Hawaii, and in 1982-84 she announced the Bruins games at UCLA. After working the 1984 Olympics with ABC in Los Angeles, she was seen on Sportsvision in 1985-87, on CBS-TV in 1991, and on WTBS in 1986 and again in 1990. Her other network af-

filiations encompass WNBA-NBC, Fox Network, ESPN, and ESPN2. She provided color coverage of Women's NCAA Basketball tournaments in the 1990s, and covered the basketball regional games and final four for ESPN.

Across a two-decade span, she reported on a range of sports, including volleyball, soccer, track, baseball, and softball. At the turn of the century she was heard on both the National Broadcasting Company (NBC) and the Fox Network. She presented games for the Women's National Basketball Association (WNBA) often with the late Chick Hearn.

When Meyers and Drysdale were married in November of 1986. Drysdale had just prior, in 1984, been inducted into the National Baseball Hall of Fame in Cooperstown, New York. In 1993, with the induction of Meyers into the Naismith Memorial Basketball Hall of Fame, the couple became the first two-way Hall-of-Fame marriage in the history of sports. Additionally Meyers earned the distinction of being the first woman inductee to the hall.

In 1994 Meyers amended her long list sports firsts yet again, becoming the first woman ever to compete in the Celebrity Golf Association Championship. By virtue of her extensive career of firsts she earned a reputation in the sports world as a key role model for women athletes of the late twentieth century and into the twenty-first.

CONTACT INFORMATION

Address: c/o Lampros and Roberts, 16615 Lark Ave Ste 101, Los Gatos, CA, 95032-7645.

FURTHER INFORMATION

Books

Markoe, Arnold, and Kenneth T. Jackson, *Scribner Encyclopedia of American Lives: Sports Figures.* New York: Charles Scribner's Sons, 2002.

Woolum, Janet, *Outstanding Women Athletes: Who They Are and How They Influenced Sports in America.* Phoenix: Oryx Press, 1992.

Periodicals

Houston Chronicle (August 6, 2000): B18.

Los Angeles Times (March 5, 1999).

Los Angeles Times (May 12, 2002): D1.

Press-Enterprise (Riverside, CA) (August 20, 1999): C3.

Sports Illustrated (May 23, 1994): 14.

St. Louis Post-Dispatch (March 30, 2001): c11.

Other

"Ann Meyers Biography," www.hoophall.com/hall offamers/Meyers.htm (January 24, 2003).

"Don Drysdale," *National Baseball Hall of Fame* www.
baseballhalloffame.org/hofers_and_honorees/hofer_
bios/drysdale_don.htm (January 25, 2003).

Sketch by G. Cooksey

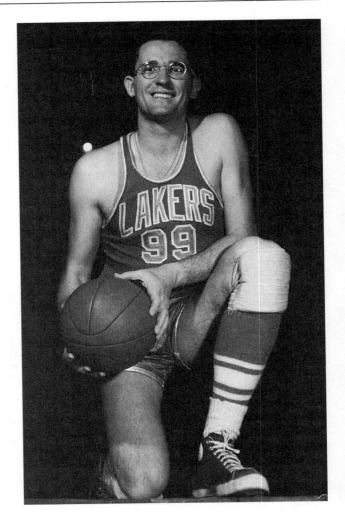

George Mikan

George Mikan
1924-

American basketball player

Destined to become one of the first of basketball's most talented big men, as a young man George Mikan was discouraged from seriously pursuing basketball because of his ungainly height and his acute nearsightedness, conditions that most coaches during the early 1940s believed would leave Mikan hopelessly clumsy. At 6 foot, 10 inches, he towered over other players of his day when smaller, quicker players dominated the game. Mikan would change all that with his shot-blocking abilities and his deadly hook shot. After four successful years of basketball at DePaul University under Hall of Fame coach Ray Meyer, Mikan entered professional basketball in 1946 and quickly became a star. Playing all but his first year of pro ball with the Minneapolis Lakers (later to become the Los Angeles Lakers), he led his team to six championship titles in seven years. His nine-year presence on the court greatly influenced the development of the modern game of basketball.

The Path to Basketball

Mikan was born on June 18, 1924, in Joliet, Illinois, the first son of Joe and Minnie Mikan, owners of a restaurant-bar where Mikan and his two brothers, Joe and Ed, worked after school. Already five feet, nine inches at the age of eight, Mikan towered over his classmates, reaching six feet by the age of 11. His unusual height made him shy, awkward, and extremely self-conscious. During a summer pickup game of basketball, Mikan broke his leg. The leg failed to heal properly, and he spent the next 18 months bedridden. During that time he continued to grow, and when he took his first steps a year and a half later, he was six feet, seven inches.

After attending Quigley Prep School, Mikan enrolled at DePaul University. Over the Christmas holidays during his freshman year, Mikan tried out for George Keogan, the famed basketball coach of the Notre Dame Fighting Irish. The tryout was an undisputed disappointment. Facing the varsity squad, who were under instructions from Keogan to throw the ball at his feet, Mikan appeared phenomenally uncoordinated and slow. Keogan's final judgment was that Mikan was hopelessly clumsy.

College Ball

Mikan returned to DePaul to discovered that the university had fired the basketball coach and hired Ray Meyer, an assistant coach from Notre Dame who had witnessed Mikan's abysmal tryout performance. Expecting Meyer's opinion to be similar to Keogan's, Mikan did not have good feelings about his chances to play for DePaul. However, on the first day of spring practice, Meyer dismissed the rest of the team to work daily for six weeks with Mikan alone. Meyer ran Mikan through a variety of drills to strengthen his coordination. He skipped rope, shadow boxed, ran, and spent hours practicing left- and right-handed hook shots and tap-ins. The long hours of practice paid off as Mikan's footwork and confidence continued to improve.

In 1944, 1945, and 1946 Mikan was named an All-American, and he led the nation in scoring in 1945 and 1946 with an average of 23.9 points per game (ppg) and 23.1 ppg, respectively. During the 1944-45 season, primarily because Mikan had become so effective at swatting the ball away from the opponent's basket that the National Collegiate Athletic Association (NCAA) instituted a new

Chronology

1924	Born in Joliet, Illinois
1942-46	Four-year letter winner at DePaul University under Hall of Fame coach Ray Meyer
1946	Leads nation in scoring, averaging 23.1 points per game (ppg)
1946-47	Plays for the National Basketball League's (NBL) Chicago Gears
1947-54	Star player for the Minneapolis Lakers
1948	Wins NBL championship with the Lakers
1949	Wins BAA championship with the Lakers; passes the Bar to become a lawyer
1950	Wins National Basketball Association (NBA) championship with the Lakers
1952-54	Wins three consecutive NBA championships with the Lakers
1954	Retires at the end of the 1953-54 season as the league's all-time leading scorer, with 11,764 points (22.6 ppg)
1955	Returns to Lakers during 1955-56 season for 37 games
1956	Retires from playing for good; runs for a congressional seat but loses election
1957-58	Coaches the Lakers for 39 games before resigning, posting a record of only 9 wins and 30 losses
1967	Becomes first Commissioner of the new American Basketball Association (ABA) league and is credited with introducing the league's trademark red, white, and blue ball.
1969	Resigns as ABA commissioner to resume law practice in Minneapolis
2000	Right leg is amputated below the knee due to complications from diabetes

rule that prohibited goaltending, namely, the ball could not be blocked on the way down toward the basket.

Despite the new goaltending rule, Mikan and his team excelled under Meyer's leadership. Reaching the 1945 NIT championship game, DePaul easily overcame Bowling Green State University, winning 71-54. During the tournament Mikan set 10 individual records, including a tremendous performance against Rhode Island at Madison Square Garden in which he scored 53 points. His total scoring for three games totaled a new record of 120 points, and he was selected for the tournament's Most Valuable Player (MVP) award. Mikan finished his college career with an average of 19.8 ppg, and over those four years, DePaul's record was 81-17.

After the 1946 collegiate season ended Mikan signed a professional contract with the National Basketball League's (NBL) Chicago Gears for $60,000 over five years plus a $25,000 signing bonus, making Mikan the highest paid pro basketball player to date. In the same year he married Patricia Lu Deveny; they had four sons and two daughters. Joining the team in mid-season, Mikan played in 25 games, averaging 16.5 ppg. The Gears won the 1947 NBL championship, and Mikan was named to the All-NBL Team. However, the following year the Gears franchise folded, and the team's players were distributed among the NBL teams.

The First Basketball Dynasty

The Minneapolis Lakers had first shot at signing Mikan. Although he intended his trip to Minneapolis a

Related Biography: Basketball Coach Ray Meyer

Known for his passion for the game and his ability to teach and motivate his players, Ray Meyer served as the head basketball coach of DePaul's Blue Demons from 1942 to 1984. His record of 724 wins and 354 losses included 37 winning seasons, thirteen National Collegiate Athletic Association (NCAA) post-season appearances and eight National Invitational Tournament (NIT) appearances, twelve 20-win seasons, two NCAA Final Four appearances (1943 and 1978), and a NIT title (1945).

Meyer, who played college basketball for the Irish, led his team to a 40-6 record during his junior and senior years. After graduating, Meyer spent two years as a social worker before returning to Notre Dame as an assistant coach. Meyer arrived at DePaul in 1942, the same year that young George Mikan came to the school. Meyer, who had encountered Mikan the previous year during the gangly young man's failed attempt to try out for the Notre Dame team, recognized Mikan's potential. Using drills such as jumping rope and shadow boxing, Meyer helped Mikan improve his coordination and guided him on his way to becoming one of the game's most influential players.

mere formality, as he did not want to live in Minnesota, Mikan ended up signing a one-year contract for $12,500. As a member of the Lakers, Mikan helped establish the first dynasty in the history of professional basketball. At the end of his first season with the team, he led the league in scoring with 1,195 points in 56 games, for an average of 21.3 ppg. The Lakers were 51-19 for the year and won the NBL championship, taking the best-of-five game series against the Rochester Royals. Mikan, who averaged 27.5 ppg in the finals, was the unanimous choice for MVP.

In 1948 the Lakers were among four NBL teams to join the Basketball Association of America (BAA), a growing and competitive league. Despite being edged out of the BAA's Western Division title by Rochester, who also made the league switch, the Lakers reached the finals of postseason play, beating **Red Auerbach**'s Washington Capitols in the best-of-seven series. Despite playing with a broken wrist in the final two games, Mikan averaged over 30 ppg in the series. He finished the season as the league's leading scorer, averaging 28.3 ppg.

In 1949 Mikan, who had been attending law school in the off season, passed the bar. In the same year the BAA merged with the American Basketball Association to form the National Basketball Association (NBA). During the first year of NBA's existence, Mikan, along with the support of several exceptional teammates that included Vern Mikkelson, Jim Pollard, Arnie Ferrin, and Slater Martin, took the Lakers to another championship title. The Lakers' NBA championship in 1950 was the franchise's third title in three years, each in a different league. Mikan led the NBA in scoring during the 1949-50 season with an average of 27.4 ppg.

During the 1950-51 NBA season Mikan was once again the leading scorer, with 28.4 ppg, but the Lakers failed to earn their fourth title when the Rochester Roy upended them in the semifinals of postseason play. Mikan was slowed down during the series by a fractured

Career Statistics

Yr	Team	GP	FG	FT	PTS	P/G
1946-47	Chicago	25	147	119	413	16.5
1947-48	Minneapolis	56	406	383	1195	21.3
1948-49	Minneapolis	60	583	532	1698	28.3
1949-50	Minneapolis	68	649	567	1865	27.4
1950-51	Minneapolis	68	678	576	1932	28.4
1951-52	Minneapolis	64	545	433	1523	23.8
1952-53	Minneapolis	70	500	442	1442	20.6
1953-54	Minneapolis	72	441	424	1306	18.1
1954-55	Minneapolis	37	148	94	390	10.5
TOTAL		520	4097	3570	11764	22.6

Chicago: Chicago Gears; Minneapolis: Minneapolis Lakers.

Awards and Accomplishments

1946	Named National Player of the Year
1947	National Basketball League (NBL) championship with the Chicago Gears
1947-48	Named to the All-NBL First Team
1948	NBL championship with the Minneapolis Lakers
1948	Named NBL's Most Valuable Player
1949	Basketball Association of America (BAA) championship with the Lakers
1949	Named to the All-BAA First Team
1950	National Basketball League (NBA) championship with the Lakers
1950	Named basketball's greatest player of the half-century
1950-54	Selected as an NBA All-Star
1952-54	NBA championship with the Lakers
1953	NBA All-Star Game Most Valuable Player
1959	Inducted into the Naismith Memorial Basketball Hall of Fame
1970	Named to the NBA 25th Anniversary All-Time Team
1980	Named to the NBA 35th Anniversary All-Time Team
1996	Named to the NBA 50th Anniversary All-Time Team

At the time of his retirement in 1954, Mikan was the league's all-time leading scorer with 11,764 points, averaging 22.6 points per game.

leg. The following year the Lakers managed to regain the NBA title, but Mikan finished second in scoring with 23.8 ppg, behind Philadelphia's Paul Arizin. The Lakers remained the dominant force in the NBA for the next two years, winning championships again in 1953 and 1954, the team's second three-peat. In his last two full seasons of play, Mikan averaged 20.6 and 18.1 ppg, respectively.

In 1954 Mikan shocked his teammates and Laker fans by announcing his retirement. Wanting to quit while he was still at the top of his game, Mikan decided to pursue the practice of law. Nonetheless, he soon found himself drawn back to the game and team he loved, agreeing to serve as the Lakers' general manager for the next year and a half. However, during the 1955-56 season, in response to a significant decline in attendance due primarily to his absence on the court and the Lakes' subsequent slump, Mikan came out of retirement to play 37 games. But, out of shape and out of practice, he averaged under 11 ppg and retired from playing for good at the end of the season.

Mr. Basketball

Despite the lack of any overwhelming name recognition by today's basketball fans, Mikan is considered one of the most influential basketball players in the history of the NBA. Known as "Mr. Basketball," Mikan's dominance on the floor led to the rule change that widened the three-second lane from six to twelve feet and goaltending rules were revised. Mikan is also credited with the institution of the twenty-four-second shot clock, which was eventually put in place after the Fort Wayne Pistons (now the Detroit Pistons) stalled an entire game against the Lakers in 1950 to remove Mikan's scoring threat. Although he still managed to put in fifteen points, the Lakers lost the game 19-18, the lowest score in NBA history. As evidence of his tenacious play, during his career Mikan suffered ten broken bones and took 166 stitches.

Not only was Mikan the league's first dominating big man, he was the first player to become a major drawing card to bring fans to the NBA. His fierce competitive spirit, rough-and-ready play, and affable character made him a star attraction in every city he played. As *Los Angeles Times* reporter Steve Springer noted in 2001, "Mikan was 'big' before **[Wilt] Chamberlain**. He was the master of the hook before **[Kareem] Abdul-Jabbar**. He was Superman before **Shaquille O'Neal**, Clark Kent before Kurt Rambis. He brought winning times to the Lakers before **[Magic] Johnson** was born and put the NBA on the map half a century before **Michael Jordan** took it into the stratosphere." Perhaps the greatest tribute to Mikan's talent and influence on professional basketball came on December 13, 1949, in a game between the Lakers and the New York Knicks. The marquee over Madison Square Garden, where the game was to be played, read "GEO. MIKAN VS. KNICKS."

Mikan, who established a successful business and law practice in Minneapolis, made two other brief returns to professional basketball. During the 1957-58 season he served as the team's head coach, but after the team won only 9 of its first 39 games with Mikan at the helm, he stepped aside. When the now-defunct American Basketball Association organized in 1967, Mikan accepted an offer to become the league's first commissioner, a position he held for two years.

Mikan remained in Minneapolis until the 1990s when he and his wife moved to Scottsdale, Arizona. Diagnosed with diabetes when he was 62 years old, Mikan had his right leg amputated below the knee in early 2000. A prosthesis allowed him to regain his mobility, but he must undergo dialysis treatment three times every week. In 2001 Mikan was honored at the halftime of a game between the Lakers and the Minnesota Timberwolves, and a nine-foot bronze statute was unveiled outside the Target Center, the Timberwolves' arena. Mikan is a member of the Naismith Memorial Hall of Fame and was selected as the greatest basketball player of the first half of the twentieth century.

CONTACT INFORMATION

Address: Scottsdale, Arizona.

FURTHER INFORMATION

Books

Great Athletes. Englewood Cliffs, NJ: Salem Press, 2001.

Hickok, Ralph. *A Who's Who of Sports Champions: Their Stories and Records.* Boston: Houghton Mifflin, 1995.

Hollander, Zander, ed. *The Modern Encyclopedia of Basketball.* 2d ed. rev. New York: Dolphin Books, 1979.

Jares, Joe. *Basketball: The American Game.* Chicago: Follett Publishing, 1971.

Joyce, Dick. "George Mikan: Basketball Revolutionist." In *The Sports Immortals,* edited by Will Grimsley. Englewood Cliffs, NJ: Prentice-Hall, 1972.

Mendell, Ronald L. *Who's Who in Basketball.* New Rochelle, NY: Arlington House, 1973.

Nelson, Murray R. "George Lawrence Mikan, Jr." In *The Scribner Encyclopedia of American Lives, Sports Figures,* Volume 2, edited by Arnold Markoe. New York: Charles Scribner's Sons, 2002.

Pepe, Phil. *Greatest Stars of the NBA.* Englewood Cliffs, NJ: Prentice-Hall, 1970.

Periodicals

Barreiro, Dan. "Before Wilt, Kareem and Shaq, There was Mikan." *Minneapolis-St. Paul Star Tribune* (December 23, 1999).

Barreiro, Dan. "Mikan Hanging Tough, Despite Diabetes." *Minneapolis-St. Paul Tribune* (April 6, 2001).

"The Battle of Baskets." *Time* (February 14, 1949): 73-74.

Fay, Bill. "Inside Sports." *Collier's* (December 25, 1948): 42.

Fimrite, Ron. "Big George." *Sports Illustrated* (November 6, 1989): 128-139.

"George Mikan." *Sports Illustrated* (August 22, 1994): 52.

Hartman, Sid. "A Great Career had Rough Start." *Star Tribune* (Minneapolis, MN) (April 8, 2001): C3.

Hartman, Sid. "Remembering the George Mikan Era." *Minneapolis-St. Paul Star Tribune* (April 6, 2001).

Springer, Steve. "Lakers Neglect Roots." *Los Angeles Times* (October 29, 2001): pt. 4, p. 1.

Tulumellos, Mike. "Basketball's Babe Ruth Carried Infant NBA." *East Valley Tribune* (Mesa, AZ) (June 15, 2001).

Wolf, Bob. "NBA Champs: Era of Excellence Minneapolis Lakers (1948-55)." *Los Angeles Times* (June 15, 2002).

Other

Lakers Web.com. http://www.lakersweb.com/players/ georgemikan.shtml/ (October 31, 2002)

Naismith Memorial Basketball Hall of Fame. http:// www.hoophall.com/halloffamers/Mikan.htm/ (October 31, 2002)

NBA Legends. http://www.nba.com/history/players/ mikan_bio.html. (October 31, 2002)

Sketch by Kari Bethel

Stan Mikita
1940-

Canadian hockey player

Playing his entire career (1959-80) with the Chicago Blackhawks, Stan Mikita was a complete player on the ice, a team leader, and multiple award winner for his playing accomplishments. Often overshadowed by his more flamboyant, goal scoring teammate **Bobby Hull**, Mikita was nonetheless known for his outstanding abilities as a scorer, stickhandler, and passer, as well as on defense. As Stan and Shirley Fischler wrote in *Fischler's Hockey Encyclopedia,* "If any single player can be described as the guts of a hockey team, Stan Mikita, the shifty Chicago Black Hawk center, is precisely that man." After overcoming a penchant for fighting and penalties in his early career—a feisty attitude which earned him the nickname "Le Petit Diable" ("The Little Devil")—Mikita began playing intelligent hockey and using his skills. He went on to be the first player to win the Lady Byng Trophy (for gentlemanly play), the Ross Trophy (as the leading scorer in the National Hockey League (NHL)), and the Hart Trophy as most valuable player in one season (1966-67). He repeated the feat the following season. Mikita was also an innovator in hockey equipment, among the first to use a curved stick as well as an early wearer of a helmet, donned after a head injury. Mikita also was active in the teaching of hockey to hearing impaired young people, which led to the founding of the U.S. National Deaf Hockey Team.

Early Years

Mikita was born Stanislas Gvoth in Sokolce, Czechoslovakia, on May 20, 1940. His father, also named Stanislas, was a textile factory worker, while his mother worked in the fields. Soon after the end of World War II,

Stan Mikita

Czechoslovakia was taken over by the Communists. To give their middle child, Mikita, a better life away from the Communists, they allowed him to be adopted by a childless aunt and uncle, Joe and Anna Mikita, who had lived in Canada for the past 20 years.

When Mikita was eight years old, the Mikitas took him to their home in St. Catharines, Ontario, Canada. The young Mikita did not want to leave his parents and home behind, going so far as to plot how he was going to throw himself off the train that was taking him out of the country and run back. However, Mikita was foiled and he arrived in Canada just before Christmas in December 1948. When Mikita came to his new country, he did not speak any English and knew nothing about hockey.

Introduction to Hockey

During the first days in Canada, Mikita saw some boys in the street playing hockey, and began playing with them. Though he hit one of the boys with his stick, he soon began playing the game. The first words he learned in English were related to hockey: "push, stick, and goal." But the language and cultural adjustments remained hard. Before hockey, Mikita thought about joining the Air Force so he could steal a plane and go back home to Czechoslovakia.

Mikita was put in third grade in the local public school, but because he did not speak English, he was put in a kindergarten class to help with the language adjustments. It took several years before Mikita was comfortable in his new country and language. His foreign background also lead to Mikita being teased and ethnically slurred by classmates and others. He would use his fists to defend himself, and became something of a street fighter. He also stole and was involved in petty larceny.

But by the time Mikita was nine years old, hockey became a focus. Playing this sport and others made him feel like he belonged in North America and gave him a way of relating to his peers. When he was nine, Mikita lied about his age and joined a team of 12 year olds. He was dedicated to practicing from an early age, going to practice at 5 or 5:30 a.m. before school. Mikita's athletic skills were not limited to hockey. He also played basketball, football, lacrosse, soccer and baseball. He was so good in baseball as a catcher that he was offered major league tryouts as a teenager. But hockey was his game, and he later credited it with saving his life.

Mikita played junior A hockey in St. Catharines. Beginning in 1956, he was a player on the St. Catharines Teepees of the Ontario Hockey Association (OHA). This was the leading junior farm team for the Chicago Blackhawks of the NHL, used to develop talent for the perpetually underachieving team. While Mikita was already overshadowed by future teammate Bobby Hull, he did regularly lead his team in scoring. When he was 16, he was named the OHA's most valuable player, and soon dropped out of high school to devote all his attention to hockey.

Joined the Blackhawks

At the end of the 1958-59 season, Mikita joined the Blackhawks for three games, and the following season jointed the Blackhawks full time. In his first years in the NHL, Mikita played an antagonistic style of hockey. He tried to make up for his small stature (only 5'9" and 165 lbs.) and lack of scoring output in his first full season (only eight goals) by fighting, tripping, and hooking all the time. In his first full season with Chicago, Mikita had 119 penalty minutes. He was soon given the nickname "La Petite Diable" ("The Little Devil") for his belligerent personality on the ice.

Mikita was not the only Blackhawk who played like that. The team had a reputation for using physical force to make up for lack of scoring. But the team was on the rise, improving because of their farm system, good trades, and a skilled general manager in Tommy Ivan. Though Mikita had a problem with penalties, as he matured in his game he showed he was a passionate competitor who wanted to win and inspired his teammates. He played on the so-called "Scooter Line" with Ken Wharram and Ab McDonald, a checking line that could score, for nearly ten years. Mikita also used his brain. As William Barry Furlong wrote in *Sports Illustrated* in 1962, "Not as burly as Montreal's big Center Jean Beliveau, not as fast as Montreal's little Center Henri Richard, Mikita brilliantly compensates with terror, wit and perception.... Mikita not only thinks well but well ahead." With Bobby Hull, Mikita was responsible for reviving the undistinguished franchise.

Won Stanley Cup

During Mikita's true rookie season, it was only the second season in many years in which Chicago made the playoffs. The following year, the 1960-61 season, Mikita played with two broken toes and racked up 100 penalty minutes in the regular season. But in the playoffs, Mikita was a leading offensive force. The Blackhawks had momentum going into the playoffs, and defeated five-time defending champions the Montreal Canadiens. In the finals, the Blackhawks faced the Detroit Red Wings, lead by Mr. Hockey **Gordie Howe**. Chicago won in six games to capture their first Stanley Cup since the late 1930s.

At the time, it was believed that Mikita and the Blackhawks would be winning several more Cups with their lineup. The team did make the finals in 1962, but lost in six games to the Toronto Maple Leafs. This series showed their vulnerability on defense. But Mikita still made big plays and set a playoff scoring record with 21 points (six goals and 15 assists). Chicago's playoff performance went downhill from there, losing in the semifinals in 1963, then the first round in 1964.

Used Curved Blade

Though the Blackhawks' post-season fortunes were not great despite quality players, Mikita had his best years in the mid to late 1960s. In about 1963, Mikita made a discovery that added to his scoring prowess. Mikita claimed that he cracked an old blade and did not want to get another one from the dressing room during a practice. He saw that the puck reacted differently, and he and Hull began experimenting with curves on their blades. The puck would be like a knuckleball in baseball—moving unexpectedly, fooling the goalie. Though Andy Bathgate of the New York Rangers claimed to be the first to use a curved blade, credit was generally given to Mikita. Despite the fact that Mikita scored much because of it, he later claimed it was an error because backhands were essentially eliminated.

Won Numerous NHL Awards

In 1963-64, Mikita began competing with teammate Hull for the league's scoring title. Mikita won the Ross Trophy by scoring 39 goals and 50 assists, while Hull had 43 goals but fewer assists. The following season, Mikita led the league in scoring again with 87 points, but also had 154 penalty minutes. Mikita added 53 additional penalty minutes in the playoffs. He changed his penalty-prone attitude after the 1965-66 season when his four-year-old daughter Meg (one of four children he had with wife Jill) asked why he had to got to the penalty box away from his teammates all the time. In this and the six seasons before it, he led the league in penalty minutes for centers. But Mikita realized as more players were bigger that could not fight everyone, but he could be more effective as a scorer.

In the 1966-67 season, Mikita set a league record with 62 assists, and tied Hull's record of 97 total points in a season. His biggest number was his smallest: he had only 12 penalty minutes on the year. Though opponents tried to goad him into fighting and taking other dumb penalties, Mikita resisted. For his restrained on-ice attitude, Mikita was awarded the Lady Byng Trophy, given for gentlemanly play. He also won the Ross Trophy, for winning the scoring title, and the Hart Trophy for most valuable player. This marked the first time a player had won all three. He repeated his triple crown in 1967-68, though he had 52 penalty minutes.

Despite these kind of numbers and awards, Mikita always played second fiddle to Bobby Hull in terms of

Career Statistics

Yr	Team	GP	G	A	PTS	+/−	PIM
1958-59	Chicago	3	0	1	1	—	4
1959-60	Chicago	67	8	18	26	—	119
1960-61	Chicago	66	19	34	53	—	100
1961-62	Chicago	70	25	52	77	—	97
1962-63	Chicago	65	31	45	76	—	69
1963-64	Chicago	70	39	50	89	—	149
1964-65	Chicago	70	28	59	87	—	154
1965-66	Chicago	68	30	48	78	—	58
1966-67	Chicago	70	35	62	97	—	12
1967-68	Chicago	72	40	47	87	−3	14
1968-69	Chicago	74	30	67	97	+17	52
1969-70	Chicago	76	39	47	86	+29	50
1970-71	Chicago	74	24	48	72	+21	85
1972-73	Chicago	74	26	39	65	+16	46
1972-73	Chicago	57	27	56	83	+31	32
1973-74	Chicago	76	30	50	80	+24	46
1974-75	Chicago	79	36	50	86	+14	48
1975-76	Chicago	48	16	41	57	−4	37
1976-77	Chicago	57	19	30	49	−9	20
1977-78	Chicago	76	18	41	59	+18	35
1978-79	Chicago	65	19	36	55	+3	34
1979-80	Chicago	17	2	5	7	+2	12

Chicago: Chicago Blackhawks.

Stan Mikita Hockey School for the Hearing Impaired

In 1974, Mikita was approached by Chicago businessman Irv Tiahny-bik in a restaurant one night and convinced the hockey star to help teach hearing impaired children how to play hockey. Tiahnybik's young son Lex had played the game for several years, but had recently had a bad experience with a coach who did not want to deal with the young deaf player. Together they founded the American Impaired Hearing Association for deaf and hard of hearing youth, and its related Stan Mikita Hockey School for the Hearing Impaired. The school held an annual summer camp to teach the game to young deaf players, and give them a way to relate to the hearing world. At first, Mikita was unsure how to deal with his students because he had no experience with the hearing impaired. Mikita told Brad Herzog of the *Sports Illustrated*, that when he moved to Canada and knew no English, "I could hear the words, but I had no idea what they meant. Although I wasn't shut out by the hearing world, I was basically being shut out by my peers." Mikita and a host of other NHL professionals, college coaches and players, and others have taught the young hockey players how to play the game and host a tournament every summer in Chicago. Though the camp's focus is hockey, it is also about supporting its young players by providing hearing aids, speech therapies, counseling, and financial support for families. By 1995, over 80 campers were there; in 1997, over 100. The annual camp has lead to the formation of the U.S. National Deaf Hockey Team which won the silver medal at the Winter Games for the Deaf in 1991, gold in 1995, and silver in 1999.

publicity, money, recognition, and from fans. But Mikita maintained the pair did not feud personally. A more important issue was the fact that Blackhawks could not win another championship despite having such quality players. The team as a whole was seen as choking.

Injuries Plague the Last Decade of His Career

While Mikita again scored 97 points in 1968-69, he finished fourth in the league in scoring behind **Phil Esposito**, Howe, and Hull. Mikita suffered a severe back injury in 1969 and had to wear a back brace for much of the rest of his career. A few years later, Mikita suffered a bad head injury and had a suspension helmet specially designed for him by an engineer. This led to his involvement in the helmet manufacturing business. Mikita correctly predicted that the NHL would someday make helmets mandatory, though it was only after a player, Bill Masterson, was killed in a game.

Though Mikita was slowed by his injuries, he remained a consistent scorer and team leader during a tumultuous time. A rival to the NHL, the World Hockey Association (WHA), formed in the early 1970s and paid huge salaries to lure such stars as Hull, Pat Stapleton, and Ralph Backstrom away. Though Mikita also received offers, he was not tempted to jump to the WHA because of his family and his belief that money was not everything. Mikita was dedicated to the concept of being a Blackhawk for life.

Played for Canada

In 1972, Mikita played a marginal role in the Summit Series, which pitted Team Canada against the strong Soviet team in Russia. Though Mikita played in only two of the eight games in the series because Canada had so much depth at center, the trip had more meaning to Mikita who was finally able to play hockey in front of his birth family. After the Summit Series ended, the Canadian team played an exhibition against the Czechoslovakian national team in Prague. For the game, Mikita was named team captain, though he did not score in the game.

Returning to the Blackhawks, Mikita was frustrated by the team's struggles in the mid-1970s and considered retiring. Still, in 1973-74, he lead his team in scoring with 80 points (30 goals and 50 assists), but the team lost to Boston in the semi-finals of the Stanley Cup playoffs. The Blackhawks showed its appreciation for Mikita's long tenure by having a Mikita night at Black Hawks' Stadium in February 1974. Mikita did not want any gifts for himself as were usually given at such events. Instead, he wanted the funds to go into a scholarship fund at Illinois' Elmhurst College. He also gave back to the community in other ways. After being approached by the father of a deaf player in 1974, Mikita was the co-founder of the American Impaired Hearing Association and Stan Mikita Hockey School for the Hearing Impaired. These groups taught hockey to deaf and hearing impaired youngsters and started a deaf hockey movement in the United States and Canada. In 1976, Mikita's contributions to the game in the United States led his being awarded the Lester Patrick Trophy.

The last few years of Mikita's career were marked by a new attitude in the Blackhawks organization. By the 1977-78 season, the team was taken over by Bob Pulford as coach. Pulford turned them into division champions, and Mikita started to have fun again. Mikita was still a force on the Blackhawks, regularly winning face-offs which were always a strong point for him.

Retired from Professional Hockey

Chronic back problems ended Mikita's career on November 30, 1979, though he did not formally retire until April 14, 1980, at the end of the season. Over the course of his career, Mikita played in 1394 regular season games, scoring 541 goals and 926 assists. He also played in 155 playoff games, with 59 goals and 91 assists. In October 1980, the team retired his No. 21 jersey, the first Blackhawks jersey to be retired. After retiring, Mikita turned to another sport, and became a golf pro at the Kemper Lakes Golf Club outside of Chicago for seven years. He also continued to work with deaf hockey players, and later founded his own business. In 1983, Mikita was elected to the Hockey Hall of Fame. He later received an honorary doctorate from St. Catherine's Brock University.

Though Mikita was not the flashiest player, his steadfast play and loyalty to his team showed the true definition of his character. A Blackhawk to the end, Mikita contributed to the franchise's only Stanley Cup since the 1930s and lead his team by his example of tough, smart play. While goalies may not have liked seeing shots from the curved blade he helped popularize, this innovation changed the game, adding a new dimension to scoring. Mikita also brought the game to a new audience, the hearing impaired, with whom he identified after coming to Canada as a non-English speaking eight year old. Mikita's own evolution from a thug type scorer to Lady Byng winner was an example for hockey players to come. As Stan Fischler wrote in *The All-New Hockey's 100,* "it was hard to think of any one player who was able to combine all his skills and achieve such a level of proficiency as Mikita. He was the embodiment of the consummate hockey player."

CONTACT INFORMATION

Online: www.stanmikita.com.

SELECTED WRITINGS BY MIKITA:

I Play to Win, 1969.

FURTHER INFORMATION

Books

Beddoes, Richard, Stan Fischler, and Ira Gitler. *Hockey! The Story of the World's Fastest Sport.* New York: Macmillan, 1973.

Diamond, Dan, and Joseph Romain. *Hockey Hall of Fame: The Official History of the Game and Its Greatest Stars.* New York: Doubleday, 1988.

Fischler, Stan. *The All-New Hockey's 100: A Personal Ranking of the Best Players in Hockey History.* Toronto: McGraw-Hill Ryerson Ltd., 1988.

Fischler, Stan. *Golden Ice: The Greatest Teams in Hockey History.* New York: Wynwood Press, 1990.

Fischler, Stan and Shirley. *Fischlers' Hockey Encyclopedia.* New York: Thomas Y. Crowell Company, 1975.

Fischler, Stan, and Shirley Walton Fischler. *The Hockey Encyclopedia: The Complete Record of Professional Ice Hockey.* New York: Macmillan Publishing Company, 1983.

Hickok, Ralph. *A Who's Who of Sports Champions: Their Stories and Records.* Boston: Houghton Mifflin Company, 1995.

Kariher, Harry C. *Who's Who in Hockey.* New Rochelle: Arlington House, 1973.

Periodicals

"Beliveau, Mikita Honored," *The Record* (October 16, 1990): C4.

Cherner, Reid. "Check out Mikita in Wayne's movie," *The Record* (September 19, 1991): 2C.

Dupont, Kevin Paul. "Communicating hockey skills; US deaf players deliver message to a world forum," *Boston Globe* (March 1, 1995): 37.

Fachet, Robert. "Capitals Face 'Hungry' Mikita," *Washington Post* (March 22, 1978): C2.

Furlong, William Barry. "'A couple of hi-hos and here we go'," *Sports Illustrated* (April 30, 1962): 58.

Herzog, Brad. "Breaking the Silence," *Sports Illustrated* (August 24, 1992): 6.

"Hotheaded Hawk," *Newsweek* (February 4, 1963): 55.

Leggett, William. "The Black Hawks' No. 2 Tries Harder," *Sports Illustrated* (January 31, 1966): 35.

"Mikita gets health scare," *The Toronto Star* (January 8, 2000).

"Mikita's Number Retired," *New York Times* (October 20, 1980): C6.

Oberhelman, David. "Hockey star replays mentors by teaching Mikita camp for deaf finishes its 26th year," *Daily Herald* (June 24, 1999): 1.

Pruner, Larry. "Mikita: From Scrapper to Scorer," *Vancouver Sun* (January 17, 1998): E3.

Rappoport, Ken. "Hats off to Stan? Not on your life," Associated Press (February 23, 1997).

Rosen, Byron. "Mikita Ends 21 Years in the NHL, Becomes Golf Pro," *Washington Post* (April 15, 1980): D5.

Salter, David. "Bathgate Claims He's Father of Curved Stick," *Hockey News* (February 5, 1999): 4.

"Stan the Man recovering well," *Calgary Herald* (January 8, 2000): E3.

Wahl, Grant. "Catching up with … Blackhawks' center Stan Mikita," *Sports Illustrated* (May 26, 1997): 5.

Other

"Canada vs. Czechoslovakia: Sept. 29, 1972 at Prague: Team Canada 3-Czechoslovakia 3." 1972 Summit Series: A September to Remember. http://www.1972 summitseries.com/czechoslovakia.html (September 26, 2002).

"Hockey Legend." http://www.stanmikita.com/ hockeylegend.html (October 7, 2002).

"Induction Showcase." Legends of Hockey—Induction Showcase-Selection Committee. http://www.legends ofhockey.net/html/indselect.htm (September 26, 2002).

"Stan Mikita." http://www.hockeysandwich.com/mikita. html (September 26, 2002).

"Stan Mikita: Team Canada # 21." The Summit in 1972: Players Info. http://www22.brinkster.com/chidlovski/ h_playersca.asp?fname-Sta (September 26, 2002).

"#21 Stan Mikita." 1972 Summit Series: A September to Remember. http://www.1972summitseries.com/ mikita.html (September 26, 2002).

Sketch by A. Petruso

Reggie Miller
1965-

American basketball player

In the history of the National Basketball Association (NBA), there's never been a three-point shooter like Indiana Pacers guard Reggie Miller, undoubtedly the most persistent and productive three-point prodigy of all time. Miller was the first NBA player to sink 2,200 three-pointers and also holds the NBA record for most consecutive seasons with at least 100 three-pointers (13 and counting). What Miller is most remembered for, however, is his long list of post-season heroics. By the end of the 2001-2002 season, the five-time NBA All-Star had competed in 109 playoff games, averaging 23.5 points per game. Once, Miller scored twenty-five points in a single playoff quarter; another time, he scored eight points in the final 8.9 seconds of a playoff game for a victory. For all his effort, Miller has yet to win an NBA championship. To this end, Miller spends his free time coaching the team's younger players, hoping to mold the Pacers into a championship franchise.

Reggie Miller

Perfected Basketball Skills to Beat Sister

Reginald Wayne Miller was born with a hip defect on August 24, 1965, in Riverside, California, to Carrie and Saul Miller. "I came out with my legs and hips all contorted and twisted, like somebody had tried to tie me in a knot," Miller recalled in his book, *I Love Being the Enemy.* "The doctors said I might not ever walk."

To correct the problem, Miller endured leg braces his first four years and used a wheelchair or crutches to get around. The fourth of five children, Miller spent his days stranded indoors with his mom, yearning to get outside and play with his sports-minded siblings. Throughout the ordeal, his mother, a nurse, offered encouragement.

When the braces came off, Miller made quick use of his legs and began hanging out with his sister Cheryl. Their father, a computer systems analyst and former collegiate basketball star, taught them the game. Miller, however, couldn't compete against his taller, more-practiced sister. Whenever he drove to the basket for a lay-up, she'd reach up behind him and thwart his shot.

Miller's ambition in life became to beat his sister, and he began taking 500 to 700 shots a day. He stepped onto the family's backyard court and shot relentlessly until he mastered a ten-foot shot. Next, he drilled himself on twelve-footers. In time, Miller stood back in his mother's rose bushes, dropping in twenty-plus footers. Then, his sister's height didn't matter. Instead of dribbling to-

Chronology	
1965	Born on August 24 to Saul and Carrie Miller
1983	Graduates from Riverside Polytechnic High School
1983	Enters UCLA (University of California-Los Angeles)
1987	Taken by Indiana Pacers as 11th draft pick
1992	Marries Marita Lynn Stavrou on August 29, 1992
1995	Makes cameo appearance alongside Billy Crystal in *Forget Paris*
1998	Makes cameo appearance in Spike Lee's *He Got Game*
2001	Divorces wife
2001-02	Donates $1,000 for every three-pointer made to a September 11th relief fund, raising $206,000

Awards and Accomplishments	
1984-85	Led UCLA to the National Invitation Tournament (NIT) championship; named tournament MVP
1985-86	Averaged 25.9 points per game, fourth among college players nationwide
1986-87	Ended college career with 2,095 points while leading UCLA to the Pac-10 conference title
1987	Chosen by the Indiana Pacers as the 11th pick in the NBA draft
1987-88	Dropped in 61 three-pointers, an NBA rookie season record; named to NBA All-Rookie second team
1990	Named to NBA All-Star team
1990-91	Led NBA in free throws made (551)
1992-93	Scored 57 points in one game; led NBA with 167 three-pointers
1993-94	Scored his 10,000th career point to become the Pacers' leading scorer of all time; set NBA playoff record with five three-pointers in one quarter
1993-94	Named co-captain of the United States' Dream Team II; won gold medal with the U.S. team at the 1994 World Basketball Championships
1994	Set NBA playoff record for most three-pointers in one quarter (5)
1995	Named to the NBA All-Star team
1996	Starred on U.S. Olympic basketball team during Olympics in Atlanta; earned a gold medal
1996-97	Led NBA in three-pointers (229)
1998	Inducted into the UCLA Hall of Fame and named to NBA All-Star team
1998-99	Led NBA in free-throw percentage (.915) and free throws made (226)
2000	Named to NBA All-Star team
2000-01	Led NBA in free throws made (323)
2001-02	Led NBA in free-throw percentage (.911) and free throws made (296)
2002	Won NBA Community Assist Award for charity fund-raising
2002	Named USA Basketball Male Athlete of the Year

ward the basket, Miller retreated and nailed one of his far-flung jumpers. In this way, Miller developed his signature long-range jump shot, which he later made famous in the NBA.

Miller's favorite sport, however, was baseball, which he played his freshman year at Riverside Polytechnic High School. He wanted to be a star like his older brother, Darrell, who was on his way to becoming a catcher for the California Angels. Miller spent several long, lonely afternoons in the outfield, then decided he should try a more action-packed sport like basketball. The game suited him well, and he led Polytechnic to the state high school championship in both his junior and senior years.

Drafted by Indiana Pacers

In 1983, Miller joined the University of California-Los Angeles (UCLA) basketball team. His sophomore year, he led the Bruins to the 1985 National Invitation Tournament (NIT) championship and was named tournament MVP for nailing nearly 60 percent of his shots.

His junior year, Miller averaged 25.9 points per game, fourth-highest in the nation. His senior year, Miller led UCLA to the Pac-10 Conference title. When he graduated in 1987, he was the school's second-leading all-time scorer (2,095 points) behind **Kareem Abdul-Jabbar**.

Miller was drafted by the Indiana Pacers in the 1987 NBA draft. During his first year in the pros, Miller dropped in sixty-one three-pointers, breaking **Larry Bird**'s rookie record. By 1989-90, his third season, Miller averaged 24.6 points per game, becoming the Pacers' leading scorer. He also made his first All-Star game appearance. In 1992-93, Miller led the NBA in three-pointers (167) and also scored a career-high fifty-seven points in one game.

Known for 'Trash-Talking' on Court

Besides shooting baskets, Miller is known for shooting off his mouth. Miller spends his games chattering at his opponents, hoping to get inside their heads and distract them from the game. Miller's on-court antics, such as making a "choke" sign around his neck when the other team can't perform, regularly make the sports highlights.

Pacers president Donnie Walsh understands that the talking helps Miller, scrawny by NBA standards, compete in the league. As Walsh noted in a Knight Ridder/Tribune News Service article, "You see him on the court and he has to be like that with his body type (6 feet 7 inches and about 180 pounds) or he'd be the biggest target who ever came into the NBA. He can't fight back physically. It's his way of dealing with the situation, psyching himself. If he did not have that attitude, he wouldn't survive."

In his adopted hometown of Indianapolis, Miller's presence is felt outside the basketball arena. He visits local schools to promote reading and started the Reggie Miller Foundation, which raises money for fire victims and for a burn unit at the local children's hospital. Miller became interested in the charity after his house burned down in 1997. Following the 9/11 tragedy, Miller pledged $1,000 for every three-pointer he made, from preseason to postseason, to a New York City fire company that lost eight men in the World Trade Center tragedy. He raised $206,000.

Will be Remembered as Consistent Shooter

While Miller isn't the most polished player in the NBA, he's certainly one of the toughest and most consis-

Career Statistics

Yr	Team	GP	PTS	FG%	3P%	FT%	RPG	APG	SPG	BPG	TO	PF
1987-88	IND	82	822	.488	.355	.801	2.30	1.6	.65	.23	101	157
1988-89	IND	74	1181	.479	.402	.844	3.90	3.1	1.26	.39	143	170
1989-90	IND	82	2016	.514	.414	.868	3.60	3.8	1.34	.22	222	175
1990-91	IND	82	1855	.512	.348	.918	3.40	4.0	1.33	.16	163	165
1991-92	IND	82	1695	.501	.378	.858	3.90	3.8	1.28	.32	157	210
1992-93	IND	82	1736	.479	.399	.880	3.10	3.2	1.46	.32	145	182
1993-94	IND	79	1574	.503	.421	.908	2.70	3.1	1.51	.30	175	193
1994-95	IND	81	1588	.462	.415	.897	2.60	3.0	1.21	.20	151	157
1995-96	IND	76	1606	.473	.410	.863	2.80	3.3	1.01	.17	189	175
1996-97	IND	81	1751	.444	.427	.880	3.50	3.4	.93	.31	166	172
1997-98	IND	81	1578	.477	.429	.868	2.90	2.1	.96	.14	128	148
1998-99	IND	50	920	.438	.385	.915	2.70	2.2	.74	.18	76	101
1999-00	IND	81	1470	.448	.408	.919	3.00	2.3	1.05	.31	129	126
2000-01	IND	81	1527	.440	.366	.928	3.50	3.2	1.00	.19	133	162
2001-02	IND	79	1304	.453	.406	.911	2.80	3.2	1.11	.13	120	143

IND: Indiana Pacers.

tent shooters. During the eleven seasons between 1989-1990 and 1999-2000, Miller averaged between 18.1 points and 24.6 points per game.

Because Miller has consistently put up points throughout his career, he entered the 2002-2003 season tied for 17th place for most career points (22,623) in the NBA. At the start of the season, Miller was sweating it out with players a decade younger, yet he continued to make a difference and electrify fans with his outside shooting. The confident veteran has clearly become one of the game's most well-liked figures—his jersey, after all, sells in the top 10. A player can't get much more popular than that.

CONTACT INFORMATION

Address: c/o Indiana Pacers, 125 S. Pennsylvania St., Indianapolis, IN 46204. Fax: (317) 917-2599. Phone: (317) 917-2500. Email: PacersInsider@Pacers.com. Online: http://www.nba.com/pacers/news/fan_mail.html.

SELECTED WRITINGS BY MILLER:

(With Gene Wojciechowski) *I Love Being the Enemy: A Season on the Court with the NBA's Best Shooter and Sharpest Tongue,* Simon & Schuster, 1995.

FURTHER INFORMATION

Books

Cox, Ted. *Reggie Miller: Basketball Sharpshooter: A Season on the Court with the NBA's Best Shooter and Sharpest Tongue,* Chicago: Children's Press, 1995.

Miller, Reggie, with Gene Wojciechowski. *I Love Being the Enemy: A Season on the Court with the NBA's Best Shooter and Sharpest Tongue.* New York: Simon & Schuster, 1995.

Rappoport, Ken. *Guts and Glory: Making it in the NBA.* New York: Walker and Company, 1997.

Periodicals

Horrow, Ellen J. "Sports Was Game to Give." *USA Today* (September 10, 2002).

"Reggie Miller's Place in NBA History." *Indianapolis Star* (October 27, 2002).

Smith, Sam. "Taking a Fresh Look at Reggie Miller." Knight Ridder/Tribune News Service (January 21, 2002).

Other

"Reggie Miller." USA Basketball. http://www.usabasketball.com/biosmen/reggie_miller_bio.html (January 3, 2003).

"Reggie Miller Bio." NBA.com. http://www.nba.com/playerfile/reggie_miller/bio.html (December 20, 2002).

"Reggie Miller Player Info." NBA.com. http://www.nba.com/playerfile/reggie_miller/ (January 1, 2003).

"Reggie Miller Printable Stats." NBA.com. http://www.nba.com/playerfile/reggie_miller/printable_player_files.html (December 20, 2002).

Sketch by Lisa Frick

Shannon Miller
1977-

American gymnast

Shannon Miller is the most decorated American gymnast. Over the course of her thirteen-year career as a

Shannon Miller

Chronology

1977	Born March 10, 1977 in Rolla, Missouri
1977	Moves with family to Edmond, Oklahoma
1977	Wears braces to straighten legs
1981	Begins ballet lessons
1982	Begins gymnastics lessons
1984	Passes United States Association of Independent Gymnastics Clubs tests
1985	Travels to Houston to Bela Karolyi's gymnastics camp
1986	Travels to Soviet Union for gymnastics camp
1986	Begins training with Steve Nunno
1988	Begins competing internationally
1989	Wins first place for uneven bars and third place for all-around at Junior National Championships
1990	Begins competing at senior level
1992	Wins five medals at Olympic Games
1993-94	Wins all-around gold at World Championships
1994	Graduated with honors from Edmond North High School
1995	Begins college at the University of Oklahoma
1996	Wins team and individual gold at the Olympic Games
1998	Writes motivational book
1999	Marries Chris Phillips
2000	Fails to make U.S. Olympic team
2001	Retires from gymnastics
2002	Works as a gymnastics instructor and motivational speaker

gymnast, Miller won fifty-nine international medals and forty-nine national medals. Over half of these medals were gold. She competed in two Olympics, in 1992 and 1996, and won a total of seven Olympic medals—two gold, two silver, and three bronze. She was a member of the "Magnificent Seven" women's gymnastics team that won the first team gold in gymnastics for the United States in 1996. Miller is also the only American to win the World Championships for two consecutive years, in 1993 and 1994. Miller retired from gymnastics in 2001 and has become an author and a motivational speaker.

An Energetic Child

Shannon Lee Miller was born on March 10, 1977 in Rolla, Missouri. She was the second of three children born to Ron Miller, a college physics professor, and Claudia Miller, a bank executive. When Miller was four months old, her family moved to Edmond, Oklahoma where her father accepted a job at the University of Central Oklahoma. Around the same time Miller's pediatrician noticed a problem with the development of her legs - they seemed to be turning in rather than growing straight. To correct the problem, an orthopedic surgeon recommended that Miller wear leg braces for a year. Her parents and doctors thought that this problem might delay her learning how to crawl and walk, but Miller developed normally.

As a young child Miller looked up to her older sister, Tessa, and wanted to do everything that she did. At age four Miller started taking ballet lessons because her sister had. Within a year both girls had become bored with dancing and they set their sights on gymnastics. In 1982 they asked for a trampoline for Christmas. Their parents reluctantly bought them one, and the girls were thrilled. Their parents, however, were frightened by some of the flips the girls were doing. They suggested that the girls take gymnastics lessons so that they would not hurt themselves on the trampoline at home. The sisters started taking lessons once a week. The instructor, Jerry Clavier, noticed potential in the girls and asked them to come for lessons one hour a day, five days a week. Older sister, Tessa, was not interested in the extra commitment and she decided to take art lessons instead. However, Shannon was up to the challenge.

Miller steadily increased her time at the gym and she progressed through the higher levels of gymnastics classes, despite her young age and small size. By the time she was seven years old, Coach Clavier had her preparing for the United States Association of Independent Gymnastics Clubs (USAIGC) testing program. Miller and five other girls from the gym passed the rigorous tests. As a reward, the team traveled to Houston to attend a training camp held by the legendary gymnastics coach, **Bela Karolyi**. When Miller was barely nine years old she had an opportunity to travel with an American and Canadian delegation to the Soviet Union for a gymnastics camp. Miller was often frustrated by her inability to complete the difficult tasks set forth by the Soviet coaches, but at the same time she was impressed by the skills of their gymnasts and she was determined to became as good as they were.

Awards and Accomplishments

1989	First place uneven bars and third place all-around, Junior National Championships
1990	First place all-around, vault, balance beam, and floor exercise, and second place uneven bars, Catania Cup
1991	First place balance beam and third place vault, United States Gymnastics Championships
1991	Second place team and uneven bars, World Gymnastics Championships
1992	First place all-around, United States Olympic Trials
1992	Second place all-around and balance beam, third place team, uneven bars, and floor exercise, Olympic Games
1992	Named Oklahoma Ambassador of Goodwill
1992	Named Edmond Citizen of the Year
1992	First female recipient of the Steve Reeves Award by the New York Downtown Athletic Club
1992	Received Jim Thorpe Award by the Oklahoma Amateur Athletic Union
1992	James E. Sullivan Award nominee by the Amateur Athletic Union
1993	First place team, all-around, vault, balance beam, and floor exercise, and second place uneven bars, United States Olympic Festival
1993	First place all-around, vault, uneven bars, and floor exercise, McDonald's American Cup
1993	First place all-around, uneven bars, and floor exercise, World Gymnastics Championships
1993	James E. Sullivan Award nominee by the Amateur Athletic Union
1993	Received Governor's Youth Award by the State of Oklahoma
1993	Named Female Athlete of the Year by the National March of Dimes
1993	Received Presidential medallion by USA Gymnastics
1994	First place all-around and balance beam, World Gymnastics Championships
1994	First place balance beam and floor exercise, second place all-around, vault and uneven bars, Goodwill Games
1994	James E. Sullivan Award nominee by the Amateur Athletic Union
1994	Received Dial Award for National High School Athlete/Scholar
1994	Named Athlete of the Year by the USA Gymnastics Congress
1994	Received Henry P. Iba Citizen Athlete Award
1994	Team Xerox Olympian
1994	Received Master of Sport Award
1994	Received Jim Thorpe Award by the Oklahoma Amateur Athletic Union
1995	James E. Sullivan Award nominee by the Amateur Athletic Union
1996	First place team and balance beam, Olympic Games
1996	James E. Sullivan Award nominee by the Amateur Athletic Union
1997	Co-Grand Marshal of the Rose Bowl Parade with Carl Lewis
1997	First place all-around, second place team, World University Games
2000	First place vault, Mississauga Gymnastics Challenge
2000	Second place uneven bars, John Hancock United States Gymnastics Championships
2002	Inducted into the Oklahoma Sports Hall of Fame

Where Is She Now?

Although Miller retired from gymnastics in 2001, she still remains involved in the sport. She works with children of all ages at summer gymnastics camps and also teaches specialized balance beam clinics. She has toured in exhibition performances and has served as a television sports analyst for gymnastics competitions. Miller also travels extensively as a motivational speaker, lecturing about how to set goals in life and how to overcome obstacles. In 1998 she also wrote a book with Nancy Ann Richardson called *Winning Every Day: Gold Medal Advice for a Happy, Healthy Life!* Miller is also finishing her Bachelor's degree in marketing and entrepreneurship. Additionally, she dedicates considerable time to charity work, particularly as a spokesperson for the Children's Miracle Network and the Special Olympics, as well as for muscular dystrophy, Alzheimer's disease, Drug Free Youth, the Make-A-Wish Foundation, and the Pediatric AIDS Foundation.

frustrated by how easily Miller cried when she was not performing her best, but he also recognized that she was extremely talented and dedicated. "The most important characteristic that she has is her work ethic," Nunno told Krista Quiner in *Shannon Miller America's Most Decorated Gymnast*. "I mean, she is just a meticulous worker, that everything that she does, she does to perfection and she does over and over and over to get it prefect without any qualms about it."

At the age of ten Miller started competing in meets and only a year later she was winning medals. In 1988 she finished second in the all-around and third in the balance beam at the Junior Pan American Games in Ponce, Puerto Rico. A year later she finished sixth in the all-around competition at the International Junior Gymnastics Competition in Yokohama, Japan. That same year she won first place for the uneven bars and third place for the all-around competition at the United States Olympic Festival held in Oklahoma City, Oklahoma.

In 1990 Miller qualified for the senior United States National Team at the age of only thirteen. In her first United States Gymnastics Championship she finished eighth in the all-around. In 1991 she was part of the United States team that competed in the World Gymnastics Championships in Indianapolis, Indiana. She finished fourth in the all-around, while teammate Kim Zmeskal became the first American to win an all-around world championship. Miller also helped the United States win a silver medal for the team competition and she tied for second place on the uneven bars.

Olympic Champion

Miller's accomplishments as a gymnast are even more amazing given the numerous injuries she has battled throughout her career. In 1992 when she was preparing for the Olympics, Miller dislocated her elbow. She underwent surgery and returned to competition within a month. She finished first in the all-around competition at the Olympic trials. At the 1992 Olympic Games in Barcelona, Spain, Miller captured five medals. She won a bronze medal for the team competition, un-

Competitive Spirit

When Miller returned to Oklahoma she realized that she would have to change coaches in order to compete against the elite gymnasts. She started training with Steve Nunno, who had also been part of the delegation that traveled to the Soviet Union, at his Dynamo Gymnastics program in Norman, Oklahoma. Nunno was

even bars, and floor exercise, and a silver medal for the balance beam and the uneven bars. During much of her early competitions Miller was in the shadow of America's best gymnast, Kim Zmeskal. The 1992 Olympics, however, were a turning point for Miller. She finished second in the all-around competition, while Zmeskal only finished tenth because of a fall on the uneven bars. It was finally Shannon's time for the spotlight. Miller had the best finish for an American woman gymnast in a non-boycotted Olympics. Although American **Mary Lou Retton** won gold for the all-around in 1984, the Soviets did not participate in those games and they were usually the toughest competition.

Miller continued to dominate women's gymnastics after the Olympics. In 1993 she won the United States championships for the all-around, uneven bars, and floor exercise. She also won gold medals for the all-around, uneven bars, and floor exercise and the World Gymnastics Championships. She became only the second American to become a World Champion. In 1994 Miller repeated her gold medal for the all-around and also won a gold for the balance beam at the World Championships. She became the only American to win consecutive World Championships.

In 1995 Miller was eighteen years old and she was already the most decorated American gymnast. She faced a difficult decision of whether to retire from gymnastics or continue training for the next Olympics. She had graduated from Edmond North High School in 1994 and she was attending college at the University of Oklahoma. She not only had trouble finding the motivation to train, but she also had to adjust to her more mature body. She also had more injuries to overcome, particularly an ankle injury that hampered her performance at the World Championships.

Member of the "Magnificent Seven"

Miller decided to stick with gymnastics for another try at the Olympics. She won first place in the all-around at the United States National Championships, but she injured her wrist in the competition. She had to sit out of the Olympic trials, but her scores at the national championships were enough to earn her a spot on the Olympic team. The Olympic team consisted of Miller, Amanda Borden, Amy Chow, **Dominique Dawes**, Dominique Moceanu, Jaycie Phelps, and **Kerri Strug**. They were nicknamed the "Magnificent Seven" because they were the first American women's team that stood a real chance of capturing the team gold medal for the first time in history. The team lived up to this expectation and won the team gold in dramatic fashion. Miller also became the first American gymnast to win a gold medal for the balance beam, bringing her total number of Olympic medals to seven.

Miller competed occasionally after the 1996 Olympics. In 1997 she won first place in the all-around

at the World University Games. She then took a few years off from competitive gymnastics to focus on her education and her personal life. In 1999 she married Chris Phillips, an ophthalmology student from Oklahoma. In 2000 Miller tried to make a comeback in gymnastics to compete at the 2000 Olympics at the age of 23. She finished second on the uneven bars at the United States Gymnastics Championships. However, she did not qualify for the Olympic team. Miller officially retired from the sport in December of 2001. She remains the most accomplished American gymnast of all time with seven Olympic medals, eight World Championships medals, and numerous other national and international medals. Even more surprisingly, Miller excelled in her sport while also earning an "A" average in school and maintaining a healthy and balanced family life.

CONTACT INFORMATION

Address: Shade Global, 250 West 57th Street, New York, New York 10019. Phone: (212) 307-5128.

SELECTED WRITINGS BY MILLER:

(With Nancy Ann Richardson) *Winning Every Day: Gold Medal Advice for a Happy, Healthy Life!*, Bantam Doubleday Dell, 1998.

FURTHER INFORMATION

Books

Cohen, Joel. *Superstars of Women's Gymnastics*. New York: Chelsea House Publishers, 1997.
Great Women in Sports. Detroit: Visible Ink Press, 1996.
Green, Septima. *Top 10 Women Gymnasts*. Berkeley Heights, NJ: Enslow Publishers, Inc., 1999.
Kleinbaum, Nancy H. *The Magnificent Seven*. New York: Bantam Books, 1996.
Miller, Claudia. *Shannon Miller, My Child, My Hero*. Norman, OK: University of Oklahoma Press, 1999.
Quiner, Krista. *Shannon Miller America's Most Decorated Gymnast*. NJ: Bradford Book Company, 1997.
Sports Stars, Series 1-4. U•X•L, 1194-1998.

Periodicals

Gillis, Stephanie. "Diary of a Champion." *Teen Magazine* (September 2000): 48.
Parrish, Paula. "Two of Magnificent Seven are Sydney Bound." Knight Ridder/Tribune News Service (August 20, 2000).
"Shannon Miller: All-Star Attitude." *Teen Magazine* (April 1993): 78-79.
"Shannon Miller & Chris Phillips." *People* (July 5, 1999): 80.

Starr, Mark. "Hands Together, Feet Apart: Not Bubbly, Just Incredibly Focused." *Newsweek* (June 10, 1996): 80.

Swift, E.M. "Growing Pains." *Sports Illustrated* (March 13, 1995): 40-41.

Other

Shannon Miller. http://shannonmiller.com (January 24, 2003).

"Shannon Miller." Distinguished Women of Past and Present. http://www.distinguishedwomen.com/biographies/millersh.html (January 24, 2003).

The Shannon Miller-Phillips Dedication Page. http://webinspiring.net/shannon/smaddy.htm (January 24, 2003).

USA Gymnastics Official Biography: Shannon Miller. http://www.usa-gymnastics.org/athletes/bios/m/smiller.html (January 14, 2003).

Sketch by Janet P. Stamatel

Billy Mills

Billy Mills
1938-

American track and field athlete

Lakota Sioux runner Billy Mills was responsible for one of the greatest upsets in Olympic history. A complete unknown in the track-and-field world, Mills outran a field of international track stars to win the gold medal in the 10,000-meter race in the 1964 Olympic Games in Tokyo. Mills's win was the first gold medal by any American in this event, and was a particular source of pride for Native Americans. Interestingly, the only other American ever to medal in the event was another Native American, Louis Tewanima, a Hopi Indian, who won silver in 1912.

"Live Your Life as a Warrior"

Born William Mervin Mills on the Pine Ridge Indian Reservation in South Dakota in 1938, Mills was one of eight children. The reservation, then as now, was one of the poorest districts in the United States, and residents often struggled with hunger, diabetes, alcoholism, and other health conditions. Mills's family was no exception. His mother, who was one-quarter Lakota Sioux, died when he was seven years old. His father, a boxer who was three-quarters Lakota, died when he was twelve. After being orphaned, Mills was sent to the Haskell Indian School in Lawrence, Kansas. This was a boarding school run by the Bureau of Indian Affairs.

At the school, Mills became involved in sports. His father had told him to live his life as a warrior. This meant combining physical and mental toughness with assuming responsibility for one's actions, being humble, and giving back to others. Mills wanted to be like his father, so he tried out for the boxing team, and he also played football. He was small and thin, 5 foot 2 inches tall and only 104 pounds, but he liked the discipline that football involved. He was not interested in track, and thought of it as a sport for sissies. However, he eventually tried running, and found that it involved a level of discipline, training, and mental focus as rigorous as that needed for football. In addition, his build was more suited to running. He soon became a top runner, and when he graduated from Haskell in 1958, he received a full athletic scholarship to the University of Kansas.

At Kansas, Mills had little contact with his long-scattered siblings, and he was lonely and isolated. According to a writer in *Contemporary Heroes and Heroines* Mills later said that this loneliness fueled his running: "I was running from rejection, from being orphaned. . . . The Indians called me mixed blood. The white world called me Indian. I was running in search of my identity. I was running to find Billy." In his first 10,000-meter race, Mills set a conference record. In 1958 and 1959 he was All-American in cross country; in 1960 he won the individual title in the Big Eight Conference cross-country tournament; and in 1961 he was conference champion in the 2-mile. The Kansas team won the NCAA outdoor national championships in 1959 and 1960.

Chronology

1938	Born June 30, on the Pine Ridge Indian Reservation, South Dakota
1958-62	Attends University of Kansas in Lawrence; becomes a top runner
1958-59	All-American in cross-country; Kansas team wins NCAA outdoor national championships
1960	Winner, individual title in Big Eight Conference cross-country tournament
1960	Attempts to qualify for Olympics, but does not make the team
1961	Conference champion, 2-mile race
1962	Marries his college sweetheart, Pat
1962	Joins Marine Corps
1964	Makes Olympic team, but his achievements are largely ignored
1964	Wins Olympic gold medal in Olympics, in a startling upset; sets new Olympic record
1965	Sets world record in 6-mile run with a time of 27:11.6; sets American records in the 10,000 meters and the 3-mile run
1968	Attends Olympic trials and beats the "winner" by 13 seconds, but is disqualified because of application form errors
1983	*Running Brave*, a film version of Mills's life, is released
1984	Inducted into U.S. Olympic Hall of Fame
1980s-present	Works as motivational speaker, author, and philanthropist
1997	Inducted into Sports Humanitarian Hall of Fame
1999	Inducted into Distance Running Hall of Fame

Awards and Accomplishments

1958-59	All-American in cross-country; Kansas team wins NCAA outdoor national championships
1960	Winner, individual title in Big Eight Conference cross-country tournament
1961	Big Eight Conference champion, 2-mile race
1964	Wins Olympic gold medal in Olympics, in a startling upset; sets new Olympic record
1965	Sets world record in 6-mile run with a time of 27:11.6; sets American records in the 10,000 meters and the 3-mile run
1984	Inducted into U.S. Olympic Hall of Fame
1997	Inducted into Sports Humanitarian Hall of Fame
1999	Inducted into Distance Running Hall of Fame

Despite these wins, Mills did not receive any recognition. He did not qualify for the 1960 Olympics, and he lost his motivation, running poorly, sometimes dropping out of races.

At the end of his senior year, in 1962, Mills married his college girlfriend, Pat. At the same time, he became an officer in the U.S. Marine Corps, based at Camp Pendleton, north of San Diego. In the Marines, his running was encouraged, and he increased his training from 40 miles a week to 100 miles a week. With this grueling regimen, he won the inter-service 10,000-meter race in Germany. His time was 30.08. He also ran 4:08 in the mile, a personal record.

In 1964, Mills went to the Olympic Trials, finishing second, behind Gerry Lindgren. His time, 29:10.4, was the best he had ever run in the event, but it was almost a minute slower than that of the other runners who qualified for the event. Although Mills made the Olympic team, no one paid much attention to him.

"My Indianness Kept Me Striving"

Later that year, Mills went to Tokyo, Japan to compete. No one in the track world had heard of this Native American Marine, and he was not considered as competition by any of the world-famous runners there. In addition, no American athlete had ever won a distance race in the Olympics. Even the American coach did not expect Mills to win, and was not sure if any American athletes would even place in the event. Ironically, Mills was actually ranked eighth in the world at the time, an immense achievement that should have forewarned coaches and competitors. In an interview with *Runner's World*, Mills said that he was overlooked as a runner because of the prejudices of his time: "I was caught, as a Native American, in that complexity of how society deals with someone who's different. Because of that, no coach, trainer, or anyone in the media knew that I went to the Olympic Games ranked eighth in the world."

Indeed, the U.S. Olympic Committee initially refused to provide Mills with shoes for the race; according to an article on the Sports Humanitarian Web page, one official said, "We only have enough for those we expect to do well." Mills borrowed shoes and got ready for the race.

Of all the thirty-six runners in the event, Australia's Ron Clarke was expected to win. Tunisian Mohamed Gammoudi was expected to place second, and any of the other runners could have taken the bronze medal. Clarke and Gammoudi were the only runners who were believed capable of winning.

Mills, who believed in the value of positive mental imagery, ignored these predictions. During his training, he had visualized a young Native American runner winning the 10,000 meters, over and over again, erasing any images of loss.

As the runners lined up on the wet track, Mills continued to focus on winning. After the starting gun sounded, Clarke and Gammoudi took first and second place, with the other runners behind them in a mixed pack. Mills stayed up with the rest of the pack, and as the group entered the last 300 yards, Mills took the lead. Gammoudi jostled Clarke, and Clarke elbowed Mills, forcing him to stumble and lose 20 yards.

The crowd watched, cheering, as Clarke and Gammoudi continued in the lead, as predicted.

According to **Bud Greenspan** in *100 Greatest Moments in Olympic History,* Mills decided he still had a chance to win. "So I started driving. They were fifteen yards in front of me, but it seemed like fifty yards. Then I kept telling myself, 'I can win . . . I can win . . . I can win . . .' Mills surged forward, passing Gammoudi and Clarke, and the crowd fell silent, shocked at this unexpected comeback.

Running Brave

Billy Mills's life story was dramatized in the 1983 film *Running Brave.* Starring Robby Benson as Mills, the movie is a powerful statement not only about Mills's Olympic achievement, but also the effects of racism on Native Americans. In *CultureDose.com,* John Nesbit wrote, "There really is a special feeling, a sense of pride that occurs within Native Americans when one of their own succeeds in the white world, and *Running Brave* captures this well."

The film opens at a high school track meet, where Mills's performance impresses white University of Kansas coach Bill Easton. When Mills accepts the track scholarship Easton offers, he finds himself isolated and uprooted on the predominantly white campus. Mills relies on his own inner sense of pride and the will to achieve to get through this tough time.

As Mills moves on to compete and win in the Olympic 10,000 meters, the film accurately depicts the race and its outcome; as Nesbit wrote, "even the incredible final finish mirrors archive footage."

Where Is He Now?

In addition to his own speaking work, Mills is also the national spokesperson for Running Strong for American Indian Youth, a charitable organization that helps poor Native American people meet their needs for food, health care, clothing, water, and shelter, and teaches them how they can become self-sufficient and take pride in their heritage. In addition, the organization sponsors young Native American runners and encourages them to succeed. On the Running Strong for American Indian Youth Web page, an article about Mills explained, "In Lakota culture, someone who has achieved success would have a 'giveaway' to thank the support system of family and friends who helped him achieve his goal. Billy's work with Running Strong is his way of giving something back to American Indian people." In *People,* a reporter quoted Mills as saying, "I've designed my life so that I can continue to give."

In addition to his work as a speaker, Mills teamed up with writer Nicholas Sparks to write *Wokini: A Lakota Journey to Happiness and Understanding.* In the book, which is a parable of a young man's spiritual journey, a young man is given a mysterious scroll by his father after his sister dies. Through the teachings in the scroll, he learns to move through his grief and pain and find happiness and spiritual insight. In *Booklist,* reviewer Pat Monaghan called it "an optimistic book likely to appeal widely." By 2002, the book had gone through four printings.

Mills finished three yards ahead of Gammoudi, who took second place, with a time of 28:24.4, a new Olympic record, forty-six seconds better than his best time to date. A writer in *Contemporary Heroes and Heroines* quoted Mills as saying later, "My Indianness kept me striving to take first and not settle for less in the last yards of the Olympic race. I thought of how our great chiefs kept on fighting when all the odds were against them as they were against me. I couldn't let my people down."

After the race, according to Mark Bloom in *Runner's World,* reporters asked Clarke if he had been worried about Mills beating him. Clarke replied, "Worried about him? I never heard of him." And, according to an article about Mills on the Sports Humanitarian Web site, he was so little-known that an official approached Mills after the race and asked, "Who are you?"

Mills' win was voted the Associated Press "Upset of the Year" for 1964. That was the same year that African-American boxer Cassius Clay (who later changed his name to **Muhammad Ali**) beat **Sonny Liston** for the heavyweight title, an event often considered one of the biggest upsets of all time; the fact that Mill's win took precedence over Clay's shows the impact it had on sports reporters at the time.

Although Mills also ran the Olympic marathon, he finished in 14th place. He told a *Runner's World* writer that he thinks he had the potential to do well in that event, but that he did not do the right type of training. In addition, during the race, he did not drink enough water. Although he was in fourth place at mile 21 of the 26.2-mile race, he became dehydrated, and when he did drink, his specially concocted beverage tasted so bad that he couldn't swallow it. By mile 24.5 he was badly dehydrated, and hit what marathoners call "the wall," a state of exhaustion in which the athlete struggles to run at all, let alone with any speed.

Makata Taka Hela

Mills reacted modestly and with great dignity to all the media attention that was focused on him after his 10,000-meter win. He took a tour to more than fifty countries, emphasizing his drive to win and his pride in his Native American heritage. In an article in *Biography Resource Center,* Mills said, "I wanted to make a total effort, physically, mentally, and spiritually. Even if I lost, with this effort I believed that I would hold the greatest key to success."

In response, Mills's tribe, the Lakota, honored him with traditional gifts, made him a warrior, and gave him a Lakota name, Makata Taka Hela, which means "respects the earth" or "loves his country." He became a hero for Native American youth on his home reservation at Pine Ridge. Mills typically downplayed his own accomplishments, often saying that other Native American people were more talented than he was, and simply needed opportunity to achieve their goals.

After his Olympic win, Mills continued to train. He set a world record in the six-mile run in 1965, with a time of 27:11.6, and set American records in the 10,000-meter run and the 3-mile run. He also continued to serve in the Marines. At the time, the Vietnam War was at its height. Mills felt that he could not indulge himself in running for sport when his contemporaries were fighting and being killed. Although the Marines never sent him to Vietnam, he was deeply saddened by the deaths of men in his unit. He finished his Marine career as a captain, then worked for the Department of the Interior.

In 1968, Mills tried out for the Olympic team, but missed making the team because of a technical flaw on his application form. He still ran in the qualifying race, and beat the official "winner"—who did go to the Games—by thirteen seconds.

This experience left Mills bitter at the fact that red tape could keep him out of the Olympics. However, as

Billy Mills, left, crossing finish line

before, he moved on with his life instead of remaining discouraged. According to a writer in *Contemporary Heroes and Heroines* he said, "A man has a lot to do with deciding his own destiny. I can do one of two things—go through life bickering and complaining about the raw deal I got, or go back into competition to see what I can do."

Mills' Olympic win was the inspiration for a 1983 movie, *Running Brave,* which Mills wrote with his wife Pat. The film, starring Robby Benson as Mills, was produced by Englander Productions.

In 1984, Mills was inducted into the U.S. Olympic Hall of Fame. He told Jay Weiner in the Minneapolis *Star Tribune,* "The first thing I think of when I think Olympics is that it shows how there can be unity through diversity. It's such a powerful thing."

Mills eventually moved to Sacramento, California, with his wife, Pat, and their three daughters, Christy, Lisa, and Billie JoAnne. He became a successful insurance salesperson, and then became a motivational speaker, running his own organization, the Billy Mills Speakers Bureau. Through this bureau, he works with many charities, such as the Christian Relief Services and the Native American Sports Council.

In addition to his charitable work, Mills has become a quiet advocate for political change. He sees the reservation system under which many Native Americans live as a form of apartheid, and believes that the way Native Americans elect senators and congressional representatives should be reorganized in order to give them fair representation.

However, Mills was opposed to an idea presented by some Native American sports advocates. They suggested that Native Americans have their own sports team that would compete as an independent nation at the Olympics. Mills told Weiner, "As long as we benefit from being citizens of the United States we should compete for the U.S. team."

In 1997, Mills was made a member of the Sports Humanitarian Hall of Fame, and in 1999, Mills was inducted into the National Distance Running Hall of Fame in Utica, New York. Of his induction, he told a *Runner's World* reporter, "I feel very fortunate and very thrilled, because I'm aware of the people who are in there already."

CONTACT INFORMATION

Address: Billy Mills Speakers Bureau, 7760 Winding Way, Suite 722, Fair Oaks, CA 95628 . Phone: (916) 965-5738.

SELECTED WRITINGS BY MILLS:

(With Nicholas Sparks), *Wokini: A Lakota Journey to Happiness and Self-Understanding,* Crown, 1994.

FURTHER INFORMATION

Books

"Billy Mills." *Contemporary Heroes and Heroines, Book III,* edited by Terrie M. Rooney. Detroit: Gale Group, 1998.

"Billy Mills." *Encyclopedia of World Biography, Supplement, Volume 19.* Detroit: Gale Group, 1999.

"Billy Mills." *Notable Native Americans.* Detroit: Gale Group, 1995.

Greenspan, Bud. *100 Greatest Moments in Olympic History.* General Publishing Group, 1995.

Periodicals

"Billy Mills." *People* (July 15, 1996): 84.

Bloom, Mark. "The Greatest Upset." *Runner's World* (August, 1991): 22.

Monaghan, Pat. "Wokini: A Lakota Journey to Happiness and Self-Understanding." *Booklist* (April 1, 1994): 1407.

Weiner, Jay. "Where Are They Now? After Making His Mark in '64, He's Been Quiet Indian Leader." *Star Tribune* (Minneapolis, MN) (August 2, 1996): 2S.

Other

"Billy Mills." *Christian Relief.* http://www.christian relief.org/ (November 15, 2002).

"Billy Mills." *Running Strong for American Indian Youth.* http://indianyouth.org/billy.html (November 19, 2002).

"Billy Mills." *World Sports Humanitarian Hall of Fame.* http://www.sportshumanitarian.com/ (November 15, 2002).

"Billy Mills' Story Inspires." *Canku Ota (Many Paths)* (November 2, 2002). http://www.turtletrack.org/ (November 15, 2002).

Distance Running Hall of Fame. http://www.distance running.com/ (November 19, 2002).

Gambaccini, Peter. "A Brief Chat with Billy Mills." *Runner's World* (June 11, 1999), http://www.runners world.com/dailynew/archives/1999/June/990611. html (November 15, 2002).

"Running Brave." *CultureDose.com.* http://www. culturedose.com/ (November 19, 2002).

Sketch by Kelly Winters

Fu Mingxia
1978-

Chinese diver

Chinese diver Fu Mingxia had international success at such a young age that she prompted world diving

Fu Mingxia

officials to create rules requiring divers to be fourteen before they could appear in major competitions. At her first Olympic appearance in 1992, she was only thirteen, but was credited with advancing the difficulty of dives being performed in competitions. Mingxia went on to become the first female diver to win gold medals at three consecutive Olympics, where she has competed in ten-meter platform, three-meter springboard, and three-meter synchronized diving events. Known as the Queen of Diving in her homeland, her fans have watched her change from a slim, giggling child into a sophisticated, womanly figure. Following the 1996 Olympics, she suffered from burnout and temporarily left the sport to begin studying economics, but returned in time to compete in the 2000 Olympics. Now retired from diving, Mingxia has become wealthy appearing in advertisements. She is also serving on China's 2008 Olympic Bid Committee.

Mingxia was born in 1978 in Wuhan, Hubei province, China. She was not considered flexible enough for gymnastics, which she had begun learning as a pre-schooler, and was introduced to diving at age seven. Her training began before she knew how to swim, causing her coach to tie a rope around her waist so that she could be pulled from the water. Her father would teach her how to swim after work. Mingxia was sent away to diving school in Beijing at age nine. After the move she rarely saw her parents, a factory worker and an accountant. The training program was extremely rigorous. Diving students practiced up to ten hours per day,

seven days a week, while also going to school. Mingxia was very scared when first learning platform diving, but the rules forbid her from climbing back down the steps.

Despite Mingxia's initial fears, she soon developed exceptional skills. In 1990 she began diving in international competitions. That year she won the Alamo Invitational at age eleven; in the Goodwill Games, she won a gold medal in platform diving. When she placed third in the 1990 Asian Games, Mingxia revised her routines and came back even stronger. In 1991 she became the youngest woman to win gold at the World Championships and youngest world champion ever in aquatic sports. This led diving's international governing body to change their regulations, requiring divers to be fourteen to compete in the World Cup, World Championships, and Olympics. Thus, Mingxia was prohibited from competing in the 1991 World Cup, but a loophole allowed her to dive in the 1992 Olympics in Barcelona.

A slim thirteen-year-old who was known to brush the platform with her closely-cut hair, Mingxia performed more difficult dives than were normally seen when she appeared at the 1992 Olympics. Winning gold in the ten-meter event, she became the youngest platform diver to win an Olympic gold medal. Her future successes, however, would be hard won. The years of training between Barcelona and the 1996 games in Atlanta, Georgia were very difficult for Mingxia. She had considerable trouble keeping slim, a great advantage in diving, after she was fifteen and remembers vividly feeling hungry all the time. Mingxia won a gold medal at the 1994 World Championships, but she was unhappy. She says she often cried while training for Atlanta and that music was one thing that soothed her.

Mingxia's troubles were not evident when she won two gold medals in Atlanta, in the platform and three-meter events. At the previous Olympics she had been five-feet tall and ninety-eight pounds; now she was two inches taller and almost thirty pounds heavier. Although she was heavier, she was also stronger and incredibly consistent. In the competition, she was the only diver to receive more than sixty points on each of her dives. Her

Awards and Accomplishments	
1990	Won Alamo Invitational
1990	Gold medal in platform diving at the Goodwill Games
1991	Gold medal in platform diving at World Championships
1992	Gold medal in platform diving at Olympics
1994	Gold medal in platform diving at the World Championships
1996	Gold medals in platform and springboard diving at the Olympics
1996	Nominated for Women's Sports Foundation Sportswoman of the Year
1999	Gold medals in platform and springboard diving at the University Games
2000	Silver medal in springboard diving at World Cup
2000	Gold medal in springboard diving at Olympics

victories made her the first woman to win both events at one Olympics since Ingrid Kramer had done so in 1960. Along with Ziong Ni, who won gold in the men's springboard event, Mingxia led a dominant Chinese diving team. Their success was attributed in part to the fact that they practiced more than their rivals. However, Mingxia suffered from mental exhaustion after the Olympics, and at age nineteen received permission to retire from the Physical Culture and Sports Commission of China.

Amidst criticism that she had deserted her team, Mingxia began studying economics at Qinghua University in Beijing. She did not dive for two years, but came to practice with the university's diving team because she wondered if she could still dive and enjoy it. Finding her skills, if not fitness intact, she was able to follow a more limited training schedule, working half-days with weekends off. She proceeded to win two gold medals at the 1999 University Games and a silver in the springboard event at the 2000 FINA Diving World Cup.

At the 2000 Olympics in Sydney, Australia, Mingxia was just twenty-two years old. She now had long, streaked hair and was seen as rebelling in other small ways, such as appearing at interviews without a handler. When she won a gold medal in springboard diving she reached the same plateau as divers **Greg Louganis** and **Pat McCormick**, who were previously the only divers to hold four Olympic gold medals. At the same time, Mingxia became the first female diver to win gold at three consecutive Olympic games. Remarkably, she also won a silver medal competing in the new event of synchronized diving with partner Guo Jingjing.

Fu Mingxia retired in 2001, having cemented her status as China's diving queen and as a model of excellence for divers everywhere. Her exceptional grace, flexibility, and strength allowed her to execute the most difficult dives with seeming ease. Beginning with her gold-medal winning performance at the 1992 Olympics, she dominated women's diving for more than eight years. While her earliest experiences in the sport were frightening and lonely, she came to love diving and would return from retirement in order to satisfy herself

rather than others. Mingxia ended her career as one of the most successful divers ever.

FURTHER INFORMATION

Periodicals

"Fu Mingxia: Unretired, newly inspired, "big sister" may teach kids a lesson." *Time* (September 11, 2000): 78.

Montville, Leigh. "Fu's Gold." *Sports Illustrated* (August 12, 1996): 66.

Pucin, Diane. "Sydney 2000/Summer Olympic Games; Fu Makes a Splash in Record Books, Not Much in Pool." *Los Angeles Times* (September 29, 2000): U-4.

Yingzi, Tan. "Sports Stars Start Gold Rush." *China Daily* (January 7, 2002).

Other

Biography Resource Center Online. Gale Group, 2000.

Muzi News/Lateline News. http://news.beststar.com/ (July 31, 2002).

New Beijing Great Olympics. www.beijing-olympic.org/ "Meet Athletes" (January 16, 2003).

Sin-mi Hon, May. "Fu Mingxia applies to become an SAR student." Asia Africa Intelligence Wire (September 7, 2002).

Sketch by Paula Pyzik Scott

Dave Mirra
1974-

American BMX rider

American Dave Mirra is a dominant BMX freestyle rider who won a number of extreme sports competitions, winning at least thirteen medals at the X Games, the most of anybody in his sport to date. Nicknamed "Miracle Boy," Mirra has suffered a number of injuries but continues to ride.

Mirra was born April 4, 1974, in Syracuse, New York, and grew up in Chittenango, New York, outside the city. His father was a VCR and television repairman, while his mother was a surgical technician. Mirra began riding a bike when he was four. After witnessing his first BMX freestyle demonstration when he was ten, he began using his own bike to do tricks, turns, and flips in the air, often off a ramp.

Mirra soon became obsessed with the sport, and did not pay attention in school. Many kids were doing BMX

Dave Mirra

Chronology	
1974	Born on April 4 in Syracuse, New York
1987	Begins competing professionally in BMX stunt riding
1992	Given nickname of Miracle Boy
1993	Suffers accident that could have ended career—hit by drunk driver while crossing street
1995	Has spleen removed; moves to Greenville, North Carolina
1999	Signs endorsement deal with Acclaim Entertainment; founds the Dave Mirra Woodward Scholarship Fund
2001	Signs endorsement deal with DC Shoes
2002	Signs sponsorship deal with Bell Sports

at the time, making it a popular, if underground, phenomenon. Mirra told Kevin Gray of the *Morning Call,* "It became an addition. I didn't really choose stunt riding. It was just what I did." Mirra would show up at a local bike shop's ramp and do tricks other kids could not do. Lance Stonecipher, the co-owner of Bike Loft told Laura Lee of *New York Times,* "He came in here and could do all of these tricks that kids were seeing on video and magazines. Everybody was like, 'Who is this kid?'"

Began Competing

In 1987, when Mirra was only thirteen years old, he began competing and had a sponsor, Haro Bikes. It was already a career for the teen. Haro gave him a bike and paid for him to go to competitions. As ESPN2 started airing BMX stunt competitions on the air, the sport exploded in popularity, and Mirra was one of its best known young riders.

Mirra was given the nickname of Miracle Boy in 1992 because he did tricks that observers thought could not be pulled off as well as the ability to make the tricks look easy. Mirra invented moves like the half-hairspin tailwhip, which has not been repeated. Describing what it feels like to ride in vert (tricks done on a half pipe), one of the BMX events Mirra competed in, Steven Daly wrote in *Rolling Stone,* "Take the most cursory of spins on a BMX bike and you'll discover just how sensitive the handlebars are; look directly down one of those

eleven-foot half-pipes and your stomach will do a half-barspin tailwhip. To even think about hurling yourself off the edge with forty pounds of BMX between your legs brings home the spleen-shattering reality of Dave Mirra's chosen profession."

Suffered Injuries

In 1993 (some sources say 1994), Mirra suffered a serious injury when he was struck by a drunk driver as he was crossing a street in Syracuse. He was sent to the hospital with a dislocated shoulder, fractured skull, and blood clot on the brain. Mirra returned to the bike within six months of the accident, after doctors said he would not ride again.

Mirra also suffered injuries in his sport. In 1995, he was injured while doing a performance on the vert ramp, and had to have his spleen removed. That same year, he moved to Greenville, North Carolina. By the mid-1990s, Mirra was considered the best and most dominant rider in his sport, and contributed to making the sport popular. Such attention was unexpected by Mirra.

Advent of the X Games

BMX stunt riding had another high profile venue with the advent of the Summer X Games in 1996. These games, aired on ESPN, featured a number of extreme sports. At the 1996 games, Mirra won gold in street (doing stunts on an urban-like street course) and silver in vert (on the ramp). In 1997, he won golds in both street and vert. In 1998, he won three gold medals in vert, street, and vert doubles. That year, Mirra was named X-Games Male Athlete of the Year.

Mirra continued to do well in 1999. That year, he won gold in street at Summer X Games, first in vert at B3, gold in vert at Gravity Games, and the BS Series Year End title in vert. He was voted Freestyler of the Year by *BMX Plus Magazine.* That year, he also signed an endorsement deal with Acclaim Entertainment, to develop video games based on him. His Dave Mirra Freestyle BMX was a leading seller in 2000.

Mirra would sign a number of endorsement deals in this time period. In 2001, he signed three-year endorse-

Awards and Accomplishments

1996	At Summer X Games, won gold in street and silver in vert
1997	Won golds in street and vert at Summer X Games
1998	Won three gold medals at the X Games, in bicycle stunt vert, street, and vert doubles; named X-Games Male Athlete of the Year; won BS Series Year End Title in street and vert
1999	Won gold in street at Summer X Games; won first place in vert at B3; won gold in vert at Gravity Games; won BS Series Year End Title in Vert; voted Freestyler of the Year by *BMX Plus Magazine*
2000	Voted favorite rider by readers of *Ride and Snap BMX Magazine*; won gold at Japan X Games in vert; won gold in vert at Gravity Games; won gold in street and silver in vert at X Games
2001	Named ESPN Action Sports and Music BMX rider of the year; placed second at Vans Triple Crown of BMX; at B3 Event in Anaheim placed first in vert and park; at B3 Event in Louisville, Kentucky, placed first in park and 13th in vert; at UGP Roots Jam placed first in park
2002	At Gravity Games, placed first in park and second in vert; at EXPN Invitational, placed second in vert and tenth in park

ment deal with DC Shoes, and developed a signature line of shoes. In addition, he also had deals with Haro Bicycles, Fox Racing, Slim Jim, and Arnett Opticals. Mirra also appeared in television commercials for Burger King and AT&T. In 2000, Mirra appeared on an episode of *The Jersey* on the Disney Channel. By 2001, he was making $1 million a year. But Mirra did not forget his past. He sponsored scholarships to Woodward Camp where action sports are taught to kids.

In 2000, Mirra won gold in Japan X Games in vert, won gold in vert at the Gravity Games, and won gold in street and silver in vert at the X Games, but he sat out the Gravity Games in 2001 because of injuries. Mirra would do this as his situation warranted. He rebounded in 2002, placing first in park (stunts done on a skatepark or skatepark-like course) and second in vert at Gravity Games, and second in vert at the EXPN Invitational.

Mirra plans on riding as long as he can. He told Mokhshin Abidin of *New Straits Times*, "I don't call it training because it is something which I love doing, riding and gym work, I never really think about it. I just want to ride every day."

CONTACT INFORMATION

Online: http://www.expn.com/bmx/mirra.

FURTHER INFORMATION

Periodicals

Abidin, Mokhshin. "Legendary Mirra just loves doing it anyway." *New Straits Times* (February 2, 2002): 3.
"BMX Legend: Dave Mirra." *News Journal* (August 15, 2002): E9.

Business Wire (June 29, 1999).
Business Wire (October 2, 2000).
Business Wire (January 5, 2001).
Business Wire (February 13, 2001).
Business Wire (August 13, 2002).
Daly, Steven. "Dave Mirra Champion '99." *Rolling Stone* (June 11, 1999): 111.
"Gravity Games 2001—The Ones to Watch." *Providence Journal-Bulletin* (September 5, 2001): D9.
Gray, Kevin. "He and His Bike Fly, Spin, Twist, Sometimes Break." *Morning Call* (February 11, 1999): C10.
Hendrickson, Brian. "Recreation Focus: Cycling star and X-Games gold medalist Dave Mirra." *Morning Star* (May 3, 2001): 1C.
LaRue, William. "Mirra Is Pull for Gravity." *Post-Standard* (November 3, 2002): D2.
Lee, Laura. "Adventure Sports; Same Tricks, More Costly Bikes." *New York Times* (August 14, 2001): D4.
Smartschan. "BMX Star Mirra Shows His Sport at Shimerville." *Morning Call* (February 11, 2001): C4.
Thamel, Pete. "Real Life Action Figure." *Herald American* (August 12, 2001): C1.
"X Games close with Mirra tops." *Press-Enterprise* (June 29, 1998): C3.

Sketch by A. Petruso

Patty Moise
1961-

American race car driver

Patty Moise's racing career spanned fifteen years. The daughter of a stock car racer, Moise later married fellow racer Elton Sawyer in 1990. During her career she faced three major challenges. First, Moise had to prove that a woman could succeed in a sport dominated by men. Second, she had to prove herself on the track, not as a woman, but as a driver. Third, Moise had to convince sponsors to fund her racing career. On the first two counts, Moise came through with flying colors, but securing adequate and ongoing sponsorship was her nemesis that ultimately forced her into early retirement.

Woman Driver

Patty Moise was born in 1961 in Jacksonville, Florida. Her father, Milton, was a veteran stock car driver and avid racing fan. Moise followed in his footsteps. Although she was never big on sports, she loved speed and accumulated so many tickets and accidents as a teenager that the family's automobile insurance was revoked. Moise attended Jacksonville University, earning a de-

Patty Moise

gree in business, but her heart was always in racing. "I'm an adrenaline junkie," she explained to *Cosmopolitan.* "I like to do things that involve danger."

Moise began racing in 1981, under the guidance of her father. She started out driving road races the first five years of her career. In 1986 Moise switched to oval tracks. Because she was unable to secure adequate sponsorship, during her first three NASCAR seasons she was only able to race part-time. In 1987 she became the first woman to ever lead a Busch event (Road Atlanta), and in 1988 she became the first woman to win a Busch qualifying race (Talladega).

Moise got a break in 1990 when Mike Laughlin, a Simpsonville car builder and team owner, took her on as a full-time driver for the entire season. In the same year she married fellow driver, Elton Sawyer, whom she had met at an auto show. Also in 1990 Moise turned in a NASCAR record fastest lap on Talladega's 2.66-mile track. She shattered the old record by nearly five miles per hour, making the trip around clocked at 217.498 miles per hour. Because Moise completed the lap on a closed course, the previous record of 212.809 miles per hour set by Bill Elliott in 1987 during a qualifying lap remains the official NASCAR record.

Sponsorship Ups and Downs

NASCAR racing is a fickle business in which finding and retaining sponsorship is the key to success. When

Moise failed to make enough good starts in 1990, the following year she returned to part-time racing. From 1991 to 1993 she lined up for a total of only twenty races. In 1994 both Moise and Sawyers secured sponsorship on the Busch Grand National level, a step below the Winston Cup. During the year they often raced against one another, drawing attention from the press. "I think it's great for us to be able to work together," Moise admitted to a NASCAR representative. "As for racing on the track with Elton, this sport takes such a high level of concentration that you really don't have time to think of other drivers, including my husband. But deep down inside I can tell you that passing Elton for a win would make for some interesting conversations during the ride home from the race." In 1995 Moise completed the best finish by a woman to date, running seventh at Talladega.

In 1996 Sawyer made it briefly into the Winston Cup circuit, driving the David Blair Motorsports Ford, and Moise was racing in the Busch Grand National with a Dial-Purex Ford that she and Sawyer had purchased together. On the racing circuit the pressure to perform, to provide value to sponsors' funding venture, is constant. "You can't compete at this level without the sponsors," Moise told *USA Today.* "And once you get a sponsor, you are an advertising mechanism—you are working for someone else, and you feel the pressure to do well." Again losing sponsoring after the 1996 season, Moise only started one race in 1997, working with limited sponsorship from Pure Silk, whose parent company also sponsored Sawyer under its Barbasol label. On May 31, 1997, Moise completed five laps at Busch Grand National Series race at Dover Downs International Speedway in Dover, Delaware, before crashing and subsequently finished last. She tried but failed to make the field for the Watkins Glen road race.

Moise's future brightened at the end of her dismal 1997 season when she secured a commitment to drive for Michael Waltrip and his wife Buffy. Her car was sponsored by Rhodes Furniture, with associate sponsorships coming from the companies that provide Rhodes' product lines, including Simmons, Kroehler Company, Berkline, La-Z-Boy, Kincaid Furniture, and Sealy. Moise sold her-

Awards and Accomplishments

1987	First woman to ever lead a Busch event (Road Atlanta)
1988	First woman to win a Busch qualifying race (Talladega)
1990	Recorded unofficial fastest lap at Talladega (217.498 miles per hour)
1995	Records best finish by a woman to date, running seventh at Talladega

self to Rhodes by pointing out that forty percent of racing fans are women, who in turn make most household decisions. "We all felt that giving a woman the opportunity to compete on a level playing field with adequate funding to support a first-rate team was the right thing to do," George A. Buck, executive vice president of Rhodes told the *Associated Press*. "Of course," he added, "we also believe it would be good for business."

Retires

Moise raced on the Busch Grand National circuit full-time during 1998, but once again funding dried up at the season's end. This led the forty-year-old to decide to retire and focus on her husband's racing future. "Moise should still be racing," Jerry Bonkowski of ESPN noted. "She wasn't just a good female racer, she was a good racer first and foremost, regardless of gender." Following her retirement, Moise declined interviews, preferring that reporters talk to Sawyer whose career was also on hold due to a lack of sponsorship.

During her on-again, off-again racing career, Moise made 133 starts. She was, at the time, only one of six women to ever race on the Busch Grand National circuit. Moise became comfortable with being a woman in a sport dominated by men, but acknowledged that on the track she saw herself as a race car driver, not a female race car driver. She was asked so often how it felt to race as a woman, she began tossing back in response a humorous rebuttal, "You mean, as opposed to when I used to be a man?"

FURTHER INFORMATION

Books

Christensen, Karen, Allen Guttmann and Gertrud Pfister, eds. *International Encyclopedia of Women and Sports*. New York: Macmillan Reference Group, 2001.
Great Women in Sports. Visible Ink Press, 1996.

Periodicals

Arneson, Erik. "Married Team Races for Future Sawyer, Moises Share, Compete." *USA Today,* (May 24, 1996): 10.
Mehegan, Sean. "Pfizer Inks Moise as Pure Silk Companion to Barbasol Nas-car." *Brandweek,* (April 28, 1997): 4.

O'Malley, Anne. "Breaking Gender Barriers (and Records), These High-Speed Pioneers Have Rocketed to the Top of Their Professions!" *Cosmopolitan,* (October 1996): 238-239.

Other

"Out of Sponsors, Out of Racing." ESPN.com, May 14, 2002. www.espn.com (January 8, 2003).
"Patty Moise." NASCAR.com, December 22, 2002. http://www.nascar.com/2002/kyn/women/02/02/Moise/ (January 8, 2003).
"Patty Moise." *A Woman a Week*. www.awomanaweek.org (January 8, 2003).
"Patty Moise announces return to full-time NASCAR BGN Series Racing for 1998." The Auto Channel, October 5, 1997. http://www.theautochannel.com (January 8, 2003).

Sketch by Kari Bethel

Art Monk
1957-

American football player

Throughout his sixteen-year professional football career, Art Monk developed a reputation for quiet determination and fearless play. The longtime Washington Redskins' receiver was known primarily as a receiver who could gain tough yardage over the middle, rather than a deep play threat. His personal records and longevity, however, were always secondary to his teams' success. After spending the majority of his career in Washington, Monk played for both the New York Jets and the Philadelphia Eagles bringing with him the experience and leadership of a successful veteran. Despite being riddled with self-doubt, Monk went on to become one of the most productive receivers in National Football league (NFL) history.

The Early Years

Born James Arthur Monk in White Plains, New York, on December 5, 1957, he learned early on the value of family and religion. "I really enjoyed my childhood," Monk told *Sports Illustrated*. "We didn't have a lot of money, but enough to be happy with - to be clothed and with a roof over our heads. I can never remember want or struggle. I mean, we never had a color TV but we had a car, and there was always food on the table." Raised by hard working parents, Monk's father, a welder, was also a first cousin of jazz great Thelonious Monk and as a child Art was encouraged to pursue music. His natural

Art Monk

Chronology

1957	Born December 5 in White Plains, New York
1980	Drafted in the first round by the Washington Redskins
1982	Makes first Super Bowl appearance
1983	Makes second Super Bowl appearance
1984	Appears in first of three consecutive Pro Bowls
1987	Makes third Super Bowl appearance
1991	Makes fourth Super Bowl appearance
1992	Sets NFL career receptions record
1994	Signs with the New York Jets
1995	Signs with the Philadelphia Eagles
1996	Retires from football

Career Statistics

Yr	Team	Rec	Yds	Avg	TD
1980	WAS	58	797	13.7	3
1981	WAS	56	894	16.0	6
1982	WAS	35	447	12.8	1
1983	WAS	47	746	15.9	5
1984	WAS	106	1372	12.9	7
1985	WAS	91	1226	13.5	2
1986	WAS	73	1068	14.6	4
1987	WAS	38	483	12.7	6
1988	WAS	72	946	13.1	5
1989	WAS	86	1186	13.8	8
1990	WAS	68	770	11.3	5
1991	WAS	71	1049	14.8	8
1992	WAS	46	644	14.0	3
1993	WAS	41	398	9.7	2
1994	NY	46	581	12.6	3
1995	PHI	6	114	19.0	0
TOTAL		940	12721	13.5	68

NY: New York Jets; PHI: Philadelphia Eagles; WAS: Washington Redskins.

ability was surpassed only by his passion for sports and in particular football. His high school football coach saw his potential despite a lack of production on the field and recommended him to visiting scouts. With good grades and the support of his coach, Monk won a full scholarship to Syracuse University.

During his first year at Syracuse, Monk struggled again on the field. "I couldn't catch a cold," Monk said of his freshman season at Syracuse. "I don't know why. It was just a disaster. I remember practices where they'd throw the ball to me and it would hit my hands and I couldn't catch it. I knew I was better than that. I got really depressed and down on myself. And I just made up my mind that this wasn't going to happen again." His determination, however, forced him to develop a strict training regiment that helped him become one of the best pass receivers in college football by his senior year. His play caught the attention of one of his childhood heroes, Washington Redskins' scout, Charley Taylor. To his surprise, Monk was drafted in the first round of the NFL draft by Washington, where he began a long and productive career.

The Redskins

In Washington, Monk was a member of a tremendously successful team in the league's most competitive division. Although his production wasn't great in either game, Monk went to the Super Bowl with the Redskins in 1982 and 1983. Continuing his relentless training

regiment, Monk was the league's top receiver by 1984. The Redskins' won the Super Bowl again in 1987 and Monk's popularity in the nation's capital began to swell. The team, however, was in decline and this and a lack of satisfaction in his personal performance drove Monk to take matters into his own hands the following season. "I just wasn't happy with the way my life was going," he said. "I had an empty feeling inside, like something was missing. I was always reaching for something to make me happy or feel good - cars and money and houses. But whatever it was out there, it wasn't doing it. I really struggled for a while." He began attending Bible studies with teammates and recommitted himself to the religion in which he was raised. The serenity he discovered helped him prioritize and rededicate himself to the team. A revitalized Monk then challenged his teammates to do the same. In 1990, after taking a more visible leadership role on the team, the Redskins' advanced into the playoffs. The following year they posted a 17-2 record and defeated the Buffalo Bills in the Super Bowl.

Art Monk

Periodicals

"A Monk's Existence." *Sports Illustrated* (September 7, 1992):32.

"If You Throw It, He Will Catch It." *Time* (October 26, 1992): 26.

"Monk, Manley and Gibbs Added to Ring of Fame." *Washington Business Journal* (September 15, 2000): 33.

"The Art of Receiving." *Sports Illustrated* (December 3,1990): 104.

Sketch by Aric Karpinski

Retirement

Monk played a season with the New York Jets and one with the Philadelphia Eagles after leaving the Redskins, bringing experience and leadership to both teams. Although he retired as the second all-time leading receiver only sixty catches short of 1,000 career receptions, Monk was without regret. "I consider myself more fortunate than most who have played the game," he said. "By God's grace, I have achieved far more than I ever could have imagined. I've had a wonderful career and I will miss the game."

Art Monk's career was unusual for its longevity and productivity. It was his own self-doubt and passion for the game that drove him to work harder and achieve more than most. "I do two important things in my life," Monk said. "I play football, and I spend time with my family. Most everything else is a distraction." Although he shunned the attention of the national press, he was voted the most popular Redskin of all time in a fan poll conducted during the team's 50th anniversary season. His achievements were considered for induction to the Pro Football Hall of Fame in 2001.

FURTHER INFORMATION

Books

Newsmakers. Detroit: Gale Group, 1993.

Joe Montana
1956-

American football player

One of the most successful quarterbacks in National Football League (NFL) history, Joe Montana led the San Francisco 49ers to victory in four Super Bowls, including back-to-back wins in 1989 and 1990. The rise of the 49ers to football dominance during the 1980s was due in large measure to Montana's brilliance as a quarterback and team leader. Throughout his sixteen-year career in the NFL, Montana picked up Most Valuable Player (MVP) honors twice for his efforts in the regular season and three times for his Super Bowl exploits. Montana's skills as a quarterback won him the respect of both his teammates and the players of opposing teams. Of Montana, Chris Collinsworth, former wide receiver for the Cincinnati Bengals, said: "Joe Montana is the greatest quarterback to ever play the game. Joe Montana is not human." Making his accomplishments all the more impressive is the fact that Montana came out of nowhere to make football history. When he entered the NFL draft in 1979, he was not considered a leading prospect and, in fact, was not drafted by the 49ers until late in the third round, the 82nd player to be selected overall. Incredibly, Mon-

Joe Montana

Chronology

1956	Born June 11 in New Eagle, Pennsylvania
1974	Graduates from Ringgold High School in Monongahela, Pennsylvania
1975	Marries high school sweetheart Kim Moses (later divorced)
1978	Earns bachelor's degree in marketing from Notre Dame University
1979	Selected by San Francisco 49ers in NFL draft
1981	Marries flight attendant Cass Castillo (divorced in 1983)
1984	Marries former model Jennifer Wallace
1993	Traded by 49ers to Kansas City Chiefs
1995	Retires from professional football on April 18

A shy child with strangers, Montana had a few friends as a child, but his fondest memories are of playing backyard ball with his dad. At the age of eight, he got into peewee football when his father listed his age as nine on the application form. But his love of sports was not limited to football. In the spring, he pitched for a local Little League team, and in the winter came his favorite game, basketball. His father started a local basketball team that practiced and played in the local armory and toured the region to compete in tournaments. So passionate was Montana about basketball that as a senior in high school, he almost accepted a basketball scholarship to North Carolina State University on the promise that strings would be pulled so that he could play both basketball and football. Eventually, Montana bowed to his region's preoccupation with football and accepted a scholarship to play the game at Notre Dame University, which his childhood idol, Terry Hanratty, had attended.

A Small Fish in a Big Pond at Notre Dame

When Montana arrived at Notre Dame, he found that his status as a high school hotshot counted for little amid the wealth of gridiron talent assembled in South Bend. During Montana's years with the Fighting Irish, a total of forty-six Notre Dame players were drafted into the NFL. Montana saw no varsity action at all his first year at Notre Dame and got only minimal playing time in freshman games. Late in his sophomore season, he managed to pull out two games in the fourth quarter. He then repeated the feat in his junior year, helping power Notre Dame's drive to the national college championship of 1977. Still, he bristled at coach Dan Devine's seeming reluctance to play him more often.

The NFL showed little interest in Montana before his senior year, which proved to be his breakthrough year. In two key games—against Pittsburgh and Southern California—he engineered almost miraculous fourth-quarter rallies to erase significant deficits. The Fighting Irish finished the season with a record of 8-3, winning them an invitation to face off against the University of Houston in the Cotton Bowl. This proved to be the greatest game of Montana's college career. With Notre

tana very nearly didn't get into football at all. While still a senior in high school, he almost accepted a basketball scholarship to North Carolina State University but in the end was persuaded to play football for Notre Dame instead.

Born in New Eagle, Pennsylvania

He was born Joseph C. Montana Jr. in New Eagle, Pennsylvania, on June 11, 1956. The only child of Joseph C. and Theresa M. Montana, he was raised in the football stronghold of western Pennsylvania, which is also home to steel mills and soft coal mines. This same region has provided professional football with some of its most legendary players, including George Blanda, Johnny Lujack, **Dan Marino**, **Johnny Unitas**, **Joe Namath**, Chuck Fusina, and Terry Hanratty. While still an infant, Montana showed signs of his budding athleticism. "He used to wreck his crib by standing up and rocking," his mother Theresa told *Sports Illustrated*. "Then he'd climb up on the side and jump to our bed. You'd hear a thump in the middle of the night and know he hit the bed and went on the floor." His father, who told *Sports Illustrated* that as a child he'd never had anyone to take him to the backyard for a game of catch. "Maybe that's why I got Joe started in sports. Once he got started, he was always waiting at the door with a ball when I came home from work." Montana's father tried to instill in him a basic grounding in the fundamentals of football and worked with him on techniques.

Career Statistics

Yr	Team	GP	ATT	COM	YDS	COM%	Y/A	TD	INT
1979	SFO	16	23	13	96	56.5	4.2	1	0
1980	SFO	15	273	176	1795	64.5	6.6	15	2
1981	SFO	16	488	311	3565	63.7	7.3	19	2
1982	SFO	9	346	213	2613	61.6	7.6	17	11
1983	SFO	16	515	332	3910	64.5	7.6	26	12
1984	SFO	16	432	279	3630	64.6	8.4	28	10
1985	SFO	15	494	303	3653	61.3	7.4	27	13
1986	SFO	8	307	191	2236	62.2	7.3	8	9
1987	SFO	13	398	266	3054	66.8	7.7	31	13
1988	SFO	14	397	238	2981	59.9	7.5	18	10
1989	SFO	13	386	271	3521	70.2	9.1	26	8
1990	SFO	15	520	321	3944	61.7	7.6	26	16
1992	SFO	1	21	15	126	71.4	6.0	2	0
1993	KAN	11	298	181	2144	60.7	7.2	13	7
1994	KAN	14	493	299	3283	60.6	6.7	16	9
TOTAL		192	5391	3409	40551	63.2	7.5	273	139

KAN: Kansas City Chiefs; SFO: San Francisco 49ers.

Dame trailing Houston 34-12 at the midpoint of the fourth quarter, Montana pulled off one of his most amazing comebacks ever. In roughly seven and a half minutes, Notre Dame erased the deficit and won the game, 35-34, thanks to a Montana touchdown pass with two seconds left on the clock.

Picked by 49ers in Third Round of Draft

Despite his heroic comeback in the Cotton Bowl, Montana was not considered a particularly hot prospect going into the NFL draft of 1979. Not until the third round was he drafted by San Francisco 49ers, the 82nd player to be selected overall. During his rookie season in San Francisco, he spent most of his time on the bench absorbing lessons in technique from veteran quarterback Steve DeBerg. The 49ers ended the regular season with a dismal record of 2-14. In 1980, he split quarterbacking duties with DeBerg, but Montana clearly outshone the veteran, throwing for 1,795 yards and fifteen touchdowns and completing sixty-five percent of his passes—the best in the NFL. Coach Bill Walsh rewarded Montana by naming him starting quarterback for the 1981 season, which turned out to be the best in 49ers' history up to that point. San Francisco finished the regular season with a 13-3 record and went on to win the National Football Conference championship, 28-27, against the Dallas Cowboys. In the Super Bowl, playing against the Cincinnati Bengals, Montana completed fourteen of twenty-two passes for 157 yards to lead the 49ers to a 26-21 victory. For his contribution, Montana received the first of his three Super Bowl MVP trophies.

The 1982 season was cut short by a players' strike, and the 49ers missed the playoffs, but the team bounced back in 1983 with a record of 10-6. Montana threw for 3,910 yards and 26 touchdowns during the regular sea-

son. In the post-season, San Francisco advanced to the NFC championship game, which it lost to the Washington Redskins, 24-21 despite another fourth-quarter rally led by Montana. Montana had tied up the game, 21-21, with three fourth-quarter touchdown passes but lost when Redskins player Mark Mosley kicked a 25-yard field goal in the final moments of the game. The 49ers enjoyed one of their best seasons ever in 1984, losing only one game for a record of 15-1. Montana during the regular season threw for 3,630 yards and 28 touchdowns, completing sixty-five percent of his passes. Facing the Chicago Bears in the NFC championship game, San Francisco rolled to an easy victory of 23-0. Almost as much of a runaway was the 49ers' 38-16 Super Bowl win over the Miami Dolphins. Montana earned his second Super Bowl MVP Trophy by throwing for 331 yards (a Super Bowl record at the time) and two touchdowns. He rushed for another touchdown.

Bounces Back from Back Injury

In 1985 Montana turned in another brilliant performance, throwing for 3,653 yards and twenty-seven touchdowns, but it wasn't enough to return the 49ers to the Super Bowl. In the first round of the playoffs, San Francisco was knocked out of the competition by the New York Giants, 17-3. The beginning of the 1986 season was particularly ominous for Montana, who suffered a severe back injury that doctors at first feared might end his career. He confounded the medical professionals by returning to the game within two months. The 49ers went on to win the NFC Western Division title but fell again to the New York Giants in the first round of the playoffs, 49-3. Labor troubles once again intervened in 1987, cutting the regular season to fifteen games, of which Montana played in thirteen. The quarterback, however, managed to throw for 3,054 yards and a ca-

Related Biography: Coach Dan Devine

Joe Montana didn't always see eye to eye with coach Dan Devine during their years together at Notre Dame, but in the years before Devine's death in 2002 the two had established an uneasy peace. For his part, Devine made it clear that he thought Montana was the greatest quarterback ever to play the game. Montana, however, still harbored a degree of resentment toward Devine for what he believes was the coach's failure to give him his fair share of playing time. One thing is clear. Despite any lingering hard feelings, the two proved a powerful combination that fueled Notre Dame's drive to the national college championship in 1977 and a memorable Cotton Bowl victory over the University of Houston in 1979.

Devine was born in Augusta, Wisconsin, on December 23, 1924. He earned a bachelor's degree in history from the University of Minnesota at Duluth in 1948 and a master's degree in guidance counseling from the University of Michigan. He began his football coaching career at Arizona State University in 1955, where he compiled a record of 27-3-1 over three seasons. He next moved on to the University of Missouri, where he coached for thirteen seasons, compiling a record of 93-37-7 and winning for his team six bowl appearances and two Big Eight championships. He jumped to pro ball in 1971, taking over the reins at Green Bay. Although he coached the Packers to a NFC Central Division championship in 1972, his other three seasons with the team was disappointing, and fans turned against Devine.

In 1975 Devine replaced legendary Notre Dame coach Ara Parseghian and over five seasons at the helm of the Fighting Irish compiled a record of 53-16-1. The brightest moments came in 1977, when Notre Dame won the national college championship, and in a brilliant come-from-behind victory against Houston in the Cotton Bowl. Montana figured prominently in both those victories.

Devine left coaching in 1980 and returned to Arizona State as executive director of the Sun Angel Foundation, a fund-raising group. In 1987 he

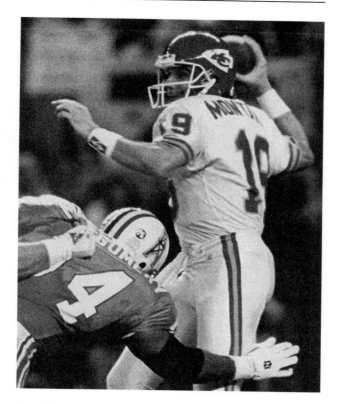

Joe Montana

reer-high thirty-one touchdowns. He also set an NFL record by completing twenty-two consecutive passes. San Francisco once again won the NFC Western Division title but fell in the first round of the playoffs, this time at the hands of the Minnesota Vikings.

As 49ers coach Walsh began giving more playing time to **Steve Young** during the 1988 season, rumors began to circulate that Montana might be traded. He later told the *Boston Globe*: "I've never doubted myself, but sometimes you wonder a little." Montana resolved to do whatever it took to hang on to his job as starting quarterback. In the end, he kept his job and led the 49ers to still another Super Bowl game after blow-out wins against the Minnesota Vikings and the Chicago Bears in the playoffs. In January 1989, the 49ers once again faced off against the Bengals in the Super Bowl. Of his third trip to the Super Bowl, Montana told the *San Jose Mercury News*: "This trip to the Super Bowl is more gratifying than the others because the road has been harder." In classic Montana form, the quarterback came to the rescue in the final minutes of the game to lead San Francisco to a 20-16 victory over the Bengals.

Siefert Takes Over as 49ers' Coach

After the retirement of coach Walsh in early 1989, coaching duties were turned over to defensive coach George Siefert. It was a good year for both Montana and the 49ers. Montana completed 70.2 percent of his passes

for 3,521 yards and twenty-six touchdowns, helping to power San Francisco into the playoffs once again. The 49ers handily disposed of their three playoff opponents with a combined score of 126-26 to win another trip to the Super Bowl. Montana, who led his team to a landslide 55-10 victory over the Broncos with a record five touchdowns, received his third Super Bowl MVP Trophy. Hoping to win their third Super Bowl in as many years, San Francisco compiled a sterling record of 14-2 during the regular season in 1990. Montana provided plenty of help, throwing for a career-high 3,944 yards and twenty-six touchdowns. With nine minutes to go in the NFC championship game, the 49ers were leading the Giants by a score of 13-9 when Montana broke his finger. Young took over the ball, performing well, but a fumble by running back Roger Craig gave the Giants the break they needed to win the game, 15-13.

Montana injured his elbow at the 49ers' 1991 training camp and missed all but one game of the 1991 and 1992 seasons. Although he performed well in the final game of the 1992 regular season, it was apparent that the job of starting quarterback had passed to Young. In April 1993 Montana asked to be traded to the Kansas City Chiefs. In his first year, he proved a welcome addition to the Chiefs, which had won only one playoff game since 1970. Despite missing at least part of six games because of a variety of injuries, Montana managed to throw for 2,144 yards and thirteen touchdowns, powering the

Awards and Accomplishments

1977	Helped lead Notre Dame to national college championship
1981, **1983-85,** **1987, 1989,** **1993**	Selected to play in Pro Bowl
1982	Led 49ers to Super Bowl victory over Cincinnati Bengals, winning MVP Trophy
1985	Led 49ers to Super Bowl victory over Miami Dolphins, winning MVP Trophy
1989	Led 49ers to Super Bowl victory over Cincinnati Bengals
1989	Named *Sporting News* Player of the Year and Man of the Year
1989	Named NFL's Most Valuable Player
1990	Led 49ers to Super Bowl victory over Denver Broncos, winning MVP Trophy
1990	Named NFL's Most Valuable Player
1990	Named *Sports Illustrated* Sportsman of the Year

The Ultimate Winner

So is he the greatest quarterback of all time or not? A large body of players and coaches, including [former 49ers coach Bill] Walsh, votes yes. The ones who say no point to the new era of football, the freer passing lanes, the bump-and-run restrictions, the elimination of head-slapping by defensive linemen. They say that a Johnny Unitas or a Norm Van Brocklin playing in this era would do the same things Montana does. "Yeah, I know. I've heard it," [Montana's high school quarterback coach Jeff] Petrucci says. "How would Joe do in the other era? How would he do against the Steelers in that two-deep zone, when they'd roll their corners up and it was over? Well, in my mind, he'd be the greatest in any era because he's the ultimate winner. Somehow he finds a way to get it done."

Source: Zimmerman, Paul. *Sports Illustrated* (August 13, 1999).

Chiefs to a season record of 11-5. They won their first and second playoff games against the Pittsburgh Steelers and the Houston Oilers, respectively, but fell to the Buffalo Bills in the AFC championship game. With Montana's help, Kansas City made it into the playoffs again in 1994 but lost to the Dolphins in the first round. Although it had been an excellent season for Montana, who threw for 3,283 yards and twenty-two touchdowns, he was increasingly troubled by injuries, particularly to his knees. On April 18, 1995, he announced his retirement from professional football.

A master of the come-from-behind victory, Montana will be forever remembered as one of the great quarterbacks of all time. The Pennsylvania native won the NFL's passing title in both 1987 and 1989 and topped the NFC in passing five times (1981, 1984, 1985, 1987, and 1989). In an incredible thirty-nine games, Montana passed for 300 yards or more. He also holds the career playoff records for attempts, completions, touchdowns, and yards gained passing. In 2000 he was enshrined in the Pro Football Hall of Fame. Looking back on his career, Montana told the *Detroit Free Press*: "I must admit that I've been very fortunate. It's been like living a dream for me. . . . The fortunate thing for me is that all that became a reality."

CONTACT INFORMATION

Address: Joe Montana, c/o IMG New York, 825 7th Ave., New York, NY 10019. Fax: (212)246-1596. Phone: (212)774-6735.

SELECTED WRITINGS BY MONTANA:

(With Bob Raissman) *Audibles: My Life in Football,* Morrow, 1986.

(With Alan Steinberg) *Cool under Fire,* Little Brown, 1990.

(With Dick Schaap) *Montana,* Turner, 1995.

(With Richard Weiner) *Joe Montana's Art and Magic of Quarterbacking,* Holt, 1997.

FURTHER INFORMATION

Books

"Joe Montana." *American Decades CD-ROM.* Detroit: Gale Group, 1998.

"Joe Montana." *Contemporary Authors.* Detroit: Gale Group, 2001.

"Joe Montana." *Encyclopedia of World Biography,* 2nd ed. 17 Vols. Detroit: Gale Group, 1998.

"Joe Montana." *Sports Stars,* Series 1-4. U•X•L, 1994-98.

Periodicals

Zimmerman, Paul. "Born to Be a Quarterback." *Sports Illustrated* (August 13, 1999).

Zimmerman, Paul. "The Ultimate Winner." *Sports Illustrated* (August 13, 1999).

Other

"Dan Devine, 1924-2002." SportsEncyclopedia.com. http://www.sportsencyclopedia.com/memorial/irish/devine.html (November 25, 2002).

"Joe Montana: Biography." Pro Football Hall of Fame. http://www.profootballhof.com/players/enshrines/jmontana.cfm (November 25, 2002).

"Joe Montana Joins SportsHabitat.com Inc." Snowboard Network.com. http://www.snowboardnetwork.com/sports/joe_Montana_joins_sportshabitat.htm (November 2, 2002).

"Joe Montana, Quarterback." Pro-Football-Reference.com. http://www.football-reference.com/players/MontJo01.htm (November 2, 2002).

Sketch by Don Amerman

Warren Moon
1956-

American football player

Although Warren Moon was overlooked time and again throughout his career, his perseverance led to an unusually long and extremely successful stint as a quarterback in the National Football league (NFL). In addition to having to fight against the perception that he didn't have what it takes to lead an NFL team, he also had to fight against prejudice in a league that had few black quarterbacks. After being passed over by the NFL, Moon went to Canada and led his team to five Grey Cups before being the subject of a bidding war among NFL teams. He would play professional football for twenty-three years and become the first quarterback to pass for over 60,000 yards in his career. Moon was the first forty-year-old to throw five touchdowns in a game and pass for 400 yards. He is also the oldest player in NFL history to score a touchdown. Although he never accomplished his goal of winning a Super Bowl, Moon's distinguished career earned him the respect of his teammates and a place in the record books.

Born Harold Warren Moon, November 18, 1956, in Los Angeles, California, he was the middle child in a family of seven children. His father died of liver disease when Moon was seven years old. He was raised, along with his six sisters, by a mother who insisted on providing her children with all the perks of the middle-class. A serious young man, Moon decided early on that football would be his sport and quarterback his position. He even went as far as enrolling, under a false address, at Hamilton High School—which had a better academic and athletic reputation than his neighborhood high school.

Struggle and Strength

Without the size or speed for football, Moon's secret weapon was his arm strength. It impressed his high school coaches enough to make him the starter on the varsity team in his senior year. He led his team to the city playoffs and was named to the all-city team in 1973. Despite his performance, he was overlooked by college recruiters and enrolled at West Los Angeles Junior College. Moon excelled immediately and began sending game tapes to major universities. The tapes got him in the door and on the field at the University of Washington. Moon had to wait for an opportunity and got it in his junior year when he was named the starting quarterback. He took the brunt of the fans' frustration after a 5-6 season but turned it around the following year. Moon, in his senior season, led his team to a Rose Bowl victory over the favored University of Michigan in 1978.

Chronology

1956	Born November 18 in Los Angeles, California
1973	Leads high school team to city playoffs
1973	Named to all-city team
1977	Leads University of Washington to conference championship
1978	Leads team to Rose Bowl victory
1978	Wins first of five consecutive Grey Cup trophies in the CFL
1983	Named MVP of CFL
1984	Joins the Houston Oilers
1987	Leads Houston to NFL playoffs
1988	Named All-Pro
1994	Signs with the Minnesota Vikings
1997	Signs with the Seattle Seahawks
1997	Becomes oldest starting quarterback in NFL history
2001	Retires as a Kansas City Chief

Canadian Success

He was overlooked by the NFL and signed with the Edmonton Eskimos of the Canadian Football League (CFL). In Canada, Moon didn't feel the prejudice he did as a black quarterback in America. He played six seasons in the CFL and became a star. He led his team to five Grey Cup championships and his 5,648 passing yards in 1983 set an all-time record for professional football. His success was finally noticed by the NFL and he was soon the subject of a bidding war between NFL teams. He signed with the Houston Oilers in 1984 after they made him the highest paid player in the league.

Pressure and Prejudice

Before Moon there were very few black quarterbacks in the NFL. He and Doug Williams, of the Washington Redskins, were among the first to find real success. His longevity and reputation for professionalism and success were factors in his eventual acceptance in the league. He and his family, however, were subjected to racist jeers by fans throughout his career when things were not going well for his team. Moon never succumbed to the pressure and always handled himself with discipline and pride.

While with the Oilers, Moon was never able to advance his team past the second round of the playoffs and became a scapegoat for the team's mediocrity. Although he set many team records and his personal performance was continually recognized, he was traded after ten years to the Minnesota Vikings where he believed he would have a more legitimate shot at the Super Bowl. In Minnesota, however, Moon was no more successful. Always a contender and never a winner, the Vikings and Moon suffered a similar fate as his Oilers had in the first ten years of his NFL career. His stay in Minnesota ended after the 1996 season. Injuries limited his abilities and his backup Brad Johnson asserted himself as the quarterback of the future.

Career Statistics

Yr	Team	Passing							
		Att	Com	Yds	COM%	TD	INT	SK	RAT
1984	HOU	450	259	3338	57.6	12	14	47	76.9
1985	HOU	377	200	2709	53.1	15	19	46	68.5
1986	HOU	488	256	3489	52.5	13	26	41	62.3
1987	HOU	368	184	2806	50.0	21	18	25	74.2
1988	HOU	294	160	2327	54.4	17	8	12	88.4
1989	HOU	464	280	3631	60.3	23	14	35	88.9
1990	HOU	584	362	4689	62.0	33	13	36	96.8
1991	HOU	655	404	4690	61.7	23	21	23	81.7
1992	HOU	346	224	2521	64.7	18	12	16	89.3
1993	HOU	520	303	3485	58.3	21	21	34	75.2
1994	MINN	601	371	4264	61.7	18	19	29	79.9
1995	MINN	606	377	4228	62.2	7	9	19	68.7
1997	SEA	528	313	3678	59.3	25	16	30	83.7
1998	SEA	258	145	1632	56.2	11	8	22	76.6
1999	KC	3	1	20	33.3	0	0	0	57.6
2000	KC	34	15	208	44.1	1	1	5	61.9
TOTAL		6823	3988	49325	58.4	291	233	458	80.9

HOU: Houston Oilers; KC: Kansas City Chiefs; MINN: Minnesota Vikings; SEA: Seattle Seahawks.

Awards and Accomplishments

1973	Named to all-city team at Hamilton High School
1978	Named Rose Bowl Most Valuable Player
1978	Named Pacific 8 Conference Player of the Year
1978-82	Grey Cup trophy
1980	Named Grey Cup Most Outstanding Offensive Player
1982	Named Grey Cup Most Outstanding Player
1983	Jeff Nicklin Memorial Trophy
1988	Named to NFL's All-Pro team
1990	Named NFL's Offensive Player of the Year
1997	Named to ninth NFL Pro Bowl
2001	Inducted to Edmonton Eskimos Wall of Fame

Longevity and Retirement

Moon's desire to win a championship kept him from retiring and he signed as a backup with the Seattle Seahawks in 1997. It was with Seattle that Moon would prove he still had something to offer despite his age. After the starter was injured in the first game of the season, Moon became the oldest starting quarterback in NFL history at the age of forty-one. His performance that season would lead to an appearance in the Pro Bowl where he earned the Most Valuable Player award. Moon retired as a Kansas City Chief in 2001.

His excellence on the field was matched by his reputation as a family man. In 1995, he was arrested after a domestic dispute between him and his long time wife. His wife didn't press charges and he was never convicted. They ultimately divorced in 2001, after nineteen years of marriage.

Moon overcame the obstacles of prejudice and paved the way for black quarterbacks in the NFL. A Super Bowl was the only thing Moon failed to achieve. He was active in his community and the winner of popularity polls during his time in Texas. Moon's arm strength, endurance and mental toughness carried him through a career that exceeded expectations.

FURTHER INFORMATION

Books

Contemporary Black Biography. Detroit: Gale Research, 1994.

Newsmakers. Detroit: Gale Group, 1991.

Periodicals

"Age is Only a Number for NFL Star Quarterback Warren Moon." *Jet* (November 2, 1998): 48.

"A Waning Moon." *Sports Illustrated* (September 11, 1995): 74.

"Blacks Star as Quarterbacks." *Jet* (November 13, 1995): 46.

"Father Moon." *Sports Illustrated* (September 27, 1993): 60.

"Felicia Moon, Wife of Ex-NFL Star Warren Moon, Files for Divorce." *Jet* (March 5, 2001):14.

"Is Moon the Man?" *Sporting News* (May 23, 1994): 34.

"The Moon Also Sets." *Sports Illustrated* (October 25, 1993): 64.

"Texas Jury Acquits Football Star Warren Moon of Assaulting his Wife." *Jet* (March 11,1996): 51.

"The Tribulations of a Mean Season." *Sporting News* (November 1, 1993): 9.

"Vikings Star Warren Moon Apologizes for Assaulting Wife." *Jet* (August 14,1995): 49.

Sketch by Aric Karpinski

Archie Moore

Archie Moore
1913-1998

American boxer

Archie Moore was one of the most colorful and respected figures in the modern history of boxing. His professional career, which included well over 200 bouts, spanned from 1936 to 1963 and included matches against **Rocky Marciano**, Cassius Clay (as **Muhammad Ali** was then called), and **Floyd Patterson**. The world light-heavyweight champion from 1952 to 1962, Moore's most notable match came on December 10, 1958, when he boxed against Yvon Durelle in the Montreal Forum in defense of his title. After being knocked down three times in the first round and again in round five, Moore regained control of the bout and eventually knocked Durelle out to take the fight in the eleventh round. He triumphed over Durelle in a rematch in 1959 and still held the light-heavyweight title through 1962, when it was taken away from him by the New York Boxing Commission and European Boxing Union for inactivity. Indeed, by that time Moore had moved on to a career as a trainer, author, actor, and philanthropist. During his retirement from professional boxing, which began in 1964, Moore devoted most of his time to the Any Boy Can (ABC) program, which he founded to help at-risk youth in San Diego. At the time of his death in 1998, Moore was hailed as "an American original" by Dave Kindred of *The Sporting News,* who wrote, "No deal with the devil is necessary to write about Archie More because anyone writing about the great man writes a celebration of life."

Grew Up in St. Louis

Archibald Lee Wright was born on December 13, 1913 in Benoit, a small town in the Mississippi Delta. His parents, Lorena and Thomas Wright, worked as farm laborers and separated not long after their son was born. Taken in by his aunt, Willie Pearl Moore, and her husband, Cleveland, he moved to St. Louis to live with the couple and took their surname as his own. The Moores eventually raised Archie, his older sister, Rena, and their half-brothers, Samuel and Louis. Around 1930 two tragedies struck the Moore family in quick succession. First, Cleveland Moore was paralyzed after an initiation ritual into a fraternal organization went awry. He eventually died from the injury. Shortly thereafter, Moore's newlywed sister, Rena, died while giving birth to twins. One of the twins also died and the surviving child was brought up by Willie Pearl Moore. The loss of Cleveland Moore's income plunged the family into economic hardship, which was compounded by the effects of the Great Depression.

With the loss of his uncle and sister, Moore entered into a period of rebellion. An indifferent student at racially segregated Lincoln High School in St. Louis, he began stealing in his neighborhood and even from his own family. As Moore recalled in his 1960 autobiography *The Archie Moore Story,* the theft and sale of two oil lamps from his aunt's house paid for his first set of boxing gloves. "I should have worn the boxing gloves the clock around," he wrote, "But I became adept at light-fingered lifting along with the rest of my gang." Moore progressed from stripping the copper wiring from abandoned houses to sell to scrap metal dealers to running onto streetcars and stealing the change box while a friend distracted the operator. After being arrested three times for theft, the authorities lost their patience with

Chronology

1913	Born December 13 in Benoit, Mississippi to Lorena and Thomas Wright
1934	Completes twenty-two month term in Missouri Training School
1935	Works in Civilian Conservation Corps
1936	Makes professional debut as boxer
1940	Marries for the first of five times
1940	Boxes on international circuit
1941	Suffers from perforated ulcer
1942	Resumes boxing career
1943	Wins California Middleweight Title in bout against Jack Chase
1952	Wins light-heavyweight boxing title in match against Joey Maxim
1955	Fails to win heavyweight boxing title against Rocky Marciano
1956	Fails to win heavyweight boxing title against Floyd Patterson
1958	Retains light-heavyweight boxing title in match against Yvon Durelle
1960	Appears in *The Adventures of Huckleberry Finn*
1962	Light-heavyweight title taken away for inactivity
1965	Ends professional boxing career
1966	Inducted into Boxing Hall of Fame
1974	Coaches George Foreman in fight against Muhammad Ali in Zaire
1981	Named by President Reagan to the Project Build sports program
1990	Inducted into International Boxing Hall of Fame
1998	Dies in San Diego on December 9

Moore and a trial resulted in a three-year sentence in the Missouri Training School in Boonville.

Moore subsequently spent twenty-two months in the Missouri Training School and the experience turned his life around. As he wrote in *The Archie Moore Story,* "The reform school was my personal crossroads. I had burned the bridge of formal education behind me and I now had a choice of which way to go and what to do. The feeling of shame that came over me when I thought of how my auntie must feel made the good she had built into me come forth." Hearing that professional fighters could earn up to $750 for a night's work, Moore decided to pursue boxing as a career. He began training in the school's facilities and scored sixteen knockout wins in his first year of intramural matches.

After nearly two years in reform school, Moore earned an early release and returned to St. Louis in the depths of the Great Depression. After struggling to find regular employment, Moore entered the Civilian Conservation Corps (CCC), a New Deal program set up by the administration of President Franklin D. Roosevelt to give employment to young men. Moore was sent to work on a forestry project in Poplar Bluff, Missouri and the hard work helped to build his muscle mass. He practiced his boxing moves every day, often improvising his workouts while he performed his duties. Moore also organized boxing matches for his CCC camp and helped to train some of the other fighters. As an amateur, Moore made his debut in an April 1935 match against Julius Kemp in St. Louis, which he lost in three rounds. Moore triumphed over Kemp in their second meeting with a third round knockout. Moore's other fight in his first year as an amateur took place in Poplar Bluff, where he won by a knockout in the second round over Billy Sims.

Makes Professional Debut

Moore continued to box as an amateur through much of 1936, when he fought in St. Louis and Cleveland with mixed results. In mid-1936 he turned professional and claimed his first win against Kneibert Davidson in two rounds. The following year a string of knockout victories earned Moore the reputation as a powerful and skillful fighter. At five-feet, eleven inches tall, Moore maintained his weight around 160 pounds as a middleweight fighter. Later, as a light-heavyweight, he would weigh in at just under 175 pounds. As impressive as his punching abilities were, it was his defensive moves that allowed him to outlast his opponents. Moore's quick reflexes eventually led him to claim the nickname "The Old Mongoose" after the fast-acting animal.

After leaving the CCC, Moore worked on a federal Works Progress Administration road crew around St. Louis in 1937. Inspired by the promise of bigger prize money, Moore moved to San Diego, California in early 1938. He continued to fight around the country, but San Diego became Moore's permanent address. On New Year's Day, 1940, he married Mattie Chapman, but the union did not survive the long separation entailed by Moore's eight-month absence to fight in Australia, where he was booked in a series of bouts with some of the country's best-known boxers. Moore enjoyed the publicity surrounding his trip, although the financial rewards seemed to be less than what his manager had promised. Based on the experience, Moore started to take a more active role in managing his own career.

Upon his return to the United States, Moore separated from his wife; the couple had been married less than one year. Moore also encountered a setback to his boxing career in February 1941 when he was disabled by a perforated ulcer that required extensive surgery. Moore was unconscious for five days after the operation and carried a long scar, shaped like a hockey stick, on his stomach as a reminder of the ordeal. His weight dropped from 163 to 108 pounds during his hospitalization.

With his recovery delayed by an appendicitis attack, it took the boxer almost a year to regain his health. Taking a job as a night watchman at a San Diego shipyard, Moore exercised regularly to retrain his muscles and increase his strength. Before reentering the ring against Bobby Britt in Phoenix in January 1942, Moore slipped a metal license plate into his high-waisted foul cup to protect his injured stomach from his opponent's punches. Moore won the fight by a knockout in the third round and continued with a string of knockout victories throughout the year. He ended 1942 with a loss against Eddie Booker in ten rounds. His bout against Jack Chase in May 1943, on the other hand, resulted in a fifteen-round win for Moore. Moore also walked away from the match with the California Middleweight title, which he held until August 1943, when Chase took the title back in a fifteen-round fight.

Over the next several years, Moore compiled an impressive record of wins, with many of his victories coming by knockout punches. Considered a leading contender for the light-heavyweight boxing title by 1946, Moore attempted in vain to set up a title match with any of the successive titleholders of the day, Freddie Mills, Gus Lesnevich, and Joey Maxim. "I took matters in my own hands, as much as I could," he wrote in *The Archie Moore Story*, "I began a letter-writing campaign to sports writers all over the country. I pleaded, I cursed, I demanded a shot at Maxim's crown." In December 1952, at the age of thirty-nine, Moore finally got his light-heavyweight title bout with Maxim.

Wins Light-Heavyweight Title in 1952

The Maxim-Moore fight took place in St. Louis and the hometown support helped Moore take thirteen of the fight's fifteen rounds, winning by a unanimous decision. Moore defended the title against Maxim in a June 1953 fight in Utah, which he won in another fifteen-round decision. In their third and final meeting, Moore repeated the feat and retained the title by decision after fifteen rounds. Moore subsequently retained the light-heavyweight title in bouts against Harold Johnson in August 1954; Carl "Bobo" Olson in June 1955; Yolande Pompey in June 1956; and Tony Anthony in September 1957.

As he held on to the light-heavyweight crown, Moore made a number of attempts to claim the heavyweight title as well. His first heavyweight title bout came against Rocky Marciano in a fight staged at Yankee Stadium on September 21, 1955. After knocking down Marciano in the second round, it looked like Moore would take the title. Yet Marciano came back to deliver a knockout blow to Moore in the ninth round that ended the fight. After Marciano retired and vacated the heavyweight title, Moore met Floyd Patterson in a match to decide who would get the crown. The November 1956 bout ended when Patterson knocked Moore out in the fifth round. It was Moore's final attempt to win the heavyweight title.

Although he was disappointed in his quest for the heavyweight crown, Moore retained his light-heavyweight title throughout the 1950s in a series of contests. The most notable challenge to his title came in a fight against Yvon Durelle at the Montreal Forum on December 10, 1958. Cheered along by the crowd, Canadian Durelle seemed to have the advantage on in the fight, especially after sending Moore to the canvas three times in the first round and again in the fifth round. Moore's endurance and defense training were crucial in the remaining rounds, as he sent Durelle down in the seventh round and again in the tenth. In the eleventh round

Awards and Accomplishments	
1943	Wins California middleweight title
1952	Wins light-heavyweight championship from Joey Maxim
1958	Named Fighter of the Year by the Boxing Writers Association
1966	Inducted into the U.S. Boxing Hall of Fame
1968	Awarded Key to the City, San Diego, California
1985	Inducted into the St. Louis Boxing Hall of Fame
1987	Awarded Rocky Marciano Memorial Award
1990	Inducted into the International Boxing Hall of Fame

Overall professional record: 181 wins; 24 losses.

Moore knocked Durelle down for good with a punch that ended the fight. Moore's perseverance had led to one of the most impressive comebacks in boxing history. In recognition of his feat, the Boxing Writers Association named him the Fighter of the Year. His victory over Durelle also marked his 127th victory by a knockout, which set a record for the sport. In a rematch with Durelle in August 1959 in Montreal, Moore retained his title with a knockout victory in the third round.

Author, Actor, and Philanthropist

After four divorces, Moore married Joan Hardy in August 1955; the couple remained married for the rest of Moore's life. With the money from his title fights—the bout against Marciano alone brought in over $270,000—Moore invested in his own training camp located just northwest of San Diego, which he christened "The Salt Mine." Among the fighters who trained there were Cassius Clay (as future world heavyweight champion Muhammad Ali was known in the early 1960s) and **George Foreman**. Clay's stint at the Salt Mine was a brief one, as he refused to do the chores that were part of Moore's training regimen. Moore later fought against Clay in a November 1962 fight that left him reeling from a fourth-round, knockout punch. Moore had just one more professional fight after that, a March 1963 bout with Mike DiBiase that he won by a knockout in the third round. In 1964 Moore announced his retirement and fought just one exhibition match after that, a bout against Nap Mitchell in August 1965 when he was fifty-one years old. In all, his professional career, which began in 1936, spanned twenty-seven years. Although Moore's erratic career made statistical information difficult to verify, most sources counted 181 wins and 24 losses in his professional career. Moore himself claimed 193 victories in 228 bouts, with 140 knockout wins. In 1966 he was inducted into the United States Boxing Hall of Fame; an induction into the International Boxing Hall of Fame followed in 1990.

As Moore's boxing career drew to a close, he received an unexpected offer to star in the film adaptation of Mark Twain's classic novel *The Adventures of Huckleberry Finn* in the role of Jim, the runaway slave. When it was released in 1960 the film received lukewarm reviews,

Archie Moore

with Moore's performance judged to be better than the movie itself. Coinciding with the release of *The Adventures of Huckleberry Finn*, Moore wrote an autobiography that was published as *The Archie Moore Story* by McGraw-Hill in 1960. The book detailed Moore's hard-luck childhood, his battles with physical and emotional adversity, and his eventual triumph in the boxing ring. The work also gave readers extensive physical training advice, including Moore's own "secret diet" that instructed its followers to drink sauerkraut juice every day and chew, but not swallow, the meat portions of their meals. His film appearance and autobiography made him into perhaps the best-known boxer of his generation.

Moore remained active as a trainer in the 1960s and 1970s. His most notable client was George Foreman, whom Moore accompanied to the famous "Rumble in the Jungle" fight with Muhammad Ali in 1974. In addition to his work as a trainer at the Salt Mine, Moore also devoted much of his time to philanthropic work after he retired from the ring. In 1967 he founded the Any Boy Can (ABC) program in San Diego to give underprivileged youth the chance to participate in sports programs. Moore took an active role in the ABC program as a mentor, coach, and inspirational speaker to its participants. In 1968 the mayor of San Diego awarded Moore the Key to the City in recognition of his work through the ABC program. Along with Leonard B. Pearl, Moore wrote a book detailing the ABC program, published in 1971 as *Any Boy Can: The Archie Moore Story*. The volume also discussed Moore's lengthy career and the development of his interests in civil rights. As he concluded the work, "I am doing what I can to bring about civil rights, to help the young and the old, to erase poverty, war and civil unrest, and then, when I see all

these things come about, then, and only then, will I be able to say that I am *the* happiest man in the world."

Moore's Legacy

After the ABC program was opened to female participants, it changed its name to Any Body Can and continued to serve the youth of San Diego through the 1970s. In 1981 President Ronald Reagan appointed Moore to the Project Build program, which brought sports programs to public-housing residents. He was also honored with the Rocky Marciano Memorial Award in 1987. Moore suffered from declining health in the 1990s and underwent heart surgery that took away much of his physical prowess. In late 1998 he fell into a coma for two weeks and died in a San Diego hospice facility on December 10. He was survived by his wife, Joan, and eight children.

For his record of knockout punches—estimated between 129 and 144 knockouts in all—Moore was recognized as one of the greatest boxers the sport had ever seen. Although the number of knockout wins was impressive, most critics agreed with Moore's own claim that he was a consummate boxer who thought on his feet, not just a slugger like Rocky Marciano, **Rocky Graziano**, or **Jake LaMotta**, to name just a few of his contemporaries. Moore's career was also notable for its sheer length, lasting for twenty-seven years and including ten years as light-heavyweight champion. Unlike many former champions, Moore found lasting satisfaction in his post-professional days as a trainer and philanthropist. "Here I am, my ring days over, gray and balding, teaching young boys, doing what I can to fight juvenile delinquency, doing what I can to make this a better America for all of us," he wrote in *Any Boy Can: The Archie Moore Story.* "And when one of my boys makes it big I'm proud of him. I'm happy to have been given the opportunity to help. . . . That is what I am proudest of."

SELECTED WRITINGS BY MOORE:

The Archie Moore Story, New York: McGraw-Hill, 1960. (With Leonard B. Pearl) *Any Boy Can: The Archie Moore Story,* Englewood Cliffs, NJ: Prentice-Hall, 1971.

FURTHER INFORMATION

Books

Douroux, Marilyn. *Archie Moore: The Ole Mongoose.* Boston: Branden Publishing Company, 1991.
Moore, Archie, and Leonard B. Pearl. *Any Boy Can: The Archie Moore Story.* Englewood Cliffs, NJ: Prentice-Hall, Inc., 1971.
Moore, Archie. *The Archie Moore Story.* New York: Mc-Graw-Hill Book Company, 1960.

Periodicals

Hirsley, Michael. "Archie Moore Dies at 84." *Chicago Tribune* (December 9, 1998).
Katz, Michael. "Light Heavyweight Archie Moore Dies in San Diego." *New York Daily News* (December 10, 1998).
Kindred, Dave. "A Celebration of Life." *Sporting News* (December 21, 1998): 62.
Lyon, Bill. "Archie Moore Treated Boxing with Reverence." *Philadelphia Inquirer* (December 11, 1998).
O'Brien, Richard, with Mark Mravic. "A Smiling Champion." *Sports Illustrated* (December 21, 1998): 30.

Other

"Cyber Boxing Champion Archie Moore." The Cyber Boxing Zone Encyclopedia,. http://www.cyberboxing zone.com/boxing/amoore.htm (September 25, 2002).

Sketch by Timothy Borden

Joe Morgan
1943-

American baseball player

Joe Morgan

Joe Morgan was the heart and soul of the Big Red Machine, the Cincinnati Reds team of the 1970s that some baseball observers consider the greatest team of all times. Morgan was that rarest of combinations: a five-time Gold Glove second baseman who could hit for average and power, and one of the premier base stealers of his era. He was also the field leader of the Reds, with such deep baseball knowledge that, unlike most batters, he was given no signals from the bench when he hit-he decided himself what to do on each pitch. Furthermore he knew how to win. During his career, Morgan played on no less than eight divisional champs, five pennant winners, and two World Series champions. When he quit baseball, his 268 career home runs led all other second basemen. In 1990 he was the first second baseman to be elected to the National Baseball Hall of Fame since **Jackie Robinson** entered in 1962. Since his retirement as an active player, Joe Morgan has remained intimately involved with baseball. He is a prize-winning color commentator for ESPN's baseball broadcasts. He has co-authored a number of books on baseball, including *Baseball for Dummies* and *Joe Morgan: A Life in Baseball.*

Growing Up

Joseph Leonard Morgan was born in 1943 in Bonham Texas. The first of six children born to Leonard and Ollie Morgan, he would later call his family the main source of this strength. While Joe was still a child, the Morgans left Texas and settled in a neighborhood in

Chronology

1943	Born in Bonham Texas
1963	Plays with Modesto Reds and Durham Bulls
1964	Plays with San Antonio Bullets, named Most Valuable Player, Texas League
1964	Joins Houston Colt 45s
1971	Traded to Cincinnati Reds
1975-76	Named Most Valuable Player, National League
1975-76	Won World Series with Cincinatti
1980	Signs with Houston Astros as free agent
1981	Joins San Francisco Giants
1982	Joins Philadelphia Phillies
1983	Traded to Oakland As
1984	Retires as active baseball player
1984	Founds Joe Morgan Investments
1985	Does color commentary on ESPN's college baseball broadcasts
1986-90	Member of San Francisco Giants broadcast team
1988	Assaulted at Los Angeles International Airport by LA undercover police
1990	Elected to National Baseball Hall of Fame
1990-present	Color commentator on ESPN baseball broadcasts
1993	LA City Council awards Morgan $796,000 in damages

Awards and Accomplishments

1964	Most Valuable Player, Texas League
1970, 1972-79	National League All-Star team
1973-77	Gold Glove, second baseman
1975-76	Most Valuable Player, National League
1990	Inducted into National Baseball Hall of Fame
1990	CableAce Award
1997	Sports Emmy
1998	ASA Sportscaster of the Year
1999	ASA Sportscaster of the Year

Oakland, California. Morgan was soon an avid player of "Army Ball," a three player variant of stickball. He and his family were also enthusiastic baseball fans. In particular, they became devoted followers of the Oakland Oaks, the town's Pacific Coast League team whose park was just blocks from the Morgan home. As a teenager Morgan played **Babe Ruth** League and high school ball. He entered Oakland City College intending to study business and played on the school team there. Morgan was already showing a knack for playing on successful teams. His high school team won the Oakland Athletic League championship and his college team won its divisional title.

Oakland was a hotbed of young baseball talent in the middle 1950s, and Morgan, a leading hitter and base stealer on his teams, should have quickly attracted the attention of a major league team. However, he had one major disadvantage in the eyes of most scouts—Morgan was barely five feet seven inches in height. He seemed much too short to be a serious prospect and only one team showed any interest, an expansion team, the Houston Colt 45s, who would eventually be renamed the Astros. In 1963, Houston offered Morgan a $500-a-month minor league contract, together with an unspectacular bonus of $3,000. Morgan was nonetheless delighted by the chance to play big league ball. His father, a former semi-pro ballplayer, was pleased for his son, but Morgan's mother took a more practical view. She was concerned that once Joe left college to play ball he would never return. Morgan promised her that he would eventually finish college. More than 25 years later, he kept the promise. He got his college degree in 1990, the same year he was elected to the Baseball Hall of Fame.

Morgan advanced quickly through the minors, from the instructional league in Moultree Georgia, to the Modesto (California) Reds , to the Durham (South Carolina) Bulls. In his first at bat with Durham in 1963, he hit a game-winning home run. While playing in Georgia and South Carolina Morgan experienced for the first time in his life the ugly racism of segregated hotels, restaurants, and drinking fountains, and obscene racist insults. It so shocked him that he briefly considered leaving baseball to escape it. Only his unflagging devotion to perfecting his baseball skills and the thought that he would be letting down his parents gave Morgan the strength to continue.

Playing with Houston

Morgan started the 1964 season with Houston's AA team in San Antonio where he was named the Texas League's Most Valuable Player with a .323 average, 90 runs batted in, 12 homers and 47 stolen bases. At the end of 1964 he played a few games with Houston . One of his hits helped knock the Philadelphia Phillies out of the pennant race. In the Phillies clubhouse after the game, manager Gene Mauch overturned a table full of food. "Mauch stood there, his face reddening," according to the *Houston Chronicle*'s Mickey Herskowitz, "and screamed at his startled players: 'Have you no shame? You just got beat by a guy who looks like a Little Leaguer!'"

Morgan skipped AAA ball completely and jumped directly to the Astros in 1965. The team had just moved to its new ballpark, the Astrodome, the first domed park in baseball and the first to use Astroturf instead of natural grass. Morgan realized that a player with his speed and hitting ability was the type most suited to playing in such a park with its vast spaces and fast artificial grass surface. After his good rookie year, batting .271 with 14 home runs, 40 RBIs and 20 stolen bases, the *Sporting News* named him their Rookie of the Year. But it was Morgan's bearing that impressed his teammates most. "To me he was never really a rookie," Jimmy Wynn, Morgan's roommate on the Astros recalled to Mickey Herskowitz of the *Houston Chronicle*. "The way he handled himself, his poise, his knowledge . . . he had the look of a veteran player." Morgan played with the Astros until 1971 when conflicts with Houston manager Harry

Career Statistics

Yr	Team	AVG	GP	AB	R	H	HR	RBI	BB	SO	SB	E
1963	HOU-C	.240	8	25	5	6	0	3	5	5	1	3
1964	HOU-C	.189	10	37	4	7	0	0	6	7	0	3
1965	HOU-A	.271	157	601	100	163	14	40	97	77	20	27
1966	HOU-A	.285	122	425	60	121	5	42	89	43	11	21
1967	HOU-A	.275	133	494	73	136	6	42	81	51	29	14
1968	HOU-A	.250	10	20	6	5	0	0	7	4	3	2
1969	HOU-A	.236	147	535	94	126	15	43	110	74	49	18
1970	HOU-A	.268	144	548	102	147	8	52	102	55	42	17
1971	HOU-A	.256	160	583	87	149	13	56	89	52	40	12
1972	CIN	.292	149	552	122	161	16	73	115	44	58	8
1973	CIN	.290	157	576	116	167	26	82	111	61	67	9
1974	CIN	.293	149	512	107	150	22	67	120	69	58	13
1975	CIN	.327	146	498	107	163	17	94	132	52	67	11
1976	CIN	.320	141	472	113	151	27	111	114	41	60	13
1977	CIN	.288	153	521	113	150	22	78	117	58	49	5
1978	CIN	.236	132	441	68	104	13	75	79	40	19	11
1979	CIN	.250	127	436	70	109	9	32	93	45	28	12
1980	HOU-A	.243	141	461	66	112	11	49	93	47	24	7
1981	SFG	.240	90	308	47	74	8	31	66	37	14	4
1982	SFG	.289	134	463	68	134	14	61	85	60	24	8
1983	PHI	.230	123	404	72	93	16	59	89	54	18	17
1984	OAK	.244	116	365	50	89	6	42	66	39	8	10
TOTAL		.271	2649	9277	1650	2517	268	1133	1865	1015	689	245

CIN: Cincinnati Reds; HOU-A: Houston Astros; HOU-C: Houston Colt .45s (Texas League); OAK: Oakland Athletics; PHI: Philadelphia Phillies; SFG: San Francisco Giants.

Walker came to a head and he was traded. Morgan regretted leaving the Astros, but his *real* career was just beginning—with the Cincinnati Reds.

The Big Red Machine

Morgan would later call the Reds the best defensive team that ever played, and it had Gold Glove players up the middle in catcher **Johnny Bench**, Morgan, shortstop Dave Concepcion, and centerfielder Cesar Geronimo. But it also had astonishing hitting power in Bench, Tony Perez, George Foster, and **Pete Rose**. Joe Morgan, however, was the spark plug of the Big Red Machine. He was its lead-off man, a batter who averaged .290 or better and more than 100 walks during most of his seasons with the team, and a perennial threat to steal—he had 434 stolen bases in his eight years with Cincinnati. Morgan flourished with the Reds. Reds manager **Sparky Anderson** had such confidence in Morgan that he was allowed to bunt and steal at will. He was named the National League's Most Valuable Player in both the Reds' world championship years: in 1975 when he batted .327, hit 17 homers, knocked in 94 runs and stole 67 bases, in and 1976 when he hit .320, hit 27 homers, knocked in 111 runs and stole 60 bases. In the 1975 World Series against the Boston Red Sox, a series some consider the most exciting in baseball history, Morgan got the late innings hit that gave the Reds the championship.

By the end of the 1970s, the glory days of Cincinnati's Big Red Machine were past. In 1980, Joe Morgan returned as a free agent to the Houston Astros, leading them that same season to their first divisional championship. However, Houston manager Bill Virdon came to resent Morgan's strong leadership role on the Astros. Virdon started pinch hitting for Morgan late in games and took him out of the last game of the playoffs, after which the second baseman said he would not play for the manager any longer. The following year, he went to the San Francisco Giants. In 1983 he joined the Philadelphia Phillies, where he and his old Reds teammates Pete Rose and Tony Perez went to one last World Series together. At the end of the 1984 season, spent with the Oakland As, Morgan retired as a player.

Award-Winning Broadcaster

Although he was no longer playing, Joe Morgan was still a regular presence at ballparks across the country, as a television announcer. In 1985 he started working as a color commentator for ESPN's broadcasts of college baseball, and joined the San Francisco Giants broadcast team from 1986 until 1990. Since then he has been a fixture on ESPN, providing some of the most intelligent, insightful baseball analysis available on any network. His television work has garnered him various awards, including the Ace Award and an Emmy.

Despite his success and visibility as an athlete and sports commentator, Morgan has on occasion come face-to-face with the grim realities of racial conflict in the United States. In 1988, at Los Angeles International

Airport, he was accosted by two undercover members of the LA police department, who accused him of being a drug dealer and took him into detention while refusing to allow him to identify himself. The police eventually realized their mistake and Morgan was released. When the LAPD refused to allow Morgan to file a formal complaint, he brought a civil suit. In 1993 the Los Angeles City Council voted to pay Morgan $796,000 to end the suit. The incident brought home the situation of other black people in the United States.

In 1990, in his first year of eligibility, Morgan was elected to the National Baseball Hall of Fame, only the seventh second baseman to be enshrined and the first in almost thirty years. When Joe Morgan retired he left the game not only as one of the greatest second basemen—some would say *the* greatest—ever to play the game, but as a *complete* player. He retired with 268 home runs—at the time the most ever hit by a second baseman—a .271 batting average, 1,133 runs batted in, 689 stolen bases and five Gold Gloves. Add to that, the fact that he was a thinking man's player and the penultimate team player, and he probably ranks as one of the greatest players in baseball history.

SELECTED WRITINGS BY MORGAN:

(Edited by Joel H. Cohen) *Baseball My Way.* New York: Atheneum , 1976.

(With David Falkner) *Joe Morgan: A Life in Baseball.* New York: W. W. Norton & Co., 1993.

(With Richard Lally) *Baseball for Dummies.* Foster City, CA: IDG Books, 1998.

(With Richard Lally) *Long Balls, No Strikes: What Baseball Must Do to Keep the Good Times Rolling.* New York: Crown, 1999.

FURTHER INFORMATION

Periodicals

Atkin, Ross. "Joe Morgan Has a Nose for Baseball Nuance." *Christian Science Monitor,* October 6, 1997.

Bass, Mike. "Morgan: Had To Work A Little Harder." *St. Louis Post-Dispatch,.* January 9, 1990.

Cohen, Joel H. *Joe Morgan: Great Little Big Man.* New York: G.P. Putnam's & Sons., 1978.

Eldridge, Larry. "Joe Morgan Lines Up With the Astros." *Christian Science Monitor,* April 2, 1980.

Herskowitz, Mickey. "A Big-Time Player, This Little Joe." *Houston Chronicle,* May 17, 1999.

Moran, Malcolm. "Joe Morgan Stretches Out His Career." *New York Times,* October 13, 1983.

Oller, Rob. "Reds Fans Will Always Find Comfort In Lil' Joe." *Columbus Dispatch.,* June 7, 1998.

Ryan, Joan. "Success Is His Trademark." *San Francisco Chronicle,* April 17, 1995.

Swan, Gary. "A Big Year for Little Joe." *San Francisco Chronicle,* August 2, 1990.

Sketch by Gerald E. Brennan

Jim Morris
1964-

American baseball player

The relief pitcher Jim Morris became one of baseball's oldest rookies in 1999, when at age 35 he signed with the Tampa Bay Devil Rays. A high school science teacher and baseball coach who had formerly played in the minor leagues, Morris stunned the Devil Rays' talent scouts with his 98-mile-per-hour fastball. Although he played for only two seasons and pitched in only 21 major league games, Morris captured baseball fans' imaginations with his Cinderella story, which took him from the classrooms and baseball diamond of a Texas high school to the national arena of a big league stadium. His made-for-Hollywood tale became a major motion picture, *The Rookie,* starring Dennis Quaid, in 2002.

James Samuel Morris Jr. was born on January 19, 1964, in Brownwood, Texas. His father was in the U.S. Navy, so his family moved often. For young Morris, baseball became a way to make friends in new towns. It was also his passion and the source of his aspirations, as he dreamed of playing in the major leagues one day.

At age 18, Morris was selected by the New York Yankees in the first round of the major league baseball draft. He chose to continue his education first, but turned down football scholarships from Penn State and Notre Dame because he wouldn't be allowed to play college baseball. Instead he enrolled at Angelo State University on an academic scholarship. In 1984 Morris attended major league tryouts again and was recruited by the Milwaukee Brewers.

Derailed by Arm Injuries

As a pitcher in the Brewers' minor league farm system, Morris was plagued by a series of arm injuries. Chronic pain in his pitching arm led to several opera-

Jim Morris

tions, including one that involved replacing a tendon in his left elbow with one from his right ankle. But the surgeries failed to alleviate the pain, and Morris was forced to retire from baseball in 1988, at age 24, before he had graduated from Class A of the minor leagues.

Leaving baseball behind, Morris set out to pursue a career in teaching. He obtained a bachelor's degree, and took a job as a high school science teacher and baseball coach in Big Lake, Texas. With his wife, Lorri, whom he'd married in his minor league days, he raised three children in the town of San Angelo. Over the years, Morris kept fit and participated in many sports. When he was 27 he became an All-American punter in college football. He played baseball in the local "beer leagues" and pitched at batting practice to the high school team he coached.

Morris challenged his young ballplayers with fast pitches, and his Reagan County High School Owls became strong hitters. After batting practice Morris would sometimes ask students to stay and catch for him so he could keep his arm in shape. It was here that the former minor league player let loose his powerful fastballs. "He'd just unleash, balls coming so hard and so fast, it hurt my hand sometimes," one young player told Dawn Fratangelo NBC-TV's *Dateline*. The Owls began to suspect that their coach had the talent for the major leagues.

As the Owls prepared for the 1999 season, Morris urged them to try to make the playoffs that year. While he was giving a pep talk one day, his players interrupted him. "They stopped me mid-speech," Morris told *Date-*

Chronology

1964	Born on January 19 in Brownwood, Texas
1982	Attends Angelo State University on an academic scholarship
1984	Drafted by Milwaukee Brewers; plays in minor league farm system
1988	Retires from minor leagues after series of arm injuries
1991	Plays football for Angelo State
mid-1990s	Becomes science teacher and baseball coach at Reagan County High School
1999	Drafted by Tampa Bay Devil Rays; begins pitching in minor league farm system
1999	Pitches first major league game, September 18
2000	Traded to Los Angeles Dodgers
2001	Retires from baseball
2001	Publishes autobiography, *The Oldest Rookie: Big-League Dreams from a Small-Town Guy*
2002	Disney film *The Rookie* debuts nationwide

line, "and they said, you know, 'Wait a minute. You're sitting her preaching to us and telling us all this stuff that we need to do, and yet, you're sitting here coaching and teaching and not trying to play baseball, and you throw harder than anybody we've ever seen.'" That day, Morris made a deal with his players. If they made the playoffs that year, he would try out for the next major league team that passed through the area.

Tried Out for Major Leagues

The Owls did make it to the playoffs, and then it was Morris's turn. On a 103-degree Saturday in June, the 35-year-old science teacher drove two hours with his children to a Tampa Bay Devil Rays tryout camp. Surrounded by 20-year-old wannabe baseball players, the left-handed pitcher lied about his age so the scouts would give him a chance. When it was his turn at the mound, Morris threw a 94-mile-per-hour pitch, followed by several 98-mile-per-hour throws. He was as dumbfounded as the scouts; after ten years of retirement and four arm surgeries, Morris's fastball had increased in speed by about ten miles per hour.

The Devil Rays signed Morris almost immediately, and he spent the summer in a minor league farm camp. After three months of intense work, which kept him away from his family and focused completely on pitching, Morris was called to the major leagues, becoming baseball's oldest rookie pitcher in nearly 30 years. His first game was on September 18, 1999, in the home stadium of the Texas Rangers. Morris's family took a seat in the audience, and his wife burst into tears when she saw her husband in his baseball uniform. When he was called in to pitch, he struck out the first batter, Royce Clayton.

Morris's big league career was brief, but every moment was a gift for the Devil Rays' pitcher. "I wake up some mornings, and it hits me that I'm 36 years old and getting to do what I wanted to do when I was 5," he told Richard Justice of the Montreal *Gazette*. "It's an amaz-

Awards and Accomplishments	
1991	Became All-American athlete as a college punter
1999	Became baseball's oldest rookie in nearly 30 years

Career Statistics

Yr	Team	W	L	ERA	IP	H	ER	BB	SO	SV
1999	TB	0	0	5.79	4.7	3	3	2	3	0
2000	TB	0	0	4.35	10.3	10	5	7	10	0

TB: Tampa Bay Devil Rays.

ing feeling. This wasn't supposed to happen for me. God gave this to me." Morris went on to pitch for the Devil Rays in the 2000 season, and signed with the Los Angeles Dodgers before retiring from baseball in 2001. He had served as a relief pitcher in 21 major league games, was 0-0 with a 4.80 Earned-Run Average (ERA), and had logged 13 strikeouts.

In April 2001 Morris published his autobiography, *The Oldest Rookie: Big-League Dreams from a Small-Town Guy,* co-written with Joel Engel. Almost a year later, on March 29, 2002, *The Rookie,* the motion picture depicting Morris's life, opened in theaters across the country. Aware that his story had inspired many people to follow their dreams, Morris became a motivational speaker after his retirement from baseball in 2001.

The Rookie

The Rookie, directed by John Lee Hancock, told the tale of Jim Morris's rise from a small-town high school science teacher and coach to a major league baseball player. It was Morris's sports agent, Steve Cantor, who had convinced the pitcher that his story could make a Hollywood movie. Walt Disney picked up the project, casting actor Dennis Quaid in the starring role. The actress Rachel Griffiths, of HBO's *Six Feet Under,* played Morris's wife, Lorri.

The Disney film remained faithful to the pitcher's real-life story, beginning with his Navy brat childhood in Texas and exploring Morris's relationships with his father, wife, children, and students. "The message we wanted to convey was that it's not a baseball movie. It's a family-oriented movie," Morris told ESPN.com. "It entails relationships with high school kids and adults, adults and adults, adults with children. Baseball just happened to be the dream that I pursued." A box-office success, *The Rookie* received favorable reviews as one of the best family and "feel-good" movies of the year.

SELECTED WRITINGS BY MORRIS:

(With Joel Engel) *The Oldest Rookie: Big-League Dreams from a Small-Town Guy.* Boston: Little Brown & Company, 1991.

FURTHER INFORMATION

Periodicals

Justice, Richard. "Tale of Ancient Reliever." (Montreal) *Gazette* (May 2, 2002): E1.

Lawson, Terry. "Pitcher Jim Morris' Personal Field of Dreams." *Toronto Star* (March 27, 2002): F4.

Other

Dateline. NBC News (April 27, 2002).
"Jim Morris: Biography." Jim Morris Official Web Site. http://www.jimmorrisjr.com/bio.html (November 13, 2002).
"Jim Morris Statistics." BaseballReference.com. http://www.baseball-reference.com/m/morrija03.shtml (November 30, 2002).
"Ten Burning Questions for Jim Morris." ESPN.com. http://espn.go.com/page2/s/questions/jimmorris.html (November 13, 2002).

Sketch by Wendy Kagan

Edwin Moses
1955-

American track and field athlete

Hurdler Edwin Moses is a four-time world-record holder in the 400-meter hurdles. He first set a new record with a time of 47.63 in 1976, and reduced it to 47.45 in 1977 and 47.13 in 1980. In 1983, he cut his time to 47.02. He was a two-time world champion, in 1977 and 1987, and won gold medals in the Olympics in 1976 and 1984.

"Track Was Almost Incidental"

Moses grew up in Dayton, Ohio, the middle son of Gladys and Irving Moses. Irving Moses had been a football center during his college career at Kentucky State, and later taught math and science and was principal of an elementary school. Gladys Moses was a supervisor of instruction for the Dayton public school system. Naturally, Moses' parents emphasized academic achievement, particularly in science, and sports came in a distant second. Moses, who like his father had a scientific mind, often read the encyclopedia for

Edwin Moses

1955	Born August 31, in Dayton, Ohio
1974-78	Attends Morehouse College in Atlanta, Georgia; graduates with B.S. degree in physics and engineering
1976	At U.S. Olympic Trials, sets new American record in 400-meter hurdles
1976	Wins Olympic gold medal and sets world record of 47.63 in 400-meter hurdles
1977	Sets new world record of 47.45 in the 400-meter hurdles
1977	Wins world championship in 400-meter hurdles
1978-79	Works as aerospace engineer for General Dynamics
1980	U.S. boycotts Moscow Olympics; no U.S. athletes compete
1980	Sets new world record of 47.13 in 400-meter hurdles
1982	Marries Myrella Bordt
1983	Sets new world record of 47.02 in 400-meter hurdles
1983	Receives Sullivan Award for best U.S. amateur athlete
1984	Named *Sports Illustrated* Sportsman of the Year
1984	Wins second Olympic gold medal
1987	Streak of 107 consecutive wins is broken
1987	Wins second world title in Rome
1988	Wins Olympic bronze medal in 400-meter hurdles
1989	Becomes member of U.S. Olympic Committee's substance abuse committee
1989-91	Trains with U.S. bobsled team, but the team does not compete in 1992 Olympics
1991	Moses and Myrella Bordt divorce
1994	Inducted into National Track and Field Hall of Fame
1994	Receives master's degree in business administration from Pepperdine University
1994	Founding member of the Platinum Group business management firm
1990s	Works for Salomon Smith Barney investment bank
2001-present	Volunteers with Laureus Group and many other charitable and nonprofit organizations

fun as a child. When he was older, he and his brothers Irving Jr. and Vincent dissected frogs, launched home-made rockets, and made models of volcanoes and cars. Moses also played the saxophone and enjoyed creating art.

When his local school auditorium was set on fire, probably by students, Moses chose to be bused to another school four miles away, where he was one of only 20 African Americans in a student body of 800. In summer school, he took science and math courses for extra credit, and often tutored other students. Although he was on the track team, he was small—5'8" and 135 pounds—and was not considered a potential athlete. "Track was almost incidental," he told Curry Kirkpatrick in *Sports Illustrated.*

Moses attended Morehouse College in Atlanta, Georgia, a traditionally African-American institution, on an academic scholarship. He studied physics and engineering, and he was also on the track team. Unfortunately, the school had no track, and the athletes had to train wherever they could. At college, he was called the "Bionic Man" because of the intensity of his training, as well as the intensity of his studying; he would later apply his scientific, mathematical and analytical talents to his athletic career. While at college he grew, eventually reaching 6'2". His legs were fully half of his height, a trait runners call "split high," and this trait would later help make him a world-record hurdler.

In 1975, Moses began talking about going to the Olympics. He did not yet have a plan; his talk was more intuition than anything else. And in March of 1976, at the Florida Relays, Moses ran times of 13.7 in the high hurdles, 46.1 in the 400 meters, and 50.1 in the intermediate hurdles. Although he didn't win any of these races, his ability was obvious to Olympic coach Leroy Walker, who attended the race. Walker told Kirkpatrick, "His size and speed; his base, the ability to carry the stride; his 'skim,' what we call the measurement of the stride over the hurdle—he had it all."

One secret of Moses' success was his stride, and his ability to run with the same stride length even when he tired at the end of a race. Hurdlers try to make their steps between hurdles smooth and even, so that as the runner approaches the hurdle, he soars over it without breaking stride or "chopping" his steps. Moses' long legs and 9-foot, 8-inch stride, as well as his endurance, gave him the unique ability to run thirteen strides between hurdles throughout a 400-meter race, even at the end, while all other hurdlers ran thirteens at the beginning of a race, shortening their steps and increasing to fourteen or fifteen strides between hurdles as they became tired. In addition, Moses' long legs allowed him to simply float over the hurdles; as his wife, Myrella Moses, later told Kirk-

Awards and Accomplishments

1976	At U.S. Olympic Trials, sets new American record in 400-meter hurdles
1976	Wins Olympic gold medal and sets world record of 47.63 in 400-meter hurdles
1977	Sets new world record of 47.45 in the 400-meter hurdles
1977	Wins world championship in 400-meter hurdles
1980	Sets new world record to 47.13 in 400-meter hurdles
1983	Sets new world record of 47.02 in 400-meter hurdles
1983	Receives Sullivan Award for best U.S. amateur athlete
1984	Named *Sports Illustrated* Sportsman of the Year
1984	Wins second Olympic gold medal
1987	Wins second world title in Rome
1988	Wins Olympic bronze medal in 400-meter hurdles
1994	Inducted into National Track and Field Hall of Fame

patrick, "Edwin's advantage is that the other fellas actually have to jump over the hurdles."

At the NCAA Division III championships, held in Chicago in 1976, Moses fell when his sunglasses fogged up. Later in the year, he ran at the AAU meet at UCLA against top hurdlers. He was in the lead, flying along, and tried to look back to see where the other runners were. That one moment of distraction made him hit the seventh and ninth hurdles and stumble over the tenth—but he finished in fourth place, with a time of 48.99. From then on, he never again looked back during a race.

"Edwin Was Like the Lone Ranger"

At the trials for the 1976 Olympics, Moses set an American record in the 400 hurdles. And at the Olympics, held in Montreal, he set a world record with a time of 47.63, and won a gold medal.

At the time, Moses was not well known and was viewed as an enigma by the press and the public. His eyes had been sensitive to sunlight since the fifth grade, and he had to wear prescription sunglasses during competition so that he could see the hurdles. However, observers claimed that he wore the sunglasses as a political or social statement. In *Sports Illustrated,* Hurdler Andre Phillips told writer Curry Kirkpatrick that he recalled seeing Moses "with the [sweat suit] hood up and the glasses. The dude had come out of nowhere and there he was and you still couldn't see him. No face. Edwin was like the Lone Ranger. . . . He was—like, wow!—hands off, alone, cool. I really got into the hurdles after that."

After his Olympic win, Moses did not receive the recognition he thought he would. He told Kirkpatrick, "I guess I expected to be recognized or doors would open or lights would flash or something. But it was like . . . nothing. The race, the gold, the Olympics. [It was like] None of it . . . had . . . ever . . . happened." He returned to Morehouse to complete his education, and for the next few years he was criticized for not running indoor events, for not running other outdoor events, for not hav-

ing a coach, and for not joining a track club. After graduating with a 3.5 average and a degree in physics and engineering, Moses moved to California, where he worked as an aerospace engineer for General Dynamics from 1978 to 1979. He also continued to run, although he was bored with the lack of true competition against him, and even more frustrated when the United States boycotted the 1980 Moscow Olympics for political reasons and he, like all other American athletes, lost his chance to compete there.

In 1977, Moses lowered his world record to 47.45. He also won the world championship title.

Moses met his wife, Myrella Bordt, in West Berlin in the summer of 1980. She was a movie set and costume designer, and a track fan—in fact, she was such a fan of Moses that she had his photo on her bedroom wall. She told Kirkpatrick, "I knew this was the guy. He was gorgeous going over the hurdle—the look, the form, the mood it portrayed. He was compelling." In that same year, Moses set a new world record in the 400-meter hurdles: 47.13. In 1982, he and Bordt were married.

Moses applied his scientific mind to his training, using a heart rate monitor and athletic watch to guide his workouts. He tracked his training sessions on his home computer, analyzing the numbers and using them to plan future efforts. In *Sports Illustrated,* Kenny Moore wrote, "His workouts take two or three hours. He was educated to be an engineer. He is also an engine. He knows all his working parts. If something takes time, he gives it time."

A Prophetic Dream

At the end of August in 1983, Moses dreamed he saw the numbers "8-31-83" then, repeatedly, the numbers "47.03." "8-31-83" was his 28th birthday, and "47.03" was a very good time in the 400-meter hurdles—so good, in fact that it was a tenth of a second better than the world record Moses had set in 1980.

"8-31-83" was also the date of a race Moses was due to run in Koblenz, West Germany. At the race, he was relaxed—so relaxed that he went to the starting line without socks and still wearing his watch, which he customarily took off before racing. In the weeks before the race, he had run 47.37 and 47.43 in the 400-meter hurdles. His relative slowness in these runs was due to the fact that he had gone out so fast and with such intensity that he ran up on the first hurdles in twelve strides, had to chop his steps to get over the hurdles, and lost momentum and speed. At the race in which he ran 47.43, he told Kenny Moore in *Sports Illustrated,*, "Everything was bad. I lost at least three-tenths [of a second], chopping, and I got tired awfully early."

So, at Koblenz, Moses decided to relax. Europeans are great fans of track and field, and the stadium was filled with 22,000 spectators. At the starting gun, Moses took off and cleared the first hurdle perfectly. He chopped at the second, third, and fifth hurdles, running even with American Andre Phillips. At the seventh hurdle, Moses accelerated. Phillips told Moore, "I saw him take a little look over his shoulder. And he just took off!" For the last 90 meters, Moses flew, not chopping, running seamlessly. His time was 47.02, a world record by .11 of a second—and a hundredth of a second faster than the time in his dream. As a result of his world record, Moses received the 1983 Sullivan Award for Best Amateur Athlete.

At the time, only three other runners had ever run the 400-meter hurdles faster then 48 seconds: Moses, Harald Schmid, John Akii-Bua, and Andre Phillips. Schmid accomplished the feat three times, and Akii-Bua each did it once. By July of 1984, Moses had done it twenty-seven times.

When Moses set that new record, he became instantly famous. Interviews in the media, advertising contracts, and other promotions changed the way the public viewed him. Moses told Kirkpatrick that before his record, interviewers focused on numbers and statistics: How many hurdles were there in the race? How fast could he run them? Moses commented that reporters didn't ask him personal questions, and assumed that because he often wore dark glasses and was an analytical person, reporters assumed, he said, "that I was aloof and distant and unapproachable and—I loved this one—radical. I felt like going around saying, 'I didn't do it.'" In contrast to this image, he said, "I've always made friends easily."

Another Gold Medal

Moses gradually improved his public image, and by 1984, was noted for speaking out against the use of performance-enhancing drugs in sports. As a member of the 1984 U.S. Olympic team, he was chosen to represent the other athletes and recite the Olympian oath, in which athletes pledge to compete fairly and with honor. He kept his winning streak going during these Olympics, winning his second gold medal in the 400-meter hurdles.

In June of 1987, his streak of 107 consecutive wins in over nine years was finally broken. Twenty-one-year-old Danny Harris beat the 31-year-old Moses at a race in Madrid, Spain. Moses, who had felt increasing pressure as his winning streak grew longer, was actually relieved that he could now simply concentrate on running fast rather than on winning. Nevertheless, he went back to winning, taking his second world title in Rome in 1987. In that race, he beat Harris by two hundredths of a second.

At the 1988 Olympics, held in Seoul, Korea, Moses came in third in the 400-meter hurdles, winning the bronze medal with a time of 47.56. After the final race, he and the other winners gathered at the interview area, waiting for the press, and out of long habit, Moses sat in the middle seat, traditionally the place of the gold medal

winner. That winner, American Andre Phillips, was horrified when a Korean official told Moses to move over and give Phillips the center seat. Phillips told Pat Putnam in *Sports Illustrated,* "I mean a chair is a chair. I was just going to come in and plop down." He said that he did not ask Moses how he felt about being asked to move over, but noted, "It was a strange moment." An ironic twist to this event was that in order to win the bronze, Moses ran faster than he had for either of his previous Olympic gold medals.

In 1989, Moses became a member of the U.S. Olympic Committee's substance abuse committee. He also switched sports and began training with the U.S. bobsled team, hoping to compete in the 1992 Winter Olympics. Those hopes fell through, and he also did not qualify to run the hurdles at the 1992 Summer Olympics. After that, he worked with the Special Olympics, Montana State Games, Goodwill Games, and the Olympic Festival. On July 4, 1991, Moses and Myrella Bordt divorced.

Sports Illustrated writer Frank Deford wrote that at his peak, Moses, "was not only a hero to the world, but also, within his own subculture, an adviser, a spokesman, a counselor, a mediator, a diplomat.... No athlete in any sport is so respected by his peers as Moses is in track and field." Moses' brother Irving told Kirkpatrick, "Edwin is hurdling, body and soul."

CONTACT INFORMATION

Address: c/o Laureus World Sport Award, 15 Hill Street, London W1J 5QT, England. Email: media@laureus.com. Online: www.worldsport.com.

FURTHER INFORMATION

Books

"Edwin Moses." *Biography Resource Center*. Detroit: Gale Group, 2001.

Periodicals

Deford, Frank. "Rising to New Heights." *Sports Illustrated* (December 24, 1984): 32.

"Former Olympian Edwin Moses Says Education Key to His Success." *Jet* (July 22, 1996): 18.

"Hurdler Edwin Moses Named to Track and Field Hall of Fame." *Jet* (December 26, 1994): 46.

Kirkpatrick, Curry. "The Man Who Never Loses." *Sports Illustrated* (July 30, 1984): 52.

Moore, Kenny. "He Gave Himself a Birthday Present." *Sports Illustrated* (September 12, 1983): 16.

Moore, Kenny. "A Streak on the Line." *Sports Illustrated* (June 9, 1986): 30.

Putnam, Pat. "Moses Move Over: Andre Phillips Thwarted Edwin Moses' Try for More Hurdles Gold." *Sports Illustrated* (October 3, 1988): 40.

Schmidt, Beth. "Push-Off: Edwin Moses Finds the Sledding Tough in Lake Placid." *Sports Illustrated* (July 22, 1991): 9.

Swift, E. M. "Ice Follies." *Sports Illustrated* (February 4, 1991): 52.

Will-Weber, Mark. "Victory Lap." *Runner's World* (December, 2000): 44.

Yen, Yi-Wyn. "Edwin Moses, Hurdler: September 12, 1983." *Sports Illustrated* (March 11, 2002): 20.

Other

Schwartz, Larry. "Gone With the Wind." *ESPN.com.* http://www.espn.go.com/ (November 13, 2002).

Sketch by Kelly Winters

Randy Moss
1977-

American football player

Minnesota Vikings receiver Randy Moss is one of professional football's star players, but he remains "the National Football League's biggest enigma," as *New York Times* writer Judy Battista described him. Though Moss's talents on the gridiron are extraordinary, his off-the-field escapades and pronouncements have landed him in trouble on more than one occasion dating back to his high-school days.

Expelled from School

Moss was born in 1977 and grew up in a small West Virginia mining town called Rand. As a student in the nearby Belle school system, Moss emerged as a phenomenally gifted young athlete. He led the DuPont High School Pan-

Randy Moss

thers to two state football titles, and as a basketball player was named West Virginia's high school player of the year. He even excelled in baseball and won track titles at the state level. Legendary Notre Dame University coach Lou Holtz called him "the best high school player I've ever seen," according to *Sport*'s Curry Kirkpatrick, and duly signed him to play for the legendary Fighting Irish after graduation. The full scholarship was rescinded, however, when Moss became involved in a school brawl and spent a month in jail after rupturing a fellow student's spleen.

Holtz suggested Moss to the Florida State University Seminoles, who allowed him to play as a "red shirt," or an off-the-roster player, during his freshman year in 1995. The following spring, Moss returned to Charleston to serve out the remainder of his sentence for malicious wounding on a work-release program, but tested positive for marijuana use. He was jailed again, and Florida State kicked him off the team. From there Moss enrolled at Marshall University in Huntington, West Virginia, and helped make their football team, the Thundering Herd, a leader in its collegiate I-AA division. Moss's receiving and running talents led the team through a spectacular two seasons, and he was a fourth-place candidate in the Heisman Trophy voting for the best American college football player after his sophomore season.

Rookie of the Year Honors

Moss decided to quit school and enter the National Football League draft for 1998. He was widely consid-

Career Statistics

Yr	Team	Receiving				Rushing			
		REC	YDS	AVG	TD	ATT	YDS	AVG	TD
1998	VKG	69	1313	19.0	17	1	4	4.0	0
1999	VKG	80	1413	17.7	11	4	43	10.8	0
2000	VKG	77	1437	18.7	15	3	5	1.7	0
2001	VKG	80	1233	15.0	10	3	38	12.7	0
2002	VKG	82	1015	12.4	10	5	26	5.2	0
TOTAL		390	6411	16.4	58	16	116	7.3	0

VKG: Minnesota Vikings.

ered to be a top-five pick, and heralded as the best receiver out to come out of the college level in thirty years. But Moss skipped the important scouting combine, claiming he suffered from an abscessed wisdom tooth, and rumors arose that he was avoiding the mandatory drug test. Wary that he had not yet shed his troublemaker reputation, nineteen NFL teams bypassed him in the draft, but the Vikings selected him and offered a $1.4 million rookie contract.

Moss began his career with Minnesota as a third-string receiver, after Jake Reed and **Cris Carter**. Then, at a nationally televised Dallas Cowboys game on Thanksgiving Day, Moss caught three touchdown passes, each for more than 50 yards. The Vikings trounced Dallas 46-36, and Moss became an overnight celebrity. By the end of his rookie season, he led the NFL with touchdown receptions, and racked up several other impressive statistics, and the Vikings had a 15-1 season. He was named Rookie of Year by several publications, and his No. 84 became the best-selling Vikings jersey nationwide. "Beyond that," noted *Sports Illustrated* writer Jack McCallum, "Moss has—not single-handedly, to be sure, but preeminently—galvanized and glamorized the Vikes, giving them the league's highest phat factor."

Troubles On and Off the Field

There was much pre-season hype before the start of the 1999 Vikings year, with many predicting they could make it to the Super Bowl. Yet Moss's performance was spotty that year, and he paid a team fine for squirting an official with a water bottle. In 2000, the team finished 11-5, a small improvement over the past season. The onset of the 2001 football year began badly for Moss and the Vikings, when his teammate and friend Korey Stringer died of heat exhaustion after a pre-season practice. Moss stunned reporters when he wept openly about the loss. Then, a few weeks into the season, he was again fined for insulting the executives of some of the team's corporate sponsors over a seat on the bus. His most infamous moment of the 2001 season, however,

came in November when he told Minneapolis *Star Tribune* writer Sid Hartman, "I play when I want to play." The remark was widely reported in the national media, but Hartman had written in the preceding paragraph that Moss's "veteran teammate, Cris Carter, will tell you there is not a player who goes 100 percent all of the time." As Moss reflected after his soon-to-be-infamous statement was made, "Do I play up to my top performance, my ability every time? Maybe not. I just keep doing what I do and that is playing football. When I make my mind up, I am going out there to tear somebody's head off," he told Hartman.

Moss's boast "made him the poster child last season for all that is wrong with professional sports," noted *Sports Illustrated* writer Michael Silver, and Vikings fans began to boo him on the field. The team finished the season with a dismal 5-11 record. The tension between Moss and Vikings coach Dennis Green was said to be the reason that Green did not finish out the 2001 season, and the team's offensive line coach, Mike Tice, advanced to the job. The Vikings failed to re-sign Carter for the 2002 season as well. Had Vikings owner Red McCombs been convinced by Tice that he could reign in Moss and make him the **Michael Jordan** of football, he was asked? "No," Moss told Silver in *Sports Illustrated.* "Mike Tice got the job because he and Randy Moss can get along. Nobody controls me but my mama and God."

"Bumped" Officer with Lexus

A few games into the 2002 season, Tice had already heralded what he termed the "Randy Ratio"—a vow that forty percent of the team's passes were to be caught by Moss. The receiver seemed to have settled down and showed far more leadership promise than in past seasons, but at the end of September, Vikings quarterback Daunte Culpepper screamed at Moss on sidelines for failing to go after a pass with both hands. Two days later, Moss spent a night in jail after disobeying a traffic control officer in downtown Minneapolis. The officer, on foot, attempted to stop Moss in his Lexus sedan from making an illegal turn, and he was said to have nudged

Chronology

1977	Born in Rand, West Virginia
1995	School brawl leads to malicious wounding charge
1995	Loses Notre Dame scholarship
1995	Plays one season with Florida State University Seminoles
1996	Violates terms of probation, spends 90 days in West Virginia jail
1996-98	Plays two seasons for Marshall University
1998	Makes dramatic catches in Vikings' Thanksgiving Day game
1999	Fined by team for assaulting NFL official
2001	Fined by team for insulting corporate sponsors
2001	Fined by league for taunting opposing team
2002	Spends night in Minneapolis jail over traffic incident, drug possession

Awards and Accomplishments

1995	West Virginia's Mr. Basketball award
1997	Heisman Trophy finalist
1998	Named to NCAA first team All-American team
1998	Fred Biletnikoff Award
1998	NFL Offensive Rookie of the Year
1998-2000	Named to Pro Bowl Team

her with the car until she fell over. Authorities found marijuana in the car, and Moss was charged with misdemeanor drug possession.

Moss remains one of the Vikings' most talented players, though skeptics note he has not yet lived up to the promise of his athletic prowess. He claims to have learned to speak more carefully, as he told *Sports Illustrated*'s Silver. "I guess that I'm a bad guy, which I'm not," he says. "I know I have a reputation to protect, and it's not just me—I'm also representing a multimillion-dollar franchise and my family. So if sometimes I say things I regret, I've got to pay for it."

CONTACT INFORMATION

Address: c/o Minnesota Vikings, Winter Park Administrative Offices, 9520 Viking Dr., Eden Prairie, MN 55344. Phone: (952) 828-6500. Email: info@vikings.com. Online: http://www.vikings.com.

FURTHER INFORMATION

Periodicals

Attner, Paul. "Ugly solution to Moss hysteria." *Sporting News* 225 (January 15, 2001): 18.

Battista, Judy. "Moss Presents a Challenge To Jets and Vikings Alike." *New York Times* (October 17, 2002): D3.

Hack, Damon. "Officials Find No Felony Against Moss." *New York Times* (September 26, 2002): D4.

Hartman, Sid. "Moss: I play when I want to play." *Star Tribune* (Minneapolis, MN) (November 23, 2001): 3C.

Kirkpatrick, Curry. "Does this guy look like trouble?" *Sport* (October 1997): 58.

McCallum, Jack. "Moss Appeal." *Sports Illustrated* (January 18, 1999): 54.

"Moss Fined $15,000 Last Month." *New York Times* (December 14, 2001): S6.

Pompei, Dan. "Trying to get answers on Moss is like pulling teeth." *Sporting News* (February 16, 1998): 51.

Scott, David. "Moss Hysteria." *Sport* (August 1999): 50.

Silver, Michael. "How Good Can Randy Moss Be?" *Sports Illustrated* (September 2, 2002): 68.

"Traffic Arrest for Randy Moss." *New York Times* (September 25, 2002): D4.

"Vikings Star Admits Nudging Officer with Car." *New York Times* (December 12, 2002): D4.

Sketch by Carol Brennan

Shirley Muldowney
1940-

American race car driver

Professional drag racing driver Shirley "Cha Cha" Muldowney is not just "good for a girl." Though she was the first woman to accomplish many feats in the sport, many of her records and claims are for the sport as a whole, regardless of gender—she is one of the most successful drag racers in history. She is second all-time in National Hot Rod Association (NHRA) history winner with seventeen titles, including three Top Fuel world championships. In her prime, she was a threat to many of the greatest names in drag racing, including Conrad "Connie" Karlitta, Don Garlits, and Tommy Ivo. In her sixties, she continues to race, though not competitively. As a fan favorite and history maker, she is popular at exhibition races.

Muldowney was born Shirley Roque on June 19, 1940, in Burlington, Vermont. She grew up in Schenectady, New York, with her father, Belgium Benedict, a taxicab driver and professional boxer, and mother, Mae, who worked in a laundry. As a girl, she showed no indication for her penchant for racing. Though she was agile and well coordinated, Muldowney was more interested in dancing, dating, and wearing pretty clothes than she was in any sport, let alone car racing. In fact, she dropped out of high school at age sixteen and married Jack Muldowney, a drag racer and mechanic, in 1956. When she married, Shirley Muldowney did not even know how to drive a car.

Shirley Muldowney

Chronology

1958	Begins racing
1965	Becomes first woman licensed by National Hot Rod Association (NHRA) to drive a dragster
1975	Becomes first woman to advance to the finals of an NHRA national event in a professional category
1975	Becomes first woman to break the 6.00 second barrier
1976	Qualifies in top spot with quickest time (6.03) and speed (249.30 MPH), becomes the first women to win a professional title in national event competition
1976	Qualifies first and wins NHRA Winston World Finals
1976	Posts best elapsed time (5.77) and top speed (249.30 MPH) for the entire NHRA Season.
1977	Becomes first woman to claim Winston World Championship, drag racing's most prestigious title
1977	Becomes first Top Fuel driver to win three NHRA national events back-to-back
1980	Wins Winston World Championship, becoming the first person in history to claim title twice
1981	Becomes first woman to win AHRA World Championship; and first woman to win March Meet
1982	Wins Winston World Championship, becoming the first person in history to claim title three times
1983	*Heart Like a Wheel* is released
1989	Drives all-time best time of 4.97 at 284 MPH
1993	Sets track record at Fuji International Speedway, Fuji, Japan (5.30 sec. at 285 MPH); sets new IHRA speed record at 294.98 MPH
1997	Sets new IHRA speed record at 303.71 MPH
1999	Drives full race schedule with no sponsorship; advances to the semi-final round at IHRA Northern Nationals.
2000	Qualifies in third place with time of 4.78; sets new track and IHRA national speed record at 310 MPH; qualifies first at IHRA Nationals with time of 4.74 and a career best speed of 319.22 (Both were track records); qualifies in NHRA U.S. Nationals and World Finals
2001	Qualified 12th at the NHRA Mac Tools U.S. Nationals; runs career best of 4.64 \ time at 320.20 MPH
2002	Drives five national events with sponsorship from Action Performance Companies and MAC Tools

Like Husband, Like Wife

Jack Muldowney's longtime interest in high-performance cars began to wear off on his young bride. She began by attending races with her husband, and cheering him on when he raced. He taught her to drive after they were married, and Shirley became intrigued with the world of drag racing, and very familiar with all aspects of the sport, from the technical requirements of driving to the particulars involved with getting a car on the track. Drag races usually run on a quarter-mile track, and are paired head-to-head; the faster of two racers wins the race, which is over in less than fifteen seconds. The cars come to a stop with the aid of a parachute that ejects from behind to slow them down. Drag racing is so-named because drivers "drag" out through each gear shift.

Muldowney soon asked her husband to let her race, and he gave her her first car, a 1940 Ford running on a Cadillac V-8 engine. She entered local competitions in the regular stock car category and, though she did not win, she occasionally made it to the finals. She became more competitive in the early 1960s with her next two cars, a 348 tri-powered Chevrolet and then a 1963 Super Stock Plymouth. She hit just over 100 mph when racing, while drivers who raced low slung, specially-outfitted drag cars were reaching speeds of 170-180 mph. Her husband built her a Chevy-powered dragster and she soon caught up.

Muldowney had no problem proving herself on the track in amateur races. But drag racing's sanctioning bodies, including the NHRA and American Hot Rod As-sociation (AHRA), had reservations about granting professional status to a woman. Muldowney and fellow female racers Judi Boertman, Paula Murphy, and Della Woods launched a campaign to be allowed to race professionally. In 1965, Muldowney was the first woman to receive her license to drive dragsters. There were naysayers who predicted one serious crash or fire would spook Muldowney off the track, but after several, she was always ready to get back in the car. She escaped what could have been a very serious crash in 1967 at the Orange County International Raceway without a scratch, and with a great deal of respect in the sport.

Funny Cars—Not So Funny

Toward the late 1960s, cars were being designed from scratch specifically for drag racing. Because of their odd proportions—a long, skinny front end and a jacked-up behind—the cars are called "funny cars." In the driver's seat of her own Plymouth, Muldowney was finishing at the front of the pack in funny car races in the early 1970s, reaching speeds over 200 mph and finishing the quarter-mile track in seven or eight seconds.

Awards and Accomplishments

1971	First place, NHRA Southern Nationals in Nitro Funny Car Class
1972	Second place, NHRA Southern Nationals in Nitro Funny Car Class
1975	Second place, NHRA Spring Nationals
1975	Voted first woman member of Auto Racing All-America team by American Auto Racing Writers and Broadcasters Association (AARWBA).
1976	First place, NHRA Spring Nationals and NHRA Winston World Finals; named *Drag News* Top Fuel Driver of the Year; voted to Auto Racing All-American Team
1977	First place, Winston World Championship; Outstanding Achievement Award, U.S. House of Representatives; named *Drag News* Top Fuel Driver of the Year; named Person of the Year, *Car Craft* magazine
1978	Voted to Auto Racing All-America Team
1979	Voted into the 250 MPH Club
1980	First place, Winston World Championship; second place, American Hot Rod Association (AHRA) World Championship
1981	First place, AHRA World Championship; voted to Auto Racing All-America Team; voted to *Car Craft* All-Star Team, and Top Fuel Driver of the Year
1982	First place, Winston World Championship; voted to Auto Racing All-America Team; voted to *Car Craft* All-Star Team, and Top Fuel Driver of the Year; Jerry Titus Memorial Award, AARWBA
1986	Comeback Driver of the Year, AARWBA
1989	Wins NHRA Fall National
1992	Mildred "Babe" Didrikson Zaharias Courage Award for courageous action in overcoming adversity to excel in sport, U.S. Sports Academy
1996	Named to the AARWBA All-American second team; second place, International Hot Rod Association (IHRA) Championship Series
1997	Third place, IHRA National Championship; voted one of Top 25 Professional Female Athletes (1972-1997), U.S. Sports Academy; named to the AARWBA All-American second team
1998	Named one of thirty Women of Distinction, New York State Senate
2000	First place, Autofest 2000 New Year's Eve race against rival Don Garlits; Second place, IHRA Performance Parts Nationals

In 1971, Muldowney held her own against the best funny-car drivers, beating many of them. In September, she made the finals of the prestigious NHRA Nationals held at Indianapolis Speedway in Indianapolis, Indiana. Any driver who could cover the track in less than seven seconds was considered elite at the time, and Muldowney did it in 6.76 seconds, reaching 215.31 mph. Her car broke down in the final round, but Muldowney was considered a threat to any driver on the track.

The Muldowneys divorced in 1972, and Shirley moved to Mt. Clemens, Michigan, to be closer to the Midwestern racing scene. Funny cars are inherently dangerous and fire prone, so Muldowney chose to switch to the top drag racing category, called Top Fuel. She won the 1974 U.S. Nationals at 241.58 mph, and was the first woman to advance to the finals in Top Fuel, coming in second place at the 1975 NHRA Spring National in Columbus, Ohio, and at the NHRA U.S. National. She was the first woman to break the five-second barrier with 5.98 seconds at the Popular Hot Rodding Championships in August. A successful season ended

with her being voted to the prestigious "All-American Team" by the American Auto Racing Writers and Broadcasters Association (AARWBA).

Comeback of the Year

In 1976, Muldowney became the first woman to win a Pro class at an NHRA event when she won the Spring Nationals. She also won the World Finals that year and finished the season fifteenth in the points. The next great obstacle before Muldowney was to win the NHRA Winston Top Fuel Championship, which she did in 1977, 1980, and 1982, becoming the first person to claim more than one title. Muldowney's competitive nature and fierce determination were captured in the 1983 feature *Heart Like a Wheel.*

In 1984, a front-tire failure caused her car to veer off the track and into a ditch at 250 mph during qualifying at Le Grandnational in Montreal, Canada. Her legs were so badly broken they required numerous surgeries and months of grueling physical therapy before she could even walk again. She won the AARWBA's "Comeback Driver of the Year" award in 1986 after her triumphant return to the track. 1989 marked Muldowney's final NHRA win, at Fall Nationals. She also broke the four-second barrier with a time of 4.97 seconds at 294.98 mph.

Muldowney then switched her focus to the match race scene, where contestants are guaranteed a fee. She drives in events for the International Hot Rod Association (IHRA), and is swarmed by autograph-seeking fans wherever she goes. She married Rahn Tobler—her former crew chief—in 1988, and lives in Armada, Michigan. She continues to set track records on racing circuits around the world.

CONTACT INFORMATION

Email: webmaster@muldowney.com .

FURTHER INFORMATION

Books

Stambler, Irwin. *Women in Sports.* New York: Doubleday, 1975.

Periodicals

Kovac, Maria. "Women of Detroit." *Hour Detroit.* (November 1999).

Other

"No. Five, Shirley Muldowney." National Hot Rod Association Web site. http://www.nhra.com (January 15, 2003).

Offical Shirley Muldowney Web site. http://www.Muldowney.com (January 15, 2003).

"Shirley Muldowney: A Lifetime of Devotion." Racer-
chicks.com. http://www.racerchicks.com (January
15, 2003).

Sketch by Brenna Sanchez

Tori Murden
1963-

American transatlantic rower

Tori Murden's list of firsts is remarkably disparate, involving unprecedented accomplishments in transatlantic rowing, mountain climbing and cross country
skiing. In 1988, she became the first woman and first
American to reach the top of Antarctica's Lewis Nunatuk
Summit. The following year, she became the first woman
and first American to ski to the geographic South Pole. A
decade later, in an astonishing three-month quest, she became the first woman and first American to row across
the Atlantic Ocean singlehandedly. "It is my own particular flaw," Murden once said, "that I am best able to find
what it means to be a human being when I'm off alone in
some hostile place."

Early challenges

Murden's family moved thirteen times when she was
a child. The youngest of three children, she was regularly drawn into fistfights in defense of her mentally
handicapped brother, Lamar. "The things that happened
to me were nothing compared to the things that happened to Lamar," Murden told *Women's Sports & Fitness* magazine. "I learned how invisible a person can be
if they're in the margins of society." After graduating
from high school in Louisville, she earned a bachelor's
degree from Smith College and a Master of Divinity degree from Harvard. Along the way, she worked in
Boston as a chaplain at a city hospital and the director
of a residential center for homeless women. In the
1990s, Murden earned a law degree and held community service jobs in Louisville.

At the same time, she developed an adventurer's
heart. Murden climbed mountains on five continents—
including her groundbreaking trek to the top of Antarti-
ca's Lewis Nunatuk. There also were ice-climbing
expeditions on Alaska's Brooks and Muldrow Glacier,
and sea kayaking excursions on Prince William Sound
and the Indian Ocean. While enrolled in The National
Outdoor Leadership School, Murden lived with a Masai
tribe in Kenya. At Harvard, she wrote her master's thesis
on the "theology of adventure."

Tori Murden

Relentless competitor

In 1989, Murden took off three months from her divinity studies at Harvard to join the International South
Pole Overland Expedition. She was its youngest member.
As part of a nine-member team, she skied cross-country
750 miles in fifty days to the geographic South Pole—
the first woman and first American to do so. A couple
years later, Murden trained intensely to earn a spot on the
1992 U.S. Olympic rowing team, but was forced to drop
out of the final qualifying heat after breaking two ribs in
a car crash. That would not, however, be the end of Tori
Murden's competitive rowing career.

In October 1997, Murden and Louise Graff, an old
high school friend and an experienced kayaker, set out
as the only American entry and only all-female team in
the Port St. Charles Atlantic Rowing Race. The 3,000
mile east-to-west trek from the Canary Islands to Barba-
dos is considered the "downhill route" across the Atlantic, with fair weather and favorable winds. Within
hours of launch, Murden and at least two other competitors were afflicted with severe food poisoning. She spent
several days semi-conscious in the hospital, then insisted on rejoining the race. She and Graff made good
progress for two days before their electrical system
failed, forcing them to abort the effort.

A second attempt

Sector Sport Watches, an Italian company, was sponsoring French rower Peggy Bouchet's solo attempt to

cross the Atlantic in early 1998 when they contacted Murden. Bouchet was traveling westward from the Canaries; Sector wanted to back Murden in an attempt to cross the North Atlantic from west to east—a much longer, more dangerous route. "Eager to crack the U.S. market, Sector turned to Murden," reported *Women's Sports & Fitness.* "With her Ivy League pedigree and Wheaties-box grin, she was a corporate sponsor's dream—a gifted public speaker who relished giving inspirational talks to schoolkids and volunteered in a rowing program for disabled youth." Murden initially rejected the idea as too dangerous, but she relented a few days later.

She set out upon the 3,600-mile, 100-day journey from Nags Head, North Carolina, on June 14, 1998. Her boat, American Pearl, was 23-feet long and built from plywood reinforced with fiberglass and covered in Kevlar. The craft capsized a week later, damaging Murden's communications system. The boat automatically righted and bailed itself, as it was built to do, but Murden spent the next 78 days unable to communicate with the outside world or obtain a weather report. On Day 85, still 950 miles from her destination in France, Murden collided with Hurricane Danielle and its 50-foot waves. Murden sealed herself inside her coffin-sized cabin; the boat capsized fifteen times. Murden did not activate her

distress beacon until the three-day storm passed, because she did not want people risking their lives in a rescue attempt. She was suffering from a dislocated shoulder and a concussion when she finally was picked up by the bulk carrier Independent Spirit. Months later, the American Pearl washed up off the shore of Portugal.

An unprecedented achievement

Bouchet also had failed in her attempted crossing, so the elusive record was still to be claimed. On September 13, 1999, a year after she eluded death in the North Atlantic, Murden set out again. This time, however, she would travel the safer east-to-west route from the Canary Islands to the West Indies. For two months, her odyssey went smoothly. By mid-November, she was 430 miles from Guadeloupe, on pace to beat the record time for a solo crossing—just over seventy-three days—set by Sidney Genders of Great Britain in 1970. Then came tropical storm Lenny. "It passed directly over her, capsizing the boat once and sending it on a violent, nauseating roller-coaster ride that lasted for hours," said *Women's Sports & Fitness.* "The thunder was constant and cacophonous, and Murden spent the night with her fingers in her ears, singing hymns at the top of her lungs to distract herself. By dawn, the worst was over, and within a couple of days, favorable winds returned."

On December 3, after rowing 3,333 miles in eighty-two days, Murden arrived at Bas-du-Fort, Guadeloupe. "There are times (alone at sea) that are incredibly sublime, and you feel like you're at once that puny speck of nothing and part of a grand universe," she told CNN upon her arrival. "There are other times when it's frightening and just lonely. And so along the roller coaster there are grand moments and sad moments, but I wouldn't trade them for anything."

Following her historic journey, Murden returned to Louisville and married Charles "Mac" McClure, a retired forester to whom she proposed during a satellite phone call from the middle of the Atlantic. She went on to become active in civic affairs, first as development director for the Muhammad Ali Center, an arts and education complex, and later as a Spalding University trustee and a member of the task force facilitating the merger of the Louisville and Jefferson County governments.

CONTACT INFORMATION

Email: tori@adept.net.

FURTHER INFORMATION

Periodicals

Barnette, Martha. "The Unsinkable Tori Murden." *Women's Sports & Fitness* (June 2000).

Mims, Bob. "Women Urged to 'Chase Your Dreams'; Adventurer Tells YWCA Forum of Harrowing Atlantic Crossing." *Salt Lake City Tribune* (September 30, 2000).

Moss, Deborah. "Victory at Sea: Last Week Tori Murden Became the First Woman to Row Across the Atlantic." *Sports Illustrated* (December 13, 1999).

Smolove, Jill. "Fantastic Journey: Braving High Seas and Solitude, Tori Murden Rows Across the Atlantic." *People* (December 20, 1999).

Stahl, Linda. "A Year Later, Rower has Eased off to Enjoy Life; Murden-McClure Free to do 'What I Feel Like Doing.'" *Louisville Courier-Journal* (January 1, 2001).

Stahl, Linda. "Rower Gives Youths Hands-On Lesson; Murden-McClure Spends Time With Visually Impaired," *Louisville Courier-Journal* (June 14, 2001).

Sketch by David Wilkins

Stan Musial

Stan Musial
1920-

American baseball player

The greatest baseball player in one of the greatest baseball towns in the United States, Stan "The Man" Musial spent his entire career twenty-three-year career with the St. Louis Cardinals, including sixteen consecutive seasons when he hit .300 or better. Musial was a first-ballot Hall of Famer, one of the best hitters of all time, and one of the game's great ambassadors. A retiring country gentleman who transcended humble beginnings but never completely overcame his stuttering, Musial constantly expressed gratitude and love for the game—and he embodied the straightforward, no-frills attitude of America's baseball heartland. Being a player was far more important to Musial than being a celebrity.

The Longshot

Stanislaus Musial was born in 1920 in Donora, Pennsylvania, three years after another Hall of Famer from an immigrant family in southwestern Pennsylvania, **Honus Wagner**, retired from active play. The parents of Musial's mother, Mary Lancos, had emigrated from Czechoslovakia. His father, Lukasz Musial, was a Polish immigrant who worked in the shipping department of the mill in Donora. The Musials had four daughters before Stanislaus was born, and later had another son, Ed, who would go on to play baseball in the minor leagues.

Stan Musial took to baseball at an early age, excited by a neighbor who played semipro ball. A natural left-handed hitter and thrower, Musial made an important refinement in his batting skills while playing for the local Donora Zinc Works company team. Their home field had a short left-field fence with a trolley track behind it, and Musial adapted his stroke so he could hit to the opposite field. His ability to hit to all fields made him very difficult to get out.

Musial's adeptness with the bat was overshadowed in his teen years by his powerful throwing arm. He threw very fast, but his pitching was unpolished. The Pittsburgh Pirates, Wagner's team, never showed any interest in Musial, but the St. Louis Cardinals did. The Cardinals' owner, **Branch Rickey**, had developed a far-flung scouting system. After Musial played basketball for Donora High School over the winter of 1937-38, he left school before graduating after signing a professional contract with St. Louis. The Cardinals assigned him to Williamson, West Virginia, in the Class D Mountain League, the lowest

Chronology

1920	Born December 20 in Donora, Pennsylvania
1937	Hones opposite-field stroke playing in park with short left field fence
1938	Begins professional career as pitcher for Class D Williamson
1939	Career saved when he is moved to outfield to replace injured player
1941	Makes Major League debut for St. Louis
1942	Leads Cardinals to World Series victory over New York Yankees
1945	Serves in U.S. Navy as ship repairman at Pearl Harbor
1946	Returns to lead league in hitting and take Cardinals to World Series
1948	Leads National League in nine offensive categories
1949	Opens popular St. Louis restaurant
1958	Has last of sixteen consecutive .300 seasons
1962	At age forty-one, plays left field and hits .330
1963	Retires as an active player and gets two hits in final game
1967	Serves as general manager of the St. Louis Cardinals

Awards and Accomplishments

1942-44, 1946	Plays in World Series
1943-44, 1946-63	National League All-Star
1943, 1946, 1948, 1950-52, 1957	Leads National League in batting average
1943, 1946, 1948	National League Most Valuable Player
1943, 1948, 1951, 1957	*The Sporting News* National League Player of the Year
1943-44, 1946, 1948, 1950, 1952	Leads National League in slugging percentage
1943-44, 1946, 1948-49, 1952	Leads National League in hits
1943-44, 1946, 1948-49, 1952-53	Leads National League in doubles
1943-44, 1948-49, 1953, 1957	Leads National League in on-base percentage
1943, 1946, 1948-49, 1951	Leads National League in triples
1946	Leads National League in at-bats
1946, 1948, 1951-52, 1954	Leads National League in runs
1946, 1951, 1957	*The Sporting News* Major League Player of the Year
1948, 1956	Leads National League in runs batted in
1953	Leads National League in walks
1954	On June 2, becomes first major leaguer to hit five home runs in a doubleheader
1964	Named director of the National Council on Physical Fitness
1969	Inducted into National Baseball Hall of Fame
1972	Poland's Merited Champions Medal
2000	Named to Major League Baseball's All-Century team

level of the minors. There Musial spent the 1938 and 1939 seasons and did not impress anyone. His strong arm was erratic, and Williamson's manager, Harrison Wickel, reported to the parent organization that he was the wildest pitcher he'd ever seen. The statistics bear out that judgment: in 1939, Musial walked eighty-nine batters (while striking out eighty-five) in ninety-one innings.

Wickel recommended that Musial be released, but luckily for Musial a Williamson outfielder was injured, and he was pressed into service as an everyday hitter. He batted .352, and that saved his career. The next season, the Cardinals moved Musial to Daytona Beach in another Class D league, the Florida State League. For Daytona Beach, he pitched and played outfielder between his pitching starts. During one game, playing center field, Musial tried to make a diving catch and injured his left shoulder. That pretty much ended his pitching career, but his .311 batting average prompted the Cardinals to give him a second chance.

Meteoric Rise

In 1941, Musial turned around his lagging career, rising from the low minors to the major leagues during the course of a single remarkable season. To start the year, the Cardinals promoted him one level to a Class C farm team in Springfield, Missouri. There, in eighty-seven games, he hit twenty-six home runs and batted .379. That earned him a midseason promotion to Rochester, New York, a Class B Cardinals farm club, where he hit .326 in fifty-four games. In September, Musial was called up to the Cardinals and was an immediate sensation, getting six hits in a doubleheader and batting .426 in his twelve-game stint. His standout performance earned him the starting left field job for the 1942 season.

The 1942 Cardinals had a team of young, inexperienced players like Musial. They were a loose, carefree bunch, including many young men with rural backgrounds, all corralled by Rickey's sterling scouting network. "They horsed around more [than older players], cut up with hillbilly songs and musical instruments," recalled Musial in his autobiography, *Stan Musial: "The Man's" Own Story.* "I never had the courage to try my harmonica outside my hotel room, but I could make my share of noise with the slide whistle and coat hanger. I always thought it helped to laugh it up before a game, not to become too tense." The Cardinals laughed their way through the National League, surprising everyone by winning 106 games, including forty-three of their final fifty-two. In the World Series, the New York Yankees were heavy favorites, but the Cardinals rolled by them in five games, though Musial hit only .222.

Led by Musial's hitting, the Cardinals won the National League pennant again in 1943, and Musial hit .357 to win the first of his seven league batting champi-

Stan Musial, swinging bat

onships. He also led the league in slugging percentage (.562), on-base percentage (.425), hits (220), doubles (48), and triples (20), and was named the Most Valuable Player (MVP) in the National League. In the World Series, however, the Yankees turned the tables and beat St. Louis. The following year, Musial hit .347 and led the league in on-base and slugging percentages, hits (197), and doubles (51). The Cardinals won their third straight league pennant and lost the World Series to the St. Louis Browns, with Musial hitting .304 in the series.

In 1945 Musial was drafted and joined the Navy but he was saved from combat duty. He served as a mechanic on a ship repair unit at Pearl Harbor in Hawaii and played baseball every afternoon to entertain other servicemen and women. The Cardinals missed Musial during the 1945 season and finished in second place.

With World War II over, Musial returned in 1946 and led the Cardinals to yet another pennant. St. Louis had finished first in each of Musial's first four full seasons, but they would never do so again throughout his long career. He again led the league in batting with a .365 average, and also topped the league in slugging, hits (228), runs (124), doubles (50), and triples (20). He was again named the league's MVP. Musial, who was a competent but not spectacular outfielder, was shifted from left field to first base, and played most of his games at his new position. In the World Series, the Cardinals faced the Boston Red Sox, and the matchup featured a showdown between each league's best hitter—Musial and Boston's

Ted Williams. Neither slugger hit much in the series (Williams batted .200 and Musial .222) but the Cardinals won the series in seven games. It would be Musial's last appearance in a World Series.

Stan the Man

Musial acquired the nickname "Stan the Man" from Brooklyn Dodgers fans who would groan when he came up to bat with runners on base, yelling: "Oh no! Here comes that man again." Because he concentrated so much and was such an apt learner, "Stan the Man" was very difficult for pitchers to figure out. He rarely was fooled on a pitch. "If I freed my mind of all distracting thoughts, I could tell what a pitch was going to be when it got about halfway to the plate," Musial wrote in his autobiography. He told the *Sporting News*: "I had a sixth sense. I don't know what else you call it, but it never deceived me." Musial feasted on fastballs, and always seemed to know when one was coming. But early in his career pitchers started throwing him breaking pitches, and he learned how to hit them too.

Musial didn't look like a fence-busting hitter. He dug his left foot into the back line of the batter's box and crouched down in a drastically closed stance. He held his bat back until the last possible moment, then unwound like a corkscrew and quickly slashed at the ball with the thin-handled, lightweight bats he preferred to use (he would scrape the bats to make the handles even thinner). He punched many of his hits to the opposite

Career Statistics

Yr	Team	AVG	GP	AB	R	H	HR	RBI	BB	SO	SB	E
1941	STL	.426	12	47	8	20	1	7	2	1	1	0
1942	STL	.315	140	467	87	147	10	72	62	25	6	5
1943	STL	.357	157	617	108	220	13	81	72	18	9	7
1944	STL	.347	146	568	112	197	12	94	90	28	7	5
1946	STL	.365	156	624	124	228	16	103	73	31	7	15
1947	STL	.312	149	587	113	183	19	95	80	24	4	8
1948	STL	.376	155	611	135	230	39	131	79	34	7	7
1949	STL	.338	157	612	128	207	36	123	107	38	3	3
1950	STL	.346	146	555	105	192	28	109	87	36	5	8
1951	STL	.355	152	578	124	205	32	108	98	40	4	10
1952	STL	.336	154	578	105	194	21	91	96	29	7	5
1953	STL	.337	157	593	127	200	30	113	105	32	3	5
1954	STL	.330	153	591	120	195	35	126	103	39	1	5
1955	STL	.319	154	562	97	179	33	108	80	39	5	9
1956	STL	.310	156	594	87	184	27	109	75	39	2	8
1957	STL	.351	134	502	82	176	29	102	66	34	1	10
1958	STL	.337	135	472	64	159	17	62	72	26	0	13
1959	STL	.255	115	341	37	87	14	44	60	25	0	7
1960	STL	.275	116	331	49	91	17	63	41	34	1	3
1961	STL	.288	123	372	46	107	15	70	52	35	0	1
1962	STL	.330	135	433	57	143	19	82	64	46	3	4
1963	STL	.255	124	337	34	86	12	58	35	43	2	4
TOTAL		.331	3026	10972	1949	3630	475	1951	1599	696	78	142

STL: St. Louis Cardinals.

field, but he was impossible to defense. He might deliver a blooping single to any field, a screaming line drive down either foul line or up the gap for a double or triple, or a wicked liner at an infielder—and most opposing infielders quivered when he came to bat. He was a very tough man to strike out; he never had more than forty strikeouts in a season and for his career averaged one strikeout for every 158 at-bats. Although he was not primarily a power hitter, he ended up with 475 career home runs because his prodigious line drives often cleared the fences. He feasted on all types of pitching and always relaxed mentally and physically before entering the batter's box. Disciplined and consistent, Musial rarely fell into slumps and was reliably productive.

In 1947, Musial "slipped" to a .312 average—mostly because he suffered from appendicitis and put off surgery until the season's end—and spent the entire year playing first base. It was the only time during his first twelve full seasons that he failed to lead the league in any offensive category. In 1948, Musial switched back to left field and had his best season. He led the league with 230 hits, forty-six doubles, eighteen triples, 135 runs, 131 runs batted in, a .376 batting average, .450 on-base percentage, and .702 slugging percentage. These were all his career best marks except for the doubles and triples. It was one of the most dominating seasons in baseball history, and it included thirty-nine home runs—one short of league leader Johnny Mize. Musial had a home run taken away from him when one of his blasts hit a speaker at Philadelphia's Shibe Park, bounced back on the field, and was ruled a double. Another home run came in a

game that was rained out before completion, so it also did not count. In recognition of his achievements, Musial was named the league's MVP for the third time.

Baseball Ambassador

In 1949, Musial opened his own restaurant in St. Louis. In a few years he had become one of the city's most prominent figures, and he would remain an outstanding citizen long after his playing career ended. Generally quiet, as a player he avoided controversy and stayed out of the public eye. He never was thrown out of a game. But when the Cardinals tried to take advantage of his easygoing nature to keep down his salary, he fought back by staging several holdouts during spring training. In those days, with players bound by the reserve clause which tied them to teams for life, it was the only weapon players had to leverage their salaries.

In the era after World War II, many "franchise" players stayed with teams for their entire careers. Many of these stalwarts played away from the media spotlight, in the working class towns of middle America. Besides Musial, they included **Al Kaline** of the Detroit Tigers, **Ernie Banks** of the Chicago Cubs, and **Roberto Clemente** of the Pittsburgh Pirates. None of these steady performers achieved the status of nationally known superstars. If Musial had played in New York, he would have been known widely as the greatest hitter of his generation. As it was, he was content to let his play speak for itself.

And his numbers speak volumes. Besides his seven batting titles, Musial led the National League in slugging percentage six times, in on-base percentage six times, in hits six times, in doubles eight times, in triples five times, in runs five times, in RBIs twice, and in walks once. For sixteen consecutive seasons, from 1942 through 1958, he batted over .300 (not including his short stint in 1941)—only **Ty Cobb** had a longer streak of .300 batting averages.

After failing to hit .300 in 1959, Musial considered retiring. The Cardinals had a new young first baseman, Bill White. But Musial's bat was still potent. "I was having too much fun hitting to want to quit," Musial recalled in his autobiography. Instead, he switched back to left field and played four more seasons, though sitting out frequently because of age and injuries. At age 41, in 1962, he hit .330 with nineteen home runs and eighty-two RBIs. Following the 1963 season, he hung up his spikes after twenty-two years with St. Louis. On the last day of the season, he was honored in pre-game ceremonies and gave a speech, then had two hits in the game.

In 1964, President Lyndon Johnson named Musial the director of the National Council on Physical Fitness. In 1967, Musial served one season as general manager of the St. Louis Cardinals. With his friend Red Schoendienst as manager, the Cardinals won the National League championship and beat the Boston Red Sox in the World Series.

In 1969, Musial was elected to the National Baseball Hall of Fame in his first year of eligibility. Like Williams, Musial was a consummate hitter who lacked the speed and defensive abilities to be considered as one of the greatest all-round players in baseball history. But it could be argued that Musial was a more accomplished pure hitter than Williams, who is usually considered the game's best hitter. In almost every offensive category, Musial has much higher all-time totals than Williams. Musial is fourth all-time in career hits with 3,630, eighth in runs scored with 1,949 (Williams had 1,798), third in doubles with 725, fifth in RBIs (1,951), second in total bases (6,134), second in extra-base hits (1,377), sixth in games played (3,026), ninth in at-bats (10,972), and 11th in walks (1,599). Musial is tied for 19th in triples with 177, but he is first in triples among players who played after World War II. And since Musial stopped playing, only **Tony Gwynn** retired with a higher career batting average than Musial's .331.

After his retirement from playing, Musial became one of baseball's greatest ambassadors. He appeared frequently at the annual Hall of Fame induction ceremonies and at other important baseball events. When Busch Stadium opened, local baseball writers held a testimonial dinner for Musial and raised $40,000 to erect a statue of him outside the ballpark. The statue says: "Here stands baseball's perfect warrior. Here stands baseball's perfect knight."

Musial continued to express gratitude for his long career. "I was a poor boy who struck it rich in many ways through the wonders of baseball," he said in his autobiography. "I believe baseball was a great game, is a great game, and will be a great game."

SELECTED WRITINGS BY MUSIAL:

(With Bob Broeg) *Stan Musial: "The Man's" Own Story, as told to Bob Broeg*, Doubleday, 1964.

FURTHER INFORMATION

Books

The Baseball Encyclopedia. New York: Macmillan, 1997.
Broeg, Bob, and Stan Musial. *Stan Musial: "The Man's" Own Story, as told to Bob Broeg*. New York: Doubleday, 1964.
Thorn, John and Pete Palmer. *Total Baseball*. New York: Warner Books, 1989.

Periodicals

American Heritage (October 1992).
Boys' Life (August 1999).
"Living Legends."*Sports Illustrated.*July 30, 2001.
"The Naturals: Stan Musial, Tony Gwynn." *Sporting News* (July 28, 1997).

"Stan Musial: 1948: a season worth another look."
Baseball Research Journal (2001): 99.

Other

baseball-reference.com. http://www.baseball-reference.
com (November 7, 2002).

"Musial was gentleman killer." *ESPN classic*. http://
espn.go.com/classic/biography/s/Musial_Stan.html.
(November 7, 2002).

"Stan Musial." *baseball library.com*. http://www.
pubdim. net/baseballlibrary/ballplayers/M/Musial_
Stan.stm. (November 7, 2002).

"Stan Musial." *The Baseball Page.com*. http://www.
thebaseballpage.com/past/pp/musialstan/default.htm.
(November 7, 2002).

Sketch by Michael Betzold

Dikembe Mutombo

Dikembe Mutombo
1966-

American basketball player

At seven-feet-two-inches, Dikembe Mutombo is a force to be reckoned with under the basket. Known for his strong defense and exceptional shot-blocking abilities, Mutombo is the only player in the history of the National Basketball Association (NBA) to be named Defensive Player of the Year four times. After playing in Denver, Atlanta, and Philadelphia, Mutombo was traded to the New Jersey Nets in 2002.

Growing Up in Africa

Dikembe Mutombo, whose full name is Dikembe Mutombo Mpolondo Mukamba Jean Jacque Wamutombo, was born on June 25, 1966, in Kinshasa, Congo (formerly known as Zaire). Mutombo grew up in a six-bedroom home in a comfortable neighborhood with his four brothers and two sisters. As members of the Luba tribe, Mutombo's family belonged to Zaire's upper class. His father, who was educated at the Sorbonne in France, was the director of the city's high schools. Kinshasa, the capital city of 2.5 million, had a very high poverty and crime rate, and Mutombo's parents raised their children in a strict environment that stressed education, respect, and faith.

Growing to nearly seven feet tall during his high school years, Mutombo gave little consideration to playing basketball. He excelled as a soccer goalie and also practiced martial arts. Finally his father insisted that Mutombo try basketball, which the teenager did with re-

luctance. However, after cracking his chin on the concrete court during his first practice, leaving him with a still-visible scar, Mutombo was ready more than ever to quit. Only after losing an intense argument with his parents did Mutombo return to the court. Later, he would heap praise on his parents for insisting that they knew what was best for their son.

Overcoming his initial awkwardness on the court, Mutombo was soon playing for the Zaire national team with his brother Ilo. For two years Mutombo traveled with the national team and learned the game. He came to the attention of a U.S. Embassy employee while he was reading the newspapers posted in the windows of the embassy. Herman Henning, a former coach, introduced Mutombo to John Thompson, the coach of the Georgetown University Hoyas. Soon, Mutombo was on his way to Washington, D.C.

Develops Basketball Skills

Mutombo was offered an academic scholarship to Georgetown, where he planned to study medicine, become a doctor, and return to the Congo. During his first year in Washington, D.C., he did not play basketball, instead focusing his energies on learning English. During his sophomore year he joined the team, but played second fiddle to future NBA star Alonzo Mourning. Mutombo began to develop into a legitimate basketball player during his junior year, averaging 10.7 points per game and leading his team in rebounds. By his senior year, Mutombo, now seven-feet-two-inches tall, was garnering the attention of NBA scouts. He finished his final year averaging 15.2 points and 12.2 rebounds per game and was named the Big East Defensive Player of the Year. Dikembe, who speaks English, French, Spanish, Portuguese and five African dialects, graduated with a degree in linguistics and diplomacy.

In 1991 25-year-old Mutombo, the oldest player in the NBA draft, was selected as the fourth overall pick by the Denver Nuggets. Because he lacked experience on the floor, critics doubted that Mutombo could play at the professional level, at least not for several years. The Nuggets were willing to take that chance, and it proved to be a very wise gamble. During his rookie year Mutombo finished third in the NBA in rebounding, with an average of 13.2 boards per game. The only rookie to play in the NBA All-Star game, Mutombo came in second to Charlotte Hornets' Larry Johnson in voting for Rookie of the Year.

Developing into one of the best defensive players in the nation, Mutombo was named NBA Defensive Player of the Year in 1995, after leading the league in blocked shots for two consecutive years. And still, he continued to improve, especially on the defensive end, finishing the 1995-96 season as the league's third leading rebounder (11.8 per game) He led the league in blocked shots for four consecutive seasons, from 1992-93 to 1995-96, with 3.5, 4.1, 3.9, and 4.5 blocks per game, respectively. Despite his unmatched success on the defensive end, Mutombo was growing increasing unhappy in Denver. Each year his scoring declined slightly until by the end of the 1995-96 season he was only averaging 11 points per game.

Defensive Genius

Frustrated with being ignored as an offensive force, coupled with another dismal season that produced only thirty-five wins and no playoff berth, at the end of the 1995-96 season Mutombo exercised his free agency and signed a five-year, $56 million contract with the Atlanta Hawks. In his first year with the Hawks he averaged 13.3 points per game and finished second in the NBA in rebounds (11.6) and blocks (3.3) per game. In 1998, racking up 11.4 rebounds and 3.4 blocks per game on the season, Mutombo was singled out as the league's best defensive player for the second consecutive year and for the third time in his career. In the same year, Mutombo was named as a starter for the NBA All-Star game for the first time in his career. The following year he reached a career high season average of 14.1 rebounds per game.

Mutombo played with the Hawks until traded to the Philadelphia 76ers just before the trading deadline in February of 2001. Joining an already successful team, Mutombo continued to dominate on defense. In May of 2001 he became the first player in NBA history to receive a fourth Defensive Player of the Year award. In the same year the 76ers made it into the finals of the NBA playoffs but fell to **Shaquille O'Neal** and the Los Angeles Lakers. It was the first time in Mutombo's career that he played in an NBA championship series.

Philanthropic Efforts

In August of 2002, Mutombo was traded to the New Jersey Nets. Having played most of his career injury-free, Mutombo suffered a torn ligament in his right hand, which required surgery in early December, and placing the center on the injured list for the a good share of the remainder of the season. Before being sidelined, Mutombo had racked up a career total of more than 10,000 rebounds, 2,800 blocked shots, and 10,000 points.

Mutombo's success on the court has not made him forget his family or his homeland. He and his wife Rose have a daughter, Carrie Biamba Wamutumbo, and a son, Jean Jacques Dikembe Mutombo Mplombo, Jr. They are the adoptive parents of four children, belonging to two of Mutombo's deceased brothers. Along with caring for his family financially, Mutombo also gives generously

Career Statistics

Yr	Team	GP	PTS	P/G	FG%	3P%	FT%	RPG	APG	BPG	TO
1992	DEN	71	1177	16.6	.493	.000	.642	12.3	2.2	3.0	252
1993	DEN	82	1131	13.8	.510	.000	.681	13.0	1.8	3.5	216
1994	DEN	82	986	12.0	.569	.000	.583	11.8	1.5	4.1	206
1995	DEN	82	946	11.5	.556	.000	.654	12.5	1.4	3.9	192
1996	DEN	74	814	11.0	.499	.000	.695	11.8	1.5	4.5	150
1997	ATL	80	1066	13.3	.527	.000	.705	11.6	1.4	3.3	186
1998	ATL	82	1101	13.4	.537	.000	.670	11.4	1.0	3.4	168
1999	ATL	50	541	10.8	.512	.000	.684	12.2	1.1	2.9	94
2000	ATL	82	942	11.5	.562	.000	.708	14.1	1.3	3.3	174
2001	ATL/PHIL	75	749	10.0	.484	.000	.725	13.5	1.0	1.9	144
2002	PHIL	80	920	11.5	.501	.000	.764	10.8	1.0	2.0	156
TOTAL		840	10373	12.3	.522	.000	.679	12.3	1.4	3.4	1938

ATL: Atlanta Hawks; DEN: Denver Nuggets; PHIL: Philadelphia 76ers.

to his homeland. In 1994 he traveled Africa as an international spokesperson for CARE, and in 1999 he established the Dikembe Mutombo Foundation to provide funding for humanitarian assistance in Congo. Already a national hero, his popularity increased in 1996 when he donated the money to provide the Congo national women's team with uniforms for the Olympic Games. In 1999 he contributed $3 million to help establish a new hospital in the country and provided $250,000 in medical supplies to existing hospitals.

CONTACT INFORMATION

Address: New Jersey Nets, 390 Murray Hill Parkway, E. Rutherford, New Jersey 07073. Email: fans@njnets.com.

FURTHER INFORMATION

Books

Contemporary Black Biography, Volume 7. Detroit: Gale Group, 1994.

Sports Stars. Series 1-4. Detroit: U•X•L, 1994-98.

Who's Who Among African Americans, 14th ed. Detroit: Gale Group, 2001.

Periodicals

Araton, Harvey. "Wings of a Dove." *Sport* (November 1998): 70.

Burns, Marty. "Don't Bogart That Joint." *Sports Illustrated* (March 15, 1999): 79.

Deveney, Sean. "Staring Down Superman." *Sporting News* (June 18, 2001): 24.

Geffner, Michael P. "The Guardian." *Sporting News* (March 25, 1996): 40.

Guss, Greg. "Gentle Giant." *Sport* (April 1998): 74.

Jinkner-Lloyd, Amy. "Being Dikembe Mutombo." *Basketball Digest* (April 2001): 72.

"NBA's Top Defender." *Jet* (May 14, 2001): 46.

Schoenfeld, Bruce. "Dikembe Mutombo." *Sport* (March 1995): 80.

"Telander, Rick. "World Class." *Sports Illustrated* (November 7, 1994): 150.

"Terms of Endearment." *Sports Illustrated* (August 1, 1994): 9.

Thomsen, Ian. "Playoff Players: Dikembe Mutombo Vindicated a Hotly Debated Trade by Powering the 76ers Past the Bucks and into the Finals." *Sports Illustrated* (June 11, 2001): 64.

Other

"Dikembe Mutombo." National Basketball Association. http://www.nba.com/ (December 11, 2002)

"Dikembe Mutombo." Sports Stats.com. http://www.sportsstats.com/national/players/1990/Dikembe_Mutombo (December 11, 2002)

Sketch by Kari Bethel

James Naismith
1861-1939

Canadian physical education teacher

The Canadian-born physical education instructor James Naismith made an indelible mark on sports history when he invented the game of basketball in Springfield, Massachusetts, in December 1891. With a soccer ball, two peach baskets, a ladder, and ten written rules, Naismith created the sport within two weeks, after he was asked to come up with an indoor game to keep students active during the severe New England winter. Word about "basket ball," as it was originally called, spread quickly, and by 1900 the game had gained popularity at universities across the country. Although Naismith had played the game only a handful of times, he lived to see his brainchild become an international sport, making its Olympic debut in 1936, three years before his death.

Combined Sports and Spirituality

The eldest son of Scottish immigrant John Naismith and his Scottish-Canadian wife, Margaret, James Naismith was born on November 6, 1861, near Almonte, Ontario, Canada. One of three children, eight-year-old Naismith moved with his family to a milling community in Grand Calumet, where his father took work as a sawhand. Loss was a theme of his early childhood, as he was orphaned at age ten, when his parents succumbed to typhoid fever within three weeks of each other. Naismith and his siblings then lived in the Upper Canadian village of Bennie's Corners with their maternal grandmother. When she died only two years later, an uncle, Peter Young, took over care of the Naismith children.

Young Naismith, whose athletic strength surpassed his early academic performance, attended Bennie's Corners' one-room schoolhouse. He attended Almonte High School initially for only two years, and dropped out, but four years later he returned and eventually graduated. Before and after school he worked on the Young family farm, and passed his free time playing sports with friends. In the winter, he and his peers enjoyed snow-

James Naismith

shoeing, ice hockey, skating, and tobogganing; in summer, they swam in the Indian and Mississippi Rivers.

In 1883 Naismith entered McGill University in Montreal, Quebec, where he applied himself to his studies and became a strong student. To keep fit, he participated in football, rugby, lacrosse, and gymnastics. Completing a Bachelor of Arts degree in Philosophy and Hebrew, he graduated in the top ten in his class in 1887, and went on to study at McGill's theological school, Presbyterian College. Although he was a good theological student and won scholarships for his achievements, Naismith aggravated his professors by continuing to participate in sports. The theologians disapproved particularly of lacrosse, which some even referred to as "legalized murder." Yet Naismith held to his belief that one could pursue both an athletic and a spiritual life.

Chronology

1861	Born November 6 in Almonte, Ontario, Canada
1890	Arrives in Springfield, Massachusetts, to take courses in spiritual and physical development at a Y.M.C.A. training school at the School for Christian Workers (now Springfield College)
1891	Invents the game of basketball at the Y.M.C.A. in Springfield
1894	Marries Maude Shermann
1895	Becomes PE director at a Y.M.C.A. in Denver, Colorado
1898	Obtains medical degree from University of Colorado Medical School
1898	Becomes assistant gymnasium director at Kansas University
1909	Becomes a professor and doctor at Kansas University
1914	Serves as captain in Kansas First Infantry regiment
1915	Becomes a Presbyterian minister
1917	Serves 19-month post in France as Y.M.C.A. Secretary
1919	Becomes director of Kansas University's PE section
1925	Takes American citizenship
1936	Sees basketball become an official international sport at the Olympic Games in Berlin
1939	Dies on November 28 in Lawrence, Kansas

Awards and Accomplishments

1885	Silver medal for best all-around athlete, McGill University
1887	Gold medal for best all-around athlete, McGill University
1890	Silver medal for work in theology, Presbyterian College, Montreal
1910	Honorary Master's Degree in Physical Education, Kansas University
1939	Honorary Doctor of Divinity Degree, Presbyterian College, Montreal
1941	Posthumously elected to the American Academy of Physical Education
1959	Enshrined as the first member of the Naismith Memorial Basketball Hall of Fame

Living in Montreal, Naismith became acquainted with the Young Men's Christian Association (Y.M.C.A.), which had been founded in London around 1800 and established branches in Montreal and Boston in 1851. At the Montreal Y.M.C.A., Naismith approached the administrators with a desire to become an instructor who combined spirituality and athletics in a program for young athletes. The general secretary, D. A. Budge, told Naismith about an international training school in Springfield, Massachusetts, which trained Y.M.C.A. youth leaders. After obtaining his diploma from McGill's Presbyterian College of Theology, and becoming an unordained minister, Naismith departed for Massachusetts in the late summer of 1890.

Created a New Indoor Sport

At the Y.M.C.A. International Training School in Springfield, Naismith took courses that combined his two chief interests: spiritual and physical development. He also taught physical education to local youths, and played rugby with the Y.M.C.A.'s team. In the summer months, Y.M.C.A. youths enjoyed a wide range of sports, including football, baseball, and track and field, which peaked in interest in the 1870s and '80s. But the athletes' winter options—mainly calisthenics, gymnastics, and drills—were much more limited.

In the winter of 1891, during his second year with the Springfield Y.M.C.A., Naismith found himself in charge of the indoor physical education program. His students consisted primarily of bored, troublemaking youths and of mature men who had begun to tire of the indoor sports options. Realizing that interest in the indoor program was beginning to wane, the head physical education instructor, Luther Gulick, charged Naismith and his co-trainees with the task of developing new indoor games. Gulick gave the trainees two weeks to come up with their new games, and to submit proposals for them. Naismith rose to the challenge.

To create a new sport, Naismith looked for inspiration to outdoor sports like soccer, lacrosse, and football, and attempted to modify them to suit an indoor format. But since the game would be played on a hardwood floor, sports involving excessive running, tackling, and rough-housing were out of the question. Brainstorming for other ideas, Naismith recalled a childhood game called "duck on the rock," which involved throwing balls into empty boxes or baskets. Realizing that the baskets or boxes, placed at opposite ends of a court, would make good goals, he adopted them for his new game. To pose more of a challenge to players, and to emphasize skill instead of force as a key to winning, Naismith decided to raise the goals above the players' heads.

His new game was beginning to take shape, and the head instructor, Gulick, was beginning to take notice. In fact, Gulick chose Naismith's plan over the other trainees' proposals, and helped him develop some rules for a promising new indoor sport. Four basic rules were the among the first to be adopted: (1) no running with the ball in hand (hence the practice of "dribbling"), (2) no tackling or rough body contact, (3) a horizontal goal above players' heads, and (4) freedom of any player to obtain the ball and score at any time.

With the help of a janitor, Naismith found two empty peach baskets that were about 15 inches in diameter around the top. With a hammer and nails, he secured them to the rails of two lower balconies on opposite ends of the gymnasium, about ten feet above the floor. (In these early days, the basket retained its bottom, and a step ladder was placed next to the basket for retrieval of the ball.) He was then ready to try out his new game with his students, who at the time did not realize they were making sports history. On that day in December 1891, they were players in the first-ever game of basketball. The new sport was an instant hit.

News about the game spread quickly, as the Y.M.C.A.'s nationwide newspaper, the *Triangle*, printed an article about the new game, along with thirteen formal rules, in January 1892. American military and naval academies also adopted the game, and arranged tournaments at home and abroad. And since the Springfield Y.M.C.A. was an international training school, trainees from around the world got wind of "basket ball," and took the game with them to their home countries. Within only two years, basketball had made its debut in more than a dozen countries.

Recognized as the Father of Basketball

Always humble and never self-promotional, Naismith avoided drawing attention to himself as the inventor of a popular new sport. Although his students had suggested he dub the game "Naismith-ball," their instructor laughed off the idea, choosing the simpler name of basket ball. Mainly a coach and teacher, Naismith played only two official basketball games in his lifetime: a public match in Springfield in 1892, and a game at the University of Kansas, where he became the assistant gymnasium director, in 1898.

After setting his new sport in motion, Naismith went on to pursue the career he had envisioned for himself, combining fitness and spirituality for a healthy body and a healthy mind. After completing his training in Springfield, he served as the physical education director at a Y.M.C.A. in Denver, Colorado. Here he attended University of Colorado Medical School, obtaining a medical degree in 1898. With his wife, Maude, he then relocated to the University of Kansas, where he first directed activities at the gymnasium, and then became a professor and doctor. Among the academic papers he published was his 1911 piece, "A Modern College."

Upon American involvement in the First World War, Naismith served as a captain in the Kansas First Infantry regiment from 1914 to 1917. Becoming an ordained Presbyterian minister in 1915, he soon added "chaplain" to his army responsibilities. In 1916 he and his regiment served for four months on the Mexican border. Upon the war's end, Naismith was nominated Y.M.C.A. Secretary, and served a nineteen-month post in France before returning to Kansas University in 1919. He became an American citizen in 1925, and he served as Kansas University's director of physical education until 1937.

Before Naismith died at age seventy-eight in 1939, he witnessed basketball's acceptance as an official international sport at the 1936 Olympic Games in Berlin. Although he generally shied away from public acknowledgement, Naismith accepted an invitation to the Games' inaugural ceremony, and agreed to throw the ball for the Games' first-ever basketball match.

Naismith never sought fame or fortune for his invention of the popular sport, and it was not until after his death that this accomplished figure—who over his lifetime received degrees in philosophy, religion, physical

---

The Early Days of Basketball

The uniform on that historic day in December was long gray trousers, short sleeved jerseys and a pair of gym shoes. The team consisted of nine players—a goalkeeper, two guards (right and left), three centres (right centre, left centre, and centre), two wings (right and left) and a home man, stationed in this order from the goal. . . . The rules called for a referee and an umpire. With the bottoms remaining in the basket, a step ladder was placed beside the basket for retrieval.

From the eighteen members of his class, Naismith soon organized a team of nine, led by Frank Mahan as captain, for competition against teams in the eastern states. This group of nine is usually recognized as the first basketball team in history.

Source: The Early Days of Basketball." Canada's Digital Collections. http://collections.ic.gc.ca/naismith/james/basketball/early_days.htm (October 15, 2002).

---

education, and medicine—achieved true recognition for his contribution to sports history. In 1941 he was posthumously elected to the American Academy of Physical Education, and in 1959 Naismith, his name now synonymous with the Father of Basketball, was enshrined as the first member of the Naismith Memorial Basketball Hall of Fame.

FURTHER INFORMATION

Other

"Dr. James Naismith." Canada's Digital Collections. http://collections.ic.gc.ca/naismith/ (October 15, 2002).
"Dr. James Naismith." Kansas Sports Hall of Fame Web Site. http://www.kshof.org/inductees/naismith.html (October 15, 2002).
"James Naismith." Basketball Hall of Fame Web Site. http://www.hoophall.com/halloffamers/Naismith.htm (October 15, 2002).
"James Naismith: Canadian Inventor of Basketball." http://www.allsands.com/Entertainment/People/jamesnaismith_byx_gn.htm (October 15, 2002).
"Naismith's Sport Resulted in 'Basket Ball Fever.'" HawkZone.com. http://www.hawkzone.com/stories/111500/bas_fever.shtml (October 15, 2002).

Sketch by Wendy Kagan

Joe Namath
1943-

American football player

Joe Namath's bold guarantee before Super Bowl III made him an instant legend in the world of profession-

Joe Namath

al football, but it was his glamorous image off the field that made him a celebrity and an icon to the rest of the world. In the sporting world of the 1960's, Namath represented the counterculture in a way that no athlete had before. While some athletes used their platform to advance their political views, such as **Muhammad Ali**, Namath seemed disinterested in playing any role other than the one that earned him the nickname, "Broadway Joe." His love of the nightlife and women brought youth culture to the normally conservative world of football. Starring for the New York Jets, owned by entertainment mogul Sonny Werblin, Namath indulged in the high life and made no excuses for his behavior. His celebrity lifestyle, however, never seemed to interfere with his performance on the field and was the reason his actions were not only tolerated, but celebrated. His guarantee of victory over the Baltimore Colts in the third Super Bowl helped make the game the media event that it continues to be today. It also helped secure the reputation of the competing AFL, which was considered inferior to its rival league the NFL, and proved a victory for underdogs all over the country.

Born Joseph William Namath on May 31, 1943, in Beaver Falls, Pennsylvania, he was the youngest of five children. His parents divorced when he was in the sixth grade and because of a lack of money the athletically gifted child learned to hustle to get by. Namath had little interest in going to college and was set on following his brother into a military career. His mother's wish that her son get an education along with the fifty-two offers he received from colleges desiring his passing skills, how-

ever, would ultimately determine his fate. Namath decided to go to Maryland, but failed to score high enough on the college board exams, so settled in at the University of Alabama, where he played for legendary coach Bear Bryant. Bryant would later call Namath, "the greatest athlete I have ever coached."

The College Years

His quarterbacking skills were so great while at Alabama that coach Bryant eventually changed his offense to accommodate his star player during Namath's sophomore year. Things did not always go as smoothly for the handsome college football star, being benched for two games for directing traffic while intoxicated was one such incident. His reputation for hijinks, however, would be quickly erased when he returned to take his team to the 1964 national championship. The injuries he would endure during his college days would continue to plague him throughout his professional career and would lead him to later claim that he left his game in college.

Coming out of Alabama with a reputation and a freshly repaired knee, Namath was far from a sure thing. He was drafted by both the St. Louis Cardinals of the NFL and the New York Titans of the AFL. In New York, the team had a new owner and soon a new name, the New York Jets. The offer he received set records and proved too much to turn down. Owner Sonny Werblin gave Namath a contract worth $427,000, which led to legendary Green Bay Packers' coach **Vince Lombardi**'s public outrage. This not only signaled the arrival of a

Career Statistics

Yr	Team	GP	ATT	COM	YDS	COM%	TD	INT
1965	NYJ	14	340	164	2220	48.2	18	15
1966	NYJ	14	471	232	3379	49.3	19	27
1967	NYJ	14	491	258	4007	52.5	26	28
1968	NYJ	14	380	187	3147	49.2	15	17
1969	NYJ	14	361	185	2734	51.2	19	17
1970	NYJ	5	179	90	1259	50.3	5	12
1971	NYJ	4	59	28	537	47.5	5	6
1972	NYJ	13	324	162	2816	50.0	19	21
1973	NYJ	6	133	68	966	51.1	5	6
1974	NYJ	14	361	191	2616	52.9	20	22
1975	NYJ	14	326	157	2286	48.2	15	28
1976	NYJ	11	230	114	1090	49.6	4	16
1977	LA	6	107	50	606	46.7	3	5
TOTAL		143	3762	1886	27663	50.1	173	220

LA: Los Angeles Rams; NYJ: New York Jets.

new star but also an escalation in the amount professional athletes could demand. In addition to his salary, Namath was rewarded with a number of lavish bonuses and jobs for his brothers.

Instant Celebrity

His first few years in New York were more notable for his antics than his play. Namath quickly became a fixture in New York's nightlife partying until the wee hours with Johnnie Walker Red and filtered cigarettes. His dalliances with numerous women were the talk of the town. He grew a Fu Manchu mustache, invested in a Manhattan club called Bachelors III and claimed that he'd "rather go to Vietnam than get married." Although his behavior may not have been so different than that of his peers, Namath was as unafraid in the public eye as he had been on the field which led to greater press coverage of his lifestyle. In contrast to old-fashioned NFL superstars, such as **Johnny Unitas**, Namath's white shoes and unruly hair scared the establishment and foretold things to come. Throughout his thirteen year career, Namath would be seen with everyone from Dean Martin and Frank Sinatra, to Raquel Welch and Elvis. "I used to drink with Sinatra and Dean Martin and Sammy Davis at Jilly's in New York," he'd remember years later. "Those guys were crazy. They stayed up all night. Every night. They didn't have anything to do in the morning. Didn't have to get up. Me, I had to go to practice. The good thing, though, was that the Jets practiced late. I didn't have to be there until noon. I could stay up pretty late and still get some sleep before practice started." At the age of twenty-six, he would title his autobiography *I Can't Wait Until Tomorrow...'Cause I get Better Looking Everyday* and would even make it onto President Richard Nixon's enemies list.

Highs and Lows

In 1967, Namath earned his money becoming the first player to pass for over 4,000 yards, but his team was far from championship caliber. His fearlessness of play was overshadowed only by the pain he played through from his ailing knees. "I never played a down of pro football with a good knee. My game was left in college," Namath would recall. "Dr. Nichols of the Jets didn't see my knee until I'd hurt it for the fifth time. I'd had it go out and ripped five times before he operated on it the first time." Because of his reputation as a playboy, with his New York penthouse, white llama-skin rug and enormous oval-shaped bed, he wouldn't get credit for the courage and toughness he displayed until he proved himself the following year.

The Guarantee and Super Bowl III

After his record setting performance in 1967, Namath followed with a more conservative approach that had sportswriters scratching their heads. With a more complete supporting cast the Jets were poised to make a run for the Super Bowl. The game, a new phenomenon resulting from an agreement between the two leagues to match their two best teams in a battle for bragging rights, was the first step toward their eventual merger. The AFL, however, was considered the lesser league because of its wide-open style of play and characters like Namath. The league had suffered defeats in both of the previous Super Bowls to Lombardi's Packers and with Namath's Jets pitted against the ultraconservative powerhouse Baltimore Colts in Super Bowl III it was widely considered a foregone conclusion. The Colts, with crewcut quarterback Johnny Unitas, represented the old NFL and the Jets with their young brash quarterback, the flashier AFL.

The Jets were seven-point underdogs going into the game in January 1969. Namath, frustrated with the lack of respect given to his team, guaranteed a victory before the game. "I try to explain that it wasn't an arrogant line, it was an angry one," Namath has said. "I was at the Miami Touchdown Club dinner at the Miami Springs

---

Hall of Fame Introduction Speech: Delivered by Larry Bruno

Thank you, Jim. Members of the clergy, Honorable Mayor, newly inducted members of the Hall of Fame, distinguished guests and ladies and gentlemen. I am sure it is the dream of every professional football player to some day be inducted into the Hall of Fame. Today that dream comes true. Gentlemen from the City of Champions, Beaver Falls, PA., let me congratulate all of you. Joe, the people of Beaver Falls and Beaver Valley want you to know they are very proud of you especially for not forgetting where you were born and raised. I am also sure the late Coach Paul Bryant is somewhere up there looking down today wearing his famous hounds tooth hat and if he could send you a message he probably would say in his deep southern voice, "way to go Joe, be brave." Joe, I want to publicly thank you for selecting me to introduce you today. This was one of the greatest events of my life. Again, thanks Joe.

If I had to choose one word to describe the fabulous career of Joe Namath, that word would be confidence. When Joe played football for Beaver Falls High School, the entire football team believed whatever play Joe called it would work, they would make it work because they knew Joe had confidence in them. A few years later, when Joe was playing professional football for the New York Jets, and the Jets were playing the Baltimore Colts in Super Bowl III, Joe made this statement, "I guarantee we will beat the Colts." This was not a cocky, or brass statement. The Jets were a 17-point underdog, but again, when Joe said we could win, his teammates believed they could win.

Just like in high school. The Jets did win that Super Bowl III and pulled one of the greatest upsets in modern football. Incidentally, the quarterback of the Colts that day was Johnny Unitas, Joe's idol in high school. Joe even wore number 19 in high school and that jersey will be included in the Hall of Fame, thanks to the late Athletic Director, Bill Ross. If Joe continues to have that same kind of confidence in his new field of entertainment, maybe someday we will be watching the Academy Awards program and the emcee will say, "the envelope please and the winner is ladies and gentlemen, Joe Namath."

Source: "Joe's Hall of Fame Speech." Sportsline.com.http://ww1.sportsline.com/u/fans/celebrity/namath/super/hallfame.htm(November 23, 2002).

Joe Namath

Villa, and I was up at the mike, and someone yelled something nasty from the back and I said, 'Wait a minute, let's hold on. You Baltimore guys have been talking all week, but I've got news for you, buddy. We're gonna win the game. I guarantee it.'" The quote set off a media storm and the stage for what has become one of the most memorable Super Bowls in the game's history

The Jets made good on Namath's promise picking apart the Colts for a 16-7 victory in which he completed seventeen of twenty-eight passes for 206 yards. His offense dominated the Colts and the defense sealed the victory intercepting the Colts three times in the first half. The image of "Broadway Joe" trotting off the field after his team's shocking victory would be forever burned into the memories of football fans everywhere. "I got letters from a lot of high school coaches who told me they used the game as a motivator," Namath said. "Maybe it motivated some other people, too. There are a lot of underdogs in the world. Maybe it meant something to the underdogs in life."

The AFL and the NFL merged during the off-season and Namath once again made the papers. He was offered an ultimatum by Football Commissioner, **Pete Rozelle**. Rozelle demanded that he sell his nightclub, because of the "undesirables" that frequented the establishment, or face indefinite suspension. Namath responded by announcing his retirement from football at the age of 26, saying he had to follow his conscience. Although he would reconsider and sell the club in time to participate in training camp, he felt the agreement went against his instincts.

Namath would stay with the Jets through the 1976 season without ever again reaching the heights he had achieved so early in his career. Because of chronic injuries and his advancing age the Jets placed their superstar quarterback on waivers after that season. Picked up on waivers by the Los Angeles Rams, he played for one more season before retiring at the age of thirty-four.

Retirement

With his celebrity status intact and his continuing success as a corporate pitchman, Namath concentrated on a career as an actor in the late seventies. So enthralled with the craft he took acting classes to improve his abilities, he eventually gave it up under the strain of going from the top of his field to the bottom of another. Namath would continue to invest in business opportunities and enjoy a short stay on ABC's *Monday Night Football*. His main focus would become his family once the confirmed bachelor settled down and married a woman he met at a voice class in 1983. After having two daughters, Namath virtually dropped out of the public eye, moving to Florida because of the beneficial effects of warm weather on his still troublesome knees. "I have four dogs, two cats, two daughters and a wonderful wife," Namath said. "I wouldn't exactly call that quiet. Different, I guess." His picture perfect life would be disrupted, however, in 1999 when his wife of fourteen years filed for divorce.

Although Namath was not a perennial winner, playing for only four winning teams in his thirteen-year career, he was one of the game's greatest superstars. He achieved the highest honors possible during his career while continually making waves in the press. He gave a face to a struggling football league and nearly single-handedly created the art of pre-Super Bowl hype. With his heroic play on the field and his sex-symbol status off the field, Namath was an athlete that appealed to both men and women. Because of what he represents, perhaps even more than what he achieved, Namath continues to be larger than life even to fans too young to remember his impossible victory.

FURTHER INFORMATION

Books

St. James Encyclopedia of Popular Culture. Detroit: St. James Press, 2000.

Periodicals

"Broadway Joe Doesn't Sell Here Anymore." *Forbes* (June 2, 1986): 206.

"Guaranteed Cool." *Sports Illustrated* (January 28, 1991): 72.

"Jilted Joe." *People* (April 19, 1999): 64.

"Joe Namath." *Sports Illustrated* (September 19, 1994): 96.

"Joe Namath and the Jets Changed the Game." *The Providence Journal* (January 29, 2002).

"Joe Namath is Intercepted for the Last Time." *People* (November 26, 1984): 50.

"Off Broadway Joe." *Sports Illustrated* (July 14, 1997): 76.

"Revolutionaries." *Sports Illustrated* (August 17, 1999): 78.

"The Sweet Life of Swinging Joe." *Sports Illustrated* (October 31, 1994): 50.

Sketch by Aric Karpinski

Martina Navratilova
1956-

Czech tennis player

Martina Navratilova won 56 Grand Slam tennis championships, including 18 in women's singles and a record nine at Wimbledon. Her rivalry with Chris Evert helped popularize women's tennis. But Navratilova, who defected from Czechoslovakia in the mid-1970s, was just as influential off the court as an icon for female and gay athletes. In 1999, the cable network *ESPN* placed her 19th on its list of the top athletes of the 20th century, one of only two females in its top 20.

It took years for the public, who perceived Navratilova as physically imposing and cold, to embrace her. But she retired from active singles play amid a tearfully appreciative crowd at New York's Madison Square Garden in November, 1994. By then, she was a first-name-only celebrity. "I think people thought of her as a villain because physically she was so strong," Evert said on *ESPN Classic*'s SportsCentury series. "There's Chrissy and Tracy Austin and **Evonne Goolagong** and then along comes Martina, who's working out and there's veins popping out of her arms and who's really strong. And people were taken back. They were intimidated by this. But she's a kitten."

Navratilova, it seemed, was always against the grain. "How gratifying it must have been for her to have achieved so much, triumphed so magnificently," wrote Frank Deford, author and longtime *Sports Illustrated* writer. "Yet always to have been the other, the odd one, alone: lefthander in a right-handed universe, gay in a straight world; defector, immigrant; the [last?] gallant volleyer among those duplicate baseline bytes. When she came into the game, she was the European among Americans; she leaves as the American among Europeans—and the only grown-up left in the tennis crib. Can't she ever get it right?"

Behind the Iron Curtain

She was born in Prague as Martina Subertova. Her father killed himself when she was very young, and when her mother remarried, to Marislav Navratil, Martina took her stepfather's name, adding the feminine suffix "ova." She was capable in many sports, including

Martina Navratilova

hockey and skiing. Growing up in the suburb of Revnice, and competing against boys was no big deal. "I'm not very psychologically oriented and I have no idea how I was affected by my real father's abandonment, the secrets and the suicide, or my feeling about being a misfit, a skinny little tomboy with short hair," she wrote in her autobiography, *Martina*. "In Czechoslovakia, nobody ever put me down for running around with boys, playing ice hockey and soccer."

She began playing tennis at age six, on the slow clay courts of Czechoslovakia. She won the Czech national championship at age 15. "Navratilova eschewed the polite, baseline-anchored woman's game," Larry Schwartz for the *ESPN.com* web site. "With a wicked serve, a rush to the net and a ferocious volley, she was a full-court drama, complete with emotional outbursts." She turned pro in 1973, at age 16, and for her first two professional years, experienced a taste of life outside the Iron Curtain. "For the first time in my life I was able to see America without the filter of a Communist education, Communist propaganda. And it felt right," she wrote in her autobiography.

She drew on her clay-court experience by defeating clay specialist Nancy Richey at the 1973 French Open and, though unseeded, she reached the quarterfinals at Roland Garros. Later that year she lost to Evert in an indoor match in Akron, Ohio, the first of 80 matches against Evert.

After Czech sports federation authorities tried to limit her travel in 1975, feeling she was becoming too Americanized, Navratilova decided to defect. After losing to Evert in the semifinals in the 1975 U.S. Open at Forest Hills, New York, Navratilova visited the Immigration and Naturalization Service in Manhattan and got her green card. She became a U.S. citizen in 1981 and for years, the Czech media refused to print or broadcast the results of her matches. (She returned to her homeland in 1986, amid media hype, and embarrassed the Czech government by leading the U.S. Federation Cup team to victory).

But Navratilova gained weight in the late 1970s, unable to control her liking for American fast food. Her game suffered when she ballooned to 167 pounds; tennis writer Bud Collins labeled her "the Great Wide Hope." She eventually got her diet under control and undertook a training regiment that included weightlifting, running sprints and studying all aspects of tennis. She also became one of the first athletes to use a personal trainer and one of the first female tennis players to work heavily on muscle tone.

Prominence, Rivalry with Evert

Navratilova won her first Grand Slam event in 1978, at Wimbledon, the first of nine titles at Centre Court. Still overweight, she overcame Evert 2-6, 6-4, 7-5. Her final one, in 1990, broke the record of eight held by **Helen Wills**. "Navratilova made extreme fitness her trademark in chasing and overcoming Evert, who became her good friend," Collins wrote in *Bud Collins' Modern Encyclopedia of Tennis*. Navratilova overcame a 21-4 deficit in matches against Evert to end up 43-37 against her rival. She also eclipsed Evert's record of 157 consecutive pro singles tournament victories. No. 158 came against Jana Novotna, against two match points.

Navratilova won Wimbledon six straight years, from 1982-87. In other Grand Slams, she took four U.S. Opens, three Australian Opens and two French Opens. It took 11 tries for Navratilova to take the U.S. Open. She finally did so in 1983, beating Evert. The closest she came to a single-season Grand Slam came in 1983 and 1984. She went 86-1 throughout 1983, falling only to Kathy Horvath in the fourth round of the French Open. In 1984, Helena Sukova beat her in the final Grand Slam, the Australian.

Awards and Accomplishments

1977-79	WTA Tour Doubles Team of the Year (1977 with Betty Stove, 1978-79 with Billie Jean King)
1978-79	Wimbledon champion
1981	Australian Open champion
1981-89	WTA Tour Doubles Team of the Year with Pam Shriver
1982	French Open champion
1982-84	Women's Sports Foundation Sportswoman of the Year
1982-87	Wins six straight Wimbledon championships
1983	U.S. Open and Australian champion
1983	Associated Press Female Athlete of the year
1984	French Open and U.S. Open champion
1985	Australian Open champion
1986	U.S. Open champion
1987	U.S. Open champion
1987	Women's Sports Foundation Flo Hyman Award
1989	Named female athlete of the decade by National Sports Review, Associated Press and United Press International
1990	Wins ninth Wimbledon singles championship, breaking Helen Wills Moody's record
1996	WTA's David Gray Award for contributions to tennis
1999	Ranked No. 19 in ESPN SportsCentury's Top 50 athletes
2000	Inducted into Hall of Fame.

Martina Navratilova: Class of 2000

Oakland was her last tour stop prior to (Madison Square) Garden in 1994, and Martina's last final on her own. She lost narrowly and gamely to Arantxa Sanchez Vicario ... despite leading 4-1 in the second, and serving for it at 5-3 in the third. "It would have been nice to have said goodbye to the tour with a win," she sighed.

Source: Collins, Bud. *Bud Collins' Modern Encyclopedia of Tennis,* reprinted by International Tennis Hall of Fame.

Navratilova's rivalry with Chris Evert became a matter of legend among tennis afficionados. "If you tried to make the perfect rivalry ... we were it," Navratilova said in a 1998 *Washington Post* interview about the Evert matches. "Most of the time, one of us was number one in the world, the other one was number two." Off court, however the two maintained a cordial relationship. Navratilova, in fact, introduced Evert to former Olympic skier Andy Mill, who married Evert in 1988. The two tennis greats even played as doubles partners for a while, but the competition to be No. 1 in singles got to be too much.

Since 1973, Navratilova has played in the most singles tournament (380) and matches (1,650), won the most titles (167) and sporting a won-loss record of 1,438-212. Her prize money, $20.3 million, ranks her only behind men's players **Ivan Lendl** and **Pete Sampras**. "Her doubles feats, attesting to a grandeur of completeness, were as sparkling," Collins wrote. She won 31 women's doubles and seven mixed doubles titles.

Navratilova's landmark 1990 Wimbledon win, over Zina Garrison in the final, was her last Grand Slam victory. She was runner-up to **Monica Seles** at the U.S. Open in 1991 and to Conchita Martinez at Wimbledon in 1994, her final year. She did return to Wimbledon in 1995 to capture the mixed doubles title with Jonathan Stark.

Her singles finale came at the season-ending WTA Championships in New York; she dropped her only match, 6-4, 6-2 to **Gabriela Sabatini**. "Thousands cheered and wept saying goodbye and thanks for the memories," Collins wrote. "She had done so much in New York, winning that prime championship eight times in singles (five times runner-up), 10 times in doubles, plus four singles and 11 doubles titles across the East River at the

U.S. Open." Her last singles final came in the previous tournament, in Oakland, when she dropped a lengthy, three-set match to **Arantxa Sanchez Vicario**.

Speaks Out for Gays

When reports of her sexual orientation surfaced in the media, she did little to hide her homosexuality. "I never thought there was anything strange about being gay," she said in her autobiography. "Even when I thought about it, I never panicked and thought, 'Oh, I'm strange, I'm weird, what do I do now?'" Her more publicized lesbian relationships involved author Rita Mae Brown and former women's basketball standout Nancy Lieberman. Though Navratilova's public declaration probably cost her millions in endorsement dollars, others praised her for her forthrightness. She remains active today with charities that help gay rights, disadvantaged children and animal rights.

Unhappy About Game Today

Navratilova attempted a singles comeback that month at the Eastbourne grasscourt championships, an annual Wimbledon tuneup. Playing at age 45 in her first tour singles match in eight years, she defeated Tatiana Panova to become the oldest woman to win a WTA match. In the next round she lost to 19-year-old Daniela Hantuchova—both matches went the full three sets. Navratilova also competed in doubles at the January, 2003 Australian Open with Svetlana Kuznetsova of Russia. They reached the third round before losing to the Williams sisters, 6-2, 6-3 in a match that lasted barely over an hour. In a sign of changing times in women's tennis, Navratilova, once the prototype of the power game, whom Newark *Star-Ledger* writer Brad Parks four months earlier said had "arms that could shame most high school football players," found herself overwhelmed.

Many in the media, meanwhile, long for the days of the Martina-Chrissie rivalry. While Navratilova vs. Evert involved a study of so many contrasts, the sister duels of today's Williams sisters, Serena and Venus, is an all-in-the-family affair. "Tennis stadiums fill with groans now, whenever the Williams sisters engage in their methodical marches through opposite ends of Grand Slam tournament brackets," Mike Vaccaro write in the Newark *Star-Ledger* while covering the 2002 U.S. Open. "This

is why fans feel so numb, and why they instantly throw their support around anyone with a different surname.

"You'll never hear Venus say of Serena, 'I'll follow that sonofagun to the ends of the earth,' the way **Jimmy Connors** once vowed to hunt down **Bjorn Borg**," Vaccaro added. "You will surely never see the ice-cold contempt that used to cleave **John McEnroe** and Ivan Lendl, or even the sweet cold wars that Martina Navratilova and **Chris Evert** used to wage regularly."

Navratilova Legacy

"Nobody, ever, has had such a glittering trove of numbers," Collins wrote. Yet Navratilova was about far more than just numbers. "Through all her transformations-of body, hair, clothes, glasses, nationalities, coaches, lovers-the one thing, ever the same, ever distinct, is her voice, which is pitched to shatter a champagne flute," Deford said. "It brought forth sounds of decency and forthrightness, leavened with wit and compassion. Tennis was very blessed to have such a voice for so long, for these times."

Navratilova, who still competes in Grand Slam doubles, drew a crowd of admirers at the 2002 U.S. Open in New York, many of whom referred to her as "Granny." "I don't think 45 is an age," she said. "It's just a number."

Saying that no rule says "grannies" can't win tennis matches, Navratilova then added, "You know, people have been putting limitations on me for a long time. First I was too young, then I was too old. It was a very short period of time that I was just right … You can't go based on what anyone else says. If I did that, I would never have left Czechoslovakia and you would have never heard of me."

SELECTED WRITINGS BY NAVRATILOVA:

(With Mary Cirillo) *Tennis My Way*. New York: Penguin, 1984.

(With George Vescey) *Martina*. New York: Knopf, 1985.

(With Liz Nickles) *The Total Zone*. New York: Villard, 1994.

(With Liz Nickles) *Breaking Point*. New York: Villard, 1996.

(With Liz Nickles) *Killer Instinct: A Jordan Myles Mystery*. New York: Villard, 1997.

FURTHER INFORMATION

Books

Collins, Bud and Zander Hollander, eds. *Bud Collins' Modern Encyclopedia of Tennis*. Detroit: Visible Ink Press, 1994.

Martina Navratilova

Elstein, Rick and Mary Cirillo Bowden. *Rick Elstein's Tennis Kinetics with Martina Navratilova*. With an introduction by Martina Navratilova. New York: Simon and Schuster, 1985.

Periodicals

Knight, Athelia. "Chrissie vs. Martina, Cont'd: Greatest Rivalry in Women's History Now on Legends Tour." *Washington Post* (May 21, 1998).

"Navratilova Sees Singles Return End." *Los Angeles Times* (June 20, 2002).

Parks, Brad. "Ageless Navratilova Has Foes Doubled Up." *Star-Ledger* (September 1, 2002): 14.

Vaccaro, Mike. "This Is No Sizzling Rivalry … It's a Boring Sister Act." *Star-Ledger* (September 8, 2002): 6.

Other

Gale Group. http://www.galegroup.com/free_resources/whm/bio/navratilova_m.htm, (January 18, 2003).

"Martina Navratilova: 2000 Enshrinee." International Tennis Hall of Fame. http://www.tennisfame.org/enshrinees/navratilova.html, (January 17, 2003).

"Martina Was Alone at the Top." ESPN Classic. http://www.espn.go.com/classic/biography/s/Navratilova_Martina.html, (January 13, 2003).

"Serena Suits Herself." SFGate.com, http:www.sfgate.com/cgi.bin/, (January 16, 2003).

"Sports Illustrated Feeling Heat from Steamy Kournikova Cover." SportsForWomen.com, http://www.caaws.ca/Whats_New/jun00/sicover_jun10.htm, (June 5, 2000).

"Starstruck: Martina Navratilova." PlanetOut.com, http://www.planetout.com/pno/entertainment/starstruck/feature/splash.html?sernum=124, (January 18, 2003).

"Tennis Notes: Williams Sisters Too Much." Toronto Star, http://waymoresports.thestar.com/, (January 19, 2003).

"Thousands March in Washington for Gay Rights." CNN.com, http://www.cnn.com/2000/US/04/30/gay.march.03, (April 30, 2000).

Women's Sports Legends Online, http://www.wslegends.com/legends_martina_navratilova.htm, (January 14, 2003).

Sketch by Paul Burton

Cam Neely
1965-

Canadian hockey player

Cam Neely, although forced into an early retirement by leg injuries, is widely recognized for the innova-

Cam Neely

Chronology

1965	Born June 6 in Comox, British Columbia
1982	Drafted by the Vancouver Canucks
1986	Traded to the Boston Bruins
1987	Mother, Marlene, dies of cancer
1991	Suffers left leg injury during playoffs, on May 11
1994	Father, Michael, dies of cancer
1996	Retires from hockey September 5
1997	Neely House opens
1998	Attempts comeback, but retires again November 17

falls apart. It teaches you an awful lot about your priorities, about what really counts."

Neely was a good, crowd-pleasing player in Boston for several seasons. He set no records, but was an all-star in 1988, 1990, and 1991. Then, in a playoff game on May 11, 1991, Neely suffered a major injury to his left leg. Neely collided with Pittsburgh Penguins player Ulf Samuelsson, and Samuelsson's knee drove into Neely's thigh with such force that it caused a rare condition called myositis ossificans. The myositis ossificans caused the injured muscle to turn to bone; as a result, Neely now carries around a brick-sized chunk of bone in his left thigh muscle. He also suffers from knee problems that doctors think were caused in part by the same collision.

Perseverance

Neely sat out much of the 1991-92 and 1992-93 seasons dealing with his injuries. He admits that not being able to play drove him crazy at the time, but since he spent much of this period watching and studying games, he learned a great deal, particularly from studying the efficiency with which famed Boston defenseman Ray Borque did his job. Earlier in his career Neely had been famous for his dashing all over the ice, which was effective—in two of his seasons with the Bruins before his injury, Neely had reached the fifty goal mark—but not very efficient.

Armed with this new "work smarter, not harder" philosophy, Neely returned to the Bruins lineup at the end of the 1992-93 season and almost immediately established himself as a star. He scored his first goal less than five minutes into his first game back in early March of 1993, and by the end of the season, despite only playing in thirteen games, he had racked up twenty-two goals. In the 1992-93 season, Neely scored fifty goals in his first forty-four games, putting himself in an exalted category with **Mario Lemieux**, who also reached fifty goals in forty-four games, and **Wayne Gretzky**, who did it in thirty-nine.

Neely's 1992-93 season also ended in injury, when he tore a ligament in his knee. He came back and had two more solid seasons, but then arthritis in his right hip forced him to retire in 1996. He acknowledged to himself that it was over when he pulled up lame after an im-

tions he brought to the role of hockey forward. Neely was the prototypical "power forward," a class which also includes such players as the Detroit Red Wings' Brendan Shanahan and the Pittsburgh Penguins' Kevin Stevens. Power forwards are defined by their size and power, which give them an uncommon ability to drive through defensemen and get to the net. However, for many people Neely is most respected for aspects other than his skating: for his perseverance in the face of injuries and personal problems and for his work with cancer patients and their families.

"What Really Counts"

Neely started his National Hockey League (NHL) career with the Vancouver Canucks, his hometown team: Neely's family lived in nearby Maple Ridge, British Columbia. He was drafted in 1982 at age seventeen and started appearing in the Canucks lineup the very next season. Then, when he was twenty-one, Vancouver traded him to the Boston Bruins.

Only months after Neely was traded to Boston, both of his parents were diagnosed with cancer. "[The Canucks] weren't using me very much, so my career wasn't going anywhere, but my personal life was wonderful. Everyone could come to games all the time, and everyone was healthy," Neely told *Sports Illustrated* reporter Leigh Montville. "I go 3,000 miles across the country, and my career takes off, but my personal life

Career Statistics

Yr	Team	GP	G	A	PTS	+/−	PIM
1983-84	VC	56	16	15	31	0	57
1984-85	VC	72	21	18	39	−26	137
1985-86	VC	73	14	20	34	−30	126
1986-86	BB	75	36	36	72	+ 23	143
1987-88	BB	69	42	27	69	+ 30	175
1988-89	BB	74	37	38	75	+ 14	190
1989-90	BB	76	55	37	92	+ 10	117
1990-91	BB	69	51	40	91	+ 26	98
1991-92	BB	9	9	3	12	+ 9	16
1992-93	BB	13	22	7	18	+ 4	25
1993-94	BB	49	50	24	74	+ 12	54
1994-95	BB	42	27	14	41	+ 7	72
1995-96	BB	49	26	20	46	+ 3	31
TOTAL		726	395	299	694	+ 82	1241

BB: Boston Bruins; VC: Vancouver Canucks.

promptu foot race with a ten-year-old relative: "I kind of realized that if I can't run to the corner, I probably can't play professional hockey," Neely was quoted as saying in the *Buffalo News*. He briefly attempted a comeback in 1998, after rest and intensive rehabilitation had improved his knee and hip, but after only three practices the pain proved too great and he retired for good.

"If I Can't Play Again, So What?"

Neely's mother died of her cancer in 1987, shortly after Neely was traded to Boston, and his father succumbed to his late in 1993. Those experiences gave Neely perspective as he struggled with injuries towards the end in his career. "If I couldn't play hockey again, it wouldn't be the worst thing in the world," Neely told David Rattigan of *Sporting News* during the 1994-95 season. "It would be disappointing, but it wouldn't even come close to what happened with my parents.... [I]f I can't play again, so what? I can still do something else."

After his retirement, Neely, maintaining that attitude, turned his attention to helping other families that were struggling with cancer. Working with his brother Scott Neely, who also lives in Boston, Neely founded the Cam Neely Foundation, and in August of 1997 the Neely House opened its doors. Its sixteen apartments (up from eight when it first opened) are a low-cost, supportive place for cancer patients and their families to stay while undergoing treatment at the New England Medical Center in Boston.

Neely has appeared in five movies—*Monument Ave.*; *Dumb and Dumber*; *Mighty Ducks II*; *Me, Myself and Irene*; and *What's the Worst that Could Happen?*—and written a book, *Hockey for Everybody: Cam Neely's Guide to the Red-Hot Game on Ice,* since retiring from hockey. Written for new fans, the book attempts to explain the fundamentals of hockey to people who enjoy watching the game but don't necessarily understand all of the intricacies of play.

"[Neely] puts his heart and soul into everything he does," fellow Bruins player and friend Don Sweeney told *Boston Herald* reporter Joe Gordon shortly after Neely abandoned his 1998 comeback attempt. "Whether it be off the ice with the Neely Foundation or on the ice with what he accomplished or the injury situation with what he fought against.... He's a testament in his character to what people should strive to be about."

SELECTED WRITINGS BY NEELY:

(With Brian Tarcy) *Hockey for Everybody: Cam Neely's Guide to the Red-Hot Game on Ice,* Chandler House Press, 1998.

FURTHER INFORMATION

Periodicals

"Farewell, Cam." *Sports Illustrated* (September 16, 1996): 20.

Felger, Michael. "No More Tears: Neely Says 'Bye without Regrets." *Boston Herald* (November 18, 1998): 110.

Frei, Terry. "Fate Unfriendly to Cam Neely." *Denver Post* (May 5, 1996): C-05.

Gordon, Joe. "One Last Cam-eo for Neely: Failed Comeback Bid Marks True End of Inspiring Career." *Boston Herald* (November 22, 1998): B22.

Harris, Stephen. "Sorry, it's No Cam Do: Neely Abandons His Comeback Attempt." *Boston Herald* (November 17, 1998): 92.

"Injuries Force Bruins' Neely to Retire." *Houston Chronicle* (September 6, 1996): 2.

Awards and Accomplishments	
1988	Named National Hockey League Second-Team All-Star
1990	Named National Hockey League Second-Team All-Star
1991	Named National Hockey League Second-Team All-Star
1994	Named National Hockey League Second-Team All-Star
1994	Wins Bill Masterton Trophy for perseverance

Montville, Leigh. "Day-to-Day for Life." *Sports Illustrated* (January 31, 1994): 56-59.

"Neely's Hockey Career Ends in Sad Farewell." *Buffalo News (Buffalo, NY)* (September 6, 1996): C2.

"Neely Writes with New Fans in Mind." *Seattle Times* (October 18, 1998): C3.

"Pain Proves Too Much as Neely Ends Comeback Bid." *Buffalo News (Buffalo, NY)* (November 17, 1998): D4.

Rattigan, David. "Cam a Lot." *Sporting News* (March 13, 1995): 51-52.

Scher, Jon. "Cam Neely." *Sports Illustrated* (March 8, 1993): 44.

Other

"1986-87: The Cam Neely Trade." Canucks Almanac. http://www.canucksalmanac.hispeed.com/trade history/camneely_trade.htm (November 7, 2002).

Buccigross, John. "Why Cam Neely Should Be in the Hall of Fame." ESPN.com. http://msn.espn.go.com/nhl/columns/buccigross_john/1455825.html (November 7, 2002).

"Cam Neely." Hockey Sandwich. http://www.hockey sandwich.com/neely.html (November 7, 2002).

Cam Neely Foundation. http://www.camneely foundation.com (November 15, 2002).

Sketch by Julia Bauder

Paula Newby-Fraser
1962-

Zimbabwean triathlete

Paula Newby-Fraser is an eight-time Ironman Triathlon winner, and has won 23 Ironman Championships, more than twice the number won by the next-greatest triathlon champions, Mark Allen, Erin Baker, and Dave Scott. The *Los Angeles Times* and ABC's "Wide World of Sports" have hailed Newby-Fraser as "The Greatest All-Around Female Athlete in the World."

Paula Newby-Fraser

"Competing Touched a Spark in Me"

Newby-Fraser was born in Harare, Zimbabwe, in 1962. She was the younger of two children. Her father, a wealthy industrialist, moved the family to South Africa when Newby-Fraser was still young; he owned a large paint factory there. Newby-Fraser grew up with wealth and privilege, and as a child took ballet lessons and swimming classes. She showed a talent for swimming early, winning a South African national ranking while she was still in high school.

In college, Newby-Fraser decided to take a break from sports, and as a consequence, gained quite a bit of weight. However, she felt she needed a break from her intense training, and was glad to spend time with her friends, studying and relaxing. After graduating in 1984, Newby-Fraser began working full-time. She decided to lose the weight she had gained, and began running, talking aerobics classes, and lifting weights. At the end of that year, she heard about a triathlon that was going to be held in her hometown. This event, which combines swimming, bicycling, and running, is a true test of endurance. A full-length, or "Ironman," triathlon includes a 2.4-mile swim, a 112-mile bicycle ride, and a full running marathon—26.2 miles—all in one day. The triathlon she heard about was almost full-length, and the winners would go to Hawaii to compete in that year's Ironman Triathlon.

Newby-Fraser and her boyfriend went to watch the competition. Her initial reaction was that it was a ridiculous thing to do. However, her boyfriend convinced her to give the event a try in the following year, and they bought bicycles and began training. Eight weeks after buying the bicycle, Newby-Fraser entered her first triathlon. She not only finished, but won, setting a new women's record for the course. She also finished among the top 10 athletes, male or female. Three months later, she won the women's division of the South African Triathlon, and won a free trip to Hawaii to compete in the famed Ironman Triathlon there. She told Judith P. Josephson in *Children's Digest*, "Competing touched a spark in me that had not been there for several years. It felt like coming home."

Newby-Fraser did not train very hard for this event. She had never even bicycled 112 miles in a week, let alone in a day, and she had never run a marathon. Her plan was simply to finish the race and learn from the experience. When she arrived in Hawaii and began doing training runs there, she ran into unforeseen difficulties. She had trouble with the heat and with the sunburn she built up from being out all day. However, she persisted, and came in third in the world-class race.

Becomes a Professional Triathlete

Realizing that she was only five or six minutes behind the winner, Newby-Fraser knew that if she trained harder, she could win the event. She also noted that the winners of the race were professional athletes who could make a living from their sport. After talking it over with her parents, she moved to southern California and hit the racing circuit. In her first year of competition, she won $25,000.

In California, Newby-Fraser began working with trainer Paul Huddle, who taught her how to train harder. In the 1986 Hawaii Ironman, she came in second, behind Patricia Puntous. Puntous was later disqualified because she had drafted during the bicycle portion of the race, and Newby-Fraser was declared the winner.

In 1987, Newby-Fraser came in third in the Hawaii Ironman. For the next eight years, though, she won the women's Hawaii Ironman seven times, missing first place only in 1995, and broke records in the bicycle and marathon portions of the course. She also set a world record time of 8:50:24, which is still unbroken. In 1993, despite having taken six months off to heal a stress fracture in her ankle, she won again.

She won the Hawaii Ironman again in 1994, and said that the 1995 competition would be her last. As she approached the finish line in 1995, she collapsed 200 feet away. Slowly and painfully, she dragged herself to the finish, crossing the line 22 minutes later. Even with that painful delay, she still came in fourth. In 1996, Newby-Fraser came back to the Hawaii Ironman, finishing first with a time of 9:06:40, a great end to her Hawaii Ironman career.

Chronology

1962	Born in Harare, Zimbabwe
1976-80	In high school, competes as a nationally ranked South African swimmer; also dances
1980-84	Attends college; does not participate in sports
1985	Enters and wins her first triathlon; wins South African national Ironman; comes in third in Hawaii Ironman
1985-present	Competes as professional triathlete
1987	After winning eight Hawaii Ironman titles, begins running ultramarathons
1989	Founds Multi-Sport School of Champions

"Running Is My Passion"

In 1997, Newby-Fraser began running ultramarathons, races of 50 km or more. In the Los Angeles *Daily News,* she told Ronni Ross, "Running is my passion, my favorite of the three sports. You always have to come back to what you love to do, what motivates you and drives you." She noted that the sport of triathlon had become increasingly commercialized: "There's the money, the politics, it's [now] an Olympic sport." She said that she had recently worked as part of the support crew for her fiancee, Paul Huddle, while he ran the famed Western States 100, a 100-mile endurance race that is run over trails. "At Western States," she said, "People were not there for the recognition or money; they were there for the pure challenge of it." The purity of the event was attractive to Newby-Fraser. She entered the Ridgecrest High Desert 50K in April of 1997, and won, setting a course record of 4 hours and 6 minutes. Although she won, she said she still had a lot to learn about running ultras. "I'm getting a real appreciation and a good deal of humility out there," she told Ross.

Newby-Fraser continued to compete in Ironman Triathlons, and by 2002 had won 23 in all. In that year, she won the Ironman Japan competition at the age of 39, making her the oldest person ever to win an Ironman. Realizing that she could not continue competing and winning forever, Newby-Fraser branched out into other areas of her sport that were not as physically demanding. With John Howard and John Duke, Newby-Fraser founded the Multi Sport School of Champions in 1989. In 2000, Newby-Fraser and Duke joined with the coaching team of Paul Huddle and Roch Frey to form Multisports.com, which provides individualized training and also runs training camps for triathletes.

"A Self-Driven Sport"

Newby-Fraser told Josephson that an important part of being a world-class triathlete is self-discipline and motivation. "It's a self-driven sport. Triathletes spend many hours alone. If I'm going to stay on top of the sport, I need to get out of bed and do the training. It's up to me." She also told Ken McAlpine in *Runner's World* that it's also important to balance intense effort with recovery time: "Before you become injured or miserable or burned out, take a break. When you come back, you'll be fresh and eager to train. You have to learn to read yourself, to distinguish real exhaustion from just plain laziness. I take days off all the time.... Everyone needs that."

CONTACT INFORMATION

Address: c/o Multisports.com, P.O. Box 235150, Encinitas, CA 92023-5150. Fax: 760-943-7077. Phone: 760-635-1795. Online: www.multisports.com.

SELECTED WRITINGS BY NEWBY-FRASER:

(With John M. Mora) *Paula Newby-Fraser's Peak Fitness for Women,* Human Kinetics, 1995.

FURTHER INFORMATION

Books

"Paula Newby-Fraser," *Great Women in Sports,* Visible Ink Press, 1996.

Periodicals

Beck, Martin, "Training Camp," *Los Angeles Times* (March 7, 2001): D11.

Hilgers, Laura, "Out of the Slammer and Into the Swim," *Sports Illustrated* (November 4, 1991): 7.

Josephson, Judith P., "Paula Newby-Fraser," *Children's Digest* (September, 1995): 15.

McAlpine, Ken, "Tips From the Top," *Runner's World* (June, 1991): 46.

Ross, Ronni, "Pain Plan: Out of Triathlon, Into Ultramarathon Fire," *Daily News* (Los Angeles, CA), (December 18, 1997): S10.

"Van Lierde, Newby-Fraser Bag Wins," *Buffalo News* (October 27, 1996): C12.

Other

Multisports.com. http://www.multisports.com/ (January 20, 2003).

"Newby-Fraser Wins Ironman Japan for 23rd Career Ironman Win," *Triathlete Magazine,* http://www.triathletemag.com/ (January 20, 2003).

Sketch by Kelly Winters

Jack Nicklaus
1940-

American golfer

For over four decades Jack Nicklaus has been one of the greatest players to ever pick up a club. The man known as the Golden Bear is one of only five golfers to ever win all four major tournaments. But more than that, Nicklaus remained dominant in the sport for nearly three decades, with twenty-five years separating his first and last Masters win. He consistently returned to top form and won an incredible 20 major victories in his career. By the time he left the professional tour, Nicklaus amassed an amazing 71 PGA tour wins, with 58 second place and 36 third place finishes. He has also been voted PGA Tour Player of the year five times (1967, 1972-73, 1975-76).

Growing Up

Jack William Nicklaus was born on January 21, 1940 in Columbus, Ohio, to Louis Charles, Jr. (a pharmacist) and Helen Nicklaus. The young Jack first took up the game of golf when he was ten, and it took scarcely any time for people around him to realize that there was something special about his golf game. He won the first tournament he entered at the Scioto Country Club Juvenile Championship in Columbus, and soon thereafter began lessons with the local club pro, Jack Grout, who became one of the major influences on Nicklaus, both the man and the golfer. By the time he was 13, Nicklaus had already broken 70 for eighteen holes and held a 3 handicap (better than many serious adult golfers ever achieve).

As an amateur player in Ohio he took home every major trophy he could, winning the Ohio State Junior Championship in 1953, 1954 and 1955, as well as the Ohio State Open Championship in 1956. When he took his first shot at the United States Amateur Championship in 1955 (and many critics rank the U.S. Amateur

Jack Nicklaus

Awards and Accomplishments	
1962	PGA Rookie of the Year; *Golf Digest*'s Rookie of the Year
1964-65, **1967,** **1972-73,** **1975**	*Golf Digest* Byron Nelson Award for Tournament Victories
1967, **1972-73,** **1975-76**	PGA Player of the Year
1972, **1975-76**	Golf Writers Association of America (GWAA) Player of the Year
1974	Inducted into PGA/World Golf Hall of Fame
1975	Wins United States Golf Association (USGA) Bobby Jones Award
1975-77	Awarded Seagram's Seven Crowns of Sports Award
1978	*Sports Illustrated* Sportsman of the Year; wins GWAA Richardson Award
1980	Named the 1970s Athlete of the Decade
1980	Receives the Comeback of the Year Award
1982	Wins Card Walker Award for Outstanding Contributions to Junior Golf
1985	Wins Golf Family of the Year award, presented by the National Golf Foundation
1988	Named the Golfer of the Century
1993	Earns *Golf World*'s Golf Course Architect of the Year award
1996	*Golf Monthly*'s "Golfer of the Century"
1999	Wins Father of the Year Award, presented by the Minority Golf Association of America

right up there with the "majors" on the PGA Tour), Nicklaus failed to win, but he returned to the championship in 1959, winning the U.S. Amateur that year.

Nicklaus played his collegiate golf at Ohio State, remaining in his hometown and majoring in pre-pharmacy. His world seemed to be falling into place. At school he met Barbara Bash, whom he fell in love with and ended up marrying in 1959 (together they would eventually have five children). Nicklaus won most of his college tournaments, and then won his second U.S. Amateur in 1961.

The Next Challenge

The blond, pudgy young golf phenom from Ohio became a United States Professional Golf Association member in November of 1961, but he would be no stranger to the PGA tour. His amateur reputation preceded him, and many professionals were in awe of his play. One player in particular, who only four years earlier had become a major superstar in his own right, had just cause to be concerned.

Arnold Palmer is often uttered in the same sentence when the debate over the "Greatest Golfer of All Time" begins. As much as their careers seemed to overlap, it's amazing how relatively little these two actually competed against each other when considering the longevity of Nicklaus' career on the PGA Tour. When they did compete, however, the matches were memorable.

In the 1962 U.S. Open at Oakmont Country Club, which just happens to be a stone's throw from where

Palmer grew up—and therefore one of the hotbeds of Palmer fandom—Jack and Arnold squared off in their first heated major tournament. As the tournament wound down on that final Sunday, Nicklaus and Palmer wound up tied at the end of regulation play. In the ensuing playoff, Nicklaus—a young upstart whom fans had heard of but who could not hold a candle to their hero Arnie—took the playoff and the Open championship from Palmer.

"Arnie's Army" was collectively devastated, and rather than helping Nicklaus usher in his era as one of golf's finest, it set up a split between the two. Nicklaus became the bad guy, the one to beat, and Arnold Palmer (known as The King) was the fallen hero, the one people still rooted for. There are many reasons for the Nicklaus-Palmer split among fans of golf, one of which might simply be that Palmer was there first. Another might be that Palmer, the handsome, tall and tan professional, was one of the crowd, every person's movie star. And they loved him. Nicklaus, on the other hand, was boyish and pudgy, and fans did not like him stripping away the glory from the man they had gone through so much with.

In 1962, as Nicklaus began his career as one of the finest golfers ever to walk the fairways, fans of Palmer were vocal in their opposition. Nicklaus came back and won the 1963 Masters (a tournament most thought of as Palmer's) and that season's PGA Championship also went to Nicklaus. Then, following the last major victory by Palmer (in 1964), Nicklaus obliterated the competition at the 1965 Masters Tournament, beating the field by nine strokes in what **Bobby Jones** called "the greatest

Chronology

1940	Born Jack William Nicklaus on January 21		**1971**	Wins PGA Championship
1950	Plays golf for the first time, winning his first tournament later in the year		**1972**	Wins Masters and U.S. Open
			1973	Wins PGA Championship
1953	Wins Ohio State Junior Championship		**1973**	Becomes the first player to reach $2 million in tournament earnings
1953	Breaks 70 for 18 holes and holds a three handicap			
1954	Repeats as Ohio State Junior Champion		**1973**	Fourth son Michael born on July 24
1955	Wins Ohio State Junior Championship yet again; loses his first United States Amateur Championshiop in first round		**1975**	Wins Masters and PGA Championship
			1977	Becomes the first player to reach $3 million in tournament earnings
1956	Wins Ohio State Open Championship		**1978**	Wins British Open
1957	Enters Ohio State University		**1980**	Wins U.S. Open and PGA Championship
1959	Wins the U.S. Amateur (repeats in 1960 and 1961); member of Walker Cup Team		**1983**	Becomes the first player to reach $4 million in tournament earnings
1960	Marries Barbara Bash on July 23		**1986**	Wins the Masters when he's 46 years old. Oldest winner in event's history
1961	Has first child with wife Barbara—Jack II—on September 23			
1961	Wins NCAA Championship		**1987**	Captains the U.S. Ryder Cup at Muirfield Village
1961	Turns professional in November		**1988**	Becomes the first player to reach $5 million in tournament earnings
1961	Member of Walker Cup Team			
1962	Graduates from Ohio State		**1989**	Leaves the PGA Tour with an incredible 71 tournament victories
1962	Earns first pro victory, defeating Arnold Palmer in an 18-hole playoff at the U.S. Open (first of a career-record 18 major championship victories)		**1990**	Joins Senior Tour, winning in his debut at The Tradition
			1991	Wins U.S. Seniors Open
1962	Wins the U.S. Open		**1993**	Wins U.S. Seniors Open
1962-78	Records the most consecutive years with a victory (17), winning at least once per year		**1996**	Plays his 10,000 hole at the U.S. Open
			1997	Breaks Sam Snead's record for most rounds played in the Masters (147)
1963	Wins his first Masters. Youngest winner at the time; wins the PGA Championship(23)			
			1998	Suffers increasing pain in left hip and has difficulty playing much of the year
1963	Second son, Steve, born on April 11			
1965	Daughter Nancy born on May 5		**1999**	Undergoes hip replacement surgery
1965	Wins Masters Tournament		**2000**	Named co-chair with Juli Inkster of The First Tee's Capital Campaign, More Than A Game, in November
1966	Wins Masters and British Open			
1967	Wins U.S. Open		**2001**	Records two top-ten finishes
1969	Son Gary born on January 15		**2002**	Jack Nicklaus Musuem opens on campus of Ohio State in Maysidebar text
1969	Plays in first Ryder Cup and concedes a two-foot putt to Tony Jacklin—results in the first tie in the Ryder Cup history			
1970	Wins British Open			

performance in golf history." Nicklaus shattered, by three strokes, the great Jones' previous Masters record of 274.

As Palmer tried repeatedly to win another major, Nicklaus always seemed right there to pull it out from under him. The more Nicklaus won, the more he slowly gathered in his own followers. But "Arnie's Army" could not be drawn to the enemy's side, and the Golden Bear (the nickname he earned for his yellow hair and pudgy features) often was heckled as he bent over a putt, the crowd's stares and attempts to will him out of his concentration palpable on the links. Palpable to everyone but Nicklaus.

A Golfing Mind

Nicklaus' concentration—his ability to focus on the task at hand—is legendary. Indeed, many critics point to his phenomenal mental acuity and ability to focus as a major part of his success. Palmer, who in his young days was famous for his comeback victories, was now getting the comebacks pulled on him by a man who methodically sucked the leaders back in before propelling himself on to victory.

In 1967, in one of their last famous duels, Nicklaus drew close to Palmer as the final round of the U.S. Open waned. Then Nicklaus began to pull away. He was soon four strokes ahead of the field, his final margin of victory. Palmer faded into the background of the PGA Tour (although, it must be noted, he never faded from his celebrity), and Nicklaus, three years into his professional life, had many records to shatter.

Golf—in spite of the jokes to the contrary—is a physically demanding game for tour professionals. Professionals appear on the links for four days straight on weeks of tournaments, playing 18 holes each of those days, as well as practicing before and after each round. And they do this week in and week out, throughout the season, while at the same time dealing with the media and with the other pressures that arise from traveling the country and the globe. So if a player gets just a bit out of rhythm in his swing, it can throw off the entire game.

Nicklaus was unwavering in his focus. He was a powerhouse of a player who drove the ball farther than almost anyone he encountered; he mastered the putter, sinking long putts as if he were tapping the ball in from three feet; and his iron play and his shots from tough situations were as good than any other professionals he encountered. With his razor-sharp focus, he became very difficult to beat.

Yet he also became an ambassador for the game of golf. During the 1969 Ryder Cup play at Royal Birkdale, Nicklaus performed one of the true gestures of good faith in the game, conceding a short putt to Britain's Tony Jacklin, giving him the match, which in turn gave America the victory but allowed England to keep the Ryder Cup trophy one more year. Many consider it one of the best gestures in the history of sport, and though it was controversial at the time (teammate Sam Snead was upset that Nicklaus had conceded), the heart with which Nicklaus made the gesture showed his true colors.

Determined to change the way the public perceived him, Nicklaus emerged the next year as a leaner and more fit player. As the 1970s began, Nicklaus had changed his drab wardrobe for brighter colors and sought to make himself into an all-around player, one worthy of admiration for more than just his stellar play. He soon released books on how to play better golf, collaborating with his mentor Jack Grout as well as with his longtime writing ally Ken Bowden. Nicklaus' body of work itself is a veritable library of golf knowledge.

During the seventies, Nicklaus continued to accumulate tournament victories. He left the 60s with thirty victories, and added 36 more during the seventies, winning his fifth Masters in 1975 in thrilling fashion by sinking a forty-foot putt to pull one stroke ahead of Tom Weiskopf.

In 1979, however, Nicklaus stumbled. He went winless for the first time, finishing 71st on the money list. Some felt this was the beginning of his decline. After all, he had been dominating for at least fifteen seasons, and it was time for newcomers like **Tom Watson** to step up. (Palmer's dominance lasted a mere seven seasons, although some argues that it was not even that long.)

But Nicklaus, like the phoenix from the ashes, came back in the 1980s and helped usher in a new decade, proving that it was his decade as much as any other golfer's. With new major victories in the U.S. Open and the PGA Championship early on, many thought that he

Jack Nicklaus

was finally slowing down when he went several seasons without a major. Nicklaus had been the youngest winner of the Masters when he first won the tournament in 1963, but he needed to endcap his record. In 1986 he became the oldest player, at 46, to win a Masters green jacket.

CONTACT INFORMATION

Address: Home: 11397 Old Harbour Rd., North Palm Beach, FL 33408. Office: 11780 U.S. Highway No. 1, North Palm Beach, FL 33408.

SELECTED WRITINGS BY NICKLAUS:

My Fifty-Five Ways to Lower Your Golf Score. Simon & Schuster, 1964.
Take a Tip From Me. Simon & Schuster, 1968.
(With Herbert Warren Wind) *The Greatest Game of All: My Life in Golf.* Simon & Schuster, 1969.

(With Ken Bowden) *Jack Nicklaus' Lesson Tee*. Simon & Schuster, 1972.

(With Bowden) *Golf My Way*. Simon & Schuster, 1974.

The Best Way to Better Golf, Numbers 1-3. Fawcett, 1975.

(With Bowden) *Jack Nicklaus' Playing Lessons*. Golf Digest, 1976.

(With Bowden. *On and Off the Fairway*. Simon & Schuster, 1979.

(With Bowden) *Play Better Golf with Jack Nicklaus,* Volume 1: *The Swing from A to Z*. Simon and Schuster, 1980.

(With Bowden) *Play Better Golf with Jack Nicklaus,* Volume 2: *The Short Game and Scoring*. Simon and Schuster, 1981.

(With Bowden) *Play Better Golf with Jack Nicklaus,* Volume 3: *Short Cuts to Lower Scores*. New York: Simon and Schuster, 1983.

(With Bowden) *Jack Nicklaus' the Full Swing in Photos*. Golf Digest, 1984.

My Most Memorable Shots in the Majors. Golf Digest, 1988.

My Story. New York: Simon and Schuster, 1997.

FURTHER INFORMATION

Books

Argea, Angelo, and Jolee Edmondson. *Bear and I: The Story of the World's Most Famous Caddie*. New York: Atheneum, 1979.

Periodicals

"A Bear Necessity." *Sports Illustrated* (July 19, 1993): 6.

Biography News (August 1974).

Boston Globe (April 11, 1996).

Business Week (February 15, 1988).

Creighton, Brian. "Greatest Sporting Moments No. 21: Jack's gimme was proudest moment in the history of golf." *Sunday Mail* (Glasgow, Scotland) (September 1, 2002).

Golf Magazine (September, 1988).

"Jack Nicklaus." *Sports Illustrated* (September 19, 1994): 100.

Los Angeles Times (March 24, 1996).

Maclean's (May 16, 1994).

Newsweek (April 25, 1966; July 18, 1966; February 6, 1967; March 20, 1972; April 24, 1972; July 3, 1972; July 24, 1972; August 27, 1973; April 14, 1975; March 27, 1978; July 24, 1978; June 30, 1980).

New York Times (February 2, 1992).

New Yorker (August 13, 1966; November 5, 1966; July 8, 1967; July 8, 1972; July 14, 1980; May 30, 1983).

Sports Illustrated (April 4, 1966; April 18, 1966; July 18, 1966; December 19, 1966; January 30, 1967; June 26, 1967; October 14, 1968; April 14, 1969; May 19, 1969; October 27, 1969; November 7, 1969; December 8, 1969; June 15, 1970; July 20, 1970; August 3, 1970; March 8, 1971; May 3, 1971; June 28, 1971; August 9, 1971; November 8, 1971; January 24, 1972; April 3, 1972; April 17, 1972; June 26, 1972; September 4, 1972; February 19, 1973; June 11, 1973; August 20, 1973; October 15, 1973; October 14, 1974; February 3, 1975; June 16, 1975; August 18, 1975; September 22, 1975; December 22, 1975; June 7, 1976; September 13, 1976; May 30, 1977; July 18, 1977; March 27, 1978; July 24; 1978; December 25, 1978; March 31, 1980; April7, 1980; June 23, 1980; August 18, 1980; September 1, 1980; April 21, 1986; April 9, 1990).

Swift, E.M. "Long Live the King." *Sports Illustrated* (April 9, 1990): 32.

Verdi, B. "'I Had My Century': His Most Personal Interview: Jack Nicklaus on Life, Love, Beer, Business—and Winning the Big Ones." *Golf Digest* (July 2000).

Other

"Jack Nicklaus." http://www.nicklaus.com (January 15, 2003).

"Jack Nicklaus." Player Biography. http://www.golfweb.com/players/00/18/69/bio.html (January 20, 2003).

Sketch by Eric Lagergren

Hideo Nomo
1968-

Japanese baseball player

Pitcher Hideo Nomo, nicknamed "Tatsumaki" (the Tornado) for his unusual windup delivery, was the first Japanese major league baseball player to join the American major leagues. After playing four years with Japan's Kintetsu Buffaloes, he joined the Los Angeles Dodgers, in 1995. He was voted Rookie of the Year with the Dodgers and led the National League in strikeouts. Already popular in Japan, Nomo became a superstar during his first year with the Dodgers, drawing thousands of Asian fans to Dodger games. He reached the 1,000 career strikeout mark faster than any other player in the history of Japanese professional baseball. Nomo is only the fourth pitcher to have pitched no-hitters in both the National League and the American League, joining Hall of Famers **Cy Young**, Jim Bunning, and **Nolan Ryan**.

Super Tornado

Hideo (pronounced He DAY oh) Nomo was born August 31, 1968, in Osaka, Japan, the oldest son of Shizuo (a postal worker) and Kayoko Nomo. The name "Hideo" means "a superman" in Japanese. The American sport of

Hideo Nomo

Chronology

1968	Born August 31, in Osaka, Japan
1986	Graduates from Seijyo Kogyo High School, where he played baseball and developed his trademark pitching windup
1988	Leads the Japanese baseball team to the Olympic silver medal win in Seoul, South Korea
1989	Is chosen by the Kintetsu Buffaloes professional team in the Japanese Pacific League in first round of free-agent draft
1990-94	Plays with the Kintetsu Buffaloes
1991	Marries wife, Kikuko; they will have two children, Takahiro and Yoshitaka
1994	Injures arm and is limited to 114 innings
1995	Signs with the Los Angeles Dodgers on February 8, becoming the first Japanese major league player to move to the American major leagues and only the second Japanese to play in the American major leagues
1995	Appears onstage with American music group the Eagles at a concert in Tokyo on November 15; on New Year's Eve, Japanese television runs a 12-hour special on Nomo
1996	Signs new contract with Dodgers
1997	Is hit in elbow with a ball and requires surgery to remove bone fragments at end of season; pitching record drops to 14-12; teaches at Nike instructional baseball clinics throughout Asia during baseball offseason
1998	Is traded to the New York Mets in June
1999	Asks for release from Mets in March; is signed by the Chicago Cubs one week later; Cubs trade him to Milwaukee Brewers after only two outings
2000	Signs one-year contract with Detroit Tigers as a free agent; signs with Boston Red Sox at end of season
2001	Signs two-year contract with Los Angeles Dodgers on December 20 for $13 million

baseball was extremely popular in Japan, and many Japanese boys aspired to be major league ballplayers. Nomo graduated from Seijyo Kogyo High School in 1986, where he developed his unusual pitching windup resembling a whirling tornado. In 1988 he pitched for the Japanese team that brought home the Olympic silver medal from Seoul, South Korea.

Nomo, 6'2" and 210 lbs., was drafted by the Kintetsu Buffaloes in the Japanese Pacific League in the first round of the 1989 free-agent draft. In his first season, 1990, he led the Pacific League in wins and strikeouts, a pattern he would repeat for three consecutive years. He won Rookie of the Year and Most Valuable Player awards in 1990, finishing the season 18-8, with an earned run average (ERA) of 2.91.

Nomo won Japan's equivalent of the Cy Young Award for the league's best pitcher, the Sawamura Award. His teammates gave him the nickname "Tatsumaki" (the Tornado) for his unique pitching windup that confuses and terrorizes batters. A right-handed pitcher, Nomo first raises his arms slowly, high over his head, and arches his back. Then he turns to put his back toward the plate, with his left foot pointing toward second base. He pauses and then whirls, releasing a 90-mile-per-hour fastball or forkball, his trademark pitches.

Nomo was considered one of Japan's best pitchers, but a dream to play in the American major leagues was kindled when he pitched 1-1 against a U.S. All-Star team on tour in Japan. After a salary dispute with the

Buffaloes in 1994 and an arm injury that some thought would permanently reduce his effectiveness, Nomo was signed as a free agent by the Los Angeles Dodgers on February 8, 1995, with a $2 million bonus. He became the first professional Japanese player to join an American major league team and only the second Japanese player to play in the American major leagues.

L.A. Dodger, Japanese Superstar

When Dodgers manager **Tommy Lasorda** saw Nomo pitch, he told his coaches, "Don't touch a thing with this kid's motion or his delivery. The batter doesn't know what he's doing out there, but he does." Nomo himself, speaking through a translator because he speaks little English, told *People* in 1995 that he does not know how he developed his windup. "I just wanted to pitch," he said. "Every part came naturally."

After signing with the Dodgers, Nomo became a superstar in Japan. Asian fans came to Dodger games in record numbers, and busloads of Japanese tourists arrived to watch their hero play or to buy Nomo memorabilia. When Nomo was named starting pitcher for the All-Star Game in 1995, some fifteen million people watched the televised game in Japan. The pressure on him was great, but Nomo told his fans, "I will not disappoint." In 1995 he won the National League Rookie of the Year Award, even though he had played professional baseball in Japan.

Career Statistics

Yr	Team	W	L	ERA	GS	CG	SHO	IP	H	R	BB	SO
1995	LA	13	6	2.54	28	4	3	191.3	124	14	78	236
1996	LA	16	11	3.19	33	3	2	228.3	180	23	85	234
1997	LA	14	12	4.25	33	1	0	207.3	193	23	92	233
1998	LA	2	7	5.05	12	2	0	67.7	57	8	38	73
	NYM	4	5	4.82	16	1	0	89.7	73	11	56	94
1999	MIL	12	8	4.54	28	0	0	176.3	173	27	78	161
2000	DET	8	12	4.74	31	1	0	190.0	191	31	89	181
2001	BOS	13	10	4.50	33	2	2	198.0	171	26	96	220
2002	LA	16	6	3.39	34	0	0	220.3	189	26	101	193
TOTAL		98	77	3.96	248	14	7	1569	1351	690	713	1625

BOS: Boston Red Sox; DET: Detroit Tigers; LA: Los Angeles Dodgers; MIL: Milwaukee Brewers; NYM: New York Mets.

On September 17, 1996, Nomo made baseball history by pitching a no-hitter against the Colorado Rockies at their Coors Field, known as a hitter's paradise. Nomo was the first Dodger pitcher to strike out more than 200 batters in his first two seasons. In 1997, however, batters began to catch on to his delivery, and his record and ERA dropped to 14-12 and 4.25. Late in the season he was hit in the elbow with a ball and had arthroscopic surgery to remove bone fragments. In mid-1998, the Dodgers revamped their team and traded Nomo to the New York Mets.

Traveling Years

His fastball dropping to about 86 miles per hour, Nomo finished his year with the Mets 6-12, with a 4.92 ERA. In March 1999, Nomo asked to be released from the team. One week later, he was signed by the Chicago Cubs, who traded him to the Milwaukee Brewers after just two outings. Nomo's pitching improved in Milwaukee, and the team offered him a two-year contract, but he instead signed as a free agent with the Detroit Tigers. He finished 8-12 and in 2001 signed a one-year deal with the Boston Red Sox.

The highlight of his year with Boston came on April 4, 2001, when he pitched his second no-hitter, against the Baltimore Orioles. Nomo became the fourth player to pitch no-hitters in both the National and the American Leagues.

Return to the Dodgers

In December 2001 the Dodgers signed their former pitcher to a new two-year contract. With a total ERA of 3.39 for the 2002 season, Nomo made a comeback with the Dodgers. His drive to stay on the mound in spite of difficulties during a game led his teammates to nickname him "The Warrior" for his fighting spirit.

Hideo Nomo is known for his calm, almost otherworldly ability to concentrate while on the pitcher's mound. He has proved quite capable of carrying the burden of great expectations and has maintained his dream to play in the American major leagues. By signing with the American majors, Nomo paved the way for other Japanese baseball players to join U.S. teams, including **Ichiro Suzuki**, Kazuhiro Sasaki, and Shigeki Maruyama.

CONTACT INFORMATION

Address: c/o Los Angeles Dodgers, Dodger Stadium, 1000 Elysian Park Avenue, Los Angeles, CA 90012. Email: fanfeedback@dodgers.mlb.com. Online: http://losangeles.dodgers.mlb.com/.

FURTHER INFORMATION

Books

Newsmakers, Issue 2. "Hideo Nomo." Detroit: Gale Group, 1996.

Periodicals

Dougherty, Steve. "Tornado Watch: Dodger Ace Hideo Nomo Comes from Japan, but His Fastball Is Making It Big in the U.S.A." *People* (July 17, 1995): 103.

Schmuck, Peter. "Mets Take a Risk on Nomo, but It's One Worth Taking." *Sporting News* (June 15, 1998): 30.

Other

Baseball-Reference.com. "Hideo Nomo." http://www.baseball-reference.com/ (December 14, 2002).

Green, Adam. "Hideo Nomo." BaseballLibrary.com. http://www.pubdim.net/baseballlibrary/ballplayers/ (November 27, 2002).

Los Angeles Dodgers Web Site. "Hideo Nomo." http://losangeles.dodgers.mlb.com/ (November 27, 2002).

McAdam, Sean. "Nomo's No-Hitter Lifts Red Sox's Spirits." ESPN.com. http://espn.go.com/mlb/columns/mcadam_sean (December 14, 2002).

Awards and Accomplishments

1988	Pitcher for Japanese baseball team winning silver medal in Olympics in Seoul, South Korea
1990	Won Sawamura Award, Japanese baseball's equivalent to the American Cy Young Award for the Pacific League's best pitcher; won Rookie of the Year and Most Valuable Player Awards with Kintetsu Buffaloes of Japanese Pacific League
1990-93	Led Japanese Pacific League in strikeouts
1995	Named National League Rookie Pitcher of the Year by *Sporting News*; named National League Rookie of the Year by the Baseball Writers Association; strikeout leader in the National League; became first Japanese player to be selected All-Star Game; set Dodger record for most strikeouts by a rookie (236); on December 1 became only the second athlete to receive Japan's Kikuchi Award, given to individuals who play an important role in introducing Japanese culture to other countries; was chosen top sports story and third biggest news event of 1995 in Japan by Kyodo News Service and the *Daily Yomiuri*;
1996	Pitched a no-hitter against Colorado Rockies at Coors Field on September 17; first Dodger pitcher to strike out more than 200 batters in first two seasons
2001	On April 4, pitched a no-hitter against the Baltimore Orioles, becoming fourth player to pitch a no-hitter in both American and National Leagues

Morris, Sarah. "Sarah's Take: Hideo Nomo." Dodgers. com. http://mlb.mlb.com/ (November 27, 2002).

Whicker, Mark. "Nomo's Second Time with Dodgers as Good as the First." Knight Ridder/Tribune News Service. (September 16, 2002).

Sketch by Ann H. Shurgin

Greg Norman
1955-

Australian golfer

Greg Norman is professional golf's all-time leading money winner. He was the first golfer to reach $10 million in earnings and from 1986 through 1990, was ranked number one four times. He won the British Open in 1986 and 1993. Norman, nicknamed the "Great White Shark," during the 1981 Masters tournament, is extremely popular with the public and the media.

Yet Norman's knack for failure in many big tournaments, particularly the Masters, is legend, and he has lost a playoff in each of the four major tournaments. In 1993, he actually led all four major tournaments entering the final round but only captured the British Open. In 1996, he led the Masters by six strokes only to shoot 78 in the final round losing to **Nick Faldo** by five strokes. Fate worked against him again in 1987 when Larry Mize

beat him for the Masters championship with a miracle chip shot. "Norman remains an enigmatic figure, a man whose talent was never questioned but whose heart often was," Ron Flatter wrote in a sports-century biography for *ESPN.com*. "Much the same way as (baseball's) Bill Buckner and (football's) Scott Norwood are remembered for singular plays, Norman's good name is underscored by eye-popping failures."

Two British Titles, Many Failures

Norman was raised in Mount Isa, Queensland, an Australian mining town, and caddied for his mother for six years. He earned his first professional victory in 1976, his first year as a pro, when he captured the West Lakes Classic outside Adelaide. He won about 20 tournaments overseas before his first victory in the United States, the Kemper Open outside Washington, D.C. in 1984.

His first disappointment in a major tournament came two weeks later at Winged Foot Golf Club in Mamaroneck, New York. After forcing an 18-hole playoff with a 40-foot putt-inducing Fuzzy Zoeller to wave a white "surrender" handkerchief-he shot 5-over par in the playoff and lost to Zoeller.

Norman won his first major title, in 1986, when he captured the British Open. He rode a second-round 63 to a five-stroke victory at Turnberry, but he blew the other three majors in what Flatter called the "Saturday Slam." (Golf tournaments hold the next-to-last rounds on Saturdays). In the Masters, it was less of a Norman fold than a Jack Nicklaus charge. Nicklaus was in ninth place entering the last 18 holes and shot a 30 on the back nine holes; still, Norman fell to Nicklaus by missing a 15-foot putt on the final hole.

At Shinnecock Hills in Southampton, N.Y. that summer, Norman fell all the way to 12th with a 5-over-par 75 the last day as Ray Floyd became the oldest U.S. Open champion. He also stumbled at the PGA Championship at Inverness in Toledo, Ohio, ending with a 76. Tway won with an against-all-odds chip shot from a greenside bunker and prevailed by two strokes.

Ironically, Norman engineered one of the great final rounds in major championship history when he took the 1993 British at Royal St George's. Starting the last day one stroke behind co-leaders Faldo and Corey Pavin, Norman shot a 6-under par 64 to offset a 67 by defending champion Faldo. Norman triumphed by two strokes. "Yeah, I would like to say I beat Bob Tway. I would like to say I beat Larry Mize and those other guys, too," Norman said. "I didn't. But I hung around, and I came back."

Agony at Augusta

Three frustrating finishes in 1986 paled in comparison to Norman's nightmarish defeat in the 1987 Masters. "As if losing one major to an unlikely shot were not punishment enough, Norman would experience golf's

Greg Norman

version of the cruel and unusual in the very next Grand Slam tournament," wrote Flatter. In the second playoff hole, Mize's pitch shot from 45 yards rolled down a slick green and into the hole. Norman missed a 30-foot birdie putt. Norman cried when he returned to his Florida beach home that night

Norman's other loss at Augusta in 1996 drew an avalanche of public sympathy. He led by six strokes entering the last 18 holes, only to suffer an 11-stroke turnaround. "Golf is the cruelest game, because eventually it will drag you out in front of the whole school, take your lunch money and slap you around. Golf can make a man look more helpless than any other endeavor," *Sports Illustrated*'s Rick Reilly wrote of Norman. "I don't know many people who watched the final round of The Masters and enjoyed what they saw," Billy Faires wrote. "Well, except for the sports reporters, who covered it like the media hounds who covered the Jessica Dubroff flight—in the hopes that she would crash and they would have a great front-page story.

Even the man in the green jacket, symbolic of a Masters triumph, was sympathetic. "I don't know what to say," Faldo told Norman in an emotional gathering. "I just want to give you a hug. I feel horrible about what happened. I'm so sorry." Still, others questioned Norman's killer instinct. Said former caddie Bruce Edwards about Norman on *ESPN Classic*'s Sports Century series: "We were walking up the 17th fairway, and Greg turns

Chronology

1955	Born in Mt. Isa, Queensland, Australia
1976	Turned professional
1984	Ties U.S. Open on 40-foot putt but loses 18-hole playoff to Fuzzy Zoeller
1986	Leads all four major tournaments entering final round but wins only British Open
1987	Larry Mize miracle chip shot in playoff proves decisive as Norman drops Masters by one stroke
1993	Leads all four majors entering final day but wins only British Open
1996	Blows six-hole lead on final day of The Masters; Nick Faldo wins tournament.
2002	Competes in only 13 PGA Tour events; announces late in year that he will rejoin PGA Tour in 2003.

to me and says, 'I guess it's better to be lucky than good.' And I was stunned. Faldo had outplayed him all day. And so I turned to Greg and said, 'I just want to caddie for someone who has heart.'"

Still Hugely Successful

Despite his legendary near misses, Norman can boast of 20 PGA Tour victories, including his two British Opens, and 66 international titles. He played a lighter schedule in 2002, competing in only 13 Tour events, making the cut 10 times and withdrawing once. A year earlier, he won $1 million at the 2001 Skins Game, shutting out **Tiger Woods**, Colin Montgomerie and Jesper Parnevik. And, in 2000, despite playing less because of medical reasons (his right hip has bothered him for several years), he was 84th on the money list. His last victories were the St. Jude Classic and the World Series of Golf, both in 1997. He was third in the Masters in 1999.

Norman, in a recent interview with the *The Golf Channel,* echoed the concern of many PGA Tour players as professional golf tournaments, just coming off a growth cycle, scramble for sponsors amid a sluggish economy. "I see the bubble growing at such an exponential rate—about 10 to 13 percent a year since 1999—that it's going to burst. Everything else is on the drop, but we're on the up, so when you have this disparity going on, it doesn't take too long before you get sailing close to the edge."

Norman, also a highly successful businessman, is chairman of Great White Shark Enterprises, a multi-national corporation whose ventures range from golf course design to clothing and yachts. "The shark logo-a multicolored image of a shark—and the Norman name are among the most potent business symbols in the world," Adam Schupak wrote on the *PGA.com* Web site. He is also an active course architect and has a strain of turfgrass named after him.

The Normans, who married in 1981 and live in Hove Sound, Florida, have two children, Morgan-Leigh and Gregory. He and his wife, Laura, are active in many charities and have received the Hands of Hope Award from the National Childhood Cancer Foundation. Norman's hobbies include hunting, fishing and scuba diving.

SELECTED WRITINGS BY NORMAN:

Norman, Greg and Don Lawrence. *Greg Norman: My Story,* London, England: Harrap, 1983.

Norman, Greg and George Peper. *Shark Attack: Greg Norman's Guide to Aggressive Golf,* New York, NY: Simon & Schuster, 1988.

Norman, Greg and George Peper. *Greg Norman's Instant Lessons,* New York, NY: Simon & Schuster, 1993.

Advanced Golf/Greg Norman, Rutland, Vt.: Journey Editions, 1996.

FURTHER INFORMATION

Periodicals

Litke, Jim. "Shark Shakes Loser's Stigma." *Daily Freeman* (July 19, 1993): 14.

"Stormin' Norman: Shark Attacks Past, Wins British Open." *Daily Freeman* (July 19, 1993): 13.

Other

Berlet, Bruce. "Title Search: Tour Sponsor Situation a Growing Concern." Hartford Courant, http://www.ctnow.com/sports, (December 15, 2002).

Faires, Billy. "On Greg Norman's Fall at The Masters, 1996." McCallie School, http://www.mccallie.org/bfaires/columns/norman.html, (December 17, 2002).

Feherty, David. "Feherty's Mailbag: Spectator Mounds." CNN-Sports Illustrated, http://sportsillustrated.cnn.com/golfonline/columns/feherty/email/2003/0103, (January 3, 2003).

Flatter, Ron. "Major Failures Overshadow Norman's Conquests." ESPN.com, http://espn.go.com/classic/biography/s/Norman_Greg.html, (December 29, 2002).

"Greg Norman." PGA.com, http://www.golfweb.com/information/norman_indepth.html, December 29, 2002).

"Greg Norman-Biographical Information." http://www.golfweb.com/players/bios/1876.html, (December 16, 2002).

"Greg Norman Biography." www.shark.com/sharkwatch/biography (December 27, 2002).

Oliver, Darius. "The Great White Shark: Greg Norman." Ausgolf, http://www.ausgolf.com.au/theshark.htm, (December 27, 2002).

Reilly, Rick. "The 1996 Masters Tournament," CNN Sports Illustrated.com, http://sportsillustrated.cnn.com/augusta/history/online_coverage/1996/, (April 17, 1996).

Sketch by Paul Burton

David O'Connor
1962-

American equestrian

With a family tradition in the saddle, a wife who is also his teammate, and a barn full of talented horses, equestrian David O'Connor seemed destined for eventing success. A longtime representative for the United States in international competition, O'Connor reached a new peak in 2000 when he took home an individual gold medal at the Olympic summer games in Sydney, Australia, having posted record scores in the demanding, sometimes dangerous, three-day event.

Born in Gaithersburg, Maryland, O'Connor got into riding through his mother, the British-born dressage judge Sally O'Connor. Sally put David and his brother, Brian, on their first ponies as young children; at age eight, David made his eventing debut mounted on his pony mare, Bramble, who got him disqualified from a dressage class when she ran out of the ring. Just a few years later, the O'Connors embarked on a memorable mission: Sally, Brian, and David rode horseback from Maryland to Oregon, a three-month trek that provided invaluable riding experience. Just as important, O'Connor has noted, the trip exposed the eleven-year-old to all facets of American life.

Eventing's New Star

As an adult O'Connor rose through the ranks of international eventing's CCI trials, graduating to the elite CCI*** ("three-star") and Olympic-qualifying CCI**** events such as the Fair Hill and Rolex trials in America, and the esteemed Badminton trials in England. Along the way he met and married Karen Lende, a world-class rider like her husband and a fellow member of the U.S. Equestrian Team. O'Connor also had the fortune to be paired with gifted eventing horses, including Wilton Fair, On a Mission, Rattle & Hum, and his two Olympic mounts, Giltedge and Custom Made.

After being named an alternate to the 1988 eventing team at the Olympic summer games in Seoul, Korea, O'Connor rode for the U.S. at the 1996 games in At-

David O'Connor

lanta, where he partnered Giltedge to a team silver. High placements in the World Equestrian Games and the Pan Am Games led to another Olympic berth, in Sydney, Australia, September, 2000.

Olympic equestrian competition dates back to 1900, when military officers entered jumping classes. Dressage and the three-day event were added for the 1912 summer games in Stockholm, but it would be another forty years before civilians, and then women, were encouraged to participate. Today, equestrian competition is one of just two Olympic sports in which men and women compete as equals (the other being sailing, which features open competition as well as men-only and women-only races). Team and individual events are offered to qualified riders; O'Connor chose Giltedge as his team partner, and Custom Made as his individual mount.

Chronology

1962	Born January 18, in Gaithersburg, Maryland
1973	Completed cross-country horseback trip with mother and brother
1986	Began competing internationally with the United States Equestrian Team
1986	Named alternate, World Champion CCI***
1988	Named alternate, Olympic Games in Seoul, Korea
1990	Represented U.S. at World Equestrian Games in Stockholm, Sweden
1991	Moved to England to continue training
1993	Married teammate Karen Lende
1994	Relocated to The Plains, Virginia
1994	Named alternate, World Equestrian Games
1996	Represented U.S. at Olympic Games in Atlanta, Georgia
2000	Represented U.S. at Olympic Games in Sydney, Australia
2002	Represented U.S. at World Equestrian Games in Jerez, Spain

Awards and Accomplishments

1986	Named alternate, World Champion CCI***
1990	Winner, Rolex CCI***
1992	Highest-placed American (seventh), Badminton CCI****
1993	Winner, Fair Hill CCI***
1995	Winner, Fair Hill CCI*** and Rolex CCI***
1996	Team silver medal, Olympic Games, Atlanta, Georgia
1997	Winner, Fair Hill International CCI*** and Mitsubishi Motors Badminton CCI****
1998	Team bronze medal, World Equestrian Games, Rome, Italy
1999	Individual silver and Team gold medal, Pan Am Games, Winnipeg, Manitoba, Canada
2000	Highest-placed American (second), Rolex CCI****
2000	Individual gold and Team bronze medal, Olympic Games, Sydney, Australia
2000	Named American Horse Show Association Equestrian of the Year
2001	Winner, Fair Hill International CCI*** and Rolex CCI****
2002	Team gold medal, World Equestrian Games, Jerez, Spain

In a three-day event, each rider must stay with the same horse for all three days. Day one belongs to dressage. A discipline derived from a horse's training for military purposes, modern dressage is often compared to ballet on horseback. Following a set pattern, horse and rider execute intricate changes of direction, gait, and tempo. Judges score the pair on fluidity of performance, correctness and obedience of the horse, and the pair's ability to meet each portion of the test.

On day two, horse and rider tackle the cross-country portion. The pair will cover as much as twenty miles in that one day, divided into four different classes of varying difficulty. The day culminates in the cross-country jump, considered the ultimate challenge of horse and rider. It can span several miles and contain as many as thirty-six jumping efforts. Because the obstacles are as solid as they are imposing, this phase is considered the most dangerous of all Olympic sports; a misjudged approach, imperfect takeoff, or awkward landing can send horse and rider sprawling. Day three of competition involves show-jumping, a test of timing and endurance after the rigors of the cross-country.

A Custom Made Victory

O'Connor's strong performance with Giltedge helped the four-member American squad secure team bronze in Sydney. As he did in Atlanta, David shared the podium with his wife, Karen, a formidable competitor on her horse, Biko. Then O'Connor readied himself for the individual title. With Custom Made (known fondly as "Tailor"), a towering thoroughbred, O'Connor entered the dressage arena. Intended to highlight the horse's suppleness, strength and obedience, dressage—French for "training"—in its quiet way is a demanding equestrian sport. When they completed their pattern, O'Connor and Custom Made had set a new Olympic record, posting the best-ever score, 29 penalties, for three-day event dressage.

Day two found O'Connor and Custom Made continuing their streak, posting a clean (no-penalty) round over the roads-and-tracks, steeplechase, and cross-country jump. Not everyone was so fortunate; only 23 of the original 38 eventing duos remained for show jumping on the final day of competition.

Going into show jumping as the leader, O'Connor knew the gold medal was within his grasp. His main competition came from Australia's Andrew Hoy, a veteran rider. Jumping in reverse order of standings, Hoy preceded O'Connor into the stadium and moved from fourth place to provisional first with a clean jumping round. To win, O'Connor would have to complete the twisting, thirteen-jump course with no more than 10.8 penalty points, which can be accrued through rail knockdowns of five points each. Points could also accumulate if the horse and rider exceed the course's 90-second time limit.

O'Connor vs. the Wall

Navigating the technically demanding stadium, O'Connor jumped clean over the first five fences. Clearing fence six, the big horse brushed the top rail, which made a rapping noise but did not fall. Then O'Connor made a potentially disastrous tactical mistake: He turned to glance back at fence six. When he faced forward again, O'Connor had temporarily lost track of his place in the course. He slowed Custom Made as he looked about. Members of the capacity crowd, sensing his distress, shouted, "the wall!," cueing O'Connor to the fence seven, a breakaway wall. He did not hear them.

To have bypassed that jump—going "off course"—would have resulted in O'Connor's elimination. In a matter of moments, though, he had regained his bearings, leapt cleanly over the wall, and continued the pattern correctly, accruing five points with one rail down.

Though the slip had cost him valuable seconds, O'Connor had still completed his round in the time allowed, and the gold medal was his in a new Olympic record of just 34 penalty points over three days. It was the first individual gold for the U.S. in that sport since 1984.

A documentary film by Olympics chronicler **Bud Greenspan** caught O'Connor muttering, "stupid, stupid" to himself as he exited the arena. "My head is still sore from being on a swivel looking for the next fence," he was quoted in an Associated Press article posted on ESPN.com. "There was a moment there of words that can't be printed." To make such an error with the stakes so high continued to dog O'Connor even after he accepted his prize: "I was so upset about the missed turn that I still thought about it during the victory gallop." Still, O'Connor's gallop, gold medal around his neck, American flag waving in his right hand, was a widely seen image of the Sydney summer games.

Subsequent to his Olympic victory, O'Connor continued to dominate international eventing. In 2001 he again took the Fair Hill CCI*** aboard The Native. And in September 2002 O'Connor (on Giltedge) joined Kim Severson, Amy Tryon, and John Williams to take the U.S. team's first gold medal at the World Equestrian Games held in Jerez, Spain. However, the future of Olympic eventing lay in doubt. The International Olympic Committee Programme Commission issued a recommendation eliminating this sport, citing cost, danger, and other factors. O'Connor spoke up for eventing, telling *Practical Horseman* that "horse sports are growing in popularity, and we're growing with them." He added: "You have people who're there and supporting you just because you're from their nation. They don't know a lot about your sport, but they're going to support you just because you're an American or a Canadian or whoever you are. And that's quite a special feeling." In November 2002, the IOC accepted the International Equestrian Federation's proposal to retain eventing in a modified form. For the 2004 games in Athens, the competition will retain dressage, cross-country and show-jumping, but eliminate the roads-and-tracks and steeplechase courses.

For O'Connor, the fascination of his sport begins and ends with the horse. "I really like the communication with the horse," he noted in his O'Connor Event Team Web site. "Watching them become confident and discover the amazing things they can do. There's definitely a personal kind of closeness between you and the horse. There's a connection between your personalities."

FURTHER INFORMATION

Periodicals

Eldridge, Annie. "An Eventful Life." *Horse Illustrated.* (May, 2001).

"Forecasting Eventing's Future." *Practical Horseman.* (January, 2003).

"How Sweet It Is." *Practical Horseman.* (November, 1999).

Jaffer, Nancy. "This WEG Was a Wow." *Practical Horseman.* (December, 2002).

Other

"David O'Connor Is Cool." HorseDaily. http://www. horsedaily.com/olympics/9-6-diana8.html (December 16, 2002).

O'Connor Event Team. http://www.oconnoreventteam. com (December 16, 2002).

"O'Connor Loses Just One Rail." ESPN.com. http:// espn.go.com/oly/summer00/news/2000/0921/765067. html (December 18, 2002).

Sketch by Susan Salter

Al Oerter
1936-

American discus thrower

One of the great figures in Olympic track and field history, Al Oerter was the first athlete to win gold medals in four consecutive Olympic competitions. Between 1956 and 1968, Oerter dominated the discus event at the Olympics, and he continued to maintain his high level of competition into the 1980s—as he approached his fiftieth birthday and long after he had been inducted into various halls of fame.

Alfred Oerter was born in Astoria, New York (a neighborhood in the borough of Queens) on August 19, 1936. His discus career had an almost mythical beginning: while running on his high school track (Oerter began his high school track and field career as a miler), an errant discus, which weighs two kilograms or nearly four and-a-half pounds, fell at his feet. When Oerter threw it back his toss went so far that the coach immediately talked him into competing as a discus thrower. In those days before video, or even readily available film of competitions, Oerter refined his technique in perhaps the most unusual way of all: he studied a flip book of a discus thrower. In 1954 Oerter set the U.S. high school record for the discus. Oerter's career blossomed at the University of Kansas under legendary track and field coach Bill Easton. Easton guided Oerter in his early amateur career that included making the United States Olympic team in 1956.

Al Oerter

Chronology

1936	Born in Astoria, New York City
1954	Enters University of Kansas
1956	Wins first Olympic gold medal in Melbourne
1957, 1959-60, 1962, 1964, 1966	U.S. National Champion
1959	Pan-American champion
1960	Wins second Olympic gold medal in Rome
1962	Breaks U.S. record three times; world record twice
1963-64	Breaks U.S. and world records
1964	Wins third Olympic gold medal in Tokyo
1968	Wins fourth Olympic gold medal in Mexico City, retires
1974	Inducted into USA Track & Field Hall of Fame
1976	Comes out of retirement to train for 1980 Olympics
1976	Personal best discus toss: 227 feet, 10¾ inches
1980	Finishes fourth in Olympic trials for three-man team; US boycotts the Moscow Olympics
1983	Inducted into Olympic Hall of Fame

First Olympic Success

The Olympics transformed Oerter into an athlete of international stature. In *The Olympics: 80 Years of People, Events and Records,* edited by Lord Killanin and John Rodda, it was acknowledged that Oerter has been "often cited as the Supreme Olympic athletics competitor..." (Here the term "athletics" refers to track and field events.) In 1956 the summer Olympics were held in Melbourne, Australia. Down through the years the United States had always fielded a strong discus team and that year Oerter's colleagues in the event included Fortune Gordien and Desmond Koch. Gordien had won the bronze medal in the 1948 Olympics and was the world record holder. The twenty-year-old Oerter stunned the world when he not only won the gold medal, but in doing so set a new Olympic record with a throw of 56.36 meters (184 feet, 10½ inches). The U.S. swept the discus competition that year: Fortune won the silver medal and Koch the bronze. Oerter would improve on his winning distance in each of the three succeeding Olympics.

Sets World Records

Oerter was just hitting his stride. In the years between the Melbourne Olympics and the 1960 Olympics in Rome he captured the U.S. national championship for discus three times: 1957, 1959, and 1960. In 1959 Oerter also won the gold medal in the Pan-American Games.

Although he again wasn't necessarily the favorite, nor the world record holder (Poland's Edmund Piatkowski had set the new mark of 59.91 meters in 1959), Oerter easily defended his gold medal in the 1960 Rome Olympics with a winning throw of 59.18 meters (194 feet, 1½ inches) as the United States once again swept the discus competition: Richard Babka won the silver medal and Dick Cochran the bronze.

Having established his Olympic credentials once and for all, Oerter dominated the sport of discus throwing on the international scene over the next four years. In a flurry of amazing competitiveness, beginning with a meet in Los Angeles in May 1962, Oerter accomplished the one goal in his sport that had eluded him—he set the world record with a throw of 61.10 meters (200 feet, 5½ inches); Oerter was the first person to throw the discus 200 feet. Oerter's record was short-lived. Two and a half weeks later Vladimir Trusenyov set the new standard (61.64 meters) in a meet in Leningrad (now St. Petersburg), Russia. Oerter recaptured the world record with a throw of 62.44 meters in July 1962 in Chicago. In April 1963 he bettered his mark with a throw of 62.62 meters (205 feet, 5½ inches). Almost exactly a year later, in April 1964, he set the mark again with a throw of 62.94 meters (206 feet, 6 inches). However, by the time the 1964 Olympics came around Oerter's record had been shattered by Ludvik Danek of Czechoslovakia, who, in a meet in August 1964, threw the discus 64.55 meters.

Pain and Triumph

When the 1964 Olympics took place in October in Tokyo, Oerter, the two-time reigning Olympic discus champion, was once again not the favorite. Not only was Danek the world record holder, but he had won an incredible forty-five consecutive competitions. To make matters worse for Oerter he was forced to wear a neck brace because of what was described as a "chronic cervical disk injury." That injury was far from the extent of Oerter's physical woes that season. About a week before the start of the Olympics, Oerter slipped and fell while practicing on a wet field. He tore cartilage in his rib cage. As he recounted to **Bud Greenspan** in *100 Greatest Moments in Olympic History*, "I was bleeding internally, I couldn't move, I couldn't sleep and I consumed bottles of aspirin to alleviate the pain. I went through ice treatments to minimize the bleeding and the doctors ordered me not to compete. But these are the Olympics and you die before you don't compete in the Olympics."

Oerter competed with his rib cage heavily taped and packed with ice, and not even three shots of Novocain could dull the pain. After four rounds (each competitor gets six throws or rounds) Oerter was in third place-a remarkable enough achievement given the circumstances, but still more than seven feet short of Danek's best throw. Acknowledging he was in too much pain to try a sixth toss, Oerter decided to go for broke in the fifth round. His throw of sixty-one meters (200 feet, 1⅓ inches) was a new Olympic record and nearly half a meter better than Danek's best toss. Oerter never saw the discus land. He was lying on the ground, doubled up in pain.

Oerter continued competing; for him the intervening years were primarily warm-ups for the Olympics. However he did win his sixth U.S. National championship in 1966 (besides the aforementioned three national championships, Oereter was also national champion in 1962, 1964).

By the time 1968 Olympics, held in Mexico City, rolled around, the world record holder was fellow American, Jay Sylvester, who had topped Danek's mark with a toss of 66.54 meters in May of that year. Sylvester extended his record in September with a throw of 68.4 meters. But it was Oerter who once again made the Olympics his special stage. His throw of 64.78 (212 feet, 6 inches) was good enough to win his fourth consecutive Olympic gold medal; Lothar Milde of the German Democratic Republic took the silver medal while Danek captured the bronze medal. Oerter's winning throw was a personal best, but more important, his four consecutive gold medals in the same event was a feat no other track and field athlete had ever duplicated. However, it was overshadowed by the controversial "black power salute" by African American track stars **Tommie Smith** and John Carlos who were protesting against racism in the United States. Smith and Carlos took the gold and bronze medals, respectively, in the 200 meter event.

The Later Years

Although he had hoped to win five consecutive gold medals for discus Oerter decided to retire after the 1968 Olympics. Injuries were taking their toll on him, and at that time track and field was far less lucrative. Oerter earned his living as a computer engineer. In 1976 Oerter had a change of heart, he came out of retirement and began training for the 1980 Olympics. He freely admitted that that year (1976), he tried steroids to bulk up but quickly gave up on the experiment when his blood pressure rose too high. He afterward became a vocal opponent of steroids and drugs. In 1976 Oerter set his own personal record discus throw of 227 feet, 10¾ inches. In 1980 the 44-year-old Oerter finished fourth in the Olympic trials, but the United States boycotted the summer Olympics that year (held in Moscow), so it was all a moot point.

In 1996 Oerter was further honored for his Olympic feats as the final torch bearer in Atlanta.

Oerter continued to compete until the mid-1980s, long after his legacy as one of the great discus throwers of all time was secured, courtesy of his four Olympic gold medals and his four world records. In addition, there was the Pan-American championship and the five U.S. records that he held. In 1974 Oerter was inducted into the USA Track & Field Hall of Fame and in 1983 he was inducted in the Olympic Hall of Fame.

FURTHER INFORMATION

Books

Greenspan, Bud. *100 Greatest Moments in Olympic History.* Los Angeles: General Publishing Group, 1995.

Killanin, Lord, and John Rodda, eds. *The Olympic Games: 80 Years of People, Events and Records.* New York: Macmillan Publishing Co., Inc., 1976.

Laing, Jane, Ed., et al. *Chronicle of the Olympics, 1896-1996.* New York: Dorling Kindersley, 1996.

Periodicals

Associated Press (July 17, 1996).
Christian Science Monitor (April 2, 1990).
Milwaukee Journal Sentinel (May 27, 1996).

Other

"Al Oerter." USA Track & Field. http://www.usatf.org/athletes/hof/oerter.shtml (January 9, 2003).

"Al Oerter." http://vm.mtsac.edu/relays/Hall Fame/Oerter.html (January 8, 2003).

"Millard 'Bill' Easton." USA Track & Field. http://www.usatf.org/athletes/hof/easton.shtml (January 21, 2003).

"M.E. 'Bill' Easton." Kansas Sports Hall of Fame. http://www.kshof.org/inductees/easton.html (January 21, 2003).

"World Record Progression-Throwing." Sportsfacts.net. http://www.geocities.com/loki314285/history/athletics/world_records/throwing_world_records.html (January 13, 2003).

Sketch by F. Caso

Sadaharu Oh

Sadaharu Oh
1940-

Japanese baseball player

Undoubtedly the greatest hitter in Japanese baseball, Sadaharu Oh holds the all-time record for most home runs in his career-an astonishing 868, surpassing the U.S. record of 755 held by **Hank Aaron**. Oh won 9 Gold Glove awards and 9 most valuable player awards, and played on 11 championship-winning teams and in 18 All-Star games. He combined martial arts, Zen, and baseball to achieve his poise, stamina, and phenomenal sports record, all chronicled in his autobiography, *A Zen Way of Baseball.* A long-time player for the Yomiuri Giants, upon retirement Oh became manager of the team, then went on to manage the Fukuoka Daiei Hawks. Today, Oh promotes good health.

Sadaharu Oh overcame shyness and his heritage to shine as Japan's all-time greatest hitter. His love for baseball began when he pitched for his Waseda High School baseball team, which won Japan's National Invitation High School Tournament.

In 1959 Oh joined the professional team, the Yomiuri Giants, where he would spend his 22-year career. The year he joined, he signed a $60,000 bonus as a pitcher. This move, compounded with his being the son of a Chinese father and a Japanese mother, made him seem like an outsider to Japanese fans. The rookie left-handed pitcher and first baseman hit .161 that first year. He was switched to first base because he had difficulty hitting curveballs. Oh was also plagued by a hitch in his swing.

Zen and the Art of the Flamingo Stance

Giants' batting coach Hiroshi Arakawa guided Oh to perfect his swing. The two began a training method that involved Zen and martial arts to master mental, physical, and spiritual focus. Oh took samurai sword lessons so he could hit curveballs. He studied aikido for patience, practiced kendo for hip action and a downward swing, and focused his *ki* (life energy) from his shoulders to the bat.

To counter Oh's hitch and gain balance when he swung, Arakawa and Oh developed Oh's foot-in-the-air

Chronology

1940	Born May 20 in Tokyo, Japan
1959	Joins Yomiuri Giants as a pitcher
1960	Switches to first base
1962	Develops his famous "flamingo" style of batting
1980	Retires from Yomiuri Giants
1984-88	Manages the Yomiuri Giants
1984	Writes his autobiography, *A Zen Way of Baseball*
1988	Works with Hank Aaron to promote baseball to children
1995	Joins the Fukuoka Daiei Hawks as manager
2000	Leads Hawks against Yomiuri Giants in Japan Series
2002	Joins Cypress Systems' public health education program

Awards and Accomplishments

1963	Begins an eight-year streak of hitting over .300
1964	Sets the Japanese record of 55 home runs in a 140-game season
1965-73	Leads Yomiuri Giants to nine straight championships
1972	Sets Japanese record of seven home runs in seven consecutive games
1974	First player in Japanese baseball to hit 600 home runs
1974-75	Wins Triple Crown
1977	Achieves a career high of 124 runs batted in one year
1978	Breaks Hank Aaron's major-league 755 home runs record
1980	Upon retirement, Oh has a lifetime batting average of .301, 2,786 hits, and 2,170 runs batted in
1994	Is voted into Japanese Baseball Hall of Fame
1999	Fukuoka Daiei Hawks win the Japan Series Championship

stance with his right foot raised as the ball reached home plate. This "flamingo" batting style was similar to American Mel Ott's, yet each was developed independently. Oh was known to practice his batting 30-40 minutes per day.

It has been reported that no one before Oh or since has duplicated this famous stance. With it, Oh was able to begin his amazing streak of batting records. After gaining new balance, his first two times at bat he singled and struck a home run.

Home Run Record

Oh's string of records and achievements made him the toast of Japanese baseball in the 1960s and 1970s. From 1963 to 1970, he hit 40 or more home runs per year. His personal best of 55 home runs in the 140-game 1964 season was a Japanese record. His batting average was .305 in 1963 and remained above .300 for the next seven years.

With Oh's performance on its side, the Giants saw 12 Japan Series crowns and from 1965 to 1973 won nine consecutive championships, an accomplishment never achieved in any other sport. Oh won triple crowns for both 1974 and 1975. He and the Giant's other batting sensation, Shigeo Nagashima, were Japan's equivalent of **Babe Ruth** and **Lou Gehrig**. During their joined career, the so-called O-N Cannon team of Oh and Nagashima hit home runs in the same games 106 times.

Oh broke many Japanese records. In 1972 he hit a record seven home runs in seven consecutive games. Two years later, he reached the 600 home run mark. Oh won 13 consecutive home run titles.

What put Oh in the history books was his surpassing of American Hank Aaron's home run record of 755 in 1978, and his achievement of a 22-year career total of 868 home runs. Oh hit 113 more home runs than Aaron in 448 fewer games.

Overall, Oh was named the Central League's most valuable player 9 times, played on 18 All Star teams, and won 9 Gold Glove awards. His career consisted of 868 home runs, 2,786 hits, 2,170 runs batted in, 1,967 runs, 2,390 walks, and a slugging percentage of .634. His lifetime batting average was .301.

From Player to Manager to Hall of Fame

Oh retired from professional baseball after the 1980 season. In 1984 he returned to his Yomiuri Giants as manager. That same year he wrote his autobiography, *A Zen Way of Baseball,* with David Falkner. In his four-year stint as Giants manager, Oh brought the team to one pennant win but no championships. He joined Hank Aaron in 1988 in working with children to foster good sportsmanship.

In 1994 Oh was voted into the Japanese Baseball Hall of Fame. At the start of the twenty-first century, heated discussions and an Internet debate at Baseballguru.com led by Japanese baseball expert Jim Albright were pushing for Oh's induction into the Baseball Hall of Fame in Cooperstown, New York.

Oh returned to managing baseball when he joined the Fukuoka Daiei Hawks in 1995. The southern Japanese team went from the bottom of the Pacific Coast League to winning the Japan Series Championship in 1999, the first time for the team since 1964. A year later, the Hawks returned to the series playing against Oh's former team, the Yomiuri Giants, which was managed by Oh's former teammate Nagashima. The Giants won.

In January 2002, Cypress Systems Inc., a leading biotechnology company, announced that Sadaharu Oh, along with American baseball Hall of Fame great **Harmon Killebrew**, was joining its public health education campaign called "Step Up to the Plate and Take Control of Your Health." The campaign focused on the prostate health benefits to men over 40 derived from supplementing their diet with SolenoExcellS High Selenium Yeast, Cypress's flagship product. In addition to participating in advertising campaigns designed to raise awareness of high selenium yeast, Oh and Killebrew also worked to educate consumers about general cancer prevention and health related issues.

Career Statistics

Yr	Team	AVG	GP	AB	R	H	HR	RBI	BB	SB
1959	YG	.161	94	193	18	31	7	25	24	3
1960	YG	.270	130	426	49	115	17	71	67	5
1961	YG	.253	127	396	50	100	13	53	64	10
1962	YG	.272	134	497	79	135	38	85	72	6
1963	YG	.305	140	478	111	146	40	106	123	9
1964	YG	.320	140	472	110	151	55	119	119	6
1965	YG	.322	135	428	104	138	42	104	138	2
1966	YG	.311	129	396	111	123	48	116	142	9
1967	YG	.326	133	426	94	139	47	108	130	3
1968	YG	.326	131	442	107	144	49	119	121	5
1969	YG	.345	130	452	112	156	44	103	111	5
1970	YG	.325	129	425	97	138	47	93	119	1
1971	YG	.276	130	434	92	120	39	101	121	8
1972	YG	.296	130	456	104	135	48	120	108	2
1973	YG	.355	130	428	111	152	51	114	124	2
1974	YG	.332	130	385	105	128	49	107	158	1
1975	YG	.285	128	393	77	112	33	96	123	1
1976	YG	.325	122	400	99	130	49	123	125	3
1977	YG	.324	130	432	114	140	50	124	126	1
1978	YG	.300	130	440	91	132	39	118	114	1
1979	YG	.285	120	407	73	116	33	81	89	1
1980	YG	.236	129	444	59	105	30	84	72	0
TOTAL		.301	2831	9250	1967	2786	868	2170	2390	84

YG: Yomiuri Giants.

Although some might dispute how Sadaharu Oh would have fared in the American professional baseball arena, none can overlook the records Oh racked up in his home country of Japan, including the world record for 868 home runs. Oh should also be remembered for his longevity with the Yomiuri Giants, his intense practice schedules, and his skill in leading his league to victory.

CONTACT INFORMATION

Online: http://www.sadaharuoh.com.

SELECTED WRITINGS BY OH:

(With David Falkner) *Sadaharu Oh: A Zen Way of Baseball*. New York, NY: Random House, 1984.

FURTHER INFORMATION

Books

Lincoln Library of Sports Champions. Columbus, OH: Frontier Press, 1989.

Shatzkin, Mike, ed. *The Ballplayers*. New York, NY: Arbor House, 1990.

Other

Cypress Systems. http://www.cypsystems.com/mroh/ press_release.html (December 15, 2002).

Nippon Professional Baseball. http://www.npb-bis.com/ player/index.html (December 15, 2002).

Sadaharu Oh. http://www.sadaharuoh.com (December 15, 2002).

Sketch by Lorraine Savage

Apolo Anton Ohno
1982-

American speed skater

Short-track speed skater Apolo Anton Ohno was the darling of American sports fans during the 2002 Salt Lake City Olympics. The 19-year-old heartthrob with the soul patch was heavily favored to finish with medals in four events at those games. Although in the end he left with only two-a gold and a silver-he was inspiring for his athleticism, for the difficulties that he had to overcome, and for his good sportsmanship in the face of contested races and death threats.

Rebellion

Ohno's father, Yuki Ohno, grew up in Tokyo, Japan, but he left the country in the early 1970s, at the age of 18. He became a hairdresser, and after traveling the world he settled down in Seattle, Washington in 1980,

Apolo Anton Ohno

Chronology

1982	Born May 22 in Seattle, Washington
1983	Ohno's parents separate
1994	Begins skating after seeing on television short-track skating at the Lillehammer Olympics
1996	Begins training at the Olympic Training Center in Lake Placid, New York
1997	Becomes the youngest U.S. short-track champion ever
1998	Finishes last at the U.S. Olympic trials
2002	Featured on the cover of *Sports Illustrated*
2002	Named one of the 50 most beautiful people of 2002 by *People Weekly*

opened his own shop, Yuki's Diffusions, and married an American named Jerrie Lee. Apolo was born in 1982, but his mother left a year later and since then has not had any contact with Apolo.

Yuki Ohno struggled to raise his son alone, but despite his best efforts by the time Apolo reached his early teens he was already getting into serious trouble. At the same time, Apolo was interested in sports and was an accomplished swimmer and inline skater. Yuki did everything possible to encourage his son to choose sports over crime, so when Apolo saw short-track speed skating on television at the 1994 Lillehammer Olympics and wanted to try it, Yuki drove him to competitions all across the country.

Opportunity

At one competition in 1995 Patrick Wentland, a speed-skating coach from the Olympic Training Center in Lake Placid, New York, saw Apolo Ohno skate and persuaded the center to bend its rules and admit Ohno even though he had not reached the minimum age of 15. Yuki Ohno was thrilled at this opportunity, but Apolo Ohno was not so sure. When, in June 1996, Yuki took Apolo to the airport to catch a flight to Lake Placid, Apolo called one of his friends to come pick him up as soon as he was out of Yuki's sight. A few weeks later, Yuki took Apolo to Lake Placid himself.

Apolo Ohno was not interested in the tough exercise regimen that he was supposed to be following at the

Olympic Training Center. In fact, whenever the skaters went out on a 5-mile run, Ohno would slip away from the group and go to Pizza Hut. Then, in August, the speed skaters were given the results of their body fat tests, and Ohno's was the highest of the group. Wentland recalled to *Sports Illustrated*'s S. L. Price that after that, "He came up to me and said, 'I don't want to be the fattest, I don't want to be the slowest, I want to be the best.' Every workout from then on, he had to win. I'd never seen that kind of turnaround so fast." A year later, at age 14, Ohno became the youngest U.S. short-track speed-skating champion ever.

Disappointment

Ohno was a favorite going into the 1998 Olympic trials, but he finished sixteenth-last-at that competition and nearly quit skating. Yuki drove him up into the mountains near Seattle and left him alone in a secluded cabin for a week to consider what he wanted to do. One day he was running in the pouring rain for his third workout of the day. "I had a hole in my shoe and I was getting a huge blister and I was just so tired. I stopped and sat on a rock on the side of the road," he told Lynn Zinser of the *Knight Ridder/Tribune News Service*. He sat and thought and "realized that if I really desired to keep speedskating that I would keep running. I got back up and kept running." Ohno reclaimed his national title the next year.

Two Controversial Medals

Short-track races are often won not by the fastest skater, but by the skater most skilled at avoiding the sport's frequent crashes, and Ohno's first event at the 2002 Olympics, the 1,000 meter, was no different. In the final heat Ohno was leading only meters from the finish when four racers tangled up and all crashed. Australian skater Steven Bradbury had been in last place, far enough behind all of the other skaters that he was able to avoid them and win his country's first Winter Olympic gold ever. Ohno crawled across the finish line for a silver, rode to the podium in a wheelchair, and then went to get stitches to close a gash on his thigh where he had collided with another skater's blade. Ohno declined to request a rerace and accepted his misfortune with a shrug, saying, "That is short track."

Awards and Accomplishments

1997, 1999, 2001-02	U.S. short-track champion
1999	World junior short-track champion
2001	World Cup overall, 500-meter, 1,000-meter, and 1,500-meter champion
2001	World Short Track Championships, 3,000-meter and 5,000-meter relay
2001	Sets the American record for 500 meter, 41.628 seconds, December 21
2002	Wins gold medal in 1,500 meter and silver medal in 1,000 meter at Olympics

Four days later Ohno raced in the final heat of the 1,500-meter event. He finished second, behind South Korean Kim Dong-Sung, but Kim was disqualified for cross-tracking, defined as illegally skating in front of another skater (in this case Ohno) to prevent him from passing, and Ohno was awarded the gold. This decision, although well received by the largely American crowd, raised a fuss in the rest of the world. Kim threw his South Korean flag to the ice and stormed out, and another racer, Italy's Fabio Carta, suggested that "we should use a rifle on Ohno." Enough threatening e-mails, some of which referred to the 1,000-meter crash as well, were sent to Ohno through the U.S. Olympic Committee Web site to crash its server for nine hours. The South Koreans threatened to boycott the closing ceremonies and to sue, but the International Skating Union refused to reconsider its decision.

Ohno failed to win a medal in his final two events, the 500-meter and the 5,000-meter relay. He was disqualified during the semifinals of the 500 meter for pushing another racer, Japan's Satoru Terao, when he tried to pass him, and the American relay team finished fourth after one member, Rusty Smith, caught his skate on a lane marker block and fell.

Future Hopes

When the Winter Olympics are held in 2006, Ohno will be only 23 years old. The average speed skater peaks at 24. Ohno's legion of fans should have many more years of spectacular performances to look forward to, but even if Ohno never wins another race, he will still be remembered for the inspiring stories he provided in 2002.

CONTACT INFORMATION

Address: c/o Nick Paulenich, Public Relations Director, U.S. Speedskating, Utah Olympic Oval, 5662 South 4800 West, Kearns, UT 84118. Email: apolofanmail@yahoo.com.

FURTHER INFORMATION

Periodicals

Armstrong, Jim. "Ohno's Big Finish Slips Away . . . Twice." *Denver Post* (February 24, 2002): C-01.

———. "S. Korea Raises Stink on Skating Lawsuit: Boycott Threatened if Ohno's Gold Not Stripped." *Denver Post* (February 22, 2002): A-13.

Borzilleri, Meri-Jo. "It's Showtime for Apolo." *Knight Ridder/Tribune News Service* (February 15, 2002): K3850.

———. "It's Time for Ohno's Star Power to Start Shining." *Gazette* (Colorado Springs, CO; February 16, 2002): Olympics3.

———. "Ohno Misses Medals: Disqualification, Fourth Place Fail to Add to Collection." *Gazette* (Colorado Springs, CO; February 24, 2002): Olympics1.

———. "Unsportsmanlike Conduct: Anti-Ohno E-mails Flood Olympic Web Site in Wake of Controversy." *Gazette* (Colorado Springs, CO; February 22, 2002): Olympics5.

Duenwald, Mary. "American Gold." *Teen People* (February 1, 2002): 82+.

Hummer, Steve. "Wipeout!: Gold Gives U.S. the Slip as Skaters Fall in a Heap." *Atlanta Journal-Constitution* (February 17, 2002): A1.

Justice, Richard. "On the Right Track." *Houston Chronicle* (February 16, 2002): 3.

Lopez, John P. "Reversal of Misfortune: Korean's Disqualification Becomes a Touch of Gold for Ohno." *Houston Chronicle* (February 21, 2002): 1.

Price, S. L. "Launch of Apolo." *Sports Illustrated* (February 4, 2002): 122+.

———. "Speed Thrills." *Sports Illustrated* (February 25, 2002): 46+.

"Stars on Ice Show City the Need for Speed." *Europe Intelligence Wire* (December 3, 2002).

Zinser, Lynn. "A Long Road to Olympic Short-Track." *Knight Ridder/Tribune News Service* (December 15, 2001): K7239.

Other

"Apolo Anton Ohno." U.S. Speedskating. http://www.usspeedskating.org/rosters/Ohno.html (January 5, 2003).

Poitevent, Evelyn. "Q & A: Apolo Anton Ohno." USA Weekend.com. http://www.usaweekend.com/02_issues/020407/020407whosnews_ohno.html (January 5, 2003).

Sketch by Julia Bauder

Hakeem Olajuwon
1963-

American basketball player

Hakeem Olajuwon

Although Olajuwon instantly loved basketball, learning to play was difficult because basketball games were not televised in Nigeria, and soccer dominated the nation's sports news. Nonetheless, under the tutelage of coach Richard Mills, 17-year-old Olajuwon quickly became a leader on the Nigeria national basketball team, which took third place in the All-African tournament in 1979. The following year Olajuwon traveled to the United States to visit colleges. Disdaining the cold wind that greeted him when he arrived in New York in October of 1980, Olajuwon enrolled in the University of Houston, which offered him both a place on the basketball team and a much more familiar climate.

Two Trips to the Final Four

Olajuwon's adjustment American basketball was not easy. After sitting out the first year as a redshirt freshman, Olajuwon joined the Houston Cougars for the 1981-82 season, but, now seven feet tall, he suffered from frequent back spasms, caused by growing pains and simply being out of shape. Still learning the game, he was also consistently in foul trouble, but from the start he was a natural shot blocker. Throughout the season he worked on increasing his weight with lots of steak and ice cream and worked one-on-one with Houston Rockets star **Moses Malone** to improve his defensive skills and learn the more aggressive-style of American basketball.

By his second season, Olajuwon had become one of the best college basketball players on the court. The trio of Olajuwon, Clyde Drexler, and Larry Micheaux, known as the "Phi Slamma Jamma," tore through the season, posting a record of 31-3. Favored to win the National Collegiate Athletic Association (NCAA) tournament in 1983, Houston lost, 54-52, in the final seconds of the last game when North Carolina State University threw up a buzzer-beater shot, a play that still earns a place on sports highlight films two decades later. Despite losing, Olajuwon was named the tournament's Most Valuable Player. With Drexler and Micheaux gone the next season, Olajuwon became a one-man show, averaging fifteen points per game and leading the nation with 13.5 rebounds per

Seven-foot Hakeem "The Dream" Olajuwon has a rare combination of strength, footwork, and speed that put him on the short list of the best big men to ever play in the National Basketball Association (NBA). On the defensive end, his shot blocking abilities are legendary, and on the offensive end he can score with a dunk, a jump hook, a drop step, and a fade away. After playing seventeen years of his eighteen-year career for the Houston Rockets, and winning two NBA titles during the 1990s, Olajuwon announced his retirement from professional basketball on December 2, 2002.

From Handball to Basketball

Hakeem Olajuwon was born on January 21, 1963, in Lagos, Nigeria. His parents, Salaam and Abike Olajuwon, owners of a concrete business, raised Olajuwon along with his four brothers and one sister in a one-story, three-bedroom red concrete house in a neighborhood inhabited by Nigeria's relatively small middle class. During his childhood, Olajuwon played soccer as a goalie and excelled as a team handball player. He did not play basketball until he was a high school senior at Moslem Teacher College, after a Nigerian basketball coach spotted the six-foot-nine-inch, 170-pound Olajuwon on the soccer field and talked him into trying the game.

Career Statistics

Yr	Team	GP	PTS	P/G	FG%	3P%	FT%	RPG	APG	SPG	BPG	TO
1985	HOU	82	1692	20.6	.538	.000	.613	11.9	1.4	1.2	2.7	234
1986	HOU	68	1597	23.5	.526	.000	.645	11.5	2.0	2.0	3.4	195
1987	HOU	75	1755	23.4	.508	.200	.702	11.4	2.9	1.9	3.9	228
1988	HOU	79	1805	22.8	.514	.000	.695	12.1	2.1	2.0	3.1	243
1989	HOU	82	2034	24.8	.508	.000	.696	13.5	1.8	2.6	3.4	275
1990	HOU	82	1995	24.3	.501	.167	.713	14.0	2.9	2.1	4.6	316
1991	HOU	56	1187	21.2	.508	.000	.769	13.8	2.3	2.1	3.9	174
1992	HOU	70	1510	21.6	.502	.000	.766	12.1	2.2	1.8	4.3	187
1993	HOU	82	2140	26.1	.529	.000	.779	13.0	3.5	1.8	4.2	262
1994	HOU	80	2184	27.3	.528	.421	.716	11.9	3.6	1.6	3.7	271
1995	HOU	72	2005	27.8	.517	.188	.756	10.8	3.5	1.9	3.4	237
1996	HOU	72	1936	26.9	.514	.214	.724	10.9	3.6	1.6	2.9	247
1997	HOU	78	1810	23.2	.510	.313	.787	9.2	3.0	1.5	2.2	281
1998	HOU	47	772	16.4	.483	.000	.755	9.8	3.0	1.8	2.0	126
1999	HOU	50	945	18.9	.514	.308	.717	9.6	1.8	1.6	2.5	139
2000	HOU	44	455	10.3	.458	.000	.616	6.2	1.4	0.9	1.6	73
2001	HOU	58	689	11.9	.498	.000	.621	7.4	1.2	1.2	1.5	81
2002	TOR	61	435	7.1	.464	.000	.560	6.0	1.1	1.2	1.5	98
TOTAL		1238	26946	21.8	.512	.202	.712	11.1	2.5	1.8	3.1	3667

HOU: Houston Rockets; TOR: Toronto Raptors.

game. Although Houston once again made it into the final game of the NCAA tournament, the Cougars failed to win the title, losing 84-75 to another future superstar center, **Patrick Ewing**, and his Georgetown Hoyas.

Hakeem "The Dream"

Foregoing his final year of college eligibility, Olajuwon was selected as the number one overall pick of the 1984 NBA draft by the Houston Rockets. Olajuwon, paired with seven-foot-four-inch Ralph Sampson in the front court, had a stellar rookie year, averaging 20.6 points and 11.9 rebounds per game, and finished second to Jordan in the Rookie of Year voting. During the 1985-86 season Olajuwon averaged 23.5 points and 11.4 rebounds per game and led his team to face the Boston Celtics in the NBA finals, but lost the series four games to two.

The next several years of Olajuwon's career proved frustrating. Although his personal statistics remained impressive, Olajuwon struggled with injuries and an overall weak team that failed to produce playoff wins. By the end of the 1991-92 season, Olajuwon was demanding that Houston management trade him. Instead, Houston brought in a new coach, Rudy Tomjanovich, who worked to keep Olajuwon in a Rockets uniform. The year proved to be a turning point for Olajuwon and the Rockets. Under Tomjanovich the team began to once again post wins, making it into the second round of the NBA playoffs before losing to the Seattle Supersonics in seven games. Personally, Olajuwon found new focus in the Islamic faith. After making his first trip to Mecca in 1992, he began to pray daily, carrying a prayer rug and compass (to find Mecca) wherever he went.

NBA Title Times Two

By the 1993-94 season Olajuwon was at the peak of his career. His undefendable fade-away jump shot, combined with his powerful dunks and tenacious defense under the basket proved a nearly unstoppable combination. Posting a season average of 27.3 points, 11.9 rebounds, and 3.7 blocks per game, Olajuwon was named the NBA Most Valuable Player (MVP). Facing star center Ewing and the New York Knicks in the NBA finals, Olajuwon won his first NBA title, defeating the Knicks in seven games. He was also named the MVP of the finals. The following season the Rockets, who were plagued by injuries throughout the regular season, surprised many by returning to the NBA finals, this time facing center **Shaquille O'Neal** and the Orlando Magic. Olajuwon dominated at both ends of the floor, and the Rockets took the seven-game series in four games. Olajuwon, once again named the NBA Finals MVP, ended the season with his second championship title.

Retirement and Beyond

In 1996 33-year-old Olajuwon married 18-year-old Dalia Asafi under the traditional Islamic custom of a prearranged marriage. As Olajuwon aged, his minutes on the court and statistics took a natural decline, and Houston management began planning a future beyond his presence on the court. During the 2000-01 season Olajuwon was diagnosed with a blood clot in his leg and benched while he took a series of blood thinners. At the end of the season Olajuwon's contract expired, and Houston management decided to free themselves of Olajuwon's hefty salary and traded their premiere center to the Toronto Raptors. Olajuwon already has plans for life after the NBA. He has significant real estate investments in Houston, which he operates under his company Palladio Development Ltd.

A shoo-in to the NBA Hall of Fame, Olajuwon matched up against some of the best centers to ever play the game, including **Bill Walton**, **David Robinson**, Ewing, and O'Neal. His ability to perform in the company of such talent proves his place in the NBA history books. Upon his retirement in 2002, the Houston Rockets announced that a life-size statue of Olajuwon would greet fans outside the team's new downtown arena.

SELECTED WRITINGS BY OLAJUWON:

Living the Dream: My Life and Basketball, Little Brown, 1996

FURTHER INFORMATION

Books

Contemporary Black Biography, Volume 2. Detroit: Gale, 1992.
Contemporary Newsmakers 1985, Issue Cumulation. Detroit: Gale, 1986.
Sports Stars. Series 1-4. Detroit: U•X•L, 1994-98.
Who's Who Among African Americans, 14th ed. Detroit: Gale Group, 2001.

Periodicals

Blinebury, Fran. "Hakeem Olajuwon." *Sport* (January 1994): 42.
Bloom, Barry M. "Dream Fulfilled: Two Straight Titles Have Rocketed Hakeem Olajuwon into Another Dimension." *Sport* (November 1995): 22.
D'Alessandro, Dave. "If This is It for Olajuwon, Basketball is Losing an Artist." *Sporting News* (March 26, 2001): 18.
D'Alessandro, Dave. "Olajuwon Must Alter His Game for Good of the Team." *Sporting News* (November 22, 1999): 52.
"Dressing Down." *Sports Illustrated* (February 20, 1995): 14.
Gietschier, Steve. *Living the Dream: My Life and Basketball* [book review]. *Sporting News* (February 19, 1996): 8.
Kirkpatrick, Curry. "The Liege Lord of Noxzema." *Sports Illustrated* (November 28, 1983): 106.
Lee, Spike. "Slam Dunk." *Interview* (February 1994): 66-67.
McCallum, Jack. "A Dream Come True." *Sports Illustrated* (March 22, 1993): 16.
McEntegart, Pete. "4 Toronto Raptors: Surrounded by a Young and Deep Supporting Cast, Hakeem Can Dream about Another Shot at a Championship." *Sports Illustrated* (October 29, 2001): 126.

Awards and Accomplishments

1983	Voted Most Outstanding Player of the National Collegiate Athletic Association (NCAA) Final Four
1984	Named First Team All American; selected first overall in the National Basketball Association (NBA) draft by the Houston Rockets(
1985	All Rookie Team
1985-90, 1992-97	NBA All Star
1987-89	First Team All NBA
1987-90, 1993-94	NBA First Team All Defense
1993	IBM Award
1994	NBA Most Valuable Player; NBA championship with Houston Rockets
1994-95	Won back-to-back NBA championship titles; named Most Valuable Player of the NBA Finals
1996	Selected as one of the 50 Greatest Players in NBA History; "Dream Team" Olympic gold medal

---

Montville, Leigh. "The Stuff of Dreams." *Sports Illustrated* (June 12, 1995): 28.
Sarnoff, Nancy. "Center of Attention." *Houston Business Journal* (January 26, 2001): 14.
Starr, Mark. "Good Enough to Dream: After Two NBA Titles, Hakeem Olajuwon is Running out of Worlds to Conquer." *Newsweek* (November 6, 1995): 70-71.
Wulf, Steve. "The Dream is Again Sweet for the Rockets." *Time* (June 19, 1995): 63-64.

Other

"Akeem [Hakeem] Olajuwon." Sports Stats.com. http://www.sportsstats.com/bball/national/players/1980/Akeem_Olajuwon/ (December 11, 2002).
"Hakeem Olajuwon." National Basketball Association. http://www.nba.com/ (December 11, 2002).

Sketch by Kari Bethel

Barney Oldfield
1878-1946

American race car driver

Originally famed for his speed in bicycle racing, Barney Oldfield became one of the pioneers of automobile racing. From 1902 to his retirement in 1918, his name was synonymous with speed and daring on the road. He was the first person to drive faster than 60 miles per hour. According to his obituary in the Toledo, Ohio *Blade,* the inventor of the automobile, Henry Ford, said of Oldfield, "The man did not know what fear was."

Barney Oldfield

Obsessed with Speed

Berna Eli Oldfield was born in a farmhouse outside Wauseon, Ohio, in 1878. His father, Henry Clay Oldfield, and his mother, Sarah Oldfield, worked the farm and struggled to provide for Oldfield and his older sister, Bertha. The severe winter of 1889 was too much for them however, and they decided to move the family to Toledo, Ohio, where Henry could find work. He took a job at a local mental hospital, and Oldfield, then eleven, attended school in Toledo.

At the time, the bicycle was a new invention, and cycling became a national craze. The young Oldfield was fascinated by the machines, and by the time he was fourteen he was obsessed with getting one for himself. During his summer vacation, he got a job as a water boy for a railroad construction crew, earning a dollar a day, hoping he could save some of it for a bicycle. On Sunday, his day off, he spent the time at the local firehouse, hoping for a fire: as firehouse mascot, he was allowed to ride the horse-drawn fire wagon as it sped through the streets of Toledo. Thus, although he didn't yet own a cycle, he could fuel his love of speed.

According to William Nolan in the Toledo *Blade,* Oldfield told his parents, "Some day I'll own the fastest cycle in the whole wide world. People will come from a thousand miles away just to watch me ride it!"

By 1893, however, times were still hard, and Oldfield had to quit school and take a job with his father at the

mental hospital, working as a kitchen helper. He disliked this job, and soon found a new one as a bellhop at the Boody House hotel in Toledo. Oldfield's outgoing and optimistic manner soon earned him plenty of tips. He also earned the nickname that he would use for the rest of his life, Barney, when the bell captain told him Berna was a "sissy" name and Barney was better. Oldfield's family began calling him Barney, and when he became an elevator operator at the Monticello Hotel in Toledo, his paychecks were made out to Barney Oldfield.

Oldfield was finally able to buy a bicycle, but it was heavy. The lightweight cycles used by racers were still too expensive for him. However, he soon discovered that a tenant of the Monticello Hotel had a lightweight cycle, and stored it in the hotel basement. Each night, Oldfield "borrowed" the cycle from its unsuspecting owner, and sped through the dark streets of Toledo. At the age of sixteen, in 1894, he entered his first cycle race. As an unknown beginner in a field of well-known riders, he didn't receive much attention. but as the race progressed, he moved up steadily from the back of the pack to second place. His prize was a $25 diamond ring, which he pawned to finance his next race.

That race was a failure, but it and others to follow were learning experiences for Oldfield, who learned about training, pacing, and tactics, as well as the physical danger of racing: he broke his collarbone twice, and his parents, who had bought a small ice cream parlor in Toledo, begged him to quit racing and join them in the business. Oldfield told them that he understood that they wanted to be proud of him, but that he would earn their praise his own way: through racing. Officials from the Dauntless bicycle factory had asked him to ride for them in the Ohio state championship, and he had agreed.

Although Oldfield came in second in that race, it was a turning point in his life. As a result of his exposure, he was hired as a parts sales representative for the Stearns Bicycle Company, and he met his future wife, Beatrice Lovetta Oatis.

Oldfield and bicycle racer Fred Titus formed the Racycle Racing Team, and toured throughout the South and Midwest, barely making a living by pawning their

Awards and Accomplishments

1903	Indiana Fairgrounds one mile dirt track, first circular mile under 60 seconds in US :59.6
1903	Columbus, OH, five mile exhibition, :05:00.6
1904	World's Records made in Peerless Green Dragon II: 1 mi. :00:51.2 70 mph; 5 mi. :04:30.0 66.5 mph; 10 mi. :09:12.0 65.0 mph; 15 mi. :14:05.0 63.7 mph; 20 mi. :18:45.4 64 mph; 25 mi. :23:38.6 63.2 mph; 30 mi. :28:38.8 62.9 mph; 35 mi. :33:36.6 62.2 mph; 40 mi. :38:31.6 62.4 mph; 45 mi. :43:29.0 62.4 mph; 50 mi. :48:39.2 62 mph
1909	Indianapolis, IN, Indianapolis 2 1/2 mi. Macadam Motor Speedway (Inaugural)—1 mi. speed trial, :43.0, in a Benz
1910	Daytona-Ormond Beach, FL, 1 mi. straightaway record, :27.33, in a Blitzen Benz; 5 mi. straightaway record, in a Blitzen Benz
1912	Cleveland, OH, 2 mi. track, :1:35.8, in a Christie
1913	Bakersfield, CA, dirt track, 1 mile in :46.4, in a Christie
1916	Indianapolis, IN, Brickyard Record: first over 100mph at Indy, in a Christie
1917	St. Louis, Missouri, 1 mi. dirt track noncompetitive speed records: 1 mi. :00:45.00, 80 mph; 2 mi. :01:30.40, 79.5 mph; 3 mi. :02:17.60, 78.5 mph; 4 mi. :03:05.60, 77.5 mph; 5 mi. :03:53.60, 77.2 mph; 10 mi. :07:56.20, 75.5 mph; 15 mi. :12:00.80, 75.0 mph; 20 mi. :15:52.20, 75.5 mph; 25 mi. :19:57.60, 75.4 mph; 25 mi. :19:57.60, 75.4 mph; 50 mi. :40:47.60, 73.5 mph
1990	Inducted into Motorsports Hall of Fame

How It Feels to Drive Under the Minute on a Circular Track

It doesn't thrill me a bit to drive a 1:05 clip, and though I might win races without having to drive under the minute, I just have to let it out to get another thrill. You just clamp your teeth on your cigar and get down to your work so that you know to an inch how much the car will swing on the turns, and you get more fun out of the ride than a whole stand full of people.

I haven't any mania for speed, and I don't lose my head and do the mad-man act or anything like that, but I do like to feel the car jump and feel the power of being able to guide the machine so nicely, no matter how quick the turns come.

My car is so well balanced and I know it so well, that I know just how to take those skids. A little too much turn of the front wheels would throw the back wheels out so far that the car would not right itself; then there would be something doing.

Source: Barney Oldfield, interviewed in *Automobile.* August 1, 1903, p. 116.

medals and trophies. In 1896, Oldfield and Oatis were married. They did not know each other well, and the marriage would not be a happy one. In the meantime, Oldfield continued to tour as a bicycle racer.

Becomes an Automobile Racer

In 1902, Oldfield raced a gasoline-powered bicycle in Salt Lake City, where he also met automobile inventor Henry Ford. Ford asked Oldfield if he would like to drive one of Ford's cars, and Oldfield agreed. When he got to Grosse Point, Michigan, where the race was to be held, neither of Ford's two cars would start. Ford sold both of them to Oldfield and his partner, Tom Cooper, for $800.

Oldfield's new car, called the "999," had no springs or shocks, and was steered by a tiller, not a wheel. Cooper found that the unwieldy machine, almost impossible to turn or control, needed "a wrestler more than a driver," according to Timothy Messer-Kruse in *Toledo's Attic.* This role was perfect for Oldfield, and, as Messer-Kruse wrote, in the Manufacturer's Challenge Cup, "Oldfield wrenched the car around the turns in a sliding cloud of dust that became his trademark and discovered his talent at last." He beat defending champion Mexander Winton by a half-mile in his first race.

On Memorial Day in 1903, Oldfield became the first person to drive a mile in a minute flat, and won another race. Two months later, he drove a mile in 55.8 seconds, leading his former competitor, Winton, to hire Oldfield to drive for him. Oldfield was given a salary, expenses, and free cars. He toured the United States, doing match races and speed runs; one year, competing for the Peerless company, he competed on twenty different tracks in

eighteen weeks. He gave four exhibition runs and won sixteen match races in a row. When asked by a reporter from *Automobile* what it felt like to drive a mile in less than a minute, Oldfield said, "There is an exhilaration in driving fast that I cannot resist: it is like intoxication."

In 1910, Oldfield bought a Benz and broke all speed records for the mile, two miles, and the kilometer at Ormond Beach, Florida. With the fame these feats brought him, he began charging $4,000 for each personal appearance.

Oldfield's Legacy to the Sport

Because automobiles at the time were handmade and thus very expensive, most owners were extremely wealthy. Automobile clubs catered to this clientele, with selective membership policies; most owners and drivers were millionaires. The sport was well on its way to becoming the province of the rich, much like yachting or polo. Very few drivers came from the working class, and those who did, such as famed racer Ralph DePalma, did all they could to make the wealthy owners of their cars feel comfortable. DePalma, for example, wore the clothing of a chauffeur, and gave the owner of the car credit for his victories.

Oldfield, on the other hand, refused to wear uniforms, chewed cigars while he drove, and was not particularly loyal to sponsors—if a better offer came along, he took it. He talked loudly, swore often, spent time in bars, and did not show extra respect to the rich. He also took his machines, named the Blitzen Benz, the Green Dragon, the Golden Submarine, and others—out to county fairs and other venues and gave rural people a show they would never forget. Messer Kruse wrote, "For many Oldfield's cars were not the first they had ever seen, but they were the first they had ever seen driven by someone they could recognize as one of their own."

Naturally, the members of the racing elite were offended, and tried to exclude Oldfield from racing.

Knowing that Oldfield's strength was in fast skidding turns, they organized straightaway races where skill did not matter, as well as road races that simply favored the fastest machine, not the best driver. They also created racing rules that excluded Oldfield from competitions because he had broken these rules—for example, in 1911 he was barred from the famed Vanderbilt Cup races because he had raced in unofficial exhibitions at county fairs. In 1912 he was banned for life from the Indianapolis Brickyard because he had given an exhibition race against his partner Bob Burman. Burman, who also participated in the race, was not banned.

Oldfield was reinstated at Indianapolis in 1914, and his best finishes there were fifth in 1914 and 1918. In addition, he was the first driver in Indianapolis history to complete a lap at 100 miles per hour.

However, when Oldfield retired from competition in 1918 and became manager of the Firestone racing team, the A.A.A. refused to let him enter a track even if his own team was racing. Eventually he was reinstated, but by then he had lost many opportunities.

As Messer-Kruse noted, the officials of the A.A.A. had also lost opportunities, although they never realized it. At the time, most Americans viewed cars as dangerous, frightening machines, playthings of the rich. Many drivers were cursed at, had stones thrown at them, or were forced off the road by horse-drawn farm wagons. In addition, many communities passed impossibly low speed limits, intended to keep automobiles out. Messer-Kruse commented, "The millionaires in control of the A.A.A. never understood that Oldfield was the best weapon they had to batter down popular resistance to the growth of their sport." Oldfield was so well-known that police officers arresting speeders often asked, "Who do you think you are, Barney Oldfield?"—which, as Messer-Kruse wrote, made Oldfield "clearly someone who struck a chord with the common folk."

On May 10, 1946, Oldfield died in his sleep, apparently of a heart attack; the evening before, he had complained of neck pains. He is buried in Beverly Hills, California.

In 1990, Oldfield was inducted into the Motor Sports Hall of Fame. Driving at speeds almost unheard of at the time, Barney Oldfield was a pioneer and one of the fathers of modern racing.

SELECTED WRITINGS BY OLDFIELD:

Barney Oldfield's Book for the Motorist, Small, Maynard and Co., 1919.

FURTHER INFORMATION

Periodicals

"Great Racer Dies." *Toledo Blade* (October 5, 1946).

Nolan, William. "Barney Oldfield: He Got a Fast Start in Toledo." *Toledo Blade* (November 12, 1961).

Oldfield, Barney. "How It Feels to Drive Under the Minute on a Circular Track." *Automobile* (August 1, 1903): 116.

"Oldfield Got Lust for Speed on Toledo Bike." *Toledo Blade* (October 5, 1946).

Other

"Barney Oldfield," *International Motorsports Hall of Fame.* http://www.motorsportshalloffame.com/ (November 5, 2002).

"Barney Oldfield: Toledo and Wauseon's Speed King." *Toledo's Attic.* http://www.attic.utoledo.edu/ (November 5, 2002).

Sketch by Kelly Winters

Merlin Olsen
1940-

American football player

He excelled at the toughest of positions in the roughest of sports and was part of a unit called the "Fearsome Foursome," yet Merlin Olsen played a gentlemanly priest on television and so visibly endorsed flowers, people named him the "Flower Man." He worked five Super Bowls as part of a broadcast team one critic called "wholesome." And when he was enshrined in the Pro Football Hall of Fame after fifteen years at defensive tackle, Merlin Olsen was credited for his cerebral approach to the game.

"It was Olsen's career-long quest to master the intellectual side of football, and he achieved his goal during a marvelous 15-year career," Anthony Holden wrote in *CBS SportsLine.com.* "The key to consistency of performance is concentration," Olsen once said. "I probably held my ability to concentrate over a longer period of time than some athletes. Each game, at the beginning of each play, I thought of it as the most important play of the year. I went into every play as if the game depended on it."

Olsen missed just two games in twenty-two years of scholastic, college and National Football League (NFL) ball, and played his last 198 consecutive games. He qualified for the Pro Bowl, the NFL's all-star game for fourteen straight seasons. "Going to the Pro Bowl 14 times adds up to an entire season of play," Olsen said.

After ending his career with his only pro team, the Los Angeles (now St. Louis) Rams, after the 1976 season, Olsen embarked on a broadcasting and acting ca-

Merlin Olsen

Chronology

1940	Born September 15 in Logan, Utah
1959-61	Plays three years at defensive tackle for Utah State University.
1962	Drafted in first round by Los Angeles Rams of National Football League and Denver Broncos of American Football League; signs with Rams.
1976	Retires as player after fifteen seasons
1977	Begins career as announcer and actor with NBC; broadcasts five Super Bowls and stars in such TV shows/movies as "Little House on the Prairie" and "Father Murphy"
1983	Becomes national spokesman for FTD Florist Inc.

reer which including working National Football games with Dick Enberg on NBC and appearing on such popular television shows as "Little House on the Prairie" and "Father Murphy."

Outland Trophy Winner

Olsen grew up the eldest of nine children in Logan, Utah. "Everything was planned," Olsen said in an interview with *Sports Illustrated*. "We'd drive a truck up into Idaho and haul back a ton of potatoes. We'd can 1,600 quarts of peaches a season, buy 100 chickens at a time."

After playing football and running hurdles for the track and field team at Logan High School, Olsen, who then stood at 6-foot-4, 225 pounds, earned a scholarship at Utah State University, also in Logan. Olsen, called the "Gentle Giant" for his soft, off-field personality, helped lead the Aggies to a Sun Bowl appearance in 1960 and the Gotham Bowl a year later. In 1961, he earned All-America at defensive tackle and received the Outland Trophy as the nation's best collegiate interior lineman. He excelled academically, earning Phi Beta Kappa honors, and would go on to earn a master's degree in economics. The Rams made Olsen their first pick in the 1962 NFL draft, as did the Denver Broncos of the upstart American Football League (AFL). Olsen signed with Los Angeles.

"Fearsome Foursome"

The Rams were building into a contender and doing so around their defense. Olsen's arrival coincided with that of

Roosevelt Grier, in a trade with the New York Giants. Olsen and Grier were the tackles, and mainstays David "Deacon" Jones and Lamar Lundy at defensive end. Team publicist called them the "Fearsome Foursome." "The Fearsome Foursome changed the way football was played and watched," Michael Gershman wrote on the Colosseum Web site. "They invented stunting and looping techniques, coined the term 'sack,' and made defense a focal point of football." Olsen said the four communicated well. Jones, for instance, charged quickly off the start of a play and was effective at stuffing the run, but often left areas uncovered. "So I accepted the responsibility of covering that territory," Olsen said. "That's how we got the job done."

"I constantly look for new ways to improve my performance," Olsen once said. "I critique myself, I say to myself, 'maybe there's a better way to rush the passer or fight off a blocker.' Just because you've been doing it a certain way for 50 years doesn't mean there can't be a better way." Added former lineman and assistant coach Tony Torgeson: "Merlin had some of the test techniques of any lineman ever. He had great leverage and balance, and never was in a bad position. He was always ready to make a play."

The Rams made the National Football Conference (NFC) playoffs six times in a ten-year span from 1967-1976, but in three consecutive seasons, 1974-76, Los Angeles lost the NFC Championship game and fell one victory short of reaching the Super Bowl. Olsen retired after the 1976 season. He bridged two eras, having played against Hall of Fame running backs **Jim Brown** and **Walter Payton**.

Transition to Broadcasting, Acting

Olsen joined Dick Enberg in the NBC booth and "won plaudits for his insight and precision." He effectively countered the exuberant Enberg, whose trademark call was "Oh, my!" They became NBC's top broadcast team and worked five Super Bowls, several American Football Conference championship games and major college bowls such as the Rose and Orange.

Making, as German wrote, "a more difficult transition to acting," Olsen achieved popularity as Jonathan

Career Statistics

Yr	Team	FR	INT	TD
1962	LAR	0	1	1
1963	LAR	0	0	0
1964	LAR	0	0	0
1965	LAR	1	0	0
1966	LAR	2	0	0
1967	LAR	1	0	0
1968	LAR	1	0	0
1969	LAR	0	0	0
1970	LAR	0	0	0
1971	LAR	0	0	0
1972	LAR	0	0	0
1973	LAR	0	0	0
1974	LAR	0	0	0
1975	LAR	1	0	0
1976	LAR	1	0	0
TOTAL		7	1	1

LAR:Los Angeles Rams.

Awards and Accomplishments

1961	Wins Outland Trophy as best college football interior lineman as a senior at Utah State
1962	Selected National Football League Rookie of the Year
1970	Named to Rams' all-time team
1982	Enshrined in Pro Football Hall of Fame
1994	Named to NFL 75th Anniversary Team

Garvey in the NBC show "Little House on the Prairie." He also starred on both "Father Murphy," in which he played a prospector-turned-clergyman and saves the orphanage he founded, and "Aaron's Law." Olsen has also been a nationwide spokesman for FTD Florist.

Olsen Legacy

Olsen, who also gives motivational speeches to businesses and makes appearances on behalf of charities, has succeeded in many endeavors and has parlayed his affability into professional success.

Possibly his best attribute was his consistency. "Olsen played for five different head coaches during his days with the Rams," Holden wrote, "and though they had different styles and philosophies, those five men had one thing in common: Olsen never had a bad year, a bad game or a bad play." Ex-players recall how nurturing he was as a teammate. "If I hadn't had Merlin beside me those first three, four, or five years, I probably would not have turned out to be the football player that I did," former Rams linebacker Jack Youngblood said. Olsen presented Youngblood into the Hall of Fame in 2001.

Olsen, still a spokesman for FTD Florist, is a motivational speaker, working with some of the largest corporations in the United States. He lives in California. Utah

State players in August 2002 received a surprise visit from Olsen, who gave a pep talk to the Aggies. "We talked about a couple of things that might help them individually to improve their performance during the year," said Olsen. Added linebacker Jesse Busta: "Anytime you have one of the best players to ever play here and in the NFL, it is inspirational."

FURTHER INFORMATION

Other

"End of an Era in Television," Courier Houma. http://www.houmatoday.com/sports/columns/stories/10237 sportscolumnrowone.html, (January 26, 2002).

"Merlin Olsen." CBS SportsLine.com, http://cbs.sports line.com/ (December 9, 2002).

"Merlin Olsen." CBS SportsLine.com, http://cbs.sports line.com/ (December 9, 2002).

"Merlin Olsen Biography." Pro Football Hall of Fame, http://www.profootballhof.com/players/enshrinees/molsen.cfm (2001).

"Merlin Olsen Drops by Football Practice." USU Athletics. http://www.fansonly.com/schools/ust/sports (August 19, 2002).

"Merlin Olsen: Gentlemanly Giant." Colosseum Web site, http://www.geocities.com/Colosseum/ (December 9, 2002).

"Merlin Olsen: NFL Hall of Famer & 14-Time Pro Bowl Selection." Speakers.com, http://speakers.com/molsen.html (December 9, 2002).

Sketch by Paul Burton

Lisa Olson
1964-

American sports journalist

Lisa Olson sent the arena of sports journalism spinning when she reported a harrowing incident she experienced when interviewing a player in the locker room in 1990. Her strong sense of righteousness allowed her to stand up and take note. This was not acceptable behavior and Olson wanted to make sure her attackers knew it, as well as the rest of the world. Unfortunately her world was turned upside down as a result of her actions. Although Olson was a victim of her circumstance, many believe she forged the way for other female journalists, giving them a voice for what they had quietly endured for years.

Lisa Olson

The *Sports Illustrated* Reading Program

For Lisa Olson becoming a sports journalist was not a whim. "She almost learned to read with *Sports Illustrated* and her brothers' *Boy's Life,*" reported Leigh Montville in *Sports Illustrated*. When Olson was seven she would report on the sporting events in her neighborhood in a newsletter she created. Of course when she started high school she was on the school newspaper and continued into college.

While Olson was in graduate school she approached Bob Sales of the *Boston Herald* about any kind of sports writing work available. Sales gave her a chance writing the anonymous daily sports summary. Sales could see Olson's excellent style shining through and decided to move her onto sports coverage of the local schools. Sales commented to *Sports Illustrated,* "She did nice stories portraying athletes as human beings.... These were stories about high school volleyball players and swimmers, and she made you want to read them. I like what she did a lot."

By this point, Olson had proven her stellar capabilities to Sales and he gave her an opportunity to cover the Boston Bruins hockey team when his regular reporter became ill and was unable to cover the beat. She really knew her sports and it came through in her writing. Olson's talent was taking her to high places in the *Boston Herald*. After a year and a half of reporting for the Bruins, a spot opened up for covering the New Eng-

land Patriots. This was an excellent opportunity for Olson and she jumped at the chance.

Ex-Patriots

The first few months on the Patriot's beat Olson had not had an incident. She was enjoying her new position. In September Olson had started working on a piece featuring Maurice Hurst. When she asked him for an interview, "Hurst said he would do the interview after practice, in the locker room, where Olson had been only twice before," commented Montville. She did not like to do interviews in the locker room, but Hurst made it clear that she had to come to him, rather than him meeting her in the pressroom. After practice on September 17, 1990, Olson went to see Hurst, who was apparently icing down an injury he had endured that day. While she was asking him questions for her piece, Robert Perryman, Michael Timpson and Zeke Mowatt surrounded them and directed crude comments at her while gesturing with their genitals. Olson, attempted to ignore them and continue her interview with Hurst, but she was too flustered and ended up leaving the locker room briskly. She ran to her car and drove home quickly, all the while crying and hitting her fist upon the steering wheel, expressing her rage.

Once she arrived home Olson immediately called Sales to tell him of the incident. They "intended to confront privately the Patriot's management about the incident, but the item was published three days later by the *Boston Globe,*" according to Mark Fitzgerald of *Editor & Publisher*. The players did not step forward to apologize before the incident was published, but when their reputations were at stake, the Patriots' owner, Victor Kiam, took out an apology ad in the paper. It was too little to late. The damage to Olson's life had already been made. Eventually an investigation into the altercation was performed, and the guilty parties were fined for their wrongdoing.

Olson ended up having to move out of the country to Australia because of the harassment she received following the story. "The people who run the NFL must have felt this was an acceptable solution, because they did nothing to change it," said Mike Celezic of the *Record*. Sadly, the event didn't have the life-changing effect it should have. "I don't think it helped women," said Andrea Kremer to the *Denver Rocky Mountain News*. She continued, "I would never second-guess anything she did. I haven't stood in her shoes. My instinct is you try to defuse everything with humor, but there was nothing humorous about this." Celezic added, "The women, knowing what happened to Olson, cringe and suffer in silence rather than lose their access and their jobs."

Higher Standard

Johnette Howard for *Newsday* stated, "One of the powerful things that came out of Lisa Olson's case was

Chronology

1964	Born
1986	Approaches Bob Sales with the *Boston Herald* for a job
1987	Begins covering scholastic sports
1988	Begins covering the Boston Bruins hockey team
1990	Covers Superbowl
1990	Begins covering the New England Patriots
1990	Confronted by several players in locker room
1991	Files suit against the Patriots, Kiam, Pat Sullivan, Jimmy Oldham, Mowatt, Perryman and Timpson
1991	Moves to Sydney, Australia to work for the *Melbourne Age* and *Sydney Morning News*
1997	Returns to the United States to work for *New York Daily News*

that teams and leagues have said adamantly that they won't tolerate that kind of behavior ... before that, I think women thought ritual hazing was part of the job they had to get through." Olson agrees, stating, "Things have changed dramatically since I was new on the Patriots' beat."

Nine years later Olson is back in the States reporting for the *New York Daily News.* In her column she relays that she has received disgusting hate mail since her return, but will not back down from the job she loves. Olson explains why women continue in the field of sports journalism saying, "we do it because we love writing and producing and filming and talking sports." Many people have tried to come up with solutions to this prominent problem as more and more women enter the field. "Reporters wish the athletes would keep their uniforms on long enough to be interviewed, and that would eliminate all problems," said Holli Armstrong for the *University Wire.* Olson has no problem doing her job in the professional manner in which she has always conducted herself.

FURTHER INFORMATION

Periodicals

Celizic, Mike. "Sport. Professional. Athlete. Woman. Behavior. Discrimination." *Record,* (October 15, 1991): 01.

Dougherty, Pete. "The Grass Ceiling Women Sports Reporters Take the Field." *Denver Rocky Mountain News,* (October 4, 1998): 15C.

Fitzgerald, Mark. "Lisa Olson Redux." *Editor & Publisher,* (January 25, 1997): 11.

Galloway, Paul. "Female Sportswriter Showing Another Kind of Grace." *St. Louis Post-Dispatch,* (July 10, 1994): 07F.

Jenkins, Sally. "There's No Room for this View." *Washington Post,* (October 29, 2000): D01.

King, Peter. "Inside the NFL: Shame on the Patriots." *Sports Illustrated,* (October 1, 1990): 54.

Kunen, James. "Up front: Sportswriter Lisa Olson Calls the New England Patriots Out of Bounds for Sexual Harassment." *People,* (October 15, 1990): 40.

"Letters: Congatulations to Leigh Montville and SI on Your Story About the." *Sports Illustrated,* (June 3, 1991): 4.

"Mail: Lisa Olson." *People,* (November 5, 1990): 4.

Montville, Leigh. "The Early Morning, at Five or Six O'clock, is When Sportswriter." *Sports Illustrated,* (May 13, 1991): 60.

Myers, Donald. "The Locker Room / The Women Who Enter to Interview Male Athletes Find They're Still Not Always Welcome." *Newsday,* (June 8, 1999): B06.

Whitaker, Leslie. "SPORT: Trouble in the Locker Rooms More Women Reporters Face Hostility that Threatens their Access." *Time,* (October 15, 1990): 97.

Other

Armstrong, Holli. "Women Still Battling for Level Playing Field in Sports Journalism." University Wire. (March 12, 2002).

"GRID: Life Down Under Not All as it Seems." AAP Sports News (Australia). (August 8, 1999).

Sketch by Barbra J Smerz

Shaquille O'Neal
1972-

American basketball player

Shaquille O'Neal represents professional basketball in the third millennium. At seven-feet-one-inch tall and 335 pounds, he dominates a basketball court with little effort. His combination of size, strength, height, and speed is rare. His hulking presence is distinctive and unmistakable even among his peers, the so-called big men of basketball. A giant of a man, he put a new slant on the celebrity status of living large, when as a 19-year-old draft pick in the National Basketball Association (NBA) he signed the largest rookie contract in the history of professional basketball. Yet without spending a dime of his NBA salary, he embarked on a luxurious lifestyle funded exclusively from endorsement contracts and personal ventures. O'Neal, who moonlights as a recording artist, movie star, and television director, is an Olympic gold medallist and on multiple occasions a most valuable player (MVP) honoree. By his eleventh year in the league he was sporting three NBA championship rings. Off the court he is known to flash an ear-to-ear grin and to emote the unflappable personality of a 12-year-old boy.

Shaquille O'Neal

Chronology

1972	Born in Newark, New Jersey, on March 6
1988-89	Leads Cole High School of San Antonio, Texas, to undefeated season; Texas Class AAA state title
1989	Enrolls at LSU
1989-92	Averages 21.6 points, 13.5 rebounds, and 4.6 blocks per game at LSU
1990	Averages 24.5 points and 13.8 rebounds at National Sports Festival
1990-91	Averages 27.6 points and 14.7 rebounds, shoots .628 from the floor; leads the nation in collegiate rebounding average
1992	Goes to the Orlando Magic as the first pick in the NBA draft on June 24; signs for over $40 million
1992-93	Leads Magic to more than double its previous year win record
1993	Sets career-high totals of 28 rebounds and 15 blocked shots on November 20 against the New Jersey Nets
1993-94	Leads Orlando to its first playoff appearance
1994-95	Leads Orlando to the NBA Finals after going 57-25 to lead the Eastern Conference
1995-96	Leads Orlando to Eastern Conference finals
1996	Signs with the Los Angeles Lakers, for seven years and $120 million on July 18 in the largest free agent move in NBA history
1998	Achieves 10,000 career points on February 10
2000	Scores career-high 61 points versus Los Angeles Clippers on March 6
2000	Leads Lakers to their first NBA title since 1988
2001	Leads Lakers to back-to-back NBA titles
2002	Leads Lakers to a third championship; marries Shaunie Nelson on December 26

Shaquille Rashaun O'Neal was born in Newark, New Jersey, on March 6, 1972. He weighed an unremarkable 7-pounds-13-ounces and was named for an Islamic phrase that means "Little Warrior." His parents, Lucille O'Neal and Joe Toney, never married. Toney, who was a student at Seton Hall University at the time of O'Neal's birth, parted ways with his new family soon afterward. O'Neal then lived with his mother at the residence of his grandmother, Odessa Chamblis, at 100 Oak Street in Jersey City. As the three generations lived together, Chamblis worked as a nurse, and her daughter worked at city hall.

When O'Neal was two years old his mother married Philip Harrison, a sergeant in the U.S. Army. The new Harrison family bonded firmly. With O'Neal as the eldest sibling, Harrison's daughters Ayesha and Lateefa became step-sisters to O'Neal; a younger brother, Jamal was born later to the Harrisons. The family moved often, going from Newark to Bayonne when O'Neal was only five, then on to Eatontown. He was in the fifth grade when they arrived at Ft. Stewart, California. When he was in junior high school the family moved overseas, to Europe. After a brief stay in Wiesbaden, Germany, they spent a few years in Wildflecken.

Can't Stop Growing

As a child O'Neal was not a natural athlete. He was in reality an eternal mischief-maker, hot-tempered, and quick to create altercations. Around the time that he entered junior high school, he began to grow very rapidly, and his parents encouraged him to become involved in sports in order to channel his youthful energy and to keep him out of trouble. While attending a youth basketball clinic in Germany, O'Neal—because of his height—caught the eye of Louisiana State University (LSU) Coach Dale Brown. Brown was pleasantly surprised to learn that O'Neal, at more than 6-feet-6-inches tall, was not an adult member of the military (as appeared to be the case). The coach was even more pleased to discover that O'Neal was merely a freshman in high school—and still growing. Brown contacted O'Neal's father and urged him to keep in touch and to consider sending O'Neal to LSU.

As it happened, O'Neal was cut from his ninth grade basketball team because of his clumsiness. He was nonetheless already determined to become a professional basketball player. By the time the Harrison family returned to the United States, O'Neal was already 6-feet-10-inches tall and his size 17 shoes were too small. He was an imposing presence for a high school athlete.

Upon the family's return in 1987, Sgt. Harrison was assigned to Ft. Sam Houston, Texas, and the family moved to San Antonio where O'Neal enrolled as a sophomore at Robert G. Cole High School. There he nurtured his dreams of fame and even practiced signing his name, as if doling out autographs for imaginary fans.

Athletes and Music

Some of the tightest bonds are between jocks and hip-hoppers, who have taken up the rock-and-roll mantle of fame-flaunting, drug-touting behavior. The rap game has seduced many professional athletes, the most prominent of whom, Lakers center Shaquille O'Neal, released his fifth CD last September. "When you watch MTV, you can tell all the musicians want to be athletes, and when you watch ESPN, you can tell all the athletes want to rap," O'Neal says. "Remember, a lot of us came from the same place...."

Some rappers believe O'Neal is fronting, that he owes his success (including that of his platinum debut CD, Shaq Diesel) to slick production and marketing. In 1995 rapper Coolio told Vibe magazine that O'Neal should "stay on the court; he can't rap." It's a decent bet, however, that none of those critics has expressed that sentiment in person to the 7'1", 315-pound dunkmeister. O'Neal, who entitled his latest CD Respect because he wants to be accepted as a legitimate rapper, says, "I'm just the first person to conquer both worlds. I'm not stupid; I know not to pick [bad] beats."

Source: Silver, Michael, *Sports Illustrated,* May 24, 1999.

Awards and Accomplishments

1990	Sets a collegiate conference record of 115 blocked shots
1990-91	Named national Player of the Year in media polls
1991	Wins the Adolph Rupp Trophy and the John Wooden Award as college basketball player of the year
1992	Picked first in the first round overall of the National Basketball Association draft
1993	Named National Basketball Association Rookie of the Year; named to National Basketball Association All-Rookie First Team
1993-98	Named to National Basketball Association All-Star
1996	Won a gold medal with the US Olympic Basketball Team; selected as one of the 50 Greatest Players in National Basketball Association history; included as one of only four athletes among the 100 most powerful people in sports, *Sporting News* (December 30, 1996)
1999	Named Most Valuable Player for the league
2000	Named most valuable player for the league; named most valuable player for the finals; named most valuable player for the All-Star game; jersey Number 33 retired by Louisiana State University athletic department
2001	Named most valuable player for the league finals
2002	Named most valuable player for the league finals

Named by the NBA as one of the league's 50 greatest players of all time.

At 250 pounds, O'Neal was a formidable center for his high school team. During his junior year the school recorded only one loss for the season as they went 32-1. The following year the team was undefeated, at 36-0. O'Neal averaged 32 points per game, 22 rebounds, and 8 blocked shots for his last two years of high school. By high school graduation in 1989 O'Neal was fully grown. He stood 7-feet-1-inch tall, wore a size 22 shoe, and was recruited intensively by coaches from major colleges. O'Neal opted to play with Coach Brown and the Tigers at LSU in Baton Rouge.

O'Neal, playing at center, was named to the All-American first team during his freshman year at LSU. He averaged more than 12 rebounds per game and set a conference record of 115 blocked shots. Although not the strongest among shooters, his game matured with practice, and he perfected his jump and hook shots. His feats were largely overshadowed that year by the talents of LSU power forward Stanley Roberts. Also a seven-footer, Roberts was faster, more experienced, and more confident.

During the summer of 1990 O'Neal went to the National Sports Festival where he represented the South. At the festival he averaged 24.5 points and 13.8 rebounds per game. Also during the summer break, through intensive conditioning he increased his vertical jump from 16 to 42 inches, which enabled him to reach more than two feet beyond the rim of the basket.

When O'Neal returned to LSU as a sophomore in the fall of 1990, the forward Roberts had left school to play professional ball. He spent the rest of the decade in the NBA playing for the Magic in 1991, and later for the Clippers, Timberwolves, Rockets, and Spurs. O'Neal easily inherited Roberts' reputation as the premiere varsity player at LSU, earning recognition as the biggest of the big men in the National College Athletic Association (NCAA) of that era.

O'Neal doubled his scoring average that season to 27 points per game, and in one contest against Arizona O'Neal scored 29 points—including 16 points in the final six minutes. *Contemporary Black Biography* cited *Sports Illustrated* in quoting Georgia coach Hugh Durham's remark at that time, that "'Shack' [O'Neal] may be unguardable." O'Neal furthermore increased his rebound average to 14.6 per game. He led the NCAA and earned the College Player of the Year distinction from *Sports Illustrated,* the Associated Press, and United Press International respectively.

NBA Bound

College, for O'Neal, became confining. Always quick to unleash the uninhibited side of his nature, he was evicted from the dormitory at LSU for rowdy behavior shortly before the beginning of his junior year. He took a reprimand on another occasion for possessing an illegally funded cell phone, which (as it turned out) was a phony—a toy he carried to impress co-eds. In April, 1992, rather than re-enroll for his senior year, O'Neal announced his availability for the NBA draft.

On June 24, the day of the draft, he was picked first in the first round. Drafted by the Orlando Magic, he signed with that team for $41 million for seven years. His was the largest rookie contract in the history of professional basketball.

O'Neal was named player of the week after his first week as a rookie. It was a first-time occurrence in the NBA, and he was named as a starter in the All-Star game—another rare feat for a rookie. His rebounds, blocks, and starts ranked as team highs for the season, and averaged 23.4 points per game. That year the Magic more than doubled its win record from the previous year. The team went to a 41-41 record, which was 20 wins more than the previous season.

With 50 wins for the 1993-4 season, the Magic went to the playoffs for the first time in franchise history. O'Neal already had dunked 709 times in his first two years as a pro. As he made strides in his professional career, he continued taking college courses through an independent studies programs at LSU during the off-seasons. On December 15, 2000, he graduated with a general studies degree and a minor in political science. When O'Neal flew to Baton Rouge for the commencement he was honored by the school with a ceremony to retire his LSU jersey, Number 33.

L.A. Lakers

In 1996 O'Neal signed with the Los Angeles Lakers as a free agent. Again his contract made NBA history. At more than $120 million over seven years it was the largest free agent move in league history. O'Neal that summer won an Olympic gold medal with the U.S. basketball team.

In 2000 he led his new team to its first NBA championship since 1988. O'Neal earned the league MVP trophy and was named MVP of the All-Star game also that year. After leading the NBA in both scoring and field goal percentages for the season, he managed to score 41 points in the decisive championship game, a feat that earned him the MVP trophy for the 2000 NBA finals. With the finals MVP in his pocket, he had succeeded in sweeping all three of the 2000 MVP awards. It was only the third time in history that all three honors fell to the same player. He reaffirmed his contract option through the 2005-06 season that year.

The 2000-01 season brought a repeat of the previous year, with a championship title for the Lakers and the finals MVP trophy for O'Neal. After back-to-back championships, the Lakers in 2002 accomplished a so-called three-peat NBA championship win, with O'Neal three-peating his MVP honor.

Moonlighting Magic

O'Neal earned an estimated $30 million from endorsements alone in his first year as a professional athlete. As he peddled carbonated beverages, athletic shoes, sports equipment, and trading cards, his endorsement income swelled to an estimated $70 million by 2001.

After finalizing his first contract out of college, he relished in spending one million dollars for the first time. He managed easily to unburden himself of the money in the space of a few days. "My first check was for a million dollars, which came to about $600,000 [after taxes] … I spent it all in about 15 minutes," O'Neal bemoaned to S. L. Price in *Sports Illustrated.* O'Neal then ex-

Shaquille O'Neal

plained that in addition to his many purchases of expensive clothes and an ostentatious Mercedes Benz with custom wheel rims and speakers, he paid some debts for his parents and purchased a Mercedes apiece for each of them. "Then the bank called and said, 'You're $200,000 in the hole,'" O'Neal recalled.

O'Neal branched also into recording, entertainment, and other industries. His personal entrepreneurial ventures include a record label and a clothing line. TWisM, by which he identifies his business projects, is an acronym for O'Neal's personal motto, "The World Is Mine." Overall, he lives a high-stakes lifestyle, which he funds exclusively from his outside ventures—according to O'Neal, he never spends his NBA earnings.

Shaq-Fu Skillz

When O'Neal initiated his career as a rap musician in 1993, his debut single, "I Know I Got Skillz," was certified gold by December of the year. A debut album, *Shaq Diesel,* appeared also in 1993 and featured cameos by other popular artists and rap stars. It was certified platinum in 1994 (over 1,000,000 sold). His sophomore album, whimsically titled *Shaq-Fu: Da Return,* appeared in 1994 and was certified gold by January of 1995. A "best of" album appeared in 1996 and provided advance publicity for an all-new follow-up album, called *You Can't Stop the Reign,* which was released one week later. On this album O'Neal shared a track with a colleague, the late gangsta' rapper Christopher "Biggie Smalls" Wallace. In March 1997 the friendship came to

Career Statistics

Yr	Team	GP	PTS	FG%	3P%	FT%	RPG	APG	SPG	BPG	TO	PF
1992-93	ORL	81	1893	56.2	0.0	59.2	13.9	1.9	0.7	3.5	307	321
1993-94	ORL	81	2377	59.9	0.0	55.4	13.2	2.4	0.9	.9	222	281
1994-95	ORL	79	2315	58.3	0.0	53.3	11.4	2.7	0.9	2.4	204	258
1995-96	ORL	54	1434	57.3	50.0	48.7	11.0	2.9	0.6	2.1	155	193
1996-97	LAL	51	1336	55.7	0.0	48.4	12.5	3.1	0.9	2.9	146	180
1997-98	LAL	60	1699	58.4	0.0	52.7	11.3	2.4	0.7	2.4	175	193
1998-99	LAL	49	1289	57.6	0.0	54.0	10.7	2.3	0.7	1.7	122	155
1999-00	LAL	79	2344	57.4	0.0	52.4	13.6	3.8	0.5	3.0	223	255
2000-01	LAL	74	2125	57.2	0.0	51.3	12.7	3.7	0.6	2.8	218	256
2001-02	LAL	67	1822	57.9	0.0	55.5	10.7	3.0	0.6	2.0	171	199
Total		675	18634	57.7	5.0	53.3	12.3	2.8	0.7	2.6	1943	2291

LAL: Los Angeles Lakers; ORL: Orlando Magic.

a tragic end with the murder of Wallace not long after he and O'Neal shared a stage in West Hollywood.

O'Neal, having gained legitimacy for his recording career, returned in 1998 with another album, *Respect*. In 2001 he released an album for the new millennium, called *Shaq O'Neal Presents His Superfriends*. Because O'Neal takes his identity in part from the ghetto life of his early years and in part from his life as an army brat, the rap albums brought validation to his image as a ghetto-child/rap icon and opened a new dimension to his persona.

"Ow!" a Toe

Excessively flippant and off-the-wall, O'Neal's outrageous personality and diverse interests keep his fans highly entertained. In his 2001 memoir, *Shaq Talks Back* from St. Martin's Press, he explains in his own words, "Where I Came from and How I Got So Damn Big." With a projected NBA salary of $21 million, O'Neal's player paycheck is the second highest in the league. With a net worth of $171 million in 2002 he was listed at number 22 among *Fortune*'s "40 richest under 40."

Nicknamed Big Aristotle by some fans, O'Neal's teammates know him at times rather as Big Moody. When a toe injury to his size 22 foot kept him off the court after the 2002 NBA finals through November of the new season, he was unabashedly vocal about how he felt. He minced no words and chided to reporters that his pain was not to be taken lightly. Regardless, O'Neal's personal confidence may well be as large as his feet. Biographer Jack McCallum reported in *Sports Illustrated* that during the 2002 NBA Western Conference Playoffs, O'Neal sent the opposing coach Rick Adelman of the Sacramento Kings a piece of poetry that read, "Don't cry/Dry your eyes/Here comes Shaq/With those four little guys." O'Neal later bared the bottom of his backside to Kings fans after the Lakers won the conference title.

McCallum defended the impact of O'Neal as a player, although he seems at times to be larger than life. "[His] influence on his team is so profound, because he has worked so hard at becoming a complete player and because he has played through so much pain, he bristles whenever it is suggested that his oversized body is the primary reason for his success—a suggestion that is made every night of the season," said the writer.

O'Neal, who published his first autobiography, *Shaq Attack,* with Hyperion in 1993, and branched into children's literature in the late 1990s with *Shaq and the Beanstalk and Other Very Tall Tales*. Following his rookie year in Orlando, he earned $1 million for his role as Nick Nolte's co-star in the feature film *Blue Chip*. O'Neal starred three more feature films—*Kazaam* in 1996, *Steel* in 1997, and *The Wash* in 2001. O'Neal, who directed the cable television series *Cousin Skeeter,* has expressed an interest in appearing in more action roles. He has appeared many times as himself on network television situation comedies and talk shows. A self-professed "Jersey guy," he anticipates a second career in law enforcement when his athletic prowess fades.

O'Neal is the father of two daughters and one son. He owns mansions Beverly Hills, California, and near Orlando, Florida. On December 26, 2002, he wed Shaunie Nelson, his friend of several years. Together the couple have four children, including one each from previous relationships and two together.

CONTACT INFORMATION

Address: Agent: c/o Leonard Armato, William Morris Agency, 151 South El Camino Dr., Beverly Hills, CA 90212-2775. Phone: (310) 859-4000. Address: c/o Staples Center, 1111 South Figueroa, St, Los Angeles, CA 90015. Phone: (213) 742-7333. Address: c/o Office, LA Lakers, 3900 W Manchester Blvd, Inglewood, CA, 90305-2200.

SELECTED WRITINGS BY O'NEAL:

(With Jack McCallum) *Shaq Attack,* New York: Hyperion Press, 1993.

Shaq and the Beanstalk and Other Very Tall Tales, New York: Scholastic, 1999.

Shaq Talks Back, New York: St. Martin's Press, 2001.

FURTHER INFORMATION

Books

Dougherty, Terri, *Jam Session: Shaquille O'Neal,* Edina (MN): ABDO Publishing Co., 2001.

Jackson, Kenneth T. and Arnold Markoe, *The Scribner Encyclopedia of American Lives: Sports Figurers,* New York: Charles Scribner's Sons, 2002.

O'Neal, Shaquille, *Shaq Talks Back,* New York: St. Martin's Press, 2001.

"Shaquille O'Neal," *Contemporary Black Biography,* Volume 30. Edited by Ashyia Henderson. Gale Group, 2001.

Periodicals

Sports Illustrated, May 24, 1999, p.97; June 17, 2002, p. 32; December 23, 2002, p. 64.

Sketch by G. Cooksey

Buck O'Neil
1911-

American baseball player

The gentlemanly and charismatic John "Buck" O'Neil became, in 1962, the first black baseball coach hired by a major league team. In the Negro Leagues during the 1940s and 1950s, he played on nine championship teams and in two Negro League World Series, managed five East-West All-Star Classics, and won a Negro National League batting title. Always an ambassador for the game and its black heritage, he enjoyed a resurgent interest in his story since the airing of Ken Burns' *Baseball* documentary series, for which O'Neil served as narrator. To preserve the legacy of black baseball, O'Neil co-founded the Negro Leagues Baseball Museum in Kansas City, Missouri, and currently serves as its chairman.

Dreaming Big

Growing up in the celery fields of Florida, John Jordan O'Neil, Jr. dreamed big. His father, a saw mill worker, played for local baseball teams and soon, young

Buck O'Neil

John took a liking to the game. He first played semi-professional baseball in 1923 with the Sarasota Tigers.

Although he was not allowed to attend Sarasota High School because he was black, he eventually obtained a high school diploma. Later, he earned a baseball and football scholarship to Edward Waters College in Jacksonville, Florida. In 1934, he toured professionally with the Miami Giants, who named him Buck after one of the team's owners, Buck O'Neal.

O'Neil flitted between several teams in his early career, playing for the New York Tigers, Shreveport Acme Giants, Memphis Red Sox, and the barnstorming team Zulu Cannibal Giants between 1934 and 1937. The Negro American League's Memphis Red Sox signed him after seeing him play in Shreveport and paid him $100 a month.

In 1938, O'Neil finally rested with the Kansas City Monarchs, an elite team of the Negro Leagues, with whom he would stay as player and manager until 1955. O'Neil began with the Monarchs as a first baseman and became a consistent hitter with good extra-base power. The Monarchs won four consecutive Negro American League (NAL) pennants from 1939-42, and won against the Homestead Grays in the first World Series played between the NAL and the Negro National League. O'Neil made three appearances for the West squad in the East-West All-Star Classic in 1942, 1943, and 1949.

```
┌─────────────────────────────────────────────────────┐
│ Chronology                                          │
│                                                     │
│  1911    Born November 13 in Carrabelle, Florida    │
│  1923    Semi-professional with Sarasota Tigers     │
│  1930    Graduates from Edward Waters College        │
│  1934    Plays for Miami Giants                      │
│  1935    Plays for New York Tigers                   │
│  1936    Plays for Shreveport Acme Giants           │
│  1937    Plays for Memphis Red Sox                   │
│  1937    Plays for Zulu Cannibal Giants             │
│  1938-43, Plays for Kansas City Monarchs            │
│  1946-55                                            │
│  1943-45  Military service during Wold War II       │
│  1946    Marries Ora Lee Owen                        │
│  1994    Narrator in Ken Burns' PBS documentary Baseball │
│  1996    Publishes memoirs, I Was Right on Time     │
└─────────────────────────────────────────────────────┘
```

```
┌─────────────────────────────────────────────────────┐
│ Awards and Accomplishments                          │
│                                                     │
│  1938    Started with Kansas City Monarchs           │
│  1939-42 Monarchs won four consecutive Negro American League │
│          pennants                                   │
│  1940    Won Negro League batting title with a .345 average │
│  1942    Appearance in the West All-Star game        │
│  1942    First World Series played between the Negro American League │
│          and the Negro National League              │
│  1946    Led Negro National League with a .353 batting average │
│  1947    Career best batting average of .358         │
│  1948-55 Named manager of Kansas City Monarchs       │
│  1950    Monarchs won the Western Division Championships │
│  1951-54 Managed East-West all-star teams            │
│  1956    Signed with the Chicago Cubs as a scout     │
│  1962    First black coach hired by a major league   │
│  1981    Joined Baseball Hall of Fame Veterans Committee │
│  1988    Became scout for Kansas City Royals         │
│  1990    Co-founded Negro Leagues Baseball Museum in Kansas City │
│  1996    Received honorary degree from University of Missouri-Kansas │
│          City Bloch School of Business              │
│  1998    Named Midwest Scout of the Year             │
│  1999    Kansas State College Lifetime Leadership Award │
└─────────────────────────────────────────────────────┘
```

O'Neil took a two-year absence from baseball in 1943 to fight in World War II. Trained for the US Navy, he was shipped out to Subic Bay in the Philippines to work loading ships.

Returning to the Monarchs and to his superb performance as a first baseman and hitter, O'Neil led the 1946 NAL with a batting average of .353, leading his team to another pennant. He scored two home runs and a .333 average in the Black World Series against the Newark Eagles. That same year he married Memphis school teacher Ora Lee Owen.

In addition to the Monarchs, O'Neil played in winter leagues and on barnstorming teams throughout his career. He teamed with the legendary **Satchel Paige** to tour with Bob Feller's All-Stars, playing numerous exhibition games in the late 1940s. He played winter ball with Almendares in the Cuban League and with Obregon in the Mexican winter league. Overall in his career, O'Neil had a career batting average of .288 including four .300-plus seasons.

O'Neil as Manager, Scout, and First Black Coach

In 1948, O'Neil was named manager of the Monarchs, experiencing mixed success at first. With divisional play in 1949, he led the Monarchs to the first-half title in the Western Division. Finally in 1950, the Monarchs won both halves of the Western Division. Between 1948 and 1955, O'Neil managed to propel the Monarchs to five pennants, two Black World Series, and four straight All-Star wins.

The Chicago Cubs noticed O'Neil and signed him as a scout in 1956. During his stint with the Monarchs, O'Neil brought more than three dozen baseball players to the Major Leagues. As a scout, he recognized talent and recommended the signing of greats **Ernie Banks**, a Monarchs slugger, and **Lou Brock** to their first professional contracts. Also on his roster were Joe Carter, Oscar Gamble, Elston Howard, Lee Smith, and Hank Thompson.

O'Neil made history in 1962 when the first major league team, the Cubs, hired an Africa-American as its coach. Eventually O'Neil realized the Cubs did not want to make him a big-league manager, so he returned to scouting. He stayed with the Cubs for thirty-three years, leaving in 1988 to return to Missouri to scout for the Kansas City Royals.

Remembering the Negro Leagues

Buck O'Neil became a member of the 18-person Baseball Hall of Fame Veterans Committee of Cooperstown, New York, in 1981. With the intense desire to preserve the memory of the Negro Leagues, he raised money and co-founded the Negro League Baseball Museum in Kansas City in 1990. For more than a decade, he has lectured about the history and accomplishments of the Negro Leagues around the country, at schools, at conferences, on radio programs, and on television.

O'Neil experienced a resurgence of popularity in 1994 with the release of Ken Burn's PBS documentary *Baseball*. O'Neil narrated the program's segment highlighting the Negro Leagues. After the show's airing, he appeared on national interviews and late night talk shows such as *Late Night with David Letterman*.

Bringing his memories and words to a new generation, the new celebrity published his autobiography in 1996, *I Was Right on Time: My Journey from the Negro Leagues to the Majors,* co-written with *Sports Illustrated* editors Steve Wulf and David Conrads. O'Neil continues to recommend Negro League players to the Baseball Hall of Fame and advocates pensions for surviving Negro League players.

The long-time Kansas City resident holds no resentment or bitterness about the past segregation and racism

Career Statistics

Yr	Team	Avg	GP	AB	H	2B	3B	HRS	B
1937	MEM	.091	3	11	1	0	0	0	0
1938	KC	.258	27	89	23	5	2	1	7
1939	KC	.257	30	101	26	7	2	2	3
1940	KC	.345	30	113	39	5	3	1	6
1941	KC	.239	23	88	21	3	2	0	3
1942	KC	.247	–	182	45	6	1	1	0
1943	KC	.222	–	99	22	1	1	2	1
1946	KC	.350	58	197	69	1	1	2	1
1947	KC	.358	46	162	58	–	–	–	–
1948	KC	.253	42	162	41	6	1	1	3
1949	KC	.330	45	109	36	–	–	–	–
1950	KC	.253	31	83	21	5	2	1	5
TOTAL		.288	335	1396	402	39	15	11	29

KC: Kansas City Monarchs; MEM: Memphis Red Sox.

he encountered. O'Neil's ability to forgive is reflected in his warm smile and sense of humor. His intention is that the Negro League museum he co-founded be more about hope and progress than about inequality. An audio program, *The Best of Buck,* compiles twenty-three stories of baseball history in the Negro Leagues told by Buck O'Neil; proceeds go to museum.

At the age of eighty-nine, O'Neil said in an interview in *Home and Away* magazine, "I want the young people to know the wonderful changes that's happened in this country. I'm old enough to see these wonderful changes… This is what we're trying to do—teach every kid about the Negro Leagues and that era."

SELECTED WRITINGS BY O'NEIL:

(With Steve Wulf, and David Conrads) *I Was Right on Time: My Journey from the Negro Leagues to the Majors,* Touchstone, 1996.

FURTHER INFORMATION

Books

Dewey, Donald. *The Biographical History of Baseball.* New York: Carroll and Graf Publishing, 1995.

Riley, James A. *The Biographical Encyclopedia of Negro Baseball Leagues.* New York: Carroll and Graf Publishing, 1994.

Shatzkin, Mike. *The Ballplayers.* New York: William Morrow & Co., 1990.

Other

African American Publications. Gale Group. http://www.africanpubs.com/Apps/bio/0076ONeilBuck.asp (January 24, 2003).

Baseball Library. http://www.pubdim.net/baseballlibrary/excerpts/buck_oneil.stm (January 24, 2003).

Home and Away Magazine. "Local Legend Buck O'Neil." http://www.homeandawaymagazine.com/webstories_buck_oneil.html (January 24, 2003).

Negro Leagues Baseball Museum. http://www.nlbm.com/oneil.bio.html (January 24, 2003).

Pitch Black Negro League. http://www.pitchblackbaseball.com/nlotmbuckoneil.html (January 24, 2003).

Sketch by Lorraine Savage

Susan O'Neill
1973-

Australian swimmer

Susie O'Neill's sweet exterior easily cloaks a determined champion. She has won more titles than any Australian swimmer in the history of that country. Every record and medal she has set her sights on has eventually come to be hers. Her 1996 gold medal win at the Atlanta Olympics was the first for an Australian woman in sixteen years and the first ever for an Australian woman in Olympic competition in the 200-meter butterfly. At the end of her swimming career she stood as the reigning champion of the 200-meter butterfly from Australia's Commonwealth games to the Olympics, from the Pan Pacific Championships to the Olympics.

Taking to Water

Susan O'Neill was born in Mackay, Queensland, Australia, on August 2, 1973. O'Neill grew up surrounded by

Susan O'Neill

the beaches and waterways of this coastal city located on the northeast side of Australia. She first began swimming when she was eight years old. By the time she was twelve she had won an Australian title for her age group. It was about this time that she started swimming in the event that would become her specialty, the butterfly.

She missed a chance to make the Australian Olympic team in 1988 and in 1989 made her debut in international competition at the Pan Pacific Championships in Tokyo, Japan. She didn't place, but that same year she won her first Australian championship in the 50-meter butterfly.

When O'Neill first began swimming, it was under the expert eye of Bernie Wakefield. Wakefield had established himself previously as a coach for Australian Olympic swim teams as well as Commonwealth Games and other world championship teams. O'Neill swam with Wakefield as her coach through the early years as she established herself as a world class competitor. He was her coach when she won her first Olympic medal at the Barcelona Olympics in 1992 for the 200-meter butterfly.

New Coach Raises Stakes

In 1994, O'Neill switched from Wakefield to Scott Volkers. She had just won bronze medals for the 100-meter and 200-meter butterfly in the world championship meets in Rome and felt she wasn't capable of achieving much better. She told Wayne Smith of the *Sunday Tas-*

Chronology

1973	Born August 2 in Mackay, Queensland, Australia
1981	Begins swimming
1987	Starts competing in butterfly
1989	Begins competitive career at Pan Pacific Championships in Tokyo; wins first Australian championship in 50-meter butterfly
1992	Competes in 1992 Barcelona Olympics
1993	Almost breaks world record for time in 200-meter butterfly
1994	Switches from coach Bernie Wakefield to Scott Volkers
1996	Scott Volkers banned from attending swim meets due to dosing controversy, overturned in time for Atlanta Olympics
1998	Marries opthamologist Cliff Fairley on October 2; wins 30th Australian national title
2000	Loses 200-meter butterfly at Sydney Olympics, first loss in the event in six years; voted onto the International Olympic Commission
2000	Announces retirement from swimming

manian, "I thought I had reached my plateau." She was wrong. Volkers helped O'Neill continue on an upward curve that led her to win a gold medal for the 200-meter butterfly in the 1996 Atlanta Olympics.

O'Neill was lucky to have Volkers by her side after her win in Atlanta because an earlier doping scandal had made him ineligible to attend. Volkers was banned for one year by La Federation Internationale de Natation (FINA) when one of his swimmers and O'Neill's very good friend, Samantha Riley, tested positive for a banned painkiller. He appealed the decision at the Court of Arbitration for Sport in Lausanne, Switzerland. The court approved his appeal and Volkers was with his team during the competitions in Atlanta, Georgia.

After her win at the 1996 Olympics, O'Neill continued to excel. She explained to the *Sunday Tasmanian,* "I don't want to fall into the trap of other gold medallists.... I want to keep improving." O'Neill did not let herself or her fans down. In 1997, she broke the Australian record for the 200-meter butterfly with a time of 2:8.90. She had won enough Australian titles by this time that she was quickly approaching the record previously set by Sir Frank Beaurepaire. In May of 1998, she won her 30th national title. She thought she had broken Beaurepaire's record, but four more wins were discovered, making his total wins thirty-three, not the previously held twenty-nine. It took her two more years, but at the Olympic trials held in 2000, O'Neill surpassed Beaurepaire's record with her thirty-fourth title. By the time she retired, O'Neill had thirty-five Australian titles to her name.

One goal that continually eluded O'Neill was breaking **Mary T. Meagher**'s 1981 world record for the 200-meter butterfly. Meagher's speed was the longest standing record in international swimming history. O'Neill had broken the Australian record in 1997. That same year she was the fastest swimmer of the 200-

meter butterfly in the world for the year. Her times were often faster than Meagher's during the first 150 meters of the race, but O'Neill's early attacks would lead to exhaustion during the last fifty meters, where she always lost her lead.

World Fastest, Australia's Best

While focusing on breaking the 200-meter butterfly record, O'Neill managed to set a new record as part of the 4x200-meter freestyle relay team. Not long afterwards, at a World Cup meet in Malmo, Sweden, she broke Meagher's record for the 200-meter butterfly short course with a time of 2:04.16. She went on to win her tenth consecutive national open title in the 100-meter butterfly, and then break the Commonwealth record for the 200-meter freestyle with a time of 1:59.11.

The day after O'Neill surpassed Beaurepaire for the most Australian swimming titles, she finally became the fastest 200-meter butterfly swimmer in the world. On May 17, 2000, with fifteen seconds to spare, O'Neill broke a record that had existed for almost twenty years and one that had been a personal goal of hers for three years with a time of 2:05.81.

Hoping to maintain the momentum gained from having set a world record in her sport, O'Neill represented her country in the 2000 Olympics held in Sydney, Australia. She had already won gold medals for the 200-meter butterfly in two previous Olympics and set her sights on defending that title. Unfortunately, O'Neill was defeated by an American swimmer, her first loss in that particular race in six years. Despite the blow, O'Neill could remain proud for having won the gold for her country in the 200-meter freestyle, and also contributing to the bronze medals won by the 4x200-meter freestyle and the 4x100-meter medley teams.

Two months after the 2000 Olympics, O'Neill announced her retirement. One of her main reasons for retiring was to focus on her marriage and her husband. She had married long-time boyfriend, Cliff Fairley, in late 1998. His work as an opthamologist ended up taking him to Sydney while O'Neill remained in Brisbane to train. She felt that she had spent enough time concentrating on swimming and had achieved the goals she set.

After she announced her retirement from swimming, O'Neill dedicated herself to working for the International Olympic Committee (IOC). Her primary focus is educating athletes regarding doping issues. She is an active member of the World Anti-Doping Agency, a group that advises the IOC as well as governments and international sports organizations regarding doping regulations. She is ambassador for various companies and organizations including SAAB, Kellogg's, the Fred Hollows Foundation. She also has her own line of swimsuits that is sold in Target stores throughout Australia.

Awards and Accomplishments

1990	Silver for 100-meter butterfly, Commonwealth Games
1992	Bronze for 200-meter butterfly, Barcelona Olympics
1994	Gold for 200-meter butterfly in Commonwealth Games; bronze for 100-meter butterfly and 200-meter butterfly, World Championships, Rome
1995	Telstra Australian Swimmer of the Year
1996	Gold for 200-meter butterfly, silver for 4x100-meter medley, bronze for 4x200-meter freestyle, Atlanta Olympics; Telstra Australian Swimmer of the Year; Australian Female Athlete of the Year; Amateur Athletic Foundation World Trophy
1997	Gold for 200-meter butterfly, Pan Pacific Games; Order of Australia
1998	Gold for 200-meter butterfly, World Championships, Perth, Australia; gold for 200-meter freestlye, 400-meter freestyle, 200-meter butterfly, 4x100-meter, 4x200-meter, 4x100-meter medley, Commonwealth Games,; 4x200-meter freestyle relay team sets new record (8:03.73); Australian Female Athlete of the Year
1999	Gold for 200-meter butterfly, World Cup, Malmo, Sweden; breaks world record for 200-meter butterfly short course; gold for 200-meter freestyle, 100-meter butterfly, 200-meter butterfly and bronze for 4x100-meter freestyle, 4x100-meter medley, 4x200-meter freestyle, Pan Pacific Games; Australian Swimming Awards for female sprint freestyle swimmer and female butterfly swimmer
2000	World record for 200-meter butterfly (2:05.81), sets Australian record for 200-meter freestyle (1:57.47), places 2nd in 100-meter butterfly, Telstra 2000 Trails; silver for 200-meter butterfly, gold for 200-meter freestyle, bronze for 4x200-meter freestyle and 4x100-meter medley, Sydney Olympics; becomes winningest Australian swimmer in history with 35 titles; Australian Swimming Awards for female middle-distance freestyle, female butterfly, female shortcourse, and female sprint freestyle; Telstra Swimmers' Swimmer of the Year
2001	Outstanding Contribution to Swimming Award
2002	Inducted into Sport Australia's Hall of Fame

Susie O'Neill left her sport at her peak. She holds more swimming titles than any other Australian swimmer ever. She set national and world records in several events from relays to freestyle to butterfly. While she maintained her determination and focus, she also presented a positive attitude that the Australian public took to their hearts. Australians not only recognized the valuable contribution that O'Neill made to the sport of swimming but also her contribution as a representative of their country to the world. She will be remembered as she had hoped when she told the *Sunday Mail*, "I want to be known as one of Australia's greatest athletes."

CONTACT INFORMATION

Address: c/o Athletes Commission, Château de Vidy, 1007 Lausanne, Switzerland. Fax: (41.21) 621 62 16. Phone: (41.21) 621 61 11.

SELECTED WRITINGS BY O'NEILL:

(With Fiona Chappell) *Choose to Win*, Sydney Pan Macmillan, 1999.

FURTHER INFORMATION

Periodicals

"O'Neill Keeps Focus on Future." *Sunday Tasmanian* (August 10, 1997): 40.

"O'Neill Smashes 200m Butterfly Record." *Sunday Tasmanian* (October 12, 1997): 29.

Smith, Wayne. "Decade of Madame Butterfly." *Advertiser* (March 22, 1999): 76.

Smith, Wayne. "The Greatest; Super Susie Now Our No. 1 Title-holder." (May 17, 2000): 128.

Smith, Wayne. "Simply Susie." *Sunday Mail* (May 10, 1998): 71.

Smith, Wayne. "Susie Stops the Rot." *Sunday Tasmanian* (July 28, 1996): 2.

Other

Australian Swimming. http://www.swimming.org.au/news/news_item.cfm?ObjectID=993 (January 28, 2003)

"Pieter the Great Rules; Hyman Stuns O'Neill." Rediff.com. http://www.rediff.com/sports/2000/sep/20hogie.htm (January 22, 2003).

"Swimmer Biography: Susie O'Neill (AUS)." FINA. http://www.fina.org/bio_Oneil.html (January 22, 2003).

Sketch by Eve M. B. Hermann

Bobby Orr

Bobby Orr
1948-

Canadian hockey player

Bobby Orr is widely regarded as the greatest defenseman in hockey history. From the time he joined the Boston Bruins at the age of eighteen, Orr revolutionized the way hockey was played. Prior to that time, defensive players had confined themselves to playing defense. They guarded the approaches to the net and cleared the puck from the defensive zone, leaving the scoring to the front line. Orr played the game differently. He kept possession of the puck rather than simply clearing it, and he frequently crossed the blue line to participate in offensive plays. Orr shattered the scoring records for defensemen, and for two seasons he was the leading scorer in the entire National Hockey League (NHL).

The Young Champion

Orr started his professional hockey career young. The Boston Bruins first took notice of him when he was twelve and playing in a bantam-league hockey All-Star game, to which the Bruins had sent scouts to check on some older players. Orr played all sixty minutes of the game, minus two minutes spent in the penalty box, and already displayed an ability to control the puck and the game that he would later be notable for in his professional career.

At the age of fourteen the Boston Bruins signed Orr into their organization for $2,800. They arranged for him to play in Canada's Junior A hockey league, which was populated mostly by nineteen- and twenty-year-olds with strong hopes of making it to the NHL. Orr continued to live in his hometown of Perry Sound, Ontario, a three-hour commute from the rink where his team, the Oshawa Generals, played and practiced. Orr in fact did not practice with the team, and only played in home games, but he still made the second all-star team in his first year. He made the first all-star team every year after, and, at age sixteen, he appeared on the cover of Canada's national magazine, *Maclean's*.

At eighteen, the youngest age at which a person was allowed to play in the NHL, Orr signed a record-breaking two-year contract with the Bruins. Orr would be making $25,000 a year, plus an undisclosed signing bonus estimated to be $25,000 to $35,000 itself. The previous record for a rookie contract was $8,000 a year, and at that time only three players in the entire NHL, all tested veterans, were making more than $25,000 a year.

Boston fans quickly pinned their hopes for a Stanley Cup, a prize which had eluded them for twenty-five years, on this fresh-faced, buzz-cut young star. He would not disappoint them.

Bobby Orr's most memorable hockey moment—the most memorable moment in all of hockey history, many say—is without a doubt "The Goal," as it is still referred to reverentially more than thirty years later by hockey fans in Boston and around the country. It was May 10, Mothers' Day, 1970, twenty-nine years since the Bruins had last won a Stanley Cup, and Boston was playing the St. Louis Blues in the fourth game of the championships. It was hot and humid inside Boston Garden, and the game had just gone into overtime. Thirty seconds into the fourth period, Orr stripped the puck from Blues player Larry Keenan and passed it to his teammate, Derek Sanderson. Orr sprinted towards the net and Sanderson passed the puck back to him. Just as Orr took his shot, Blues defenseman Noel Picard used his stick to trip Orr, sending him flying. The goal went in, and *Boston Record American* photographer Ray Lussier snapped the famous picture of Orr flying through the air, parallel to the ice, with arms outstretched and a look of sheer joy on his face. He had just brought the Stanley Cup back to Boston.

"A Man with Class"

In an era where hockey players were often known for their carousing as much as for their playing, Orr was known for his class. Former referee Wally Harris recalled in an interview with *Boston Herald* reporter Joe Fitzgerald a night where Harris ejected Orr from a game in Boston. "It took twelve policemen to get me out of there," Harris said. "That night my phone rang and a voice asked, 'Wally, did you get back all right?' It was Orr. Let me tell you, there was a man with class."

This is not to say that Orr didn't have a tough streak. He was a frequent and capable participant in hockey's typical on-ice brawls, and spent plenty of time in the penalty box paying for them. But Orr still displayed modesty in his relations with opponents. Don Cherry, Bruins coach in the mid-1970s, recalled in an interview with Craig MacInnis for the book *Remembering Bobby*

Orr that Orr went out of his way not to humiliate losing teams. "I saw him pass up goals and points because we were playing expansion teams. Once we'd get up 4-1 or 5-1 he would not want to embarrass the other teams. . . . After a great goal, he'd put his head down. He felt embarrassed for the other team."

A Disappointing End

Orr played in Boston (or "Orr Country," as a popular bumper sticker of the time dubbed it) for six more seasons after that first Stanley Cup. He helped bring the Stanley Cup back to the city in 1972, again scoring the winning goal, and he remained a favorite of Bruins fans.

A bizarre twist marred the end of Orr's hockey career for many Bostonians. In 1976 Orr's long-time agent, Alan Eagleson, was negotiating a new contract for him. Orr wanted to remain with the Bruins, and the Bruins desperately wanted to keep him, offering him an 18.5% ownership stake in the team, worth millions, if he would stay. However, Eagleson had unethical ties with Chicago Blackhawks owner Bill Wirtz, who also wanted Orr. Eagleson concealed Boston's offer from Orr and convinced him that Boston didn't want him to stay. Orr signed the deal with Chicago.

Orr was at that time struggling to play at all. He had suffered from knee problems ever since colliding with a teammate in a charity-benefit game in 1967. By 1976, he had already had multiple operations on his left knee, but in the days before artificial knees there was little that the doctors could do. There was nearly no cartilage remaining in the joint, and the sensation of bone rubbing against bone was excruciatingly painful. After playing only twenty-six games in just over two seasons with Chicago, Orr announced his retirement in a tearful news conference on November 8, 1978. Later that season, he

Career Statistics

Yr	Team	GP	G	A	PTS	+/−	PIM
1966-67	BOS	61	13	28	41	—	102
1967-68	BOS	46	11	20	31	+ 30	63
1968-69	BOS	67	21	43	64	+ 65	133
1969-70	BOS	76	33	87	120	+ 54	125
1970-71	BOS	78	37	102	139	+124	91
1971-72	BOS	76	37	80	117	+ 86	106
1972-73	BOS	63	29	72	101	+ 56	99
1973-74	BOS	74	32	90	122	+ 84	82
1974-75	BOS	80	46	89	135	+ 80	101
1975-76	BOS	10	5	13	18	+ 10	22
1976-77	CHI	20	4	19	23	+ 6	25
1978-79	CHI	6	2	2	4	+ 2	4
TOTAL		657	270	645	915	—	953

BOS: Boston Bruins; CHI: Chicago Black Hawks.

received an eleven-minute standing ovation from the crowd in Boston when his #4 was retired. That same year, 1979, Orr became the youngest player ever to enter the Hockey Hall of Fame.

Orr's troubles with Eagleson did not end with his retirement. Eagleson, who had been representing Orr before he signed his first contract with the Bruins, had mismanaged Orr's finances in a way that left him in deep trouble with both the Canadian and the American tax agencies. Between back taxes and legal bills, Orr was essentially bankrupt by 1980. The full extent of Eagleson's crimes, however, would not become apparent for many more years. In 1992, Eagleson was indicted in the United States on thirty-two counts of racketeering, fraud, and embezzlement related to the time he spent heading the NHL players' league. He eventually served an eighteen month sentence. After Eagleson's conviction, Orr was one of eighteen members of the Hall of Fame who threatened to quit the hall if Eagleson, also in the Hall of Fame, was not removed. (He was.)

Orr's Legacy

Although Orr has not skated professionally for over twenty years, his influence can still be seen on the game. He is still the only defenseman ever to lead the league in scoring even once, let alone twice, but the idea of defensive players participating in offensive plays is now seen across the NHL. His legendary puck-handling moves, which included a trademark 360 degree evasive spin, continue to inspire, and his thirty second and longer penalty-killing games of keep-away remain legendary. Yet, as much as Orr is imitated, no one has ever matched his combination of defensive and offensive prowess. Although players with longer careers have surpassed him in number of goals scored, his career averages of 1.39 points per regular season game and 1.24 per playoff game seem certain to stand as records for a defensive player for years to come.

SELECTED WRITINGS BY ORR:

(With Dick Grace) *Orr on Ice,* Prentice-Hall, 1970.

FURTHER INFORMATION

Books

MacInnis, Craig, editor. *Remembering Bobby Orr.* Toronto: Stoddart, 1999.

Periodicals

"Blues Playbook: Bobby Orr's Goal." *St. Louis Post-Dispatch* (January 20, 2002): C8.

"Bruins Flew to '70 Cup on the Wings of Orr's Dramatic Goal." *Washington Times* (May 13, 2002): C11.

Cashman, Wayne, and O'Donnell, Chris. "Wayne Cashman." *Hockey Digest* (March, 2001): 78.

Conway, Russ. "Eagleson's 'Slick Trick' Didn't Work: Sinden." *Eagle-Tribune* (Lawrence, Massachusetts) (April 14, 1998).

Deford, Frank. "Hello Again to a Grand Group." *Sports Illustrated* (August 5, 1985): 58-70.

Dupont, Kevin Paul. "Flash Points: Inimitable Orr Ignited Boston and NHL." *Boston Globe* (December 29, 1999): D01.

Fitzgerald, Joe. "Orr: Best in Ages." *Boston Herald* (March 20, 1998): 112.

Goold, Derrick. "Tonight's Goal: Letting Memories Take Flight." *St. Louis Post-Dispatch* (January 18, 2002): E1.

Gordon, Joe. "Orr's Historic Flight Lives On: 'The Goal' Still Classic 30 Years Later." *Boston Herald* (May 10, 2000): 119.

Kennedy, Kostya. "This Date in Playoff History: May 11, 1972, Bruins vs. Rangers." *Sports Illustrated* (May 11, 1998): 108.

Lefton, Terry. "MasterCard Campaign Takes NHL Tack with Orr, Stojko on Ice." *Brandweek* (November 9, 1998): 16.

"Orr Says He'll Quit Hall of Fame if Eagleson Stays." *Rocky Mountain News* (Denver, Colorado) (March 16, 1998): 16C.

"Orr Shrugs off 'Greatest Moment': Ex-Bruin Reflects on Career." *Houston Chronicle* (June 11, 1996): 1.

Silver, Jim. Review of *Game Misconduct: Alan Eagleson and the Corruption of Hockey,* by Russ Conway. *Canadian Dimension* (July-August, 1996).

Swift, E. M. "Bobby Orr." *Sports Illustrated* (September 15, 1994): 124-126.

Van Voorhis, Scott. "Orr Could Play Shorthanded—Woolf Exit May Deplete Client Base." *Boston Herald* (March 6, 2002): 031.

Wharnsby, Tim. "Hockey Great Happy in His New Career." *Boston Globe* (December 29, 1999): D01.

Wigge, Larry. "Orr Provided a Blueprint for Offensive Defensemen." *Sporting News* (June 17, 1996): 35.

Other

"Bobby Orr: A Worthwhile Investment." Boston Bruins History. http://www.bostonbruins.com/history/bobby orr.html (October 8, 2002).

BobbyOrr4.com. http://www.bobbyorr4.com (October 14, 2002).

Martin, Mary. "Remembering #4, Bobby Orr." All-Sports.com. http://www.allsports.com/cgi-bin/showstory.cgi?story_id=30470 (October 14, 2002).

"Moments to Remember." CBS Sportsline. http://cbs.sportsline.com/u/ce/feature/0,1518,1486831_60,00.htlm (October 14, 2002).

Murdoch, Jason. "1-on-1 with #4." CBC Sports Online. http://cbc.ca/sports/indepth/focus/orr2.html (October 8, 2002).

"Say It Ain't So: Transactions That Broke Our Hearts." CNNSI.com. http://sportsillustrated.cnn.com/hockey/nhl/news/2001/02/15/sayitaintso_bruins/ (October 14, 2002).

Schwartz, Larry. "Orr Brought More Offense to Defense." ESPN.com. http://espn.go.com/sportscentury/features/00016391.html (October 14, 2002).

Schwartz, Larry. "Orr's Great Goal." ESPN.com. http://espn.go.com/sportscentury/features/00016392.html (October 14, 2002).

Sketch by Julia Bauder

Sonia O'Sullivan
1969-

Irish track and field athlete

Irish middle distance runner Sonia O'Sullivan has mastered the 5,000 meter race. In addition to her wins in the 5,000 meter, she established several records over the years, running the 2,000 meter in 5:25:63 (world record), the 3,000 meter in 8:21:64 (European record), and setting the record for the two mile. Gaining international visibility through her participation in the Olympic Games beginning with the 1992 Games in Barcelona, Spain, O'Sullivan has won every track and field award in her native Ireland and is considered one of her country's greatest athlete.

Born in the island town of Cobh, in County Cork, Ireland, O'Sullivan enjoyed running as a young girl and raced with a group of teens who had formed a small track club. She soon quit participating in races, however. A bit of a perfectionist, O'Sullivan was discouraged by the club's faster members and came to believe that her own running would never improve beyond the mediocre. Instead, it was her tendency to leave for school at the last possible moment each morning that helped her to develop her speed: every day she sprinted the half-mile from her front door to her classroom, building the muscles that she would later need as a professional middle-distance runner.

O'Sullivan returned to running in secondary school, training in the evenings either alone or with members of the track club. Her performance earned her an athletic scholarship to Pennsylvania's Villanova University in 1987, but when the red-haired runner arrived there on shaky ground—injured and on crutches—she had her hopes of freshman success dashed by injuries caused by overtraining. Determined to live up to the expectations Villanova coach Marty Stern had of her, O'Sullivan established a healthy balance between classes and running. She earned her degree while also making her mark in collegiate sports as part of the Villanova Wildcats running team and gaining personal honor as National Collegiate Athletic Association 3,000-meter champion in 1990. As Coach Stern recalled to Mark Will-Weber of *Runner's World:* "Sonia is as talented as any runner I've ever coached, and she loves to run. That's a tough combination to beat. Sometimes, she actually has a smile on her face when she's running a workout."

After graduating from Villanova with a degree in accounting and returning to Ireland in 1991, O'Sullivan began to devote all her time to her career as a track and field athlete. A rigorous training schedule required her to work out either on distance runs or on the track every

Sonia O'Sullivan

day, regardless of the weather; because training allowed for no down-time, she even relocated to Australia when it was too cold or snowy at home.

Endowed with natural speed, O'Sullivan has worked since her days on the Villanova cross-country team to develop her physical stamina, and is also capable of mentally outmaneuvering her opposition on the track. Competing in her first Olympic Games in Barcelona, Spain in 1992, she placed fourth in an elite field in the 3,000 meters, repeating her fourth-place performance the following year at the 1993 World Track and Field Championships held in Stuttgart, Germany. In Stuttgart she also walked away with the silver medal for the 1,500 meters, topping that performance at the European Championships the following year by capturing the gold for the same distance. Demonstrating her versatility, O'Sullivan won the mile in Cologne, Germany in 1995 over defending world champion Hassiba Boulmerka.

Although O'Sullivan's record on the shorter distances is commendable, it is at the 5,000 meters that she really excels. By the mid-1990s wins like the first place trophies at the 1995 World Championships caused running fans to sit up and take notice. As time rolled around for the 1996 Olympic Games in Atlanta, Olympic veteran O'Sullivan was favored for the gold in the 5,000 and perhaps even the 10K. Frustratingly, the stress of training for the race combined with ill-

ness did her in, leaving her with a career almost on its way out.

Fortunately, the plucky O'Sullivan rebounded. With a new coach in the person of Alan Storey, she altered her training regimen and competed in a variety of smaller races rather than focusing all her training on one major running competition. O'Sullivan also took time out to establish a steady personal relationship with Australian Nick Bideau and have the first of their two daughters, Ciara, in 1999 (their second daughter, Sophie was born in December of 2001).

The year 1998 proved to be a banner one for O'Sullivan in running the 5,000 meters: in that year alone she took home the gold at both the European Track and Field Championships in Budapest and South Africa's World Cup. She also mastered the 10K, chalking up a second gold in Budapest in 1998 and was named World Cross-Country Champion in Morocco after winning back-to-back competitions in the 8,000 and 4,000 meters.

In 2000 O'Sullivan focused on the Olympic Games scheduled for Sydney, Australia. Qualifying to run in the 1,500, 5,000 and 10K, the 30-year-old Irishwoman gave up the gold to in the 5,000 to Romanian runner Gabriela Szabo by only .23 seconds, walking away with the silver with a finish time of 14:41:02. A second-place win might have disheartened O'Sullivan in the past, but she had other things to focus on; namely, maintaining a balance between her running and her responsibilities as a mother . . . and a mother-to-be.

In 2002 O'Sullivan sidestepped the mold of middle-distance runner to take on an entirely different athletic challenge when she trained for and raced in the New York City Marathon. Completing the 26.2-mile run through New York's five boroughs in 2 hours and 36 minutes, she found the experience challenging but not necessarily pleasant. As she told an interviewer for *AS-*

APSports.com: "I just wanted it to end . . . and just get to the finish line." After the marathon she was eager to return to her family in Melbourne, Australia, and work toward her next goal as a professional athlete: the 2004 Olympics.

CONTACT INFORMATION

Address: c/o Kim McDonald, 201 High St., Hampton Hill, Middlesex TW12 1NL, England. Phone: 020 8941 9732. Online: http://www.soniaosullivan.com.

FURTHER INFORMATION

Books

Great Women in Sports. Detroit, MI: Visible Ink Press, 1996.

Periodicals

Fairplay Sport and Leisure, April/May, 2002.
Runner's World, April, 1991:131.

Other

ASAPSports.com, http://www.asapsports.com/ marathon/2002nycmarathon/110302SO.html (November 3, 2002).
BBC Sport Online, http://news.bbc.co.uk/sport1/low/ northern_ireland/941234.stm (September 25, 2000).
Sonia O'Sullivan Web site, http://www.soniaosullivan. com (January 15, 2003).

Sketch by Pamela L. Shelton

Jesse Owens
1913-1980

American track and field athlete

Few athletes have transcended their sports to become a symbol of an era as did Jesse Owens. Enduring a childhood marked by grinding poverty in Alabama, Owens became a star athlete in high school after his family moved to Cleveland, Ohio. His achievements earned Owens several lucrative offers to attend college as a track-and-field athlete, and he enrolled at Ohio State University in 1933. On May 25, 1935, Owens made national headlines for setting five world records and tying another record at the Big Ten Intercollegiate Championships in Ann Arbor, Michigan. Although many historians consider Owens's performance that day the greatest achievement by any track-and-field athlete in a single day, his participation in the 1936 Berlin Olympic Games made him into a legend. After winning one team and three individual Olympic Gold Medals in an atmosphere charged with German Chancellor Adolf Hitler's declarations of Aryan racial superiority, Owens became an American hero. Although his professional career endured several struggles after his retirement as an amateur athlete, the public's admiration of Owens never dimmed. In the last decades of his life, the former star athlete became a sought-after public speaker. Using his own life's experience as a model, Owens preached the values of hard work, self-esteem, and patriotism. Prior to his death in 1980, Owens was awarded the Presidential Medal of Freedom and in 1983 was inducted posthumously into the US Olympic Committee Hall of Fame.

Part of the Great Migration

Jesse Owens was born in the rural hamlet of Danville in northern Alabama on September 12, 1913. He was the youngest of the ten children of Henry and Mary Emma (Fitzgerald) Owens who had survived childhood. Like most of his African-American neighbors, Henry Owens struggled to provide for his family as a sharecropper and barely managed to keep his children fed and clothed. After their daughter, Lillie, moved to Cleveland during World War I, Mary Owens encouraged her husband to move the family North to take advantage of the higher wages, steadier work, and personal freedom that their daughter had described to them. Henry Owens took two of their older sons to Cleveland after the war and found conditions promising enough to bring the rest of the family to the city around 1922.

In their decision to move North to escape the poverty, limited opportunity, and virulent and sometimes violent racism of the South, Mary and Henry Owens were part of one of the greatest movements of people in American history, a phenomenon known as the Great Migration.

Jesse Owens

Given a labor shortage in the North induced by World War I and a halt to European immigration, a massive wave of African Americans from the rural South took place to keep America's northern industries running. Between 1915 and 1920 at least 400,000 African Americans left for the North, and as many as one million joined them in the following decade. By 1920 an estimated 65,000 African Americans from Alabama alone had made the journey northward.

Life indeed was different for the Owens family in the North—so different that a fearful Mary Owens kept the drapes closed in the family's modest apartment for several months after they moved in. The family's east-side neighborhood was racially diverse and economically disadvantaged; after Henry Owens and three of the older Owens sons gained employment in local steel mills, the family nonetheless made a promising start in Cleveland. The youngest Owens enrolled in Bolton Elementary School on the East side, where he was initially placed in the first grade with students much younger than himself. After proving that he could read and write, Owens advanced to the second grade. He also took on a new name, although not by choice. Named James Cleveland at birth, Owens went by his initials "J.C." for the first several years of his life. He adopted the name by which he would become famous after his first teacher in the North failed to understand his southern drawl and put his name down as "Jesse." Too modest to correct his teacher, Owens kept the name.

Athletic Success as a Teenager

Owens enrolled in Cleveland's Fairmount Junior High School around 1927 and quickly attracted the attention of a mentor who would prove crucial in his future athletic success. Charles Riley worked at the school as a physical education teacher and track-and-field coach and immediately realized that Owens was a naturally gifted athlete who had not yet taken up serious training. Riley started a rigorous training program for Owens in special morning sessions before school. Within a year, Owens was running the 100-yard dash in eleven seconds and in 1928 he set two world records for his age group in the high jump, at six feet, and the long jump, at twenty-two feet, eleven and three-quarters inches. Under Riley's instruction to run as though the track were on fire, Owens also improved his times on the track. Of the seventy-nine races he entered in high school, Owens won seventy-five of them. Owens also formed a warm personal relationship off the track with Riley, who continued to coach him after he entered East Technical High School in 1930. After Henry Owens suffered a traffic accident in 1929 and experienced extended periods of unemployment in the Great Depression, Riley's role as a surrogate father was especially important to the young athlete.

As an East Tech track-and-field sensation, Owens became a nationally renown athlete while still in his teens. Although he failed to make the national team in his tryout for the 1932 Olympic Games to be held in Los Angeles, his performance at the June 1933 National Interscholastic Championship, held in Chicago, was stunning. Winning the long jump, 220-yard dash, and

100-yard dash, Owens set and tied the world records in the latter two events. When he returned to Cleveland, the nineteen-year-old was honored with a parade. Several universities competed to offer Owens a place on their track-and-field squads, but Ohio State University (OSU) came up with the best offer. In exchange for an undemanding job as a page in the Ohio State Legislature and the promise of a weekly stipend for attending local civic functions, Owens enrolled at OSU in the fall of 1933. The school also agreed to overlook Owens's lack of a high school diploma, as he had left East Tech before completing all of his required courses.

Now earning a substantial sum of money during the depths of the Depression, Owens sent much of funds back to his parents as well as to longtime girlfriend, (Minnie) Ruth Solomon, who had given birth to their daughter on August 8, 1932. The couple married on July 5, 1935, allegedly after a Cleveland newspaper reporter threatened to publish a photo of their daughter along with an unflattering portrait of the athlete's personal life. The Owenses subsequently had two more daughters. Although talk about his infidelities persisted throughout their union—including his siring of a child by another woman—the couple remained married up to the time of Jesse Owens's death in 1980. Ruth Solomon Owens died in 2001 at the age of eighty-six.

Owens indeed had a lot to lose in a scandal, as he had vaulted into the front ranks of Olympic hopefuls with his masterful performance at the Big Ten Track and Field Championship held in Ann Arbor on Mary 25, 1935. Suffering from a sore back in the early stages of the meet, Owens surprised everyone in the final rounds of the competition. His 220-yard dash, 220-yard hurdles, 200-meter dash, and 200-meter low hurdles times were all new world records—as was his winning broad jump effort—and his time in the 100-yard dash tied the existing world record of 9.4 seconds. Owens's achievement stands as perhaps the best single-day accomplishment of any track-and-field athlete in the history of the discipline.

For his feats at the 1935 Big Ten Championship, Owens seemed certain of winning the James E. Sullivan Award, given annually by the Amateur Athletic Union (AAU) to the country's best amateur athlete. When it was revealed that OSU sponsors had paid some of the athlete's travel expenses in the guise of reimbursing him for his job in the State Legislature, however, Owens was taken off the list of candidates for the award. More troubling to his future, he had also been threatened with being stripped of his amateur status altogether by the AAU. In the end, the AAU decided that Owens's offense was unintentional. Owens faced another challenge when he was placed on academic probation by OSU for his continuing poor performance in his course work. Owens managed to continue as a full-time student through 1936, but later took classes only intermittently; in 1941 he left OSU altogether without completing a degree.

Star of the 1936 Berlin Olympics

Along with boxer **Joe Louis**, Owens was one of the best-known African-American athletes by 1936. Owens was also one of the most popular athletes for the sportsmanship he demonstrated on the field. In one competition in mid-1936, Owens offered to run a 50-yard dash again when he learned that a competitor, Eulace Peacock, had suffered from a faulty starting block; the race was conducted again, and Owens came in second to Peacock. He did not contest the outcome and earned public praise for his sense of fair play. Thus, when he earned a place on the U.S. track-and-field delegation to the 1936 Olympics, Jesse Owens was the most admired and talked-about athlete in the contingent.

Jesse Owens

Owens surpassed all expectations of his performance at the Berlin Games. On August 3, 1936, he took the Gold Medal in the 100-meter dash; his time of 10.3 seconds set a new world record in the event. Owens also set Olympics records in his winning long jump of twenty-six feet, five-and-one-quarter inches and Gold Medal 200-meter dash of 20.7 seconds. Owens's fourth Gold Medal came in the 400-meter relay race; not originally part of the team, Owens and Ralph Metcalfe had been enlisted for the relay in place of two Jewish runners, Marty Glickman and Sam Stoller. Glickman immediately accused the U.S. track coaches of giving into the prevalent anti-Semitism of Nazi Germany, although he held Owens blameless for the decision. The relay team won the race in a world- and Olympic-record setting time of 39.8 seconds.

That Owens won four Gold Medals at the Berlin Olympics was astounding; yet his feat also represented a rebuke to the Nazi Party's theories of Aryan racial superiority. Owens later capitalized on his triumph over Nazi ideology by claiming that Adolf Hitler was so upset by his achievements that he refused to congratulate him as he had the other winning athletes. In reality, Hitler only met personally with Gold Medal winners on the opening day of the games; any deliberate snub was unplanned. Yet Owens went on to retell the story of "Hitler's Snub" so many times that it became reported as fact. What was undeniable was that Owens emerged from the games as an American hero.

Checkered Post-Athletic Career

Owens gave up his amateur status after the 1936 Berlin Games and took on numerous paid speaking engagements, including appearances for Republican presidential nominee Alf Landon in the 1936 election, for which he earned $10,000. Owens put some of his earnings into a dry cleaning business in Cleveland, which soon went out of business. With the Internal Revenue Service (IRS) filing suit against Owens for unpaid taxes from his 1936 earnings, Owens declared bankruptcy in May 1939 and struggled to pull his finances together. He took a position in the personnel department of the Ford Motor Company, where he worked from 1943 to 1945, and then pursued a short-lived venture with a sporting goods business in Detroit. In 1946 Owens moved with his family to Chicago, where he started his own public relations agency and remained active in Republican Party politics. After polishing his skills as a public speaker, Owens was able to make a comfortable living as a motivational speaker and his political connections helped him gain an appointment with the Illinois State Athletic Commission in 1953.

As a public relations executive and motivational speaker, Owens finally hit his stride in his post-athletic career. He also began a lucrative association with the Atlantic Richfield Company, which began sponsoring the Jesse Owens Games for Chicago youth in 1965. The next year, however, Owens was convicted for tax evasion. The IRS revealed that Owens had failed to file tax returns between 1954 and 1962 and he was ordered to pay restitution in the amount of $3,000 in addition to his back taxes. Owens emerged from the scandal with his reputation fairly intact. Yet he courted controversy again when he criticized the protest of two African-American athletes at the 1968 Mexico City Olympic Games. The athletes had given a "Black Power" salute of raised fists on the awards podium, which Owens deemed inappropriate. In 1970 Owens published a book that chided Black Power activists, *Blackthink: My Life as a Black Man and White Man,* although he offered a more conciliatory tone in his 1972 book *I Have Changed.*

The Legend of Jesse Owens

The last decade of Owens's life brought him renewed acclaim. In 1974 he was inducted into the USA Track and Field Hall of Fame and in 1976 President Carter honored him with the Presidential Medal of Freedom. Taking up retirement in Scottsdale, Arizona, Owens suffered from physical ailments brought on by his pack-a-day smoking habit. The habit resulted in a diagnosis of lung cancer for Owens in 1979. He died in Tucson, Arizona on March 31, 1980 from the disease, leaving behind his wife, Ruth Solomon Owens, and three daughters. He was honored posthumously by an induction into the US Olympic Committee Hall of Fame in 1983.

One of the first African-American athletes to emerge as a truly national hero, Jesse Owens was an important figure in the sporting history of the United States. His participation in the 1936 Berlin Olympic Games resulted in four Gold Medals, two with new world records and two with new Olympic records. Indeed, his achievements demanded recognition from sports fans regardless of his ethnicity and inspired future generations of African-American athletes to pursue their own dreams of Olympic greatness. Although his post-Olympic career generated some negative publicity for his business troubles, Owens remained an Olympic legend for the rest of his life. His eventual work as a corporate spokesman and motivational speaker allowed him to burnish this legend to the point where the 1936 Olympics seemed to be all about a confrontation between Owens and Hitler. In the

---

I Have Changed

For my whole life was wrapped up, summed up—and stopped up—by a single incident: my confrontation with the German dictator, Adolf Hitler, in the 1936 Olympics. The lines were drawn then as they had never been drawn before, or since. The Germans were hosting the Games and, with each passing day, were coming to represent everything that free people have always feared.

To me and my American buddies, most of the German athletes, the German officials, even the hundreds of thousands of German citizens who crammed the stadium those days in Berlin, weren't really our enemies. How could Lutz Long—the Nazi record-breaking broadjumper—be an enemy after he came over and put his arm around my shoulder and told me what I needed to do when I was on the verge of fouling out of that key event and maybe blowing the entire Olympiad?

But Hitler—he was something else. No one with a tinge of red, white, and blue doubted for a second that he was Satan in disguise. Not that I was *too* involved with Hitler in the beginning. I'd spent my whole life watching my father and mother and older brothers and sisters trying to escape their own kind of Hitler, first in Alabama and then in Cleveland, and all I wanted now was my chance to run as fast and jump as far as I could so *I'd* never have to look back. . . .

If I could just win those gold medals, I said to myself, the Hitlers of the world would have no more meaning for me. For *anyone,* maybe.

Source: Jesse Owens with Paul Neimark, *I Have Changed,* William Morrow, 1972.

---

end, his accomplishments alone were enough to rebut all the Nazi claims of Aryan superiority; the legend of Jesse Owens's performance did not need embellishment.

SELECTED WRITINGS BY OWENS:

(With Paul G. Neimark) *Blackthink: My Life as Black Man and White Man,* William Morrow, 1970.
(With Paul Neimark) *I Have Changed,* William Morrow, 1972.

FURTHER INFORMATION

Books

Baker, William J. *Jesse Owens: An American Life.* New York: Free Press, 1986.
Guttmann, Allen. *The Olympics: A History of the Modern Games.* Urbana: University of Illinois Press, 1992.
Owens, Jesse, with Paul Neimark. *Blackthink: My Life as Black Man and White Man.* New York: William Morrow and Company, 1970.
Owens, Jesse with Paul Neimark. *I Have Changed.* New York: William Morrow and Company, 1972.

Periodicals

Bennett, Jr., Lerone. "Jesse Owens' Olympic Triumph Over Time and Hitlerism." *Ebony* (April 1996): 68.
Hemhill, Gloria Owens. "Humiliating Hitler." *Newsweek* (October 25, 1999): 53.

Kelley, Timothy. "Stealing Hitler's Show." *New York Times Upfront* (September 4, 2000): 32.

Litsky, Frank. "Jesse Owens Dies of Cancer at 66; Hero of the 1936 Berlin Olympics." *New York Times* (April 1, 1980).

Taylor, Phil. "Flying in the Face of the Fuhrer." *Sports Illustrated* (November 29, 1999): 137.

Sketch by Timothy Borden

Satchel Paige
1906-1982

American baseball player

L eroy Robert "Satchel" Paige, one of the game's true natural talents, was an African-American man living during the height of the Jim Crow days in a South where the color-barrier was thick and seemingly insurmountable. Yet in spite of the odds, Paige transcended place, time, and sport, and became one of the greatest players baseball has ever seen. The first black pitcher to play in the major leagues, the oldest major league rookie, and a man who pitched—and won—more games than any other baseball player in history, many of Paige's accomplishments stand on their own. But many of his feats exist as part of the mythology that preceded him in life, and now—since his death from a heart attack in 1982—follow Paige's legend wherever it goes. As Mark Ribowsky noted in his 1994 book *Don't Look Back: Satchel Paige in the Shadows of Baseball*: "If Paige hadn't existed, someone in art or literature would have invented him. . . . Wherever [he] went, something important happened in the evolution of baseball."

Satchel Paige

Growing Up

Leroy Robert Paige was born on July 7, 1906, in Mobile, Alabama, the third son and seventh child in a family that would eventually run to 12 children. Born to Robert and Lula Paige, Satchel came into the world in the back room of a rundown shack he would later describe as a "shotgun shack"—meaning, he said, that if someone were to shoot a shotgun through the front door, it would carry right on through and out the back door. Although this date is now widely recognized as Paige's official birthday, there is still some dispute as to when he was actually born. Integration was unheard of in the South at that time and most blacks in Mobile weren't born in hospitals. Therefore, no public records exist to back up—or deny—the circumstances surrounding Paige's birth.

The confusion around his birth gave Satchel fodder for his tall tales. Until the day he died he would never give a straight answer—even going so far as to have question marks engraved on his tombstone where the birth date normally appears. "Age is a question of mind over matter," he would say. "If you don't mind, age don't matter." Paige told reporters that he was born in "nineteen-ought." He said the family goat ate the Bible in which they stored his birth certificate.

With so many children to look after, Satchel didn't receive much attention at home. His mother did the cooking, the washing, and the cleaning for the family, while Satchel's father, described as a "sometimes-gardener," was not around and gave little support to Lula and the children. Driven by necessity to earn money for the family, Paige took a job as a baggage handler at the local railroad station. He was seven-years-old.

He and the other boys who worked at the station earned their money in tips, scrambling, as the trains pulled in, to be chosen to carry the businessmen's lug-

Chronology

1906	Born July 7 in Mobile, Alabama, to Josh and Lula Paige
1913	Works as baggage handler at local railroad station where he gains nickname "Satchel"
1918	Sentenced to five-and-a-half years at the Industrial School for Negro Children in Mt. Meigs, Alabama. Baseball becomes part of his life
1924	Joins the Mobile Tigers, a local black baseball team
1926	At 19 years old makes professional baseball debut with Chattanooga Black Lookouts
1929	Plays winter baseball in West Indies and Latin America
1934	Joins Bismarck team in North Dakota. Marries Janet Howard, a nineteen-year-old waitress
1934	Pitches two no-hitters on July 4 in two different cities on the same day (Pittsburgh and Chicago)
1936	Returns east to play for Pittsburgh Crawfords
1937	Accepts offer to play for Trujillo Stars in the Dominican Republic
1938	Pitches in the Mexican League and suffers shoulder injury
1938	Joins B team of Kansas City Monarchs
1939	Pitching arm improves, becomes ace pitcher for Monarch's A team (they win Negro American League title in 1939, '40, and '41)
1942	Paige becomes the highest-paid player in all of baseball
1943	Janet Howard and Satchel Paige divorce
1947	Marries Lahoma Brown, with whom he eventually fathers eight children
1948	Signs contract with Cleveland Indians, at 42 years old, becomes oldest rookie, and first African American to pitch in American League as a reliever
1948	Becomes first African American to pitch in the World Series
1951	Returning to Major League ball for first time since 1949, signs with St. Louis Browns
1956	Signs with Birmingham Black Barons (Negro League), at age 50, to play and manage
1966	Makes final big league appearance for Kansas City Athletics
1968	Runs for seat in Missouri state legislature and loses
1969	Atlanta Braves put Paige on their roster to allow him a sufficient number of days for a major league pension
1971	Inducted into the Baseball Hall of Fame
1979	Installed in the Missouri Sports Hall of Fame
1982	Dies of a heart attack at his Kansas City home, June 8

Awards and Accomplishments

1952	Voted to appear in Major League All-Star game
1953	Voted to appear in Major League All-Star game
1971	Named to Baseball Hall of Fame
1979	Inducted into the Missouri Sports Hall of Fame

broke and ran with it. That fella caught him and slapped him hard, in the face, and took it back. That's when I named him Satchel, right on that day." Hines, aware of the many versions of how Paige earned his nickname, added, "All those years he said he got the name 'cause he carried satchels. Hell no—it's 'cause he *stole* 'em!"

Paige's tendencies towards mischievous behavior at the train yards followed him through childhood, and by the age of ten, he was a budding thief. Stealing bicycles or toys, throwing bricks or rocks, or getting in fights—if there was something to be done to thwart authority, Paige was first in line. He understood that in order to survive as a black youth in Mobile, he had to have an attitude and make himself known. And he wanted to be known. He wanted to be the kid others looked up to or avoided or talked about.

In *Maybe I'll Pitch Forever*, Paige reflects with a "profound eloquence" on the antisocial tendencies of his youth. "Maybe I got into all those fights," he recalled, "because I found out what it was like to be a Negro in Mobile. Even though you're only seven, eight, or nine, it eats at you when you know you got nothing and can't get a dollar. The blood gets angry." Paige wanted out of Mobile, but he wasn't sure how to get there.

The life of petty crime came to an end when, at 12-years-old, he was caught stealing rings from a jewelry store and sentenced to five-and-a-half years at the Mount Meigs Negro Reform School. His mother, who could do no more for him, gave in to the police's recommendation that Satchel be sent away. Although he'd wanted to get out of the city, this was not what he had in mind. While at the Meigs school, however, Paige would discover his passion and gift for baseball. He'd played some ball at the W.H. Council School in Mobile and spent some time in the ballparks back home, but that was mostly sweeping the grandstands or mowing the grass for extra money. At the Meigs School, Satchel would embark on a baseball path that defined the rest of his life.

gage from the platform to the nearby hotels. Satchel soon realized that style and charisma were the things that got a person noticed. Even with his ability to carry more bags than the other boys, it wasn't enough. Showmanship was a skill he honed, and soon, with talents superior to those of the other boys, he had his arms full.

During his years as a baggage-handler, Paige earned his now-famous nickname "Satchel." Always eager for more, young Leroy Paige would soon step outside the bounds of the law. Most accounts of the "Satchel" nickname origin say Paige earned it because, often carrying many bags at once, his friends told him he looked like a "satchel tree." But as with most stories surrounding his life, it's often difficult to determine what is true and what is part of the Satchel Paige mythology. Mark Ribowsky wrote in *Don't Look Back* that one of Satchel's childhood friends, Willie Hines, came up with the famous moniker.

As Hines recalled, "One day [Paige] decided to run off with one of the bags. The man gave it to him and he

Played in the Negro Leagues

The Industrial School for Negro Children in Mount Meigs, Alabama, provided Paige with the education he'd been lacking and gave him his first true introduction to baseball. Initially a first basemen, he soon became the starting pitcher. That same Willie Hines—the one who'd witnessed Satchel's dead-on accuracy when he'd thrown rocks and bricks back in Mobile—told the coach Satchel could pitch better than any guy they had up there. Though Paige wasn't a refined pitcher by any means, the Mount Meigs coach, Edward Byrd, worked with Satchel and helped turn him into one of the greatest pitchers the game has ever known. He taught Satchel the beginnings of moves that became characteristic of Paige's style: the high front foot kick, "so it looked like I blocked out the sky," and the release of the ball at the last possible moment. He taught him to study not only the batter's eyes, but also his knees, "like a bullfighter. A bullfighter can tell what a bull is going to do by watching its knees."

When he was released from the Mount Meigs School, Paige returned to Mobile unsure of what to do next. Seeking the next chapter in his life, wandering the streets for answers, he came across some black men playing baseball. In 1923, the popularity of baseball was beginning to rise in the South. Satchel Paige soon began playing with the local team, but word of his talents as a pitcher spread, and in 1926 he signed with the Chattanooga, Tennessee Black Lookouts.

Paige's mother wasn't happy that her son would probably be playing baseball on Sundays, but was pleased that baseball had finally given him a ticket to get out of Mobile. Paige would end up staying with the Black Lookouts through the 1927 season, touring a South he'd never seen, and concentrating on sharpening his talents and expanding his pitching repertoire.

Paige's fastball had always been—and would continue to be—his principal pitch. Yet as he matured he developed an arsenal of pitches. Almost as famous as his fastball would be his "hesitation pitch," a delayed pitch in which the hurler strides forward, holds back a second, then lets go of the ball at the very last moment. On the mound Paige's reputation preceded him and some batters were so unnerved by his appearance that they would swing their bats before he even released the ball.

"I got bloopers, loopers, and droopers," Paige would say, describing his many pitches. "I got a jump-ball, a be-ball, a screw ball, a wobbly ball, a whipsy-dipsy-do, a hurry-up, a nothin' ball and a bat dodger." This "be-ball," he explained, "is a be-ball 'cause it 'be' right where I want it, high and inside. It wiggles like a worm." He would also, in typical Paige fashion, assert at other times that this was a "bee" ball because of the buzzing noise it made as it rocketed past batters.

As when he toted luggage, Paige soon saw that being successful in baseball—especially in the Southern Negro Leagues, which were considered inferior to the majors— took more than just being a great ballplayer. The emptiness and poverty of growing up in Mobile turned Paige into an opportunist. The boy who carried luggage from the train platform was now a man standing on the mound. Yet he still wanted the most attention, and so, in addition to being a phenomenal ballplayer, Satchel became an entertainer, a spectacle who drew the fans to the ballparks.

Satchel Paige

Although he was all seriousness when he took hold of the ball, Satchel gave the audience what they came for, and they almost always left with stories to tell. Paige might signal to the outfielders to leave the field early, or at the very least, tell them to sit down because he planned to strike out the side. Or he might announce beforehand that he would fan the first nine batters—and then do it!

Satchel Paige packed 'em in. In fact, in his first three starts in the major leagues, in 1948, he drew over 200,000 fans and set nighttime attendance records in Chicago and Cleveland.

Paige was always open to discussions with other teams who were willing to pay him more, and he participated in exhibition games to bring in more cash. This itinerant nature is one of the reasons it is so difficult to pin down statistics on him during his years in the Negro leagues, and why often some of the statistics can't be found. Paige moved often from team to team, as well as being "loaned" out to other clubs from his parent club, always going where the money was. It has been estimated that towards the end of his life, he'd pitched in well

---

Baseball: A Film by Ken Burns

Documentary filmmaker Ken Burns's *Baseball* is a twenty-hour tribute to the sport, broken up into nine "innings," or chapters, and narrated by John Chancellor, joined by testimonials from a diverse group chosen for their love of the game, including former Negro league player Buck O'Neil, editor Daniel Okrent, historian Doris Kearns Goodwin, Mickey Mantle, comedian Billy Crystal, and sportscaster Bob Costas. It is periodically aired on public television. Burns has referred to his trilogy of films: *The Civil War, Baseball, and Jazz,* as a trilogy about race in the United States. Baseball contains ongoing commentary on race, especially about the treatment of African-American baseball players before, during, and after Paige's lifetime. The film covers the development of the Negro leagues and the star players emerging from them. It also covers the struggle of blacks to break into the major leagues, overcoming a color barrier that had kept them out for decades. The film shows the heroism of not only Jackie Robinson but such players as Satchel Paige, Josh Gibson, Hank Aaron, Rube Foster, Curt Flood, Bob Gibson, and Frank Robinson.

---

over 2500 games, winning about 2000 of them-with 300 shutouts and 55 no-hitters.

After leaving the Chattanooga Black Lookouts, he signed with the Alabama Birmingham Black Barons, in 1927, for $275 a month. He then began to bounce around the country "globetrotting" to demonstrate his talents. In 1928 he played for the Nashville Elite Giants and spent the off-season touring with a group of barnstormers—something he would continue to do throughout his career in the Negro and semi-pro leagues. During these exhibitions, he played against the white ballplayers he wasn't allowed to join in the majors.

Babe Ruth headed up one of the exhibition teams Paige would play on, though he never pitched against Ruth. Whenever Satchel was on the mound, the Babe was always conveniently riding the bench. Paige was able to fan the best hitters in the majors, and in one particular game, on the west coast during those barnstorming days, he struck out 22 major leaguers, which would have been a big league record.

In early 1931 he joined the Pittsburgh Crawfords for $750 a month, a great salary at that time, and he stuck with this ball club during six regular seasons. In 1934, he married Janet Howard, a waitress who worked in a restaurant he frequented, and she moved with him out west, where he spent a season earning top dollar with an all-white team in Bismarck, North Dakota. At one point during this time, he set a never-to-be-duplicated record of pitching 29 games in a single month.

After a year in North Dakota, however, Paige returned to the Pittsburgh Crawfords. Life out west was difficult, and he couldn't find housing for him and his wife—in fact, they were forced to live in an abandoned railroad freight car. In his autobiography, *Maybe I'll Pitch Forever*, he says he was a wandering man, "but Janet was against all that wandering. She wanted a man who ran a store or something and came home every night, a guy who'd never leave her and if he had to go

somewhere he'd be the kind to take her with him. I wasn't that kind at all back in those days," Paige wrote. He didn't want to be tied down, and with a reputation for carousing, drinking, staying out late and free spending, Janet and Satchel wouldn't see much of each other in the nine years they were married.

When he returned to the Crawfords, however, Paige discovered that he had been banned from the Negro Leagues for breaking his contract with the Pittsburgh ball club. The ban would last only a year, and in 1937 Paige headed to the Dominican Republic to play with the Trujillo Stars for a salary of $30,000, equivalent to the best the major leagues were offering at the time. In spite of the money, however, Paige found himself with financial problems. He spent too much on his wife, on clothes and cars, and on shotguns and fishing. Things seemed to be steadily declining, and in 1938, while playing in the Mexican Leagues, Paige suffered a career-threatening injury to his shoulder while pitching in Mexico City.

Unsure about what to do, he sought coaching jobs with teams around the Negro Leagues, but his lackluster reputation as a rabble-rouser preceded him. Ralph Wilkinson, owner of the Kansas City Monarchs, decided to buy out the remainder of Paige's contract and invited him to travel with the Monarchs B-team throughout the northwest and Canada. In 1939, with his shoulder better, he joined the Monarchs A-team as their ace pitcher, leading them to the Negro League World Series—and the series titles—in 1939, 1940, and 1941.

For Paige, there never really was an off season. Back then, as is still common today, pitchers would throw every four to five days, then rest at the season's end. Throughout his career, Paige would continue on the exhibition circuit, playing year-round to earn extra money, barnstorming in small towns, and facing many great major-leaguers before they were famous (men such such as **Dizzy Dean** and **Joe DiMaggio**).

In The Big Leagues

In 1946, the Brooklyn Dodgers signed **Jackie Robinson** to play in the majors, at long last breaking the color barrier. Other teams soon followed suit and two years later, Bill Veeck, the owner of the Cleveland Indians, signed Satchel Paige to a contract. He was 42 years old, and many critics believed this was a publicity stunt designed by Veeck to bring more fans into the stadium.

The Indians were in the middle of a pennant race, and Veeck saw Paige as a valuable asset. Satchel had become the seventh black player recruited into the majors, and, in his debut start, in spite of his age and the skepticism of many critics, Paige pitched a 5-0 shutout over the Chicago White Sox. The savvy of Paige as an entertainer, and the hype surrounding the Indians' owner in recruiting Satchel, paid off. He went 6-1 in his first ever major league season, with a 2.47 earned run average (ERA), helping the Indians into the World Series.

Career Statistics

Yr	Team	W	L	ERA	GP	GS	CG	SHO	IP	H	BB	SO
1927	BBB	8	3	—	20	9	6	3	93	63	19	80
1928	BBB	12	4	—	26	16	10	3	120	107	19	112
1929	BBB	11	11	—	31	20	15	0	196	191	39	184
1930	BBS	11	4	—	18	13	12	3	120	92	15	86
1931	PC	5	5	—	12	6	5	1	60	36	4	23
1932	PC	14	8	—	29	23	19	3	181	92	13	109
1933	PC	5	7	—	13	12	10	0	95	39	10	57
1934	PC	13	3	—	20	17	15	6	154	85	21	97
1935	PC	0	0	—	2	2	0	0	7	0	0	10
1936	PC	7	2	—	9	9	9	3	70	54	11	59
1937	TS	1	2	—	3	3	2	0	26	22	6	11
1940	KCM	1	1	—	2	2	2	1	12	10	0	15
1941	KCM	7	1	—	13	11	3	0	67	38	6	61
1942	KCM	8	5	—	20	18	6	1	100	68	12	78
1943	KCM	5	9	—	24	20	4	0	88	80	16	54
1944	KCM	5	5	—	13	—	—	2	78	47	8	70
1945	KCM	3	5	—	13	7	1	0	38	22	2	23
1946	KCM	5	1	—	9	9	1	0	68	65	12	48
1947	KCM	1	1	—	2	2	2	0	11	5	—	—
1948	CLE	6	1	2.48	21	7	3	2	72.7	61	25	45
1949	CLE	4	7	3.04	31	5	1	0	83.0	70	33	54
1951	SLB	3	4	4.79	23	3	0	0	62.0	67	29	48
1952	SLB	12	10	3.07	46	6	3	2	138.0	116	57	91
1953	SLB	3	9	3.53	57	4	0	0	117.3	114	39	51
1965	KCA	0	0	0.00	1	1	0	0	3.0	1	0	1

BBB: Birmingham Black Barons (Negro Leagues); BBS: Baltimore Black Sox (Negro Leagues); CLE: Cleveland Indians (American League); KCA: Kansas City Athletics (American League); KCM: Kansas City Monarchs (Negro Leagues); PC: Pittsburgh Crawfords (Negro Leagues); SLB: St. Louis Browns (American League); TS: Trujillo Stars (Negro Leagues).

Paige played only two seasons with the Indians, soon becoming a burden on the team, missing meetings, trains, warm-ups, and falling mostly on his old habits from the Negro League days when he answered, essentially, to no one. When Paige was nearly 60, the Kansas City Athletics signed him to a contract in what most people also considered a publicity stunt. This was 1965, and he would pitch only three innings that season, with the promise of one more season, so that he could earn his big league pension. The Athletics failed to honor their word, however, and let Satchel go. He would eventually get his pension in 1969, while working as a pitching coach with the Atlanta Braves. The team put him on the roster so he could retire with a major league pension.

Though he rarely showed any anger over segregation, Paige felt all along—and rightly so—that he belonged in the majors. Indeed, he had countless off-seasons of pitching to, and decimating, many major league ballplayers. Mark Ribowsky wrote, "For all of his outward gaiety and nonchalance, Paige was deeply offended by the color line that kept him from playing in the major leagues." A *New York Times* correspondent, Dave Anderson, stated, "To the end, Satchel Paige had too much dignity to complain loudly about never being in the big leagues when he deserved to be."

Paige had married Lahoma Brown, a longtime friend, in 1947, a woman who brought stability to his life. Following his playing years he spent some time in the minor leagues as a coach with the Tulsa Oilers. Eventually he settled down in Kansas City with his wife and eight children.

Due Recognition

Satchel Paige was inducted into the Major League Baseball Hall of Fame in 1971. Today, Paige's plaque sits alongside the other great major leaguers who grace the halls in Cooperstown. Though he never played major league ball in his prime, Paige will stand in his rightful place forever as one of the greats. "Baseball turned Paige from a second-class citizen to a second-class immortal," he said in his induction speech.

Paige was one of the game's true talents, and in spite of almost insurmountable odds, he dominated a sport and was instrumental in helping break down the color barriers—not through any activism, but by sheer talent, showmanship and determination. The first black pitcher to play in the major leagues and a man who pitched—and won—more games than any other baseball player in history, Paige's accomplishments and his contributions to making baseball what it is today will not be forgotten.

SELECTED WRITINGS BY PAIGE:

(With Hal Lebovitz) *Pitchin' Man.* Meckler Publishing, 1992.

(As told to David Lipman) *Maybe I'll Pitch Forever.* University of Nebraska Press, 1993.

FURTHER INFORMATION

Books

Cline-Ransome, Lesa and James Ransome (Illus.). *Satchel Paige.* New York: Simon & Schuster, 1999.

Contemporary Black Biography, Vol. 7. Detroit, MI: Gale, 1998.

Costas, Bob, and Sterry and Eckstut, eds. *Satchel Sez: The Wit, Wisdom, and World of Leroy 'Satchel' Paige.* New York: Crown, 2001.

Holway, John. *Josh and Satch: The Life and Times of Josh Gibson and Satchel Paige.* Westport: Meckler, 1992.

Humphrey, Kathryn L. *Satchel Paige.* New York: Franklin Watts, 1988.

"Leroy Robert Paige." *The Scribner Encyclopedia of American Lives, Volume 1: 1981-1985.* New York: Charles Scribner's & Sons, 1998.

Macht, Norman L. *Satchel Paige.* New York: Chelsea House, 1991.

Paige, Leroy, as told to David Lipman. *Maybe I'll Pitch Forever: A Great Baseball Player Tells the Hilarious Story Behind the Legend.* Lincoln: University of Nebraska Press, 1993.

Paige, Leroy, as told to Hal Lebovitz. *Pitchin' Man: Satchel Paige's Own Story.* Westport: Meckler, 1993.

Reisler, Jim. *Black Writers/Black Baseball: An Anthology of Articles from Black Sportswriters Who Covered the Negro Leagues.* Jefferson, N.C.: McFarland & Co., 1994.

Ribowsky, Mark. *Don't Look Back: Satchel Paige in the Shadows of Baseball.* New York: Simon and Schuster, 1994.

Riley, James A. *Biographical Encyclopedia of the Negro Baseball Leagues.* New York: Carroll and Graf Publishers, 1994.

Rubin, Robert. *Satchel Paige: All-Time Baseball Great.* New York: G.P. Putnam's & Sons, 1994.

"Satchel Paige." *Encyclopedia of World Biography, 2nd ed.* Detroit, MI: Gale, 1998.

"Satchel Paige." *Notable Black American Men.* Detroit, MI: Gale, 1998.

"Satchel Paige." *St. James Encyclopedia of Popular Culture. 5 vols.* Detroit, MI: St. James Press, 2000.

Shirley, David. *Satchel Paige.* New York: Chelsea House, 1993.

Thorn, John, and Pete Palmer, eds. *Total Baseball: The Ultimate Encyclopedia of Baseball. 3rd ed.* New York: HarperPerennial, 1993.

Periodicals

Durso, Joseph. "Satchel Paige, Black Pitching Star, Is Dead at 75." *New York Times* (June 9, 1982): D-20.

Ebony (September 1982): 74-8.

Greene, James "Joe" and John Holway. "I Was Satchel's Catcher." *Journal of Popular Culture.* (1972) (6)1: 157-70.

Holway, John B. "The Kid Who Taught Satchel Paige A Lesson." *Baseball Research Journal* (1987) 16:36-44.

Newsweek (June 1, 1981): 12.

Reader's Digest (April 1984): 89-93.

Sports Illustrated (June 21, 1982): 9.

Other

"The Official Satchel Paige Homepage." http://www.cmgww.com/baseball/paige/index.html.

"Paige, Leroy Robert." BaseballLibrary.com. http://www.pubdim.net/baseballlibrary/ballplayers

"Paige, Leroy Robert." Baseball-Reference.com. http://www.baseball-reference.com.

Sketch by Eric Lagergren

Arnold Palmer
1929-

American golfer

Arnold Palmer wrote in his 1997 autobiography, *A Golfer's Life,* that his father gave him a big piece of advice that served him well through the years. He said, "Get the right grip. Hit the ball hard. Go find the ball, boy, and hit it hard again."

Palmer found the right grip, hit the ball hard, and—more often than not—often found the ball in the bottom of the cup. The little boy that "Deacon" Palmer gave the advice to went on to become one of the greatest golfers of the twentieth century. But not only was Palmer a great golfer, he was and is the game's great ambassador. Many believe that Arnold Palmer single-handedly helped resurrect the game from the stodgy upper classes, making it a spectator sport for the common man, and making it a game that all sorts and kinds could play and enjoy.

Growing Up

Arnold Palmer was born in Youngstown, Pennsylvania on September 10, 1929, to Milfred "Deacon" Palmer and Dorris Palmer. Soon after he was born, the family moved to Latrobe, Pennsylvania (where Palmer still has a home and chooses to reside most of the year). He was born into a golfing household, with his father as the greenskeeper and teaching professional at the Latrobe Country Club. Palmer learned much of what he knows about the game from his father, who made a set of clubs for Arnold when the boy was three years old.

Arnold Palmer

Chronology

1929	Born September 10 in Latrobe, Pennsylvania
1933	Father gives Arnold his first set of golf clubs when he's three
1938	Playing regularly with the older caddies on Latrobe's nine hole golf course
1941	Becomes a caddy at age 11 on Latrobe's course
1947	Enters Wake Forest University
1950	Leaves Wake Forest and for his military/wartime service joins U.S. Coast Guard
1953	Upon leaving Coast Guard, returns to Wake Forest but doesn't complete his degree (he will be awarded an honorary degree years later)
1954	Wins United States Amateur Championship
1954	Marries Winnifred Walzer on December 20(they would have two daughters, Peggy and Amy)
1954	Turns professional after signing with Wilson Sporting Goods
1955	Wins his first important professional tournament, the Canadian Open
1958	Wins his first Masters
1960	Wins Masters for a second time; wins first and only U.S. Open
1960	Founds Arnold Palmer Enterprises
1961	Wins his first British Open
1962	Wins third Masters Tournament; wins second British Open
1964	Wins fourth Masters
1968	Becomes first player in PGA Tour History to reach $1 million in official earnings, on July 21, with a tie for 2nd at the PGA Championship
1970	Awarded honorary LL.D. from Wake Forest University
1971	Becomes president and owner of Latrobe Country Club
1974	Becomes president of Arnold Palmer Cadillac in Charlotte, North Carolina
1980	Enters Senior Tour and wins the PGA Seniors Championship
1981	Wins the USGA Senior Open (first player to claim both U.S. and Senior U.S. Open titles)
1984	Wins his second PGA Seniors Championship
1992	Establishes major annual fundraiser for Latrobe Area Hospital
1994	Plays in final U.S. Open
1996	Captains the U.S. team to victory in the President's Cup
1997	Undergoes surgery for prostate cancer
1999	Co-authors his autobiography, *A Golfer's Life* with James Dodson
1999	Wife Winnie dies of cancer on November 20
2000	Plays in 1000th tour event
2002	Matches his age (73) in the final round of the Napa Valley Championship
2002	Makes record 48th consecutive start at the Masters (his final Masters Tournament)

With immense natural talent and his father's tutelage, Palmer soon developed his own distinctive game, creating a style that would last him a lifetime. Though it wasn't pretty, the trademark Palmer swing and quick method of play later became part of the appeal that brought him millions of fans. His swing, an awkward and fundamentally flawed hack at the ball, forced Palmer as a boy to swing so hard he "often toppled over."

Comes of Age on the Links

As a kid he was only allowed on the Latrobe course (which he later ended up purchasing) before the members arrived in the morning or after they'd gone home in the evenings. On the links, he started playing the older boys, and when he was eight he consistently defeated the 12 year olds; soon he played regularly with the older boys—the caddies on the golf course—and waited until the day he would be allowed to caddie himself.

While he was in high school Palmer began winning tournaments with ease. In four years on the Latrobe High School golf team, he lost only once. He also added to his list of accomplishments three Western Pennsylvania Amateur titles. A friend of Palmer's, Bud Worsham (whose brother Lew was a professional golfer) convinced Arnold to accept a golf scholarship to Wake Forest College in North Carolina, where he went in 1947. Palmer was soon dominating college tournaments just as he had dominated tournaments in high school.

To Paint or Play

Palmer ended up leaving Wake Forest a year early to join the Coast Guard. He fully intended to return to school to earn his degree. He did return to Wake Forest, but he never completed the degree. (Wake Forest would later award him an honorary doctorate in the humanities.)

He was unsure of what to do, and when Palmer left school, he was tempted to turn pro right away. But that was not an easy decision to make. Though being a professional golfer enticed the young Palmer, professional golf promised no financial stability in the 1950s. In fact, Palmer's popularity after his entrance into the world of professional golf, in 1954, brought about the higher winnings and larger purses players are familiar with

---

Awards and Accomplishments

1957	*Golf Digest*'s Byron Nelson Award for Tournament Victories
1960	Awarded the Hickok Belt
1960	Earns PGA Player of the Year honors
1960-63	*Golf Digest*'s Byron Nelson Award for Tournament Victories
1961-62	Awarded the PGA's Vardon Trophy
1962	Earns PGA Player of the Year honors
1964	Awarded the PGA's Vardon Trophy
1967	Awarded the PGA's Vardon Trophy
1969	Golf Writers Association of America awards Palmer the Richardson Award
1970	Associated Press Athlete of the Decade (for the 1960s)
1972	United States Golf Association Bobby Jones Award
1974	Charter Member of World Golf Hall of Fame
1975	*Golf Digest* Man of Silver Era
1976	GWAA Charlie Bartlett Award
1978	Awarded the Herb Graffis Award
1980	Inducted into the PGA Hall of Fame
1983	Old Tom Morris Award
1989	American Senior Golf Association National Award
1991	Ambassador of Golf Award, World Series of Golf
1992	National Sports Award, Washington D.C.
1996	Named Golfer of the Century

---

today. Many professionals still call Palmer "The King" because they realize that were it not for Palmer's decision to turn pro the game would never have taken off.

To Play

After turning pro in November of 1954 and signing a contract with Wilson Sporting Goods, Palmer married his Winnie Walzer, with whom he would have two daughters. Palmer and Winnie were a great team, and they stayed together until she passed away from cancer in 1997.

In 1955 he won his first big tournament, the Canadian Open, earning $2,400 as the top prize. He continued to add victories over the next few years, winning three in 1956 and then adding four more victories in 1957. But he would have to wait for the major he wanted until the 1958 Masters Tournament in Augusta, Georgia. A victory in this tournament secures your name in golf's book of legends, but Palmer was just getting started.

1960 would be a banner year for Palmer, a season in which "Arnie's Army" materialized and his fan base became legion. At the beginning of the season, in the first major, Palmer took a stunning victory away from Ken Venturi in the Masters after birdieing the final two holes. People all over the country tuned in, and thousands more were on the course to watch the spectacle. During the late fifties, golf coverage on television became more and more commonplace, and most weekends Americans found this tall, average-looking guy named Arnold Palmer on their screen. He was, as *Sports Illustrated* put it, "earthy and sexy and tan" all at once. The average American found in Palmer a player whose "emotion leaked out of him from every pore." They identified with him. Golf has always carried the stigma for being "a rich man's game," but when working-class people saw Palmer out on the course, a cigarette in his mouth, an awkward (and far from textbook) swing, and his shots ending up in the rough more often than not, they figured that if he could do it, so could they.

Fans began calling themselves "Arnie's Army," a nickname that came about when Palmer played in a tournament near Fort Gordon. According to the *News-Press* of Fort Myers, soldiers from the base who were working the scoreboards held up signs declaring their allegiance to Arnie. His "soldiers were so devoted," the article said, "that it was not unusual for one to let himself be hit by a Palmer missile to keep it from bounding over the green and into trouble." The signs fans held up would later be banned, but the idea of a following that considered itself an army never died. In fact, it only grew, and soon the "Army" began to irritate Palmer's competitors.

Palmer won the 1960 U.S. Open with a final round of 65—another come-from-behind victory—and people began to believe that there was no deficit from which Arnie couldn't return. His power to capture the hearts of Americans over seemed unstoppable. As did his golf game. He won the British Open in 1961 and 1962, and repeated at The Masters again in 1962. Palmer continued to win some of the regular tournaments on tour, but in 1964 he claimed his last major victory with a win in The Masters.

What Defines Great?

Many say that Palmer was more of a celebrity than he was a great golfer. While indeed he had fantastic performances on the course and won many majors, as well as taking home PGA Player of the Year awards, he won all his honors in less than seven seasons (from 1957 to 1964). Did his competitive drive fizzle, or was he bored and wanting to become more involved with his businesses? He had founded Arnold Palmer Enterprises in 1960 and had started opening golf courses around the country. In addition to that, he also opened up a car dealership and was fascinated by flying and spent much time in the air.

Many also wonder if he was unable to compete with a new superstar by the name of **Jack Nicklaus**. Palmer's critics often cite the span of Nicklaus's career when discussing the two. Yet in spite of the criticism, over the years people devotedly followed the swift Palmer as he, in turn, followed his ball onto the green. Like a well-tuned military machine, Arnie's Army continues to pull in recruits, and he often draws large crowds at the Seniors Tour events. Some even speculate that he has as many fans today, in his seventh decade, as he did when he was thirty. "I'd just like to think that the people got to know me," he told the Ft. Myers *News-Press*.

A Hero's Last Masters

This contemporary following, almost twenty-five years after he left the PGA tour, could be seen at the

Arnold Palmer

2002 Masters tournament, which Palmer had declared to be his last a few weeks before playing in the tournament. He made the cut, thanks in large part to a heavy rain that day, that kept him in the tournament for the weekend, and by that Sunday afternoon, people were lined up twenty deep in some places to get a view of The King as he made his final walk up the 18th fairway at Augusta in tournament play.

According to *Sports Illustrated,* Palmer brought golf "to the truck drivers and the mailmen and the women trying to make three no-trump in their neighborhood bridge groups." What Palmer's presence on the golf course, and in the millions of living rooms each weekend, did was to make golf a little less "prissy" and took some of the high society country club attitude out of the game.

Great players have always been a part of the game, from **Bobby Jones** to Walter Hagen and from Sam Snead to **Ben Hogan**, but according to *Sports Illustrated,* players such as Hogan, true standouts in the game, were "about as lovable as a border guard, an automaton who walked down the middle of the fairway without looking left or right." Palmer engaged the audience. Audiences felt they knew him, that they, in fact, might be Palmer if only circumstances had been a little different. When he was on the course, Palmer didn't make it feel like a rich man's game. Instead, he "walked fast, let his hair get mussed and bummed cigarettes from the gallery."

CONTACT INFORMATION

Address: Home and office—Box 52, Youngstown, PA 15696. Agent—International Literary Management, Inc., 767 Fifth Ave., New York, NY 10022.

SELECTED WRITINGS BY PALMER:

Arnold Palmer's Golf Book: Hit it Hard. Ronald Press, 1961.
Portrait of a Professional Golfer. Golf Digest, 1964.

My Game and Yours. Simon and Schuster, 1965.
Situation Golf. McCall Publshing Co., 1970.
(With William Barry Furlong) *Go For Broke.* Simon and Schuster, 1973.
(With Bob Drum) *Arnold Palmer's Best 54 Golf Holes.* Doubleday, 1977.
Arnold Palmer's Complete Book of Putting. Atheneum, 1986.
Play Great Golf: Mastering the Fundamentals of Your Game. Doubleday, 1987.
Arnold Palmer: A Golfer's Life. Random House, 1999.
Playing by the Rules: All the Rules of the Game, Complete with Memorable Rulings from Golf's Rich History. Pocket Books, 2002.

FURTHER INFORMATION

Books

McCormack, M.H. *Arnie.* New York: Simon and Schuster, 1967.
Palmer, Arnold. *Arnold Palmer's Golf Book: Hit it Hard.* Ronald Press, 1961.

Palmer, Arnold. *Portrait of a Professional Golfer.* Golf Digest, 1964.

Palmer, Arnold. *My Game and Yours.* New York: Simon and Schuster, 1965.

Palmer, Arnold. *Situation Golf.* McCall Publshing Co., 1970.

Palmer, Arnold and William Barry Furlong. *Go For Broke.* New York: Simon and Schuster, 1973.

Palmer, Arnold and Bob Drum. *Arnold Palmer's Best 54 Golf Holes.* Doubleday, 1977.

Palmer, Arnold. *Arnold Palmer's Complete Book of Putting.* New York: Atheneum, 1986.

Palmer, Arnold. *Play Great Golf: Mastering the Fundamentals of Your Game.* Garden City, New York: Doubleday, 1987.

Palmer, Arnold. *Arnold Palmer: A Golfer's Life.* New York: Random House, 1999.

Palmer, Arnold. *Playing by the Rules: All the Rules of the Game, Complete with Memorable Rulings from Golf's Rich History.* New York: Pocket Books, 2002.

Periodicals

"Arnold Palmer." (personal profiles). *Sports Illustrated* (September 19, 1994): 60.

Deacon, J. "Return of the King: Arnold Palmer May Be Golf Royalty, But He is also a Man of the People." *Maclean's* (May 6, 1996).

Dienhart, T. "Palmer Won't Coast Into Retirement." *Sporting News* (June 3, 2002): 60.

"The End of an Era." *Golf World* (April 19, 2002).

New York Times Book Review (April 11, 1965; May 1, 1977).

Reilly, Rick. "Seven ahead, nine to go, and then…" *Sports Illustrated* (June 15, 1987).

Soffian, Seth. "A Master's Farewell." *News-Press (Fort Myers, FL)* (April 14, 2002): 1.

Sports Illustrated (June 27, 1966; April 4, 1966; December 19, 1966; March 6, 1967; October 30, 1967; October 14, 1968; August 3, 1970; June 11, 1973; February 18, 1974; June 20, 1977; June 19, 1978).

Other

"Arnold Palmer" biography. http://www.sandhills online.com/plantation/palmer.htm. (January 21, 2003)

"Arnold Palmer." Player biography. http://www.golfweb. com/players/00/19/10/bio.html. (January 21, 2003)

Sketch by Eric Lagergren

Shaun Palmer
1968-

American extreme athlete

Shaun Palmer

When it comes to sports, Shaun Palmer likes them extreme. If he doesn't get an adrenaline rush from it, it's not worth doing. He started with skateboarding and snowboarding as a boy and over time has tried his hand—quite successfully, it turns out—at mountain biking and motocross racing. He's had this insatiable appetite for speed since his childhood. As his mother told *People* in 1999, "Whether it was on wheels or on a board, it had to be superfast—he had no fear. I remember once when he was 13, I had grounded him. Well, he jumped out of his second-floor bedroom window, got on his bike and took off. He was like that—always pushing the limits." Never one to hide his light under a bushel, Palmer bristles with self-confidence. In an interview with Pam Lambert and Ron Arias of *People,* he boasted: "I think I'm the greatest athlete in the world. **Michael Jordan** just had a basketball. I'm on a bike going down a mountainside. Or on a board flying over 60-foot cliffs. I know there are injuries in football, basketball, and baseball, but it's not, like, death-defying."

Born in San Diego

The son of Tim and Jana Palmer, he was born in San Diego, California, on November 12, 1968. His father left shortly after he was born, and Palmer was raised by his mother and his maternal grandmother, Perky Neely, who watched him while his mother worked at an assortment of odd jobs. With his beloved Perky, young Palmer watched the Winter Olympics on TV and dreamed of

Chronology

1968	Born November 12 in San Diego, California
1980	Makes his first snowboard
1985	Enters first junior pro snowboard race
1992	Begins drinking heavily after the death of his grandmother
1995	Founds Palmer Snowboards
1997	Signed by Mountain Dew-Specialized Bicycles team

Awards and Accomplishments

1997	Gold medal in downhill biking and boarder X competitions at Winter X Games
1998	Gold medal in boarder X competition at Winter X Games
1999	Placed first in Swatch Boardercross Tournament
1999	Gold medal in boarder X competition at Winter X Games
1999	Won dual slalom biking event at NORBA National championship
2000	Won Pike's Peak Hill Climb auto race
2000	Gold medal in skier X competition at Winter X Games
2001	Named Action Sports Athlete of the Year by ESPN
2001	Gold medal in ultracross competition at Winter X Games
2002	Won skiercross event at Gravity Games

someday becoming a downhill ski racer. As a boy he showed a talent for skiing and baseball but was most interested in the relatively new sport of snowboarding. Never formally schooled in the sport, he taught himself to board. "I didn't watch tapes or study other guys—I just figured out what felt right," Palmer told *People*. By the time he was twelve, he had made his first snowboard.

In his teens, Palmer, then estranged from his mother, was living in South Lake Tahoe, California, with his grandmother. He dropped out of high school at the age of fifteen to join the junior snowboarding tour. "And I've been on the tour ever since," he told an interviewer for *Swatch.com*. For the next few years he was reigning junior world champion. In 1989, at the age of twenty, he won the world championship at Breckenridge, Colorado, a feat he duplicated in 1990.

Starts Mountain Biking in 1995

In 1995 Palmer borrowed a friend's mountain bike and began spending time with veteran mountain bikers, watching their moves, learning their techniques, and beginning to race now and then. He proved to be a quick study. In the second World Cup race of the 1996 season, held in Nevegal, Italy, Palmer, the new kid on the block, shocked veteran mountain biking observers by finishing the downhill event in seventh place. In July 1996, he won first place in the downhill at the NORBA Championships in Big Bear Lake, California. The event drained Palmer so completely that he could hardly speak after winning. Marti Stephens, mountain biking editor of *Racer X Illustrated*, told Rob Buchanan of *Outside*: "He pushed his body to the max, and at the finish line he was bent over, moaning, 'Oh . . . I gotta get in shape.'" By the end of the biking season, Palmer was number five in the World Cup rankings and seventh in the NORBA National Championship Series. So impressive was his debut that in 1997 he was signed by the Mountain Dew-Specialized Bicycles team to a long-term contract.

Long before he got into biking, Palmer had fallen in love with motocross, racing in local events in Carson City, Nevada, ever since he was a boy. Soon he was competing in extreme snowboarding, mountain biking, and motocross events in Winter X Games competition. At the Winter X Games of 1997, Palmer finished first in the downhill biking competition and first in the boarder X snowboard competition. He successfully defended his

boarder X title at the 1998 games. He entered the snocross snowmobile competition and skier X skiing competition at the 1999 Winter X Games, finishing 15th and sixth, respectively. At the same games in 1999, he placed 14th in the biker X competition and first in the boarder X snowboard competition. At the Winter X Games of 2000, Palmer showed a vast improvement in his skiing skills, finishing first in the skier X competition and fourth in the boarder X contest. At the 2001 games, he won gold in the ultracross competition and placed 12th in the boarder X contest. At the 2002 games, Palmer first sixth in the boarder X snowboard competition.

One of the greatest athletes in extreme sports, Palmer also has expanded into business, opening Palmer Snowboards in 1995. He serves the Minnesota-based company as chief executive officer and also captains the company's snowboarding team. The team's members include Andy Finch, Abe Teter, Alisa Mokler, Chris Nelson, Jonnel Janewicz, and Brandon Ruff. Palmer also serves as a consultant to Activision Inc. in the development of extreme sports video games. His "bad boy" attitude has brought Palmer his fair share of negative press. The fans may love his rebellious spirit, but it's worn a little thin with some of his fellow sportsmen and the media. Helping to redeem him in the eyes of knowledgeable observers is Palmer's undeniable talent. As Rob Buchanan wrote in *Outside*, "Palmer would have remained nothing more than a minor footnote in the annals of sports thuggery if not for one critical fact. Behind all the posturing and acting out, he was, and is, an extraordinary talent."

CONTACT INFORMATION

Address: Shaun Palmer, c/o Palmer Snowboards, 7150 Boone Ave. N., Brooklyn Park, MN 55428.

FURTHER INFORMATION

Books

"Shaun Palmer." *Biography Resource Center Online*. Detroit: Gale Group, 1999.

Periodicals

Lambert, Pam, and Ron Arias. "Going to Extremes: Sports You Wouldn't Try on a Bet, Shaun Palmer Risks His Life and Limb for." *People* (February 22, 1999): 67.

Ruibal, Sal. "Is This the World's Greatest Athlete? Free-Wheeling Punk Rocker Excels in Emerging Sports." *USA Today* (May 1, 1998): 1A.

Ruibal, Sal. "Palmer Parks Bike to Fish Bass, Chase Olympic Gold; King of Extreme Has Unfulfilled Dreams." *USA Today* (March 24, 2000): 12C.

Other

"Shaun Palmer." EXPN.com. http://expn.go.com/athletes/bios/PALMER_SHAUN.html (February 2, 2003).

"Shaun Palmer." Palmer Snowboards. http://www.palmerusa.com/about/shaun_palmer.asp?cat=about (February 2, 2003).

"Shaun Palmer: Perhaps the World's Greatest Natural Athlete." MountainZone.com. http://classic.mountainzone.com/snowboarding/99/interviews/palmer/ (February 1, 2003).

Sketch by Don Amerman

Bill Parcells

Bill Parcells
1941-

American football coach

Not everyone liked Bill Parcells, but he won. Parcells, a football turnaround specialist, took two struggling football franchises and coached them to Super Bowls, and nearly did so with a third.

Parcells' New York Giants won the Super Bowl, the National Football League's (NFL) championship game, in 1987 and 1991. He brought the New England Patriots to the title game in 1997. And the New York Jets, under his tenure, fell one victory short of reaching the Super Bowl in 1998.

Parcells, who espoused old-school football, motivated by fear. "Parcells could be difficult, but those players who responded to his barbs earned his loyalty for a lifetime," Mike Puma wrote in *ESPN.com*. "Numerous players followed him to different coaching stops." "When we were playing real well as a team, [Parcells] was miserable because he needs friction," said Phil Simms, the quarterback most of Parcells' years with the Giants, during an interview on *ESPN*'s Sports Century

series. "He lives on that friction. He needs adversity, and he's got to have a spat going with a player. If there's no adversity, he'll create it."

Raised in New Jersey

Born as Duane Charles Parcells, he began calling himself Bill, after a lookalike, as an early teen in Oradell, New Jersey. At River Dell High School, Parcells excelled in football, basketball and baseball. "His temper was sometimes a problem, but never his work ethic," Puma wrote.

Parcells spent a year at Colgate, but transferred after one year to Wichita State. There, he was an All-Missouri Valley Conference as a linebacker. The NFL's Detroit Lions drafted him in the seventh round in 1964 but cut him shortly after training camp began. Parcells then coached as an assistant at several colleges including Army, where he befriended men's basketball coach **Bobby Knight,** whose own career would be highly successful, though stormy. In Parcells' first head coaching job, in 1978, Air Force lost eight of eleven games.

He agreed to become the Giants' linebacker coach in 1979, but he and his family didn't want to move again; then, after a year of selling real estate in Colorado, Parcells became a New England Patriots' assistant under Chuck Fairbanks. In 1981, he joined Ray Perkins' New York Giants staff.

Parcells, Nicknamed

In 1986, "Parcells changed little about the team from the previous year, relying on a fearsome defense and ball-control attack on offense," Puma wrote. The Giants sported a league-best 14-2 record during the regular season, then dominated San Francisco and Washington in the playoffs for the franchise's first National Football Conference (NFC) championship since 1956, when it was the pre-merger NFL. In the NFC title game against the Redskins, Parcells opted for New York to kick off to start the game rather than receive, but with a 30 miles-per-hour wind at its back in the first quarter. New York dominated early and won 17-0. In Super Bowl XX at the Rose Bowl in Pasadena, California, the Giants scored 30 second-half points to defeat the AFC champion Denver Broncos 39-20.

Parcells, whom the Giants denied permission to speak to Atlanta about a coaching vacancy shortly after wining the title, returned the team to the Super Bowl in January, 1991. At Tampa Stadium, the Giants knocked off the Buffalo Bills, 20-19. Though most remember Super Bowl XXV ending on Scott Norwood's missed 47-yard field goal attempt for the Bills, Parcells and his staff, especially defensive coordinator Bill Belichick, got credit for limiting Buffalo's high-powered offense. New York held the ball for two-thirds of the game.

Bill Belichick, as New York Giants defensive coordinator, helped Bill Parcells win two Super Bowls. Fired as head coach by the Cleveland Browns in 1995, Belichick rejoined Parcells in New England, where the two, in the same roles, went to another Super Bowl; then, they nearly went back with a third team, the New York Jets.

Patriots Beckon

Parcells quit the Giants after that Super Bowl, worked the broadcast booth for two years and had heart surgery. Then, New England owner James Orthwein beckoned Parcells. Taking over in 1993 a team in disarray and rumored to be moving out of town, Parcells re-built it around quarterback Drew Bledsoe, whom he drafted out of Washington State. The Patriots made the playoffs in 1994, Parcells' second year; two years later they played in Super Bowl XXXI, losing 35-21 to the Green Bay Packers.

But Parcells' tenure there was stormy. Bob Kraft purchased the team from Orthwein, kept it in New England, and feuded with Parcells over personnel decisions. "If they want you to cook the dinner," Parcells said, "at least they ought to let you shop for some of the groceries."

Kraft overruled Parcells in the 1996 draft, siding with personnel director Bobby Grier's preference for Ohio State wide receiver Terry Glenn. In training camp that year, Parcells referred to Glenn as "she" at a press conference, incurring the wrath of women's groups. That Kraft's wife, Myra, entered the fray, calling Parcells' comment "disgraceful," reflected the rift between Parcells and the owner. After the Super Bowl, Parcells did not fly back to New England with the team. A week later, Parcells accepted an offer from the New York Jets, who had to surrender four draft choices to the Patriots.

Returns to New York

Parcells took over a Jets team coming off a 1-15 season and produced a 9-7 record in 1997, the team just missing the playoffs. One year later, Parcells, armed with some of his former New England and New York Giant players and assistants, went 12-4 in the regular season. In the AFC Championship game, the Jets led 10-0 at halftime but the Broncos rallied to win 23-10 in Denver. In 1999, his final coaching season, the Jets missed the playoffs but managed a 9-7 record despite having lost starting quarterback Vinny Testaverde for the season to injury on opening day. Parcells stayed in the Jets' front office for a while before returning to broadcasting. He spent the 2002 season as a studio commentator on *ESPN*.

Parcells Legacy: Hovering Presence

Parcells' services are constantly in demand. He rejected a three-year, $18 million offer from the Tampa Bay Buccaneers after the 2001 season and in December, 2002, was linked to the University of Alabama opening.

In January of 2003, Parcells signed on as head coach of the Dallas Cowboys.

Like him or not, Parcells knew how to win. Howard Troxler wrote in the *St. Petersberg Times:* "His method was to ride players hard, with the de facto motto: 'You stink. Now prove to me that you don't.' Sometimes his former players bad-mouthed him, but that didn't change the fact a team's record usually was worse the year before he took over and worse the year after he left."

SELECTED WRITINGS BY PARCELLS:

(With Mike Lupica) *Parcells: Autobiography of the Biggest Giant of Them All,* Bonus Books, 1987.
(With Jeff Coplon) *Finding a Way to Win: The Principles of Leadership, Teamwork, and Motivation,* Doubleday, 1995.
Talkin' Tuna: The Wit and Wisdom of coach Bill Parcells, compiled by Jefferson Davis, ECW Press, 1999.
(With Will McDonough) *Final season: My Last Year as a Head Coach in the NFL,* Morrow, 2000.

FURTHER INFORMATION

Other

"2002 Finalist-Bill Parcells." Pro Football Hall of Fame. http://www.profootballhof.com (December 11, 2002).
"Baying the Bill." *SouthCoast Today.* http://www.s-t.com (January 28, 2000).
"Bill Parcells, Psychologist." Psychology of Sports. http://www.psychologyofsports.com/parcells.htm (August 19, 1997).
"Brady-Bledsoe Foremost among QB Controversies." ESPN.com. http://espn.go.com/chrismortensen (November 23, 2001).
"First a Scare, Then Parcells' Bombshell." *SouthCoast Today.* http://www.s-t.com (January 30, 1997).
"Kraft Blisters Parcells." *SouthCoast Today.* http://www.s-t.com (August 28, 1996).
"New York, You Got Off Easy." *SouthCoast Today.* http://www.s-t.com (January 7, 2000).
"Parcells Made Struggling Franchises into Winners." ESPN Classic. http://www.espn.go.com/classic/biography/ (January 7, 2000).

Sketch by Paul Burton

Derek Parra
1970-

American speed skater

Derek Parra

Derek Parra turned his back on his successful career as an inline skater to hit the ice in hopes of making the Olympic Games as a speed skater. After an awkward transition, he was good enough to qualify for the 1998 Olympics, but a technicality prevented him from competing. Parra came back in 2002 to win a gold and silver medal from the Olympic Games in Salt Lake City, Utah, breaking a world record and becoming the first Mexican-American to win gold at a winter Games.

Parra was born in San Bernadino, California, and raised by his single father, who worked at a prison. He was an avid roller skater at the nearby Stardust Roller Rink, where Cokes were given to the fastest skaters. Life was tough for Gilbert Parra and his two sons. His father did not understand Parra's desire to skate, but finally came around after the Olympics. Parra credits his family, friends, and blue-collar background for his strength of character. His gold, he is quoted as saying in *USA Today,* "Shows that a working man can be on the podium."

Parra quickly switched from the Stardust rink to the inline racing circuit, and became a champion there. He was a three-time national champion, two-time overall world champion, two-time world-record holder, and won eighteen individual gold medals. At the 1995 Pan-Am Games, Parra survived a collision with the pace car during a 26-mile race and went on to place first in the event. He also took home four other golds, two silvers, and a bronze medal, becoming the most decorated athlete of the Games. He earned his living as an inline skater, about $50,000 per year.

Inline skating is not an Olympic sport, so Parra switched to the ice in 1996 with visions of competing in an Olympiad. He had a tough time adjusting to the ice. "I came from being number one in the world [as an inline skater] to being beaten at first by girls that were twelve years old," he recalled in an interview with *Vibrant Life*. His first races on ice were forgettable, but by 1997 he won first place in the American Cup championships, and in 1998 he qualified as an alternate for the 1998 Olympics in Nagano, Japan. Ranked 41st in the world, Parra knew he was not a serious medal contender, but was excited at the chance to race.

Parra did not get his chance that year. The skater he had replaced decided to skate at the last minute, and Parra was bumped. After having traveled to Nagano and getting his hopes up, Parra felt as if the rug had been pulled out from under him. It was such a blow he almost retired. Instead of retiring, Parra moved to Utah to train, leaving his wife Tiffany behind. He worked in the floor and wall sales department at a Home Depot there, which has a flexible-job program for Olympians.

Parra's training regimen is rigorous, even when compared to other Olympic athletes. "I know it's for a purpose," Parra told Tom Weir in an interview with *USA Today*. "It's a confidence builder … knowing that I've suffered through that. I always come to the starting line knowing I have trained the hardest." At five-feet-four-inches tall, Parra is by far the shortest skater in a sport dominated by tall, lanky athletes. Their longer legs make for longer strides, which means Parra had to gain his edge by beating them with technique. He is known by his taller competitors as "the little man with the big strokes," according to writer Paul Oberjuerge in the Los Angeles *Daily News*. He has developed leg power sufficient to get him down the straightaways of the 400-meter oval with the same number of strokes as a taller skater. Parra spent just five weeks with his wife during her pregnancy, and was able to take just one week away from training to be with his her and their first child, Mia Elizabeth, after her birth in December 2001.

Parra's hard work paid off. He was one of eight Olympians chosen to carry the World Trade Center flag

into the opening ceremonies of the 2002 Olympic Games, and was told by President George Bush, "You make us proud." Parra went on to skate the races of his life. He held the world record (6:17.98) for thirty minutes after competing in the men's 5,000-meter race, coming away with a silver medal in the event. A few days later, all eyes were on the shortest skater in the field as he took the ice to skate the 1,500-meter event. Before the race, he found his wife in the crowd and mouthed the words "I love you" to her. Then, he raced like never before, setting a world record (1:43.95) and beating his own fastest time by almost fifteen seconds. Parra's dynamic time earned him the gold medal in the event, and made him the first Mexican-American to win gold in the Winter Games. And although he knew he was not a medal contender for it, Parra raced in the grueling 10,000-meter event.

Despite his golden accomplishment and all the media attention that surrounded him, Parra maintained his humility during the Games, which became a focus of commentators and the media. Through it all, Parra let his emotions flow. "It shows what people can do," he told Paul Oberjuerge in the Los Angeles *Daily News*. "Anybody. If you have faith, if you believe in yourself, if you have people behind you that support you, anything in possible." He cried openly during his victory laps and at the medal ceremonies. Olympic gold also meant increased financial security for Parra and his family—his wife was barely able to afford to travel to see him race. Sponsorships, endorsements, and speeches by the skater likely replaced his Home Depot job. Parra continued to skate after his Olympic triumph. After losing the 500-meter race, he won the gold in the 1,500-meter event at the World Cup in Germany in November 2002.

FURTHER INFORMATION

Periodicals

Cazeneuve, Brian. "Scorecard." *Sports Illustrated* (February 19, 2002): 5.

Lambert, Pam. "Fellowship of the rings." *People* (March 11, 2002): 62.

Mellskog, Pam. "Racing for gold with God: Derek Parra and Caroline Lalive." *Vibrant Life* (January-February 2002): 10.

Oberjuerge, Paul. "Parra excellence; San Bernadino speed skater captures silver." *Daily News* (February 10, 2002): N1.

"Parra captures 1,500-meter race." *New York Times*. (November 17, 2002): 11.

Sandomir, Richard. "Getting there via hardware and lumber." *New York Times*. (February 21, 2002): 2.

Weir, Tom. "Blue-collar Parra skates to surprising silver." *People* (March 11, 2002): 62.

Weir, Tom. "Parra doesn't want to come up short; U.S. speed skater stands tall with extra hard work." *People* (March 11, 2002): C7.

Wong, Edward. "Parra turns tables and zips to gold in 1,500." *New York Times*. (February 20, 2002): D1.

Other

"Athlete profile: Derek Parra." U.S. Olympic Team Home Page. http://www.usolympicteam.com/athlete_profile/v_Parra.html (January 15, 2003).

"Derek Parra." U.S. Speedskating Home Page. http://www.usspeedskating.org/rosters/Parra.html (January 15, 2003).

"Latino community embraces Olympic champion." Latino Legends in Sports. http://www.latinosports legends.com/2002/parra_Latino_community_embraces_him-101102.htm (January 15, 2003).

Sketch by Brenna Sanchez

Joe Paterno

Joe Paterno
1926-

American college football coach

Joe Paterno is a living legend. With his thick glasses, khaki slacks (always a bit too short), and his Penn State windbreaker, Paterno is one of the most recognizable coaches in this history of football—college or professional. And he deserves the recognition. Since taking over the head coaching position at Pennsylvania State University in 1966, he has amassed five undefeated seasons, more bowl wins than any coach in college football (including three national championships), and risen to earn the title "the winningest active coach in college football." Paterno has also been voted coach of the year an amazing four times by the American Football Coaches Association.

But he is more than just a coach. He is a tenured professor, too, and to his players he is like a father, more so than most coaches could even dream of being. He instills in every member of his team that being well-rounded supercedes singular successes on the football field. "In an era of college football in which it seems everybody's hand is either in the till or balled up in a fist," writes Rick Reilly in *Sports Illustrated*, "Paterno sticks out like a clean thumb."

Growing Up

Joseph Vincent Paterno was born in Brooklyn, New York, on December 21, 1926, to Italian parents who pressed upon him early the importance of education. His father worked hard, and eventually obtained his law de-

Chronology

1926	Born Joseph Vincent Paterno on December 21 in Brooklyn, New York
1932	Learns early on the value of education over sports—but plays touch football as much as he can
1942	Enters Brooklyn Prep High School
1946	Enters Brown University where he plays quarterback and also returns punts and kickoffs
1949	Brown goes 8-1 with Paterno at the helm
1950	Becomes an assistant coach at Penn State
1962	Marries Suzanne Pohland (together they'll have five children: Diana Lynne, Mary Kathryn, David, Joseph Vincent Jr., and George Scott)
1966	Appointed as head coach of the Nittany Lions on February 19
1968	Records first of five unbeaten seasons at Penn, going 11-0 and beating the University of Kansas in the Orange Bowl
1977	Misses the second kickoff in his career as a coach when his son is seriously injured in an accident; the first was due to the death of his father, in 1955 (hasn't missed a kickoff since)
1982	Captures first National Championship, beating the University of Georgia in the Sugar Bowl
1986	Wins second National Championship, beating Miami in the Fiesta Bowl
1992	Attends opening ceremonies of the Joe Paterno Child Development Center on the campus of Nike, Inc., in Beaverton, Oregon
1993	Penn becomes a part of the Big Ten conference
1993	Brown honors its alum with the scholarship presented in his honor, the Joe Paterno Male Outstanding Freshman Athlete Award
1995	Guides Penn to an undefeated season and a victory in the Rose Bowl. It was to that point the first Big Ten team with an undefeated season in 26 years
1995	Penn State is ranked first as being the college program that best prepares players for the NFL
1997	The Paterno family donates $3.5 million to Penn State to endow faculty positions and scholarships
2001	Earns win 324, which puts him as the career leader in Division I-A football, surpassing previous record holder Bear Bryant

Awards and Accomplishments

1972	Named Coach of the Year by the Walter Camp Football Foundation and the Football Writers Association of America
1978	Football Writers Association of America Coach of the Year
1986	Football Writers Association of America Coach of the Year
1986	*Sports Illustrated* Sportsman of the Year
1991	National Football Foundation and Hall of Fame Distinguished American Award
1994	Receives the Ernie Davis Award, presented by Leukemia Society of America
1996	Earns National Education and Leadership Award by The Sons of Italy
1997	Honored with Duff Daugherty Memorial Award by Michigan State University
1997	Vince Lombardi Foundation Coach-of-the-Year Award

After graduating from college, Paterno was offered a job as an assistant football coach at Pennsylvania State University. Although he was initially unsure if he should accept the position, he soon fell in love with the people of the community and stayed.

Happy in Happy Valley

Paterno remained an assistant coach at Penn State for the next sixteen years. He had started a family with wife Suzanne (they would have five children, all of whom attended Penn State) and felt at home in Happy Valley. When head coach Rip Engle retired in 1966, Paterno was asked to be the new head coach. He had a rocky start, going 5-5 in his first year, but the following season he turned it around and compiled an 8-2-1 record, making an appearance in the Gator Bowl (the first in a long, long line of bowl appearances).

As the seventies progressed, Paterno made the Nittany Lions a dominant force in college football, following back-to-back undefeated seasons (the streak ended at 31 games). Yet in spite of his consistent excellence on the field, Paterno's teams never got the recognition he felt they deserved. For instance, after they went 12-0 in 1973, the team went on to beat Louisiana State University in the Orange Bowl. When the final polls came out, the Nittany Lions were ranked 5th in the nation. Paterno—to put it mildly—was furious with the results, and he paid to have championship rings made for every player on his team.

When Penn State finally won a national championship and earned number one status in 1982, Paterno refused bask in the glory of his hard-won national title. According to *Sports Illustrated*'s Rick Reilly, Paterno "marched into a meeting of [Penn State] University's board of trustees and, in effect, scolded them. He urged the board to raise entrance requirements and to spend more money on the library.... It may go down as the only time in history that a coach yearned for a school its football team could be proud of."

gree when he was forty years old, while at the same time supporting a family with his full time job. The drive and determination of his father rubbed off on Joe.

Growing up, Paterno spent most of his time either playing touch football or with his nose in a book. His parents encouraged friendly debates, and the family spent much of their dinner hours engrossed in heated discussions about one topic or another. According to *Sports Illustrated*, "At the dinner table we were allowed to talk about anything. And we did. You name it, we'd argue about it. Kids from the neighborhood would walk into our kitchen, unannounced, and sit in, just to listen."

Initially Paterno considered—like his father, whom he idolized—practicing law. But when he graduated from Brooklyn Prep High School and then spent a year in the military, his focus began to change. He ended up at Brown University on a football scholarship where he played quarterback. Though he was not an outstanding player, he was quick and very intelligent, able to outwit defenses and able to inspire his teammates to victory. In 1949 he led the Brown Bears to an 8-1 record.

Moving On Up

In the late eighties Penn State—based in large part on Paterno's exceptional tenure with the school and the reputation he had brought the football program—was invited to play in the Big Ten, college football's powerhouse. The school accepted, entering the Big Ten officially in the early nineties, and giving Paterno the opportunity he'd been longing for: to win the Rose Bowl.

After only two seasons in the Big Ten, Paterno led the Nittany Lions to an appearance in the Rose Bowl against Oregon, following an undefeated season. Penn State was victorious, defeating Oregon 38-20. Paterno ended up taking his team through the nineties with an incredible record of 97-26 and attaining 300 wins for his career. "There's no secret to how we do things here," he told *Newsday.* "The kids have to understand they're part of a certain tradition here, and one that doesn't just involve football. I'm old-fashioned enough to believe that these kids want you to give them structure. They want it individually and they want it as a team. So if they go to school at Penn State and play football for me, they know there's going to be a certain structure. I know what's succeeded here, and I'm reluctant to give it up."

Tough Times

But as the millennium turned, so too did the program. Or so it seemed. For the first time in Paterno's career, he posted back-to-back sub-.500 seasons (5-7 in 2000, 5-6 in 2001). In the fall of 2001, despite having an overall sub-par season, Paterno did surpass Bear Bryant's record for coaching victories, with 324 gridiron triumphs at that point.

In the 2002 season the Lions got back on track, going 9-4 and making it to the Capital One Bowl, where they lost to Auburn. Paterno's record at the end of the 2002 season stood at 336 wins, 99 losses and three ties.

Leaving His Legacy

Throughout his career, Paterno has not been without his detractors, many of whom in recent years called for him to step down, due in part to his age and in part to the losing seasons of 2000 and 2001. He has also come under scrutiny for holding closed practices and not allowing fans to watch. But Paterno is a private individual, and he has never been a big fan of media attention.

What he has done for the university, the community, and his players, however, often silences the critics. Dick Frasca, a pizza shop owner on College Avenue in Pennsylvania, told *Sports Illustrated,* "Before Paterno they couldn't get city kids and suburban kids to come here. Look at how he's grown the place." Indeed, he has been a key factor in Penn State's enrollment increasing from just over 12,000 in the year he signed on as head coach to over 40,000 today. Beaver Stadium (Penn State's football stadium) now holds over 100,000 fans on Nittany Lions game days.

Indeed, he has taken the idea of a college football player and made it something special. Paterno's program consistently ranks in the top tier, if not #1, for preparing football players for the NFL. But it also prepares them for an MBA, or any other graduate degree they want to pursue. Paterno stresses academic excellence, and thus far the Nittany Lions have produced 21 All-Americans in addition to their nearly forty first-round NFL draft picks. He is critical of athletes who arrive at college for the sole purpose of playing a sport. "We've lost a generation and a half of people who were potential lawyers, doctors, teachers and what have you," he told *Sports Illustrated,* "because they were all caught up in bouncing a basketball and running with a football....We were supposed to be educating those kids. Instead, we conned them for 15 years and then, when they were through playing pro football or pro basketball, they knew they'd been conned; they knew they'd been had."

He also cares for his players—though it may be a form of "tough love" that keeps many from getting too close to him. Nonetheless he has their best interests at heart. "I don't care if my players like me," he told *Sports Illustrated,* "I want them to like me when it's important they like me, when they're out in the world, raising families, using their degrees. I want them to like me when it hits them what I've been trying to say all these years."

During their lackluster 2000 season, Penn State cornerback Adam Taliaferro was hit hard during a game at Ohio State. The accident frightened Paterno, who had a similar scare years earlier when his son hurt himself on a trampoline. After Taliaferro, who might have been totally paralyzed, made a miraculous recovery, the athlete told *Sports Illustrated*'s Rick Reilly that "You see this man on television.... but you don't know him. I know him now. His caring isn't an act."

Paterno also cares about the school, giving of himself both donating millions to the school (a new library wing was named after him) and raising millions more for academic programs, all the while living a rather humble life.

He "lives in a home far below what he can afford," writes Reilly. "He takes no salary for his weekly TV show. When the Paternos give one of their regular dinner parties for 40 or so, there's no catering. For two days Sue [Paterno's wife] cooks manicotti and lasagna and freezes it all."

In an uncharacteristic style, Paterno has of late taken issue with some of the officiating he has seen in college football. After a recent game against conference rival Michigan in which a Penn State receiver was called out when the replay clearly showed him in bounds, Paterno, according to Michael Bamberger of *Sports Illustrated,* had Penn State athletic director Tim Curley write a letter to the Big Ten commissioner "calling for a top-to-bottom review of conference officiating." He later told Bamberger, "In 50 years I've never been in the position I'm in now, in a controversy over whether a guy is a good official or a lousy official and who is appointing them."

No Signs of Stopping

Asked by *Sporting News* reporter Tom Dienhart before the 2002 season began if he would ever take it easy, Paterno replied: "If I feel as I do now, I'm gonna keep coaching. I'm enjoying it… It's a little tougher job than maybe it was 20 years ago because of the environment that's out there now—the exposure and the attention… I'd like to say [I'll coach] maybe five more years. It could be 10 more years. I really don't know."

When Bamberger of *Sports Illustrated* recently reminded him that nobody lives forever, Paterno said, "You only say that because nobody's ever done it." Regardless of what happens in the last years of Paterno's tenure at Penn State, he has turned around the two-year hiccup in the program of back-to-back losing seasons. His five undefeated seasons, his statistic of more bowl wins than any coach in college football (including those three national championships), his claim as the "winningest active coach in college football," and his greatness seem to speak for itself. Add to that his relationship with his players and his ability to turn young men into outstanding adults, and Paterno remains as one of the greatest coaches the game has known.

CONTACT INFORMATION

Address: Office—234 Recreation Building, Pennsylvania State University, University Park, PA 16802.

SELECTED WRITINGS BY PATERNO:

(With Bernard Asbell) *The Paterno Principle.* Random House, 1989.

(With Asbell) *Paterno: By the Book.* Berkeley Publishing, 1991.

(With Brice Durbin) *Portrait of an Athlete.* Human Kinetics Press, 1991.

Joe Paterno

(With Bob Reade) *Coaching Football Successfully.* Human Kinetics Press, 1993.

(With L. Budd Thalman) *Quotable Joe: Words of Wisdom by and About Joe Paterno, College Football's Coaching Icon.* Towlehouse Publishers, 2000.

(With Mickey Bergstein) *Penn State Sports Stories and More.* Rb Books, 2000.

FURTHER INFORMATION

Books

Hyman, Mervin D. and Gordon S. White. *Joe Paterno: "Football My Way."* New York: MacMillan, 1978.

"Joe Paterno." *Newsmakers 1995,* Issue 4. Farmington Hills, MI: Gale Research, 1995.

O'Brien, Michael. *No Ordinary Joe: The Biography of Joe Paterno.* Rutledge Hill Press, 1998.

Paterno, George. *Joe Paterno: The Coach From Byzantium.* Sagamore Publishing, 1997.

Paterno, Joe and Bernard Asbell. *The Paterno Principle.* Random House, 1989.

Paterno, Joe and Bernard Asbell. *Paterno: By the Book.* Berkeley Publishing, 1991.

Paterno, Joe and Mickey Bergstein. *Penn State Sports Stories and More.* Rb Books, 2000.

Paterno, Joe and Bob Reade. *Coaching Football Successfully.* Human Kinetics Press, 1993.

Paterno, Joe and Brice Durbin. *Portrait of an Athlete.* Human Kinetics Press, 1991.

Paterno, Joe and L. Budd Thalman. *Quotable Joe: Words of Wisdom by and About Joe Paterno, College Football's Coaching Icon.* Towlehouse Publishers, 2000.

Werley, Kenneth. *Joe Paterno, Penn State and College Football—What You Never Knew.* University of New Haven Press, 2001.

Periodicals

Bamberger, Michael. "What's Up With Joe Pa?" *Sports Illustrated* (October 28, 2002): 50.

Benestad, J. Brian. "Paterno on Vergil: educating for service." *America* (April 2, 1994): 15.

Bradley, Michael. "No ordinary Joe." *Sporting News* (October 29, 2001): 20.

Burgess, Jack. "For Football's `Joe Pa,' Third Time's the Charm." *Insight on the News* (October 4, 1999): 32.

Dienhart, Tom. "Paterno Won't Coast Into Retirement." *Sporting News* (June 3, 2002): 60.

Reilly, Rick. "The Wins That Really Count." *Sports Illustrated* (November 13, 2000): 100.

Reilly, Rick. "Not an Ordinary Joe." *Sports Illustrated* (December 22, 1986): 64.

Other

Barra, Allen. "When it's time to go." salon.com. http://www.salon.com (January 20, 2003).

"Meet Coach Paterno." Pennsylvania State University website. http://www.psu.edu/sports/football/Paterno/paternobio.html (January 22, 2003).

Online review of *No Ordinary Joe.* http://toolscart.com/cgi-bin/ebooks/1007.html (January 20, 2003).

Sketch by Eric Lagergren

Floyd Patterson
1935-

American boxer

Floyd Patterson became the youngest heavyweight champion, a record he held onto until a young fighter by the name of **Mike Tyson** entered the ring almost four decades later. A fast-moving and clever heavyweight with a snappy punch, Patterson was by no means the strongest of fighters, but he had resilience and heart, and he called upon his determination to overcome severe psychological handicaps and remain a contender in the ring for over two decades.

Floyd Patterson

Growing Up

Floyd Patterson was born on January 4, 1935, in Waco, North Carolina, the third of nine sons in a family of thirteen. He would grow up in poverty, a condition that was the catalyst for the chain of events that made him a heavyweight fighter.

In 1936, Patterson's family moved to Brooklyn so that his father could look for better paying work. Though he would find employment, he still had a difficult time making ends meet for such a large family. Construction, longshoreman, sanitation, fish market—every day Patterson's father worked any number of jobs. But every day Floyd saw the conditions in which he lived, saw his father coming home virtually empty-handed. He saw that no matter how hard his father worked, it was never enough.

The family was always on the move, so young Patterson had a difficult time keeping friends. With the lack of any money for extras, Patterson was given the hand-me-down clothes from his brothers. He grew to feel ashamed of his appearance, and he felt helpless.

Not wanting to encounter people, as a young boy Patterson skipped school often, preferring instead to remain in the dark for most of the day. He would hide out in cellars, alleyways, or the corners of subway stations; or, if he could sneak in or round up the few cents it took, hide out at the movies. He cultivated the life of a loner. Eventually he started stealing, maybe to pass the time, but

Chronology

1935	Born January 4 in Waco, North Carolina, and grows up in poverty
1936	Family moves to Brooklyn, New York
1945	Sent to Wiltwyck School for Boys for stealing
1945-49	Discovers boxing while at Wiltwyck, overcomes some of his shyness and self-esteem problems
1949	Begins association with Cus D'Amato at Gramercy Gym. D'Amato becomes his trainer
1950	Enters and wins first Amateur Athletic Union tournament bout
1951	Meets future wife Sandra Hicks
1952	Wins Golden Gloves Championship at Madison Square Garden as well as the AAU Championship in Boston
1952	Wins gold medal at the Olympics in Helsinki
1952	Turns professional and wins pro debut at age of 17
1956	Marries Sandra Hicks for the first time (would remarry her later that year after his conversion to Catholicism)
1959	Knocked down seven times in three rounds by Ingemar Johansson, Floyd's career appears to be over
1960	Returns to ring and defeats Johannson, knocking the Swede out with vicious left hook
1965	Loses to Muhammad Ali in a twelve round bid to retain the heavyweight championship
1968	Leaves the ring for two years after losing to WBA Champion Jimmy Ellis
1972	Fights Muhammad Ali in what would be his last professional fight
1972	Announces his retirement
1976	Takes an interest in 11-year old boxer named Tracy Harris, whom he'd eventually adopt
1994	Informed by Harris that he no longer wants Patterson to manage him
1995	Named athletic commissioner of the State of New York by Governor George Pataki
1998	Steps down from athletic commission, citing memory loss as reason for no longer being able to fulfill duties
1998	Moves permanently to his 17-acre farm in New Paltz, NY

Awards and Accomplishments

1950	New York City Golden Gloves Champion
1952	National Amateur Athletic Union middleweight champion
1952	U.S. Olympic Gold Medalist
1956, 1960	*Ring* Magazine Merit Award Neil Trophy
1976	Inducted in to *Ring* Magazine Boxing Hall of Fame
1987	Inducted into U.S. Olympic Hall of Fame
1991	Inducted into International Boxing Hall of Fame

also because he saw that by taking what he wanted, he could get the things his family needed, such as milk, or dresses for his mother.

A Needed Change

The conditions of his poverty, and then his stealing to try to do something about it, led to Patterson's being sent to the Wiltwyck School for Boys in 1945. This was an alternative to jail for boys aged eight to twelve. It was located north of the city in a pastoral setting, and it is while he was at the Wiltwyck School that Patterson came into his own. He relished the attention he was given from his teachers, attention that his parents, with eleven children, could rarely give him. He also noticed that he was treated as an equal with the white children.

Patterson fell in love with the countryside. He studied nature, rode horses, and acquired a fondness for snakes. His teacher, Vivian Costen, would help him overcome shyness and lack of self-confidence. Coach Walter Johnson, the school's sports director, introduced Patterson to boxing.

Under Johnson's tutelage, Patterson slipped into boxing gloves like a second skin. He won all three matches he fought while at the school, and then it was time for him to return home.

Back in the City

When he returned home, Patterson was twelve and still shy. But he had overcome his shame, and he had discovered that boxing, not stealing, was a way to earn the money his family needed.

Cus D'Amato, who would later manage Mike Tyson, ran the Gramercy Gym in Brooklyn. He would build on the fundamentals that Patterson was taught at Wiltwyck and begin to shape Patterson into a contender. But Patterson's first fight was against his brother Frank, who had been boxing for years, and he beat the heck out of Floyd. Showing early the resilience he would demonstrate throughout his career, Patterson came back in a few months for his first amateur fight.

In January of 1950, Floyd Patterson won his first Amateur Athletic Union fight in the 147 lb. weight class. The next year he moved up to the 160 lb. class. Still very young (he was sixteen), Floyd was impatient and wanted badly to turn professional. But D'Amato forbade it. He saw something in the young fighter and wanted him to maintain his amateur status so he would be viable for the 1952 Olympics in Helsinki, Finland.

After the Gold

Patterson made the Olympic team and left school to fight as a representative of the United States. He had become a member of one of greatest U.S. Olympic boxing teams ever put together, a group that won five gold medals, including the one Patterson took home. When he came back from the Olympics and turned professional, he would win three fights in his first month alone. In 1952, Patterson won the Gold Gloves Championship at Madison Square Garden and the National Amateur Athletic Union Championship in Boston. He earned the honor of "Ring Rookie of the Year," given by *Ring* magazine.

Patterson still wanted to move forward fast, but D'Amato was always there to slow him down. In his first big fight against Joey Maxim, Patterson had lost due to lack of experience. He was devastated. Later he would realize that "he had been outsmarted by the ex-champion." He learned to appreciate experience over youth, and he would develop a respect for Maxim.

Where Is He Now?

Since his resignation from the commission, Patterson has spent his days on his 17-acre farm in New Paltz, where he takes care of his animals and lives without the interruption of modern life, choosing not to even own a television.

When he came back to the ring, as was often the case after he took time off, he won his next eleven fights with straight knockouts. Among these fights was his first official heavyweight bout against Archie McBride. With his rising celebrity in the world of boxing, Patterson would merit fights on the West Coast, where he'd hobnob with stars. Yet he missed Sandra, his girlfriend back in Brooklyn. He proposed to her in 1956 and they married. Then, following his conversion to Catholicism, Patterson remarried her two years later. They moved to Mt. Vernon, New York.

The Heavyweight Title is Open

On April 12, 1956, **Rocky Marciano** retired, which left the heavyweight division wide open. Patterson, who wanted badly to have the belt, fought Tommy "Hurricane" Jackson at Madison Square Garden for a purse of $50,000 on his road to a title fight. In spite of a broken hand that gave Patterson trouble throughout the match, he won the fight in a split decision.

He was now free and clear to fight for the heavyweight championship. D'Amato signed him to fight **Archie Moore**, whom he knocked out in the fifth round. The fight took place on the same night Patterson's wife was in labor with their first child, and after the fight, in the dressing room, Patterson was shown a picture of his daughter, Seneca.

In 1960, in a bout to defend his Heavyweight Title, Patterson took on Ingemar Johannson, from Sweden, who was undefeated in twenty-one fights, with thirteen knockouts of his opponents. In the weeks leading up to the fight, Patterson was duped by Johannson's claim of a bad right hand, and lulled into believing it was true. During the fight, however, Patterson began leaving his left side open. Johannson took advantage of it, puncturing Patterson's left ear drum, which left him dazed. The referee finally stopped the fight. Patterson fell to the mat an amazing seven times, but each time he always got back up.

After the loss to Johannson, and losing the World Heavyweight title, Patterson fell on hard times. He endured sleepless nights full of self doubt and pity. This in turn became a fierce, burning desire to rematch Johannson, which he did later that same year at the Polo Grounds in New York. Patterson literally knocked Johannson senseless during the match. Yet after the fight, Patterson realized that his motivation for winning wasn't something he liked. In fact, he hated his motivation. He later told *Sports Illustrated,* "I was so filled with hate. I would not ever want to

be like that again." Patterson fought Johannson one more time, and though he struggled, he eventually won.

As long as Patterson fought, he would hear from critics. They claimed he wasn't fighting true contenders for the crown. Then **Sonny Liston**, an ex-convict who was dominating opponents came along. D'Amato didn't believe Patterson should fight Liston, and his feelings were backed up when the NAACP expressed their desires that Patterson avoid Liston because of his ties to organized crime. In 1962, in Chicago, Patterson and Liston fought. Liston, twenty-five pounds heavier, bludgeoned Patterson, knocking him out in the first round.

Patterson, as had been his style with Johansson, wanted a rematch. Again, the results were similar. Liston knocked down Patterson three times, and then KO'd him in round one. Many thought Patterson's career was over after his first two formidable defeats by Liston. He was twenty-nine, and though not old by boxing standards, he'd taken a beating. He kept coming back, returning to fight **Muhammad Ali** in 1965. Then, in 1968, after losing to Jimmy Ellis in a title fight in Sweden, he left the ring for two years.

Patterson made one last go of it in 1970, lending credence to his critics' harassment that he was fighting mostly has-beens. He had one last chance to prove them wrong, against Ali in 1972. Ali, who wanted to stay in shape for his rematch with **Joe Frazier**, agreed to fight Patterson on Sept. 20, 1972. A cut over Patterson's right eye prompted the ring doctor to stop the fight in the 8th round. It was his last fight, and he would finish his career at 55-8-1 with forty knockouts. The defeats, however, when they came, were often to formidable opponents and gained him more publicity than his wins.

Tough Time As A Black Fighter

Though he was firmly in control of his own destiny in the world of boxing, and at twenty-one should have felt that the sky was the limit, his impressive status didn't matter at all when he'd visit the segregated south. America was still functioning under heavily racist tendencies, and Patterson encountered many hardships while he traveled on his fighting circuit. He was unable to get meals in Baltimore, or eat inside a restaurant in Kansas City. Fed up with the racism, Patterson, "vowed that he would never box in front of a segregated crowd again. He insisted that promoters desegregate seating and avoid scheduling him to train in segregated towns."

Patterson became a proponent of desegregation. He fought for his rights both inside and outside of the ring. He even fought for those of his wife, whom he joined to become part of an anti-discrimination lawsuit filed against a beauty parlor that refused service to her.

Archie Moore, the man he'd defeated for the heavyweight championship. He resigned from the commission the following month.

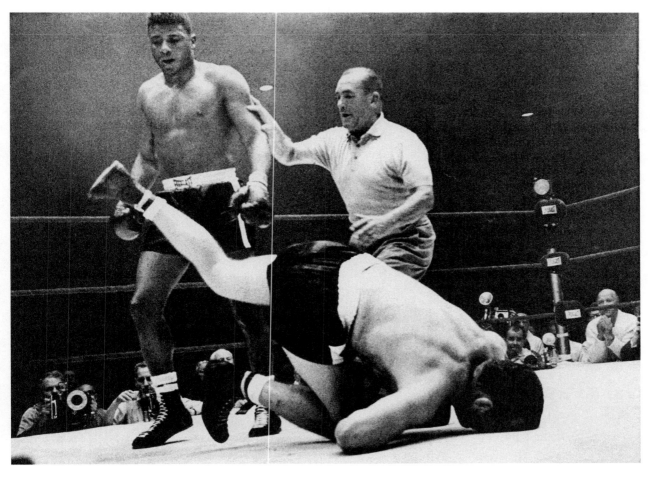

Floyd Patterson, standing at left

"Boxing has given me everything," Patterson said in 1994, in an article in the *Colorado Springs Gazette.* "Without it I'd be nothing."

CONTACT INFORMATION

Address: Floyd Patterson, c/o CMG Worldwide, 8560 Sunset Boulevard 10th Floor Penthouse, West Hollywood, CA 90069.

SELECTED WRITINGS BY PATTERSON:

(With Milton Gross) *Victory Over Myself,* Bernard Geis Associates, 1962.

FURTHER INFORMATION

Books

Brooke-Ball, Peter. *The Great Fights: 80 Epic Encounters from the History of Boxing.* Southwater Publishers, 2001.

Fleischer, Nat, and Sam Andre. *An Illustrated History of Boxing, 6th ed.* New York: Citadel Press, 2002.

"Floyd Patterson." *Great Athletes, vol. 6.* Farrell-Holdsclaw. Hackensack, NJ: Salem Press, Inc.

Levinson, David, and Karen Christenson, eds. *Encyclopedia of World Sport: From Ancient Times to Present.* New York: Oxford University Press, 1999.

Mullan, Harry. *The Ultimate Encyclopedia of Boxing: The Definitive Illustrated Guide to World Boxing.* Edison, NJ: Chartwell Books, 1996.

Newcombe, Jack. *Floyd Patterson, Heavyweight King.* New York: Bartholomew House, 1961.

Patterson, Floyd, and Milton Gross. *Victory Over Myself.* New York: Bernard Geis Associates, 1962.

Schulman, Arlene. *The Prize Fighters: An Intimate Look at Champions and Contenders.* New York: Lyons and Burford, 1994.

Periodicals

D'Amato, Constantine "Cus," and Murry Olderman. "Everybody Wants a Piece of Patterson." *True* (October 1956): 34.

"Floyd Patterson resigns as NY State Athletic Commission chairman citing memory loss. *Jet* (April 20, 1998): 46.

Graham, Frank Jr. "Prizefight Prodigy." *Sport* (April 1954): 20.

Gross, Milton. "The Floyd Patterson Story." *New York Post* (September 9-11, 1957).

Licis, Karl. "Patterson happiest teaching young boxers." Knight-Ridder/Tribune News Service. (February 4, 1994).

Sports Illustrated (March 22, 1993): 70.

Sports Illustrated (November 18, 1996): 4.

The Sporting News (April 1, 1988).

Other

"Floyd Patterson Biography." http://www.cmgw.com/sports/patterso/bio.html/ (November 10, 2002).

"Floyd Patterson." http://www.cyberboxingzone.com/ (November 10, 2002).

Sketch by Eric Lagergren

Gary Payton
1968-

American basketball player

Gary Payton

In 1999 Seattle SuperSonics point guard Gary Payton was dubbed "the best player on the planet" by no less of a basketball authority than superstar **Charles Barkley**. Payton has won two Olympic gold medals and is one of only eight players in National Basketball Association (NBA) history to compile a career total of over 15,000 points, 6,000 assists, and 1,000 steals. Despite this, Payton, who has spent his entire career with the SuperSonics, has yet to win an NBA championship ring.

One Tough Player

Payton grew up playing street basketball in Oakland, California. From a young age, the other young men he played with there taught him how to be tough. "You learned that you can be friends before the game and after the game. But once the game starts, it's all about business. No jive," he told *Sports Illustrated* contributor L. Jon Wertheim in 1999. "[T]hat's one reason I love it and go back to visit every summer." Then, when he was in high school, Payton's school played in a league where it often took several carloads of police to get the opposing team out of the building safely after games. What those experiences did not teach him, his father, Al Payton, a man who drove a car with the vanity plate "MR MEAN," did. Even today, the elder Payton will call his son after watching his NBA games on the television to critique his performance.

Only rarely does Al Payton have reason to criticize his son, who leads the NBA in technical fouls, for not being tough enough. Gary Payton's on-court persona is legendary. His "conversational tone in the heat of battle is as soft as a loan shark's," Dave D'Alessandro wrote in the *Sporting News*. Even when playing against the Chinese team in the 2000 Olympics, Payton trash-talked the entire time, despite the fact that the most of the Chinese players did not understand a word of his insults. "I'm always gonna be talkin'," Payton told Wertheim. "It's nothing personal, but it's at the point where if I change, people will say, 'Oh, he's soft now.' That ain't never gonna happen like that."

Playing in the NBA

After he was graduated from Oregon State University, where he was the best college basketball player in the country according to *Sports Illustrated*, Payton was drafted by the Seattle SuperSonics. The Sonics then had their star in power forward **Shawn Kemp**, but Payton quickly established himself as a key member of the team as well. Behind Kemp and Payton, the Sonics emerged as one of the powerhouse teams of the Western Conference during their regular seasons in the early and mid-1990s. They won at least 55 games per

---

Career Statistics

Yr	Team	GP	Pts	FG%	3P%	FT%	RPG	APG	SPG	TO	PF
1990-91	SEA	82	588	.450	.077	.711	2.9	6.4	2.0	180	249
1991-92	SEA	81	764	.451	.130	.669	3.6	6.2	1.8	174	248
1992-93	SEA	82	1110	.494	.206	.770	3.5	4.9	2.2	148	250
1993-94	SEA	82	1349	.504	.278	.595	3.3	6.0	2.3	173	227
1994-95	SEA	82	1689	.509	.302	.716	3.4	7.1	2.5	201	206
1995-96	SEA	81	1563	.484	.328	.748	4.2	7.5	2.9	260	221
1996-97	SEA	82	1785	.476	.313	.715	4.6	7.1	2.4	215	208
1997-98	SEA	82	1571	.453	.338	.744	4.5	8.3	2.3	229	195
1998-99	SEA	50	1084	.434	.295	.721	4.8	8.7	2.2	154	115
1999-00	SEA	82	1982	.448	.340	.735	6.4	8.9	1.9	224	178
2000-01	SEA	79	1823	.456	.375	.766	4.5	8.1	1.6	209	184
2001-02	SEA	82	1815	.467	.314	.797	4.9	9.0	1.6	209	179

SEA: Seattle SuperSonics.

Chronology

1968	Born July 23 in Oakland, California
1986-90	Attends Oregon State University
1990	Drafted second overall by the Seattle SuperSonics
1996	Establishes the Gary Payton Foundation for underprivileged children
1996	Plays in the NBA finals against the Chicago Bulls
1999	Publishes a children's book, based on his life, *Confidence Counts*

Awards and Accomplishments

1990	Named *Sports Illustrated*'s College Player of the Year
1994-98, 2000-01	Selected for the All-Star Team (as a starter in 1997 and 1998)
1994-2001	Selected to the All-Defensive First Team
1996, 2000	Earns gold medal in Olympics (with Team USA)
2000	Mayor of Seattle declares June 6 Gary Payton Day

---

season for six years in a row, something that only two other teams have achieved in the history of the NBA. But somehow the Sonics always fell apart during the playoffs. They made a good run in 1993, coming within 13 points of making it to the championships, but Barkley and the Phoenix Suns defeated them in game seven to win the Western Conference Finals. Only once, in 1996, did the Sonics make it the whole way to the NBA Finals, where they lost to the Chicago Bulls in six games.

Olympic Victories

Only months after losing to Chicago, Payton helped win a different championship: the 1996 Atlanta Olympics. He was a late addition to "Dream Team III," replacing **Glenn Robinson** after an injury forced him to withdraw. Payton contributed to Team USA's drubbings of all eight of its opponents by leading the United States in assists.

When Payton returned to the Olympics in 2000, he proved to be a stand-out player for one important reason that had nothing to do with ball-handling skills: He was the team's moral leader. Not only did he make sure that all of the other players were fired up for games in which the outcome was never really in question, he also required that all of his teammates be good representatives of their country by not skipping the Opening Cere-

monies. Once again Team USA easily defeated all of the other teams they played, even winning two games by margins of close to 50 points.

Rocky Relations

Payton and the SuperSonics seemed destined to part ways after the 2001 season. Despite having plenty of good players, the team never seemed to be able to jell into a championship-winning organization, and Payton was getting frustrated. With a limited number of years left to play, he wanted the Sonics to either get serious about winning or trade him to a team that was. The Sonics would have been happy to trade him, but between the NBA's salary cap and Payton's impending free agency (his contract was set to expire at the end of the 2002-03 season), no deals could be reached and Payton was forced to return to a weak Sonics team.

When the Sonics started to struggle in the middle of the 2002-03 season, rumors about impending trades began to circulate again, and it seemed highly unlikely that Payton would be playing in a Sonics uniform in the 2003-04 season. Payton's contract would be expired, and the Sonics seemed unwilling to re-sign him even if Payton wanted to remain. Sonics general manager Rick Sund told *Seattle Times* reporter Percy Allen that the team was focusing on "rebuilding." He explained, "We try to use the word transition, but we recognize that we've really emphasized the youth (movement) the last two years."

"You've Got to Learn the Game First"

Payton still remembers the first time he played against his idol, **Magic Johnson**. It was 1990, Payton's rookie season, and the Los Angeles Lakers creamed the Sonics. As Payton recalled to the *Denver Post*'s Adam Schefter, Johnson told him: "You're going to be good. But you've got to learn the game first." Payton certainly did prove to be "good," even great, as his seven selections to the NBA All-Star team and his eight consecutive years on the NBA All-Defensive First Team show. Even if Payton were to retire without an NBA championship ring, he would still be remembered as one of the best point guards of all time.

CONTACT INFORMATION

Address: c/o Seattle SuperSonics, 351 Elliott Ave. W., Suite 500, Seattle, WA 98119.

SELECTED WRITINGS BY PAYTON:

(With Greg Brown) *Confidence Counts*. Dallas, TX: Taylor, 1999.

FURTHER INFORMATION

Periodicals

Allen, Percy. "Sonics Listen as Record Plunges: Most Trade Talk Involves Payton." *Seattle Times* (January 14, 2003): D1.

D'Alessandro, Dave. "Payton Has Molded Sonics in His Bickering Image." *Sporting News* (December 4, 2000): 57.

———. "Sonics, Even with Payton, Don't Scare the Competition." *Sporting News* (April 5, 1999): 27.

Deveney, Sean. "Payton's Flight from Seattle Is Delayed." *Sporting News* (July 30, 2001): 56.

Kelley, Steve. "Sonics Lack Big Man, Have Large Problems." *Seattle Times* (January 15, 2003): D1.

———. "Sonics, Payton Need to Part Ways." *Seattle Times* (January 10, 2003): D1.

Kirkpatrick, Curry. "'Gary Talks It, Gary Walks It.'" *Sports Illustrated* (March 5, 1990): 30-33.

"Payton Named to Dream Team after Robinson Goes down with Injury." *Jet* (July 15, 1996): 53.

Schefter, Adam. "Know Him from Adam." *Denver Post* (January 5, 2003): C-04.

Smith, Sam. "Payton's New Place: Try the Indiana Pacers." *Knight Ridder/Tribune News Service* (January 12, 2003): K0436.

Taylor, Phil. "Still Dreaming: The Other Dominant U.S. Team Had Nothing to Kick About." *Sports Illustrated* (September 25, 2000): 58.

———. "Talk Show." *Sports Illustrated* (May 13, 1996): 38-41.

Wertheim, L. Jon. "The Hustler." *Sports Illustrated* (December 20, 1999): 92+.

Other

"Gary Payton." NBA.com. http://www.nba.com/player file/gary_payton/ (January 7, 2003).

The Gary Payton Foundation. http://www.gpfoundation. org (January 7, 2003).

"Gary Payton Statistics." ESPN.com. http://sports.espn. go.com/nba/players/statistics?statsID=259 (January 7, 2003).

"Seattle SuperSonics History." NBA.com. http://www. nba.com/sonics/history/sonics_history.html (January 20, 2003).

Sketch by Julia Bauder

Walter Payton
1954-1999

American football player

Walter Payton, nicknamed "Sweetness" in college for his sweet and graceful moves on the football field, never lost that sweetness, even after he left the game. Never were Payton's qualities of grace and dignity more evident than in his final days, as he struggled unsuccessfully against a rare liver disease that progressed to the cancer of the bile duct that eventually took his life. Only 45 when he died in November 1999, Payton was, until the fall of 2002, the leading National Football League (NFL) rusher of all time, with a career total of 16,726 yards. Payton spent the final weekend of his life with former teammate Mike Singletary, who later told the *Washington Times*, "With all the greatest runs, the greatest moves I saw from him, what I experienced this weekend was by far the best of Walter Payton I've ever seen. As a person, he was a bright spot for any darkness that appeared." Payton's intensity and ferocity on the football field were balanced by a generosity of spirit and magnanimity off the field that were no less impressive. In his tribute to Payton, NFL Commissioner Paul Tagliabue probably summed it up best: "Walter exemplified class, and all of us in sports should honor him by striving to perpetuate his standard of excellence. Walter was an inspiration in everything he did. The tremendous grace and dignity he displayed in his final months reminded us again why 'Sweetness' was the perfect nickname for Walter Payton."

Walter Payton

Born in Columbia, Mississippi

He was born Walter Jerry Payton in Columbia, Mississippi, on July 25, 1954. The son of Peter (a factory worker) and Alyne (a homemaker) Payton, Walter Payton grew up in what he later called "a kid's paradise," close to the Pearl River and several factories where he and his siblings enjoyed playing hide and seek. His Baptist parents instilled both a strong religious faith and a desire to strive for excellence in all their children. As a boy, Payton often ran afoul of their strict rules, but he later described them as firm but fair disciplinarians. Years later, Payton told Philip Koslow, author of *Walter Payton*: "My parents spent a lot of time with us and made us feel loved and wanted. I didn't care much about what went on around me, as long as I was in solid at home."

By the time Payton was eight-years-old, his father, who worked in a nearby factory manufacturing packs and parachutes for the federal government, had saved enough money to move the family into a new home that had separate rooms for each of his children. Only a block away was the John J. Jefferson School, a segregated school attended by all of Columbia's African American children from grades one through twelve. Walter was a better than average student, but his greatest love was music, on which he spent more time than either his studies or sports. Much to the chagrin of his parents, he'd sometimes duck his chores at home so that he could dance or sing instead.

Chronology

1954	Born in Columbia, Mississippi, on July 25
1971	Graduates from Columbia High School where he starred in football
1971-75	Attends Mississippi's Jackson State College
1972	Scores 46 points in a single game
1975	Picked by Chicago Bears in first round of NFL draft
1976	Marries college sweetheart Connie Norwood on July 7
1985	Leads Chicago Bears to Super Bowl Championship
1987	Retires from professional football
1993	Inducted into Pro Football Hall of Fame
1999	Develops rare live disease and later cancer of the bile duct
1999	Dies at the age of 45 in South Barrington, Illinois, on November 1

Joins Track Team as Long Jumper

Payton's interest in sports picked up in the ninth grade when he joined Jefferson's track team as a long jumper. He also played drums in the school's band. Although he was drawn to football, he didn't go out for the school team, on which his older brother, Eddie, was the star running back, because he didn't want his mother worrying about both her sons getting hurt. After Eddie graduated, Jefferson's football coach asked Payton, then a sophomore, to try out for the team. After winning a promise from the coach that he could stay in the band, Payton agreed. In his very first high school game, he ran 65 yards for a touchdown. In 1969, all-black Jefferson merged with all-white Columbia High School, and Payton quickly became the unchallenged star of the school's football team, scoring in every game of his junior and senior years. Looking back on Payton's high school football career, Columbia coach Tommy Davis said he could always count on Walter when the team needed to score. Three years in a row, Payton was named to the all-conference team, and in his senior year he led the Little Dixie Conference in scoring and was selected for the all-state team.

After his graduation from Columbia High, Payton joined older brother Eddie at predominantly black Jackson State College where together the siblings were stars in the college football team's backfield. At the end of Payton's freshman year in college, Eddie graduated and moved on to the NFL, leaving Walter alone in the spotlight. Payton proved himself a versatile player, serving as Jackson State's halfback, punter, and place kicker. He ended his sophomore year as the nation's second highest collegiate scorer. That same year he broke college records by amassing the highest number of points—46—in a single game. As a junior, Payton ran for a total of 1,139 yards and led the country in scoring with 160 points.

Named NCAA Leading Scorer of All Time

After a grueling summer of training with brother Eddie in 1973, Payton, now a senior, returned to Jackson State stronger than ever. At the end of his senior year in football,

Awards and Accomplishments

1974	Named Little All-American after setting nine school records at Jackson State College
1975	Tops 100 yards rushing for Chicago Bears for the first time
1976	Named *Sporting News* NFC Player of the Year and picked to play in Pro Bowl
1976-81	Rushes for 1,000 yards or more each season
1977	Sets single-game rushing record with 275 yards vs. Minnesota on November 20
1977	Named NFL Player of the Year and *Sporting News* NFC Player of the Year
1977	Named NFL Offensive Player of the Year
1978-81, 1984-87	Selected to play in Pro Bowl
1984	Breaks Jim Brown's NFL career rushing record
1985	Named NFL Player of the Year
1993	Inducted into Pro Football Hall of Fame

Lessons in Greatness

Payton was not the greatest running back in history, but he was close. Jimmy Brown and O.J. Simpson were better, but no one player in NFL history at any position has forced more from his body and driven himself as relentlessly as Payton. This is Payton's first lesson: Never settle for less than you can possibly be. . . .

"I'm always fearful I'm not in the best shape I can be in," Payton once told me. "My goal is to be able to play all out 60 minutes every game. Since you might have the ball only 30 minutes, I figure I've got enough left to go all out every play."

Source: Attner, Paul *Sporting News* (November 15, 1999): 8.

he was named the National Collegiate Athletic Association's (NCAA) leading scorer of all time with 464 points. Somehow, through it all, Payton managed to keep up with his studies, earning his bachelor's degree in special education in only three and a half years. It was during his college years that Payton picked up the nickname "Sweetness," which was to stay with him for the rest of his life.

In the first round of the 1975 NFL draft Payton was chosen by the Chicago Bears, making him the fourth player to be drafted overall. He successfully pushed for a signing bonus larger than that the Bears paid four years earlier to Archie Manning, a quarterback from the University of Mississippi. In the end, the Bears paid Payton $126,000. The Bears, which had had their last winning season in 1967, were hoping that Payton could help turn things around for them. Sadly, the dreams of a quick turnaround were not to materialize. Even with Payton energizing the Bears lineup, the team lost six of its first seven games. Slowed by an ankle injury, Payton played only sporadically in the first half of the season and missed one game altogether—the only missed game of his career.

Payton snapped back in the second half of his rookie season as his ankle healed. At season's end, he led the NFL in kickoff returns and had amassed a total of 679 yards rushing, the highest for any Bears runner since 1969. During the summer following his first season with the Bears, Payton married Connie Norwood, his college sweetheart at Jackson State, on July 7, 1976. During Payton's second season, the Bears fared better than they had in eight years, with an even split of seven wins and seven losses. Had it not been for an injury he suffered in the final game of the season, Payton almost certainly would have won the NFL rushing title for the year—and he did lead the National Football Conference (NFC) in yards gained with a total of 1,390.

Breaks Single-Game Rushing Record

Payton's breakthrough year came in 1977. In the opening game of the Bears' season, Payton gained 160 yards, and six weeks later he posted the first 200-yard game in his pro career. Three weeks later, Payton broke **O.J. Simpson**'s single-game rushing record when he ran for 275 yards. Freezing rain during the Bears' final game of the season held down Payton's rushing yardage for the year to 1,852, just 151 yards short of Simpson's season rushing record of 2,003 yards.

As his performance on the football field grew steadily more impressive, armchair fans across the country became increasingly familiar with Payton's unique running style-running on his toes with short, stiff-legged strides. Payton also seemed to derive genuine pleasure from blocking for other running backs and protecting the Bears quarterback against blitzing linebackers. Interviewed by *Esquire*, legendary Bears running back **Gale Sayers** commented on this side of Payton's game: "That's what sets him head and shoulders above other running backs, the maximum effort he puts into other phases of the game." Payton also showed his appreciation to the offensive linemen who blocked for him by handing the football to one of them after he had scored a touchdown.

Negotiates Lucrative Contracts

Having proved his worth to the Bears, Payton in 1978 negotiated contracts that guaranteed him $400,000 for the 1978 season, $425,000 for 1979, and $450,000 plus incentive bonuses for 1980. However, despite the front office's high hopes, Payton's 50 pass receptions and 1,395 yards in rushing yardage were not enough to keep the Bears from another losing season. They ended the 1978 season with a 7-9 record. Payton and fullback Roland Harper, with 992 rushing yards, accounted for 72 percent of the Bears' offense in 1978.

Hampered by a painful pinched nerve in his shoulder through much of the 1979 season, Payton nevertheless managed to rush for 1,610 yards, the best in the NFC. With a 10-6 record, the Bears made it into the playoffs, but they were eliminated in the first round. With a season total of 1,460 yards, Payton snagged his fifth consecutive NFC rushing title in 1980, but it was not enough to keep the Bears from a dismal 7-9 record. The following year was even worse for the Bears, who fin-

Walter Payton

ished the season with a record of 6-10. Slowed for much of the 1981 season by a sore shoulder and cracked ribs, Payton managed to rush for only 1,222 yards for the season, failing to win the NFC rushing title for the first time in several years.

Signed to 3-Year, $2 Million Contract

In advance of the 1982 season, Payton negotiated a three-year contract worth $2 million with the Bears. To beef up its chances, the Bears' owners brought in **Mike Ditka** as coach. But the season as marred by a players' strike, and the Bears finished the shortened season with a disappointing record of 3-6. In 1983 the Bears brought in Jim McMahon as quarterback. Thus strengthened, the team finished with an 8-8 record. Payton alone accounted for more than a third of the Bears' offense, running for 1,421 yards and catching 53 passes for 607 yards. Payton's performance in 1984 was electrifying. Early in the season, he broke Jim Brown's 19-year-old NFL career rushing record of 12,312 yards and ended the year with a season total of 1,684 yards. The Bears ended the regular season with a record of 10-6. In the first game of the playoffs, Chicago defeated the Washington Redskins by a score of 23-19 but fell to the San Francisco 49ers in the NFC title game.

Payton's dream of making it to the Super Bowl finally came true in 1985. The Bears compiled a stunning record of 15-1 in the regular season and handily polished off its two playoff opponents in home games to power its way into Super Bowl XX. It was a storybook finish for the Bears as they demolished the New England Patriots, 46-

10, in the big game. The following year, the Bears finished the season with a blazing 14-2 record but stumbled in its first playoff game, losing to the Redskins, 27-13. In 1987, the season was once again marred by a player strike. However, the Bears performed strongly in the regular season, finishing with a record of 11-4 and making it into the playoffs again. Paired off against the Redskins, the Bears' post-season march was stopped in its tracks. Not long after the end of the season, Payton, now 33, decided it was time to call it quits and announced his retirement from pro football.

After his retirement, Payton focused most of his attention to the operations of Walter Payton Inc., his personal holding company with investments in restaurants, timber, and real estate. He managed, however, to find time to race cars and boats. In July 1993, Payton was inducted into the Pro Football Hall of Fame. In making the presentation to his father, Payton's son, Jarrett, said: "Not only is my dad an exceptional athlete, he's a role model; he's my biggest role model and best friend. We do a lot of things together. . . . I'm sure my sister will endorse this statement: we have a super dad."

In February 1999 Payton called a press conference to reveal that he was suffering from a rare liver disease called primary sclerosing cholangitis (PSC) that causes the bile ducts to close, backing up bile, and permanently damaging the liver. Only three months later, he learned that he had developed bile duct cancer as a result of the

Career Statistics

Yr	Team	GP	Rushing				Receiving			
			Att	Yds	Y/A	TD	Rec	Yds	Y/R	TD
1975	CHI	13	196	679	3.5	7	33	213	6.5	0
1976	CHI	14	311	1390	4.5	13	15	149	9.9	0
1977	CHI	14	339	1852	5.5	14	27	269	10.0	2
1978	CHI	16	333	1395	4.2	11	50	480	9.6	0
1979	CHI	16	369	1610	4.4	14	31	313	10.1	2
1980	CHI	16	317	1460	4.6	6	46	367	8.0	1
1981	CHI	16	339	1222	3.6	6	41	379	9.2	2
1982	CHI	9	148	596	4.0	1	32	311	9.7	0
1983	CHI	16	314	1421	4.5	6	53	607	11.5	2
1984	CHI	16	381	1684	4.4	11	45	368	8.2	0
1985	CHI	16	324	1551	4.8	9	49	483	9.9	2
1986	CHI	16	321	1333	4.2	8	37	382	10.3	3
1987	CHI	12	146	533	3.7	4	33	217	6.6	1
TOTAL		190	3838	16726	4.4	110	492	4538	9.2	15

CHI: Chicago Bears.

PSC. On November 1, 1999, surrounded by his family and close friends, he died at his home in South Barrington, Illinois.

Records are made to be broken, and so it was with Payton's career rushing record. In late October 2002, **Emmitt Smith** of the Dallas Cowboys amassed a total of 16,743 career yards to surpass Payton's 16,726. But Payton was so much more than just a rushing record. In the hearts of his fellow players, coaches, and football fans everywhere, he lives on as one of the game's greatest players. Former teammate Dan Hampton probably said it best: "No one on this football team and no one in the NFL is actually in Walter Payton's league."

SELECTED WRITINGS BY PAYTON:

(With Jerry B. Jenkins) *Sweetness*, NTC/Contemporary Publishing, 1978.
(With Don Yaeger) *Never Die Easy: The Autobiography of Walter Payton*, Random House, 2001.

FURTHER INFORMATION

Books

"Mike Singletary." *Contemporary Black Biography*, Volume 4. Detroit: Gale Group, 1993.
"Walter Payton." *Contemporary Black Biography*, Volume 25. Detroit, MI: Gale Group, 2000.
"Walter Payton." *Encyclopedia of World Biography Supplement*, Volume 20. Detroit, MI: Gale Group, 2000.
"Walter Payton." *Newsmakers 2000*, Issue 2. Detroit, MI: Gale Group, 2000.
"Walter Payton." *St. James Encyclopedia of Popular Culture*. five volumes. Detroit, MI: St. James Press, 2000.

Periodicals

Attner, Paul. "Lessons in Greatness." *Sporting News* (November 15, 1999): 8.
Pierson, Mark. "American Football: NFL Mourns Loss of Walter 'Sweetness' Payton." *Independent* (November 3, 1999): 27.
"Walter Payton." *Washington Times* (November 7, 1999): B2.
"Walter Payton Timeline." *USA Today* (November 2, 1999).

Other

"Remembering Walter Payton, 1954-1999." SportingNews.com. http://www.sportingnews.com/archives/payton (November 6, 2002).
"Walter Payton: Running Back." Football-Reference.com. http://www.football-reference.com/players/PaytWa00.htm (November 2, 2002).

Sketch by Don Amerman

Pele
1940-

Brazilian soccer player

The greatest and most famous soccer player in history, Brazil's Pele revolutionized the game with his electrifying, creative and athletic style of play. He was such an appealing player that he transcended national boundaries in a sport that is almost synonymous with nationalism. Pele became a global ambassador of the sport, bringing increased attention to soccer in many countries, especially the United States.

Kicking the Sock

In October 1940, in the poor town of Tres Coracoes in the state of Minas Gerais in Brazil, soccer player Dondinho and his wife Celeste Nascimento gave birth to their first child. They christened him Edson Arantes de Nascimento. Two years later another son, Zoca, was born (he was briefly a pro soccer player before becoming a lawyer). His parents couldn't afford to buy Edson a soccer ball, so his father took an old sock and stuffed it with rags, and the child would run shoeless through the streets and kick the sock.

When Edson was six, his family moved to the larger town of Bauru, a railroad junction in southern Brazil. He often skipped school to practice soccer in the fields. To try to earn money for a soccer ball, Edson shined shoes and sold roasted peanuts outside movie theaters. With his friends, he formed a team called the Shoeless Ones. They played barefooted soccer — which later became known as "pelada," after Pele — on the streets or vacant lots. Pele developed many of his feints and unorthodox dribbling maneuvers playing these rough-and-tumble street games.

Pele left school for good after fourth grade, expelled when the head schoolmaster caught him playing soccer during the school day. He took a job as a cobbler's apprentice for $2 a day. His family called him Dico, but his friends bestowed the nickname Pele, which means nothing in Portuguese or any other language. At first he resisted the name because he thought it was an insult, but then he embraced it. In pickup games around Bauru Pele was often the youngest player.

At age 11, Pele was discovered by Waldemar de Brito, one of Brazil's top players. De Brito took him under his wing and trained him in secret. When Pele was 12, de Brito placed him on the local junior club, Baquinho. Pele danced home the day he got his own uniform, because finally he was a real soccer player like his father. "It may not seem such a big deal to some, but to me it was one of the thrills of my life," Pele later revealed to biographer Joe Marcus. He scored many goals for Baquinho, using both his feet and his head to drive balls into the net. Pele's scoring, dribbling and passing skills made him the talk of Brazilian junior soccer.

National Prodigy

When Pele was 15, de Brito brought him to the directors of Santos, a top club team, and told them, "This boy will be the greatest soccer player in the world." In an exhibition game on September 7, 1956, Pele entered the game in the second half for Santos and within a few minutes scored his first goal as a professional. He began earning about $60 a month playing for Santos. In his

Pele

second season Pele became a starter on the team and started scoring from everywhere on the field. He was the top scorer in the league and became a national hero by scoring three goals in a game pitting the top players from Santos and another Brazilian club against the Belenenses club from Portugal. Late in 1957, Pele was picked for the National Team

In 1958, between playing on Santos and on the national team, Pele scored 87 goals and assisted on at least another 100. He also brought Brazil glory. Though soccer was a national obsession in Brazil, the country had never won a World Cup. At 17, Pele was the youngest player in the World Cup tournament and a virtual unknown. He rode the bench for the first two games to recuperate from a knee injury he had suffered in a qualifying game. The doctors cleared Pele to play in the final game of the opening round, and he assisted on one goal and hit the goal post on a shot of his own as Brazil won 2-0. In the next match, a quarterfinal game against Wales, Pele scored the only goal.

In the semifinal game, Pele was the sparkplug of the team. After France scored a game-tying goal early in the first half, he snatched the ball out of the net and raced upfield, yelling at his teammates to get going. Pele went on to score three goals in Brazil's victory, a feat which made him famous worldwide. In the final game, he scored two goals and Brazil won the World Cup for the first time by beating Sweden, 5-2. One of his goals became legendary:

he caught a long pass by trapping it in his chest, sent it into the air with his left foot without letting it touch the ground, flipped it over his shoulder, and then pivoted and kicked the ball while it was still in the air.

Pele, still a teenager, quickly cemented his reputation as the world's best player. While serving in the army, he played on the national team and on Santos and scored a record 127 goals in 1959. European teams started trying to lure Pele away with offers of more than a million dollars, though no team up until then had ever paid more than $100,000 for a player. Though he could have left Santos to play with an Italian club and still have played for the national team of Brazil, Santos refused to sell him. President Janio Quadros declared Pele "a national treasure" who could not be exported.

While Pele was on the team, Santos won 11 league championships. In 1960, he slipped to 78 goals because he was constantly being double- and triple-teamed by defenders. Pele was happy just to pass the ball off to teammates, making Santos even more successful. In 1961 he scored 110 goals. Pele scored more than 400 goals before he turned 20 years old.

In the 1962 World Cup, held in Chile, Brazil was a favorite to win, but Pele pulled a leg muscle in the second game and sat out all the games until his country reached the championships. Doctors refused him permission to play, but Brazil was so strong it won the cup without him. In 1962, Pele won the Brazil scoring championship for the fifth straight year.

The Black Pearl

Pele wore uniform number 10 and played left inside forward. With his agility, speed and incredible ball-handling skills, he revolutionized soccer, instigating a creative, all-out attack that became the Brazilian style and was much more exciting for casual fans than the traditional defense-oriented game. During Pele's career, he scored five goals or more in a game on six occasions, scored four goals in 30 games, and had 92 games with three goals. Three times he scored more than 100 goals in a season.

Pele acquired several nicknames during his career: "Gasoline" for his energy, "The Executioner" for his bril-liant ability to finish an offensive drive and put the ball in the net, and, most popularly, "The Black Pearl," because he was precious. On the field, his joy at playing the game he loved was obvious and infectious. Pele would salute the crowd after scoring a goal and, on many occasions, the goalkeeper he had just beaten would wave or bow to him. If a keeper stopped his shot, Pele would often shake hands with him. When he scored, thousands of fans would stand and chant his name.

Pele had countless tricks to get around defenders. He developed incredible shots, including a swerving shot from 40 yards out that would curve away from the goalie at the last second, and a drop shot that would appear to be going over the crossbar and then dip into the net. Often, defenders would be all over Pele, and he would be fouled and harassed. After years of tolerating this treatment, he began to retaliate and draw yellow cards hinmself. After an Argentinian player repeatedly kicked him and spat at him, Pele kicked back.

The first soccer player to become a millionaire, Pele was overwhelmed with offers to make personal appearances and sign business deals, but he refused to endorse cigarettes or liquor. "I know that I have influence on youngsters and I don't feel that I want them to think if I should endorse these products I want them to use them," he said, according to Marcus's book.

The King of Soccer

In 1964, Pele scored only 60 goals, because most teams were playing six men back on defense against his team. At the end of the season, however, he scored eight goals in a game. In 1965, he bounced back and scored 101 goals. In 1966, Brazil played Bulgaria in the opening game of the World Cup, and Bulgaria fouled Pele brutally and repeatedly. He had to sit out a game to recover, and he returned to action as Brazil faced Portugal needing to win to stay alive in the tournament. With Portugal leading 2-0, a player tripped Pele and then stepped on his knee. No foul was called though Pele was severely injured, and Brazil lost the World Cup. He vowed never to play in another World Cup.

Later that year, Santos made the first of many tours of the United States and played several exhibition games in New York, drawing record crowds at a time when soccer was not popular in the United States. When the National Professional Soccer League was formed in 1967, its president Bob Hermann spoke of wanting to buy Pele, but the Brazilian star said he would never play for any team except Santos or the Brazilian national squad.

In 1969, Pele bowed to pressure and agreed to play in the World Cup in Mexico City, Mexico, in 1970. Brazil won every game, beating Italy in the finals, and Pele became the first person ever to play on three World Cup champions.

Pele

Awards and Accomplishments

1956, **1958**, **1960-62**, **1964-65**, **1967-69**, **1973**	Plays on Sao Paulo state champion team
1957-65, **1969**, **1973**	Top goal scorer in Sao Paulo league
1958, **1962**, **1970**	Plays on FIFA World Cup champion team
1959	Top goal scorer in Copa America
1961	Plays in Copa Liberatadores
1962-63	On World Club champion team
1962-65, **1968**	On Brazilian Cup winner
1966	Plays in FIFA World Cup
1977	North American Soccer League champion team, Cosmos
1978	International Peace Award
1993	National Soccer Hall of Fame
1999	Athlete of the Century, National Olympic Committee
1999	World Sports Awards
2000	Second place, Sportsman of the Century award

With his global notoriety and interest in humanitarian causes, Pele became a freelance goodwill ambassador. In 1967, both sides in Nigeria's civil war declared a cease-fire so they could together watch him play an exhibition game in Lagos. Pele toured throughout the world with his Santos club, adding to his all-time goal-scoring record and his reputation as the king of soccer. He also signed contracts to teach soccer to young children in 115 countries and made soccer training films for Pepsi, as well as doing endorsements for coffee and sporting-goods products. Pele was a multimillionaire and a hugely successful businessman, with interests in construction, rubber and coffee products. He was also a noted philanthropist who gave money especially to support children's causes.

Heeding his father's advice, Pele decided to retire while he was still a top player. In 1971, he retired from the national team, playing his 111th and last game for Brazil on July 18, even though the Brazilian government kept trying to persuade him to play in the 1974 World Cup. Pele later said he quit playing partly to protest human rights abuses by Brazil's military government. His 97 goals in international matches were an all-time record.

Signing a final two-year contract with Santos, Pele donated his final year's salary to children's charities. He retired at age 34, taking the ball and kneeling at midfield during his final game. Pele had scored 1,280 goals in 1,362 matches, second only to Brazil's Arthur Freidenreich.

Several European teams tried to talk him into playing for them. Instead, Pele, who was facing some financial problems, eventually agreed to play for the North American Soccer League (NASL), signing a contract with the New York Cosmos for at least $4.5 million for three years, plus incentives. In the off season, Pele learned English and studied business management, invested in real estate, and gave soccer clinics. He also received many offers to coach in Europe and Brazil, "but there's no way I can stand on the side of the field," he admitted to *Time* magazine.

Pele's entrance into the struggling NASL boosted Americans' interest in soccer. Within two years, players registered in the U.S. Soccer Federation increased from slightly over 100,000 to nearly 400,000. NASL attendance soared, and by 1977 a Cosmos playoff match drew 77,000 fans. Pele retired again after that season, playing a final exhibition game before 75,000 fans broadcast to 38 nations. In a speech before the game, Pele pleaded for the world's children and made everyone shout in the stadium after him: "Love! Love! Love!" The game pitted Cosmos against Santos, with Pele playing for the Cosmos and scoring a goal in the first half, and then playing the second half for Santos.

After the 1977 season, Pele wrote in the *New York Times*: "It seems that God brought me to Earth with a mission to unite people, never to separate them." When a movie was made about his life in 1977, titled *Pele*, he composed the sound track.

After leaving Brazil, Pele wasn't always popular in his native country. In 1988, Brazil, Morocco and the United States were named as the finalists for the 1994 World Cup, and he endorsed the United States, inspiring wrath in Brazil but helping to earn the games for the U.S. In 1994, Pele became sports minister of Brazil, and he spoke out against corrupt practices in the country's football confederation.

Few athletes in any sport commanded global notoriety like Pele. In the 20th century, Pele's only athletic rival for worldwide fame was boxer **Muhammad Ali**. He was the most exciting and productive soccer player in history, and he brought the game vastly increased attention, especially in countries such as the United States that were not already soccer-crazy. Pele also epitomized joy in sport, because he showed emotion openly on the field and was never aloof or distant. He was loved, admired, and respected worldwide, and his genuine honesty and humility made him an appealing role model.

SELECTED WRITINGS BY PELE:

(With Robert L. Fish) *My Life and the Beautiful Game.* Doubleday, 1977.

FURTHER INFORMATION

Books

Harris, Harry and Joseph S. Blatter. *Pele: His Life and Times.*Welcome Rain, 2002.
Marcus, Joe. *The World of Pele.*Mason/Charter, 1976.

Periodicals

"Ali, Pele And Carl Lewis Honored At World Sports Awards Of The Century Gala." *Jet,* 97 (December 13, 1999): 48.
"Facing Football's Bald Facts: Brazil." *The Economist (US),* 345 (December 20, 1997): 33.
Hersch, Hank. "Pele (Forty for the Ages)." *Sports Illustrated,* 81 (September 19, 1994): 122.
"International: 141 Aids Pfizer in Viagra Awareness." *PR Week (UK),* (April 5, 2002): 6.
Kissinger, Henry A. "The Phenomenon: Pele." *Time,* 153 (June 14, 1999): 110.
"On a New Kick." *Time,*158 (October 8, 2001).
"Panamerican Pele." *Multichannel News International.* 7 (April 2001): 12.
Swift, E.M. "A dream come true."*Sports Illustrated,* 80 (June 20, 1994): 86.
Thomsen, Ian. "A Great Revolution Was Afoot." *Sports Illustrated,* 91(November 29, 1999): R36.

Other

"Edson Arantes 'Pele' Nascimento." *Latino Sports Legends* http://www.latinosportslegends.com/Pele_bio.htm(January 3, 2003).
"Pele." *International Football Hall of Fame.* http://www.ifhof.com/hof/pele.asp (January 3, 2003).
"Pele - O Rei, The King, El Rey." *360 Soccer.*http://www.360soccer.com/pele/(January 3, 2003).
"Pele to Advertise Viagra." *On-line Pravda*http://english.pravda.ru/fun/2002/02/01/26160.html (January 3, 2003).
"Play Soccer with Pele." *360 Soccer.*http://www.360soccer.com/pele/peleplay.html (January 3, 2003).

Sketch by Michael Betzold

Roger Penske
1937-

American race team owner

Following a short-lived but distinguished career as a race-car driver in the early 1960s, resulting in Sports Car Driver of the Year awards from, respectively, the periodicals *Sports Illustrated,* the *New York Times,* and the *Los Angeles Times,* Roger Penske established Penske Racing. In IndyCar competition, Penske Racing has won more Indianapolis 500 races than any other team. In addition, Penske Racing has posted championships in such automotive racing circuits as Canadian-American Challenge Cup, and Sports Car Club of America (SCCA) Trans-Am, as well as posting wins on the National Association of Stock Car Racing (NASCAR)and Grand Prix Formula One tours. In addition, Penske organized the Championship Auto Racing Teams (CART) circuit in 1978, and owns the Michigan and Nazareth (Pennsylvania) International Speedways, North Carolina Speedway, and California Speedway, as well as coordinates the Cleveland Grand Prix IndyCar race. As a businessman, Penske is no less successful: Penske Corporation employs more than 30,000 people and generates estimated annual revenues of $11 billion through such businesses as Penske Truck Leasing, Penske Automotive, Penske Capital Partners, and the automotive retailer UnitedAuto Group. Penske is estimated to be one of the top-500 wealthiest individuals in the United States.

Roger Penske

Early Years

Roger Penske was born February 20, 1937, in Shaker Heights, Ohio, near Cleveland. His father was a corporate executive. In his early years, Penske bought and owned thirty-two cars over a span of ten years—cars that he raced and sold at a profit. These cars included an MG TD, MG TC, a Maserati, a Corvette, a Porsche, and a Jaguar Cooper. While he was in college at Lehigh University in Pennsylvania, he entered his first race at the Akron Speedway. He entered SCCA competition in 1958 at Sebring, driving an RS Porsche. The following year, he bought a Porsche RSK from racer Bob Holbert, and battled Holbert to win an SCCA class title the same year. In 1960, he won the SCCA F Modified class title. One year later, he obtained sponsorship from Zerex, bought and modified a Maserati renamed the Telar Special, and set a speed record at Road America. Penske's deal with Zerex is often considered groundbreaking for its introduction of corporate sponsorship into the world of motorsports.

Professional Racer

Penske graduated from college in 1962, and went to work for the aluminum company Alcoa. He also abandoned his status as a semi-professional racer to turn professional. He bought a Cooper-Climax Formula One race car, which he converted into a two-seater sports car. He outfitted the car's chassis with a lightweight aluminum body, and named it the Zerex Special. He took the Special to earnings of $34,350 in 1962, which also

Chronology

1937	Born February 20 in Shaker Heights, Ohio
1958	Drives first official race in the SCCA National at Marlboro Motor Raceway, Maryland
1959	Wins first race at SCCA Regional at Lime Rock, Connecticut
1963	Wins NASCAR Grand National race
1964	Wins Nassau Trophy, Nassau Tourist Trophy, and Governor's Trophy
1965	Retires from race-car driving to run dealership in Philadelphia
1966	Launches Penske Racing; debuts as team owner at Sebring
1969	Penske Racing wins 24 Hours of Daytona
1972	Penske Racing wins first Indianapolis 500
1973	Team Penske wins first NASCAR race at Riverside, California
1974	Penske Racing enters Grand Prix Formula One racing
1975	Mark Donohue, Penske's driver, dies in crash during Formula One practice; Penske Racing wins both NASCAR races at Darlington
1976	Penske Racing wins Austrian Grand Prix with driver John Watson
1976	Penske abandons Formula One to focus on IndyCar racing
1979	Penske driver Rick Mears wins pole position for every oval track in IndyCar racing as well as wins Indianapolis 500
1981	Penske driver Bobby Unser wins Indianapolis 500
1984	Mears wins second Indianapolis 500 of career, fourth for Penske Racing
1985	Penske driver Danny Sullivan wins team's fifth Indianapolis 500
1987	Al Unser wins Indianapolis 500 with car chassis taken from a hotel-lobby display
1988	Mears wins Penske Racing's seventh Indianapolis 500
1991	Mears becomes one of three drivers to win four Indianapolis 500s
1993	Penske driver Emerson Fittipaldi posts team's ninth Indianapolis 500 win
1994	Al Unser, Jr., wins pole position and wins Indianapolis 500; Penske drivers post top-three finishes in five races, win twelve of sixteen races, and earn ten pole positions
2001	de Ferran wins second CART FedEx Series Championship; Penske drivers Helio Castroneves and de Ferran post top-two finishes at Indianapolis 500; Penske announces this will be last year Penske Racing will compete in CART
2002	Racing in the Indy Racing League (IRL), Castroneves wins Penske Racing's twelfth Indianapolis 500

earned him the title "Driver of the Year" in the *New York Times*. Penske entered the 1963 NASCAR Grand National Series in 1963, winning five races driving a Corvette Chaparral GS. In 1964, Penske set the motorsports world on fire. Competing at the Bahamas Speed Week, he drove a Corvette Grand Sport to win the Nassau Tourist Trophy. He then drove a Jim Hall Chaparral to defeat contenders Bruce McLaren, Dan Gurney, and **A. J. Foyt** for the Nassau Trophy. He retired from racing at this point, buying a Chevrolet dealership in Pennsylvania. He returned to racing briefly, entering the 1966 Sebring race in a Corvette Grand Sport.

Team Owner

In 1966, Penske bought a Lola T70 and hired Mark Donohue as his fulltime driver, inaugurating Penske Racing. Fielding Chevrolet Camaros and, later, AMC Javelins, in Trans-Am competition; Porsche 917-10 and 917-30 Turbopanzers in Canadian-American Challenge Cup competition; and the Lola in such races as the 24 Hours of Daytona, Penske Racing became a force to be

Awards and Accomplishments

1961	Wins SCCA National D Modified championship and is named Sports Illustrated SCCA Driver of the Year
1962	Named New York Times Driver of the Year, wins U.S. Auto Club's road-racing championship
1967	Penske Racing wins United States Road Racing Championship (USRRC)
1968	Penske Racing won USRRC championship
1968-73	Penske Racing won SCCA Trans-Am
1981	Penske driver Rick Mears wins national CART points championship
1982	Mears wins national CART points championship
1983	Penske driver Al Unser wins national CART points championship
1988	Sullivan wins CART championship
2001	Penske driver Gil de Ferran wins second CART FedEx Series Championship

reckoned with by securing championships in the USRRC series in 1967 and 1968, and SCCA Trans-Am championships in 1968, 1969, and 1971, 1972, and 1973.

In 1971, Penske Racing entered IndyCar racing. Donohue qualified for the pole at the Sears Point 150 in April that year, and scored the team's first victory at the Pocono 500 in July. The following year, Donohue won the Indianapolis 500, the first of twelve wins that Penske Racing would earn before 2003, with such drivers as **Al Unser, Sr.**, **Bobby Unser**, **Rick Mears**, Danny Sullivan, **Emerson Fittipaldi**, Paul Tracy, Gil de Ferran, and Helio Castroneves. By 2001, the team had amassed a staggering eleven national championships in IndyCar racing.

Penske's efforts in the international Grand Prix Formula One series were less successful. Following a crash during practice session for the 1975 Austrian Grand Prix, Donohue died. Penske persevered, however, and posted a win in the 1976 Austrian Grand Prix with John Watson driving a PC4-Ford. This would be Penske Racing's only Formula One win, however, as he decided to quit the series at the end of the 1976 season. Penske Racing's win marked only the third time that a team from the United States won a Formula One event.

In the mid-1970s, Penske Racing also began fielding cars in the NASCAR circuit. Driver Bobby Allison drove an AMC Matador to two wins at Darlington Speedway in 1975. Penske Racing's streak of NASCAR successes extended into the twenty-first century with driver Rusty Wallace.

Series Co-Founder and Track Owner

One of the most successful team owners in the history of IndyCar racing, Penske co-founded Championship Auto Racing Teams (CART) in 1978 with fellow team owner U. E. "Pat" Patrick. Both founders were unhappy with the management of the IndyCar series, prompting them to start CART. By 1981, CART was offering more prize money than its competitor and became the domi-

nant IndyCar competitive series. In 2002, Penske abandoned CART and threw his support, his drivers, and his cars into the Indy Racing League (IRL).

In addition to being a winning team owner in several motorsports series, Penske also has been adept at the business end of the sport. As owner of Michigan International Speedway, Pennsylvania International Speedway, North Carolina Speedway and Carolina Speedway, Penske has generated millions of dollars in revenues. In 1999, he merged Penske Motorsports, Inc., with International Speedway Corporation in a deal that was estimated to control more than one hundred motorsports events, 800,000 seats, and 400 suites.

Honored for Motorsports Achievements

In 2001, Porsche honored Penske and other former Porsche drivers and team owners at a Porsche Rennesport Reunion at Connecticut's Lime Rock Park. As part of the festivities, Penske drove the Porsche 917/30 that Mark Donohue drove during the 1973 Canadian-American Championship Cup tour. In 1995, Penske was inducted into the Motorsports Hall of Fame and Museum of America. The Hall of Fame' Web site includes the following assessment of Penske's accomplishments: "Few men have cast as large a shadow over their respective fields as Penske. Even as a privateer, he always insisted that his cars look impeccable. And nobody ever earned the Unfair Advantage as often as he did, whether it be by turning a Formula I wreck into a world-beating sports car, building special refueling rigs for lightning-fast Trans-Am pit stops, introducing turbocharging to the Can-Am series, or developing an entirely new engine to win a single race, the 1994 Indy 500."

FURTHER INFORMATION

Other

"Grand Prix Drivers: Roger Penske." Grand Prix.com. http://www.grandprix.com (January 18, 2003).

"Roger Penske." International Motorsports Hall of Fame. http://www.motorsportshalloffame.com/halloffame/1998/Roger_Penske_main.htm (January 18, 2003).

"Roger Penske." Motorsports Hall of Fame and Museum of America. http://www.mshf.com/index.htm?/hof/penske_roger.htm (January 18, 2003).

Sketch by Bruce Walker

Gaylord Perry
1938-

American baseball player

Gaylord Perry

Chronology

1938	Born September 15 in Williamston, North Carolina
1958	Drafted by San Francisco Giants
1962	Played three games in the Major Leagues
1963	Batting-practice and game pitcher, San Francisco Giants
1964	Pitched in famous 23-inning game against New York Mets
1971	Traded to Cleveland Indians
1974	Traded to Texas Rangers
1978	Traded to San Diego Padres
1979	Traded back to Texas Rangers
1980	Traded to New York Yankees
1980	Became a free-agent, signed with Atlanta Braves
1982	Signed with Seattle Mariners
1982	Ejected from a game for doctoring the ball
1983	Played for Kansas City Royals
1983	Ended Major League playing career
1986	Filed for bankruptcy protection after farm fails

Gaylord Perry has held many distinctions—in 1982, he was the oldest player in the major leagues; he was also the fifteenth pitcher in the game's history to record 300 lifetime victories. He's played in All-Star games representing both the American and National leagues, taken home two **Cy Young** Awards (the first player to do so in both leagues), and in 1991 was inducted into the Baseball Hall of Fame. But if the right-hander were remembered in no other way, Perry could well go down in baseball history as the "king of the spitballs."

A native of Williamston, North Carolina, Perry was preceded in birth by his brother, Jim, who also ended up in the Major Leagues. The young family resided in a tenant farming community, where the baseball-happy brothers spent their after-school time either harvesting in the fields or practicing their pitches. "We just pitched until we got tired," Perry later wrote in his book, *Me and the Spitter: An Autobiographical Confession* "And a desire to win just developed naturally. I believe the long hot hours in the fields gave Jim and me a physical and mental discipline that has helped us on the mound."

Perry was introduced to organized ball in high school. As a member of the Williamston High team in his freshman year, he threw two shutouts on the way to winning the state championship. The youngster continued to develop over the next few years; by the time he was a junior, Perry had completed five no-hitters and allowed not a single earned run. Lured to the semipros be-

fore his senior year, Perry played in Alpine, Texas, where he developed some new moves, including his curve and a side-arm delivery. On his graduation in 1958, Perry was signed by the San Francisco Giants for what was then a record amount for a rookie: $91,000. He quickly sent $30,000 to his parents to help them pay for their home, devastated by a hurricane a year earlier.

Minor Setbacks

The young pitcher reported to the Giants' farm club in St. Cloud, Minnesota, where he posted a 9-5 win-loss record. At the end of the 1958 season Perry, who wished to explore a college career, enrolled in Campbell Junior College in Buies Creek, North Carolina. At six-foot-four, Perry had been admitted on a basketball scholarship, but Perry was soon compelled to leave the school after the Giants decreed that he could not play basketball while a member of their organization.

So Perry took to the road, following his franchise into the minor leagues. Four years of developing his arm in the minors led him to San Francisco, where in 1962 Perry was given his first shot at a Major League game. He won three games for the Giants before being sent back to Tacoma, Washington, to complete the '62 season. But by 1963 Perry was back in San Francisco in what he described as his worst season. In thirty-one games he posted only one win, with a relatively high 4.03 earned-run average (ERA).

The year 1964 turned out to be a watershed one for Perry: it was the year he learned the spitball. Illegal in the majors, a spitball has the pitcher coating the ball with saliva or some other slick substance. The doctored ball will thus become an extreme "sinker" as it approaches the plate. Bob Shaw, a spitball expert, had joined the Giants organization and instructed Perry in the basics, which include how to hide the presence of the banned ball from "four umpires, three coaches, and

Awards and Accomplishments

1958	Signed with San Francisco for highest sum yet paid for a rookie
1961	Named Pacific Coast League Pitcher of the Year
1966	Winning pitcher, All-Star game
1968	Led National League in innings pitched
1970	Led National League in shutouts.
1970	With brother, Jim Perry, became first brothers to play All-Star game in same year
1971, 1974	Cy Young Award
1972	Member of American League All-Star team
1979	Member, National League All-Star team
1991	Inducted into Baseball Hall of Fame

Where Is He Now?

Gaylord Perry's retirement from baseball took the former pitcher and his family to Martin County, North Carolina. Perry began a new life as a farmer, as his parents had been, growing corn, soybeans, tobacco and peanuts. Unfortunately, the widespread misfortune endured by many farmers in the 1980s affected Perry; in 1986 he filed for Chapter 7 bankruptcy protection, explaining simply, "It's a farm situation." On a brighter note, in 1991 Perry was elected into the Baseball Hall of Fame in Cooperstown, New York.

twenty-five players on the field as well as spying executives up on the box seats," as he later wrote in his autobiography. The key, Perry noted, was in the use of the fingers: "Those days you were allowed by the rules to lick your fingers as long as you wiped them dry. A great decoy was going to the resin bag after licking your first and second fingers. You bounced the dusty bag all around in your pitching hand, but those two fingers never got a touch of dry resin."

The Spitball Artist

Among the 1964 games that featured a Perry spitball was the notable "longest day," a marathon May 31 double-header pitting the Giants against the New York Mets that culminated in a twenty-three-inning second-game tiebreaker. After taking the mound in the thirteenth inning, Perry began wetting his fingers in the fifteenth inning. In the twentieth inning, an unidentified Giants player slipped Perry a round, brown tablet. "That was my first taste of slippery elm," Perry later wrote. "The juice in my mouth was slicker than an eel's." With the Mets unable to claim a run off the juiced-up baseball, the Giants won the game 8-6.

At the same time, Perry's legitimate pitching improved. He finished 1964 with a 12-1 record, and after a 1965 slump of 8-12, came back even stronger in 1966, posting twenty-one wins in twenty-nine games and serving as the winning hurler in that year's All-Star game. The next year brought a challenge to Perry's signature spitball: the new league rules banned wetting the fingers before a throw. That led to the "greaseball," a collection of liquids and semisolids intended to make Perry's pitches even more intimidating. There was the mudball, the sweatball, the K-Y (jelly) ball, and the Vaseline ball; Perry claimed he must have "tried everything on the old apple but salt and pepper and chocolate-sauce topping."

By the late '60s the athlete, at age thirty, was firmly established on the mound. Never known for his batting prowess, Perry nonetheless made good on an unusual prediction. In 1962, according to a *Sports Illustrated* article, Giants then-manager Alvin Dark predicted "there will be a man on the moon" before Perry hit a home run.

On August 4, 1969—thirty-four minutes after the U.S. manned spacecraft *Apollo 11* made its historic first moon landing-Perry hit his first home run.

In 1971 Perry was traded to the Cleveland Indians—the first of many transfers that would later mark his career. He pitched for Cleveland starting in 1972, posting a 24-16 record. Over the next three seasons his performance varied, from a 19-19 record in 1973 to a less-than-stellar 2-9 record in 1975, during which time Perry was traded to the Texas Rangers. His game improved initially (12-8 during the remainder of '75), then slumped in subsequent seasons to 15-14 in 1976 and 15-12 in 1977.

Time Catches up with a Pitcher

In 1978 Perry was pushing forty—an old pro in a young man's game. He was traded to the San Diego Padres and quickly put to rest any implication that he was past his prime, pitching a 21-6, 2.72 ERA season and leading the National League in wins. But Perry reportedly wasn't happy with San Diego, a team he regarded as lacking in ambition. The pitcher responded in kind, letting his win-loss record slow to 12-11 in 1979. Over the next year the pitcher ping-ponged from San Diego, back to Texas, then to the New York Yankees, who acquired Perry in late 1980.

Perry became a free-agent in late 1980, and chose to sign with the Atlanta Braves; a players' strike that year shortened his season to 8-9, with a 3.93 ERA. He was released from that team at the end of the 1981 season. By now nearly forty-four years old, branded as a spitball artist, and known for a fiery temperament that sometimes alienated his teammates, Perry seemed an uncertain prospect for future employment. But in 1982 Seattle Mariners did sign the pitcher at a cost of $50,000, a fraction of what Perry had earned playing for Atlanta.

The year turned out to be one of highs and lows for Perry. He recorded his 300th career win on May 6, after beating the New York Yankees 7-3. But the occasion was also notable for three inspections of Perry's baseball looking for signs of tampering. No evidence was found that day, but two months later, in a game against the Boston Red Sox, an umpire ruled that Perry had doctored the ball, fining him $250 and suspending him for ten days. But Perry's signature spitballs did have an influence on the Mariners, helping lift the struggling team

Career Statistics

Yr	Team	W	L	ERA	GS	CG	SHO	IP	H	BB	SO
1962	SFG	3	1	5.23	7	1	0	43.0	54	14	20
1963	SFG	1	6	4.03	4	0	0	76.0	84	29	52
1964	SFG	12	11	2.75	19	5	2	206.3	179	43	155
1965	SFG	8	12	4.19	26	6	0	195.7	194	70	170
1966	SFG	21	8	2.99	35	13	3	255.7	242	40	201
1967	SFG	15	17	2.61	37	18	3	293.0	231	84	230
1968	SFG	16	15	2.44	38	19	3	291.0	240	59	173
1969	SFG	19	14	2.49	39	26	3	325.3	290	91	233
1970	SFG	23	13	3.20	41	23	5	328.7	292	84	214
1971	SFG	16	12	2.76	37	14	2	280.0	255	67	158
1972	CLE	24	16	1.92	40	29	5	342.7	253	82	234
1973	CLE	19	19	3.38	41	29	7	344.0	315	115	238
1975	CLE	6	9	3.55	15	10	1	121.7	120	34	85
1975	TEX	12	8	3.03	22	15	4	184.0	157	36	148
1976	TEX	15	14	3.24	32	21	2	250.3	232	52	143
1977	TEX	15	12	3.37	34	13	4	238.0	239	56	177
1978	SDP	21	6	2.73	37	5	2	260.7	241	66	154
1979	SDP	12	11	3.06	32	10	0	232.7	225	67	140
1980	TEX	6	9	3.43	24	6	2	155.0	159	46	107
1980	NYY	4	4	4.44	8	0	0	50.7	65	18	28
1981	ATL	8	9	3.94	23	3	0	150.7	182	24	60
1982	SEA	10	12	4.40	32	6	0	216.7	245	54	116
1983	SEA	3	10	4.94	16	2	0	102.0	116	23	42
1983	KCR	4	4	4.27	14	1	1	84.3	98	26	40
TOTAL		314	265	3.11	690	303	35	5350.3	4938	1379	3534

CLE: Cleveland Indians; KCR: Kansas City Royals; NYY: New York Yankees; SDP: San Diego Padres; SEA: Seattle Mariners; SFG: San Francisco Giants; TEX: Texas Rangers.

from the ratings basement to land in fourth place in the American League West.

If Perry's best days were behind him—he hadn't posted an ERA under 3.0 since 1978—he continued to show his determination, playing for Seattle and, in late 1983, for the Kansas City Royals. *Time* writer Tom Callahan characterized Perry, at nearly forty-five, as "the most elderly player in either league." But the pitcher had few doubts about his ability to keep playing. "For me, it's a pretty good job and it pays well—that's why I'm still playing," he remarked to Callahan. At the end of the 1983 season Perry retired from professional play, having posted 314 wins in twenty-two years in big-league baseball representing both the American and National leagues. He and his brother, Jim, held a record as the winningest pitching siblings until 1987, when brothers Phil and Joe Niekro took the title.

CONTACT INFORMATION

Address: c/o Baseball Hall of Fame, P.O. Box 590, Cooperstown, NY 13226-0590.

SELECTED WRITINGS BY PERRY:

Me and the Spitter: An Autobiographical Confession, Saturday Review Press, 1974.

FURTHER INFORMATION

Books

(With Bob Sudyk) *Me and the Spitter: An Autobiographical Confession*. Saturday Review Press, 1974.

Periodicals

Callahan, Tom." As Good as Anyone Ever." *Time*. (August 22, 1983).
"Dark Prophecy." *Sports Illustrated*. (July 19, 1993).
Wulf, Steve. "Commotion in the Hall." *Sports Illustrated*. (January 21, 1991).

Sketch by Susan Salter

Duane Peters
1961-

American skateboarder

Skateboard champion and punk-rock vocalist Duane Peters has been an idol of the underground skate-punk movement for nearly three decades. Known among

Chronology

1961	Born in Anaheim, California
1975	Drops out of high school as a ninth-grader; discovers underground skateboarding culture
late 1970s	Invents own skateboarding tricks; begins earning money performing at skate shows
1978	Discovers punk rock music
1980s	Sings vocals in punk bands; performs in skateboarding competitions
1994	Forms punk band the U.S. Bombs
late 1990s	Launches recording label Disaster Records
1999	Forms punk band Duane Peters & the Hunns

his fans as the Master of Disaster, Peters is largely credited with pioneering the counterculture that unites skateboarding and punk music. Skin-headed, missing his two front teeth, and festooned with tattoos and safety-pin earrings, he has been skateboarding since the late 1970s, and has led such punk bands as the U.S. Bombs and The Hunns. A heroin user in his earlier days, Peters renounced drugs in his mid-30s. Peters, who turned 40 in 2001, remains a strong presence in extreme sports and alternative music.

Peters's parents divorced when he was a child in Anaheim, California, and Peters went to live with his father, a used-car salesman, in nearby Newport Beach. A rebellious youth, Peters often skipped school. Hoping to discipline his son, his father sent Peters to live for a year with relatives on a farm in Michigan. "I went to school every day that year because there was nothing else to do," Peters told Rich Kane of *OC Weekly*.

Returning to live with his father, Peters dropped out of school at age 14. By then he had discovered the underground skateboarding scene of the mid-1970s. Not having the money to buy a skateboard, he made one for himself by sawing off a piece of wood and nailing on roller-skate wheels. He spent his days skate-surfing the sidewalks of Newport Beach and nearby Balboa. "I just wanted to skate all the time and didn't want to have to go to work," he told Kane of *OC Weekly*. "I didn't want to grow up."

Invented Skateboarding Tricks

In the days before skate parks, youths such as Peters and his friends liked to practice skating in empty swimming pools. Breaking into neighbors' backyards, they skateboarded in underground pools until the police chased them out. In pools and empty half-pipes, Peters honed his skills and started inventing his own signature skateboarding tricks. Like his idol, motorcycle stunt rider Evel Knievel, Peters often injured himself, earning the nickname Master of Disaster. At 16, practicing in a 14-foot pipe, he perfected an upside-down, 360-degree loop, a stunt that seemed to defy gravity. With this trick he caught the attention of *Skateboarder* magazine; soon

he was offered money to perform in skate shows, and even made a skateboarding appearance on the 1970s television show *That's Incredible!* A regular winner in skating contests, Peters had developed a reputation in the skateboarding subculture.

In 1978, Peters, then 17, discovered punk rock. Hearing a recording of punk band The Ramones, he took an instant liking to the music. Soon he was collecting records by such punk groups as Generation X, the Dead Boys, and the Sex Pistols. Peters and some of his friends cut their hair in punk styles and started frequenting punk clubs such as the Cuckoo's Nest in Costa Mesa, California. Eventually Peters and his cohorts started forming their own bands and performing in Southern California clubs. Out of the skateboarding subculture, a new punk-skate subculture was born, with Peters at the center.

"A lot of us were from broken homes," Peters told John Roos of the *Los Angeles Times*. "We were freaks and misfits. That's why we found punk rock, and it took us in.... We suddenly had somewhere to go."

Influenced by drug-using punk-idol Sid Vicious, Peters and his friends started experimenting with heroin. It didn't take long for the skate-punker to become hooked. For the next 15 years, he struggled with addiction, spending all of his skateboarding prize money on drugs. As a junkie, he was often in trouble with the law, charged with drug possession and trafficking. In and out of jail throughout his 20s and 30s, his time behind bars amounted to six or seven years. Peters quit using heroin in his mid-30s, substituting alcohol for drugs. When he developed liver problems, he eventually quit drinking, too. Living a clean, drug-free lifestyle, Peters became more active in music and skateboarding.

Fronts '90s Punk Bands

In 1994 Peters formed his punk band, the U.S. Bombs, with guitarists Kerry Martinez and Chuck Briggs, bassist Wade Walston, and drummer Chip Hanna. Signing with Alive records in 1996, the group released its first album, *Garibaldi Guard*. In his husky voice, Peters barked out angry lyrics he had penned himself; many of his songs conveyed defiant political and social messages. As a concert performer, Peters became known for his highly physical onstage manner. Fusing his skateboarding style with his musical performance, he would pull stunts and turn flips, often deliberately abusing his body.

After five years with the U.S. Bombs, Peters put the band on hold to form a new group, Duane Peters & the Hunns (later known simply as The Hunns). This punk-rock quintet released its first album, *Unite,* in June 2000 on Disaster Records, a recording label that Peters had co-founded with independent record executive Patrick Boissel. The same year, he announced his engagement to longtime girlfriend Trisha Maple. The couple did not marry, however; by 2002 Peters had a new squeeze, Hunns bassist Corey Parks.

Peters lives in Huntington Beach, California, and continues to perform with his two punk bands, the U.S. Bombs and The Hunns. In January 2002 The Hunns released a third album, *Wayward Bantams,* on Peters' recording label Disaster Records. With his record company, he has assembled a roster of punk bands, such as the Crowd, Smogtown, and the Pushers. Peters also continues to participate in professional skating competitions, pulling such stunts as lay-back roll-outs, sweepers, and tail-slide reverts. "I feel good about being 40," he told *OC Weekly* in June 2001. "I'm still skating better than most 25-year-olds. I still look alive onstage. I don't see me slowing down. I'm just trying to get wiser."

Maintains Hardcore Following

Through his drug addictions and rehabilitations, and during his long and varied punk music career, Peters has continued skateboarding. As a member of the skateboarding club Beer City, he has participated in contests nationwide through his late 30s and into his early 40s. Within the skate-punk subculture, he has maintained a devoted following, and is celebrated as a pioneer.

FURTHER INFORMATION

Periodicals

Kane, Rich. "Duane's Addictions." *OC Weekly* (Orange County, California; June 22, 2001): 21.

Libes, Howard. "How the Skate Punks Conquered Europe." *Los Angeles Times* (August 11, 2002): I-16.

Roos, John. "Skateboarding, Punk Inspire a Hunn's Salvation." *Los Angeles Times* (December 5, 2000): B6.

Other

"Duane Peters Interview." Skaterock.com. http://www.skaterock/com/features/duanepeters.html (January 24, 2003).

"Duane Peters & the Hunns." Disaster Records. http://www.disasterecords.com/Hunns.html (January 24, 2003).

Sketch by Wendy Kagan

Viktor Petrenko
1969-

Ukrainian figure skater

An Olympic champion with a heart of gold, figure skater Viktor Petrenko is known for his finesse on skates and for the finesse of his heart. With his trademark grace and poise on the ice, he skated to gold-medal championships in international amateur competition and generously used his influence to raise funds and otherwise assist with worthy causes both internationally and at the personal level. Following the breakdown of his national identity, the Soviet Union in 1991, Petrenko broke new ground as an international representative of the newly recognized independent Ukraine. In the mid 1990s he immigrated to the United States where he raises a family, performs, teaches, and maintains close ties with his homeland.

Petrenko was born in the Black Sea port city of Odessa on June 27, 1969. His parents, Tamara and Vassily were engineers. Petrenko, the eldest of their two sons, was never athletic by nature. He was, in fact, a sickly child, but he enjoyed soccer, and his parents encouraged him to skate at the local rink so that he might develop more stamina and strength. He also studied classical dance and was an accomplished student of ballet.

A Rising Star

Petrenko, having begun skating at age five, was ten years old when he first caught the notice of coach Galina Zmievskaya. In observing him on the ice, she recognized his potential as a figure skater and took him and his brother, Vladimir, under her charge. Petrenko, an able student, managed his first triple jump at age eleven.

By his mid teens Petrenko was a world-class skater. He won the Junior World Championship at age fourteen and placed on the Soviet national team. With practice he matured admirably as a skater, unusually graceful and very smooth, he was notable for his layback spins. He has been called the Baryshnikov of the rink for his grandeur and eloquent flourish on ice.

Petrenko advanced in his skill, and in 1984 he performed internationally on tour. In 1988 he emerged as a major international presence on ice when he took the bronze medal in the men's individual figure skating competition at the Olympics in Calgary, Canada. He took another bronze that year—at the World Championships in Budapest—and by the end of the season was the number one ranked skater in the world. Petrenko had mastered the triple axel at age sixteen but was never completely comfortable with quadruple spins. In practicing to perfect his quadruple toe loop after the Skate Canada meet in 1988 he tore a muscle in his pelvis and spent weeks away from the ice in a painful recuperation.

Viktor Petrenko

The injury left him unable to sit, and after missing the European championships altogether he returned to competition, but placed a disappointing sixth at the World Championships.

Once healed he made his presence felt when he returned to the ice for the 1989-90 season. That year he took the first of his two consecutive European Championships and finished with a silver medal at the Worlds and a silver from the Goodwill Games. He went on to win the Skate America competition and back-to-back trophies from the Japan Skating Foundation (NHK). At the World Championships in 1990-91 he accomplished the second of back-to-back silver medals.

With the breakup of the Soviet Union in 1991, Petrenko shed the weight of an outer core of national identity. No longer a member of the Soviet National team, he now skated for his homeland, Ukraine, a member of the Commonwealth of Independent States (CIS), a more intimate association with a greater commonality. Now a Ukrainian national, Petrenko, it seemed, burst out from his holding pattern and let loose with a never-before-seen vigor in his competitive demeanor. After a second place finish at the European championships, he skated to Olympic gold in Albertville, France, and then to gold again, at the World Championships in Oakland, California. Enjoying the view from the pinnacle of international competition, he embarked triumphantly on the Tour of Champions.

With his career in first place he pushed his professional life aside to focus on personal matters. After completing the tour he returned to Odessa for his wedding to Nina Melnik on June 19. Melnik, the daughter of Zmievskaya, had been a companion of Petrenko since childhood. They and their families had grown close, and a week-long wedding celebration ensued, capped by an Israeli honeymoon for the pair.

Professional Turned Amateur

With Olympic and world championships in his pocket, Petrenko made the decision to skate professionally. He moved with his family to Las Vegas where he trained with Karin Doherty at the Santa Fe ice rink. Unprotected by the rigorous demands of amateur competition, the professional circuit proved tumultuous for Petrenko.

Beginning in 1994 the Olympics was staggered into a biennial schedule with the winter Olympics scheduled for 1994 and at four-year intervals thereafter. To encourage greater competition for the transitional winter games in Lillehammer in 1994, the International Skating Union (ISU) passed a one-time-only resolution allowing professional athletes to reclaim amateur status that year for the purpose of Olympic competition. Then twenty-five years old, Petrenko accepted the ISU offer and returned to Odessa to train and qualify for the competition. He made his appearance at the games, this time skating for the fully independent Ukraine, not the CIS. Although a medal eluded him, Petrenko placed fourth and left Lillehammer gratified for the experience.

Up close and personal, Petrenko befriended the hard-knocks Olympian Oksana Baiul and convinced Zmievskaya to take the young figure skater into her

Awards and Accomplishments	
1983	Won the Junior World Championships
1986	First place, Golden Spin
1988	Bronze medal at the Calgary Olympics
1989-90	First place, Skate America; Japan Skating Foundation Trophy
1990-91	Won the European Championships
1992	Gold medal at the Albertville Olympics; gold medal at the Worlds Championships; first place, Miko Masters
1993	First place, Skate America; first place, Nations Cup
1994	First place, European Championships; first place, North American Open; first place, Skate America
1995	First place, Challenge of Champions
1996	First place, Men's Pro Championships
1997	First place, U.S. Pro Championships; first place, Ice Wars

home when the loss of family became an overwhelming burden for the girl. On his return to the United States, he resumed professional status and moved with his family to Simsbury, Connecticut, where a colleague, Bob Young, had built the International Skating Center. Petrenko made the move along with Melnik, her mother, and Baiul. They were joined in Connecticut by **Ekaterina Gordeeva**, her husband Sergei Grinkov, and the couple's daughter. Soon afterward, to Petrenko's sadness, Grinkov died an untimely death of a heart attack in 1995. Petrenko's daughter, Viktoria, was born on July 21, 1997.

With Melnik teaching dance classes at the Skating Center, Petrenko supplemented his professional touring schedule as a skating pro at Young's ice center and went on tour with the "Nutcracker on Ice" in 1994-95. Despite an unfortunate slipped disk he managed to recuperate after seeking treatment in Odessa, and competed in the Tournament of Champions that season. In addition to purchasing a home in Simsbury in 1996, he assumed the role of Beast in Disney's "Beauty and the Beast" on ice. In competition at the Winter Open on December 17, 1999, he finished in second place.

His ongoing humanitarian efforts and personal kindness are as much a part of his life as his skating accomplishments. Early in his career, as an amateur skater in Moscow in April of 1986, he became overwhelmed with concern upon hearing of the explosion and meltdown at the Chernobyl nuclear power plant. In the 1990s, after making a name for himself as a skater, he became closely affiliated with a New Jersey-based relief fund, called Children of Chernobyl. He used his celebrity to raise funds for the organization, and made follow-up contacts to insure that the funds were being used effectively.

CONTACT INFORMATION

Address: c/o International Skating Center of Connecticut, 1375 Hopmeadow Street, P. O. Box 577, Simsbury, CT 06070. Online: www.geocities.com/Colosseum/Midfield/3907/CelebVik.htm.

FURTHER INFORMATION

Periodicals

Hartford Courant (January 6, 2002): H1.

Other

"Biography." www.geocities.com/Colosseum/Midfield/3907/longbio.htm (February 6, 2003).
"Viktor Petrenko." *Biography Resource Center Online.* Gale Group, 1999. www.galenet.com/servlet/BioRC (February 6, 2003).
"Viktor Petrenko." www.geocities.com/Colosseum/Midfield/3907/art17.htm (February 6, 2003).

Sketch by G. Cooksey

Lee Petty
1914-2000

American race car driver

Lee Petty was a key figure in the early development of stock car racing and the National Association for Stock Car Auto Racing Inc. (NASCAR). He contributed to the evolution of the sport from an illegal, back road event, to dirt tracks at local fairgrounds and other sites throughout the South and Midwest, to the latter-day super-speedways at Daytona, Florida, Charlotte, North Carolina, and other cities. By the time Petty retired—after sixteen years behind the wheel and 427 NASCAR starts—he had racked up fifty-five wins, an all-time high that stood until his son **Richard Petty** passed him on his way to 200 NASCAR victories, a record that still stands. Lee Petty was the first NASCAR driver to win three national championships; he finished fifth or better 231 times. Besides being one of the best drivers in NASCAR history, Lee Petty played a significant role in the transformation of stock car racing from a sport to a business, testified most clearly by the continuing success of the family firm he founded, Petty Enterprises.

Hard Times in the Rural South

Lee Petty was born in 1914 in rural North Carolina. His parents scraped out a living on the family farm and Petty grew up dirt poor. With the hard times of the Great Depression in the 1930s, Petty accepted whatever jobs were available in order to support his young wife, the former Elizabeth Toomes, and his two sons, Richard and Maurice. For a time he was a biscuit salesman and later he owned a small trucking company. Hard luck, however, was never far away. In 1943, after a freak wood stove

Lee Petty

accident, the family house burned to the ground in front of the horrified eyes of his wife and sons. Petty and his family saw their way through the catastrophe and soon converted a trailer into a new house.

Petty was something of a natural athlete. He played minor league baseball as a young man, and in his retirement became a scratch golfer. His passion, however, was automobiles, driving them and working on them. He was constitutionally unable to leave a car alone and much to the chagrin of his wife, he was always tinkering with the family vehicle. He was "improving it," he told her.

In the 1930s and early 1940s stock car races were nothing more than illegal drag races held on back roads; the only prizes were whatever wagers one was able to win. By the time World War Two ended, informal but legal meets were being held on dirt tracks throughout the South. In 1948, when he was already in his mid-thirties, Lee entered—and won—a race in Danville Virginia in a 1937 Plymouth he and his brother Julie had rebuilt. He came in second in his next race, an event in Roanoke Virginia. From the very beginning he possessed the remarkable consistency that would be a hallmark of his racing career, finishing in the top five in more than half the races he entered.

Petty's success was due as much to his temperament as to his ability on the track. At a time when stock car racing was populated by men out for a good time, drivers who thought nothing of partying into the wee hours, be-

Chronology

1914	Born March 14 in North Carolina
1948	Wins first race
1949	Founds Petty Enterprises
1949	Helps organize NASCAR event at Charlotte North Carolina
1953	First driver to install a roll bar on his car
1954, 1958-59	Wins NASCAR championship
1960	Wins last race when he protests would-be first time victory of Richard Petty
1961	Critically injured in qualifying heat for the Daytona 500
1964	Retires from stock car racing
1969	Inducted into National Motorsports Press Association's Hall of Fame
1990	Inducted into International Motorsports Hall of Fame
2000	Dies following stomach surgery

fore and after a race, Petty was different. Racing was much more than merely a hobby for him and he approached it with seriousness, calculation, and a singular determination to win. In his book *King Richard I* Petty's son Richard recalled his father telling him. "There ain't no second place, you win or you lose. That's the only two parts there are to racing." Petty had more than a fierce will to win. He also recognized that only the winners would be able to pay their way in 1940s racing, where expenses often ran into several thousand dollars while winner's purse rarely totaled more than $1000.

A NASCAR Pioneer

When NASCAR was founded in December 1947, the purpose of the association was to promote stock car racing—races that used standard car makes rather than the special Formula One automobiles driven at other established races. The first NASCAR event was held on December 16, 1948 at the old Daytona Beach track, a course that made its way through the streets of the city before heading out onto the sands of the beach itself. Petty was there, but he was unable to win the race. Not long after, he and Julie took part in organizing the first NASCAR event in Charlotte North Carolina, held on June 19, 1949 with a purse of $6000. Leading up to the race, Petty did not have a car of his own, so he called an unsuspecting friend and asked to borrow his 1948 Buick Roadmaster for the weekend. His sons, Richard, age eleven, and Maurice, age ten, acted as his pit crew at Charlotte. Petty was well-placed near the front of the pack and was challenging to win when his radius bar broke. The car went into a barrel roll. When the dust cleared, Petty had suffered a minor cut on his face but the borrowed car was wrecked beyond repair. To make matters worse, the Petty family had no vehicle to drive home. The incident taught Petty two important lessons. First, he began towing his race car with another car so he would never again be stranded. Second, he learned to do whatever he had to do to win—but to always save the car. He had learned the hard way: If the car didn't finish the race, you can't win.

Petty finished up the eight-race 1949 season second in points only to Red Byron. After the first Charlotte race, Petty bought the first of several Plymouths he would race. Plymouths didn't have the horsepower of other makes, but they were highly dependable, maneuverable, and one of the lightest cars on the market. After he won his first race in a Plymouth at Heidelburg, Pennsylvania, the make became a trademark of Petty's for several years. He started winning in them regularly, to the dismay of drivers in more powerful cars, like Cadillacs. "He used to take those little old Plymouths and just outthink people," Mark Bechtel quoted Richard Petty in *Sports Illustrated*,. "When they got him in Oldsmobiles, he won races. He won championships. He was blowing people away." In 1953 he switched to Dodges, a car with twice the horsepower. He also installed a roll bar on his Dodge—the first one in NASCAR. Whatever he drove he won or came very close. Between 1949 and 1959, he finished no lower than fourth place in any NASCAR Grand National event and was the first driver ever to win three Grand National titles.

Petty impressed almost everyone who saw him drive. "There wasn't any better driver than Lee Petty in his day," legendary stock-car racer **Junior Johnson** told the Associated Press's Estes Thompson. "There might have been more colorful drivers, but when it came down to winning the race, he had as much as anyone I've ever seen." Glen Wood told Rea McLeroy of the *Richmond Times Dispatch* "He was one of the toughest competitors there was at that time." His desire to win could border on mania at times. At one race, Petty pulled out of a pit stop before he realized his son Richard was still on the hood wiping off the windshield. Already back on the track, Lee signaled his son to hold on. He did—for dear life—as his father roared around the track once and back into the pits to drop him off. Petty did whatever he thought necessary to win. Most infamously, he attached his door plates with bare bolt ends sticking out inches, designed to tear into opponents bodies or, better, their tires, reminding drivers and spectators of a 20th century version of the race in the film *Ben Hur*.

The First Daytona 500

In 1959 Petty entered the inaugural running of the Daytona 500, NASCAR's answer to the Indianapolis 500. The race was held on a brand new track, the highly banked Daytona International Speedway. The race was a nail-biter that ended in a three-way photo finish between Petty, Johnny Beauchamp and Joe Weatherly. NASCAR officials immediately declared Beauchamp the winner. Petty was infuriated, particularly after he heard that a dozen newsmen unanimously thought Petty had won. Petty remained in Daytona for three days after the conclusion of the 500, campaigning for the victory. Finally, after reviewing the photos for days, NASCAR changed its ruling and named Lee Petty the winner. The victory marked the highlight of Petty's career.

Awards and Accomplishments	
1950	Mechanic of the Year
1954, 1958-59	NASCAR champion
1959	Winner Daytona 500
1969	Inducted into the National Motorsports Press Association's Hall of Fame
1990	Inducted into International Motorsports Hall of Fame

Two years later, Petty nearly lost his life in a qualifying race at Daytona. While attempting to avoid another driver who had gone into a spin Petty and Johnny Beauchamp hit each other. Lee's car was sent flying 150 feet over a wall and into a parking lot. Richard Petty witnessed the crash and described the aftermath in his autobiography: "There wasn't anything left of either car. There was blood everywhere, and they had just taken Daddy out of the car and were putting him in the back of an ambulance. He was lifeless." Petty suffered a crushed chest, punctured lung, fractured collarbone, and a broken leg, among other injuries. After days in a coma, Petty managed to pull through. He spent the next four months in a hospital bed.

Petty explained the accident, according to *Sports Illustrated*'s Mark Bechtel, by saying "It was a left turn, and we went straight." However, he was never the same afterwards. His son Richard noticed the difference the next time Lee drove. "It sure wasn't the Lee Petty of old," Richard wrote in his autobiography, "he didn't charge into the turns and he wasn't smooth. That's the part I noticed most." Petty drove in six more races, but his winning days were behind him, admitting in 1989 to the *Sporting News*'s Richard Sowers "That wreck in '61 took the desire out of me." His last win came in 1960 in Jacksonville Florida. He hung on until 1964, then retired after a race in Watkins Glen, New York, telling his sons it was not fun anymore.

Lee Petty always supported the racing ambitions of his son Richard, who began his career while Lee was still active. When the two drove against each other, Richard experienced first-hand what a hard-boiled competitor his father was. In one of Richard's very first races, Lee took his son into the wall in order to pass him. Richard thought he had recorded his first victory at a race in 1960—until a protest was filed claiming that Richard was actually a lap short at the finish. The protest, made by Lee Petty, was upheld and a new victor was named, also Lee Petty. "I would have protested even if it was my mother," Lee Petty said, according to Joseph Slano of the *New York Times*.. That race turned out to be his last win.

A Complicated Man

For some who knew him Lee Petty was uncommunicative, tight-fisted, and a dirty competitor. Others,

---

Related Biography: Racecar Driver Adam Petty

When seventeen-year-old Adam Petty, Lee Petty's great-grandson, drove his first race on April 11, 1998, he was writing the beginning of another chapter in the Petty family's book of records. It was the first time four generations of a single family had participated in a professional sport. From the start it was clear that he was cut from the same mold as his grandfather (Richard Petty) and great-grandfather. He won his first race just two months after his debut, the youngest winning driver ever in the American Speed Association, and won in his first Winston Cup race in 2000 before the assembled Petty clan. Three days later, Lee Petty passed away. Even as an amateur, Adam seemed to have a penchant for getting into wrecks. In May 2000, just five weeks after his great-grandfather's death, a bad crash ended Adam Petty's brief NASCAR career tragically. In a preliminary at the New Hampshire International Speedway, the 19-year-old lost control of his car and was killed when it hit the wall. The Petty dynasty had apparently come to an unexpected sudden end.

---

however, found that he was also a gentleman. Driver Ned Jarrett was close behind Petty for ten laps with no way to get past in one race. Finally Jarrett bumped Petty's car. After the race Petty pulled Jarrett aside and advised him to learn some manners when driving. However a few days later, when the two met at another track and Petty learned Jarrett didn't have a car to race, he told him that if he had known he would have brought one for him. "I learned right then that I'd got the man's respect," Jarrett said, according to Estes Thompson of the Associated Press. Those who knew Petty in his hometown of Level Cross, North Carolina felt that success and fame never changed him. Petty lived out his life in the same home he built for his family after their house burned down.

In his retirement, Lee Petty continued as head of Petty Enterprises. In his later years he became a fanatic golfer, playing often four times a week. In February 2000 he underwent surgery for a stomach aneurysm. He never recovered. On April 5, 2000 he passed away at Moses Cone Hospital in Greensboro, North Carolina.

Lee Petty left behind a legacy that is unique in professional sports. In addition to being a pioneer of NASCAR and one of its greatest drivers, and to compiling a record of wins that is still number six on the all-time NASCAR list—doubly remarkable considering he didn't start racing until he was already thirty-five—he started a formidable racing dynasty. His son Richard is the all-time leader in wins, his grandson Kyle drove, and—until his tragic death at 19—so did his great-grandson Adam Petty. It was the first time that four generations from a single family participated in a professional sport. It is unlikely sport will witness the likes of Lee Petty or his family again.

FURTHER INFORMATION

Books

Chapin, Kim. *Fast As White Lightning*. New York: Dial Press, 1981.

Petty, Richard, with William Neely. *King Richard I*. New York: Macmillan Publishing, 1986.

Periodicals

Bechtel, Mark. "The Patriarch: Lee Petty 1914-2000." *Sports Illustrated* (April 17, 2000): 26.

McLaurin, Jim. "Lee Petty, First Winner of Daytona 500, Dies in Greensboro, NC." *State* (April 6, 2000): 26.

McLeroy, Rea. "Racing Pioneer Dies; Lee Petty turned Family Business into Dynasty." *Richmond Times Dispatch* (April 6, 2000): C-1.

Siano, Joseph. "Lee Petty, 86, Racing Family Patriarch Dies." *New York Times* (April 7, 2000): B12.

Sowers, Richard. "Patriarch of His Sport's First Family." *Sporting News* (July 24, 1989): 59.

Woods, Skip. "Kings of the Road—Four Generations of Pettys." *Richmond Times Dispatch* (February 15, 1998): E-1.

Other

"Lee Petty March 14, 1914-April 5, 2000" http:// www. pettyracing.com/www2/main/drivers/lee.shtml (January 5, 2003).

"Lee Petty Nascar Win Career: 1949-64" http://www. nascar.com/2002/kyn/history/drivers/02/02/lpetty/ (January 5, 2003).

Thompson, Estes. "Lee Petty, Racing Family Patriarch, Dies at 86." http://www.detnews.com/2000/sports/ 0004/06/20000406-31608.htm (April 6, 2000).

Sketch by Gerald E. Brennan

Richard Petty
1937-

American race car driver

Richard Petty's thirty-four years of winning competition on the National Association of Stock Car Auto Racing (NASCAR) circuit—during most of which he was the overwhelmingly dominant force—earned him the fitting nickname "The King." His record is unprecedented and unlikely ever to be equaled: 200 wins in NASCAR competition; seven Winston Cup championships; a record 700 top ten finishes. In 1967 alone, he won twenty-seven races, and in 1971, twenty-one. Petty won at least one race in eighteen consecutive seasons, from 1960 until 1977. When he retired in 1992, his racing winnings totaled $7,757,964. But more than the winningest driver in NASCAR history, Richard Petty was far and away its most popular figure. He was a man of

Richard Petty

Chronology	
1937	Born July 2 in Level Cross, North Carolina to Lee and Elizabeth Petty
1949	Becomes Lee Petty's crew chief at age twelve
1958	Drives in his first NASCAR event
1959	Wins his first NASCAR race at Columbia Speedway
1960	Richard, Maurice, and Lee Petty race in the same event for the first and only time
1965	Pettys and Chrysler boycott NASCAR for part of the season when it bans their hemi-engine; Richard wins a national drag racing event
1967	Passes his father, Lee, for most career wins
1967	Wins ten consecutive races and 27 for the season
1970	Helps develop window net for stock cars after nearly losing his life in crash in race at Darlington, South Carolina
1973-74	Wins Daytona 500 two years in a row
1983	Celebrates 25 years in professional racing
1984	Wins 200th and final career race at Firecracker 400 at Daytona
1986	Makes 1000th career start
1988	Nearly loses his life in crash at Daytona 500
1991	Announces retirement
1992	Makes Fan Appreciation Tour
1995	Makes debut as color commentator on televised racing events
1999	Petty Enterprises celebrates 50th anniversary

the people who thought nothing of devoting eight or more hours to signing autographs for the legions of fans who turned out to see him wherever he appeared. Nine times fans voted him Winston Cup's most popular driver, and by the 1980s his fame had spread as far as Europe and Asia. It was Petty's common touch, far more than his dominance of the sport, that won NASCAR the following it enjoyed as the 1990s ended.

Richard Petty ranks in the pantheon of motor racing. He stands alone in stock car history: His 127 pole positions is a record, as are his twenty-seven victories in one season, his ten victories in a row, his 513 consecutive starts, and his 1,185 total starts. In addition, he has won seven Winston Cup championships, seven Daytona 500s, and was voted NASCAR's most popular driver in nine different years. What's more, Petty was an active participant in NASCAR history from its earliest inception when as a twelve-year-old, he was his father's pit crew chief into its period of greatest popularity in the 1970s, 1980s, and 1990s—popularity fueled by his own popularity among race fans. As NASCAR President Bill France Jr. told *USA Today* when Petty retired, "Richard Petty is NASCAR Winston Cup racing." That was no exaggeration.

Growing Up With Cars

Richard Petty was born on July 2, 1937 in Level Cross, North Carolina. He was the son of three-time NASCAR Grand National champion driver **Lee Petty** and

his wife Elizabeth. In 1943, after a fire that destroyed the Petty home, the family moved to Randleman where Petty and his brother Maurice attended elementary and high school.

Cars were an integral part of Petty and Maurice's lives from the time were old enough to be aware. Lee Petty was constantly repairing, rebuilding and racing automobiles. By the time the two boys were about to become teenagers, they were members—sometimes the only members—of their father's pit crew at races mounted by the nascent NASCAR. Racing was in Richard Petty's blood, whether it was wagons, bicycles or cars. Even as a young boy, he seized every advantage over his opponents. When he was eight, Richard, Maurice, and a friend were racing wagons. "I had a plan," he wrote in his autobiography, *King Richard I,* "I went straight to the reaper shed and got a can of axle grease from the shelf, and I took off each wheel and greased the daylights out of the axles.... Dale and Maurice didn't know they were in a race; they thought they were just playing, but I meant business. I beat them both by a country mile." Petty concluded: "*Racing Lesson Number One:* If you can get an advantage, take it." Unfortunately the other two boys caught on to his trick, teaching him that the secrets of such advantages had to be held close to the vest.

Petty was just eight when an uncle let him drive an old 1938 Ford pickup for farm chores for the first time. In the meantime, he was learning what made a car run from his father, who besides being one of the great drivers of his day, was a master mechanic. He loved fixing cars almost as much as driving them fast and when folks asked what he planned to be when he grew up, he would answer: his father's mechanic car-builder. "They always looked at me

---

Awards and Accomplishments

1959	NASCAR Grand National Rookie of the Year
1962, 1968, 1974-77	Most Popular Driver, Nascar
1964, 1966, 1971, 1973-74, 1979, 1981	Daytona 500 victory
1964, 1967, 1971-72, 1974-75, 1979	Winston Cup
1971	NASCAR Driver of the Year
1973	Inducted into North Carolina Sports Hall of Fame
1992	Awarded the Medal of Freedom by President Bush
1992	Inducted into Daytona's Stock Car Racing Hall of Fame
1997	Inducted into Motor Sports Hall of Fame

The King's Last Lap

Lee didn't so much encourage Richard to drive as not stand in his way. As he lay in a hospital bed, with a punctured lung, fractured chest, and broken left thigh, he told Richard the family car was now his to ride. He wondered if his boy's blood bubbled the same as his.

By then, the speed-way era was in full swing. The debut of the 2.5-mile Daytona Speed-way was followed by 1.5-mile tracks in Charlotte and Atlanta. Racing was about two-hundred-mile-per-hour speeds. It needed a new, more calculating driver. Lee bluntly drove the bullrings. His son decided to try something different. He seduced the speedways.

Richard drove closer to the wall than anyone, which is like leaning into a Mike Tyson punch, except that the wall hits harder. But Richard got along well with the wall. He was economical, deliberate, patient. When he saw that your tires were getting bald after all your foolish banging, he'd come down off the high groove like the devil himself, and you'd be passed, son.

"When they start the next race," he says matter-of-factly, "I won more than all them put together. Next was David Pearson. Then Bobby Allison. Dale Earnhardt may have won seven championships, but he ain't won but seventy-four races. He ain't but an honorable mention. After that, there's guys who won ten. And I won two hundred." How did that two hundredth feel, coming on July 4, 1984, with fireworks and a personal embrace by President Ronald Reagan? "Just another day in the life of Richard Petty," he says.

Source: Shaun Assael. *Esquire,* March 1997, p. 102.

---

like I was a little on the strange side, but it was the truth," he reported in *King Richard I,* "I wanted to see what made a car run; I didn't want to drive it." He was such a good mechanic that when he was just twelve years old, Lee made him his crew chief during races. Straight out of high school, Petty took a full-time job at his father's new racing company, Petty Engineering.

Joins the NASCAR Circuit

A day after he turned twenty-one, Petty let it be known that he was interested in racing. With an old Oldsmobile that Lee gave him, Petty drove in his first event in 1958, and followed the circuit across the country looking for his first win. Lee, in his own tight-lipped way, helped Petty learn the ropes. In his autobiography Petty reported the most important piece of advice that Lee gave him early on: "Richard, if you expect to make it in anything, you gotta put all you've got into it…. you have to work harder than the next guy if you expect to be a success." On the track, however, Lee treated his son in his usual take-no-prisoners racing fashion. In one early race, he forced Petty into the wall on a curve. In another, in 1959, Petty believed he had his first NASCAR victory—until Lee protested to a NASCAR official that Richard's laps had been miscounted. One lap short, Petty's victory was nullified and given to the second place finisher—Lee Petty.

In July 1959, when Petty finally won his first pro race at Columbia Speedway, his fabulous career was underway. He was named the NASCAR Grand National Rookie of the Year that same year. In 1960, he won his first Grand National event. In August 1960, for the first and only time, all three Pettys—Richard, Lee, and Maurice—took part in the same race, finishing second, third and eighth respectively. Petty won three races altogether that year, but finished in the Top ten thirty times, in the Top five sixteen times, and second in the NASCAR points standings. His years of watching his father and other racers up close was paying off. He knew how to drive strategically out on the track, and how other drivers used their cars. Petty was apparently an astonishingly relaxed driver. A physician who did a study of drivers' heart rates after driving hundreds of miles at dangerously high speeds with other drivers often only inches away, found that most exhibited wildly increased heartbeats. Petty's alone was virtually unaffected. The strain showed in other ways though. Years later ulcers ate away half of Petty's stomach, and the thunderous noise of the track had seriously impaired his hearing.

Between 1961 and 1964, Richard Petty came into his own as a driver. He won forty-five of the 262 NASCAR events in which he ran, finished in the Top five on a remarkable 147 occasions, and took home $317,536 in prize money. He recorded his first superspeedway win at the Daytona 500 in 1964 driving a Chrysler with a powerful 426-cubic-inch hemi-head engine. "The first time I cranked it," Petty told Bill Robinson of the *Atlanta Journal and Constitution,* "I thought it was gonna suck the hood into the engine." He won that Daytona after leading 184 of the race's 200 laps, an achievement Bill Robinson called "the most lopsided achievement in big-track history in American racing." In response to the overwhelming superiority of Petty's automobile to others, NASCAR banned the use of hemi-head engines. The Pettys protested the ban by pulling out of NASCAR briefly in 1965. For the first part of the season, Petty participated only in drag racing. He returned to NASCAR later in the summer after a mechanical failure in one of his cars caused an accident in which a young boy was killed.

By 1967, bad crashes had long since driven both Lee and Maurice out of racing. It was Richard's greatest

Richard Petty, sitting in car

year, however. He won twenty-seven of his forty-eight events, including ten consecutive wins, and his second NASCAR championship. His most unexpected victory that season came in Nashville Tennessee. He was in the lead until a blown tire caused him to crash. By the time his crew had him ready to go again he was ten laps behind the leaders. He made up ground doggedly, however, and ended up winning by five laps. Early in the 1967 season he scored his 55th career win, overtaking his father Lee as the NASCAR's all-time win leader. 1967 was also the year when Petty was given the nickname by which he is best known. "A bunch of reporters got together, sitting around drinking their Budweisers, and got to talkin'," he told Bruce Lowitt of the *St. Petersburg Times*. "If my name had been Dale or Kyle or Darrell, it wouldn't have sounded like much. I mean, King Dale? But Richard was just a natural to go with King. They just throwed it in there. They'd been trying to name me the Randleman Rocket, all kinds of names. Never took hold. But first time anybody saw King Richard, it stuck."

Petty continued to show why he was the King in the 1970s. He became the first NASCAR driver to pass $1 million in career earnings in 1971. That same year he won his third Daytona 500—the Super Bowl of NASCAR—and his fourth and fifth two years in a row

in 1973 and 1974. He won the 500 again just before the decade ended in 1979. Petty's most memorable Daytona 500, however, was in 1976—when he finished second. Petty was leading the race until its final lap when he was passed by David Pearson. When Petty attempted to get past Pearson on the last of Daytona's high-banked turns, he careened into Pearson's car and both spun off the wall and down toward the finish line. "For a bizarre moment," wrote the *Washington Post*'s Dave Kindred, "it seemed Petty would win his game's biggest prize spinning backward under the checkered flag." His car stopped short, however, its engine dead while Pearson inched his car across the finish line at about ten miles per hour. Petty survived a number of other serious accidents in the course of his career. He looked to be dead at the Darlington Speedway after hitting the wall on a turn, then pinwheeling end over end into the pit wall. Fortunately he suffered no more than a dislocated shoulder, but after the Darlington wreck Petty helped develop the window net, that keeps drivers from flying out the window during crashes.

When Petty's son Kyle won his very first race in 1979 it seemed the torch was being passed to a new generation of Pettys. In the 1980s, Richard Petty won fewer races, two in 1980, three 1981, three in 1983, and two in 1984, including Petty's seventh Daytona 500 win and a win at the Firecracker 400, which would be the last of his career. In 1989 his record string of 513 consecutive starts that stretched back to 1969 ended when he missed a race at Richmond Virginia. He continued to take home purses throughout the eighties, however, winning $3.79 million between 1980 and his retirement in 1991, more than he won during his first twenty-eight years when he was having his heyday.

Those figures hint at the popularity that NASCAR racing had achieved by the 1980s, a popularity for which Richard Petty was almost single-handedly responsible. "Richard's been one of the people who's brought racing from when it wasn't a very respectable sport to where it is today," **Junior Johnson**, a former NASCAR star told Darrell Fry of the *St. Petersburg Times*. "He's contributed more to the sport than any other individual." As much as for his wins, Petty was famous for his friendliness to fans, remaining at tracks for hours after races to sign autographs and press the flesh. His feather-laden cowboy hats, wraparound sunglasses and fabulous smiles were still synonymous with stock car racing in 2002, thanks in part to his long-time commercial endorsements of STP. Just before the start of the 1992 NASCAR season Petty announced his retirement. He fittingly dubbed his final season the "Fan Appreciation Tour." Tens of thousands turned out across the country to see his last runs. He didn't win a single race, but it was clear he was still the most beloved driver on the circuit.

After he hung up his helmet, Petty devoted himself to running the family business, with its stable of drivers—which by the end of the 1990s included Petty's grandson Adam—Petty Enterprises, as well as overseeing The Richard Petty Driving Experience. The venture, founded in 1990, gave amateurs an opportunity to drive a stock car on a real NASCAR track. In February 1995 Petty made his TV debut as color commentator for a CBS broadcast of the Daytona 500.

CONTACT INFORMATION

Address: Petty Enterprise, 311 Branson Mill Rd., Randleman, NC 27317. Online: http://www.pettyracing.com/.

SELECTED WRITINGS BY PETTY:

(With William Neely) *King Richard I,* Macmillan Publishing Company, 1986.

FURTHER INFORMATION

Books

Bledsoe, Jerry. *The World's Number One, Flat-Out, All-Time Great, Stock Car Racing Book.* New York: Doubleday, 1975.

Howell, Mark D. *From Moonshine to Madison Avenue: A Cultural History of the NASCAR.* Bowling Green, OH: Bowling Green State University Popular Press, 1997.

Periodicals

Bisher, Furman. "'King' Richard's reign." *Atlanta Journal and Constitution* (November 15, 1992).

Cawthon, Raad. Richard's Last Ride: The Making Of A Legend." *Atlanta Journal and Constitution* (November 15, 1992).

Clark, Ian M. "Petty born to race. Petty family goes from glory to tragedy." *Manchester Union Leader* (May 13, 2000).

Coble, Don. "Hometown hero hasn't forgotten his roots." *USA Today* (November 13, 1992).

Fry, Darrell. "The King." *St. Petersburg Times* (November 15, 1992).

Glick. Shav. "For Richard Petty, it's been a long, fun ride." *Houston Chronicle* (November 15, 1992).

Hudgens, Dallas. "Minutes of Thunder." *Washington Post* (June 28, 1998).

Kindred, Dave. "It Will Take a Heap of Booze-Running to Top Petty." *Washington Post* (February 19, 1978).

Minter, Rick "'Not retired, just recycled'." *Atlanta Journal and Constitution* (November 12, 1993).

Perrone, Vinnie. "Petty Goes Out With Blaze, Kulwicki Gets Glory." *Washington Post* (November 16, 1992).

"Richard's Last Ride: A Special Thank You To Fans." *Atlanta Journal and Constitution* (November 15, 1992).

Robinson, Bill. "Richard's Last Ride: The Races He Has Won Remembering Richard." *Atlanta Journal and Constitution* (November 15, 1992).

Thomy, Al. "Petty's first victory snatched away by father." *Atlanta Journal and Constitution* (November 15, 1992).

Tuschak, Beth. "Farewell To The King." *USA Today* (November 13, 1992).

Tuschak, Beth. "Royal sendoff begins for Petty." *USA Today* (February 14, 1992).

Williams, Robert. "Richard Petty a Daytona Rookie—in TV Booth." *Omaha World Herald* (February 17, 1995).

Sketch by Gerald E. Brennan

Mike Piazza
1968-

American baseball player

Although many people once believed that Mike Piazza was only in the big leagues due to his connection with **Tommy Lasorda**, he has certainly proven them wrong throughout his career. He has made a name for

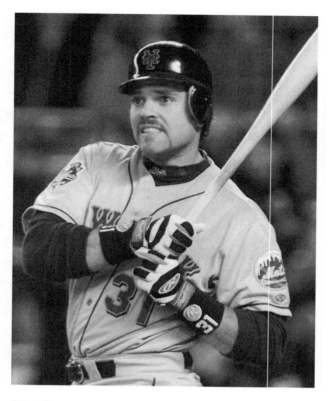

Mike Piazza

himself in baseball with his remarkable batting, and has made an impact on the world, using his celebrity status. Baseball did not come easy for him, but he has always loved the game so much, he was willing to pay any price to get to the major leagues. He is known for his hot temper when it comes to his performance, but also has a reputation for his compassion and laid back attitude off the field. Although he has had a handful of altercations with other players, most players express only admiration for him and his ability on the field.

Batter Up

Mike Piazza grew up living and breathing baseball. His focus was fueled by his father's passion for the game. From an early age he began to practice his batting. In an interview with *Sports Illustrated* Piazza said, "I would come home from school, get a snack, watch cartoons then hit. Every spring I would see I was hitting the ball farther and farther." Piazza would act as a bat-boy when the Dodgers were in town, due to his father's connection with Tommy Lasorda. In his senior year at Phoenixville High School he broke the schools record for career home runs. It was obvious his practice was paying off. Although Piazza's stats were good, the talent scouts did not seem to find him remarkable. He was passed up for any opportunities to break into the major leagues. Fortunately, having Lasorda as a family friend proved to be invaluable. Lasorda arranged a spot for Piazza with the University of Miami Hurricanes. He did

Chronology

1968	Born September 4 in Norristown, Pennsylvania
1986	Breaks Phoenixville High School's record for career home runs
1986	Plays for the University of Miami Hurricanes
1987	Transfers to Miami-Dade Community College
1988	Drafted by the Los Angeles Dodgers
1989	Plays his rookie season in Arizona on Dodger's instructional league team
1989	Attends Campo Las Palamas in Dominican Republic to hone his catching skills
1991	Catches full time with Class A Bakersfield
1992	Plays his first major league game for the Dodgers
1993	Hits the most home runs for a rookie catcher
1993	Offered a three-year contract with the Dodgers
1995	Suffers knee injury taking him out of the game
1995	Becomes first Dodger to hit more than twenty home runs in each of first three seasons
1998	Traded to the Florida Marlins
1998	Traded to the New York Mets

not do well in the single season he played with the Hurricanes and decided to transfer to Miami-Dade Community College. He was unable to play most of the season with the school due to a hand injury, so Lasorda once again stepped in to help Piazza out by influencing the Dodgers to draft the young Piazza, who was picked last in the 62nd round. When Piazza consistently blew the balls out of the ballpark for the Dodgers scouting director, Ben Wade, he knew they would find a place for him. Lasorda worked with Wade to come up with a way for Piazza to make it with the Dodgers. Wade finally agreed when Lasorda suggested that Piazza play the position of catcher. Wade was hooked, and offered Piazza a $15,000 signing bonus. Piazza gladly accepted the offer, remarking that he could have cared less about the money and would have paid for the opportunity.

Catcher if He Can

Piazza had never played the position of catcher, so in order to learn the position, he requested to be sent to Campos Las Palmas, which is the training camp for Latino recruits, in the Dominican Republic. The conditions at the training camp were not ideal, as Piazza was out of his element. He did not speak the language, and endured squalor living conditions. As usual, Piazza was willing to do anything to improve his game. He put up with a lot of razzing by teammates due to his association with Lasorda. Bob Nightengale with the *Sporting News* stated, "He still was considered Tommy's boy and clearly paid the price." Everything he battled was made worthwhile when he was catching full time for the Class A Bakersfield team, and was called up to play with the Dodgers for a game against the Chicago Cubs on September 1, 1992. He did not take this opportunity lightly, showing everyone what he had to offer. The next year with the Dodgers he hit thirty-five home runs, which was the most any rookie catcher had ever hit, influenc-

Awards and Accomplishments

1986	Broke record for career homeruns at Phoenixville High School
1993	Hit the most home runs for a Major League rookie catcher
1993	Named National League Rookie of the Year
1993-2002	Awarded Silver Slugger award, honoring the best offensive players
1993-2002	Elected to All Star team
1995	Becomes first Dodger to hit more than twenty home runs in first three seasons
1996	Named Major League All-Star MVP

ing the decision to name him National League Rookie of the Year in 1993. It also resulted in a contract with the Dodgers for three years. The contract was for $4.2 million, which was a far cry from his original signing bonus of $15,000. He had finally made it in the big leagues. It was a proud moment, not only for him, but for his father, whose dream had come true. Piazza realized what a gift he had been given for the opportunity to play with the Dodgers and expressed, "I'll never take this game for granted, never. I have worked too hard to get here," when speaking with Bob Nightengale for the *Sporting News*. He went on to talk about his celebrity, saying, "I'm only known because of my success on the ballfield. Nobody knew who I was three years ago." He wanted to make it quite clear that although a favor was called in for him to have a chance, he worked for everything he had achieved.

In 1998 everything Piazza knew was about to change. He thought he would be playing for the Dodgers for the rest of his career. Little did he know that in the span of two weeks he would be traded twice. He was first traded to the Florida Marlins, then to the New York Mets. It is with the Mets that he remains, but it wasn't without a lot of hard work proving himself. In the *Palm Beach Post* Julius Whigham wrote, "He struggled to live up to high expectations in New York early on and heard about it." Piazza stated in the article, "I chose to embrace it and go with it and be accountable and not make excuses." John Franco, a pitcher for the Dodgers, believed he just had to acclimate to the New York state of mind. He said, "Once he got used to being around, the rest is history." Once Piazza settled in he not only was accepted into the Mets fan base, he was embraced. In *The Record* Pete Caldera explained that the "Mets can't bear to think of life without him."

Piazza is Everywhere

Piazza enjoyed his celebrity. His charm off the field landed him cameo appearances as well as several guest appearances on TV shows like *Baywatch* and *Mar-*

ried...with Children. He has also been seen in commercials, notably several for Pert shampoo and 10-10-220. He is known and admired for his drive, as well as his attitude towards life in general. In 1995, he donated $100 for every home run he hit to a fund for all the Dodger Stadium employees who were not paid during the baseball strike.

Piazza was impacted by the September 11th attacks, and after visiting "ground zero" was so touched by the experience he wanted to do something to help. One of the firehouses, Ladder 3, found out about this and hooked him up with the Carroll family. Mike Carroll was a huge fan of Piazza, and was teaching his son Brendan to hit "like Piazza," according to an interview with the Carroll family in *Sports Illustrated*. Mike Carroll was one of the many New York Fire Fighters who lost his life in the World Trade Center on September 11th. The day before Thanksgiving that year Piazza met with Brendan and his mom, Nancy. Brendan was ecstatic to get to ask his father's favorite player questions about his life. During the barrage of questions Brendan asked if Piazza knew him and his dad were at the game where **Roger Clemens** hit him in the head with a pitch. It was at that point that Brendan broke down and cried. According to the article in *Sports Illustrated* Piazza did not move, but rubbed Brendan's shoulders saying, "You'll be alright, buddy, you'll be alright." He then invited Brendan and his mother back to his place to hang out. He and Brendan played a video football game while Nancy looked on. Nancy noted that "Brendan is hanging out with Mike Piazza, in Mike Piazza's apartment, and Mike thinks it's the funniest thing in the world." She knew her husband Mike would have been ecstatic knowing that Brendan had this opportunity, because he knew what an outstanding person Piazza was. Piazza stated in an interview with Julius Whigham of the *Palm Beach Post*, "I enjoy the triumph of the human spirit. To see the inspiration of how you come through it ... through the challenges and pressures of life and death." It is obvious that Piazza lives this idea, and has truly made an impact on a little boy named Brendan.

Feet on the Ground

Piazza has every opportunity to become smug in his ability and celebrity, but he has never been one to flaunt

Career Statistics

Yr	Team	Avg	GP	AB	R	H	HR	RBI	BB	SO	SB
1992	LA	.232	21	69	5	16	1	7	4	12	0
1993	LA	.318	149	547	81	174	35	112	46	86	3
1994	LA	.319	107	405	64	129	24	92	33	65	1
1995	LA	.346	112	434	82	150	17	93	39	80	1
1996	LA	.336	148	547	87	184	36	105	81	83	0
1997	LA	.362	152	556	104	201	40	124	69	77	5
1998	LA	.282	37	149	20	42	9	30	11	27	0
1998	NYM	.348	109	394	67	137	23	76	47	53	1
1998	FLA	.278	5	18	1	5	0	5	0	0	0
1999	NYM	.303	141	534	100	162	40	124	51	70	2
2000	NYM	.324	136	482	90	156	38	113	58	69	4
2001	NYM	.300	141	503	81	151	36	94	67	87	0
2002	NYM	.280	135	478	69	134	33	98	57	82	0
TOTAL		.321	1393	5116	851	1641	347	1073	563	801	17

LA: Los Angeles Dodgers; FLA: Florida Marlins; NYM: New York Mets.

it. He is known for having high expectations for himself, but only on a personal level, not in comparison to others. Besides **Barry Bonds**, he has received the most votes for MVP for the National League. With numbers like that, it's no wonder he is feared in the realm of baseball. Todd Pratt, who is Piazza's backup said, "I don't understand why anybody would pitch to him. He's that good," when questioned by *Sports Illustrated*. But through all the accolades, Piazza remains loyal to the game and realizes what a precious gift that has been handed to him. It is because of his respect for the game that he understands this lesson stating, "This game is humbling. It has a way of keeping your feet on the ground," in an interview with Gregory Schutta with *The Record*. Piazza remains at the top of his game and looks forward to many more years of playing the game he loves.

CONTACT INFORMATION

Address: Mike Piazza, c/o New York Mets, 12301 Roosevelt Ave., Flushing, NY 11368.

FURTHER INFORMATION

Books

Newsmakers 1993. Detroit: Gale Group, 1998.

Noble, Marty. *Mike and the Mets*. Champaign, IL: Sports Publishing Inc., 1999.

Sports Stars. Series 1-4. U•X•L, 1994-98. Detroit: Gale Group, 2002.

Periodicals

Bamberger, Michael. "Like so many other New York City Firefighters who died on September 11 Mike Carroll was a dedicated athlete and loyal teammate whose indomitable spirit led him to embrace his final heroic mission. His young son would find comfort in the company of Mike Piazza." *Sports Illustrated* (December 24, 2001): 106.

Bamberger, Michael. "Baseball: playin' the Dodger blues in the course of a few traumatic days, Mike Piazza's world turned upside down—and SI was there when he heard the news that his L.A. days were over." *Sports Illustrated* (May 25, 1998): 32.

Caldera, Pete. "Iron Mike: Piazza shows true grit." *Record* (Bergen County, NJ) (August 29, 2000): S05.

Jacobson, Steve. "Comfortable Piazza a giant in Big Town." *Newsday* (July 2, 2000): C07.

Nightengale, Bob. "Piazza's attitude and discipline keep him on top." *Sporting News* (April 24, 1995): 38.

Plaschke, Bill. "The man in the gold mask." *Sporting News* (March 16, 1998): 9.

Schutta, Gregory. "Piazza awes teammates." *Record* (Bergen County, NJ) (July 3, 2000): S03.

Shenolikar, Sachin, and Schwartz, Alan. "Pudge Vs. Piazza see how two of baseball's toughest characters stack up." *Sports Illustrated For Kids* (July 3, 2000): 42.

Verducci, Tom. "Catch this! Mike Piazza isn't just the best-hitting backstop of all time. He's also the leading man on baseball's hottest team." *Sports Illustrated* (August 21,2000): 38.

Whigham, Julius. "The man behind the mask: from Valley Forge to New York, Mike Piazza knows his history." *Palm Beach Post* (February 21, 2001): 1C.

Other

baseball-reference.com. http://www.baseball-reference.com/p/piazzomi01.shtml (November 17, 2002).

"Bonds, Piazza win 10th Silver Slugger awards." *Associated Press* http://foxsports.com/content/view?contentId=741946 (November 11, 2002).

ESPN. http://sports.espn.go.com/mlb/players/stats?
    statsId=4928 (November 17, 2002).

FOXSports. http://foxsports.com/content/view?
    contentId=603032 (November 11, 2002).

"Piazza reacts to Butler's comments by saying he leads in
    his own way." *AP Press Online* (March 3, 1998): 38.

Sketch by Barbra J Smerz

Mary Pierce

Mary Pierce
1975-

French tennis player

At five-feet-ten-inches and 150 pounds, Pierce has a powerful ground stroke that can overwhelm even her toughest opponents. She has won 15 tournaments, including two Grand Slam singles titles, the Australian Open in 1995 and the French Open in 2000. During the first half of her career Pierce's accomplishments on the court were often been overshadowed by antics of her overzealous and abusive father in the stands, who was banned from attending his daughter's tennis tournaments in 1993 by the Women's Tennis Council (WTC).

A Tennis Natural

Mary Pierce was born on January 15, 1975, in Montreal, Quebec, Canada, to an American father and a French mother. Soon after her birth her parents, Jim and Yannick (Adjani) Pierce, married. The following year Pierce's brother, David, was born. The family moved to Florida, where her father, an ex-Marine with a criminal record, made and sold jewelry. In his first attempt at the classic middle-class American life, Pierce's father joined the local country club and took up golf, and Pierce was persuaded to join the club's junior tennis clinic. After just a couple of sessions of watching the already athletic ten-year-old Pierce strike the ball, her father's attention turned from golf to his daughter's future in tennis.

Just two weeks after picking up a racket for the first time, Pierce, who also participated in gymnastics and ballet as a child, defeated the twentieth ranked local player in a 12-and-under division tournament. By the age of 12, Pierce was the No. 2 player in the United States in the 12-and-under division. Although he had no experience in tennis, Pierce's father studied the game until he was ready to take over as his daughter's coach. Everything in the Pierce family began to revolve around Pierce's tennis. They sold their house and replaced two cars with one, and in 1986, when Pierce was in sixth grade, Jim Pierce pulled Pierce and her brother out of school so they would be free to travel the amateur cir-

cuit. The children were taught by their mother, and both children took correspondence courses to complete their high school education.

Father's Effect

As quickly as Pierce was earning a reputation for her hard-hitting forehand, her father was becoming infamous for his abusive and berating behavior. He bragged about how hard he worked his daughter, telling *The Sporting News* in 1993, "For seven years, eight hours a day, I hit 700 serves at Mary. We usta work until midnight. My young son slept by the net. I wouldn't let Mary leave until she got it right. Sure, she cried. I cried, too. So what?" He controlled everything, including her diet, her workouts, and her friends. Pierce told *Sports Illustrated* "He was always very tough, but the more and more I was winning, the better I was doing, the tougher he got." Even early in her career, Pierce's father was openly abusive both to his daughter and anyone else who happened to be in his line of fire. In 1987 Pierce was playing 12-year-old Magdalena Maleeva in a tournament when her father screamed from the stands, "Mary, kill the bitch!" In response, Pierce threw h! er racket in her father's direction. As a result the Florida Tennis Association banned Jim Pierce from attending its tournaments for six months.

In 1988 the highly regarded Harry Hopman Tennis Academy in Wesley Chapel, Florida, refused to renew

Chronology

1975	Born in Montreal, Quebec, Canada
1985	Begins to play tennis at the age of 10
1987	Withdraws from school to travel to tournaments; ranked No. 2 in the United States among 12-and-under girls
1989	Turns professional soon after her fourteenth birthday
1990	Moves to France after the United States Tennis Association (USTA) withdraws its financial support
1990-92	Plays with French Federation Cup Team
1991	Wins first professional tournament in Palermo, Italy
1992	Competes in Olympic Summer Games for France; Pierce's father punches two fans at the French Open
1993	Pierce's father is banned from attending tournaments; Pierce fires her father as her coach; hires body guards and seeks restraining orders
1994-97	Plays with French Federation Cup Team
1995	Wins first Grand Slam, the Australian Open; attains No. 3 ranking (January 30-June 11; July 31-August 6)
1996	Competes in Olympic Summer Games for France
2000	Wins second Grand Slam, the French Open; regains No. 3 ranking (June 12-July 9)
2001	Withdraws from matches due to injury
2002	Returns to tour; reaches quarterfinals of the French Open

Awards and Accomplishments

1994	Reaches final of French Open
1995	Wins Australian Open
1997	Wins Italian Open
2000	Wins French Open, singles and doubles
2002	Wins Sanex Fans Award as most natural and nicest player at the French Open

Pierce's scholarship because of her father's behavior. Pierce turned professional just three months after her fourteenth birthday in 1989. At the time she was the youngest professional ever. (The following year **Jennifer Capriati** turned pro at the age of thirteen.) In 1990 the United States Tennis Association (USTA), who had been working to provide Pierce with financial and coaching support, withdrew funding because of Jim Pierce's volatile and abusive behavior that routinely included courtside tantrums and verbally berating his daughter, lines judges, opponents, and fans. Claiming that he was fed up with the USTA's lack of support, Jim Pierce moved the family to France where Pierce and her French-born mother had citizenship. Pierce received financial support in exchange for playing on the French Olympic and! Federation Cup teams.

The Jim Pierce Rule

Although Pierce, who spoke little French, had difficulty adjusting to the move, her tennis game continued to improve. She won her first tournament in Italy in 1991, but winning only seemed to fuel her father's fanatical behavior. When Pierce, playing for France in the 1992 Olympics in Barcelona, Spain, lost in the second round, her father screamed at her so much that she ran to the locker room in tears. Later, still enraged, he totaled his rental car. During the 1992 French Open, in which Pierce reached the fourth round, he punched two fans who were ridiculing Pierce's play. As Pierce walked off the court after losing to an unseeded player in the Italian Open, Jim Pierce threw an equipment bag at her. He then followed her into the parking lot and was seen slapping her. The next week, 17-year-old Pierce withdrew from the tournament. Later Pierce would admit that her father was physically as well as verbally abusive.

As the pressure to win every point became more and more unbearable, Pierce began to show signs of cracking. She was nervous and ill-at-ease on the court. Sometimes she would lose on purpose or simply forfeit, feigning an injury. The situation reached a climax during the 1993 French Open. Jim Pierce became enraged when he saw his daughter in the stands chatting and laughing with her 22-year-old cousin, Olivier. He attacked Olivier, choking him badly enough that he required medical attention. Jim Pierce's excuse was that the cousin was distracting Pierce, who was supposed to be scouting an upcoming opponent. Later, when Pierce was playing a match, her father began yelling at her, and tournament officials ejected him.

As a result the WTC enacted a new rule, known as the Jim Pierce Rule, that allows a player's disruptive family members or coaches to be banned from attending tournaments. Jim Pierce was denied entrance to tournaments in which his daughter played. At the same time, Pierce finally decided to break ties with her father and fired him as her coach. Her mother also began divorce proceedings. However, Jim Pierce did not go quietly; he made physical threats and stalked his daughter around the country. Tournament officials and ticket booths were supplied with his picture to prevent him from getting into a tournament. Pierce, fearing for her safety, hired bodyguards and requested restraining orders against her father.

Two Grand Slam Singles Titles

Pierce's break from her father proved to be a turning point in her career. In 1994 she reached the quarter finals of the U.S. Open and the finals of the French Open. In 1995 she won her first Grand Slam tournament by beating **Arantxa Sanchez Vicario**, 6-3, 6-2, in the Australian Open. Feeling the pressure from fans to continue winning, Pierce's game slumped for the remainder of the year and into 1996. By 1997 she was back on track, reaching the finals of Australian Open and the fourth round in the U.S. Open, the French Open, and Wimbledon. In 1998 she was once again in the top ten, with a No. 6 ranking.

Pierce won the French Open in 2000, giving her a second Grand Slam singles title. Seeded sixth in the tournament, Pierce beat third and first seeds, **Monica Seles** and **Martina Hingis**, and then overcame Conchita Martinez, 6-2, 7-5, in the final round. She also won the doubles championship at the 2000 French Open, teaming with Hingis. An injury forced Pierce to sit out much of the 2001 season, but she returned in 2002; her best finish was the quarter finals of the French Open.

In 2001 Pierce forged a partial reconciliation with her father. He sporadically helped her train, but Pierce has yet to ask the WTC to lift the ban on her father's attendance courtside. Pierce has refused to answer questions regarding her father, maintaining that their relationship is a private matter. In November 2001, Pierce ended her engagement to professional baseball player, **Roberto Alomar**. She lives in Sarasota, Florida, with her two long-haired Chihuahuas, Gilbert and Ginger. Over the course of her dramatic and often melodramatic career, Pierce has earned more than $6 million on the court.

CONTACT INFORMATION

Address: IMG Center, 1360 E. 9th Street, Ste. 100, Cleveland, Ohio 44114.

FURTHER INFORMATION

Books

The Complete Marquis Who's Who. New York: Marquis Who's Who, 2001.
Great Women in Sports. Detroit: Visible Ink Pres, 1996.
Newsmakers 1994, Issue 4.Detroit: Gale Research, 1994.
Sports Stars. Series 1-4. Detroit: U•X•L, 1994-98.

Periodicals

Cunningham, Kim. "The Love Game." *People Weekly,* (September 7, 1992): 59-60.
Jenkins, Sally. "Persona Non Grata." *Sports Illustrated,* (August 23, 1993): 28+.
Jones, David. "The Return of Jim Pierce." *Campaign,* (May 12, 2000): 160.
Jordan, Pat. "A Family Tragedy in the Name of Love." *The Sporting News,* (November 15, 1993): 10.
Leand, Andrea. "Working Out with Mary Pierce." *Tennis,* (November 2000): 58.
Malinowski, Mark. "The World According to Mary Pierce." *Tennis,* (September 2000): 20.
Reed, Susan. "Breaking Away: A Year After Firing Her Abusive Father as Her Coach, a Happy, Confident Mary Pierce Soars Toward the Top in Women's Tennis." *People Weekly,* (June 27, 1994): 43-5.
Wertheim, L. Jon. "Hail Mary." *Sports Illustrated,* (June 19, 2000): 48+.
"Withdrawal Symptoms." *Sports Illustrated,* (June 27, 1994): 13.

Other

"Mary Pierce." ESPN.com. http://www.espn.com (January 22, 2003).

"Mary Pierce." Sanex WTA Tour. http://www.sanexwta. com (January 8, 2003).

Sketch by Kari Bethel

Lou Piniella
1943-

American baseball player

After nearly four decades as a winning baseball player and manager, Lou Piniella finally went home in late October 2002, accepting a job as manager of his hometown Tampa Bay Devil Rays. Born and raised in Tampa, Piniella had his work cut out for him, trying to put the Devil Rays on a winning track. Since first taking to the ball field in the spring of 1998, the Devil Rays had compiled one of the most dismal records in the history of major league baseball. Tampa Bay area fans and team executives were hopeful that Piniella could do for the Devil Rays what he did for the Seattle Mariners-turn them into winners. As for Piniella himself, it was clear that he was glad to be back home again. "I would enjoy winning here more than anyplace else," Piniella told the *St. Petersburg Times.* "This is my hometown. This is where I'm going to live the rest of my life. This is where I'm going to die. This is where I'd like to get it done. I know we have a challenge ahead. I'm not naive enough to think this will be an overnight sensation. But at the same time, it's something that can be done. And it's something that when it's done, I'll take tremendous pride in. And I didn't say if, I said when."

Born in Tampa, Florida

He was born Louis Victor Piniella in Tampa, Florida, on August 28, 1943. The grandson of Spanish immigrants, he spoke Spanish until he began school, but even before school he had begun to play ball. His mother, Margaret, told Bruce Lowitt of the *St. Petersburg Times* that Piniella's first bat was a trimmed-down broom handle, swung at a tape-wrapped cork. "Lou was just 3 years old, but you should have seen the way he hit that ball." When he was five years old, his family moved to a new home, conveniently located across the street from a playground, which quickly became Piniella's home away from home. "There were times I had to drag him off the field," his mother told the *St. Petersburg Times.* "He would come home from school, do his homework, and then go to the playground and play baseball. He always wanted to be a baseball player." The Tampa neighborhood Piniella grew up in also produced other baseball greats, including Ken Suarez, Tino Martinez, and Tony La Russa.

Lou Piniella

Baseball remained Piniella's passion throughout his boyhood. He played the game while a student at St. Joseph's Catholic School and later at Jesuit High School. He also played on Colt League and American Legion teams. After high school, Piniella attended the University of Tampa for a year, playing baseball and basketball while there. In 1962, at the age of 18, Piniella was signed as an outfielder by the Cleveland Indians. For the next two years he played for minor league teams in Cleveland's farm system. In 1964 Piniella was traded to the Baltimore Orioles for pitcher Buster Narum. He first played for an Orioles' minor league team in Aberdeen, South Dakota, making his major league debut on September 4, 1964. He played only four games for the Orioles before being sent back to the minor leagues, playing for an Orioles' farm team in Elmira, New York. In 1966 Piniella was traded back to the Indians and assigned to the team's top farm team, the Portland Beavers, for whom he played until 1968. After six games for the Indians, Piniella was selected in the expansion draft of 1968 by the Seattle Pilots, which traded him to the Kansas City Royals in the spring of 1969.

Wins AL Rookie of the Year Award

In 1969, his first season with the Royals, Piniella batted .282 and won the American League (AL) Rookie of the Year Award. He spent five seasons with the Royals, compiling a batting average of .285 in his years with the team. Piniella in 1974 was traded to the New York Yan-

kees, a once-dominant team that had not won a pennant in nine years. The presence of Piniella and other players acquired by trade helped to energize the Yankees. During his first year in the Bronx, he batted .305 with 70 runs batted in. During his 11 seasons with the team, Piniella batted over .300 in five seasons. With the help of Piniella and others, the team finally snagged a pennant again. Things got even better in 1977 and 1978, when the Yankees not only won the AL pennant but back-to-back world championships. With batting averages of .330 in 1977 and .314 in 1978, Piniella earned the nickname Sweet Lou.

Piniella continued to play with the Yankees through the 1984 season, retiring with a lifetime average of .291 and a total of 1,705 base hits. During Piniella's 11 seasons with the Bronx Bombers, the Yankees four times won the AL pennant and twice were victors in the World Series. After leaving the Yankees, Piniella returned briefly to Tampa but was back in New York the following year to sign on as manager of the Yankees. He piloted the team through the seasons of 1986 and 1987 but was replaced by **Billy Martin** after the 1987 season ended. Piniella was moved to general manager but in June 1988 replaced Martin as manager, only to be fired at season's end.

Hired to Manage the Reds

Marge Schott of the Cincinnati Reds hired Piniella as manager in 1989, setting the stage for one of the high points of the Tampa native's managerial career. He guided the Reds to a world championship in 1990, his first sea-

Career Statistics

Yr	Team	Avg	GP	AB	R	H	HR	RBI	BB	SO	SB
1964	BAL	.000	4	1	0	0	0	0	0	0	0
1968	CLE	.000	6	5	1	0	0	1	0	0	0
1969	KCR	.282	135	493	43	139	11	68	33	56	2
1970	KCR	.301	144	542	54	163	11	88	35	42	3
1971	KCR	.279	126	448	43	125	3	51	21	43	5
1972	KCR	.312	151	574	65	179	11	72	34	59	7
1973	KCR	.250	144	513	53	128	9	69	30	65	5
1974	NYY	.305	140	518	71	158	9	70	32	58	1
1975	NYY	.196	74	199	7	39	0	22	16	22	0
1976	NYY	.281	100	327	36	92	3	38	18	34	0
1977	NYY	.330	103	339	47	112	12	45	20	31	2
1978	NYY	.314	130	472	67	148	6	69	34	36	3
1979	NYY	.297	130	461	49	137	11	69	17	31	3
1980	NYY	.287	116	321	39	92	2	27	29	20	0
1981	NYY	.277	60	159	16	44	5	18	13	9	0
1982	NYY	.307	102	261	33	80	6	37	18	18	0
1983	NYY	.291	53	148	19	43	2	16	11	12	1
1984	NYY	.302	29	86	8	26	1	6	7	5	0
TOTAL		.291	1747	5867	651	1705	102	766	368	541	32

BAL: Baltimore Orioles; CLE: Cleveland Indians; KCR: Kansas City Royals; NYY: New York Yankees.

son as manager. Shortly after the end of the 1992 season, Piniella was hired to manage the Seattle Mariners and three years later led the team to its first division title ever, coming out on top of the AL West. For this accomplishment Piniella was honored with the AL Manager of the Year Award, which he again received in 2001. In Seattle Piniella was reunited with fellow Tampan, Tino Martinez, who grew up in a home across the street from Piniella.

Piniella returned to Tampa Bay confident that in time he could groom the hapless Devil Rays into a championship team. Though many had their doubts, Paul Straub, Piniella's basketball coach at Jesuit High School, voiced optimism that Sweet Lou was the right man for the job. He told the *Tampa Tribune:* "Having a local man like Lou will give hope he can bring them back. They need that right now."

CONTACT INFORMATION

Address: c/o Tampa Bay Devil Rays, Tropicana Field, 1 Tropicana Dr., St. Petersburg, FL 33705. Phone: (727) 825-3137.

SELECTED WRITINGS BY PINIELLA:

(With Maury Allen) *Sweet Lou.* New York: Putnam's, 1986.

FURTHER INFORMATION

Books

"Tino Martinez." *Sports Stars,* Series 1-4. U•X•L, 1994-98.

Periodicals

Carter, Scott. "Lou's Rooted Here." *Tampa Tribune* (October 29, 2002).

Carter, Scott. "Piniella Inspires Winners." *Tampa Tribune* (October 29, 2002).

Gaddis, Carter. "Safe at Home." *Tampa Tribune* (October 29, 2002).

Henderson, Joe. "Love of Family, Love of the Game Bring Lou Piniella Home." *Tampa Tribune* (October 29, 2002).

Lowitt, Bruce. "Piniella's Passion, Pride Took Root in Tampa." *St. Petersburg Times* (October 27, 2002).

Topkin, Marc. "Can He Save the Rays?" *St. Petersburg Times* (October 29, 2002).

Other

"Lou Piniella: Batting." Baseball-Reference.com. http://www.baseball-reference.com/p/pinielo01.shtml (December 2, 2002).

"Lou Piniella." *Biography Resource Center Online.* Farmington Hills, MI: Gale Group, 2002.

"Lou Piniella: Managerial Record." Baseball-Reference.com. http://www.baseball-reference.com/managers/pinielo01.shtml (December 3, 2002).

"Piniella Timeline." Tampa Bay Online. http://rays.tbo.com/rays/MGA1WRD8V7D.html (December 3, 2002).

Sketch by Don Amerman

Scottie Pippen

Scottie Pippen
1965-

American basketball player

Chronology	
1965	Born September 25 in Hamburg, Arkansas
1983	Begins stint as team manager and point guard while student at University of Central Arkansas
1987	Drafted fifth overall by Seattle SuperSonics and immediately traded to Chicago Bulls
1988	Moves to starting lineup of Bulls in point forward position
1990	Divorces first wife Karen McCollum after two-year marriage
1991	Named to first of many NBA All-Star teams
1992	Member of U.S. Olympic Basketball "Dream Team" in Barcelona, Spain
1993	Breaks string of consecutive games with suspension for throwing a punch at an opposing player
1993	Takes on-court leadership role of Bulls after Jordan temporarily retires
1994	Refuses to play final 1.8 seconds of Game 3 against New York Knicks in Eastern Conference semifinals
1995	Ordered by court to pay model Sonya Roby $10,000 for maternity costs involved in bearing his twin daughters in 1994
1995	Arrested on charge of domestic battery filed against him by ex-fiancee Yvette DeLeone
1996	Member of gold medal-winning U.S. Olympic basketball team in Atlanta, Georgia
1996	Earns $7 million in product endorsements with Ameritech, Frito Lay, Ginsana, Mazda, Nike, and others
1997	Wins fourth national basketball championship with Chicago Bulls
1997	Lands role on NBC Wednesday-night sitcom *Chicago Sons*
1997	Marries second wife, a former model
1997	Undergoes surgery to correct a sports-related injury to his left foot
1998	Signs 5-year contract for $67.2 million with Houston Rockets
1999	Charged with misdemeanor DWI in Harris county, Texas and released after posting $500 bail
1999	Traded to Portland Trailblazers
2002	Finishes college degree in kinesiology begun in 1983

Considered one of the top basketball players of all time, point forward Scottie Pippen made news both on and off the court throughout his decades-long career as a professional athlete. Beginning in 1987 with the Chicago Bulls, Pippen has gone on to demonstrate his multiple talents in shooting, passing, blocking, and rebounding, as well as in defense strategy, and has become known even among non-basketball fans for his performance as part of the U.S. basketball "Dream Team" that took the gold at the Olympic Games in Barcelona, Spain, and Atlanta, Georgia.

Contributing to his reputation as one of the greatest forwards in professional basketball was Pippen's talent for complementing Bulls teammate **Michael Jordan** while Jordan rose to superstardom during the 1990s. Overshadowed by Jordan throughout his tenure with the Bulls, Pippen also exhibited a sometimes erratic performance, moodiness, and a trouble-tinged personal life, all of which made his role as a top player somewhat controversial. His career was characterized by some as a balancing act between moments of athletic genius and spats of uncooperativeness and immaturity. However, in the broad view the balance falls on the plus side, at least in the opinion of the National Basketball Association (NBA) which voted the 6'8", 228-pound Pippen among the fifty top basketball players of all time in 1996.

Born in 1965 in Hamburg, Arkansas, Pippen was one of twelve children born to Preston and Ethel Pippen. Growing up in a rural hometown, the six Pippen brothers spent much of their time playing basketball, their family dogged by poverty after Preston, a paper mill worker suffered a debilitating stroke the year Pippen entered high school. Although he enjoyed basketball, Pippen's unremarkable stature—he did not attain his full height of 6'8" until he reached college—did little to hint at his future career. As a student, math was his favorite subject due to its practicality; basketball was simply recreation until his sophomore year, when he joined the school team and doubled as the football team equipment manager. As a high school senior the 6'1", 150-pound Pippen played starting point guard, but was unable to attract the attention of college scouts or scholarship monies. Convinced that basketball would provide the young man perhaps his only chance at furthering his education, Pippen's high school coach located a work-study arrangement at the University of Central Arkansas

Awards and Accomplishments

1991	NBA All-Defensive Second Team
1992	U.S. Olympic basketball team; NBA All-Star Team; NBA All-Defensive First Team
1993	NBA All-Defensive First Team; NBA All-Star Team
1994	NBA All-Defensive First Team; NBA All-Star Team and MVP
1995	NBA All-Star Team; All-NBA First Team
1996	Gold medal as part of U.S. Olympic basketball team; NBA All-Defensive First Team; NBA All-Star Team; named among NBA's 50 greatest basketball players of all time
1997	NBA All-Defensive First Team; NBA All-Star Team
1998	All-NBA Third Team
1999	NBA All-Defensive First Team; NBA All-Star Team
2000	NBA All-Defensive Second Team

whereby Pippen could continue to play point guard and be team manager. Pippen enrolled at Central Arkansas in 1983, intending to major in industrial education and find a job as a factory manager.

Fortunately, Pippen began to gain some height following high school graduation, and by September he was 6'3". During his sophomore year he started a weight-training program, gained another two inches, and watched his game noticeably improve. Impressed, his coach had Pippen play not only forward but other positions as well. Viewed as the team's best all-around player during his last year at Central Arkansas, Pippen now averaged 23.6 points, 10 rebounds, and 4.3 assists per game. While his impressive performance at Central Arkansas registered slightly with Chicago Bulls general manager Jerry Krause, Pippen's equally impressive performance at a college all-star event in Portsmouth, Virginia transfixed Krause, who made a deal whereby Pippen was the number-five draft choice of the Seattle SuperSonics in late 1986 and immediately traded to the Chicago Bulls with a six-year contract worth over $5 million.

During the 1987-88 season the Bulls were led by coach Doug Collins and player Michael Jordan, who dominated Collins's starting lineup. As backup point forward Pippen averaged 7.9 points per game before becoming sidelined by a herniated disk that required back surgery. Missing the 1988-89 preseason as well as the first eight games that followed, he advanced to the starting lineup in late December by averaging 14.4 points per game. During the Eastern Conference playoffs Chicago downed their first two rivals before facing the Detroit Pistons. Suffering a concussion at the start of game six against Detroit, Pippen was forced from play and could only watch as the Bulls were downed in a hard-fought match.

The appointment of **Phil Jackson** to the Bulls' head coach spot at the start of the 1989-90 season was a boon for Pippen. Jackson's three-point offensive strategy allowed him greater freedom on the court. Scoring an average of 16.5 points per game, Pippen found himself on

the NBA All-Star team for the first time. "He handles the ball well enough to be virtually a third guard," explained *Sports Illustrated* contributor Leigh Montville of Pippen, "dribbling up the floor in the Bulls offense. He is a point forward, . . . the modern all-purpose basketball part. . . . Guard him high, and he will take you low. Guard him low, and he will take you high. Don't guard him for a moment? He is gone, rising over the basket and depositing the ball with a house-call efficiency that makes you remember Dr. **Julius Erving** himself." Eerily echoing the previous year's playoffs, the Bulls again faced Detroit, and fans again saw Pippen play poorly before being pulled from Game 7, this time due to migraine headaches. Chicago's 74-93 loss was put squarely on Pippen's shoulders by many fans, many of whom did not realize that the point forward was also mourning the recent death of his father, who had passed away during the playoffs.

Pippen returned for the Bulls' 1990-91 season a more focused player. After a heated contract dispute he ended the season with a guaranteed annual salary of $3.5 million through 1997-98. Pippen's efforts on the court justified the increase as he led the Bulls to a sweep of the conference championship series against the Pistons by scoring 17.8 points per game, 595 rebounds, 511 assists, and 193 steals. The Bulls went on to beat the Los Angeles Lakers in the world championship.

Pippen's stats during the 1991-92 season earned him a spot on both the 1992 All-Star game and the U.S. Olympic "Dream Team" alongside Jordan, **Magic Johnson**, and **Larry Bird**. He also continued to lead his team in assists. Ironically, considering these honors, in a playoff game against the New York Knicks his sprained ankle and injured wrist cost the team points and sparked renewed grumblings among Bulls fans. This time, however, the Bulls were victorious, and Pippen entered the final games of the playoffs in top form, then traveled to Barcelona, Spain to help the Dream Team take the 1992 gold medal.

The 1992-93 season found Pippen at the top of his game; he spearheaded a drive to the top of the Eastern Conference by beating the Knicks in the playoffs 4-0 and helped the Bulls become the first team to win three consecutive league titles since 1966. At the close of the season teammate Jordan announced that he was retiring to begin a second career in baseball, and Pippen filled the void by taking on a more active role on the court.

During the 1993-94 season an ankle injury kept Pippen out of the first ten games before he returned to boost the Bulls' standings with an average of 22 points, 8.7 rebounds, and 5.6 assists per game. He bagged NBA Most Valuable Player honors in the All-Star game by posting 29 points, 11 rebounds, and 4 steals before his now-characteristic fall from grace during the May, 1994 playoffs. During the final, crucial 1.8 seconds of the Bulls' third game against the Knicks, Pippen refused to return to the

Career Statistics

Yr	Team	GP	Pts	FG%	3P%	FT%	RPG	APG	SPG	BPG	TO	PF
1987-88	CHI	79	7.9	46.3	17.4	57.6	3.8	2.1	1.2	0.7	1.7	2.7
1988-89	CHI	73	14.4	47.6	27.3	66.8	6.1	3.5	1.9	0.8	2.7	3.6
1989-90	CHI	82	16.5	48.9	25.0	67.5	6.7	5.4	2.6	1.2	3.4	3.6
1990-91	CHI	2	17.8	52.0	30.9	70.6	7.3	6.2	2.4	1.1	2.8	3.3
1991-92	CHI	82	21.0	50.6	20.0	76.0	7.7	7.0	1.9	1.1	3.1	3.0
1992-93	CHI	81	18.6	47.3	23.7	66.3	7.7	6.3	2.1	0.9	3.0	2.7
1993-94	CHI	72	22.0	49.1	32.0	66.0	8.7	5.6	2.9	0.8	3.2	3.2
1994-95	CHI	79	21.4	48.0	34.5	71.6	8.1	5.2	2.9	1.1	3.4	3.0
1995-96	CHI	77	19.4	46.3	37.4	67.9	6.4	5.9	1.7	0.7	2.7	2.6
1996-97	CHI	82	20.2	47.4	36.8	70.1	6.5	5.7	1.9	0.5	2.6	2.6
1997-98	CHI	44	19.1	44.7	31.8	77.7	5.2	5.8	1.8	1.0	2.5	2.6
1998-99	HOU	50	14.5	43.2	34.0	72.1	6.5	5.9	2.0	0.7	3.2	2.4
1999-00	POR	82	12.5	45.1	32.7	71.7	6.3	5.0	1.4	0.5	2.5	2.5
2000-01	POR	64	11.3	45.1	34.4	73.9	5.2	4.6	1.5	0.5	2.4	2.5
2001-02	POR	62	10.6	41.1	30.5	77.4	5.2	5.9	1.6	0.6	2.8	2.6
2002-03	POR	12	8.2	51.2	31.2	83.3	2.3	3.2	0.9	0.1	1.8	1.9
TOTAL		1104	15.0	47.5	32.9	70.0	6.5	5.3	1.99	.83	2.8	2.9

CHI: Chicago Bulls; HOU: Houston Rockets; POR: Portland Trailblazers.

game after a time-out. Angered that teammate Toni Kukoc had been awarded both a lucrative contract and the final shot of the game, Pippen stubbornly sat out the final seconds, during which Kukoc's shot saved the game for the Bulls. Despite his subsequent apologies, Pippen found this action would haunt him as fans blamed him for the Bulls' ultimate loss of the series to New York.

Pippen's dissatisfaction with his team flooded over into his private life, and his name began to appear on more than just the sports pages during the 1993-94 season. In January 1994 he was arrested for possession of a firearm, although the charges were later dropped after the basketball star intimated allegations of racism on the part of the arresting officers. Subsequent reports revealed a domestic abuse charge by then-fiancee Yvette Deleone and a paternity suit by model Sonya Roby that cited Pippen as the father of her daughter, a surviving twin, and cost the athlete $10,000 despite his denial of the charge.

Although Pippen illustrated his continuing frustration with the 1994-95 season by throwing a chair onto the court in response to a call by officials during a game in January 1995, he finally gave Bulls fans something to cheer about the following February when he joined a returning Jordan and the recently acquired former Piston **Dennis Rodman** to propel the team to fifty wins in their first fifty-six games. Pippen managed to keep his legal problems off the court during the remainder of the 1995-96 season and averaged over nineteen points per game. Named to the All-NBA First Team for the third year in a row, he also walked away with a gold medal for his role in the 1996 U.S. basketball Olympic team. Bulls teammates Jordan, Pippen, and Rodman also became the first trio of teammates in thirteen years to make the NBA's All-Defensive Team.

The 1996-97 season, marking the end of Pippen's contract with the Bulls, was highlighted by his inclusion as one of the NBA's fifty greatest players. Taking advantage of his on- and off-court fame, the savvy athlete supplemented his annual salary of $2.25 million with $7 million from product endorsements and appearances on television programs such as *ER* and *Chicago Sons*. Pippen's biggest endorsement, with shoe manufacturer Nike, earned him between $2.5 to $3.5 million. The athlete's name recognition only improved when he led the Bulls to their fifth world championship, averaging 19.2 points and 6.8 rebounds in nineteen playoff games despite being hobbled with an injury to his left foot.

At the start of Pippen's tenth pro season, 1997-98, the thirty-two year old was sidelined for three months while recovering from foot surgery while rumors of his planned departure from the Bulls began to circulate. Undergoing more back surgery in July to repair two herniated disks, Pippen then accepted a deal whereby he was traded to the Houston Rockets after signing a five-year contract with the Bulls worth $67.2 million. Pippen ended his Bulls career with per-game averages of 18 points, 6.8 rebounds, and 5.3 assists.

During his first season with the Rockets, Pippen clearly welcomed the change in team affiliation. Joining fellow player **Charles Barkley** on the starting lineup, he adopted the new defensive system of Houston coach Rudy Tomjanovich, and led his new team in assists. However, by the following spring Pippen openly expressed frustration over the shortcomings of his teammates—particularly Barkley—and his own inability to be cast in scoring positions, telling a *Jet* interviewer, "Playing the minutes I'm playing [without scoring] . . . makes the game not any fun anymore. My next step is to find out why this organization wanted me." As before, off-court troubles followed on-court troubles, and in May 1999 Pippen was arrested for driving while intoxicated, although the charges were later dropped

Because of his growing dissatisfaction with Houston, Pippen requested that he be traded, and in October of 1999 he found himself signed with the middle-ranked Portland Trailblazers. Although he helped Portland into the Western Conference finals in both 2000 and 2001, Pippen averaged only 11.3 points during the 2000-01 season. Exhibiting a playing style characterized by *Chicago Tribune* reporter Sam Smith as "toned down" and "quieter," the now-veteran Pippen's performance was praised by fellow teammate Steve Kerr as that of a player who "knows how to find you where you want the ball." Despite his fall from the national spotlight, Pippen expressed his satisfaction at playing on a team noted for its camaraderie and love of the game.

Although his accomplishments have been somewhat overshadowed by ups and downs in his personal life, Pippen developed into one of the greatest forwards in professional basketball, his success inspired in no small part by the straightened circumstances of his childhood. His pairing with superstar Jordan proved to be a double-edged sword: while he fueled Jordan's rise to stardom and helped make the Chicago Bulls a force to be reckoned with during most of the 1990s, his own abilities were often overshadowed. Determined to achieve a modest fortune in addition to professional success, Pippen has remained wise to the vagaries of professional sports, lending his name to a variety of products and appearing on several television programs while his name held value for commercial sponsors. Joining the Portland Trailblazers as a mature player, Pippen has continued to distinguish himself, his confidence and authority among younger, less experienced athletes bolstered by his multiple NBA records, Olympic wins, and countless other accolades.

CONTACT INFORMATION

Address: Office, Portland Trailblazers, One Center Ct., Suite 200, Portland, OR 97227. Online: http://www.nba.com/blazers.

FURTHER INFORMATION

Books

Bjarkman, Peter C. *Sports Great Scottie Pippen.* Springfield, NJ: Enslow Publishing, 1996.

Periodicals

Chicago Tribune (December 28, 1989).
Chicago Tribune (June 5, 2000).
Chicago Tribune (May 8, 2001).
Chicago Tribune (November 30, 2001).
Jet (June 12, 1995): 27.
Jet (March 18, 1996): 52.
Jet (April 15, 1999): 48.
People (May 6, 1996): 238-240.
Sporting News (February 6, 1995): 42.
Sporting News (December 8, 1997): 68.
Sporting News (February 8, 1999): 32.
Sporting News (May 22, 2000): 20.
Sporting News (May 29, 2000): 42.
Sports Illustrated (November 30, 1987): 67-71.
Sports Illustrated (March 25, 1991): 68.
Sports Illustrated (February 24, 1992): 74-84.
Sports Illustrated (June 13, 1993): 40.
Sports Illustrated (March 14, 1994): 72.
Sports Illustrated (December 13, 1999): 80.
Washington Post (June 16, 1993): D1.

Sketch by Pamela L. Shelton

Jacques Plante
1929-1986

Canadian hockey player

A pioneer hockey goaltender on several fronts, Jacques Plante changed the position forever when he became the first wear a goalie mask in games on a regular basis after a serious injury to his face. Though Plante took much grief for wearing the mask, it became standard gear for goaltenders within a decade. He also became the first goalie to regularly leave his crease to play the puck to a teammate, and was a pioneer of the butterfly style of goalie technique. Plante is considered one of the best goalies to ever play the game. He played the majority of his career with the Montreal Canadiens, winning five Vezina Trophies as best goalie in the NHL, and one Hart Trophy as league's most valuable player, an award rarely given to goalies. Though Plante was a recognized winner, he was also known as eccentric, arrogant, and difficult.

Plante was born on January 17, 1929, in Shawinigan Falls, Quebec, Canada, the oldest of eleven children born to Xavier and Palma Plante. His father was a machinist, while his mother did knitting piecework. Plante learned to knit from her and would later use the skill to relax him as a player.

Plante began skating at the age of three, and played hockey on outdoor rinks as a youngster. Originally Plante was a defenseman, but asthma prevented him

Jacques Plante

Chronology

1929	Born on January 17, in Shawinigan Falls, Quebec, Canada
c. 1931	Begins skating
1944	Plays goal on a factory team for money
1949-53	Plays goal for the Montreal Royals of the Quebec Senior League
1952-54	Plays minor hockey league hockey with the American Hockey League's Buffalo Bison
1953	Called up by the Montreal Canadiens; wins his first Stanley Cup with the Montreal Canadiens
1954	Becomes the first-string goalie with the Canadiens
1959	Becomes first goalie to regularly wear face mask in games
1963	Traded to the New York Rangers
1965	Retires from hockey for two years
1967	Returns to hockey, playing in goal for the St. Louis Blues, an expansion team
1970	Traded from the Blues to the Toronto Maple Leafs
1972	Plays for the Boston Bruins
1973	Retires from the National Hockey League
1974	Plays in a few games for the Edmonton Oilers in the World Hockey Association
1975-86	Works as part-time goaltending coach
1986	Dies on February 26 of stomach cancer in Geneva, Switzerland

from being an effective skater. He then concentrated on learning the goalie position.

By the 1944-45 season, Plante was talented enough as a goaltender to play goal for a factory team for money. He also played junior hockey for Quebec City and the Montreal Junior Canadiens until 1949. From 1949-53, Planted was playing in the Quebec Senior League for the Montreal Royals and he was seen as a leading young goaltender. Though this was an amateur league, Plante was paid for his play.

Played Professional Hockey

Plante officially became a professional hockey player in the early 1950s. Signed by the Montreal Canadiens, he began his career in the minor leagues. He first played for the Buffalo Bisons in the American Hockey League, for part of the 1952-53 and much of the 1953-54 season. Plante had a big break during the 1953 playoffs, when he was called up to the Canadiens.

In the 1953 Stanley Cup semi-finals against the Chicago Blackhawks, the Canadiens were losing the best of seven series three games to two. The Canadiens number one goalie, Gerry McNeill, was playing on a broken ankle, and needed to be replaced in the last two games. Using his unconventional technique,

Plante won both games. In the finals against the Boston Bruins, McNeill and Plante split up games. The Canadiens won in five games. Plante was later reprimanded for criticizing McNeill's goaltending, breaking an unwritten rule.

It was during his playoff appearances against Chicago that Plante demonstrated his innovative way of playing the puck, alarming his coach Dick Irvin. Because Plante was an excellent skater, he would roam away from the crease to play the puck to a teammate to start the rush. Though Plante was not the first player to do this (New York Ranger Chuck Rayner did in the 1940s), he was the first to do it on a regular basis on a successful team and it rarely backfired on him. Plante also had another uncommon goalie technique that involved coming out of the net to the top of the crease to cut down on the angle of slapshots. This would mean the puck would come at his chest not at his head.

Plante's success in the playoffs led to his being named the number two goaltender for the Canadiens in the 1953-54 season, backing up McNeill. Plante played in 17 games, but when McNeill lost in the seventh game of the Stanley Cup, he lost his number one job. Plante was the number one goalie in the 1954-55 season, and McNeill basically retired from the game.

Plante remained Montreal's number one goalie for nearly a decade until he was traded. These were some of the best years for Plante and Montreal. He won five straight Vezina Trophies as the league's best goaltender from 1956 to 1960. His goals against was low, but began going up by 1958. These were same years that Montreal won five straight Stanley Cups. While both Plante and the Canadiens were winning, there was ten-

Career Statistics

Yr	Team	GP	W	L	T	GAA	TGA	SHO
1952-53	Canadiens	3	2	0	1	1.33	4	0
1952-53	Bisons	33	13	19	1	3.42	114	2
1953-54	Bisons	55	32	17	6	2.64	148	3
1953-54	Canadiens	17	7	5	5	1.59	27	5
1954-55	Canadiens	52	31	13	7	2.14	110	5
1955-56	Canadiens	64	42	12	10	1.86	119	7
1956-57	Canadiens	61	31	18	12	2.02	123	9
1957-58	Canadiens	57	34	14	8	2.11	119	9
1958-59	Canadiens	67	38	16	13	2.16	144	9
1959-60	Canadiens	69	40	17	12	2.54	175	3
1960-61	Royals	8	3	4	1	3.00	24	0
1960-61	Canadiens	40	23	11	7	2.80	112	2
1961-62	Canadiens	70	42	14	14	2.37	166	4
1962-63	Canadiens	56	22	14	19	2.49	138	5
1963-64	Rangers	65	22	36	7	3.38	220	3
1964-65	Rangers	33	10	17	5	3.37	109	2
1964-65	Clippers	17	6	9	1	3.01	51	1
1968-69	Blues	37	18	12	6	1.96	70	5
1969-70	Blues	32	18	9	5	2.19	67	5
1970-71	Maple Leafs	40	24	11	4	1.88	73	4
1971-72	Maple Leafs	34	16	13	5	2.63	86	2
1972-73	Maple Leafs	32	8	14	6	3.04	87	1
1972-73	Bruins	8	7	1	0	2.00	16	2
1974-75	Oilers	31	15	14	1	3.32	88	1
TOTAL		837	435	247	145	2.38	2390	89

Bisons: Buffalo Bisons (AHL); Blues: St. Louis Blues (NHL); Bruins: Boston Bruins (NHL); Canadiens: Montreal Canadiens (NHL); Clippers: Baltimore Clippers (AHL); Maple Leafs: Toronto Maple Leafs (NHL); Oilers: Edmonton Oilers (WHA); Rangers: New York Rangers (NHL); Royals: Montreal Royals (EPHL).

sion between Plante and his coach and former teammate **Toe Blake**, which was heightened by Plante's use of a goalie mask.

Began Wearing Goalie Mask

In 1959, Plante became the first goalie to wear a mask in games on a regular basis. (Clint Benedict of the Montreal Maroons had 29 years earlier, but it was short-lived experiment.) Many goalies of the era wore masks in practice, including Plante, but after his nose was broken by a hard shot in a game on November 1 in New York, he refused to come back in without his fiberglass face mask. Since there was no backup goalie with the team, Blake gave in. Plante insisted on wearing it in games from that day forward. While there were many detractors, including his own coach and teammates, Plante played better with it on. In the first 11 games in which he played with the mask, he only gave up 13 goals. Within a decade, the goalie mask became standard equipment in the NHL.

Though Plante had the mask and was still one of the leading goalies in the NHL, Montreal struggled (relatively) in the early 1960s. The team did not win another Stanley Cup with Plante in goal. In 1962, Plante won the Hart Trophy as the NHL's most valuable player. His record was 42-14-14 with a 2.37 goals against average. In the 1962-63 season, the Canadiens finished only third overall, though Plante played well.

Traded to the Rangers

In 1963, Plante was traded as part of a seven player deal to the New York Rangers, where he spent the next two seasons. Though Plante was still considered a leading goalie, he was traded in part because he of his inflexible attitude. Because the Rangers were a losing team, Plante had a high goals against average and his team never made the playoffs. He retired after the 1964-65 season, during which he was demoted to their minor league team, the Baltimore Clippers.

During his retirement, Plante worked as a salesman for Molson's. He had previously been their goodwill ambassador during his off-seasons. Plante's tenure as a salesman was short-lived. He returned to hockey in 1967, when he was signed by the St. Louis Blues, an expansion team. That year, he and **Glenn Hall** back-stopped the team to the Stanley Cup finals. Together, the pair won the Vezina Trophy in 1969; Plante's goals against average that season was 1.96. His skills and ability to play the angles had not diminished much with age.

In 1970, Plante was traded to the Toronto Maple Leafs for future considerations. He played for the team through most of the 1972-73 season. Though Plante generally was solid in net, he was accused of only playing the easy games to increase his goals against average to the disfavor of his backup, Bruce Gamble.

Awards and Accomplishments

1953	Won his first Stanley Cup with the Montreal Canadiens
1956	Won Vezina Trophy as best goalie in the NHL; All-Star (First Team); Won Stanley Cup
1957-58, 1960	Won Vezina Trophy; All-Star (Second Team); Won Stanley Cup
1959	Won Vezina Trophy; All-Star (First Team); Won Stanley Cup
1962	Won the Hart Trophy, as NHL MVP; Won Vezina Trophy; All-Star (First Team)
1969	Won Vezina Trophy (with Glenn Hall)
1971	All-Star (Second Team)
1978	Elected to the Hall of Fame

Plante: Just Who Was That Masked Man?

In his time, Jacques Plante was called a lot of things, not all of them complimentary. Iconoclastic? Yes. Hypochondrical? At times. Idiosyncratic? Yes. Superstitious? Definitely. But, above all, Frere Jacques was a unique individual, a marvelous teacher, ahead of his time, and the man who quite literally changed the very face of hockey.

Source: Halligan, John. *New York Times*, March 16, 1986, section 5, p. 2.

Retired from NHL

Plante's final NHL stop was the Boston Bruins. The Leafs traded him to the Bruins in 1972 for a draft choice. Over the course of his career, he had 434 career wins, a 2.38 goals against average, and 82 shutouts. His playoff record, based on 112 games, included a 2.17 goals against average.

Though Plante retired from playing in the NHL, he remained active in the game. In 1973-74, he served as the general manger-coach of the Quebec Nordiques in the World Hockey Association. Though he had a ten-year contract, he only lasted one year because he did not have the skills for the job.

Plante did play in goal again. During the 1974-75 season, he appeared in 31 games for the Edmonton Oilers in the World Hockey Association. He had a 3.31 goals against average, which was good for this high scoring league. Plante also intended to play in the 1975-76 season, and went to the team's training camp though he was 45 years old. However the suicide of one of his children contributed to his decision to retire as a player for good.

After his retirement, Plante was connected to the game by serving as a goaltending coach for a number of teams on a part-time basis, including the Philadelphia Flyers, Montreal Canadiens, and the St. Louis Blues. Plante continued to coach goaltenders until his death from stomach cancer on February 26, 1986, in Geneva, Switzerland, where he was receiving treatment for his illness.

Elected to Hockey Hall of Fame in 1978, Plante's legacy was not just as a great goaltender but someone who fundamentally changed how the position was played, especially because of the mask. As he told Dave Anderson of the *Saturday Evening Post*, "For stopping the puck, the mask doesn't help me. But I am a better goalkeeper now because I can laugh at getting hit in the face."

SELECTED WRITINGS BY PLANTE:

(With Andy O'Brien) *The Jacques Plante Story,* McGraw-Hill Ryerson, 1972.
Goaltending, New York: Collier, 1972.

FURTHER INFORMATION

Books

Fischler, Stan. *The All-New Hockey's 100: A Personal Ranking of the Best Players in Hockey History.* Toronto: McGraw-Hill Ryerson Ltd, 1988.

Fischler, Stan and Shirley. *Fischlers' Hockey Encyclopedia.* New York: Thomas Y. Crowell, 1975.

Hickok, Ralph. *A Who's Who of Sports Champions: Their Stories and Records.* Boston: Houghton Mifflin Company, 1995.

Hunter, Douglas. *A Breed Apart: An Illustrated History of Goaltending.* Chicago: Triumph Books, 1995.

Kariher, Harry C. *Who's Who in Hockey.* New Rochelle, NY: Arlington House, 1973.

McGovern, Mike. *The Encyclopedia of Twentieth-Century Athletes.* New York: Facts on File, Inc., 2001.

Periodicals

Anderson, Dave. "Hockey's Masked Marvel." *Saturday Evening Post* (December 17, 1960): 25.

Associated Press (February 27, 1986).

Bonventure, Peter. "The Iceman Stayeth." *Newsweek* (March 3, 1975): 47.

Falla, Jack. "A brash act 20 years ago became a tribute to the late Jacques Plante." *Sports Illustrated* (November 17, 1986): 90.

Frei, Terry. "Goalie legends leave lasting memories." *Denver Post* (October 18, 2000): D7.

Halligan, John. "Plante: Just Who Was That Masked Man?" *New York Times* (March 16, 1986): Section 5, p. 2.

Hofmann, Rich. "Hockey's First Masked Man Had Guts—Jacques Plante Donned Mask, Changed Game." *Seattle Times* (January 7, 1990): C6.

"Jacques Plante Dies; All-Star Goaltender Played 18 Seasons." *New York Times* (February 28, 1986): A20.

Johnson, George. "Facing the Past/It's Been 40 Years Since Jacques Plante Made NHL History." *Calgary Sun* (November 14, 1999): S19.

LeBrun, Pierre. "Plante the best goalie ever: That's the word according to a computer formula used by magazine." *Gazette* (December 3, 1999): E3.

Neff, Craig, and Robert Sullivan. "Jacques Plante: 1929-86." *Sports Illustrated* (March 10, 1986): 10.

Perley, Warren. "Hockey great Plante dies of cancer at age 57." United Press International (February 27, 1986).

Zurkowsky, Herb. "The other man behind the mask; Bathgate shot at Plante and changed the face of hockey forever." *Ottawa Citizen* (April 25, 1993): C7.

Other

"Joseph Jacques Omer 'Jake the Snake' Plante." http://ucsu.colorado.edu/~norrisdt/bio/plante.html (November 2, 2002).

"The Legends: Players: Jacques Plante: Biography." Legends of Hockey. http://www.legendsofhockey.net:8080/LegendsOfHockey/jsp/Legen… (November 2, 2002).

"The Legends: Players: Jacques Plante: Career Statistics." Legends of Hockey. http://www.legendsofhockey.net:8080/LegendsOfHockey/jsp/Legen… (November 2, 2002).

Sketch by A. Petruso

Lilia Podkopayeva

Lilia Podkopayeva
1978-

Ukrainian gymnast

As an Olympic champion, Lilia "Lily Pod" Podkopayeva affirmed her status as the premiere women's gymnast with gold medal wins in the European Championships, Worlds, and the Olympics. At age seventeen and holding the top titles at every level of competition, Podkopayeva was the first athlete ever to win multiple medals while representing the Ukraine. Known best for her amazing floor exercise routines, Podkopayeva is the only woman in the world to execute an Arabian double front brani out in her routine.

Podkopayeva was born on August 15, 1978, in Donetsk in the Ukraine, which at that time was a part of the former Soviet Union. The second of two children, she lived in a household of three generations, with her parents and grandparents. Her father abandoned the family when she was two years old. After that time she lived with her mother, brother, and grandparents, although it was her grandmother who took responsibility and raised her. At age five Podkopayeva was enrolled in gymnastics classes at the Dynamo Gym. There she worked with coach Ulla Pugacheva, who recognized the girl's natural ability.

Soon Podkopayeva was training with Galyna Losinska. With the gymnasium located in Donetsk, and the home of Podkopayeva's grandparents situated outside of town, Podkopayeva faced a three-hour round trip to gymnastics class. Commuting six days per week and practicing four hours daily, her dedication to her sport was exceptional.

When she won her first age-group competition at age six, Podkopayeva enjoyed the flowers and attention that accompanied the victory. Her determination was reaffirmed, and she set for herself a personal goal to become the number one gymnast in the world.

Podkopayeva was first named to the Ukrainian national team in 1988 at age eleven. She then spent five years with Losinska at a gymnastics training camp in preparation for her planned Olympic competition in 1996. Along with other Olympic hopefuls the two lived at the camp, living and training together. Podkopayeva's career at the international level was launched in earnest in 1992. At the European Cup the following year she took second place in the all-around competition and won a bronze medal on the balance beam. She won her first gold medal in the all-around competition at the Ukrainian Cup and took the gold on the vault at the Hungarian International competition.

She followed with a gold in the floor exercise and on vault at the 1994 European Championships and Goodwill Games respectively. With the exception of a silver medal on balance beam at the World Championships, she won a string of golds worldwide. She took first

Chronology

1978	Born August 15 in Donetsk, Ukraine
1981	Is abandoned by father during parents' divorce
1983	Enrolls at the Dynamo Gym in Donetsk
1985	Wins an age-group competition at age six
1988-92	Enters regional competitions in Ukraine, Belarus, and Moscow
1990	Wins a spot on the Ukraine National Team at age 11

Awards and Accomplishments

1992	Gold medal in Brussels
1993	Gold medals at the Hungarian Internationals and Ukrainian Cup
1994	Gold medals at the European Championships and at the Good Will Games; won silver at the World Championships in Brisbane, Australia
1995	All-around gold medal at the World Championships
1996	All-around gold medals at the European Championships and at the Atlanta Olympics

Podkopayeva was the first multiple medal winner ever from the Ukraine.

place in the all-around competition at the 1995 Worlds, the subway World Challenge, and at the Kosice and Bymnix Internationals.

As she approached her teens, the Soviet Union underwent a period of unrest and the Union dissolved altogether in 1991. The Republic of the Ukraine that year declared its independence. Representing the Ukraine, she won two golds and a silver at the Atlanta Olympics in 1996. By virtue of the wins she earned a place in Ukrainian sports history as the first multiple Olympic medallist. Her victory in the Olympic all-around competition came impressively in the wake of a broken rib earlier in the season.

Known for her innovative and very difficult choreography in her floor exercise routines, her double front summersault variations are most impressive. At the 1996 European Championships in Birmingham, England, she executed a tucked double-front somersault with half-twist. The move helped clinch her gold medal win in the all-around competition. Despite winning two additional golds in the apparatus finals at the Birmingham competition that year, she expressed displeasure with her performance and vowed to improve in time for the upcoming Olympics in late summer of the year.

In the competition for the all-around championship at the Atlanta Olympics, Podkopayeva bested Romanian Lavinia Milosovici on the floor exercise by a score of 9.887-9.812. Podkopayeva went on to win the contest with a total score of 39.255, topping the Romanians who tied with a score of 39.067 each and shared the bronze. The Olympic gold capped gold medal wins at the European and World Championships and confirmed her status at age seventeen, as the best women's gymnast worldwide. Her gold medal performances at the 1996 Olympics were enhanced by gold in the European Championships and at the Grand Prix of Rome. With the Olympic win, Podkopayeva brought back-to-back women's all-around championships to the Ukraine, which produced 1992 gold medallist Tatyana Gutsu. Furthermore Podkopayeva became the first woman gymnast since Lyudmila Turischeva to cap a World Championship title with an Olympic all-around gold medal.

After learning of the death of her devoted grandmother in 1996 just prior to the Olympic competition,

Podkopayeva performed with championship precision while dedicating her performance to her grandmother. In recognition of the Olympic success Podkopayeva was honored by the Ukrainian President and by the national Parliament. The Ukrainian government awarded her a car and a house in Donetsk.

After Atlanta, Podkopayeva appeared at an exhibition in Brussels before setting out on a tour of the United States with the John Hancock Tour of World Champions. As she toured, Losinska arranged with Coach Viktor Savitsky for the two to move to Tampa, Florida. According to the agreement, Losinska was hired as a coach at Rocky Strassberg's Gemini School of Gymnastics where Podkopayeva would also train.

After her arrival in Florida in January of 1999, Podkopayeva began to prepare for the 2000 Olympics in Sydney, Australia. In March she appeared before 4,000 gymnasts at the three-day Gasparilla Classic gymnastics meet in Tampa.

In 2000, hampered by back and ankle injuries, 21-year-old Podkopayeva did not compete in the Sydney Olympics. After her gold medal Olympic performances, Podkopayeva achieved considerable fame in her native Ukraine and was worshipped like a hero for her legendary accomplishments. With future plans focused on choreography, she made plans to return to the Ukraine to study at the Kiev Sports University.

CONTACT INFORMATION

Address: c/o Gemini School Of Gymnastics, 401 Douglas Rd. E., Oldsmar, FL 34677-2907 . Phone: (813) 855-3737.

FURTHER INFORMATION

Periodicals

Sports Illustrated (July 26, 1996): 26.
Tampa Tribune (January 30, 1999).
Time (June 3, 1996): 18.

Other

"USA Gymnastics International Athlete Biography: Lilia Podkopayeva." www.usa-gymnastics.org/athletes/intlbios/p/lpodkopayeva.html (February 5, 2003).

Sketch by G. Cooksey

Alain Prost
1955-

French race car driver

Formula One auto racing (F1) is the most elite, well funded, avidly followed, and competitive sport in the world. The drivers of F1 are among the most talented racing car drivers in the world, and Alain Prost retired in 1993 as the greatest driver in F1 history. Known for his seemingly effortless ability, Prost won a record-breaking fifty-one races in his career, with a style so understated that it was joked he lacked verve. "He can go stunningly fast without looking as if he's trying," Frank Williams, head of the Williams F1 team once said, according to *Sports Illustrated*. He was considered "a master strategist on the racecourse and a cunning opportunist off it," according to *Sports Illustrated,* a reputation that earned him his nickname, "The Professor."

Prost was born in 1955 in Lorette, France, to Andre and Marie-Rose (Karatchian) Prost. He aspired to becoming a professional soccer player until he began kart racing as a teen. He quickly emerged as a competitive talent by winning the 1973 Karting World Championship. After graduating to cars, Prost clinched the 1976 European Formula Renault series, and the 1979 European Formula 3 championship. His impressive win that season at Monaco—one of F1's most prestigious circuits—foretold his bright future in the F1 series.

Built Reputation in Junior Formulae

It wasn't long before Prost's success in the junior series earned him the attention of a leading F1 team. Prost was on a losing streak when McLaren team director Teddy Mayer offered him a chance to test in a McLaren car. After just three laps, Prost's talents were obvious; Mayer was ready to offer the young driver a contract to drive in the most prestigious auto racing series in the world. He actually offered Prost a ride in the final race of the 1979 series, but Prost turned him down—had no interest in racing F1 without adequate preparation. It was a move that would become characteristic of the calculating Professor. Prost debuted in 1980 as McLaren's

Alain Prost

second driver alongside British F1 veteran John Watson at the Argentine Grand Prix. He drove flawlessly, finishing in sixth place, and followed up two weeks later with a fifth place in the Brazilian Grand Prix.

Prost's sunny picture began to cloud before the third race of the season. The suspension broke in his McLaren during practice before the South African Grand Prix, resulting in a crash. He suffered a broken wrist and missed the next two races. Car failure led him to crash again that season, during practice for the United States Grand Prix. Prost was disgusted with McLaren team management. They had a falling out over his lack of confidence in the team's engineering standards. He broke his contract with McLaren to join Renault, France's national racing team. He challenged McLaren to sue, leaving the two teams to settle the matter legally.

High Hopes for Frenchman on French Team

The pressure was high for Prost to become the first French World Champion driving a French car. He won his first F1 Grand Prix in France in 1981, and finished the season in fifth place for the World Championship, a respectable finish for a second-year driver. Prost began the 1982 season with impressive back-to-back wins, but the season quickly disintegrated for him. He took the top spot on the podium at the South African Grand Prix. He was third crossing the finish line at the Brazilian Grand Prix, but won the race when the first and second-place cars, dri-

Chronology

1955	Born February 24 in Lorette, France
1973	Wins Karting World Championship
1976	Begins racing professionally and wins Formula Renault Challenge series
1977	Wins Formula Renault Europe title and begins racing the Formula 3 series
1979	Wins French and European Formula 3 titles
1979	Signed to race the F1 series for McLaren team
1980	Places sixth and fifth, respectively, at first two Grand Prix races; breaks wrist before third
1980	Returns in May to score points at British and Dutch Grand Prix
1980	Frustrated by McLaren car failures, breaks contract to drive for Renault Sport; challenges McLaren to sue
1981	Finishes fifth in the 1981 F1 Championship
1982	Finishes fourth in the 1982 championship, but is plagued by car reliability problems
1983	Loses World Championship by two points; is fired by Renault
1984	Returns to drive for McLaren
1984	Loses World Championship by one-half of a point to teammate Niki Lauda
1985	Wins five Grands Prix and first World Championship
1986	Wins second World Championship, over Nigel Mansell and Nelson Piquet
1987	Finishes fourth in World Championship
1988	Loses World Championship to teammate Ayrton Senna
1989	Wins World Championship, but tension with Senna leads Prost to defect to Ferrari team
1990	Loses World Championship after controversial crash with Senna
1991	Fired from Ferrari for criticizing team
1992	Sits out 1992 season
1993	Returns to drive for Williams-Renault, wins fourth World Championship, breaks world record with fifty-one Grand Prix wins
1993	Announces retirement when Williams hires Senna
1994	Works for French television and as representative for Renault
1994	Works as consultant for McLaren team
1997	Buys Liegier team, renamed Prost Grand Prix
1998	Debut chassis proves unreliable, team has disappointing season
1999	Peugot engine proves too heavy too win
2000	Sells share of team after third losing season
2002	Begins liquidation of Prost Grand Prix team

Awards and Accomplishments

1973	Karting World Championship
1976	Formula Renault Championship
1977	Formula Renault Europe Championship
1979	French and European F3 Championships
1981	Fifth place, F1 World Championship
1982, 1987	Fourth place, F1 World Championship
1983-84, 1988, 1990	Second place, F1 World Championship
1985-86, 1989, 1993	F1 World Championship
1993	World record for 51 Grand Prix wins

as the hero. Furious at the turn of events, Prost was fed up and even considered retiring from F1. He moved his family from France to Switzerland not long after.

After his strong performance in 1982, Prost was a legitimate contender for the 1983 World Championship. He finished "in the points," or in the top six, in nine of the first eleven races. The Brabham team became a serious threat halfway through the season, however, after engineers improved the BMW engine. Prost clearly saw that Brabham's Nelson Piquet could succeed in upsetting him on the points table. He stressed to Renault engineers that an immediate improvement was necessary to remain competitive, but Renault did not consider the Frenchman's pleas seriously. Prost's fears played out. He was the points leader until the very end of the season, when Piquet and his new engine narrowly edged him out. Feeling Renault had miserably mismanaged the season, Prost again found himself in an adversarial position with an F1 team. In an unforeseen turn, Renault responded by replacing him.

Nasty Rivalry With Teammate

In the years since Prost had abandoned the team, McLaren had taken on new management and was fast becoming a competitive force in F1. Teamless, Prost had little bargaining power to resist an offer from the team's ambitious new director, Ron Dennis. Dennis hired Prost as partner to Niki Lauda for a reported $500,000 season retainer, a pittance in F1. McLaren's new turbo V6 engine by Porsche proved to be a competitive move for the team. Prost had accumulated six wins and Lauda five coming into the final Grand Prix of the 1984 season, in Portugal. Prost went into the race knowing that even if he won, and Lauda came in second, Lauda would win the World Championship by one-half a point. Prost took an early lead in the race, while Lauda got caught behind in the middle of the pack. Lauda was persistent, however, and managed to finish the race in second behind Prost, winning the Championship. Prost was near tears when he took the podium. In a show of incredibly good-natured sportsmanship and compassion, Lauda remarked to Prost, "Forget it. Next year, the

ven by Nelson Piquet and Keke Rosberg, were disqualified. His winning streak ended in Brazil. Renault's turbocharged engine technology was quickly becoming eclipsed by that of the Ferrari and Honda teams. Prost's most searing disappointment of the year was personal. He was second behind teammate René Arnoux in the French Grand Prix when it was agreed that Arnoux would give Prost the lead, as Prost was closer to a Championship than his teammate. Arnoux reneged and held Prost in second, leaving him to finish third in the 1982 World Championship.

In the highly competitive world of F1, the deal made on the track in France between Prost and Arnoux was not an unusual one. When a race comes down to being won by one of two teammates, it is common to let the one who has scored the most Championship points during the season move ahead. In a fickle turn of publicity, however, Prost was villainized, and was characterized as a poor sportsman. Arnoux, in comparison, was depicted

---

Where Is He Now?

Prost tested for the 1994 McLaren team, but decided not to race. He appeared as a commentator for French television and represented Renault in an attempt to secure an F1 engine deal for the manufacturer. Unable to sell the Renault engine to an F1 team, Prost quit the company to work as a consultant for McLaren F1 team. During this time, he was trying to organize his own F1 team, and negotiated a deal with Peugeot to build engines for him from 1998-2000. He purchased the Ligier team, renaming it Prost Grand Prix, but the first Prost chassis, which ran in the 1998 season, proved unreliable. By the next year, the Peugeot engine had become to heavy to be competitive, and Prost had another disappointing season. The 2000 season was an outright disaster. The team's relationship with Peugeot had fallen apart, and Prost ended up running with Ferrari engines, which were not successful. In an attempt to keep the team afloat, Prost sold a share of the team. "Prost as a team owner was not in the same league as Prost the driver," according to GrandPrix.com. The team went into liquidation in January 2002.

Championship is yours," according to *Grand Prix Champions* by Alan Henry. Even Lauda knew the Championship could just as easily have gone to Prost.

Lauda was right. Prost won both the 1985 and 1986 World Championships, becoming the first driver to retain a title since Jack Brabham in 1960. Prost won his twenty-eighth career race in 1987, beating **Jackie Stewart**'s 1973 record, but falling short of the Championship. McClaren came back the next year with a more competitive turbo engine, and Prost found himself driving alongside Brazilian driver Ayrton Senna, whose mission to best his teammate fueled one of the bitterest rivalries in motorsports. There was no friendly competition between the teammates. Senna was aggressive and impulsive on the track and beat Prost to the 1988 World Championship with eight wins to seven. While Senna thrived on the confrontational rivalry, Prost did not. The fire was stoked further when Prost won the 1989 World Championship after the two McLarens collided during the penultimate race of the season, in Suzuka, Japan, taking Senna out of Championship contention.

Retired With World Record

Prost was driving for Ferrari a year later when Senna returned the favor upon their return to Suzuka. Senna deliberately ran Prost off the track going into the first corner of the race, taking the 1990 Championship from him. Prost raced with Ferrari until one race before the end of the 1991 season, when he was fired for publicly criticizing the team. The driver took the 1992 season off, but returned in 1993 to take a seat with Williams-Renault. Prost won the 1993 World Championship, but announced his retirement when Williams announced its intention to sign Senna. Prost cited the politics of F1 as his motivation to quit. "It is full of hypocrisy," he told *Sports Illustrated*. "You never know if the hand slapping you on the back has a dagger in it."

Prost took home his fourth and final World Championship in 1993, and retired as the winningest F1 driver

in history, with a career fifty-one race wins. He held the title until it was broken in 2002 by **Michael Schumacher**. His long-standing win record is testament to his careful strategies on the track. To this day, the Professor is legendary in F1 as one of the most calculating and cunning drivers in the sport's history.

CONTACT INFORMATION

Address: Alain Prost, Federation des Sports automobiles, 136 rue de Longchamp, Paris 75116, France.

FURTHER INFORMATION

Books

Henry, Alan. *Grand Prix Champions: From Jackie Stewart to Michael Schumacher.* Motorbooks International, 1995.

Periodicals

Laushway, Ester. "Paris: From cockpit to pit wall." *Europe* (June 1997): 36-37.
"Sports people: Alain Prost." *Sports Illustrated* (November 15, 1993): 88.

Other

"Alain Prost." Formula One Art & Genius. http://f1-grandprix.com (October 30, 2002).
"Alain Prost." Formula One Database. http://f1db.com (October 30, 2002).
"Grand Prix drivers: Alain Prost." GrandPrix.com. http://www.grandprix.com (October 30, 2002).

Sketch by Brenna Sanchez

Kirby Puckett
1960-

American baseball player

Baseball player Kirby Puckett played twelve seasons with the Minnesota Twins, from 1984 to 1996, helping his team win the World Series in 1987 and 1991. A superstar beloved of Minnesota fans, he was given the nickname "Puck" for his short stature and jovial nature. He was forced to retire as a player at age thirty-six after losing the sight in his right eye to glaucoma. Puckett finished his career with a .318 batting average, the best by a right-handed hitter since **Joe DiMaggio**. He set a record with 2,040 hits in his first ten seasons. Puckett was

Kirby Puckett

named to the American League All-Star team for ten consecutive years, from 1986 to 1995. Among many other awards, he was inducted into the Baseball Hall of Fame in 2001, at age forty-one.

Humble Beginnings

Kirby Puckett was born March 14, 1960 (some sources say 1961), in Chicago, Illinois, the son of postal worker William Puckett and his wife, Catherine. He was the youngest of nine children. The family was poor, making their home in the Robert Taylor housing project on Chicago's South Side. As a boy, Puckett loved baseball and played his early games using aluminum-foil bats and balls made from rolled-up socks. He played ball whenever and wherever he could, scratching out makeshift baseball diamonds and scrounging a team from among neighborhood playmates. Puckett considers his parents heroes because they supported him in his interest and made life in the projects bearable.

Short and stocky, Puckett began body building at Calumet High School in Chicago. He played baseball there and for the semipro Chicago Pirates, at third base. By the time he graduated, however, no major league scouts had made him an offer. He went to work in a Ford Motor Company plant and later worked as a census taker. One year after graduation, he was offered a scholarship to Bradley University in Peoria, Illinois, after trying out for the Kansas City Royals.

Discovered by the Twins

After his first year at Bradley, however, Puckett's father died, and he moved back to Chicago to be closer to his mother. He attended Triton Community College, where he continued to play baseball. By this time, he could bench press 300 pounds and was hitting .472, with forty-two stolen bases. A Minnesota Twins scout picked him out, and the Twins drafted him in the first round in January 1982. He started his career on the Twins' minor league team in Elizabethton, Tennessee, in the Appalachian League, where he led the league in seven categories. The following season he was sent to Visalia, California, and chosen best major league prospect. By the spring of 1984, Puckett was moved up to the majors. He made his debut with the Minnesota Twins on May 8, 1984, when he had four hits in five times at bat. As good as his batting was, however, Puckett could not seem to hit home runs, prompting **Reggie Jackson** to refer to him as "a Punch and Judy hitter."

During spring training in 1986, new Twins manager Tom Kelly and batting coach Tony Oliva helped Puckett overcome his fear of being hit by the ball and trust his strength and speed at the plate. By the start of the season he had found his powerful, accurate swing and hit thirty-one home runs, with ninety-six runs batted in (RBI), in the 1986 season as a lead-off hitter. The same season, he won his first Gold Glove award as a centerfielder.

Awards and Accomplishments

1982	Named Minor League Player of the Year by *Baseball America*
1984	Topps Major League All-Rookie Team; voted Rookie of the Year by Minnesota Twins
1985	Calvin Griffith Award as Minnesota Twins' Most Valuable Player
1986	American League Silver Slugger Team; Most Valuable Player, Twin Cities Chapter, Baseball Writers Association of America
1986-95	American League All-Star Team
1986-89, 1991	Gold Glove Award
1987	Minnesota Twins won World Series
1987-89	Silver Slugger Award
1991	Minnesota Twins won World Series
1993	Branch Rickey Award
1995	Chosen one of five most caring athletes by *USA Weekend*
1996	Roberto Clemente Award
2001	Inducted into Baseball Hall of Fame, the third youngest living player to be so honored

The Branch Rickey Award is given by the Rotary Club of Denver to Major League Baseball's top community volunteer.

The Roberto Clemente Award is given to the Major League player who best represents baseball through community service.

Where Is He Now?

Retired from the Minnesota Twins as a player since 1995, Kirby Puckett has remained with the club as executive vice president. He has kept a fairly low profile, according to his former teammates. They say he seems to prefer spending time with his family and fishing to being in the public eye, although he remains tremendously popular with his fans. He also devotes a good deal of time to charity work. However, after a great year in 2001, in which he was inducted into the Baseball Hall of Fame, 2002 was a difficult one for Puckett. His wife, Tonya, filed for divorce in February, citing domestic violence and an "irretrievable breakdown" in their marriage. She sought sole custody of their two children. Then, in September, Puckett was charged with felony false imprisonment and misdemeanor criminal sexual conduct. Puckett declared that he was innocent of the charges. He remained free on his own recognizance, and a pretrial was set for late November.

In 1987, Puckett batted .332, with twenty-eight home runs and ninety-nine RBIs. The Twins won the World Series, and Puckett was third in Most Valuable Player (MVP) voting. He finished third again in 1988, his best season, after batting .356, with twenty-four home runs and a total of 234 hits. In 1991, Puckett was named MVP of the Twins' Championship victory over the Toronto Blue Jays. In game six of the World Series, Puckett proved himself a superstar when he had three RBIs in the first inning, made astounding plays in the third, fifth, and eighth innings, and hit a game-winning home run in the eleventh inning. This forced a seventh World Series game, which the Twins also won, taking the World Series championship for the second time in five years.

Puckett passed up a chance to earn more money elsewhere in 1992 and decided to stay with the Minnesota Twins for the rest of his career. His loyalty and his humility—coupled with his outstanding playing ability, short stature, and friendly demeanor—made him a favorite of Minnesota fans. He began shaving his head before the baseball season, which made him look even more like a storybook character, and he always drove to ball games in an old pickup truck. In 1995 he turned down his chance to become a free agent and settled in for a long career in Minneapolis. He had married Tonya Hudson in 1986, and they had a young daughter. He told *Esquire,* "I'm living out my dream every day." Then, in September of 1995, everything began to change.

Injury and Glaucoma

On September 28, 1995, Puckett was hit in the face by a fastball. The blow shattered his jaw and put him out of play for the rest of the season. At spring training camp the following March he was batting well, but on March 28 he woke up unable to see out of his right eye. Doctors discovered he had glaucoma. The problem could not be corrected, even after four surgeries, and on July 12, 1996, he announced his retirement as a player. Puckett told his fans that he was happy with the twelve seasons he had been able to play, including two World Series championships and ten All-Star games. The Twins kept him on as executive vice president of the club, and he and his family were able to stay in Minneapolis, the adopted city they loved.

During his playing years and after retirement, Puckett established and worked for a number of charities, including serving as a national spokesperson for the Glaucoma Foundation and making public appearances to encourage people to get eye exams for the disease. He and his wife hosted an annual invitational pool tournament to raise money for the Children's HeartLink in Minneapolis, to help those in need pay for life-saving heart surgery. Both of Puckett's parents died of heart attacks. As an executive with the Minnesota Twins, he chaired the club's Community Fund committee. He won both the **Wesley Branch Rickey** Award and the **Roberto Clemente** Award for service to the community.

Hall of Fame

Puckett was inducted into the Baseball Hall of Fame in Cooperstown, New York, in 2001. He was the third youngest player still living at the time of induction to receive the sport's highest honor, behind only **Lou Gehrig** and **Sandy Koufax.** Twelve busloads of fans from Minneapolis-St. Paul came to support their favorite son at the ceremony, many wearing Puckett's Number 34 jersey. At his acceptance speech, he told the crowd, "Don't feel sorry for yourself if obstacles get in your way. I faced odds when glaucoma took the bat out of my hands, but I didn't give in or feel sorry for myself. It may be cloudy in my right eye, but the sun is shining very brightly in my left eye."

Career Statistics

Yr	Team	Avg	GP	AB	R	H	HR	RBI	BB	SO	SB
1984	MIN	.296	128	557	63	165	0	31	16	69	14
1985	MIN	.288	161	691	80	199	4	74	41	87	21
1986	MIN	.328	161	680	119	223	31	96	34	99	20
1987	MIN	.332	157	624	96	207	28	99	32	91	12
1988	MIN	.356	158	657	109	234	24	121	23	83	6
1989	MIN	.339	159	635	75	215	9	85	41	59	11
1990	MIN	.298	146	551	82	164	12	80	57	73	5
1991	MIN	.319	152	611	92	195	15	89	31	78	11
1992	MIN	.329	160	639	104	210	19	119	44	97	17
1993	MIN	.296	156	622	89	184	22	89	47	93	8
1994	MIN	.317	108	439	79	139	20	112	28	47	6
1995	MIN	.314	137	538	83	169	23	99	56	89	3
TOTAL		.318	1783	7244	1071	2304	207	1085	450	965	134

MIN: Minnesota Twins.

Kirby Puckett followed his dream as a young boy growing up in the inner city of Chicago, and it led him to stardom. He appears to have remained humble throughout the process, however, and thankful for the years he had as a player as well as for the years ahead. As a young player he did not let his short stature prevent him from becoming a strong and gifted hitter and fielder. Instead of becoming discouraged, he hung a photo of an even shorter player, Hall of Famer Hack Wilson at 5'6" and 190 pounds, for inspiration. While playing award-winning ball games, Puckett still found time to give back to his community, and even after losing part of his eyesight continued to serve in an uplifting way.

CONTACT INFORMATION

Address: Kirby Puckett, c/o Minnesota Twins, Metrodome, 34 Kirby Puckett Place, Minneapolis, MN 55415. Phone: 612-375-1366. Email: fanfeedback@twins.mlb. com. Online: http://minnesota.twins.mlb.com/.

SELECTED WRITINGS BY PUCKETT:

(As told to Greg Brown) *Be the Best You Can Be,* Waldman House Press, 1993.
I Love This Game!: My Life and Baseball, HarperCollins, 1993.
(With Andre Gutelle) *Kirby Puckett's Baseball Games,* Workman, 1996.

FURTHER INFORMATION

Books

Contemporary Black Biography. Volume 4. "Kirby Puckett." Detroit: Gale Group, 1993.

Who's Who Among African Americans. 14th edition. "Kirby Puckett." Detroit: Gale Group, 2001.

Periodicals

Swanson, William. "Kirby without Tears." *MPLS-St. Paul Magazine* (June, 2000): 84.
"When It Comes to Helping Kids, Kirby Puckett Is All Heart!" *Sports Illustrated for Kids* (May, 1997): 19.
"Winfield, Puckett Head Baseball's Class of 2001 Hall of Fame Inductees." *Jet* (August 20, 2001): 52.
"Zorich, Puckett & Johnson among Most Caring Athletes." *Jet* (February 20, 1995): 47.

Other

Baseball Reference.com. "Kirby Puckett." http://www. baseball-reference.com/ (October 31, 2002).
Boone, Matthew. "MLB Hall of Famer Kirby Puckett Divorcing Wife." SportsScoops.com. http://www. sportsscoops.com/ (February 22, 2002).
Major League Baseball Official Info: Community Programs. http://mlb.mlb.com/ (November 1, 2002).
Minnesota Twins Official Web Site. http://minnesota. twins.mlb.com/ (November 1, 2002).
National Baseball Hall of Fame. "Kirby Puckett." http:// www.baseballhalloffame.org/ (November 1, 2002).
Ramstad, Evan, Associated Press. "Puckett Declares Innocence after Appearing at County Jail." Yahoo! Sports. http://sports.yahoo.com/ (October 21, 2002).
"Rotary Club Releases Branch Rickey Award Finalists." BizJournals.com. http://www.bizjournals.com/ Denver/ (August 6, 2002).
Yahoo! Sports. "Hall of Famer Puckett Charged with Sexual Assault." http://sports.yahoo.com/ (October 18, 2002).

Sketch by Ann H. Shurgin

John Randle
1967-

American football player

Playing for the Minnesota Vikings and the Seattle Seahawks, John Randle was a leading defensive tackle in the 1990s. Though small for a defensive tackle in this time period (only 6'1" and 267 lbs.), he once played in 176 consecutive games and started in 140 consecutive games. Randle also had eight consecutive seasons in which he had at least ten quarterback sacks, and was selected to play in the Pro Bowl six times.

Randle was born on December 12, 1967, in Hearne, Texas, where he and his older brother Ervin (who was also a football player who played for the Tampa Bay Buccaneers from 1985-92) were raised by their single mother, Martha. His mother was employed as a maid, and Randle grew up very poor. The family lived in a shack until he was a senior in high school.

It was not until Randle began attending Hearne High School that he began to play football, following in the steps of his brother. At Hearne High, he was both an offensive and defensive lineman. Randle was also a member of the track team. Because of his poor SAT scores, however, he had to go the junior college route.

Plays College Football

After spending two years at Trinity Valley Community College, Randle entered Texas A & M in Kingsville, a Division II school. As a senior in 1990, he earned Little All-America honors, and graduated with a degree in sociology.

Signs With the Vikings as Free Agent

During the 1990 NFL draft Randle was not selected in part because of his small size for the position he played. His play at Texas A & M did merit a workout with the Atlanta Falcons, but they declined to sign him because they believed he was out of shape. A week later, the Minnesota Vikings invited him to training camp, and Randle was later signed to a free agent contract. He played his heart out to prove his value to the team.

John Randle

It took several seasons for Randle to emerge as a defensive force. In 1990, he only had one quarterback sack. In 1991, Randle started eight games and had 8.5 sacks. By 1992, he established himself as solid player and began his consecutive game start streak. Randle proved his worth as a leader in quarterback sacks and forcing fumbles.

Though Randle continued to post improved numbers in the mid-1990s, it was not until 1996 that he had a break-out season. This was due in part to a coaching change, but also to Randle's emerging approach to the game. He began to trash talk more on the field, getting into his opponents' heads. Randle also would paint his face, and developed his own physical pre-game ritual.

Randle continued to improve in 1997, with a career-high 15.5 sacks, the most in the NFL that season. Though he was a great defensive player, he had more to offer with his instinctual, relentless play that wore down offenses. Paula Parrish in the *Star Tribune* wrote, "his bigger contributions, according to teammates and his defensive coordinator, continued to be the intangibles— his leadership, his electricity, his experience."

In 1998, Randle became a free agent, but was the Vikings' designated transition player. (That is, Minnesota had the right to match any offer Randle received.) He had a hard time getting a deal done with the Vikings, and considered signing with the Miami Dolphins, among other teams. Randle ended up signing a five-year deal worth $32.5 million with $20 million guaranteed. This was the largest contract ever for a defensive lineman.

During the first season of his contract, Randle only had 10.5 sacks (his lowest number in years) and was not chosen to play in the Pro Bowl. In 2000-01, Randle was still playing relatively well, but had a disappointing season with only eight sacks and 31 tackles. Though he was sometimes double and triple-teamed, some observers believed his skills were in decline.

Randle believed his career was incomplete without a Super Bowl ring and believed that Minnesota was not progressing in that direction. Because the Vikings wanted to give him a pay cut, he asked to be traded. Instead, the team released him. When his career in Minnesota ended after 2000-01 season, he had recorded the third most sacks, with 114, and the third most fumbles caused, with 24, in team history.

Signs with Seattle

In 2001, Randle was signed by the Seattle Seahawks. The team's coach and general manager, **Mike Holmgren**, had previously been the coach of the Green Bay Packers, a team Randle excelled against. Randle signed a five-year deal worth $25 million, including a $5 million signing bonus.

Randle immediately proved his worth, with a great 2001 season. He had 11 sacks, and went to the Pro Bowl. He began the 2002 season on the injured list recovering from knee surgery—his first major injury—but played well during the rest of the season. The injury brought his consecutive game streak to an end at 140. Randle led the Seahawks with seven sacks in 12 games.

Randle's stretch of eight consecutive seasons where he recorded ten or more sacks was the second most in NFL history after **Reggie White**. Coach Holmgren told Chuck Carlson of the *Capital Times,* "He's got a lot of energy. He's the type of player you want on your team because his motor is so great, his heart is so great and he goes 150 percent all the time. Everybody wants guys like that."

CONTACT INFORMATION

Address: c/o Seattle Seahawks, 11220 NE 53rd St., Kirkland, WA 98033.

FURTHER INFORMATION

Periodicals

Allen, Percy. "Knee Injury Ends Randle's Streak at 140." *Seattle Times,* (November 12, 2001): D6.

Allen, Percy. "Seahawks Quickly Get Handle on Randle." Knight Ridder/Tribune News Service, (March 4, 2001).

Banks, Don. "A Method to His Madness." *Star Tribune,* (January 3, 1998): 1C.

Banks, Don. "Randle Becomes $32.5 Million Man." *Star Tribune,* (February 18, 1998): 1C.

Banks, Don. "Randle Visits Eager Dolphins." *Star Tribune,* (February 17, 1998): 4C.

Banks, Don. "Unsettled, Randle proves to be Quite Unsettling." *Star Tribune,* (September 22, 1998): 1C.

Barreiro, Dan. "Randle has Reasons to Smile These Days." *Star Tribune,* (July 26, 2000): 1C.

Bruscas, Angelo. "Can't Hold Candle to Randle." *Seattle Post-Intelligencer,* (December 30, 2002): D8.

Bruscas, Angelo. "Energizer Charging Hawks Randle's Return Should Provide Lift for Defense." *Seattle Post-Intelligencer,* (October 12, 2002): D4.

Carlson, Chuck. "Vikings' Randle Backs Talk." *Capital Times,* (November 28, 1997): 1B.

Ditrani, Vinny. "Vikes' Lineman Has a Big Bite." *The Record,* (December 27, 1997): S2.

Farnsworth, Clare. "Randle is Too Hard to Handle." *Seattle Post-Intelligencer,* (July 31, 2001): C1.

Hartman, Sid. "Randle Says It's Time to Start Over." *Star Tribune,* (March 4, 2001): 3C.

Career Statistics

Yr	Team	Tackles				Fumbles		Interceptions	
		TOT	SOLO	AST	SACK	FF	BK	INT	TD
1990	MIN	21	12	9	1	1	0	0	0
1991	MIN	58	32	26	9.5	2	0	0	0
1992	MIN	56	45	11	11.5	0	0	0	0
1993	MIN	59	54	5	12.5	3	0	0	0
1994	MIN	42	32	10	13.5	3	0	0	0
1995	MIN	44	34	10	10.5	1	0	0	0
1996	MIN	46	36	10	11.5	4	0	0	0
1997	MIN	58	48	10	15.5	2	0	0	0
1998	MIN	41	30	11	10.5	3	0	0	0
1999	MIN	38	30	8	10.0	4	0	1	0
2000	MIN	26	25	1	8.0	2	0	0	0
2001	SEA	35	26	9	11.0	4	0	0	0
2002	SEA	15	13	2	7.0	0	0	0	0
TOTAL		539	408	131	132.0	29	0	1	0

MIN: Minnesota Vikings; SEA: Seattle Seahawks.

Jensen, Sean. "Roving Randle Keeps Vikings' Opponents Guessing." Knight Ridder/Tribune News Service, (October 10, 2000).

King, Peter. "Home Free." *Sports Illustrated,* (March 2, 1998): 74.

Parrish, Paula. "Randle Again Looms Large." *Star Tribune,* (September 23, 1996): 12C.

Powell, Jaymes. "John Randle's Sack Milestone Just Part of a Package." Knight Ridder/Tribune News Service, (November 13, 1999).

Reusse, Patrick. "High Expectations Not New for Randle." *Star Tribune,* (August 8, 1998): 1C.

Reusse, Patrick. "Randle: He Keeps Going and Going…" *Star Tribune,* (November 19, 1998): 1C.

Williamson, Bill. "Randle Seeks Trade After Poor Season." Knight Ridder/Tribune News Service, (January 31, 2001).

Williamson, Bill. "Vikings Expected to Release Randle." Knight Ridder/Tribune News Service, (February 28, 2001).

Youngblood, Kent. "One Speed." *Star Tribune,* (August 2, 1999): 1C.

Youngblood, Kent. "Positively Pumped Up." *Star Tribune* (April 29, 2000): 1C.

Youngblood, Kent. "Stats Don't Reflect Randle's Solid Play." *Star Tribune,* (September 13, 2000): 1C.

Other

"Green, Vikings Agree to Buyout." ESPN.com. http://sports.espn.go.com/espn/print?id=1305597&type=news (January 25, 2003).

"John Randle." ESPN.com. http://sports.espn.go.com/nfl/players/stats?statsId=1422 (January 13, 2003).

"John Randle." NFL.com. http://www.nfl.com/players/playerpage/4128/bios (January 13, 2003).

Sketch by A. Petruso

Steve Redgrave
1962-

British rower

S ir Steve Redgrave is the greatest competitive rower in history, one of the greatest Olympians ever and, arguably, Britain's greatest sportsman of the twentieth century. His feats as an oarsman are legendary—gold medals at five consecutive Olympic Games; nine World Championships; a string of four unbeaten seasons; and countless awards in Thames River competitions. "Most of us dream of winning one gold medal, but to do it at five Olympics is something else," Australian rower Bo Hanson told *Time International*. "It's just a shame he had to race against us."

Pursuing his Passion

Redgrave, the son of a carpenter, was a frustrated, dyslexic student when he left school at age sixteen to become a rower—and began more than two decades of six-day-a-week, five-hour-a-day training sessions. "When you're dyslexic, you are always trying to get around situations, to find another way to do some things," Redgrave told Diane Pucin of Knight-Ridder Newspapers. "If you find something you are quite good at, then you tend to stick with it. Some people call me obsessive, but I think it was just that, at a time in life when you need to fit in, I found something that I was good at."

Redgrave claimed his first Olympic gold medal at the 1984 Games in Los Angeles in the coxed four race. Two years later, in 1986, he won the first of his nine World Champion gold medals and won three gold medals in

Steve Redgrave

the Commonwealth Games: in the single sculls, coxless pairs and coxed four events. At the 1988 Olympics in Seoul, Redgrave teamed with Andrew Holmes and they blew away the field to win gold in coxless pairs. The next day, on a whim, they rowed in the pair with coxswain race—and won the bronze medal.

Relentless

Holmes retired after the Seoul Games; Redgrave teamed with Matthew Pinsent, an Oxford-educated vicar's son, in 1990. "The two shared nothing but a love of rowing, yet that was enough to make them inseparable," Brian Cazeneuve wrote in *Sports Illustrated.* "When fans would ask Redgrave, who is dyslexic, to write a special inscription with his autograph, he sometimes called on Pinsent to watch over him so he wouldn't reverse the letters." The pair was relentless on the water, going undefeated for five years and winning gold medals in coxless pairs in four World Championships and the 1992 Olympic Games in Barcelona.

The 1996 Games in Atlanta offered Redgrave a shot at his fourth consecutive Olympic gold medal and a place in the history books. Danish sailor Paul Elvstrom had won gold medals at four consecutive Olympic games from 1948 to 1960 and Americans **Al Oerter** (1956-1968) and **Carl Lewis** (1984-1996) matched that mark in track and field. The Hungarian fencer Aladar Gerevich leads all athletes with six golds in consecutive games between 1932 and 1960 (no games were held in

1940 or 1944.) Redgrave downplayed the distinction of joining this elite group as he headed into the 1996 games. "I row to do my very best," he told Pucin, "and it is silly to think about pressure. There isn't a lot of hype in this sport. It is filled with good people who are never arrogant, and so the people who win will have done their best. That's what's important. If I win another gold, that is wonderful. If not, then that is too bad, but that's all."

A Brief Retirement

Redgrave and Pinsent won the coxless pairs in Atlanta; Redgrave's place in history was secure, but he was physically and mentally exhausted. "If anyone sees me go near a boat again," he gasped after racing to his fourth Olympic gold, "they have my permission to shoot me." Redgrave's rash retirement did not last, however. Four months later, he was back in training. "He has lived with the job so long now he doesn't know any other way," said his wife, Ann, a physician with the British rowing team. "My training as a doctor tells me people just can't switch off like that."

Redgrave, Pinsent, Jim Cracknell and Tim Foster began preparations for the 2000 Olympics in Sydney, Australia, where they would compete in the coxless four. Some commentators suggested the move to a four-man race was due to Redgrave's dwindling abilities. The team worked hard, however, averaging "370 kilometers a week on the water, plus weights sessions in the gym," *Time International* reported. "About 65 percent of the rowing time is just grinding out the kilometers at 18-20 strokes a minute, at a heart rate of 140. Two or three times a week they do more intensive exercises to up the heart rate, and once a week get up to competitive pace of 36 strokes a minute, which has the heart racing nearer to 170-180 beats a minute. It would be a grueling schedule for an athlete in perfect health. But Redgrave, 38, is not." Redgrave was diagnosed with colitis, appendicitis, and diabetes after the 1996 Olympics. To manage his diabetes while in training, he consumed 6,000 calories a day in six meals, each followed by an insulin shot. "There are no athletes who compete in an endurance sport with diabetes," he said, "so there's no form guide."

A Lasting Legacy

The Britons prevailed in Sydney, and Redgrave had Olympic gold medal number five. He was the second athlete ever—and the first in an endurance sport—to win gold medals at five successive Olympics. "Steve told us, 'Remember these six minutes the rest of your life,'" Foster said. At the medal ceremony, Redgrave received his gold from Princess Anne of Britain, and International Olympic Committee President **Juan Antonio Samaranch** presented him with a special medal commemorating his fifth straight gold medal.

Redgrave lives in Marlow, England, with his wife, Ann, and their three children. He is off the water, but he's pushing as hard as ever. Redgrave has launched his own line of men's sportswear and has secured endorsement deals for a cholesterol-lowering spread, a brand of snack foods, and the luxury carmaker Jaguar. Also, the Sir Steve Redgrave Charitable Trust has a goal of raising £5 million over five years for philanthropic efforts focused on children's health. In *Sports Illustrated,* Cazeneuve summarized Redgrave's legacy: "If rowing has given value to Redgrave's life, he in turn has ennobled the gentleman's pursuit with his workingman's dedication."

CONTACT INFORMATION

Address: Marlow, Buckinghamshire, England. Online: Steve Redgrave Web site: http://195.172.104.2/.

SELECTED WRITINGS BY REDGRAVE:

(With Nick Townsend) *A Golden Age: Steve Redgrave, the Autobiography,* BBC Worldwide, 2000.

FURTHER INFORMATION

Periodicals

"Britain's Redgrave Gets Special Reward." *New York Times* (December 30, 2000).

Cazeneuve, Brian. "Never Say Never: Britain's Steve Redgrave, the Greatest Oarsman Ever, Isn't the Retiring Type." *Sports Illustrated* (October 9, 2000).

Noble, Kate. "On Golden Ponds." *Time International* (July 10, 2000).

Noble, Kate. "Steve Redgrave." *Time* (October 2, 2000).

Awards and Accomplishments

1984	Gold medal in coxed four, Olympic Games in Los Angeles, California
1986	Gold medal, coxed pairs, World Championships
1986	Gold medal in single sculls, coxless pairs, and coxed four, Commonwealth Games
1987	Silver medal in coxed pairs, World Championships
1987, 1991, 1993-95	Gold medal in coxless pairs, World Championships
1988	Gold medal in coxless pairs and bronze medal in coxed pairs, Olympic Games in Seoul, South Korea
1989	Silver medal in coxless pairs, World Championships
1990	Bronze medal in coxless pairs, World Championships
1990	Indoor World Rowing Champion, World Rowing Championships
1992	Gold medal in coxless pairs, Olympic Games in Barcelona, Spain
1996	Gold medal in coxless pairs, Olympic Games in Atlanta, Georgia
1997-99	Gold medal in coxless four, World Championships
1997, 1999	Gold medal in coxless four, World Cup
2000	Gold medal in coxless four, Olympic Games in Sydney, Australia
2000	Voted BBC Sports Personality of the Year
2001	Knighted by Queen Elizabeth II, receiving Commander of the Order of the British Empire status

---

Pucin, Diane. "Redgrave Ready to go for Fourth Rowing Gold." *Knight-Ridder/Tribune News Service* (July 20, 1996).

Vecsey, George. "Five Games, Five Medals for a Determined Briton." *New York Times* (September 23, 2000).

Ware, Michael. "Kings' Row: Britain's Steve Redgrave Strokes His Way to Immortality, While New Zealand's Rob Waddell Doesn't Miss a Beat." *Time International* (October 2, 2000).

Sketch by David Wilkins

Gabrielle Reece
1970-

American volleyball player

Gabrielle Reece is not only known for her physical prowess, but also for her beauty. She has made a name for herself in the world of sports by merely being herself, and she has graced the world with her beauty by modeling to make a living while doing what she truly loves, which is playing volleyball. Reece has made great strides in challenging the world's perception of femininity and size, being 6'3" and weighing 160-170 pounds. She has never been ashamed to tell people her weight,

Gabrielle Reece

and it is obvious why, as she is quite fit. Reece's goal in life is to change people's perceptions of what it is to be a woman and an athlete. She is not one to mince words and her straightforward communication is refreshing. Reece continues to intrigue the world, with her latest pursuit being golf. It is clear she is a woman of many talents and is always up for the challenge.

Around the World in 15 Years

"Sometimes I think the only reason my mother was put on earth was to give birth to me," says Reece in her book *Big Girl in the Middle*. It was clear to her early in life that if things were going to get done, it would have to be by herself, as she found her mother to be unreliable. After being born in California and spending the first two years of her life in Trinidad, she was abandoned by her mom in Long Island at the age of three. Reece's mother left her with friends who were reliable, but unfortunately at the age of seven, her mother requested she come live with her and her new husband. This was devastating for Reece. From there she lived in Puerto Rico then on to St. Thomas in the Caribbean. All of this turmoil caused Reece to act out with frustration. Her mother had the insight to realize her daughter was going nowhere good living in St. Thomas, so they uprooted and moved to Florida.

That was the best move she could have made, because that is where Reece finally found an outlet for all her tension through sports. At the Catholic high school she attended in St. Petersburg, Florida, she was recruited

for basketball and volleyball simply due to her height. Reece eventually realized she really enjoyed playing and had found her niche in the world.

Florida is also where Reece was led into the modeling scene. A friend of the family encouraged her to get some portraits done and take some modeling classes. That same friend sent Reece's photos to an agent who was ready to fly her off to Paris, France immediately. Her mother put the breaks on that, as at seventeen she felt her daughter was too young. Looking back, Reece concurs with her mother's decision, as she was not ready for that kind of life. Staying in Florida allowed her to really develop her skills in volleyball and learn some self-discipline. After Reece was in college the agent called on her again, and that is when she took off as a model. She had an agreement with the volleyball coach at Florida State that when she was playing volleyball, that should be the focus, but the off-season was her choice. This caused some problems with the other players who would train during the off-season, but obviously this did not phase Reece.

Once Reece's college career had ended, she was at a loss for what to do with her life. She did some modeling, but she knew that was not where her passion was. In an interview with the *Daily Paragraph*, Reece stated, "modeling was a vehicle for me and I never viewed it as anything else but that. Sport felt instinctively like the right place to go." A friend intervened and suggested she try beach volleyball. She went professional in 1992 and left modeling behind for good. She became quite accomplished in the four-person beach volleyball circuit, earning many awards. During this time she became known for her risk-taking personality. This won her a few hosting positions for MTV. She hosted a show called *The Extremists* and *MTV Sports*. She took time off from volleyball from 1997 until 1999, during which she wrote a book and married husband Laird Hamilton. In 1999 she went back to the beach to play two-player volleyball. Two-player volleyball was a lot more work, and she discovered she was not as well suited for it.

Developed Passion for Golf

Reece was approached by David Lee, a former PGA Tour journeyman, about a "nontraditional teaching method" for golf according to Alan Shipnuck with *TL Golf*. Lee proposed that she agree to work on this method for a year and a half. Reece states in the article "my greatest strength in all of this, besides my discipline, is my curiosity." It is this curiosity and discipline that helped her realize she liked the challenge of golf, but was not satisfied with the training techniques of the Gravity Golf program. In January 2001 she began working with the Butch Harmon Golf School. Butch Harmon's school takes a much more traditional, yet high-tech approach to training golf. They examine your strokes through computer models to see where improvements needs to be made. Reece has been working with them for the past couple years and intends to train for the LPGA Qualifying School in 2004.

Unfortunately when Reece quit volleyball, her life became askew. Her new passion for golf invaded her life and took over every facet. That left no space for her husband Laird. Reece filed for divorce in January of 2001. Fortunately time heals all wounds. After nearly a year apart, the couple reconciled and have been together ever since. She feels the same way about her pursuit of golf. "I've never quit anything in my life. I started this, and I need to finish it. Even if I'm a bust, I have to finish this journey," she stated to Shipnuck.

Reece was interviewed for the cable channel Lifetime's program *Intimate Portrait*, where she was able to share in her own words the story of her life. Lifetime named her as "one of the 20 most influential women in sports" and "a new female idol." The program outlined Reece's amazing attitude and how she is able to accomplish anything she puts her mind to. She shares how her early life was quite turbulent. Reece was able to express how participating in sports turned her life around and gave her focus. She also explains how she survived the tumultuous years and admitted that it made her a better person because she had to learn to rely upon herself. Reece feels that everything she has is due to her hard work and love and relationships she has encountered along the way are the perks.

Awards and Accomplishments

1992	Named Most Valuable Player, 4-woman Pro Beach Volleyball Tour
1994-95	Awarded Offensive Player of the Year, 4-Woman Pro Beach Volleyball Tour

---

Through all of these journeys, Reece has remained true to herself and who she is. She concedes to the issues she addresses saying, "The thing I don't like about this fear of being big is that it feeds into this general female thing of wanting to be less – less powerful, less assertive, less demanding, less opinionated, less present, less big," Reece wants to make it clear that it is okay to show all sides of yourself. She encourages people to be whom they truly are to make a better life for themselves, rather than living up to what everyone else is expecting. Barbara Harris with *Shape* states, "She is leading us in a direction not only of someone with a healthier body image, but of also being your own person." In an article about her book for *Newsday,* Reece expressed, "I'm hoping the book is motivating for younger girls, to give them a wake up call." She shares that she regrets not getting involved in sports earlier than age 15. Reece wants to give that chance to other girls. She is obviously making some sort of impact, as she was ranked the ultimate fitness role model by *Shape* readers two years in a row.

CONTACT INFORMATION

Address: Gabrielle Reece, c/o Crown, 201 East 50th St., New York, NY 10022.

SELECTED WRITINGS BY REECE:

(With Karen Karbo) *Big Girl in The Middle*. New York: Crown Publishers, Inc., 1997.

FURTHER INFORMATION

Books

"Gabrielle Reece." *The Complete Marquis Who's Who*. Marquis Who's Who, 2001.
"Gabrielle Reece." *Sports Stars*. Series 1-4. U•X•L, 1994-98.

Periodicals

Blauvelt, Harry. "Spikes Now on Feet Volleyball Star Reece Shoots for LPGA tour." *USA Today,* (April 26, 2001): 01C.
Coats, Bill. "Ruling at the Net Gabrielle Reece Makes Her Point in Beach Volleyball." *St. Louis Dispatch,* (June 30, 1996): 01F.

Davies, Gareth. "Sport: Modeling Took Second Place to Sport." *Daily Telegraph,* (February 2, 1998).

"The 50 Most Beautiful People in the World 1992: Gabrielle Reece." *People,* (May 4, 1992): 74.

Fish, Mike. "Women in Sports: Growing Pains: Selling of Female Athletes: Sponsors Struck with Reece's Looks, Not Skills." *Atlanta Constitution,* (September 25, 1998): D01.

Reed, Susan and Meg Grant. "Lookout: Volleyball, Anyone? Model Gabrielle Reece's Favorite Spikes are Not on Her Heels." *People,* (October 16, 1989): 97.

Silver, Michael. "Big Girl in the Middle." Scorecard – Book Reviews.*Sports Illustrated,* (August 25, 1997): 20.

Skotnicki, Monique. "When You Fish Upon a Star." *Newsday,* (August 9, 2002): 03.

"Super Power: Super Strong, Superfit: Adrienne Shoom Gets a Look at the Body According to Pro Beach Volleyball Superstar Gabrielle Reece." *Flare,* (May 1, 1998): 118-23.

Other

"Gabby scores (again)." *Shape.* http://www.shape.com/shapelife/p/2038.jsp?requestedPage=4. (December 15, 2002).

"Gabrielle Reece." *Lifetime Intimate Portrait.* http://www.lifetimetv.com/shows/ip/portraits/9820/9820_index.html. (January 2, 2003).

"Gabrielle Reece." Volleyball.org. http://www.volleyball.org/people/gabrielle_reece.html. (December 15, 2002).

"Gabrielle Reece Dove 80 Feet in Search of the Rare Shovel-Nose Shark." *Discovery Channel.* http://dsc.discovery.com/convergence/sharkweek2002/celebrities/celebrities.html. (1/2/2003).

"Model Gabrielle Reece seeks divorce." *AP Online.* (March 9, 2001).

Shipnuck, Alan. "The Glorious Quest of Gabrielle Reece: Can a World-Class Cover Girl and Superstar Athlete Find Success and Happiness on the LPGA Tour? This One is Determined to Try." *TLGolf.* http://www.tlgolf.com/features/0701reece.html. (December 15, 2002).

Sketch by Barbra J Smerz

Pee Wee Reese

Harold "Pee Wee" Reese
1918-1999

American baseball player

Major League Baseball player Harold "Pee Wee" Reese was considered one of the greatest of all Brooklyn Dodger players. A superb defensive shortstop, a capable hitter, and a student of baseball who used his intelligence as much as his athletic abilities to beat opponents, Reese, however, earned his place in baseball history for far more than his ball playing talent. Ultimately he will be remembered as the man whose courage, and sense of justice and fair play greatly helped smooth the entry of **Jackie Robinson** onto the 1947 Brooklyn Dodgers. Reese's support of Robinson hastened the integration of African-Americans into major league baseball at a time when it was still pervaded by racism.

Youth in Kentucky

Harold Henry Reese was born on July 23, 1918 in Ekron, Kentucky. His father, Carl, was a railroad detective, and his family lived for the most part in Louisville. Harold was a small boy growing up, but it was not his stature that brought him his famous nickname. Folks started calling him "Pee Wee" when the fourteen-year-old Reese won a national marbles tournament. A "pee wee" is a kind of marble.

Despite providing Reese with the trappings of a normal boyhood, Louisville was still a segregated city in the American South. "When I was growing up, we never played ball with blacks because they weren't allowed in the parks," Reese told Ira Berkow of the *New York Times.* "And the schools were segregated, so we didn't go to school with them." Reese later admitted he had never shaken the hand of a black man until he greeted Jackie Robinson on the first day of the Dodger's 1947

Chronology

1918	Born July 23 in Ekron, Kentucky
1937	Plays for New Covenant Presbyterian Church team
1938-39	Plays for Louisville Colonels of American Association
1939	Acquired by Boston Red Sox
1940	Sold to Brooklyn Dodgers
1941	Plays in first World Series
1942, 1947-54	National League All-Star
1943-45	Serves in U.S. Navy
1947	Jackie Robinson joins Brooklyn Dodges as first African American in major league baseball
1949, 1952-53, 1955-56	Plays in World Series
1954	Bats career high .309
1955	Brooklyn celebrates "Pee Wee Reese Night"
1958	Retires from baseball
1959	Coach for Los Angeles Dodgers
1984	Elected to National Baseball Hall of Fame at Cooperstown
1984	Elected to Brooklyn Dodgers Baseball Hall of Fame
1997	Diagnosed with lung cancer
1999	Dies in Louisville

Awards and Accomplishments

1932	National Marbles Champion
1943, 1947-54	National League All-Star
1947	Leads National League with 104 bases on balls
1949	Leads National League with 132 runs scored
1952	Leads National League with 30 stolen bases
1952	Reaches base safely three times in one inning, a National League record
1953	Leads National League with 15 sacrifice hits
1984	Elected to National Baseball Hall of Fame and Brooklyn Dodgers Baseball Hall of Fame

spring training. Kentucky had much darker secrets than segregation. When Reese was about ten-years-old, his father took him to a tree and solemnly told the boy that black men had been lynched on the tree. The story impressed Reese deeply, and when he became a father himself, Reese showed his own sons the same tree.

Reese did not play on his high school baseball team, probably because of his size. After he graduated and took a job as a cable splicer for the local phone company, however, Reese joined the New Covenant Presbyterian Church team. In the church league, Reese proved to be a talented shortstop and at the end of the 1937 season he was signed by the Louisville Colonels of the minor league American Association (AA). By the end of his second season with the Colonels, Reese had become the star of the team. He was a sterling infielder, with a fielding average of .943 whose speed and smarts enabled him to lead the league in both triples and stolen bases. In 1939 Reese was acquired by the Boston Red Sox who, unable to find a place for him in their line-up, sold him the following year to the Brooklyn Dodgers of the National League (NL) for $75,000. He joined the team for the 1940 season. He had an unremarkable rookie season, but Reese came into his own in 1941, and under his field leadership, the Dodgers won the National League pennant.

In 1942 Reese married Dorothy Walton, with whom he would have two children, a daughter Barbara and a son Mark. Shortly after their marriage, Reese enlisted in the Navy in 1943 and shipped out to fight in the Pacific theater of the Second World War. Like many another ball-players in the early 1940s, Reese lost some of the best years of his playing life in the service of his country in the Second World War. Sailing home from

Guam in 1945, a shipmate brought Reese the news that the Dodgers had just become the first team in the major leagues to sign a black player, Jackie Robinson. Reese was unfazed, till he learned that Robinson was a shortstop. "My God, just my luck, Robinson has to play my position!" Reese told Berkow of the *New York Times*. "But I had confidence in my abilities, and I thought, well, if he can beat me out, more power to him. That's exactly how I felt." Reese held onto his shortstop position. Robinson was used at first base, and later moved to second.

Playing with Jackie Robinson

In spring 1947, when Brooklyn brought Robinson up from its Montreal farm club, tensions were high at the Dodger training camp. Reese took the lead in making a place for Robinson on the team despite resentments. Reese was the first to shake Robinson's hand and the first to play cards with him in the clubhouse. Not long after spring training began, a group of southern players, led by Dixie Walker, circulated a petition stating that they would not play if Robinson were allowed on the team. Reese, the team captain and a Southerner himself, bluntly refused to sign it. That action, many believe, effectively put an end to the uprising.

That was not the end of attacks on Robinson however. Once the season began, Robinson's presence gave rise to virulent racist provocation at ball parks throughout the United States. Witnessing a particularly violent eruption of racist heckling against Robinson in Cincinnati, Ohio, Reese walked onto the field and put his hand on Robinson's shoulder, a powerful expression of solidarity. "Pee Wee kind of sensed the sort of hopeless, dead feeling in me and came over and stood beside me for a while," Robinson is quoted in Arnold Rampersad's biography *Jackie Robinson*. "He didn't say a word but he looked over at the chaps who were yelling at me . . . and just stared. He was standing by me, I could tell you that. I will never forget it."

Reese became Robinson's closest friend on the Dodgers, as well as his mate in a deadly double-play tandem after Robinson was switched to second base.

Career Statistics

Yr	Team	Avg	GP	AB	R	H	HR	RBI	BB	SO	SB	E
1940	BRO	.272	84	312	58	85	5	28	45	42	15	18
1941	BRO	.229	152	595	76	136	2	46	68	56	10	47
1942	BRO	.255	151	564	87	144	3	53	82	55	15	35
1946	BRO	.284	152	542	79	154	5	60	87	71	10	26
1947	BRO	.284	142	476	81	135	12	73	104	67	7	25
1948	BRO	.274	151	566	96	155	9	75	79	63	25	31
1949	BRO	.279	155	617	132	172	16	73	116	59	26	18
1950	BRO	.260	141	531	97	138	11	52	91	62	17	26
1951	BRO	.286	154	616	94	176	10	84	81	57	20	35
1952	BRO	.272	149	559	94	152	6	58	86	59	30	21
1953	BRO	.271	140	524	108	142	13	61	82	61	22	23
1954	BRO	.309	141	554	98	171	10	69	90	62	8	25
1955	BRO	.282	145	554	99	156	10	61	78	60	8	23
1956	BRO	.257	147	572	85	147	9	46	56	69	13	25
1957	BRO	.224	103	330	33	74	1	29	39	32	5	19
1958	LA	.224	59	147	21	33	4	17	26	15	1	10
TOTAL		.269	2166	8058	1338	2170	126	885	1210	890	232	407

BRO: Brooklyn Dodgers; LA: Los Angeles Dodgers.

Playing next to Jackie Robinson seems to have spurred Reese to the finest performances of his career. Beginning in 1947, Reese appeared in eight consecutive All-Star games. He had his best all-around season in 1949, batting .279 and leading the National League in runs scored. In 1954, he batted for a career high average of .309. Under Reese's captainship, the Dodgers won five National League pennants between 1949 and 1956. It wasn't until 1955 that Brooklyn finally managed to win the World Series, thanks in great measure to a spectacular play in the deciding game, in which Reese cut off a throw from the outfield after a fly out, spun blind and fired the ball to first to double off a runner there. The play helped preserve the Dodger's lead.

Reese hung up his spikes at the close of the 1958 season. When he retired, the Dodgers offered him the job of manager, a position he had already turned down twice as a player. He declined the job a third time, preferring to work with the team as a coach, a position he held for a single season. He subsequently worked as a baseball broadcaster for NBC and CBS, and as a representative for Louisville Slugger, the country's most respected maker of baseball bats. Reese underwent surgery for prostate cancer in the 1980s and in 1997 was diagnosed with lung cancer. He died on August 14, 1999 at his Louisville home.

As an eight-time All Star who led the Dodgers to seven pennants and one World Series victory, Pee Wee Reese would have won a place in the hearts of Brooklyn Dodger fans whatever else he had done. His courageous public support of Jackie Robinson earned him a more important spot not just in the history of baseball but in the history of the civil rights movement of the mid-century. Joe Black, a black pitcher who joined the Dodgers a couple years after Robinson, told *Jet* magazine, "When

I finally got up to Brooklyn, I went to Pee Wee and said, 'Black people love you. When you touched Jackie, you touched all of us.' With Pee Wee, it was No. 1 on his uniform and No. 1 in our hearts."

FURTHER INFORMATION

Books

Golenbock, Peter. *Teammates.* Gulliver Books, 1990.

"Harold "Pee Wee" Reese." *Contemporary Heroes and Heroines,* Book IV. Detroit: Gale Group, 2000.

Kahn, Roger. *The Boys of Summer.* New York: Harper & Row, 1971.

Schoor, Gene. *The Pee Wee Reese Story.* New York: J. Messner, 1956.

Periodicals

Berkow, Ira. "A Baseball Celebration—Standing Beside Jackie Robinson; Reese Helped Change Baseball." *New York Times* (March 31, 1997): C1.

Block, Hal. "Pee Wee Reese remembers the start of a baseball revolution." Associated Press (March 30, 1997).

Independent (August 19, 1999): 6.

Kindred, Dave. "An artist at life." *Sporting News* (August 30, 1999): 62.

"Pee Wee Reese Has Lung Cancer." *Newsday* (March 9, 1997): B12.

Weil, Martin. "Shortstop Pee Wee Reese Dies; Brooklyn Dodger Admired for His Support of Jackie Robinson." *Washington Post* (August 15, 1999): C6.

Sketch by Gerald E. Brennan

Dan Reeves
1912-1971

American football executive

One of football's greatest innovators, the American entrepreneur Dan Reeves is credited with bringing the first major sports team to the West Coast. After purchasing the Cleveland Rams in 1941, Reeves moved the team to Los Angeles five years later, paving the way for other Pacific Coast sports teams. Reeves was also the first modern day National Football League (NFL) owner to sign an African American player, halfback Kenny Washington, who joined the Rams in 1946. After the trendsetting Reeves established the first full-time scouting staff, other NFL team owners followed suit. A New York-born businessman, Reeves was also known for founding a "Free Football for Kids" program at the Rams' stadium. He was inducted into the Pro Football Hall of Fame in Canton, Ohio, in 1967.

Born in New York City on June 30, 1912, Daniel F. Reeves was the son of Irish immigrants James Reeves and Rose Farrell. His father and an uncle, Daniel, had risen from fruit peddlers to owners of a grocery-store chain, bringing wealth to the family. Young Reeves attended the Newman School in Lakewood, New Jersey, where he captained the football team. But rather than desiring to play football professionally, Reeves dreamed of becoming a football team owner. Upon graduating in 1930, he received the Newman School's General Excellence Medal.

Reeves attended Georgetown University but left before completing his degree. He then worked in the family business, and married Mary V. Corroon, a friend of a Georgetown classmate, on October 25, 1935. The pair had six children.

After the family's grocery-story chain merged with Safeway Stores in 1941, twenty-eight-year-old Reeves set out to fulfill his childhood dream of owning a football team. He bid unsuccessfully for the Pittsburgh Steelers and the Philadelphia Eagles franchises before purchasing two-thirds of the Cleveland Rams. In addition to this NFL team, Reeves also acquired holdings in an American Professional Football Association team, the Jersey City Giants.

During the Second World War, the sports entrepreneur served as a second lieutenant in the Army Air Corps. Joining the service in 1942, he relocated with his family to army bases in upstate New York. By the following year, a manpower shortage during the war led to a temporary disbanding of the Cleveland Rams franchise. Reeves remained with the army and was promoted to captain before his discharge in 1945. That same year, the Rams took the NFL championship title in a 15-

Dan Reeves

14 game against the Washington Redskins. Rookie quarterback Bob Waterfield, who had led the team to victory, was named NFL Player of the Year.

Brought First Major Team to West Coast

The Rams' championship game was to be their last played in Cleveland, as it was Reeves' decision to relocate the team to Los Angeles for the 1946 season. Poor attendance among the Ohio fans, as well as a high rental fee at the Cleveland stadium, had impelled Reeves to look for a new home for the team. In choosing Los Angeles—which was then 2,000 miles away from the nearest NFL city—the Rams' owner generated heated controversy. Though the city boasted college football, Los Angeles had no pro-football tradition. (A former NFL team, the Los Angeles Buccaneers, had played a road schedule but had never established a home stadium.) Although they pronounced the move financially irresponsible, Reeves' fellow NFL owners eventually conceded, and the Los Angeles Rams were established.

Once in Los Angeles, Reeves made another major contribution to professional football when he employed the NFL's first full-time scouting staff. This network of scouts specialized in visiting universities and evaluating the major-league potential of college athletes. Before long, every other major-league team had copied Reeves' idea, and scouting staffs became standard NFL team fixtures.

In another innovative move, Reeves became the first post-war NFL owner to sign an African American player, halfback Kenny Washington, who joined the team in 1946. A few months later, he hired a second African American player, Woody Strode. It was no coincidence that two major changes—the Rams' move west and its racial integration—had come at the same time. The Los Angeles Coliseum had stipulated that the team must racially integrate if the coliseum was to serve as the Rams' home stadium. Reeves readily agreed, and some credit the Rams owner for helping to inspire racial integration in all American pro sports. A year later the Brooklyn Dodgers signed **Jackie Robinson**, the first African American major-league baseball player. (Incidentally, Washington and Robinson had been roommates at the University of California at Los Angeles.)

Also in 1946, Reeves opened his own Wall Street firm, Daniel Reeves & Co., with offices in Beverly Hills and New York City. He had become a member of the New York Stock Exchange in 1943, through the firm of Adler, Coleman and Co. Yet the dual responsibilities of his firm and his football team proved too much. In 1947 Reeves transferred his seat to L. Morton Stern, a member of his New York office.

Meanwhile, the Rams encountered serious financial difficulties. During their first years in Los Angeles, the team had to compete for ticket sales with the Los Angeles Dons, who were part of the new All-America Football Conference. Using his business acumen to draw fans to the stadium, Reeves created the "Free Football for Kids" program. By encouraging children's attendance, Reeves invested in a future audience for the Rams. By 1949 the All-America Football Conference had folded, removing the competition for Los Angeles football fans. In another positive move, Reeves hired **Pete Rozelle** as the Rams' publicity director. Rozelle, who became Reeves' protégé, would later serve as commissioner of the NFL.

Yet the Rams' financial troubles were not over. A year earlier, Reeves' team had suffered a deficit of $250,000, and he was forced to take partners. These in-

cluded the oil mogul Edwin Pauley—who, along with Reeves, owned one-third of the team—as well as Fred Levy, Hal Seley, and the entertainer Bob Hope. With larger funding, the team was able to increase its promotional campaigns. Crowds soon swelled at Los Angeles Coliseum, which hosted the first NFL game attended by more than 100,000 spectators.

Hired Coach George Allen

The Rams won NFL championship titles in 1951 and 1955, during a high point of the team's history. But by 1956 a personality clash between Reeves and co-owner Pauley was beginning to have a detrimental effect on the Rams. In 1962 a solution was finally reached when Reeves bought out Pauley and other owners for $4.8 million. Meanwhile, the Rams' performance had dipped. After seven consecutive losing seasons, Reeves hired a new coach to pull the Rams out of their slump.

The new coach was the flamboyant, talented George Allen, who would later gain a reputation for transforming losing teams into consistent winners. Once a former assistant coach for the Rams, Allen was hired in 1966 as head coach. His effect on the team was immediate. The Rams became contenders once again, thanks to Allen's creation of the "Fearsome Foursome"—a defensive line that included future Hall of Famers **Merlin Olsen** and Deacon Jones.

Despite Allen's stellar winning record, the head coach clashed with Reeves. The Rams owner disapproved of some of Allen's tactics, which included spying on other teams and publicly criticizing the Rams' opponents after defeats. Reeves fired Allen in December 1968, but rehired the popular coach when the players threatened to strike. Two years later, Allen's contract expired and Reeves failed to renew it.

During the early 1960s tension had mounted between the NFL and its rival, the American Football League (AFL). When the two leagues finally merged in 1966-67, Reeves took a key role in representing the NFL team owners. It was Reeves' general manager, **Tex Schramm**, who negotiated on behalf of the NFL during the historic negotiations.

Reeves died on April 15, 1971, in New York City. The cause of death was Hodgkin's disease. He was fifty-eight years old. Four years before his death, he was inducted into the Pro Football Hall of Fame in Canton,

Related Biography: Head Coach George Allen

Born on April 29, 1918, in Detroit, Michigan, George Allen approached coaching with passion and a determination to win. He attended Alma College, Marquette University, and the University of Michigan before becoming a coach at Morningside College in Sioux City, Iowa, in 1948. Three years later he moved to Whittier College in California, and in 1957 he joined the NFL as an assistant coach to the Rams' Sid Gillman. After joining the Chicago Bears as a defensive assistant, Allen returned to the Rams in 1966 in his first job as head coach. After lifting the Rams out of a losing slump, Allen was named NFL Coach of the Year in 1967. Moving to the Washington Redskins in 1971, Allen worked a similar magic. In his twelve years of coaching, he never had a losing season, and was ranked tenth in NFL history upon his retirement. Allen died on December 31, 1990, at age 72.

Mary Lou Retton

Ohio. He will be remembered for his historic contributions to the game, including his essential role in football's cross-country expansion to the West Coast.

FURTHER INFORMATION

Books

"Daniel F. Reeves," *Dictionary of American Biography, Supplement 9: 1971-75*. New York: Charles Scribner's Sons, 1994.

Other

"Dan Reeves." Pro Football Hall of Fame. http://www.profootballhof.com/players/enshrinees/dreeves.cfm (December 9, 2002).

"Dan Reeves Moves West." Professional Football Researchers Association. http://www.footballresearch.com/articles/frpage.cfm?topic=reeves (December 9, 2002).

"George Allen." Pro Football Hall of Fame. http://www.profootballhof.com/players/mainpage.cfm?cont_id=94070 (December 9, 2002).

"St. Louis Rams Team History." NFL Archives. http://www.nflarchives.com/ramsHistory.htm (December 9, 2002).

Sketch by Wendy Kagan

Mary Lou Retton
1968-

American gymnast

Mary Lou Retton burst onto the gymnastic front with all the vivaciousness she could muster, and in doing so, took the world by storm. She changed the way people thought of a gymnast, not having the typical physique for the sport. Retton was very muscular, a change from the petit, smaller gymnasts fans were used to seeing catapulting off the balance beam and swinging around the uneven bars. She also changed the world simply by her exuberance. Retton's infectious smile captured the hearts of people everywhere during the 1984 Olympics. It is that smile that continues to inspire people to this day.

Inspired By Nadia

Mary Lou was born to Lois and Ronnie Retton. She was the youngest of five children. Growing up in the Retton household meant you were going to be very active. All five of the children would participate in various sports at any given time. Lois described her children as hyper and wanted to channel that energy into something positive. She would take Mary Lou and her sister Shari to West Virginia University for gymnastics once a week. "I would sleep in my leotard on Friday nights because I was so excited about gymnastics on Saturday mornings," Retton shared with Skip Hollandsworth of *Texas Monthly*. Her first pining for Olympic Gold came at the age of four when watching **Olga Korbut** during the 1972 Olympics. Korbut was gutsy and full of vim and vigor. Retton could identify with Korbut's spirit. Retton was also intrigued with the way Korbut expressed emotion, during the time when the Cold War forced most Russian athletes to show no emotion. When Retton was seven she watched **Nadia Comaneci** compete in the Olympics and enchant the world with her skill and force. Retton

Chronology

1968	Born in Fairmont, West Virginia
1975	Begins taking gymnastics at University of West Virginia
1980	Enters Class I Nationals
1982	Meets coach Bela Karolyi at a meet in Las Vegas, Nevada
1982	Moves to Houston to train with Karolyi<.
1983	Fractures wrist at U.S. Gymnastics Championships in Chicago, Illinois, forcing her to miss the World Gymnatics Championships that year
1984	Competes in the Olympics in Los Angeles, California
1986	Retires from full-time gymnastics
1986	Writes a book with Karolyi about her road to the gold
1990	Marries Shannon Kelley
2000	Writes an inspirational book on how to achieve happiness
2000	Begins production for the children's show created by her and her husband

Mary Lou Retton

It came down to the final event. For almost a week, 16-year-old Mary Lou Retton, America's best female gymnast, had sparred with Romania's Ecaterina Szabo for the gold medal in all-around gymnastics in the 1984 Olympic Games in Los Angeles. The winner would bear the title of finest woman gymnast in the world.

The competition had been nip and tuck. Then Szabo, a solid international star who rarely made a mistake, twirled around the uneven bars with her usual brilliance, earning a score of 9.90.

Now it was Mary Lou's turn on the vault, the last chance for the 4-foot 9-inch, 92-pound dynamo to take home the gold.

As Mary Lou waited her turn, her personal coach, Bela Karolyi, leaned across the barricade that separated him from the contestants and handed her a piece of paper. On it he had done some arithmetic: "Score a 9.95 and you will tie Szabo for the gold. Score a perfect 10 and you will be the all-around champion. Anything less than 9.95 means second place."

Source: Sullivan, George. *Mary Lou Retton*. New York:Julian Messner, 1985.

knew she wanted to one day stand on the podium and receive a gold medal.

Retton eventually got to the point where she outgrew the training she was receiving in West Virginia. In 1982 she left home for Houston, Texas. Retton had met **Bela Karolyi** when competing in Las Vegas, Nevada, and he encouraged her to come train with him. Retton's parents were reluctant at first, believing she was too young to be away from her family. It took a lot of pushing for Retton to convince them that if she did not go to Houston, her career as a gymnast may never come to fruition. Her parents decided she was right, and wanted her to be all she could be.

Retton stayed with a family in Houston whose daughter was in the same program at Karolyi's school. At this point she was training eight to ten hours a day, which left little time for schoolwork. Retton ended up taking correspondence courses, which allowed her to complete her studies at a pace that adhered to her training schedule.

Karolyi the Bear

Karolyi had been known for his harsh training style when in Romania. When he defected to the United States with his wife they opened their gymnastic school in Houston. Since being in the States Karolyi had mellowed considerably. He had become "an enthusiastic cheerleader, constantly shouting words of encouragement during competitions, clapping his gymnasts on the back, and rewarding displays of excellence with big bear hugs. Mary Lou responded well to this type of treatment. It psyched her up," wrote George Sullivan in his biography of Retton's life, titled *Mary Lou Retton*. Karolyi was enamored with Retton's innate ability in gymnastics and could see the energy within her. In Sullivan's book he expressed, "Mary Lou is a little volcano on the floor."

After only one month of Karolyi's tutelage Retton won the all-around title at the Caesar's Palace Invitational. When her team was to attend the McDonald's American Cup Competition at Madison Square Garden, she had not ranked high enough yet to be invited. Retton

went with the team as a substitute. Her big break would happen when one of her teammates suffered an injury, rendering her unable to compete. Karolyi put Retton in her teammate's position. "Not only did she win the competition, but she set a meet record of 9.95 points in the vault event," wrote Sullivan. It was this win that put her in contention for the 1984 Olympics, but the months prior to the Olympics would prove to be harrowing ones.

Olympic Visions

A mere six weeks before the Olympics Retton suffered a major knee injury that required surgery. Her parents consulted with the most skilled physician they could find, who flew in to do arthroscopic surgery. The surgery was minimally invasive, and allowed Retton to walk immediately and begin training again a week later, after doing physical therapy to ensure the knee was healing properly. By the time she was to go off to the Olympics she had fully recovered and was stronger than ever. "In the weeks before the Olympics, Mary Lou often lay in her bed with her eyes closed and let her imagination romp. She would visualize herself on each piece of equipment, performing her best routines and hitting every move perfectly," described Sullivan. Retton even went as far as to imagine receiving the gold medal, while hearing the "Star Spangle Banner" booming in the background. Her creative visualization would prove to be prophetic.

The U.S. Women's team performance at the Olympics got off to a rocky start, with several of the girls making critical mistakes during their routines. Fortunately Mary Lou Retton was on their team, who would not accept anything other than a perfect performance. With Retton's perfect 10s along with her teammate Julianne McNamara's perfect performances, they were able to bring the teams score up to medal winning status. These performances lead the team to a silver medal victory. A medal had not been won by the U.S. Women's

Gymnastic team since 1948, when they had earned a bronze. The performance was somewhat tainted by the fact that the Soviet Union and their allies (except Romania) had boycotted the Games.

Retton's greatest competition in the all-around competition was Romanian Ecaterina Szabo. They each would compete in a rotation cycle, with Szabo always performing first, which allowed people to compare their scores. Szabo did extremely well on the balance beam, earning a prefect 10. Retton was a little behind due to her routine on the uneven bars, earning a paltry 9.85. This caused her and Szabo to be neck and neck, and tensions were high. With another costly stumble on the balance beam, Retton's chances at a gold were diminishing. She was a fraction of a point behind Szabo. Karolyi, who was in the photographer's area, was cheering Retton on the whole way – and at this point Retton went over to tell her coach that she was going to "stick it." This meant she was going to do her last event, the vault, perfectly to win the gold. She waited in position until the green light on the scoreboard flashed. "Mary Lou raised her right arm to the crowd, then bounded down the runway, rocketed off the springboard to fly some 14 feet. In the air, she combined a back somersault with a double twist, her body stretched out flat like a knife blade. And then she stuck it, landing upright and rock still," writes Sullivan in his account of the moment. Although Retton waited anxiously for her score to be posted, she knew it would be a 10. When it was announced she had received a 10 she ran to the runway and waved at the crowd excitedly. Retton wasn't done though, as Olympic rules state that she had to complete another vault. She did just that, and to prove that she was worth her weight in gold, she did another perfect 10 vault. Karolyi said after the event, "Very few have her power to keep going like a bulldozer to get what they want and go on to win."

Dreams Do Come True

What Retton had envisioned years ago at seven years old, while watching Nadia Comaneci, had come to fruition. She had won the gold she had longed for. In addition to the gold for the all-around competition, Retton also earned a silver medal on the vault, and bronze medals in the uneven bars and floor exercise. She came home from the 1984 Olympics having earned the most medals any athlete had received that year. Once her competition was done Retton decided to go home to Fairmont, as she had not been home for over ten months, and due to security issues, there was not much she could do at the Games. She planned to fly back to Los Angeles for the closing ceremonies. Upon her arrival back home, Retton got a homecoming she never had expected in her wildest dreams. The town had been notified when her plane was to touch down, and there was a crowd of people waiting for her at the airport, holding signs and cheering for her. Retton was whisked away from the airport in a convertible, which was taken

Awards and Accomplishments	
1981	Named to the US junior national team
1983	Wins American Cup Championship
1983	Becomes American Classics Champion
1983	Wins Chunichi Cup Championship
1984	Wins American Cup Championship
1984	Wins the title of American Classics Champion for second time
1984	Becomes U.S. Champion and Gold Medallist for All-Around
1984	Brings home one Gold, two Silver, and two Bronze medals from Summer Olympics in Los Angeles, California
1984	Named *Sports Illustrated's* "Sportswoman of the Year."
1984	Named "Amateur Athlete of the Year" by *Associated Press*
1984	Becomes first woman to be spokesperson for Wheaties and be featured on the box
1985	First person to win American Cup Championship three times
1985	Inducted into the United States Olympic Champions Olympic Hall of Fame
1993	Named as "Most Popular Athlete in America" by Associated Press' national survey
1997	Inducted into the International Gymnastics Hall of Fame

to a parade arranged for her through the streets of Fairmont. "Quickly made banners and signs had gone up all over town. Several said: We love you, Mary Lou, and Fairmont's Golden Girl. Precious Gifts Come in Small Packages another declared," said Sullivan. It was quite a sight. Retton participated in many celebrations following the Olympics, including one in New York with a ticker tape parade. She said it was nothing compared to the celebration put on by her home town.

Retton did not realize what a celebrity she had become. Everyone knew who she was and had fallen in love with her contagious smile. Retton was requested for a plethora of television engagements, including the *Tonight Show,* where she chatted excitedly with Joan Rivers who was filling in for Johnny Carson at the time. "She won a nation's heart with spunk and a high-wattage smile," reports Steve Wieberg for *USA Today.* Retton could not go anywhere without being recognized. She tried to disguise herself by wearing sunglasses, but when you are a 4' 9" dynamo, it is hardly a disguise. Every girl in America wanted to be just like Retton to have her "winning combination of power and personality," as conveyed in *Teen Magazine*. In the same article Retton shared, "I thought I'd go to the Olympics, do my best, see what happened, then go back to normal life. But it didn't work out that way."

Retton trained two more years with Karolyi, going on to win a third McDonald's American Cup Competition, which no one had done before. About her accomplishments she stated, "you have to have dedication. And you have to get the proper coaching." She continued by expressing her gratitude to Karolyi for his part in her success, saying "I couldn't have done it without him." Karolyi has nothing but good things to say about Retton as well saying "I have been teaching gymnastics 25 years, and had many world and Olympic champions, but

Mary Lou Retton

I have never coached anybody more positive and dedicated than this little girl." Retton returned the compliment to Karolyi, sharing "He gave me a confidence that I never would have had without him." She retired from full-time gymnastics in 1986, but has remained close to Karolyi.

Before Retton retired from full-time gymnastics she had already become involved in doing various endorsements for various products. The most notable was Wheaties, as she was the first woman to grace the infamous box. Retton continued to do her endorsements while attending the University of Texas. It was there she met her husband, Shannon Kelley. Kelley and Retton married in December of 1990. Kelley said "I know it sounds like a fairy tale, but when I first saw Mary Lou on television, I told my mom I had the strangest feeling that someday I would meet her and we would get married." It was only ten months later that the wheels went into motion to bring them together. Retton is now a mother to three children and continues to do motivational speaking across the country. "Retton's vivacity remains a breathtaking phenomenon," said Hollandsworth. Retton wrote an inspiring book in 2000 sharing her methods for happiness. "What I've been doing my whole life, from being in the Olympics to getting married and being a mother, is training for my own personal happiness. Now what I want to do is share my formula

for happiness," she explained to Janice Lloyd of *USA Today*. In the book, she explains, "I tell people how to leave the comfort zone and meet life's challenges." Her and husband Shannon submitted a proposal for a program called *Mary Lou's Flip Flop Shop* which is now shown on FamilyNet, as well as several other networks. She explained, "My show will create a foundation for kids – teach them the values of honesty and respect. We will educate and entertain through the use of physical movement. This will be an interactive program that will be both educational and fun."

Mary Lou Retton showed the world that it is possible to aspire to something and with dedication and a great attitude, go on to achieve your dreams. She has helped people to see one can truly be happy simply being the best person each individual is called to be. Retton wants everyone to be able to accomplish the happiness she has. She shared "I smile because I am truly, fundamentally happy" That big smile on the outside comes from a place deep within me—and I want others to know how to find that place within themselves." Retton continues to inspire people, making public appearances, and doing her show for children. Sullivan sums up Retton's future best, stating "Mary Lou will survive. Her pretty face and winning smile, her charm, her cheerful, upbeat matter will be there for us to see for years to come."

CONTACT INFORMATION

Address: Mary Lou Retton, c/o Washington Speakers Bureau, 1663 Prince Street, Alexandria, VA 22314. Phone: (703) 684-0555.

SELECTED WRITINGS BY RETTON:

(With Bela Karolyi and John Powers) *Mary Lou: Creating an Olympic Champion.* McGraw–Hill Book Company, 1986.

(With David Bender) *Gateways to Happiness: 7 Ways to a More Peaceful, More Prosperous, More Satisfying Life.* New York: Broadway Books, 2000.

FURTHER INFORMATION

Books

"Mary Lou Retton." *Contemporary Newsmakers 1985.* Issue Cumulation. Gale Research, 1986.

"Mary Lou Retton." *Great Women in Sports.* Visible Ink Press, 1996.

Sullivan, George. *Mary Lou Retton.* New York: Julian Messner, 1985.

Woolum, Janet. *Outstanding Women Athletes: Who They Are and How They Influenced Sports In America.* Vol.1. "Chapter 3, Outstanding Women Athletes Who Influenced American Sports: Mary Lou Retton." Oryx Press, 1992.

Woolum, Janet. *Outstanding Women Athletes: Who They Are and How They Influenced Sports In America.* Vol.1. "Chapter 3, Outstanding Women Athletes Who Influenced American Sports: Olga Korbut." Oryx Press, 1992.

Periodicals

Becker, Debbie. "Retton Still Flips Over Her '84 Heroics." *USA Today,* (July 23, 1996): 06E.

Calkins, Laurel Brubaker. "'10' Again." *People,* (July 15, 1996): 65-71.

Hersch, Hank. "Beaming Again." *Sports Illustrated,* (October 27, 1992): 13.

Hollandsworth, Skip. "Change of Routine." *Texas Monthly,* (September 2000): 130.

Huzinec, Mary. "Passages." *People,* (November 28, 1994): 148.

Lloyd, Janice. "Retton's 'Gateways' Provide Her Balance Olympic Gymnast Discusses Her Life Since 1984 Gold." *USA Today,* (April 6, 2000): 03F.

"Mary Lou Retton: Life After the Olympics." *Teen Magazine,* (May 1985): 94.

Montville, Leigh. "Return of the Pixies Olympic Champion gymnast Olga Korbut and Mary Lou Retton Showed They Still Have A Lot of their Old Magic During a Crowd-Pleasing, Eight-City Tour." *Sports Illustrated,* (November 27, 1989): 34.

Torpy, Bill and Beth Warren. "Salt Lake City 2002: Gymnastics Legend Slips from Glory to Humiliation." *Atlanta Journal and Constitution,* (February 10, 2002): A1.

"Up Front: Mary Lou Retton Revels in Texas in Houston the Former Olympian Goes the Whole Nine Yards – of Tulle – as She Vaults into the Big Event, Grinning as Usual." *People.* (January 14, 1991):50.

Weiner, Jay. "Where are They Now? Chernobyl Disaster Changed Korbut's Life and Her Location." *Minneapolis Star Tribune.* (August 1, 1996): 02S.

Wieberg, Steve. "Retton Reflects on Her Decade of Fame." *USA Today,* (August 3, 1994): 02.

Other

"Mary Lou Retton." http://www.ighof.com/honorees_marylou.html (January 6, 2003).

"Mary Lou Retton has Three More Reasons to Smile." Business Wire (March 7, 2000).

"Olga Korbut." http://www.olgakorbut.com/biogr.htm (January 6, 2003).

Reed, Susan. "Update: Golden Girl Olympic Gymnast Mary Lou Retton Delivers Yet Another Perfect 10: Her First Child." Anne Maier in Houston (January 5, 2003).

Sketch by Barbra J Smerz

Manon Rheaume
1972-

Canadian hockey player

In 1992, Manon Rheaume became the first woman to play in one of the United States' four major professional sports when she played goal for the National Hockey League's (NHL) Tampa Bay Lightning. Rheaume was also the first woman to play in a major junior hockey game. For much of her career, Rheaume played against boys and men, though she was also a member of several women's hockey teams for Team Canada.

Rheaume was born on February 24, 1972, in Lac Beauport, Quebec, Canada, the daughter of Pierre and Nicole Rheaume. Her father was a hockey coach who was in charge of the local outdoor rink. Rheaume had several brothers, including the youngest, Pascal, who later played in the NHL.

Rheaume began skating when she was three in a backyard rink her father built. She often practiced in goal at home when her father was practicing with her brothers. When she was five, she asked him if she could

Manon Rheaume

play in a tournament in which he needed a goalie. He agreed, and Rheaume loved the competition. Though she also did ballet, skied, and played baseball, she told William Plummer of *People,* "I didn't just play hockey. It was my passion."

Played on Boys Teams

As a child, Rheaume played on boys teams at school and in youth leagues. At age eleven, she played at the International Pee Wee Hockey Tournament of Quebec, the first time a girl played. In 1991, she played for Louiseville of Quebec Tier II junior hockey. For the last place team, Rheaume's goals against average was 8.88.

From an early age, Rheaume understood that getting respect of her teammates was important, and would lead to acceptance. As her Louiseville coach Yves Beaudry was quoted as saying by Brian McFarlane in *Proud Past, Bright Future,* "Manon was tough, very tough. She was a good team member. She never backed down."

On November 26, 1991, Rheaume became the first woman to play in a major junior hockey game. She played for Trois-Rivières Draveurs in the Quebec Major Junior Hockey League. In her first game, she went in mid-game of a tied game, and let three goals in on thirteen shots. Rheaume took a shot to the head, but stuck it out, though she was bleeding. This led to international attention, though she only played three games for the team.

Rheaume did not always play against males at this stage of her career. In 1992, she was in net for Canada's women team at the world championships. The team won gold, and Rheaume only gave up two goals in three games. There was some controversy over why she was on team: because she was known or because she earned it.

Trained with Lightning

In the fall of 1992, Rheaume was invited to the training camp of the expansion NHL team, the Tampa Bay Lightning. While it was done for publicity in part, she was also invited because of her talent. During one pre-season game against the St. Louis Blues, she played for one period, allowing two goals on nine shots. After the pre-season, the team offered her a contract to play in their minor league organization, the Atlanta Knights. She signed a three-year deal that ensured she would not be exploited but developed as a hockey talent.

The tryout with Tampa Bay led to lots of publicity that Rheaume did not enjoy. She also did not speak much English, so the demands of her notoriety were hard on her in other ways as well. She told Jeff Schultz of the *Atlanta Journal and Constitution,* "I did not ask for the attention, but it came to me, and it was very uncomfortable. I was there because I wanted to play hockey and make a living." The pressure led to three stomach ulcers over the next five years.

Rheaume continued to break down barriers. On December 13, 1993, she played in a regular season game for the Knights, against the Salt Lake City Golden Eagles. This was the first time a woman played in a regular season men's professional hockey game. She played for 5:49, allowing one goal on five shots. During the following season, she was given more seasoning by playing in the East Coast Hockey League. Played for Knoxville Cherokees, then traded to Nashville Knights. She earned her first professional victory with Knoxville during the season, a 9-6 victory over the Johnstown Chiefs. In three games she had a 2-0-1 record; with Nashville, a 3-0-0 record.

In 1994, Rheaume again played for the Canadian's women team at the World Championships in Lake Placid. But she continued to play primarily with men's teams as well. In 1994-95, she played for the Vegas Thunder of the International Hockey League and the Tallahassee Tiger Sharks (ECHL). During the summer of 1995, she played roller hockey with the New Jersey Rockin' Rollers, Roller International League. During summer of 1996, she again played pro roller hockey for the Ottawa Loggers and Sacramento River Rats (RHI). In 1996-97, she played for the Reno Renegades of the WCHL.

Won Olympic Silver

Though Rheaume was still a celebrity, this did not always ensure she would play on Canadian national women's teams. She was cut from the 1997 Canadian na-

Chronology

1972	Born February 24, in Lac Beauport, Quebec, Canada
1991	On November 26, becomes the first woman to play in a major junior hockey game
1992	Plays on Canada's women's national team, winning gold at the world championships; invited to training camp of the NHL's Tampa Bay Lightning; first woman to play in professional game when she plays in a pre-season game for the Lightning
1993	On December 13, becomes first woman to play in regular season game; played for the Knights against Salt Lake City Golden Eagles
1994	Plays in the East Coast Hockey League for Nashville and Knoxville
1994	Plays on Canada's women's national team at world championships, winning gold
1994-95	Plays with the Vegas Thunder (IHL) and the Tallahassee Tiger Sharks (ECHL)
1995	Plays for the New Jersey Rockin' Rollers (RHI)
1996	Plays for the Ottawa Loggers and Sacramento River Rats (RHI); wins gold as member of the Canadian women's team at the Pacific Rim Three Nations Cup
1996-97	Plays for the Reno Renegades (WCHL)
1998	Plays for Team Canada at the Winter Olympics; wins silver medal; marries Gerry St. Cyr
1998-99	Sits out season due to pregnancy
1999	Gives birth to son Dylan; named goaltending coach for the University of Minnesota-Duluth women's team
2000	Retires as a goalie; begins working for Mission Hockey

Awards and Accomplishments

1992, 1994	Played on Canada's women's national team, winning gold at the world championships
1996	Won gold as member of the Canadian women's team at the Pacific Rim Three Nations Cup
1998	Played for Team Canada at the Winter Olympics; won silver medal

tional women's team before the world championships. The coaches did not think she was hungry enough. Rheaume also had to readjust to the demands of the women's game; she played a more stand up style against men, butterfly against women. This cut forced her to improve her game, and led to her being chosen for the Olympic team. In 1998, she played for Team Canada at the Olympics in Nagano. Rheaume and the Canadian women won the silver medal, losing to the United States.

Rheaume sat out the 1998-99 season when she was pregnant with her son. She was married to Gerry St. Cyr, a roller hockey player and minor league hockey player, whom she later divorced. She remained connected to the game as she served as goaltending coach for the University of Minnesota-Duluth women's team. She also continued to practice with high level teams near her home. Originally, Rheaume planned on playing on the Canadian women's national team in 2000, but did not make team. She then retired from international play, and essentially her career as a goalie.

Rheaume was hired by Mission Hockey as head of global marketing for women's hockey. There, she helped develop hockey skates for women. She later became manager of apparel and special events for the company. Rheaume also coached a team of girls, the Mission Bettys, to the Quebec International Pee Wee Tournament.

After retiring as a goalie in 2000, Rheaume still played as a forward in a woman's professional league, the Montreal Wingstars of the National Women's Hockey League, for a short time. She continued to play recreational hockey as a forward. Of her most famous stint in hockey, with the Lightning, she told Martin Fennelly of the *Tampa Tribune,* "I just wanted to play. I didn't think about what it meant. Now I do."

SELECTED WRITINGS BY RHEAUME:

(With Chantal Gilbert) *Manon: Alone in Front of the Net,* HarperCollins, 1993.

FURTHER INFORMATION

Books

Athletes and Coaches of Winter. New York: Macmillan Reference USA, 2000.

Johnson, Anne Janette. *Great Women in Sports.* Detroit: Visible Ink, 1996.

McFarlane, Brian. *Proud Past, Bright Future: One Hundred Years of Canadian Women's Hockey.* Stoddart, 1994.

Woolum, Janet. *Outstanding Women Athletes: Who They Are and How They Influenced Sports in America.* Oryx Press, 1998.

Periodicals

Adams, Alan. "Rheaume tends to a new job." *Ottawa Citizen* (October 8, 1999): B7.

Blackmar, Trisha, and Mark Bechtel. "First and fearless." *Sports Illustrated* (July 15, 2002): 116.

Bradley, Jeff. "Women's work." *Sports Illustrated* (December 30, 1991): 10.

Cleary, Martin. "Manon leaves net to have baby." *Calgary Herald* (October 6, 1998): D5.

Fennelly, Martin. "Rheaume's goal simply was to play hockey." *Tampa Tribune* (October 9, 2002): 1.

Long, Wendy. "Rheaume at home with Olympic team." *Vancouver Sun* (January 17, 1998): E2.

Plummer, William. "The puck stops here." *People* (September 28, 1992): 85.

"Rheaume hangs up pads." *Gazette* (July 9, 2000): B5.

Scanlon, Wayne. "Not just a pretty face." *Gazette* (February 14, 1998): C2.

Schultz, Jeff. "Groundbreaker in goal finds comfort out of the spotlight during Games." *Atlanta Journal and Constitution* (February 7, 1998): 2G.

Stubbs, Dave. "Rheaume trades pads for Pampers."
Gazette (July 25, 1999): B5.
Vecsey, George. "The Goalie Who Just Wants to Improve."
New York Times (October 18, 1992): section 8, p. 9.

Sketch by A. Petruso

Jerry Rice
1962-

American football player

When you mention "the greatest football player ever," you will find many different ideas about who that might be. Jerry Rice, however, will always be near the top of the list. Playing the bulk of his years with the San Francisco 49ers, a powerhouse of a team that won a record five Super Bowls over the past twenty years, Jerry Rice is still a force to be reckoned with.

A man who has dominated the record books, his accomplishments could fill up an encyclopedia. The most prolific pass receiver in professional football, Rice forces teams to change their defense and double-team him, because he's not only a threat to catch the ball, but he's liable to tack on major yards once he pulls the ball in.

Growing Up

Jerry Rice was born on October 13, 1962, in Crawford, Mississippi, to Joe Nathan and Eddie B. Rice. His father was a mason, and as a kid, Jerry Rice helped haul bricks and mortar when his father had too much work. He grew up with five brothers, with whom he began playing sports, and learned early on the value of playing and having fun, but also about hard work, thanks to his father's insistence that he give it his all.

Like many kids, when Rice got bored, he wasn't immune to getting into trouble. This penchant for trouble is what eventually led him to a career in professional football. Were it not for his attempt to skip school one day, we might never know Jerry Rice's potential. He told the *Los Angeles Times* that he had "never had any intention of playing football" until the vice principal caught him sneaking out of the school and then, after catching Jerry in a footrace, hauled him back to the gym. As punishment for his attempted truancy, Rice was ordered to go to participate in football practice. "He made me go out for the team," Rice told the *Los Angeles Times*, "and that's how I started playing the game."

As a high school student, Rice he was a versatile player, moving around on the field and trying out most every position. Not many colleges showed interest in him as he entered his senior year, however. Except for Archie Coo-

Jerry Rice

ley, with Mississippi Valley State (MVS), a small NAIA school in Itta Bena, Mississippi. He thought he saw something in Rice, and he wouldn't be disappointed.

Rice attended MVS and majored in auto-technology. During his college career he caught an amazing fifty-one touchdown passes, and over the course of his junior and senior seasons would average two touchdown receptions per game. In his best and final season, 1984, Rice put up statistics that he'd rival in the pros. That senior season, he pulled down 112 passes, netting 1845 yards, with an unbelievable 28 of those catches for touchdowns. He accomplished this in only eleven games (Rice's team averaged over fifty-nine points a game that year).

Superstar in the Making

Some say Rice wasn't fast enough to be a star receiver in the National Football League (NFL), but San Francisco 49ers coach Bill Walsh selected Rice as the 16th pick of the first round. "Jerry's movements were spectacular for a pass receiver," Walsh told the *Los Angeles Times*. "He'd been catching 100 passes year after year. We felt that if they'd throw to him that much.... he must have the basic instincts for the job."

Yet in his first few games, people wondered about Walsh's decision. In Rice's rookie season, he dropped fifteen passes, but this was due to the complicated 49ers offense, and soon, after he got over the learning curve, he started hanging onto the passes. By the end of the

Chronology

1962	Born October 13 in Crawford, Mississippi, to Joe Nathan and Eddie B. Rice
1981	Enters Mississippi Valley State University
1985	Selected in 1st round of NFL draft by San Francisco 49ers; sets rookie team record with 927 yards
1986	Sets then-49er record with 1,570 yards receiving; begins string of eleven straight pro-bowls
1987	Sets NFL record for receiving touchdowns (22) and touchdown catches in consecutive games (13)
1987	Daughter Jaqui Bonet born to Jerry and wife Jackie on June 7
1988	Catches longest pass of his career, 96-yarder from Joe Montana for a touchdown
1989	Key member of 49ers Super Bowl Victory over Cincinnati Bengals
1990	Gets his second Super Bowl Ring in 49er victory over the Denver Broncos
1991	Son Jerry Jr. born on July 27
1994	Breaks Jim Brown's record for career touchdowns in first game of the season
1994	Gets his third Super Bowl ring as 49ers win record fifth Super Bowl victory over the San Diego Chargers
1995	Considers retiring from football, then decides to keep playing
1995	Breaks two all-time receiving records, for total yards in a single season (1,848) and he becomes the NFL's most prolific pass receiver with 942 receptions and 14,040 yards
1995	Sets single game career high with 289 yards receiving in a game against the Minnesota Vikings
1996	Daughter Jada Symone born on May 16
1996	Catches the 1,000th pass of his career
1997	Suffers a serious injury to left knee in first game of the season. Misses a game for the first time in nineteen seasons
1997	Makes remarkable recovery and returns December 15th. Re-injures knee on a touchdown reception, breaking bone in kneecap. Out for rest of season
1998	Overcomes two surgeries on left knee and injury on right to complete the season and make it to his 12th Pro Bowl
2001	Released by San Francisco 49ers and acquired by the Oakland Raiders
2002	Voted to Pro Bowl at age 40 (13th appearance)

Related Biography: Coach William Earnest "Bill" Walsh

From 1979 until his retirement in 1989, Bill Walsh led his team, the San Francisco 49ers, to three Super Bowl victories. He created an NFL team that came to be known as "team of the eighties," adding, in the middle of the decade, Jerry Rice to an already successful formula. With one Super Bowl victory secure, the addition of Rice to the mix netted the 49ers two more championships before the Walsh decade expired.

Walsh, a native of Los Angeles, California, was born on November 30, 1931. Though he has been in sports his entire life, he wasn't a standout athlete by any measure but played football at San Jose State University in the early 1950s. After service in the military, he returned to complete a graduate degree in Education while working as an assistant coach for the football team.

Bill Walsh began his pro football coaching career as an offensive backfield coach for the Oakland Raiders in 1966. From 1968-75, he would spend eight seasons with the Cincinnati Bengals as their quarterbacks and receivers coach. Then, after a few seasons at the college level, as Stanford's head coach, he took on the position as head coach with the 49ers, in 1979, giving rise to an era of dominance that has been matched by few teams in the history of the league.

With license to build the team the way he saw fit, Walsh invented an incredible team. He led his 49ers to the National Football Conference (NFC) Championship in only his second season as head coach. Then, following the 1984 season, piloted the franchise to its first championship with a victory in Super Bowl XIX over the Miami Dolphins. His team that season went 18-1, the second best in NFL history, setting Super Bowl records in several categories.

Jerry Rice, coming out of Mississippi Valley State University, wasn't heavily favored in the 1985 NFL draft. But Walsh saw something in the receiver and drafted him. Walsh has been labeled a football genius by many (though he denies it) and told the *Los Angeles Times* that, "Jerry's movements were spectacular for a pass receiver, no matter the level."

When Walsh retired from the NFL after the 49ers' third Super Bowl victory in 1989, he returned to Stanford for several seasons. In 1999 he made his way back to the 49ers, this time as their General Manager. After the 2001 season, he stepped down as GM and now serves as a consultant for the organization.

season, Rice had caught passes for 927 yards and three touchdowns, on the way breaking the 49ers single game receiving record with a 241-yard game. He earned a spot on the NFL's All-Rookie Team.

Rice continued his dominance in the NFL, teaming up with **Joe Montana** to become one of the most successful quarterback/receiver duos in the history of the game. The 49ers had won the Super Bowl the season before Rice joined the team, and Rice wanted to be a part of that. He wanted a ring of his own.

He wouldn't have to wait long. His team, with two Super Bowls in the past six seasons, would become "the team of the '80s," as the 49ers returned to the Super Bowl after the 1988 season, beating the Bengals 20-16 in Super Bowl XXIII. Rice was voted the game's Most Valuable Player.

That was the third Super Bowl for the 49ers in the 1980s, but it wouldn't be their last. In the next season, Rice led all NFL receivers with seventeen touchdowns, and helped his 49ers, which had amassed a 14-2 regular season record, return to Super Bowl XXIIV, which they

won. Scoring the most points ever in the most lopsided victory in Super Bowl History, Rice and his teammates blew away the Denver Broncos 55-10. Jerry Rice caught seven passes for 148 yards in the game.

Rice and his team would fall one victory short of making it to the next Super Bowl, but that season he led the NFL in catches (100) and receiving yards (1,502) as well as receiving touchdowns (13). After Joe Montana hurt his back, the 49ers continued to pile up winning records, but for several years they seemed to fall just short of the Super Bowl.

Then, Rice and the 49ers returned to Super Bowl XXIX in 1995, facing off against the San Diego Chargers. Though Rice had been sick the night before the game, and although still weak before game time, he played, and went on to catch ten passes for 149 yards and three touchdowns as his team won a record fifth Super Bowl, 49-26. This put Rice in the record books as the man with the most Super Bowl touchdowns (7) in the history of the NFL.

Rice considered retiring after that third Super Bowl ring, but thought better of it and came back in '95. He continued to put up great stats, and soon became the all-

Career Statistics

Yr	Team	Receiving				Rushing				Fumbles	
		Rec	Yds	Avg	TD	Att	Yds	Avg	TD	Fum	Lst
1985	SF	49	927	18.9	3	6	26	4.3	1	1	0
1986	SF	86	1570	18.3	15	10	72	7.2	1	2	0
1987	SF	65	1078	16.6	22	8	51	6.4	1	2	0
1988	SF	64	1306	20.4	9	13	107	8.2	1	0	0
1989	SF	82	1483	18.1	17	5	33	6.6	0	1	0
1990	SF	100	1502	15.0	13	2	0	0.0	0	1	0
1991	SF	80	1206	15.1	14	1	2	2.0	0	1	0
1992	SF	84	1201	14.3	10	9	58	6.4	1	2	0
1993	SF	98	1503	15.3	15	3	69	23.0	1	3	0
1994	SF	112	1499	13.4	13	7	93	13.3	2	1	1
1995	SF	122	1848	15.1	15	5	36	7.2	1	3	3
1996	SF	108	1254	11.6	8	11	77	7.0	1	0	0
1997	SF	7	78	11.1	1	1	-10	-10.0	0	0	0
1998	SF	82	1157	14.1	9	0	0	0.0	0	2	2
1999	SF	67	830	12.4	5	2	13	6.5	0	0	0
2000	SF	75	805	10.7	7	1	-2	-2.0	0	3	2
2001	OAK	83	1139	13.7	9	0	0	0.0	0	0	0
2002	OAK	92	1211	13.2	7	3	20	6.7	0	0	1
TOTAL		1456	21597	14.8	192	87	645	7.4	10	25	9

OAK: Oakland Raiders; SF: San Francisco 49ers.

time NFL reception leader with 942 catches. In 1996 he caught his 1,000th pass, still at the top in a sport where he should have been entering the twilight of his career. In 1997 it seemed his luck had run out when he injured his left knee in the first game of the season. Rice needed surgery, and it looked like he would be out for the season. But he hated the injury, and the cast bothered him so much that at one point, wrote Gary Swan of the *San Francisco Chronicle*, he "went into his garage at 3 am.... took a saw and cut the cast off."

Still Going Strong

Rice returned to the field at the end of that 1996 season in a December game against the Denver Broncos. It had been a remarkable recovery, and even more remarkable when Rice caught a touchdown pass, putting him over 1,000 points for his career. But the tackle in the end zone cracked his kneecap, and he was out of commission once more. He would return full-strength in 1998.

After the 2000 season, Rice left the 49ers, much to the chagrin of fans who'd spent fifteen years watching his every move on the field. Rice moved across the Bay and began the final years of his career with the Oakland Raiders. But neither the move nor age has seemed to slow down Jerry Rice, who, in 2002, was selected for his 13th Pro Bowl Appearance.

CONTACT INFORMATION

Address: Jerry Rice, c/o The Oakland Raiders, 1220 Harbor Bay Parkway, Alameda, CA 94502.

SELECTED WRITINGS BY RICE:

(With Michael Silver) *Rice,* St. Martin's Press, 1996.

FURTHER INFORMATION

Books

Dickey, Glenn. *Sports Great Jerry Rice.* Hillside, N.J.: Enslow Publishers, 1993.

Evans, J. Edward. *Jerry Rice: Touchdown Talent.* Minneapolis: Lerner Publications, 1993.

"Jerry Rice." *Sports Stars.* Series 1-4. U•X•L, 1994-98.

Rice, Jerry, and Michael Silver. *Rice.* New York: St. Martin's Press, 1996.

Periodicals

Chi, Samuel. "Rice comes of age (40) with Pro Bowl No. 13." *Denver Post* (December 20, 2002).

Fresno Bee (January 28, 1990).

Los Angeles Times (December 13, 1987).

Los Angeles Times (November 4, 1996).

Los Angeles Times (December 15, 1997).

King, P. "Rice suits Raiders fine: a star is reborn." *Sports Illustrated* (August 20, 2001): 68.

Sports Illustrated (September 28, 1987).

Sports Illustrated (December 15, 1997).

Sports Illustrated (November 29, 1999).

Swan, Gary. "Rice Wants to Cast Off Doubts." *San Francisco Chronicle* (September 20, 1997).

USA Today (November 4, 1996).

Washington Post (January 22, 1989).

Awards and Accomplishments

1985	Unanimous choice for NFL All-Rookie team
1985	NFC Offensive Rookie of the Year and NFC Offensive Rookie of the Year
1986	Voted *Sports Illustrated* Player of the Year
1986-96, 1998, 2002	Selected to Pro Bowl
1987	Voted NFL's Most Valuable Player; wins Len Eshmont Award
1987	*Sporting News* and NFL Player of the Year
1989	Superbowl XXIII MVP
1990	Named once again as the *Sports Illustrated* Player of the Year
1990	NFL Player of the Year
1993	Named AP, NFL and *Sports Illustrated* Offensive Player of the Year
1994	Voted to NFL 75th Anniversary All-Time Team

Washington Post (January 23, 1989).
Washington Post (September 1, 1989).

Other

"Farewell Jerry Rice." List of accomplishments as a 49er. http://www.49erswebzone.com/rice/. (December 29, 2002).
"Jerry Rice." NFL.com. http://www.nfl.com/players. 1291_bios.htm (December 20, 2002).
"Jerry Rice." http://pro-football-reference.com (December 20, 2002).

Sketch by Eric Lagergren

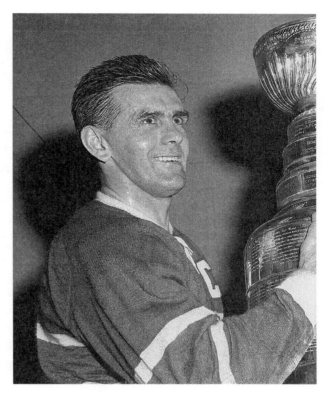

Maurice Richard

Maurice Richard
1921-2000

Canadian hockey player

When Maurice Richard—universally known by his nickname, "The Rocket"—died in Montreal on May 27, 2000, the entire nation of Canada went into mourning. One of the greatest players in the history of hockey, Richard's legendary exploits on the ice helped the Montreal Canadiens win eight Stanley Cup championships during his eighteen years with the team. The leading goal scorer in the National Hockey League (NHL) five times, Richard was also the first player to score fifty goals in one season. Yet Richard's true importance to his fans lay not in his impressive statistics and career longevity, but rather in what he symbolized. To many people in the province of Quebec, Richard was the epitome of French-Canadian pride. Indeed, Richard's professional career from 1942 to 1960 paralleled the growth in Quebecois consciousness that culminated in the so-called Quiet Revolution of the 1960s, when the province's social, political, and economic landscapes transformed the Canadian nation.

Native Son of Montreal

Joseph Henry Maurice Richard was born on August 4, 1921 in Montreal, Quebec. The oldest child of Onesime, a carpenter for the Canadian Pacific Railway, and Alice Richard, Maurice grew up in a rough neighborhood in Montreal's north end, where the Richard family house sat next to a city jail. Richard began playing hockey in his neighborhood when he was about four years old and played in the city's athletic leagues through his teens. After playing in junior hockey leagues while studying to be a machinist at the Montreal Technical School, Richard joined the Montreal Canadiens organization in 1940 and was sent to play for its minor-league affiliate, the Montreal Royals. Although he scored a goal in his first game with the team, Richard suffered a broken ankle when his skate got caught in a rut on the ice. He sat out the rest of the season.

Returning to the Royals for the 1941-42 season, Richard lasted thirty-one games before another injury—this time, a broken wrist—put him out of action. He had healed sufficiently to rejoin the team for the playoffs, where he scored six goals. The performance was impressive enough to get Richard called up to the Canadiens for the start of the 1942-43 season. Signed as a free agent in October 1942, he was again made inactive

Richard's thirty-two regular season goals helped the Canadiens finish the 1943-44 season in first place. In the team's first game of the Stanley Cup finals, Richard scored five goals to give the Canadiens the win. The team subsequently swept the series to claim their first NHL victory since the league assumed sponsorship of the Stanley Cup in 1926. Although the Canadiens did not make it to the finals the following season, Richard topped the NHL for goals scored in the 1944-45 season, with fifty goals in fifty games. It was the first time any player had reached that number; the record was not surpassed until 1966. Richard went on to lead the league in goal scoring in four more seasons: 1946-47; 1949-50; 1953-54; and 1954-55, when he shared the honor with Montreal's Bernie Geoffrion. Richard also won the Hart Trophy as Most Valuable Player in the NHL at the conclusion of the 1946-47 season; it was the only Hart Trophy he received in his career, much to the disappointment of his fans.

With his own weekly newspaper column, which he often used to criticize NHL officials and administrators, Richard became Quebec's best-known athlete by the early 1950s. Although he was often criticized himself for his rough tactics on the ice, Richard's rivalry with Detroit Red Wings star **Gordie Howe** delighted fans of both teams. Montreal emerged as the NHL champion at the end of the 1952-53 season, but the Red Wings held the edge in the first half of the 1950s, when the team won the Stanley Cup four times.

The Richard Riot

After losing to Detroit in the 1954 championship by one game, the Canadiens were determined to turn the tables the following year. Richard was especially pleased to welcome his younger brother, Henri, to the lineup of the Canadiens for the 1954-55 season, which promised to be one of the Rocket's finest. Yet Richard's season ended in one of the most controversial episodes in sports history. In Boston on March 13, 1955, Richard was struck on the head by Bruins defenseman Hal Laycoe during a third-period power play that left the Bruins short-handed. Richard retaliated by hitting Laycoe with his own stick and, after a linesman took that away, with two other sticks that he managed to grab. Finally restrained by linesman Cliff Thompson, Richard hit the official twice before leaving the ice. Richard left the game to receive five stitches to a head wound caused by Laycoe, and Laycoe received a five-minute penalty for high sticking.

when he broke his ankle after just sixteen games. Given the recurring injuries, Canadiens general manager Tommy Gorman had doubts about Richard's future on the team. In the midst of World War II, however, there was a lack of available players to join the roster; Richard himself had attempted to enlist twice in the Canadian Armed Forces but was deferred because of his numerous injuries. With the Canadiens mired in fourth place in the then-six-team NHL at the end of the season, there was little choice but to let Richard rejoin the team for the 1943-44 season.

First of Eight Stanley Cup Victories in 1944

For the 1943-44 season, Richard began wearing the number-nine jersey in honor of his first child, daughter Huguette, who had been born to his wife, Lucille, weighing in at nine pounds. The couple eventually had seven children and remained married up to the time of Lucille Richard's death in 1994. In addition to picking up a new number for the 1943-44 season, Richard also earned a new nickname, "The Rocket," bestowed upon him by teammate Ray Getliffe. The moniker was a testament to the left-handed, right wing's speed and power on the ice, as well as for his explosive temperament that often resulted in fights with his opponents. Although his size was modest—at just five feet, ten inches tall and weighing between 170 and 180 pounds—Richard had the ability to intimidate his opponents just by staring them down. "What I remember most about the Rocket were his eyes," said goalie **Glenn Hall** in a remark later reprinted in Richard's Associated Press obituary, "When he came flying toward you with the puck on his stick, his eyes were all lit up, flashing and gleaming like a pinball machine. It was terrifying."

Maurice "Rocket" Richard

Of course, he was much more than "just a hockey player." It wasn't just that he was a winner during his eighteen seasons with the Canadiens, it was the way he won. He could lift a team, a province, and at times even a country into a frenzy of winning. He pushed himself to the brink, and when he and the team won, "his people" imagined themselves winners as well—even if it was for only a little while. When he was Number One, they were too. When he lost, they lost. It's why "his people" erupted into what will always be remembered as the Richard Riot on March 17, 1955. The reason? After clubbing Hal Laycoe of the Boston Bruins with his stick, Richard had been suspended for the last few games of the regular season and for the entire playoffs.

With Richard, the eyes had it. They were coal-black, wet, and shining with the intensity he brought to every game. No wonder he lit up every arena in which he performed. It was the menace implicit in him each time he swooped in on an opposing goaltender, often with another player clinging to his back. It was in his arms and in the barrel of his chest which threatened to burst his sweater at any moment. It was in the tight line of his mouth, and in the snarl it formed when he was challenged.

Source: Red Fisher, *Hockey, Heroes, and Me*, McClelland & Stewart, 1994.

Career Statistics

Yr	Team	GP	G	A	Pts	PIM
1942-43	Canadiens	16	5	6	11	4
1943-44	Canadiens	46	32	22	54	45
1944-45	Canadiens	50	50	23	73	46
1945-46	Canadiens	50	27	21	48	50
1946-47	Canadiens	60	45	26	71	69
1947-48	Canadiens	53	28	25	53	89
1948-49	Canadiens	59	20	18	38	110
1949-50	Canadiens	70	43	22	65	114
1950-51	Canadiens	65	42	24	66	97
1951-52	Canadiens	48	27	17	44	44
1952-53	Canadiens	70	28	33	61	112
1953-54	Canadiens	70	37	30	67	112
1954-55	Canadiens	67	38	36	74	125
1955-56	Canadiens	70	38	33	71	89
1956-57	Canadiens	63	33	29	62	74
1957-58	Canadiens	28	15	19	34	28
1958-59	Canadiens	42	17	21	38	27
1959-60	Canadiens	51	19	16	35	50
TOTAL		978	544	421	965	1285

Canadiens: Montreal Canadiens (NHL).

NHL president Clarence Campbell was outraged by Richard's treatment of the game officials. In a hearing held in Montreal on March 16, 1955, the league announced that Richard would be suspended for the rest of the regular season and any playoff games as well. The decision shocked Canadiens fans for its severity; not only would it put Richard out of the race for that year's top scorer award, but it would also jeopardize the team's chances for a Stanley Cup victory. Many French-speaking Canadians also saw Campbell's decision as a slap in the face by the English-speaking elites who then dominated the country's economic and political spheres.

Although he had received numerous death threats for issuing the suspension of Richard, Campbell insisted on attending the game between the Canadiens and the Red Wings at the Montreal Forum the day after the decision was announced. He was greeted with jeers and insults and after he took his seat, a variety of objects began raining down on him. At the end of the first period, one spectator walked up to Campbell as if to shake his hand; instead, he started punching the NHL president. Another fan later made his way up to Campbell and threw tomatoes at him. Despite the assaults, Campbell remained in his seat until another protester threw a tear gas canister into the audience. The bomb exploded and sent the Forum crowd scrambling toward the exits. No one was injured in the incident and the game was immediately canceled; the victory was awarded to the Red Wings, who were leading by a score of three to one.

What happened next turned the event into the Richard Riot. As fans fled the Forum, a restless crowd started to gather on the streets. Outraged by Campbell's seeming arrogance, the mob turned violent and began smashing windows and looting stores in downtown Montreal. It was not until 3:00 am that the crowd of about 10,000 people was finally dispersed, some six hours after the event began. Richard immediately went on the radio to ask his fans to restore order, and calm prevailed the next day. Privately, however, Richard blamed Campbell for deliberately inciting the crowd with this appearance at the Forum. *L'affaire Richard,* as the event was also known, not only ended Richard's season but contributed to the loss by the Canadiens to the Red Wings in the Stanley Cup finals by a single game.

Five Consecutive Stanley Cup Victories

The infamous conclusion of the 1954-55 season fueled Richard's desire for another Stanley Cup victory. The Canadiens indeed won the 1956 championship over the Red Wings in a four-to-one game series. Thus began one of the greatest hockey dynasties in the sport's history, as the team went on to win five consecutive championships. In all Richard contributed to eight Stanley Cup victories by the Canadiens in his eighteen years with the team.

Ironically, the Canadiens' success from 1956 to 1960 occurred when Richard's skills were being dimmed by age. At the conclusion of the 1959-60 season, Richard announced his retirement. Within a year, in contradiction of the rule mandating a five-year waiting period for retired players, Richard was inducted into the Hockey Hall of Fame. He continued to work for the Canadiens for a brief period, but tensions with the team's owners left him disillusioned. He instead worked as a sporting goods salesman for several years until the Canadiens lured him back with an offer to serve as the team's goodwill ambassador.

A Nation Mourns

Richard's last major public appearance occurred at the closing of the old Montreal Forum on March 11,

1996, where he was given an extended standing ovation by the audience. Suffering from abdominal cancer and Parkinson's disease, Maurice Richard died on May 27, 2000. An estimated 50,000 people waited in line to pay their respects at a public showing held in the Molson Centre hockey arena before Richard's funeral at the Notre-Dame Basilica in Montreal.

Acknowledged as one of the best players in the sport's history, Maurice Richard's significance reached beyond the hockey rink. As the most popular member of the Canadiens in the 1940s and 1950s, he symbolized the aspirations of a province that often felt slighted by the Anglo-dominated institutions that prevailed in the Canada of that era. Although his fans' passions sometimes boiled over, as in the infamous riot that followed his 1955 suspension, they also contributed to the newfound pride of French-speaking Canadians in their language and heritage that led to a cultural renaissance in the province in the 1960s and beyond.

FURTHER INFORMATION

Books

Fisher, Red. *Hockey, Heroes, and Me.* Toronto: McClelland and Stewart, 1994.

McFarlane, Brian. *The Habs.* Toronto: Stoddart Publishing, 1996.

Periodicals

Bird, Heather. "Adieu, M. Richard." *Toronto Sun* (June 1, 2000).

Bird, Heather. "A Family Member Lost." *Toronto Sun* (May 31, 2000).

McRae, Earl. "'He Was Everything to Us.'" *Ottawa Sun* (June 1, 2000).

Other

Flatter, Ron. "The Rocket Lit Up Hockey." ESPN Classic Web site. http://espn.go.com/classic/biography/s/Richard_Maurice.html (October 20, 2002).

"Maurice Richard Dead at 78." Canoe Web site. http://www.canoe.ca/HockeyRocketRichard/may27_dead.html (October 17, 2002).

"Maurice Richard: 'The Rocket.'" Joy of Hockey Web site. http://www.joyofhockey.com/xRet1Maurice Richard.html (October 21, 2002).

"Prime Minister Chretien Speaks Out." Canoe Web site. http://www.canoe.ca/HockeyRocketRichard/may27_pm.html (October 17, 2002).

"Rocket Remembered for His Emotion, Determination." Canoe Web site. http://www.canoe.ca/HockeyRocket Richard/may27_roc.html (October 17, 2002).

Sketch by Timothy Borden

Dot Richardson
1961-

American softball player

Two-time Olympic softball gold medalist Dot Richardson is much more than just a star shortstop. Richardson, who hit the first home run ever in Olympic softball, became an orthopedic surgeon while simultaneously training for the U.S. Olympic team. Richardson chronicled her success in a memoir, *Living the Dream.*

Dreams of Olympic Gold

Richardson, known as "Dr. Dot," experiencd a defining moment as youth when, in 1968, she watched Olympic highlights on television. That night, she dreamed of standing on the podium, cloaked in Olympic gold. Twenty-eight years later, that dream came true.

Despite her talent, opportunities were limited. Richardson was born in the 1960s, a decade before Title IX opened the pathways for women in sports. The best she could do was be a bat girl for her brothers' baseball team, which at least allowed her the opportunity to practice with the team. At 10, Richardson mesmerized a baseball coach with her throwing arm and was offered a chance to pitch, as long as she cut her hair and answered to "Bob."

"As quickly as I had gotten excited, I became crushed," Richardson recalled in her memoir. "I wanted to play, but I didn't want to pretend to be a boy.... I told him, 'Thanks but no thanks. If I have to hide who I am, I don't feel it's right.'"

Luckily that afternoon, the coach of a local women's fast-pitch team saw Richardson and offered the gangly 10-year-old a chance to join her team.

Outshines Elders

By 1975, Richardson had joined the Orlando Rebels, an Amateur Softball Association fast-pitch team. Barely a teen, Richardson was competing in softball's "major league." She became the youngest player in the ASA since its founding in 1933, holding her own against women twice her age.

In 1979, just hours after graduating from Colonial, Richardson left to try out for the U.S. team that would compete at the 1979 Pan American Games, where softball was being played the first time. Richardson made the team. It was the first of many times she would earn the right to wear U.S.A. across her chest. The youngest U.S. starter on the squad, Richardson earned her first gold medal in international play. Over the years, she collected three more golds in Pan American play (1987, 1995, and 1999).

Dot Richardson

Chronology	
1961	Born September 22 in Orlando, Florida
1975	Joins Orlando Rebels, an Amateur Softball Association (ASA) fast-pitch team
1979	Graduates from Orlando's Colonial High School
1984	Leaves Orlando Rebels and joins the Raybestos Brakettes, another ASA fast-pitch team
1984	Graduates with a bachelor's degree in kinesiology from UCLA
1988	Graduates with a master's degree in exercise physiology from Adelphi University
1993	Graduates from the University of Louisville School of Medicine and begins residency in orthopedic surgery at the Los Angeles County/University of Southern California Medical Center
2001	Becomes medical director of the USA Triathlon National Training Center in Clermont, Florida
2001	Marries Bob Pinto

That fall, Richardson entered Western Illinois University and played several sports, including softball. Her .480 batting average led the nation. The following year, she transferred to the University of California, Los Angeles (UCLA). As a junior, Richardson led the Bruins to the 1982 National Collegiate Athletic Association (NCAA) title.

Struggles to become Doctor, Olympian

After earning a master's degree in exercise physiology from Adelphi University in 1988, Richardson entered the University of Louisville School of Medicine and kept up the frenetic pace of softball and academics. Merging her two passions began to prove problematic. During Richardson's second year of medical school, she concentrated so fiercely on making the USA World Championship team that she failed her boards and had to repeat the year. During her repeat year, she concentrated more on school and failed to make the U.S. Pan American team.

Just as Richardson contemplated giving up softball, the International Olympic Committee announced that the sport would become at Olympic event at the 1996 Summer Olympic Games in Atlanta. Richardson couldn't quit now.

Richardson stepped up her softball training and simultaneously began her demanding residency in orthopedic surgery at the Los Angeles County/University of Southern California Medical Center. By now, Richard-son was playing for the Raybestos Brakettes, a softball team based in Stratford, Connecticut. It was common for Richardson to finish a shift at the hospital, then fly across the country to join her team for a doubleheader.

Richardson found it increasingly hard to train. She purchased a treadmill for her residence and also set up a net and a pitching machine in her bedroom so she could practice her hitting at night. It wasn't long before she received a letter asking that she train for the Olympics at a more reasonable hour. Her work, however, paid off, and Richardson made the Olympic team.

Golden Olympic Moment

At the 1996 Olympics in Atlanta, Richardson hit the first softball home run ever in the Games. In the gold medal game against China, Richardson whacked a two-run homer that put the U.S. ahead 2-0 en route to a 3-1 victory. She hit three homers and drove in seven runs in nine Olympic games, and batted .273 (9-for-33). The outgoing Richardson became a media darling; her picture was splashed across newspapers and television broadcasts, which showed her at the medal ceremony, joyously weeping during the national anthem.

Richardson again represented the U.S. at the 2000 Olympics in Sydney, Australia. In the gold medal game, Richardson hit a sixth-inning, bases-empty homer and Lori Harrigan pitched the first Olympic no-hitter ever as the Americans defeated Canada, 6-0.

Richardson's Olympic performance brought more respect to women's softball. Broadcaster and author **Bob Costas** noted in the foreword to her memoir that Richardson helped the sport's audience grow because her pure love for the sport stood out.

Lives up to Dreams

Richardson lives in Clermont, Florida, with her husband, Bob Pinto, whom she married in 2001. A licensed orthopedic surgeon in Florida, Richardson serves as medical director for the USA Triathlon National Training Cen-

Awards and Accomplishments

1979	Wins gold medal as member of U.S. softball squad at Pan American Games
1980s	Named NCAA Softball Player of the Decade
1981	Wins USA Softball's MVP award
1981-83	Named three-time NCAA All-American at UCLA
1982	Win's NCAA softball championship with UCLA
1983	Wins UCLA's All University Athlete Award as co-winner with Jackie Joyner-Kersee
1987	Wins gold medal at as member of U.S. squad at Pan American Games
1989-90	Won USA Softball's MVP award
1995	Wins gold medal as member of U.S. squad at Pan American Games
1996	Wins the U.S. Olympic Committee's Athlete of the Year award, the Amateur Athletic Foundation's Southern California Athlete of the Year award, and USA Softball's MVP award; also, inducted into the UCLA Hall of Fame
1996, 2000	Wins Olympic gold medal as member of U.S. softball team
1999	Wins gold medal as member of U.S. squad at Pan American Games
1999	Inducted into State of Florida Hall of Fame
2003	Saint Leo University Women in Sports Achievement Award

ter, a part of South Lake Hospital in Clermont. She is retired from softball but hopes to spend the 2004 Olympics as a commentator. Richardson spends her free time holding softball clinics. She also oversees the Dot Richardson Softball Association, an instructional, not-for-profit league. In addition, Richardson coaches an 18-and-under girls team called "Dot's Diamonds." Richardson has said she is interested in starting a family. Her ambitions include becoming head coach of the U.S. Olympic softball team, and someday, head U.S. Olympic team physician.

Richardson, a sought-after speaker nationwide, addressed the Republican National Convention in 1996. As Saint Leo University basketball coach Kerri Reaves told the *Tampa Tribune,* "This is a woman who sets a great precedent, which goes to show you can excel in both aspects of life, athletics and academics." Richardson's story testifies to the power of personal volition.

CONTACT INFORMATION

Address: c/o Dot Richardson Softball Association, 614 E. Highway 50, Suite 211, Clermont, Florida, 34711. Fax: (352) 243-0585. Phone: (352) 243-7395. Online: http://www.drsa.org.

SELECTED WRITINGS BY RICHARDSON:

(With Don Yaeger) *Living the Dream,* New York: Kensington Books, 1997.

FURTHER INFORMATION

Books

Richardson, Dot and Don Yaeger. *Living the Dream.* New York: Kensington Books, 1997.

Periodicals

Frey, Jennifer. "Dr. Dot Dispenses Sports Medicine; Lessons from an Olympic Gold Medal Serve Resident Richardson." *Washington Post* (February 2, 1997).

Hoppes, Lynn. "At Home Today: Dot Richardson, Softball Player." *Orlando Sentinel* (August 5, 2001).

Moritz, Amy. "Diamond Vision; Olympian Dot Richardson is an Inspirational Ambassador of Softball." *Buffalo News* (February 21, 2001).

Norrie, David. "Saint Leo to Honor Richardson with Women in Sports Award." *Tampa Tribune* (December 26, 2002).

Other

"Athletic Awards." Dot Richardson Enterprises Inc. http://www.dotrichardson.com/all%20about%20dot/awards.htm (January 13, 2003).

"Just the Facts." Dot Richardson Enterprises Inc. http://www.dotrichardson.com/all%20about%20dot/facts.htm (January 13, 2003).

Sketch by Lisa Frick

Wesley Branch Rickey
1881-1965

American baseball executive

The names Rickey and Robinson will always be linked in the annals of sport because of their respective roles in breaking major league baseball's "color line," a seminal event which is regarded as having had a monumental effect — perhaps most of all symbolically, but also in a practical sense — on the Civil Rights movement. Wesley Branch Rickey's determination, in the face of opposition from other baseball owners, to sign a black player and desegregate professional baseball; his recruitment and signing of **Jackie Robinson**; and his orchestration of Robinson's debut in the major leagues opened the door for blacks in baseball and helped change the course of American history.

Raised on a Farm

Wesley Branch Rickey was born in 1881 in southern Ohio, the son of Jacob Franklin Rickey, a Wesleyite Methodist, and raised on a farm. Rickey was greatly influenced by his mother, Emily, who helped to give him a sense of moral purpose and a strong religious faith. Rickey attended school in a one-room schoolhouse in Rush Township, Ohio and later in the nearby town of Lucasville but was unable to earn a high school diploma

Wesley Branch Rickey

(since the school didn't offer one). After completing his schooling, Rickey, who was then in his late teens, was encouraged by James Finney, a school superintendent and coach, to take an exam to become a schoolteacher. After a course of intensive self-study, Rickey earned a teaching certificate and taught for two years in a school in Scioto County. Rickey learned early that he had to show his command of the class by standing up to rowdy students, which he did on two notable occasions, using his fists to put strong, older boys in their place.

In March 1901, Rickey enrolled at Ohio Wesleyan University (OWU) in Delaware, Ohio, a Methodist school. He had not been expected to go to college and had to talk his father into letting him attend. Rickey played on the OWU football and baseball teams in his freshman year. To help pay school costs, he also played baseball during summer vacation for a local semipro team, earning $25 a game. When he returned to school, Rickey found to his surprise that playing for money had caused him to lose his athletic eligibility. The president of OWU, Dr. James W. Bashford, gave Rickey a way to get back his eligibility by suggesting that he sign a paper denying the charges that he had played for money, but Rickey said he could not do so and attest to something that was false. In the spring of 1903, the OWU baseball coach resigned and Bashford, who had been impressed by Rickey's honesty and character in the loss of eligibility incident, asked Rickey, who was in his sophomore year, to take over as the school's baseball coach. During his first season, Rickey witnessed a couple of no-

table instances of overt racism against the only black player on the OWU team, first baseman Charles Thomas. These incidents made an "indelible" impression on him.

Tentative Steps in the Big Leagues

Rickey graduated from OWU in 1904 with a B.Litt. degree. Meanwhile, he had become a professional baseball player during the summer months, when on vacation from college. He played minor league baseball for two consecutive seasons and at the end of the 1904 season was promoted from the Dallas team in the Texas League to the Cincinnati Reds, who were in need of help at Rickey's position, catcher. He joined the Reds in September, but was sent packing (and never got into a game) after the manager found out that Rickey, because of religious scruples, refused to play baseball on Sundays. Rickey made it to the major leagues again in 1905 and played parts of two seasons as a catcher for the St. Browns. He also played in 1907 for the New York Highlanders (the team that eventually became the Yankees), but an injury sustained during the offseason while throwing a ball in the OWU gymnasium had impaired Rickey's throwing ability and ended his playing career prematurely.

Becomes Major League Executive

While playing professional baseball, Rickey continued to coach at the college level. He spent two years as football and baseball coach at Allegheny College in Meadville, Pennsylvania. In 1906, he was married to Jane Moulton.

In 1907, Rickey enrolled in the University of Michigan Law School, from which he earned a law degree in 1911 while also coaching the university's baseball team. In 1911, he set up a short-lived law practice in Boise, Ohio with two former OWU fraternity brothers, but the practice foundered, and Rickey soon returned to the University of Michigan, where he took up coaching again. His University of Michigan team included the future Hall of Famer George Sisler, whom Rickey would later sign to a contract with the St. Louis Browns.

Rickey was hired in 1912 by Browns owner Robert Lee Hedges (who had known Rickey from his playing days with the Browns) as a scout and then, shortly thereafter, in 1913, became an executive assistant in the Browns' front office. Rickey was also appointed field manager at the end of the 1913 season and served in that capacity for the next two seasons before being replaced by the Browns' new owner, Philip De Catesby Ball, who retained Rickey in a front office role. In 1917, Rickey accepted a higher-paying job as president of the Browns' national league counterparts, the St. Louis Cardinals. The Browns' owner, Ball, objected to Rickey's departure and undertook legal action in an unsuccessful attempt to enforce provisions of Rickey's contract with the Browns. Rickey volunteered to serve in the First World War, was commissioned a major, and served in France during 1918

Chronology

1881	Born December 20 in Little California (later renamed Stockdale), Ohio
1901	Enrolls at Ohio Wesleyan University
1903	Becomes baseball coach at Ohio Wesleyan. Plays minor league baseball during summer at Terre Haute, Indiana and Le Mars, Iowa
1904	Earns B.Litt. from Ohio Wesleyan
1904-05	Plays for Dallas of Texas League. Signs contact with Cincinnati Reds; dismissed for refusing to play Sundays. Contract returned to Dallas. Traded to Chicago White Sox and, subsequently, to St. Louis Browns. Plays part of 1905 season with Browns
1904-06	Coaches football and baseball at Allegheny College in Meadville, Pennsylvania, plus teaching
1906	Earns B.A. from Ohio Wesleyan. Marries Jane Moulton in June. Plays 65 games for Browns and has his best year as a player, batting .284, third highest on team. Sold to New York Highlanders in December
1907	Plays 52 games for Highlanders. On June 28, Washington Nationals (later known as Senators) steal a record 13 bases on Highlanders catcher Rickey (who had been pressed into service despite a bad shoulder), setting a record. Enters law school at University of Michigan in fall
1909	Diagnosed with tuberculosis; spends time at sanatorium in Saranac Lake, New York
1910-13	Coaches baseball at University of Michigan. Earns J.D. degree in 1911
1913-16	Serves in executive capacity for St. Louis Browns, with responsibility for acquiring players and making trades. Also serves as team's field manager from September 1913 to end of 1915 season
1916	Hired as president by St. Louis Cardinals
1918	Serves in Chemical Warfare Unit of U.S. Army
1919	Becomes field manager of Cardinals (retaining title of president)
1920	Sam Breadon buys a controlling interest in Cardinals, takes over as president, and demotes Rickey to vice-president
1925	Rogers Hornsby is named player-manager of Cardinals, replacing Rickey, who remains as vice-president and business manager
1942	Resigns as Cardinals GM and becomes president of Brooklyn Dodgers
1944-45	Rickey and associates Walter O'Malley and John Smith acquire controlling interest in Dodgers
1945	Rickey announces plan (later acknowledged to be a ruse to obscure his real intentions) to form Brown Dodgers team as Brooklyn's entry in proposed new Black United States Baseball League
1945	Signs Kansas City Monarchs shortstop Jackie Robinson to minor league contract
1947	Announces that Dodgers have purchased Robinson's contract from Montreal farm team
1950	Resigns as president of Dodgers. Named executive vice-president and general manager of Pittsburgh Pirates
1955	Steps down as Pirates GM and moves into advisory role with team
1959	Resigns as CEO of Pirates and becomes president of proposed Continental League (which disbands in 1960 without playing a game)
1962	Rejoins Cardinals as senior consultant for player development
1964	Fired from consulting job with Cardinals
1965	Collapses on November 13 while giving speech in Columbia, Missouri and dies on December 9

---

with ballplayers such as **Ty Cobb** and Christy Mathewson in the Army's Chemical Warfare Unit.

Develops Farm System

Rickey served for twenty-six years as an executive of the Cardinals, and he was also the team's field manager for over six seasons during this period. In 1922, a controlling interest in the Cardinals was purchased by a wealthy St. Louis businessman, Sam Breadon. Although Breadon and Rickey were temperamental opposites, they combined to create one of baseball's most successful franchises. The heart of the Cardinals operation was the much maligned but ultimately successful "farm system" (at first called by its detractors "chain store" or "chain gang" baseball), which was copied in due course by every major league team. Although the idea of a farm system was not entirely new, Rickey almost single-handedly put it into execution and brought it to fruition. By forging working agreements with minor league clubs at various levels, Rickey could develop talent without having to worry that the owner of a rival team would outbid him for a player (as had happened in earlier days, when minor league owners made it a practice to sell their marquee players to the highest bidder).

Signs Robinson

In October 1942, in the midst of a deteriorating relationship with Breadon, Rickey resigned from the Cardi-

nals and shortly thereafter was named general manager of the Brooklyn Dodgers. The stands at Sportsman's Park in St. Louis, where the Cardinals played, were segregated, but in New York City, the chances for successfully integrating a major league team seemed much better. In 1943, while reporting to the Dodgers board of directors on his plan to set up a mass scouting system, Rickey mentioned that he "might include a Negro player or two"; the idea met with tacit approval. Rickey then engaged his scouts in a mission to find the "right man" to break baseball's color line. Rickey announced publicly in 1945 that he intended to establish a new Negro league called the United States League, which would include a Brooklyn franchise called the Brown Dodgers. Rickey then had Dodger scouts intensively scout players in the existing Negro Leagues, including Robinson, who were presumably being scouted to play for the Brown Dodgers. The new Negro league team was actually a smokescreen, Rickey later conceded, invented as a ruse to mask his real intentions.

On August 18, 1945, Rickey met with Robinson, who had been scouted by a Dodger scout, Clyde Sukeforth, and was immediately impressed with Robinson's intelligence, character, and demeanor. Rickey delivered to Robinson an impassioned discourse on the abuse Robinson would face as baseball's first black player and why he believed Robinson had to take the abuse without retaliation. "You will symbolize a crucial cause," Rickey said. "One incident, just one incident, can set it back twenty years.... I'm looking for a ballplayer with enough guts not to fight back." On October 23, 1945, Rickey signed Robinson to a contract with the Dodgers' minor league affiliate in Montreal. On April 10, 1947, he made the epochal announcement that Robinson, after an outstanding year at Montreal, was being promoted to the Dodgers roster.

Post-Dodger Years

Rickey's tenure with the Dodgers lasted until 1950, when he was forced out by a fellow owner, Walter O'Malley, who became the team's president (and who ultimately moved the team to Los Angeles, earning O'Malley the enmity of Brooklyn fans). One month after leaving the Dodgers, Rickey became the general manager of the Pittsburgh Pirates, a second division club with whom he was less successful (although he did acquire players such as **Roberto Clemente** who provided a foundation for the Pirates' later success). Rickey stepped down as Pirates general manager in 1955 and remained in an advisory role with the team until 1959. He was then named president of a proposed new third league in Major League baseball, the Continental League. The Continental League never became a reality. But it was a key factor in spurring the expansion of major league baseball into two 10-team leagues.

On July 23, 1962, Rickey attended Jackie Robinson's induction into the National Baseball Hall of Fame. Rickey himself was elected to the Hall in 1967 by a unanimous vote of the Committee on Baseball Veterans. He is one of twenty-three men elected to the Hall of Fame as "executives" or "pioneers," and one of only four inductees in that category whose primary role was serving in a day-to-day executive capacity as general manager. His Hall of Fame plaque sums up his contribution to baseball integration and Civil Rights simply and matter-of-factly by stating, "BROUGHT JACKIE ROBINSON TO BROOKLYN IN 1947."

Rickey's Legacy

Rickey was a genuine innovator who had a good bit of the college professor in him. His chief innovation, of course, was the farm system concept, which enabled teams like the Cardinals to compete against teams bankrolled by deeper-pocketed owners. Rickey was continually coming up with newfangled ideas, such as sliding pits, "pitching strings," and batting tees; he hired the first statistician in baseball (the Dodgers' Allan Roth) and used mathematical formulas to predict a team's success in offensive and defensive categories (and to question some commonly held assumptions about whether factors such as strikeouts are a reliable predictor of a team's ability to prevent runs). Rickey was interested in his players' moral welfare, and he always made it a point to inquire about a boy's character and family cir-

---

> ### *Baseball: An Illustrated History*
>
> In the spring of 1903, Ohio Wesleyan was scheduled to play Notre Dame at South Bend, Indiana. Rickey's star was the first baseman, Charles "Tommy" Thomas, an African American equally skilled at baseball and football....
>
> [When] Rickey and his team filed into the lobby of the Oliver Hotel at South Bend, the clerk told Rickey that while he and the rest of the team were welcome, Thomas was not. Thomas, humiliated, suggested that he just quietly return to Ohio Wesleyan and forget about playing.
>
> Rickey wouldn't hear of it; he took Thomas to his own room. When the manager protested, Rickey threatened to take his whole team elsewhere if he didn't cooperate. The manager backed down.
>
> Many years later, Rickey remembered what happened after he sent for the team captain to come to his room and talk over strategy for the big game: "Tommy stood in the corner, tense and brooding and in silence. I asked him to sit on a chair and relax. Instead, he sat on the edge of the cot, his huge shoulders hunched and his hands clasped between his knees. I tried to talk to the captain, but I couldn't take my gaze from Tommy. Tears welled, ... spilled down his black face. ... Then his shoulders heaved convulsively, and he rubbed one great hand over the other with all the power of his body, muttering, 'Black skin, ... black skin. If I could only make 'em white.' He kept rubbing and rubbing as though he would remove the blackness by sheer friction."
>
> Rickey did his best to reassure Thomas, but "whatever mark that incident left on Charles Thomas, it was no more indelible than the impression made on me." The memory never left him and the conviction slowly grew that he would someday try to see to it that such things never happened again.
>
> Source: Ward, Geoffrey C. and Ken Burns. *Baseball: An Illustrated History.* New York: Alfred A. Knopf, 1994.

---

cumstances before deciding whether to sign him. He often spoke before the YMCA and other civic groups and was an early sponsor and supporter of the Fellowship of Christian Athletes. Sports, Rickey believed, exemplified the moral percepts that make American great and that help to mold individual character.

Rickey had a genuine aesthetic appreciation of baseball and an almost evangelical faith in its place in American life. He was motivated by two guiding principles in challenging baseball's pre-World War II apartheid policy: a fundamental respect for democratic principles and "fair play"; and a religious conviction that it was not only the right time to break baseball's color line but was the right thing to do.

SELECTED WRITINGS BY RICKEY:

(With Robert Riger) *The American Diamond: A Documentary of the Game of Baseball,* Simon & Schuster, 1965.

FURTHER INFORMATION

Books

Barber, Red. *1947: When All Hell Broke Loose in Baseball.* Garden City, NY: Doubleday, 1982.

Awards and Accomplishments

1967	Elected to National Baseball Hall of Fame

Burk, Robert F. *Much More Than a Game: Players, Owners, and American Baseball Since 1921.* Chapel Hill, NC: University of North Carolina Press, 2001.

Chalberg, John C. *Rickey and Robinson: The Preacher, the Player, and America's Game.* Wheeling, IL: Harlan Davidson, 2000.

Cohen, Stanley. *Dodgers! The First 100 Years.* New York: Carol Publishing Group, 1990.

Dictionary of American Biography: Supplement Seven, 1961-1965. New York: Charles Scribner's Sons, 1981.

Dorinson, Joseph, and Joram Warmund, Eds. *Jackie Robinson: Race, Sports, and the American Dream.* Armonk, NY: M. E. Sharpe, 1998.

Frommer, Harvey. *Rickey and Robinson: The Men Who Broke Baseball's Color Barrier.* New York: Macmillan, 1982

Golenbock, Peter. *The Spirit of St. Louis: A History of the St. Louis Cardinals and Browns.* New York: HarperCollins, 2000, 1995.

Helyar, John. *Lords of the Realm: The Real History of Baseball.* New York: Villard Books, 1994.

Herzog, Brad. *The Sports 100: The One Hundred Most Important People in American Sports History.* New York: Macmillan, 1995.

Honig, Donald. *Baseball America: The Heroes of the Game and the Times of Their Glory.* New York: Macmillan, 1985.

Lieb, Frederick G. *The St. Louis Cardinals: The Story of a Great Baseball Club.* New York: G. P. Putnam's Sons, 1944.

Mann, Arthur. *Branch Rickey: American in Action.* Boston: Houghton Mifflin, 1957.

Martinez, David H. *The Book of Baseball Literacy.* New York: Penguin, 1996.

Monteleone, John J., ed. *Branch Rickey's Little Blue Book: Wit and Strategy from Baseball's Last Wise Man.* New York: Macmillan, 1995.

Obojski, Robert. *Bush League: A History of Minor League Baseball.* New York: Macmillan, 1975.

O'Toole, Andrew. *Branch Rickey in Pittsburgh: Baseball's Trailblazing General Manager for the Pirates, 1950-1955.* Jefferson, NC: McFarland, 2000.

Parrott, Harold. *The Lords of Baseball: A Wry Look at a Side of the Game the Fan Seldom Sees—the Front Office.* New York: Praeger, 1976.

Polner, Murray. *Branch Rickey: A Biography.* New York: Atheneum, 1982.

Rampersad, Arnold. *Jackie Robinson: A Biography.* New York: Alfred A. Knopf, 1997.

Skipper, John C. *A Biographical Dictionary of the Baseball Hall of Fame.* Jefferson, NC: McFarland, 2000.

Stockton, J. Roy. *The Gashouse Gang and a Couple of Other Guys.* New York: A. S. Barnes, 1945.

Sullivan. Neil J. *The Dodgers Move West.* New York: Oxford University Press, 1987.

Tygiel, Jules. *Baseball's Great Experiment: Jackie Robinson and His Legacy.* New York: Oxford University Press, 1997

Tygiel, Jules, Ed. *The Jackie Robinson Reader: Perspectives on an American Hero.* New York: Dutton, 1997.

Voigt, David Quentin. *American Baseball, Volume II: From the Commissioners to Continental Expansion.* Norman, OK: University of Oklahoma Press, 1970.

Periodicals

"Branch Rickey, 83, Dies in Missouri." *New York Times* (December 10, 1965): 1.

Dexter, Charles. "Brooklyn's Sturdy Branch." *Collier's* (September 15, 1945): 116.

Graham, Frank, Jr. "Branch Rickey Rides Again: The Return of the Mahatma." *Saturday Evening Post* (March 9, 1963): 66-68.

Other

"Baseball Library.com: Branch Rickey." http://www.pubdim.net/baseballlibrary/ballplayers/R/Rickey_Branch.stm (November 30, 2002).

"the BASEBALL page.com: Branch Rickey." http://www.thebaseballpage.com/past/pp/rickeybranch/default.htm (November 30, 2002).

"BrainyQuote: Branch Rickey." http://www.brainyquote.com/quotes/authors/b/a125843.html (November 30, 2002).

"Breaking the Color Line: 1940-1946." http://memory.loc.gov/ammem/jrhtml/jr1940.html (December 16, 2002).

"A Jackie Robinson Society Exclusive Interview with Branch B. Rickey [grandson of Branch Rickey]." http://www.utexas.edu/students/jackie/robinson/rickey.html (November 30, 2002).

The Jackie Robinson Story [film]. Dir. Alfred E. Green. Perf. Jackie Robinson, Ruby Dee, Minor Watson, Louise Beavers, Richard Lane. MGM, 1950.

Lurie, Mike. "Rickey As Much a Pioneer As Robinson." CBS SportsLine, May 28, 1997. http://cbs.sportsline.com/u/baseball/robinson/notes/luriem52897.htm (December 16, 2002).

"National Baseball Hall of Fame: Branch Rickey." http://www.baseballhalloffame.org/hofers_and_honorees/hofer_bios/rickey_branch.htm (November 30, 2002).

Pappas, Doug. "Only four GMs in Hall of Fame." ESPN.com. June 26, 2002. http://espn.go.com/mlb/columns/bp/1399247.html (December 7, 2002).

Transcript of interview with Branch Rickey by Davis J. Walsh [1955?]. Library of Congress, Manuscript Di-

vision, Branch Rickey Papers. http://memory.loc.
gov/ammem/jrhtml/davis.html (November 30, 2002).

West, Jean. "Branch Rickey and Jackie Robinson (Interview Essay)," by Jean West. http://www.jimcrow
history.org/resources/pdf/hs_in_robinson_rickey.pdf
(November 30, 2002).

Sketch by Roger W. Smith

Libby Riddles
1956-

American dogsledder

Libby Riddles

The 13th annual Iditarod Trail Sled Dog Race in 1985
was particularly grueling—"jinxed from the start by
bad weather, bad trail and bad luck," according to Associated Press reports. Temperatures plunged to -50 degrees Farenheit and storms twice forced race officials to
halt the competition, for a total of eighty-seven hours,
and fly in emergency rations of dog food. So it looked
like more of the same when, after two weeks of racing,
an oncoming blizzard compelled dogsledders to hunker
down on a Sunday night in Shaktoolik, an Eskimo village on the coast of northwest Alaska.

It wasn't more of the same for 28-year-old Libby
Riddles, however. For Riddles, it was an opportunity to
rise up and write a new page in Iditarod history.

Into the Storm

With her competition pinned down in Shaktoolik, Riddles and her thirteen dogs plunged boldly into the storm
and onto the sea ice of Norton Sound. The daring move
soon looked like a colossal miscalculation. After three
hours running against the forty-knot winds, Riddles' team
was exhausted. For the next twelve hours, the dogs slept
on the snow and Riddles huddled in her sleeping bag. The
blinding storm was still raging as the dogs awoke, but the
team was rested and ready to run. They never relinquished the lead and, three days later, Riddles rode into
Nome and across the finish line—the first woman to win
the Iditarod. She covered the 1,135-mile trail in eighteen
days, twenty minutes, and seventeen seconds—three
hours faster than the second-place finisher. "When I started out across the Sound, it just really looked pathetic because you couldn't even tell one marker from another,"
Riddles said after the race. "But I figured if it does pan
out, it might help me win the race. So I'm going to try it
even if it's crazy. . . . I thought I had the team to do it. I
didn't know if I could keep up my end of it."

Riddles had not distinguished herself in two previous
Iditarod runs, finishing 18th and 20th. Unable to attract

sponsors for the 1985 race, she covered her costs by
sewing and selling fur hats and giving sled dog exhibitions for tourists. Once the race began, her team ran away
with her sled, she broke a sled brake, and some of her
dogs succumbed to an energy-draining virus. Tough
competition cemented Riddles' role as the quintessential
underdog. Favorites to win the race included Rick Swenson, a four-time champion, and **Susan Butcher**, who had
twice placed second and was widely expected to become
the first woman to win the Iditarod. Butcher had to drop
out of the race, however, when a moose killed two of her
dogs and injured several others, and Swenson was
pinned down in Shaktoolik with the rest of the field
when Riddles drove into the blizzard on Norton Sound.

Heading North

Riddles was born April 1, 1956, in Madison, Wisconsin, and grew up in St. Cloud, Minnesota. An animal
lover as a child, she dreamed of a life as a cowgirl or
farmer. After graduating from high school, she followed
a boyfriend, Dewey Halverson, to a homesteader's life
in Alaska. The young couple lived in a cabin near Anchorage and Riddles helped Halverson train sled dogs.
"I learned real quick it's not much fun to help somebody
else drive dogs," Riddles told *Women's Sports & Fitness.* "I wanted to do it myself."

She entered the Iditarod in 1980, finishing in 20th
place. The following year, she finished 18th—and met
dogsledder Joe Garnie. Riddles soon joined Garnie in

Teller, a remote Alaskan village with a population of 250. They lived in a trailer without plumbing, fished and hunted for food, and bred and trained sled dogs. Riddles continued racing. In 1982, she placed 7th in the Kusko 300 Sled-Dog Race. She followed up with a 5th place finish in 1984.

Caretaker

In addition to winning the Iditarod in 1985, Riddles won the Humanitarian Award given to the Iditarod musher who takes the best care of his or her dogs. Riddles treated her team with equal parts discipline and tender loving care. "I feel like I'm a real expert at keeping my dogs happy," she said. "If I had to treat (them) like soldiers, it would just take the fun out of it. But when things get serious, they listen to me, too. You've got to be strict with them. . . . When I'm out there racing, I'm racing as much as anybody to win. But I'm also out there because I enjoy being with my dogs and I love what I'm doing."

Riddles, whose victory earned her $50,000, has never come close to winning the Iditarod again. She was scratched from the field in 1987, placed 16th in 1989, and finished 32nd in 1995. Susan Butcher, meanwhile, became the second woman to win the Iditarod in 1986, the year after Riddles' winning run. Butcher covered the course in record time—eleven days, fifteen hours, six minutes. The old record, set by Swenson in 1981, was twelve days, eight hours, forty-five minutes, and two seconds.

Libbymania

Riddles' dramatic victory in 1985 generated an unprecedented level of press coverage and brought Riddles—and the Iditarod—instant fame. "Being the first woman to win, and winning in such bold fashion, caught people's attention," reported the *Anchorage Daily News*. "She was a phenomenon, sparking a nationwide burst of Libbymania.... President Ronald Reagan sent her a telegram of congratulation. *Vogue* ran her picture. The Women's Sports Foundation made her its Professional Sportswoman of the Year." In addition, March 21, 1985 was proclaimed Libby Riddles Day in Alaska. "Her win and her grace afterwards led to a tremendous increase in nationwide and worldwide publicity for the race," said race official Tim Jones.

Riddles lives near Anchorage, Alaska, where she continues to raise and train sled dogs. In 2002, Sasquatch Books celebrated the 30th anniversary of the Iditarod by publishing a revised edition of Riddles' book, *Storm Run: The Story of the First Woman to Win the Iditarod Sled Dog Race*. The book, written for children, recounts Riddles' winning ride. "We moved into the blackest of nights," she writes. "I couldn't make out any runner tracks. In fact, I could barely see the trail. I was either lost—or in first place."

CONTACT INFORMATION

Address: P.O. Box 872901, Wasilla, AK, 99687-2901.

SELECTED WRITINGS BY RIDDLES:

(With Tim Jones) *Race Across Alaska: First Woman to Win the Iditarod Tells Her Story*, Stackpole Books, 1988.

(With Shelley Gill, and illustrator Shannon Cartwright) *Danger: The Dog Yard Cat*, Paws IV Publishing, 1995.

(With Shannon Cartwright) *Storm Run*, Paws IV Publishing, 1996.

(With Shannon Cartwright) *Storm Run: The Story of the First Woman to Win the Iditarod Sled Dog Race*, Sasquatch Books, 2002.

FURTHER INFORMATION

Periodicals

"Alaskan Sled Dog Race Won Again by a Woman." *Chicago Tribune* (March 14, 1986).

Esser, Doug. "The Last Great Race on Earth." Associated Press Wire Service (March 2, 2002).

"Facts and Figures of the Race." *USA Today* (March 3, 1995).

Foster, David. "Woman Wins Dog Sled Race." Associated Press Wire Service (March 20, 1985).

"Libby Riddles, 1997 Iditarod." *Anchorage Daily News* (February 23, 1997).

Livadas, Greg. "Champion Libby Riddles Promotes Faith in Oneself." *Rochester Democrat and Chronicle* (October 11, 2002).

Upicksoun, Martha J. "Woman Takes Iditarod by Crossing Sea Ice in Blizzard." Associated Press Wire Service (March 21, 1985).

Wergeland, Kari. "Nonfiction Evolves into Truly Creative New Works, From Everest to Iditarod." *Seattle Times* (May 4, 2002).

"Woman, for First Time, Wins Alaska Sled Race." *New York Times* (March 21, 1985).

Sketch by David Wilkins

Cathy Rigby
1952-

American gymnast

Cathy Rigby

Before **Mary Lou Retton**, before **Nadia Comaneci**, even before **Olga Korbut** came the gymnast whose prodigious talent and upbeat personality served to make her a representative of her sport. America's Cathy Rigby never won an Olympic medal, but she was much-honored in international competition and helped boost gymnastics in the United States. Following her competitive career, Rigby remained in the public eye, recreating herself as a musical-comedy actress best known for her athletic portrayal of the boy who would not grow up, Peter Pan. At the same time, Rigby became an advocate for healthy eating, freely discussing her own battles with anorexia and bulimia.

Talented, But Torn

Born in Long Beach, California, to two aerospace specialists, Cathy Rigby was a spirited child who turned first to ballet to channel her energy. At age nine she discovered gymnastics—still a relatively low-profile activity in the early 1960s. Rigby showed early talent at tumbling, but found herself in the midst of a power struggle between her father and her coach. Each man wanted to direct the child's talent, but fate intervened when Rigby's father, Paul, an alcoholic, lost his job. "Life was hell for a long time," Rigby recalled in a *People* interview with Mark Goodman. "Gymnastics was a way to be away from home, but it too had its problems."

Chief among those problems was the issue of Rigby's weight. Though decidedly on the petite size—she stood four-foot-eleven—the teenager was informed that her ideal weight was not to exceed 89 pounds, far less than her normal weight. At first Rigby attempted to control her size through diet. "Sometimes I ate only one meal a day, even though I was practicing eight hours a day and needed food to be strong" she noted in a cautionary article she wrote for *Sports Illustrated for Kids*. "Some-

times I didn't eat for a week and drank only apple juice. I often felt tired and dizzy. Sometimes I felt so weak, I fainted. But I lost weight."

At sixteen a maturing Rigby gained ten pounds. Weighing in at 105, the gymnast felt, she told Goodman, that "my identity was threatened." A bout with anorexia (curtailing eating) led to a case of bulimia (purging food before digestion). It was the beginning of a vicious cycle that lasted more than a decade. At her lowest point, Rigby weighed only 79 pounds and was hospitalized twice with coronary episodes.

Off to the Olympics

None of this information was made available to Rigby's fans at the time. She was far better known the embodiment of health and fitness, the youngest and smallest member of the U.S. gymnastics team competing in Mexico City in 1968. Competing in the four divisions of gymnastics—floor exercise, balance beam, vaulting, and uneven bars—Rigby finished sixteenth, the best-ever placement of an American in a sport more commonly dominated by Eastern European women.

Rigby's success in Mexico City heralded a four-year streak of gymnastics championships in the U.S. and abroad. The young woman took home honors in various contests, most notably in 1970 when Rigby became the first American of either gender to win a gold medal at the World Championships held in Yugoslavia. As her profile increased, Rigby increasingly became known as the woman to beat in the 1972 Olympic games in Munich, Germany. At nineteen, Rigby was again an Olympian, even though she could not curtail her binging and purging. Olympic glory, however, was not in her future. When the scores were tallied, gold medalist Korbut had stolen the spotlight as gymnastics' newest gamine. But even though Rigby had again set the record as the highest-placed American, finishing tenth, the pre-Olympics publicity—including a *Life* cover story—led her to feel like a failure. She retired from competition and married Tommy Mason, himself an ex-athlete.

Hiding a Painful Secret

Now a recognizable figure, Rigby embarked on a new career as a gymnastics commentator while she started her family. The early days of post-athletic training proved difficult, she related in a 1984 *People* article. "I no longer had a goal and all I was doing was eating and throwing up. Everybody thought I had the most successful life: I had a career working with ABC Sports, I was doing TV movies … and commercials, and the money was coming in." Rigby struggled to maintain this "perfect" image, saying she hid her condition from her husband and secretly consumed 10,000 calories a day in fast food. "I took a voice lesson every week," she told the *People* reporter, "and I can tell you where every McDonald's and Jack-in-the-Box was along the way—and every bathroom where I could get rid of the food."

During Rigby's pregnancy with her first son, Bucky, the former athlete gained only eleven pounds. Though she was praised for her self-discipline, some internal damage was done. Rigby's son was born small, and because of her lack of body fat Rigby could not produce enough milk to nurse him for more than a month. After landing in the hospital with an electrolyte balance problem, Rigby determined to improve her health in time to have her next child. She gained twenty-five pounds this time and was

able to successfully nurse her second son, Ryan, for four months. But Rigby's bulimia recurred shortly after.

At the same time, Rigby was considering her professional future. "When I got out of gymnastics and retired at the age of [nineteen], I thought, What else am I going to do with my life?" she said in a *Back Stage West* interview with Rob Kendt. "I started doing episodic television, where I'd always play the Russian gymnast or whatever, and someone recommended I take voice and acting lessons. I studied for seven years before I had the courage to really step onstage." Rigby approached acting as she did gymnastics. "I knew I could get better if I just worked at it," she told Goodman. "It's that athlete's obsessiveness—the need to prove yourself and work harder than anyone else."

Flying High as Peter Pan

As her performing talent developed Rigby was finding herself cast in musicals where she could display her range. She starred in such shows as *Meet Me in St. Louis, They're Playing Our Song,* and *South Pacific.* But her best-known role came with a lavish revival of *Peter Pan* that made it to Broadway in 1991 (she had done an arena version of the show as early as 1974). The title role seemed tailor-made for Rigby, who not only mastered the strenuous flying sequences but also added her own signature flourishes, such as using a stairway railing as a balance beam. Critics were impressed: Martin Schaeffer of *Back Stage* commented on Rigby's "surprisingly strong performance." Rigby's voice "is strong," he noted, "and she's able to muster the needed degree of poignancy for such evergreens as [the ballad] 'Neverland.'" An "all-around delight" is how Nelson Pressley of *Washington Times* saw Rigby in a 1998 tour. "She is more than merely cute as Peter Pan. She knows the magical boy is a bit of a brat and deeply lonely, and these darker qualities come through easily." Rigby was nominated for the 1991 Tony Award as best musical actress, the first Olympian to be so recognized.

There seemed but one hurdle left for the athlete—conquering her eating disorder. In 1981, with her marriage to Mason dissolving, Rigby met fellow actor Tom McCoy, who encouraged her to face her problem. Part of his intervention was based on pure "vanity," as Rigby noted in *People.* "He said, 'You [have] circles under your eyes, your hair is falling out and you look older.' For the first time I listened to somebody." Rigby and McCoy married, and with psychiatric help she finally was cured of her bulimia. The couple went on to have two daughters, Theresa and Kaitlin, while Rigby added health advocate to her credentials. To that end, she took a role in a 1997 television movie *Perfect Body,* playing a gymnastics coach who warns a young girl of the dangers of starving herself to attain an unreasonable weight. She also narrated a video, *Cathy Rigby on Eating Disorders.*

Awards and Accomplishments

1968	Highest-placed American (sixteenth), Olympic summer games
1968	World Cup gold medalist
1970	U.S. Championships gold medalist
1970	World Championships silver medalist
1971	World Cup gold medalist and champion
1971	Riga Cup gold and bronze medalist
1971	South African Cup all-around champion
1971	U.S.-U.S.S.R. Dual Meet champion, floor exercise
1972	Highest-placed American (tenth), Olympic summer games
1972	U.S. Championships gold, silver, and bronze medalist
1972	Appeared on cover of *Life* magazine
1991	Tony Award nomination, *Peter Pan*
1998	Inducted into International Gymnastics Hall of Fame
2001	Ovation Award, Theatre L.A. board of governors

By 1998 Rigby—healthy and accomplished—had been performing on-and-off in *Peter Pan* for twenty years. But even after two decades "she never seems to be going through the paces as she charms the Darling children and the audience with her tough-talking, good-hearted attitude," according to *Variety* reviewer Christopher Isherwood. "Her affection for the role seems freshly minted, and her exuberant singing is wining. The show really takes wing whenever she does." Rigby admitted in Kendt's article, "I love doing long runs, because some nights you go out there and … it just happens. You're just alive, and no matter how you feel that day, it works."

CONTACT INFORMATION

Address: McCoy Rigby Entertainment, 110 East. Wilshire Ave., Ste. 200, Fullerton, CA 92832. Phone: (714) 525-8388.

FURTHER INFORMATION

Books

St. James Encyclopedia of Popular Culture. Gale, 2002.

Periodicals

Churnin, Nancy. "Cathy Rigby Finds Her Inner Child in 'Peter Pan.'" *Knight-Ridder/Tribune News Service.* (October 4, 2000).

Goodman, Mark. "Cathy Rigby, Flying High." *People.* (May 6, 1991).

Kelleher, Terry. "Perfect Body." *People.* (September 8, 1997).

Kendt, Rob. "Local Heroes." *Back Stage West.* (November 8, 2001).

Life. (May 5, 1972).

Pressley, Nelson. "Rigby Lifts 'Peter Pan' to Satisfying Heights." *Washington Times.* (February 13, 1998).

Rigby, Cathy. "The Worst Day I Ever Had." *Sports Illustrated for Kids.* (August, 1994).

Where Is She Now?

After playing 2,500 performances of *Peter Pan*, Cathy Rigby committed her production to video in 2000. When not acting, she holds the title of Artistic Producing Director for McCoy Rigby Entertainment, a stage production company she runs with her husband, Tom McCoy, in Fullerton, California. Rigby's contribution to theatre was recognized with the 2001 Ovation Award from Theatre L.A. In 2002, approaching age fifty, she showed no sign of slowing down, taking the part of the mischievous Cat in the Hat in the Broadway and touring companies of *Seussical: The Musical.*

Rigby, Cathy. "A Onetime Olympic Gymnast Overcomes the Bulimia That Threatened Her Life." *People.* (August 13, 1984).

Roberts, Terri. "Peter Pan." *Back Stage West.* (December 7, 2000).

Schaeffer, Martin. "Peter Pan." *Back Stage.* (January 4, 1991).

Sketch by Susan Salter

Pat Riley
1945-

American basketball coach

Currently president and head coach for the Miami Heat basketball team, Pat Riley has been an NBA coach for more than 20 years. He started as a coach for the Los Angeles Lakers before moving to the New York Knicks, and finally to the Miami Heat. His NBA regular season win-loss record in 2002 stood at a remarkable 1,085-502. Those 1,085 wins were second only to coach **Lenny Wilkens**. His record of 155 post-season wins was bettered only by **Phil Jackson** in the history of the NBA. Riley's 255 postseason games are an all-time NBA record. During the 1996-97 season, Riley was named one of the Top 10 Coaches of All-Time by a panel of sports journalists.

Riley's other accomplishments include 16 divisional championships, eight conference championships, and a total of four NBA championships. Named NBA coach of the year three times, Riley is the only NBA coach ever to have received this honor as coach of three different teams. From 1982 to 2001, Riley coached 19 playoffs in a row, a league record. He is also tied for the most playoffs for one coach. Riley has also coached nine NBA All-Star games. In addition, Riley has won 50 games in a single season and NBA record-breaking 17 times. He has taken his teams to victory 60 times in one season seven times, at least once with each of the three NBA teams he has coached.

Pat Riley

Riley reached a major milestone in the 2000-01 season when he became fastest the coach or manager to reach 1,000 wins—not just in the NBA, but in all four of the professional sports in North America.

A Family of Athletes

Patrick Riley was born in 1945 in Schenectady, New York, where he attended Linton High School. His was an athletic family; his father, Leon "Lee" Riley, was a professional baseball player. He played catcher and outfielder for the Philadelphia Blue Jays in 1944. Leon Riley went on to become a manager for the Blue Jays organization in the minor leagues. Pat Riley's brother Lee was also an athlete. He played football for the National Football League's Detroit Lions, the Philadelphia Eagles, and the New York Giants from 1955-60. Lee also played for the American Football League's New York Titans in 1961-62.

In high school, Pat Riley excelled in both baseball and basketball. After graduating from high school, Riley went on to the University of Kentucky in 1963, where he became a star basketball player, earning the school team's Most Valuable Player award three times. He graduated from Kentucky in 1967.

After graduating from college, Riley was picked in the first round of selections to play for the San Diego Rockets basketball team during that team's first season, 1967-68. He played with the Rockets for three seasons before joining the Los Angeles Lakers in the 1970-71

Chronology

1945	Born in Schenectady, New York
1963	Graduates from high school, attends University of Kentucky
1967	Graduates from University of Kentucky
1967	Becomes basketball player with the San Diego Rockets
1970	Becomes a player for the Los Angeles Lakers
1975	Becomes a player for the Phoenix Suns
1977	Becomes a TV broadcaster for the Lakers
1979	Becomes assistant coach for the Lakers
1981	Becomes head coach for the Lakers
1990	Earns Coach of the Year Award
1990	Leaves the Lakers to become co-host of NBC show *NBA Showtime*
1991	Becomes head coach for the New York Knicks
1993	Earns NBA Coach of the Year award
1995	Becomes head coach for the Miami Heat
1996	Earns NBA Coach of the Year award
1997	Earns NBA Coach of the Month award
2001	Passes 1,000-win mark

season; he played with the Lakers for five years. During his first season with the Lakers, the team won 33 games in a row, at the time an NBA record. The Lakers also went on that year to win the NBA championship. In 1976, Riley spent his last year as a player with the Phoenix Suns.

From Basketball Player to Coach

After retiring as a player, Riley worked as a television broadcaster for the Lakers beginning in 1977. He stayed in this post until 1979. At the start of the 1979-80 season, Riley accepted an offer from Paul Westhead, the head coach of the Lakers to become his assistant coach.

Riley took over as head coach of the Los Angeles Lakers early in the 1981-82 season. In his very first season in the top coaching position, the Lakers won the NBA Championship. During the nine years Riley was head coach for the Lakers, the team won four NBA titles in seven NBA Finals appearances. Riley also led the Lakers to 60 wins four seasons in a row (1984-85 through the 1987-88 season). Under Riley, the Lakers won every division title, and won 50 or more games in each of the nine seasons Riley led them. The Lakers' win-loss record under Riley was 533-194. In 1990, Riley earned the first of his Coach of the Year awards. He told the *Washington Post*'s Anthony Cotton after winning the award, "I don't want to belittle the award—it does mean something—but I think I became a good coach when I stopped worrying about things like recognition."

A Winning Philosophy

Asked during this time to describe his winning philosophy that helped the Lakers perform so well, Riley told Cotton, "When I came in, I'd never coached anywhere before, so what I started doing was teaching a

Awards and Accomplishments

1963-67	Wins University of Kentucky basketball team Most Valuable Player award three times
1982, 1985, 1987-88	As head coach, leads Lakers to NBA championship
1990, 1993, 1997	Wins Coach of the Year Award
1992	Wins Miami Project Sports Legend Award
1997	Wins Coach of the Month Award
1998	Wins Boys and Girls Clubs Miami Person of the Year Award
2001	Becomes fastest coach or manager in any professional team sport in North America to reach 1,000 wins

philosophy that I didn't know I'd even had. There were never any ABCs, but over the years there's definitely been a definitive series of things I believe in." One of those things that he believes in, is something Riley has consistently promoted at each of the three NBA teams he has coached—the power of teamwork. Not one to believe in individual grandstanding, his style of coaching has each team member pulling for the others to create a whole that is greater than the some of its parts. "I'm a tremendous believer in peer pressure," he told Cotton. "I look at our team as a big circle with 12 parts and I'm on the perimeter just trying to make sure it stays enclosed. It's okay for a player to have space and to get out on a limb at times, but he has to be aware of the others and that they will pull him back in."

Riley left the Lakers in 1990, going to work for the NBC television network as co-host of a show called *NBA Showtime*. He held this job only until 1991, when he went to work for the New York Knicks as head coach. During his four years with the Knicks, Riley led the team to four playoffs in a row, concluding his time with a .680 winning percentage, the best in the history of the team. His 50 wins in each of his four years with the team also set a record for the team. In 1994, Riley led the Knicks to the NBA finals. It was the first time the team had made it to the finals since the 1972-73 season. His work with the Knicks earned him recognition as NBA Coach of the Year in 1993. It was the second time he had won the honor.

Riley moved from the Knicks to become head coach of the Miami Heat in September, 1995. One of his first moves on taking charge was to bring in center Alonzo Mourning, who subsequently became the team's star player. In the 1996-97 season Riley received his third NBA Coach of the Year honor, becoming the first to be named Coach of the Year while with three different teams. In December, 1997, Riley also earned Coach of the Month honors.

One of Riley's major accomplishments with the Heat has been to lead his team to a remarkable recovery from the devastating loss of Alonzo Mourning. Mourning had

to drop out of the game in 2000 because of kidney disease. Analysts wrote off the rest of the season for the Heat, but Riley successfully juggled his remaining players to lead his team to a 50-32 win-loss record to finish second in the Atlantic Division.

Active Beyond Baseball

In addition to coaching basketball, Riley is a highly successful motivational speaker, traveling around the United States speaking to corporate executives about how better to manage their "teams" of employees. He is also the author of two books, *Show Time,* and *The Winner Within.*

Riley and his wife Chris are also actively involved in many charitable organizations, including the Miami Heat Family Outreach, which they founded in 1997, and which provides funds to community service organizations in the South Florida area, the Kids for Kids organization of the Pediatric AIDS Foundation, which they founded in 1992, the YMCAs of Los Angeles, New York, and Miami, and the Boys and Girls Clubs. Riley's honors in connection with these activities include the Miami Project Sports Legend Award, which he received in 1992, and the Boys and Girls Clubs Miami Person of the Year Award, which he received in 1998.

SELECTED WRITINGS BY RILEY:

Show Time: Inside the Lakers' Breakthrough Season. New York: Warner Books, 1988.
The Winner Within: A Life Plan for Team Players. New York: Putnam's Sons, 1993.

FURTHER INFORMATION

Periodicals

Cotton, Anthony. "Riley Directs a Quality Production; Coach Has Lakers Right on Cue, Drops Curtain on Personal Accolades." *Washington Post* (June 14, 1987): C4.
"Pat Riley Profile." *Chicago Sun-Times* (May 20, 1993): C4.

Other

"Lee Riley Statistics." Baseball Almanac. http://www.baseball-almanac.com/players/player.php?p=rileyle01 (December 13, 2002).

"Lee Riley Statistics." Baseball-Reference.com. http://www.baseball-reference.com/r/rileyle01.shtml (December 13, 2002).

"Pat Riley Coach Info." NBA.com. http://www.nba.com/coachfile/pat_riley/?nav=page (December 9, 2002).

"Ten Minor Leaguers for the Ages." EricEnders.com. http://www.ericenders.com/minorleaguers.htm (December 13, 2002).

Sketch by Michael Belfiore

Cal Ripken, Jr.

Cal Ripken, Jr.
1960-

American baseball player

Merely going on his playing accomplishments—a much-admired all-around slugger/shortstop, several Golden Glove and Player of the Year honors—Cal Ripken, Jr. may well be placed among professional baseball's elite. But beyond his talent, Ripken demonstrated a devotion to his game and to his team, the Baltimore Orioles, that moved him into the pantheon of sport's most notable figures. He became an embodiment of dedication by missing not a single game from his start in 1983 until 1995, when he broke Lou Gehrig's longstanding record of consecutive games played at 2,131. It would be another five hundred consecutive games before Ripken would finally "sit out" a Major League contest. "You gotta play as many games as you can," he told Ralph Wiley in a 1990 *Sports Illustrated* interview. "Since there are so many possible plays, you can't get it all unless you're there every day. You can't get it from a book. You play games."

All in the Family

Ripken began "playing games" early in life. His father, for whom Ripken was named, preceded his son onto the Orioles, beginning as a minor-league catcher in 1957. For decades thereafter, Cal Sr. would be a figurehead in the organization as player, coach, and manager of farm teams in Wisconsin, South Dakota, and North Carolina, and the Orioles proper in Baltimore. Calvin Edward Ripken, Jr. was born in Havre de Grace, Maryland, on August 24, 1960. While the Ripkens made their home in Aberdeen, Maryland, their house was often empty as the family—including two brothers and a sister—traveled with their mother to wherever Cal Sr. was coaching or managing that summer. But even with the elder Ripken based in Baltimore, the family was still an often-divided one: "Baseball took my dad away from me," Cal Jr. told Wiley. "He left at one o'clock every day on the days he was at home, and he was gone completely half the time, on the road. I learned very early that if I wanted to see my dad at all, I would have to go to the ballpark with him."

Baseball became a centerpiece in the boy's life. Ironically, the largest influence in that area was Cal's mother, Viola Ripken. With Cal Sr. away so often, it was Viola who supplied the coaching, the cheers, and the consolation while her son learned his game. Even the elder Ripken was quick to acknowledge his wife's contribution: "I didn't get to see many of [Cal's] games in Little League," he remarked in a *People* article. "So [his mother] taught him to hit. She was a pretty good hitter herself, and I'm not talking about fanning the kids' behinds."

Entering his teens, Ripken turned his attention toward the minor leagues where his father was coaching. He became a fixture in Asheville, North Carolina, studying the games and peppering Cal Sr. with questions about pitching and hitting strategy. "I always wanted to know why he did something," Ripken was quoted by *Sports Illustrated*. "By the time I was ready to play, I knew the proper way to do things." Ripken made his mark as a student-athlete, playing in the **Mickey Mantle** World Series in 1977 and winning the Harford County batting title with a .492 average in his senior year.

Career Statistics

Yr	Team	Avg	GP	AB	R	H	HR	RBI	BB	SO	SB
1981	BAL	.128	23	39	1	5	0	0	1	8	0
1982	BAL	.264	160	598	90	158	28	93	46	95	3
1983	BAL	.318	162	663	121	211	27	102	58	97	0
1984	BAL	.304	162	641	103	195	27	86	71	89	2
1985	BAL	.282	161	642	116	181	26	110	67	68	2
1986	BAL	.282	162	627	98	177	25	81	70	60	4
1987	BAL	.252	162	624	97	157	27	98	81	77	3
1988	BAL	.264	161	575	87	152	23	81	102	69	2
1989	BAL	.257	162	646	80	166	21	93	57	72	3
1990	BAL	.250	161	600	78	150	21	84	82	66	3
1991	BAL	.323	162	650	99	210	34	114	53	46	6
1992	BAL	.251	162	637	73	160	14	72	64	50	4
1993	BAL	.257	162	641	87	165	24	90	65	58	1
1994	BAL	.315	112	444	71	140	13	75	32	41	4
1995	BAL	.262	1441	550	71	144	17	88	52	59	0
1996	BAL	.278	163	640	94	178	26	102	59	78	1
1997	BAL	.270	162	615	79	166	17	84	56	73	1
1998	BAL	.271	161	601	65	163	14	61	51	68	0
1999	BAL	.340	86	332	51	113	18	57	13	31	0
2000	BAL	.256	83	309	43	79	15	56	23	37	0
2001	BAL	.239	128	477	43	114	14	68	26	63	0
TOTAL		.276	3001	11551	1647	3184	431	1695	1129	1305	36

BAL: Baltimore Orioles.

The Road to Baltimore

The youth had set his sights modestly, however, revealing in his high-school yearbook that his goal was to become "a minor league baseball player." On graduation in 1978, Ripken appeared destined to achieve that goal. He was selected as a second-round draft choice by his beloved Baltimore, and assigned to a farm team in Bluefield, West Virginia. It was here that the young man was inaugurated as a shortstop (Ripken was also a pitcher in high school). Though he had talent, Ripken also had some maturing to do, as evidenced by his less-than-stellar first year batting average of .264; he also led the league in errors that season. With his move to the Orioles' Florida Instructional League, Ripken was able to strengthen his hitting until he reached a .303 average.

By 1979 Ripken had improved enough to be placed on an Orioles AA team in Charlotte, North Carolina. Over the next two seasons he was given increasingly more innings; by 1980 Ripken had a .276 batting average and had hit twenty-five home runs, nearly three times the number of homers from the year before. After being named the Southern League's all-star, he was promoted to a AAA team in Rochester, New York, in 1981. Finally, in August 1981, Ripken got the call to join the Orioles. He stepped up to the plate in his first Major League game on Opening Day 1982.

If the early 1982 season were any indicator, Ripken may well have moved back to the minors. In his first game he impressed with a home run, but then slipped, finishing with a 7-for-60 hitting record over the next seventeen games. By May 1, Ripken's batting average had dropped to a dismal .117, leading to a serious crisis of confidence. The young batter sought help from a master, in this case California Angels star **Reggie Jackson**. It was Jackson who provided these words of advice, as quoted from *Baseball Digest:* "The Orioles traded away a fine player [third baseman Doug Decinces] so they could bring you up. They know you're going to be great. So just do what you know you can do, not what everybody else tells you to do." Ripken rallied and ended the season with an average of .264.

The Orioles' fortunes rose in 1983, as the team became favorites to win the World Series. Ripken had grown into his game and had become a formidable hitter. He led the majors with 211 hits and forty-seven doubles, and led the American League with 121 hits, including twenty-seven home runs and a .318 batting average. With Ripken's bat leading the way, the Orioles bested the Chicago White Sox in the American League Championship Series. Within the hoopla over the Pennant win, it was also noted that Ripken had played every inning of every game in the 1983 season; it was the quiet beginning of a streak that would help make him a household name. As the Orioles faced the Philadelphia Phillies for the 1983 World Series, Ripken fell into an uncharacteristic slump, batting only .167; still, his team took the crown four games to one.

Seasons of Change

Seasons 1984 through 1986 were ones of challenge for the Orioles. The team finished second in the American League in 1984; two seasons later the former World Series champions occupied the bottom rung of the standings. Ripken, however, continued to rack up accomplish-

Chronology

1960	Born August 24 in Havre de Grace, Maryland
1978	Second-round draft choice, Baltimore Orioles
1982	Makes Major League debut
1990	Sets record for 95 consecutive non-error games
1994	Joins professional players' strike
1995	Plays in 2,131st consecutive game, a national record
1996	Extends playing streak to 2,216 games, a world record
1998	Sits out first game in 2,632 games
1999	Signs a contract extension through 1999 season
2001	Retires from professional play

Excerpts from Ripken's Speech on Breaking the Record

This year has been unbelievable. I've been cheered in ballparks all over the country. People not only showed me their kindness, but more importantly, they demonstrated their love of the game of baseball. I give my thanks to baseball fans everywhere.... There are, however, four people I want to thank specially. Let me start by thanking my dad. He inspired me with his commitment to the Oriole tradition and made me understand the importance of it.... My mom—what can I say about my mom? She is an unbelievable person. She let my dad lead the way on the field, but she was there in every other way—leading and shaping the lives of our family off the field.... When I got to the big leagues there was a man—Eddie Murray— who showed me how to play this game, day in and day out. I thank him for his example and for his friendship.... As my major league career moved along, the most important person came into my life—my wife Kelly. She has enriched it with her friendship and with her love. I thank you, Kelly, for the advice, support, and joy you have brought to me, and for always being there. You, Rachel, and Ryan are my life."

ments, including a setting an American League record for shortstops with 583 assists (a play that leads directly to an out being recorded). From 1985 to 1986, he hit twenty-six and twenty-five home runs respectively and batted .282 each season. All the while, he continued to be a part of every inning, every game. In 1987 another Ripken—brother Billy—joined the Orioles at second base. With Cal Sr. serving as team manager, the franchise set a record for the most sons on the same team at once.

That season didn't turn out as successful as the Ripkens may have hoped. The team finished 1987 in sixth place; Cal Sr. was dismissed as manager (though he stayed with the organization as third-base coach). Cal Jr. also fell back a bit, finishing with a .252 average, but increasing his home run count to twenty-seven. With misfortune following Baltimore into 1988, Ripken was notable mainly for being a bright spot in a losing team, batting .264 with twenty-three homers. Though Ripken's playing streak was still in effect, his father insisted that Cal Jr. sit out part of a losing game in 1987, marking a few innings off his otherwise perfect record; he still maintained his presence in every game, however.

The 1989 season marked Ripken's eighth in the Major Leagues; with his twenty-one home runs that season, he became the first shortstop to post eight consecutive seasons of at least twenty home runs. No less impressive was his fieldwork, particularly because, at six-foot-four and 230 pounds, Ripken was decidedly larger in stature than the average shortstop. In a position where players traditionally must grab, pivot, and throw quickly, Ripken instead focused on the action at the mound and the plate for his success. "While a shortstop like Ozzie Smith ... dazzles the crowds with his acrobatic moves," noted *Baseball Digest* writer Kevin Cowherd, "Ripken relies on the situation—the pitcher working in front of him that inning, the count on the batter, and the tendencies of the batter-to get a jump on the ball and make the play." As a result, Ripken often seemed miraculously at the place the ball was hit, affording him more time to complete his play.

Game after Game

By 1990 it was becoming clear that Ripken was no ordinary player. In an era of free-agents, the shortstop was "completely loyal to his team and old-fashioned in his values," as *Gentleman's Quarterly* writer Thomas Boswell stated. Ripken also went against the tide of the aloof, inaccessible star; he remained approachable to his fans and the press. "A lot of people are hesitant to come up to me," he told *Sports Illustrated,* but they shouldn't be. I'm a fan too, I enjoyed the game when I was sitting in the stands." Nor was money the driving force in Ripken's life, though he did benefit from his position in the Orioles. Even after he signed a four-year, $4 million contract, Ripken admitted to *Newsweek:* "I don't want to run down this contract, but the satisfaction that you get from playing, from catching the last out of the World Series ... those feelings are a lot greater than this."

Awards continued to follow Ripken through the seasons. In 1991 he was named Most Valuable Player at the All-Star game on the strength of a three-run homer that won the game for the American League. By the end of that season, Ripken had posted an unprecedented season for a shortstop, batting .323, knocking out thirty-four home runs, with 114 runs batted in (RBIs). He struck out only forty-six times. The same year, Ripken won his first Gold Glove for fielding, and though the Orioles did not make the playoffs, their slugger/shortstop was named the American League MVP. His hitting flagged a bit in 1992, a period that saw Ripken at odds with management over contract issues. Though a free agent, he chose to stay with the Orioles, who offered him an unprecedented five-year, $30.5 million contract. By 1993, Ripken was back to form, hitting .300.

All the while, Ripken continued playing in every game. The professional players' strike of 1994 interrupted the action, cutting the season to only 148 games and canceling the World Series. When the players suited up again it was 1995, and Ripken was quickly closing in on the consecutive-game record set by the beloved **Lou**

Cal Ripken, Jr.

Awards and Accomplishments

1977	Played in the Mickey Mantle World Series
1980	Named Southern League All-Star
1982	Voted American League Rookie of the Year
1983	Baltimore Orioles win World Series
1983	Voted American League Most Valuable Player (MVP)
1990	Set records for fewest errors and highest fielding percentage by a shortstop
1991	American League Most Valuable Player; *Sporting News* Major League Player of the Year; All-Star Game MVP, and Gold Glove
1995	Associated Press and United Press International Male Athlete of the Year; *Sporting News* Major League Player of the Year; *Sports Illustrated* Sportsman of the Year; *Newsweek* newsmaker; *People* Most Intriguing People.
1996	Opened Ripken Museum, Aberdeen, Maryland
1997	Published autobiography, *The Only Way I Know*
2001	Made farewell address at Camden Field, September 9

Where Is He Now?

Having retired from play in 2001, Cal Ripken, Jr.—a family man whose wife, Kelly, and children Rachel and Ryan, figure largely in his life—has left a legacy of community service. He founded the Kelly and Cal Ripken, Jr., Foundation, which supports adult and family literacy, youth recreation, and health-related programs in the greater Baltimore area; the couple are also benefactors of the Baltimore Reads Ripken Learning Center, the Kelly G. Ripken Program for thyroid education at Johns Hopkins University; and the Baltimore School for the Arts. In 1995, the Cal Ripken, Jr./Lou Gehrig ALS Research Fund was established at Johns Hopkins. "Because We Care," a program funded by Ripken, donates tickets to Baltimore home games to the underprivileged. In April 2002, GoodMark Foods entered into a promotion featuring lunch with Ripken as the grand prize of a sunflower-seeds contest.

Gehrig. The "Pride of the Yankees," Gehrig had faced up to an incurable disease with such grace that he became a symbol of dignity long after his death. Indeed, there were those who suggested to Ripken that in Gehrig's honor, he should sit out the tie-breaking game and resume the next day with a new "streak." But Ripken was following his own path: "I wasn't doing this for a record in the first place, so I wasn't going to not do it for the record either," he was quoted by Richard Hoffer in a *Sports Illustrated* piece.

A Record Tied, a Record Set

With more than 2,000 consecutive games under his belt, Ripken—dubbed the "Iron Man" of baseball—was scheduled to tie Gehrig's record on September 5, 1995. The media build-up to that day was intense, and the shortstop found himself checking into hotels under false names to protect his privacy. The evening of September 5, Ripken played the game that brought his streak to 2,130, tying with Gehrig. The next day, September 6, Ripken's appearance at Baltimore's Camden Yards was met by a capacity crowd roaring its approval. When the record became official in the fifth inning, Ripken was acknowledged to have played a record-breaking 2,131 games, missing not a single game since 1983. A postgame speech revealed Ripken's humility over the landmark event: "Tonight I stand here, overwhelmed, as my name is linked with the great and courageous Lou Gehrig. I'm truly humbled to have our names spoken in the same breath."

Even after the cheers had died down, Ripken continued in his work ethic. In 1996 he posted game number 2,216, surpassing the world record set by Sachio Kinusaga of Japan. A 1997 move from shortstop to third base did not slow the Baltimore icon at all; in fact, the Orioles made the playoffs that year, with Ripken hitting .385 in the postseason. Finally, on September 20, 1998, Ripken sat out a game, ending the streak at 2,632. But his appeal had hardly faded: Ripken was showcased in a variety of commercials playing off his "Iron Man"

image: such trademark lines as Chevrolet's "Like a Rock" and Coca-Cola's "Always" took new meaning when paired with Ripken's image.

On Sunday, September 9, 2001, Ripken made his final appearance as a Baltimore Orioles player. At forty-one, he was a senior member of the organization and had served his team with consistency and conviction. Once more Ripken stepped up to address his fans. "As a kid I had this dream," he said. "And I had the parents that helped me shape that dream. Then, I became part of an organization, the Baltimore Orioles, to help me grow that dream." As he continued, on that night "we close a chapter of this dream: my playing career. But I have other dreams. . . . My dreams for the future include pursuing my passion for baseball. Hopefully I will be able to share what I have learned." He had played 3,001 games for the same team over twenty years.

"There are three words which aptly describe Cal Ripken, Jr., both as a player and a person," noted a *CBS Sportsline* writer: "Excellence; dependability; and consistency." For all his acclaim, however, the athlete long ago recognized his responsibility to his fans. "As a baseball player you are instantly a role model," he told *Sport*. "Some people don't accept that. I choose to accept it because I remember vividly what baseball players meant to me and how they influenced my life."

SELECTED WRITINGS BY RIPKEN:

Ripken: Cal on Cal, Summit, 1995.
(With Greg Brown) *Count Me In*, Taylor, 1995.
(With Mike Bryan) *The Only Way I Know*, Viking, 1997.
(With Mike Bryan) *Cal Ripken, Jr.: My Story*, Dial Books for Young Readers, 1999.

FURTHER INFORMATION

Books

Contemporary Newsmakers 1986. Detroit: Gale, 1987.
Encyclopedia of Popular Culture. Detroit: St. James Press, 2000.

Encyclopedia of World Biography. Detroit: Gale, 1998.

Ripken, Cal, Jr., with Greg Brown. *Count Me In.* Taylor, 1995.

Ripken, Cal, Jr., with Mike Bryan. *Cal Ripken, Jr.: My Story.* Dial Books for Young Readers, 1999.

Ripken, Cal, Jr., with Mike Bryan. *The Only Way I Know.* New York: Viking, 1997.

Ripken, Cal, Jr. *Ripken: Cal on Cal.* New York: Summit, 1995.

Rosenfeld, Harvey. *Iron Man: The Cal Ripken, Jr. Story.* New York: St. Martin's, 1995.

Periodicals

Baseball Digest (June, 1983).
Baseball Digest (March, 1986).
"Cockeyed Coup." *Time* (September 7, 1992).
Gentleman's Quarterly (April, 1984).
Newsweek (April 1, 1984).
People (October 21, 1983).
Podesta, Jane. "Cal-ligraphy." *People* (June 30, 1997).
Reyes, Sonia. "GoodMark Goes Nuts for Sunflower Seeds as Chaser to Slim Jim Success." *BrandWeek* (April 8, 2002).
Sport (May, 1992).
Sports Illustrated (June 18, 1990).
Sports Illustrated (June 25, 1990).
Sports Illustrated (June 10, 1991).
Sports Illustrated (July 29, 1991).
Sports Illustrated (June 8, 1992).
Sports Illustrated (May 31, 1993).
Sports Illustrated (June 28, 1993).
Sports Illustrated (August 7, 1995).
Sports Illustrated (September 11, 1995).
Sports Illustrated (September 18, 1995).
Sports Illustrated (December 18, 1995).
Sports Illustrated (August 4, 1997).
Sports Illustrated (September 7, 1998).
Sports Illustrated (September 28, 1998).

Sketch by Susan Salter

Fatuma Roba
1973-

Ethiopian marathon runner

The first African woman to ever win an Olympic marathon, Fatuma Roba walked away with the gold in 2000 after crossing the marathon finish line in Olympic Stadium in 2:26.05 and beating silver medalist Valentina Yegorova of Russia by two minutes. A native of Ethiopia, Roba made similar history in her first attempt at the historic Boston Marathon in 1997, becom-

Fatuma Roba

ing the first African woman to win the race. Victories in the next two Boston Marathons made her the first woman to win that great race in three successive years.

A Fan of Abebe Bikila

Born in 1973 and raised in the village of Cokeji in Ethiopia's mountainous southern region—also home to internationally known 10K champion Derartu Tulu—Roba was one of seven children born to a farming couple who raised and herded cattle. Like most children growing up in rural Africa, if she wanted to go somewhere, the quickest way to get there was to run. The daily run to and from her school—much of it going up and down hills—trained the young Roba in the art of sprinting. As a child her hero was 1960 and 1964 Olympic marathon champion Abebe Bikila, a fellow Ethiopian. After completing school, the five-foot-five-inch Roba decided to train to become a police officer after her performance at a national cross-country championship caught the attention of members of the Adis Ababa prison police athletic team.

Roba first gained an international profile in 1990 when at age 18 she placed fourth in the 3,000 meter and 10K competition during the African Championships. Three years later she decided to attempt the 26.2-mile marathon distance in her home town of Addis Ababa, and had reached a personal best time of 2 hours 35 minutes 25 seconds by 1995. Roba continued to reduce her marathon time throughout the spring

Chronology

1973	Born in Arsi, Ethiopia
1990	Runs first international race at African Championships
1993	Runs first marathon in Adis Ababa, Ethiopia
1996	Wins gold in women's marathon at Atlanta Summer Olympics
1997	Runs and wins first Boston Marathon in April
1997	Withdraws from World Championship marathon due to injury
1998	Wins second Boston Marathon
1999	Runs personal best of 2:23:25 at Boston Marathon in winning race for third successive year
2000	Ninth-place female finisher in Olympic Marathon in Sydney, Australia

Awards and Accomplishments

1996	Wins Rome Marathon in 2:29:05.
1996	Wins Olympic women's marathon in 2:26:05.
1997	Wins Boston Marathon in 2:26:23
1998	Wins second straight Boston Marathon in 2:23:21
1999	Wins third straight Boston Marathon in 2:23:25.
1999	Places second in Tokyo Marathon.
2000	Places third at Boston Marathon.
2000	Finishes ninth in Olympic Marathon in Sydney, Australia.
2001	Wins Kyoto City Half-Marathon in 1:09:19.

of 1996, helped along by the coaching of Yilma Berta. To train to excel at the 26.2-mile marathon distance, the 22-year-old Roba logged an average of 125 miles a week, most of it at high altitude, thereby forcing her body to use its resources of oxygen efficiently. She ran and won two marathons early in 1996, the first in January at Marakech and the second in Rome, Italy, two months later.

When Roba joined the field of the 1996 Olympic women's marathon in Atlanta, Georgia, in July of 1996, she was ranked only 29th among the elite women athletes assembled there. Surprising almost all onlookers of that years' Summer Games, she managed consistent five-minute miles, gained the lead by mile 13, and left behind Japanese runner Yuko Arimori, who had won the silver at the 1992 Summer Olympics in Barcelona, Spain. At mile 19 timers clocked her race pace at 5:21; relaxed and alert, Roba waved as she passed, the crowds cheering on the first woman in the pack. She went on to cross the line in 2:26:05, her lead a remarkable two minutes. "This is not only a special thing for me but also for my country and all African women," Roba was quoted as commenting by Amanda Mays in the *Philadelphia Inquirer*. "The Ethiopian women are coming up in the marathon. This was the breakthrough and now we are ready to challenge the others."

Roba's success in Atlanta was balanced by an equally notable performance in 1997 at the 101st Boston Marathon. She gained and held an easy lead by mile 20 to win in 2:26:23. The first African woman ever to win the historic Boston race, Roba bested an elite field that included defending champion Uta Pippig, Japan's Junko Asari, and South African runners Colleen de Reuck and Elana Meyer. "She ran with the same smooth stride and placid, dispassionate look on her face that she carried through the Olympic race," reported *Runnersworld.com*. "Race commentator (and fellow Olympic marathon champion) Frank Shorter called her 'The most relaxed-looking runner I have ever seen.'" Roba's performance at the World Championship Marathon held in Athens, Greece, the following fall was a disappointment when she was forced to leave the course after being injured.

In 1999 the 25-year-old Roba took her third straight win at Boston, her time a personal best of 2:23:25 that set a new women's overall course record. She won the silver at the Tokyo Marathon with a time of 2:27:05, but at the World Championships in Seville, Spain she finished a disappointing fourth. Roba's winning streak at Boston ended in 2000, when she fell to third, barely losing the Boston gold to Kenyan runner Catherine Ndereba in one of the closest finishes in Boston Marathon history. Like Seville, the summer heat in Sydney, Australia proved hot enough to stall Roba, who finished a disappointing ninth at September 2000's Sydney Olympics with a time of 2:27:38.

Like her hero Abebe Bikila, Roba has become a role model for African runners, women runners in particular. Her own younger sister, Sennaito Tekru, has followed in her path, and has embarked on a course as a competitive marathon runner. With her grace and seemingly effortless performances, Roba has broken the barrier for African women with her triumphs at both the Olympic Games and the Boston Marathon. Despite her disappointment in Sydney, she has continued to rank among elite women marathoners, handily winning the San Diego Marathon in 2001 with a time of 2:27:22.

FURTHER INFORMATION

Periodicals

Boston Herald, April 13, 2001.
New York Daily News, July 28, 1996.
New York Times, April 17, 2000.
Philadelphia Inquirer, July 28, 1996.
Runner's World, November 1996; July 1997; July 1998.

Other

Boston.com, http://search.boston.com/sports/marathon/101.htm (January 17, 2003).
Made in Ethiopia, http://www.madeinethiopia.net/ethopiasport/MARATHON/women_sMarathon/ (January 14, 2003).
Runnersworld.com, http://www.runnersworld.com/events/boston/news/womenrac.html (April 11, 1997).

Sketch by Pamela L. Shelton

Oscar Robertson

Chronology

1938	Born November 24 in Charlotte, Tennessee
1942	Family moves to Indianapolis
1952	Enters Crispus Attucks High School and joins basketball team
1955-56	Leads Crispus Attucks Tigers to 45-game winning streak and two Indiana state championships
1956	Named Indiana's Mr. Basketball
1956	Enters University of Cincinnati as recruit for the Bearcats
1959-60	Leads team to NCAA Final Four
1960	Co-captains U.S. Olympic basketball team and wins gold medal
1960	Signs with Cincinnati Royals
1960	Marries Yvonne Crittenden on June 25
1961	Named NBA's Rookie of the Year
1961-62	Averages triple-double for entire season
1964	Named league MVP
1964	Becomes president of NBA players' union
1970	Traded to Milwaukee Bucks
1971	With Lew Alcindor (Kareem Abdul-Jabbar), leads Bucks to NBA championship
1974	Leads Bucks to NBA Finals
1974	Retires amidst pressure from team management
1976	Settles union lawsuit with league, resulting in "Oscar Robertson Rule" regarding free agency
1979	Named to Naismith Memorial Basketball Hall of Fame
1997	Again makes national headlines after donating kidney to daughter Tia

Oscar Robertson
1938-

American basketball player

Oscar Robertson is known as one of the greatest basketball players of all time. A standout at the University of Cincinnati, he went on to become a star National Basketball Association (NBA) player for the Cincinnati Royals (now the Sacramento Kings) and the Milwaukee Bucks, and a co-captain of an Olympic team considered by some to be the greatest group of amateurs ever assembled for the games. Known for his versatility, Robertson is the only professional player to ever accomplish an entire season of triple-doubles—double digits in scoring, rebounds and assists. In addition to his on-court challenges, Robertson, an African American, faced many obstacles his white teammates could have never imagined. Rather than turn his back, however, Robertson became an outspoken advocate for civil rights. He was also active in securing fair treatment of players, serving as president of the NBA players' union for a decade.

Defying the Odds

Growing up in Indianapolis, where his family moved when Robertson was four years old, Robertson learned the game of basketball at a run-down neighborhood court known as the "dust bowl." Robertson's father worked for the city sanitation department and his mother worked as a maid. Their salaries were small and they could not afford a basketball for their son, so he threw tin cans and old tennis balls through the hoop at the dust bowl. When he was eleven his mother gave him a basketball that one of her employers had planned to throw away, and his career began in earnest.

Robertson joined the basketball team at Crispus Attucks High School and found he still had to improvise— the all-African American school had no gym. His self-taught skills and ability to adapt, coupled with sound lessons in the basics from coach Ray Crowe, set Robertson up as a team leader early on. In his junior and senior years, he led the team through a 45-game winning streak and two state championships, making Crispus Attucks the first African American high school to capture that honor. In 1956 Robertson was named Indiana's "Mr. Basketball" and he was recruited by more than thirty colleges.

On to Cincinnati

Robertson elected to stay close to home and attend the University of Cincinnati. He took the team by storm, leading them to the NCAA Final Four during his junior and senior years, although each time the team lost to the University of California. Still, Robertson, who came to be known as "The Big O," set fourteen NCAA records during this time and averaged nearly thirty-four points per game. He was the NCAA's top scorer three years straight, and was named both an All-American and College Player of the Year in his last three seasons. He was the first play-

Awards and Accomplishments

1958-60	*Sporting News* College Player of the Year
1958-60	*Sporting News* All-Star First Team
1960	Gold medal, U.S. Olympic basketball team
1961	NBA Rookie of the Year
1961-69	All-NBA First Team
1961, 1964, 1969	NBA All-Star Game MVP
1964	NBA MVP
1979	Named to Naismith Memorial Basketball Hall of Fame
1980	NBA 35th Anniversary All-Star Team
1984	Named to Olympic Hall of Fame
1994	Oscar Robertson statue erected at University of Cincinnati
1998	College Player of the Year award renamed Oscar Robertson Trophy
1999	Named one of *Sports Illustrated*'s Greatest Athletes of the 20th Century
1999	Named Indiana Living Legend
1999	Named one of ESPN's 50 Greatest Athletes of the Century
1999	Ohio Governor's Award

Where Is He Now?

When Oscar Robertson returned to the Cincinnati area following his retirement from basketball in 1974, he applied the same drive he had displayed on the court in the business world. Today, he is principal owner of three successful companies: ORCHEM, which sells chemical used for industrial cleaning; ORPACK, a corrugated box manufacturer; and ORDMS, a firm that helps companies reduce their paper flow. He also serves on the boards of community groups and is active in charity events. Often quoted on matters related to both basketball and civil rights, Robertson made headlines again in 1997 when he donated a kidney to his daughter Tia, who suffered from lupus. While Robertson and his daughter attempted to keep the medical procedure quiet, they faced a media onslaught when they left Cincinnati's University Hospital following the successful transplant. Robertson broke down as he spoke to the press. "I'm no hero," he told them, as quoted in *People*. "I'm just a father."

er to ever win the latter award three times in a row and in 1998 it was renamed the Oscar Robertson Trophy.

All was not smooth for Robertson, however. As the first African American to play for Cincinnati, he was subject to intense racism, especially when the team traveled in the south. As a matter of fact, he had originally wanted to attend Indiana University, but after meeting with coach Branch McCracken, suspected he was not welcome because of his color. He often was not permitted to stay with the team at their hotel during away games, and instead had to stay alone in dorm rooms at nearby black colleges. At a game at North Texas State, the crowd threw programs at him. Back in Cincinnati, he was often barred from theaters and restaurants. Robertson felt his teammates and coach, George Smith, were unsupportive as well and, at one point, he considered leaving Cincinnati and joining the Harlem Globetrotters. Instead, he decided to stay and graduated with a degree in business in 1960.

Olympic and NBA Star

After graduation Robertson joined the U.S. Olympic basketball team as a co-captain with University of West Virginia's **Jerry West**. Many regard this team as the best group of amateur men's basketball players ever assembled. The team captured a gold medal and Robertson emerged as a standout. Following the victory, he was offered a $100,000 three-year contract with the Cincinnati Royals.

Robertson proved equally valuable to the Royals' organization. He was named Rookie of the Year for the 1960-61 season and received Most Valuable Player honors for his first of twelve consecutive appearances at the NBA All-Star game. The following season Robertson achieved his legendary season tripledouble when he averaged 30.8 points, 12.5 rebounds and 11.4 assists per game. This feat has yet to be matched by another professional player. He fell just shy of repeating his accomplish-

ment the next four years. Other players marveled at the ease with which Robertson appeared to accomplish such feats. "It took me five or six years to become an accomplished player," West told *Sports Illustrated*. "But from the first game Oscar played, he looked as if he had been in the league for 10 years. There was nobody like him."

In 1964 Robertson was named league MVP and he won MVP honors at the All-Star game as well. That same year he became president of the NBA players' union, a post he held until he retired a decade later.

Moves to Milwaukee

When **Bob Cousy** took over the Royals during the 1969-70 season, he wanted to trade Robertson to the Baltimore Bullets. Robertson staged a two-week hold out and was instead sent to the Milwaukee Bucks. There, he joined teammate Lew Alcindor, later known as **Kareem Abdul-Jabbar**, to lead the Bucks to an NBA championship in 1971. The pair also spearheaded the team's second visit to the Finals in 1974, where they eventually lost to the Boston Celtics in a seven-game series. Robertson retired at the end of that season, giving into what he saw as pressure from team officials. The "Oscar Robertson Night" staged by the team appeared to be a request for him to say farewell, Robertson claimed.

Active Retirement

Even off-court, Robertson continued to make his mark on the NBA. In 1976, a lawsuit he had filed against the NBA when he was still union president was settled. The lawsuit sought, among other things, removal of a clause that essentially prevented free agency. The ruling in Robertson's favor is today known as the Oscar Robertson Rule. Robertson also became president of the retired players' union.

Returning to Cincinnati, Robertson became a successful businessman and became involved with several community and charity organizations. He also remains an outspoken champion of civil rights—both in word and in practice. In 1999 he refused an endorsement offer from Converse, reasoning "Converse was there for a lot

Career Statistics

Yr	Team	GP	Pts	FG%	FT%	RPG	APG	PF
1960-61	CIN	71	2165	.473	.822	10.1	9.7	219
1961-62	CIN	79	2432	.478	.803	12.5	11.4	258
1962-63	CIN	80	2264	.518	.810	10.4	9.5	293
1963-64	CIN	79	2480	.483	.853	9.9	11.0	280
1964-65	CIN	75	2279	.480	.839	9.0	11.5	205
1965-66	CIN	76	2378	.475	.842	7.7	11.1	227
1966-67	CIN	79	2412	.493	.873	6.2	10.7	226
1967-68	CIN	65	1896	.500	.873	6.0	9.7	199
1968-69	CIN	79	1955	.486	.838	6.4	9.8	231
1969-70	MIL	69	1748	.511	.809	6.1	8.1	175
1970-71	MIL	81	1569	.496	.850	5.7	8.2	203
1971-72	MIL	64	1114	.472	.836	5.0	7.7	116
1972-73	MIL	73	1130	.454	.847	4.9	7.5	167
1973-74	MIL	70	888	.438	.835	4.0	6.4	132
TOTAL		1040	26710	.485	.838	7.5	9.5	2931

CIN: Cincinnati Royals; MIL: Milwaukee Bucks.

of white athletes when I was playing, but they never came to Oscar Robertson." He also told *Sports Illustrated* that he believes his race and his involvement with the players' union precluded careers in broadcasting or coaching. While Robertson provided color commentary for CBS after retirement, he was fired after one year.

In 1997 Robertson lamented the fact that his off-court legacy to contemporary players seems to have been diminished. "The players today don't know anything about racism," he told *People*. "So few of today's players have any idea what he fought for, what he stood for," Robertson's wife, Yvonne, told *Sports Illustrated*.

As for his contributions on the court, though, Robertson still remains a legend. As the year 2000 approached, numerous sports writers named him among their greatest athletes of the 20th century. "He was so smart on the court that whatever he told you to do you just did it," former teammate Adrian Smith recalled for *Sports Illustrated*. "It always seemed to be the right thing. I guess he made mistakes from time to time, but I don't remember any."

CONTACT INFORMATION

Address: c/o Orchem Corp, 4293 Mulhauser Rd., Fairfield, OH 45014-5450. Online: www.thebigo.com.

SELECTED WRITINGS BY ROBERTSON:

The Art of Basketball, Oscar Robertson Media Ventures, 1999.

FURTHER INFORMATION

Books

"Oscar Robertson." *Contemporary Black Biography*, Volume 26. Edited by David G. Oblender. Detroit: Gale Group, 2000.

Periodicals

Jerome, Richard. "A Father's Gift." *People* (May 26, 1997): 52.

McCallum, Jack. "King Without A Castle." *Sports Illustrated* (July 15, 2002): 78.

Sketch by Kristin Palm

Brooks Robinson
1937-

American baseball player

Brooks Robinson was one of baseball's greatest third basemen. Many say that he single-handedly turned the Baltimore Orioles from a no-name team into a legitimate contender year after year. Off the field, Robinson was kind and gentle, a true ambassador of the game, while on the field he was known primarily for his fielding. Opposing teams would try and keep the ball away from him. He won sixteen consecutive Gold Gloves, played in 2,870 major league games in a career that spanned twenty-three years. Brooks Robinson is an integral part of baseball culture and a fixture in the minds of the people in Baltimore.

Growing Up

Brooks Robinson was born on May 18, 1937, in Little Rock, Arkansas, the son of Brooks Calbert Robinson and Ethel Mae Robinson. His father was a firefighter and mother a homemaker. Oddly enough, the man who would become one of the best defensive infielders in baseball did not play much as a child. His high school

Brooks Robinson

Chronology

1937	Born May 18 in Little Rock, Arkansas, to Brooks Calbert and Ethel Mae Robinson
1951	Plays baseball with local church team because high school has no baseball team
1955	Plays for the first time with the Orioles baseball system
1956-57	Attends Little Rock University (now University of Arkansas at Little Rock)
1958	Hits into first triple play of a record four for his career
1960	Goes 5-5, hitting for the cycle
1960	Marries Constance Louise Butcher on October 8
1962	Becomes 6th major leaguer to hit grand slams in back to back games
1963	Benched for poor hitting, streak of 463 straight games playing third base comes to a halt
1967	Plays in longest All-Star game, 15 innings (three hours and 41 minutes)
1970	Hits 2,000th major league hit, a three-run homer
1971	Ties World Series record by reaching base five straight times on three hits and two walks
1977	Retires from baseball
1978	Becomes color commentator for Orioles games
1979	Takes position as assistant to management for Crown Central Petroleum Corporation
1979	Works with Shapiro & Robinson, a consulting firm
1979	Becomes vice-president of Baltimore Orioles
1983	Elected to Baseball Hall of Fame in landslide election

didn't have a team, and he was actually discovered while playing second base for his local church league.

The Early Years

Robinson started with the Baltimore Orioles in 1960. In his first season he hit .294, belted fourteen home runs, and drove in eighty-eight runs. He won his team's Most Valuable Player award, as well as receiving his first gold glove. He would miss winning the American League MVP and take third in the voting.

During his second season, his numbers improved. In 1961 he hit .303 and knocked twenty-three home runs. His offense, though never stellar, peaked during the 1964 season. He knocked in 118 runs (leading the league in RBIs), hit .317 and slugged twenty-eight homers. Even though it was only his fourth season and he would play ball for nineteen more years, these would be his offensive career highs. He garnered the Most Valuable Player award and was voted Major League Player of the Year by the *Sporting News* for his 1964 season.

Though his batting average would fluctuate during his long career, Robinson's fielding remained superb.

One Man Show

In 1970, Robinson had three career milestones: he collected his 2,000th hit, his 1,000th RBI and 200th home run. The Orioles would also make it into the World Series, again, but this time the fall classic would be referred to by many as "The Brooks Robinson Show." His bat got hot again, and his glove, always hot, would blaze.

Robinson made some of the most memorable plays in World Series history in 1970, many of which went to put down Cincinnati rallies. Reds relief pitcher Clay Carroll talked about one of his fielding plays as follows: "He was going toward the bullpen when he threw to first. His arm went one way, his body another, and his shoes another." Reds manager **Sparky Anderson** said that the Orioles didn't beat the Reds, Brooks Robinson beat the Cincinnati Reds. "I'm beginning to see Brooks in my sleep," he said. "If I dropped this paper plate, he'd pick it up on one hop and throw me out at first."

Hanging it Up

On August 21, 1977, the Orioles dropped Robinson from their roster. Rick Dempsey, coming off the disabled list, filled into the space and Robinson decided it was time to retire. He was inducted into the Hall of Fame in 1983, on the first ballot. It was a landslide election.

For fifteen straight seasons, Robinson was the American League's starting All-Star third baseman. He led American League third basemen in assists eight times, and led in fielding eleven times. Robinson holds almost every lifetime record for third basemen, often by a large margin. He holds

Career Statistics

Yr	Team	Avg	GP	AB	R	H	HR	RBI	BB	SO	SB	E
1955	BAL	.091	6	22	0	2	0	1	0	10	0	2
1956	BAL	.227	15	44	5	10	1	1	1	5	0	2
1957	BAL	.239	50	117	13	28	2	14	7	10	1	3
1958	BAL	.238	145	463	31	110	3	32	31	51	1	22
1959	BAL	.284	88	313	29	89	4	24	17	37	2	13
1960	BAL	.294	152	595	74	175	14	88	35	49	2	12
1961	BAL	.287	163	668	89	192	7	61	47	57	1	14
1962	BAL	.303	162	634	77	192	23	86	42	70	3	11
1963	BAL	.251	161	589	67	148	11	67	46	84	2	12
1964	BAL	.317	163	612	82	194	28	118	51	64	1	14
1965	BAL	.297	144	559	81	166	18	80	47	47	3	15
1966	BAL	.269	157	620	91	167	23	100	56	36	2	12
1967	BAL	.269	158	610	88	164	22	77	54	54	1	11
1968	BAL	.253	162	608	65	154	17	75	44	55	1	16
1969	BAL	.234	156	589	73	140	23	84	56	55	2	13
1970	BAL	.276	158	608	84	168	18	94	53	53	1	17
1971	BAL	.272	156	589	67	160	20	92	63	50	0	16
1972	BAL	.250	153	556	48	139	8	64	43	45	1	11
1973	BAL	.257	155	549	53	141	9	72	55	50	2	15
1974	BAL	.288	153	553	46	159	7	59	56	47	2	18
1975	BAL	.201	144	482	50	97	6	53	44	33	0	9
1976	BAL	.211	71	218	16	46	3	11	8	24	0	6
1977	BAL	.149	24	47	3	7	1	4	4	4	0	0
TOTAL		.267	2896	10654	1232	2848	268	1357	860	990	28	264

BAL: Baltimore Orioles.

the records for most games played, for best fielding percentage (.971), most putouts (2,697), most assists (6,205), most chances (9,165) and most double plays (618).

His uniform, #5, was officially retired on opening day 1978. In 1999, Robinson was named to the ESPN All-Century Team, honoring the best twenty-five players in baseball during the 20th century.

His Legacy

At the end of the 1964 season, *Washington Post* columnist Shirley Povich wrote: "It is not quite proper to say that the Baltimore Orioles have brought Robinson's talents to notice with their resolute pennant rush. It is Robinson who has taken Baltimore to its present eminence."

Brooks Robinson's consistent superlative presence at the third base spot, year in, year out, is perhaps only a small reason that even today he's well known in baseball lore. He added a new dimension to the third base position, often forcing teams to change their plans if they'd wanted to bunt. He had skill and flare, and his highlight-reel playmaking took the Orioles from obscurity to a major presence in professional baseball. A truly generous and decent individual, everyone seemed to like Brooks, and no one said anything bad about him. With his wife Connie and their four children, he's a staple in the Baltimore area and more than a few people in Baltimore have named their children after Robinson.

As Robinson neared retirement, due to some naive business dealings, he was having financial difficulty, and the Orioles kept him on those last few seasons, in part, to help him out. When he finally left the playing field, he entered broadcasting. In addition to doing color commentary for the Baltimore Orioles, he also serves as vice-president of Personal Managment Associates, a company that provides athletes comprehensive counseling and support in their professional, financial, and personal lives. Robinson is also is a special assistant with the Crown Central Petroleum Company.

CONTACT INFORMATION

Email: info@brooksrobinson.com. Online: brooksrobinson.com.

SELECTED WRITINGS BY ROBINSON:

(With Fred Bauer) *Putting It All Together,* Hawthorn, 1971.

(With Jack Tobin) *Third Base Is My Home,* Word, Inc., 1974.

(With Fred T. Smith) *Brooks Robinson's Baseball Quiz,* privately printed, 1979.

(With Jerry Coleman, Ernie Harwell, Ralph Kiner, Tim McCarver, and Ned Martin) *The Scouting Report: 1983,* ed. by Marybeth Sullivan, Harper, 1983.

(With Dave Campbell, Denny Matthews, and Duke Snider) *The Scouting Report: 1984,* edited by Marybeth Sullivan, Harper, 1984.

Awards and Accomplishments

1960-74	American League All-Star Team
1960-75	American League Gold Glove Award
1964	American League most valuable player; *Sporting News* American League Player of the Year
1966	All-Star Game most valuable player
1970	World Series most valuable player; Hickok Belt
1977	Joe Cronin Award
1983	Inducted into National Baseball Hall of Fame
1999	MLB All-Century Team; Uniform number 5 retired by Baltimore Orioles

(With Dave Campbell, Denny Matthews, and Duke Snider) *The Scouting Report: 1985,* ed. by Marybeth Sullivan, Harper, 1985.

(With Dave Campbell, Harmon Killebrew, and Duke Snider) *The Scouting Report: 1986,* ed. by Sullivan, Harper, 1986.

(With Ted Patterson) *The Baltimore Orioles: Four Decades of Magic from 33rd Street to Camden Yards,* Taylor, 2000.

FURTHER INFORMATION

Books

Davis, Mac. *100 Greatest Baseball Heroes.* New York: Grosset, 1974.

Hirshberg, Al. *Greatest American Leaguers.* New York: Putnam, 1970.

Libby, Bill. *Heroes of the Hot Corner.* New York: Watts, 1972.

Peary, Danny, ed. *We Played the Game: Memories of Baseball's Greatest Era.* New York: Black Dog & Leventhal Pub, 1994.

Robinson, Brooks, with Ted Patterson. *The Baltimore Orioles: Four Decades of Magic from 33rd Street to Camden Yards.* Taylor Publishers, 2000.

Robinson, Brooks, with Fred Bauer. *Putting It All Together,* Hawthorn, 1971.

Robinson, Brooks, with Jack Tobin. *Third Base Is My Home.* Word, Inc., 1974.

Robinson, Brooks, with Fred T. Smith. *Brooks Robinson's Baseball Quiz,* privately printed, 1979.

Robinson, Brooks, with Jerry Coleman, Ernie Harwell, Ralph Kiner, Tim McCarver, and Ned Martin. *The Scouting Report: 1983,* ed. by Marybeth Sullivan. New York: HarperCollins, 1983.

Robinson, Brooks, with Dave Campbell, Denny Matthews, and Duke Snider. *The Scouting Report: 1984,* edited by Marybeth Sullivan. New York: HarperCollins, 1984.

Robinson, Brooks, with Dave Campbell, Denny Matthews, and Duke Snider) *The Scouting Report: 1985,* ed. by Marybeth Sullivan. New York: HarperCollins, 1985.

Robinson, Brooks, with Dave Campbell, Harmon Killebrew, and Duke Snider) *The Scouting Report: 1986.* ed. by Marybeth Sullivan. New York: HarperCollins, 1986.

Zanger, Jack. *The Brooks Robinson Story.* New York: Messner, 1967.

Periodicals

Los Angeles Times (August 1, 1983).
National Observer (October 12, 1964).
News-American (Baltimore) (April 6, 1975).
Newsweek (February 3, 1971).
Newsweek (September 5, 1977).
New York Times (July 17, 1966).
New York Times (September 25, 1977).
New York Times (August 29, 1982).
New York Times (January 13, 1983).
New York Times (July 31, 1983).
New York Times (August 1, 1983).
O'Shea, Tim. "Tips on Third Base Defense Shared by Brooks Robinson. *Baseball Digest* (no. 6, 1995).
People (May 23, 1983).
Sport (June, 1972).
Sporting News (January 24, 1983).
Sporting News (August 1, 1983).
Time (October 26, 1970).

Other

"Brooks Robinson." http://www.baseball-reference.com/ (November 10, 2002).
"Brooks Robinson." http://www.pubdim.net/baseball library/ (November 10, 2002).
"The Official Brooks Robinson Homepage." http://www.brooksrobinson.com/ (November 10, 2002).

Sketch by Eric Lagergren

David Robinson
1965-

American basketball player

David Maurice Robinson, known as "The Admiral," did not play his first professional basketball game until he was twenty-four years old, after serving two years in the U.S. Navy. A member of the San Antonio Spurs for his entire career, Robinson has established himself as one of the best big men to ever play in the National Basketball Association (NBA). Consistently posting solid offensive numbers, at the height of his career, Robinson was known as a defensive stopper with excellent shot-blocking abilities. Robinson is also well

David Robinson

Chronology

1965	Born August 6 in Key West, Florida
1983-87	Attends the U.S. Naval Academy
1987	First overall National Basketball Association (NBA) draft pick by the San Antonio Spurs
1987-89	Serves as an engineer in the U.S. Navy
1989	Joins the Spurs; named NBA Rookie of the Year
1991	Marries Valerie Hoggatt
1992	Establishes the David Robinson Foundation
1997-98	Misses all but 15 games of the season due to injury
2002	Announces his retirement following the 2002-03 season

known as a stellar role model who gives generously to his community.

Growing Up and Up

David Robinson was born on August 6, 1965, in Key West, Florida. His father, Ambrose, was a naval officer, and his mother, Freda, a nurse. When Robinson was still young, his father was transferred to Virginia Beach, Virginia, where Robinson grew up with his two siblings. He attended schools for gifted children since the age of six and, as a high school senior, scored among the top five percent nationally on the Scholastic Aptitude Test. He was active in sports, including tennis, golf, and baseball. Although he joined the basketball team as a freshman, he soon quit because he spent most of his time warming the bench.

After growing from five-feet-nine-inches as a freshman to six-feet-seven-inches as a senior, Robinson decided to give basketball another try. Although he became a star center for Osbourn Park High School in Manassas, Virginia, he lacked the exposure and experience to attract the attention of top college recruiters. Robinson, who was more concerned with getting good grades, wasn't worried about a future in basketball and enrolled at the U.S. Naval Academy. Robinson joined the Naval Academy team as a freshman, but played little. However, during the summer between his freshman and sophomore years, he grew five inches, to seven feet. When he was finally done growing, Robinson stood seven-feet-one-inch

tall. For the first time, Robinson considered the possibility of pursuing basketball on a professional level.

As a junior Robinson led his team to the Elite Eight of the National Collegiate Athletic Association (NCAA) tournament. During the year Robinson averaged 22.7 points and thirteen rebounds per game and dominated on the defensive end, setting NCAA records for most blocks in a game (14), most blocks in a season (207), and most career blocks (372). Robinson's game continued to improve, and he was named to the Associated Press All-American Team in both 1986 and 1987. In his senior year he also received the Naismith Award as the College Player of the Year.

Soon after graduating in 1987 Robinson was drafted as the number one overall pick by the San Antonio Spurs. At first reluctant to play in San Antonio, Robinson was swayed by the offer of an eight-year, $26 million contract. The Spurs, however, would have to wait two years while Robinson completed his service obligation to the Navy before he could join the team. For the next two years, the future NBA star worked as an engineer at the Kings Bay Naval Submarine Base in Georgia.

Promoted to "Admiral"

In 1989 Robinson donned a Spurs uniform and became a member of a team that had won only twenty-one games the previous year. However, with the added support of the 1989 College Player of the Year, Sean Elliot of the University of Arizona, Robinson, who soon became known as "the Admiral," helped turn the team around. In his rookie year he averaged 24.3 points, twelve rebounds, and 3.9 blocks per game, leading his team to fifty-six wins, the biggest one-season turnaround in league history. Robinson was the unanimous choice as NBA Rookie of the Year.

Over the next seven years Robinson became one of the premiere players in the NBA. He played in the NBA All-Star Game from 1990 to 1996 before missing the All-Star Game and all but five Spurs games in the 1997-98 season due to a strained back and broken foot. Despite his impressive performance, which earned him the scoring title in 1994 with an average of 29.8 points per

Career Statistics

Yr	Team	GP	Pts	P/G	FG%	3P%	FT%	RPG	APG	SPG	BPG	TO
1990	SA	82	1993	24.3	.531	.000	.732	12.0	20.	1.7	3.9	257
1991	SA	82	2101	25.6	.552	.143	.762	13.0	2.5	1.6	3.9	270
1992	SA	68	1578	23.2	.551	.125	.701	12.2	2.7	2.3	4.5	182
1993	SA	82	1916	23.4	.501	.176	.732	11.7	3.7	1.6	3.2	241
1994	SA	80	2383	29.8	.507	.345	.749	10.7	4.8	1.7	3.3	253
1995	SA	81	2238	27.6	.530	.300	.774	10.8	2.9	1.7	3.2	233
1996	SA	82	2051	25.0	.516	.333	.761	12.2	3.0	1.4	3.3	190
1997	SA	6	106	17.7	.500	.000	.654	8.5	1.3	1.0	1.0	8
1998	SA	73	1574	21.6	.511	.250	.735	10.6	2.7	0.9	2.6	202
1999	SA	49	775	15.8	.509	.000	.658	10.0	2.1	1.4	2.4	108
2000	SA	80	1427	17.8	.512	.000	.726	9.6	1.8	1.2	2.3	164
2001	SA	80	1151	14.4	.486	.000	.747	8.6	1.5	1.0	2.5	122
2002	SA	78	951	12.2	.507	.000	.681	8.3	1.2	1.1	1.8	104
TOTAL		923	20244	21.9	.519	.250	.737	10.8	2.6	1.4	3.1	2334

SA: San Antonio Spurs.

game and the NBA's Most Valuable Player award in 1995, Robinson's detractors weren't sure that he had the leadership ability and passion it would take to propel his team to an NBA championship. Robinson, a devout Christian since 1991 who listened to classical music, didn't party. He read the Bible, and took seriously his job as a role model, and was considered by some as simply too nice to win big.

The Twin Towers

Robinson's chances for an NBA championship improved greatly in 1997 when the Spurs, after a disappointing 1996-97 season with Robinson sidelined by injury, drafted seven-footer **Tim Duncan**, a highly regarded center from Wake Forest. Quickly dubbed the "Twin Towers," Robinson and Duncan dominated under the basket on both ends of the court. Yet despite the team's regained success, Robinson struggled personally with his changing role on the team. For the first time in his NBA career, he was asked to step aside from the center focus of the team to support Duncan as the team's new go-to man. Despite the blow to his pride and a decline in his playing time and numbers, Robinson accepted his new place, for which he earned the praise of the sports press and fans alike.

The following season the Spurs finally reached the NBA finals, beating the New York Knicks in five games to win the 1999 championship. It appeared that Robinson had finally quieted those who thought him to be too soft, especially come playoff time. In 2000 the Spurs lost in the first round of the NBA playoffs, primarily because Duncan was out with an injury. During the summer of 2000 Robinson cut short his vacation in Hawaii, returning early to talk Duncan into foregoing his free agent option of moving to another team. When Duncan re-signed with the Spurs, Robinson was given much of the credit. In 2002 Robinson announced that he would retire following the 2002-03 season.

Giving Back

In the twilight of his career, Robinson struggled with his nagging bad back and knees. Although his stats declined due to his changing role on the team, he continued to contribute positively to his team. Regardless of his on-court performance, the Admiral has proven himself to all that he is an exceptional person. In 1991 he made a pact with ninety-one fifth-graders from Gates Elementary School in San Antonio that if they finished high school, he would donate $2,000 to each of their college educations. In the same year he married Valerie Hoggatt; they have three sons. The following year he and his wife established the David Robinson Foundation, which provides funding grants to schools, homeless, and children's charities, including a $9 million gift in 1997 to build a prep school in San Antonio. Robinson, who signs autographs for free with his name, number 50, and reference to a Bible verse, has a simple explanation for his generosity: "We do the right things because that's what God told us to do."

CONTACT INFORMATION

Address: San Antonio Spurs, 100 E. Market St., San Antonio, Texas 78203. Phone: (210) 554-7773.

FURTHER INFORMATION

Books

Newsmakers 1990, Issue 4. Detroit: Gale, 1990.

Phelps, Shirelle, ed. *Contemporary Black Biography,* Volume 24. Detroit: Gale Group, 2000.

Sports Stars. Series 1-4. Detroit: U•X•L, 1994-98.

Who's Who Among African Americans, 14th ed. Detroit: Gale Group, 2001.

Awards and Accomplishments

1986	Led nation with 13 rebounds per game and 5.9 blocks per game
1987	National Player of the Year and First Team All American; first overall pick in the National Basketball Association (NBA) draft by San Antonio Spurs
1990	Rookie of the Year, All Rookie Team, Second Team All Defense, and Third Team All NBA
1990-91, 1994-96	Received IBM Award
1990-96, 1998, 2000-01	NBA All Star
1991-92	First Team All NBA and First Team All Defense
1992	Defensive Player of the Year; First Team All Defense
1994	Won NBA scoring title, averaging 29.8 points per game
1995	Selected as NBA's Most Valuable Player
1995-96	Named to First Team All NBA
1996	Named one of the 50 Greatest Basketball Players in NBA History
1998	Inducted into the Sports World Humanitarian Hall of Fame
1999	NBA championship as member of San Antonio Spurs; received the Montblanc de la Culture Award
2000	Received the Patriot Award from the Congressional Medal of Honor Society

Periodicals

Bailey, Scott. "Spurs Brass Get Caught Between an Admiral and a Hard Place." *San Antonio Business Journal* (July 20, 2001): 23.

Clancy, Frank. "Twin Engines." *Sporting News* (December 15, 1997): 52.

Jerome, Richard. "Hoop Dreamer." *People* (December 1, 1997): 99.

MacMullan, Jackie. "Robinson's Helping Hand." *Sports Illustrated* (March 23, 1998): 48.

Montville, Leigh. "Trials of David." *Sports Illustrated* (April 29, 1994): 90.

Reilly, Rick. "Spur of the Moment." *Sports Illustrated* (June 14, 1999): 106.

Smith, Stephen A. "Robinson Playing Young Now But Will He Be Old for the Playoffs?" Knight Ridder/Tribune News Service (November 14, 2002).

Smith, Stephen A. "Time for Robinson to Say Adios." Knight Ridder/Tribune News Service (May 18, 2002).

Taylor, Phil. "Here's to You, Mr. Robinson." *Sports Illustrated* (July 7, 1999): 20.

Taylor, Phil. "Rear Admiral." *Sports Illustrated* (April 12, 1999): 40.

Taylor, Phil. "Spur of the Moment." *Sports Illustrated* (March 7, 1994): 58.

Other

"David Robinson." National Basketball Association. http://www.nba.com/ (December 11, 2002)

"David Robinson." Sports Stats.com. http://www.sportsstats.com/bball/players/NPOYS/David_Robinson/ (December 11, 2002)

Sketch by Kari Bethel

Frank Robinson

Frank Robinson
1935-

American baseball player

Frank Robinson was a ballplayer whose career was so outstanding that he starred in both major leagues, both as a player and as a manager. In 21 seasons as an active player, primarily with the Cincinnati Reds and the Baltimore Orioles, Robinson hit for both power and average, with a career average of .294, 586 home runs, and 1812 runs batted in. Until injuries slowed him down in the mid-1960s, he was a threat on the base paths as well, averaging just over 17 stolen bases a year between 1957 and 1965. Along the way he helped his teams to five pennants and two World Series titles. Just as much as his prowess on the field, Frank Robinson will be remembered for his role in integrating baseball management. In 1975 he became the first African-American to manage a major league team, the Cleveland Indians of the American League; five years later he was the first black to manage a National League team, the San Francisco Giants. In 2000, he was named a vice president of Major League Baseball.

Early Life

Born in 1935 in Beaumont, Texas, Frank Robinson was the youngest of Ruth (Shaw) Robinson's ten chil-

Chronology

1935	Born to Frank Robinson and Ruth Shaw in Beaumont, Texas
1953	Signed by Cincinnati Reds, plays with Ogden team in Pioneer League
1954	Plays AA ball in Tulsa, Oklahoma, and A ball in Columbia, South Carolina
1956	Called up to majors by Cincinnati Reds, wins Rookie of the Year Award
1961	Marries Barbara Ann Cole in Los Angeles
1961	Cincinnati wins National League pennant, named National League's Most Valuable Player
1965	Traded to Baltimore Orioles
1966	Baltimore wins World Series, named American League's Most Valuable Player
1968-75	Manages winter ball in Puerto Rico
1971	Traded to Los Angeles Dodgers
1972	Traded to California Angels
1974	Traded to Cleveland Indians
1975-77	Player-manager of Indians
1978	Manages minor league Rochester Red Wings
1981-84	Manages San Francisco Giants
1985-87	Coach for Baltimore Orioles
1988-91	Manages Baltimore Orioles
1991-97	Assistant general manager for Baltimore Orioles
1997	Appointed director of baseball operations of Arizona Fall League
2000-02	Named vice president for on-field operations for Major League Baseball
2002-	Manages Montreal Expos

Awards and Accomplishments

1956	National League Rookie of the Year
1957, 1959, 1961-62, 1965	National League All-Star
1961	Named National League's Most Valuable Player
1966	Named American League's Most Valuable Player
1966	Named World Series' Most Valuable Player
1966	Babe Ruth Award
1966	Associated Press Male Athlete of the Year
1966	Hickock Professional Athlete of the Year
1966	Sid Mercer Award
1966	Clark Griffith Award
1966	Rogers Hornsby Award
1966-71, 1974	American League All-Star
1968	Named Puerto Rico Winter League Manager of the Year
1971	Most Valuable Player, All-Star Game
1982	Inducted into National Baseball Hall of Fame
1982	Named National League's Manager of the Year
1989	Named American League's Manager of the Year

dren. After her third husband Frank deserted her, Ruth took her children, including four-year-old Frank Jr, and moved to Oakland, California. By the time he was a teenager, baseball was the focus of young Frank's life. His mother was poor and he was fourteen before he owned his own baseball glove. But that did not prevent Robinson from playing baseball all day long every day in the summer, coming home for dinner only after there was no more light for the game. Just after his fourteenth birthday, his batting talent caught the eye of one of his school teachers, George Powles, who invited Robinson to join his Doll Drug Company team, and a year later his championship American Legion team. After Robinson joined, the team—which would eventually send 14 of its 25 players into professional ball—won another title. Robinson continued under Powles' mentorship at Oakland's McClymonds High School, where he was in the class just a year behind future basketball great **Bill Russell**'s.

Robinson had told a high school counselor at McClymonds that he intended to play major league ball. The dream started coming true after his graduation in 1953 when he was signed by the Cincinnati Reds organization. Though he grew up poor, Robinson had lived in an integrated neighborhood in Oakland that was remarkably free of racial strife. This changed dramatically when he played for the Reds' minor league teams in Ogden, Utah, and Columbia, South Carolina. "Ogden was in a Mormon state, and though I didn't know it, at that time the Mormon religion insisted that Negroes

were inferior beings," he recalled in his book *Extra Innings*. "I got my first taste of racial bigotry in Ogden." He could not use the hotels or restaurants frequented by white players; he was not allowed in movie theaters; he had to wait for special black cabs to ride to the ballpark. On top of it all, he had to endure the racial taunts and obscenities shouted by fans and opponents. The situation was no better in Columbia.

Joining the Big Leagues

Robinson finally got the call to the majors in 1956, joining the Reds at a annual salary of $6,000. In his first major league at-bat, he drilled a fastball off the outfield wall for a double. By the time that first season had ended, Robinson had turned in one of the most remarkable rookie years in major league history, hitting .290, driving in 83 runs and slugging 38 home runs, a performance that earned him recognition as the National League's Rookie of the Year. Over the next ten years, Robinson crafted the foundation of a Hall of Fame career, hitting consistently for both average and power, topping .300 five times, batting in more than 100 RBIs four times and hitting 25 or more homers eight times. In 1961, when he led the Reds to a National League pennant, Robinson was voted National League Most Valuable Player.

Early in his career, Frank Robinson got a reputation as a problem player who was prey to sudden, inexplicable mood swings. His fierce playing style, particularly on the base paths, got him labeled a dirty player who would go out of his way to spike opposing infielders. Robinson defended himself in *Extra Innings:* "I never relaxed on a ball field. I have always believed in going all out all the time. The baseline belongs to the runner, and whenever I was running the bases, I always slid hard. If the second baseman or shortstop was in the

Career Statistics

Yr	Team	AVG	GP	AB	R	H	HR	RBI	BB	SO	SB	E
1956	CIN	.290	152	572	122	166	38	83	64	95	8	8
1957	CIN	.322	150	611	97	197	29	75	44	92	10	6
1958	CIN	.269	148	554	90	149	31	83	62	80	10	6
1959	CIN	.311	146	540	106	168	36	125	69	93	18	18
1960	CIN	.297	139	464	86	138	31	83	82	67	13	10
1961	CIN	.323	153	545	117	176	37	124	71	64	22	3
1962	CIN	.342	162	609	134	208	39	136	76	62	18	2
1963	CIN	.259	140	482	79	126	21	91	81	69	26	4
1964	CIN	.306	156	569	103	174	29	96	79	67	23	3
1965	CIN	.296	156	582	109	172	33	113	70	100	13	5
1966	BAL	.316	155	576	122	182	49	122	87	90	8	1
1967	BAL	.311	129	479	83	149	30	94	71	84	2	2
1968	BAL	.268	130	421	69	113	15	52	73	84	11	7
1969	BAL	.308	148	539	111	166	32	100	88	62	9	5
1970	BAL	.306	132	471	88	144	25	78	69	70	2	4
1971	BAL	.281	133	456	82	128	28	99	72	62	3	11
1972	LAD	.251	103	342	41	86	19	59	55	76	2	6
1973	CAL	.266	147	534	85	142	30	97	82	93	1	1
1974	CAL	.251	129	427	75	107	20	63	75	85	5	0
1974	CLE	.200	16	50	6	10	2	5	10	10	0	1
1975	CLE	.237	49	118	19	28	9	24	29	15	0	0
1976	CLE	.224	36	67	5	15	3	10	11	12	0	0
TOTALS		.294	2808	10006	1829	2943	586	1812	1420	1523	204	103

BAL: Baltimore Orioles; CAL: California Angels; CIN: Cincinnati Reds; CLE: Cleveland Indians; LAD: Los Angeles Dodgers.

way, coming across the base trying to turn a double play, I hit him hard."

He was just as often on the receiving end of the spikes. In one incident Robinson got slashed on the leg and required 30 stitches. In 1967, playing with Baltimore, he was hit so hard in the head by an infielder's knee, that he was knocked unconscious for five minutes. As a result, he missed a month of the season and suffered from impaired vision of varying degrees for much of the rest of his career. His equally aggressive batting stance—he leaned his head out over the plate to get a good look at pitches as they came in and to protect the outside corner—made him the regular league leader in being hit by pitches.

At the end of the 1965 season, assuming that at 30 years of age Robinson was well past his prime, Cincinnati traded him to the Baltimore Orioles. The season that followed was one of the greatest of Robinson's career. He won the Triple Crown—the batting, home run and RBI titles—led the Orioles to a triumph in the World Series, and was named the American League's Most Valuable Player, becoming the first and only player to be voted MVP in both major leagues. Robinson batted .316 in 1965, hit 49 home runs, and drove in 122.

With Robinson in the line-up, the Orioles would win three more pennants and another World Series. In 1966 Robinson was named World Series MVP after he led Baltimore to a four-game sweep of the Los Angeles Dodgers. During the Series he batted .286, hit two home runs, and drove in three runs.

Robinson stayed with the Orioles through the 1971 season, then was traded to the Los Angeles Dodgers for the 1972 season. This began an odyssey that saw him play for the Dodgers, Angels, and the Cleveland Indians over the next five seasons. Robinson retired as a player in 1976.

The First Black Manager

While playing with the Orioles, Robinson had set his sights on becoming a major league manager. He knew the odds were against him. Despite integration of players, there was still a de facto color barrier at the management level in the majors. No black or Hispanic had ever managed a big league team, much less made it into the executive ranks. Knowing of Robinson's ambition, Baltimore manager Earl Weaver helped him obtain an entry level managing job with the Santurce Cangrejeros in the Puerto Rican winter leagues, a job he held from 1968 to 1975. The team won the pennant in 1968 and Robinson was named Manager of the Year.

In 1975, in a historic move, he was named the Cleveland Indians' player-manager. The appointment came with a hitch, however: Much to Robinson's displeasure, the Indians refused to give him even a token raise over his player's salary. "If they were to release me right now, I would get $180,000 over the next year," he relates telling his agent. "If I take the job to manage the ballclub, and also play, I get the same amount. But they've put me in a position where they know I almost can't refuse their offer. If I refuse, there's no telling when I will ever get another chance to manage in the major leagues—or if I will. If I turn the job down, that would just give other owners an excuse not to hire me or other blacks." Robinson ultimately took the Cleveland job, becoming the first African-American manager in baseball. He kept the job a little over a year.

In 1980 Robinson became the first black manager in the National League when he took over the San Francisco Giants. The team played so well in 1982, going 87-75, that Robinson was named the National League's Manager of the Year. However, conflict on the Giants bench, combined with Robinson's impatience with some young players, and an uncooperative front office led to his being fired in 1984. He returned to his old home, the Baltimore Orioles, as a coach in 1985, and in 1988 was appointed manager there. In 1989 he led the team, which had come in last the previous year, to an 87-75 record and surprising second-place finish, just two games behind pennant-winning Toronto. At the season's end, he was the unanimous choice for the American League's Manager of the Year. He was the first manager to win the award in both leagues. When the team faltered in 1990, Robinson was replaced, but not fired. He was promoted to assistant general manager of the Orioles.

In 2000 Robinson became one of the highest-placed blacks in organized baseball when Commissioner **Bud Selig** created a position for him, the vice president for on-field operations. A large part of Robinson's responsibility was disciplining players involved in on-field altercations. His hard-line approach thrust him back into the public eye. After one brawl between the Dodgers and Cubs, Robinson levied fines totaling $72,000 and suspended 16 players and three coaches for a total of 84 games, a major league record. Once one of the fiercest, most unrelenting players in the major leagues, Robinson was determined to put an end to the disturbing trend of violence on major league baseball diamonds.

Frank Robinson's life in baseball has been one of unremitting commitment to excellence, as witnessed by his Rookie of the Year, two MVP, and two manager of the Year awards, his presence on 12 All-Star teams in both major leagues, and his first ballot induction into baseball's Hall of Fame. His outspoken courage in criticizing baseball's discrimination against people of color and his own success in overcoming racial barriers have earned him an equally important place in the sport's history.

CONTACT INFORMATION

Address: c/o Montreal Expos, P.O. Box 500, Station "M", Montreal, QC H1V 3P2, Canada.

SELECTED WRITINGS BY ROBINSON:

(With Al Silverman) *My Life Is Baseball*. New York: Doubleday, 1968.

(With Dave Anderson) *Frank*. New York: Holt, Rinehart, Winston, 1976.

(With Berry Stainback) *Extra Innings*. New York: McGraw Hill, 1988.

FURTHER INFORMATION

Periodicals

Anderson, Dave. "Frank Robinson's Return." *New York Times,* January 15, 1981: D21.

Chass, Murray. "After Spending His Life Inside the Game, Robinson Finds Himself Out of It." *New York Times,* April 20, 1997:. H7.

Chass, Murray. "Latest Literary Battle: Robinson vs. Ueberroth and Edwards." *New York Times,* April 24, 1988: H3

Cooper, Tony. "Enigmatic Frank Robinson Has Mellowed." *San Francisco Chronicle,* May 16, 1991: D1.

Dolgan, Bob. "Explosive Tenure Began With Bang."*Cleveland Plain Dealer,* May 19, 1997: 5C.

Durso, Joseph. "Aaron, Robinson Inducted And Honored As Pioneers." *New York Times,* August 2, 1982: C7.

Elderkin, Phil. "Frank Robinson stresses basics for the Giants." *Christian Science Monitor,.* March 18, 1981: 14.

Elderkin, Phil. "Robinson Takes Accumulated Baseball Knowledge to Giants Manager Job." *Christian Science Monitor,*January 19, 1981: 12.

"Frank Robinson: Baseball's Dean Of Discipline." *Ebony.,* August, 2000: 48.

Graeff, Burt. "Robinson Still Fearless At The Plate." *Cleveland Plain Dealer,* August 7, 2000: 1D.

Justice, Richard. "Baseball Names F. Robinson VP." *Washington Post,* February 26, 2000: D01.

Justice, Richard. "Frank Robinson Sets to Work." *Washington Post,* April 17, 1988, D1.

Justice, Richard. "Robinson 'Recharged,' Eager to Manage Again." *Washington Post,* July 1, 1987: B1.

Kjos, Les. "Another Black Manager? Not Soon, Says Robby." U.P.I. March 23, 1985.

Leavy, Jane. "Frank Robinson, at Ease."*Washington Post,* June 21, 1988: D1.

"Robinson Wins By A Landslide." *St. Louis Post-Dispatch.* November 2, 1989: 6D.

Stubbs, Dave. "Still Blazing a Trail." *Montreal Gazette,* July 13, 2002: D1.

Other

Expos Year in Review, December 26, 2002. Available at: http://montreal.expos.mlb.com/NASApp/mlb/mon/news/mon_news.jsp?ym20021226&contentid=187360&vkeynews_mon=mon&fextjsp

Sketch by Gerald E. Brennan

Glenn Robinson
1973-

American basketball player

The odds may not have looked good for NBA star Glenn Robinson. Born January 10, 1973, to Christine Bridgeman, an unmarried teenager, Robinson had little contact with his father, who often found himself in trouble with the law. Robinson's neighborhood in Gary, Indiana, was riddled with crime and drugs, but under Bridgeman's guidance, Robinson stayed straight. Once, Bridgeman pulled Robinson off the high school basketball team when she thought his grades were too low. The fledgling basketball star carried tools and worked at an air-conditioning and refrigeration shop to earn money.

Not a Natural

While basketball may have been Robinson's ticket to a more posh life, the sport did not come easy to the player now known as "Big Dog." In seventh grade, he refused to try out for the team, and with good reason, according to his future high school coach Ron Hefflin. "He wasn't very good," Hefflin told *Sports Illustrated*. "People don't understand how hard that kid worked. He hasn't always been a good ballplayer."

The hard work paid off; in his freshman year at Gary's Roosevelt High School, Robinson made the junior varsity team and he made varsity the following year. By his senior season in 1991, Robinson was averaging 25.6 points and 14.6 rebounds per game, statistics good enough to lead his team to a 30-1 record and a state championship. That year he was named Indiana's Mr. Basketball and shared National High School Player of the Year honors with the Sacramento Kings' **Chris Webber**, who attended Detroit Country Day High School in Michigan.

Sits Out Freshman Year

Despite all his hard work on the court, Robinson did not achieve a high enough score on the Scholastic Aptitude Test to qualify for an athletic scholarship. He entered Purdue University under Proposition 48, which allowed him to receive a scholarship provided he met the school's academic standards while sitting out his freshman year. Robinson honed his skills by playing against other future National Basketball Association (NBA) stars such as **Tim Hardaway** and Kevin Duckworth in the Malcolm X summer league in Chicago and he returned for his first season with the Boilermakers in top form.

While Robinson took the court by storm, finishing in the top ten in the conference in scoring, rebounding, steals, blocked shots, field goal percentage and free throw percentage, his team's overall performance was less stellar. The Boilermakers finished their season with an 18-10 record and were eliminated from the NCAA tournament in the first round.

Robinson had the option to turn pro after his sensational season, but he decided to stay another season at Purdue. He had both his team and himself in mind, Robinson explained in *Sports Illustrated*. He didn't want to leave his teammates in the lurch and he didn't feel he was mature enough for the big leagues. "I wasn't ready to go off into that big world yet," he explained. "Out there you have to be able to deal with girls, agents, people trying to give you drugs, all that stuff."

He led the team to a Big Ten championship and the NCAA tournament semifinals, where Purdue lost to Duke. The awards came pouring in. In addition to receiving the Naismith and Wooden awards, Robinson was named National College Basketball Player of the Year. Although he had a good chance at an NCAA championship if he stayed on, Robinson opted to enter the NBA draft, where he was the first pick. After being chosen by the Milwaukee Bucks, Robinson held out for a 10-year, $68.15 million contract, which he signed just one hour before the Bucks' first game of the season. The

Career Statistics

Yr	Team	GP	PTS	FG%	3P%	FT%	RPG	APG	SPG	BPG	TO	PF
1994-95	MIL	80	1755	.451	.321	.796	6.40	2.5	1.44	.28	3.91	2.90
1995-96	MIL	82	1660	.454	.342	.812	6.10	3.6	1.16	.51	3.44	2.90
1996-97	MIL	80	1689	.465	.350	.791	6.30	3.1	1.29	.85	3.36	2.80
1997-98	MIL	56	1308	.470	.385	.808	5.50	2.8	1.23	.61	3.57	2.90
1998-99	MIL	47	865	.459	.392	.870	5.90	2.1	.98	.87	2.26	2.40
1999-00	MIL	81	1693	.472	.363	.802	6.00	2.4	.96	.51	2.75	2.60
2000-01	MIL	76	1674	.468	.299	.820	6.90	3.3	1.13	.82	2.88	2.50
2001-02	MIL	66	1366	.467	.326	.837	6.20	2.5	1.47	.62	2.64	2.60

MIL: Milwaukee Bucks.

Awards and Accomplishments

1991	Indiana Mr. Basketball
1991	National High School Player of the Year (tie with Chris Webber)
1994	Big Ten championship
1994	Naismith Award
1994	Wooden Award
1994	National College Basketball Player of the Year
1995	NBA All-Rookie Team
1996	Named to U.S. Olympic men's basketball team (sits out due to injury)
2000-01	NBA All-Star Team

holdout was of such interest to the media that U.S. Senator Herb Kohl, who owns the Bucks, fielded questions about it during his campaign.

Big Dog with the Bucks

Due to the holdout, Robinson missed training camp. As a result, his start with the Bucks was shaky. His recovery was quick, however, and by the end of the season he led all rookie scorers with 21.9 points per game and finished second in the voting for Rookie of the Year. In 1996 he was named to the Olympic "Dream Team III," although he opted to fully recover from the Achilles tendonitis that had plagued him during the season rather than play.

During his time off, Robinson worked on conditioning, footwork and ballhandling. "I want to be known as a complete player," he told *The Sporting News*. "The emphasis was on my offense the first two years, but I want to be known for all aspects of the game." Coach Chris Ford took notice, and named Robinson co-captain in the 1996-97 season. It took some time, but the Bucks finally made the postseason in 1999 and again in 2000. In 2001 Robinson led the Bucks to the Eastern Conference finals.

In July 2002 Robinson made headlines for his off-court behavior. After an altercation with his former fiancée, he was arrested for domestic battery, assault and possession of a firearm. The next month, following a sea-son in which the Bucks did not make the playoffs, the team traded Robinson to Atlanta. Robinson, who has risen above defeat and disappointment so often in the past, told *Sports Illustrated* he was thrilled with the move. "I've always thought about living and playing in Atlanta," he said. "I'm in my prime, and this is a new beginning."

CONTACT INFORMATION

Address: c/o Atlanta Hawks, One CNN Center, Atlanta, GA 30303. Email: hawks.fanmail@turner.com.

FURTHER INFORMATION

Books

Sports Stars, Series 1-4. U•X•L, 1994-98.

Periodicals

Anande, J.A., Greg Hoffman and Radd Cawhorn. "Looking Out for Number One." *Sporting News* (February 10, 1997): 9.

Ballard, Chris. "9 Atlanta Hawks." *Sports Illustrated* (Oct. 28, 2002): 112.

Sketch by Kristin Palm

Jackie Robinson
1919-1972

American baseball player

Jackie Robinson is most remembered as the player who broke baseball's color barrier. By stepping into the white baseball world, the black Robinson changed the face of not only baseball, but the United States.

Jackie Robinson

Robinson integrated baseball during a time when schools, buses, restaurants, hotels, and drinking fountains remained segregated. His actions helped touch off the Civil Rights movement. That Robinson even produced during his baseball years is amazing, given the climate in which he played. After joining the Brooklyn Dodgers in 1947, Robinson faced death threats, vulgar insults, and hate-filled fans, along with beanballs aimed at his head and sharp, shiny spikes at his face as opponents slid into his tag at second base. Despite the pressure, Robinson earned a reputation as a dead-solid ballplayer through his no-nonsense fielding, reliable line drives, and his mastery of the tricky steal of home. After baseball, Robinson committed his life to ensuring fairer chances for African-Americans. He marched with Martin Luther King, raised funds for the National Association for the Advancement of Colored People, and politically supported candidates he thought would help the cause of his people.

Born to a Sharecropper

Robinson, the grandson of a slave, was born on a plantation shack in Cairo, Georgia. He was the youngest of five children born to Mallie and Jerry Robinson. Just months after Robinson's birth, his father, a sharecropper, ran off with a neighbor's wife, and the plantation owner ordered the Robinsons off the land. Seeking a better life for her children, Mallie Robinson moved the family to California, where her brother, Burton McGriff, lived.

Chronology

1919	Born January 31 in Cairo, Georgia
1920	Relocates to California with mother and siblings
1937	Graduates from John Muir Technical High School and enters Pasadena Junior College
1939	Enters the University of California at Los Angeles (UCLA)
1941	Leaves UCLA a few credits shy of his degree
1942	Joins U.S. Army
1944	Receives honorable discharge from Army
1945	Plays for the Negro League's Kansas City Monarchs; signs to play with the Montreal Royals, an all-white Brooklyn Dodgers-affiliated farm team
1946	Marries Rachel Isum in February; debuts with Montreal Royals in April
1947	Breaks major league baseball's 20th century color line by taking the field for the Brooklyn Dodgers on April 15
1956	Plays last season of baseball; joins Chock Full O' Nuts restaurant chain as vice president
1963	Marches with Martin Luther King in Birmingham, Alabama
1972	Dies October 24 in Stamford, Connecticut

Mallie Robinson found work washing and ironing and by 1923 had purchased a house in Pasadena, on Pepper Street. As the only black family on the street, the Robinson children were singled out as troublemakers. Neighbors filed false reports with the police claiming the boys were throwing rocks and vandalizing the area. Soon, the neighborhood united to buy them out. However, when some key wealthy families refused to support the plan, instead favoring the Robinsons' right to live there, the rest of the neighbors gave up, and the family stayed.

As he grew up amid poverty and racial prejudice, Robinson learned he could gain acceptance with his athleticism. In grammar school, kids would share their lunches with Robinson if he agreed to join their team. Robinson found that at least on the playing field, white students counted him as their equal.

During his childhood, Robinson befriended an interracial group called the Pepper Street Gang, which consisted of poor black, Japanese, Mexican, and caucasian boys. They roamed the streets challenging more affluent, mostly white boys to football matches, or other sports, betting modest amounts of money they'd win. Robinson sharpened his skills on the streets, then put them to use at John Muir Technical High, where he starred on the baseball, football, basketball, and track teams.

Multi-Sport Star

In 1937, Robinson enrolled at Pasadena Junior College, moving from football, to basketball, to baseball, and track, at times competing in two sports simultaneously. One day, Robinson set a junior college broad jump record of 25 feet, 6½ inches, then raced across town to a baseball game to help Pasadena win the league championship. Though baseball was never Robinson's best sport, he stood out on the diamond. His first year at

The Negro Leagues: A Brief History

Following the Civil War (1861-1865), baseball boomed as a popular pastime among both black and white athletes. In 1867, the National Association of Base Ball Players was formed, but from its inception, the league voted to bar black players.

A few years later, the National Association of Professional Baseball Players did not outright bar African-American players, although there was a "gentleman's agreement" among owners not to allow blacks.

With blacks yearning for a league of their own, the Negro National League was organized in 1920, followed by the Eastern Colored League in 1923. In 1924, the first all-black World Series took place.

A Negro League season consisted of about 60 to 80 league games. In addition, the teams each averaged 100 exhibition games, generally against other semi-pro squads, small-town teams, and teams with a few white major-leaguers.

Black ballplayers enjoyed exhibitions against major league teams or those with major league players. According to *The Negro Baseball Leagues* by David K. Fremon, from 1900 to 1950, Negro League teams playing against teams with white major-leaguers won 268 such contests. The major league-stocked teams won 168. In 1912, Smokey Joe Williams shut out the New York Giants and New York Yankees within a two-week period. In the early 1920s, the baseball commissioner, Judge Kennesaw Mountain Lands, outlawed such intra league games.

Negro Leagues' innovations included night games. By 1930, the Monarchs began traveling with a set of portable floodlights. Attendance nearly tripled because day laborers could come. White major league baseball introduced night games in 1935.

By the early 1960s, the last Negro League club had folded. The Baseball Hall of Fame was under pressure to recognize the talents of Negro League players who, undoubtedly, would have made the Hall had they been allowed to play. In 1971, Satchel Paige became the first Negro Leaguer enshrined.

Pasadena, Robinson played shortstop, hit .417, and stole 25 bases in 24 games.

His second year at Pasadena, Robinson ran for more than 1,000 yards to score 17 touchdowns and lead the football team to 11 straight victories. He even returned a kickoff for a 104-yard touchdown. In basketball, he averaged 19 points per game and led Pasadena to the California Junior College championship. That spring, Robinson was named Southern California Junior College MVP after leading the baseball team to the league title, all the while running and jumping for the track team.

Colleges took note of Robinson, and in 1939, he accepted a scholarship to the University of California at Los Angeles (UCLA). He was a dazzling runner in the open football field. His first season at UCLA, he led the nation with an average of 12.24 yards per carry.

During his time at UCLA, Robinson became the school's first four-letter winner, playing baseball, football, basketball, and track. While at UCLA, he met nursing student Rachel Isum, his future wife.

In spring 1941, seeing no future in athletics or college, Robinson left UCLA. "I was convinced that no amount of education would help a black man get a job," Robinson noted in his autobiography, *I Never Had It Made*. "I felt I was living in an academic and athletic dream world."

The fate of his older brother, Mack, may have prompted Robinson's disenchantment. Mack Robinson participated in the 1936 Olympics in Berlin, Germany, finishing second in the 200-yard dash behind **Jesse Owens**. When he returned home with his silver medal, Mack Robinson's achievement went mostly unnoticed, and the only work he could find was street sweeping.

After leaving college, Robinson was drafted into the Army in 1942 as the United States became more involved in World War II. Robinson achieved the rank of lieutenant and became a morale officer for a black unit at Fort Hood, Texas, where the Army's policy of segregation finally got the best of him. One day in July 1944, a bus driver at Fort Hood instructed Robinson to move to the back of the bus. Robinson declined and drew a court-martial. Because of Robinson's stature as a respected athlete, the black press took up his cause. Eventually, the Army dropped the charges and granted Robinson an honorable discharge.

In 1945, Robinson joined the Kansas City Monarchs as a shortstop. The Monarchs, led by fireballing pitcher **Satchel Paige**, were a marquee Negro League team. Little did Robinson know, Brooklyn Dodgers general manager **Branch Rickey** was monitoring his performance.

Part of Noble Experiment

In August 1945, Rickey brought Robinson to Brooklyn and offered him a chance to play baseball for the Montreal Royals, the Dodgers' principal minor league team. Rickey told Robinson that if he succeeded, he could play in the major leagues. The watershed meeting lasted hours, as Rickey interrogated Robinson and tested his ability to turn the other cheek. Rickey, a devout Methodist who despised profanity, turned to role-playing, and, posing as an unwelcoming hotel clerk, or a Southern sportswriter, berated Robinson with every racist insult he could muster.

Rickey taunted and teased Robinson until, at one point, according to Glenn Stout's book, *Jackie Robinson: Between the Baselines,* an aggravated Robinson called out, "Mr. Rickey, what do you want? Do you want a ballplayer who is afraid to fight back?"

"I want a ballplayer with guts enough not to fight back," Rickey replied.

Rickey understood that character would weigh more heavily in baseball's integration that batting average. Rickey envisioned a peaceful infiltration and told Robinson that he could, under no circumstances, fight back or he'd ruin his chances. Thus, baseball's "noble experiment" began.

Before joining the Montreal Royals for spring training in 1946, Robinson married Rachel Isum. The honeymoon soon ended when Robinson arrived in Daytona Beach and found himself barred from the whites-only Riviera seaside motel where his teammates stayed. Not

Career Statistics

Yr	Team	Avg	GP	AB	R	H	HR	RBI	BB	SO	SB	E
1945	KAN	.387	47	163	36	63	5	23	–	–	13	–
1946	MON	.349	124	444	113	155	3	66	92	27	40	10
1947	BRO	.297	151	590	125	175	12	48	74	36	29	16
1948	BRO	.296	147	574	108	170	12	85	57	37	22	15
1949	BRO	.342	156	593	122	203	16	124	86	27	37	16
1950	BRO	.328	144	518	99	170	14	81	80	24	12	11
1951	BRO	.338	153	548	106	185	19	88	79	27	25	7
1952	BRO	.308	149	510	104	157	19	75	106	40	24	20
1953	BRO	.329	136	484	109	159	12	95	74	30	17	6
1954	BRO	.311	124	386	62	120	15	59	63	20	7	7
1955	BRO	.256	105	317	51	81	8	36	61	18	12	10
1956	BRO	.275	117	357	61	98	10	43	60	32	12	9
*TOTAL		.311	1382	4877	947	1518	137	734	740	291	197	117

BRO: Brooklyn Dodgers; KAN: Kansas City Monarchs (Negro League); MON: Montreal Royals (International League).
*Total reflects his 10 years with the Brooklyn Dodgers (excludes play in Negro League and International League).

that it mattered—Robinson's teammates didn't care for him, because the attention he drew made them leery. Also, Robinson's presence cut into their playing time. Many communities canceled exhibition games with the Royals because local law prohibited race-mixing. While playing in Sanford, Florida, Robinson singled, stole second base, then scored on a hit only to find the sheriff waiting in the dugout with handcuffs. He was removed from the game. When Robinson got the chance to play, he faced attacks from opponents, who slid into base with their spikes flashing toward his face or shins. Pitchers threw beanballs at his head. But Robinson didn't complain.

Amid the tension, Robinson won the International League batting title with a .349 average. That season, he drove in 66 runs to help his team win the pennant. He was named the league's Most Valuable Player.

In time, Robinson was promoted to the Brooklyn Dodgers. On April 15, 1947, Robinson shattered baseball's color barrier when he played first base for the Dodgers against the Boston Braves. He wore uniform No. 42, which today, has been retired from every ballclub in deference to Robinson.

Being the only black player in a white baseball world proved tough for Robinson. His teammates passed a petition to have him removed from the roster. Rickey, however, told the players that if they didn't adjust their thinking, he would be glad to let them go. In addition, Robinson and his family faced death threats.

Opponents were cruel to Robinson, too, and throughout games hurled race-baiting taunts at him. In addition, crowds showered Robinson with trash, tomatoes, and watermelon slices. The abuse got so bad Robinson's teammates eventually rallied around him. Pitchers knocked him down. He barely survived the first few months, then channeled his anger into his play and began

to thrive, winning 1947 Rookie of the Year honors and leading the Dodgers to the National League pennant.

In 1948, Robinson switched from first base to second base and came alive. His 1949 season proved phenomenal, and Robinson led the league with a .342 batting average and 37 stolen bases. Voted the league's Most Valuable Player, Robinson also appeared in his first of six consecutive All-Star games.

One of Robinson's best weapons was his base-running finesse. With his cheetah-fast speed, Robinson could turn a single into a double. Once on base, Robinson would dance around and rattle the pitcher. He was particularly dangerous on third base, stealing home 19 times over his career. This became his signature play. Though he didn't do it often, the threat remained. His most famous steal of home came in Game 1 of the 1955 World Series in New York, off Yankees star pitcher Whitey Ford. Historic footage showed the steal, followed by catcher **Yogi Berra**'s heated argument with plate umpire Bill Summers.

Between 1948 and 1953, Robinson's batting average was .323; he averaged 108 runs scored, 91 RBI, and 13 stolen bases. Only **Stan Musial** and **Ted Williams** played close to his average during this period. In addition, Robinson led second basemen with double plays from 1949 to 1952.

The Dodgers clinched the National League pennant six times during Robinson's 10 years with the team, winning the World Series for the first time in 1955.

By 1956, however, the struggles were beginning to slow Robinson. His hair had grayed, and he was heavier. He was also battling diabetes. Traded to the archrival New York Giants at the end of the 1956 season, he decided to retire, and in 1962, was inducted into baseball's Hall of Fame.

Jackie Robinson, sliding into home plate

Following baseball, Robinson became vice president of Chock Full O' Nuts, a restaurant chain that marketed its coffee nationwide. Robinson then became more involved in trying to make integration a social and economic reality. He was integral in founding Harlem's Freedom National Bank, marched with Martin Luther King in Birmingham, Alabama, and raised funds for the NAACP's "Freedom Fund Drive."

Disabled by diabetes that impeded his mobility and nearly blinded him, Robinson died on October 24, 1972, in Stamford, Connecticut, leaving behind a wife and two surviving children. His eldest son, Jackie Robinson, Jr., had died in a car crash in 1971.

Receives Hero's Funeral

About 2,500 people turned out for Robinson's funeral at New York's Riverside Church on October 27, 1972. Rev. Jesse Jackson enthusiastically recounted the events of Robinson's life and delivered the eulogy to a crowd that cheered more as though it was celebrating a ninth-inning home run than a funeral.

According to the *Boston Globe,* Jackson said, "When Jackie took the field, something within us reminded us of our birthright to be free. And somebody without re-

minded us that it could be attained. There was strength and pride and power when the big rock hit the water, and concentric circles came forth and ripples of new possibility spread throughout the nation."

"… For a fleeting moment, America tried democracy, and it worked. For a fleeting moment, America became one nation under God. This man turned the stumbling block into a stepping stone." Jackson also noted that Robinson's tombstone read "1919-1972. On that dash, is where we live," according to Stout's book. "And for everyone there is a dash of possibility, to choose the high road or the low road, to make things better or worse."

Even in his death, Robinson remained an inspiration to African-Americans. He was buried at the Cypress Hills Cemetery in Brooklyn, the area of the city where he fought the hardest to make a difference.

Remembered as Superhuman Hero

When Robinson cracked baseball's color line in 1947, he also cracked open the United States and helped catapult the Civil Rights movement. Before Rosa Parks and Martin Luther King, there was Robinson. For blacks

<table>
<tr><td colspan="2">**Awards and Accomplishments**</td></tr>
<tr><td>1939</td><td>Named Southern California Junior College Most Valuable Baseball Player</td></tr>
<tr><td>1946</td><td>Named Most Valuable Player of the International League while playing for the Montreal Royals, a Brooklyn Dodgers-affiliated farm team</td></tr>
<tr><td>1947</td><td>Integrates major league baseball by joining the Brooklyn Dodgers; led league with 29 stolen bases; named Rookie of the Year</td></tr>
<tr><td>1949</td><td>Leads league with highest batting average (.342) and most stolen bases (37)</td></tr>
<tr><td>1949</td><td>Named National League Most Valuable Player</td></tr>
<tr><td>1949-54</td><td>Selected for All-Star team</td></tr>
<tr><td>1952</td><td>Leads league with an on-base percentage of .440</td></tr>
<tr><td>1962</td><td>Inducted into the Baseball Hall of Fame on July 23</td></tr>
</table>

fighting the fight, Robinson was a hero who showed superhuman endurance could pull you through.

Robinson remained a hero because he never quit fighting, even after he'd won the baseball battle. In his autobiography, *I Never Had It Made,* Robinson wrote, "I cannot possibly believe I have it made while so many of my black brothers and sisters are hungry, inadequately housed, insufficiently clothed, denied their dignity as they live in slums or barely exist on welfare."

Because of Robinson, blacks united, seeking an end to segregation in areas other than baseball. His victory in baseball served to unite African Americans who, following Robinson's lead, began to fight to be free.

SELECTED WRITINGS BY ROBINSON:

Baseball Has Done It, Philadelphia: Lippincott, 1964.
(With Alfred Duckett) *Breakthrough to the Big League: The Story of Jackie Robinson,* E.M. Hale, 1968.
Jackie Robinson's Little League Baseball Book, Englewood Cliffs, NJ: Prentice-Hall, 1972.
(As told to Alfred Duckett) *I Never Had It Made,* Hopewell, NJ: Ecco Press, 1972.

FURTHER INFORMATION

Books

Craft, David. *The Negro Leagues: 40 Years of Black Professional Baseball in Words and Pictures.* New York: Crescent, 1993.
Fremon, David K. *The Negro Baseball Leagues.* New York: Macmillan, 1994.
Simon, Scott. *Jackie Robinson and the Integration of Baseball.* Hoboken, New Jersey: John Wiley & Sons, Inc., 2002.
Stout, Glenn and Dick Johnson. *Jackie Robinson: Between the Baselines.* San Francisco: Woodford Press, 1997.

Periodicals

"1947-1997: the 50th Anniversary of the Jackie Robinson Revolution." *Ebony* (April 1997): 87.

Other

"Jackie Robinson Statistics." Baseball-Reference.com. http://www.baseball-reference.com/r/robinja02.shtml (January 26, 2003).
"Opening a New, Wide World: Robinson's Impact Felt Well Beyond the Chalk Lines." *Boston Globe*. http://www.boston.com/globe/specialreports/1997/mar/robinson/ (January 29, 2003).

Sketch by Lisa Frick

Shawna Robinson
1964-

American race car driver

As a woman stock car racer, Shawna Robinson has a long list of "firsts" behind her name, including being the first woman to start a NASCAR Winston Cup race since **Patty Moise** did so in 1989 and the first woman to finish a Winston Cup race since **Janet Guthrie** in 1980. Yet, she has said she is more interested in being remembered as a winning driver than as the first of her gender to accomplish racing feats. Competing primarily against men on the racetrack, Robinson has faced prejudice and even outright hostility from some drivers. She also struggles with finding sponsorship for competitions. Robinson started her career in Great American Truck Racing (GATR) tours. She turned to racing in the National Association for Stock Car Auto Racing (NASCAR) in 1988, at age twenty-three, winning the AC Delco 100 race, which made her the first woman ever to win a major NASCAR Touring Series event. Still racing in 2002, Robinson is a single mother of two children.

Racing Family

Shawna Robinson was born November 30, 1964, in Des Moines, Iowa, the daughter of Richard "Lefty" Robinson and his wife, Lois, who drove a race car until she flipped it and her husband asked her to stop racing. "Lefty" Robinson was an amateur diesel truck racer and promoter who worked on vehicles in his home garage. Shawna was the youngest of the Robinsons' five children. She and her siblings were taught they could do anything they set their mind to, and they raced minibikes, snowmobiles, and motorcycles until they were old enough to drive cars. As a teen, she looked up

Shawna Robinson

to racecar drivers **A. J. Foyt**, Steve Kinser, and Sammy Swindell. By her early twenties she admired Janet Guthrie as her interests turned to stock car racing.

When Shawna turned eighteen, her dad taught her to drive the 14,000 lb. diesel truck cabs he raced as an amateur. Only 5'6" and 110 pounds, young Shawna began racing the big rigs on short tracks, competing against male racers, who often resented her. At age nineteen, she became the first woman to win a GATR major super speedway points race, the Milwaukee Mile Bobtail 100, and was voted GATR Rookie of the Year. She went on to race big rigs at the Paul Ricard Grand Prix Truck Race in France the following year and finished second in the Grand Prix of Trucks in Mexico City in 1986. In 1987, Robinson won the GATR Big Rig 100 at Flemington, New Jersey. Then she set her sights on NASCAR racing.

Dash Division Debut

Robinson made her debut as a stock car racer in the spring of 1988, finishing third in the Charlotte/Daytona

Dash Series Florida 200 in Daytona. That June, she made history by winning the AC Delco 100 NASCAR Dash Series race in Asheville, North Carolina, the first woman to win a major NASCAR Touring event. She also won her first race in the Goody's Dash series that year and was voted NASCAR Dash Series Most Popular Driver and Rookie of the Year. She won the Most Popular Driver award again in 1989.

In her first two years in NASCAR, Robinson started all thirty Charlotte/Daytona Dash Series races. She won three of them and finished in the top ten a total of twenty-one times. By 1991, she was ready to move up to the Grand National Division, competing in the Busch Series, in which full-size, eight-cylinder cars reach up to 200 miles per hour.

Pole Position History and Crash

In 1994, Robinson became the first woman ever to win the pole position in the Busch Series, by setting a Grand National track record lap speed of 174.330 mph, at Atlanta Motor Speedway. At the race two days later, however, as Robinson started from her prime position in the first lap, racer Mike Wallace pulled in between her car and that of racer Joe Nemechek, taking air off Robinson's spoiler and causing her to bump Nemechek's car broadside. Both cars then slammed into the retaining wall. After her pit crew removed most of the damaged front of her Chevrolet, Robinson went on racing for sixty-three laps before radiator damage forced to her withdraw. Nemechek never finished the first lap and made public charges that Wallace had planned the aggression against Robinson. Wallace denied it, however, and NASCAR officials, after a review, issued a statement that no one was to blame for the crash.

Temporary Retirement

After the Atlanta race, Robinson continued to compete in the Grand National division. Her best finish in a Busch Series race was a tenth place, and she retired temporarily to start a family in 1995. Married and giving birth to a son, Tanner, in 1996 and a daughter, Samantha, in 1997, Robinson worked in Charlotte, North Carolina, as an interior decorator, where many of her clients were involved with NASCAR.

ARCA Comeback

By 1999, she was ready to return to racing and began her comeback with the Automobile Racing Club of America (ARCA) Series. With a second place finish at Daytona and a fourth place in Charlotte in ARCA races that year, she won the STP-Prestone Highest Finishing Rookie Award.

She raced in ARCA again in 2000, taking the Talladega (Alabama) Pole Award at the Bondo/Mar-Hyde Series race on June 10, in Michigan, where she broke the track record with a lap speed of 184.606 mph. As she started the race, however, she crashed coming out of a turn and was briefly hospitalized with a broken right shoulder and two broken ribs. She again took home the Prestone Highest Finishing Rookie Award at Talladega on October 14, 2000. Robinson scored in the top ten finishes in approximately half of her ARCA starts.

Winston Cup

By the 2001 season, Robinson was ready to get back into NASCAR racing. She came back with a bang, as the first female driver to start a prestigious Winston Cup Series race since Patty Moise in 1989. Robinson finished her first series race in Brooklyn, Michigan, on June 10, 2001, making her the first woman to do so since Janet Guthrie in 1980. "That was my goal, that's all they asked of me today," Robinson said after finishing the race in 34th place. She spun the car around in Turn 2 but regained control without hitting anything, thinking, "Oh no, just hold onto it" as it happened.

In October 2001, Robinson began racing with BAM Racing, owned by Beth Ann and Tony Morganthau. Robinson started in seven Winston Cup Series races in 2002. She qualified for the Daytona 500 based on her qualifying speed of 182.66 mph from the Time Trials on February 9. She started the race in the 36th position, becoming only the second female driver ever to race the 500. Guthrie finished it in 1977 and 1980, in 12th and 11th places, respectively. Robinson finished the race in

Awards and Accomplishments	
1984	Voted Great American Truck Racing (GATR) Rookie of the Year
1986	Second place finish in Grand Prix of Trucks Mexico City Race
1987	Won GATR Big Rig 100 at Flemington (New Jersey) Speedway
1988	Won AC Delco National Association for Stock Car Auto Racing (NASCAR) race in Asheville, North Carolina; third place finish in overall Dash point standings; named NASCAR Dash Series Rookie of the Year and Most Popular Driver; her winning Pontiac Sunbird was donated to the International Motorsports Hall of Fame
1989	First woman to win a NASCAR pole position, in the Goody's Dash Series at Florence, South Carolina; set new track record, captured pole, and won at Myrtle Beach (South Carolina) Speedway; named NASCAR Dash Series Most Popular Driver for second year in a row; was nominated for Sportswoman of the Year by the Women's Sports Foundation
1990	Qualified second for Florida 200 at Daytona
1992	Runner-up in Busch Series Rookie-of-the-Year standings
1994	Captured outside pole in Goodwrench 200 at North Carolina Speedway on February 26; set new Busch Series track-speed record of 174.330 mph at Atlanta Motor Speedway, qualifying for Busch Light 300-in that race on March 12 she became the first woman in NASCAR history to win a pole position in Busch Series, Grand National Division; finished in top ten on June 25 at Watkins Glen, New York
1999	Second place finish in FirstPlus Financial Automobile Racing Club of America (ARCA) 200 at Dayton, Florida; fourth place finish at ARCA Bondo/Mar-Hyde Series in Charlotte, North Carolina; won STP-Prestone Highest Finishing Rookie honor
2000	Voted Highest Finishing Rookie at Xenia, Ohio, on May 26; won Talladega Pole Award at ARCA Bondo/Mar-Hyde Series Event at Michigan Speedway on June 10, breaking track-speed record with speed of 184.606 mph; won Prestone Highest Finishing Rookie Award at Talladega, Alabama, on October 14
2001	Was first woman to start a Winston Cup race since 1989 when she began race at Brooklyn, Michigan, on June 10; was first woman to finish a NASCAR Winston Cup race since Janet Guthrie did so in July 1980

24th place, racing a No. 49 Dodge. She finished the season 52nd in Winston Cup standings.

Slow Season

By the fall of 2002, at age thirty-seven, Robinson had begun to feel her career was in jeopardy because she was driving so few races. The constant search for a sponsor and the introduction of new drivers to BAM had given her less time in the driver's seat. She told Tim Packman of Turner Sports Interactive that she was spending lots of time with her two children, becoming involved in their sports and school activities. She also continued to serve as a speaker for women's associations and business groups and had made several television appearances. BAM was planning to put her into some Busch Series races as well. "I really just want to race," she told Packman. "I would love to run the Busch Series, Truck Series or even the ARCA Series. I know I can drive."

Robinson has indeed proven she can drive. With the ambition and focus to become not just a great woman racecar driver but a great driver regardless of gender, she has overcome many barriers in her twenty years behind the wheel. She told Kesa Dillon of *Sports Illustrated*

Related Biography: Racing Executive Michael Kranefuss

Michael Kranefuss is one of the racing business's top executives. He spent twelve years as head of Ford Motor Company Europe's international racing programs, directing races in national programs as well as in Formula One, the World Rally Championship, and International Sports Car Racing. He helped to establish Ford as a winner in every motorsport in which it competed.

After leaving Ford, Kranefuss became an executive in the United States, as co-owner, with Ken Anderson, of MK Racing. His drivers, which included Jeremy Mayfield, have participated in numerous successful NASCAR Winston Cup, Busch Grand National Series, and ARCA races.

In his mid-sixties and following numerous attempts to retire, in 2001, Kranefuss and three-time Winston Cup champion Cale Yarborough, along with several other investors and directors, created the Team Racing Auto Circuit (TRAC), a new major stock car series to begin racing with the 2003 season. Two-car teams will be represented by cities and race on oval tracks.

MK Racing has also announced that it will be one of only three chassis builders to supply Falcon Cars to the Indy Racing League for 2003-2005 specifications. The step toward manufacturing race cars is a natural one for both Kranefuss and Anderson.

When Shawna Robinson was offered a contract with Kranefuss after returning to racing in 2000, following the birth of her second child, she reentered the arena as part of his ARCA RE/MAX race team. By the spring of 2001, she was ready to race a Kranefuss car in the Winston Cup.

Robinson stayed with Kranefuss until October 2001, when she was offered a car by BAM Racing and asked to be released from her contract.

Women in November 2002, "I'm an athlete. I've always wanted to compete, and I want to win. Whatever car I'm in, whatever series I'm running, whatever track I'm racing—I want people to know Shawna Robinson was there."

CONTACT INFORMATION

Address: c/o Shawna Robinson Fan Club, 545-C Pitts School Rd. NW, Concord, NC, 28027. Online: http://www.shawnarobinson.com.

FURTHER INFORMATION

Books

Great Women in Sports. "Shawna Robinson." Detroit: Visible Ink Press, 1996.

Periodicals

Dillon, Kesa. "Shawna Robinson: The NASCAR Winston Cup Tour's Lone Female Driver on Racing Daytona, Meeting Ali and Going after What She Really Wants." *Sports Illustrated Women* (November 1, 2002): 118.

Lieber, Jill. "Shawna Robinson." *Sports Illustrated* (March 21, 1994): 78.

Other

Akers, Shawn A. "Crash Doesn't Wreck Robinson's Dream." Racing One.com. http://www.racingone.com/ (February 16, 2002).

Benjamin, Rick. "Way Off TRAC." SpeedFX.com. http://www.speedfx.com/ (May 19, 2001).

Falcon Cars.com. "An Interview with Michael Kranefuss." http://www.falconcars.com/ (January 30, 2003).

Falcon Cars.com. "MK Racing Selected to Manufacture in the IRL." http://www.falconcars.com/ (January 30, 2003).

Kelly, Kevin. "On the Brink of History: Shawna Robinson Wants to Become the Next Pioneer Female Driver." *St. Petersburg Times* Online. http://www.sptimes.com/ (April 28, 2001).

NASCAR.com. "Driver Profile: Shawna Robinson." http://www.nascar.com/drivers/ (January 8, 2003).

NASCAR.com. "Shawna Robinson." http://www.nascar.com/2002/kyn/women/ (December 22, 2002).

Packman, Tim (Turner Sports Interactive). "Robinson Completes Race, Finishes 34th." NASCAR.com. http://www.nascar.com/2001/NEWS/ (June 10, 2001).

Robinson, Shawna, as told to Tim Packman (Turner Sports Interactive). "Insider's View: Shawna Robinson." NASCAR.com. http://www.nascar.com/2002/news/features/insiders_view/ (October 3, 2002).

Shawna Robinson.com. "Shawna." http://www.shawnarobinson.com/ (January 8, 2003).

Utter, Jim. "Sadler Shaken up in Final Practice: Robinson Hurt in Steele's ARCA Win." Knight Ridder/Tribune News Service. Galenet. http://galenet.galegroup.com/ (June 10, 2000).

Williams Company of America. Shawna Robinson Press Releases. "California 500: First NASCAR Winston Cup Female Driver in 12 Years." http://www.williamscompany.com/ (May 5, 2001).

Yahoo! Sports. "NASCAR: Shawna Robinson." http://sports.yahoo.com/rac/nascar/drivers/ (January 8, 2003).

Sketch by Ann H. Shurgin

Sugar Ray Robinson
1921-1989

American boxer

Five-time middleweight champion of the world, Sugar Ray Robinson is remembered as the greatest boxer ever produced by the sport. He won Golden Gloves championships in both featherweight and welterweight classifications and retired undefeated as the world welterweight champion in 1952. He managed also a brief career as a tap dancer, and his Ray Robinson Enterprises spanned the better part of a city block in New York City on 7th Avenue, between 123rd and 124th Streets. Known also for his great generosity and his concern for children, Robinson holds a special place in boxing history.

Walker Smith, Jr.

Born Walker Smith Jr. on May 3, 1921, Robinson was the son of Leila (Hurst) and Walker Smith Sr. The Smiths had moved from Dublin, Georgia, to Detroit, Michigan, along with their two daughters, Marie and Evelyn, just weeks before Robinson's birth. In Detroit, Robinson's father worked as a ditch-digger and moonlighted laying sewers. Leila Smith, who found work as a chambermaid at Detroit's Sheraton Hotel, later supported her family by working as a seamstress. Robinson attended Balch Elementary School where during his early years he was known by all as Junior.

When his parents separated in 1927, Robinson's mother took him and his sisters to stay with their grandmother in Greenwood, Georgia, then returned to Michigan to handle the divorce. She returned after one year and brought the children back to Detroit where the four of them lived on Palmer Street, pending finalization of the divorce. In Detroit, Robinson spent his free time at the Brewster Recreation Center, where he met and idolized the young **Joe Louis**, still an unknown at that time.

With the divorce papers finalized, in November of 1932 Robinson's mother brought her children to live with her in New York City. There the family rented an apartment near Times Square, at 419 W. 53rd Street. The neighborhood, an ethnic ghetto, was known during the Great Depression as Hell's Kitchen. To stay busy after school Robinson and his sisters went to the Ray Scott Studio for tap dancing lessons. After a year the family moved to Harlem, where Robinson attended Cooper Junior High School; he earned spending money by working at a fruit stand.

Smitty the Flyweight

In June of 1936, at the invitation of Reverend Frederick Cullen, Robinson began to frequent the Salem-Crescent Gym and Athletic Club in the basement of Salem Methodist Church, at 129th Street and 7th Avenue. At the club Robinson learned to box under the guidance of George Gainford, the top man of the time on Harlem's amateur boxing scene. Boxing, according to Robinson, was the only youth sport that could be played in those days without costly fees. Equipment and facilities were all available free of charge.

At age fifteen Robinson weighed 111 pounds and qualified as a flyweight boxer. He was known to his friends as Smitty. He traveled regularly to meets and tournaments with other amateur boxers from the area, but according to his mother's wishes, never fought a match.

Finally one day in Kingston, New York, Gainford needed a fill-in fighter for a flyweight bout. Although qualified by weight, Robinson was not registered with the Amateur Athletic Union (AAU) and could not fight for Gainford as a result. Determined to remain in the competition, Gainford resolved the issue by flipping through a stack of AAU identification cards that he held

Sugar Ray Robinson

for his fighters. He turned up a card belonging to Ray Robinson, a fighter who had been inactive on the boxing circuit for some time. Gainford then submitted the card to the officials and instructed fifteen-year-old Walker Jr. to answer the call for Ray Robinson to fight. Smith Jr.— fighting under the name of Ray Robinson that day—won his first-ever boxing match by a unanimous decision.

Sugar Ray Robinson

Using Ray Robinson's AAU card, Smith Jr. continued to fight on the so-called bootleg circuit. It was a bootleg operation because the fighters, who were presumed to be amateurs, pocketed $10 per win. Still fighting under the alias of Ray Robinson, Smith Jr. picked up the nickname of Sugar when a local sports editor in Watertown, New York, remarked of Robinson "That's a sweet fighter you've got there...," to which a fan rejoined, "As sweet as sugar." Still growing, and training in earnest, Robinson brought his weight up to 118 pounds and continued undefeated throughout his years as an amateur boxer. Thus, the career of Sugar Ray Robinson was born.

In 1939 then eighteen-year-old Robinson, weighing just under 116 pounds, defeated Louis (Spider) Valentine for the featherweight championship in the Golden Gloves competition. In 1940, at 126 pounds, Robinson won his second Golden Gloves championship, this time as a lightweight. Leaving behind an amateur record of eighty-five undefeated bouts, including sixty-nine

Chronology

1921	Born on May 3 in Detroit, Michigan
1932	Moves with mother and sisters to New York City
1936	Trains with George Gainford at Salem-Crescent Gym and Athletic Club; assumes the name Ray Robinson as an alias in order to compete in AAU
1940	Makes a professional debut, against Joe Echeverria on October 4 at Madison Square Garden
1941	Fights in a main event for the first time, against Sammy Angott on July 21
1942	Beats Jake LaMotta for the first time in New York City on October 2
1943	Loses first fight ever on February 5, to LaMotta in Detroit; enters basic training as a U.S. Army draftee; marries Edna Mae Holly on May 29; beats Henry Armstrong in New York City on August 27
1947	Knocks out Jimmy Doyle (who dies from injuries) in round 8 of a title bout on June 24 in Cleveland
1950	Beats Robert Villemain in Philadelphia, for Pennsylvania middleweight title; beats Charley Fusari in final welterweight defense, on August 9 in Jersey City; tours Europe in November and December
1951	Knocks out LaMotta in 13 rounds in Chicago, on February 14 for the middleweight championship; loses middleweight title to Randy Turpin in London on July 10; beats Turpin by a knockout for the middleweight title, on September 12 in New York City
1952	Loses to Joey Maxim in New York City on June 25 in a light heavyweight title bout; announces retirement on December 18
1954	Returns to ring in an Ontario exhibition against Gene Burton on November 29
1955	Beats Carl "Bobo" Olson for the middleweight title, on December 9 in Chicago
1957	Loses middleweight title to Gene Fullmer on January 2 in New York; beats Fullmer for the middleweight title, on May 1 in Chicago; loses middleweight title to Carmen Basilio on September 23 in New York; beats Basilio for the middleweight title, on March 25 in Chicago
1958	Loses middleweight title to Paul Bender on January 22 in Boston
1965	Retires on December 10 after 202 total bouts, 109 knockouts, 66 winning decisions, 6 draws, 18 losses by decision and 1 loss by knockout
1989	Dies on April 12

knockouts—with forty in the first round—he hired Curt Horrmann as a manager and turned professional that year. Sugar Ray Robinson made his debut as a welterweight on October 4 at Madison Square Garden in a bout against Joe Echeverria. Robinson won by a knockout in the second round of the scheduled four-round fight, and took a purse of $150. Just four days later he defeated Silent Stefford in Savannah, and once again it was a second-round knockout for Robinson.

Robinson earned a modest reputation and on July 21, 1941, he fought in a main event for the first time, in a contest with Sammy Angott, the reigning lightweight champion of the National Boxing Association. Angott had agreed to the fight only in a non-title bout. Robinson as a result had to weigh more than 136 pounds in order to be heavier than a lightweight. After tipping the scale at 136½ pounds at weigh-in, Robinson won the ten-round decision and pocketed a $6,000 purse for the affair. He finished the calendar year with three more knockouts and two ten-round decisions in his favor.

In 1942 Robinson signed with agent Mike Jacobs who wasted no time in contracting a fight with **Jake La-Motta** on October 2, 1942 in New York City. Robinson took the 10-round decision but four months later suffered the first loss of his career, in a re-match with La-Motta in Detroit on February 5. After defeating Jackie Wilson two weeks later in New York, Robinson dealt LaMotta a second defeat on February 26 in Detroit in a ten-round decision. On February 27 Robinson reported for induction to the U.S. Army as Private Walker Smith Jr., in compliance with a call to the draft.

Sergeant Smith

After basic training at Fort Dix, New Jersey, Robinson reported for duty as a corporal and was assigned along with Joe Louis to entertain the troops. It is worthy of note that Robinson, because of his forthright manner and conscientious regard for fair play, successfully accomplished the integration of otherwise segregated troops during those military exhibitions in which he appeared. He received an honorable discharge from the army on June 3, 1944, after taking a fall and suffering amnesia for more than one week. Robinson by the end of his military career had attained the rank of sergeant.

Six months after his induction, on August 27, 1943, Robinson went up against former three-way world champion Henry Armstrong, then thirty years old. Robinson, at age twenty-two, was greatly honored to box against one of his own boyhood heroes. The ten-round fight, arranged by Jacobs, would be the final contest of Armstrong's career. Although Robinson won by decision and was later accused of holding back in the bout, he retorted ambiguously that, "The only guys who went the distance with me were the guys I just couldn't knock out.... And I just *couldn't* knock out Henry Armstrong either."

Won the Welterweight Belt

Robinson racked up a fourth and fifth defeat of LaMotta in February and September of 1945, after which a scheduled title bout between Robinson and world welterweight champion Marty Servo was cancelled when Servo retired unexpectedly. Robinson subsequently prevailed in a ten-round decision against Angott in March 1946, and that fight proved instrumental in setting the conditions for a December 20 title bout versus Tommy Bell in New York City for the vacant welterweight championship. Robinson won the title in a 15-round decision.

After knockouts of Bernie Miller, Fred Wilson, and Eddie Finazzo, Robinson won a ten-round decision against George Abrams in New York City on May 16, 1947. All were non-title bouts, with Robinson's first welterweight title defense scheduled against Jimmy Doyle on June 24 in Cleveland. On the day of the fight Robinson tried to cancel the bout because of a dream he had the night before. In the dream, according to Robinson, he dealt a fatal blow to Doyle. Representatives from the boxing commission, and even from the Roman Catholic clergy, counseled Robinson and urged him to consider that the dream was a mere nightmare. Reluctantly he agreed to proceed with the fight.

In an eighth round knockout by Robinson, Doyle hit the mat. He raised one arm momentarily, instinctively seeking the rope, but never regained consciousness and was transported to the hospital. Jimmy Doyle died on the day after the fight, after undergoing surgery. Robinson was shaken by the event and considered ending his career. He came back cautiously over the course of that year, with five knockouts, including a sixth-round knockout in a title defense against Chuck Taylor in Detroit.

Despite a busy fight schedule, title bouts for Robinson were increasingly sparse due to a dearth of contenders. After a title defense against Bernard Docusen in June 1948 and a July 1949 defense against Kid Gavilan, Robinson gained weight and moved into middleweight contention. After a June 5, 1950, defeat of Robert Villemain for the Pennsylvania middleweight tile, Robinson just barely lost the weight necessary to defend his welterweight crown on August 9 in Jersey City against Charley Fusari. The match would be the last welterweight fight of Robinson's career.

Five-time Middleweight Champion

After defeating Fusari and subsequently defending the Pennsylvania middleweight title against Jose Basora and Carl "Bobo" Olson, Robinson spent the final weeks of 1950 on a European tour. On the Continent he fought a series of middleweight opponents and drew an immense following. During the tour he knocked out Jean Stock and Robert Villemain in Paris, Luc van Dam in Brussels, and Hans Stretz in Frankfort. He fought also in Geneva, winning a ten-round decision against Jean Walzack.

Robinson returned to the United States prepared to challenge then middleweight champion LaMotta for the belt. On February 14, 1951, Robinson defeated LaMotta by a technical knockout in the thirteenth round. He returned to Europe—more triumphant than before—in possession of the middleweight belt.

In a title defense in London on July 10, 1951, Robinson relinquished the middleweight title to Randy Turpin in a 15-round decision. After reclaiming the belt in a rematch against Turpin on September 12 in New York City, Robinson defended the title in San Francisco on March 13, 1952, against Olson. He won by a unanimous decision, and fought a second defense on April 16 against **Rocky Graziano**, defeating the contender by a knockout in the third round.

After suffering the second defeat of his career at the hands of Joey Maxim in a contention for the light heavyweight title on June 25, 1952, Robinson retired from boxing on December 18. He spent 1953 tending to a series of business enterprises and entered the performing arts as a tap dancer.

Related Biography: Boxer Henry Armstrong

Born Henry Jackson, on December 12, 1912, in Mississippi, and raised in St. Louis, Missouri, Armstrong was the only boxer ever to hold simultaneous world championship titles in three classifications: featherweight, lightweight, and welterweight.

Armstrong boxed professionally in two bouts in 1931, scoring one win, and one loss by knockout. At that time he appeared under the assumed name of Melody Jackson in order to maintain the amateur status necessary to compete in the 1932 Olympics. As it happened, he failed in his bid for the Olympic team, went to California instead, and embarked on a professional career, changing his name to Armstrong in the process.

After losing his first two professional bouts, he improved steadily and went 52-10-6 in 1936. His 27-0 record in 1937 included twenty-six knockouts. He took the featherweight title on November 19, 1937, by a technical knockout in round six, over Petey Sarron. In 1938 he went 14-0, winning the welterweight title from Barney Ross in a 15-round decision on May 31. Just weeks later, on August 17, he took the lightweight crown from Lou Ambers, also by decision after 15 rounds.

Armstrong, who earned the nicknamed Hurricane Hank for his all-out boxing style, attempted a comeback in 1943 at age 30, but retired soon after losing to Sugar Ray Robinson on August 27.

Robinson announced his return to boxing on October 20, 1954 and fought a six-round exhibition bout against Gene Burton in Hamilton, Ontario on November 29. He spent 1955 making the steady climb up the ladder of worthy opponents, in an effort to position himself in contention for a middleweight title bout against Olson, who held the belt at that time. Robinson's sixth-round knockout of Joe Rindone in Detroit on January 5 was followed by a loss to Ralph "Tiger" Jones on January 19 in Chicago. Robinson then won a ten-round decision against Johnny Lombardo in March, knocked out Ted Olla in April, and won a ten-round decision against Garth Panter in May. After defeating Rocky Castellani on July 22 in San Francisco, Robinson was scheduled to challenge Olson on December 9 in Chicago. The fight was a route, with Robinson reclaiming the title in a second-round knockout.

After successfully defending the title in a rematch with Olson in Los Angeles on May 18, 1956, Robinson lost to Gene Fullmer in New York on January 2, 1957, after fifteen rounds. Robinson reclaimed the middleweight belt for a fourth time, knocking out Fullmer in five rounds in Chicago on May 1, only to lose to Carmen Basilio in New York on September 23, in the first defense of his fourth middleweight title.

On March 25, 1958, in a rematch against Basilio, Robinson—at age 36—regained the middleweight title for an unprecedented fifth time in a 15-round decision. With no contenders, he held the title for nearly two years, until January 22, 1960, on which day he lost the belt to Paul Bender.

Although he never held another title, Robinson fought nearly fifty times more over the course of the next five years, losing in only twelve of these contests. When he celebrated his final retirement from boxing on

Sugar Ray Robinson, right

December 10, 1965, at age forty-four, he was joined ceremonially in the ring by Basilio, Fullmer, Olson, and Turpin—four of the five men who relinquished the middleweight belt to him.

Side Glimpses

Robinson, in his 1969 autobiography, professed to drinking beef blood for vitamin fortification. Perhaps it worked, because he endured a 25-year career, having fought a total of 202 bouts, of which 109 ended in knockout. He won sixty-six by decision, posted six draws and only nineteen losses—with only one loss by knockout. Critics concur that he was the most capable boxer in the history of the sport.

Robinson, who stood 5-feet-11-inches tall, never finished junior high school, having slowly abandoned his studies as his amateur boxing career materialized. Just before he dropped out of school altogether, an adolescent fling with a schoolmate led to a teenage marriage and the birth of his first son, Ronnie. The marriage was later annulled according to the wishes of the girl's parents.

On May 29, 1943, soon after his induction into the Army, Robinson married Edna Mae Holly, a dancer, in Chicago. Holly, a college graduate, proved to be a great asset for Robinson. In addition to her attractive appearance and sincere devotion to him as a partner, she encouraged him to become well spoken, an asset that greatly enhanced his public image. Their son, Ray Jr., was born on November 19, 1949. Although the two stayed together for many years, Robinson by his own admission was not the most faithful of husbands. In 1963 Holly obtained a Mexican divorce. Robinson married Mildred Wiggins Bruce on May 25, 1965.

Over the course of his professional career Robinson earned an estimated $4 million dollars and was known for his generosity as much as for his fighting ability. Following his ill-fated bout with Doyle in 1947, he gave several thousand dollars to Doyle's mother and later set up a small annuity for her. Similarly, on August 9, 1950, he donated all but one dollar of one prize purse to cancer research, in memory of Valentine, who had died of cancer and was a friend and Golden Gloves opponent to Robinson.

Awards and Accomplishments

1935-40	Fought in 85 amateur bouts; scored 69 knockouts, including 40 in the first round
1939	Won Golden Gloves (featherweight division)
1940	Won Golden Gloves (lightweight division)
1946	Won vacant World Welterweight Championship
1950	Won the Pennsylvania middleweight title; won final welterweight defense
1951	Won the world middleweight title for the first and second time
1955	Won the world middleweight title for the third time
1957	Won the world middleweight title for the fourth and fifth time

Robinson retired on December 10, 1965, after 202 total bouts, 109 knockouts, 66 winning decisions, 6 draws, 18 loss by decision and 1 loss by knockout

After a final farewell to boxing in 1965, Robinson retired to Los Angeles where he founded the Sugar Ray Robinson Youth Foundation in 1969. He died from heart problems on April 12, 1989, having suffered from Alzheimer's disease for several years prior. He lays buried in Inglewood Cemetery in Los Angeles.

SELECTED WRITINGS BY ROBINSON:

(With Dave Anderson) *Sugar Ray,* Viking Press, 1969.

FURTHER INFORMATION

Books

Markoe, Arnold, ed., and Kenneth T. Jackson. *Scribner Encyclopedia of American Lives.* New York: Charles Scribner's Sons, 2002.
Robinson, Sugar Ray, with Dave Anderson. *Sugar Ray.* New York: Viking Press, 1969.

Other

"IBHOF/Sugar Ray Robinson." www.ibhof.com/robinson. htm (February 3, 2003).
Sugar Ray Robinson: Pound for Pound. Big Fights Inc. (1978) (video).

Sketch by G. Cooksey

John Rocker
1974-

American baseball player

John Rocker caused a tempest among New York Mets fans and the general public in 1999 when he publicly

John Rocker

vented his feelings over what he saw as character flaws of the people of New York City. In his comments, originally published in a *Sports Illustrated* article, Rocker took umbrage at the city's immigrants, single mothers, homosexuals, and, of course, Mets fans. The nationwide reaction that erupted not only resulted in Rocker's temporary suspension from Major League Baseball, but also sparked a debate on the definition of free speech versus political correctness in America.

Hometown Talent Drafted by Braves

By most other accounts, Rocker at his prime was considered one of the premier "closers" in late-1990s baseball. Born in Statesboro, Georgia, Rocker came by his pitching talent early in life. He attended Presbyterian Day High School, reportedly graduating with a 3.5 grade point average. By his senior year there, Rocker, a starting pitcher, had posted three intra-school no-hitters and a pair of sixteen-strikeout games. But it was his 95-mile-per-hour fastball that caught the baseball scouts' attention.

Rocker was drafted by the Atlanta Braves in the eighteenth round of the June 1993 amateur draft. Bypassing college ball, the young pitcher instead hit the road with a Class A team. Even in the early days, Rocker earned a reputation as a temperamental eccentric, biting baseballs and letting throws from the catcher hit him in the chest. "He can get crazy," fellow Atlanta pitcher Kerry Ligtenberg told *Sports Illustrated* reporter Jeff Pearlman in the article that sparked the controversy. "He's got a real short fuse. When it goes off, it's probably better not to be around."

Though Rocker eventually enrolled in Macon, Georgia's Mercer University and finished two semesters during the off-season, baseball took precedence over his studies. By 1997 the pitcher still hadn't hit his stride, posting a 5-6 won-loss record and a 4.86 Earned Run Average (ERA) in Double-A play. The Braves sent Rocker to the Arizona Fall League, where the young man learned a lesson about playing in the big leagues: "I used to worry over every pitch, every batter," Rocker was quoted in Pearlman's article. "The coaches in Arizona talked to me about just going out and throwing. Don't worry, throw."

That advice seemed to work; on May 5, 1998, Rocker made his big-league debut with the Braves. By the end of the 1999 season, Rocker, a reliever, was throwing stronger, lowering his ERA to 2.49 and amassing thirty-eight saves and 104 strikeouts in more than seventy-one innings. His talent helped the Braves reach the National League Championship Series against the New York Mets—and that's where the trouble began.

At Full Blast

When the Atlanta team hit New York City for a series of pennant playoff games, Rocker found a partisan crowd of Mets fans greeting his appearance at Shea Stadium with boos, insults, and even thrown objects. This didn't sit well with the emotional left-hander, and he made his feelings known in the *Sports Illustrated* piece titled "At Full Blast."

First, he talked to Pearlman about the likelihood that he would ever accept a position on a New York team. "I would retire first," Rocker said. "It's the most hectic, nerve-wracking city." That was a benign comment compared to what came next. On the city's residents: "The biggest thing I don't like about New York are the foreigners. I'm not a very big fan of foreigners." Then there's the experience of riding a New York City subway: "Imagine having to take the [Number] 7 train to the ballpark ... next to some kid with purple hair next to some queer with AIDS right next to some dude who just

got out of jail for the fourth time right next to some 20-year-old mom with four kids. It's depressing." He was no more charitable to his Atlanta teammates, calling one black player a "fat monkey."

But, according to Pearlman, "Rocker reserves a special place in his heart for Mets fans, whom he began badmouthing during the regular season." Said Rocker: "Nowhere else in the country do people spit at you, throw bottles at you, throw quarters at you, throw batteries at you.... I talked about what degenerates they were, and they proved me right."

But in the court of media opinion, it was Rocker who was found guilty of being degenerate. Talk-show hosts, politicians, and sports columnists took him to task, some calling for his dismissal from the game; Rocker responded by quickly issuing a public apology, though in the view of *New York Times Upfront* writer George Vecsey, the prepared statement's "coherence and maturity make it impossible to have been written by [Rocker]. The ghostwritten mea culpa will not work." Indeed, Rocker—who told ESPN television "The last thing I wanted to do was offend people"—was fined $20,000 and suspended from play until May 2000.

His union, the players' association, filed a grievance to overturn the suspension, calling the act "without just cause," as union representative Shaym Das noted in an Associated Press wire story, which also pointed out that Rocker's punishment was more typical of a player who used drugs or engaged in similar malfeasance. Rocker's New York-based insults "[were] crude, stupid, and could've been left unsaid," wrote *Baseball Digest*'s John Kuenster, "but it was hardly deserving of a lengthy suspension from the Braves. Take a subway train in most any big city in this diverse land of ours, and you're going to see some unusual creatures sitting right across from you. So what else is new?"

A Nationwide Argument

"Off His Rocker" and "Screwball" screamed the headlines of New York's tabloid newspapers, the *Post* and *Daily News*. The papers were responding to the report that the pitcher was ordered by Major League Commissioner **Bud Selig** to undergo psychological testing and sensitivity training. This decision led pundits to wonder if Rocker's case had become one of political correctness

Career Statistics

Yr	Team	W	L	ERA	IP	H	R	ER	BB	SV
1998	ATL	1	3	2.13	38.0	22	10	9	22	2
1999	ATL	4	5	2.49	71.1	47	24	20	37	38
2000	ATL	1	2	2.89	53.0	33	23	17	48	24
2001	CLE	3	7	5.45	34.2	3	23	21	25	4
2001	ATL	2	2	3.09	32.0	25	13	11	16	19
2002	TEX	2	3	6.66	24.1	29	19	18	13	1
TOTAL		13	22	3.40	254.3	198	112	96	161	88

ATL: Atlanta Braves; CLE: Cleveland Indians; TEX: Texas Rangers.

run amok. Allan Barra of *Salon* called Rocker a "whipping boy" who "got toasted by the media for saying the same things about New York [in public] that a lot of baseball executives say to each other about New York in private." Another *Salon* columnist, Peter Collier, castigated the "politicization" of modern sports, characterizing as hypocritical the sports writers who called for Rocker's ouster. "The fact that Rocker had lived with Braves' star Andruw Jones and other black and Hispanic teammates, in his own family house, for several years counted for little," said Collier. Nor was the media satisfied with the level of Rocker's public remorse, he added. The pitcher, Collier said, had "merely apologized instead of abjectly abasing himself and crying ... and agreeing to shed his raunchy joie de vivre and spend the rest of his life as a pilgrim walking the rocky road of racial reconciliation."

Others felt Rocker got what he deserved. "The point is," wrote Clarence Page in *Philadelphia Business Journal,* "that Rocker's sentiments, expressed in a rude and crude attempt at humor, were unacceptable in a civilized society, let alone the entertainment industry known as professional sports." Rocker was returned to the Triple-A league while serving out his suspension.

An independent arbitrator cut Rocker's suspension in half, and the pitcher rejoined the Braves in training camp in March 2000. Some of his teammates angrily confronted him, leading Rocker to plead, "Please, guys, let me play." After settling some scores with his fellow ballplayers, Rocker appeared before spectators in central Florida. Some of their reactions were generous: "We still love you, John!" one woman shouted. In June Rocker returned to the mound and seemed to struggle, surrendering five runs and eight walks in his first five innings. By the end of that month, however, he seemed to have returned to form, and in a generally peaceful return to Shea Stadium, Rocker retired all three batters in the one inning he pitched against the Mets.

Though he finished the 2000 season with a 2.89 ERA, Rocker's days with the Braves were numbered. He was traded first to the Cleveland Indians, then to the Texas Rangers, who called him back from Triple-A play in Okla-

homa. Rocker's 2002 season with the Rangers was cut short by a bout with bursitis that put him on the disabled list for several weeks. He was not out of the headlines, however: Rocker reportedly got into a flap outside a Dallas restaurant in August of that year, prompting another public apology. The athlete also turned actor, taking a bit part in a Georgia-filmed horror movie, *The Greenskeeper.*

Whether or not Rocker's arm proves dependable, he will likely be remembered not so much for his throwing ability as for his temperament, which became a catalyst for public debate. Indeed, wrote David Martinson in *High School Journal,* Rocker's *cause celebre* can provide educational value: "John Rocker—paradoxical as it may be—has done the secondary school social studies teacher a genuine favor by bringing a specific example of controversial speech into a popular culture context."

FURTHER INFORMATION

Periodicals

Blum, Ronald. "Grievance Filed on Rocker Suspension." *Associated Press* (February 1, 2002).

Bowman, John. "John Rocker and the Price of Free Speech." *Business Journal* (February 11, 2000).

Elliott, Michael. "The Lesson of the Streets." *Newsweek International* (January 17, 2000).

Hoffer, Richard. "A Rocker, Sock 'Em Affair." *Sports Illustrated* (July 10, 2000).

"John Rocker, under Fire." *Economist* (June 10, 2000).

Kinsley, Michael. "Call Him Closer Outrageous." *Sporting News* (October 25, 1999).

Kuenster, John. "Politically Incorrect Remarks Can Land Today's Players in Deep Trouble." *Baseball Digest* (September, 2000).

Leo, John. "Dissing John Rocker." *U. S. News and World Report.* (February 14, 2000).

Martinson, David. "Freedom of Speech and John Rocker." *High School Journal* (October-November, 2001).

Page, Clarence. "John Rocker's Rights vs. Respect for Others." *Philadelphia Business Journal.* (January 28, 2000).

Pearlman, Jeff. "At Full Blast." *Sports Illustrated* (December 27, 1999).

Quindlen, Anna. "Ignore Them off the Field." *Newsweek* (January 31, 2000).

"Rocker's Wild Pitch." *Newsweek* (June 19, 2000).

Rushin, Steve. "Spinning Their Wheels." *Sports Illustrated* (January 24, 2000).

Vecsey, George. "Baseball's Bigmouth." *New York Times Upfront* (January 31, 2000).

Other

Barra, Allen. "John Rocker, Whipping Boy." *Salon*, http://www.salon.com (November 14, 2002).

Collier, Peter. "Mark Fuhrman in Cleats?" *Salon*, http://www.salon.com (November 14, 2002).

Sketch by Susan Salter

Knute Rockne
1888-1931

American college football coach

Knute Rockne

Knute Rockne holds college football's record for career wins as a coach. Rockne led Notre Dame's "Fighting Irish" team for 13 seasons before his untimely death in 1931, and made the Indiana school a powerhouse in the game during its day. Known for his spirited, if sometimes truth-stretching, team pep talks, Rockne helped popularize the sport at the college level and bring it—and his team—to national prominence. He revolutionized the game by introducing new strategies and techniques, still in use more than seventy years after his death.

Rockne was a native of Norway, born in a town called Voss in 1888, and came with his family to the Chicago area when he was five. They settled in a heavily Scandinavian neighborhood near Logan Square, and as a teen Rockne emerged as a star high-school athlete, though he was not particular impressive in size. He played football and baseball, and was a standout on the track team as a pole vaulter as well. He left school without graduating in 1905 after facing disciplinary measures for cutting class in order to practice track. He worked in the Chicago post office for four years as a mail handler and dispatcher, and when two friends enrolled at Notre Dame University in South Bend, Indiana, they encouraged him to join them at the Catholic school. A gifted student, Rockne worked as a janitor in the chemistry department to help pay his expenses, and began playing for its football team in 1911 as a fullback and left end.

Rockne captained the Notre Dame team during his senior year, leading the team to its third undefeated season. In one of college football's most famous plays, he and his roommate, Gus Dorais, used an impressive forward pass in a game against Army that made gridiron history. With the West Point Cadets heavily favored to win, Rockne faked a limp on the field, and when Dorais threw a forward pass, he caught it running. "In 1913, you did two things with a football: You ran with it or you kicked it," explained *Los Angeles Times* writer Earl Gustkey, and described the passing-and-running plays the two completed as "football's first all-out air attack." Notre Dame won the game, 35-13.

After he graduated magna cum laude in 1914 with a pharmacy degree, Rockne's application to enter the medical school at St. Louis University was rejected, and he took a job instead as a chemistry teacher at Notre Dame and assistant football coach. He became head coach in 1917, and though the team's first full season under him was a dismal one, with many top players serving in the U.S. military as the country entered World War I, Rockne's 1919 team finished its first unbeaten season under his watch. They repeated the feat the next year, and for the 1921 contest against rival Army, a record crowd of 20,000 turned out.

In all, Rockne would have five unbeaten, untied seasons as Notre Dame coach, and he modernized the game of football along the way. Prior to his era, teams huddled in compact groups and fought for the ball in contests of physical strength. Rockne introduced the box formation and influence blocking, and made the game more exciting for spectators with a strategy that emphasized deception and speed. He instituted what came to be called the "Notre Dame shift," also known as the precision backfield move. These and other moves perfected under Rockne were such crowd-pleasers— and so effective in eliminating opponents—that other coaches banded together and attempted have some of them barred from the official rulebook. He also began what developed into platoon football, using groups of players in various formations in an attempt to wear down the opposing team.

Notre Dame alumni and American Catholics became some of the Fighting Irish's most devoted fans. "Rock," as he was called, was regularly celebrated in newspapers and magazines for his coaching abilities, but his ability to turn a good phrase also made him famous. He was one of the first coaches to cultivate and publicize star players like George Gipp, an all-purpose back. In his 1924 season—the first in which Notre Dame finished with a national championship title—Rockne relied heavily on a quartet of players trumpeted by sportswriters as the "Four Horsemen of Notre Dame," Harry Stuhldreher, Don Miller, James Crowley, and Elmer Layden.

The 1928 season proved the Fighting Irish's worst under Rockne, with a 5-4 season finish. In one showdown that year-yet again against Army-Rockne allegedly told his losing team at halftime to "win one for the Gipper," a phrase that later gained currency through a 1940 film that starred Ronald Reagan as the gridiron hero Gipp. That day, the Irish rallied and routed Army in a game that ended 12-6. The team won two more national titles, in 1929 and 1930. By then Rockne had become Notre Dame's athletic director and designed a new stadium to hold the record home crowds.

Rockne was one of the most celebrated Americans of his era. He wrote a regular newspaper column and authored two books; he also began a second career as a motivational speaker under contract with the Studebaker Corporation, a South Bend auto maker, to deliver inspirational speeches to its sales force. Rockne even launched his own automobile company in 1931, but movie offers also came his way, and Rockne was on his way to Los Angeles to discuss one project when the plane carrying him crashed in a Kansas wheat field. The March 31, 1931 accident killed all aboard. International condolences poured in, and even U.S. President Herbert Hoover sent a telegram that called his death "a national loss."

Rockne was survived by a wife and four children. He was inducted into the National Football Foundation Hall of Fame in 1951. His every successor as Notre Dame coach has endured the inevitable comparisons. During the 2002 season, Rockne's mythic greatness

Chronology	
1888	Born in Voss, Norway
1893	Emigrates to United States and settles in Chicago, Illinois
1905	Leaves high school without a diploma
1907	Passes civil service examination and becomes mail handler at Chicago post office
1910	Begins courses at Notre Dame University
1914	Graduates from Notre Dame with a bachelor of science degree in pharmacy
1914	Marries Bonnie Skiles in Sandusky, Ohio
1914	Becomes assistant football coach and chemistry instructor at Notre Dame
1917	Advances to head coach of Notre Dame's team
1919	Finishes first unbeaten season as coach
1924	Fighting Irish win first national college football championship title
1925	Converts to Roman Catholicism
1925	Becomes athletic director at Notre Dame
1930	Finishes fifth unbeaten season and team wins third national championship title
1931	Dies in plane crash near Bazaar, Kansas on March 31

was still a vivid presence: students and supporters of the Fighting Irish, elated about the wins under a new coach Tyrone Willingham—the first African-American to hold the job at the school—took to wearing t-shirts emblazoned with one of Rockne's famous phrases, "Return to Glory."

SELECTED WRITINGS BY ROCKNE:

The Autobiography of Knute K. Rockne. Edited, with prefatory note, by Bonnie Skiles Rockne (Mrs. Knute K. Rockne) and with introduction and postscript by Father John Cavanaugh, C.S.C.; illustrated from photographs. Indianapolis: Bobbs-Merrill, 1931.

Coaching: The Way of the Winner. New York: Devin-Adair, 1931.

FURTHER INFORMATION

Books

"Rockne, Knute." *Encyclopedia of World Biography,* 2nd edition. Detroit: Gale, 1998.

Wallace, Francis. *Knute Rockne.* New York: Doubleday, 1960.

Periodicals

Drape, Joe. "Return to Glory? For Notre Dame, the Answer Just Might Be Yes." *New York Times* (September 15, 2002): 1.

Gustkey, Earl. "A Day-by-Day Recap of Some of the Most Important Sports Moments of the 20th Century." *Los Angeles Times* (January 6, 1999): 6.

Gustkey, Earl. "Rockne's Last Game Produced National Title." *Los Angeles Times* (December 6, 1999): D14.

Awards and Accomplishments

1919	Leads Notre Dame to its first undefeated season
1924	Notre Dame wins first national college football title
1925	Notre Dame beats Stanford 27-0 in Rose Bowl game
1929	Notre Dame wins second national college football title
1930	Notre Dame wins third national college football title
1930	Ends 13th season with 105-12-5 record, or .881 average
1951	Inducted into National Football Foundation Hall of Fame

Heller, Dick. "When Notre Dame Learned How to Win one for the Gipper." *Washington Times* (November 13, 2000): 14.

Sketch by Carol Brennan

Dennis Rodman

Dennis Rodman
1961-

American basketball player

Bad Boy of Basketball Dennis Rodman is perhaps more famous for his exploits off the court (as well as a few key incidents while *on* the court) than he is for his superlative play. Rodman's physical appearance is as hard to miss as the rumors and gossip that surround him. Known for his multi-hued, everchanging hair color and a penchant for adding a new tattoo at a moment's notice, as well as any number of piercings, Dennis Rodman (known also as "The Worm") is in fact one of the greatest rebounders to ever set foot on the hardwood. A student of the game who led the National Basketball Association (NBA) in rebounding for four straight years, Rodman was a key factor in bringing home championships for the Detroit Pistons and the Chicago Bulls.

Growing Up

Dennis Rodman was born in Trenton, New Jersey, on May 13, 1961. His father, Philander, would end up deserting the family when Rodman was only three, leaving his mother Shirley to try to raise her son and his two younger sisters without a father figure. As a kid, Rodman played sports, but given his small size, there was nothing fantastic about his athletic childhood. As Rodman often says, he was just regular.

When Rodman graduated from high school, he was only five foot eleven, and had failed, throughout four years, to make the varsity basketball squad. He couldn't find a place to fit in, and bounced from job to job. At one point he worked as a janitor for the Dallas-Fort Worth Airport, and on a dare from a friend, stuck the handle from his mop through a gift shop grate and stole fifteen watches. According to Mark Seal in *Playboy*, "he was arrested, jailed for a night and released after he told the cops where the watches were." The incident passed, but it contributed to the problems Rodman was having with his slacker lifestyle. The arrest infuriated his mother, who was tired of her son's inability to grow up. She threatened Rodman with an ultimatum. He had a choice: he could go to college, find another job, or, following in the footsteps of his father, enter the military. Rodman didn't choose. Getting no response, his mother packed his bags and kicked him out of the house.

Better Late Than Never

About this time, Rodman was truly "blooming late." He is said to have grown over a foot in one year, hitting an incredible growth spurt that ended up propelling his final height in the stats sheets to six foot eight (Rodman later admitted that he's really only six foot six). With his new outlook on life, Rodman entered Cooke County Junior College in Dallas, where he played basketball for a year, just long enough for him to be recognized by the coach at Southeastern Oklahoma State University, where he entered on a basketball scholarship in 1983. While at Oklahoma, he led the National Association of Intercollegiate Athletics (NAIA) in rebounding, averaging over sixteen boards per game in 1985 and almost eighteen per contest in 1986.

Chronology

1961	Dennis Keith Rodman born May 13 in Trenton, New Jersey, to Philander and Shirley Rodman
1982	Plays basketball for a year at Cooke County Junior College in Dallas
1983	Wins basketball scholarship to Southeastern Oklahoma State University
1986	Drafted in the second round of NBA draft by Detroit Pistons
1989	Has daughter, Alexis, with Annie Banks
1992	Misses opening of Pistons' training camp, saying his pending divorce and departure of coach Daly sapped his desire to play. Misses all of camp
1993	Marries Annie Banks. They'll divorce within three months
1993	Signs a 3-year contract with the San Antonio Spurs
1995	Traded to Chicago Bulls for Will Perdue
1996	Wins third NBA championship and first as a member of the Bulls; shares Finals record of 11 offensive rebounds in a game, doing so twice in Finals
1996	Signs a 20-show deal with MTV to star in series *The Rodman World Tour*
1996	*Bad As I Wanna Be* becomes a best-seller
1997	Heads Mr. Blackwell's 37th Annual Worst-Dressed Men List, a roll-call of fashion misfits
1997	Grabs 10,000th rebound of his career on January 14
1997	Suspended by NBA and fined $25,000 for kicking a courtside television photographer
1997	Takes role of "Deacon 'Deke' Reynolds" in TV show *Soldier of Fortune*
1998	Picked up by Los Angeles Lakers but only plays 23 games for the team
1999	After showing up late to a morning Los Angeles Lakers practice, Rodman sent home and let go from the team that night
2000	Cut from Dallas Mavericks before season ends. Retires from basketball
2000	Plays "Randy 'Turbo' Kingston" in feature film *Cutaway* with Tom Berenger and Stephen Baldwin
2002	Makes uncredited appearance in movie *Undercover Brother*

Awards and Accomplishments

1985-86	NAIA rebound leader
1986	All-American
1989-91	NBA Defensive Player of the Year
1989-93, 1996	NBA All-Defensive Team
1990, 1992	NBA All-Star Team
1991-94, 1997-98	Led the league in defensive rebounds
1992-98	Had 7 consecutive seasons where he led the league in total rebounds and rebounds per game

The Professional Dennis

The Detroit Pistons picked up Rodman in the second round of the 1986 NBA Draft. Coach **Chuck Daly** already had a team with aggressive players, and Rodman, whether they knew it or not, fit right in. In no time at all the Pistons took control of the league, winning back-to-back national championships in 1989 and 1990. Rodman garnered Defensive Player of the Year honors in 1990 and 1991, and it seemed that he'd found his groove.

Then the team began to disband, and when some of Rodman's teammates were traded, he became skeptical of the whole business aspect of basketball. He was vocal about the way the NBA handled its players, telling the *St. Louis Post Dispatch* that "this business is rotten." He would shortly leave the Pistons and head back to his home state to play for the San Antonio Spurs, where he helped yet another team make it to the playoffs, again leading the league in rebounding (1993-95).

On the heels of his disenchantment with the National Basketball Association, Rodman seems to have been unable to deal with the pressures and reality of the game.

Regardless of whether or not he believed that once he got to the pros it would be all roses, he began cultivating the image of troublemaker once he had announced his frustration with the system. While dyeing his hair, getting tattoos and piercings were not a reason to label Rodman a problem, he voiced his problems with the league in front of the media, and he began to act out, getting into altercations with referees (at one point head-butting a referee and getting suspended from the league for eleven games), and interrupting the play of his teammates with unnecessary technical fouls.

In 1995, Rodman was traded to the Chicago Bulls for Will Perdue, and for three seasons he continued his superlative play in the Windy City as a rebounder for **Michael Jordan** and **Scottie Pippen**. Here he would earn another championship ring (1997). But his off-the-court persona was growing rapidly at this time. Rodman, always in a high-profile relationship, had been dating Madonna, but broke it off when she allegedly wanted him to marry her and he refused. He picked up with *Baywatch*'s Carmen Electra (Rodman had a guest appearance on the program), whom he married in 1998 (they would divorce shortly thereafter).

Basketball Takes a Backseat

His desire to move his star above and beyond the basketball court pushed Rodman into the world of professional wrestling in 1997, when he joined the WCW (World Championship Wrestling). That same year he took his first major film role in a movie titled *Double Team* (he'd had a bit part in *Eddie* with Whoopi Goldberg in 1996). Though it was a less than steller debut, Rodman wasn't deterred. He followed with roles in *Simon Sez* in 1999 and *Cutaway* in 2000. Along with the big screen, he joined the cast of a small television series, *Soldier of Fortune* in 1997, and signed a deal with MTV for twenty episodes of a show that followed him around.

All of these extra-curricular activities were obviously taking their toll on Rodman's presence on-court. Add to the mix a bestseller (*Bad As I Wanna Be*) in 1996, and yet another book (*Walk on the Wild Side*) in 1997, and not many would argue that Rodman was wearing himself thin.

Career Statistics

| Yr | Team | GP | PTS | FG% | 3P% | FT% | Rebounds | | | | |
							OFF	DEF	APG	SPG	BPG
1986-87	DET	77	500	.545	.000	.587	163	169	0.7	0.49	0.62
1987-88	DET	82	953	.561	.294	.535	318	397	1.3	0.91	0.55
1988-89	DET	82	735	.595	.231	.626	327	445	1.2	0.67	0.93
1989-90	DET	82	719	.581	.111	.654	336	456	0.9	0.63	0.73
1990-91	DET	82	669	.493	.200	.631	361	665	1.0	0.79	0.67
1991-92	DET	82	800	.539	.317	.600	523	1007	2.3	0.83	0.85
1992-93	DET	62	468	.427	.205	.534	367	765	1.6	0.77	0.73
1993-94	SAN	79	370	.534	.208	.520	453	914	2.3	0.66	0.41
1994-95	SAN	49	349	.571	.000	.676	274	549	2.0	0.63	0.47
1995-96	CHI	64	351	.480	.111	.528	356	596	2.5	0.56	0.42
1996-97	CHI	55	311	.448	.263	.568	320	563	3.1	0.58	0.35
1997-98	CHI	80	375	.431	.174	.550	421	780	2.9	0.59	0.23
1998-99	LAL	23	49	.348	.000	.436	62	196	1.3	0.43	0.52
1999-00	DAL	12	34	.387	.000	.714	48	123	1.2	0.17	0.08
TOTAL		911	6683	.521	.231	.589	4329	7625	1.8	0.67	0.58

CHI: Chicago Bulls; DAL: Dallas Mavericks: DET: Detroit Pistons; LAL: Los Angeles Lakers; SAN: San Antonio Spurs.

In 1998, Rodman was picked up by the Los Angeles Lakers, who saw a need for his rebounding talents. But his personality didn't fit in with the team (in fact, his personality by this point didn't fit in with many NBA organizations), and after only twenty-three games, he was cut when the head office ran out of patience. In 2000 he joined the Dallas Mavericks, finally returning full-circle to the town where he grew up, but the team released him after only twenty-nine days. Rodman ended up retiring from basketball.

Greatness Can't Be Denied

Dennis Rodman loves his outsider image. He believes that as much as he is an athlete, he is first and foremost an entertainer. "I tried something bold," he told *Playboy* magazine, referring to his lifestyle. "I created something that everyone has been afraid of … the Dennis Rodman I was born to be."

Regardless of what basketball fans or critics think of Rodman's behavior, whether they find it reprehensible or, as Rodman hopes, entertaining, the numbers he amassed as a rebounder during his fourteen seasons in the NBA speak for themselves. He's been compared in his rebounding skills with such greats as **Wilt Chamberlain**, **Moses Malone**, and **Bill Russell**, all of whom had a height and weight advantage over the shorter, slimmer Rodman.

"I'm something I shouldn't have been," Rodman told the *St. Louis Post-Dispatch*. "I should have been an average Joe Blow, nine to five."

SELECTED WRITINGS BY RODMAN:

(With Pat Rich and Alan Steinberg) *Rebound: The Dennis Rodman Story,* Crown, 1995.

(With Tim Keown) *Bad as I Wanna Be,* Dell Books, 1997.

(With Michael Silver) *Walk on the Wild Side,* Delacorte Press, 1997.

(With David Whitaker) *Words from the Worm: An Unauthorized Trip Through the Mind of Dennis Rodman,* Bonus Books, 1997.

(Author of forword) *The Exotic Erotic Ball: Twenty Years of the World's Biggest Sexiest Party,* SPI Books, 2002.

FURTHER INFORMATION

Books

Bickley, Dan. *No Bull: The Unauthorized Biography of Dennis Rodman.* New York: St. Martin's Press, 1997.

"Dennis Rodman." *Contemporary Black Biography.* Volume 12. Detroit: Gale Group, 1996.

"Dennis Rodman." *Newsmakers 1996.* Issue 4. Detroit: Gale Research, 1996.

"Dennis Rodman." *St. James Encyclopedia of Popular Culture.* Detroit: St. James Press, 2000.

Hanson, David, and Christopher Erckmann (illustrator). *Dumb as I Wanna Be: 101 Reasons to Hate Dennis Rodman.* New York: Avon Books, 1998.

Mann, Perry (with introduction by Dennis Rodman). *The Exotic Erotic Ball: Twenty Years of the World's Biggest Sexiest Party.* SPI Books, 2002.

Rodman, B. Anicka. *Worse Than He Says He Is: White Girls Don't Bounce.* New York: Dove Books, 1997.

Rodman, Dennis, and Tim Keown. *Bad As I Wanna Be.* New York: Dell Books, 1997.

Rodman, Dennis, and Michael Silver. *Walk on the Wild Side.* New York: Delacorte Press, 1997.

Rodman, Dennis, and David Whitaker. *Words from the Worm: An Unauthorized Trip Through the Mind of Dennis Rodman.* Bonus Books, 1997.

Steinberg, Alan. *Rebound: The Dennis Rodman Story.* New York: Crown Publishers, 1995.

Periodicals

Associated Press (March 19, 1996).
Atlanta Journal and Constitution (February 22, 1996).
Chicago Sun Times (October 4, 1995).
Chicago Tribune (February 29, 1996): 1.
Detroit News (May 18, 1995): D1.
New Yorker (June 10, 1996): 84-88.
People (May 15, 1995): 137-138.
Philadelphia Daily News (January 11, 1996): S6.
Playboy (January 1996): 98.
Publishers Weekly (December 20, 1993): 57.
Reilly, Rick. "A nose ring runs through it." *Sports Illustrated* 86 (May 12, 19978): 116.
Sports Illustrated (March 4, 1996): 30.
USA Today (May 26, 1995): A1.
Wolff, Alexander. "Mr. Manners." *Sports Illustrated* 88 (May 25, 1998): 64-67.

Other

"Dennis Rodman." NBA.com http://www.nba.com/ playerfile/dennis_rodman.html (January 2, 2003).
"The Official Dennis Rodman Homepage." http:// lonestar.texas.net/~pmagal/rodman.html (January 2, 2003).

Sketch by Eric Lagergren

Alex Rodriguez
1975-

American baseball player

At a very young age, Alex Rodriguez was being compared to the greatest shortstops in baseball history. Few if any shortstops had ever combined consistent and slick fielding with powerful offensive production the way Rodriguez did in his early years. At age 26 he established a new all-time record for home runs by a shortstop in a single season, and the following year he broke his own record. He also set new standards for athletic compensation. Rodriguez's $252 million, ten-year contract with

Alex Rodriguez

the Texas Rangers in December 2000 was the most lucrative in the history of professional sports, and it caused headlines worldwide. Rodriguez became the foremost example of the well-paid modern athlete, as well as a popular and handsome celebrity. Entering his prime years and steadily increasing his power production, Rodriguez was considered a candidate to eventually become baseball's all-time career home run champion.

Great Expectations

The son of immigrants from the Dominican Republic, Alex Rodriguez was born in New York City in 1975. His parents moved him and his two siblings, Joe and Susy, to the Dominican Republican when Alex was four, and then moved again to the Miami, Florida, area when he was eight. When Alex was in fifth grade, his father, Victor, a shoe salesman and a catcher in the Dominican pro baseball league, left the family, and his parents divorced. His mother, Lourdes Navarro, worked two jobs, as a secretary and a waitress, so that she could send Alex to private school. She and the three children lived in Kendall, Florida, a suburb of Miami.

Having learned baseball from his father, Rodriguez as a child idolized major league players Dale Murphy of the

Atlanta Braves and **Cal Ripken, Jr.** of the Baltimore Orioles. At Westminster Christian High School in Miami, he was an honor roll student, devoutly religious, popular, and a sharp dresser—as well as an exceptional sports star, playing quarterback on the football team, point guard on the basketball team, and shortstop on the baseball team. In his junior year, Rodriguez batted .450 and his team won the national championship. He later credited coach Rich Hofman with teaching him to stop swinging at bad pitches. Rodriguez's baseball teammate Doug Mientkiewicz, who went out to play with the Minnesota Twins, told the *Minneapolis Star-Tribune* in 1999 that Rodriguez's greatness was already obvious in high school: "He would hit a ball hard enough to kill people." While Rodriguez was still a sophomore, scouts were projecting him as an eventual number one pick. As a senior, he hit .505 and stole 35 bases without being caught once.

The Seattle Mariners had the first pick in the amateur draft in June 1993, and they selected Rodriguez because he was the most exciting "five-tool" prospect in years: he could hit for average, hit for power, run fast, throw well, and play great defense. Agent Scott Boras, who represented many of the major league's top players, took charge of negotiations. It took more than two months to get a contract signed, a $1.3 million, three-year deal that included a stipulation that Rodriguez be called up to the major leagues no later than September 1994.

In 1994, Rodriguez played in 65 games at Class A Appleton, hitting .319, and 17 games at Class AA Jacksonville, batting .288. In mid-season, at the urging of Mariners manager **Lou Piniella**, he went directly to the major leagues. Still only 18 years old, he debuted on July 8, 1994, the youngest player in an American League starting lineup since Toronto's Brian Milner in 1978. Superstar **Ken Griffey, Jr.** insisted that Rodriguez be given a locker next to his, and from that time on Griffey both teased and advised Rodriguez. At 6 foot 3 and 195 pounds, the new kid was unusually big for a shortstop and exuded incredible confidence. "I know I'm ready," he revealed to Tom Verducci of *Sports Illustrated*. A right-handed batter, Rodriguez was hitless in three at-bats in his debut but had his first two major league hits the following day. Later that year Rodriguez was sent down to Class AAA Calgary. After the 1994 season, he played winter ball in the Dominican Republic and hit only .197, later describing it to Verducci as "the toughest experience of my life." Rodriguez returned for another call-up in 1995 after spending most of the year at Class AAA Tacoma. The Mariners knew he could play great defense, but he showed no signs of being a powerful hitter in his first two partial seasons, and when the Mariners played in two post-season series, Rodriguez stayed on the bench except for two at-bats.

Breakthrough to Stardom

In 1996, his first full year, Rodriguez put together an incredible season, becoming the youngest player since Detroit's **Al Kaline** in 1955 to win a batting championship. He hit .356, the highest batting average by a right-handed batter in the major leagues in 57 years, and scored 141 runs, with 23 home runs and 54 doubles, a new single-season record for two baggers by a shortstop. On August 29, he had five hits in a game. His 379 total bases for the season tied the all-time record for shortstops set by **Ernie Banks**. Rodriguez won the Silver Slugger Award as the best-hitting shortstop in the league, an honor he would get almost annually thereafter. Because of his earlier stints in the two previous seasons, Rodriguez was not eligible for the American League Rookie of the Year award, which went to the New York Yankees' shortstop Derek Jeter. He also narrowly lost the Most Valuable Player Award to Juan Gonzalez of Texas but was named Major League Player of the Year by the *Sporting News*.

Baseball pundits proclaimed that Rodriguez's ceiling was unlimited, and magazines gushed over his poster-boy good looks. Well-mannered, well-read, and quiet, he still made his home with his mother, and made it clear that his goal was to treat people with respect, like his idol Ripken. In the off-season, Rodriguez took classes in writing and political science at Miami-Dade Community College. He also played golf regularly.

The following year Rodriguez—who had acquired the nickname "A-Rod" to distinguish him from other players with the same last name, such as Texas's Ivan Rodriguez—experienced a "sophomore slump." But a subpar year for Rodriguez would be considered a career year for most players: he hit .300 with 23 homers and 84 runs batted in. On June 5 he became the first player in Seattle Mariners history to hit for the cycle in a nine-inning game.

In 1998, "A-Rod" became the third player in major league history up to that point to hit at least 40 home runs and steal at least 40 bases in a season, with 42 home runs and 46 steals to go with a .310 batting average and 124 runs batted in. He set an American League single-season record for home runs by a shortstop, and he became the fourth-youngest player in history to hit 100 career home runs. In April, he equaled the American

Awards and Accomplishments

1996	American League batting champion
1996	Sets all-time single-season records for doubles, matches record for total bases by a shortstop
1996	Leads American League in doubles
1996, 1998-2001	Leads American League in runs
1996, 2001-02	Leads American League in total bases
1996, 2002	Sporting News Major League Player of the Year
1996-2002	Silver Slugger Award, best-hitting American League shortstop
1996-1998, 2000-02	American League All-Star Team
1997	Hits for the cycle in game against Detroit
1998	Leads American League in hits
1998	Leads American League in at-bats
1998	Sets American League single-season record for home runs by a shortstop
2001	Leads American League in extra-base hits
2001	Sets major league single-season record for home runs by a shortstop
2001-02	Leads American League in home runs
2001-02	Leads American League in games played
2002	Leads American League in runs batted in
2002	Sporting News Major League Player of the Year
2002	Gold Glove, American League
2002	Hank Aaron Award, American League's top batter
2002	Breaks own major league record for home runs by a shortstop
2002	Player of the Year, Players' Choice Awards
2003	Wins Ted Williams Award as the major league's top hitter in 2002

League record of eight extra base hits in three consecutive games. On August 18, he had another five-hit game.

During spring training in 1999, Rodriguez tore cartilage in his knee doing an agility exercise. He underwent knee surgery and missed the first month of the regular season, yet he still managed to equal his previous high of 42 home runs and also drove in 111 runs. In August he homered in five consecutive games. However, the knee injury and a subsequent second knee injury slowed down Rodriguez on the bases, and his stolen base totals declined dramatically from 46 in 1998 to only nine in 2002.

Griffey, threatening to leave Seattle as a free agent, was traded to Cincinnati over the off-season, and in 2000 opposing pitchers refused to give Rodriguez much to hit. For the first time in his career Rodriguez had 100 walks, but he still managed 41 home runs and 132 RBI. On Sept. 30, Rodriguez had five hits, including two home runs, and drove in seven runs.

Record Contract

Rodriguez made $4.3 million in 2000 for the Mariners and was eligible to become a free agent after the season ended. Negotiations in which Rodriguez reportedly asked for perks such as the use of a private jet tarnished his image as a wholesome, hard-working player. Seattle could not afford to keep Rodriguez, and he used Boras to negotiate the richest contract in sports history, signing a $252 million, ten-year deal with the Texas Rangers in December 2000. It was more money than any baseball player had earned in an entire career and more than the assessed value of 18 of the 30 major-league teams. The quarter-billion-dollar contract became international news and fueled countless commentaries about how salaries for professional sports indicated priorities were misplaced in the United States. The deal also became a rallying cry for baseball executives who wanted to institute contract changes to get spending under control.

Seattle felt betrayed, and its fans expressed their unhappiness with Rodriguez's decision to forsake the team that had given him his start. When Texas played the Mariners in Seattle on April 16, 2001, fans threw phony dollar bills all over the field.

"I never dreamed I'd be making this kind of money," said Rodriguez. "I'm embarrassed to talk about it." He was not too embarrassed, however, to make lucrative endorsement deals with Nike, Armani, and Radio Shack. But he also did public service announcements in a national campaign for the Boys & Girls Clubs of America; as a child, Rodriguez had spent a lot of time at Miami's club after his parents' divorce.

Ironically, without its best player, Seattle won the most games of any team in baseball in 2001, while the Rangers finished in last place. Rodriguez expressed no regrets about leaving Seattle and spoke about his admiration for previous players who broke baseball's old reserve clause which bound players to one team for life. "Not one day goes by when I don't remind myself how grateful I am for those who came before me over the last 25 years," Rodriguez explained to Verducci.

While he was skewered among fans and non-baseball commentators, among those in the game Rodriguez continued to be held in high regard. "Every big league player should aspire to be like Alex Rodriguez, and I'm not just talking about his talent," Baltimore manager Mike Hargrove told Verducci. "I'm talking about the way he goes about his business, his attention to detail and his re-

Career Statistics

Yr	Team	AVG	GP	AB	R	H	HR	RBI	BB	SO	SB	E
1994	SEA	.204	17	54	4	11	0	2	3	20	3	6
1995	SEA	.232	48	142	15	33	5	19	6	42	4	8
1996	SEA	.358	146	601	141	215	36	123	59	104	15	15
1997	SEA	.300	141	587	100	176	23	84	41	99	29	24
1998	SEA	.310	161	686	123	213	42	124	45	121	46	18
1999	SEA	.285	129	502	110	143	42	111	56	109	21	14
2000	SEA	.316	148	554	134	175	41	132	100	121	15	10
2001	TEX	.318	162	632	133	201	52	135	75	131	18	18
2002	TEX	.300	162	624	125	187	57	142	87	122	9	10
TOTAL		.309	1114	4382	885	1354	298	872	472	869	160	123

SEA: Seattle Mariners; TEX: Texas Rangers.

spect for the game." And Texas manager Jerry Narron said in the same article: "He is without a doubt the best player in baseball, but that's not what impresses me the most. I only hope that someday he might be as good a player as he is a person."

With Texas, Rodriguez continued to expand his power while playing in all 162 games in each of his first two seasons as a Ranger. On May 12, 2001, he hit his 200th home run, becoming the fifth-youngest player to reach that mark. In 2001, Rodriguez set a new major league single-season record for home runs by a shortstop. He finished with 52 home runs and 135 RBI while batting .318. Rodriguez became a clubhouse leader, trying to inspire the lesser talents around him into better performances. He also deferred several million dollars of his salary to try to help Texas become a more competitive team.

In 2002, Rodriguez had another great, batting .300 with a league-leading 57 home runs and 142 RBI despite a slow start. He finished the season with 298 career home runs. At age 27, he had established himself as probably the best all-around player in baseball, winning his first Gold Glove in 2002 despite stiff competition from the league's other premiere shortstops, such as Jeter, Nomar Garciaparra of the Boston Red Sox, Omar Vizquel of the Cleveland Indians, and Miguel Tejada of the Oakland A s. Though having clearly the finest offensive season in the league, A-Rod finished second in the Most Valuable Player voting to Tejada, because many of the baseball writers who vote on the MVP refused to give top honors to players from teams with losing records.

Rodriguez was one of many players of his era to change the image of shortstop from that of a light-hitting, slick-fielding player to an overall offensive and defensive powerhouse. Despite all his remarkable batting feats, Rodriguez insisted to *Baseball Digest*'s Evan Grant: "The way I can most help my team win is with defense." Studious, movie-star handsome, quiet, and hard-working, Rodriguez might have been held in higher regard as a model athlete if he had not also been the symbol of the modern athlete's apparently unbridled greed. No matter the size of his contract, however, it appeared certain that Rodriguez would fulfill the greatness that had been predicted for him since he was in high school.

FURTHER INFORMATION

Books

The Baseball Encyclopedia. Macmillan, 1997.

Periodicals

"Alex Rodriguez (The 25 Most Intriguing People 2000." *People.* 54 (December 25, 2000): 75.

Antonen, Mel. "Alex Rodriguez: Master of Baseball Arts."*Baseball Digest.* 59 (December 2000): 60.

"Baseball: A-Rod at the Double as Players' Votes Make Him Baseball's No. 1."*European Intelligence Wire.*(October 18, 2002).

Berardino, Mike. "Looks Like A-Rod Can't Win for Losing."*Knight Ridder/Tribune News Service (South Florida Sun-Sentinel,* (September 9, 2002): K6848.

Callahan, Gerry. "The Fairest of Them All."*Sports Illustrated,* 85 (July 8, 1996): 38.

Coppola, Vincent. "At Bat for the Boys & Girls Clubs." *Adweek.* 23 (February 18, 2002): 4.

Grant, Evan. "Texas' Alex Rodriguez: A Complete Package of Talent."*Baseball Digest.* 61 (March 2002): 24.

Hein, Kenneth. "Radio Shack Shacks Up with New Pitchmen." *Brandweek,* 42 (July 2, 2001): 8.

Hickey, John. "Mariners' Shortstop Alex Rodriguez Not a Typical Superstar." *Baseball Digest.* 59 (July 2000): 40.

Kaplan, Ben. "Boy Wonder!"*Sports Illustrated for Kids,* 9 (July 1997): 36.

Knisley, Michael. "All A-Rod All the Time."*Sporting News,* 223 (June 28, 1999): 12.

Morrissey, Rick. "Seattle Fans Go Too Easy on Rodriguez."*Knight Ridder/Tribune News Service (Chicago Tribune),* (July 9, 2001): K7804.

Rains, Rob. "A New Standard."*Sporting News,* 220 (October 14, 1996): 19.

"Ready for His Close-Up: After Signing his Megadeal, A-Rod is Living like a Megastar." *Newsweek,* (April 9, 2001): 54.

Verducci, Tom. "Early Riser." *Sports Illustrated,* 81 (July 18, 1994): 39.

Verducci, Tom. "The Lone Ranger."*Sports Illustrated,* 97 (September 9, 2002): 34.

Other

"Alex Rodriguez." *Baseball Library.com,* http://www. pubdim.net/baseballlibrary/ballplayers/R/Rodriguez_ Alex.stm (December 26, 2002).

"Alex Rodriguez." *CNNSI.com Baseball,* http://sports illustrated.cnn.com/baseball/mlb/players/3099/ latest_news.html (December 26, 2002).

baseball-reference.com, http://www.baseball-reference. com (December 26, 2002).

"Ken Griffey Jr." *Baseball Library.com,* http://www. pubdim.net/baseballlibrary/ballplayers/G/Griffey_ Ken.stm (December 27, 2002).

Sketch by Michael Betzold

Chi Chi Rodríguez

Chi Chi Rodríguez
1935-

American golfer

Professional golfer Chi Chi Rodríguez has entertained generations of golf fans with his powerful drives, his victory dances, and his wisecracks. Rodríguez has been declared the longest-driving golfer ever on a pound-for-pound basis: The five-foot-seven-inch golfer, who weighed 117 pounds when he began playing on the Professional Golfers' Association (PGA) Tour in his mid-twenties, has been known to hit drives as far as 350 yards and consistently hit over 250 yards. Although he has not won a tour event since 1993 and suffered a major heart attack in 1998, Rodríguez continues to play on the Senior PGA Tour.

Disadvantaged Childhood

Life was hard for Rodríguez's family when he was a child. Rodríguez was the one of six children, and he was the sickliest. He suffered from rickets, a disease caused by vitamin deficiencies, and tropical sprue, and he nearly died of them when he was a preschooler. He still has brittle and sensitive bones as a result, but this did not stop him from participating in sports. In fact, before he became a professional golfer Rodríguez boxed and was a pitcher in a semiprofessional baseball league that in-

cluded such skilled players as **Roberto Clemente**. (Baseball gave Rodríguez the nickname "Chi Chi": he borrowed the name from another player, Chi Chi Flores, who was noted for his hard-working attitude.)

Rodríguez's parents separated when he was seven, and the children stayed with Rodríguez's father, Juan Rodríguez, Sr. He was a manual laborer who never earned more than $18 a week, but the younger Rodríguez remembers how his father shared their meager food with other hungry children. Rodríguez credits his father's example for his own generosity: After he became successful Rodríguez started his own foundation to help disadvantaged children, and he often passes up lucrative sponsored events to appear at charity benefits.

Hard Work

Rodríguez started working in the sugarcane fields for a dollar a day when he was seven, but he soon realized that better, easier money could be made working at the country club nearby. He was too small to carry a full bag of clubs, so he became a fore-caddy, a boy who watched where the customers' balls fell so that they did not have to search for them. For this job he earned 35 cents per round. As soon as he was old enough, Rodríguez became a full caddie and started playing golf himself.

Rodríguez joined the army for two years when he was 19, and then after he was discharged he came back to Puerto Rico and worked as a caretaker on a psychiatric ward. Along the way, he kept improving his golf game, even winning a base championship at Fort Sill, Oklahoma, one year. In 1957 he was hired as head caddie at the Dorado Beach resort in Puerto Rico. A professional golfer named Pete Cooper, who had won ten events on the PGA Tour, was the course pro there, and he recognized Rodríguez's natural talent and worked with him to improve his game.

After three years under Cooper's tutelage, Rodríguez was ready to try the PGA Tour himself. In 1960 Laurance Rockefeller, who was, among other things, one of the owners of Dorado Beach, gave Rodríguez $12,000 to get started, and he and Cooper headed to Michigan to play in the 1960 Buick Open. To everyone's amazement, the newcomer was tied for the lead after the open's ninth hole. His performance slipped at the end and he did not win, but he finished in the money.

The PGA Tour's Leading Comic

In the 25 years that he spent on the PGA tour, Rodríguez won a mere eight tournaments and a little over $1 million, but because of his attitude on the course Rodríguez was better known than his record would indicate. At a time when many golfers' idol was the silent, serious **Ben Hogan**, Rodríguez wisecracked for his gallery and did victory dances when he sank a putt.

His first signature victory dance, which involved throwing his ubiquitous snap-brimmed Panama hat over the hole, stemmed from an incident that happened when he was playing golf as a caddie. He and another boy were betting on a round. Rodríguez sank a 40-foot putt, but there was a toad in the hole and when the ball hit it, the toad hopped out, taking the ball with it and causing Rodríguez to lose a stroke. So Rodríguez started throwing his hat over the hole so the ball would not hop back out.

Some players on the PGA Tour, however, claimed that Rodríguez's hat messed up the turf around the hole, and he was asked to find another way to celebrate. This was the origin of his matador dance: Rodríguez "slays" the hole with his putter, wipes off the imaginary blood, and slides it with a flourish into his imaginary scabbard.

Into the Sunset with a Swing

In 1985 Rodríguez graduated to the Senior PGA Tour and almost immediately found much more success there than he had on the regular tour. He credits much of this improvement to a putting tip given to him by famed golf teacher Bob Toski, whom he bumped into in an airport in May 1986. Rodríguez has always been an excellent driver, but his putting was never very accurate. Toski told him to stand up straighter and to hit the ball with more downward force when he putts, which helps to eliminate sidespin. After getting that tip Rodríguez went on to win three tournaments in 1986, and in 1987 he won seven, including four in a row, and set the money-winning record for the senior tour. He would never have a year quite as good as 1987 again, but Rodríguez remained one of the dominant players on the senior tour through the early 1990s.

Despite suffering a major heart attack in 1998, Rodríguez continues to play competitive golf and to do all of the charitable work that he can, especially with the 450 abused and neglected children who are served each year by the Chi Chi Rodríguez Youth Foundation. In the grand scheme of things he sees the latter as more important, as he said in an interview with *Golf Digest* in 2000: "I don't care about how many tournaments I won. Winning tournaments is very important for your ego, but winning the people is very important for your soul. . . . I want to be remembered as a guy who was the kids' pal."

SELECTED WRITINGS BY RODRÍGUEZ:

Chi Chi's Secrets of Power Golf. New York: Viking, 1967.

(With Chuck Fitt) *Everybody's Golf Book.* New York: Viking, 1975.

(With John Andrisani) *101 Supershots: Every Golfer's Guide to Lower Scores.* New York: Harper & Row, 1990.

(With John Anderson) *Chi Chi's Golf Games You Gotta Play.* Champaign, IL: Human Kinetics, 2003.

FURTHER INFORMATION

Periodicals

"Chi Chi: On Helping Kids, the Death of Showmanship, and Why He Just Can't Stop the Music." *Golf Digest* (March 2000): 178.

Diaz, Jaime. "Chi Chi Has a Last Laugh." *Sports Illustrated* (November 23, 1987): 38-42.

Friedman, Jack. "At 51, Chi Chi's Still Laughing: Now It's on His Way to the Bank." *People Weekly* (September 21, 1987): 51-53.

McCoy, Doris Lee. "Golf's Good Samaritan." *Saturday Evening Post* (March, 1989): 52-53.

Other

"Chat Transcript: Chi Chi Rodriguez." PGATour.com. http://www.pgatour.com/u/ce/multi/pgatour/ 0,1977, 3657960,00.html (January 7, 2003).

Awards and Accomplishments

1963	Denver Open Invitational
1964	Lucky International Open
1964	Western Open
1967	Texas Open Invitational
1968	Sahara Invitational
1972	Byron Nelson Golf Classic
1973	Greater Greensboro Open
1979	Tallahassee Open
1981	Given Ambassador of Golf Award
1986	Senior Tournament Players Championship
1986	United Virginia Bank Seniors
1986	Given Hispanic Achievement Recognition Award
1986	Recipient of Horatio Alger Award for humanitarianism
1986-88	Digital Seniors Classic
1987	General Foods PGA Seniors' Championship
1987	Vantage at the Dominion
1987	United Hospitals Senior Golf Championship
1987	Silver Pages Classic
1987	Senior Players Reunion Pro-Am
1987	GTE Northwest Classic
1988	Doug Sanders Kingwood Celebrity Classic
1988	Named Hispanic Man of the Year by *Replica*
1989	Crestar Classic
1990	Ameritech Senior Open
1990	Sunwest/Charley Pride Classic
1990-91	Las Vegas Senior Classic
1991	GTE West Classic
1991	Vintage Arco Invitational
1991	Murata Reunion Pro-Am
1992	Inducted into the PGA's World Golf Hall of Fame
1992	Ko Olina Senior Invitational
1993	Burnet Senior Classic
1994	Inducted into the World Humanitarian Sports Hall of Fame

"Chi Chi Rodriguez: Biographical Information." PGA-Tour.com. http://www.golfweb.com/players/00/20/15/bio.html (January 7, 2003).

Chi Chi Rodriguez Youth Foundation. http://www.chichi.org (January 7, 2003).

"Juan 'Chi-Chi' Rodriguez." Latino Legends in Sports. http://www.latinosportslegends.com/chi-chi.htm (January 7, 2003).

Sketch by Julia Bauder

Pete Rose
1941-

American baseball player

Baseball's all-time leader in hits, singles, at-bats, and games played, Pete Rose has often been compared to the legendary **Ty Cobb**, whose decades-old hitting record Rose broke on September 11, 1985. Curiously, the com-

Pete Rose

parisons between Rose and Cobb don't end with their outstanding hitting abilities. Late in their respective careers, both men were accused of betting on their own teams. Cobb escaped relatively unscathed, when Kenesaw Mountain Landis, who was baseball's first commissioner, helped to cover up the allegations against him. In 1936, Cobb was one of the first players to be voted into the National Baseball Hall of Fame. Sadly, Rose may never be so honored. Because of the gambling allegations, Major League Baseball Commissioner Bart Giamatti in early 1989 suspended Rose from baseball for life. Vehemently denying the charges, Rose battled against Giamatti's ban for several months before finally agreeing in August 1989 to accept the lifetime suspension.

Born in Cincinnati

He was born Peter Edward Rose in Cincinnati, Ohio, on April 14, 1941. One of four children of Harry and LaVerne Rose, he grew up in nearby Anderson Ferry, Ohio. His father, who had once played semi-professional football, pushed Rose into sports at an early age. According to one story, Harry Rose one day went downtown to shop for a pair of shoes for his daughter but returned instead with a pair of boxing gloves for Pete. Rose spent much of his childhood playing baseball with neighborhood friends and later joined the local Little League team. At Western Hills High School in Cincinnati, he played both football and baseball but excelled particularly in the latter sport. Shortly after his

Chronology

1941	Born April 14 in Cincinnati, Ohio
1960	Begins pro baseball career with Geneva (NY) Red Legs
1963	Makes major league debut with Cincinnati Reds
1970	Becomes baseball's first singles hitter to sign six-figure contract
1989	Major League Baseball launches probe into Rose gambling charges on March 6
1989	Bart Giamatti announces Rose's suspension from baseball for life on August 24
1990	Sentenced to five months in jail on tax charges
1991	Moves from Cincinnati to Boca Raton, Florida
1997	Applies for reinstatement to baseball
2003	Commissioner Bud Selig considers reinstating Rose, if Rose admits to gambling on baseball

Related Biography: Baseball Player Ray Fosse

Pete Rose figured prominently in one of the more memorable moments of catcher Ray Fosse's baseball career. In the 12th inning of the 1970 All-Star Game, the score was tied 4-4. As Rose charged toward home base with the run that would win the game for the National League, Fosse blocked his way. Never one to be put off, Rose barreled right over Fosse, fracturing the catcher's right shoulder. Fosse, whose nickname was "Mule," played out the rest of the season despite the broken shoulder.

Born in Marion, Illinois, on April 4, 1947, Fosse was the number-one pick of the Cleveland Indians in the first-ever June 1965 free agent draft. After a couple of years in the Indians' farm system, Fosse made his major league debut for the Indians late in the 1967 season. He was injured a number of times during his years in professional baseball, missing all or parts of several seasons. He was traded in March 1973 to the Oakland Athletics, for whom he played through 1975. Back with the Indians in 1976 and the first part of 1977, Fosse played out the end of the 1977 season in Seattle, missed all of 1978 because of injury, and spent his final year with the Milwaukee Brewers in 1979. With a career batting average of .256, the injury-prone Fosse left baseball in 1979 and became an Oakland executive and broadcaster.

graduation from high school, Rose was signed to a contract by the Cincinnati Reds. Under his contract with Reds, he was first assigned to play for the Geneva Red Legs, a Reds farm team in upstate New York.

As his game improved, Rose was promoted through the ranks of the minor league teams in the Reds farm system, putting in time with teams in Tampa, Florida, and Macon, Georgia. By the start of the 1963 season, the Reds decided that Rose was ready for the big time. During spring training that year, Rose earned the nickname "Charlie Hustle" that would stick with him throughout his career. In an exhibition game against the New York Yankees, Rose won a base on balls. Rose ran out the walk, eliciting laughter from the Yankees. Yankee pitcher Whitey Ford dubbed the rookie "Charlie Hustle."

Makes Major League Debut

On April 8, 1963, Rose made his major league debut playing second base for the Reds. He played nearly every game his rookie season. With a batting average of .273 and forty-one runs batted in, Rose was named National League (NL) Rookie of the Year. In his second season with the Reds, Rose's batting average slipped slightly to .269 and his RBIs totaled only thirty-four, but he barreled back in 1965 with a batting average of .312 and an impressive eighty-one RBIs. For the next eight seasons, through 1973, Rose posted batting averages of .300 or higher every year and in 1969 hit a career-high eighty-two RBIs. In 1967, after four years at second base, Rose was switched to outfield to make room for **Joe Morgan** at second base. At the end of the 1969 season, Rose and **Roberto Clemente** were tied for the NL batting title going into the final game of the year. In his last at-bat of the season, Rose bunted for a base hit to beat out Clemente and win the title.

For the first seven years of the 1970s, the Reds were the most successful team in the National League, and Rose clearly played a major role in powering the team's climb to the top of the league. In the 1970 All-Star Game, Rose's trademark hustle pushed the NL to victory.

In the process, Rose roughed up Ray Fosse, catcher for the Cleveland Indians, in one of the most memorable plays in All-Star history. With the game tied 4-4 in the 12th inning, Rose came charging home with the winning run of the game, barreling over Fosse and separating the catcher's shoulder. After the end of the regular season, Rose fueled the Reds' drive to the NL championship in a sweep over the Pittsburgh Pirates. In the first game of the series, Rose drove in a run to break a scoreless tie in the 10th inning. He then singled during the eighth-inning rally that produced the winning run in the third game.

Leads Reds to NL Championship

In 1972 Rose, now playing left field, led the NL in hits (198) and at-bats (645), finishing the regular season with a batting average of .307. In the post-season, he batted .450 in the NL championship series against the Pirates but slipped to only .214 in the World Series, which the Reds lost to the Oakland Athletics in seven games. For Rose personally, 1973 was the best season ever. With a batting average of .338, he won his third and final batting title, was named the NL's most valuable player, and collected a career-high total of 230 hits. The Reds, however, did not fare quite as well, losing the NL championship series to the New York Mets, despite Rose's best efforts. Those best efforts included his eighth-inning homer that tied the first game of the series and a 12th-inning homer that won Game Four. Ironically, the Mets may well have been energized in their quest for the league championship by a fight Rose had in the third game with Mets shortstop Bud Harrelson.

Rose's batting average slipped below .300 in 1974 to .284, but he still managed to lead the league in runs scored with 110. He bounced back in 1975, batting .317 and knocking in a total of seventy-four runs for the season. To make room for rookie outfielder Ken Griffey, Rose moved to third base. He also led the Reds to the first of two back-to-back World Series victories. In the

Career Statistics

Yr	Team	AVG	GP	AB	R	H	HR	RBI	BB	SO	SB
1963	CIN	.273	157	623	101	170	6	41	55	72	13
1964	CIN	.269	136	516	64	139	4	34	36	51	4
1965	CIN	.312	162	670	117	209	11	81	69	76	8
1966	CIN	.313	156	654	97	205	16	70	37	61	4
1967	CIN	.301	148	585	86	176	12	76	56	66	11
1968	CIN	.335	149	626	94	210	10	49	56	76	3
1969	CIN	.348	156	627	120	218	16	82	88	65	7
1970	CIN	.316	159	649	120	205	15	52	73	64	12
1971	CIN	.304	160	632	86	192	13	44	68	50	13
1972	CIN	.307	154	645	107	198	6	57	73	46	10
1973	CIN	.338	160	680	115	230	5	64	65	42	10
1974	CIN	.284	163	652	110	185	3	51	106	54	2
1975	CIN	.317	162	662	112	210	7	74	89	50	0
1976	CIN	.323	162	665	130	215	10	63	86	54	9
1977	CIN	.311	162	655	95	204	9	64	66	42	16
1978	CIN	.302	159	655	103	198	7	52	62	30	13
1979	PHI	.331	163	628	90	208	4	59	95	32	20
1980	PHI	.282	162	655	95	185	1	64	66	33	12
1981	PHI	.325	107	431	73	140	0	33	46	26	4
1982	PHI	.271	162	634	80	172	3	54	66	32	8
1983	PHI	.245	151	493	52	121	0	45	52	28	7
1984	MON	.259	95	278	34	72	0	23	31	20	1
	CIN	.365	26	96	9	35	0	11	9	7	0
1985	CIN	.264	119	405	60	107	2	46	86	35	8
1986	CIN	.219	72	237	15	52	0	25	39	31	3
TOTAL		.303	3562	14053	2165	4256	160	1314	1566	1143	198

CIN: Cincinnati Reds; MON: Montreal Expos; PHI: Philadelphia Phillies.

first, against the Boston Red Sox, Rose, batting .370, piled up a total of ten hits, earning him the title of MVP for the 1975 World Series. The following year, Rose turned in a brilliant performance during the regular season with a batting average of .323 and sixty-three RBIs. In the post-season, the Reds swept the Yankees in the World Series, although Rose's personal stats were far less impressive with a series batting average of only .188.

Turns in Batting Average of .311

In 1977 Rose turned in a batting average of .311 and knocked home sixty-four runs. In 1978, he mounted the last serious threat to **Joe DiMaggio**'s 56-game hitting streak, pushing his personal total to forty-four consecutive games, the most for a NL player in the 20th century. Early in the season, on May 5, Rose became the youngest player ever to reach 3,000 hits. At season's end, he turned free agent, setting off a frenzied bidding war for his services. In the end, he signed with the Philadelphia Phillies and was assigned to play first base, his fifth position since his 1963 debut with the majors. In his first season with the Phillies, Rose turned in a batting average of .331 and knocked home fifty-nine runs. The following year his batting average slipped to .282 during the regular season, but he played well enough to help Philadelphia win its first-ever World Championship. In the ninth inning of the sixth game of the World Series, the Phillies were leading 4-1, but the Kansas City Royals had loaded the bases.

Royal Frank White's pop-up foul bounced out of catcher Bob Boone's glove but was caught by Rose to prevent a possible tragedy. The Phillies took the series, four games to two.

During the 1981 season, shortened by a players' strike, Rose had his last .300 season and led the NL in hits. Already forty years of age, it was clear that Charlie Hustle's career was winding down, but attention remained focused on Rose as he edged ever closer to Ty Cobb's career hitting record of 4,192 hits. The night after the players' strike ended in August, Rose passed **Stan Musial** as the NL's all-time leading hitter. At the end of the 1981 season, Rose's total stood just shy of 3,700 hits, less than 500 from the magic mark. In 1982, his batting average slipped to .271, but he managed to add another 172 hits, bringing his total to within 323 hits of Cobb's record. During 1983, the final year of his contract with the Phillies, Rose batted only .245, but he helped the Phillies make a return visit to the World Series, which Philadelphia lost to the Baltimore Orioles in five games. By season's end, Rose's career hit total had moved up to 3,990, only 202 hits away from the magic mark.

Signed by Montreal Expos

In 1984 the Montreal Expos, looking for a marquee name to energize the team's home ticket sales, signed Rose, who celebrated his 43rd birthday a day early by

Pete Rose

Awards and Accomplishments

1963	Named National League Rookie of the Year
1964	Hits only grand slam of career on July 18
1965,	Voted to All-Star Team
1967-71,	
1973-82,	
1985	
1966	Hits home runs right- and left-handed in a single game on August 30
1969	Edges out Roberto Clemente to win NL batting title
1969	Wins NL Gold Glove Award as outfielder
1970	Wins NL Gold Glove Award as outfielder
1973	Collects 2,000th hit on June 19
1973	Named NL Most Valuable Player
1975	Named World Series MVP
1978	Collects 3,000th hit on May 5
1978	Hitting streak ends at 44 games
1981	Breaks Stan Musial's all-time hitting record
1985	Breaks Ty Cobb's all-time hitting record with 4,193rd hit

posting the 4,000th hit of his career. However, by July the Expos had benched Rose because of his failure to hit consistently. On August 16, Charlie Hustle was traded back to the Reds, this time as player-manager. Rose repaid the Reds for their vote of confidence by batting .365 for the remainder of the season. As the 1985 season began, Rose's all-time hitting record stood at 4,097, less than 100 hits away from Cobb's 4,192. Excitement mounted as Rose marched inexorably toward a new hitting record. The hitter's hometown of Cincinnati in 1985 named a street near the city's Riverfront Stadium in Rose's honor. Late in the season, on September 11, Rose, batting left-handed, hit a single to the left off San Diego Padres pitcher Eric Show, landing himself in the record books with his 4,193rd hit. Rose managed to collect nearly a quarter of his career hits after the age of thirty-eight.

As player and manager, Rose helped guide the Reds to a second-place finish in the NL West in both 1985 and 1986, his last year as an active player. In his final appearance as a major league player on August 17, 1986, Rose, batting as a pinch hitter, struck out against pitcher Goose Gossage of the Padres. To make room for pitcher Pat Pacillo, Rose was officially dropped from the Reds' 40-man roster on November 11, 1986. He returned as manager in 1987 and 1988 but was suspended for thirty days by Baseball Commissioner Bart Giamatti in May 1988 after a headline-grabbing shoving incident. Rose's shoving match with umpire Dave Pallone caused a near-riot in Cincinnati. But the worst was yet to come.

Faces Charges of Betting on Baseball

The gambling scandal that was to forever mar Rose's baseball career began to take shape in 1984, when the Cincinnati hitter started to spend an increasing amount of time with a group of men he'd met at a gym in Cincinnati. This group introduced Rose to some bookmakers, and over time he allegedly developed a gambling habit that ultimately reached $15,000 a day and included bets on baseball, including games played by his own team. After reports of Rose's alleged gambling activities reached the offices of Major League Baseball, an investigation into the charges was launched early in 1989. Finally, after the probe was concluded, Commissioner Giamatti on August 24, 1989, permanently banned Rose from major league baseball. A five-page document signed by both Giamatti and Rose included no formal findings, but Giamatti said he considered Rose's acceptance of the ban to be a no-contest plea to the charges.

Whether Major League Baseball ever relents and eases its sanctions against Rose is anybody's guess. Early in 2003, Commisioner of Baseball **Bud Selig** was considering reinstating Rose, if the former player admitted to gambling on his own team, something Rose had always refused to admit to. Reportedly, Rose was willing to "come clean" if it meant possible reinstatement. In the meantime, the ban and the reasons for its imposition have tainted one of the most brilliant careers in baseball history and in the process given the "Charlie Hustle" nickname an alternate and less than wholesome alternate meaning.

However, nothing in the gambling allegations against Rose can alter the monumental performance of Charlie Hustle on the ball field. Nearly two decades after he set the new hitting record, Rose's career 4,256 hits stands as a mark for other ambitious batters to shoot for. And even when Rose's record falls, as eventually it almost certain-

---

Agreement and Resolution In the Matter of: Peter Edward Rose "2"

Therefore, the Commissioner, recognizing the benefits to Baseball from a resolution of this matter, orders and directs that Peter Edward Rose be subject to the following disciplinary sanctions, and Peter Edward Rose, recognizing the sole and exclusive authority of the Commissioner and that it is in his interest to resolve this matter without further proceedings, agrees to accept the following disciplinary sanctions imposed by the Commissioner:

   a. Peter Edward Rose is hereby declared permanently ineligible in accordance with Major League Role 21 and placed on the Ineligible List.

   b. Nothing in this Agreement shall deprive Peter Edward Rose of the rights under Major League Rule 15 to apply for reinstatement. Peter Edward Rose agrees not to challenge, appeal, or otherwise contest the decision of, or the procedure employed by, the Commissioner or any future Commissioner in the evaluation of any applications for reinstatement.

   c. Nothing in this agreement shall be deemed either an admission or a denial by Peter Edward Rose of the allegation that he bet on any Major League Baseball game.

Source: Office of the Commissioner of Baseball, "Agreement and Resolution," August 23, 1989.

---

ly will, he will be remembered as one of baseball's greats, whether or not he is ever enshrined in the National Baseball Hall of Fame.

CONTACT INFORMATION

Address: Pete Rose, c/o Pete Rose Ball Park Café, 1601 N. Congress Ave., Boynton Beach, FL 33426. Email: whg222@aol.com. Online: http://www.peterose.com.

SELECTED WRITINGS BY ROSE:

The Official Pete Rose Scrapbook: The Life, Times, and Record-Smashing of Charlie Hustle, Prentice Hall, 1975.
(With Bob Hertzel) *Pete Rose's Winning Baseball,* McGraw-Hill, Contemporary Books, 1976.
Pete Rose: My Life in Baseball, Doubleday, 1979.
(With Hal Bodley) *Countdown to Cobb: My Diary of the Record-Breaking 1985 Season,* Sporting News, 1985.
Pete Rose: My Story, MacMillan, 1989.
(With Roger Kahn) *Ballplayer! The Headfirst Life of Peter Edward Rose,* Warner Books, 1990.

FURTHER INFORMATION

Books

"Pete Rose." *American Decades CD-ROM.* Detroit: Gale Group, 1998.
"Pete Rose." *Encyclopedia of World Biography Supplement,* Vol. 21. Detroit: Gale Group, 1998.
"Pete Rose." *St. James Encyclopedia of Popular Culture,* 5 vols. Detroit: St. James Press, 2000.

Other

"Agreement and Resolution." DowdReport.com. http://http://www.dowdreport.com/agreement.pdf (November 16, 2002).
"Biography." Pete Rose's Official Web Site. http://www.peterose.com/bio.htm (November 1, 2002).
"Chronology of Rose Case." Cincinnati.com. http://reds.enquirer.com/2001/08/08/red_chronology_of_rose.html (November 16, 2002).
"Pete Rose." Baseball-Reference.com. http://www.baseball-reference.com/r/rosepe01.shtml (November 1, 2002).
"Ray Fosse." BaseballLibrary.com. http://www.pubdim.net/baseballlibrary/ballplayers/F/Fosse_Ray.stm (November 18, 2002).

Sketch by Don Amerman

Patrick Roy
1965-

Canadian hockey player

One of the greatest goalies to ever play the game, Patrick Roy was a dominant goalie from his rookie season in Montreal in which he lead the Montreal Canadiens to a Stanley Cup. In addition to winning four Stanley Cups with Montreal and the Colorado Avalanche, Roy also won three Conn Smythe Trophies as playoffs most valuable player. Roy also surpassed **Terry Sawchuk** as the NHL goalie with the most regular season wins.

Roy was born on October 5, 1965, in Quebec City, Quebec, Canada, the son of Michel and Barbara Roy. His father was the vice president of the Quebec Automobile Insurance Board, while his mother was a real estate agent who was also a champion synchronized swimmer and swim coach. Roy's brother Stephanne was a forward who was drafted in the pros. Roy himself began playing hockey as a child, and decided to be a goalie when he was seven.

Drafted by the Canadiens

In 1984, Roy was drafted by the Montreal Canadiens with the 51st pick. At the beginning of the season, he remained in major junior hockey, playing with the Granby Bisons in the Quebec Major Junior Hockey League. This was a very bad team, and Roy's goals against average was 5.55 in forty-four games. He was then called up to the Sherbrooke Canadiens in the American Hockey League. The team won Calder Cup with Roy in net. Fi-

Patrick Roy

nally, he joined the Montreal Canadiens at the end of the 1984-85 season playing in one game, a win.

Won Stanley Cup

In 1985-86, Roy was one of the two goalies (the other being Brian Hayward) carried by the Canadiens during the regular season. He posted a respectable regular-season record of 23-18-3 with goals against of 3.35, and carried much of the load during the playoffs. Though a rookie, Roy played like a veteran. During the playoffs, he had a record of 15-5 with a 1.92 goals against average. Montreal defeated the Calgary Flames to win the Stanley Cup. Roy was named playoff MVP, the youngest player to ever win the honor. He made $80,000 for the season. Roy was one of the keys to Montreal's success, but he also had a great defense in front of him. He was still developing his butterfly style of play. He had some flaws in his style, included angles and puck handling, but corrected them. It was also revealed that Roy had some goalie quirks, including that he talked to his goalposts telling them they will all play well and no pucks will go in.

Describing his goaltending style, Robin Finn of the *New York Times* wrote, "the lanky Roy shimmies and shivers in his crease like a twitching stork. While his positioning is usually impeccable, he rarely remains statuesque for long, and tends to flail his way to the ice in pursuit of rebounds."

Roy could not immediately follow-up this success. In 1987 and 1988, he put much pressure on himself to repeat with the Stanley Cup, instead of focusing on winning in the first round of the playoffs. Though he was nominated for the Vezina Trophy, the award given to the best goalie in the NHL, he had more improvement in 1988-89 as he became more consistent in the regular season.

Roy finally won his first the Vezina Trophy in 1989, a year in which he lead the league with a 2.47 goals against average. He also won the Vezina in 1990 and 1992. In 1991-92, Roy lead the league with a 2.36 goals against average, but the Canadiens lost in the second round to the Boston Bruins.

Won Second Cup with Montreal

Though Roy had a relatively poor regular season in 1992-93, posting a career high goals against of 3.20, and was not even nominated for the Vezina, he rebounded in the playoffs. Backstopping the Canadiens to another Stanley Cup, Roy won ten straight overtime games in the playoffs. He had a playoff record of 16-4, with a 2.13. Montreal defeated the Los Angeles Kings to win the Stanley Cup. Roy was again awarded the Conn Smythe Trophy.

Traded to Colorado

Roy did not live up to the expectations of the rabid Montreal fans and media, especially when the team missed the playoffs in 1995. Already known for having a temper, during a game in December 1995, Roy acted out when the first-year Montreal coach Mario Tremblay did not take him out of a game in which he was losing badly, something that was generally done. Roy declared he would never play for the Canadiens again. He was suspended, then traded to the Colorado Avalanche. This blowup was not the only reason he was traded. Roy was making the highest salary in Montreal—$2.8 million per season—on a team that had money issues.

Though Roy was traded, he went into a good situation. The Avalanche won the Stanley Cup in 1996, defeating the upstart Florida Panthers. Roy was in net as

Career Statistics

Yr	Team	GP	W	L	T	GAA	TGA	SV	SV%	TSA
1984-85	Montreal	1	1	0	0	0.00	0	2	1.000	2
1985-86	Montreal	47	23	18	3	3.35	148	1037	.875	1185
1986-87	Montreal	46	22	16	6	2.93	131	1079	.892	1210
1987-88	Montreal	45	23	12	9	2.90	125	1123	.900	1248
1988-89	Montreal	48	33	5	6	2.47	113	1115	.908	1228
1989-90	Montreal	54	31	16	5	2.53	134	1390	.912	1524
1990-91	Montreal	48	25	15	6	2.71	128	1234	.906	1362
1991-92	Montreal	67	36	22	8	2.36	155	1651	.914	1806
1992-93	Montreal	62	31	25	5	3.20	192	1622	.894	1814
1993-94	Montreal	68	35	17	11	2.50	161	1795	.918	1956
1994-95	Montreal	43	17	20	6	2.97	127	1230	.906	1357
1995-96	Montreal	22	12	9	1	2.95	62	605	.907	667
1995-96	Colorado	39	22	15	1	2.68	103	1027	.909	1130
1996-97	Colorado	62	38	15	7	2.32	143	1718	.923	1861
1997-98	Colorado	65	31	19	13	2.39	153	1671	.916	1825
1998-99	Colorado	61	32	19	8	2.29	139	1534	.917	1673
1999-2000	Colorado	63	32	21	8	2.28	141	1499	.914	1640
2000-01	Colorado	62	40	13	7	2.21	132	1381	.913	1513
2001-02	Colorado	63	32	23	8	1.94	122	1507	.925	1629
TOTAL		966	516	300	118	2.61	2409	24221	.900	26630

Colorado: Colorado Avalanche (NHL); Montreal: Montreal Canadiens (NHL).

the Avalanche went to the playoffs each year 1997-2001, but did not repeat as Stanley Cup champions until 2001. Roy again won the Conn Smythe Trophy. In 2002, Roy again had great a regular season with a 1.94 goals against. While he kept team going in the 2002 post-season, he lost to Detroit in Western Conference Finals, letting in six goals in the seventh and deciding game of the series. The defeat did nothing to shake his confidence, and Roy did not plan on retiring in the near future.

Roy is generally recognized as a great goalie who changed the position and how it is played, refining the butterfly style. He also owns two significant records that cemented his reputation. In October 2000, in a game against the Washington Capitals, he bested Terry Sawchuk's record for regular season wins by a goalie with 448 plus and counting. He already held the record for playoff wins with 121 (before the 2001 playoffs). As Michael Farber wrote in *Sports Illustrated*, "outside the box of numbers and awards ... Roy is the most important goalie in history."

CONTACT INFORMATION

Address: c/o Colorado Avalanche, Pepsi Center, 1000 Chopper Circle, Denver, CO 80204.

FURTHER INFORMATION

Books

Hickok, Ralph. *A Who's Who of Sports Champions: Their Stories and Records.* Boston: Houghton Mifflin Company, 1995.

Periodicals

Bloom, Barry M. "Montreal's avalanche." *Sport* (January 1997): 63.

Dater, Adrian. "Avs' Roy faces former team." *Denver Post* (December 6, 2002): D9.

Dater, Adrian. "Deconstructing Patrick Roy." *Sporting News* (April 29, 2002): 52.

Dater, Adrian. "'Motown Meltdown' is long over." *Denver Post* (October 9, 2002): E4.

Dater, Adrian. "Roy plans to play a few more years." *Denver Post* (June 23, 2002): C1.

Farber, Michael. "Canada's net result." *Sports Illustrated* (February 23, 1998): 100.

Farber, Michael. "King no more." *Sports Illustrated* (December 18, 1995): 42.

Farber, Michael. "King of the Ice." *Sports Illustrated* (April 8, 2002): 64.

Farber, Michael. "Now or Never." *Sports Illustrated* (April 16, 2001): 42.

Farber, Michael. "St. Patrick." *Sports Illustrated* (May 28, 2002): 58.

Finn, Robin. "2 Pillars of Humility." *New York Times* (May 19, 1989): B19.

Frei, Terry. "Avalanche notes: Roy likes current workload." *Denver Post* (October 25, 2002): D7.

"Inside the NHL." *Sports Illustrated* (October 23, 2000): 90.

Kravitz, Bob. "King of the Kiddie Corps." *Sports Illustrated* (October 13, 1986): 38.

Paige, Woody. "Greatest athlete, period." *Denver Post* (September 20, 2002): D1.

"Roy Captures No. 400 for Red-Hot Colorado." *Washington Post* (February 6, 1999): D6.

Awards and Accomplishments

1985	Was in net for the Sherbrooke Canadiens (AHL) when the won the Calder Cup
1986	*Sport Magazine*'s playoff MVP
1986, 1993	Won Stanley Cup with the Montreal Canadiens
1986, 1993, 2001	Conn Smythe Trophy as playoff MVP
1989-90, 1992	Vezina Trophy as league's outstanding goalie
1996, 2001	Won Stanley Cup with the Avalanche
2002	All-Star (first team)

Swift, E.M. "The Habs Have a Hot One." *Sports Illustrated* (May 19, 1986): 32.

Swift, E.M. "Saving Grace." *Sports Illustrated* (June 21, 1993): 26.

Tyrangiel, Josh. "People." *Time* (October 30, 2000): 107.

Other

"Bob Hartly: Head Coach." Colorado Avalanche Web Site. http://ww.coloradoavalanche.com/team/hartley.html (December 16, 2002).

"Patrick Roy," ESPN.com. http://sports.go.com/nhl/players/statistics?statsId=440 (December 14, 2002).

Sketch by A. Petruso

Pete Rozelle

Pete Rozelle
1926-1996

American football commissioner

For nearly three decades, Pete Rozelle guided professional football as the commissioner of the National Football League (NFL). Under his direction, pro football attained unprecedented popularity with the American public, as well as a level of profitability that far exceeded anything seen before Rozelle. He engineered the merger of the rival American Football League (AFL) into the NFL, paving the way for the annual Super Bowl, a face-off between the best in the American Football Conference (AFC) and the National Football Conference (NFC). Upon Rozelle's death in 1996, Lamar Hunt, owner of the Kansas City Chiefs, told *USA Today*: "I think his greatest achievement was to supervise and organize growth at a time when other sports were battling and fighting among themselves. He had the ability to create compromise and make things work." A Gallup Poll in 1960, the year Rozelle took over the reins of the NFL, showed that thirty-four percent of Americans named baseball as their favorite sport, while twenty-one

percent preferred football. In just the first twelve years of Rozelle's leadership of the NFL, the game's popularity skyrocketed. In another Gallup Poll taken in 1972, thirty-six percent of Americans picked football as their favorite sport, while baseball had fallen to a popularity rate of only twenty-one percent.

Born Near Los Angeles

He was born Alvin Ray Rozelle in South Gate, California, near Los Angeles, on March 1, 1926. His uncle gave him the nickname "Pete" when Rozelle was only five years old. Raised in nearby Compton, Rozelle showed an early interest in sports, playing tennis and basketball for Compton High School. He graduated from Compton High in 1944 with World War II still raging in Europe and the Pacific. Fresh out of high school, Rozelle enlisted in the U.S. Navy, in which he served until 1946. After leaving the Navy, he returned to California and enrolled at Compton Junior College, where he served as the school's athletic news director. Rozelle also worked briefly as an assistant to the public relations director of the Los Angeles Rams, which had selected the junior college's athletic fields for its training camp. After completing two years at the junior college, he headed north to continue his studies at the University of San Francisco (USF). He remained close to sports at USF by editing the Rams' game programs in his spare time. While still a student at USF, Rozelle married Jane Coupe of Chicago, whom he had met while in the Navy.

Chronology

1926	Born in South Gate, California, on March 1
1944	Graduates from Compton (CA) High School
1944-46	Serves in U.S. Navy
1946-48	Attends Compton Junior College
1949	Marries Jane Coupe of Chicago (later divorced)
1950	Graduates from University of San Francisco and becomes university's athletic news director
1952	Goes to work for Los Angeles Rams as public relations director
1955	Joins public relations firm of P.K. Macker in San Francisco
1957	Replaces Tex Schramm as general manager of the Rams
1960	Elected commissioner of National Football League
1974	Marries Carrie Cooke
1989	Retires from NFL
1996	Dies of cancer in Rancho Santa Fe, California, on December 6

Awards and Accomplishments

1960	Moved headquarters of NFL to New York City
1961	Won antitrust exemption allowing NFL to negotiate TV contracts collectively
1966	Engineered merger of American Football League into the NFL and subsequent organizational changes
1969	Negotiated contract with ABC-TV creating "Monday Night Football"
1977	Negotiated four-year TV deal with ABC, CBS, and NBC
1982	Negotiated five-year, $2.1 billion contract with ABC, CBS, and NBC
1985	Elected to Pro Football Hall of Fame
1985	Won Tuss McLaughry Award of the American Football Coaches Association

The couple, who eventually divorced, had a daughter, Anne Marie, born in 1958.

After graduation in 1950, Rozelle went to work for USF as its athletic news director. In that job, he attended a broad range of sporting events, building a network of contacts that would serve him well in the years to come. In 1952, **Tex Schramm**, general manager of the Rams, hired Rozelle as the team's public relations director. He stayed with the Rams for three years until 1955 when he left to join the San Francisco public relations firm of P.K. Macker. When Schramm left the Rams in 1957 after conflicts with some of the team's owners, NFL Commissioner **Bert Bell** asked Rozelle to take over as general manager of the Rams. The new general manager's ability to resolve conflicts within the Rams organization was particularly impressive to **Dan Reeves**, who owned fifty percent of the team.

Replaces Bell at Helm of NFL

After the sudden death of Bell in 1959, NFL team owners met in 1960 to find a successor and also map a strategy against the rival AFL. When owners deadlocked on Bell's replacement, Reeves offered Rozelle as a compromise candidate. Over the opposition of some of the league's most influential owners, Rozelle was elected the new NFL commissioner. He set to work immediately to convince NFL team owners to pool all media revenues and share them equally among all teams, putting each franchise on an even footing with the others. The rival AFL had already announced its intentions to follow a similar policy, and Rozelle thought the NFL needed to do the same to ensure its competitiveness against the new league. He also urged that the NFL provide a united front for the teams by bargaining collectively with the television networks for coverage contracts. To accomplish the latter, Rozelle was forced to argue before Congress for an exemption from the Sherman Antitrust Act. In September 1961 Congress approved such an exemption for the NFL.

As its television exposure grew, football attracted more and more fans. In 1962 Rozelle negotiated a $9.3 million contract with CBS TV. Football's growing popularity benefited not only the NFL but the rival AFL. The two leagues became locked in a costly bidding war for new players during the first half of the 1960s. By 1966, the situation had become untenable. Rozelle consulted with team owners in both leagues to promote the idea of a merger between the rival organizations. He also went back to Congress to argue for another exemption from antitrust law to make such a merger possible. He was successful on both fronts, and the AFL was merged into the NFL in 1966. The AFL became the American Football Conference (AFC), while the NFL teams were grouped in the National Football Conference (NFC). The merger and related organizational changes paved the way for the first Super Bowl, which was played between the Green Bay Packers of the NFC and the Kansas City Chiefs of the AFC in January 1967. A few years later, in 1969, Rozelle negotiated a contract with ABC TV creating "Monday Night Football." In 1974, Rozelle married Carrie Cooke, the former daughter-in-law of Washington Redskins owner Jack Kent Cooke.

New Challenges Emerge

Despite the rapid ascendancy of the NFL under Rozelle's leadership, new challenges continued to emerge. A new rival, the World Football League, was launched in 1972 but was disbanded only three years later for lack of adequate financial support. Over the objections of Rozelle and the city of Oakland, California, the Oakland Raiders in 1980 moved to Los Angeles when it was able to negotiate a more favorable lease on a stadium in Southern California. The NFL and Oakland asked the courts to block the Raiders' move but were rebuffed when the courts ruled that such NFL constraints on teams' ability to move would violate antitrust laws. Another challenge arose over the matter of players' contractual rights. For most of its history, NFL rules forced players to renegotiate only with their team rather than

Related Biography: NFL Commissioner Paul Tagliabue

Like his predecessor as NFL commissioner, Paul Tagliabue's boyhood passion was basketball and not football. After he was sidelined by a ligament tear in his sophomore year at Georgetown, he began spending more time on academics, leading him eventually into a career in law. It was as a lawyer that Tagliabue first came into close contact with the NFL.

He was born Paul John Tagliabue in Jersey City, New Jersey, on November 24, 1940, the third of four sons born into a working-class family with roots in Italy. As a boy, he excelled in both academics and sports, playing three sports at his Jersey City high school. It was his prowess at basketball, however, that eventually won him a scholarship to Georgetown University in Washington, D.C. After graduating from Georgetown, he studied law at New York University. He began his career as a law clerk in the U.S. Claims Court in 1965. In 1969 he joined Covington & Burling, where he gradually took on more and more of the firm's NFL account. In the 1980s, Tagliabue became a managing partner at the firm and was made its lead lawyer on NFL matters. The decade saw an explosion of litigation involving the NFL, during which Tagliabue became a close adviser to NFL Commissioner Pete Rozelle.

Ironically, the flood of litigation that brought Tagliabue closer to the NFL and Rozelle are believed to have played a large part in Rozelle's decision to retire from the league in 1989. Tagliabue was tapped as Rozelle's successor. Of Tagliabue's qualifications for the job, Minnesota Viking President Mike Lynn told the *St. Paul Pioneer Press*: "He's a forward-thinking man. He's a man of ideas who can take us into the next century."

Tagliabue and his wife, Chandler, whom he married in 1965, live in New York City, which is also home to the headquarters of the NFL. The couple has two children, Drew and Emily.

offer their services to all NFL teams. After the merger of the AFL into the NFL, Rozelle had instituted what came to be known as the Rozelle Rule. The rule required any team that signed a player that previously belonged to another team to pay compensation for the lost player, and it had a chilling effect on the signing of free agents within the league. Players struck in 1982 and 1987 to win some form of free agency. Eventually the Rozelle Rule was suspended, and a controlled form of free agency was put into effect, along with a salary cap

With Rozelle skillfully leading negotiations, the NFL's television revenues continued to climb steadily through the 1970s and into the 1980s. In 1982 the NFL signed a five-year, $2.1 billion contract with ABC, CBS, and NBC to televise all regular season and post-season games. In 1987, the league and the three broadcast networks concluded a three-year contract worth just over $1.4 billion. That same year the NFL signed its first contract with a cable television network, agreeing to let ESPN broadcast thirteen prime-time games over the course of a three-year contract.

Elected to Hall of Fame

Rozelle in 1985 won some long overdue recognition when he was inducted into the Pro Football Hall of Fame while still active in professional football. This was a unique honor in that most Hall of Fame candidates are not inducted until after the end of their football career. Despite all that Rozelle had done to strengthen professional football and increase its popu-

larity, the latter half of the 1980s saw a gradual erosion of faith in his leadership among NFL team owners. In 1989, with two years remaining on his contract, Rozelle reluctantly stepped down as NFL commissioner. He served briefly on the board of directors of NTN Communications Inc. of Carlsbad, California, but spent most of his time at his home in Rancho Santa Fe. A heavy smoker for much of his life, Rozelle died of cancer on December 6, 1996.

Probably no single person has had as profound an effect on a sport as Rozelle had upon football. After his death at the age of seventy, friends and professional colleagues alike were lavish in their praise of Rozelle's contributions. Lifelong friend Don Klosterman told *USA Today*: "He was the most incredible person I've ever met. Given that power, he never had an ego. A lot of people can't live with success. He was so easy with it. He was never a showboat." One of the highest tributes came from Paul Tagliabue, Rozelle's successor as NFL commissioner. Tagliabue told the *Minneapolis Star Tribune:* "No one was more responsible for the success of the National Football League and public passion for the NFL game than Pete Rozelle. Though he would credit others, Pete was the driving force in changing the face of professional sports in this country. His vision, integrity, and commitment made him the ideal leader."

SELECTED WRITINGS BY ROZELLE:

The Super Bowl, Random House, 1991.
(With Joseph Hession) *Forty Niners*, Foghorn Press, 1993.

FURTHER INFORMATION

Books

Harris, David. *League: The Rise and Decline of the NFL*. New York: Bantam Books, 1986.
"Paul Tagliabue." *Newsmakers 1990*. Issue 2. Detroit: Gale Group, 1990.
"Pete Rozelle." *Encyclopedia of World Biography Supplement,* Volume 19. Detroit: Gale Group, 1999.
"Pete Rozelle." *Newsmakers 1997*. Issue 4. Detroit: Gale Group, 1997.

Periodicals

Celizic, Mike. "More Than a Visionary, Rozelle Exuded Class." *Record* (Bergen County, NJ) (December 8, 1996): S13.
Forbes, Gordon. "Deft Negotiating Touch Good as Gold for NFL." *USA Today* (December 9, 1996): 4C.
Glauber, Bob. "1926-1996: Rozelle Got Last Word In on Detractors." *Newsday* (December 8, 1996): B6.

Jones, Del. "League Community Mourns Former Leader's Death." *USA Today* (December 9, 1996): 4C.

Kindred, Dave. "Most Significant Developments This Century: No. 4, Pete Rozelle Becomes NFL Commissioner." *Sporting News* (April 21, 1999).

Lewis, Michael. "TIME 100: High Commissioner Pete Rozelle." *Time* (December 7, 1998): 188.

"NFL Visionary Pete Rozelle Dies." *Minneapolis Star Tribune* (December 7, 1996): 1C.

Wilbon, Michael. "Visionary Pete Rozelle Left NFL Monumental Legacy." *St. Louis Post-Dispatch* (December 15, 1996): 1F.

Other

"Pete Rozelle." Pro Football Hall of Fame. http://www.profootballhof.com/players/mainpage.cfm?cont_id=100119 (October 17, 2002).

"Rozelle Was NFL Innovator." ESPN Classic. http://espn.go.com/classic/s/add_rozelle_pete.html (October 17, 2002).

Sketch by Don Amerman

Barbara Jo Rubin

Barbara Jo Rubin
1949-

American jockey

Barbara Jo Rubin overcame polio as a child and prejudice as an adult to become a pioneer in sports. In 1969 Rubin was a member of the charter class of young women seeking work as professional jockeys—no small accomplishment in Thoroughbred racing, long known as the "sport of kings" and a male-only bastion. In the space of just one year of racing, Rubin accomplished several "firsts" and topped it off by becoming the first female jockey to retire from the track.

Though her parents were Floridians—father Robert Rubin ran the Golden Sands Lounge in Miami—Barbara Jo was born in Illinois, during a visit to Rubin's mother's family. The girl grew up in an atmosphere of diversity, describing her family to the New York *Post* as "a little bit of everything," British, Jewish, German and other ancestral ties. At age six Rubin contracted polio, a scourge of children in the United States from the 1940s into the '50s, when a vaccine developed by Dr. Jonas Salk finally conquered the spread of the debilitating disease. Fortunately for Rubin, her case was a mild one; the family doctor recommended sports as therapy for the child's affected knees.

Horses—The Sure Cure

The young girl chose her sport as soon as she saw the 1944 movie *National Velvet* on television. "From that time on," she told the *Post,* "I set my heart on riding horses." At that time Robert Rubin ran a gas station and kept a pony on the lot to entertain customers' children. Barbara Jo, however, was the main rider, and as she grew, the girl developed into not only an equestrian but also a horse trader, swapping each consecutive pony for a larger equine. A brief stint as a junior rodeo competitor ended when Rubin took a nasty spill; her mother, Maxine, declared calf-roping and bull-riding off-limits.

A winning rider at horse shows during her teen years, Rubin set her sights on something a little more thrill-packed: racing. While she was a taller than average jockey, Rubin was determined to make her way onto the track. With the encouragement of her father, Rubin—a student at Broward Junior College—left school in 1968 to take a job at Miami's Tropical Park racetrack. Paying dues for Rubin meant hours of daily tasks like mucking out stalls and rubbing down horses before she was permitted a twenty-minute workout with a Thoroughbred. By that summer Rubin was galloping horses in New England, earning three dollars per workout. During those early days, the young athlete caught the eye of a man who went on to become a mentor—trainer Bryan Webb.

The Quest to Be the First

Webb, who was working out of Charles Town, West Virginia, at the time, urged Rubin to apply for a jockey's license. Others were not so supportive. After obtaining her license by the Florida State Racing Commission, Rubin was scheduled to make her professional debut on Webb's horse Stoneland at Tropical Park in January, 1969. But a group of male jockeys protested her presence, and threatened to boycott the track should Rubin be allowed to ride. The pressure forced Rubin's withdrawal, especially after someone threw a brick through the window of a trailer she was using for a changing room. The nineteen-year-old was philosophical about the ruckus: "If I were a boy I'd probably fight this thing too," she told *Parade* reporter Linda Gutstein. "It's been a man's sport for so long—well, it's traditional. I guess I don't blame them for fighting it."

Instead of provoking further confrontation, Rubin found another way to ride. She left the U.S. for Nassau, Bahamas, where the young woman was welcomed onto the Hobby Horse Hall track. There she posted her first race—and her first win, aboard the heavily favored Fly Away. Following the three-length victory, as George Gipe wrote in his *Great American Sports Book,* Rubin "galloped triumphantly into the winner's circle, where she was greeted by her parents and a contingent of Miami supporters."

Into the Winner's Circle

Returning to the United States, Rubin took her credentials in West Virginia on February 18, 1969. Four days later, riding Cohesion in Charles Town, she made history as the first woman to win in a pari-mutuel (betting) race on a major U.S. track. (Rubin missed being the first woman to ride a U.S. pari-mutuel by a two weeks; jockey Diane Crump preceded her at Hialeah on February 7.) But that race, and subsequent others, brought out emotions in her competitors and the bettors. "Get married!" shouted one spectator at Aqueduct. "At Pimlico," she told Stan Isaacs in a 1969 *Newsday* piece, "somebody told me to go home and cook spaghetti. I don't pay any attention. They boo other people."

So Rubin concentrated on riding effective races. The catcalls turned to cheers when the rookie brought home two winners in two days at Aqueduct in March. And while racing, already a dangerous undertaking, did not get any easier, there was more of a sense of acceptance about the young woman. Isaacs described a race in which "the other jocks cut over on Rubin and made it rough for her, not because she is a girl, but because that's the way the game is played." Jockey Angel Cordero commented to Isaacs that if he saw Rubin taking the lead, he would ease his horse in front of her "because that's the way I would do it against everybody. Everybody else thinks of her as a girl. I think of her as a jockey." Rubin won eleven of her first twenty-two starts. Her style, according to Audax Minor of *New Yorker,* was characterized by "balance, good control and sensitive hands, because of which horses run well for her."

The owner of a stakes-running horse, Picnic Fair, thought enough of Rubin to offer her the mount for the 1969 Kentucky Derby. She would have entered the history books as the first woman to run a Triple Crown race; however, Picnic Fair was scratched from the race. But neither the Derby nor other major races had seen the end of women jockeys. Overcoming tremendous obstacles, Crump, Tuesdee Testa, Robyn Smith, Cheryl White, and Mary Bacon were the riders who, like Rubin, opened the door to athletes such as **Julie Krone**, who earned $81 million in her career and in 1993 became the first woman to win a Triple Crown race.

As for Rubin, the realities of her own body caught up with her dream of riding. Her height, five-foot-six, made keeping racing weight difficult; Rubin's knees, still sensitive from her bout with polio, did not let her maintain the strength she needed to control a 1,200-lb. Thoroughbred at top speed. Rubin retired from racing in January, 1970. The Barbara Jo Rubin Stakes, run in Charles Town, is named in her honor. "I don't feel I've done anything special," Rubin said to Isaacs in 1969. "I feel I've just been riding a horse, which is all I want to do."

FURTHER INFORMATION

Books

Almanac of Famous People. Gale, 1998.

Gipe, George. *The Great American Sports Book*. Dou-
    bleday, 1978.
Women's Firsts. Gale, 1997.

Periodicals

Connelly, Mary. *New York Post* (March 22, 1969).
Gutstein, Linda. *Parade* (March 30, 1969).
Isaacs, Stan. "Barbara Jo: A Girl to Fall in Love With."
    Newsday (March 20, 1969).
Minor, Audax. *New Yorker* (March 22, 1969).

Sketch by Susan Salter

Wilma Rudolph

Wilma Rudolph
1940-1994

American track and field athlete

Wilma Rudolph made Olympic history in 1960
when she became the first American woman ever
to win three gold medals in track and field events. Her
achievement would have been remarkable for any athlete, but it was even more impressive because Rudolph
had spent her childhood in leg braces and special shoes;
doctors had told her family that she would never walk
normally.

Early Obstacles

Wilma Glodean Rudolph was born June 23, 1940, in
Bethlehem, Tennessee, to a poor and very large family.
Her father, Ed Rudolph, had eleven children by an earlier marriage, and had eight more with Wilma's mother,
Blanche Rudolph. Wilma was the fifth of this second set
of children. When she was born, she weighed only four
and a half pounds.

During Rudolph's infancy, the family moved to a
house on Kellogg Street in Clarksville, Tennessee,
where her father worked as a railroad porter and did odd
jobs, and her mother worked six days a week as a maid
in the homes of wealthy white families in Clarksville.

When Rudolph was four years old, she contracted
polio, for which there was no immunization or curative
treatment. The illness weakened her, and she also suffered through double pneumonia and scarlet fever,
which almost killed her. Although she survived, her left
leg remained paralyzed from the polio. Her parents took
her to a specialist at Meharry Medical College in
Nashville, Tennessee, who told them that in order for
Rudolph's leg to regain strength, they would have to do
therapeutic massage. For the next two years, Wilma and

her mother visited Meharry each week for heat and
water therapy. Every other day of the week, Rudolph's
mother, with three of her older siblings, took turns mas-
saging the crippled limb at least four times a day.

During her weekly trips to Nashville, Rudolph saw
the deep segregation of races that existed at that time in
the South. Traveling on a Greyhound bus, she noted that
the African-American passengers had to sit in the back,
and that there were separate ticket windows, waiting
areas, and restrooms for African Americans. In addition,
if white passengers did not have seats, African Americans were expected to give up their seats and stand in
the aisle for the duration of the trip.

When Rudolph was five years old, her doctors fitted
her with a steel brace on her left leg. She was supposed
to wear the brace from the moment she got up until she
went to bed at night. She hated the brace, because it was
a visible sign that she had a physical problem, and she
wanted to be like everyone else. When her parents were
not around, Rudolph often took off the brace and tried to
walk without a limp. In her autobiography, *Wilma,* she
wrote that even as a child she was aware that, "From
that day on [when she walked normally], people were
going to start separating me from that brace, start thinking about me differently, start saying that Wilma is a
healthy kid, just like the rest of them." This knowledge,
and the desire to walk like everyone else, became a driving force in her life.

In 1947, at the age of seven, Rudolph entered Cobb Elementary School in Clarksville. Her poor health had forced her to miss kindergarten and first grade, so she entered at the second-grade level. The school, which enrolled only African-American students, included all grades from elementary through high school, and its facilities, curriculum, and materials were inferior to those of local white schools. However, Rudolph loved school, and found that it changed her life. From being a sickly, often-teased child, she became accepted by other children. "I needed to belong, and I finally did," she wrote in *Wilma*.

At Cobb Elementary, the students were taught some African-American history, with an emphasis on African American achievements, but did not discuss prejudice or oppression. Rudolph wrote, "The object of it was to give us black kids somebody to be proud of, not to tell us we were still oppressed."

Interestingly, Rudolph had red, sandy hair and light skin, and in her autobiography, she wrote that next to some of her darker-skinned brothers and sisters, she "felt like an albino." Her awareness of her appearance, coupled with her growing awareness in the disparities in American culture's treatment of African Americans and whites, made her believe as a child that "all white people were mean and evil." As she grew up, her anger about society's treatment of African Americans would be tempered by her Christian religious beliefs, which taught tolerance and forgiveness.

Rudolph's teacher, Mrs. Allison, was a kind, generous woman who boosted Rudolph's self-esteem and confidence. A later teacher, Mrs. Hoskins, who taught fourth grade, was a martinet who once spanked Rudolph and who was known, Rudolph wrote, as the "meanest, toughest teacher in the whole school." However, Rudolph came to respect her because she "had no pets in class, no favorites, and treated everybody equally." Hoskins taught Rudolph to go out and work to achieve her goals, rather than simply daydreaming about them. This attitude would later fuel Rudolph as she worked on her athletic training.

Not Just Walking, But Running

When Rudolph was eleven, her family's persistence with her physical therapy, her long training without the brace, and her determination paid off: she took off the brace and was able to walk normally without it. She progressed rapidly from then on, and not only walked, but outran her peers. According to a writer in *Great Women in Sports,* Rudolph told a *Chicago Tribune* writer, "By the time I was twelve, I was challenging every boy in our neighborhood at running, jumping, everything."

In seventh grade, Rudolph entered Burt High School, a new school for African American children. Everything in their community revolved around the school, and Rudolph begged her high school coach to play basketball. She was allowed to play only because the coach wanted her older sister to play. The following year, Rudolph's basketball coach, Clinton Gray, decided to invite girls who were on the basketball team to join the track team. Rudolph joined, although she continued to play basketball until the ninth grade. In her first season, at the age of thirteen, she ran five different events—the 50-meter, 75-meter, 100-meter, 200-meter, and the 4 X 100 relay. In twenty different races, she won every event.

In her sophomore year on the basketball team, Rudolph scored 803 points in 25 games, then a state record in girls' basketball, and her team made it to com-

Wilma Rudolph

petition in the Middle East Tennessee Conference championship. Although they lost in the second game of the playoffs, the championship was a pivotal event in Rudolph's life because one of the referees was also a track coach at Tennessee State University. This coach, Ed Temple, noticed Rudolph's running ability and told her that she had the talent to become a great runner. He encouraged her to attend his university when she finished high school.

In that same year, Rudolph attended her first big track meet, held at Tuskegee University in Alabama. Girls from all over the South traveled there to compete, and in this wider field of competition, Rudolph did not win a single race. The losses were devastating to her, but in the long run, made her realize that her innate talent was not enough: she also had to work to improve her training and ability. She became determined to go to the meet again the following year and beat everyone there.

The next summer, Rudolph attended a track camp run by Ed Temple, where the girls ran long cross-country distances every day in order to build up their endurance. At the end of the summer, Temple's team went to the National Amateur Athletic Union (AAU) meet in Philadelphia. Rudolph entered nine races and won all of them. At the meet, she met and was photographed with baseball greats **Jackie Robinson** and Don Newcomb. Rudolph looked up to Robinson as her first African-American hero.

Wins Bronze at Melbourne Olympics

Although Rudolph had never even heard of the Olympics until high school, she attended the Olympic trials in Seattle and qualified for the 1956 Olympics in Melbourne, Australia at the age of sixteen, as a high school junior. The youngest member of the American team, she was excited to go on her first airplane flight. At Melbourne, she was eliminated from the 200-meter event and did not make the final race, but she ran the third leg of the 4 x 100-meter relay and won a bronze medal.

According to *Great Women in Sports*, she told a reporter for the *Chicago Tribune*, "I remember going back to my high school this particular day with the bronze medal and all the kids that I disliked so much or thought I disliked . . . put up this big huge banner: 'Welcome Home Wilma.'" And I forgave them right then and there . . . They passed my bronze medal around so that everybody could touch, feel and see what an Olympic medal is like. When I got it back, there were handprints all over it. I took it and I started shining it up. I discovered that bronze doesn't shine. So, I decided, I'm going to try this one more time. I'm going to go for the gold."

During her senior year of high school, Rudolph underwent a routine physical and found out that she was pregnant. Her parents and coach supported her, and she finished high school and kept up with her training as much as she could. A month after graduating, she gave birth to a daughter, Yolanda. Her parents, who wanted her to attend college, took care of the baby until she was able to do so.

In 1958, Rudolph entered college at Tennessee State University, majoring in elementary school education and psychology. Surprisingly, she did not have an athletic scholarship, although she did work two hours a day, five days a week, as part of the school's work assistance program. Another little-known facet of her college career was that when she was not on the track, she never hurried anywhere, and was often late for class.

Wins Gold in 1960 Olympics

In 1960, Rudolph went to Corpus Christi, Texas, for the National AAU meet. The winners of the meet were invited to the Olympic Trials, held two weeks later at Texas Christian University. At the trials, she set a world record in the 200 meter race that would stand for the next eight years, and qualified for the Olympic team in the 100 meter, 200 meter, and 4 x 100 relay.

At the 1960 Olympics in Rome, she went for the gold, and won it—three times, becoming the first American woman ever to accomplish this feat. In the 100-meter dash and the 200-meter dash, she finished at least three yards in front of her closest competitor. In the 100-meter dash, she tied the world record, and she set a new Olympic record in the 200. As a member of the 4 x 100-meter relay team, she brought the team from behind to

first place. A reporter for *Time* magazine wrote, "Running for gold medal glory, Miss Rudolph regularly got away to good starts with her arms pumping in classic style, then smoothly shifted gears to a flowing stride that made the rest of the pack seem to be churning on a treadmill." Her wins were even more amazing because on the day before the 100-meter semifinal event, she stepped in a hole and twisted her ankle. It swelled and became painful, but Rudolph ran anyway, and won all of her events.

Personally, Rudolph was thrilled by her gold medals because she had repeated the achievement of another of her heroes, famed African American athlete **Jesse Owens**, who won three gold medals at the 1936 Olympics in Germany, in front of notoriously racist Nazi officials.

After the Olympics, Temple took Rudolph and the other members of the team to the British Empire Games in London. Rudolph won every event she ran in. The team continued to travel throughout Europe, and Rudolph kept winning.

Her achievements brought her instant fame, and crowds gathered wherever she ran. President John F. Kennedy invited her to the White House, she received ticker tape parades, and she was invited to dinners, awards, and television appearances. Her homecoming parade in Clarksville was attended by over 40,000 people, and was the first racially integrated event in the history of the town—at her insistence, since she refused to participate in the segregated event that the white town officials originally proposed. In 1961, she was given the Sullivan Award as the top amateur athlete in the United States, and won the Associated Press's Female Athlete of the Year Award. She also became the first woman to be invited to compete in some of track's most prestigious events, including the New York Athletic Club Meet, the Millrose Games, the *Los Angeles Times Games,* the Penn Relays, and the Drake Relays. Rudolph also traveled with evangelist Billy Graham on a trip to French West Africa and with the Baptist Christian Athletes on a trip to Japan.

"You Can't Go Back to Living the Way You Did Before"

Despite all the awards and praise, Rudolph received little or no money for her success, and though she had to work for a living, she found it hard to fit back into her old life. According to *Great Women in Sports,* she told a reporter for *Ebony,* "You become world famous and you sit with kings and queens, and then your first job is just a job. You can't go back to living the way you did before because you've been taken out of one setting and shown the other. That becomes a struggle and makes you struggle."

Although Rudolph could have competed in the 1964 Olympics, she decided not to. She was not sure she could win gold medals again, and didn't want to look like a fading athlete in the eyes of the public. She retired from competition in 1963, the same year she graduated from Tennessee State University, and became a second-grade teacher and girls' track coach at her childhood school, Cobb Elementary in Clarksville, where she was paid $200 a month. She also married her high school sweetheart, Robert Eldridge, but was later divorced from him and raised her four children—two daughters, Yolanda and Djuana, and two sons, Robert, Jr. and Xurry—on her own. She lived in Evansville, Indiana, where she was a coach at DePauw University, and later moved to Boston, where she worked for the Job Corps program in Poland Springs, Maine.

In 1967, Rudolph was invited by Vice President Hubert Humphrey to work on a program called "Operation Champion." This program took well-known athletes into poor inner-city areas, where they trained young people in sports. When this project was complete, the Job Corps transferred Rudolph to St. Louis; after that, she went to Detroit, where she taught at Palham Junior High School. In 1977 she spent time in Clarksville, Tennessee, before going back to Detroit.

Rudolph's autobiography, *Wilma,* was published in 1977. In that same year, the NBC network produced a television film titled *Wilma,* starring Cicely Tyson as Rudolph. In 1991, Rudolph served as ambassador to the European celebration that marked the fall of the Berlin Wall. Rudolph also founded the Wilma Rudolph Foundation, a nonprofit organization dedicated to promoting amateur athletics.

Rudolph has been inducted into the U.S. Olympic Hall of Fame, the National Track and Field Hall of Fame, the Helms Hall of Fame, the Women's Sports Foundation Hall of Fame, and the Black Athletes Hall of Fame. A street in Clarksville, Tennessee, is named in her honor. In 1987, she was the first woman to receive the National Collegiate Athletic Association's Silver Anniversary Award. In 1993, she was honored as one of "The Great Ones" at the first National Sports Awards.

A year later, on November 12, 1994, Rudolph died of brain cancer in Nashville, Tennessee. She was buried with the Olympic flag draped over her casket.

Rudolph's achievements as an athlete were remarkable for many reasons. She was a woman and an African American in a time when fewer opportunities existed for both groups, and she also overcame serious childhood illness and disability to not only walk normally, but win gold medals in national and Olympic competition. In the *Kansas City Star,* Claude Lewis summed up Rudolph as "an athletic queen who mesmerized the international sporting world through personal achievement, physical heroics, and a stunning elegance that dwarfed her impoverished beginnings." A writer in *Contemporary Heroes and Heroines* quoted Rudolph's hero, Jesse Owens, who wrote, "Wilma Rudolph's courage and her triumph over her physical handicaps are among the most inspiring jewels in the crown of Olympic sports. . . . She was speed and motion incarnate, the most beautiful image ever seen on the track."

SELECTED WRITINGS BY RUDOLPH:

Wilma: The Story of Wilma Rudolph, New American Library, 1977.

FURTHER INFORMATION

Books

Biracree, Tom. *Wilma Rudolph.* Philadelphia: Chelsea House, 1988.
Great Women in Sports, Detroit: Visible Ink Press, 1996.
Jackson, Linda. *Wilma Rudolph,* Eric Corp., 1975.
Lewis, Dwight, and Susan Thomas. *A Will to Win,* Cumberland Press, 1983.
Newsmakers 1995, Issue 4, Detroit: Gale, 1995.
Notable Black American Women, Book 1, Detroit: Gale, 1992.
Rudolph, Wilma. *Wilma: The Story of Wilma Rudolph,* New York: New American Library, 1977.
Straub, Deborah Gillian, editor. *Contemporary Heroes and Heroines,* Detroit: Gale, 1992.

Periodicals

"Ahead of Their Time," *Runner's World,* (June, 1993): 50.
"Fast Train from Clarksville [Obituary]," *Sports Illustrated,* (November 21, 1994): 13.
Heller, Dick. "Rudolph Had Bumpy Path to Greatness as Olympic Sprinter," *Washington Times,* (September 25, 2000): 16.
Lewis, Claude. "Wilma Rudolph [Obituary]," *Kansas City Star,* (November 22, 1994).
"Olympic Gold Medal Runner Wilma Rudolph, 54, Succumbs [Obituary]," *Jet,* (November 28, 1994): 58.
Reed, Susan, "Born to Win: Speed Was of the Essence for Wilma Rudolph, Who Beat Polio to Win Three Olympic Gold Medals [Obituary]," *People* (November 28, 1994): 62.

Other

"A Lifetime of Achievement: Edward Stanley Temple," Tennessee State University Web Site, http://www.tnstate.edu/library/temple/templebio.html (September 30, 2002).
Percentie, Chanella. "Edward Stanley Temple—1927," NCT American Collection, http://www.nctamerican collection.org/litmap/temple_Edward_tn.htm (September 30, 2002).

Roberts, M.B. "Rudolph Ran and World Went Wild," ESPN.com, http://espn.go.com/sportscentury/ features/00016444.html (September 24, 2002).

Sketch by Kelly Winters

Bill Russell

Bill Russell
1934-

American basketball player

Bill Russell, the Boston Celtics' Hall of Fame center who almost single-handedly redefined the game of basketball, was, in the words of *Basketball's Big Men* by David Klein, "the standard against whom all others will be judged." A big man who specialized in defense rather than scoring, Russell was the ultimate winner. After winning two National Collegiate Athletic Association (NCAA) titles at the University of San Francisco, and an Olympic gold medal in 1956, he led the Boston Celtics to eleven league championships in thirteen years, a string that is virtually unparalleled in professional sport, including eight consecutive National Basketball Association (NBA) titles between 1959 and 1966, and two in 1968 and 1969 while himself the Celtics coach. On an individual level—a level Russell largely disdained in favor of team performance—he was named the NBA's Most Valuable Player five times. The first African American to coach in the NBA—indeed he was the first to coach a major sport at the professional level in the United States—Bill Russell was also an impassioned and intelligent advocate of civil rights both on and off the basketball court for blacks and America's other minorities.

Growing Up

Bill Russell was born to Charles Russell and Katie King in Monroe, Louisiana in 1934. Racism was pervasive in Louisiana at the time, and a dangerous confrontation with a white man led Russell's father—who was known as Mr. Charlie—to move his family to the North. After a brief stop in Detroit, Michigan, Russell, his parents and his older brother Charlie, settled in Oakland, California's black ghetto. Mr. Charlie set up his own trucking company, and Russell and his brother entered Oakland's public schools. When he was twelve, tragedy struck. Russell's mother passed away after a brief illness. Mr. Charlie gave up his company to be with his children while Russell retreated into the solace of books at the public library. A book about the life of Henri Christophe, a slave who led an insurrection and became emperor of Haiti, made an impression that remained with him throughout his life.

Russell first played basketball on Oakland's playgrounds. As a child and teen, he gave the impression of being a uniquely untalented athlete. His brother was making himself a star player at Oakland Tech, a mostly white high school; in grade school Bill, however, could not make the basketball team, the football team or even the cheerleading squad. When his studies faltered after the death of his mother, Bill was unable to gain admission to Oakland Tech, and had to enroll instead in a neighborhood school, McClymonds High. Although he washed out of the junior varsity basketball team a freshman, attending McClymonds was a stroke of good fortune for Bill Russell. Despite his apparent ineptitude, the junior varsity basketball coach, George Powles, saw something in Russell and kept him as the 16th man of a 15-man-squad. In his book *Go Up For Glory* Russell described the importance of that gesture. "I believe that man saved me from becoming a juvenile delinquent. If I hadn't had basketball, all my energies and frustrations would surely have been carried in some other direction." Powles also encouraged Russell to work on his game at the local Boys' Club. Even as a senior member of McClymonds team he wasn't turning heads. However, he turned in a very strong performance at a game being watched by a scout from the University of San Francisco (USF). The scout was so impressed that he offered Russell a scholarship instead of the player he had come to observe. It was the only scholarship offer Russell received and he accepted it gratefully.

After his graduation, Russell was asked to join the California High School All-Stars—he was invited to join only because the team was desperate for graduates and he had finished high school in January. The team

jumper who specialized in blocking opponent's shots and deflecting those of his teammates' into the basket. So dominant did Russell become under the basket that the NCAA doubled the width of the lane to 12 feet, and made it a violation to touch a ball once it had begun its descent toward the basket. Russell was named the Most Valuable Player of the NCAA tournament in 1955, and was named an All-American in both 1955 and 1956. He was also a world-class high-jumper in college who came within a hair of breaking the world record.

Russell had come a long way from the days when he wasn't even wanted as cheerleader. As a graduating senior he was one of the players most coveted by NBA and other teams. The Harlem Globetrotters—who he considered more a degrading vaudeville act than basketball—offered him a $32,000 contract. Although the Boston Celtics had a low pick in the college draft, coach **Red Auerbach** wanted Russell badly enough to trade two of the Celtics star players to St. Louis for their pick. Russell did not accept the Celtics $19,500 offer right away. He wanted to maintain his amateur status in order to compete in the 1956 Olympics in Melbourne, Australia. With Russell in the line-up, the U.S. team won the gold medal. Days after his return from Australia, in December 1956, Russell married his girlfriend, Rose Swisher. They would have three children together, William Jr., Karen Kenyatta, and Jacob, before divorcing in 1973.

played exhibition games throughout the Pacific Northwest and British Columbia. While on the tour, Russell became obsessed with basketball, discussing it whenever he could. When he wasn't talking the game, he was analyzing in his head other players' plays as well as his own which he'd made or failed to make. Envisioning each play on the inside of his eyeballs, he imagined what he *should* have done, or something new he wanted to try out. "If I had a play in my mind but muffed it on the court, I'd go over it repeatedly in my head, searching for details I'd missed," he wrote in *Second Wind*. "It was like working a phony jigsaw puzzle, one piece in the completed picture was slightly imperfect, and I had to find out which one it was." Without grasping what he was on to, Russell had discovered on his own the visualization techniques that would become standard practice in professional sports in and after the 1980s.

College Champion

Using his newfound technique, Russell's game improved by leaps and bounds. He was well on his way to becoming a dominant player when he entered USF in the fall of 1952. Russell joined the varsity team, the Dons, as a sophomore. He and his roommate, K.C. Jones—who would play with Russell on the great Celtics teams of the 1950s and 1960s—discussed basketball incessantly. In Russell's junior year, the Dons caught fire, running off a string of 55 straight victories that extended well into his senior year, and included two NCAA championships.

Although Russell was a big player—he was nearly seven feet in height—he was not a high scorer. Instead he was developing into a defensive genius. Russell could out-think most of his opponents and he was a spectacular

Celtics Star

In early 1957, Russell joined the Celtics. Despite its potential—besides being coached by Auerbach, it included **Bob Cousy** and Tommy Heinsohn—the Celtics team Russell joined had never won an NBA championship. Few in Boston thought they would do so with Russell. Writers complained that the team had given up two proven players for a player who would never make it as a pro. But Russell's defensive play was the piece the Celtics needed to win the NBA title in his first full year with the team. As if to emphasize his importance, when a fractured ankle forced him out of the championship series the following year, the Celtics lost. Beginning in 1959, Boston reeled off eight straight NBA championships, a feat unmatched before or since. So crucial was Russell's role in these victories, his time with Boston has come to be known as the "Bill Russell Era."

Bill Russell

What Russell brought to the Celtics, and to pro basketball in general, was a new emphasis on defense and teamwork. He showed that a player did not have to be a high scorer to dominate the game. In fact, Russell scoffed at individual statistics, such as the scoring title. The only important stat, he said, was winning. By that measure alone Bill Russell was the greatest. When he retired, he had not only his two NCAA titles and the Olympic gold, but eleven NBA championship rings, an unparalleled achievement.

When Red Auerbach decided to retire at the end of the 1965-66, he selected Russell as his replacement. It was a natural choice—he had been a thoughtful, analytical student of the game since his tour with the California All-Stars, and after years in the NBA he knew the other teams inside out. Russell's appointment also marked a landmark in American sports history. It was the first time a black had ever been named to lead a professional team in any major sport. In his three years as player-coach, the Celtics won two more championships.

Russell retired at the end of the 1969 season. To all appearances he was done with pro basketball, which he described as men playing a child's game. Before three years had passed, though, he returned as coach and general manager of the Seattle SuperSonics from 1973 until 1977. He took the Sonics to the playoffs in his second year at the helm, but the team was wracked by dissension that Russell was unable to quell and he resigned. He joined the Sacramento Kings organization, serving

first as coach in the 1987-88 season, and then as president of basketball operations through 1989. He was a regular color commentator on basketball broadcasts on NBC and CBS in the 1970s and early 1980s.

Civil Rights Advocate

Despite his fierce dedication to basketball during his career as a player and coach, Bill Russell was keenly aware that there was a world beyond the court. Beginning in the late 1950s, he was an active participant in the struggle by American blacks for full civil rights. Early in his career Russell charged the NBA with maintaining a de facto quota system which limited the number of blacks on each team. In 1963, at the height of the civil rights struggle in the American South, he accepted, uneasily and at great personal risk to himself, a request to travel to Jackson, Mississippi, to organize and lead integrated basketball clinics. Russell was one of the few professional athletes in the United States, black or white, to speak out on civil rights in such a dramatic way in the 1960s. Around the same time, he was the target of racist attacks when he bought a home in white suburban Boston.

Bill Russell has taken stands that have been controversial among fans. For example, he refuses to sign autographs, preferring to shake hands and speak directly to fans and well-wishers. Russell resisted having his number retired by the Celtics in 1972, until Red Auerbach agreed to hold the ceremony without any fans present. In 1974 when he became the first black to be elected to the Basketball Hall of Fame, Russell at first refused to accept the honor. "Aside from racism or my own feelings about the cheers and boos in sports, I don't respect it [the Basketball Hall of Fame] as an institution," he wrote in *Second Wind*. "Its standards are not high enough. It's too political, too self-serving." He was inducted despite his objections.

Despite the passing of years and the increasing number of fans who never saw him play, Bill Russell remains a basketball icon. In 1980 the Professional Basketball Writers Association named Bill Russell the "Greatest Player in the History of the NBA." In 1996 the NBA voted him one of the top 50 players of all-time. In 1999 cable broadcaster ESPN named him one of the fifty top athletes of the 20th century. Bill Russell was more than simply the greatest defensive player in the history of the basketball, he was an intelligent, thoughtful, deeply honest man, who spoke out when he saw injustice. His courage and dedication provide an example for young athletes everywhere.

Career Statistics

Yr	Team	GP	PTS	FG%	FT%	RPG	APG	PF
1956-57	BOS	48	706	42.7	49.2	19.6	1.8	143
1957-58	BOS	69	1142	44.2	51.9	22.7	2.9	181
1958-59	BOS	70	1168	45.7	59.8	23.0	3.2	161
1959-60	BOS	74	1350	46.7	61.2	24.0	3.7	210
1960-61	BOS	78	1322	42.6	55.0	23.9	3.4	155
1961-62	BOS	76	1436	45.7	59.5	23.6	4.5	207
1962-63	BOS	78	1309	43.2	55.5	23.6	4.5	188
1963-64	BOS	78	1168	43.3	55.0	24.7	4.7	190
1964-65	BOS	78	1102	43.8	57.3	24.1	5.3	204
1965-66	BOS	78	1005	41.5	55.1	22.8	4.8	221
1966-67	BOS	81	1075	45.4	61.0	21.0	5.8	258
1967-68	BOS	78	977	42.5	53.7	18.6	4.6	242
1968-69	BOS	77	762	43.3	52.6	19.3	4.9	231
TOTAL		963	14522	44.0	56.1	22.5	4.3	2592

BOS: Boston Celtics.

SELECTED WRITINGS BY RUSSELL:

(With Bob Ottum) "The Psych ... and My Other Tricks." *Sports Illustrated*, October 25, 1965: 32—34.

(With William McSweeny) *Go Up for Glory*. New York: Berkely, 1966.

(With Tex Maule) "I Am Not Worried about Ali." *Sports Illustrated*, June 19, 1967: 18—21.

(With Taylor Branch) *Second Wind: The Memoirs of an Opinionated Man*. New York: Ballantine Books, 1979.

FURTHER INFORMATION

Books

Klein, Dave. *Pro Basketball's Big Men..* New York: Random House, 1973.

Shapiro, Miles. *Bill Russell*. New York: Chelsea House Publishers, 1991.

Periodicals

MacQuarrie, Brian. "Russell Makes Peace With City That Brought Glory And Pain." *Boston Globe*, November 12, 2000.

Moss, Irv. "Russell Remembers Very Good Old Days." *Denver Post*, March 18, 2001.

Ryan, Bob. "Pride Of The Celtics."*Boston Globe*, May 26, 1999.

Sandomir, Richard. "Russell Redux: A Private Man Bursts Back Into the Public Eye." *New York Times*, June 16, 2000.

Tuttle, Dennis. "Solving An Enigma." *Washington Post*, April 16, 2000.

Sketch by Gerald E. Brennan

Babe Ruth
1895-1948

American baseball player

As befitting his legendary status in American popular culture, Babe Ruth's exact birth date is a matter of debate. For most of his life Ruth, himself, believed he had been born in Baltimore, Maryland, on February 7, 1894, but when he applied for a passport, the date on his birth certificate read February 6, 1895. Ruth continued to celebrate his birthday on the 7th, and as Robert W. Creamer wrote in *Babe: The Legend Comes to Life*, "The 1895 birth date is not necessarily the right one. The birth record in Baltimore says only that a male child was born on that day to George and Katherine Ruth." However February 6, 1895 has been recognized as the birth date of George Herman Ruth, Jr. the son of George Herman and Katherine Schamberger Ruth. He was the eldest of eight children though only he and a sister, Mary Margaret, lived past infancy.

George Ruth, Sr. worked at a variety of jobs including a horse driver, a salesman, a streetcar gripman, and a bartender. After working in his own father's saloon (both of Babe Ruth's grandfathers were saloon owners) he eventually ran his own bar on West Camden Street, near the present Camden Yards baseball stadium, home of the Baltimore Orioles.

At age seven Ruth's parents sent him to live at the St. Mary's Industrial School for Boys (whose other notable student was singer Al Jolson), which at that time was both an orphanage and a reform school. Ruth, who was admitted as an incorrigible, spent two separate one-month terms at St. Mary's in 1902, and was a frequent inmate over the next dozen years. In fact, the Xaverian

Babe Ruth

Chronology

1895	Born in Baltimore, Maryland
1902-14	Attends St. Mary's Industrial School for Boys; member of its baseball team
1914	Signs first professional contract with minor-league Baltimore Orioles
1914	Contract sold to the Boston Red Sox
1914	Marries Helen Woodford
1915-17	Premier left-handed pitcher in the American League
1918	Sets record with 29 consecutive shutout innings
1919	Sets single season home run record of 29
1919	Contract sold to the New York Yankees
1920	Sets single season home run record of 54
1921	Sets single season home record of 59
1923	Leads Yankees to first world championship
1923	Wins American League Most Valuable Player (MVP) award
1926	Hits three home runs in a World Series game vs. the St. Louis Cardinals
1927	Sets single season home record of 60
1928	Hits three home runs in a World Series game vs. the St. Louis Cardinals
1929	Wife Helen dies in a fire; marries Claire Hodgson
1932	Hits so-called "called shot" home run off Charley Root of the Chicago Cubs in the World Series
1935	Signs contract to play for the Boston Braves of the National League
1935	Retires from baseball
1936	Becomes a charter member of the Baseball Hall of Fame
1938	Signs contract in June to coach the Brooklyn Dodgers through the end of the season
1948	Dies of cancer in New York City

Brothers who ran St. Mary's actually had custody of Ruth during his youth. In 1904 he reentered St. Mary's where he remained for the next four years. After his mother's death on August 23, 1910, Ruth returned to the Home (as St. Mary's was known) for a year. In 1912 he was again back in St. Mary's where he stayed until 1914 when he signed a contract to play professional baseball.

At St. Mary's, Ruth worked in the shirt factory putting collars on the shirts, a piecework job that earned him six cents per shirt. He also came under the spell of the six foot six inch Brother Mathias, the school disciplinarian and the man Ruth, without irony, later claimed had the greatest influence on him. Ruth played his first organized baseball at St. Mary's; the school teams had major league names and Ruth coincidentally played for the Red Sox. He started out as a catcher, but soon switched to pitcher. By the time he was in his late teens he was not only the school's star player but his name was beginning to become known around Baltimore.

Becomes a Professional Ballplayer

On February 27, 1914, at age 19, Ruth signed his first professional contract with the Baltimore Orioles of the International League (a high-level minor league). The man who signed him was Jack Dunn, a former major leaguer and the owner and manager of the Orioles. After leaving St. Mary's for good Ruth spent some time with his father before embarking with the other pitchers and

catchers to Fayetteville, North Carolina for his first spring training. It was at this time the veteran Oriole players hung the name "Babe" on him, because of his youth. Yet Ruth impressed those veterans with his pitching prowess and with his hitting, especially his power. Legend has that he hit the longest home run hit in Fayetteville up to that time, some 60 feet farther than the previous local record hit by **Jim Thorpe**. So impressive was Ruth against major league teams that when the team returned to Baltimore to begin the season his legend had already begun.

Ruth played for three teams during the 1914 season. He spent the first half of the season with the Orioles, his 14 wins helping to lead them to first place in the International League standings. But these were the years of the Federal League, an unofficial third major league that had signed stars from the American and National leagues and even drawn players from the International League. The Federal League had placed a team in Baltimore, the Terrapins, who played across the street from Dunn's Orioles and continually outdrew them. Dunn quickly felt the financial squeeze and attempted to move his team to Richmond, Virginia, but the Virginia League demanded too high an indemnity payment. Dunn then attempted to persuade the major league owners to halt their drafting of International League players, but to no avail. His only recourse was to sell off some of his players to keep the team afloat. As a result Babe Ruth made

Career Statistics: Batting

Yr	Team	AVG	GP	AB	R	H	HR	RBI	BB	SO	SB	SLG
1914	BOS	.200	5	10	1	2	0	2	0	4	0	.300
1915	BOS	.315	42	92	16	29	4	21	9	23	0	.576
1916	BOS	.272	67	136	18	37	3	15	10	23	0	.419
1917	BOS	.325	52	123	14	40	2	12	12	18	0	.472
1918	BOS	.300	95	317	50	95	11	66	58	58	6	.555
1919	BOS	.322	130	432	103	139	29	114	101	58	7	.657
1920	NYY	.376	142	458	158	172	54	137	150	80	14	.847
1921	NYY	.378	152	540	177	204	59	171	145	81	17	.846
1922	NYY	.315	110	406	94	128	35	99	84	80	2	.672
1923	NYY	.393	152	522	151	205	41	131	170	93	17	.764
1924	NYY	.378	153	529	143	200	46	121	142	81	9	.739
1925	NYY	.290	98	359	61	104	25	66	59	68	2	.543
1926	NYY	.372	152	495	139	184	47	146	144	76	11	.737
1927	NYY	.356	151	540	158	192	60	164	137	89	7	.772
1928	NYY	.323	154	536	163	173	54	142	137	87	4	.709
1929	NYY	.345	135	499	121	172	46	154	72	60	5	.697
1930	NYY	.359	145	518	150	186	49	153	136	61	10	.732
1931	NYY	.373	145	534	149	199	46	163	128	51	5	.700
1932	NYY	.341	133	457	120	156	41	137	130	62	2	.661
1933	NYY	.301	137	459	97	138	34	103	114	90	4	.582
1934	NYY	.288	125	365	78	105	22	84	104	63	1	.537
1935	BB	.181	28	72	13	13	6	12	20	24	0	.431
TOTAL		.342	2503	8399	2174	2873	714	2213	2062	1330	123	.690

BB: Boston Braves; BOS: Boston Red Sox; NYY: New York Yankees.

his debut with the Boston Red Sox after only half a season of professional baseball.

Ruth was used sparingly by the Red Sox manager, Bill Carrigan, because the team already had good left-handed pitching at that time. He compiled a 2-1 record but actually did not pitch for nearly four weeks in July and August. When he did pitch he was used in two mid-season exhibition games (which he won). Yet Ruth was such a prospect that he was sent down to the minor league Providence Grays to help them win the International League pennant. After Dunn had sold his star players the Orioles had quickly fallen out of the pennant race, replaced by the Providence and Montreal teams. Ruth won nine games in less than two months for Providence (not counting an exhibition victory), and the Grays did indeed win the pennant. That season, 1914, Ruth's International League record was 23-8; his major league record was 2-1; and his exhibition record was 3-0. His total record for his first year of professional baseball was 28-9.

During his time in Boston that first season Ruth frequented Landers' Coffee Shop where he met and fell in love with a young waitress named Helen Woodford. The two were married on October 17, 1914 at St. Paul's Roman Catholic Church in Ellicott City, Maryland.

Ruth was a full-time member of the Red Sox pitching rotation in 1915 and he responded with an 18-8 record and a 2.44 earned run average (ERA). The Red Sox were the American League (AL) pennant winners, but despite his outstanding season Ruth did not pitch in the World Series against the Philadelphia Phillies. Ruth's only appearance in the Series was a pinch hit at bat against **Grover Cleveland Alexander** in the first game. He grounded out to first base. Even without Ruth the Red Sox won the Series in five games.

World Series Hero

In 1916 the Red Sox repeated as league champs with Ruth's record improving to 23-12 and a 1.75 ERA. He also pitched nine shutouts. Ruth had become the premier lefthander in the American League, and many consider him to have been the best pitcher in the league for the 1916 season. He started the second game of the World Series against the Brooklyn Dodgers and went the distance in a 14-inning 2-1 pitchers' duel. After giving up an inside-the-park home run in the first inning, he pitched 13 scoreless innings. It was the only game Ruth appeared in, as the Red Sox once again won the Series in five games.

When the war in Europe, which had been raging since 1914, finally involved the United States in 1917, many ballplayers enlisted in the reserves or were subject to the military draft. For a time Ruth was exempt from the draft because he was married, but a later ruling exempted only men whose jobs were vital for the national effort, which baseball was not. He later joined a reserve unit. The Red Sox failed to win the league pennant in 1917, but Ruth's pitching continued to dominate the hitters. He posted a 24-13 record, a 2.01 ERA, and six

Awards and Accomplishments	
1923	American League MVP
1933-34	American League All-Star Team
1936	Baseball Hall of Fame
1999	Associated Press Athlete of the Century
1999	Major League Baseball All-Century Team
1999	Sporting News Greatest Player of All-Time

shutouts. In an era when relief pitchers where used sparingly Ruth completed 35 of the 38 games he started that year. He also batted for a .325 average.

In 1918 the Red Sox were once again the AL pennant winners. The season was also a critical one for Ruth as it marked the beginning of his transformation from a star pitcher to a star hitter—the man who more than anyone else influenced (and some contend saved) the game of baseball. That year he started only 19 games as a pitcher, completing 18. His record was 13-7; his ERA was 2.22 and he pitched one shutout. As a batter that season, Ruth compiled 317 at-bats (his previous high was 136). He hit 11 home runs—most of them of the towering kind that sportswriters would take to describing as "Ruthian," drove in 66 runs and hit for a .300 average. What's more, Ruth made it known to his manager, Ed Barrow, that he preferred hitting to pitching. In time, the fans would agree.

In the World Series against the Chicago Cubs, Ruth was used as a pitcher (he had only five at-bats) and he responded masterfully. He won the first game 1-0, pitching a complete game. Ruth then pitched in the fourth game (the Red Sox held a 2-1 Series lead) and shutout the Cubs for seven innings before being relieved in the ninth inning. The Red Sox won the game 3-2. The seven shutout innings, combined with the nine he had pitched in the Series opener and the 13 he had pitched in the 1916 Series, gave him 29 consecutive scoreless World Series innings, a new record. Christy Mathewson had set the previous record of 28 in 1905. Of all his baseball achievements Ruth claimed he was proudest of this record.

The 1918 season had not been a rosy one for Ruth, who never really got along with manager Ed Barrow. Arguments between the two flared up often, and at one point in the season Ruth jumped the team and threatened to play for a semiprofessional team sponsored by the Chester Shipyards in Chester, Pennsylvania. But Harry Frazee, the Red Sox owner, threatened a lawsuit and Ruth came back into the fold. The following year, after Ruth threatened to punch Barrow in the nose, the manager suspended his star player. A contrite Ruth apologized and had his first important season as a hitter.

1919 was the last year Ruth pitched with any regularity, though he did compile a 5-0 record with the Yankees over the years. His indifference to pitching now showed.

The Colossus

Babe Ruth died of cancer 50 years ago this week, on Aug. 16, 1948. More than 63 years have passed since he made his last appearance as a player, in a Boston Braves uniform, yet he remains the purest original ever to have played big league baseball. For all that he did in his 22 seasons in the majors, surely nothing left a deeper imprint on the game than the force and flair he brought to bear in striking the ball.

In the late teens of [the twentieth century] Ruth was the best left-handed pitcher in the American League. As a member of the Boston Red Sox, he pitched 29 2/3 consecutive scoreless innings in World Series play, a record until Whitey Ford broke it more than 40 years later. But Ruth's pitching feats are footnotes, gathering dust among his batting records.

The irony is that 1927 [Ruth's most memorable year] wasn't his most productive year. No player in history ever had a season like Ruth's in '21. In addition to his 59 homers, he batted .378 and led the league in runs (177), runs batted in (171) and walks (144, many of them intentional), and his colossal slugging percentage of .846 was just a tick behind his 1920 mark of .847, a record that still stands. Yet it's '27 that became Ruth's year, the enduring symbol of the man and his myth. By that season he had altered the balance of the game, raising the home run from its relatively modest role into baseball's most dramatic event and a significant force in determining the outcome of games. ...

Unlike in 1920, when the Babe was just making his name as a power hitter, in '27 he was the Show. His home run quest was a one-ring traveling circus, the merriest entertainment in sport...

Source: Nack, William. *Sports Illustrated, August 24, 1998, p. 58.*

In 1919 Ruth appeared in only 17 games as a pitcher, 15 of which he started. He had a mediocre (for Ruth) 9-5 record, but his ERA was a respectable 2.97. He also saved a game.

As a hitter he wowed the fans. Ruth smacked a record 29 home runs and drove in 114 runs while batting .322. He also hit four grand slams (home runs with the bases loaded) that year which was another record. It stood as the AL standard for 40 years.

Joins the New York Yankees

Following his tremendous 1919 season Ruth sought a salary increase from $10,000 per season to $20,000. Frazee, however, still owed the previous Red Sox owner, Joseph Lannin, money for his purchase of the team, and his credit was no longer as solid as it had been a few years earlier. Frazee, a New York theatrical producer, was also good friends with Colonel Tillinghast L'Hommedieu Huston, a partner in the Yankees ownership, and when Ruth kept pressuring for more money Frazee decided to sell his star for $100,000 plus a $300,000 loan from the other Yankee owner, Colonel Jacob Ruppert. The collateral on the loan was Fenway Park, where the Red Sox played ball.

In subsequent years Frazee was demonized for selling Ruth to finance the Broadway show *No, No Nanette,* but in reality the musical did not open until 1925 (and was successful). Because the Red Sox (as of the 2002 season) had not won another World Championship, the selling of Ruth has taken on mythic proportions of its

Career Statistics: Pitching

Yr	Team	W	L	ERA	GS	CG	SHO	IP	H	ER	BB	SO
1914	BOS	2	1	3.91	3	1	0	23.0	21	10	7	3
1915	BOS	18	8	2.44	28	16	1	217.7	166	59	85	112
1916	BOS	23	12	1.75	41	23	9	323.7	230	63	118	170
1917	BOS	24	13	2.01	38	35	6	326.3	244	73	108	128
1918	BOS	13	7	2.22	19	18	1	166.3	125	41	49	40
1919	BOS	9	5	2.97	15	12	0	133.3	148	44	58	30
1920	NYY	1	0	4.50	1	0	0	4.0	3	2	2	0
1921	NYY	2	0	9.00	1	0	0	9.0	14	9	9	2
1930	NYY	1	0	3.00	1	1	0	9.0	11	3	2	3
1933	NYY	1	0	5.00	1	1	0	9.0	12	5	3	0
TOTAL		94	46	2.28	148	107	17	1221.3	974	309	441	488

BOS: Boston Red Sox; NYY: New York Yankees.

own and has become known as "The Curse of the Bambino." Indeed, for ten of the next twelve years, Ruth outhomered the entire Red Sox team, which finished in last place most of that time.

During the next two seasons Ruth cemented his legend as the game's greatest slugger. In 1920 he batted .376 with 54 home runs and 137 RBIs. That year he was the first player to hit 30, 40 and 50 home runs in a season. As good as he was in 1920, in 1921 Ruth was even better. His batting average was .378 and he slugged 59 home runs and drove in 171 runs. Only his slugging percentage decreased—and that by one point, from .847 to .846. On July 15, 1921, Ruth slammed his 25th home run of the season, but it was the 138th of his career. That made him the all-time home run champion and every home run he hit for the rest of his career added to his record. (Ruth's all-time record was surpassed in 1975 by Henry Aaron.) Unfortunately for Ruth during these years, there was no Most Valuable Player Award (MVP). It had been awarded in both leagues from 1911 to 1914 (when it was known as the Chalmers Award), but from 1915 to 1921 no award was given. The Chalmers Award was revived in 1922 as the league MVP awards.

In 1920 the Yankees finished in third place, but in 1921 Ruth led them to their first league pennant. New York had its first Subway Series that year with the New York Giants winning the National League (NL) pennant. The Giants, who were the landlords at the Yankees' ballpark, the Polo Grounds, won the World Series five games to three. (Between 1919 and 1921 the World Series was a best five-out-of-nine affair.) Ruth hit .312 with a home run and four RBIs.

The Yankees repeated as AL champions in 1922 with Ruth again leading the way, although his average and power numbers were down from the previous two years. He slugged 35 home runs, had 99 RBIs, and hit for a .315 average. It was the first time since 1918 Ruth had not led the league in home runs (Ken Williams of the St. Louis Browns had 39), and the first time since 1919 he was not the RBI leader. (Williams drove in 155 runs.) Still, the Yankees were the champs and once again faced the Giants, who took the Series 4-0. Ruth had a miserable Series hitting just .118 with no home runs and just one RBI.

As if to make up for his poor World Series performance Ruth tore up the league in 1923. It was the inaugural season for the Yankees' new ballpark in the Bronx, Yankee Stadium—or as it came to be known, "The House That Ruth Built." Fittingly he hit the first home run in the Stadium. That season, Ruth led the league in home runs with 41 and RBIs with 131, and was second in hitting with a .393 average. For his efforts he was awarded the AL MVP. Unfortunately, until 1930 previous MVP award winners were ineligible, which probably deprived Ruth of several more awards during the 1920s. For the third year in a row the Yankees met the Giants in the World Series, but this time the outcome was different. Ruth hit three home runs, all solo homers for his only RBIs of the Series, but he batted .368 and scored eight times. The Yankees took the Series 4-2, and for the first time in their fabled history were champions. And Ruth was the king of them all, the Sultan of Swat.

Ruth followed up his MVP season with another tremendous year in 1924, but the Yankees finished in second place. It was a disappointment that presaged the collapse of 1925. Ruth reported to spring training that year even more overweight than usual and with a fever. But after the fever subsided and his wife went back to New York, Ruth returned to his carousing ways. However, by the time the Yankees broke camp to head north, a nagging stomach ache finally forced Ruth out of the lineup and into a hospital. Ruth took a separate train to New York where the pain grew so intense emergency surgery was required for an abscess in his intestine. It went down in Ruthian legend as the Big Bellyache, which sportswriters attributed to too many hotdogs.

Babe Ruth, swinging bat

Ruth didn't really get going until midseason and had only 25 home runs and 66 RBIs that season. As Ruth went so went the Yankees and the team finished seventh.

The Sultan of Swat

But the greatest player could not be held down for long. Over the next seven seasons Ruth averaged 49 home runs, 151 RBIs and a .353 batting average. During that span of time the Yankees won four league pennants and three World Series. The Yankees of these years also boasted future Hall of Famers **Lou Gehrig**, who joined the team in 1925 and Tony Lazzeri, who became a Yankee in 1926.

In the midst of this run was the magnificent 1927 team, still considered by many as the best baseball team ever assembled. That season Ruth set a single season home run record of 60 that stood for 34 years. He also drove in 164 runs and batted .364 as the team cruised to the pennant and swept the Pittsburgh Pirates in the World Series. During the 1926 World Series and again in 1928, both times against the St. Louis Cardinals, Ruth hit three home runs in a single game.

Throughout these years, at the height of his fame, Ruth's constant womanizing led to an estrangement from his wife, Helen, and their adopted daughter, Dorothy. While Ruth lived in New York his family remained on the farm Ruth had purchased years ago in the Boston suburb of Sudbury, Massachusetts. By 1929 Helen, still married to Ruth, was living in Watertown, Massachusetts with Dr. Edward Kinder. On the night of January 11, 1929, an electrical fire broke out in their home while Kinder was away and Dorothy at boarding school; Helen died of smoke inhalation. Three months later Ruth married Claire Hodgson, a widow with a daughter of her own. Ruth and his new wife each adopted the other's child.

In 1930 Ruth signed a two-year contract that paid him $80,000 per year, more than the president of the United States was paid. When told this he replied in typical Ruthian fashion: "Why not? I had a better year than he had."

The last great Ruthian moment to enter into baseball lore occurred during the 1932 World Series, in which the Yankees swept the Chicago Cubs. Ruth's home run off Charlie Root has gone down as "the called shot," in which he supposedly pointed to a spot in the right field stands moments before he hit the ball there. Most contemporary reports make no mention of the call, yet it has remained ensconced in the Ruth myth.

Disappointment at the End of the Line

Nearing forty years old, Ruth's skills rapidly diminished after 1933 and he began to angle for the Yankee manager's job. However, the Yankee front office wanted no part of Ruth as a manager. After the Yankees gave him his unconditional release prior to the 1935 season, he signed on with the Boston Braves of the National League in hopes of managing in 1936. It did not take long for Ruth to become disillusioned with his new team. He played only 28 games that year and called it quits, knowing he would never manage the Braves.

Over the next seven years, Ruth played in exhibition games and made public appearances while he waited for the call to manage a team. It was a call that never came, though in June 1938 he signed a contract to serve as a coach for the Brooklyn Dodgers for the remainder of the season.

In late 1946 Ruth entered the hospital to have a malignant tumor removed from around his left carotid artery. The operation was only partially successful. April 27, 1947 was declared Babe Ruth Day throughout the major leagues; Ruth himself appeared at Yankee Stadium. On June 13, 1948, a frail Ruth, leaning on a bat for support, made his final public appearance for the twenty-fifth anniversary celebration of the opening of Yankee Stadium. Ruth wore his uniform one last time, and his number three was retired that day. Ruth died of cancer on August 16, 1948.

No other player in the history of baseball affected how the game was played like Babe Ruth did. His prodigious power literally changed baseball from an "inside" little game of scratching for one or two runs to an "outside" game of power; eventually every team sought to sign men who could drive the ball over the fence. With a team's ability to suddenly score two, three, or even four runs at a time came a shift in strategy that continues to this day. In 1936, Babe Ruth was one of the first six players to be elected to the Baseball Hall of Fame. His career statistics read: 714 home runs, 2213 RBIs, a .342 batting average and a .690 slugging percentage. As a pitcher his record was 94 wins, 46 losses and a 2.28 ERA. Among his posthumous honors, Babe Ruth was named to the Major League All-Century Team, Associated Press Athlete of the Century, and *The Sporting News* Greatest Player of All-Time.

SELECTED WRITINGS BY RUTH:

The "Home-run King," or, How Pep Pindar Won His Title, New York: A. L. Burt Company, 1920.

Babe Ruth's Own Book of Baseball, New York: G. P. Putnam's Sons, 1928.
(With Bob Considine)*The Babe Ruth Story,* New York: E. P. Dutton & Co., 1948.

FURTHER INFORMATION

Books

Creamer, Robert W. *Babe: The Legend Comes to Life,* New York: Penguin Books, 1983.

Other

"Babe Ruth," http://www.baseball-reference.com (September 23, 2002).
The Official Babe Ruth Web Site, http://www.baberuth. com (September 26, 2002).
"Ruth named AP athlete of the century," *USA Today,* http://www.usatoday.com/sports/ssat1.htm (October 12, 2002).

Sketch by F. Caso

Birger Ruud
1911-1998

Norwegian ski jumper

In Norway, Birger Ruud is a national hero. He was not only a champion ski jumper; he was also a fierce patriot. He won two Olympic gold medals and one silver. In world championships, he won three gold medals and one silver. During World War II he joined the Resistance and used his skiing skills to subvert the Nazis who had invaded his country. His skill was the result of a combination of inborn athletic ability and the terrain of his homeland.

A Family of Ski Jumpers

Ruud was born on August 23, 1911, in Kongsberg, Norway. Kongsberg is a mining town situated southwest of Oslo. Ruud and his brothers Sigmund and Asbjorn grew up skiing and jumping and participating in all manner of winter sports. Something in their upbringing contributed to producing three of Norway's best ski jumpers. Sigmund and Asbjorn won many titles of their own. Of the three, Birger would make the biggest mark in the world of international competition.

In 1931 Ruud won the first of three World Championships. That year he also set the world record in ski jumping when he registered a 76.5-meter jump in Odnesbakken, Norway. His gold at the World Championships

Birger Ruud

set the stage for his performance at the 1932 Lake Placid Olympics. He surpassed the distances of his countryman, Hans Beck, and was awarded the gold medal.

After the Olympics, Ruud continued his winning streak. In 1934, while practicing jumps after competition in Planica, Slovenia, he became the first man to jump 92 meters. He also won first place in the ski jump at the Holmenkollen competition, the premier Norwegian skiing competition. In 1935, he won his second gold medal in the World Championships.

At the Garmisch-Partenkirchen Olympics, held in 1936, Ruud competed in both the Nordic and the Alpine events, an unusual choice. Most skiers at that time specialized in one or the other, rarely attempting both. His attempt was successful though. The Alpine events combined downhill and slalom and Ruud placed first in the downhill. He would have placed first in the slalom and won the event but he missed a gate and was penalized 4.4 seconds. The penalty moved Ruud from first place to fourth. Despite not placing in the Alpine events, Ruud was able to defend his medal in the ski jump.

Ruud continued to compete internationally, and in 1937 won his third gold medal in the World Championships. Norway recognized his accomplishments by awarding him the Holmenkollen Medal, the highest possible award given by Norway to skiers. In 1938, he traveled to southern California to compete in the First Annual Southern California Open Ski Jump Meet. It was the first ever such meet held on man-made snow in southern California.

The War Intervenes

In 1940, the war came to Norway. Despite repeated promises not to occupy Norway, the Germans invaded in April. Ruud opposed the occupation, as did much of the populace. One of his methods of protesting was to hold unsanctioned ski events to raise money for the resistance. For his part in these ski events, Ruud was arrested in 1943 and placed in the Grini concentration camp. After his release in 1944, Ruud began to work for the resistance. The British would drop artillery and other supplies in the mountains and countryside. Ruud would use his skill and strength as a skier to locate the dropped items.

One of the consequences of World War II was the cancellation of both the 1940 and the 1944 Olympics. Sports scholars and fans alike wonder what other awards could have come to Ruud had he had the opportunity to compete in those games. Fortunately, Ruud was able to prove his abilities one more time in the 1948 St. Moritz Olympics. By this time he was thirty-six years old, which was considered too old to compete. He went to the games as the ski jump coach, but ended up competing in the event and winning a silver medal for his effort.

After Ruud retired from Olympic competition, he spent the rest of his life promoting skiing to the youth of Norway. He was also partially responsible for establishing the Kongsberg Ski Museum. His achievements are recognized throughout Norway, where he is considered by some to be the **Jesse Owens** of ski jumping. Although his name is not common outside skiing circles or in the United States, he is a national hero to the Norwegians. His commitment and achievements in the ski jump brought notoriety to his country. His patriotism in the face of German occupation earned him the respect of his countrymen.

FURTHER INFORMATION

Periodicals

Bisher, Furman. "The Winter Olympics Lillehammer, Norway, the Games: Norwegian Ruud was durable, patriotic." *Atlanta Constitution* (February 26, 1994).

Awards and Accomplishments

1931	Breaks ski jumping record with 76.5-meter jump in Odnesbakken, Norway; triple world champion
1932	Gold medal in ski jumping at Lake Placid Olympics
1934	First place in ski jump at Holmenkollen competition; breaks his own ski jumping record with 92 meter jump in Planica, Slovenia
1935	Triple world champion
1936	Gold medal in ski jumping at Garmisch-Partenkirchen Olympics
1937	Awarded Holmenkollen Medal; triple world champion
1948	Silver medal in ski jumping at St. Moritz Olympics
1985	Inducted into Rolex International Ski Racing Hall of Fame
1999	Named one of Norway's ten best athletes of 20th century

"Norway Names Best Ten Athletes of the Century." Xinhau News Agency (January 16, 1999).

Rogers, Thomas, and Janet Nelson. "Scouting: Honoring Ruud." *New York Times* (April 6, 1985): 16.

"Ski: Norwegian Ski Jump Legend Dies." AAP Newsfeed (June 13, 1998).

Other

Alpenglow Ski History. http://www.alpenglow.org/ ski-history/notes/news/news-patrol-race.html (January 31, 2003)

"Birger Ruud." International Olympic Committee. http://www.olympic.org/uk/athletes/heroes/bio_uk. asp?heros=73289 (January 23, 2003).

International Olympic Committee. http://www.olympic. org/uk/games/past/facts_uk.asp?OLGT=2=1936 (January 18, 2003).

"A Little English." *Trolldalen Times* http://www. azstarnet.com/public/nonprofit/trollda/nlsep99.htm (January 23, 2003).

"Pac Rim Presents Ski History of California." Pacific Rim Alliance. http://www.pacificrimalliance.org/ F.PublicAffairs/SkiHistory/TimelineSoCal.html (January 18, 2003).

Sun Valley Guide: Winter 2001. http://www.sunvalley guide.com/w01/w01locallore.htm (January 31, 2003).

Sketch by Eve M. B. Hermann

Nolan Ryan
1947-

American baseball player

Baseball pitcher Nolan Ryan is the all-time strikeout king, with a career total of 5,714 strikeouts, and seven no-hitters. His career lasted 27 years, the longest

Nolan Ryan

of any major league baseball player. With a career average of 9.55 strikeouts per nine innings, he was one of only three pitchers to average a strikeout per inning. He set a major league record by striking out 10 batters in a game 215 times, and an American League record in 1974 by striking out 19 batters in a 9-inning game. In 1992, a year before his retirement, Ryan became the oldest pitcher in the major leagues to strike out more than 10 batters in a single game. His six seasons of 300+ strikeouts and 15 seasons with 200+ strikeouts are still major league records.

Two Life-Long Loves Begin

Lynn Nolan Ryan Jr. was born in 1947 in Refugio, Texas. He grew up in Alvin, Texas, where his family moved when he was less than two months old. In 1954, when Ryan was seven years old, he father bought him in his first baseball glove at the local hardware store. "That was one of my favorite memories," Ryan said many years later to Jody Goldstein in the *Houston Chronicle*. "Getting to go with my dad down to Alvin Hardware and being the last of six kids and getting to pick out, for the first time, anything new for myself and not being a hand-me-down. That was a new experience."

For Ryan, it was to be the beginning of a lifelong love affair with baseball. He joined his local Little League team soon after. To play in the youth league, Ryan told Goldstein, "That was the highest thing you

Chronology

1947	Born in Refugio, Texas
1947	Moves with his family to Alvin, Texas, forever after his home town
1954	Receives his first baseball glove
1965	Graduates from high school, signs with the New York Mets organization
1966	Plays for Mets' minor league team in Marion, Virginia
1967	Marries Ruth Holdorff
1968	Becomes a pitcher with the Mets' major league team
1969	Plays with the Mets in the 1969 World Series—the only World Series of his career
1971	Is traded to the California Angels
1973	Pitches his first two no-hitters
1979	Leaves the Angels for the Houston Astros
1988	Leaves the Astros for the Texas Rangers
1989	Strikes out his 5,000th player
1993	Retires from playing baseball
1997	Buys minor league baseball team with son Reid and other investors
1999	Elected to the National Baseball Hall of Fame
1999	Elected to the All-Century Team

Related Biography: Baseball Player Reid Ryan

Nolan Ryan's eldest son, Reid Ryan, also became a pro baseball pitcher. He played in the minor leagues for three seasons before hanging up his gloves and becoming a television broadcaster for the Texas Rangers. He missed being more actively involved in the game, though, so he brokered a business deal to purchase a minor league team in Mississippi, convincing his father to join him in the venture. Nolan and Reid brought the team to Texas in 1997, changing its name to the Round Rock Express.

Reid Ryan was born in 1976 in Southern California, where he father was pitching for the California Angels. The Ryans moved back to his parents' native Texas by the time Reid was in high school, and Reid attended his parents' high school, Alvin High. There he played on the same school team on which his father got his start, as well as on the school basketball team. After graduating from high school, he went to the University of Texas on a baseball scholarship, pitching on the school team for one year.

After his freshman year at the University of Texas, Reid transferred to Texas Christian University, where by his senior year, he was the number one starter for the school baseball team, helping the team get to the NCAA regional games for the first time in several years. Coming out of school, Reid went pro, playing for the Hudson-Valley Renegades, a member of the New York-Penn League based New York State's Hudson River Valley.

After three years in the minor leagues, Reid decided to call it quits, acknowledging that he probably lacked the power to do well in the major leagues. "I could always throw strikes," he later told the *Houston Chronicle*'s Alan Truex. "I just couldn't throw a Nolan Ryan fastball." And, "I'd have to be in the minors eight to 10 years before I'd get a cup of coffee in the big leagues."

could look forward to as a kid growing up in a small, rural town like that. To go to tryouts and stuff. That was a big event in your life." Ryan was just 15 years old when he first dated the girl who was to become his wife, Ruth Holdorff. She was 13 years old. "I still remember him asking," Ruth recalled years later to Goldstein. "He game up to me and said, 'Do you think your mom would let you go to a movie?'"

In high school, Ryan and Ruth were voted by their classmates the Most Handsome and Most Beautiful, respectively. "We love to tease them about that," their son Reese told Goldstein. "We always tell them there must not have been much to choose from." Both Ryan and Ruth excelled in athletics in high school. Ryan played basketball as well as baseball, and Ruth became a state tennis champion.

But although he stood out in athletics in high school, he did not do so well academically. He found out as an adult that he had dyslexia, a learning disability that causes one to misread words. But in high school, "one teacher thought he was stupid and wanted to fail him," Ruth later told Goldstein. "He was a C student, with a couple of D's and F's mixed in. The hardest thing for him was spelling. He also had a slight lisp, and as a result, he was shy in the classroom."

As his high school career progressed, Ryan spent more and more time playing baseball, starting to perfect the pitches for which he was to become famous. "I swear," his high school coach Jim Watson told Goldstein years later, "that ball jumped six to eight inches when it reached the plate." Ryan also developed a reputation for throwing wild balls, often hitting batters—a reputation that was to follow him into the major leagues. Some of his high school opponents even became afraid of batting

against Ryan. Said Watson, "Those kids were so scared, they'd swing at anything just to get out of there."

"The Best Arm I Have Ever Seen"

While in his junior year in high school, Ryan attracted the notice of a scout for the New York Mets, Ruff Murff. Murff said in his report on Ryan, "This skinny high school junior has the best arm I have ever seen in my life." Watson thought Murff was exaggerating until he went to see a baseball game at the Astrodome and saw that the major league pitchers there were pitching slower balls than Ryan.

Ryan graduated from Alvin High School in 1965 after helping the school team get to the state finals, and immediately signed as a player with the New York Mets. His first assignment was with the Mets' minor league team in Marion, Virginia, for which he started playing in 1966. In 1967 Ryan married Ruth. (They eventually had two sons, Reid, the eldest, Reese, and a daughter named Wendy. By 2002, Ryan and Ruth had three grandchildren, Jackson, Caroline, and Victoria.) Ryan worked his way up to the major leagues, becoming a pitcher for the Mets' major league team after three years, in 1968.

Ryan did not enjoy living in New York. As he later told the *Houston Chronicle*'s Neil Hohlfeld "I hated that place. I'd get cabin fever, sitting around the house. Then you'd drive to the ballpark and, no matter what time you went, there would be traffic and people getting in fights, honking, flipping people off, yelling." In addition to the shock of moving from the open spaces of his native

Awards and Accomplishments

1969	Wins World Series with the New York Mets
1973	Pitches two no-hitters
1973	Awarded American League's Joe Cronin Award for significant achievement
1974	Pitches third no-hitter
1975	Pitches fourth no-hitter
1981	Pitches fifth no-hitter
1983	Becomes record holder for most strikeouts
1987	Elected to Texas Baseball Hall of Fame
1989	Strikes out his 5,000th player
1989	Awarded American League's Joe Cronin Award for significant achievement
1990	Pitches sixth no-hitter
1990	Awarded Sporting News Annual Man of the Year Award
1990	Named Male Athlete of the Year Award by United Press International
1990	Awarded U.S. Sports Academy/USA Pro Sportsman of the Year Award
1991	Pitches seventh no-hitter
1991	Elected to Peter J. McGovern Little League Museum Hall of Excellence
1999	Elected to the All-Century Team
1999	Elected to the National Baseball Hall of Fame

Nolan Ryan

Texas to the densest city in the country, Ryan had the stress of proving himself for a team that had a surplus of pitchers and could therefore afford to let him go if he did not perform well enough.

On top of everything else, Ryan had military duties to fulfill, requiring absences during the baseball season. "Looking back," he told Hohlfeld, "it turned out to be one of those situations where things just didn't match up. The combination of how many good, young pitchers there were and my military obligations, that made for some problems." Nevertheless, Ryan made it along with the Mets to the World Series in 1969, defeating the Orioles 4-1 to take the title. Then, the death of his father at the age of 63 in 1970 sent Ryan to a new low. He very nearly quit baseball.

The Strikeout King

In 1971, Ryan was traded to the California Angels. It turned out to be a godsend. As he told Hohlfeld, "I went to a team that was in the building stages and I got to pitch every fourth day. My military obligation was over that year, and I went from pitching 130 innings with the Mets to 300-plus innings each year with the Angels. At that point in my career, really, that's all I was looking for." Ryan stayed with the Angels for eight years, playing from the 1972 season until 1979. These years formed the foundation of his career. It was during that time that he learned to hone his pitching skills to a razor sharpness, in 1972 leading his league in strikeouts (329). As in his early years, he developed a reputation for aggression on the mound. Of the batters who faced Ryan at this time was Tom Grieve, then a player for the Texas Rangers. He later said of Ryan to Hohlfeld, "He was the only pitcher I faced ... that fear entered into the

at-bat. He was throwing so hard, and he was wild, and you knew he was mean. He'd knock you down, and you never knew whether it was on purpose or not."

In 1973, Ryan pitched the first two of what was to be a total of seven no-hitters during his career. By 1974, Ryan's fastball was being clocked at 100.9 miles per hour. Also in 1974, he pitched his third no-hitter. He pitched his fourth no-hitter in 1975. In 1979, Ryan moved his family back to Texas, where he signed a 4-year, $4.4 million contract with the Astros. This made him the best-paid athlete in history. Ryan pitched his fifth no-hit game with the Astros in 1981, earning him the distinction of being the no-hit champion. Then 34 years old, Ryan wasn't sure that he would have the stamina to pull off this feat. "It was the one thing I wanted," he told the *Houston Chronicle*'s Bill Sullivan. "I'd had a shot at if for a long time, but because of my age, I thought I wouldn't get it." Get it he did, and he repeated this remarkable performance two more times, in 1990, playing a no-hit game with the Texas Rangers, with which he signed in 1988, and a final time less than a year later, in 1991, to complete a record series of seven no-hitters.

Career Statistics

Yr	Team	W	L	ERA	GS	CG	SHO	IP	H	R	BB	SO
1966	NYM	0	1	15.00	1	0	0	3.0	5	5	3	6
1968	NYM	6	9	3.09	18	3	0	134.0	93	50	75	133
1969	NYM	6	3	3.53	10	2	0	89.1	60	38	53	92
1970	NYM	7	11	3.42	19	5	2	131.2	86	59	97	125
1971	NYM	10	14	3.97	26	3	0	152.0	125	78	116	137
1972	CAL	19	16	2.28	39	20	9	284.0	166	80	157	329
1973	CAL	21	16	2.87	39	26	4	326.0	238	113	162	383
1974	CAL	22	16	2.89	41	26	3	332.2	221	127	202	367
1975	CAL	14	12	3.45	28	10	5	198.0	152	90	132	186
1976	CAL	17	18	3.36	39	21	7	284.1	193	117	183	327
1977	CAL	19	16	2.77	37	22	4	299.0	198	110	204	241
1978	CAL	10	13	3.72	31	14	3	234.2	183	106	148	260
1979	CAL	16	14	3.60	34	17	5	222.2	169	104	114	223
1980	HOU	11	10	3.35	25	4	2	233.2	205	100	98	200
1981	HOU	11	5	1.69	21	5	3	149.0	99	34	68	140
1982	HOU	16	12	3.16	35	10	3	250.1	196	100	109	245
1983	HOU	14	9	2.98	29	5	2	196.1	134	74	101	183
1984	HOU	12	11	3.04	30	5	2	183.2	143	78	69	197
1985	HOU	10	12	3.80	35	4	0	232.0	205	108	95	209
1986	HOU	12	8	3.34	30	1	0	178.0	119	72	82	194
1987	HOU	8	16	2.76	34	0	0	211.2	154	75	87	270
1988	HOU	12	11	3.52	33	4	1	220.0	186	98	87	228
1989	TEX	16	10	3.20	32	6	2	239.1	162	96	98	301
1990	TEX	13	9	3.44	30	5	2	204.0	137	86	74	232
1991	TEX	12	6	2.91	27	2	2	173.0	102	58	72	203
1992	TEX	5	9	3.72	27	2	0	157.1	138	75	69	157
1993	TEX	5	5	4.88	13	0	0	66.1	54	47	40	46
TOTAL		324	292	3.19	773	222	61	5386.0	3923	2178	2795	5714

CAL: California Angels; HOU: Houston Astros; NYM: New York Mets; TEX: Texas Rangers.

Ryan finished his playing career with the Texas Rangers. In his first season with the Rangers, Ryan won 16 games and struck out 301 batters It was also with the Rangers that he pitched his sixth and seventh no-hitters. Other milestones he passed with the Rangers were his 300th win and his 5,000 strikeout. "The years I spent with the Rangers were the ones that put me over the top," he told the *Houston Chronicle*'s Bill Sullivan. In particular, Ryan was proudest of his 5,000th strikeout (of the Oakland A's **Rickey Henderson**). As he told Sullivan, "It represented that many innings pitched and being able to maintain that style of pitching my entire career." Ryan retired from playing baseball in 1993, at the remarkable age of 46. He was the oldest player ever to play for the Texas Rangers.

In all, Ryan's career as a major league baseball player spanned 27 years. He played for four teams—the Mets, with which he made his pro ball debut, the California Angels, the Houston Astros, and finally, the Texas Rangers. Four decades as pro saw Ryan set or break 51 major league pitching records. Among these were seven no-hitters, and 5,714 strikeouts during the course of his career. He also played longer than any other player. He won a total of 324 games.

Ryan has had his uniform number retired by three teams, also a major league record. His number was retired by the Angels, the Astros, and the Rangers. He was elected to the National Baseball Hall of Fame in 1999, his first year of eligibility. The same year, he was elected to the All-Century Team.

Ryan still lives in his hometown, Alvin, Texas, with his wife Ruth. After retiring from baseball, he entered into several business ventures, among them ownership and management of a bank based in Alvin, two restaurants, and a group of cattle ranches. In 1997, Ryan and his son Reid headed a group of investors that bought a minor league team affiliated with the Houston Astros, moving it from its Jackson, Mississippi base to Texas and renaming it the Round Rock Express.

FURTHER INFORMATION

Periodicals

"Baseball: A Chip Off the Glorious Ryan Arm." *New York Times* (July 11, 1994): C9.

Truex, Alan. "Express Deliverer; Reid Ryan Has Found Round Rock Ready for Minor-League." *Houston Chronicle* (April 13, 2000): C9.

Other

"The Express Gets on Track." Round Rock Express Baseball. http://www.roundrockexpress.com/history. (December 11, 2002).

Where Is He Now?

After retiring from the Texas Rangers in 1993, Nolan Ryan entered into several business ventures. He became the majority owner and the chairman of the board of a bank with branches in Alvin and Danbury, Texas, the Express Bank, and opened a restaurant near Three Rivers, Texas called Nolan Ryan's Waterfront Restaurant and Brass Inn. He also owns a string of cattle ranches in South Texas.

Ryan has also been able to keep a hand in the game he loves best. In 1997, Ryan and his son Reid, a former pitcher in the minor leagues, headed a group of investors that bought a Houston Astros affiliated minor league team based in Jackson, Mississippi called the Generals. They moved the team to Round Rock, Texas, and renamed it the Round Rock Express.

Ryan is also actively involved in several civic organizations. He is on the board of directors of the Nolan Ryan Foundation, a nonprofit organization based in Alvin, Texas dedicated to honoring Ryan's baseball career. Ryan also serves of the boards of the Justin Cowboy Crisis Fund, the Texas Water Foundation, the Natural Resources Foundation of Texas, and the Alvin Community College Baseball Fund. Ryan still lives in his hometown of Alvin, Texas, with his wife Ruth.

"Express Staff: Lynn Nolan Ryan Jr." Round Rock Express Baseball. http://www.roundrockexpress.com/staff/item15528. (December 9, 2002).

"Good Deal: Despite Some Shaky Moments, California Strikes Gold." *Houston Chronicle.* http://www.chron.com/cs/CDA/plainstory.hts/special/ryan/295392. (December 9, 2002).

"A Hero's Welcome: Arlington Fans Get Hospitality Repaid." *Houston Chronicle.* http://www.chron.com/cs/CDA/plainstory.hts/special/ryan/294710. (December 9, 2002).

"Home Economics: Contract Dispute Forces Final Move." *Houston Chronicle.* http://www.chron.com/cs/CDA/plainstory.hts/special/ryan/294946. (December 9, 2002).

"Magnificent Seven: Chances of Topping this Mark Far-Flung." *Houston Chronicle.* http://www.chron.com/cs/CDA/plainstory.hts/special/ryan/294711. (December 9, 2002).

"Nolan Ryan." CNN/SI. http://sportsillustrated.cnn.com/baseball/mlb/all_time_stats/players/r/1985/. (December 9, 2002).

"Nolan Ryan Foundation." Nolan Ryan Foundation. http://www.nolanryanfoundation.org/. (December 9, 2002).

"Nolan Ryan: Journey of a Legend." *Houston Chronicle.* http://www.chron.com/content/chronicle/special/ryan/photos/scoutcard.html. (December 9, 2002).

"Nolan Ryan Statistics." Baseball-Reference.com. http://www.baseball-reference.com/r/ryanno01.shtml. (December 9, 2002).

"Slow Start: New York Doesn't Become Apple of Young Pitcher's Eye." *Houston Chronicle.* http://www.chron.com/cs/CDA/plainstory.hts/special/ryan/294770. (December 9, 2002).

"Young Gun: Solid Roots in Hometown Become Foundation for Success." *Houston Chronicle.* http://www.chron.com/cs/CDA/plainstory.hts/special/ryan/294698. (December 9, 2002).

Sketch by Michael Belfiore

Gabriela Sabatini
1970-

Argentine tennis player

Argentinean Gabriela Sabatini was a teen tennis phenomenon in the mid-1980s who, while popular on the circuit, never lived up to her potential as a player. While she had a great tennis game, she only won one grand slam singles title, the U.S. Open in 1990. Sabatini left professional tennis behind in the mid-1990s to concentrate on her work in the perfume business.

Born May 16, 1970, in Buenos Aires, Argentina, Sabatini was the daughter of Osvaldo and Beatriz Sabatini. Her father was an executive at General Motors, who later gave up his career to manage his daughter's tennis career.

Buenos Aires was the leading tennis city in South America, and Sabatini began playing when she was six years old. She wanted to play because her older brother was a junior player. Sabatini began taking private lessons a year later, and by the time she was 10 years old, she was the number one under-12 player in Argentina. From an early age, she was motivated to win and hated to lose.

Trains in Florida

Within a few years, Sabatini left Argentina to train with coach Patricio Apey in Key Biscane, Florida. In 1983, she began playing on the world junior tennis circuit. She was the youngest to win the Orange Bowl Girls 18 singles tournament. After being the number one ranked junior in the world in 1984, Sabatini felt she had nothing left to prove on the junior circuit.

Turns Professional

In 1985, Sabatini turned professional. Her first big splash was at the Family Circle Magazine Cup where she beat three ranked players. She later made the semifinals of the French Open, the youngest to do this at the time, but lost to **Chris Evert**. She finished the year ranked number 11 in the world.

Because of her young age, observers were afraid that Sabatini would burn out. She dropped out of school

Gabriela Sabatini

when she was 14 to concentrate on tennis, though she planned on completing her education later. Sabatini had no close friends, and constantly dealt only with adults. She was also isolated on the professional tour, in part because she did not speak English for the first three years.

In 1986, Sabatini made the semifinals of Wimbledon. As her star rose in women's tennis, her looks, not unlike those of a movie star/model, led to a number of endorsement deals. She ended the year ranked in the top 10, where she would remain until 1996.

In 1988, while Sabatini won a silver medal in ladies singles tennis at the Summer Olympics, won the Virginia Slims Tournament, and made the finals of the U.S. Open, she had problems with endurance during matches. She changed coaches to Angel Gimenez, who challenged her to work on her conditioning and kept her interested in the game. When she began as a professional, she was a baseline player, but later developed a potent serve-and-volley attack. The graceful Sabatini had a great backhand, but her serve was never strong.

Contemplates Quitting

In 1989, Sabatini was ranked number three, but she was generally regarded as not reaching her full potential as a player. Many tennis observers thought she could be a great rival to **Steffi Graf**, and one of the futures of women's tennis, but she never made it. Though Sabatini would appear in a semifinal of a Grand Slam every year and win a tournament every year from 1985-95 (except 1993), she did not win big.

Martina Navratilova told Robin Finn of the *New York Times,* "She's so erratic. Her game is more complicated than Steffi [Graf]'s, and she's got better ground strokes. But...." In the late 1980s, Sabatini thought about quitting, admitting that she did not have the mental edge to win.

Wins U.S. Open

Sabatini addressed these issues by working with a tennis psychiatrist and hiring a new coach, Carlos Kirmayr, after losing in the first round of the French Open in 1990. She became more aggressive on the court, and won that year's U.S. Open women's singles title. She defeated Graf 6-2, 7-6.

In the early 1990s, Sabatini reached her peak as a professional, earning $4 million on the women's tour in 1990-91. She was more interested in the game than ever and played well. In 1991 and 1992, she won both the Bausch & Lomb Championship and Family Circle Magazine Cup. She also became more social with other players.

In 1992, Sabatini began having problems with tendonitis. Her relatively weak serve began being a problem in matches. Though many of her advisors thought she should take a hiatus to recover from her injuries and mentally recharge, she elected to play through her problems. After making the semifinals of the Australian Open in 1993, she did not play well in 1993 and 1994.

She lost in the first round of the French Open in 1994. Sabatini switched coaches several times, but eventually returned to Kirmayr.

Sabatini's last win as a professional was the Virginia Slims championship in 1995. With injury problems, she retired in 1996, after winning no titles that season. When Sabatini retired, she primarily focused on the perfume business that she had been a part of since 1989. That year, she introduced her first fragrance, Gabriela Sabatini, and went on to develop at least eight others. She also had her own line of clothing, linens, and watches. Sabatini remained marginally involved in sports as an athlete representative to the IOC (International Olympic Committee). While she played in some exhibition tennis matches on occasion, she did not enjoy playing the game much.

When she retired, she was ranked 29th in the world. While she earned about $8-11 million from playing tennis, Sabatini made $20 million from endorsements. As Josh Young wrote in *The Washington Times,* "She was beautiful to watch but dull in conversation, talented but lacking killer instinct. In the end, it seems she should have gone further in tennis, but perhaps she went further than she should have."

CONTACT INFORMATION

Address: c/o Cosmopolitan Cosmetics, GmBH, Venloer Strasse 241-245, 50823 Koln Germany. Online: www.gabriela-sabatini.com.

FURTHER INFORMATION

Books

Christensen, Karen, et al, eds. *International Encyclopedia of Women and Sports.* New York: Macmillan Reference USA, 2001.

Johnson, Anne Janette. *Great Women in Sports.* Detroit: Visible Ink Press, 1996.

Layden, Joe. *Women in Sports.* General Publishing Group, 1997.

Periodicals

Arias, Ron. "Look out, Chris & Martina—Gabriela is Gunning for You." *People* (September 7, 1987): 127.

Finn, Robin. "Critics' Carping Follows Sabatini." *New York Times* (November 12, 1989): section 8, p. 11.

Finn, Robin. "Sabatini Shifts Gears and Learns to Enjoy the Ride." *New York Times* (April 13, 1992): C3.

Finn, Robin. "Shedding a Demon, Sabatini Flourishes." *New York Times* (November 15, 1990): D23.

Finn, Robin. "Unhappy Anniversary for Stumbling Sabatini." *New York Times* (May 5, 1994): B23.

Frey, Jennifer. "She's Long on Talent, Short on the Serve." *New York Times* (September 7, 1994): B17.

"Goodbye, Gaby! Farewell With Few Regrets." *The Advertiser* (October 26, 1996): 58.

Honeyball, Lee. "Don't Cry for Me." *Sunday Herald Sun* (April 7, 2002): Z14.

Honeyball, Lee. "Whatever Happened To? Gabriela Sabatini." *The Observer* (February 3, 2002): 22.

Jenkins, Sally. "A New World Order." *Sports Illustrated* (March 18, 1991): 66.

Jenkins, Sally. "Gabriela Sabatini." *Sports Illustrated* (June 6, 1994): 60.

Kervin, Alison. "Model Competitor Setting Example by Continuing to Court Success." *The Times* (July 2, 2002): 36.

Newman, Bruce. "Talk About Net Gains." *Sports Illustrated* (May 2, 1988): 52.

Penner, Degen. "Egos & Ids; Tennis, Music and Perfume on Her Mind." *New York Times* (November 14, 1993): section 9, p. 4.

Picker, Al. "Game, Set, Match: Sabatini Bows Out." *Star-Ledger* (October 23, 1996): 59.

Roberts, John. "Sweet Smell of Success Off Court for Sabatini the Underachiever." *The Independent* (January 7, 2002): 7.

"Tennis player Gabriela Sabatini." *Christian Science Monitor* (August 31, 2000): 19.

Wolff, Alexander. "Upset Time." *Sports Illustrated* (September 17, 1990): 22.

Young, Josh. "When the Competitive Fire Finally Went, So Went Sabatini." *Washington Times* (October 30, 1996): 5.

Sketch by A. Petruso

Joe Sakic
1969-

Canadian hockey player

Champion hockey player Joe Sakic has earned respect as a quiet leader and a skillful player with a

Joe Sakic

talent for stealth and a lightning-quick wrist. From his childhood in Canada, the son of Croatian immigrants, to his 2002 standing as one of the most highly paid, award-winning players in the National Hockey League (NHL), Sakic has followed his father's strict work ethic. He discovered his natural leadership ability after a tragic accident involving his high school hockey team in 1986. Sakic is honored for his kindness, loyalty to his team, and humble nature. A longtime center and team captain with the Colorado Avalanche, Sakic has led his team to two Stanley Cups.

Young Star

Joseph Steven Sakic was born July 7, 1969, in the Vancouver, British Columbia, Canada, suburb of Burnaby, the son of Croatian immigrants Marijan, a carpenter and commercial fisherman, and Slavica Sakic, a homemaker. Before Joe started school, his family spoke only Croatian at home. Learning English a little later than other students, combined with a natural shyness, probably caused him to develop the economy of words he is known for today, particularly around reporters.

Many promising young Canadian hockey players left their hometowns to play major junior hockey. Sakic and two teammates moved to Saskatchewan to play with the Swift Current Broncos when Joe was seventeen. The players lived with host families and attended Swift Current Comprehensive High School. There Joe met Debbie Metivier, who would become his wife a few years later.

Chronology

1969	Born July 7 in Burnaby, British Columbia, Canada
1985	Begins playing hockey with Lethbridge Broncos
1986	Plays with Canadian National Team
1986	Leaves home to play hockey with Swift Current Broncos in Saskatchewan and attend Swift Current Comprehensive High School; bus accident on the way to a game on December 30 leaves four team members dead
1988	Joins Quebec Nordiques after being the fifteenth pick in National Hockey League (NHL) draft
1989	Adopts jersey number 19
1992	Is named team captain of the Nordiques; gets four-year, $8.8 million contract
1993	Nordiques make playoffs for first time in six seasons; marries Debbie Metivier—they will have a son, Mitchell, and twins Chase and Kamryn
1995	Nordiques finish second overall in NHL's strike-shortened season; in June, team moves to Denver, Colorado, and changes name to Colorado Avalanche
1996	Colorado Avalanche wins Stanley Cup championship
1997	Is injured in January and misses seventeen games; Colorado Avalanche finishes first overall in NHL regular season but is defeated in playoffs by the Detroit Red Wings
1997	In August, the New York Rangers offer Sakic, now a free agent, a $15 million signing bonus plus $2 million a year for three years; Colorado Avalanche matches the offer
1998	With eight other Avalanche players, is chosen to participate in Winter Olympics in Nagano, Japan; is named captain of the Canadian team but is injured and misses last two games
1999	Scores 1,000th point on December 27
2000	Nets 400th goal on March 23
2001	Leads Avalanche to a second Stanley Cup Championship; signs five-year, $50.5 million contract with Colorado Avalanche in late June, just before scheduled to become a free agent on July 1
2002	Plays on Team Canada in 2002 Olympics

Tragedy at Swift Current

When Sakic was in his first year at Swift Current, the hockey team was traveling to a game in Regina on December 30, 1986, when it hit a patch of black ice on a highway overpass and plunged to the service road below. Four of Sakic's teammates—who had been playing cards in the back of the bus—were killed. Joe, who was unhurt, and his some of his teammates walked out the bus's broken front window. As the Broncos continued the season in memory of their lost teammates, Sakic came forward as a natural leader. Earning sixty goals and seventy-three assists, he helped the team make the playoffs and pulled his teammates through an emotionally difficult time.

Small for his age, at 5' 11" and 185 pounds, Sakic was the fifteenth pick for the Quebec Nordiques draft in the spring of 1987, but he chose to stay another year in junior hockey with Swift Current to strengthen his upper body and perhaps the spirits of his teammates as well. He finished the season with seventy-eight goals and eighty-two assists and was named Canadian Major Junior Player of the Year. The next day, he signed a contract with the Nordiques.

When Sakic joined the Nordiques in 1988, they were in a slump due to financial problems and management troubles. Although he scored more than 100 points twice during the next four years, the Nordiques did not make the playoffs until 1992-93, the season he was made team captain. Suddenly, sportswriters and the public began to take notice.

Colorado Avalanche

Sakic was the Nordiques' top scorer in 1995, when the team finished second in a season shortened by a players' strike. On June 21 of that year, the team moved to Denver, Colorado, and changed its name to the Colorado Avalanche. Sakic scored fifty-one goals, sixty-nine assists, and 120 points in the 1995-96 season, and the Avalanche won the Stanley Cup. Sakic was awarded the Conn Smythe Trophy as most valuable player on his team in the playoffs. He had scored eighteen goals and sixteen assists in twenty-two games.

On receiving the Stanley Cup, Sakic held it up to the 450,000 Colorado fans. He later said, "There is no greater satisfaction than winning the Cup . . . just thinking about it makes me speechless."

The Avalanche had another great season in 1996-97, finishing first overall and winning the President's Trophy, in spite of injuries that kept Sakic and second-line center Peter Forsberg out of seventeen games. Sakic was playing well again by the playoffs, however, and the team had a winning streak before falling prey to the Detroit Red Wings.

Career Statistics

Yr	Team	GP	G	A	PTS	+/-	PIM	SOG	SPCT	PPG	SHG
1988-89	NORD	70	23	39	62	-36	24	148	15.5	10	0
1989-90	NORD	80	39	63	102	-40	27	234	16.7	8	1
1990-91	NORD	80	48	61	109	-26	24	245	19.6	12	3
1991-92	NORD	69	29	65	94	5	20	217	13.4	6	3
1992-93	NORD	78	48	57	105	-3	40	264	18.2	20	2
1993-94	NORD	84	28	64	92	-8	18	279	10.0	10	1
1994-95	NORD	47	19	43	62	7	30	157	12.1	3	2
1995-96	AVAL	82	51	69	120	14	44	339	15.0	17	6
1996-97	AVAL	65	22	52	74	-10	34	261	8.4	10	2
1997-98	AVAL	64	27	36	63	0	50	254	10.6	12	1
1998-99	AVAL	73	41	55	96	23	29	255	16.1	12	5
1999-2000	AVAL	60	28	53	81	30	28	242	11.6	5	1
2000-2001	AVAL	82	54	64	118	45	30	332	16.3	19	3
2001-2002	AVAL	82	26	53	79	12	18	260	10.0	9	1
TOTAL		1016	483	774	1257	13	416	3487	13.9	153	31

AVAL: Colorado Avalanche; NORD: Quebec Nordiques.

Worth a Fortune

In the off-season of 1997, Sakic became a restricted free agent. He could entertain contract offers from other teams, but the Avalanche had the right to match any contract in order to keep him. In August the New York Rangers offered him a $21 million contract—$2 million per year for three years, with a $15 million signing bonus. A few days later, the Avalanche matched the offer, to the relief of Denver fans. Commenting on the generous contract, Sakic told a *Denver Post* writer, "I don't think I'm going to feel any more pressure than I have in the past.... I've always been one to put pressure on myself and do whatever I can to help the team win." Only one sore spot had come between Sakic and Avalanche general manager Pierre Lacroix: Sakic wanted a "no-trade" clause in his contract, providing him with a place on the team regardless of his success, but Lacroix did not believe in them.

In 1997, Sakic promised the team and the fans another Stanley Cup, but it was a few seasons in coming. The Avalanche came in sixth overall that year in regular play. Several members, including Sakic, had participated in the 1998 Winter Olympics in Japan. In addition, a knee injury had kept Sakic out of eighteen games in the regular season that year. In the 1998-99 season, he was out several games with a shoulder injury, but he still scored a team-best forty-one goals in seventy-three games, and the team made the playoffs.

In 1999-2000, Sakic played only sixty games, but the team went to the playoffs and he was invited to his eighth All-Star game. The following season, 2000-2001, brought the long-promised second Stanley Cup for the Colorado Avalanche. Sakic scored 118 points during the season, with twelve game-winning goals out of a total of fifty-four. He scored twenty-six points against the New Jersey Devils in the final game of the playoffs, making

him the NHL's top scorer. He showed his true team spirit when he briefly held the Stanley Cup up for the cameras then promptly handed it to retiring defenseman Ray Bourque, while applauding him.

Team Commitment

As the July 1, 2001, deadline approached for Sakic to become an unrestricted free agent, Lacroix remained hopeful that Sakic would stay with his team. In a suspenseful last-minute signing, Sakic and teammates **Patrick Roy** and Rob Blake made a commitment to stay in Denver. Sakic's five-year contract was for $50.5 million, with an optional sixth year making it $57 million. The top salary for the previous single season in the NHL had been $10 million. Lacroix said in *Sports Illustrated* of the signing, "To have athletes like Joe Sakic, Patrick Roy, and Rob Blake commit themselves to this organization and market before having a chance to be an unrestricted free agent indicates how special they are and how equally special this city and hockey environment is." The Denver fans had indeed showed their appreciation: the Avalanche's home games were sold out 295 consecutive times, including playoffs, since 1995.

Since re-signing with the Avalanche, Sakic has continued to work toward making the team the consistent best in the NHL. He scored a total of seventy-nine points during the 2001-2002 season and again played with Team Canada at the Olympics, where he scored four goals and three assists in six games.

Cultivating his quiet leadership ability, Sakic has become not only one of the most respected players in the league but also one of the most admired team captains. His numerous awards and generous contracts speak for his value as a player, and his steadfast loyalty to the Avalanche shows his dedication to the principle that

Awards and Accomplishments

1987	Western Hockey League (WHL) East Most Valuable Player; WHL Stewart (Butch) Paul Memorial Trophy; WHL All-Star Second Team
1988	Canadian Major Junior Player of the Year; Four Broncos Memorial Trophy; Bob Clarke Trophy; Canadian Hockey League Player of the Year; WHL Player of the Year
1990-94, 1996, 1998, 2001	NHL All-Star Game
1994	Gold medal, World Hockey Championships
1996	As captain of Colorado Avalanche, team won Stanley Cup; Conn Smythe Trophy; NHL All-Star Game
1997	Avalanche won President's Trophy
1998	Ranked 15th best player in NHL by *Hockey News*; participated in Winter Olympics in Nagano, Japan, with Canadian team
2000	NHL Player of the Month, November
2001	As captain of Colorado Avalanche, team won Clarence Campbell Bowl and Stanley Cup; named NHL's Most Valuable Player; Hart Trophy; Lady Byng Memorial Trophy; Lester B. Pearson Trophy; Bud Light Plus-Minus Award

Conn Smythe Trophy is given to NHL's most valuable player for his team in the playoffs

Stanley Cup is NHL hockey's championship award, given following a best-of-seven-games series between Eastern and Western Conference champions

Hart Memorial Trophy is awarded to NHL's most valuable player to his team

Lady Byng Memorial Trophy goes to player with best sportsmanship and most gentlemanly conduct, with high level of playing ability

Lester B. Pearson Trophy is awarded to the NHL's outstanding player as selected by the members of the NHL Player's Association

winning is a team effort. He once told *Sporting News,* "Pressure is part of the game. But I don't worry about it. I just go out and play the game as hard as I can."

CONTACT INFORMATION

Address: Joe Sakic, c/o Colorado Avalanche Hockey Club, Pepsi Center, 1000 Chopper Circle, Denver, CO 80204. Phone: 303-405-1100. Online: http://www.coloradoavalanche.com.

FURTHER INFORMATION

Books

Newsmakers, Issue 1. "Joe Sakic." Detroit: Gale Group, 2002.

Periodicals

"Get the Man Some Silver Polish." *Maclean's* (June 25, 2001): 46.

Habib, Daniel G. "Colorado Avalanche: Having Peter Forsberg for a Full Season Makes a Formidable Team." *Sports Illustrated* (October 14, 2002): 84.

Murphy, Austin. "Two Much." *Sports Illustrated* (December 9, 1996): 50.

Wigge, Larry. "Sneaky Good: Joe Sakic Is All Action and No Talk." *Sporting News* (January 14, 2002): 52.

Wigge, Larry. "Teams Don't Let MVPs Walk, and Sakic Won't Either." *Sporting News* (April 30, 2001): 56.

Other

Biography Resource Center Online. http://galenet.galegroup.com/. "Joseph Steven Sakic." Detroit: Gale Group, 1999.

Biography Resource Center Online. http://galenet.galegroup.com/. "Peter Forsberg." Detroit: Gale Group, 1999.

CBS Sportsline. "No. 19 Joe Sakic." http://cbs.sportsline.com/ (November 1, 2002).

Colorado Avalanche. http://www.coloradoavalanche.com/ (November 18, 2002).

"Colorado's Joe Sakic Named NHL Player of the Week." Colorado Avalanche. http://www.coloradoavalanche.com/ (November 4, 2002).

"Free-Agent Avalanche: Champs Re-sign Stars Sakic, Roy, Blake on First Day." CNN Sports Illustrated. http://sportsillustrated.cnn.com/hockey/nhl/ (July 1, 2001).

Internet Hockey Database. "Joe Sakic." http://www.hockeydb.com/ (November 14, 2002).

Sketch by Ann H. Shurgin

Jamie Sale and David Pelletier

Canadian figure skaters

It is the dream of perhaps every amateur athlete: to mount the podium and accept an Olympic gold medal. It happened for Canadian pairs skaters Jamie Sale (pronounced SA-lay) and David Pelletier (PELL-tee-ay). But in their case, the glow of the gold was tarnished somewhat by the taint of scandal that preceded it. Theirs was one of the most compelling stories to come out of the 2002 Winter Games in Salt Lake City, Utah, and raised questions about how figure skating is judged.

Growing up on Ice

Sale and Pelletier had been partners for only four years when they leaped into international headlines. The two Canada natives grew up three years in age and four provinces apart; Sale in Alberta and Pelletier in Quebec. For the young girl, skating was a creative outlet for her energy. She first got on the ice at age three, wearing double-bladed skates to help her balance. At five, Sale was enrolled in both figure skating and gymnastics, but she would make her choice two years later.

Jamie Sale and David Pelletier, right, with Russian skaters Yelena Berezhnaya and Anton Sikharulidze

Meanwhile, Pelletier was also making a choice—figure skating or hockey. He made his decision at fifteen, despite the razzing from his friends that he had entered a "girl's sport." When a coach told Pelletier's mother that the boy had no talent, David, an independent sort, responded by redoubling his efforts. Soon his practice and dedication had paid off. He began competing, first as a single, but it was in pairs that he began to realize success. He was partners with Julie Laporte when the two of them placed seventh at the 1992 world junior championships. Three years later Pelletier and new partner Allison Gaylor finished fifteenth at the 1995 world championships.

Change Partners and Skate

Sale was also making her name on the world stage. At age sixteen she and partner Jason Turner represented Canada at the Olympic Winter Games in Lillehammer, Norway, placing twelfth. That same year they placed sixteenth at the world championships in Chiba, Japan; after those two competitions Sale and Turner decided to go their separate ways. Sale embarked on a singles career, peaking at fifth in the 1995 Canadian Nationals.

Pelletier and Sale had met more than once in the past. In 1994, the two were Canadian national teammates, though she skated in the senior division and he in the juniors. Pelletier admitted to *Chatelaine* interviewer Beth Hitchcock that the thought of partnering with Olympian Sale was "intimidating." Though she was the younger of the two, "in skating you put people on a pedestal," Pelletier said. "She was the star out West; she was the future. She was a very confident, cocky little girl. Everybody in Quebec wanted to skate with Jamie Sale."

By 1996, however, Sale was on a downward track, splitting with Olympics partner Turner and struggling as a singles competitor. The first tryout of Sale and Pelletier was described as "awkward" in the *Chatelaine* piece. "To start, Sale wasn't entirely sure she wanted to leave Alberta," noted Hitchcock. Even Pelletier's coaches "were discouraged by what they saw; they advised him to look elsewhere." When Pelletier delivered an outright rejection, Sale was "devastated," as the skater told Hitchcock. "I thought he was my last hope," she remarked.

Depressed and unmotivated, Sale was delivered an ultimatum by her parents: no more funding unless her heart was truly in the sport. She "picked herself up," said Hitchcock, "hired a trainer and went to skating boot camp." Pelletier was likewise experiencing difficulty.

After learning his first partner, Laporte, had been killed in an auto accident in 1998, "I decided to take two months off my skating," Pelletier told an interviewer for Canadian television. "I sat down and wrote some criteria I wanted for another partner. I decided that if I can't find anybody, I'll just quit."

Together at Last

He and interim partner Caroline Roy hadn't performed well enough to make the Canadian senior team; after they finished a disappointing sixth in the 1998 nationals, "his coach, Richard Gautier, gave him two choices: quit or give Sale a second try," according to James Deacon in a *Maclean's* piece. "It wasn't much of a choice for either of them. Off the ice, he was serving beer at the Molson Centre in Montreal, while Sale was working as a waitress in Edmonton." The two engaged in one more tryout, during which Pelletier hoisted Sale in the air. She whispered to her coach, "Wow, I had no idea it was supposed to be like this!" A new partnership was born.

The debut of Sale and Pelletier took place at the 1998 Skate Canada finals. The pair won a bronze medal. Their skating would take a dramatic new turn with the addition of choreographer Lori Nichol, who created a routine from the theme to the movie *Love Story*. As they recreated the story of the ill-fated lovers, Sale and Pelletier began embarking on a love story of their own. Pelletier separated from his wife and the two skaters became a real-life couple, sharing a home in Edmonton, Alberta, while remaining protective of their privacy.

As Sale and Pelletier began to excel in elite competition—they were undefeated from 2000 to 2001 in international meets—their path led to the 2002 Olympic Winter Games. By the time they arrived in Salt Lake City, Utah, the two were considered "the It couple of figure skating," in the words of *Time International* reporter Mary Jollimore. "In a pursuit that rewards mirror imaging of every move," explained James Deacon of *Maclean's*, "they are uncanny mimics of one another,

gliding seamlessly around the ice, totally in sync. And they skate with such evident passion—for the sport, for the music, for each other."

Having finished second after the Olympics short program, Sale and Pelletier prepared to "trot out their straight-to-the-tear-duct long program," as *Sports Illustrated* reporter Michael Farber put it. "They were born for Love Story: Sale, with gleaming black hair and ready smile, could pass for a young Ali McGraw, and Pelletier has the boyish looks and carefree ways that evoke Ryan O'Neal bounding across Harvard Yard." But no Olympic gold is ever assured, and for Sale and Pelletier the main threat came from the much-admired Russian pair, Yelena Berezhnaya and Anton Sikharulidze. Nor were the Canadians without their critics. "Their routine was one they had performed at competitions two years ago," remarked *Time* writer Richard Lacayo in a cover story. "As music they were using the theme from [*Love Story*]. Compared to the Russians' more nuanced classical choice,. . . it sounded a bit sappy and show biz."

The Salt Lake Scandal

But on the evening of Monday, February 11, the Russian pair "did not skate their best," according to Lacayo. Berezhnaya and Sikharulidze "had as many as six flaws in their program, notably Sikharulidze's stumble on the side-by-side double Axel." By comparison, Sale and Pelletier were "a miracle of unity." Then, wrote Lacayo, "came the astonishing scores. While the Canadians posted high technical scores, the Russians beat them in the presentation category, and were placed first by five of the nine judges. "Sale and Pelletier looked briefly stunned," wrote Lacayo. "The crowd of some 16,000 at the Salt Lake Ice Center exploded in boos."

Even while the Russians were accepting the gold medal and the Canadians silver, the suspicion of fixed judging was raised. The spotlight in particular shone on the French judge Marie-Reine Le Gougne, who seemed to own the deciding vote between the Russia-China-Poland-Ukraine bloc who favored the Russians, and the U.S.-Canada-Germany-Japan judges who placed Sale and Pelletier as the winners. "Skategate" read the headlines as an investigation into judging began. In a matter of days Le Gougne admitted that she had been pressured by her sport's national federation to favor the Russian pair in exchange for the Russian judge's vote in favor of France's ice-dancing finalists. It was a world-class scandal that eventually forced a promise from the International Skating Union (ISU) to clean up their sport's judging practices.

In the midst of the controversy, both pairs strove to maintain a sense of camaraderie and sportsmanship. "We are not the bad guys, and we don't steal anything from anybody," Sikharulidze said in a *People* piece. "We have a good relationship with Jamie and David." "Anton and Yelena are our friends," Pelletier maintained in the same article. Six days after the controversy erupted, International Olympic Committee (IOC) president Jacques Rogge announced the suspension of Le Gouge and said that Sale and Pelletier would be awarded co-gold medals with Berezhnaya and Sikharulidze in a special medals ceremony.

On February 17, the Canadians and the Russians shared the podium; the two sets of friends exchanged small talk and gifts as 700 journalists and a worldwide television audience tuned in to see the dual gold medalists. But while Sale and Pelletier maintained a professional face during the Olympic uproar, there was some underlying resentment. Pelletier said he was "ready to go down the skeleton run without a helmet," according to Deacon. When Sale was asked whether the vote-tampering had denied the pair a rightful place at the top, she "left no doubt that she felt a terrible loss," Deacon added. She told him that a gold medal was "what I have dreamed for, well, for my whole life. You bet I feel cheated out of that. Big-time."

FURTHER INFORMATION

Periodicals

"15 Who Had 15 Minutes of Fame." *Time* (December 30-January 6, 2003).

Begley, Sharon. "Our Sport Has Gangrene." *Newsweek* (February 25, 2002).

Chu, Jeff. "Fun and Games." *Time International* (February 25, 2002).

Cruz, Clarissa. "The Ice Storm." *Entertainment Weekly* (March 1, 2002).

Deacon, James. "Passion Play." *Maclean's* (April 2, 2001).

Deacon, James. "Stuff the Silver." *Maclean's* (February 25, 2002).

Deacon, James. "'We Lost Control of Our Lives.'" *Maclean's* (November 18, 2002).

Farber, Michael. "High Concept." *Sports Illustrated* (February 11, 2002).

Hitchcock, Beth. "Hearts of Gold." *Chatelaine* (February, 2002).

Jollimore, Mary. "Love Is Cool." *Time International* (January 28, 2002).

Lacayo, Richard. "A Sport on Thin Ice." *Time* (February 25, 2002).

Morse, Jodie. "After a False Start, Chemistry." *Time* (February 25, 2002).

Smolowe, Jill. "Happy Ending." *People* (March 4, 2002).

Swift, E. M. "Thorny Issue." *Sports Illustrated* (February 25, 2002).

Other

Kaufman, King. "Skategate." Salon.com. http://www.salon.com/news/feature/2002/02/13/scandal/ (February 13, 2002).

Sale and Pelletier Web Site. http://www.sale-pelletier.com/ (January 16, 2003).

Sketch by Susan Salter

Borje Salming
1951-

Swedish hockey player

Anders (Borje) Salming was the first European player to achieve fame in North American professional hockey. In his sixteen seasons with the Toronto Maple Leafs, Salming galvanized a struggling team and became a crowd favorite at its legendary home venue, Maple Leaf Gardens. A six-time National Hockey League (NHL) All-Star player, Salming opened the door for a new generation of foreign-born hockey stars.

Borje Salming, left

Played in Top Swedish League

Salming was born in Sweden in 1951, and played in the minor leagues there for six years as a teen and young adult. He was first with Kiruna AIF of the Swedish Second Division, and moved to Brynas IF Gavle in the Swedish Elite League while attending technical college. At the 1972 World Championships, Salming impressed a scout for the Maples Leafs with his toughness on the ice, and he and teammate Inge Hammarstrom were acquired for $50,000 transfer fees to the Swedish Ice Hockey Federation.

Salming's first appearance in the Leafs' jersey came on October 10, 1973, in a game against the Buffalo Sabres before a crowd that included Sweden's ambassador to Canada. Salming and Hammarstrom were not the first Europeans to skate in the NHL—the year before, the Detroit Red Wings had signed a Swede, Thommie Bergman, to their roster—but there was a blatant prejudice against foreign players. The League had been dominated by Canadian-born or Canadian-raised players until the 1960s, and national pride ran high still. In the late 1950s and again in 1964, a few outstanding Swedes had been given tryouts, but they had been treated viciously on the ice. There was still a certain scrappiness to the game in the early 1970s, and the pacifist Swedes were considered too soft to play in the League. "Swedes just don't know how to fight," Salming recalled in an interview with Peter Gammons a few years later in a *Sports Illustrated* article. "In Canada kids are brought

Chronology	
1951	Born in Kiruna, Sweden
1966-73	Plays in Swedish leagues
1973	Signed by Toronto Maples Leafs
1975-80	Makes NHL All-Star Team
1986	Briefly suspended for admitting prior drug use
1989	Signs with Detroit Red Wings
1990	Retires from NHL play
1996	Inducted into National Hockey Hall of Fame

up fighting. In Sweden, never. It is the philosophy we have about the game."

Slammed and Sliced

Not surprisingly, Salming was given his own trial by fire: at the Leafs' next match, against a tough Philadelphia Flyers team whose ice style was so fierce they were nicknamed the "Broad Street Bullies," Salming was body-checked, sticked, taunted as a "chicken Swede," and even punched. At 6'1" and 190 pounds, Salming was physically imposing enough to handle the abuse, and his fortitude quickly endeared him to Toronto fans. In an article titled "New Immigration Policy: Sign a Swede" by *Sports Illustrated*'s Mark Mulvoy, even Maple Leaf coach Red Kelly admitted he had his initial doubts about signing Salming and Hammarstrom. "Then I saw them skate and many of my doubts disappeared. They did things with their feet that you can't teach players." Kelly called Salming "an outstanding shot-blocker" who once took a puck in his stomach fired from just ten feet away, and noted that there was a certain grace to his skating style as well. "When he makes a turn on the ice, he does it with the style of a figure skater, moving his upper body first, not his legs."

Salming's talents as a defenseman proved so impressive that he won the Molson Cup after his rookie NHL season. Over the next few years he made the All-Star team six times, and by 1976 had become the Leafs' most famous player, as well as the crowd favorite. That year, he was signed to a new five-year contract totaling a cool $1 million. Gammons called him "the Swedish **Bobby Orr**," equating him with the exceptional Boston Bruins defenseman and hockey's biggest star of the 1970s; both were quiet men who spoke infrequently to the press. "Like Orr, he plays with remarkable instinct and flair, displaying a recklessness that seems beyond reason or science," Gammon asserted about Salming, and noted he had become "the player around whom the Maple Leafs revolve—offensively and defensively."

Oldest Player in League

Salming played for Sweden again on several occasions during the Canada Cup game. Twice he came close to winning the James Norris Memorial Trophy for

Awards and Accomplishments

1975, 1978-79, 1981	NHL Molson Cup winner
1975-76, 1978-80	Named to NHL Second All-Star Team
1976	Canada Cup All-Star Team
1977	Swedish World All-Star Team
1977	Named to NHL First All-Star Team
1996	Inducted into National Hockey Hall of Fame

Career Statistics

Yr	Team	GP	G	A	PTS	+/-
1973-74	MPL	76	5	34	39	+38
1974-75	MPL	60	12	25	37	+4
1975-76	MPL	78	16	41	57	+33
1976-77	MPL	76	12	66	78	+45
1977-78	MPL	80	16	60	76	+30
1978-79	MPL	78	17	56	73	+36
1979-80	MPL	74	19	52	71	+4
1980-81	MPL	72	5	61	66	0
1981-82	MPL	69	12	44	56	+4
1982-83	MPL	69	7	38	45	-3
1983-84	MPL	68	5	38	43	-34
1984-85	MPL	73	6	33	39	-26
1985-86	MPL	41	7	15	22	-7
1986-87	MPL	56	4	16	20	+17
1987-88	MPL	66	2	24	26	+7
1988-89	MPL	63	3	17	20	+7
1989-90	DRW	49	2	17	19	+20
TOTAL		1148	150	637	787	139

DRW: Detroit Red Wings; MPL: Toronto Maple Leafs.

outstanding defense, and by 1980 was the Leafs' highest earner at $275,000 a year. The subsequent decade, however, proved a difficult one for Toronto, and they made continually abysmal showings. His final seasons were problematic: in September of 1986, the Leafs suspended him for the entire season after he admitted in a newspaper article that he had used cocaine; team management relented, however, and he was reinstated after eight games. The following year, he and three other teammates were ejected from a Minnesota hotel after noise complaints, and Salming again missed some games. Despite the absences, he achieved an NHL first a few months later when, in January of 1988, he became the first European player to play 1,000 games in the League. At the end of that season, he ended his Leafs career with a franchise defense record for all-time goals (148) and assists (620).

Salming played the 1989-90 season, his last, with the Detroit Red Wings. At 38 years old, he was the oldest player in the NHL at the time, and was widely rumored to be ready to retire. True to form, Salming refused to speculate on his future. "I just go year by year," he told *Detroit Free Press* sports writer Keith Gave. "I'm not saying this is the last year. But if it is, I don't want to make a big deal about it, either. I just want to leave quietly." In the end, Salming did retire and returned to Sweden with his two teenaged children and wife Margitta. He played again for the Swedish Elite League, putting in two seasons with AIK Solna Stockholm and part of third before retiring from the ice for good. His last appearance was playing for the Swedish national team during the 1992 Winter Olympic Games in Albertville, France. Four years later Salming became the first European player to be inducted into the National Hockey Hall of Fame.

Following his retirement, Salming returned to Sweden, where he owns a hockey equipment business and runs a youth hockey school. He is also involved with a Stockholm wine-import business, Bornicon and Salming.

Twenty years after Salming's star years, Scandinavian, Russian, Czech, and Slovak players had emerged as some of the NHL's most exciting players. Nicklas Lidstrom, the Wings' Swedish defenseman, won the Norris Trophy two years in a row, and in 2002 was one of forty-seven Swedes in the League. European-born players were so commonplace in the NHL that in 1998 it abandoned its format of Eastern versus Western Conference teams for the All-Star Game; instead, the contest pitted North American players against a World team.

CONTACT INFORMATION

Address: c/o Bornicon and Salming, Box 45438, S-1043 Stockholm, Sweden.

FURTHER INFORMATION

Periodicals

Gammons, Peter. "The Swedish Invasion." *Sports Illustrated* (October 18, 1976): 38.

Gave, Keith. "Salming Finds New Life with Wings." *Detroit Free Press* (September 15, 1989): 1D.

Gleason, Bucky. "Europeans Make a World of Difference." *Buffalo News* (February 6, 2000): C1.

Mulvoy, Mark. "New Immigration Policy: Sign a Swede." *Sports Illustrated* (October 29, 1973): 95.

"Salming Stays Out Despite Apology." *New York Times* (October 18, 1987): C11.

Schoenfeld, Bruce. "The NHL's most exciting players are Russians Serge Federov and Pavel Bure." *The Sporting News* (April 17, 1995): 50.

Other

Alumni Bios, http://www.torontomapleleafs.com/ tradition/alumni/alumni_salming.html (December 10, 2002).

"Borje Salming," http://www.hockeysandwich.com/ salming.html (December 10, 2002).

"Leaf Legend: Borje Salming," http://www.penaltybox.com/legends/borje_salming.html (December 10, 2002).

Sketch by Carol Brennan

Juan Antonio Samaranch
1920-

Spanish athletic administrator

In his two decades at the helm of the International Olympic Committee (IOC), Juan Antonio Samaranch worked a miraculous transformation, turning what was a largely amateur enterprise into a billion-dollar showcase for the world's finest professional athletes. Sadly, however, when he stepped down as IOC president in July 2001, he left behind an organization badly tainted by scandal, much of it generated by the charges of widespread corruption and bribe-taking in connection with Salt Lake City's successful bid for the 2002 Winter Olympics. Although he surrendered the IOC presidency to Belgian surgeon Jacques Rogge in mid-2001, Samaranch will never be far from the heart of the Olympic movement, having been named honorary president for life of the Olympic organization. And he's not the only Samaranch deeply involved in IOC affairs. Before Samaranch stepped down, his son, Juan Antonio Samaranch, Jr., known as Juanito, was elected a member of the IOC.

Born in Barcelona

He was born Juan Antonio Samaranch Torello in Barcelona, Spain, on July 17, 1920. The son of Francisco, the wealthy owner of a prosperous upholstery business, and Juana (Torello) Samaranch, he showed an early interest in sports. After graduating from the Higher Institute of Business Studies in Barcelona, he worked briefly in the family business and later became involved in the banking industry. At college Samaranch became interested in roller hockey, a sport for which he later organized the world championships. He also got involved in local and national politics, serving for a time as city councilor in Barcelona. In 1954, Samaranch was named to Spain's Olympic Committee and two years later served as his country's chief representative at the 1956 Winter Games. He also represented Spain at both the 1960 and 1964 Summer Games. In 1955, Samaranch married fellow Barcelonan Maria Teresa Salisachs Rowe, whose mother was British. The couple has one son, Juan Antonio, Jr.

In 1966 Spanish dictator Generalissimo Francisco Franco named Samaranch to a cabinet-level post overseeing sports development in Spain. Shortly thereafter,

Chronology	
1920	Born in Barcelona, Spain, on July 17
1954	Joins Spanish Olympic Committee
1955	Marries Maria Teresa Salisachs
1956	Serves as Spain's chief representative at 1956 Winter Olympics
1960	Serves as Spain's chief representative at 1960 Summer Olympics
1964	Serves as Spain's chief representative at 1964 Summer Olympics
1966	Joins International Olympic Committee (IOC) as member
1967	Elected president of Spanish Olympic Committee
1974-78	Serves as vice president of IOC
1977-80	Serves as Spain's ambassador to Soviet Union and Mongolia
1980	Elected president of IOC
2001	Steps down as president of IOC

he was elected a member of the IOC. A year after joining the IOC, Samaranch was elected president of the Spanish Olympic Committee. His involvement in Spanish politics continued, and in the late 1970s, after the death of Franco, he served as Spain's first ambassador to the Soviet Union, a country with which Spain had had a strained relationship during Franco's rule. The contacts Samaranch made with influential Soviets during his years as ambassador were to serve him well as he rose through the ranks of the IOC.

Elected President of IOC

The 1980 Olympic Summer Games in Moscow were boycotted by the United States and many of its allies. The athletes of only 81 countries participated in the Moscow Games. Against this backdrop, Samaranch, who was then serving as the IOC's chief of protocol, was elected president of the Olympic organization. A major factor in his election was Samaranch's close ties to influential political figures in both the West and the East. It was believed that he was ideally positioned to broker some sort of Olympic détente between the opposing political forces of East and West. Despite his best efforts, however, Samaranch was unable to head off a Soviet-led boycott of the 1984 Summer Games in Los Angeles, staged largely in retaliation for the 1980 U.S.-led boycott of the Moscow Games. According to the official Soviet line, the boycott was motivated by growing concerns about anti-Soviet hysteria in Los Angeles. The Soviets cited in particular the activities of the Ban the Soviets Coalition, a group formed to conduct letter-writing campaigns to Soviet officials and open safe houses where Soviet Bloc athletes could be encouraged to defect.

Although he had failed to prevent a boycott of the Los Angeles Games by the Soviet Bloc, Samaranch did manage to heal bruised feelings among all parties in time to attract a record total of 160 countries to the 1988 Summer Games in Seoul, South Korea. Under Samaranch's direction, the Olympic Games became a prize that cities

---

Awards and Accomplishments	
1988	Attracts record number of nations (160) to Seoul Summer Games
1989	Donates collection of Olympic stamps to Olympic Museum
1992	Attracts record number of nations (169) to Barcelona Summer Games
1996	Attracts record number of nations (197) to Atlanta Summer Games
1998	Opens internal IOC probe into Salt Lake City scandal
1999	Announces expulsion of six IOC members over scandal on March 17; others had resigned earlier
2000	Attracts record number of nations (199) to Sydney Summer Games

---

Related Biography: IOC President Jacques Rogge

Former Olympic yachtsman Jacques Rogge succeeded Samaranch as president of the scandal-tainted International Olympic Committee (IOC) on July 16, 2001. An orthopedic surgeon by profession, Rogge has been a delegate to the IOC since 1991. In 1998 he was elected to the organization's executive board and was a protégé of Samaranch.

Born in Ghent, Belgium, on May 2, 1942, Rogge participated in yachting competitions at the 1968 Summer Games in Mexico City, the 1972 Summer Games in Munich, and the Montreal Summer Games in 1976. Away from the Olympics, he was for a time a member of Belgium's national rugby team.

Married and the father of two children, Rogge served as president of the Belgian National Olympic Committee from 1989 to 1992. In 1989, he was elected president of the European Olympic Committees.

---

around the world competed fiercely to attract. In the process, the IOC's coffers grew accordingly. He managed to increase participation in the Olympic Games by broadening the membership of the IOC, bringing in more of the less developed countries. Critics of Samaranch pointed out that IOC delegates from the poorer nations of the world were easier for him to keep in line and manipulate.

Recruits Corporate Sponsors

Another important way in which Samaranch strengthened the Olympics franchise was through his successful recruitment of big business sponsors. In return the corporate sponsors enjoyed unprecedented worldwide marketing opportunities. At the same time he was growing the corporate sponsorship of the Olympics, Samaranch and the IOC seemed to be doing little about the problem of doping. The IOC's anti-doping enforcement measures hardly made a dent in the thriving practice, critics argued.

According to its critics, pressure to open up the IOC and make it more accountable for its actions and inaction has had little effect on the organization, which remains pretty much a closed shop. Delegates to the IOC are not elected, nor do they represent their home countries or those countries Olympic committees. Instead, they are co-opted by the IOC, ensuring that their loyalty lies with it. Upon their induction into the IOC, new members take an oath to respect the decisions of the IOC, which Samaranch considered to be nonnegotiable. Further cementing Samaranch's hold on the closed shop of the IOC was the fact that no delegate joined the committee without the express approval of His Excellency, as Samaranch was known by obedient delegates.

Guides IOC to Financial Success

Despite the criticism of certain aspects of the Olympic operation, there can be no argument with the overall success of the IOC under the direction of Samaranch. At the time he took over the reins of the organization in 1980, the IOC reportedly had only $500,000 in its treasury. In mid-2001, the committee's coffers held approximately $350 million. In 1980 worldwide televi-

sion rights brought in $122 million; the current host, NBC, paid $1.8 billion for the rights to five Olympics. According to a report in New Zealand's *Sunday Star Times,* under Samaranch's leadership, Olympic broadcast hours increased from 500 to 3,800; ticket sales swelled from $13 million to $625 million; and total income from marketing rose tenfold to $3.7 billion.

Marring the Olympic success story was the scandal related to Salt Lake City's successful bid for the 2002 Winter Games. In June 1995 the IOC announced the selection of Utah's largest city as the site for the 2002 Winter Games. A little over three years later, reports surfaced in the media alleging that the Salt Lake Organizing Committee (SLOC) had in effect bribed IOC members to win approval. In the end, the ensuing scandal cost ten IOC members their jobs. While Samaranch himself was never implicated in the scandal, he and other top IOC officials were widely criticized for their failure to thoroughly investigate earlier complaints of inappropriate behavior.

Samaranch managed to survive the Salt Lake City scandal but about seven months before the Winter Games of 2002, he stepped down as IOC president, surrendering the post to Belgian surgeon Jacques Rogge, a former Olympic sailor. But Samaranch will never stray far from the Olympic movement, having been named Honorary President for Life shortly before he stepped down. He also presided over the selection of his son, Juan Antonio Jr., as a new delegate to the IOC. In his formal farewell to IOC members, Samaranch said: "Thank you for having allowed me to serve the Olympic movement. Goodbye and hasta la vista." Despite the taint of the Salt Lake City scandal, there can be little doubt that Samaranch left the organization in far better shape than that in which he found it more than two decades earlier.

CONTACT INFORMATION

Address: Juan Antonio Samaranch, c/o International Olympic Committee, Chateau de Vidy, 1007, Lausanne,

Switzerland; 40 Bay St., Ste 300, Toronto, ON, Canada, M5J 2X2. Fax: (41 21)621-6216. Phone: (41 21)621-6111.

SELECTED WRITINGS BY SAMARANCH:

Memorias Olimpicas, Planeta Publishing, 2002.

FURTHER INFORMATION

Books

"Juan Antonio Samaranch." *Complete Marquis Who's Who.* Marquis Who's Who, 2001.

"Juan Antonio Samaranch." *Contemporary Newsmakers 1986,* Issue Cumulation. Detroit: Gale Research, 1987.

Periodicals

"IOC Hails Samaranch as a Marketing Hero." *Marketing* (September 3, 2001): 7.

"IOC's Godfather Won't Disappear Into Retirement." *Washington Times* (July 17, 2001).

"A New Lord of the Rings: Behind the Race to Run the $1 Billion Olympics Empire." *Newsweek* (July 9, 2001): 47.

Taylor, Phil. "The Lord of the Olympic Rings." *Sunday Star Times* (New Zealand) (July 22, 2001): 2.

Other

"IOC Scandal Timeline." Associated Press. http://wire.ap.org/APpackages/ioctimeline/ioc_timeline.html (January 28, 2003).

"Jacques Rogge." International Olympic Committee. http://www.olympic.org/uk/organisation/ioc/presidents/rogge_uk.asp (January 14, 2003).

"Juan Antonio Samaranch." Freelance Spain. http://www.spainview.com/people/biog23.html (January 13, 2003).

"Juan Antonio Samaranch's Donation." Olympic Collectors Commission. http://www.collectors.olympic.org/e/fipo/fipo_donation_e.html (January 13, 2003).

"Samaranch: The Biography." 112th IOC Session. http://www.moscow2001.olympic.org/en/president/bilan/annees_samaranch/biographie.html (January 13, 2003).

Sketch by Don Amerman

Pete Sampras
1971-

American tennis player

Pete Sampras

During 2002 Sampras earned his record fourteenth Grand Slam title when he won the U.S. Open. With eight titles at Wimbledon, five at the U.S. Open, and three at the Australian Open, only the clay courts of the French Open have persistently denied Sampras a Grand Slam championship. His unemotional but powerful game is built on a serve that crosses the net at up to 130 miles per hour and is backed up by excellent ground strokes and precise serve-and-volley skills. Added to his physical abilities is his single-minded determination to win, which has made him one of the greatest players in the game.

Winning Ways

Pete Sampras was born on August 12, 1971 in Washington, D.C., the third of four children. His parents, Soterios (known as Sam) and Georgia (Vroustrous) Sampras, are of Greek descent. Sampras spent his first years in Potomac, Maryland, where his father worked as a civil aerospace engineer for the U.S. Air Force. His father took a job in the aviation industry when Sampras was seven and the family moved to Rancho Palos Verdes, California.

After moving to the warmer climate, Sampras, along with his brother Gus and two sisters, Stella and Marion, decided to take up tennis. The family joined the Peninsula Racquet Club where the Sampras children began taking lessons. Sampras, whose previous tennis experience amounted to hitting a ball against the basement wall and knocking about on the local D.C. high school

Born to Win

"When I won the Open in '90, I wasn't ready. Not as a person, and not as a tennis player. I just happened to have two great weeks. That's the only way to explain it. Otherwise, I was a really green, insecure kid.

"The morning after I won, I did all these talk shows. And they made me feel intensely uncomfortable. It's tough for a kid just turning 19 to have all that attention. I was a shy, immature kid, and that came across. Suddenly, everybody always expected me to be in a good mood. But all I really wanted, like most 19-year-olds, was to find a comfort zone as a person, to fit in. And fame wasn't my idea of it. It got overwhelming trying to figure out what people wanted from me. I also saw that what I'd done would affect the rest of my life, and that was scary."

Source: Pete Sampras, in an interview with Peter Bodo. *Tennis,* 36 (September 2000): 60.

courts, took to the game quickly. When he was eight his parents, who knew little about the game, invited Peter Fischer, a pediatrician and tennis buff, to begin coaching their son. Although Fischer was inexperienced and unsalaried, he understood the game, and taught Sampras strategy. By the time he was twelve, Sampras was playing up in the 14-year-old division and winning.

When Sampras was fourteen Fischer insisted that he shift from being a baseline player to serve-and-volley player. He also convinced Sampras to change from a two-handed to a one-handed backhand. Although other professionals were brought in to help Sampras with his game, Fischer is credited with improving Sampras's monster serve. During practice, Sampras would begin his serve and only after the ball was released from his hand did Fischer call out where he wanted Sampras to place it. The drill taught Sampras to disguise his serving motion so that his opponent has no idea where the ball is going to land. Fischer, who was often more critical than sympathetic after his young student lost a match, constantly raised the bar of expectations, reminding Sampras that his competition was legendary Australian tennis player **Rod Laver**, Sampras's lifelong role model.

First Years on Tour

Throughout his teenage years, tennis dominated Sampras's life. He didn't have any close friends at school, never played any other sports, and never socialized with his age group, except for his buddies at the Jack Kramer Club where he practiced. In 1987, when he was sixteen, he entered the United States Tennis Association (USTA) Boys' 18 tournament, placing second in singles (losing to **Michael Chang** in the finals) and first in doubles. After making it to the third round of the Newsweek Champions Cup several weeks later, Sampras accepted the $7,000 prize money, which effectively changed his status from amateur to professional. Quitting school, Sampras joined the tour in 1988, beginning his career ranked No. 311 in the world.

Sampras had a rather unremarkable rookie season. His only win was a doubles title in Rome with **Jim Courier** as his partner. He entered one grand slam event, the U.S. Open, but was ousted in the first round. The follow-

ing year, Sampras made his presence known at the 1989 U.S. Open by making it into the fourth round, upsetting defending champion Mats Wilander along the way. Soon after, Sampras and Fischer parted company after a bitter argument regarding Fischer's compensation as well as Fischer's high expectations. According to *Sports Illustrated,* Fischer was upset because Sampras wasn't training hard enough. "The only acceptable rank for you is Number 1," he told Sampras. When Sampras's father retorted, "What if he wants to be Number 5?" Fischer answered, "Unacceptable." The two did not speak for three years, and thereafter had a distant and more remote friendship. (In 1998 Fischer pled guilty to charges of child molestation and spent several years in prison.) Despite their less-than-amicable parting, Sampras has long praised Fischer as being responsible for pushing him to become a champion rather than just a good tennis player.

First Grand Slam

Starting off strong in 1990 Sampras made it to the fourth round of the Australian Open in January and earned his first professional victory in February at the U.S. Pro Indoors in Philadelphia. Knocked out in the first round of his first Wimbledon, he entered the U.S. Open seeded twelfth. Riding on the strength of his overwhelming serve, Sampras walked through the early rounds. He then beat Ivan Lendl in five sets in the quarterfinals, four-time Open winner **John McEnroe** in the semifinals, and met **Andre Agassi** in the finals.

Sampras's matchup with Agassi proved to be a contrast in styles. Sampras, who modeled his behavior after an early generation of tennis greats including Laver, was subdued in his behavior, dress, and demeanor, which compared sharply with Agassi's long hair, nontraditional (nonwhite) clothing, and open personality. Agassi, however, could do little to hold up against his opponent's serve, and Sampras won in three sets, 6-4, 6-3, 6-2, becoming the youngest U.S. Open winner in history (19 years, 28 days).

Sampras followed up his 1990 U.S. Open victory by winning the first Grand Slam Cup, an event that features

---

<table>
<tr><td colspan="2">**Awards and Accomplishments**</td></tr>
<tr><td>1990</td><td>Wins U.S. Open; wins Grand Slam Cup</td></tr>
<tr><td>1991</td><td>Wins American Tennis Pro (ATP) World Championships</td></tr>
<tr><td>1993</td><td>Wins U.S. Open</td></tr>
<tr><td>1993-95</td><td>Wins Wimbledon</td></tr>
<tr><td>1994, 1997</td><td>Wins Australian Open</td></tr>
<tr><td>1995-96</td><td>Wins U.S. Open</td></tr>
<tr><td>1997-2000</td><td>Wins Wimbledon</td></tr>
<tr><td>2002</td><td>Wins U.S. Open</td></tr>
</table>

Sampras holds a record 14 Grand Slam titles (Grand Slam events are the Australian Open, French Open, Wimbledon, and the U.S. Open).

---

the 16 best finishers in the year's Grand Slam events. With numerous endorsement contracts added to his on-court earnings, Sampras netted approximately $6.5 million in 1990. During 1991, suffering under the pressure of overly high expectations as well as some physical injuries, Sampras skipped the Australian Open and was eliminated in the second round of both Wimbledon and the French Open. In his attempt to defend his U.S. Open title, he was eliminated in the quarterfinals.

Dominates Wimbledon

In 1992 Sampras began working with a new coach, Tom Gullikson, a former top-ten player. Gullikson insisted that Sampras spend more time on clay courts, where the ball has a slower kick off the clay than hard courts, making Sampras depend less on his serve and more on winning points on good strokes and strategy. During the year he reached the quarterfinals of the Australian Open. He made it as far as the semifinals at Wimbledon before being ousted by Goran Ivanesevic, another hard-serving powerhouse. At the U.S. Open Sampras overcame Courier in the semifinals, but a stomach ailment left him drained and a step slow, and he lost to Stephan Edberg in the finals in four sets, 3-6, 6-4, 7-6, 6-2. Although he failed to win a Grand Slam during the year, Sampras rounded out 1992 with five titles, 70 match wins, and over $1.5 million in earnings.

After the 1992 U.S. Open, Sampras won 19 consecutive matches over the next six months. Reaching the semifinals of the Australian Open in January 1993, in April Sampras overtook Courier in point standing and claimed the No. 1 ranking. At the French Open, Sampras was stopped in the quarterfinals, but for the first time he walked into Wimbledon as the number one seed. In a spectacular performance, Sampras overcame defending champion Agassi in the quarterfinals and three-time winner **Boris Becker** in the semifinals. He met Courier, ranked No. 2, in the finals. After four grueling sets and 22 aces, Sampras prevailed to win his first Wimbledon championship. Overcoming a post-Wimbledon slump, Sampras won his second U.S. Open, easily overtaking fifteenth-seeded Cedric Pioline in the finals.

Following his Wimbledon victory, Sampras was slammed in the London press for his subdued, unemotional presence on the court. Headlines read "Wimble-Yawn" and "Samprazzzzz." Ironically, over the course of his career Sampras's lack of controversy in his life and play became his biggest source of controversy. Following in the wake of such on-court performers as **Jimmy Connors** and McEnroe, who were known for their emotional and passionate play, Sampras's expressionless silence during his matches was bemoaned as too impassionate, too seemingly indifferent. For years Sampras struggled to understand the distain for his demeanor. He was humble, polite, professional, and provided no distasteful distractions on or off the court. He was raised, and trained, to focus on winning alone.

Sampras earned his third straight Grand Slam title, winning his first Australian Open championship in 1994. Then, for the third year in a row, he was ousted in the quarterfinals of the French Open, the only Grand Slam that he failed to dominate. Returning to Wimbledon, Sampras defended his championship, defeating Ivanisevic, 7-6, 7-6, 6-0, to take his second title on the grass courts. Coming off an ankle injury that sidelined him for six weeks, Sampras failed to play well at the U.S. Open, falling in the fourth round, but remained ranked No. 1.

Personal Tragedy

In 1995 Sampras faced a personal crisis that played out in front of the spectators at the Australian Open. Prior to his quarterfinal match with Courier, Sampras found out that Gullikson, his coach and good friend, had terminal brain cancer. Down two sets to none to Courier, according to *Los Angeles Magazine,* a fan called out "Come on, Pete do it for your coach." Sampras began to cry, then served an ace. He staged an emotional comeback to defeat Courier in five sets, and following his win, the stoic Sampras broke down and sobbed, giving a brief if uninvited glimpse into his deepest emotions. Meeting Agassi in the finals, Sampras could not pull off a victory and lost in four sets, 6-4, 1-6, 6-7, 4-6. For a period following the Open, Sampras gave over his top ranking to Agassi. After losing in the first round of the French Open, Sampras rebounded to win his third consecutive Wimbledon championship and his third career U.S. Open title, successfully regaining his No. 1 ranking.

Gullikson lost his battle with brain cancer in May 1996, and although Sampras had his career-best showing at the French Open where he reached the semifinals, he went without a Grand Slam title until the U.S. Open. Facing Chang in the finals, Sampras won in straight sets to claim his second consecutive, and third career, U.S. Open. The following year he took his second Australian Open championship and his fourth Wimbledon title. The Wimbledon win gave 25-year-old Sampras his tenth Grand Slam title, just two shy of Roy Emerson's record 12 titles and one short of **Bjorn Borg** and Laver's 11 Slam titles.

Record-breaking Career

Sampras once again won at Wimbledon in 1998. Yet, with only one Grand Slam in the year, his top spot in the rankings was threatened, and Sampras launched an obsessed, and successful, drive to hold his No. 1 ranking for a record six straight years. He defended his Wimbledon title again in 1999 and 2000, winning on the grass courts for a record four consecutive years and a career record seven titles in eight years. His 2000 victory at Wimbledon was his 13th Grand Slam victory, breaking the career record of 12 set by Roy Emerson. In 2001, suffering from injuries and a step slower, for the first time in eight seasons, Sampras went without a Grand Slam championship title, although he reached the finals of the U.S. Open.

Just as critics were calling for his retirement, Sampras proved that he still had his game by winning the 2002 U.S. Open, his fourth career Open title, and a record 14th career Grand Slam title. Once slandered as too boring for tennis, Sampras was lauded for his achievement, his heart, his persistence. He had, in effect, secured his name in the history books as one of the game's greatest players. Following the win, Sampras considered retirement, but decided to remain active for the 2003 season, although he sat out of the Australian Open to rest up for what may be his last shot at the French Open, the only Grand Slam title that has eluded him.

After spending most of his career in Florida, focused on his training, Sampras moved back to Los Angeles in 1998 to be near his family. In 2000 he married actress Bridgette Wilson, and the couple had their first child, Christian, at the end of 2002. Having committed to playing in the remaining Grand Slams in 2003, 31-year-old Sampras is unsure about how long he will stay in the game. "If I'm a betting man," Sampras told *USA Today* in January 2003, "I'm not 100% this is my last year, but it definitely could be.... But I still love playing, and I still feel I'll win another major. Once I start playing I'll know where my heart is and how far I'll take this. I already know I'm living proof that if you believe in yourself, you can do anything." Just as Sampras is thinking about signing off, he has finally achieved the acceptance that he has so long desired—to be appreciated as a great player and understood as deeply human.

CONTACT INFORMATION

Address: ATP Tour, 420 W. 45th Street, New York, New York 10036.

FURTHER INFORMATION

Books

The Complete Marquis Who's Who. New York: Marquis Who's Who, 2001.

Pete Sampras

Newsmakers 1994, Issue 4. Detroit: Gale Research, 1994.

Sports Stars. Series 1-4. Detroit: U•X•L, 1994-98.

Periodicals

Bodo, Peter. "Born to Win." *Tennis* (September 2000): 60.

Drucker, Joel. "Match Point: His Glory Days Fading, Tennis's Pete Sampras Seeks One Last Hurrah." *Los Angeles Magazine* (September 2002): 50-4.

Flink, Steve. "Tennis: Wimbledon Will Be Key to Sampras Decision." *Europe Intelligence Wire* (October 7, 2002).

Jenkins, Sally. "Natural Born Killer." *Sports Illustrated* (September 5, 1994): 19+.

Jenkins, Sally. "The Lonely Living Legend." *Tennis* (May 1999): 40.

O'Connor, Ian. "Sampras Believes He Still Has a Major Left in Him." *USA Today* (January 3, 2003): 4C.

Price, S. L. "Alone at the Top." *Sports Illustrated* (July 14, 1997): 26+.

Price, S. L. "For the Ages." *Sports Illustrated* (July 17, 2000): 36+.

Price, S. L. "A Grand Occasion." *Sports Illustrated* (September 16, 2002): 52+.

Price, S. L. "The Passion of Pete." *Sports Illustrated* (May 26, 1997): 92+

Simpson, Lisa. "Grand Slam: The Courtship of Champions." *In Style* (February 1, 2001): 330+.

St. John, Allen. "Male Player of the Year: Pete Sampras." *Tennis* (February 2001): 24.

Sketch by Kari Bethel

Arantxa Sanchez Vicario

Arantxa Sanchez Vicario
1971-

Spanish tennis player

Arantxa Sanchez Vicario had the privilege and the misfortune of playing tennis during the reign of **Steffi Graf** and **Monica Seles**. Despite playing in their long shadows, Sanchez Vicario won the French Open three times and the U.S. Open once, as well as six Grand Slam doubles titles and four Grand Slam mixed doubles titles. Her peppy, expressive personality endeared her to fans as did her tenacious play. At just five-feet-six-inches and 123 pounds, she endured and often overcame the giant strokes of her larger, stronger opponents.

Professional at Fourteen

Arantxa Sanchez Vicario was born on December 18, 1971 in Barcelona, Spain. Named after Saint Aranzazu, the patron saint of the Basque region of Spain, Sanchez Vicario was the youngest of four children. Her father, Emilio, is an engineer, and her mother, Marisa, is a teacher. Sanchez Vicario fell in love with tennis, or at least a tennis racket, when she was two years old. Because she was constantly toddling onto the court and interrupting the play of her parents and older siblings, her mother gave her a Slazenger racquet to distract and occupy her. Once Sanchez Vicario picked it up, she never put it down. The racket became her constant companion and her favorite toy.

Following in the footsteps of her older siblings, Sanchez Vicario soon became an impressive tennis player. At first she spent hours hitting balls against the wall at the country club. She then began to train with Manuel Orantes, a former top-ten player, who worked with Sanchez Vicario on the clay courts of nearby Club Real de Tenis. By the time she was thirteen, she was the top female player in Spain. She turned professional in June 1986 at the age of fourteen.

In 1987 Sanchez Vicario made a grand debut at her first Grand Slam event by reaching the quarterfinals of the French Open. She did not drop a set until losing to **Gabriela Sabatini**, ranked No. 7, in the quarterfinals. Although she was defeated in the first round at both Wimbledon and the U.S. Open, her year-end ranking had risen to from No. 124 to No. 47. In 1988 Sanchez Vicario once again did well on the clay courts at Roland Garros, where the French Open is played. She again reached the quarterfinals, this time by upsetting **Chris Evert**, ranked No. 3 at the time. She won her first singles title at the Belgian Open just a month before her seventeenth birthday.

Stuns Graf

During 1989, her third year on tour, Sanchez Vicario claimed her first Grand Slam title by winning the French Open in an upset over Graf, 7-6(8-6), 3-6, 7-5. She became the first Spanish woman to win at Roland Garros. Her defeat of seemingly unbeatable Graf, who came to the French Open having won the last five consecutive Grand Slam titles and 117 of her last 121 matches, brought Sanchez Vicario, seeded seventh, to the forefront of the tennis world. The three-hour match was marked by long rallies of 30 to 40 shots in which Sanchez Vicario chased down everything that came her way. Graf, who was suffering from a stomach ailment, made 71 unforced errors, failed to convert 10 of 11 break points, and could not put Sanchez Vicario away serving for the match at 5-3 in the third set.

Upon winning the French Open, the elated Sanchez Vicario rolled in the red clay then sprang up, rushed to Graf, giving her a heartfelt hug. According to *Sports Illustrated,* in her endearing broken English, Sanchez Vicario exclaimed, "I am very joyed. I am so exciting to win Steffi." Following her win, Sanchez Vicario and her family were granted a private audience with Spain's King Juan Carlos and Queen Sofia. After reaching the quarterfinals of both Wimbledon and the U.S. Open, Sanchez Vicario ended the season ranked No. 4.

Following her French Open win, Sanchez Vicario, who up to this point had been known simply as Arantxa Sanchez, decided to tack on her mother's maiden name so that she could honor both sides of her family and they could all see their name in the newspapers. During the 1990 season Sanchez Vicario won two singles titles, four women's doubles, and the mixed doubles title at the French Open. Her best Grand Slam finish was the semifinals of the U.S. Open. Her biggest win came at the Hamburg Open, where she finally defeated **Martina Navratilova**, ranked No. 2, after six previous losses. Advancing to the finals, Sanchez Vicario lost to Graf in three sets.

A Decade of Winning

In 1991 Sanchez Vicario returned to the finals of the French Open by defeating Graf in the semifinals, 6-2, 6-0, but lost to No. 1 ranked Seles in the finals, 6-3, 6-4. With Sanchez Vicario's help, Spain won its first Federation Cup championship in 1991. The following year the Olympics were held in Barcelona, and both Sanchez Vicario and her brother Emilio played for Spain. She won a bronze medal in the singles and a silver medal,

with countrywomen Conchita Martinez, in doubles. In the same year she managed to upset Seles to win the Canadian Open and advanced to the finals of the U.S. Open for the first time, defeating Graf in the quarterfinals, but lost in the finals to Seles. That same year she won ten doubles titles, including her first Grand Slam doubles win at the Australian Open.

Sanchez Vicario reached the semifinals of three of the four Grand Slam events (Australian Open, French Open, and U.S. Open) and made the quarterfinals of 17 of 18 singles tournaments in 1993. She ended the year with a 77-14 singles record, four singles titles, four doubles titles, the Australian Open mixed doubles title, the U.S. Open women's doubles title, and a second Federation Cup title. In 1994 Sanchez Vicario claimed two more Grand Slam singles titles. She beat hard-hitting **Mary Pierce**, 6-4, 6-4, to retake the French Open title and overcame Graf, 1-6, 7-6, 6-4, to win her first and only U.S. Open title.

Briefly holding the No.1 spot in 1995 in both singles and doubles, Sanchez Vicario lost to Pierce in the Australian Open singles finals. She also reached the finals at the French Open and Wimbledon, but on both occasions fell to Graf. Their battle at Wimbledon became known as one of the best women's finals ever to be played. Tied at a set apiece, with the score was 5-5 in the deciding third set, Sanchez Vicario and Graf battled through one 20-minute, 32-point game that finally awarded Graf her sixth Wimbledon title. Despite her eventual loss, Sanchez Vicario was highly praised for her aggressive, tenacious play.

In both 1996 and 1997 Sanchez Vicario reached the finals of the French Open and Wimbledon, but failed to walk away with another Grand Slam title. In 1997 her best finish was the quarterfinals at Wimbledon, but in 1998 she earned her third French Open championship and fourth Grand Slam title, defeating Seles in the finals. Although this was to be her last Grand Slam title, Sanchez Vicario continued to find her way through the early rounds of most of her matches. In 2000 she played in her fifth Grand Slam event at the French Open. She reached the semifinals, marking the fourteenth time in fifteen years of playing at Roland Garros that she made it into the quarterfinals or better.

Retires

Sanchez Vicario took a break after the 2000 season and skipped the Australian Open. Her best Grand Slam finish of 2001 was the third round of the U.S. Open. In 2002 she did not play at Wimbledon and did not make it beyond the first round in any other Grand Slam tournament. Although she did not win a singles title in 2002, she did win six doubles titles. In November 2002, Sanchez Vicario announced her retirement. She was a gritty player, who had no exceptional weapons in her arsenal of shots, but won nonetheless through sheer determination. Chasing down every ball, she frustrated and exhausted her opponents until the points totaled in her favor. Although other tennis greats took more Grand Slam trophies home, Sanchez Vicario took home over $16 million in prize money, making her the third highest paid female tennis player to date.

CONTACT INFORMATION

Address: c/o IMG, 1360 E. 9th Street, Ste. 100, Cleveland, Ohio 44114.

SELECTED WRITINGS BY SANCHEZ VICARIO:

Young Tennis Player: A Young Enthusiast's Guide to Tennis. New York: Dorling Kindersley, 1996.
Tennis. New York: Dorling Kindersley, 2000.

FURTHER INFORMATION

Books

The Complete Marquis Who's Who. New York: Marquis Who's Who, 2001.
Great Women in Sports. Detroit: Visible Ink Press, 1996.
Sports Stars. Series 1-4. Detroit: U•X•L, 1994-98.

Periodicals

"Arantxa Sanchez-Vicario Announces Her Retirement." *EFE World News Service* (November 12, 2002).
"Factfile on Arantxa Sanchez-Vicario." *Agence France Presse* (November 12, 2002).
Kirkpatrick, Curry. "Giant Killers." *Sports Illustrated* (June 19, 1989): 34-9.
Kirkpatrick, Curry. "The Home Team." *Sports Illustrated* (July 22, 1992): 172-5.
Lidz, Franz. "Tennis with Plenty of Bounce." *Sports Illustrated* (May 14, 1990): 10-2.
Pope, Edwin. "Game, Set, Classic." *The Sporting News* (July 17, 1995): 8.
"Sanchez Vicario Ends 17-Year Career." *The Washington Post* (November 13, 2002): D2.
Sawai, Akshay. "Smiling Face of the Fight Club." *Asia Africa Intelligence Wire* (November 19, 2002).

Other

"Arantxa Sanchez-Vicario." Sanex WTA Tour. http://www.sanexwta.com (January 8, 2003).

Sketch by Kari Bethel

Barry Sanders
1968-

American football player

One of football's greatest running backs of all time, Barry Sanders is a bundle of contradictions. His sudden departure from professional football in the summer of 1999 still has observers scratching their heads. He left the game less than 1,500 yards short of eclipsing the career rushing yardage of the late **Walter Payton**. (As of late October 2002, Sanders, with a total of 15,269 yards, fell to third leading all-time rusher when Dallas Cowboys running back **Emmitt Smith** surpassed Payton's 16,726 career yards by piling up 16,743 yards.) Although Sanders was clearly one of pro football's biggest stars, he never acted the part, preferring to take a low profile. He lived in a simple home and showed little interest in either flashy clothes or high-powered cars. A man of great wealth, he nevertheless displayed a frugality more suited to a pensioner on a limited budget, taking his dirty clothes to a coin laundry rather than entrusting them to his vacation hotel's high-price dry cleaning service.

During the decade he played for the Detroit Lions, the media almost always found him willing to talk about his team, but he never seemed particularly comfortable

Barry Sanders

Chronology	
1968	Born in Wichita, Kansas, on July 16
1986-89	Attends Oklahoma State University in Stillwater
1989	Wins Heisman Trophy
1989	Drafted third overall in NFL draft by Detroit Lions
1991	Holds out for 33 days before season starts—finally signs four-year 5.9 million dollar contract
1999	Retires from Detroit Lions shortly before beginning of 1999 season
2000	Marries Detroit TV anchor Lauren Campbell on November 11

discussing his own accomplishments. In a way, Sanders always seemed to get a certain degree of satisfaction from being a bit of a mystery. That enigmatic quality mirrored in many ways his magic on the gridiron—the ability to confound the opposing team with his very unpredictability. Even Sanders found it difficult—if not impossible—to describe his running style, but he was clear enough about what it was that kept him fired up on the football field. "I love competing," he told Paul Attner of *Sports Illustrated* late in his career. "If I wasn't playing, I'd be going to a gym somewhere and getting up a game of five-on-five. That's one of the simple things I enjoy doing. . . . The biggest joy is that I am still playing the game I have been playing since I was a kid and enjoying it more than I ever have."

Born in Wichita, Kansas

He was born Barry James Sanders in Wichita, Kansas, on July 16, 1968. Son of William (a roofer) and Shirley (a registered nurse) Sanders was one of 11 children. While still a boy, Sanders learned the importance—and value—of hard work. As soon as they could handle the tools of the trade, he and his two brothers were pressed into service as roofer's assistants by their father. Of Sanders's boyhood apprenticeship, Mitch Albom of the *Detroit Free Press* wrote: "All day they would labor, with the hammers, with the tar, sweating in the hot summer sun. You did not complain in the Sanders family. Not unless you wanted a good whupping."

As a boy, Sanders excelled in all things athletic, but his first love was basketball. His father, however, steered him toward football, believing that his son's chances of winning a college scholarship would be greater on the gridiron than on the basketball court. Although Sanders showed definite promise on the football field, he was stuck on the second string until the last half of his senior year by coaches who felt that his play was hampered by a fear of getting hit. In the last five games of his senior year, Sanders came alive, rushing for more than 1,000 yards, for a total of 1,417 yards for the year—a city-wide record. His coaches—and his opponents—were confounded by his ability to elude tackles. Despite the spectacular finish to his high school football career, only three colleges— the University of Tulsa, Iowa State, and Oklahoma State—offered scholarships to Sanders. He decided on Oklahoma State because of its strong business program.

Football's Demands Hamper Studies

Sanders wasn't fully prepared for the demands football put on him at Oklahoma State. He later told the *Sporting News*: "I remember in my freshman year we didn't have any days off. I couldn't believe it, and it never got any better. They pretended (football) wasn't the main thing you were there for, but you were doing it 50 or 60 hours a week. I fell behind in my schoolwork." During his freshman and sophomore years Sanders played second string to **Thurman Thomas**, who later played for the Buffalo Bills from 1988 to 2000. A late bloomer at college, as he had been in high school, Sanders was made a starter in his junior year and proceeded to smash 13 NCAA records—including most rushing yards (2,628) and most touchdowns (39) in a season. On the strength of this spectacular performance, Sanders was nominated for the coveted Heisman Trophy. Never one for the limelight, he had to be pressured to attend the award ceremonies in New York. In the end, he was persuaded to make the trip, where he received the trophy. He was at first inclined to continue his studies at Oklahoma State but eventually decided to enter the NFL draft instead, largely to help his family financially. Looking back on Sanders's years at OSUC, his college coach, Pat Jones, told *Sporting News*: "If someone was to ask me who the most explosive back I've coached is, that would be Barry, as far as a guy who can

Career Statistics

Yr	Team	GP	Rushing					Receiving			
			ATT	YDS	AVG	TD		REC	YDS	AVG	TD
1989	DET	15	280	1470	5.2	14		24	282	11.8	0
1990	DET	16	255	1304	5.1	13		36	480	13.3	3
1991	DET	15	342	1548	4.5	16		41	307	7.5	1
1992	DET	16	312	1352	4.3	9		29	225	7.8	1
1993	DET	11	243	1115	4.6	3		36	205	5.7	0
1994	DET	16	331	1883	5.7	7		44	283	6.4	1
1995	DET	16	314	1500	4.8	11		48	398	8.3	1
1996	DET	16	307	1553	5.1	11		24	147	6.1	0
1997	DET	16	335	2053	6.1	11		33	305	9.2	3
1998	DET	16	343	1491	4.3	4		37	289	7.8	0
TOTAL		153	3062	15269	5.0	99		352	2921	8.3	10

DET: Detroit Lions.

Related Biography: Coach Wayne Fontes

Leo Durocher claimed that nice guys finish last. Wayne Fontes, long-time coach of the Detroit Lions, proved him wrong. In the high point of his eight years at the helm of the Lions, Fontes earned the Associated Press' NFL Coach of the Year honors in 1991 after leading Detroit to the NFC championship game. Perhaps his greatest contribution to the Lions, however, was his insistence that the team draft Barry Sanders in 1989. Sanders went on to become one of the top running backs in NFL history, and he's never forgotten Fontes's guidance and support, crediting the coach for making him the player he eventually became.

The son of Portuguese-American parents, Fontes was born and raised in Canton, Ohio. He played baseball and football during his student years at Michigan State University (MSU) and later coached freshman football at MSU. After coaching assignments at Dayton, Iowa, and USC, Fontes in 1985 joined the Lions organization as defensive coordinator. He was made head coach in 1988 and remained in that post until he and his coaching staff were let go during the 1997 season.

In the mid-1990s, as the Lions hit a slump and anti-Fontes sentiment grew among Lions team members, Sanders remained a staunch supporter of the coach. Of the coach, Sanders said: "He proves that a coach can show affection and appreciation and still win."

take your breath away and is liable to score on every down. . . . I don't know that I've ever seen anyone like him with my own eyes."

Drafted third overall in the NFL draft of 1989, Sanders signed a whopping $6.1 million five-year contract with the Detroit Lions, one of the most lucrative NFL contracts ever for a rookie. Sanders wasted no time at all in proving that he was worth every penny Detroit was paying him. Although he didn't start the first two games of the 1989 season and missed parts of two others, Sanders managed to rush for a total of 1,470 yards, missing the NFL's individual season rushing record by only 10 yards. The following year, he rushed a total for a total of 1,304 yards to score 13 touchdowns.

In an interview with the *Philadelphia Daily News,* Lions coach Wayne Fontes waxed enthusiastic about his new running back's amazing ability to elude tacklers: "He just has some incredible moves. He runs into a pile of tacklers on the line, then you see his helmet come out and then some shoulder pads and then him. **O.J. Simpson** was like that." Fontes expressed the hope that Sanders could rush for 2,000 yards or more per season if he stayed healthy. For his part, the five-foot, nine-inch Sanders had a simple explanation for his slippery moves. "I was smaller than everybody else; I didn't want to take a pounding."

Shoots for 2,000 Yards a Season

Averaging 4.5 yards per rushing attempt in 1991, Sanders compiled a total of 1,548 yards and scored 16 touchdowns rushing. In 1992 his total rushing yardage slipped 1,352, and he averaged 4.3 yards per rushing attempt. Plagued by injury in 1993, Sanders managed to amass rushing yardage of only 1,115 that season, but pushed his average per rushing attempt to 4.6 yards. Sanders rushed for 1,883 yards during the 1994 season, averaging 5.7 yards per rushing attempt but scoring only seven touchdowns rushing. The next year he averaged 4.8 yards per rushing attempt for a total of 1,500 yards and 11 touchdowns rushing. In 1996 Sanders averaged 5.1 yards per rushing attempt for a total of 1,553 yards and 11 touchdowns rushing. In 1997 he fulfilled Fontes's prediction, compiling a total of 2,053 yards rushing and averaging a stunning 6.1 yards per rushing attempt. Sanders' rushing yardage slipped just below the 1,500-mark in 1998, but he averaged only 4.3 yards per rushing attempt. At the end of the 1998 season, Sanders had a career total of 15,269, trailing the career record of 16,726 set by Walter Payton by only 1,457 yards. Then, to the surprise of almost everyone, Sanders announced his retirement from football shortly before he was to report to the Lions' training camp for the 1999 season. In his announcement, Sanders said: "The reason I am retiring is simple: My desire to exit the

Awards and Accomplishments

1985	Sets city-wide Wichita high school rushing record with total of 1,417 yards his senior year
1987	Named to *Sporting News* College All-America Team
1988	Sets 13 NCAA records as running back for Oklahoma State
1989	Wins Heisman Trophy his junior year
1989	Named *Sporting News* NFL Rookie of the Year
1989-90	NFC rushing title
1989-98	Selected to play in Pro Bowl all 10 seasons in the NFL (missed 1993 due to injury)
1990-91	NFC and NFL rushing titles
1991	Named NFC's Most Valuable Player by the NFL Players Association
1997	Named *Sporting News* Player of the Year

game is greater than my desire to remain in it. I have searched my heart through and through and feel comfortable with this decision."

There seems little doubt that Sanders could have easily surpassed Payton's rushing record if he'd stayed in football, but that was not the path he chose to take. How far he might have gone is anybody's guess. But his career is no less spectacular for the absence of the rushing crown. Paul Attner of the *Sporting News* summed up Barry Sanders's career: "He gave us a style unlike any we had ever witnessed.... We will miss his grace under extreme pressure, his sportsmanship, the way he conducted himself as a marvelous onfield role model in an era stained by boorish stars.... His classy behavior combined to make him one of the league's most popular players."

FURTHER INFORMATION

Books

"Barry Sanders." *Contemporary Black Biography,* Volume 1. Detroit: Gale Group, 1992.

"Barry Sanders." *Newsmakers 1992,* Issue Cumulation. Detroit: Gale Group, 1992.

"Barry Sanders." *St. James Encyclopedia of Popular Culture,* five volumes. Detroit: St. James Press, 2000.

"Barry Sanders." *Who's Who Among African Americans,* 14th ed. Detroit: Gale Group, 2000.

Periodicals

Attner, Paul. "Man of Mystery." *Sporting News* (August 9, 1999): 40.

Attner, Paul. "Wayne's World Is Off Its Axis." *Sporting News* (November 18, 1996): 19.

"Barry Sanders Discusses a Possible Return to the NFL on His Official Website at BroadbandSports' AthletesDirect.com." *PR Newswire* (January 25, 2001).

"Barry Sanders Tells Why He Retired from Detroit Lions After 10 Seasons." *Jet* (August 16, 1999): 47.

"Football Great Barry Sanders Launches Official Website on Broadband Sports' AthletesDirect, Says 'I Don't Ever See Myself Playing Again.' "*PR Newswire* (November 14, 2000).

Other

"Barry Sander's Career Stats." SportingNews.com. http://www.sportingnews.com/archives/sanders/stats.html (November 4, 2002).

"Barry Sanders: Running Back." Football-Reference.com. http://wwwo.football-reference.com/players?SandBa 00.htm (November 2, 2002).

"Wayne Fontes: NFL Coach of the Year." Michigan State University. http://www.msu.edu/unit/msuaa/magazine/s92/wayne.htm (November 4, 2002).

Sketch by Don Amerman

Deion Sanders
1967-

American football and baseball player

The only man in professional sports history to play in both the Super Bowl and World Series, Deion Sanders has been a top-ranked athlete since his high school years. Sanders credits sports with keeping him out of trouble as a teenager. Nicknamed "Prime Time" during high school, Sanders has probably received more prime-time sports coverage than any other athlete in recent years because of his involvement in both professional football and major league baseball. He played 12 seasons in the National Football League (NFL), including stints with the Atlanta Falcons, San Francisco Giants, Dallas Cowboys, and Washington Redskins. In major league baseball, Sanders played for the New York Yankees in 1989 and 1990; the Atlanta Braves from 1991 through the first part of 1994; the Cincinnati Reds in the second part of 1994, the first part of 1995, and all of 1997 and 2001; and for the San Francisco Giants in the latter part of the 1995 season. After leaving football and baseball in 2001, Sanders joined CBS Sports as a feature reporter/contributor for the *NFL Today* television show, and the next year became a studio analyst.

Born in Fort Myers, Florida

He was born Deion Luwynn Sanders in Fort Myers, Florida, on August 9, 1967. The son of Connie Knight (a cleaning woman), he grew up in a poor neighborhood of the southwest Florida city. Active in sports as a boy, he stayed busy enough to avoid the lure of the ever-present

Deion Sanders

Chronology	
1967	Born in Fort Myers, Florida, on August 9
1988	Signed by New York Yankees
1989	Picked in first round of NFL draft by Atlanta Falcons
1993-98	Married to Carolyn Chambers
1999	Marries actress and model Pilar Biggers on May 21
2001	Announces retirement from football and baseball; joins *NFL Today* with CBS Sports

drug trade that ensnared many of his friends. Years later Sanders told *Esquire:* "It would've been easy for me to sell drugs. But I had practice. My friends who didn't have practice, they went straight to the streets and never left." At the age of eight, he joined a Pop Warner youth league football team. He also joined a local Little League team. While a student at North Fort Myers High School, Sanders played baseball and football, as well as basketball, which was his biggest passion as a teen. A high school friend dubbed Sanders "Prime Time" after he scored 30 points in a basketball game. Sanders earned all-state honors in all three sports.

In his senior year of high school, the multisport star was deluged with offers from colleges but eventually decided to attend Florida State University (FSU) in Florida's capital city of Tallahassee. At college Sanders began to focus more of his energies on football and baseball. Although he had played left-handed option quarterback in high school, he switched in college to defense and special teams. During his years at FSU, Sanders twice was named an All-American in football and scored six touchdowns on punt or interception returns. As a senior he led the country in yardage for punt returns with an average of 15.2 yards. He also won the **Jim Thorpe** Award as the best defensive back in the country. On the baseball field, Sanders continued to shine, helping to power FSU's drive to the College World Series in 1987, where the team from Tallahassee finished fifth.

Drafted by Atlanta Falcons

In the 1989 NFL draft, the Atlanta Falcons picked Sanders early in the first round, offering him a contract that would pay him $400,000. Sanders demanded $11 million, and lengthy, often bitter negotiations followed. In the meantime, however, Sanders kept busy on the baseball field, having signed with the New York Yankees in 1988. He played about 100 games for minor league teams in the Yankees' farm system before being called up by the Yankees in June 1989 to fill in for an injured outfielder. Later that summer Sanders accepted a five-year contract from the Falcons that would pay him $4.4 million in salary and bonuses. He made his professional football debut only 24 hours after blasting a home run for the Yankees in a game against the Seattle Mariners. And a flashy debut it was. Five minutes into the game, Sanders returned a punt for a 68-yard touchdown, becoming the first athlete ever to hit a home run and score a touchdown in professional games the same week. Over the next couple of years, he solidified his position as cornerback for the Falcons, winning All-Pro honors at the end of the 1991 season.

Released by the Yankees in 1990, Sanders quickly signed a contract with the Atlanta Braves. Although his contract with the Braves allowed him to play both baseball and football, Sanders soon was telling sportswriters that he wished he could focus all of his energies on baseball. Particularly irksome to Sanders was his inability to play postseason baseball because of his gridiron responsibilities. He eventually negotiated a compromise with the Falcons that kept him in football but allowed him to play postseason baseball. This cleared the way for Sanders to play in the 1992 World Series, where he batted .533 against the Toronto Blue Jays, who eventually won the championship. He missed the first three games of the football season, triggering a storm of criticism. Despite the missed games, Sanders led Pro Bowl balloting in both the cornerback and kickoff returner categories. He led the NFL with a 26.7 kickoff return average and a total of 1,067 yards.

Leads NFL in Interceptions

Batting .276 for the Braves during the 1993 regular season, Sanders was felled by a respiratory infection in August. The illness also kept him out of football for a few games at the beginning of the season, but he never-

Awards and Accomplishments

1987-88	Named All-American in college football
1988	Receives Jim Thorpe Award as best defensive back
1989	Becomes the only athlete in modern history to score touchdown and hit home run in professional play during the same week
1990	Returns interception 82 yards for touchdown, the longest touchdown play of the year in the NFL
1992	Bats .533 in World Series against Toronto Blue Jays
1992	Leads NFL with average kickoff return of 26.7 yards and total of 1,067 yards
1992-98	Selected to play in Pro Bowl

Related Biography: Bishop Thomas D. Jakes Sr.

A major influence in Sanders's life since the mid-1990s has been Bishop Thomas D. Jakes Sr., founder of the Potter's House, a nondenominational, multiracial church in Dallas, and the T. D. Jakes Ministries. In October 1997, signaling a rebirth of Sanders's Christianity, Jakes baptized Sanders and fellow Dallas Cowboys players Emmitt Smith, Omar Stoutmire, and George Hegamin. Jakes also wrote the foreword to Sanders's *Power, Money, and Sex,* published in 1998.

Jakes was born and raised in Charlestown, West Virginia, the son of Ernest and Odith Jakes. He grew up in a hillside neighborhood and "From a very young age, he was devoted to the gospel," according to Jakes's biography on the Web site of T. D. Jakes Ministries. Jakes was called to the ministry at the age of 17 and began preaching part time while studying psychology at West Virginia State University. He later took over as music director at the Charleston church he attended as a boy and in 1982 became a full-time pastor at the same church.

The first church founded by Jakes began with only ten members and was located in a storefront in Montgomery, West Virginia. Eventually Jakes's message attracted a large, racially mixed congregation and became known as the Greater Emanuel Temple of Faith. By the time Jakes relocated to Dallas in 1996, the church's membership had grown to nearly 1,000.

theless managed to lead the NFL with seven interceptions in 11 games. He was named National Football Conference (NFC) Defensive Player of the Month for November and was chosen as a Pro Bowl starter.

Sanders made some significant changes on both the baseball and football fronts in 1994. At the beginning of the baseball season, the Braves traded him to the Cincinnati Reds. When a players' strike prematurely ended the baseball season in August, Sanders was batting .283 for the Reds. In football, he signed a one-year contract to play for the San Francisco 49ers, hoping the move would increase his chances of getting to the Super Bowl. He was named NFL Defensive Player of the Year after tying the 49ers' single-season record with three interception returns for touchdowns. And his Super Bowl dream came true, as the 49ers beat the San Diego Chargers, 49-26, helped by Sanders's contribution of four tackles and an interception.

More changes were in store for Sanders in 1995. In July he was traded by the Reds to the San Francisco Giants, where he ended the season with a batting average of .268 and 8 steals. Once again a free agent in football, Sanders signed a seven-year, $35 million contract to play for the Dallas Cowboys. His debut with the Cowboys was delayed until the end of October by arthroscopic surgery on his ankle. For much of the regular season with the Cowboys, Sanders seemed to be still finding his way, but in postseason play the cornerback helped push Dallas to a Super Bowl victory. Sanders skipped the 1996 baseball season, instead focusing all his energies on football, becoming the first full-time, two-way NFL player since Chuck Bednarik, who had played from 1949 to 1962. On offense, Sanders caught 36 passes for 475 yards while continuing to prove a force to reckon with on defense. At season's end, the Cowboys reported that Sanders had been on the field for half of their offensive plays and 80 percent on defense.

Returns to Baseball

In 1997 Sanders returned to baseball, batting .273 for the Reds and accounting for a total of 23 runs batted in. He missed the first two weeks of the football season while continuing to play for the Reds. Although he missed the tail end of the baseball season, Sanders still managed to rank second in the National League with 56 stolen bases. His season with the Cowboys was further shortened by a rib injury that caused him to miss the last three games of the regular season. Despite the missed games, Sanders in 1997 was again named All-Pro and also tapped as NFC Defensive Back of the Year. One of the highlights of Sanders's football season came on September 28 when he returned a punt 83 yards for a touchdown in a game against the Chicago Bears. It was to be the longest punt return of his career and the fourth longest in team history. Sanders's accomplishments of 1997 are all the more remarkable because away from sports it was a year of great personal turmoil for him. His marriage to college sweetheart Carolyn Chambers was ending (they divorced in 1998), and Sanders later admitted that he twice attempted to commit suicide that year.

For the next three years, Sanders played no baseball at all. His football season in 1998 was cut short when he injured his toe in a game against the Arizona Cardinals. He returned to the Cowboys for the team's playoff loss to the Cardinals. Despite his injury, Sanders was named to his seventh consecutive NFC Pro Bowl squad as a cornerback and kick returner. He was also named NFL Special Teams Player of the Year by the NFL Alumni Association for his brilliant performance as a punt returner. In the spring of 1999, Sanders's personal life took a turn for the better when the two-sport star married New York model and actress Pilar Biggers in a private ceremony on Paradise Island in the Bahamas. Presiding at the marriage ceremony was Bishop Thomas D. Jakes Sr., founder of the Dallas-based T. D. Jakes Ministries and a close spiritual adviser to Sanders.

Misses First Two Games of Season

In 1999 Sanders missed the first two games of the football season while recovering from toe surgery he

Career Statistics: Football

| Yr | Team | GP | Tackles | | | Fumbles | | | Interceptions | |
			TOT	SOLO	AST	SACK	FF	BK	INT	TD
1989	ATL	15	39	28	11	0.0	2	0	5	0
1990	ATL	16	50	31	19	0.0	0	0	3	2
1991	ATL	15	49	35	14	1.0	2	0	6	1
1992	ATL	13	66	44	22	0.0	2	0	3	0
1993	ATL	11	34	27	7	0.0	1	0	7	0
1994	SFO	14	36	36	0	0.0	0	0	6	3
1995	DAL	9	25	24	1	0.0	0	0	2	0
1996	DAL	16	33	33	0	0.0	1	0	2	0
1997	DAL	13	33	30	3	0.0	0	0	2	1
1998	DAL	11	25	25	0	0.0	0	0	5	1
1999	DAL	14	42	40	2	0.0	1	0	3	0
2000	WAS	16	41	40	1	0.0	1	0	4	0
TOTAL		163	474	385	89	1.0	10	0	48	8

ATL: Atlanta Falcons; DAL: Dallas Cowboys; SFO: San Francisco 49ers; WAS: Washington Redskins.

Career Statistics: Baseball

Yr	Team	AVG	GP	AB	R	H	HR	RBI	BB	SO	SB
1989	NYY	.234	14	47	7	11	2	7	3	8	1
1990	NYY	.158	57	133	24	21	3	9	13	27	8
1991	ATL	.191	54	110	16	21	4	13	12	23	11
1992	ATL	.304	97	303	54	92	8	28	18	52	26
1993	ATL	.276	95	272	42	75	6	28	16	42	19
1994	ATL	.288	46	191	32	55	4	21	16	28	19
	CIN	.277	46	184	26	51	0	7	16	35	19
1995	CIN	.240	33	129	19	31	1	10	9	18	16
	SFG	.285	52	214	29	61	5	18	18	42	8
1997	CIN	.273	115	465	53	127	5	23	34	67	56
2001	CIN	.173	32	75	6	13	1	4	4	10	3
TOTAL		.263	641	2123	308	558	39	168	159	352	186

ATL: Atlanta Braves; CIN: Cincinnati Reds; NYY: New York Yankees; SFG: San Francisco Giants.

had undergone during the off-season. With a punt-return average of 11.5 yards, he finished fourth in the NFC for the season. The most impressive of Sanders's punt returns that season came in an October 31 game against the Indianapolis Colts, when he returned a punt 76 yards to the two-yard line. On November 25, Sanders enjoyed his fifth career two-interception game when he picked off Miami Dolphins quarterback **Dan Marino** twice. In the spring of 2000 the Cowboys cut Sanders for salary cap reasons. Once again a free agent, Sanders on June 6 was signed by the Washington Redskins to a seven-year, $56 million contract. Interviewed by *Jet,* Sanders said of his new team: "It's wonderful to be a Redskin. They've always had something special. There's nothing like these fans, this tradition." Although he turned in a credible performance for the Redskins in 2000, Sanders announced a year later that he was leaving football.

Never one to remain idle for long, Sanders in the spring of 2001 returned to baseball after an absence of more than three years. But it proved to be a very short stint indeed. After only 32 games with the Reds, Sanders, who was batting a disappointing .173, was released in late June.

Another major change in Sanders's life came in the late 1990s in the wake of the breakup of his first marriage. He renounced his flashy, hedonistic lifestyle to become a born-again Christian. In an interview with Bob Cohn of the *Washington Times,* Sanders spoke of the challenge he had faced in separating his job from his life. "Does Michael Jackson wear his glove home? Does Bill Cosby sit around and eat Jell-O at home? Is there a pulpit in the pastor's living room at home? You have to distinguish between the two—this is my job, and this is my life."

Deion Sanders

SELECTED WRITINGS BY SANDERS:

(With Jim Nelson Black) *Power, Money, and Sex*, Nashville, TN: Word Publishing, 1998.

FURTHER INFORMATION

Books

"Deion Sanders." *Contemporary Black Biography*, Volume 31. Farmington Hills, MI: Gale Group, 2001.

Periodicals

Cohn, Bob. "Prime Time Faith: He Has Money. He Has Championship Rings. And, Deion Sanders." *Washington Times* (August 31, 2000): E2.
Cook, Kevin. "Playboy Interview: Deion Sanders." *Playboy* (August 1994).
"Deion Is Done." *Sports Illustrated* (July 27, 2001).
Kirkpatrick, Curry. "'They Don't Pay Nobody to Be Humble,' So Says Deion Sanders." *Sports Illustrated* (November 13, 1989): 52.

Other

"Bishop T. D. Jakes Biography." T.D. Jakes Ministries. http://www.thepottershouse.org/BK_popup.html (January 27, 2003).
"Deion Sanders." Baseball-reference.com. http://www.baseball-reference.com/s/sandede02.shtml (December 1, 2002).
"#21, Deion Sanders." ESPN.com. http://football.espn.go.com/nfl/players/stats?statsId=589 (December 1, 2002).

Sketch by Don Amerman

I've always been able to separate the two, even when other people haven't. But I took that other person with me sometimes. I took him to nightclubs, to bars, to places where he shouldn't have been. And now, I'm murdering slowly a person that I built up to take me into prosperity and financial gain. I'm killing him slowly. I'm working on Deion now."

These days Sanders is focusing most of his energies on being a family man. He lives with his wife, Pilar, and three children in Plano, Texas, outside Dallas. He began working full-time as a studio analyst for the *NFL Today* on CBS Sports. Whether he stays retired from both baseball and football remains to be seen. But even if he never plays again, there can be no doubt that Sanders has left an indelible mark on both sports.

CONTACT INFORMATION

Address: c/o CBS Sports, 666 Third Ave., 18th Fl., New York, NY 10017. Fax: (646) 487-2597. Phone: (646) 487-1000. Online: http://www.deion-sanders.com.

Summer Sanders
1972-

American swimmer

In the early 1990s, American Summer Sanders was a dominant swimmer. She represented the United States at the 1992 Summer Olympics in Barcelona, Spain, becoming a hero for her four medal-winning performance. She also won eight national championships. After her swimming career ended, Sanders became a broadcaster, working on a number of sports-related programs.

Sanders was born on October 13, 1972, in Roseville, California, the daughter of Bob and Barbara Sanders. Her father was a dentist, while her mother was an airline

Summer Sanders

attendant. Her parents named her Summer because her older brother Trevor, born in the summer, had not been a girl. As their children became involved in swimming, Bob and Barbara Sanders became involved in the sport. Her father worked as a swim-meet official, while her mother was a part-time swim coach.

Began Swimming

Sanders's parents built a pool in their backyard, and because of concerns about their children's safety, Sanders and her brother took swimming lessons from the time they were toddlers. At first, Sanders did not seem very interested, she would often cry and not pay attention. But one day she took off her water wings and began to swim well.

When she was three years old, Sanders joined the Roseville Bears swim team. She could already swim 25 yards. Sanders soon stood out from the other swimmers. When she was four years old, she was competing against seven year olds. Still, she had moments when she was afraid to get into the water.

When Sanders was eight years old, her parents decided to divorce; Sanders found solace at the pool. Although her parents shared custody, the constant moving back and forth was hard on Sanders and her brother. Sanders did train hard at swimming throughout her childhood, but often relied more on talent than on hard work. By her late teens, she would often skip practices. Sanders

learned the importance of training hard when she performed poorly at the 1987 Long Course National Championships.

Breakthrough at Olympic Trials

In 1988 Sanders had her big breakthrough as a swimmer. She competed in the U.S. Olympic trials, in the 200- and 400-meter individual relays, and the 100- and 200-meter breaststroke. Though she had never made the finals for the nationals, she made the finals of the 400-meter individual medley (finishing eighth) and finished third in the 200-meter individual medley. Sander missed making the Olympic team by .27 of a second.

Sanders continued to train hard, and started doing well in national competition. In 1989, she won the 200-yard butterfly at the U.S. Short Course Championships. The following year, she won the 200-yard butterfly and the 400-yard individual medley at the U.S. Short Course Championships. At the U.S. Long Course Nationals that year, she won the 200-meter individual medley. Sanders, with other swimmers, was emerging as the future of women's swimming in America.

In 1990, Sanders also competed well internationally. She did well at the Goodwill Games winning three gold medals in the 200-meter individual medley, 200-meter butterfly, and 400-meter individual medley. The last race was an upset of **Janet Evans**, who had a four-year winning streak, with a time of 4:39.22. Sanders had lowered her time by almost nine seconds.

Swam for Stanford

In addition to excellence in swimming, Sanders also had strong academic credentials, entering Stanford University on an athletic scholarship in 1990. Her success as a swimmer came from her great feel for the water and being a good overall swimmer, but not the best sprinter or the best distance swimmer. She grew to an adult height and weight of five feet, nine inches tall and 125

Awards and Accomplishments

1989	Won 200-yard butterfly at the U.S. Short Course Championships
1990	Won 200-yard butterfly and 400-yard individual medley at the U.S. Short Course Championships; won 200-meter individual medley at the U.S. Long Course National Championships; won three gold medals at the Goodwill Games, in the 200- and 400-meter individual medleys and the 200-meter butterfly
1991	Set National Collegiate Athletic Association (NCAA) records in 200-yard butterfly and 400-yard individual medley; set American record in 200-yard individual medley; won 200-meter butterfly at the World Championships as well as a silver and bronze
1991-92	Named NCAA swimmer of the year
1992	Set U.S. record in 200 butterfly; set NCAA record in 400-yard medley at Olympic Games, won gold medals in 200-meter butterfly and 400-meter medley relay, silver medal in 200-meter individual medley, and bronze in the 400-meter individual medley
2002	Inducted into the International Swimming Hall of Fame

Where Is She Now?

After retiring from swimming for a second time, Sanders pursued her career in broadcast television in earnest. In the late 1990s, she hosted a game show for Nickelodeon, *Figure It Out*. Beginning in 1997, she was hired to cover the National Basketball Association (NBA) as co-host for the show *NBA Inside Stuff*. She also provided coverage of the NBA and the Women's National Basketball Association (WNBA), and was a sideline reporter for the WNBA on NBC (National Broadcasting Company). Sanders remained connected to the Olympics, when she co-hosted *Scholastics at the Olympic Games*, which aired on MSNBC and served as a special correspondent for the 2000 Summer Games in Sydney, Australia. She was also a correspondent for the 2002 Winter Olympic Games for NBC. Sanders married Mark Henderson on July 5, 1997, in Lake Tahoe, Nevada.

pounds, with a lithe build. Although freestyle was the easiest stroke for most swimmers, it was her weakest event, while the butterfly was her strongest. Richard Quick, her coach at Stanford, told Karen Rosen of the *Atlanta Journal-Constitution,* "Summer swims the butterfly like **Edwin Moses** runs the hurdles, like **Michael Jordan** plays basketball. She just flows in the pool."

Sanders did well at Stanford. In 1991, she set National Collegiate Athletic Association (NCAA) records in the 200-yard butterfly and the 400-yard individual medley, and an American record in the 200-yard individual medley. Stanford finished second in the NCAA championships, and Sanders was named NCAA swimmer of the year. That year, Sanders also competed at the World Championships, winning a gold medal in the 200-meter butterfly, as well as a silver and a bronze in other events.

At Stanford, the following year, Sanders continued to dominate. She set the U.S. record in the 200-yard butterfly and an NCAA record in the 400-yard medley. Stanford won the NCAA Championships, with Sanders earning 60 points, more than anyone else at the competition. She was again named swimmer of the year. However, it was the last time she would compete as a Cardinal. She gave up her remaining college eligibility to get sponsorships (primarily a deal with Speedo) and to train harder in preparation for the 1992 Summer Olympics.

Shined at the Olympics

In 1992, Sanders did well at the U.S. Olympic trials, then at the Olympics in Barcelona, Spain. At the trials, she won three events, and qualified for four events and the medley relay. She won the 200- and 400-meter individual medleys, 200-meter butterfly, and finished second in the 100-meter butterfly. Sanders was only the third woman to qualify for five swimming events at the Olympics.

At the Olympics, her hard work paid off when Sanders won four medals and set two U.S. records. She won gold in the 200-meter butterfly and the 400-meter medley relay. Sanders also took silver in the individual medley (with a time of 2:11.91), and bronze in the 400-meter individual medley (with a time of 4:37.58). The 400-meter individual medley and 200-meter individual medley times were American records. Sanders actually won the bronze and silver medals first, and had had doubts about winning any gold medals.

Loss of Competitive Focus

After the Olympics were over, Sanders continued to attend Stanford. Although she did not swim with their team, she did train for competitive swimming. However, she could not match her 1992 numbers, and retired in January 1994. At the time, Sanders was burned out on swimming, did not enjoy going to the pool, and was not having fun. At the time, she told Michael Flam of the *Associated Press,* "I've always been a goal-setter and I've always wanted to prove something. So I think there's something else out there, some field that I can get into, some job that I'll love."

Sanders found her career in broadcasting. After the Olympics, she appeared as a guest star on her favorite soap opera, *All My Children*. After completing her degree, she became a co-host on MTV's game show *Sandblast,* and did commentary for swimming events, speaking engagements, swimming clinics, and product endorsements for Speedo and Power Bar.

Tried to Make Olympic Team Again

In April 1995, Sanders decided to return to swimming and began training for the 1996 Olympic Games. She had been accepted to the United States Swimming Resident National Team based in Colorado, and felt she needed to begin training again. She told the *Omaha World-Herald,* "I could just fall flat on my face. But I think either way you gain something from it. It'll be a lifelong lesson."

At first, training was hard for Sanders; she could not keep up with the other swimmers. She had her own lane so that she could swim against herself, and gradually build up to swimming with the group. Coach Jonty Skinner pushed her, and she qualified for the 1995 Pan Pacific Championships. Her goal remained the 1996 Olympics, but at the Olympic trials she did not make the team, although she competed in three events. Sanders's competition was younger and hungrier than she was, and her lack of training had hurt her. Sanders retired from swimming permanently.

At the 1996 Olympic Games, in Atlanta, Georgia, Sanders was a commentator for NBC. After she failed at the Olympic trials, she told Hank Lowenkron of *Associated Press,* "Obviously I'm disappointed because you don't like your last race to be eighth place, but I'm looking beyond that. I have a new appreciation for swimming.… It took this for me to really realize and look back and remember when I won that gold medal and how special it is."

CONTACT INFORMATION

Address: c/o NBA Entertainment, Inc., 450 Harmon Meadow Blvd., Seacus, NJ 07094-3618.

SELECTED WRITINGS BY SANDERS:

(With Melinda Marshall) *Champions Are Raised, Not Born: How My Parents Made Me a Success,* New York: Delacorte Press, 1999.

FURTHER INFORMATION

Books

Johnson, Anne Janette. *Great Women in Sports.* Detroit: Visible Ink Press, 1996.

Layden, Joe. *Women in Sports: The Complete Book on the World's Greatest Female Athletes.* Santa Monica, CA: General Publishing Group, 1997.

Porter, David L., editor. *Biographical Dictionary of American Sports: 1992-1995 Supplement for Baseball, Football, Basketball, and Other Sports.* Westport, CT: Greenwood Press, 1995.

Sherrow, Victoria. *Encyclopedia of Women and Sports.* Santa Barbara, CA: ABC-CLIO, 1996.

Periodicals

Allen, Karen. "Sanders to Leave Swimming on Top." *USA Today* (January 11, 1994): 3C.

Bondy, Filip. "The Highest Season for One Summer." *New York Times* (July 19, 1992): section 8A, p. 5.

Brennan, Christine. "Swimmer Evans Suffers Rare Loss." *Washington Post* (July 22, 1990): D8.

Dial, Karla. "Sanders Is Back." *Press-Enterprise* (August 5, 1995): D6.

Dixon, Oscar. "Sanders Thrives in 'Real World'." *USA Today* (September 29, 2000): 3C.

Flam, Michael. "Sanders Stays Dry, but Still Has Her Smile." *Associated Press* (March 22, 1994).

Kensler, Tom. "Sanders Pools Her Talent Again for Summer Blast." *Denver Post* (March 9, 1996): C2.

Litsky, Frank. "Mature Sanders Wins National Championship." *New York Times* (March 21, 1990): B10.

Litsky, Frank. "Stanford Freshman Stays Busy." *New York Times* (April 7, 1991): section 8, p. 2.

Lowenkron, Hank. "Star of '92 Olympics Accepts Toll of Time." *Associated Press* (March 12, 1996).

Lowenkron, Hank. "Time Catches Up to Sanders, Thompson." *Associated Press* (March 13, 1996).

Montville, Leigh. "Summer Time." *Sports Illustrated* (June 1, 1992): 46.

Powers, John. "Summer Time at the US Trials?" *Boston Globe* (March 8, 1996): 31.

Rosen, Karen. "Sanders Back Home in Water." *Atlanta Journal-Constitution* (August 11, 1995): 1E.

Rosen, Karen. "Sanders 'Relieved' after Finally Meeting Great Expectations." *Atlanta Journal-Constitution* (August 1, 1992): E4.

Rosen, Karen. "Tonight's Main Event Just Call Them 'Summer's Olympics'." *Atlanta Journal-Constitution* (July 26, 1992): E2.

"Sanders Takes Plunge at Olympic Comeback." *Omaha World-Herald* (June 22, 1995): 25.

Schoenfeld, Bruce. "New Kids on the Blocks." *Sporting News* (December 31, 1990): 36.

Steptoe, Sonja. "Summer Heat Wave." *Sports Illustrated* (April 1, 1991): 44.

"Summer Sanders Heads Swimming Hall of Fame Class." *Associated Press* (May 10, 2002).

"Swimmer Summer Sanders Skips Stanford." *United Press International* (May 12, 1992).

Zavoral, Nolan. "Summer's Best." *Star Tribune* (October 16, 1994): 16C.

Sketch by A. Petruso

Terry Sawchuk
1929-1970

Canadian hockey player

He's been called the greatest goaltender in National Hockey League (NHL) history. He won the Stanley Cup four times, earned the Vezina Trophy for the year's best goalie four times, and his performance in a 1967 playoff game is still called the best display of goaltending ever. Goalies ever since have imitated the way he crouched in front of the goal. In a sport full of tough,

Terry Sawchuk

tenacious men who play hurt, his countless physical injuries and mental wounds still became legendary. Terry Sawchuk triumphed, faltered, raged, rebounded, and triumphed again, always in pain.

Growing Up

Terry Sawchuk was born December 28, 1929 in Winnipeg, Manitoba, Canada. Sawchuk's father, a Ukrainian immigrant, had met his mother when they were working in a burlap factory together. Sawchuk learned to skate at age four, and started playing hockey with his older brother Mitch on an ice rink at his uncle's house. Mitch and another brother died while Sawchuk was young, and Sawchuk wore Mitch's old goalie pads when he played. A Winnipeg-based scout for the Detroit Red Wings invited him to Detroit to work out with the team when he was fourteen, and he signed a contract with the Wings soon after.

Rookie of the Year

Sawchuk left home at sixteen to play in junior leagues, then spent most of three years in the minor leagues, playing for Omaha in the United States League and Indianapolis in the American Hockey League. He was named Rookie of the Year in both leagues and led Indianapolis to the AHL's Calder Cup in 1950. He played his first NHL game on January 8, 1950, at age twenty, filling in for the Red Wings' injured goalie, Harry Lumley. In seven games for the Red Wings that

year, Sawchuk was 4-3, with a goals-against average of 2.28. That proved he was ready to play goal in the NHL, so at the end of the season, the Red Wings traded Lumley to Chicago and made Sawchuk their regular goalie. He played in every Wings game in 1950-51, his first full season, shut out the Wings' opponents eleven times, compiled a GAA of 1.98, and won the Calder Trophy for NHL Rookie of the Year.

Right away, Sawchuk's stance in goal attracted attention around the league. Back then, goalies would usually bend at their knees but keep their upper bodies erect. Instead, Sawchuk bent deeply at the waist. "I found that I could move more quickly from the crouch position," he explained in an interview quoted in Chris McDonell's *Hockey All-Stars*. "It gave me better balance to go both ways, especially with my legs. Scrambles and shots from the point were becoming the style in hockey when I broke into the NHL. From the crouch, I could keep the puck in my vision much better when it was coming through a maze of players." Goalies around the league eventually adopted his stance.

The Red Wings won the Stanley Cup in Sawchuk's second full season with them. He again played every game, had twelve shutouts and a 1.91 GAA, and won the Vezina Trophy. The Red Wings swept through the playoffs, winning the semi-finals and finals four games to none. Sawchuk didn't let in a single goal in any of the home playoff games. "Sawchuk is their club," declared a frustrated **Maurice Richard** after his Montreal Canadiens lost in the finals (according to David Dupuis's book *Sawchuk*). "Another guy in their nets and we'd beat them."

For the next three seasons, Sawchuk remained at the top of his game. The Red Wings won two more Stanley Cups, and Sawchuk won the Vezina Trophy two more times. Each year, he let in an average of less than two goals per game. "The key for us was Sawchuk," Wings

Awards and Accomplishments

1950-51	All-Star First Team
1950-51	Calder Memorial Trophy
1951-52	All-Star First Team
1951-52	Vezina Trophy
1952-53	All-Star First Team
1952-53	Vezina Trophy
1953-54	All-Star Second Team
1954-55	All-Star Second Team
1954-55	Vezina Trophy
1958-59	All-Star Second Team
1962-63	All-Star Second Team
1964-65	Vezina Trophy
1970-71	Lester Patrick Trophy
1971	Inducted into Hockey Hall of Fame

defenseman Bob Goldham once said, looking back on the 1954 and 1955 Stanley Cup wins, according to Dupuis's *Sawchuk*. "He was the greatest goaltender who ever lived. We could always count on him to come up with the big save."

A Dark Temper

But even in those early years, Sawchuk revealed a dark, depressive temper. The first time Detroit sports writer Joe Falls ever saw Sawchuk in 1953, "he was raging with anger and shouting obscenities and throwing his skates at a reporter," Falls is quoted as saying in McDonell's *Hockey All-Stars*. A 1954 photograph taken at the Red Wings' Olympia Stadium shows Sawchuk climbing a metal fence to get into the crowd and confront a heckler. He got married in 1953, to Pat Morey, the eighteen-year-old daughter of a Detroit-area golf course owner, but he often took his drunken rage out on her after spending nights carousing with Detroit Lions football players. In February 1955, coach Jack Adams briefly benched Sawchuk because of his drinking and ordered him to undergo psychiatric counseling. (Adams only told the press he was resting Sawchuk.)

In 1955, Adams traded Sawchuk to the Boston Bruins. The trade shook Sawchuk's confidence. He did well during his first season in Boston, posting nine shutouts, but faltered in 1956-57. He came down with mononucleosis, missed several games, and came back to play before he was fully recovered. He didn't play as well after his return, still feeling sick and weak, and worried about his performance until he began to suffer from insomnia.

Miserable, he told the Bruins he was retiring from the game rather than let his team down on the ice—and his angry coach labeled him a quitter in the papers. He went back to his home in Detroit, where the Red Wings' team physician examined him and declared he was on the verge of a nervous breakdown. He called a press conference, explained his decision, and announced he might return to hockey if his health improved. He tried to work as a car dealer, insurance salesman, and bartender. When the Red Wings decided they wanted him back for the next season, he gladly returned to hockey. But his mental instability had become public knowledge, a famous example of the self-doubt and lonely despair that can take over a goalie's mind.

Sawchuk spent seven more seasons as the Wings' goalie, but the team wasn't quite what it once was. He was still a solid, talented goalie, but never posted the amazing statistics of his first years. During the 1960-61 season, as more teams began to carry two goalies on their rosters, he had to share goaltending duties with Hank Bassen. "It really rocked his world," his wife, Pat, told Dupuis for his book. "If he sat out a game, there are no words to describe his depression." He still drank heavily, which caused pain to flare up in his legs. He frequently lashed out at his wife and children, and his infidelities became obvious. Twice, his wife filed for divorce but reconciled with him.

In his twenty years as an NHL goaltender, Sawchuk suffered repeated injuries and was in and out of hospitals all the time. As a young player, he had multiple elbow surgeries to remove bone chips from youthful injures. In his first years in the NHL, when each team had only one goalie and no one wore a mask, games would stop if a shot or a stick cut a goalie's face, the team's trainer would quickly sew up the wound, and the goalie would keep playing. Sawchuk got an estimated 400 stitches in his face and head before he started wearing a mask in 1962. He broke bones and suffered concussions. Once, in 1963, a teammate's skate slashed his hand open. "It looked like a little cut at first," he said (accord-

Career Statistics

Yr	Team	GP	W	L	T	GAA	TGA	SHO
1949-50	Detroit	7	4	3	0	2.28	16	1
1950-51	Detroit	70	44	13	13	1.98	139	11
1951-52	Detroit	70	44	14	12	1.91	133	12
1952-53	Detroit	63	32	15	16	1.94	120	9
1953-54	Detroit	67	35	19	13	1.96	129	12
1954-55	Detroit	68	40	17	11	1.94	132	1
1955-56	Boston	68	22	33	13	2.66	181	9
1956-57	Boston	34	18	10	6	2.38	81	2
1957-58	Detroit	70	29	29	12	2.96	207	3
1958-59	Detroit	67	23	36	8	3.12	209	5
1959-60	Detroit	58	24	20	14	2.69	156	5
1960-61	Detroit	37	12	16	8	3.26	113	2
1961-62	Detroit	43	14	21	8	3.33	143	5
1962-63	Detroit	48	23	16	7	2.57	119	3
1963-64	Detroit	53	24	20	7	2.64	138	5
1964-65	Toronto	36	17	13	6	2.56	92	1
1965-66	Toronto	27	10	11	4	3.16	80	1
1966-67	Toronto	28	15	5	4	2.81	66	2
1967-68	Los Angeles	33	11	14	6	3.07	99	2
1968-69	Detroit	11	3	4	3	2.62	28	0
1969-70	NY	8	3	1	2	2.91	20	1
TOTAL		971	447	330	173	2.52	2401	103

Boston: Boston Bruins; Detroit: Detroit Redwings; Los Angeles: Los Angeles Kings; NY: New York Rangers; Toronto: Toronto Maple Leafs.

ing to Dupuis's *Sawchuk*), "then it opened up and I could see the knuckle bones." Doctors had to reattach his tendons in surgery.

Comeback

Sawchuk played his last great season as a Red Wing goalie in 1963-64. A pinched nerve put him in the hospital again during the playoffs—but he left, went to Olympia Stadium for the third game of the semi-finals, made twenty-six saves and shut out Chicago, then went back to the hospital. The Wings advanced to the finals, but lost to Toronto in seven games. Detroit hockey writers named Sawchuk the team's most valuable player of the season.

Still, Detroit let Sawchuk go in the waiver draft that year, and the Toronto Maple Leafs acquired him. The next year, he shared the Vezina Trophy with fellow Leaf goalie Johnny Bower. In 1966, he collapsed from back pain during a round of golf. Doctors discovered two herniated discs in his spine. He had surgery that fused two of his vertebrae together, and doctors warned he might not be able to play again. But that warning seemed to compel him to play even harder. His win-loss-tie record for the 1966-67 season was 15-5-4, and he achieved his 100th shutout that year.

In the 1967 semi-finals against Chicago, Sawchuk played the first four games, and won two and lost two. Exhausted, he insisted that Bower start the fifth game. But the coach put Sawchuk in to start the second period after Chicago scored two quick goals in the first period,

shaking Bower up. Many hockey writers consider Sawchuk's performance that night the best game a hockey goalie ever played. A **Bobby Hull** slap shot hit Sawchuk in his tender shoulder and knocked him down, but he kept playing through the severe pain. Sawchuk made thirty-seven saves in two periods, robbing scoring champs like Hull and **Stan Mikita**. He didn't let in a goal, and the Leafs won 4-2. They went on to win the series, then defeated Montreal in six games to win the Stanley Cup, Sawchuk's fourth.

His Last Years

The Los Angeles Kings took Sawchuk in that year's expansion draft, and the aging goalie played for three different teams in the next three years. By the time he was traded back to Detroit and then to the New York Rangers, the aging goalie was serving as a backup. Early in 1969, after more of Sawchuk's alcoholic fits of temper, his wife left him, taking their seven kids, and divorced him. He moved in with some of his teammates.

His violent temper led to his tragic death. In April 1970, Sawchuk got into an argument with roommate and teammate Ron Stewart. They got into a shoving match, then both fell to the ground. Sawchuk suffered internal bleeding, and surgeries failed to heal the injuries. He died on May 31, 1970.

Sawchuk's record of 103 shutouts may never be broken. He played in a record 971 regular-season games; he was one of the last great goaltenders from the era when goalies played every game, when their careers were one long endurance test. All goalies sacrifice their bodies, absorbing the blows of speeding pucks, and all struggle with the intense mental challenge of carrying the praise or blame for their teams' successes and failures. Sawchuk faced those trials in more games than any other goalie, and may have suffered more than anyone else. His achievements and his tragedies, his physical stamina and mental torment, make him not only hockey's best goalie, but the ultimate goaltending legend.

FURTHER INFORMATION

Books

Dupuis, David. *Sawchuk: The Troubles and Triumphs of the World's Greatest Goalie.* Toronto: Stoddart Publishing, 1998.

Fischler, Stan. *Goalies: Legends from the NHL's Toughest Job.* Toronto: Warwick Publishing, 1995.

McDonell, Chris. *Hockey All-Stars: The NHL Honor Roll.* Willowdale, Ont.: Firefly Books Ltd., 2000.

Other

Boston Bruins Legends. http://www.bruinslegends.com.

Detroit Red Wing Alumni Association Legends. http://www.redwingalumni.com.

Iovino, Jim. LCS Hockey Greats of the Game. http://www.lcshockey.com.

Sketch by Erick Trickey

Gale Sayers

Gale Sayers
1943-

American football player

Knee injuries cut short the brilliant football career of running back Gale Sayers, but not before the "Kansas Comet" was recognized by the National Football League (NFL) as the greatest running back in the first 50 years of the league's history. Although he played only 68 games in professional football, in 1977 Sayers, at the age of only 34, became the youngest player ever to be enshrined in the Pro Football Hall of Fame. Honored as the NFL's Most Valuable Player in 1967, 1968, and 1970, Sayers in 1965 became the NFL's all-time leading scorer in a single season with 22 touchdowns and retired from the game with a career gain of 6,213 yards. As well as he was known for his accomplishments on the football field, Sayers is remembered by many for his friendship with fellow running back Brian Piccolo, a relationship memorialized in two memorable made-for-television movies (the first in 1971, the remake in 2001). For many, Sayers's unwavering love and support for Piccolo during the latter's losing battle with cancer defined the essence of true friendship in its purest form.

Born in Wichita, Kansas

He was born Gale Eugene Sayers in Wichita, Kansas, on May 30, 1943. The second of three sons of Roger Winfield (an auto mechanic and car polisher) and Bernice (Ross) Sayers (a homemaker), Sayers owes his first name to his mother who was hoping her second child would be a girl she planned to name Gail. When she had a son instead, the name was retained but with a spelling modification. Sayers's father worked as a mechanic for the Goodyear Corporation in Wichita but in 1950 moved the family to his ailing father's wheat farm in Speed, Kansas. When Sayers's grandfather died in 1951, the family moved to Omaha, Nebraska, where Sayers spent the remainder of his childhood. As a boy he showed a natural athletic ability and became involved in a number of sports both in and out of school.

Sayers began playing football in a midget football league soon after his arrival in Omaha, but his interest in the game really began to blossom during his years at Omaha's Central High School, where he played middle linebacker on the school's varsity team. In his senior year at Central, Sayers was named to both the All-Mid-

Chronology

1943	Born in Wichita, Kansas, on May 30
1951	Moves with family to Omaha, Nebraska
1961-65	Attends University of Kansas
1962	Marries high school sweetheart Linda Lou McNeil (later divorced) on June 10
1965	Picked in first round of NFL draft by Chicago Bears
1971	Friendship with Brian Piccolo recounted in *Brian's Song,* a made-for-TV movie
1972	Retires from professional football
1973	Marries Ardythe Elaine Bullard on December 1
1973	Returns to University of Kansas as assistant athletic director

Related Biography: Football Player Brian Piccolo

Brian Piccolo, one of Sayers's closest friends and the subject of the made-for-television movie *Brian's Song,* was born in Pittsfield, Massachusetts, on October 21, 1943. As a young child, he moved with his family to Fort Lauderdale, Florida, where he attended high school, participating in a number of sports. But football was his first love, and after high school, he attended Wake Forest University in North Carolina on a football scholarship. As a senior at Wake Forest, he led the nation in rushing but nevertheless failed to get picked at the NFL's 1965 draft. Legendary Chicago Bears owner and coach George Halas stepped in and signed Piccolo as a free agent.

Although he now wore a Bears uniform, Piccolo spent the 1965 football season on the team's practice squad and saw no real action. Although he played in all 14 games of the 1966 season, he rushed for only 12 yards on three carries. The following year, Piccolo gained a total of 317 yards. His big break came in 1968 when Sayers, already a close friend of Piccolo's, injured his knee in the ninth game of the season, putting him out of commission for the rest of the year. For the 1968 season as a whole, Piccolo rushed for 450 yards and scored his first two touchdowns in the NFL.

Just as his football career appeared ready to take off in a big way, a physical exam and follow-up tests in 1969 revealed that Piccolo had a rare form of lung cancer. In the months that followed, Sayers grew even closer to Piccolo, providing all the support he could during this difficult period. Piccolo died on June 16, 1970.

western and All-American high school team. He also became a standout star in track and field, winning three gold medals in area competition. But football clearly was Sayers's first passion, and he was courted by dozens of top colleges interested in his gridiron skills. In the end, he decided to return to his native Kansas to play halfback for the University of Kansas Jayhawks. Before heading off to college, Sayers became engaged to his high school sweetheart, Linda Lou McNeil.

Overwhelmed by Academic Demands

An undistinguished scholar in high school, Sayers was clearly overwhelmed by the academic demands of college. Although he continued to shine on the football field, Sayers did poorly in the classroom during his freshman year, failing English and getting dangerously low grades in most of his other courses. Because of his disappointing academic performance, Sayers was forced to enroll in summer school between his freshman and sophomore years at Kansas. He got a little help with his homework from new wife Linda, whom he married shortly after the end of the spring semester. (The couple later divorced.)

With his academic situation stabilized somewhat, Sayers turned in an amazing performance on the football field during his sophomore year, rushing for 1,125 yards and averaging 7.2 yards per carry. He turned in creditable stats during his junior year, rushing for 941 yards, as well as his senior year, rushing for 678 yards, and earning All-American honors after both seasons. With a Big Eight Conference career record of 2,675 yards rushing, Sayers had truly earned his nickname of the "Kansas Comet."

Academically, Sayers finally hit his stride during his senior year at Kansas, maintaining a B average during the fall semester. With the end of the football season, however, he began to focus almost single-mindedly on a career in pro football, entertaining offers from teams in both the NFL and the rival American Football League, which was later to become the American Football Conference within the NFL. His interest in school waned, and Sayers failed to complete all the credits needed to

earn his bachelor's degree. In the NFL draft of 1965, he was drafted in the first round by the Chicago Bears of the NFL. Sayers himself negotiated a four-year contract with the Bears that paid him $25,000 a season and included a signing bonus of $50,000.

Named NFL's Rookie of the Year

Sayers made a spectacular debut in pro football, rushing for a total of 867 yards and 22 touchdowns during his rookie season. His outstanding performance earned Sayers Rookie of the Year honors as well as the NFL's scoring title for the year. The high point of Sayers's rookie season with the Bears came in a game against the San Francisco 49ers on December 12, 1965, when the running back rushed for six touchdowns on a cold and muddy football field in Chicago. He single-handedly gained 316 yards and scored 36 points, prompting teammate **Mike Ditka** to tell the *NFL Insider:* "Yeah, the mud affected the kid. If it had been dry out there, he would've scored 10 touchdowns." The rookie also managed to win a trip to the Pro Bowl.

As if to prove that his rookie season was no fluke, Sayers came back with a vengeance in 1966, rushing for a total of 1,231 yards to lead the league. Averaging 5.4 yards per rushing attempt, Sayers was once again selected to play in the Pro Bowl. The following year, he again earned All-Pro honors, rushing for 880 yards. Sayers also began to lay the groundwork for a life after football, taking a job as a stockbroker in Chicago during the off-season. In addition, he began to take a more active role in civic and humanitarian affairs, focusing particularly on programs to benefit underprivileged children.

It was also during this period that his friendship with fellow running back Brian Piccolo began to grow

Career Statistics

Yr	Team	GP	Rushing					Receiving			
			ATT	YDS	AVG	TD	REC	YDS	AVG	TD
1965	CHI	14	166	867	5.2	14	29	507	17.5	6
1966	CHI	14	229	1231	5.4	8	34	447	13.1	2
1967	CHI	13	186	880	4.7	7	16	126	7.9	1
1968	CHI	9	138	856	6.2	2	15	117	7.8	0
1969	CHI	14	236	1032	4.4	8	17	116	6.8	0
1970	CHI	2	23	52	2.3	0	1	6	6.0	0
1971	CHI	2	13	38	2.9	0	0	0	0.0	0
TOTAL		68	991	4956	5.0	39	112	1307	11.7	9

CHI: Chicago Bears.

stronger. It was in many respects a very unusual friendship indeed. Both men played the same position, which most often fuels rivalry rather than friendship. Sayers was African American and Piccolo was white. In 1967 the two roomed together during a preseason training camp in Alabama. Although they lived and practiced together, they could not go out in public and eat a meal comfortably during a period when the barriers of racial segregation had yet to be fully dismantled. When Piccolo was diagnosed with lung cancer in the fall of 1969, the bonds of friendship between the two men grew even stronger. Sayers was a pallbearer at Piccolo's funeral after his friend died on June 16, 1970.

Suffers Serious Knee Injury

During the 1968 season Sayers suffered his first serious knee injury. In a game against the 49ers, the running back was hit so hard that his knee was badly twisted, tearing ligaments and ending his season prematurely. Although he played only nine games in 1968, Sayers managed to rush for a very respectable total of 856 yards, averaging 6.2 yards per carry. Because of his knee injury, Sayers was forced to undergo extensive surgery and a lengthy period of physical rehabilitation. Although he was back for the beginning of the Bears' 1969 season, he was forced to start very slowly. The uncharacteristically conservative nature of Sayers's early play in 1969 gave rise to rumors that the running back was washed up. Despite the slow start, Sayers ended the season as the NFL's leading rusher, having piled up a total of 1,032 yards.

At the end of the 1969 season, Sayers was honored with the **George Halas** Award as "the most courageous player in professional football." When he was presented with the award at the annual dinner of the Professional Football Writers, he dedicated the award to Piccolo, saying: "You flatter me by giving me this award, but I can tell you here and now that I accept it for Brian Piccolo. Brian Piccolo is the man of courage who should receive the George S. Halas award. Mine is tonight; it is Brian

Piccolo's tomorrow.... I love Brian Piccolo, and I'd like all of you to love him, too. Tonight, when you hit your knees, please ask God to love him."

Tears Ligament in Left Knee

In a preseason exhibition game in 1970, Sayers suffered a torn ligament in his left knee. Although he underwent surgery to repair the damage, his knee was never again the same. Despite the injury and subsequent surgery, Sayers managed to play two games during the regular season, but he was unable to maneuver with the same agility and speed for which he would become famous. He finished the season with only 52 yards on 23 carries, averaging 2.3 yards per carry. He underwent two more surgeries over the next several months and even had his leg put in a cast, but it was all to no avail. In the two games he played during the 1971 season, Sayers rushed for only 38 yards on 13 carries, gaining an average of 2.9 yards per carry.

The writing was on the wall and could no longer be ignored. At the beginning of 1972 season, Sayers announced his retirement from professional football. He did not stray far from the game, however. He worked for a while as a football analyst for CBS Sports. Then in 1973 he went back to his old alma mater, the University of Kansas, to work as assistant athletic director. He also became director of the Williams Educational Fund, the principal fund-raising organization for University of Kansas athletic programs. Sayers (who had earlier been divorced from his first wife, Linda) married Ardythe Elaine Bullard on December 1, 1973. In 1976 he left Kansas to take over as athletic director at Southern Illinois University.

Enshrined in Pro Football Hall of Fame

In 1977 Sayers became the youngest player ever to be enshrined in the Pro Football Hall of Fame. In his acceptance speech, Sayers looked back on the road he had traveled to football success: "God gave me a great gift

Awards and Accomplishments

1961	Named to All-American high school football team
1963-64	Wins college All-American honors
1965	Named NFL's Rookie of the Year
1965-69	Picked to play in Pro Bowl
1966, 1969	Leads NFL in rushing
1968	Founds Gale Sayers Foundation to help young newspaper carriers
1969	Receives George S. Halas Award as "most courageous player in professional football"
1977	Becomes youngest player to be enshrined in Pro Football Hall of Fame
1977	Voted into College Football Hall of Fame
1984	Founds a computer supplies company
1999	Named to Chicago Area Entrepreneurship Hall of Fame

Gale Sayers

and I had a lot of help developing for this occasion. Reaching this point, however, is not as important as striving to get here. This is true in all professions and all of life's activities. There are doctors, lawyers, school-teachers, plumbers all who strive to do their very best with their abilities. We hear a lot today about how the American people have lost their dedication to excellence. I don't believe that is true. Each of us excels at different things, sometimes in areas that are only a hobby, more often in our life vocation. The most important thing, however, is to strive to do our very best. Nothing is more of a waste than unrealized potential." That same year the running back also was voted into the College Football Hall of Fame.

After five years as athletic director at Southern Illinois, Sayers and his wife Ardythe in 1981 returned to the Chicago area, where they continue to live today. From his two marriages Sayers has a total of six children: one daughter and five sons.

It has been more than three decades since Sayers left professional football. Many of his records have fallen by the wayside in the intervening years. But no amount of time will erase the brilliance of the running back's short but memorable career. Of Sayers's injury-shortened football career, Pulitzer Prize-winning sportswriter Red Smith later told ESPN: "His days at the top of his game were numbered, but there was a magic about him that still sets him apart from the other great running backs in pro football. He wasn't a bruiser like **Jim Brown**, but he could slice through the middle like a warm knife through butter, and when he took a pitchout and peeled around the corner, he was the most exciting thing in pro football."

CONTACT INFORMATION

Address: c/o Sayers Group, 1150 Freehanville Dr., Mt. Prospect, IL 60056. Phone: (847) 391-4040. Email: info@sayers.com. Online: http://www.sayers.com.

SELECTED WRITINGS BY SAYERS:

(With Al Silverman) *I Am Third,* New York: Viking Press, 1970.
(With Bob Griese) *Offensive Football.* New York: Atheneum, 1972.

FURTHER INFORMATION

Books

"Gale Sayers." *Contemporary Black Biography,* Volume 28. Farmington Hills, MI: Gale Group, 2001.
"Gale Sayers." *Encyclopedia of World Biography Supplement,* Volume 21. Farmington Hills, MI: Gale Group, 2001.

Periodicals

Hill, Michael E. "'Brian's Song': ABC Adds a Few Notes to a Classic." *Washington Post* (December 2, 2001): Y6.

Other

"Brian Piccolo, Bears Running Back, 1965-1969." BearsHistory.com. http://www.geocities.com/dipiccolo41/piccolo.html (November 30, 2002).
"Gale Sayers: Bio." Pro Football Hall of Fame. http://www.profootballhof.com/players/enshrinees/gsayers.cfm (November 29, 2002).

"'Kansas Comet' Disappeared Too Quickly." Pro Football Hall of Fame. http://www.profootballhof.com/players/mainpage.cfm?cont_id=26423 (November 29, 2002).

"Meet Gale." Sayers Group. http://www.sayers.com/galebio.cfm (November 30, 2002).

Roberts, M. B. "Fame Couldn't Wait for Sayers." ESPN.com. http://espn.go.com/sportscentury/features/00016460.html (January 29, 2003).

Sketch by Don Amerman

Dolph Schayes

Dolph Schayes
1928-

American basketball player

Dolph Schayes is generally credited with being the first modern basketball forward. His career began in 1948, before the formation of the National Basketball Association (NBA) in 1949. His playing career totaled 16 years with the Syracuse Nationals, which became the Philadelphia 76ers in 1964. He played for the Nationals from 1948 to 1964, and during that time, he was an All-Star twelve years in a row, became the NBA's all-time best scorer, and by the time he retired from playing, had played more games than any other player in the NBA (1,059). He was also the NBA's all-time leader in scoring, with 19,249 points to his credit, and the leader in free throws made (6,979) and attempted (8,273).

Schayes went on to become the first coach of the Philadelphia 76rs in 1964. In 1966, Schayes led the 76ers team to the NBA title, and he was named NBA Coach of the Year. Following his tenure as coach of the 76ers, Schayes became the supervisor of referees for the NBA, and then became the first coach of the Buffalo Braves in 1970. His last coaching assignments were

with the gold medal-winning U.S. men's basketball team at the Maccabiah Games in 1977, and the master's team for the Pan-American Maccabi Games in Uruguay in 1991.

Dolph Schayes was born in New York City in 1928. He attended DeWitt Clinton High School in the Bronx, graduating in 1945. In high school, he played on the school basketball team, earning letter honors three of his four years there. He was also captain of the basketball team his junior and senior year.

After graduating from high school, Schayes went on to New York University (NYU), where he excelled on the school basketball team as a center. At NYU, he earned letters all four years. His achievements on the team earned him All-American honors in 1948, and also the Haggerty Award as the best player in the New York City area. He earned All-Metropolitan honors in 1945, 1946, and 1948. He played a total of 80 games in college, earning 815 points for an average of 10.2 points per game. In his senior year at NYU, he broke the school's scoring record by scoring 356 points. In his junior year, he helped his team reach the National Collegiate Athletic Association (NCAA) finals.

Upon graduating from NYU with a degree in engineering in 1948, Schayes had offers from both the Basketball Association of America's (BAA) New York Knickerbockers (the Knicks) and the National Basket-

Career Statistics

	GP	Pts	P/G	FG%	FT%	Reb	RPG	AST	APG	PF
NBA Regular Season	1059	19249	18.2	.380	.844	11256	10.6	3071	2.9	3667
NBA Playoffs	103	1973	19.2	.390	.822	1051	10.2	257	2.5	397

Chronology

1928	Born on May 19 in New York City
1945	Graduates from high school, attends New York University (NYU)
1948	Earns All-American honors
1948	Earns Haggerty Award for being the top basketball player in the New York City area
1948	Breaks NYU's scoring record
1948	Graduates from NYU, signs with the Syracuse Nationals
1964	Retires as player; becomes coach of the Philadelphia 76rs
1966	Becomes referee supervisor for the NBA
1970	Becomes coach of the Buffalo Braves
1977	Coaches gold medal-winning U.S. men's basketball team at the Maccabiah Games in Tel Aviv, Israel
1991	Coaches master's team in Uruguay at the Pan-American Maccabi Games

Awards and Accomplishments

1949	Named NBL Rookie of the Year
1950-51, 1956, 1959-61	Named to the All-NBA Second Team
1951	Becomes NBA's top scorer and rebound leader
1951-62	Named an NBA All-Star
1952-55, 1957-58	Named to the All-NBA First Team
1955	Led the Nationals to victory in the NBA championship game
1958, 1960, 1962	Leads the NBA in free throws
1966	Named NBA Coach of the Year
1973	Inducted into the Naismith Memorial Basketball Hall of Fame
1977	Named one of the all-time top players in the NBA
1996	Named to the NBA 50th Anniversary All-Time Team
1999	Inducted into the Philadelphia Jewish Sports Hall of Fame

ball League's (NBL) Syracuse Nationals. Schayes explained years later to Dave Anderson in the *New York Times,* "I was the Knicks' first-round choice, but that year their boss, Ned Irish, had ... what amounted to a salary cap—$100,000 for the team, $5,000 for a rookie. That's all the Knicks could offer me, but Syracuse, which was then in the rival National Basketball League before the merger, offered me $7,500." The Knicks wanted Schayes badly enough to offer him another job during the off-season, but since they didn't tell him what the job would be, he decided to sign with the Nationals. He intended to play just one year and then see what his options would be. "But that one year," as he told Anderson, "turned into 16 years."

With the Nationals, Schayes moved from playing center to forward. He was named Rookie of the Year in 1949 after averaging 12.9 points per game, the same year that the two rival basketball leagues merged to form the National Basketball Association (NBA). By 1951, Schayes was the top scorer in the NBA, as well as the rebound leader, with an average of 16.4 rebounds per game.

During this time, Schayes developed an innovative way of improving his free throw shooting. He would practice with a 14-inch hoop inserted inside a regulation 18-inch hoop. This paid off for him by making him the NBA's free throw leader in three separate years, 1958, 1960, and 1962. During his time as a player with the Nationals, Schayes helped his team to several playoff games. In 1955, Schayes averaged 18.5 points and 12.3 rebounds per game. That year, the Nationals won the NBA title by defeating the Fort Wayne Pistons in seven games.

Schayes was instrumental in that win; with less than one minute on the clock, he scored on two free throws, pushing the Nationals into the lead with 91-90 points.

The Nationals moved from Syracuse to Philadelphia in 1964, changing its name to the 76rs. That year, Schayes retired as a player and became coach of the team in its new home, taking his team to two third-place Eastern Division wins, and ultimately the NBA championship. The 76ers' 55-25 record in 1966 was the best in NBA, and earned Schayes recognition as NBA Coach of the Year.

During his career as a player, Schayes scored a total of 19,249 points in 1,059 pro games, for a points per game average of 18.2. His rebound total was 11,256. His best year was 1958, in which he scored an average of 24.9 points per game. By the time he retired from playing in 1964, he was the top-scoring player in NBA history, and had played more games than anyone else in the NBA.

In 1966, Schayes became supervisor of NBA referees. He served in this post until 1970, when he became head coach of a new team, the Buffalo Braves.

In 1977, Schayes went to the Maccabiah Games, held since 1932 in Tel Aviv, Israel, as head coach of the United States men's basketball team. Playing on the team was Schayes's son Danny Schayes, who had just graduated from high school. Team USA beat the Israeli team 92-91 to take home the gold medal. Also in 1977, Schayes was named one of the top 50 players ever to play in the NBA. His last post as a coach came in 1991, when he coached the masters team, made up of players 35 years old and older, in Uruguay for the Pan-American Maccabi Games.

Dolph Schayes's son Danny Schayes also had a long career with the NBA. After the Maccabiah Games in Tel Aviv, Danny went on to Syracuse University, where he became a star player. After college, in 1981, he signed with the Utah Jazz. He played for numerous other teams before retiring during the 1999-2000 season with 18 seasons as an NBA player under his belt.

Dolph Schayes was inducted into the Basketball Hall of Fame in 1973. He is also enshrined in the International Jewish Sports Hall of Fame located in Israel. In 1999, he was inducted into the Philadelphia Jewish Sports Hall of Fame.

FURTHER INFORMATION

Periodicals

Anderson, Dave. "Sports of the Times; Old P.S.A.L. Names Reminisce a Little." *New York Times* (March 10, 2000): D4.

Other

"Dolph Schayes Biography." Basketball Hall of Fame. http://www.hoophall.com/halloffamers/Schayes.htm (December 16, 2002).

"Dolph Schayes." Philadelphia Jewish Sports Hall of Fame. http://www.pjshf.com/1999schayes.html (December 16, 2002).

"Maccabiah Games." International Games Archive. http://www.internationalgames.net/maccabia.htm (December 16, 2002).

"NBA History: Dolph Schayes." NBA.com. http://www.nba.com/history/schayes_bio.html (December 16, 2002).

Sketch by Michael Belfiore

Curt Schilling
1966-

American baseball player

At 6'4" and 215 pounds, Curt Schilling is an intimidating presence on the pitcher's mound. By 2002 the 37-year-old starting pitcher could boast 45 wins in two years with the Arizona Diamondbacks, tying Jim Palmer's record of consecutive wins set during the

Curt Schilling

1975-76 season. But those who know him well know a different Curt Schilling: a compassionate humanitarian who is dedicated to his family and actively involved in a number of charitable causes that benefit from his continued high profile as a professional athlete.

In 2001 Schilling pitched the four-year-old Diamondbacks into World Series champions, sharing mound duties—and National League Most Valuable Player (MVP) kudos—with teammate **Randy Johnson**. This achievement is all the more surprising coming on the heels of an uneventful career with the Philadelphia Phillies during the 1990s, although Schilling pitched for the Phillies in the 1993 World Series and struck out over 300 batters for his former team between 1997 and 1998. A strong-armed pitcher, he alternates between a 92-plus-mph fastball, slider, and split finger pitches, and is known for pulling out extra velocity in key situations. Embracing the technology available to 21st-century athletes, Schilling keeps a video file containing every pitch he's thrown since 1993, and he studies tapes of opposing batters prior to his games in search of an edge that will let him hold the field.

Born Curtis Montague Schilling in Anchorage, Alaska, Schilling was raised in Phoenix, where his father, Cliff Schilling, served in the Army and passed along his love of baseball. Enrolling at Yavapai Junior College in Prescott, Arizona in 1985, he pitched for the school team, then signed with the Boston Red Sox as a second

Chronology

1966	Born November 14 in Anchorage, Alaska
1986	Signs with Boston Red Sox
1987	Leads minor league with 189 strikeouts
1988	Moves to Baltimore Orioles and the major leagues
1991	Traded to Houston Astros
1991	Lecture by Roger Clemens provides inspiration to focus on game
1992	Traded to Philadelphia Phillies
1993	Pitches in his first World Series for Philadelphia
1995	Recovers from shoulder surgery
1996	Named Baseball's Most Caring Athlete by *USA Today*
1997	Starts in first All-Star game of his career
2000	Wife Shondra is diagnosed with melanoma.
2001	Perfects tandem pitching style with teammate Randy Johnson

Awards and Accomplishments

1993	National League Championship Series Most Valuable Player (MVP)
1996	Lou Gehrig award from Phi Delta Theta
1996	March of Dimes Phillie of the Year award
1997	Sets National League record for strikeouts by a right-handed pitcher with 319
1997-99, 2001-02	Named to National League All-Star Team
2000	Philadelphia Sports Writers Association Humanitarian Award
2001	Shares World Series MVP honors with teammate Randy Johnson
2001-02	Cy Young Award runner-up

round draft choice in 1986. Traded to the Baltimore Orioles in 1988, Schilling made his major league debut in September, the occasion a poignant one due to the recent death of his father. Only a year before, Cliff Schilling had been diagnosed with brain cancer, and in January of 1988, just a few months before Curt's major-league debut, his life support was finally removed. When Schilling took the mound for the Baltimore Orioles, he reserved an empty seat for his dad, as he had for the thirteen years during which his father had been his most loyal fan.

Although mounting a lackluster record with the Orioles, Schilling showed promise, and during the 1990 season he chalked up an ERA of 2.54 as a middle reliever. With his mohawk haircut streaked red and blue, his flashy Corvette, and sporting an earring and a reputation as an off-the-mound crazyman, the twenty-one year old also showed that he still had some wild oats to sew, but Orioles manager **Frank Robinson** helped set Schilling straight. In 1991 Schilling moved to the Houston Astros where he pitched 75 innings during a season that left him with three wins and five losses; in Texas he received a further attitude adjustment from Red Sox star **Roger Clemens** and started to perfect his game. Traded to the Philadelphia Phillies in early 1992, he showed his potential by pitching twenty-nine straight scoreless innings. In November Schilling settled down for good, marrying Shonda, a producer for a Baltimore sports television station with whom he would have three children.

The year 1993 was a good one for the Phillies, fueled by Schilling's 95-mph fastball and his 16-7 record as a starter. The team made it into the World Series against the ultimately triumphant Toronto Blue Jays, following a 4-2 win over the Atlanta Braves in the Eastern division playoffs. Despite his team's loss to Toronto, Schilling was named 1993 National League Championship Series MVP.

In 1994, the Phillies hit a slump, and that year's players' strike left them with 54 wins and 61 losses. Disabled twice during the season due to a bone spur in his elbow and a knee injury, Schilling followed suit with a 2-8 record and an ERA of 4.48. In 1995, during which the Phillies ranked third in their division, Schilling suffered a torn labrum and required shoulder surgery by August. He began 1996 on the disabled list, then returned to the mound throwing 97 mph after extensive rehab. Still, the Phillies remained in a slump, ending the season in fifth place.

Although Schilling topped his career average and set a new league record for strikeouts by a right-handed pitcher in 1997, with 319, as well as going 17-11 with a 2.97 ERA, the Phillies remained in the doldrums. Frustrated by his team's inability to turn things around, Schilling continued to wait it out, and was rewarded in 1998 when the Phillies finally climbed out of the hole to settle in third place in the Eastern division. He also received his second consecutive invitation to pitch in an All-Star game. The year 1998 was a good year personally as well. Haunted by his father's death to cancer, Schilling had been battling his own addiction to chewing tobacco for several years; finally a routine dentist's visit in 1998 that revealed a lesion on the inside of his lower lip convinced him to give up the habit in favor of watching his children grow up.

In 1999, Schilling pitched in his third All-Star game, this one in Boston's Fenway Park, but by season's end he was once again disabled. He underwent arthroscopic surgery on his right shoulder in December 1999, and was well on his way to recovery the following February when his wife was diagnosed with a potentially lethal melanoma. Strong enough not to let his concern for his wife overshadow his responsibilities as a player, Schilling continued to develop his career. In July of 2000, now into his final season under contract with Philadelphia, Schilling was traded to the Diamondbacks in exchange for Travis Lee, Vicente Padilla, Omar Daal, and Nelson Figueroa. After playing nine years with a team that seemed content to remain on the sidelines of victory, he was enthused about joining a young ball club. Although his first months with Arizona proved disappointing—he had 5 wins and 6 losses with a 3.69 ERA—he signed on for three years with Arizona after

Career Statistics

Yr	Team	W	L	ERA	GS	SHO	IP	H	R	BB	SO
1988	BAL	0	3	9.82	4	0	14.2	22	19	10	4
1989	BAL	0	1	6.23	1	0	8.2	10	6	3	6
1990	BAL	1	2	2.54	0	0	46.0	38	13	19	32
1991	HOU	3	5	3.81	0	0	75.2	79	35	39	71
1992	PHI	14	11	2.35	26	4	226.1	165	67	59	147
1993	PHI	16	7	4.02	34	2	235.1	234	114	57	186
1994	PHI	2	8	4.48	13	0	82.1	87	42	28	58
1995	PHI	7	5	3.57	17	0	116.0	96	52	26	114
1996	PHI	9	10	3.19	26	2	183.1	149	69	50	182
1997	PHI	17	11	2.97	35	2	254.1	208	96	58	319
1998	PHI	15	14	3.25	35	2	268.2	236	101	61	300
1999	PHI	15	6	3.54	24	1	180.1	159	74	44	152
2000	PHI/ARI	11	12	3.8	29	2	209.4	204	90	45	158
2001	ARI	22	6	2.98	35	1	256.2	237	86	39	293
2002	ARI	23	7	3.23	35	1	259.1	218	95	33	316
TOTAL		155	108	3.36	314	17	2418.0	2142	959	571	2348

ARI: Arizona Diamondbacks; BAL: Baltimore Orioles; HOU: Houston Astros; PHI: Philadelphia Phillies.

the 2000 season was over. In addition to supporting Shondra while she dealt with her cancer, he worked to hone his skills and expand his pitching repertoire, adding a splitter and slider and perfecting his curveball and fastball.

Schilling started the 2001 season strong, pitching 7.1 perfect innings during a May match with San Diego. He went on to pitch the best regular season of his professional career, but remained modest about his achievements, crediting his team as well as his partnership with Randy Johnson. Schilling ended the regular season 22-6, with 293 strikeouts, and was ranked second in the league's ERA and strikeouts, going on to win all three starts in the National League play-offs.

With Schilling and Johnson, the Diamondbacks suddenly found themselves with an almost unbeatable pitching machine that rated comparisons to 1960s tandem pitchers **Sandy Koufax** and Don Drysdale. As *Baseball Digest* contributor Phil Elderkin noted, the pair is successful due to "intimidation and few mistakes. They pitch inside just often enough to discourage even the league's best hitters from crowding the plate. And when they do give up a home run, invariably it comes with no one on base." After a win against Atlanta propelled them into the 2001 World Series and a seven-game win over the New York Yankees, Schilling was voted Johnson's runner up for the National League's prestigious **Cy Young** Award from the Baseball Writers Association of America, and was top choice for co-MVP. Following his World Series win, Schilling spent a week at Disney World with wife Shonda and their three children, Gehrig, Gabriella, and Grant. Once again on the Arizona mound in 2002, Schilling pitched a minimum of six innings in each of his twenty-six starts and seven or more innings in twenty-three starts. Continuing the trend of the year before,

teammate Johnson won his fifth Cy Young honor, with Schilling runner-up for the second consecutive year.

As is evidenced by his decision to name his first son Gehrig, Schilling loves all things baseball, including memorabilia, and is an active student of the history of the sport. Schilling's interests apart from baseball include war and strategy games, an interest he has furthered as president of game producer Multi-Man Publishing. A World War II history buff, he also helps create military board games marketed by Hasbro, Inc. and is also a PC game fan who plays EverQuest to pass the time while on the road. Because the climate is more beneficial to Shondra's condition, Schilling and his family make their permanent home in Philadelphia, but reside in Phoenix during the baseball season.

Together with his wife, Schilling also contributes to the battle against amyotrophic lateral sclerosis (ALS), a degenerative muscle ailment named for storied Yankee slugger **Lou Gehrig**, who died from the condition. Schilling told Gerry Callaghan of *Sports Illustrated,* "I met a guy … who had been diagnosed with ALS; six months later I saw him again, and he couldn't walk. I started thinking. What if that was my child or my wife, and I never got off my ass and did anything to help? How could I live with myself?" Involved in the cause since 1992 when they began Curt's Pitch for ALS under the auspices of the Curt and Shonda Schilling ALS Research Fund, the couple have earned $1.5 million to fight the disease, and have also befriended ALS patients and testified before Congress to boost research. Due to the tragedies that have touched his family, Schilling remains active in efforts to remove smokeless tobacco from baseball and funding cancer research. In 1997, 1998, and 2001 he was honored with baseball's **Roberto Clemente** Award for balancing outstanding performance with civic responsibility, and has received numerous other public service awards.

CONTACT INFORMATION

Address: Arizona Diamondbacks, 401 East Jefferson St., Phoenix, AZ 85004-2438.

FURTHER INFORMATION

Periodicals

Baseball Digest (November, 2001): 28.
Baseball Digest (October, 2002): 40
Boston Globe (October 19, 2001).
New York Times (September 29, 2002).
New York Times Magazine (September 29, 2002): 52.
People (June 1, 1998): 73.
Sporting News (October 1, 2001): 46
Sporting News (December 17, 2001): 8.
Sports Illustrated (February 2, 1998): 78.
Sports Illustrated (August 14, 2000): 5.
Sports Illustrated (November 7, 2001): 46.

Sketch by Pamela L. Shelton

Max Schmeling
1905-

German boxer

Widely vilified as a willing propaganda tool of Adolf Hitler's Third Reich, Max Schmeling was

Max Schmeling

nevertheless one of Europe's greatest boxers of all time. His professional career stretched from 1924 to 1948, during which time he compiled a career record of fifty-six wins, ten losses, and four ties. World Heavyweight Champion from 1930 to 1932, Schmeling is perhaps best remembered for his two heavyweight bouts with Alabama-born **Joe Louis**. In 1936 Schmeling, the underdog, knocked out the previously unbeaten Louis in the 12th round of a match at Yankee Stadium. The tables were turned, however, in the 1938 rematch between Louis and Schmeling. America's "Brown Bomber" exacted his revenge on Schmeling by knocking out the German in the first round. Although the highly visible Schmeling continued for years to be a symbol of Hitler's Nazi regime and the racial policies for which it became known, the boxer was not quite the ogre most Americans imagined. Years after World War II, it was revealed that Schmeling had risked his own position and freedom by sheltering the two teenaged sons of a Jewish friend during the Kristallnacht pogrom of 1938. Despite unrelenting pressure from Hitler and his top aides, Schmeling steadfastly refused to join the Nazi party and also refused Nazi demands that he fire his Jewish manager, Joe Jacobs.

Born in German Village of Uckermark

He was born Maximilian Adolph Otto Siegfried Schmeling in Uckermark, Germany, on September 28, 1905. He began boxing as a boy and by his early teens

Chronology	
1905	Born in Uckermark, Germany, on September 28
1924	Turns professional on August 2
1933	Marries Polish-born actress Anny Ondra
1938	Shelters teenaged sons of David Levin during Kristallnacht
1940	Drafted into Wehrmacht as a private
1941	Parachutes into war-torn Crete
1947	Returns to boxing
1954	Returns to America, visiting grave of Joe Jacobs in New York
1957	Buys Coca-Cola dealership in Hamburg-Wandsbek
1981	Helps to pay for costs of Joe Louis's funeral

Related Biography: Boxer Jack Sharkey

Jack Sharkey, born Josef Paul Zukauskas in Binghamton, New York, on October 26, 1907, first got into boxing while he was serving in the U.S. Navy. He engaged in more than twenty-five bouts during his military service, becoming champion of the Atlantic Fleet. In 1924, shortly before leaving the service and while stationed in Boston, he changed his name and turned professional. He won his first three professional fights, only to lose his fourth on a poor decision. Although he avenged that loss, he was knocked out by Chilean Quintin Romero-Rojas in his 10th match. He also lost decisions to Jim Maloney, Charley Weinert, and Bud Gorman, but he beat Maloney twice in rematches and defeated the highly rated Johnny Risko and Jack Renault.

On July 21, 1927, Sharkey was knocked out by Jack Dempsey, but he bounced back from that defeat to score a number of major victories, including defeats of Jack Delaney and Tommy Loughran. He also knocked out British heavyweight champ Phil Scott, earning himself a match on September 26, 1930, with Germany's Max Schmeling for the vacant world heavyweight title. After almost knocking out Schmeling in the third round, Sharkey landed a low blow in the fourth round and was disqualified, giving Schmeling the title.

Sharkey and Schmeling met again in a rematch on June 21, 1932, at the Long Island City Bowl in New York City. It was a close match, although many observers felt that Schmeling definitely had the edge. However, Sharkey won the split decision and took the championship, prompting Joe Jacobs, Schmeling's manager, to shout, "We wuz robbed!"

Sharkey married Dorothy Pike in 1925. The couple had three children. Carefully husbanding his boxing earnings, he retired from the ring in 1936. Living in Boston with his family, he managed a neighborhood bar and refereed local boxing and wrestling matches. Later in life, he and his wife moved to Epping, New Hampshire, where he lived until his death in 1994.

was competing in amateur bouts throughout his native region of Germany. In 1924, Schmeling turned professional, facing off against Kurt Czapp in Dusseldorf on August 2. He knocked out Czapp in the sixth round to win his first professional bout. For the remainder of 1924, he fought another nine matches, winning eight, six by knockout, and losing only one. On October 10, 1924, Schmeling was knocked out in the fourth round by Max Dieckmann in a match in Berlin.

In 1926, Schmeling squared off twice against Max Dieckmann in Berlin. In their second match of the year on August 24, Schmeling knocked out Dieckmann in the first round to win the German light heavyweight title. The following year, Schmeling won the European light heavyweight championship by knocking out Fernand Delarge in the 14th round of a match in Dortmund, Germany. Later that year, he successfully defended his European light heavyweight title in a match against Hein Domgorgen in Leipzig, Germany, on November 6. On January 6, 1928, Schmeling again successfully defended his European title by knocking out Italian light heavyweight champion Michele Bonaglia in the first round of a match in Berlin. Three months later, boxing as a heavyweight, Schmeling defeated Franz Diener in a 15-rounder in Berlin to capture the German heavyweight title.

Faces Off against U.S. Boxers

In 1929, realizing that the United States was rapidly becoming the center of the international boxing scene, Schmeling came to America to challenge some of the world's leading heavyweight boxers. After a couple of matches against unremarkable contenders, the German heavyweight made his mark internationally by defeating two major heavyweights, Johnny Risko and Paolino Uzcudun, earning him a number-two ranking and a shot at the world heavyweight title. On June 12, 1930, Schmeling and American Jack Sharkey faced off in New York's Yankee Stadium to fight for the vacant world heavyweight title. The German became the first heavyweight champion in history to win the title on a foul when Sharkey was disqualified in the fourth round for a low blow. It was just over a year before Schmeling fought again, successfully defending his heavyweight

title by knocking out Young Stribling in the 15th round of a match in Cleveland, Ohio. Just over two years after he'd won the world heavyweight title, Schmeling lost it in a controversial split-decision in a Long Island rematch with Sharkey.

Schmeling's two years as world heavyweight champion—the first German ever to hold that title—elevated him to heroic status in his homeland. In the wild and wicked final days of the Weimar Republic, Berlin's café society embraced Schmeling, and Schmeling, poorly educated and never more than a laborer before getting into boxing, loved it. Dark and handsome, he suddenly found himself keeping company with actors, actresses, writers, poets, artists, and dancers. He took to buying the finest tailored suits money could buy, almost all of them bought at David Lewin's justly famous Prince of Wales shop in the German capital. It was in Berlin that Schmeling met Anny Ondra, a Polish-born actress who starred in a number of motion pictures in Austria, Czechoslovakia, Germany, and Great Britain between the late teens and early fifties. Schmeling married the actress in 1933. Childless, their marriage lasted more than half a century and ended only with Anny's death in 1987.

Knocked Out by Max Baer

Three months after losing his heavyweight title to Sharkey, Schmeling battered former welterweight and middleweight champ Mickey Walker into submission in eight rounds. In his only fight in 1933, Schmeling was knocked out by Max Baer in a New York match. Next up was a February 13, 1934, Philadelphia match with Steve Hamas, which Schmeling lost. The following year in Hamburg, Hamas and Schmeling faced off again, and this time Schmeling took the match, knocking out Hamas in the ninth round. On July 7, 1935, Schmeling again defeated Paolino Uzcudun in a twelve-rounder in Berlin.

Schmeling's life through the early 1930s showed no signs of anti-Semitism. In fact, many of the people with whom Schmeling and his wife were closest were Jewish. After Hitler's rise to power, the Fuhrer and his cohorts exerted strong pressure on Schmeling to fire his Jewish manager, Joe Jacobs, who was often known by his Yiddish name, Yussel. Third Reich officials were particularly incensed by an incident that followed Schmeling's victory over Steve Hamas on May 10, 1935, in Hamburg. To honor Schmeling, spectators began to sing the national anthem, raising their arms in the Nazi salute. Jacobs, somewhat playfully, joined in, throwing up his arm as well, even though he clutched a large cigar in his hand. To top it off, Jacobs gave a big stage wink to Schmeling, as if to say, "Hey, look at me." The entire incident was captured on film, infuriating Nazi officials. The head of Hitler's Sports Ministry demanded in writing that Schmeling get rid of Jacobs, but Schmeling refused to do so.

Upsets Brown Bomber in New York

In what was undoubtedly the high point of his boxing career, Schmeling on June 19, 1936, faced off against America's unbeaten heavyweight, Joe Louis, known affectionately as the Brown Bomber. Widely thought to be washed up, Schmeling was an 8-1 underdog. Having scouted his opponent in Louis's fight against Paolini Uzcudun on December 13, 1935, Schmeling later observed: "I noticed something—a flaw in Louis's defense." In the 12th round of the fight, Schmeling found the opening he was looking for and pounded Louis with a flurry of right-hand punches, knocking him out. Two years later, in one of the briefest fights of all time, Louis knocked out Schmeling in the first round of their Yankee Stadium rematch. Despite their enmity in the boxing ring, Schmeling and Louis were to become close friends. When Louis fell on hard times later in life, struggling with tax problems and drug dependency, Schmeling extended a helping hand. After Louis died in 1981, Schmeling helped to underwrite the cost of the funeral for his one-time opponent.

One of the most revealing incidents in Schmeling's life—and one about which he modestly prefers not to talk—did not come to light until more than fifty years after the event. In November 1938, during the Nazi-engineered Kristallnacht terrorism of Germany's Jews, Jewish haberdasher David Lewin, a longtime friend of Schmeling, became worried for the safety of his two

Awards and Accomplishments	
1924	Won first professional fight, knocking out Kurt Czapp on August 2
1926	German light heavyweight title
1927	European light heavyweight title
1928	German heavyweight title—defeated Franz Diener
1930	World heavyweight title—defeated Jack Sharkey
1936	Upset Joe Louis in match at Yankee Stadium
1938	Defeated by Louis in rematch at Yankee Stadium
1992	Inducted into International Boxing Hall of Fame

teenaged sons—Henri and Werner. Lewin told the boys to go to Schmeling's suite in Berlin's Excelsior Hotel and ask him to take them in.

Risks Life to Save Lewin's Sons

For two days, Schmeling hid Lewin's sons in his hotel suite, sharing with them everything he had. Eventually, the entire Lewin family was able to escape Nazi Germany. They fled to a Jewish enclave in Shanghai, where they ended up captives of the Japanese. Finally, they were able to make their way to the United States, where the family settled. Looking back on the incident at a dinner to honor Schmeling in 1989, Henri Lewin recalled: "Max was a man of the highest quality. If they had caught him hiding us, they would have shot him. Let me tell you: If I had been Max Schmeling in Germany in 1938, I wouldn't have done it." Although Schmeling attended the 1989 Las Vegas dinner in his honor, he made it clear that he didn't like being "glorified."

Schmeling in 1939 regained the German heavyweight title by knocking out Adolf Heuser in the first round of their match in Stuttgart. Not long thereafter, Schmeling was forced to pay the price for his long-running refusal to join the Nazi party. In 1940, at the age of thirty-four, he was inducted into Wehrmacht as a private. Assigned to the paratroopers, Schmeling in May 1941 jumped into Crete, where he was knocked unconscious upon landing and captured by British troops. His failure to condemn his treatment by his British captors further infuriated Nazi officials.

Buys Coca-Cola Dealership

After the end of World War II, Schmeling fought a handful of fights in an effort to earn some much needed money. Some of those earnings were used in the 1950s to buy a Coca-Cola dealership in the Hamburg area, where he continues to live today.

A successful businessman in Hamburg for decades, Schmeling also earned a well deserved reputation as a humanitarian, contributing to a wide variety of worthwhile causes. Asked how he would like to be remembered, Schmeling told a reporter: "I would not like to be remembered as someone who amounted to so much as an athlete but who was good for nothing as a person. I couldn't stand that." There's seems little chance that will happen.

SELECTED WRITINGS BY SCHMELING:

(With George B. Von der Lippe) *Max Schmeling: An Autobiography,* Bonus Books, 1998.

FURTHER INFORMATION

Books

"Max(imilian) Schmeling." *Almanac of Famous People,* 6th ed. Detroit: Gale Group, 1998.

Periodicals

"Almost a Hero." *Sports Illustrated* (December 3, 2001): 64.
Cox, James A. "The Day Joe Louis Fired Shots Heard 'Round the World." *Smithsonian* (November, 1988): 170.
"Max Schmeling." *Publishers Weekly* (September 7, 1998): 77.
Ward, Nathan. "Max Schmeling: An Autobiography." *Library Journal* (August, 1998): 101.

Other

"Jack Sharkey." American National Biography Online. http://www.anb.org/articles/19/19-00875-article.html (October 25, 2002).
"Max Schmeling." Boxingpress. http://www.boxing press.de/records/schmeling.htm (October 25, 2002).
"Max Schmeling." IBHOF. http://www.ibhof.com/ schmelin.htm (October 25, 2002).
"Max Schmeling. Aryan Champ, Savior of Jews." Raoul Wallenberg Web Site. http://www.raoul-wallenberg. org.ar/english/opinionbarucht4.html (October 25, 2002).
"Max Schmeling: The Story of a Hero." Auschwitz.dk. http://www.auschwitz.dk/schmeling.htm (October 25, 2002).

Sketch by Don Amerman

Mike Schmidt
1949-

American baseball player

Mike Schmidt

In his eighteen-year major league baseball career, Mike Schmidt's skill helped lead his team to five division ti- tles, two National League (NL) pennant titles, and two World Series games. He was an essential part of the Philadelphia Phillies' 1980 World Series championship— the only one for that team. When he retired in 1989, he ranked seventh in all-time home runs, having hit 548 in major league play. He held major league, team career, and team season records that ranked in the double digits. In his first year of eligibility for baseball's Hall of Fame, Schmidt garnered one of the highest percentages of votes. He was the 26th player to be voted in his first time on the ballot.

From Unremarkable to Exceptional

Schmidt was born on September 27, 1949, in Dayton, Ohio, one of two children of Jack and Lois Schmidt. He was an athletic child who had interests ranging from tree climbing to more organized sports such as football, bas- ketball, and baseball. He also learned how to play golf from his father. Eventually he gave up tree climbing and opted to concentrate on baseball and basketball.

Schmidt's high school and early college years in baseball were unremarkable. He attended Ohio Univer- sity in Athens, Ohio, playing basketball and baseball. Unlike many players who look forward to a career in sports, Schmidt did not win any scholarships for his par- ticipation. A knee injury forced Schmidt to quit basket- ball, and it was then that he began to focus on baseball.

During the summer before his sophomore year of college, Schmidt took a more serious approach to the

Chronology

1949	Born September 27 in Dayton, Ohio
1971	Drafted in second round by Phillies, plays two seasons in minor leagues
1972	Called up to play for Phillies
1973	First full season in major league; meets Donna Wightman
1974	Hits one of the longest singles in major league history: 329 feet from home plate, 117 feet in the air; marries Wightman
1975	Despite striking out 180 times due to sprained left shoulder, he stills leads the National League in home runs; steals a career high 29 bases
1976	Hits four home runs in one game at Wrigley Field, helping team to a come-back win against the Chicago Cubs, 18-16
1977	Becomes a born-again Christian
1978	Daughter Jessica Rae born December 19; elected team captain
1979	Hits a career high 45 home runs
1980	Breaks his own career high by hitting 48 home runs; helps take Phillies to World Series
1981	Begins providing tickets to games to those who couldn't normally attend
1983	Becomes highest paid baseball player with a $2.1 million per year salary
1985	Begins raising money for the United Way by having companies donate $100 for every home run he hits
1986	Surpasses Lou Gehrig's 494 home runs
1988	Second year of his two-year contract not renewed by Phillies
1989	Announces retirement from baseball on Memorial Day; elected to play for the National League in the All-Star Game, but does not play
1995	Baseball Writers' Association of America votes Schmidt into the Hall of Fame with an overwhelming 96.52 percent of the vote; 26th player to be voted in his first time on the ballot
2002	Becomes commissioner for United States Professional Softball League

Awards and Accomplishments

1970	Ohio University wins NCAA District 4 title; fourth place, College World Series
1970-71	All-American Shortstop
1974, 1976-77, 1979-84, 1986-87, 1989	Elected to All-Star team
1974-76, 1980-81, 1983-84, 1986	Led league in home runs
1976	National League record for most homers, hitting 11 in April
1976-84, 1986	Gold Glove award winner
1980	Most Valuable Player; Phillies win World Series; voted World Series MVP; National League Player of the Year
1980-81, 1984	Led league in RBIs
1980-84, 1986	Silver Slugger award winner
1981	Most Valuable Player
1983	Phillies play in World Series; voted Greatest Phillies Player Ever
1986	Most Valuable Player; National League Player of the Year; became first Phillies player to ever play in 2,000 games, June 9, 1986
1990	Phillies hold a tribute night and retire his jersey
1995	Inducted into Hall of Fame; fifth place, Isuzu Celebrity Golf Challenge in Lake Tahoe
1996	Ninth place, Isuzu Celebrity Golf Challenge in Lake Tahoe

game. He played for the Dayton Summer League team after approaching the coach several times. His persistence paid off, and coach Ted Mills brought him in at shortstop. His fielding and hitting impressed Mills so much that he called the Ohio University baseball coach, Bob Wren, and told him about it. He also wrote the California Angels about Schmidt's abilities.

When Schmidt returned to play for Ohio University, his batting average had gone from .260 to .310. During his college career, Schmidt was twice named All-American Shortstop. He helped his team win the NCAA District 4 title, and place fourth in the College World Series in 1970. By the time he graduated, Schmidt had a batting average of .330 and had hit a total of twenty-seven home runs.

Building a Reputation

In 1971, Schmidt was drafted in the second round by the Philadelphia Phillies. He spent two years in the minor leagues. He played one season with the Reading (Pennsylvania) Phillies and most of the next season with the Eugene (Oregon) Emeralds. He was called up to the major leagues in September of 1972. It wasn't until 1974 that Schmidt came into his own as a Phillies player. While he led the league in strikeouts he also led the

league in home runs, and continued to do so for the next two years. That same year he hit one of the longest singles recorded in major league history. In a game against the Houston Astros at the Astrodome, Schmidt hit the ball 329 feet from home plate and 117 feet in air, smashing a speaker that hung from the ceiling. In later years, he got his swing under control and had four more seasons as the home run leader (1980-81, 1983, and 1986). In 1984, he tied for that lead.

By 1978, Schmidt was considered one of the Phillies' best players. He was reluctantly elected to the position of team captain and his game suffered many setbacks that year. He hit only twenty-one home runs and seventy-eight Runs Batted In (RBIs). He got himself back together the next season and hit a career high forty-five home runs.

For the Philadelphia Phillies, 1980 was an unforgettable year. With Schmidt's excellent fielding and batting ability the team won their only World Series championship. He was voted Most Valuable Player (MVP) in the National League (NL) that year as well as MVP for the World Series. He bested his previous career high home runs, hitting forty-eight. Schmidt related his feelings about being part of the 1980 World Series championship team to Joe O'Loughlin of *Baseball Digest*, "Every organization has a team that's really special, and

Career Statistics

Yr	Team	AVG	GP	AB	R	H	HR	RBI	BB	SO	SB
1971	RP	.211	74	237	27	50	8	31	27	66	3
1972	EE	.291	131	436	80	127	26	91	87	145	6
1972	PP	.206	13	34	2	7	1	3	5	15	0
1973	PP	.196	132	367	43	72	18	52	62	136	8
1974	PP	.282	162	568	108	160	36	116	106	138	23
1975	PP	.249	158	562	93	140	38	95	101	180	29
1976	PP	.262	160	584	112	153	38	107	100	149	14
1977	PP	.274	154	544	114	149	38	101	104	122	15
1978	PP	.251	145	513	93	129	21	78	91	103	19
1979	PP	.253	160	541	109	137	45	114	120	115	9
1980	PP	.286	150	548	104	157	48	121	89	119	12
1981	PP	.316	102	354	78	112	31	91	73	71	12
1982	PP	.280	148	514	108	144	35	87	107	131	14
1983	PP	.255	154	534	104	136	40	109	128	148	7
1984	PP	.277	151	528	93	146	36	106	92	116	5
1985	PP	.277	158	549	89	152	33	93	87	117	1
1986	PP	.290	160	552	97	160	37	119	89	84	1
1987	PP	.293	147	522	88	153	35	113	83	80	2
1988	PP	.251	108	390	52	97	12	62	49	42	3
1989	PP	.203	42	148	19	30	6	28	21	17	0
TOTAL		.267	2404	8352	1506	2234	548	1595	1507	1883	174

EE: Eugene Emeralds (Pacific Coast League, Class AAA); PP: Philadelphia Phillies; RP: Reading Phillies (Eastern League, Class AA).

the 1980 club is that team for the Phillies.... I'm honored to be on that team and be a central figure on it."

The 1980s continued to be excellent years for Schmidt. He became one of eleven players to be elected MVP two years in a row, when he was named MVP in 1981. In 1983, he helped the Phillies team to the World Series, but they ended up losing to the Orioles. That same year, he became the highest paid player in baseball with a $2.1 million per year contract. In 1986, he won his third MVP award.

In 1988, Schmidt encountered the first major injury of his career. A torn rotator cuff put Schmidt on the injured list. While he was undergoing surgery for the shoulder injury, the Phillies announced that they would not renew the second year of his two-year contract, which was worth $2.25 million. Schmidt elected to spend one more season with the Phillies, but ended up announcing his retirement on Memorial Day, 1989.

An Uneasy Fame

Despite the glowing statistics and broken records, Schmidt's years in baseball weren't always easy. He spent his entire career playing for the Phillies, becoming one the best players they ever had. Still, he had an uncomfortable relationship with Phillies fans that effected his personal life. Obsessed with succeeding, Schmidt was quiet, introspective, and superstitious. His focus on the game came at the expense of fun. Looking back Schmidt related to Frank Fitzpatrick, a Knight Ridder/Tribune News Service writer, "There's no question at all that I didn't enjoy my professional life like I wished I would have.... I didn't allow myself to enjoy it because of my obsession for succeeding, my obsession for wanting to be the best."

Schmidt was often criticized in Philadelphia newspapers and by fans for being too sensitive or for not trying hard enough. He was just as likely to be booed by Phillies fans as he was to be cheered. He stopped inviting his family to home games because people in the crowd would yell at them. Schmidt endured the criticism quietly by focusing on his game throughout his career. He told Fitzpatrick about the moment when he finally felt reconciled with Phillies fans, "It was a night at the end of '86, when I passed **Lou Gehrig**, who had 494 homers, and was getting close to 500. I got a great ovation, and there was something about that night that got me over the hump."

It took fourteen years playing in Philadelphia for that reconciliation to arrive. During most of his career he felt uncomfortable with the attention he received from fans. He felt his privacy was invaded, and avoided going out in public as much as possible. If he did appear in public, he would try and disguise himself with hats and sunglasses. That discomfort and fear of the fans lingered even when Schmidt was accepting his 1995 induction to the Hall of Fame. With an estimated 25,000 to 28,000 people in attendance, most of them Phillies fans, Schmidt was worried. He told Jayson Stark in the Knight Ridder/Tribune News Service, "I was concerned about it. Probably more than anything, I worried about catcalls or some nasty thing called out during some quiet time." Luckily for Schmidt, the fans had nothing but love and appreciation for him and fellow Phillies inductee Richie Ashburn.

CONTACT INFORMATION

Address: Mike Schmidt, 373 Eagle Drive, Jupiter, FL 33477.

SELECTED WRITINGS BY SCHMIDT:

(With Barbara Walder) *Always On the Offense,* Atheneum, 1982.
(With Rob Ellis) *The Mike Schmidt Study: Hitting Theory, Skills, and Technique,* McGriff and Bell, 1994.

FURTHER INFORMATION

Periodicals

Brookover, Bob. "Mike Schmidt Back to Play Teacher." Knight Ridder/Tribune News Service (February 25, 2002).
Brookover, Bob. "Schmidt Returns to Reality After Brief Managerial Stint." Knight Ridder/Tribune News Service (March 7, 2002).
Fitzpatrick, Frank. "Mike Schmidt Wishes He Could Have Enjoyed His Hall of Fame Career More." Knight Ridder/Tribune News Service (January 8, 1995).
Glick, Shav. "Morning Briefing: So Far, He's Been Striking Out in Efforts to Get Another Life." *Los Angeles Times* (July 10, 1992): C2.
Hayes, Marcus. "Mike Schmidt Finds His Managerial Calling in Florida." Knight Ridder/Tribune News Service (March 4, 2002).
O'Loughlin, Joe. "Mike Schmidt Interview." *Baseball Digest* (March, 2001): 60.
"Phillies Won't Take Option on Schmidt." *Washington Post* (September 9, 1988): D6.
"Sports Flash." *Newsday* (November 7, 2002): A75.
Stark, Jayson. "Schmidt Calls Induction The Greatest Day of His Life." Knight Ridder/Tribune News Service (July 30, 1995).

Other

"Hall of Fame release from Monday, January 9, 1995." *CBS Sportsline.* http://cbs.sportsline.com/u/fans/celebrity/schmidt/career/hallofame.html (December 9, 2002).
"Mike Schmidt." BaseballLibrary.com. http://www.pubdim.net/baseballlibrary/ballplayers/S/Schmidt_Mike.stm (December 9, 2002).
"Mike Schmidt's Speech, Tribute Night, Saturday May 26, 1990." *CBS Sportsline.* http://cbs.sportsline.com/u/fans/celebrity/schmidt/career/awards.html (December 9, 2002).
"Ohio University." *CBS Sportsline.* http://cbs.sportsline.com/u/fans/celebrity/schmidt/career/university.html (December 9, 2002).
"Phillies Records." *CBS Sportsline.* http://cbs.sportsline.com/u/fans/celebrity/schmidt/career/ (December 9, 2002).

Sketch by Eve M. B. Hermann

Sandra Schmirler
1963-2000

Canadian curler

S andra Schmirler, known as "the Queen of Curling" and "Schmirler the Curler" in her native Canada, dominated Canadian women's curling in the 1990s until her death from cancer in 2000, at the age of 36. She and her team (known as a "rink" in curling parlance) won the Canadian and world champions three times during the 1990s; her team went on to take the first Olympic gold medal ever awarded for curling, at the 1998 Nagano games. Their victories were more poignant because Schmirler and her rink were average women, with husbands, children, and jobs, who curled in their spare time for fun and yet still became the best curlers in the world.

Building Skills and a Team

Schmirler played many sports as a child, including volleyball, swimming, badminton, and track, but curling was her favorite. Schmirler began curling at a young age, joining the Biggar Curling Club at the age of 12. Even before that, she and her friend Anita Silvernagle threw rocks on the flooded and frozen fields of the Silvernagle farm, and as teenagers, Silvernagle and Schmirler curled together on the rink that won the 1981 Saskatchewan high school curling championships.

Schmirler continued to curl when she moved to Saskatoon to study physical education at the University of Saskatchewan, and by 1984 a rink on which she

Sandra Schmirler

Chronology	
1963	Born July 11 in Biggar, Saskatchewan
1997	Daughter Sara born
1999	Father, Art Schmirler, dies of esophageal cancer in April
1999	Daughter Jenna born June 30
1999	Diagnosed with cancer August 26
2000	Dies March 2

1992, 1995, and 1998, and surpassed their record with a fourth win in 1999.)

First Olympic Gold

Those wins in 1997 made Schmirler's rink the Canadian favorite going into the 1998 Olympics, the first Olympics at which curling would be an official medal event. Schmirler's rink won the Canadian Olympic trials in November 1997, beating nine other teams for the chance to represent Canada in Nagano, Japan. Schmirler's infant daughter, Sara, and her second husband, Shannon England, remained at home in Regina, Saskatchewan while Schmirler flew to Japan to compete. Schmirler's rink defeated Denmark to win the Olympic gold, and it was her shot in the final, tenth end (or inning) that clinched the victory. She said that when she returned to Canada, she was going to hang her gold medal over Sara's crib. "She had to sacrifice as much as I did. She didn't know it, that's all," Schmirler explained to Donna Spencer of the Canadian Press.

Fight of Her Life

In June 1999, shortly after Schmirler's father Art died of esophageal cancer, Schmirler's daughter Jenna was born. Throughout the pregnancy Schmirler suffered from digestive problems and excruciating back pains, but her doctors told her that they were pregnancy related. When the problems did not go away after Jenna was born, her doctors did further tests and found a fist-sized, malignant tumor directly behind Schmirler's heart.

Schmirler did not have the strength to compete at curling while she was undergoing chemotherapy and radiation treatment, but she remained involved as much as she could. From her sickbed she worked with the rest of her rink to coordinate the details of her comeback, making sure that they had sponsors lined up and uniform jackets picked out. "She was the Skip," Gudereit later recalled to Adrian Wojnarowski of the Bergen County, New Jersey, *Record.* "She wanted everything right when she came back."

But Schmirler never came back. She passed away early in the morning of March 2, 2000.

Canada and Curling

Schmirler, who had guarded her privacy carefully when she first became ill, had reappeared in the public

played made it to the Scott Tournament of Hearts, which is the Canadian women's curling championships. She competed on Kathy Fahlman's rink as third in the 1990 Saskatchewan championships, but the rink did not fare well. Disappointed, Schmirler decided to form her own rink. Schmirler, the "skip" or captain, recruited her friend Jan Betker, who had also curled on Fahlman's rink, to be third. Marcia Gudereit became lead, and Joan McCusker second. These four women would remain together as a rink until Schmirler's death.

World Champions

Schmirler's rink won the Scott Tournament of Hearts in 1993, only a few years after forming. They represented Canada in the world curling championships that year, and won those, too. The team repeated their wins at the Scott Tournament of Hearts and the world championships in 1994, but by 1995 the pressure of being the favorites, as well as stresses in their personal lives, began to affect the rink and they started to slump. But they pulled together, found their focus again, and in 1997 they won the Canadian and world championships for an unprecedented third time, despite the fact that Schmirler was throwing stones while five months pregnant with her first child at the world championships. At that time no other rink composed of the same four women had ever won more than two world championships. (Schmirler's perpetual competitor, the Swedish rink captained by Elisabet Gustafson, tied their record of three titles with wins at the world championships in

---

Awards and Accomplishments

1993-94, 1997	Rink wins Canadian championships
1993-94, 1997	Rink wins world championships
1997	Rink places first in Canadian Olympic qualifiers
1998	Rink wins gold medal in Olympics
1998	Rink named Team of the Year by the Canadian Press
1999	Inducted into the Canadian Curling Hall of Fame

---

eye in the weeks just before her death. She had agreed to provide color commentary for the 2000 Canadian juniors' curling championships, as well as the Scott Tournament of Hearts and the Labatt Brier, the men's championships, although her failing health allowed her only to do the first, the juniors' championships. There, on February 11, she gave an emotional press conference to discuss her battle. "I now know that losing a curling game isn't the end of the world," she said, speaking also of the importance of spending time with her family.

As an article in the Bergen County, New Jersey, *Record* recalling the life of Schmirler put it, she was "survived by a husband, two daughters, Canada, and curling." Canada as a nation certainly felt itself bereaved. In death as in life, Schmirler was treated like a queen by her country: All across Canada flags flew at half-staff, a national television station broadcast her memorial service live, and the Canadian Broadcasting Corporation was planning a television movie based on her life. The curling world also held several tributes to Schmirler. The first day of the Scott Tournament of Hearts has been permanently declared Sandra Schmirler Day, and the remnants of Schmirler's gold-medal winning rink threw a ceremonial stone in her honor to the sound of Scottish bagpipes on the Olympic ice in Utah in 2002. The Canadian Curling Association and Schmirler's friends and family also came together to create a permanent tribute, the Sandra Schmirler Foundation, which raises money to help the families of children with serious illnesses.

FURTHER INFORMATION

Books

Lefko, Perry. *Sandra Schmirler: The Queen of Curling.* Toronto: Stoddart Publishing, 2000.

Scholz, Guy. *Gold on Ice: The Story of the Sandra Schmirler Curling Team.* Regina: Coteau Books, 1999.

Periodicals

Araton, Harvey. "A Curler's Homey Legend Can Still Inspire." *New York Times* (February 12, 2002): D1.

Wallace, Bruce. "In Too Few Years a Life to Remember: Sandra Schmirler Earned Fame on the Ice, but Never

Lost Sight of the Important Things in Life." *Maclean's* (March 13, 2000): 56.

Wojnarowski, Adrian. "Curling Star's Legacy Lives On: Canadians Honor Schmirler." *Record* (Bergen County, NJ; February 12, 2002): S1.

Other

"The Life & Times of Sandra Schmirler." Canadian Broadcasting Corporation. http://www.tv.cbc.ca/life andtimes/bio2001/schmirler.htm (January 8, 2003).

"Sandra Schmirler: Celebrating Women's Achievements." National Library of Canada. http://www. nlc-bnc.ca/2/12/h12-237-e.html (January 8, 2003).

Sandra Schmirler Foundation. http://www.sandra schmirler.org (January 8, 2003).

"Schmirler Talks with Media about Fight for Her Life." Canadian Association for the Advancement of Women and Sport and Physical Activity. http://www. caaws.ca/Whats_New/feb00/schmirl_feb11.htm (January 8, 2003).

Spencer, Donna. "Canadians Felt a Part of Schmirler's Success." Canadian Association for the Advancement of Women and Sport and Physical Activity. http:// www.caaws.ca/Whats_New/mar00/schmirl_mar2. htm (February 11, 2003).

Sketch by Julia Bauder

Marge Schott
1928-

American baseball executive

Throughout the decade and a half that she was owner of Major League Baseball's (MLB) Cincinnati Reds, Marge Schott managed to offend just about everyone—including players, fans, and her fellow owners—with the use of racial slurs and other insensitive remarks. Twice suspended by the MLB for such comments, Schott remained feisty and combative until the end, which came in the early fall of 1999 when Schott sold her controlling interest in the Reds to a group headed by Carl H. Lindner. A day after handing over control of the Reds to Lindner, Schott told Michael Perry of the *Cincinnati Enquirer*: "I think I tried my best, I really do. When I came in, there wasn't much attendance … I was able to survive 15 years and turn the Reds around financially and … also we had some wins. I don't think a lot of owners have even won the World Series [her Reds did in 1990]—although I got reprimanded for sweeping. But I couldn't help that. I'm not too ashamed of what we've accomplished."

Marge Schott

Born in Cincinnati

She was born Margaret Unnewehr in Cincinnati, Ohio, on August 18, 1928. The second of five daughters born to Edward and Charlotte Unnewehr, she grew up as a fan of the Reds, Cincinnati's hometown baseball team. Her love of sports strengthened her ties to her father, who called his second daughter "Butch." Of her father, Schott told *Sports Illustrated*: "My poor father, he kept trying to have a son, and he kept getting girls." Unnewehr eventually brought Marge into the lumber business, but she stayed in the family business only briefly. Between 1950 and 1952, she attended the University of Cincinnati but dropped out after meeting and marrying Cincinnatian Charles J. Schott, heir to an industrial fortune. The couple moved to a 70-acre enclave in Cincinnati's posh Indian Hills neighborhood, where the childless Marge played mother to the family menagerie of animals and gracious hostess at scores of memorable society affairs.

Schott experienced a major personal loss in 1968 when her 42-year-old husband suffered a massive heart attack and died. With little business experience beyond the brief stint with her family's lumber business, Schott suddenly found herself the owner of Schottco Corporation, a holding company for a wide variety of businesses, including a brick manufacturing company, an insurer, a shopping center, a concrete products factory, and an automobile dealership. The dealership, one of the largest in Ohio, had never made much money, so

Chronology

1928	Born August 18 in Cincinnati, Ohio
1950-52	Attends University of Cincinnati
1952	Marries Cincinnati businessman Charles J. Schott
1968	Becomes president of Schottco Corp. after the death of her husband
1981	Becomes a limited partner in the Cincinnati Reds
1984	Becomes a general partner in the Reds
1985	Becomes president and CEO of the Reds on July 8
1993	Banned from day-to-day operations of the Reds for a year
1996	Ordered to surrender control of team through the end of 1998 season
1999	Sells controlling interest in the Reds to group headed by Carl Lindner

Schott decided to focus her energies on trying to turn Schott Buick around financially. She got little help. General Motors executives were reluctant to turn the franchise over to a woman. When she discovered that some of the dealership's managers were plotting to force her out of the business, she moved decisively, firing the managers and moving up lower ranking employees to fill their slots. Using eye-catching promotions and waving the "Buy-American" banner, Schott managed to turn things around for the dealership. In less than three years, sales at Schott Buick had jumped forty percent, convincing GM that Schott deserved to retain the franchise. By 1980, she had opened a second GM dealership, Marge's Chevrolet.

A lifelong Reds fan, Schott in 1981 became a limited partner in the baseball team. She told the *Cincinnati Enquirer* she bought her small share in the Reds "as a token of respect to my late husband." The team in the early 1980s had fallen on hard times: attendance was way down and most of the best players had been either sold or traded by the conservative Reds management. With only a small share in the team, Schott felt powerless to end the team's steady decline. She later told the *Cincinnati Enquirer*: "It was very frustrating sitting back and watching some of the stuff. It just kept getting so bad, it got to the point where finally you have to speak up." Her chance to do something came in 1984 when the Reds' general partners—William and James Williams—decided to sell the team after four consecutive years of losses. Schott was able to buy the team for $13 million "as a Christmas present to the city," she told *People*.

A little more than six months after she became a general partner in the Reds, Schott was named president and chief executive officer of the Reds organization. She seemed to revel in the celebrity of being the owner of a major league ball club. Some of her favorite moments came when she paraded around the field before game time with "Schottzie," her pet St. Bernard, greeting her own players and those of the opposing team. And she did manage to turn the Reds around, basking in the glow of some of the team's more notable successes. These included **Pete Rose**'s record-breaking 4,192nd hit on September 11, 1985; pitcher Tom Browning's perfect game on September 16, 1988; and the team's fifth world championship in 1990. In the process, she went through a total of five general managers and seven managers. One of the latter—Davey Johnson—was fired because he lived with his fiancée before marriage, while another—Ray Knight—was hired partly because Schott liked his wife, pro golfer **Nancy Lopez**.

A notorious penny-pincher, Schott closely monitored spending by the Reds organization, down to keeping track of the number of pens and pencils in the front office. She slashed spending for the Reds minor league farm system and said she hated spending for talent scouts because "all they do is watch games." Sadly, Schott's insensitive remarks largely overshadowed her positive contributions to the Reds. On February 3, 1993, Schott was fined $25,000 and banned from the day-to-day operations of the Reds for a year for usiing racial epithets.

Interviewed by ESPN in May 1996, Schott said she believed that Hitler "was good in the beginning but went too far," setting off a new round of controversy and again bringing down the wrath of Major League Baseball upon her head. On June 12, 1996, MLB Commissioner **Bud Selig** ordered that Schott relinquish control of the team through the end of the 1998 season. The suspension is later extended to include the 1999 season, during which time Schott negotiated the sale of the team to a investor group led by fellow Cincinnatian Carl H. Lindner, chairman and CEO of American Financial Group Inc. In October 1999, Schott received $67 million for her shares in the team.

A lifelong resident of Cincinnati, Schott lives there still. Although she retains some token holdings in the Cincinnati Reds, she has not been involved in the team's management since she was forced to sell her majority interest in 1999. But she will forever remain one of the biggest fans of her hometown baseball team, and she still has seats at the Reds' Cinergy Field, where she cheers on the Reds whenever she can. Since stepping down as the Reds' majority owner, Schott has been plagued by illness and injury. In 1999, she was hospitalized at Cincinnati's Jewish Hospital with a bout of seasonal allergy, and she was hospitalized several times during 2001 and 2002 with breathing problems. Schott remains active in civic affairs and has made a couple of sizeable contributions to Cincinnati's St. Ursula Academy. An animal lover, Schott again made news in early 2002 when she offered to make a home for a runaway cow at her 70-acre Indian Hill estate.

There can be no argument that Marge Schott and her business skills helped the Cincinnati Reds recover from one of their biggest slumps—in terms of both finances and morale—ever. In a statement released after the sale of the Reds was finalized, new owner Lindner said of Schott: "I've known her for a long time, including her many years as an owner of the Reds. She has always kept the fans first in her mind. For that, all of Cincinnati should thank her and join me in wishing her the very best." Unfortunately, much of the good Schott accomplished may eventually be forgotten in the shadow of some of the insensitive remarks attributed to her over the years.

CONTACT INFORMATION

Address: Marge Schott, c/o Schottco Corp., 30 E. Central Pkwy., Suite 300, Cincinnati, OH 45202-1118. Phone: (513) 721-8400.

FURTHER INFORMATION

Books

"Marge Schott." *Almanac of Famous People,* 6th ed. Detroit: Gale Group, 1998.
"Marge Schott." *Contemporary Newsmakers 1985,* Issue Cumulation. Detroit: Gale Group, 1986.

Periodicals

Bass, Mike. "Schott Down." *Sporting News* (June 16, 1996): 8.
Graham, Janet. "It's Official: Marge Selling Reds." *Cincinnati Post* (October 24, 1998).
"Marge Schott, Carl Lindner." *U.S. News and World Report* (September 27, 1999): 14.
"Marge Strikes Out: Baseball." *Economist* (December 12,1999): A35.
Perry, Michael. "Schott: A 'Heartbreaking' End." *Cincinnati Enquirer* (October 2, 1999).
Radel, Cliff. "RADEL: Marge Schott." *Cincinnati Enquirer* (February 26, 2002).

Other

"Carl H. Lindner." *Biography Resource Center.* Detroit: Gale Group, 2001.
"Marge Schott, Born: 1928." BaseballLibrary.com. http://www.pubdim.net/baseballlibrary/ballplayers/S/ Schott_Marge.stm (November 24, 2002).

Sketch by Don Amerman

Tex Schramm

Tex Schramm
1920-

American football executive

It isn't easy to measure Tex Schramm's impact on professional football, for his mark is on so much of the game as we know it today. Schramm is perhaps best known for building a little-known expansion team in Dallas into one of football's most venerable franchises, so widely popular across the nation that it came to be known as "America's team." For nearly three decades he was the general manager of the Dallas Cowboys and in 1991 became the only football executive who never owned or coached a team to be elected to the Professional Football Hall of Fame. With **Pete Rozelle**, commissioner of the National Football League (NFL), and Lamar Hunt, founder of the American Football League (AFL), Schramm engineered the merger of the two rival leagues. He's also credited with building the NFL's first bona fide scouting system and is known as well as the father of the instant replay.

Born in Southern California

He was born Texas Edward Schramm in San Gabriel, California, just outside Los Angeles, on June 2, 1920. After graduating from Alhambra High School,

Schramm, who had family ties in Texas, enrolled at the University of Texas to study journalism. As a freshman, he had a brief fling at collegiate football, playing fullback, but at only 147 pounds, he quickly decided that he'd be better off writing about football and not playing it. During his years in Austin, he covered sports for the student newspaper and also worked part-time for the *Austin American-Statesman*. After earning his bachelor's degree, Schramm served four years in the U.S. Air Force.

Returning to civilian life, Schramm was introduced to Los Angeles Rams owner **Dan Reeves**, who hired him to handle publicity for the team, which had only recently moved to Los Angeles from Cleveland. Five years later, in 1952, Reeves was promoted to assistant to the president of the Rams. Schramm became the team's general manager in 1956 but left the following year in the midst of a power struggle between Reeve and his fellow owners. Before leaving the Rams, however, Schramm recommended Pete Rozelle as his replacement.

From the Rams Schramm went to CBS-TV as assistant director of sports. Although he had no particular expertise on winter sports or the Olympic Games, Schramm had an idea. And, as he would soon begin to prove during his twenty-nine years at the helm of the Dallas Cowboys, a Schramm idea was not something to be taken lightly. Fortunately for television viewers, CBS executives liked Schramm's suggestion that the network televise competition at the 1960 Winter Olympic Games in Squaw Valley, California. And the rest is history.

Scouts Locations at Squaw Valley

After getting the green light from his bosses at CBS, Schramm scouted locations at Squaw Valley during the summer of 1959, several months before the scheduled games. Logistics for the operation were far more difficult in those days when every piece of camera equipment had to be attached by cable. For Schramm, the first order of business was the burial of miles of cable leading from the network's on-site headquarters to each of the Olympic venues. And the headquarters for CBS was hardly the plush affair to which we've become accustomed in recent years. Instead, the network's delegation was housed in the basement of a building erected for IBM, which would keep track of statistics for the competition.

Although this first coverage of the Winter Olympics was primitive by today's standards, Schramm ensured a touch of class by insisting that the format for coverage feature a central anchor desk moderating coverage from reporters at the various venues. No less a personage than Walter Cronkite occupied the anchor's chair, with such distinguished reporters as Jim McKay, **Dick Button**, Chris Schenkel, Bob Beattie, and Bud Palmer.

The Squaw Valley experience also produced a dividend that would resurface some years later and become transformed into a football tradition. At one point during the games, Olympics officials appealed to CBS for a replay of some of its tape to help verify the outcome of a contested event. Schramm filed away the idea, which returned to him years later in the form of instant replay.

Looks to Return to Football

Even before the Winter Olympics aired, Schramm had begun to look for a way to get back into pro football. When he learned in late 1959 that the NFL might soon award an expansion franchise to Dallas, he let it be known among his network of friends in football that he'd be interested in running the new team. **George Halas** of the Chicago Bears introduced Schramm to Clint Murchison Jr., a wealthy Texas oilman who'd tried for years to bring an NFL team to Dallas. The two hit it off immediately, and Murchison hired Schramm as general manager for a team that did not yet exist. For Schramm it was a dream job. "I'd always wanted, as far back as I can remember, to take a team from scratch and build it. So this was an opportunity I couldn't pass up even though we didn't know for sure that Dallas would get a team." On January 28, 1960, the dream became a reality when the NFL formally awarded the franchise to Dallas. In anticipation of winning the franchise, Schramm had already hired two key people for the team—**Tom Landry** as coach and Gil Brandt as personnel director.

Schramm firmly believed that the key to building a strong team was through the annual college draft and the signing of free agents. However, under the terms of the franchise agreement, Dallas was forced to acquire thirty-six veterans, three from each of the twelve teams in the expansion draft. With eleven losses and one tie, the Cowboys' debut season was an unmitigated disaster. Schramm stuck to his guns, building the team with young players wherever possible. A number of losing seasons followed. Impatient fans called for Landry's

---

Awards and Accomplishments

1960	Hired Tom Landry as coach and Gil Brandt as personnel director for new NFL team in Dallas
1966	Engineered merger of AFL into NFL with AFL founder Lamar Hunt
1970	Negotiated four-year contract with NFL Players Association
1977	Named NFL Executive of the Year by *Sporting News*
1978	Bert Bell Award for outstanding executive leadership in the NFL
1987	Father of the Year by Dallas Father of the Year Committee and the New York-based Father's Day Council Inc.
1991	Inducted into Pro Football Hall of Fame

---

head, but Schramm was not to be moved, signing the coach to an unprecedented ten-year contract extension in 1964. It was slow work, but by 1966 the Cowboys had finally managed to finish the season over the .500 mark. The Cowboys won their first NFL Western Conference titles in 1966 and 1967 but lost to Green Bay in the NFL championship game both years. This marked the beginning of the team's ascendancy to a football powerhouse. For the next twenty seasons, Dallas won more games than they lost, making it to the playoffs eighteen times. Over the next two decades, the Cowboys won thirteen divisional championships, five NFC titles, and Super Bowls VI and XII. The team also played in Super Bowls V, IX, and XIII but lost to their AFC opponents.

"Once our popularity got started, we wanted to keep it going," Schramm later observed. "I think we were probably more image-conscious than most other teams. We tried to do everything first class, from top to bottom." Although Schramm didn't invent the "America's team" label for the Cowboys, he was quick to exploit it in his promotion of the team. At one point, he sent out 100,000 souvenir calendars bearing the "America's team" moniker. Despite all that he did to build Dallas into one of football's most outstanding franchises, Schramm was not universally liked. Some were put off by his outspoken nature. But even those who found Schramm somewhat abrasive were forced to acknowledge his impressive accomplishments while at the helm of the Cowboys. In 1977, he was named NFL Executive of the Year by *Sporting News*; the following year he received the **Bert Bell** Award for outstanding executive leadership in the NFL.

Murchison, who had owned the team since its inception in 1960, sold the Cowboys to Bum Bright in 1984. In the latter half of the 1980s, the fortunes of the Cowboys took a marked turn for the worse. Their twenty-year winning streak ended in 1986, and two years later the team finished the season with a dismal 3-13 record. In 1988 Bright sold the team to Arkansas oil man Jerry Jones, who made it clear from the outset that he would personally manage every aspect of the Cowboys operation. The time had finally come for Schramm to move on, which he did in early 1989, leaving to become president and CEO of the new World League of American Football. Less than two years later, he stepped down from that post when he clashed with NFL officials over the future of the new league. Although he's now retired, Schramm remains active and as outspoken as ever. He's also developed a reputation as an accomplished sports fisherman, noted in particular for his competitive tag and release search for deep-sea marlin.

Schramm's role in building the Dallas Cowboys into one of professional football's most legendary teams is undeniable. And whether they love him or hate him, almost everybody in football is forced to acknowledge his contributions to the game as a whole. For his part, Schramm always hoped that he could make of the Cowboys a gridiron version of the New York Yankees in their heyday. "They were tops, first class. That's the way we want to be," Schramm once said. "Football is such a great and emotional business, and I want to look and say I was a part of greatness." Most observers would conclude that Schramm succeeded beyond his wildest dreams.

FURTHER INFORMATION

Books

St. John, Bob. *Tex: The Man Who Built the Dallas Cowboys.* New York: Prentice Hall Trade, 1988.

"Tex(as Edward) Schramm." *Almanac of Famous People,* 6th ed. Detroit: Gale Group, 1998.

Periodicals

Horn, Barry. "Schramm Was Ready to Give Game the Old College Try." *Dallas Morning News* (November 24, 1998): 4B.

Luksa, Frank. "Schramm Left His Mark with First Televised Games." *Dallas Morning News* (February 13, 1998): 18B.

Moore, David. "Unable to Lead, Schramm Left Behind." *Dallas Morning News* (February 25, 1999): 12B.

Other

"Cowboy Management." Tim's Cowboy History Page. http://users.conwaycorp.net/tstone/management.htm (October 18, 2002).

"Outstand Alumnus 1999-2000: Tex Schramm." College of Communication. http://communication.utexas.edu/alumni/outstanding.html (October 19, 2002).

"Tex Schramm." Professional Football Researchers Association. http://www.footballresearch.com/articles/frpage.cfm?topic=schramm (October 18, 2002).

"Tex Schramm: Biography." Pro Football Hall of Fame. http://www.profootballhof.com/players/enshrinees/tschramm.cfm (October 18, 2002).

Sketch by Don Amerman

Michael Schumacher

Michael Schumacher
1969-

German race car driver

Michael Schumacher reigns in the elite, highly competitive, and glamorous world of Formula One (F1) auto racing. He has broken the world records for most wins and most championship points in F1, and tied the record for most wins in 2002 with his fifth championship title. Arguably the greatest F1 driver in history, Schumacher is also one of the highest-paid athletes in the world.

Schumacher was born January 3, 1969 in Hurth, Germany. His father Rolf managed a go-kart track there and "Schumey," as he is known, got his start driving go-karts at age four. Unlike many elite drivers, Schumacher did not come from a wealthy family to back his career. Instead, he capitalized on what he had—access to a track. The Schumacher's lived meagerly, and winter was the worst time for them—there was not a huge call for go-karts in the winter. When Schumacher hit his first major payday at age twenty-one, he gave his father a suitcase of money. Despite his humble beginnings, Schumacher lives with his wife, Corinna, and their two children in Vufflens-le-Chateau, Switzerland. He earns roughly $80 million per year and travels to races in his private jet. Schumacher's younger brother, Ralf, is also an elite F1 driver for the Williams-BMW team.

Like many European racing drivers, Schumacher got his start on the go-kart circuits there. He was German junior go-kart champion in 1984 and European Kart champion in 1987. After graduating to the Formula Three (F3) league, he was German F3 champion in 1990. He got his first chance to race F1 that year as an alternate for the Jordan team. Jailed for punching a London cabbie, Jordan driver Bertrand Gachot was unable to make it to the track, and Schumacher filled in. Schumacher made his debut in the Belgium Grand Prix, qualifying in seventh position. After just one race and a legal battle, the Benetton team wrested Schumacher away from Jordan.

Schumacher won his first race back in Belgium, and finished third overall in his first year in F1, an amazing start for a rookie. He won the 1994 world championship by a single point after a controversial collision with Damon Hill in the final race. He took the title more legitimately in 1995. In 1996, he joined the Italian Ferrari team, which had not won a world championship in two decades.

Despite a season plagued by technical and dependability problems from the car, Schumacher managed to place third in the world championship in 1996. After battling for the 1997 championship with Canadian driver Jacques Villeneuve, Schumacher was disqualified from second place for trying to run Villeneuve off the track. Schumacher returned the next year to finish second behind Finland's Mika Hakkinen and the highly competitive McLaren-Mercedes team.

A crash in 1999 at the British Grand Prix at Silverstone, England almost took Schumacher out of racing. "You see the wall coming. You know the speed you do," he recalled online at CBSNews.com, "and you think, 'Oh, that's gonna hurt.'" And it did. A broken leg side-lined him for most of the season, and he considered retiring. Despite the crash, Schumacher finished the season in fifth place.

F1 is the most technically-advanced league in auto racing, with cars that are designed like jet planes and run in excess of 200 mph. Schumacher is the number-one driver and teammate Brazilian driver Rubens Barrichello is number two on the most elite team in auto racing. Estimates of what Ferrari spends each year to race its two cars range between $170 and $285 million. In comparison, other teams on leagues such as NASCAR and Indy rarely spend more than $15 million per year, per car. Ferrari employs 550 people to work exclusively on the two cars.

Schumacher is known for his remarkably smooth driving style, his control on the track, and most notably his mastery of curves. "I have this natural ability of knowing how fast I can go into this corner, without going out too often," he said online at CBSNews.com. "It's an instinct." His biggest fear is driving under wet conditions, and he has twice crashed on a wet track, but he is known for excelling in the rain. He also is impeccably fit. He works out four hours per day before going to the test track to drive.

Schumacher made a strong debut in 2000, winning the first three races of the season. After a mid-season slump, he came back with an emotional win in Italy, Ferrari's home country, and seized his third world championship title. He was the first Ferrari driver in twenty-one years to claim the championship. He won the championship again in 2001, but with a more dominant season. He won nine out of the season's sixteen races, and broke a slough of records in the process. He broke the fifty-one career-win record held by **Alain Prost**, and tied late driver Graham Hill's record of five career wins at Monte Carlo.

After achieving almost every significant record in auto racing, Schumacher finished in first place for the world championship in 2002. He holds the records for fastest laps (51) and career points earned (945). He finished in the top three in every race of the 2002 season, another record. His fifth world-championship title tied him with five-time winner **Juan Manuel Fangio.** "I always say that statistics aren't my first priority," Schumacher is quoted as saying in *Auto Racing Digest.* "But it does mean something to me to have this number on my account. Actually, I'm delighted about this, but I will enjoy it much more when I'm retired and sitting on the sofa, having a cigar and a beer, and think about it."

FURTHER INFORMATION

Books

Henry, Alan. *Grand Prix Champions: From Jackie Stewart to Michael Schumacher.* Motorbooks International, 1996.

Periodicals

Knutson, Dan. "F1: The best there ever was." *Auto Racing Digest* (February-March 2002): 36.

Schwarz, Steve. "Formula One: The 2002 Formula One season—a year of crisis." *Sports Network* (November 14, 2002).

Other

"Driver bio: Michael Schumacher." Unofficial Formula One Home Page. http://www.formula1.com/drivers/bio.html (January 15, 2003).

"F1 Driver factfiles: Michael Schumacher." CNNSI.com. http://www.cnnsi.com (January 15, 2003).

"Grand Prix drivers: Michael Schumacher." GrandPrix.com. http://www.grandprix.com/gpe/drv/schmic.html (January 15, 2003).

"Michael Schumacher: On the fast track." CBSNews.com. http://www.cbsnews.com/stories/2002/05/07/60II/printable508224.shtml (January 15, 2003).

"Schumacher wins in Monaco." CNNSI.com. http://www.cnnsi.com (January 15, 2003).

Sketch by Brenna Sanchez

Wendell Scott
1921-1990

American race car driver

Wendell Scott had a lot working against him in his career as a Grand National NASCAR (National Association for Stock Car Auto Racing) driver. He was an independent driver racing against factory-backed drivers. This meant he never drove a new car, often buying last

Wendell Scott

year's cars from competitors. He drove without sponsorship, sometimes making the trip to a race hoping to win back the expense of traveling to that particular race. His biggest obstacle though was being a black man in a white man's sport. He was blocked from some races, denied the promised compensation at others, and was sometimes run off the track because of his skin color. Scott never let this stop him, and despite the odds stacked against him he was an excellent driver who often made a showing. He won 128 races in the lower Sportsmen division. In Grand National races, he finished in the top five twenty times and won once. Shav Glick reported in the *Los Angeles Times* the following quote from Scott, "Once I found out what it was like, racing was all I wanted to do as long as I could make a decent living out of it.... I'm no different from most other people who're doing what they like to do."

Learning How to Drive a Car

Wendell Oliver Scott was born on August 29, 1921, in Danville, Virginia. Early on he was interested in cars and owned and drove his own taxi. Around 1940 he met his future wife Mary. He went into the Army around 1942 and served in the 101st Airborne division until 1945. In 1943 he and Mary were wed. They began raising their family in Danville, eventually having six children.

The Army had trained Scott as a mechanic. His skill with cars, along with a natural mechanical ability led him to become involved in the trafficking of illegal alcohol. Scott explained to Larry Edsall of *AutoWeek,*

Chronology

1921	Born August 29 in Danville, Virginia
1942-45	Serves in World War II in Army's 101st Airborne
1943	Marries
1947	Races for first time, Danville Fairgrounds; begins racing in the Dixie Circuit
1950	Opens car repair shop; makes first attempt to race in the NASCAR circuit
1954	Begins racing in the NASCAR Modified Division
1961	Debuts in NASCAR's Grand National at Spartenburg Fairgrounds in South Carolina
1973	Suffers major injuries in a pileup at Talladega Superspeedway in Alabama; retires from racing
1977	*Greased Lightning,* a film based on his life starring Richard Pryor released
1990	Dies December 23 from complications due to spinal cancer

Awards and Accomplishments

1947	Placed 3rd and won $50 in first ever race at Danville Fairgrounds
1959	Won Virginia State Championship as well as twenty-two other races in the Dixie Circuit
1961	Finished in the top ten 5 times, earning $3,240
1962	Finished in the top ten 11 times, earning $7,000
1963	Only Grand National win, Jacksonville Speedway Park, Jacksonville, Florida, on December 1
1964	Only pole position start at Grand National race in Savannah, Georgia, on July 20
1964	Set Grand National record for 40th place starter at World 600 in Charlotte, North Carolina, when he finished 9th
1965	Ranked 11th in the nation, earning $20,000
1977	Inducted into Black Athletes Hall of Fame
1994	Inducted into Jacksonville, Florida Hall of Fame
1996	Inducted into Danville Register & Bee Hall of Fame
1997	Inducted into National Sports Hall of Fame
1999	Inducted into International Motorsports Hall of Fame
2000	Inducted into Virginia Sports Hall of Fame and National Motorsports Press Association Hall of Fame
2002	Inducted into Danville Museum of Fine Arts and History Hall of Fame

"When I was young, I … started hauling whisky.… We would buy it for 55 cents a pint at Danville and sold it for $1.10 at Charlotte. But I learned how to drive a car." Transporting whiskey required Scott to drive fast and keep his car in good running shape. He was somewhat notorious in the region for being able to escape capture. The police knew who he was though, and that eventually helped him get his start in stock car racing.

Around 1947, a race promoter was trying to figure out how to get more African Americans to the racetracks. His attempts to find black racecar drivers were unsuccessful so he went to the police. Glick wrote Scott's description of the events, "He went to the county police and they told him about this 'darkie' they'd been chasing through the mountains, driving awful fast. That was me." The promoter contacted Scott and invited him to race at the Danville Fairgrounds. Scott borrowed one of his old liquor cars that he'd sold because it was beginning to be recognized by the police. In his first race, Scott placed third and won $50. He was hooked.

Facing Down Racism

Scott dedicated himself to racing. In 1950 he made his first attempt to enter a NASCAR sponsored race. Because he had light skin, officials didn't recognize that he was black. But when he went to purchase the safety belt they had asked him to buy so he could drive, his race was recognized and he was told he couldn't participate. No reason was given.

During the next few years, Scott raced in what was known as the "Dixie Circuit." These were smaller tracks—less than a mile long—than those used for NASCAR races and were held throughout the South. In 1954, he was accepted into the NASCAR Modified Division. In those years he honed his driving skills and began winning races. He ended up winning around 127 races in these lower divisions. In 1959, he won a total of twenty-two races, including the Virginia State Championship. Scott felt ready to take on the Grand Nationals.

In 1961, Scott debuted in the Grand National, now known as the Winston Cup, at the Spartenburg Fairgrounds in South Carolina. In the beginning of his Grand National career he faced racism from officials, drivers, and crowds. Drivers in races would try to force him off the track. Inspectors would demand erroneous repairs, like fixing chipped paint, before letting him race. He was once disqualified from a race because his crew was racially mixed. Sometimes he was only allowed to have his wife in the pit to help him during a race. Crowds would often jeer at him.

Scott persisted. He finished in the top ten five times in 1961, earning $3,240. He never felt like he was there to make a statement. His only desire was to race cars. He eventually won over the trust of many other drivers who were in the same situation he was, an independent driver with limited finances working hard to stay in a sport he loved. He and his wife were always willing to help as best they could any drivers who were in distress.

Scott placed consistently throughout the '60s. In 1962, he had eleven top ten finishes and earned $7,000. By 1965 he was rated eleventh in the nation and that year won $20,000 in prize money. In 1964 he set a Grand National record for a 40th place starter. At the World 600 in Charlotte, North Carolina, Scott was able to go from his 40th place start and finish ninth. No other driver had ever done that. That same year, on July 20, Scott earned his only pole position start at the Grand National track in Savannah, Georgia.

One and Only Grand National Win

His greatest accomplishment came in 1963. Scott won his first and only Grand National race. Unfortunately, his victory was marred by tampering with the

Greased Lightning

Released in 1977, *Greased Lightning* chronicled Wendell Scott's racing career from his days transporting moonshine to his astonishing success in NASCAR's Grand National races. The film starred Richard Pryor as Scott, Pam Grier as his wife, and Beau Bridges as Hutch, a former competitor who becomes Scott's close friend.

Scott served as a technical consultant on the film and was not impressed with the stunt car drivers. The film suffered from the same fate that often afflicted Scott in his career as a racecar driver—insufficient funds. Pryor is reported to have felt the proudest of this role than any other because of how Scott was able to further the cause of civil rights in the arena of sports.

scoring that was most likely the result of racist intentions. The race wasn't an easy one for Scott to make. He was in debt and needed the money he could earn from this competition. He drove from Virginia to Jacksonville, Florida, to compete at the Jacksonville Speedway Park. Exhausted from the trip, Scott couldn't make the repairs he wanted on his car. Instead he removed the shock absorbers from each corner of the car. He told Edsall, "The track was so rough … but that way (single shocked) was just perfect. I lapped the field."

Scott started in fifteenth position and easily lapped all the other racers. He was coming up on his 200th lap, the final lap, and expected to see the checkered flag waving for his first place finish. The flag remained unmoved. Scott continued on for two more laps expecting the checkered flag to signal the end of the race and his victory. Instead, the flag waved for Buck Baker, who was two laps behind Scott. The judges awarded Scott third place.

The fanfare, including the trophy and a kiss from the beauty queen, all went to Buck Baker but Scott knew he had won and he argued his case with the judges. After the crowds had gone and the supposed clerical error corrected, Scott was awarded his prize money. Unfortunately, he did not receive the original trophy. Stories differ on what happened to the trophy. One story relates that it went home with Baker, another that the trophy was stolen. Whatever the case, Scott ended up with a wooden statue that does not contain any information about his placing, the date, or the race. He did however get the money. He told Edsall, "I needed $900-some dollars to pay my bills.… I got $1000 for winning … and $150 for racing on Goodyear tires. But I really didn't have Goodyears. I had recaps."

Scott continued racing for ten more years, ever hopeful that he would get a break. In 1966 he told *Ebony*, "I don't have too many wins in the Grand National … but I have a bunch of places and shows. With a little better equipment I know I can come out on top." Scott was always driving older model cars, often bought from other racecar drivers. It was never the car itself that helped Scott place, it was his skill as a driver and a mechanic.

Career-Ending Crash

Even skilled drivers can be involved in accidents, and Scott had his fair share. Sometimes he was able to fix the car and get back out on the track to finish the race. Sometimes even the best attempts failed. Scott was never injured seriously in a wreck until 1973 when he was involved in a multiple-car pileup at the Talladega Speedway in Alabama. The resulting injuries nearly killed him. He survived the crash despite fracturing his ribs, pelvis, both knees, and one of his legs. He also needed sixty stitches to close up a wound on his arm. The wreck forced Scott to retire.

After retiring, Scott worked full-time in the auto repair shop he'd opened around 1950. The money he made from racing and the repair shop helped him send all six of his children to college. In the late '70s, he served as a consultant for the film *Greased Lightning*, which was based on his life and starred comedian Richard Pryor. Unfortunately, Scott was diagnosed with spinal cancer in mid-1990, and succumbed to its effects on December 23, 1990, after six months in the hospital. In recognition of his importance to the racing community as well as the regard in which they held him a group of racers held a show featuring racing memorabilia and an auction to raise money to help pay for the costs of his hospitalization.

The only hall of fame induction that Scott received while he was alive was into the Black Athletes Hall of Fame. Since his death, his commitment to racing and the adversity that he faced so winningly have earned him spots in national and international halls of fame. Although Scott didn't break NASCAR wide open for other African-Americans to enter, he did set an example of integrity and determination.

FURTHER INFORMATION

Books

Ashe, Jr., Arthur R. *A Hard Road to Glory: A History of the African-American Athlete Since 1946*. New York: Warner Books, 1988.

Periodicals

"Dixie's Daredevil on Wheels." *Ebony* (May 1960): 61.

Edsall, Larry. "The Speedways Remembered." *AutoWeek* (February, 8, 1988).

Glick, Shav. "Motor Racing; Scott Was Pioneer, But Nobody Followed." *Los Angeles Times* (December 27, 1990): C7.

"Stock Car Racer Reaches Bigtime." *Ebony* (May 1966): 61.

Other

"Lester Looks to Future While Respecting Past." NASCAR.com. http://www.nascar.com/2002/news/

headlines/ct/07/18/loudon_pre/index.html (January 16, 2003).

"Pole Position, One Win Under Our Belts, A Tribute to the Legendary Wendell Scott." Black Athletes Sports Network. http://www.blackathlete.net/Motorsports/motorsports072902.html (January 16, 2003).

"Scott's Historical Win Highlights Florida Racing." NASCAR.com. http://www.nascar.com/2001/NEWS/11/07/duskey_110701/index.html (January 16, 2003).

Sketch by Eve M. B. Hermann

Briana Scurry

Briana Scurry
1971-

American soccer player

As the only African-American starter on the U.S. women's national soccer team in the 1990s, Briana Scurry revolutionized the way young black children looked at soccer. Her tenacious goalkeeping and unflappable demeanor provided a rock-solid base for the women's triumphs in the 1996 Olympics and the 1999 World Cup, victories which catapulted soccer to new popularity in the United States. Scurry later was one of the founders and most popular members of the new women's soccer league, the WUSA.

Against the Odds

Ernest and Robbie Scurry had already started their large family when Hurricane Donna destroyed their home in Galveston, Texas, in 1960. They moved to Minneapolis, Minnesota, but an underground lake started undermining their home shortly after Briana, the youngest of their nine children, was born. The family then moved to Dayton, Minnesota, a nearly all-white Minneapolis suburb where they were some of the first African-Americans. But instead of prejudice, Briana found only encouragement.

"I never got singled out," Scurry later told *Sports Illustrated*. "My parents never let me think I was alone in anything. They taught me that I could do whatever I wanted to do, and the odds against that didn't matter." Her first love was football; when she was 11, she scored nine touchdowns in a boys' league. Scurry also competed in softball, basketball, and track. She first played on a soccer team when she was 12, and that was a boys' team, because there was no girls league. The coach put Scurry in goal because he thought she would be safest there, but she hated not being able to score. After one season in goal, she played the field for three years, then returned to

goal. "I realized I could control the game from the goal," she later explained to *Sports Illustrated for Kids*.

At Anoka High School, Scurry played softball, ran track, was an all-state basketball player, and became a high-school All-American in soccer. As a senior, her team won the state championship and she was voted the state's top female athlete.

Scurry earned a soccer scholarship to the University of Massachusetts, where she refined her game under coach Jim Rudy. As a sophomore, she started in goal in all 19 of her team's games, allowing just nine goals all season and recording 12 shutouts. In 1992, her junior year, Scurry posted seven shutouts in 13 starts and also played three games as a forward. To cap her collegiate career, she started all 23 games as a senior and blanked opponents another 15 times, giving her 37 shutouts in 65 starts and an average of 0.56 goals allowed per game for her college career. Scurry led her team to the semifinals of the NCAA championship tournament after winning both the Atlantic 10 conference and tournament titles. She was named to the All-New England first team and the All-Northeast Region first team and to the All-American second team. Scurry graduated in the spring of 1995 with a degree in political science and planned to go to law school, but playing soccer put those plans on hold.

After college, Scurry joined the U.S. Women's National Team, and in her first game, against Portugal on March 16, 1994, she allowed no goals. She immediately

<table>
<tr><td colspan="2">Chronology</td></tr>
<tr><td>1989</td><td>Member of state championship high school team in Anoka, Minnesota</td></tr>
<tr><td>1990-93</td><td>Stars for University of Massachusetts</td></tr>
<tr><td>1994</td><td>Blanks Portugal in first appearance for U.S. National Team</td></tr>
<tr><td>1995</td><td>Plays in Women's World Cup</td></tr>
<tr><td>1996</td><td>Plays on U.S. Olympic gold medal team</td></tr>
<tr><td>1999</td><td>Keeper for U.S. Women's World Cup champions</td></tr>
<tr><td>2001-02</td><td>Plays for Atlanta Beat in WUSA</td></tr>
</table>

became the National Team's number one goalie and kept the job for six full seasons. In her first year with the U.S. team, Scurry started 12 games and had seven shutouts, and she was named the Most Valuable Player of the Chiquita Cup.

Scurry was a stalwart in goal as the women's team won the CONCACAF World Cup qualifying championship in Montreal in 1994. In the World Cup the following year, played in Sweden, she was the keeper as the U.S. finished a disappointing third. After cup play ended, Scurry was in an auto accident and hurt her back. She was unable to play in the U.S. Women's Cup later that year.

But Scurry bounced back the following season, starting 16 games and allowing only 11 goals with two shutouts. Her team lost only one of the 17 games she appeared in. Also in 1996, she played every minute of the U.S. team's five matches at the Atlanta Olympics, allowing only three goals as the U.S. women won the gold medal.

Scurry became the player that every teammate depended on to keep the match close. One of the world's most athletic goalkeepers, she possessed quick hands, great leaping ability, and an intimidating presence. Scurry seemed to play even better under pressure. In an online chat in CNNSI.com, she said she tried to use nervousness as a tool to help her play. "I try not so much to worry about being the last line of defense, I try to stay in my game and I make the plays I can make, and a few of the ones I shouldn't, and deep breathing—that also helps." She always seemed unflappable, even in adversity. "I don't like the other team to see me upset," Scurry aadmitted to *Sports Illustrated,* "because I like to win the psychological battle in a game. Being ice cold is the way I do it."

"Playing against Briana is like rock-climbing a slap of marble," former coach Rudy revealed to *Sports Illustrated.* "There are no weaknesses in her game."

The Big Save

Scurry continued to star for the National Team, posting a team-record 12 shutouts in 1998 and 11 more in 1999. During her six-year run (1994-99) as the U.S. national team's starting keeper, Scurry started 95 of the club's 132 international matches and appeared as a substitute in three others. In more than half of those games, 54, she held the opponents scoreless, and she allowed an average of just 0.6 goals per game. During the 2000 season, Scurry became the 11th U.S. women's player and the first goalie to appear in 100 international games. She had started more than three times as many games as any other U.S. goalie.

In the 1999 World Cup Scurry played every minute of the six games, posting four shutouts and allowing only three goals. She made six saves in an incredible performance against Brazil in a crucial semifinal game, including stopping a couple of point-blank shots. Coach Tony DiCicco said "Scurry was awesome, and she was for sure the number one star for us today." Scurry called it the best game of her career.

Thanks to Scurry, the championship game against China remained a scoreless tie through regulation and two overtimes. The World Cup would be decided on five penalty kicks for each team. On China's third penalty kick, by Liu Ying, Scurry moved immediately to the right and made a save that sent the largest crowd in women's sports history, more than 95,000 fans, into a frenzy. "I went fully on instinct," she was quoted in the *Washington Times.* "I had a feeling when she was walking up that I would get that one.... And I knew I just had to make one save, because my teammates would make their shots." Recalling it later for CNNSI.com, she said: "I experienced an almost indescribable calmness during that situation. I always believed I would make at least one save. I guess you can call that being in the zone or divine inspiration of whatever you want to call it."

Replays of the save showed that Scurry appeared to move forward off the goal line just before the kicker struck the ball. A kicker is allowed to move only laterally before a penalty kick is made. But goalies are at such a severe disadvantage during penalty kicks that most of them try to "cheat" a little, and referees often allow the indiscretion.

Moving On

In 2000, Scurry battled injuries and lost her starting job to Siri Mullinix. She did not appear in the 2000 Olympics, even though she was healed from her injuries, and played in only five games all season, slipping to a 1.19 goals-against average. After that year, Scurry's career totals for the National Team included records for most appearances by a goalie (103), most wins (79) and most shutouts (54).

After the Olympics, Scurry said she wanted to try something new and seriously considered joining the Women's National Basketball Association. Instead, she became a founding member of the Women's United Soccer Association (WUSA). In its inaugural season in 2001, Scurry was assigned to the Atlanta Beat. She held opponents to 0.82 goals per game that season, the

<table>
<tr><td colspan="2">Awards and Accomplishments</td></tr>
<tr><td>1989</td><td>High school All-American</td></tr>
<tr><td>1989</td><td>Top female athlete in Minnesota</td></tr>
<tr><td>1993</td><td>All-New England, All-Northeast Region teams and second team college All-American</td></tr>
<tr><td>1993</td><td>National College Goalkeeper of the Year</td></tr>
<tr><td>1994</td><td>Most Valuable Player, Chiquita Cup</td></tr>
<tr><td>1996, 2000</td><td>Olympic Gold Medalist</td></tr>
<tr><td>1999</td><td>Member of Women's World Cup champions</td></tr>
<tr><td>2001-02</td><td>WUSA Global 11 second team</td></tr>
</table>

league's best average, and won nine games, losing three and drawing six. Her eight shutouts was the second-highest in the league, and after the season she was named goalie on WUSA's Global 11 second team. In the Founders Cup championship game, Scurry got an assist on a goal by Charmaine Hooper.

In 2002 Scurry added five more shutouts to take over the WUSA lead with 13 career shutouts. She allowed 1.33 goals per game, with nine wins, eight losses and a tie. Again, she was named to the league's second team. Scurry also played two more games for the U.S. national team, but she was unable to regain her starter's job from Mullinix.

Scurry donated volunteer time to promote awareness of AIDS and for the Make a Wish Foundation, and she visited many U.S. cities to try to spark interest in soccer among inner-city girls and boys. "I am proud of my heritage," she told *Knight Ridder Newspapers* in 1998, "and I take very seriously my role of showing African-American youth and people in general that we can excel in any sport or anything."

FURTHER INFORMATION

Books

Christopher, Matt. *In the Goal with ... Briana Scurry.* Little, Brown, 2001.

Periodicals

Foltman, Bob. "Fire goalie Zach Thornton gives his take on Briana Scurry's penalty-kick save." *Knight Ridder/Tribune News Service,* (August 2, 1999): K5608.

Hinnon, Joy Bennett. "Soccer Star Boomlet in Black America." *Ebony,* 55 (January 2000): 56.

Hruby, Patrick. "On Top of the World: Scurry Saves Day, Chastain Wins it for U.S." *Washington Times* (July 11, 1999): 1.

Ponti, James. "Get Out of My Net! A Shot has no Chance with Briana Scurry in Goal." *Sports Illustrated for Kids,* 8 (November 1996): 36.

Smallwood, John. "Goalkeeper Takes her Role as African-American Role Model Seriously." *Knight Ridder/Tribune News Service* (August 4, 1998): 804K6896.

Tunstall, Brooke. "U.S. Women Scurry into Final: Goalkeeper Brilliant vs. Brazil." *Washington Times* (July 5, 1999): 1.

"Wahl, Grant. She's a Keeper." *Sports Illustrated,* 91 (July 12, 1999): 36.

Other

"Briana Scurry." *"SoccerDivas.com.* http://www.soccerdivas.com/brianna_scurry.htm (January 19, 2003).

"Briana Scurry." *WUSA.* http://www.wusa.com/players_coaches/players/briana_scurry/(January 19, 2003).

"Chat Reel: Briana Scurry." *CNNSI.com.* http://sports illustrated.cnn.com/your_turn/news/2000/11/15/chatreel_scurry/(January 19, 2003).

"Scurry, Briana." *Women's Soccer World Online.* http://www.womensoccer.com/biogs/scurry.html(January 19, 2003).

"U.S. Teams - Goalkeeper." *SoccerTimes.com.* http://www.soccertimes.com/usteams/roster/women/scurry.htm (January 19, 2002).

Sketch by Michael Betzold

Junior Seau
1969-

American football player

Known for his dominance on the defensive side of the ball, Junior Seau entered the league in 1990 as a first-round draft pick by the San Diego Chargers and soon became a linebacker whose name was mentioned with other contemporary greats, such as **Lawrence Taylor** and **Derrick Thomas**. In a sport known for its brutality and the need for its players to maintain an air of indestructibility, Seau is a rarity in that he is truly a humanitarian, giving back as much as he gets, devoting much of his time away from the field to charitable endeavors.

Growing Up

Though fans know him as Junior Seau, he was born Tiaina Seau on January 19, 1969, in Oceanside, California. His father, Tiana Sr., and mother Luisa were natives of Samoa from the island of Aunuu, who came to America seeking medical help for Junior's older brother. Seau's father, though strict and unrelenting, had instilled early on in Junior a strong moral sense and a work ethic that Seau used during high school and then into college, propelling him to become one of the stars of today's NFL.

Growing up, Seau wanted to be a quarterback, but he led his school to the city championship as a line-

Junior Seau

Playing for the Home Team

The San Diego Chargers picked up Junior Seau in the 1990 draft and he immediately made an impact on the team. He was moved to inside linebacker, and even though this was a position he wasn't familiar with, his enthusiasm for the game wasn't diminished and he did his best to accommodate.

At USC Seau had been an outside pass-rusher. Still, he managed in that rookie season to finish second on the team in tackles, making the change in positions almost seamlessly and learning quickly how to cover running backs on pass plays.

In his second season Seau earned a trip to the Pro Bowl, beginning a long string of Pro Bowl appearances. Then in the 1992 season, with new coach Bobby Ross at the helm, Seau was the catalyst for the Chargers, who finished with an 11-5 record and the division title. In what was the biggest turnaround in NFL history, the team went from losing their first four games to finishing with an 11-1 record the rest of the season.

Seau is the leader on the team, no doubt about it. In a 1994 AFC Championship game, Seau had sixteen tackles against the Pittsburgh Steelers and helped the defense hold a late surge by the Steelers in a game that the Steelers had said they would have no problem winning. Seau and the Chargers' defense held the Steelers to only sixty-six yards rushing. The Chargers would lose the Super Bowl to the San Francisco 49ers, but Seau would have eleven tackles and one sack in the game.

Continues to Excel

Seau's impact on the field has been and continues to be great—even with a Chargers team that finished the 1990s with a struggle. In the past few years the team has turned things around, acquiring quarterback **Doug Flutie** and, most recently, Drew Brees. In 2002, Seau's Charg-

backer and tight end for Oceanside High School. He was named defensive player of the year, as well as earning all-state and USA Today All-USA honorable mention. He was an all-around outstanding athlete, excelling not only at football, but also in basketball and track, all the while doing very well in the classroom, being named to California's All-Academic team with a 3.6 grade point average.

When he graduated, he was recruited by the University of Southern California, but he did not have a very good first few years. As he recounted in *Sports Illustrated*, during his freshman year he couldn't suit up because he had scored ten points too low for the NCAA rules on his SATs. The setback only served to motivate Seau to work even harder. That spring he won USC's annual contest of strength, physical endurance and speed (known as the "Superman" contest), beating out every other player on the football team. It seemed that he was back on track, but then he injured his ankle prior to the start of the second season and was out for yet another year.

Finally, his junior year, two starters were injured, giving Seau the opportunity he needed to prove his worth. He had a great season, earning All-American Honors and the PAC-10 Defensive Player of the Year award. With only one season of college football under his belt, Seau opted to not take any more chances or risk injury and another season away from the field. He entered the National Football league (NFL) draft.

Career Statistics

Yr	Team	Tackles				Fumbles		Interceptions	
		TOT	Solo	AST	Sack	FF	BK	INT	TD
1990	SD	85	61	24	1.0	0	0	0	0
1991	SD	129	111	18	7.0	0	0	0	0
1992	SD	102	79	23	4.5	1	0	0	0
1993	SD	129	108	21	0.0	1	0	2	0
1994	SD	152	126	26	5.5	1	0	2	0
1995	SD	129	113	16	2.0	1	0	0	0
1996	SD	138	111	27	7.0	1	0	2	0
1997	SD	97	85	12	7.0	1	0	2	0
1998	SD	115	94	21	3.5	1	0	2	0
1999	SD	99	80	19	3.5	1	0	0	0
2000	SD	123	104	19	3.5	1	0	1	0
2001	SD	95	85	10	1.0	1	0	2	0
2002	SD	84	62	22	1.5	1	0	1	0
TOTAL		1481	1205	276	47.0	11	0	15	0

SD: San Diego Chargers.

Awards and Accomplishments

1989	Voted unanimous first-team All-America at University of Southern California
1991	Begins string of eight consecutive Pro-Bowl appearances
1992	Voted AFC and NFL Defensive Player of the Year, as well as first-team All-Pro
1993	Named Chargers "Edge Man of the Year"
1994	NFL's Linebacker of the Year; True Value Hardware Man of the Year
1995	NFL First team All-Pro
1996	Named AP All-Pro First Team
2000	Named to Pro Football Hall of Fame's All-Decade team for the 1990s; named NFL Alumni Association's Linebacker of the year

ers were in playoff contention up until the final game of the season. Playing in an extremely tough AFC West division, the team just missed the playoffs.

Junior Seau seems to have fun with life, taking the opportunities afforded him by football and turning them around. He told ESPN's *The Life* that his one weakness is buying sunglasses (he buys a new pair almost weekly). Other than that, he doesn't see the need to spend all of the money he earns on himself. Though he was one of the first NFL players to begin his own apparel line, the "Say-Ow" Gear, Seau's impact off the field is probably greatest in the area of philanthropy.

He started his Junior Seau Foundation in 1992, an organization developed to help out kids who, like Seau, don't always have the best opportunities growing up. The foundation's purpose, as it says on the foundation's Web site, is "to educate and empower young people through the support of child abuse prevention, drug and alcohol awareness, recreational opportunities, anti-juvenile delinquency efforts and complimentary educational programs."

Though he'll be one of the most passionate players on the field, Junior Seau's work off the field and the contributions he makes to his community put Seau at the top of the list of NFL players who give back.

CONTACT INFORMATION

Address: Junior Seau, c/o San Diego Chargers, P.O. Box 609609, San Diego, CA 92160.

FURTHER INFORMATION

Books

Notable Asian Americans. Detroit: Gale Research, 1995.
Sports Starts. Series 1-4. Detroit: U•X•L, 1994-98.

Periodicals

King, P. "Labor of Love: Junior Seau the consummate pro, pushes on for the lowly Chargers." *Sports Illustrated* (October 23, 2000): 96-98, 100.
Samson, Kamon. "Junior Achievement; Seau is still heart and soul of stout Chargers defense." *Gazette* (Colorado Springs) (October 5, 2002).
Sport (October 1994).
Sporting News (January 16, 1995).
Sporting News (January 23, 1995).
Sporting News (January 30, 1995).
Sporting News (February 6, 1995).
Sporting News (January 8, 1996).
Sports Illustrated (September 6, 1993).
Sports Illustrated (December 22, 1997).
USA Today (August 5, 1997).

Other

http://www.juniorseau.org/juniors_career.htm (December 22, 2002).

Interview with Dan Patrick. http://espn.go.com/talent/
danpatrick/s/2000/1017/822877.html (December 22,
2002).
"Junior Seau." http://www.nfl.com/players/playerpage/
4239 (December 22, 2002).

Sketch by Eric Lagergren

Tom Seaver
1944-

American baseball player

Tom Seaver

A s Tom Seaver himself put it, there was nothing like
"seeing someone do what they love, and do it so
well ... then later on being able to do it myself." For
millions of fans, Seaver was the epitome of a baseball
pitcher, and for nearly two decades they watched this
hard-working perfectionist, the first true superstar of the
New York Mets, lead that franchise to its first World Series Championship in franchise history.

Growing Up

Tom Seaver was born November 17, 1944, in Fresno,
California. He would begin little league ball at the age
of nine, and at twelve, pitch his first no-hitter. He was
also the team's leading hitter. But Seaver's little league
stardom would not last long. He was a late-bloomer, and
found himself lagging behind his teammates. He lacked
the size and strength to participate in sports, and after a
while pure talent only took him so far.

To remedy this, Seaver became a student of the game.
In fact, not hitting his growth spurt early on was one of
the best things that could ever have happened to him.
Seaver studied the art of pitching; he learned every pitch
he could get his hands on. His hero was **Sandy Koufax**.
"Seeing his concentration level was amazing," he told
author James Mauro. "I learned about pitching from
watching Koufax, even when he lost."

Even though Seaver was unable to throw as hard or
as fast as other pitchers, eventually, after some time performing manual labor, and then after serving his stint in
the Marines, Seaver at last had the physical size and
strength to accompany his vast knowledge about the art
of pitching. He earned a baseball scholarship to the University of Southern California, and was drafted into the
majors.

Once a Met

Seaver ended up with the New York Mets in 1966
when the Atlanta Braves, who made Seaver an offer

while he was still in college, found that their offer had
been declared void. Any team that could match the
Braves' offer, the commissioner of baseball declared,
could have him. The Mets won a lottery, and Seaver became a New York Met.

In his first season with the Mets he earned the nickname "Tom Terrific." Seaver won sixteen games, pitched
in the All-Star game, and began capturing the hearts of
Mets fans, who prior to Seaver didn't have much to cheer
for—and still, the team won only sixty-one games that
year. But they now had Tom, who came with a trademark
style: "The hand cocking back at almost sidearm height,"
as James Mauro described it in *Psychology Today*. "[His]
eyes sighting the catcher's mitt like a laser-guided missile launcher; right arm windmilling over the head. And
then that whole powerful, boyish body going down on
one knee almost, so that when the rocket was fired and
the target hit, there would be a smudge of dirt on the uniform where it had scraped the mound."

On April 22, 1970, Seaver struck out nineteen Padres,
a record ten in a row to end the game, which tied a then-
major league record for a nine-inning game. Seaver routinely won twenty or more games in a season, often
leading the National League in strikeouts and earned run
average (ERA). In 1973, he led the Mets to the second
national league pennant in their short history, going on
to win the **Cy Young** Award.

Seaver feels his best season was the 1971 season, in
which he compiled a 20-10 record and led the league for

Chronology

1944	Born November 17 in Fresno, California
1953	Begins playing Little League ball
1956	Pitches no-hitter at age of 12
1962	Earns baseball scholarship to University of Southern California
1966	Drafted by Braves
1966	Made free agent before career even begins, picked up by New York Mets
1969	Helps Mets to their first World Series Championship in franchise history
1970	Strikes out 19 in a win over the San Diego Padres, including ten in a row to end the game
1971	Smashes 8th inning homer in June 24th game to win his own game, 2-1
1971	Finishes season with 1.71 ERA, half the league average
1973	Leads Mets to their second National League pennant
1975	Reaches 200 strikeouts for major league record 8th straight season
1977	Traded by Mets to the Reds
1978	Throws first no-hitter for the Cincinnati Reds on June 10
1981	Stung by the players' strike and would lose in Cy Young balloting by three points
1982	Agrees to contract with Mets in a trade that sends him back to New York
1984	Stunning New York fans once more, Seaver is picked up by Chicago White Sox
1985	Sets major league record by making 15th of his 16 opening day starts
1985	Becomes 17th pitcher to win 300 games
1986	Makes his major league record 16th opening day start
1987	Abandons comeback attempt and announces his retirement
1992	Inducted to Baseball Hall of Fame with a record 98.8% of the vote
1999	Becomes broadcast booth color man for New York Mets and also serves as part-time coach for the team

Awards and Accomplishments

1967	National League Rookie of the Year
1967-73, 1975-78, 1981	National League All-Star Team
1969	Associated Press Male Athlete of the Year
1969	Named *Sports Illustrated* Sportsman of the Year
1969	Named *Sporting News* Man of the Year
1969	Awarded Hickock Bell award
1969, 1973, 1975	Winner of National League Cy Young Award
1981	National League Comeback Player of the Year
1992	Inducted into National Baseball Hall of Fame
1992	Honored by having his number, 41, retired by New York Mets

the second straight year with a 1.76 ERA and 289 strikeouts. In his ten years playing for the New York Mets, Seaver would compile an astonishing 25% of the Mets' wins. He was the 17th 300 game winner in major league history, and struck out 200 or more batters in ten seasons (nine straight seasons from 1968 to 1976). He also took home three Cy Young awards.

In the end, "Tom Terrific" won 311 games with an average 2.86 ERA over twenty seasons in the majors. His 3,272 strikeouts set a National League career record, and he struck out 3,640 batters overall. The Mets would win their first World Series in franchise history, in 1969, with the help of Seaver's awesome performances on the mound.

From Met to Red

Tom Seaver had an incredible period of undisputed dominance on the mound in the early to mid-1970s. His only off-season would come in 1974, when he developed a sore hip and finished with an 11-11 record and an ERA over 3.00 (3.20), the first time ever. Of course, the very next season he rocketed to 22-9, leading the league once again in strikeouts, wins, and winning percentage, as well winning the Cy Young.

In 1976, however, Seaver developed problems with Mets general manager, M. Donald Grant. They argued about Seaver's salary, and about how Grant ran the ballclub. In June of 1977, the Mets traded Seaver to the Cincinnati Reds for four players. Mets fans were devastated. With the Reds, Seaver would finally get his elusive no-hitter, on June 16, 1978, and go on to four winning years with the Reds.

Tom Seaver's career began to go downhill in 1982. He fell to a 5-13 mark that season, and the Reds traded Seaver back to the Mets. The Mets fans would rejoice only briefly, however. The White Sox lured him away after he was left unprotected in the free agent compensation pool. He won fifteen games for the Sox in 1984, 16 in 1985, and won his 300th game in a 4-1 complete game against the Yankees that season. On October 4, 1985, he moved past Walter Johnson and into third place on the all time strikeout list, where he finished his career.

In 1986 he pitched for the Red Sox, but an ankle injury kept him out of World Series play. The following season he was released, and ended up quitting rather than bounce somewhere else. Number 41 retired.

Since retiring from baseball, Seaver has been enjoying the perks of being a hero and one of the most recognizable names in baseball (especially to Mets fans). He insists on having fun, which is an attitude that served him well a few years ago, when in 1999 he was chosen to replace Tim McCarver as the on-air analyst for Mets baseball. The move was not one that happened without controversy. Seaver, as a total student of the game, knows more about baseball than most professional teams combined, but one of the criticisms is that he's too well-versed. It's been said that, when he talks about pitching, it's like hearing Einstein explain the theory of relativity. Regardless, Seaver now juggles among his duties his position as broadcaster and front office executive for the Mets. He often goes down to talk to the pitchers, but that's not what he's paid to do. It's more of a hobby.

In 1992, Seaver was voted into the National Baseball Hall of Fame, netting 425 votes out of 430 ballots cast.

Career Statistics

Yr	Team	W	L	ERA	GS	CG	SHO	IP	H	R	BB	SO
1967	NYM	16	13	2.76	34	18	2	251.0	224	77	78	170
1968	NYM	16	12	2.20	35	14	5	277.7	224	68	48	205
1969	NYM	25	7	2.21	35	18	5	273.3	202	67	82	208
1970	NYM	18	12	2.82	36	19	2	290.7	230	91	83	283
1971	NYM	20	10	1.76	35	21	4	286.3	210	56	61	289
1972	NYM	21	12	2.92	35	13	3	262.0	215	85	77	249
1973	NYM	19	10	2.08	36	18	3	290.0	219	67	64	251
1974	NYM	11	11	3.20	32	12	5	236.0	199	84	75	201
1975	NYM	22	9	2.38	36	15	5	280.3	217	74	88	243
1976	NYM	14	11	2.59	34	13	5	271.0	211	78	77	235
1977	NYM	7	3	3.00	13	5	3	96.0	79	32	28	72
	CIN	14	3	2.34	20	14	4	165.3	120	43	38	124
	TOT	21	6	2.58	33	19	7	261.3	199	75	66	196
1978	CIN	16	14	2.88	36	8	1	259.7	218	83	89	226
1979	CIN	16	6	3.14	32	9	5	215.0	187	75	61	131
1980	CIN	10	8	3.64	26	5	1	168.0	140	68	59	101
1981	CIN	14	2	2.54	23	6	1	166.3	120	47	66	87
1982	CIN	5	13	5.50	21	0	0	111.3	136	68	44	62
1983	NYM	9	14	3.55	34	5	2	231.0	201	91	86	135
1984	CHW	15	11	3.95	33	10	4	236.7	216	104	61	131
1985	CHW	16	11	3.17	33	6	1	238.7	223	84	69	134
1986	CHW	2	6	4.38	12	1	0	72.0	66	35	27	31
	BOS	5	7	3.80	16	1	0	104.3	114	44	29	72
	TOT	7	13	4.03	28	2	0	176.3	180	79	56	103
TOTAL		311	205	2.86	647	231	61	4782.7	3971	1521	1390	3640

BOS: Boston Red Sox; CHW: Chicago White Sox; CIN: Cincinnati Reds; NYM: New York Mets.

SELECTED WRITINGS BY SEAVER:

(With Dick Schaap) *The Perfect Game: Tom Seaver and the Mets,* E.P. Dutton, 1970.

(With S.H. Burchard) *Tom Seaver: Sports Star,* Harcourt Brace, 1976.

(With Steve A. Jacobson) *Pitching With Tom Seaver,* Prentice Hall, 1982.

(With Martin Appel) *Tom Seaver's All-Time Baseball Greats,* Wanderer Books, 1984.

(With Martin Appel) *Great Moments in Baseball,* Birch Lane Press, 1992.

(With Lee Lowenfish) *The Art of Pitching,* Morrow, 1994.

FURTHER INFORMATION

Books

Cohen, Joel H., ed. *Inside Corner: Talks With Tom Seaver.* New York: Atheneum, 1974.

Devaney, John. *Tom Seaver.* New York: Popular Library, 1974.

Great Athletes, vol. 7. Hackensack, N.J.: Salem Press, Inc. 2506-2508.

Schoor, Gene. *Seaver: A Biography.* Chicago: Contemporary Books, Inc., 1986.

Seaver, Tom, and Martin Appel. *Tom Seaver's All-Time Baseball Greats.* New York: Wanderer Books, 1984.

Seaver, Tom, and Martin Appel. *Great Moments in Baseball.* New York: Birch Lane Press, 1992.

Seaver, Tom, and S.H. Burchard. *Tom Seaver: Sports Star.* New York: Harcourt Brace, 1976.

Seaver, Tom, and Steve A. Jacobson. *Pitching With Tom Seaver.* New York: Prentice Hall, 1982.

Seaver, Tom, and Lee Lowenfish. *The Art of Pitching,* New York: Morrow, 1994.

Seaver, Tom, with Dick Schaap. *The Perfect Game: Tom Seaver and the Mets.* New York: E.P. Dutton and Company, 1970.

Shatzkin, Mike, ed. *The Ballplayers: Baseball's Ultimate Biographical Reference.* New York: Morrow

Siegel, Barry, ed. *Official Baseball Register.* (1986 & '87 eds.). St Louis: *The Sporting News,* 1986-1987.

Periodicals

Friedman, Jack. "300!." *People* (August 19, 1985): 41.

Jares, Joe. "The Mets Find a Young Phenom." *Sports Illustrated* (June 26, 1967): 64-66.

Jordan, Pat. "Tom Terrific and His Magnificent Talent." *Sports Illustrated* (July 24, 1972): 22-31.

Leggett, William. "Sportsman of the Year." *Sports Illustrated* 31 (December 22, 1969): 32-37.

Ludtke Lincoln, Melissa. "TV Radio: Making Another Kind of Pitch." *Sports Illustrated* (September 18, 1978): 58.

Mauro, James. "Mound Olympus" (interview with Tom Seaver). *Psychology Today* (July-August, 1992): 22.

Schollberg, Dan. "Tom Seaver: Perfection Was His Goal." *Baseball Digest* (1999).

Other

"Tom Seaver." http://www.baseball-reference.com/ (November 10, 2002).
"Tom Seaver." http://www.pubdim.net/baseballlibrary/ (November 10, 2002).
"Tom Seaver." http://www.thebaseballpage.com/past/pp/ seavertom/default.htm/ (November 2, 2002).

Sketch by Eric Lagergren

Secretariat
1970-1989

American racehorse

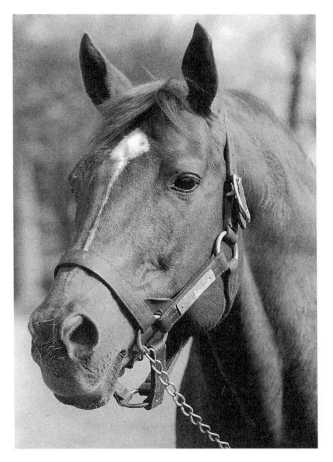

Secretariat

The headlines dubbed him "Super Horse"—and the name fit. Big, barrel-chested, and sporting a gleaming chestnut coat, the Thoroughbred Secretariat bounded into sports history with amazing performances during the 1972-73 racing seasons, culminating in a Triple Crown victory. At his peak in June 1973, Secretariat appeared on the covers of three national magazines in the same week. The colt nicknamed "Big Red" shattered racing records but was equally admired as a symbol of dignity and honesty, no small claim during a period that saw America disheartened by the Watergate scandal and discouraged by the ongoing war in Vietnam.

Secretariat was a product of equine aristocrats. His dam (mother) was Somethingroyal, a respected broodmare of Meadow Farm (also known as the Meadow Stud) of Doswell, Virginia; his sire (father) was Bold Ruler, a champion in his own right who, "sleek and haughty, … dominated racing for a decade," according to Pete Axthelm's *Newsweek* cover article. Helen (Penny) Tweedy, the daughter of Meadow Farm's founder, Christopher Cherney, was new to the racing business but passionately interested in her family's horses.

In a Word: "Wow!"

The foal by Bold Ruler out of Somethingroyal was born just after midnight on March 30, 1970. In his book, *Secretariat,* Raymond Woolfe wrote, "he was a big, handsome chestnut colt with three white feet and a star and a stripe on his forehead. He staggered to his feet within twenty minutes and began nursing in about forty-five." On a walk through the farm later on, Penny Tweedy took her first look at Somethingroyal's newborn, and made a one-word assessment in her notebook: "Wow!"

Early on, Secretariat caught the eye of farm manager Howard Gentry. "It was when he was a yearling, playing in the fields with the others, that I first suspected" the horse's potential, Gentry told Axthelm. Physically, the young Secretariat was close to textbook perfection for a thoroughbred. He had, as Gentry was quoted by Woolfe, "plenty of bone," meaning the horse sported a "solid, well-chiseled frame, not the 'mushy' or round, soft-looking joints and skimpy bone areas that spell potential trouble on lesser horses."

Beyond being physically impressive, Secretariat was also regarded as mentally and emotionally sound. Doted upon by his dam, the foal grew into a gregarious and even-tempered sort, though prone to displays of aggressive enthusiasm. "He was so precocious," Gentry told Woolfe, "that we were worried that he'd pick up the habit of getting away from men. That could mean a lot of trouble later on. For a time, we put a restraining chain on him to stop him from trying to bolt. But he was so intelligent that he caught on quickly and never developed any bad habits."

Training Trials and Tribulations

Secretariat was weaned from Somethingroyal on October 5, 1970. He spent the next winter and the following

Chronology	
1970	Born at Meadow Farm in Doswell, Virginia
1971	Begins training at Meadow Farm
1972	Moves to Florida to complete training with Lucien Laurin
1972	Competes in first race. After being brushed at the start, finishes fourth
1972	Wins first of many stakes race
1973	Syndicated for $6,080,000, a new record
1973	Becomes first Triple Crown winner in twenty-five years, setting new track records
1973	Turf-track debut in Man o' War Stakes; wins by five lengths
1973	Retires to stud at Claiborne Farm, Paris, Kentucky
1989	Diagnosed with laminitis, euthanized October 4, age nineteen.

Awards and Accomplishments	
1973	First two-year-old named Horse of the Year
1973	Winner of the Kentucky Derby in a new record time
1973	Winner of the Preakness Stakes
1973	Winner of the Belmont Stakes by thirty-one lengths, a new track and world record
1973	"Farewell to Secretariat" Day at Aqueduct Park
1974	Bronze statue unveiled at Belmont Park
1999	Named one of ESPN's fifty greatest athletes of the twentieth century

spring and summer at liberty in the Meadow Farm fields. In August 1971, the yearling received his first pair of front shoes, signaling his move to the farm's training center. Secretariat was taken under the wing of veteran trainer Bob Bailes, who made it a point to introduce his yearlings to saddle, bit, and rider gently and gradually.

But at the same time, Secretariat had developed a ravenous appetite. The big colt's weight gain and attendant clumsiness became a concern at Meadow Farm, especially after Secretariat's first track tryouts proved less than promising. But the horse was still considered a "comer." In 1971 Meadow trainer Roger Laurin, offered a job at the competing Phipps barn, turned over the Meadow youngsters to his father, respected Florida-based trainer Lucien Laurin. The elder Laurin quickly made his name at Penny Tweedy's establishment by mentoring Meadow's bay colt Riva Ridge to a Kentucky Derby win in 1972.

Secretariat was shipped to Florida to continue his education under the eye of Laurin. As a two-year-old, the chestnut was showing signs of talent, but his playful nature would get the better of him. Secretariat was given to deliberately bumping and nipping the other horses. The colt also amused himself by periodically dumping his exercise riders. But there was no malice in the horse's actions; "Everybody that had anything to do with him couldn't help loving him," jockey Ron Turcotte is quoted in *Secretariat*. "He was such a big clown."

Out of the Gate

Revisions in his diet, exercise, and training schedule cured Secretariat of his weight problems and practical joking. In June 1972, the colt impressed his handlers by "breezing" (galloping) five furlongs in a blazing 57 3/4 seconds. Later that month, Laurin pronounced the horse ready to run. Secretariat made his professional bow on July 4, 1972, at Aqueduct Park in Queens, New York. As the horses broke from the gate, a contender named Quebec ducked sharply and hit Secretariat in the side. The red colt "was slammed inward almost into the rail and out of contention," as Woolfe's book put it. "If he wasn't

so strong," jockey Paul Feliciano was quoted, "he would have gone right down."

Secretariat recovered and rallied to move from tenth position to finish fourth, less than two lengths behind the winner. Word of the talented two-year-old spread to bettors; by Secretariat's second start there, he had been made the six-to-five favorite. The horse didn't disappoint. After a clean start, Secretariat methodically breezed past his competitors, winning by six lengths.

In August 1972 Saratoga beckoned; the famed New York track was America's oldest and had hosted such champions as **Man o' War**. It was at Saratoga that trainer Laurin first teamed Secretariat with the jockey who would become most associated with the horse, thirty-one-year-old Ron Turcotte. Secretariat and Turcotte were entered in Saratoga's opening-day race, a six-furlong allowance for horses who have won fewer than two races. Secretariat broke conservatively from the gate, allowing the other thoroughbreds to establish pace. Then, at the final turn, the chestnut made his move, picking off horses one by one until he could claim a decisive victory. "He just floats," Turcotte was quoted in *Secretariat*. "You don't feel like you're goin' that fast, but then you look up and you're passin' horses like they were standin' still."

More victories followed: the $27,000 Sanford Stakes; the $86,5000 Hopeful Stakes; the $144,000 Futurity at Belmont Park; and the $146,000 Champagne Stakes, the first time Secretariat ran a mile in competition. In the latter race, the chestnut gave his fans some pause when, characteristically, he broke slowly, but then allowed the gap to widen to a daunting fifteen lengths off the lead. Turcotte urged his mount with hands and leg, but Secretariat preferred to run his own race. The horses made the final turn and, according to Woolfe, "there was an explosion" as "a copper-colored streak zoomed around the outside of the entire field and down to the finish line as if the other horses had stopped for lunch. The crowd went wild. No one had ever seen anything like this." The cheers turned to stunned silence, however, when the "inquiry" light went up on the tote board. Secretariat, the officials ruled, had illegally brushed up against another horse at the 3/16 pole. The chestnut was disqualified to second, his first defeat since his maiden race.

Jockey Ron Turcotte riding Secretariat

Run for the Roses

Secretariat earned Horse of the Year honors for 1972, the first two-year-old ever so named. As spring 1973 approached, talk turned to the Triple Crown. Though the colt's talent was well established, the grueling pace of the Kentucky Derby, Preakness, and Belmont Stakes had upset many a potential champion. In fact, it had been a long, dry spell of twenty-five years since Citation had swept all three races in 1948.

The Kentucky Derby's distance—a mile and a quarter—is longer than any race previously handled by a three-year-old. The Preakness track makes sharp turns that challenge the poise of a galloping horse. And the Belmont Stakes "is sheer, vast distance," in Woolfe's words, a mile-and-a-half oval that includes the longest homestretch in the world.

April's mile-and-an-eighth Wood Memorial is considered a key indicator of Kentucky Derby success. But here the horse now nicknamed "Big Red" (a tribute to the original "Big Red," Man o' War) proved he was not invincible. Taking command of the Wood was Meadow stablemate Angle Light, followed by Sham, a lean, dark-brown colt from Kentucky's Claiborne Farm. Perhaps hampered by an interrupted pre-race workout, Secretariat never applied the late burst of killing speed that marked his victories. He finished third. The question arose: Did this horse have the stamina for the Triple Crown?

Derby Day dawned May 5, 1973. Secretariat had drawn the number ten post position, to the outside of the field of fourteen. As the starting gates crashed open, the colt dropped far back. At the first turn "he was dead last," as William Nack wrote in a *Sports Illustrated* piece. Then Turcotte guided Secretariat to the outside. The horse made his move, passing the field until only his Wood Memorial rival, Sham, stood between Secretariat and the Derby's fabled garland of roses. The two horses raced head-to-head for one hundred yards. Secretariat put on the final burst to finish by two-and-a-half lengths. But what caused even more cheers was his time: 1:59 and 2/5, a new track and Derby record. Adding to the brilliance of Secretariat's race was the fact that the horse had run each quarter faster than the preceding one.

After the Kentucky Derby win, Secretariat had few detractors at the Preakness, run at Pimlico in Baltimore on May 19, 1973. That day, "Big Red" broke slowly, as usual, and did not let the track's tight turns intimidate him. As Nack described it, Turcotte signaled "as subtly as a man adjusting his cuff, and the colt took off like a flushed deer." Again he mastered the field in a bold stretch run, and again he passed front-running Sham to take the second jewel of the Triple Crown by 2-1/2 lengths. Due to a malfunction of the track's timer, Secretariat could not be credited with better than 1:54 and 2/5. "But two *Daily Racing Form* clockers caught Secretariat at 1:53 2/5," noted Nack, "a track record by three fifths of a second."

Related Biography: Jockey Ron Turcotte

Ron Turcotte wasn't the first man to ride Secretariat in a race. Nor was he the last. But the native of Grand Falls, New Brunswick, was the rider most closely associated with the chestnut colt's greatest turns, including the duo's history-making Triple Crown victory in 1973.

Born July 22, 1941, Turcotte came from French-Canadian heritage, the son of a lumberjack. Growing up as one of twelve children, Turcotte learned early on to fend for himself; the family home had no indoor plumbing or central heating. Short in stature (he stood five-foot-one), Turcotte proved large in determination. When logging proved too much of a physical challenge, Turcotte was put in charge of the logging camp's horses, where he learned the equestrian trade. "My father taught me to be patient with horses," he said in a *Le Forum* interview. "He taught me how to give horses confidence,"

Leaving the forests, Turcotte tried his hand at being a jockey. He ended up in Laurel, Maryland; by 1972 he was partnered with quality Thoroughbreds like 1972 Kentucky Derby winner Riva Ridge. In 1971, he was introduced to the promising yearling Secretariat. "He was the kindest of animals, but big and clumsy," Turcotte recalled. "He wasn't spooky, he was calm, like riding a big pony."

Together, Secretariat and Turcotte dominated the stakes-racing season in 1972 and 1973, culminating in a record-setting Triple Crown championship. The horse's career statistics included sixteen wins in twenty-one starts, most of them under the guidance of Turcotte. After Secretariat retired to stud in 1973, Turcotte remained on the track; in 1978 he suffered a traumatic injury in a race that ended his riding career. In August 1980, the jockey was inducted into the Canadian Sports Hall of Fame. He and his family moved back to Grand Falls, and Turcotte became a spokesman for the disabled.

"Like a Tremendous Machine!"

Now Secretariat was a beloved public figure. The week before the Belmont, *Time, Newsweek,* and *Sports Illustrated* had cover stories on the Thoroughbred dubbed "Super Horse." The charismatic colt "transcended horse racing and became a cultural phenomenon, a sort of undeclared national holiday from the tortures of Watergate and the Vietnam War," as Nack remarked.

Nack made camp at Belmont Park in Elmont, New York, to record the actions of Secretariat on Belmont Stakes day. That June 9, he reported, Secretariat greeted the day in an expressive mood. Normally docile, the colt found reason to rear and dance as he was groomed for his biggest race to date. "I had never seen a horse so fit," wrote Nack. "The Derby and Preakness had wound him as tight as a watch, and he seemed about to burst out of his coat."

A great roar came from the grandstand as Secretariat, with Turcotte up, paraded to the post. As the gates swung open, Secretariat for the first time abandoned his usual tactic of hanging back. Instead, he bounded to the lead of the pack of five, including his archrival, Sham. As jockey Laffit Pincay brought Sham up to challenge, the two colts dueled for the lead, posting split times of under twenty-four seconds.

Track announcer Chick Anderson made the now-famous call for CBS television: "It is Secretariat, Sham on the outside is also moving along strongly and now it's Sham, Sham and Secretariat are right together.... They're on the backstretch. It's almost a match race now. Secretariat's on the inside by a head.... They've opened ten lengths.... They're moving on the turn now.... For the turn it's Secretariat. He looks like he's opening. The lead is increasing. Make it three, three and a half. He's moving into the turn. Secretariat holding on to a large lead. Sham is second.... They're on the turn and Secretariat is blazing along!" In a 2002 *Harper's* article, John Jeremiah Sullivan recalled the emotion in Anderson's voice as the red horse made his final move. Anderson, wrote Sullivan, appeared to be "holding back tears of disbelief as he shouts: "It looks like he's opening ... the lead is increasing! Secretariat is *widening* now! He is moving like a TREE-MENDOUS MA-SHEEN!"

Entering the homestretch, Secretariat held such a commanding lead that the television cameras could not fit the entire field in the same shot. As the Belmont grandstand rocked with excitement, Anderson continued the call: "Secretariat has opened up a twenty-two length lead.... Here comes Secretariat to the wire. An unbelievable, an amazing performance! He hits the finish.... twenty-five lengths in front!" When the race was tallied, it turned out that Secretariat had in fact finished by an astounding thirty-one lengths, setting a new track record of 2:24. "To say that there was pandemonium in the Belmont stands would be a limp description," Woolfe noted.

A Hero's Farewell

After his Triple Crown victory, Secretariat continued to rack up wins including the Marlboro Cup and the turf-run Man o' War Stakes. After his final race before a packed crowd at Woodbine in Ontario (with jockey Eddie Maple substituting for an injured Turcotte), and a "Farewell to Secretariat" day at Aqueduct, "Big Red" retired to stud at Claiborne Farm under a syndication agreement between Tweedy and Claiborne's Seth Hancock. He was assigned the stall of his sire, Bold Ruler. In retirement Secretariat was a popular attraction, posing for tourist photos and lording over his private paddock.

As a stud, Secretariat produced several stakes winners, though none that equaled his brilliance. The progeny of "Big Red" includes 1976 Kentucky Derby runner-up General Assembly and 1986 Horse of the Year Lady's Secret. A generation later, Summer Squall raced to victory in the 1990 Preakness.

In fall 1989, the stallion began to show signs of illness. The diagnosis: laminitis, a painful and incurable degeneration of the hoof. The humane, if heartbreaking, decision was made to euthanize Secretariat. He was put down by injection on October 4, 1989, at the age of nineteen. Great racehorses are often said to have "heart," but on autopsy, Secretariat proved that point in a startling way. He heart was measured at nearly eighteen pounds, twice the size of the average thoroughbred's. "It wasn't pathologically enlarged," elaborated Dr. Thomas Swercek in Nack's article. "All the chambers and the valves were normal. It was just larger. I think it told us why he was able to do what he did." Secretariat's gravesite at Claiborne Farm was festooned with flowers from his fans; "You see all this," farm owner Dell Hancock told Nack in a 1989 *Sports Illustrated* article, "and you suddenly realize the impact he had on people."

Secretariat's legacy remains in the record books and the hearts of his fans. As of 2002, his time for the Kentucky Derby and the Belmont Stakes has not been bettered. A stakes race is named in his honor. In 1991 a bronze statue of "Big Red" was unveiled at Belmont Park, the site of Secretariat's greatest victory. And in an ESPN poll of the hundred greatest athletes of the twentieth century, Secretariat placed thirty-fifth, the only non-human in the top fifty. In Sullivan's view, Secretariat "is best described not as the greatest horse, nor as the greatest runner, nor even as the greatest athlete of the twentieth century, but as the greatest creature."

FURTHER INFORMATION

Books

Nack, William. *Secretariat: The Making of a Champion.* Da Capo Press, 1988.

Woolfe, Raymond G. *Secretariat.* Derrydale Press, 2001

Periodicals

Axthelm, Pete. "Superhorse Secretariat." *Newsweek* (June 11, 1973).

Nack, William. "Big Red (1970-1989)." *Sports Illustrated* (October 16, 1989).

Nack, William. "Pure Heart." *Sports Illustrated* (October 24, 1994).

Nack, William. "Secretariat." *Sports Illustrated* (September 19, 1994).

Sports Illustrated (June 11, 1973).

Sullivan, John Jeremiah. "Horseman, Pass By." *Harper's* (October, 2002).

"Super Horse." *Time* (June 11, 1973).

Other

"French-Canadian Jockey a Horse Racing Legend." Le Forum. http://www.happyones.com/ (October 4, 2002)./bibcit.composed

"Greatest Performance in Racing History." Chef de Race. http://www.chef.-de-race.com/ (October 4, 2002).

"Secretariat Remains No. 1 Name in Racing." ESPN Classic. http://www.espn.go.com/classic/ (October 4, 2002).

"Secretariat 1973." Second Running. http://www.secondrunning.com/ (October 4, 2002).

Secretariat.com. http://www.secretariat.com (October 4, 2002).

"Top N. American Athletes of the Century." ESPN. http://espn.go.com/ (October 4, 2002).

Sketch by Susan Salter

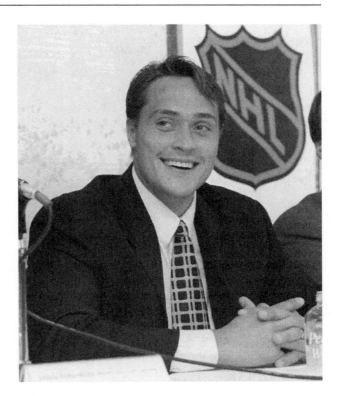

Teemu Selanne

Teemu Selanne
1970-

Finnish hockey player

Known as the Finnish Flash, right wing sharp shooter Teemu Selanne set a record by scoring seventy-six goals in his rookie season. Selanne began his career with the Winnipeg Jets (who later moved to Phoenix and became the Coyotes), before being traded to the Anaheim Mighty Ducks, and later the San Jose Sharks. During his time in Anaheim, Selanne often played on a line with another gifted scorer, **Paul Kariya**, and the pair produced much of the team's offense. Selanne is also known for his good natured personality.

Selanne was born on July 3, 1970, in Helsinki, Finland, with a twin brother Paavo, who played goal at one time. While Selanne was recognized as a great hockey talent in Finland in his youth—a player who scored on nearly every shot—the sport was not his only interest. He once played on the Finnish junior national soccer team. He also loved to race cars, and would race in Finland in off-road rallies and other races, during the NHL off season. Hockey, however, was his focus. By 1986, he was recognized as one of the best players in Finland.

Drafted by Winnipeg

Selanne's skills attracted the attention of the NHL. In 1988, he was drafted by the Winnipeg Jets as the tenth

Chronology

1970	Born July 3 in Helsinki, Finland
1988	Drafted by Winnipeg Jets in the first round
c. 1988-89	Serves in the Finnish Army
1989-92	Plays for Jokerit (Finnish team); also teaches kindergarten
1992	Plays for the Finnish national team in the Olympics; begins playing for the Winnipeg Jets (NHL)
1995	Signs five-year deal worth $14 million with Winnipeg
1996	Marries Sirpa Vuorinen on July 19; traded to the Anaheim Mighty Ducks on February 7
1997	Plays in the post-season with the Mighty Ducks (first time the team played in playoffs)
1998	Plays for Finland at the Winter Olympics, winning bronze medal
2001	Traded to the San Jose Sharks on March 5
2002	Signs a one-year deal with Sharks worth $6.5 million ($3 million less than he had made the previous season); plays for Finland at the Winter Olympics

Awards and Accomplishments

1992-93	Set rookie record by scoring 76 goals in a season for the Winnipeg Jets
1993	Calder Memorial Trophy as rookie of the year
1998	MVP of the All-Star game; played for Finland at the Winter Olympics, winning bronze medal
1999	Maurice "The Rocket" Richard Trophy for most goals scored in the season

pick in the first round. However, the team had to wait for him. Selanne had to complete his required eleven-month commitment to the Finnish Army. There, he learned marksmanship and enjoyed the experience.

After finishing up his stint in the army, Selanne played for Jokerit, a club team in Helsinki. He also had another job. While playing for the team at night, he taught kindergarten during the day. Kids were also a focus in another way. Selanne went to a children's hospital for an event when he was eighteen years old, and moved by the experience, he founded the Godfathers Foundation, which raised money for sick kids. During this time period, when Selanne was nineteen, he broke his leg. During the year-long recovery period, he was worried about his future in the NHL.

Joined the NHL

Selanne recovered fully from the injury, and played on the Finnish national team at the 1992 Olympics. By this time, he was a national figure in Finland. In the fall, Selanne finally joined his NHL team, the Winnipeg Jets. He had an outstanding rookie season in 1992-93. He scored seventy-six goals and fifty-six assists for 132 points; the goals alone were a record. For this effort, he was named Rookie of the Year. While Selanne never matched these numbers again through the 2002 season, his reputation as a sniper was cemented.

During the 1993-94 season, Selanne suffered from a serious injury, a severed Achilles tendon, from which he eventually recovered. Despite injuries, Selanne still managed an average of one goal every two games. To keep their scorer, Winnipeg signed him to a five-year deal in 1995 worth $14 million.

Traded to the Ducks

During the 1996 off-season, the Jets decided to trade Selanne to the Anaheim Mighty Ducks for Chad Kilger

and Oleg Tverdovsky. He played on a line with Kariya, which gave both of them many goals. The pair played well together. In fact, it was Kariya who had met him at the 1996 All-Star game they both played and encouraged the Duck's general manager Jack Ferreira that Selanne was a good player and might have the right personality for their team.

Of Selanne's personality and game, Johnette Howard of *Sports Illustrated* wrote "If Selanne's wit doesn't charm someone first, his unebbing enthusiasm, his slack-jawed smile or wide-eyed look of wonder probably will. His game has all the bells and whistles.... He has blazing speed and the power to shrug off defenders; he's a natural scorer and can shrewdly read a game."

During his first season with the Ducks, Selanne scored fifty-one goals and helped lead the Ducks to their first playoff berth in 1997. The following season, Selanne again scored over fifty goals. He carried the team through much of the season, though it was in last place. Kariya was out much of the season due to injury and a contract dispute. Selanne also represented his country at the 1998 Winter Olympics, winning a bronze as a member of the Finnish hockey team.

For his effort, Selanne received a contract extension of two years, $19.5 million, taking him through the end of the 2002 season. The pressure of a new deal did not hamper or change Selanne's scoring abilities. In 1999, he won the NHL's goal-scoring title, scoring a league-leading forty-seven goals.

Traded to San Jose

Though Selanne and Kariya had chemistry, the Ducks were a struggling franchise in the late 1990s and early 2000s. They only went to the playoffs twice, and rumors were rampant that the team's parent company, Disney, might sell them. Though Selanne's salary was costly, it was less than Kariya's, and he had value on the trade market. Selanne had scored more goals than anyone since coming into the NHL.

In March 2001, Selanne was traded from the Ducks to the San Jose Sharks for goalie Steve Shields, Jeff Friesen, and a conditional draft pick. His first months in San Jose were not great. Soon after the trade, he had to have arthoscopic knee surgery to remove loose cartilage. San Jose

Career Statistics

Yr	Team	GP	G	A	PTS	+/-	PIM	SOG	SPCT	PPG	SHG
1992-93	Jets	84	76	56	132	8	45	387	19.6	24	0
1993-94	Jets	51	25	29	54	-23	22	191	13.1	11	0
1994-95	Jets	45	22	26	48	1	2	167	13.2	8	2
1995-96	Jets	51	24	48	72	3	18	163	14.7	6	1
1995-96	Ducks	28	16	20	36	2	4	104	15.4	3	0
1996-97	Ducks	78	51	58	109	28	34	273	18.7	11	1
1997-98	Ducks	73	52	34	86	12	30	268	19.4	10	1
1998-99	Ducks	75	47	60	107	18	30	281	16.7	25	0
1999-2000	Ducks	79	33	52	85	6	12	236	14.0	8	0
2000-01	Ducks	61	26	33	59	-8	36	202	12.9	10	0
2000-01	Sharks	12	7	6	13	1	0	31	22.6	2	0
2001-02	Sharks	82	29	25	54	-11	40	202	14.4	9	1
TOTAL			719	408	447	855	273	2505	197	6	

Ducks: Anaheim Mighty Ducks (NHL); Jets: Winnipeg Jets (NHL); Sharks: San Jose Sharks (NHL).

was already headed for the playoffs, but when Selanne returned for the post-season, he was playing with a broken right thumb, which limited his scoring abilities. The Sharks were eliminated from the playoffs, but Selanne was finally playing with a winning organization.

In 2001-02, Selanne still struggled, only scoring three goals in his first sixteen games of the year, and twenty-nine goals for the season. While twenty-nine goals was the most on the Sharks, Selanne had fewer minutes per game than in Anaheim and was often frustrated. The Sharks did improve, making the post-season, before losing to the Colorado Avalanche in the Western Conference semi-finals. In 2002, Selanne also got to play for Team Finland at the Winter Olympics.

Though Selanne was an unrestricted free agent in July 2002, he signed a one-year deal with the Sharks worth $6.5 million, three million less than he made the previous year. While Selanne could have signed a bigger, long-term deal somewhere else, he still believed he had the scoring touch the team needed to win the Stanley Cup.

CONTACT INFORMATION

Address: c/o San Jose Sharks, 525 West Santa Clara St., San Jose, California 95113.

FURTHER INFORMATION

Periodicals

Chi, Victor. "Frustration Grows for Sharks' Selanne." *Pittsburgh Post-Gazette* (November 11, 2001): D17.

Habib, Daniel G. et al. "2 San Jose Sharks." *Sports Illustrated* (October 14, 2002): 86.

Howard, Johnette. "Top dog." *Sports Illustrated* (January 27, 1997): 52.

Hurd, Rick. "Selanne Isn't in Hurry to Re-sign." *Pittsburgh Post-Gazette* (September 23, 2001): D13.

Johnson, George. "It's time the Ducks shopped Selanne." *Calgary Herald* (February 20, 2001): D1.

Kennedy, Kostya. "Unugly Duck." *Sports Illustrated* (April 20, 1998): 36.

McKeon, Ross. "No trade secret to say Selanne isn't going anywhere." *San Francisco Chronicle* (February 12, 2002): C3.

McKeon, Ross. "San Jose's Offense Wakes Up." *San Francisco Chronicle* (March 20, 2001): E1.

McKeon, Ross. "Selanne Eyes Comeback, Cup." *San Francisco Chronicle* (March 11, 2001): C11.

McKeon, Ross. "Selanne: Money isn't everything." *San Francisco Chronicle* (September 15, 2002): B3.

McKeon, Ross. "Selanne's part of team at last." *San Francisco Chronicle* (December 16, 2001): B16.

McKeon, Ross. "Sharks Get a Fine Finn." *San Francisco Chronicle* (March 6, 2001): D1.

McKeon, Ross. "Sharks' Scout Goes Way Back with 'Flash'." *San Francisco Chronicle* (March 6, 2001): D8.

McKeon, Ross. "Teemu's thumb could cost Sharks." *San Francisco Chronicle* (April 21, 2001): E1.

Ratto, Ray. "Only sniping with Selanne is coming from his stick." *San Francisco Chronicle* (May 12, 2002): B1.

Ratto, Ray. "Selanne forever stuck with an empty feeling." *San Francisco Chronicle* (May 16, 2002): C1.

Scher, Jon. "Teemu Selanne." *Sports Illustrated* (March 29, 1993): 36.

"Selanne, Newest Shark, Faces Knee Surgery." *Dayton Daily News* (March 7, 2001).

"Selanne Staying with San Jose." *Pittsburgh Post-Gazette* (July 6, 2002): C8.

"Selanne to skate with Sharks on Friday." Associated Press (March 15, 2001).

Stevens, Neil. "Selanne swept away by trade winds."
Calgary Herald (March 6, 2001): C1.

Turula, Marius. "Selanne, Koivu lead Finns for
Olympics." Associated Press (March 23, 2001).

Wigge, Larry. "Not just a shot in the dark." *Sporting
News* (January 8, 2001): 44.

Woodburn, Graig. "Ducks send Selanne to San Jose."
Press-Enterprise (March 6, 2001): C1.

Woodburn, Graig. "Selanne's stick change helps snap
goal slump." *Press-Enterprise* (January 9, 2001): C3.

Other

"Roy Wilson is Sharks New Coach." San Jose Sharks
Web Site. http://www.sjsharks.com/sharks/news/
20021204-1039036671.htm (December 16, 2002).

"Teemu Selanne," ESPN.com. http://sports.espn.go.com
/nhl/players/statistics?statsId=500 (December 14,
2002).

Sketch by A. Petruso

Monica Seles

Monica Seles
1973-

Yugoslav tennis player

With youth, personality and talent on her side, as
well as a number one ranking and one of the
game's most memorable grunts, Monica Seles put power
into her shots and dominated tennis in the early nineties.
But when a crazed fan at a German tournament attacked
her in 1993, her subsequent two years away from the
sport left many wondering if she would ever return;
when she did return, people questioned if she'd ever
come back to full form. She did, and in spite of several
hardships that might have caused lesser players to leave
the game altogether, Seles is back, and once again she
has been ranked with the top players in the world. She
finished the 2002 season with 589 wins, 116 losses, and
53 career singles titles, with 9 Grand Slam singles titles
in her career.

Growing Up

Monica Seles was born December 2, 1973, in Novi
Sad, Yugoslavia, to Karolj and Esther Seles. Her father
worked as a cartoonist and film director and her mother
was a computer programmer. Her brother, Zoltan, also
played tennis, and Monica would take up the game
when she was six, learning from her father the style that
she uses to this day, one that consists of using both
hands to hit her forehand and backhand shots, an unorthodox method that nonetheless allows her to put

more power into her game and be precise with where
shot placement.

As a child, Seles aimed for the cartoon faces that her
father would draw onto the tennis balls. It was soon apparent that she didn't just love practicing, but that she was
somewhat of a tennis prodigy. By the time she was nine—
only three years after taking up the game—she competed
in and won the Yugoslav 12-and-under girls championship. As her youth progressed, she continued to accumulate juniors titles. winning the European 12-and-under
championship when she was ten, and then at twelve earning the title of Yugoslavia's Sportswoman of the Year.

Trip to America

Following her accolades in her home country, it
seemed there was nothing left for Seles to accomplish as
a child superstar in her own country. Soon after she won
the Sportswoman of the Year honors, her family flew to
Florida, where she competed in an American junior
tournament.

It was in Florida that she drew the attention of tennis coach Nick Bollettieri, who also coached the likes
of **Andre Agassi** and **Jim Courier**. Bollettieri offered to
coach the young standout, but like many other tennis
stars, Seles and her family had a tough decision to
make: Bollettieri would not be traveling back to Yugoslavia, and so if they wanted a standout coach for
their daughter, the Seles family would have to part ei-

Chronology

1973	Born December 2, 1973, in Novi Sad, Yugoslavia, to Ester and Karoly Seles
1980	Begins playing tennis; plays in first tournament in the spring and wins
1982	Ranked no. 1 junior player in Yugoslavia
1985	Wins the Orange Bowl in Miami, meets coach Nick Bollettieri and moves to Florida from Yugoslavia to train
1987	Ranked no. 1 junior player in the world
1988	Competes in the Virginia Slims tournament in Boca Raton, Florida (competes as an amateur)
1989	Turns professional at the age of 15
1989	Wins her first professional tournament at the Virginia Slims in Houston in April
1990	Wins her first Grand Slam event—the French Open
1991	Becomes youngest tennis professional tennis player in history to be ranked no. 1 in the world
1991	Wins the French Open, the U.S. Open and the Australian Open
1992	Withdraws from Wimbledon due to shin splints
1992	Wins the French Open, the U.S. Open and the Australian Open
1993	Wins Australian Open
1993	Stabbed in the back on April 30th in the quarterfinals of the Citizen Cup in Hamburg, Germany (she will be away from tennis for almost two years)
1994	Becomes a naturalized U.S. Citizen
1995	Makes her comeback on July 29 and rejoins WTA in August
1995-96	Named to Federation Cup Team
1996	Releases book "From Fear to Victory" in June 1996
1996	Member of U.S. Olympic Tennis Team
1996	Publishes her autobiography, *Monica: From Fear to Victory*
1996	Wins the Australian Open
1997	Wins her 40th title in August
1998	Wins the Tokyo Princess Cup with Anna Kournikova
1998-2000	Again named to Federation Cup Team
2000	Member of U.S. Olympic Tennis Team
2001	Ends season with a thirteen-match winning streak

Awards and Accomplishments

1985	Yugoslavian Sportswoman of the Year
1989	*Tennis* Magazine/Rolex Watch Female Rookie of the Year
1990	Rado Topspin Award for overall sportsmanship and dedication to the game
1990	Sanex WTATour Most Improved Player
1991	Sanex WTA Tour Player of the Year; voted ITF Women's World Champion
1991	Associated Press Female Athlete of the Year
1992	Associated Press Female Athlete of the Year
1992	Sanex WTA Tour Player of the Year; voted ITF Women's World Champion
1995	*Tennis* Magazine Comeback Player of the Year
1995	Sanex WTA Tour Comeback Player of the Year Award
1998	Sanex WTA Tour Comeback Player of the Year Award
1998	Named Female Pro Athlete of the Year by the Florida Sports Hall of Fame
1999	Named Family Circle Cup Player Who Makes a Difference
1999	Awarded the "Commitment to Community" Award by the Florida Times-Union
2000	Named Player of the Decade by ESPN at the ESPY Awards
2000	Named to *Forbes* magazine's Power 100 in Fame and Fortune list at no. 66 (no other female athletes made the list)
2000	Receives the Flo Hyman Memorial Award from the Women's Sports Foundation

then beat Graf in the German Open. Seles continued to chalk up victories, and for such a young star many wondered if she would get a Grand Slam sooner rather than later. They would not have to wait long. Seles picked up her first Grand Slam victory at the French Open, facing Graf yet again at Rolland Garros, but this time defeating her in two sets. Seles had become the youngest player to capture a Grand Slam final.

Rises Fast

From October 3, 1990, to March 18, 1992, Seles made it to the finals of 21 straight tournaments. Graf was still ranked number one in the world, but it seemed that the next great rivalry was in the works (people had loved watching Evert and Navratilova fight over number one in the early eighties). Seles took the Australian Open in 1991, once more making her mark as the youngest victor at a tournament. She repeated the event in Paris at the French Open, then in March ended Steffi Graf's streak of 188 weeks at number one, setting yet another record by becoming the youngest player, male or female, to hold the world number one ranking.

1991 was the year in which fans thought they'd see Seles do what only six other players in tennis history have done: win the Grand Slam (the Australian and French Opens, Wimbledon, and the U.S. Open) in one year. Seles, however, mysteriously pulled out of Wimbledon, citing illness as the cause. The media rumor-mill started to churn, and there was speculation that she might be pregnant. Seles didn't give the press an answer they wanted, simply asking them, "What if I am?" (She wasn't.)

ther with their country or their daughter. They chose to leave their country, giving up their jobs in Yugoslavia and moving the family to Florida. Seles's career became the entire family's focus, and she soon devoted her life to developing her game at Bollettieri's academy where she excelled both on the court and in the classroom.

Young and Professional

Seles chose to turn professional early in 1989. It was not too soon, as she won the second pro tournament she played in by defeating **Chris Evert**, who then came back to beat the 16-year-old later that year at the U.S. Open. But it was a phenomenal start to her career. While **Steffi Graf** dominated women's tennis, Seles earned her wings by playing in the majors. That first year, in addition to playing Evert in the U.S. Open, Seles reached the semifinals of the French Open but lost to the number one Graf in three sets. By the conclusion of the season she had earned a number six ranking. And her career was just beginning.

Her second year on tour didn't disappoint her fans—who were growing in number by the tournament. She won the Italian Open (defeating **Martina Navratilova**),

She returned to the U.S. Open later in the season and defeated Navratilova, who by then was twice Seles's age. The final was not Seles's toughest, but the first set looked as if Navratilova might win one more Grand Slam against the young phenom. After Seles won a grueling first set 7-6, however, she came back to easily win the second set 6-1.

As 1992 wound to a close, it appeared that Seles would reign as the queen of Women's Tennis for years to come. She was only 18, had already won a handful of Grand Slams, and had a number one ranking. She had just finished a season in which she won the Australian Open, and then faced Graf in one of the fiercest French Opens in history. The match saw the tide turn several times, and Seles won the first set 6-2, then lost the second 6-3. By the third set, Seles had flirted with defeat numerous times, but in the end came back and won 10-8, taking the match in what was the "hardest I've ever had to work for a Grand Slam title," she said in *Sports Stars*.

Bizarre Tragedy

In a bizarre incident in the spring of 1993, Seles went through what most sports stars and celebrities fear most. She was attacked on April 30, as she sat courtside at a tennis match in Hamburg, Germany, by an out-of-work German lathe operator named Gunter Parche. The man had moved up behind her and, with both hands on a knife, stabbed her in the back. He was poised to strike again when he was wrestled to the ground, but the damage had been done. At his trial, the judge determined that he no longer posed a threat to anyone, which further served to rattle the scared Seles.

Seles was quickly hospitalized. She soon became paranoid about being the object of another attack. She chose to remain out of the spotlight—and away from tennis—for the next two years. It turned out that Parche was an unstable fan of Graf's with a history of stalking the German tennis star. His intention in stabbing Seles was

to help return Graf to her number one ranking. When Seles finally returned to tennis again in July of 1995 in an exhibition match against Navratilova, she did so because she wanted to represent the U.S. in the 1996 Olympics, making her official return in August. In a move that many players felt was controversial, Seles was allowed to share a number one world ranking with Graf.

More Pain

On New Year's in 1996, Seles learned that her father's stomach cancer had returned and the tumor had metastasized. For the next year and a half she was torn between playing tennis—which her father wanted her to do—and spending time with her father. His death in 1998 was hard on her. "He was everything to her," Wertheim writes, "... parent, best friend, architect of her game. Every act reminds her of his absence."

Her father's illness was reflected in her on-court appearance, and she had lost some of the form she had worked so hard to regain since her attack. After he passed away, in May of 1998, Seles got back on the court to avoid sinking too far into despair. "I was unsure whether I would be ready emotionally and probably tennis-wise," she said in *Sports Stars*. "It was just too tough for me to stay at home. It's so much better for me to be here. It's really tough.... My dad would love me to play. This is what I want to do for the next part of my life. I wish my dad could have seen the end of my career and a lot of other things."

Seles—wearing her father's wedding ring on a chain around her neck—defeated **Martina Hingis** in the semi-finals but eventually lost to **Arantxa Sanchez Vicario** in the final (7-6, 0-6, 6-2). But it was the first time Seles had been in a finals since 1993, and the taste of the competition and center court was what she needed to realize that tennis was truly something she loved.

The match in Paris became a turning point for her following the attack and her father's death. "I don't think the real Monica ever left," she said in *Sports Stars*. "I just think that when there's so many things going on outside your life, it's very difficult to go on a tennis court and be really excited about hitting a ball. Some weeks you can't even go to hit because you're just so sad about what's going on. I was able to concentrate on tennis, which was a very nice feeling. I haven't had it in a long time."

Return to Form

In 2001 Seles reached the finals in two tournaments in California, then made it to the semifinals of the Rogers AT&T Cup in Toronto where she lost to **Serena Williams**. Seles "is playing her best tennis in recent memory," says Jon Wertheim in *Sports Illustrated*. In fact, she recently turned to a new training regimen to improve her stamina, which was never great and which

Monica Seles

had seemed to dissipate since her return from the attack. According to Wertheim, since she has been forbidden to run due to a foot injury, she started a routine that "included biking, swimming and weight training," as well as hiring a new coach, Mike Sell.

Fans love her, and Seles talks to and acknowledges her fans. In spite of the attack and the isolation she imposed on herself for several years, Seles seems more outgoing now than ever; in a sport where most players are hard to get access to, Seles is one of the more friendly and approachable stars on the circuit. It is a big part of her popularity, and it is a main reason she has the following she does. "She engages whoever stops her, grins, thanks the person, [and] asks questions," S. L. Price writes in *Sports Illustrated,* mentioning that some of Seles' closest friends were complete strangers she met in a restaurant or at a club.

Sometimes, however, those close to her—her mother, her trainers and coaches—worry that her friendliness may get her back into trouble. According to that same *Sports Illustrated* article, in 1997 she accepted a ride from the airport with someone she had only just met on the plane.

Yet true to the dynamics of her personality, she is also a solitary individual. When she craves her privacy, it is almost impossible to get her out in public. And when she wants to be outgoing, you cannot turn her off. Since the attack, however, she has been able to mitigate what the world wants with what Seles wants. "I was definitely a pleaser," she told *Sports Illustrated* in 1998. "Even until last year I always wanted everybody to like me... Then I realized: Just be who you are. You don't have to make everybody else happy if you're really not happy. I realized with my dad, when he was dying, that everything is so much a facade. The only time you're true to yourself is when you die. You have no pretensions. I don't want to wait until I'm dying to be like that."

With youth, personality and talent on her side, as well as a number one ranking and one of the game's most memorable grunts, Monica Seles put power into her shots and dominated tennis in the early nineties. But when she was attacked by a crazed fan at a German tournament in 1993, the subsequent two years away from the sport left many wondering if she had ever return; when she did return, people questioned if she had ever come back to full form.

But she did return, and in spite of several hardships that might have caused lesser players to leave the game altogether, Seles is back and once again one of the top ten players in the world. At the conclusion of the 2002 season, her career record stood at 589 wins, 116 losses, and 53 career singles titles, with 9 Grand Slam singles titles.

CONTACT INFORMATION

Address: c/o Linda Dozoretz Communications, 8033 Sunset Blvd, Suite 6226, Los Angeles, CA 90046.

SELECTED WRITINGS BY SELES:

(With Nancy Ann Richardson) *Monica: From Fear to Victory.* Harper Collins, 1996.

FURTHER INFORMATION

Books

Collins, Bud and Zander Hollander, eds. *Bud Collins' Modern Encyclopedia of Tennis,* 2nd ed. Detroit: Visible Ink Press, 1994.

Layden, Joseph. *Return of a Champion: The Monica Seles Story.* New York: St. Martin's Press, 1996.

"Monica Seles." *DISCovering Biography.* Detroit: Gale Research, 1997.

"Monica Seles." *Great Women in Sports.* Detroit: Visible Ink Press, 1996.

"Monica Seles." *Sports Stars,* Series 1-4. U•X•L, 1994-98.

"Monica Seles." *St. James Encyclopedia of Popular Culture,* 5 vols. Detroit: St. James Press, 2000.

Schwabacher, Martin. "Monica Seles." *Superstars of Women's Tennis.* Philadelphia: Chelsea House, 1997.

Seles, Monica and Nancy Ann Richardson. *Monica: From Fear to Victory.* New York: Harper Collins, 1996.

Periodicals

Detroit Free Press (June 7, 1995): C2.

Howard, Johnette. "Home Alone." *Sports Illustrated* (April 10, 1995): 44.

Los Angeles Times (May 28, 1996; June 5, 1996; June 27, 1996; September 9, 1996; September 3, 1997; May 27, 1998).

New York Times (May 27, 1991; March 19, 1995; April 30, 1995; July 9, 1995).

Price, S. L. "There's Something About Monica." *Sports Illustrated* (September 7, 1998): 56-60.

Shmerler, C. "A game of inches." *Tennis* (September 2000): 70.

Sports Illustrated (June 19, 1988; August 22, 1988; June 18, 1990; May 27, 1991; July 15, 1991; September 16, 1991; June 15, 1992; July 13, 1992; November 30, 1992; June 14, 1993; September 20, 1993; June 19, 1995; July 17, 1995; August 7, 1995; February 5, 1996; April 7, 1997).

USA Today (May 24, 1996; June 11, 1996; July 30, 1996; September 9, 1996; June 5, 1997; May 27, 1998): C2.

Wertheim, L. Jon. "New Training Regimen Pays Off." *Sports Illustrated* (August 27, 2001): 88.

Other

"Monica-Seles.com." Website for Monica Seles fans. http://www.monica-seles.com (January 22, 2003).

Monica Seles news online. http://www.wso.net/monicaseles/ (January 23, 2003).

Sketch by Eric Lagergren

Bud Selig
1934-

American baseball commissioner

As Major League Baseball (MLB) commissioner for more than a decade (the first six as acting commissioner), Bud Selig has won few friends. In fact, he seems to have an uncanny ability to do things that will enrage the maximum number of people in and around the game. Even when Selig engineered a last-minute compromise settlement between players and owners to avert a season-ending baseball strike in the late summer of 2002, he came under fire for his absence from negotiations until the eleventh hour. This only added to the list of the most recent grievances against Selig, which include his widely reviled decision to end the 2002 All-

Bud Selig

Star game after the 11th inning, a late-2001 proposal to eliminate two or more teams from MLB, and his strong support of testing to detect the use of steroids and other drugs by players. There's no question that Selig is in a delicate position. A great deal of passion surrounds the American pastime, and it's only logical that decisions that favor owners over players very likely would earn Selig the enmity of the players, or vice-versa. However, Selig in recent years has been unable to make anyone—players, fans, or even owners—very happy.

Born in Milwaukee

He was born Allan H. Selig in Milwaukee, Wisconsin, on July 30, 1934. Son of Ben (owner of a car dealership) and Marie (an elementary school teacher) Selig, he inherited his love of baseball mostly from his mother. An avid baseball fan, Marie Selig followed the exploits of the area's major league teams—the Chicago White Sox and the Chicago Cubs—on her kitchen radio. Whenever possible, young Selig tried to attend local games, and in high school he joined the baseball team, aspiring someday to get into major league ball. Before long, he accepted that his lack of any notable talent on the ball field meant he would have to try to get into the game through the front office.

In 1956, after graduating from the University of Wisconsin with a bachelor's degree in American history and political science, Selig served in the U.S. Army for two years. Returning from military service in 1958, he

Chronology

1934	Born July 30 in Milwaukee, Wisconsin
1956	Earns B.A. degree from University of Wisconsin in Madison
1956-58	Serves in U.S. Army
1969	Makes unsuccessful bid to bring the Chicago White Sox to Milwaukee
1970	The Brewers, an organization headed by Selig, acquires Seattle Pilots for $10.8 million
1977	Marries Suzanne Lappin Steinman
1992	Elected chairman of major league baseball's executive council, effectively becoming interim chairman
1998	Formally elected baseball commissioner by club owners

Awards and Accomplishments

1959	Named president of Selig Executive Leasing Company
1978	Named UPI's Major League Executive of the Year
1981	Received International B'nai B'rith Sportsman of the Year Award
1983	Named Sportsman of the Year by U.S. Olympic Committee
1989	Received August A. Busch Jr. Award for service to baseball
1994	Named Wisconsin's Top Sports Personality of Past 25 Years
2002	Engineered settlement averting players' strike

joined his father in running the family's Ford dealership. Not long thereafter, his father died, leaving the business to his son. Selig had obviously inherited a knack for business from his father, for the dealership prospered under his guidance, generating enough profit to allow him to diversify his business holdings. He made a substantial investment in Jake's, a popular Jewish deli in Milwaukee, that in time proved even more profitable than the auto dealership.

Seeks Ball Club for Milwaukee

Selig's love of baseball remained strong. When the Braves moved to Milwaukee from Boston in 1953, he became an avid supporter and eventually became the largest public investor in the team. Shortly after the Braves decamped for Atlanta in 1965, Selig formed an organization called Teams Inc., dedicated to bringing major league baseball back to Milwaukee. Teams Inc., which later changed its name to The Brewers, made an unsuccessful bid for the Chicago White Sox in 1969 but a year later got lucky when a federal bankruptcy referee awarded the failing Seattle Pilots to the organization. Shortly thereafter, Selig, the principal owner, was named president of the Brewers organization.

In sharp contrast with his current situation as baseball commissioner, Selig was widely praised for his management of the Brewers franchise. Twelve years after the team made its new home in Milwaukee, the Brewers advanced to the World Series, where they lost to the St. Louis Cardinals in seven games. The Brewers won an unprecedented three consecutive Baseball America awards in 1985, 1986, and 1987, and in 1978 Selig himself was named Major League Executive of the Year by United Press International.

Heads Major League Executive Council

In September 1992, when Fay Vincent resigned under pressure as baseball commissioner, Selig's fellow club owners named him chairman of the Major League Executive Council. Since the Major League Agreement gives the Executive Council the right to regulate baseball in the absence of a commissioner, Selig became the de-

facto commissioner. In his new post, he pressed for some sort of revenue-sharing arrangement under which the larger, more profitable teams, such as the New York Yankees, would help to subsidize smaller franchises, such as Selig's own Milwaukee Brewers. Selig also called for a cap on player salaries and an end to arbitration to settle salary disputes. His support of these issues endeared him to many of his fellow owners but won him no friends among the players.

Less than two years after taking over as acting commissioner, Selig faced his first big challenge in the form of a players strike in 1994. After the players struck on August 12, Selig worked hard to promote owner unity. As the strike dragged on into early September with no end in sight, Selig cancelled the rest of the season, including the World Series. Not until the beginning of the 1995 season was the strike ended, and then only by a court injunction ordering baseball to go back to its previous collective bargaining agreement while negotiations continued. A new contract was eventually hammered out, but the bitterness between owners and players lingered long after the settlement. And for Selig, the 1994 strike signaled an end to the two-year honeymoon he'd enjoyed with the media, which now turned on him with a vengeance. Pete Pascarelli of *Sporting News* wrote that Selig was "willing to crush the game into an unrecognizable mess," adding that baseball was "on the brink of utter ruin under his watch."

Criticism of Selig Grows

In the eight years between the 1994 strike and the threatened strike of 2002, Selig did little to redeem himself in the eyes of the media, players, and baseball fans. His stock among ball club owners even began to erode. Although some of his ideas appeared to make good sense, it seemed somehow that Selig had become the man to hate, and nothing he did could reverse his dramatic decline in popularity. After the World Series in 2001, Selig announced that it might be necessary to eliminate two or more teams in order to ensure the survival of Major League Baseball. Then came his disastrous decision to end the 2002 All-Star Game after the 11th inning. Among players, Selig won few fans with his continuing push for routine drug testing. By the end of the 2002 baseball season, calls for Selig to step down had reached a fever pitch.

Selig, a man who once said that he wanted more than anything to be liked, seemed to be holding up well in the face of the almost universal approbation he was facing early in the new millennium. Whether he draws strength from his lifelong love of the game he now administers or from a firm conviction in the rightness of his ideas, we can only speculate. But it doesn't look like Selig has plans of stepping down anytime soon.

Selig and his wife, the former Suzanne Lappin Steinman, have two daughters, Sari and Wendy. Away from baseball, both he and his wife are involved in a wide variety of humanitarian and charitable causes, including the Milwaukee Brewers Child Abuse Prevention (CAP) Fund, which Selig co-founded in December 1987.

CONTACT INFORMATION

Address: Office of the Commissioner of Baseball, 245 Park Ave., 31st Fl., New York, NY 10167. Phone: (212) 931-7800.

FURTHER INFORMATION

Books

"Bud Selig." *Newsmakers 1995,* Issue 4. Detroit: Gale Group, 1995.
"Fay Vincent." *Newsmakers 1990,* Issue 2. Detroit: Gale Group, 1990.

Periodicals

Burwell, Bryan. "With Selig at Helm, Baseball Has Lost a Lot of Its Appeal." *St. Louis Post-Dispatch* (October 28, 2002): C1.
Corliss, Richard. "In Defense of Bud Selig." *Time* (July 12, 2002).
Hyman, Mark. "Bud Selig's Turn at Bat." *Business Week* (November 6, 2000).
Le Batard, Dan. "Where Once There Was Glory, Vincent Can Only See Gloom." *Miami Herald* (July 15, 2002).
Mann, Dinn. "Behind the Scenes with Bud Selig." *MLB.com* (January 30, 2001).
Propson, David. "Opinion: Bud Selig, Reviled Savior." *Flak* (August 26, 2002).
Reaves, Jessica. "Person of the Week: Bud Selig." *Time* (August 29, 2002).
Ryan, Allan. "Not Much Respect for Baseball's Bud." *Toronto Star* (September 5, 2002).

Other

"Bud Selig: 1992-Present." Sports Encyclopedia. http://www.sportsecyclopedia.com/mlb/comish/selig.html (November 11, 2002).
"Bud Selig, Born: 1934." BaseballLibrary.com. http://www.pubdim.net/baseballlibrary/ballplayers/S/Selig_Bud.stm (November 11, 2002).
"The Secret of Bud Selig's Success." RoadsidePhotos.com. http://roadsidephotos.com/baseball/secret.htm (November 11, 2002).

Sketch by Don Amerman

Sterling Sharpe
1965-

American football player

A wide receiver for the Green Bay Packers from 1988 to 1994, Sterling Sharpe made it to five Pro Bowls with his team during his career. A receiver of exceptional ability, Sharpe is the first player in the National Football League (NFL) to make 500 catches before playing seven seasons in the NFL. In 1993, Sharpe's 112 receptions broke the record for the most number of receptions in a single season. In his last season, in 1994, his 18 touchdown receptions were the best in the league. A spinal injury he suffered in December 1994 forced an early retirement for Sharpe, and in 1995, he became an analyst for ESPN, working on the *NFL GameDay* and *NFL Prime Monday* shows.

Sterling Sharpe was born in Chicago in 1965. When he was still in elementary school, he and his family moved to farm country near Savannah, George, where their grandparents lived.

Sterling Sharpe

Sharpe knew from an early age that he wanted to play pro football. So did his brother, Shannon Sharpe, and both eventually realized their dream. As their high school football coach, William Hall told the *Star Tribune*'s Patrick Reusse, "They kind of knew what they wanted to do—those two young men. When they would come back from college in the summer, I would get a call, and I would go down and open the weight room for them. Sterling and Shannon were dedicated athletes. And, said Hall, "Sterling put us on the map for the college recruiters."

Sharpe was playing football seriously by the time he was in junior high school. While playing on his junior high school team, he attracted the notice of his future high school football coach, William Hall. Hall later told Reusse, "The first play I ever saw Sterling Sharpe was a kickoff, and he brought it back for a touchdown. That was quite an impression."

Sharpe excelled on the high school football team as well as on the track team, where he developed a reputation for playing through painful injuries. He took his track team to the state finals, where he injured a leg winning first place in the long jump. Over the protests of his coach, he immediately ran the relay, taking second place in spite of his bad leg. Shannon Sharpe, too, played on the high school football team and ran on the track team, where he broke the state long jump record for his class.

Sharpe attended college at the University of South Carolina. There he played on the school football team, breaking numerous school records, including those for career receptions (169), receiving yards (2,497), and receiving touchdowns (17).He graduated in 1988 with a double major in interdisciplinary studies and retailing.

On graduation, Sharpe was the number one draft choice of the Green Bay Packers. He became a starting wide receiver immediately, playing a total of seven years for the team—from 1988 to 1994. With an intense focus on the game, he avoided giving interviews to the media and signing autographs. His brother, Shannon told Jon Saraceno of *USA Today* in 1994 that Sharpe refused to give interviews because he felt he was treated unfairly by the press in his rookie year. "He hasn't been willing to forgive or forget."

From the beginning, Sharpe was exceptional, in his first season catching more passes, 55, than any other rookie in the history of the Packers. Even so, he felt he could do better, according to the *Milwaukee Journal*'s Bob McGinn, as reported by Saraceno the following year, "I didn't really go out with the intensity the other guys played with. I continued to play with the same college attitude. I'm going to change my work habits in practice."

In 1989, Sharpe was selected for the Pro Bowl. That year he caught 90 passes for a total of 1,423 yards. The press loved him, but still he refused to grant interviews, a practice he was to carry on throughout through his career. In a rare interview on a radio station in Green Bay, said Saraceno, Sharpe hinted that his silence was a kind of revenge for being written about unfavorably at the start of his pro career. "It's one way of me saying, 'Guys, for what you did to me back then, I'm finally getting a chance to pay you back.'"

Sharpe's younger brother Shannon Sharpe followed Sharpe into the NFL as a player for the Denver Broncos in 1990. Shannon started as a wide receiver, then switched to tight end, becoming a starter in 1991, and a Pro Bowl player in 1992. In 1992, Sharpe and his brother became the only brothers to have led their separate teams in receiving in the same year.

In 1992, Sharpe made 108 receptions, and the following year, his 112 receptions broke the NFL record for the most receptions in a single season. He eventually caught more passes than any one else in the history of the Packers. He also set a Packers' record by playing 103 straight games with at least one pass reception.

Career Statistics

Yr	Team	Receiving				Rushing				
		REC	YDS	AVG	TD	ATT	YDS	AVG	TD	FUM
1988	GB	55	791	14.4	1	4	-2	-0.5	0	3
1989	GB	90	1423	15.8	12	2	25	12.5	0	1
1990	GB	67	1105	16.5	6	2	14	7.0	0	0
1991	GB	69	961	13.9	4	4	4	1.0	0	1
1992	GB	108	1461	13.5	13	4	8	2.0	0	2
1993	GB	112	1274	11.4	11	4	8	2.0	0	1
1994	GB	94	1119	11.9	18	3	15	5.0	0	1
TOTAL		595	8134	13.7	65	23	72	3.1	0	9

GB: Green Bay Packers.

Awards and Accomplishments

1988	Set Green Bay Packers team record for most receptions by a rookie
1993	Set National Football League record for most number of receptions in a single season
1993	Set Packers record for most games in a row with at least one pass reception
1994	Led the National Football League in touchdown receptions
1994	Became first National Football League player to catch at least 100 passes two seasons in a row

In January, 1994, Sharpe was instrumental in the Packers' winning their first playoff game of the 1990s. With only a little over a minute remaining on the clock, Sharpe made a 40-yard touchdown to beat the Detroit Lions 28-24—his third touchdown of the game. Not only did he win the game for the Packers, but he became the first receiver in the history of the NFL to catch 100 or more passes two season in a row.

Sharpe's performance in 1994 was all the more remarkable considering that an injury known as turf toe kept him from practicing with his team for half of the season. Sharpe's turf toe was a painful hyperextension of his left big toe. "I wear a size 8 1/2 or size 9," he told Frank Litsky of the *New York Times,* "and I can't wear that size shoe. I have to wear a 10 on my left leg. It's very painful to go out and try to play. You're not able to do the things you're accustomed to doing. You really can't go out and be the type of player that you want to be. You've got to try and improvise."

But Sharpe's improvisation could not save his game after he suffered a debilitating injury to the top two vertebrae in his neck. The injury occurred when his neck snapped back while blocking a player in a game. Although he received a clean bill of health immediately following the incident, the injury worsened when he was tackled in the next game he played, resulting in numbness and tingling in his limbs. The team physician, Patrick McKenzie declared that Sharpe would require surgery to fuse the dangerously loose vertebrae. It was the final blow to Sharpe's career, and it forced his retirement from the game.

In 1995, the year after he retired from playing football, Sharpe became a broadcaster for ESPN, analyzing games for the *NFL GameDay* and *NFL Prime Monday* shows. Since leaving the Packers, Sharpe has also become part owner and chief executive officer of Pro Bowl Motors, an auto purchasing and selling service in Columbia, South Carolina, where he lives.

FURTHER INFORMATION

Periodicals

"Injury Could End Sharpe's Career." *New York Times* (December 29, 1994): B10.

Litsky, Frank. "For Packers' Sharpe, the Hurt Had Better Go Away Soon." *New York Times* (January 14, 1994): B9.

Reusse, Patrick. "Sharpe Brothers Make Granny Proud." *Star Tribune* (December 18, 1993): 1C.

Saraceno, Jon. "Younger Sharpe Speaks for Elder." *Star Tribune* (January 12, 1994): 4C.

Other

"All-Century Team: Sterling Sharpe." PackersNews. com. http://www.packersnews.com/archives/allcentury/ hsterlingsharp.shtml (December 16, 2002).

Pro Bowl Motors. http://www.probowlmotors.com (December 16, 2002).

"Spend a Day at ESPN's NFL GameDay!" Stargiving. com. http://www.stargiving.com/events/all_event_ info.php3?event_id=20 (December 16, 2002).

"Sterling Sharpe." Jt-sw.com. http://www.jt-sw.com/ football/pro/players.nsf/ID/06940180 (December 16, 2002).

Sketch by Michael Belfiore

Jack Shea
1910-2002

American speed skater

Jack Shea's two Olympic gold medals were only the beginning of his lifelong involvement with the Olympic Games. After his speed skating victories in his hometown of Lake Placid in 1932, Shea raised another Olympian, his son James, while staying involved in the Olympic movement. Shea was a major figure in the drive to bring the winter Olympics back to Lake Placid in 1980, and in 2001, Shea became the patriarch of the first family ever to have three generations of Olympians when James Shea's son, Jim Jr., qualified to compete in skeleton at the 2002 Salt Lake City Games.

Olympic Spirit

Shea was a sophomore at Dartmouth College when the Olympics came to Lake Placid in 1932. The winter Olympics were only eight years old then, but Lake Placid speed skaters had already made their mark: the first gold medal in the first Winter Olympics, the 1924 Chamonix, France, games, was won by a young man from Lake Placid named Charles Jewtraw. Shea dreamed of following in Jewtraw's footsteps, and hours after taking the Olympic oath on behalf of the American team he did, winning the 500-meter speed skating event, the first event of the 1932 games. Shea also took the 1500-meter, giving him one-third of the American team's six gold medals that year.

Much had changed in Shea's life by the time the 1936 Olympics rolled around. He graduated from Dartmouth in 1934, married, and spent a year at Albany Law School, but he was forced to drop out when the Depression removed his family's ability to cover the tuition. Shea returned to Lake Placid and worked at his family's market and as a mailman.

Shea was still one of the top speed skaters in the world in 1936, but he did not compete in the Olympics that year, which were held in Berlin, Germany. Shea was a political science major at Dartmouth, so he was perhaps more aware than most of the dangers posed by the Nazi ideology. Also, he knew and respected many Jewish customers who patronized his family's market, and he did not want to give legitimacy to a regime which was so anti-Semetic. Some say that the rabbi of the community asked him personally not to participate.

Although Shea would not compete in the Olympics again, he remained involved with them. Shea was active in Lake Placid community life for years, rubbing shoulders with the numerous past and future Olympians who lived and trained there. While working as the supervisor of the township which includes Lake Placid, Shea was instrumental in bringing the Olympics back to Lake

Jack Shea

Placid in 1980. Shea also raised an Olympian, his son James, who competed in several skiing events in 1964 but did not medal. In the years before his death, Shea was outspoken in his opposition to holding the 2008 Olympics in Beijing, China because of that country's checkered human rights record.

A New Olympic Record

The Shea family reached a milestone on December 20, 2001. That day, when Shea's grandson Jim Jr. qualified for the Olympic skeleton team, they became the first family ever to have three generations of Olympians. Shea was there, watching the World Cup skeleton meet in Lake Placid, when the youngest Shea qualified, and he was looking forward to watching his grandson compete at the Olympics in two months. Other Olympians and Olympic organizers were impressed with the family as well, and plans were made to honor Shea, the oldest living American to have won a gold medal at a Winter Olympics, at the Salt Lake City games. Jim Shea Jr. was selected to recite the Olympic oath for the American team, just as his grandfather had seventy years before.

But Shea would not be there to be honored, to see his grandson take the Olympic oath, or to see him come from behind on the last segment of the course to win the gold medal in skeleton by a mere five hundredths of a second. Shea was struck by an allegedly drunk driver less than a mile from his Lake Placid home on January 21, 2002. He died the next day.

Chronology

1910	Born September 7 in Lake Placid, New York
1932	Competes in Olympics in Lake Placid
1934	Graduates from Dartmouth College
1934	Marries Elizabeth Stearnes
1936	Refuses to compete in Olympics in protest of their being held in Nazi Germany
1958-78	Serves as town justice of Lake Placid
1964	Shea's son James competes in cross-country and nordic combined skiing at Olympics in Innsbruck, Austria
1974-83	Serves as township supervisor of North Elba
1980	Instrumental in bringing Winter Olympics back to Lake Placid
2001	Becomes member of only family with three generations of Olympians when grandson Jim Shea Jr. qualifies for the U. S. Olympic skeleton team in Lake Placid December 20
2001	Carries the Olympic flame in Lake Placid December 29
2002	Dies January 22 after being struck by an allegedly drunk driver on the 21st
2002	Jim Shea Jr. wins Olympic gold in skeleton February 19

Awards and Accomplishments

1929	National speedskating championships
1930	National speedskating championships
1932	Gold Medal in Olympic 500- and 1500-meter speed skating
2000	Became first recipient of U.S. Speedskating's Jack Shea Award

In a gesture of which Shea, a lifelong embodiment of the Olympic spirit, would surely have approved, Jim Shea Jr. mailed one of the runners off of his winning skeleton sled to Yoshida in return. "This is what the Olympics are all about," Jim Shea Jr. said, as quoted by Dwyre. "My grandfather loved the friendships. He loved to do nice things for the other athletes."

The Olympic Saga Continues

Shea's Olympic story did not end with his death. It did not even end with Jim Shea Jr.'s emotional victory, which Jim Jr. attributed to his grandfather's spirit riding with him that day. Shea's image rode with him as well, on a funeral card bearing the man's picture which Jim Jr. tucked into his helmet and tearfully displayed to the crowds, who were chanting "U-S-Shea! U-S-Shea!," at the end of his run. Shea's Olympic saga ended with the return of the skates which Shea wore when he skated his way to gold in 1932.

A young Japanese skier, Katsumi Yamada, also competed at Lake Placid in 1932. Shea gave his winning skates to Yamada as a gesture of international friendship, and in return, Yamada gave Shea his cross-country skis. In 1955, Yamada gave the skates to a coworker's son, Kozo Yoshida, who was an aspiring speed skater. (Coincidentally, Yamada and Yoshida's father worked together at the city hall of Sapporo, Japan, the city where the 1972 Winter Olympics were held.) Yoshida wore the skates to compete in the Japanese high school skating championships for three straight years, and then wore them occasionally for recreational skating for the next forty-odd years.

Yoshida was in his sixties when he read about Shea's death in the Japanese newspaper *Yomiuri Shimbun*. In a ceremony a few day's after Jim Shea Jr.'s winning skeleton run, the managing editor of *Yomiuri Shimbun*, Kazuhiro Takaoka, unwrapped the skates and presented them to the Jim Sheas, Jr. and Sr. Tears sprung to Jim Shea Sr.'s eyes when he saw what was on the underside of one skate. "It's my dad's signature, see right there," Jim Shea Sr. was quoted as saying by Bill Dwyre in the *Los Angeles Times*. "This is unbelievable. I'm not sure I really believed it until I saw that." Jim Shea Sr. told the assembled reporters that he planned to donate the skates and the skis to the Lake Placid Olympic Museum.

FURTHER INFORMATION

Periodicals

"After Long Journey, Shea's Skates Returned." *Buffalo News* (February 25, 2002): S7.

Barron, David. "Oldest Winter Games Gold Medalist Dies." *Houston Chronicle* (January 23, 2002): 10.

Barron, David. "Third-Generation Olympian Embraces Oath." *Houston Chronicle* (February 8, 2002): 8.

Blinebury, Fran. "Heaven Sent: Elder Shea's Spirit Alive and Golden in Grandson's Stirring Run." *Houston Chronicle* (February 21, 2002): 1.

Borzilleri, Meri-Jo. "Not How It Was Supposed to Be: Death Is Cruel End to Family's Dream." *Gazette* (Colorado Springs, CO) (January 23, 2002): SP1.

"Dead Star's Commercial Plays On." *New York Post* (January 31, 2002): 70.

Drake, Kate. Obituary for Jack Shea. *Time International* (February 4, 2002): 16.

Dwyre, Bill. "Their Greatest Gift: A Pair of Jack Shea's Skates Are Presented to His Son and Grandson, Providing Fitting Coda to Family's Inspiring Story." *Los Angeles Times* (February 22, 2002): U-4.

Gregorian, Vahe. "The Shea Family: Jim Jr. Loses His Grandfather Days Before Joining Him As an Olympian." *St. Louis Post-Dispatch* (January 27, 2002): C8.

Hersh, Philip. "1932 Gold Medalist Dies in Crash: Shea Was First of Three Generations of Olympians." *Knight Ridder/Tribune News Service* (January 22, 2002): K4724.

Kelley, Steve. "Inspiration Powers Shea Down Skeleton Course." *Knight Ridder/Tribune News Service* (February 20, 2002): K4391.

Litsky, Frank. "Jack Shea, 91; Won Two Olympic Golds in '32." *New York Times* (January 23, 2002): A16.

Meyer, John. "Holding Up Olympic Legacy: Salt Lake Would Be Third Generation." *Denver Post* (October 31, 2001): D-07.

Parrish, Paula. "Patriarch of Three-Generation Olympic Family Dies." *Rocky Mountain News* (Denver, CO) (January 23, 2002): 1C.

Pucin, Diane. "'32 Gold Medalist Shea, 91, Is Killed." *Los Angeles Times* (January 23, 2002): D-1.

Robertson, Linda. "Shea, Oldest Living U.S. Winter Olympic Gold Medalist, Killed in Car Crash." *Knight Ridder/Tribune News Service* (January 22, 2002): K4803.

"Shea Family Mourns Loss of Patriarch." *Denver Post* (February 25, 2002): D-01.

"Sheas Get Look at Family Heirloom." *Tampa Tribune* (February 25, 2002): 5.

"Spirit on Board: Skeleton Winner Says Late Grandpa Helped Push Sled to Golden Victory." *Denver Post* (February 21, 2002): A-01.

Swift, E. M. "The Olympic Family." *Sports Illustrated* (December 17, 2001): 106+.

"Third Generation Headed to Winter Games." *Capper's* (January 8, 2002): 2.

Tomasson, Chris. "Shea Wins One for His Grandfather." *Knight Ridder/Tribune News Service* (February 20, 2002): K4314.

Vaughan, Kevin. Day-by-day Olympic summary. *Rocky Mountain News* (Denver, CO) (March 2, 2002): 15S, 19S.

Other

"Shea, 91, Among Three Generations of Olympians." ESPN Classic. http://espn.go.com/classic/obit/s/2002/0122/1315383.html (January 22, 2002).

"Shea's 1932 Golden Skates Back in Family." CNN/Sports Illustrated. http://sportsillustrated.cnn.com/olympics/2002/skeleton/news/2002/02/24/shea_skates_ap/ (February 24, 2002).

United States Olympic Committee. http://www.olympic-usa.org/ (October 16, 2002).

Sketch by Julia Bauder

Gary Sheffield

happy, however, he is a consistent offensive force, combining a high batting average and on-base percentage with power. Sheffield, who at one time was the highest-paid player in the game, is a prime example of the modern baseball star: highly paid, self-protective, and more concerned about individual performance than team loyalty.

Fearless and Promising

Gary Sheffield learned to be fearless at any early age. He grew up in the tough Belmont Heights section of Tampa, Florida. His mother, Betty, was 17 when he was born, and he never knew his father. For the first seven years of his life he lived with his stepfather, Harold Jones, his mother and his mother's younger brother, Gooden. By the time Gary was six years old, he was playing ball every day with Gooden, a future star for the New York Mets. Gooden already had a menacing fastball, and Sheffield learned to catch it and hit it. Hitting against Gooden helped him develop quick hands — the most important element in a batter's arsenal. Sheffield also often swung a broomstick in his front yard and tried to hit rocks his stepfather tossed at him.

Young Sheffield also developed a quick temper. He frequently got into fights at school, in the neighborhood, and on the ball field. On one occasion in Little League, Sheffield was benched for missing a practice and chased his coach around the field with a bat. He was suspended and had to miss the league championship game. Later, Sheffield appeared in the Little League World Series

Gary Sheffield
1968-

American baseball player

One of the most feared sluggers in baseball, Gary Sheffield has had a controversial, up-and-down career. The nephew of Dwight Gooden, the once overpowering pitcher of the New York Mets, he overcame an upbringing in a rough neighborhood in Tampa and became the top high school player in the nation. Frequently traded and often injured, Sheffield has been quick to criticize management wherever he has played. When healthy and

<table>
<tr><td colspan="2">

Chronology

</td></tr>
</table>

Chronology	
1980	Plays in Little League World Series
1982	Pitches on team that wins Senior Little League World Series
1986	Drafted by Milwaukee Brewers with sixth pick overall
1988	Gets winning hit in major league debut for Milwaukee Brewers
1991	Traded to San Diego Padres
1992	Wins National League batting championship
1992-93, 1996, 1998-2000	National League All-Star team
1993	Traded to Florida Marlins
1997	Leads Marlins to World Series victory
1998	Traded to Los Angeles Dodgers
2002	Traded to Atlanta Braves

Awards and Accomplishments	
1986	USA Today's Top High School Baseball Player
1988	Sporting News Minor League Co-player of the Year
1992	Sporting News Major Legue Player of the Year
1992	Wins National League batting championship
1996	Leads National League in on-base percentage

when his junior team lost to Taiwan, 4-3, in the 1980 championship game. Two years later, Sheffield pitched his senior Little League team to the 1982 world title.

At Hillsborough High School, Sheffield was a dominant force as a pitcher and third baseman and attracted so much attention from scouts that he was named the nation's top high school baseball player by *USA Today*. As a pitcher, he displayed a 90-mile-an-hour fastball, but his hitting overshadowed his pitching, with a .500 average, 15 home runs and no strikeouts in 62 at-bats. The Milwaukee Brewers selected him as the sixth pick overall in the 1986 draft and gave him a $152,000 signing bonus. Off the field Sheffield had problems, already fathering two children by different mothers.

Sheffield rocketed through the Brewers' minor league system. In a rookie league, he batted .365 at Helena, Montana, playing mostly at shortstop, an unfamiliar position. After the season, he, Gooden and two others were arrested after a traffic stop in Tampa for fighting with a police officer and resisting arrest; Sheffield pleaded no contest and was given two years' probation.

The next season Sheffield knocked in 103 runs at Class A Stockton. In 1988 he hit a combined .327 with 28 home runs and 119 runs batted in at Class AA El Paso and Class AAA Denver. At Denver he was moved back to third base because he had made too many throwing errors at shortstop. He was named minor league co-player of the year by the *Sporting News* and was called up to Milwaukee for his big-league debut. On September 3, 1988, he broke into the majors in dramatic fashion, hitting a game-tying home run in the ninth inning and driving in the winning run with a single in the 11th. When Milwaukee's regular shortstop, Dale Sveum, was injured, Sheffield was placed there and made several dazzling plays. Manager Tom Trebelhorn told him shortstop was his position to lose the next spring.

Trouble Brewing

After such a promising beginning, things went swiftly downhill for Sheffield in Milwaukee. First, he became angry because he was shifted back to third base to make room for rookie Bill Spiers. Then Sheffield hurt his foot, but the team doctors found nothing wrong with it. He was accused of faking the injury and shipped back to Denver. Sheffield consulted his own doctor, who found a broken bone. After that, there was no trust between Brewers management and Sheffield. He often criticized his teammates, made errors at third base, and was frequently booed by fans. Sheffield crowded the plate and pitchers threw at him, and he complained that Brewers pitchers didn't retaliate. He later admitted that he sometimes purposely overthrew first base to show his disdain for the team.

During the 1990 season, Sheffield took an unauthorized leave from the team and ended up hospitalized with an unexplained illness. In spring training the next year, he was fined for refusing to run sprints. Sheffield hit .194 in 1991, playing in only 50 games because of injuries and turmoil. Finally, before the 1992 season, he was traded to the San Diego Padres, and Sheffield was overjoyed. "Everything you asked for in Milwaukee, you didn't get," he told Tim Kurkjian of *Sports Illustrated*. "Ask for good weather, you don't get it. Ask for a good playing surface, you don't get it. Ask for a first-class organization, you don't get it."

Homecoming

San Diego proved to be a much sunnier climate for Sheffield. Management let him alone, and Sheffield had his first injury-free season. It was a highly productive one: He batted .330, leading the National League, with 33 home runs and 100 RBI, nearly winning the Triple Crown, and the *Sporting News* named him Major League Player of the Year.

The Padres, however, faced a financial crisis and shipped Sheffield to Florida during the 1993 season to save on salary. The Marlins moved him from third base to the outfield, where he worked on his notoriously poor defense and began to cut down on his errors. Sheffield also dramatically increased his walk totals.

Sheffield's return to his home state landed him in plenty of off-field trouble. He was accused of threatening his son's mother. A complaint of aggravated battery was lodged against him. Sheffield's mother was the target of a murder plot. He was stalked by a female fan, was convicted of drunk driving, had an ex-girlfriend file a lawsuit against him, and he fathered a third child out of wedlock. One night, while sitting at a traffic light in Tampa, Sheffield was shot, but luckily the bullet only

Career Statistics

Yr	Team	AVG	GP	AB	R	H	HR	RBI	BB	SO	SB	E
1988	MIL	.238	24	80	12	19	4	12	7	7	3	3
1989	MIL	.247	96	368	34	91	5	32	27	33	10	16
1990	MIL	.294	125	487	67	143	10	67	44	41	25	25
1991	MIL	.194	50	175	25	34	2	22	19	15	5	8
1992	SD	.330	146	557	87	184	33	100	48	40	5	16
1993	SD	.295	68	258	34	76	10	36	18	30	12	15
1993	FLA	.292	72	236	33	69	10	37	29	34	5	19
1994	FLA	.276	87	322	61	89	27	78	51	50	12	5
1995	FLA	.324	63	213	46	69	16	46	55	45	19	7
1996	FLA	.314	161	519	118	163	42	120	142	66	16	6
1997	FLA	.250	135	444	86	111	21	71	121	79	11	5
1998	FLA	.272	40	136	21	37	6	28	26	16	4	1
1998	LA	.316	90	301	52	95	16	57	69	30	18	1
1999	LA	.301	152	549	103	165	34	101	101	64	11	7
2000	LA	.325	141	501	105	163	43	109	101	71	4	10
2001	LA	.311	143	515	98	160	36	100	94	67	10	6
2002	ATL	.307	135	492	82	151	25	84	72	53	12	4
TOTAL		.296	1727	6153	1064	1819	340	1100	1024	741	182	154

ATL: Atlanta Braves; FLA: Florida Marlins; LA: Los Angeles Dodgers; MIL: Milwaukee Brewers; SD: San Diego Padres.

grazed him. When Gooden ran into well-publicized troubles with a cocaine addiction, Sheffield was frequently searched and tested for drugs. With all these distractions, he had another bout of injuries and his playing time shrank in 1994 and 1995. At one point, though, Sheffield had eight consecutive hits during the 1995 season.

In 1996, Sheffield hired a public relations agent, started his own charity, took lessons in public speaking, posed for a fashion magazine, and moved to Miami. All these efforts at repairing his image and avoiding off-field trouble paid off on the field, as well, with his second excellent season. He hit .314 with 42 home runs and 120 runs batted in.

At the start of the 1997 season, Sheffield became the richest player in baseball by signing a six-year, $61 million contract extension. Pitchers decided to pitch around him, and Sheffield, notorious for his frequent strikeouts, decided to stop swinging at bad pitches. He slumped to .250, but he had 121 walks, 21 home runs and 71 RBI. For the rest of his career Sheffield always enjoyed high on-base percentages. He was frequently on base during the 1997 playoffs and World Series, which the Marlins won in their first and only post-season appearance, hitting .320 for the post-season with a remarkable .514 on-base percentage.

Starting Over

After the Marlins won the World Series, owner Wayne Huizenga sold the team and the new owners unloaded their high-priced players. Sheffield was sent to Los Angeles in a blockbuster trade. Through the 2001 season Sheffield was a fixture in the Dodgers' lineup. Playing left field for Los Angeles, Sheffield continued to bat over .300 with power and plenty of walks. In 2000 he had 43 home runs and 109 RBI while batting .325 with a .438 on-base percentage and a .643 slugging percentage. In 2001 he became the first player in major league history to win three 1-0 games in a season with home runs.

Yet, after three solid seasons, Sheffield demanded to be traded, saying he was unhappy in Los Angeles. In 2002, he went to the Atlanta Braves, his fourth major league team, in a trade for Brian Jordan, Odalis Perez and a minor-league pitcher. In Atlanta, Sheffield was overjoyed to be playing for Bobby Cox, a manager he'd liked ever since Cox batted him third in the National League All-Star team lineup in 1993. Sheffield seemed relaxed as he helped the Braves to a National League Eastern Division title with another outstanding season.

Sheffield's accomplishments might have given him a shot at the Hall of Fame, had he not missed so much playing time early in his career with injuries. In baseball he is widely known as one of the top offensive threats, but he has failed to achieve the superstardom once predicted for him.

FURTHER INFORMATION

Books

The Baseball Encyclopedia. Macmillan, 1997.
Shatzkin, Mike. *The Ballplayers.* William Morrow, 1990.

Periodicals

Gammons, Peter. "Street Smarts." *Sports Illustrated,* 70 (April 5, 1989): 92.
Geffner, Michael P. "A Fish Out of Water." *Sporting News,* 220 (July 1, 1996): 7.

Kurkjian, Tim. "A Blessing for the Padres."*Sports Illustrated,* 76 (April 27, 1992): 54.

Nightengale, Bob. "Diamonds are Forever for Sheffield."*Sporting News,* 221 (April 14, 1997): 37.

Nightengale, Bob. "Sheffield is Baseball's Most Tormented Player."*Sporting News.* 220 (April 15, 1996): 18.

Reilly, Rick. "Can't Take Nothin' Off Nobody."*Sports Illustrated,* 77 (September 14, 1992): 54.

Verducci, Tom. "Part of the Crowd."*Sports Illustrated,* 84 (May 27, 1996): 68.

Other

baseball-reference.com, http://www.baseball-reference. com (December 23, 2002)

"Dwight Gooden." *Baseball Library.com*http://www. pubdim.net/baseballlibrary/ballplayers/G/Gooden_ Dwight.stm (December 23, 2002).

"Gary Sheffield." *Baseball Library.com*http://www. pubdim.net/baseballlibrary/ballplayers/S/Sheffield_ Gary.stm (December 22, 2002).

"Gary Sheffield." *CNNSI.com Baseball*http://sports illustrated.cnn.com/baseball/mlb/players/2114/index. html (December 22, 2002).

Romano, John. "Sheffield Concentrates on Future." *St. Petersburg Times Online*http://www.sptimes.com/ News/031801/news_pf/Sports/Sheffield_concentrate. shtml (December 23, 2002).

Shea, John. "Latest Twist in the Sheffield Saga." *SFGate.com*http://www.sfgate.com/cgi-bin/article.cgi? file=/chronicle/archive/2001/03/11/SP139150.DTL (December 23, 2002).

Shea, John. "Sheffield Blue, But Not the Dodger Kind." *SFGate.com*http://www.sfgate.com/cgi-bin/article. cgi?file=/chronicle/archive/2001/02/261/SP150412. DTL (December 23, 2002).

Vecsey, George. "Sheffield's Bat Wins Over Atlanta." *SFGate.com*http://www.sfgate.com/cgi-bin/article. cgi?file=/chronicle/archive/2002/04/08/SP201910. DTL (December 23, 2002).

Sketch by Michael Betzold

Willie Shoemaker
1931-

American jockey

In the unlikely role of jockey, Willie Shoemaker became known throughout the world during the course of a phenomenal career. After first entering the winner's circle in 1949, he went on to set record after record.

Willie Shoemaker

Among these, Shoemaker claimed the highest total purse money among riders ten times and for twenty-nine years had the most wins ever accumulated by a jockey. Known as "Shoe" and several other nicknames, he earned his fame on the racetrack and rarely drew attention to his life outside of racing. A quiet man with the reputation of outsmarting other riders and knowing how not to get in his horse's way during a race, he has been quick to draw attention to worthy rivals. During the 1970s, fame and personal problems reduced the jockey's appearances on the track and winning percentage, but he regained his old form as was evidenced by his Kentucky Derby win on Ferdinand in 1986. A 1991 single-car accident that turned Shoemaker into a quadriplegic is the saddest chapter in his life. However, the mental toughness he exhibited as a rider has given him the strength to fight for his own recovery and to help others who are paralyzed.

Early Challenges

Shoemaker has possessed a courageous spirit since birth. He was born prematurely, weighing just one pound, thirteen ounces, and wasn't expected to live through the night. His grandmother, Maudie Harris, took charge of the situation. She washed him, put him on a pillow in a shoebox, and set it on the open door of the oven to warm. When Shoemaker was four years old, his parents Ruby and Bebe Shoemaker divorced. He and Ruby went to live on the nearby Texas ranch where his grandparents were sharecroppers. It was there that Shoe-

Chronology

1931	Born August 19 in Fabens, Texas to parents Bebe and Ruby Shoemaker
1949	Makes first professional ride on March 19
1950	Marries Virginia McLaughlin
1955	Has first Kentucky Derby victory
1957	Loses Kentucky Derby after misjudging finish line
1960	Divorced from first wife
1961	Marries Babs Bayer on November 29
1968	Breaks femur in riding accident
1969	Breaks pelvis, ruptures bladder, and damages nerves in paddock accident
1978	Divorced by second wife effective March 6
1978	Marries Cindy Barnes on March 7
1979	Wins Marlboro Cup on Spectacular Bid
1986	Wins Kentucky Derby at age fifty-four
1990	Retires from race riding
1991	Paralyzed in automobile accident

Related Biography: Jockey Eddie Arcaro

As the only jockey to win two Triple Crowns, Eddie Arcaro is one of the finest riders in racing history. He began riding thoroughbreds at age fourteen and entered his first race in 1931. Arcaro's career took off after his contract was sold to Calumet Farms, which provided his first Derby winner, Larwin, in 1938. He would become known as a strong, instinctual rider who credited his horses in his wins and earned himself the nickname "The Master."

Arcaro had seventeen wins in the legs of the Triple Crown—the Kentucky Derby, Belmont Stakes, and Preakness—including a tie with Bill Hartack for a record five Derby victories. He captured all three in one year for the first time in 1941 with Whirlaway, and then again in 1948 on Citation. When Arcaro rode Nashua in the Derby in 1955, the now senior rider placed second behind Shoemaker on Swaps. A rivalry was made despite the fact that Swaps would not appear in the subsequent Belmont or Preakness, both of which Arcaro would win on Nashua, so a special $100,000 match race was held. In this competition, Arcaro won easily.

The horse that Arcaro admired most was Kelso, with whom he paired to win twelve out of fourteen races at the end of his career. He retired at age forty-five in 1961. His record 554 stakes wins would stand until Shoemaker passed this mark in 1972. After he retired from racing, Arcaro worked as a sportscaster on radio and television. He died at age eighty-one in 1997.

maker introduced himself to riding by jumping on a pony without benefit of reins, saddle, or supervision. While picking cotton, he also began to think of his future: "I'll never pick up another hoe. There's gotta be a better way to make a living and I'm gonna find it," he said to his grandfather, according to a *Sports Illustrated* writer.

Both of Shoemaker's parents remarried, and he moved to El Monte, California with his father when he was ten. He had a perfect record competing as a boxer and wrestler in high school, but was frustrated by his small size. At just four feet, eleven inches and ninety-five pounds, Shoemaker would be small even for a jockey. At fifteen he quit school to muck out stalls and work with yearlings. Originally motivated to take the job by the need to work, more than an interest in riding, Shoemaker now considers the experience essential to his understanding of horses.

Exceptional Talents

Shoemaker had his first win on April 20, 1949 riding Shafter V at Golden Gate Fields. In his first full year, he had an impressive 219 winners. And before long, he was predicted to be a perennial winner. In a 1953 *Newsweek* article jockey Ted Atkinson remarked, "This is a real race rider.... He will go on and on." What observers like Atkinson saw was a quiet rider with gentle hands, someone who used smarts to win his races. A *Newsweek* writer explained, "They attribute to him an excellent sense of pace, an eye for a developing pattern of danger that can be avoided up ahead, and a way of first hustling his horse out of the gate and then letting the animal settle into his stride pretty much on his own until the rider feels the mechanism under him to be functioning smoothly." Nearly a decade later, the accomplished jockey Eddie Arcaro complimented him in *Time,* saying, "Willie takes such light hold of a horse ... that he could probably ride with silk threads for reins."

Quiet in the saddle, Shoemaker was also quiet when interviewed, although after decades in the media spotlight, he learned to be more communicative. In 1950 a *Newsweek* writer described him as someone who "can make a whole conversation out of a nod." At the time he was battling Italian rider Joe Culmone for the year's most wins, but when asked to identify the best jockey, he said "Eddie Arcaro." The jockey was never one to boast about his accomplishments. Shoemaker and Arcaro would in fact become good friends and Shoemaker would credit the other jockey with teaching him to relax and work with the horse rather than resort to the whip. In 1999, Shoemaker was eloquent in his appreciation of another jockey, when Laffit Pincay passed his record 8,833 career wins. He said in an interview for cbs.sportsline.com, "There has never been anyone more dedicated to their profession or sport like Pincay. To have my record broken by him is a very big honor."

Setting Records

Shoemaker's 8,833 wins represent several decades worth of excellence on thoroughbred tracks. In 1951 the jockey was the leading money winner at $1,329,890. In 1953 he beat the world record for victories in one year with 392 and ended year with 485. He had his first victory in the Kentucky Derby in 1955, when he rode Swaps to a length-and-a-half victory over the favorite Nashua. Another big race came on Jaipur in the 1962 Belmont stakes, a competition in which he nosed out Admiral's Voyage and Crimson Satan. Shoe made a rare and now notorious mistake in the 1957 Kentucky Derby when he misjudged the finish line aboard Gallant Man. The jockey thought he had won the race and stood up in the stirrups prematurely; he was passed by Iron Liege, who won the race. Shoemaker was suspended for fifteen days by Churchill Downs stewards for "gross carelessness." Other riders have marveled

Willie Shoemaker

that he was able to put this incident behind him, considering it a potentially mentally debilitating experience.

Struggle with Fame

Because he most often rode on the west coast, Shoemaker soon became a celebrity in southern California. With his ten percent cut of purse money, he was a wealthy man and his second wife Babs Bayer thoroughly enjoyed the lifestyle it afforded them. In the mid-1960s the Shoemakers moved into a Beverly Hills high-rise apartment and were attending glamorous parties. Babs dressed in expensive furs and jewelry, she did charity work, and their names appeared in society columns. Quietly unhappy with these changes, Shoemaker would later say what he thought of his Hollywood acquaintances in *Sports Illustrated:* "I never really wanted to know them. I went to their houses and I couldn't remember them now if I tried because I want to put it out of my mind." He also reflected, "An athlete's supposed to be doing a job the next day, and those people don't have anything to do. They sleep all day. It affected my riding. It affected my attitude about it a lot."

The jockey found himself fighting boredom and personal problems at the height of his career. In 1967 he helped make Damascus the horse of the year and his mounts earned more than $3 million for the first time, but the jockey suffered two serious injuries. In January of 1968 he broke his femur when a horse fell and kicked him, resulting in thirteen months of recovery. In April of the next year, a horse threw and crushed him against a paddock hedge. His pelvis was broken in several places, his bladder was torn, and nerves in his leg were damaged. After he again returned to racing, Shoemaker reached one of the greatest hallmarks of his career: in 1970 he passed Johnny Longden's record of most career wins with 6,033 victories. It had taken Longden forty years to set a record that was overturned by Shoemaker in just twenty-two years. Nevertheless, Shoemaker's performance in the saddle was diminished. By 1973 his winning percentage had dropped to seventeen percent from an average of twenty-four percent and he was increasingly absent on the job.

Shoemaker's comeback began with his getting into shape physically, but was most closely linked to a resolution in conflict at home. In February 1977 Babs filed for divorce, citing "irreconcilable differences." That summer Shoemaker became engaged to Cindy Barnes and married her in March of 1978, just a day after his divorce was official. Barnes was then twenty-seven years old and shared her husband's interests in sports and horses. Approximately two years later the couple had a daughter, Amanda.

Return to Form

On the racetrack, Shoemaker entered a new era. In 1979 he won the Marlboro Cup on Spectacular Bid,

Where Is He Now?

Shoemaker hopes that researchers will discover a way to regenerate damaged spinal chords and is concentrating on being physically prepared for new treatments. He plans to start using a voice-activated computer, which he sees as new way of keeping active and informed. He has also published several novels since his accident, including *Dark Horse: A Coley Killebrew Novel*, which appeared in 1996.

After spending five and half months in the hospital, Shoemaker returned to training horses while using a wheelchair controlled by a sip-and-puff mechanism. Shoemaker's marriage to Cindy ended three years after the accident and he retired in 1997, having decided that the work took too much time away from his physical therapy. He also serves as director of The Shoemaker Foundation, an organization that was founded to help fund his own medical expenses and which now provides financial assistance to others from the racing industry who are paralyzed. As the honorary chair of the Paralysis Project, Shoemaker uses his legendary status as a jockey to advance spinal chord research. During more than forty years in the saddle, he dazzled his fellow riders, journalists, and sports fans. While his records have been surpassed in part, his importance to thoroughbred racing is still heralded. His exceptional understanding of horses, rare modesty, and mental stamina will be far more difficult to match.

whom he would describe as the greatest horse he had ever ridden. In a 1980 *Sports Illustrated* article he explained, "He does everything like a great horse should do it. He won on every kind of track you can imagine. Carried his weight and won. He's so versatile you can move any time you want and then move again if you have to." One of the greatest events of Shoemaker's later career was his 1986 Kentucky Derby victory on Ferdinand. The rider was 54 years old and was himself amazed that he was still racing. The victory was made even sweeter because it was shared with trainer Charles Wittingham, with whom Shoemaker had collaborated in more than 200 stakes wins.

In time, however, Wittingham had to tell Shoemaker that his owners were asking for a younger rider. Having decided to retire in 1990, the jockey agreed to do an unusual, year-long world tour arranged by New Zealander Michael Watt. From the Royal Ascot in England, to Australia, to tiny venues in the American outback, Shoemaker would say good-bye to his fans across the world. According to *Sports Illustrated* writer Clive Gammon, most people in American thoroughbred racing looked down on the spectacle. But Gammon countered, "On the whole, though, it is perhaps more unsettling to consider how the exit of Shoemaker might have gone, indeed, how it might have been shamefully overlooked, if it had been left to his countrymen." The writer speculated that the jockey's international fame was second only to **Muhammad Ali** among American athletes. Shoemaker left the job of jockey having taken home about $10 million and holding a twenty-two percent winning record. He immediately turned to training horses, a role that he had begun preparing for at Wittingham's training facility.

Tragic Accident

Ironically, Shoemaker left the dangers of the race-track only to face paralysis after a single-car rollover accident in 1991. Following a round of golf and several drinks, Shoemaker lost control of his Ford Bronco on straight stretch of highway in San Dimas, California. He swerved across a nine-foot shoulder and rolled down a forty-foot embankment, where he was found with his chin on his chest, his head under the top of the steering wheel. With his spinal cord smashed, Shoemaker was left without control of his arms or legs. When Shoemaker's lawyer pursued several lawsuits seeking to prove medical malpractice and negligence by the State of California, it prompted a very negative public response. Shoemaker would not admit that alcohol played an important role in the accident, despite a bartender's testimony and a blood alcohol test of .13.

CONTACT INFORMATION

Address: Vincent Andrews Management, 315 S. Beverly Hills Dr., Suite 208, Beverly Hills, CA 90212-4310.

SELECTED WRITINGS BY SHOEMAKER:

(With Dan Smith) *The Shoe: Willie Shoemaker's Illustrated Book of Racing,* Rand McNally, 1976.
(With Barney Nagler) *Shoemaker,* Doubleday, 1984.
Stalking Horse, Fawcett, 1995.
Fire Horse, Fawcett, 1995.
Dark Horse: A Coley Killebrew Novel, Fawcett, 1996.

FURTHER INFORMATION

Periodicals

"A Way with Horses." *Time* (May 9, 1962):74.
Gammon, Clive. "The Long Goodbye: Bill Shoemaker, World's Winningest Jockey." *Sports Illustrated* (February 5, 1990):54-60.
"The Shoe." *Sports Illustrated* (June 2, 1980).

Sports Illustrated (April 19, 1993):73-82.

"Who's Arcaro?" *Newsweek* (December 11, 1950).

"Willie the Shoo-In." *Newsweek* (October 19, 1953).

Other

"Horse racing legend Bill Shoemaker." *CBS SportsLine* (April 7, 2000).

Sketch by Paula Pyzik Scott

Eunice Kennedy Shriver

Eunice Kennedy Shriver
1920-

American sports activist

Eunice Kennedy Shriver can be recognized by her name alone. That was not good enough for her, however, and she forged her own way in the world. Shriver's life was deeply touched by her older sister Rosemary, who was mentally challenged. She noticed how Rosemary struggled to keep up with her and her siblings. Shriver wanted to make a difference for others like Rosemary, showing everyone the wonderful gifts those who were mentally challenged held. Shriver changed the way people perceived those who were mentally impaired, helping those who were mentally challenged believe in themselves and inspiring them to become all they could be by exposing them to new activities.

Growing Up A Kennedy

Eunice had her life cut out for her when she was born into the Kennedy family. John Kennedy Sr. was known for his strict winning philosophy, and Eunice had a lot of competition with eight other siblings. Her older mentally-retarded sister Rosemary wasn't much of a challenge for her, but she cared deeply for Rosemary and was sympathetic to the way others treated her. For years Rosemary's condition was kept secret. It wasn't until Shriver's brother John was elected to the Presidency that she had a pulpit from which to preach her message. President Kennedy felt strongly about Rosemary as well and in 1961 requested that Shriver research the physical capacity of the mentally retarded.

There was no data to be found. What Shriver did find were people being shut away from society in institutions of despair. No one believed that mentally challenged people could do anything but lay in beds all day. People were too scared to explore anything different. Shriver knew different after seeing what her sister was able to do growing up. She decided the only way to collect the data she needed for her task was to organize her own re-

search project. Her husband, Sargent Shriver supported her and assisted her in assembling nearly 100 volunteers to help out at a day camp held at Timberlake in Rockville, Maryland, where she taught the attendees athletics, floor hockey and aquatics. Sargent was not always sure of Shriver's idea. In an interview for the *Record* he stated, "I can remember my own skepticism about this at the beginning. I didn't go around saying 'Hot dog, this is the best thing since they invented the light bulb.' When Eunice started her camp in our back yard in Maryland, I saw people doing things we had been told they couldn't do. Like riding horseback, swimming, and climbing trees. This was 1963. You have to understand, when we used to go around to institutions for the mentally retarded in the 1950s, most mentally handicapped people were not involved in any physical activity. They weren't considered strong or capable. Some places wouldn't even let them in the swimming pool for fear they might drown."

Shriver not only changed the mind of her husband, she had an effect on the way political leaders and eventually the general public viewed the mentally retarded. Sheila Dinn writes in *Hearts of Gold,* "In the summer of 1962, 100 young people with mental retardation came to Mrs. Shriver's camp to run, swim, play soccer, and ride horses. They enjoyed the camp and loved the sports they learned, and by the end of the summer they were 'faster and stronger' than ever before. The doctors and experts had been wrong!"

Chronology

1920	Born July 10 in Brookline, Massachusetts
1946	Runs Juvenile agency
1960	Eunice's brother, John F. Kennedy presides as president
1961	Works with brother John F. Kennedy to establish Presidential Committee on Mental Retardation
1962	Creates Joseph P. Kennedy Jr. Awards in Mental Retardation
1962	Creates the National Institutes for Child Health and Human Development
1963	Runs summer day camp at Timberlawn for mentally retarded
1963	Brother John F. Kennedy is shot and killed
1964	Initiates five-year public information campaign by the National Advertising Council to promote acceptance of people with metal retardation
1964	Influences changes in Civil Services regulations to allow persons with mental retardation to be hired on ability rather than test scores
1968	Helps organize the first international competition for mentally challenged, calling it the Special Olympics
1968	Special Olympics becomes an official nonprofit organization
1969	Eunice Kennedy Shriver Center founded
1970	Summer Special Olympics World Games held for first time in Chicago, IL
1977	First Winter Special Olympics World Games held in Steamboat Springs, CO
1981	Creates "Community of Caring" concept for the reduction of mental retardation among babies of teenagers
1982	Establishes sixteen "Community of Caring" model centers
1999	Home burns down causing over $600,000 worth of damage as well as loss of family heirlooms
2000	Undergoes surgery to remove benign pancreatic tumor
2001	Attends Winter Special Olympics World Games held in Anchorage, AK

Awards and Accomplishments

1973	Receives Legion of Honor, Lasker Award, Humanitarian Award A.A. M.D
1973	Receives National Volunteer Service Award
1973	Receives Philadelphia Civic Ballet Award
1974	Awarded Prix de Couronne Francais
1984	Awarded Presidential Medal of Freedom
1993	Receives Freedom From Want Medal from Roosevelt Institute
1995	Becomes the first living American woman to be portrayed on United States legal tender: the 1995 Special Olympics World Summer Games silver commemorative coin
1998	Inducted into National Women's Hall of Fame in Seneca Falls, NY
1998	Awarded Aetna Voice of Conscience® Award
1999	Receives Juanita Kreps Award
2000	Recognized at the inaugural Laureus Sports Awards with the Sport for Good Award
2000	Presented with the Noel Foundation Life award
2000	Awarded with the Greater Washington D.C. Jewish Sports Hall of Fame Humanitarian Award
2000	Receives the Phoenix Foundation for Children Champion of Children Award
2001	Awarded an Honorary Degree from the Cardinal Strich University
2002	Receives the Theodore Roosevelt Award from the National Collegiate Athletic Association

Presidential Influence

President John F. Kennedy waited for his sister's report with great anticipation. "JFK even broke away from one of the emergency meetings on the Cuban missile crisis on October 15, 1962, to receive the panel's report," according to Harrison Rainie and Katia Hetter writing for *U.S. News & World Report.* Shriver knew that with this report she would be able to influence those in the political realm, but now she needed to address the daunting task of how to influence the public. According to Rainie and Hetter, She "hammered at the issue" further with her brother, expressing that she wanted to "come out" about their sister Rosemary by writing an article for the *Saturday Evening Post.* He agreed to this, just asking that he be able to see it before she submitted it. He approved of what Shriver wrote and it was published. "I wanted to convince people if the mentally retarded were given a chance they could achieve," stated Shriver in the book *Special Olympics* by Nancy Gilbert. When a Kennedy speaks, people listen, and according to Rainie and Hetter "the change in public and scientific attitudes prompted by the article and the work of the presidential panel was striking."

Someone Believes

"She has a carefully constructed set of values and she will not budge from them. She is highly principled in ways that are more sophisticated than anyone in the family. If you ask, most of my brothers, sisters, and cousins would say they'd like to be like her," said Bobby Kennedy when speaking with Rainie about his Aunt Eunice. People with mental retardation finally had a voice. Shriver believed in them, and she would be a champion for their cause at all costs. Each summer she continued to assist in organizing camps all over the United States and in Canada where the mentally challenged could explore their physical prowess.

"In 1967 the people who ran the Chicago program decided that athletes around the city were ready to compete against one another. When they asked the Kennedy Foundation for money to help organize a city-wide competition, Mrs. Shriver decided to take the idea even further – and hold an international competition!," writes Dinn. In 1968, at Soldier Field in Chicago, Illinois, the first international competition began. The United States and Canada participated and there were over 1,000 athletes who took part. The event was so successful that the Special Olympics non-profit organization was formed that same year, to continue the development of this wonderful competition. Shriver states in Dinn's book "if those athletes had been uninterested or bored, Special Olympics probably never would have happened. You can't push people into something like this – their enthusiasm has to carry it."

Shriver inspired many mentally challenged people to believe in themselves and to work hard to achieve things people never thought possible. "Special Olympics really brings families together". It gives parents and siblings tangible evidence of what this relative who's mentally retarded can really do," according to Doug Single. Michael

Related Biography: Founder and President of Best Buddies Anthony Shriver

Anthony is the youngest of Shriver's five children, and Eunice passed on many of her principles to her son. "His mother became his role model," stated Kevin Gray for *Miami*. People would point and whisper at his Aunt Rosemary when he and his mother would take her out. "It never fazed her. Even when people were staring, she didn't care," said Anthony in the same article. When he was at Georgetown University he noticed his fellow students wasting their spare time, when they could be out making a difference. He organized a group called Best Buddies, where he paired college students with a mentally challenged person. "His goal is to integrate the mentally disabled into mainstream society through one-on-one friendships with others," according to Gray. Over time news of this organization spread throughout the country, and young Anthony would receive incessant calls asking for information on how to set up a program at their school. Shortly after graduating, what was a hobby became his career, as he now manages over "6,500 participants in 172 chapter of the Best Buddies programs around the world," cited Gray. George Zitnay of the National Head Injury Foundation stated, "People with mental retardation have been isolated for too long. Best Buddies addresses the need for valued friendship." Gray concluded that the Shriver family has created a name for themselves for "addressing the needs of the retarded."

Hearts of Gold: A Celebration of Special Olympics and Its Heroes

In the category of pure skill, there is Robert Vasquez. The twelve-year-old from Virginia, USA competed in the top level of gymnastics at the 1995 World Games. In his best event, the rings, Bobby earned a gold medal. Bobby also won four silvers: in the floor exercise, vault, pommel horse, and all-around; one bronze, in the parallel bars; and a fourth place in the high bars.

Bobby's coach Shane Revill, who also coaches non-Special Olympics athletes, considers Bobby's skill and his flexibility in a league with many regular gymnasts. The biggest obstacle to Bobby's success is his frustration when he can't do a move or when things don't go his way. "We had trouble on the first day of competition, when we got a score we didn't agree with," said Shane. "I thought Bobby would be down for the rest of the week. But the next day, he went on his own and apologized to the officials for his poor sportsmanship. Then the group he was competing with came together, almost like a team, instead of athletes competing against each other. High fives, great attitudes – it ended up being the meet of everyone's lives! Bobby ate it up and did a flawless routine on the rings to win the gold."

Source: Dinn, Sheila. *Hearts of Gold: A Celebration of Special Olympics and Its Heroes.* Woodbridge, CT: Blackbirch Press, Inc., 1996: 58-59.

Maglione's mother had never seen him ski before. She remarked in Gilbert's book, "I was terrified when I saw the size of the mountain. I was watching him come down like it was so easy, going in and out of all the poles. It was very, very thrilling." These valuable results, as well as a plethora of other attributes, have made Shriver's work so important. She truly changed the world and the way in which we conduct it when it comes to those who are mentally challenged. "In the past, parents of children with mental retardation might have felt ashamed or embarrassed. Today they can share the pride and joy of watching their children succeed," writes Gilbert. She changed the mentally challenged lives forever, not only because she petitioned for them to have recreation so that they may become active, but also to treat them as the integral part of society they are. Mike Stone, a Special Olympic competitor remarked to Dinn "Now athletes around the world all have a chance to show who they are, and what they believe in." Loretta Claiborne who competes in running for the Special Olympics shared, "Sports was and still is an outlet for me". Special Olympics is even more than sports. It helps me respect others and get respect back. And most of all it has helped me to get over so many hurdles and to say to myself, 'I am who I am, but I can be the best of who I am'."

Shriver inspired the mentally challenged to dream, and influenced them to believe that anything is possible. The athletes have taken ownership of their event. They have come up with new and exciting games in which to compete. Shriver is even impressed with what has come from Special Olympics, stating to Harrar, "the idea for the chess match came from the athletes. We have no idea how much is possible." Sue Porter, in the same article stated, "It has to change you, seeing all these amazing people doing their best." In fact, the motto of the Special Olympics is "Let me win. But if I cannot win, let me be brave in the attempt."

Those who participate in the World Games are not chosen by their abilities, but rather by picking their name out of a hat. Because of this process "the World Games are a chance for Special Olympics athletes of all abilities from all over the world to show their love of sports," as written by Tim Kennedy in his book titled *Special Olympics*. President George W. Bush honored Shriver at a holiday reception for the Special Olympics stating she "has made the Special Olympics her life's work. If you ever had any doubt about how much good one person can bring into the world, look no farther than this kind and gracious lady." President Bush continued to speak about the Special Olympics saying it "is an example of America at its best, sharing with the entire world a spirit of joy and kindness."

Still Going Strong

Although Shriver has experienced some set backs due to illness, she still makes an appearance at a variety of events that support the Special Olympics and advocates for the mentally challenged. Shriver told a Toronto reporter "I feel a sense of gratitude, a sense of admiration. I am very energized by them." That explains how she was able to attend the games of 2001 in Alaska, after suffering an acute infection following a surgery she had to remove a benign pancreatic tumor. Although Tim Kennedy, who organized the event, encouraged her to take it easy, she wouldn't miss it for the world. Although Shriver hates public speaking, she knows that it is necessary to inspire the athletes and their families as well as educate the public on the topic of mental retardation.

"With enormous conviction and unrelenting effort, Eunice Kennedy Shriver has labored on behalf of America's least powerful, those with mental retardation "Her decency and goodness have touched the lives of many," stated

President Ronald Reagan when awarding Shriver with the Presidential Medal of Honor. Shriver has received many awards for all her diligent work, but she is the last person to brag about it. She humbly shrugs off any attempts to glorify her work. Michelle Green of *People* exhorts Shriver saying "She had wooed, coaxed and, sometimes, strong-armed an entire generation of coaches, donors, and volunteers. Along the way she had convinced skeptics that the retarded, once treated as frail specimens (if not ignored altogether), could blossom on the playing field." She paved the way for the mentally challenged to become a normal, working part of society. "Simply not accepting the limitations that the world may put on people with disabilities – that is success," stated Shriver in the foreword for Dinn's book. Shriver is not an openly emotional person, but is moved to tears of joy at most events, seeing how far these athletes have come. Rainie and Hetter sum it up stating "the changes wrought by Eunice Shriver may well be seen as the most consequential. With a lot of help for her very powerful brother Jack and inspiration from her powerless sister Rosemary, Eunice Shriver helped move the nation for good and for all."

FURTHER INFORMATION

Books

Dinn, Sheila. *Hearts of Gold: A Celebration of Special Olympics and Its Heroes*. Woodbridge, CT: Blackbirch Press, Inc., 1996.

Encyclopedia of World Biography Supplement, Vol. 19. Detroit: The Gale Group, 1999.

Gilbert, Nancy. *The Special Olympics*. Mankato, MN:Creative Education, Inc., 1990.

Kennedy, Mike. *Special Olympics*. Children's Press, 2002.

Periodicals

"CAN-Do Spirit at Benefit for Autism." *Washington Times*, (July 5, 2002).

"Coin to Honor Special Olympics Founder Shriver." *Minneapolis Star*, (February 8, 1995): 2A.

Green, Michelle. "Up front: Eunice Shriver's Olympian Friends on the Playing Fields of Notre Dame, a Legion of Retarded Athletes Learn What it Means to Win." *People*, (August 17, 1987): 30.

Harrar, Sari. "At the Finish." *Record*, (August 4, 1991): I01.

"Juanita Kreps Award Presentation." *Dallas Morning News*, (November 17, 1999): 6R.

Mizejewski, Gerald. "Shriver's Mansion Burns; $600,000 in Damage Estimated." *Washington Times*, (June 10, 1999): C3.

"People." *International Herald Tribune*, (December 16, 2000).

Rainie, Harrison. "The Most Lasting Kennedy Legacy." *U.S. News & World Report*. (November 15, 1993): 44-47.

Rankin, Margaret. "Best Buddies has One in Ethel Kennedy." *Washington Times*, (October 27, 1999): C8.

"Retarded Children Deserve Life, Too." *Record*, (August 15, 1991): B06.

Schwarzbaum, Lisa. "Clan Destinies Laurence Leamer Chronicles Several Generations of the Female Side of the Kennedy Dynasty, Which Stoically Kept the Faith Despite Heartbreak and Tragedy." *Entertainment Weekly*, (August 12, 1994): 48.

Skow, John. "Heroism, Hugs and Laughter Special games for Courageous Spirits and Generous Hearts." *Time*. (August 17, 1987): 60.

Swift, E. M. "They Came Up Roses the Athletes at the Special Olympics for the Mentally Retarded Couldn't All Win Gold Medals, but the Hope and Joy They Brought to South Bend Made Them Champions in a Much Larger Scene." *Sports Illustrated*. (August 17, 1987):38.

Williams, Jeannie. "Special Olympics Goes North to Alaska." *USA Today*, (January 10, 2001): 02D.

Other

"Bushes Honor 'Special Olympians' at Black-Tie White House Dinner." AP Worldstream. (December 14, 2001).

"Bushes Host Kennedys in Special Olympics Event." Reuters. (December 13, 2001).

Droschak, David. "Special Olympians Close Out Games." AP Online. (July 5, 1999).

"Eunice Kennedy Shriver." Vol. 5, *Contemporary Women's Issues Database*, (December 1, 1998): 18.

Gray, Kevin. "Angels: Best of Buddies Anthony Shriver's Program for the Mentally Disabled Encourages People to Stop Staring and Start Sharing." AP Worldstream. (December 3, 2002).

"Remarks Honoring Eunice Kennedy Shriver at the Special Olympics Dinner." Weekly Compilation of Presidential Documents. (December 21, 1998): 2500.

Thomas, Bob. "Shrivers Produce TV Movie on Mary." AP Online. (November 13, 1999).

Sketch by Barbra J Smerz

Don Shula
1930-

American football coach

The winningest coach in professional football, Don Shula compiled an unparalleled record of 347-173-6 over thirty-three seasons coaching in the National Football League (NFL). On November 14, 1993, as coach of the Miami Dolphins, Shula broke the record of 324 wins set by the legendary **George Halas**. Shula went on to ex-

Don Shula

tend his record of wins to 347 before stepping down as coach of the Dolphins at the end of the 1995 football season. Shula began his coaching career in 1963 when, at the age of thirty-three, he took over the reins of the Baltimore Colts to become the youngest head coach in the NFL. Throughout his career, Shula led six teams to the Super Bowl, winning twice. In what was the high point of his coaching career, Shula in 1972 coached the Dolphins to a perfect record of 17-0, the only NFL team to go undefeated for an entire season.

Born in Grand River, Ohio

He was born Donald Francis Shula in Grand River, Ohio, on January 4, 1930. The son of Dan and Mary (Miller) Shula, he began playing football while still quite young and at the tender age of eleven was forbidden by his parents to play the game anymore after sustaining a bad facial cut during a neighborhood scrimmage. But Shula was not to be so easily dissuaded. In 1942 he forged his parents' signatures on a permission slip so that he could play football at school but was sidelined by a case of pneumonia just before the season began. Encouraged by an assistant coach to return to the game as soon as possible, a healthy Shula later rejoined the team but kept his football participation a secret from his parents until he was named a starter. As a senior at Thomas W. Harvey High School, Shula was named All-Ohio quarterback in 1946. He went on to become a star player at John Carroll University in Cleveland, gaining

Chronology

1930	Born January 4 in Grand River, Ohio
1951	Earns bachelor's degree from John Carroll University in Cleveland
1951-53	Plays defense for Cleveland Browns
1953-56	Plays for Baltimore Colts
1956-57	Plays for Washington Redskins
1958	Named assistant football coach at the University of Virginia
1958	Marries Dorothy Bartish on July 19
1959	Joins coaching staff at University of Kentucky
1961	Becomes defensive coordinator for Detroit Lions
1963	Named head coach of Baltimore Colts
1970	Becomes head coach of Miami Dolphins
1990	Loses wife to cancer
1993	Marries Mary Anne Stephens on October 15
1996	Steps down as coach of Miami Dolphins

125 yards in a 21-15 upset over Syracuse University. Recruited by a number of professional teams, Shula eventually signed with the Cleveland Browns for whom he played defense for the next couple of years before being traded in 1953 to the Baltimore Colts.

Shula spent three seasons with the Colts before being traded in 1956 to the Washington Redskins. His professional playing career ended in 1957. The following year he married Dorothy Bartish and joined the University of Virginia's football coaching staff as assistant coach. In 1959 he joined the coaching staff at the University of Kentucky and two years later broke into the professional coaching ranks when he signed on as defensive coordinator for the Detroit Lions. Shula spent two years with the Lions and in 1963 became the youngest head coach in NFL history when he agreed to lead the Baltimore Colts. Only thirty-three at the time, Shula wasted little time in making his mark with the Colts. In his second season at the helm of the Colts, he led the team to a 12-2 record and earned for himself the first of six Coach of the Year awards.

Coaches Colts to Super Bowl III

In their third and fourth seasons under Shula's direction, the Colts compiled still-impressive records of 10-3-1 and 9-5, respectively. In 1967 the Colts barreled back with a record of 11-1-2 but again failed to make it to the Super Bowl. Shula's dream of coaching a team into the Super Bowl came true in 1968. On the strength of an extraordinary 13-1 record in the regular season, the Colts faced off against the New York Jets in Super Bowl III but were handed an upset by the New Yorkers. In his final season with the Colts, Shula coached the Baltimore team to a winning—but disappointing—record of 8-5-1 in 1969. Looking for a new challenge, Shula turned his attention southward. In 1970 he signed on as new head coach of the Miami Dolphins, which had ended its 1969 season with a dismal record of 3-10-1.

Shula quickly turned things around in Miami, coaching the Dolphins to winning records of 10-4 and 10-3-1

Related Biography: Football Coach David Shula

David Shula has followed in his father's footsteps, spending a decade and a half coaching in the National Football League before joining his father in overseeing the day-to-day operations of the family-owned restaurant chain.

He was born in Lexington, Kentucky, on May 28, 1959, the first child of Shula and his first wife, Dorothy, who died of cancer in 1990. After earning his bachelor's degree from Dartmouth College in 1981, he spent a year playing for the Baltimore Colts. After his year with the Colts, he turned to coaching, joining the staff of the Miami Dolphins as assistant coach from 1982 until 1989. From Miami, Shula moved to Dallas, where he served as the Cowboys' assistant coach from 1989 until 1991. He was named assistant coach of the Cincinnati Bengals in 1991 and soon thereafter was promoted to head coach, a post he retained until 1996. That year, he left coaching and returned to Miami to serve as president of Shula Enterprises, holding company for the family's chain of steak restaurants. He and wife Leslie Ann have three children, Dan, Chris, and Matt.

his first two seasons with the team. The Dolphins capped off their 1971 season with a visit to the Super Bowl, where they lost, 24-3, to the Dallas Cowboys. In 1972 Shula's Dolphins turned in a perfect 14-0 regular season (with another three wins in the playoffs), an achievement that has never been duplicated in NFL history. Miami then went on to win its first Super Bowl, defeating the Redskins, 14-7. After compiling a record of 12-2 in the regular 1973 season, the Dolphins powered their way back to the Super Bowl where they crushed the Minnesota Vikings, 24-7. Shula's greatest glory as a coach came during the early 1970s as he coached the Dolphins through sixty-two consecutive games without a single back-to-back loss, earning a record of 53-9 for the period.

Dolphins Win 1974 AFC Eastern Title

The Dolphins enjoyed another winning season in 1974, winning the American Football Conference's (AFC) Eastern Division title with a record of 11-3. However, the Dolphins were eliminated from the playoffs after being narrowly defeated, 28-26, by the Oakland Raiders. Miami ended 1975 with a 10-4 record in the regular season but were edged out of the AFC Eastern title by the Baltimore Colts. The following year was not a good one for Shula and the Dolphins, which suffered their first losing season (6-8) since Shula's arrival. Miami bounced back in 1977 to finish the regular season with a record of 10-4, finishing second in the AFC Eastern Division.

In 1978 Shula coached the Dolphins to a winning record of 11-5. Miami made it into the AFC wildcard game in the playoffs, where the team lost 17-9 to the Houston Oilers. The Dolphins' 10-6 record in 1979 won the AFC Eastern Division title, but Miami fell to the Pittsburgh Steelers, 34-14, in the divisional playoffs. The following year the Dolphins broke even with a record of 8-8, placing third in the AFC Eastern Division. Things looked up in 1981 when the Dolphins again took the AFC Eastern title with a record of 11-4-1. In the divisional playoffs, Miami was narrowly defeated, 41-38, by the San Diego Chargers in overtime. In the strike-shortened 1982 season, the Dolphins captured the AFC Eastern title with a record of 7-2. Miami went on to win

the AFC championship with a 14-0 defeat of the New York Jets. In the Super Bowl, the Dolphins were overpowered, 27-17, by the Redskins.

Dolphins Return to Super Bowl in 1984

Shula's Dolphins capped off the 1984 season with a return visit to the Super Bowl, where they lost, 38-16, to the San Francisco 49ers. For the next eleven seasons, under Shula's direction, the Dolphins enjoyed break-even or winning seasons every year except 1988 when they finished with a record of 6-10. Finally in 1996, Shula at the age of sixty-six retired from professional football, leaving behind the winningest record in NFL coaching history. Only two years later, in his first year of eligibility, Shula was voted into the Pro Football Hall of Fame. At the induction ceremonies, Shula was formally presented by sons David and Michael, both of whom have spent time as coaches in the NFL.

Shula's first wife, Dorothy, died of cancer in 1990, and in 1993, he married Mary Anne Stephens. The two live in the Miami area, where Shula concentrates most of his time today on running Shula Enterprises, a holding company for his restaurant chain. Looking back on his pro coaching career, Shula told the Pro Football Hall of Fame induction ceremonies: "It's a wonderful tribute to be here, and I'm very proud of it. There have been so many memories, so many wonderful people I've been privileged to work with. I'm grateful I've had the opportunity to achieve the things I set out to do."

CONTACT INFORMATION

Address: Don Shula, c/o Shula Enterprises Inc., 16 Indian Creek Island, Miami Beach, FL 33154-2904. Online: http://www.donshula.com.

SELECTED WRITINGS BY SHULA:

(With Lou Sahadi) *The Winning Edge,* Dutton, 1973.

(With Ken Blanchard) *Everyone's a Coach,* Harper Business, 1995.

FURTHER INFORMATION

Books

"Don Shula." *Newsmakers 1992,* Issue Cumulation. Detroit: Gale Group, 1992.
"Don Shula." *St. James Encyclopedia of Popular Culture,* five volumes. Detroit: St. James Press, 2000.

Periodicals

Glauber, Bob. "NFL/Hall of Fame Inductions/Shula's Finally at Home." *Newsday* (July 27, 1997): B16.
McFarland, Sabrina. "Passages." *People* (November 1, 1993): 97.

Other

"Don Shula: Biography." Pro Football Hall of Fame. http://www.profootballhof.com/players/enshrinees/ dshula.cfm (December 30, 2002).
"Don Shula's Coaching Record." Miami Dolphins. http://www.uswebpc.com/dolphins/record.html (December 30, 2002).
"Don Shula: Highlights." Pro Football Hall of Fame. http://www.profootballhof.com/players/highlights/ dshula.cfm (December 30, 2002).
"The Gridiron: Pro Football-Miami Team Season Records and Coaches." Rauzulu's Street-NFL Team Information. http://www.rauzulusstreet.com/football/ profootball/miamiseason.html (December 30, 2002).
"Shula Career Highlights." DonShula.com. http://www. donshula.com/careerhighlights.htm (December 30, 2002).
"Shula History." DonShula.com. http://www.donshula. com/shulahistory.htm (December 30, 2002).

Sketch by Don Amerman

Roy Simmons, Jr.
1935-

American college lacrosse coach

Roy Simmons Jr. has done it all for the Syracuse University men's lacrosse team—he's served as ballboy, mascot, player, freshman coach, assistant coach and, from 1970 to 1998, varsity head coach. Simmons was born into all of these roles. His father, Roy Simmons Sr., served as a coach for the Orangemen for forty-five years

Chronology

1935	Born August 6 in Syracuse, New York
1955	Enters Syracuse University
1956	Joins Syracuse lacrosse team
1957	Named All-American
1958	Named All-American and team captain
1959	Graduates Syracuse with degree in fine arts
1959	Joins Syracuse lacrosse program as coach of freshman team
1971	Succeeds father, Roy Simmons Sr., as men's varsity lacrosse coach
1983	Captures first of five national titles
1988	Captures second national title
1989	Captures third, and second consecutive, national title
1990	Brings team to Lockerbie, Scotland to memorialize Pan Am Flight 103 victims
1990	Team wins third consecutive championship, which must later be forfeited per NCAA ruling
1993	Captures fourth national title
1995	Wins fifth and final national title
1995	NCAA determines Syracuse must relinquish 1990 championship title due to minor infractions
1998	Retires with 290-96 record

prior to his son's taking over the team. The legacy continues to this day. Simmons Jr.'s son, Roy Simmons III, is an assistant to John Desko, who assumed head coaching duties when Simmons Jr. retired in 1998.

Early Start

Having practically grown up on Syracuse's lacrosse field, it came as no surprise that Simmons elected to attend SU and play for the Orangemen once he graduated from Kimball Union Academy in New Hampshire. In three years with the team, he was named an All-American twice, in 1957 and 1958. He served as team captain in 1958 as well. After graduating with a degree in sculpture in 1959 (Simmons' artwork is featured in museums across the United States), Simmons took a job as coach of Syracuse's freshman lacrosse team. He served in this position, and as an assistant coach with his father's varsity team, for twelve years. He took over as head coach of the varsity team in 1971, following his father's retirement.

Known for stressing academics and life skills as strongly as athletics, Simmons became the only men's lacrosse coach to capture five Division I national championships during his tenure. His 290-96 record made him the winningest coach in Syracuse's history. Simmons led the Orangemen to the national semifinals for sixteen years straight—his team lost a semifinal round to Princeton just prior to his announcing his retirement—and he coached 130 All-Americans, four national players of the year and five championship MVPs.

Minor Controversy

Simmons would have had six national championships under his belt, but Syracuse was required to relinquish its 1990 title due to two minor infractions. Because Simmons' wife, who the NCAA deemed a representative of the team, co-signed a car loan for a player and because the school paid a $13.80 hotel room-service bill for two other players, NCAA officials ruled in 1995 that Syracuse must vacate the 1990 title. *USA Today* reported in 1998 that Simmons "bitterly resented" the NCAA action.

Controversy aside, Simmons's accomplishments are particularly noteworthy because, when he inherited the team, lacrosse was a sparsely funded sport, which made recruiting difficult and, consequently, his early years of coaching less statistically memorable. By 1989, though, he was coaching a team regarded by many as the greatest in the history of the game. Led by twins Paul and Gary Gait, the Orangemen boasted a 13-0 season that year and captured the national championship, the Orangemen's third under Simmons' guidance.

Beyond the Game

It was that winning 1989 team that took on a monumental off-field challenge—taking lacrosse to the suffering town of Lockerbie, Scotland. Pan Am Flight 103 was bombed over Lockerbie that year, claiming the lives of some of its residents and bringing tragedy into its midst. Thirty-five Syracuse University students were on that flight as well, and visitors from the stricken town attended a memorial service at the university. After the memorial service Simmons decided to take his team to Lockerbie.

In addition to placing a lacrosse stick on the Wall of Remembrance, a memorial erected in the town, the Orangemen ran several lacrosse clinics for youth and donated equipment to interested young players. Only women played lacrosse in Scotland, so the boys in the clinics had a great deal to learn about the game. After the visit, lacrosse soared in popularity with youth in the area. Simmons and his players returned to Scotland several times, bringing more equipment, conducting workshops and talking to physical education directors about adding lacrosse to their curricula. When Simmons visited in 1995, the Orangemen took on the newly formed Scottish national lacrosse team. Three years later, that team competed at the World Games in Baltimore, squaring off against Wales' equally new squad.

Revolutionizing Lacrosse

Simmons was credited with increasing the visibility of lacrosse at home as well. "He allowed a game that was formerly defensive to become offensive," Paul Gait told *Syracuse University Magazine*. This approach resulted in a faster-paced, more spontaneous game that drew a greater number of fans.

What Simmons is perhaps best known for, though, is the tremendous respect he generated among students, fans and even opposing coaches. "You can't help but

Awards and Accomplishments	
1957-58	Named All-American
1973-98	NCAA national semifinals
1983, 1988-89, 1993, 1995	NCAA championship winner
1992	Named to Lacrosse Hall of Fame

like him," Princeton coach Bill Tierney told *USA Today* after his team beat the Orangemen and Simmons announced his retirement. "You're watching a legend leave the game. He's been wonderful for lacrosse and for college sports."

Tearful Farewells

Simmons had kept the news of his retirement from all but a few players so his team would not feel pressure to win a championship in his honor. He told the team just after their loss to Princeton. They responded with tears before hoisting him on their shoulders so that 20,000 fans could cheer in appreciation. "I don't think anyone will be able to match what he's done," Gait told *Syracuse University Magazine* following the announcement. "There's only one Roy Simmons Jr. No one will ever forget him."

CONTACT INFORMATION

Address: c/o Syracuse University, Manley Field House, Syracuse, NY 13244-0001.

FURTHER INFORMATION

Periodicals

Canavan, Tom. "Simmons Retires After Six Title in 28 Years." Associated Press (May 23, 1998).

"Syracuse Coach Takes Sixth National Crown." Associated Press (May 30, 1995).

"Syracuse to Give Up 1990 Lacrosse Crown." (Greensboro) *News & Record (June 17, 1995): C6*.

Thamel, Pete. "Lessons of a Lacrosse Legend." *Syracuse University Magazine* (fall, 1998).

Timanus, Eddie. "Syracuse Coaching Legend Ends 'Great Ride.'" *USA Today* (May 26, 1998): 12C.

Wallace, William M. "Syracuse Lacrosse Revival Spans Three Generations." *New York Times* (May 15, 1986): D29.

Other

"Simmons Retires as Lacrosse Coach." http://www.ncaa.org/news/1998/19980608/record.html#2.

Sketch by Kristin Palm

O.J. Simpson

O.J. Simpson
1947-

American football player

O.J. Simpson's squeaky clean image and rags to riches story was the type of "only in America" success story that the sports world holds up as an example of how much can be achieved in athletics. His electrifying career with the Buffalo Bills and the endless opportunities it led to after his retirement were an inspiration to his many fans. Simpson represented an American ideal in the wake of the civil rights movement. He was accepted by white mainstream America as no other athlete had been before him and for that he enjoyed the benefit of being almost universally loved. In 1994, when he was arrested for the double murder of his ex-wife and her friend, the country became mesmerized by the unfolding events and eventually split down the dividing lines of race after his acquittal. With an overwhelmingly positive public persona and a record breaking career, O.J. Simpson's fall from grace ultimately became a sociological study in race relations and celebrity in America.

The Early Years

Born Orenthal James Simpson on July 9, 1947, in Putrero Hill, a low-income neighborhood outside of San

Chronology	
1947	Born July 9 in San Francisco, California
1967	Enrolls at the University of Southern California
1967	Marries Marguerite Whitley
1967	Named Outstanding Player in the Rose Bowl
1968	Wins the Heisman Trophy
1968	Signs television contract with ABC
1969	Joins the Buffalo Bills
1969	Named Man of the Year by Sport magazine
1973	Breaks single season rushing record
1974	Appears in *The Towering Inferno*
1975	Begins Hertz Rent-A-Car campaign
1977	Meets Nicole Brown
1978	Divorces Maguerite Whitely
1978	Traded to San Francisco 49ers
1979	Daughter Aaren drowns in backyard swimming pool
1979	Retires from football
1985	Inducted into Pro Football Hall of Fame
1985	Marries Nicole Brown
1989	Arrested for spousal battery
1992	Files for divorce from Brown
1994	Nicole Brown found murdered
1994	Arrested for murder
1995	Acquitted in criminal trial

Francisco, California, Simpson's childhood pointed to everything but a career in athletics. His father left the family while Simpson was still a toddler and his mother worked at a psychiatric ward to support her four children. Simpson developed rickets soon after birth and the disease left him pigeon-toed and bowlegged. Unable to afford surgery to correct the affliction, Simpson endured the wrath of his childhood friends who took to calling him "Pencil Pins" because of his legs. His early interest in sports was encouraged by his mother, however, and combined with his unfettered determination he would eventually achieve the excellence and acceptance he desired in his youth.

During Simpson's adolescence his experiments on the wrong side of the law would lead to a life changing meeting with San Francisco Giant hero **Willie Mays**. Simpson, along with friend Al "A.C." Cowlings, joined a local gang known as the Persian Warriors. After getting caught stealing, a neighborhood youth leader asked Mays to spend an afternoon with the teenage Simpson. He would recall it later in life as the first time he realized that he could achieve his dreams.

Simpson would quickly gain his first taste of the adulation that he would enjoy throughout so much of his life. Simpson and Cowlings were named to the all-city team in high school and were their team's star players. Simpson, however, didn't have the grades to go on to a reputable school and instead played at City College of San Francisco. At City College, Simpson quickly garnered notice averaging 9.3 yards per carry and scoring fifty-four touchdowns. Of the fifty colleges that tried to recruit him after his sophomore year, Simpson chose the University of Southern California. He married his high

Career Statistics

Yr	Team	Rushing				Receiving			
		ATT	YDS	AVG	TD	REC	YDS	AVG	TD
1969	Buffalo	181	697	3.9	2	30	343	11.4	3
1970	Buffalo	120	488	4.1	5	10	139	13.9	0
1971	Buffalo	183	742	4.1	5	21	162	7.7	0
1972	Buffalo	292	1251	4.3	6	27	198	7.3	0
1973	Buffalo	332	2003	6.0	12	6	70	11.7	0
1974	Buffalo	270	1125	4.2	3	15	189	12.6	1
1975	Buffalo	329	1817	5.5	16	28	426	15.2	7
1976	Buffalo	290	1503	5.2	8	22	259	11.8	1
1977	Buffalo	126	557	4.4	0	16	138	8.6	0
1978	SF	161	593	3.7	1	21	172	8.2	2
1979	SF	120	460	3.8	3	7	46	6.6	0
TOTAL		2404	11236	4.7	61	203	2142	10.6	14

Buffalo: Buffalo Bills; SF: San Francisco 49ers.

school sweetheart, Maguerite Whitley, and continued his climb to stardom.

USC and Beyond

At USC, Simpson enjoyed the attention of the nation playing in a national championship game and setting college football records with his uncanny abilities and charming personality. "He's not only a wonderful football player, but he's a wonderful young man," said Norman Topping, then president of USC. Simpson won the Heisman Trophy in 1968 and quickly began signing endorsement deals and branching out into television. Before signing his first NFL contract, Simpson had already signed a three-year, $250,000, endorsement deal with Chevrolet. Before he played in his first NFL game, he had already made a guest appearance on the television drama, "Medical Center."

Simpson was drafted by the Buffalo Bills with the first pick of the draft. His first few years in the NFL would be rather uneventful. He was rarely used in his rookie season, gaining only 697 yards in 1969. The following year he was sidelined with a knee-injury. It wasn't until 1971, behind an offensive line named "The Electric Company" because "they turned on the Juice," that Simpson would show off his innate ability to elude defenders and consistently break the game with long yardage runs. He was effectively a one-man team, although he was always generously deferring credit to his teammates. "There were power runners and there were escape runners, but he was a slashing-type runner," recalled former Kansas City Chief coach Hank Stram. "He had tremendous vision and excellent balance and very good timing. He would always be gauging to get where he was going. He would start off like he was looking for a hold, and BANG!, he was gone. You could contain him and contain him, and then he'd go 75 yards for a touchdown."

The Record Books

At times his teammates seemed more interested in helping him achieve the personal accolades that became important to a Buffalo team that was never a championship contender during Simpson's stay. In 1973, Simpson became the first back to rush for over 2,000 yards, breaking **Jim Brown**'s single-season rushing record of 1,863. "O.J. gives credit where credit is due," said Joe Ferguson, the Bills' rookie quarterback, in *Sports Illustrated*. "He's helped me on the field and off. Nobody here is jealous of him. He hasn't got an enemy in the world. All of us wanted to see him get the yardage." Added offensive linemen Reggie McKenzie, "A record is a collective thing, anyway. I'm just thankful to be on the offensive line that broke Jim Brown's record." What made the record even more remarkable were the back to back 200 yard games that Simpson ran in the freezing cold and snow filled fields of New England and New York.

Acting and Endorsements

The following year Simpson made his acting debut in the film, *The Towering Inferno*. It marked the beginning of what would become a fairly successful career for an athlete turned actor. Simpson, to his credit, would never take his movie career as seriously as some of his contemporaries. "I'm a realist," he said in a Knight Ridder/Tribune News Service story. "Obviously, I'm not Dustin Hoffman. I have to play an athletic type, just as Woody Allen has to play a wimp type. No matter how many acting lessons I took, the public just wouldn't buy me as Othello." Nevertheless, Simpson continued to act throughout the years following his football career, most notably in *The Naked Gun* series.

Because of his natural charisma and an almost universal acceptance, Simpson continued to field endorse-

O.J. Simpson, right

ment offers from numerous companies lured by his impeccable image. In 1975, Hertz Rent-A-Car made him the first African-American man hired for a major national corporate advertising campaign. The teaming would be wildly successful and continue long into his retirement from football. He would eventually endorse, among others, Royal Crown Cola, Schick, Foster Grant, Treesweet orange juice and Wilson Sporting Goods.

In 1978, Simpson was traded from the Buffalo Bills to the San Francisco 49ers. After an injury early in his first year there led to the discovering of a badly dam-

Where Is He Now?

Simpson moved to Florida and regained custody of the two young children he had with Nicole. He's had a few minor brushes with the law but has generally kept to himself. Playing golf and caring for his young children, Simpson continues to periodically defend his innocence and insist that he still has the public's support. Most recently, Simpson was fined $130 for speeding through a manatee zone in a powerboat near Miami.

aged knee, Simpson retired in 1979 the highest paid football player in the NFL with a salary of $806,688. He finished his career with 11,236 yards and six Pro Bowl appearances along with the numerous records and firsts.

It was also during the late seventies that Simpson's personal life began to change. In 1977, he moved to Brentwood, California with his wife and family. The struggling marriage, however, would officially end after the strain of their daughter's death in the family's swimming pool. Their divorce was finalized in 1979 and O.J. would soon move Nicole Brown, a young waitress he met in 1977, into his Brentwood estate. "She was 18," he said of Brown years later. "She was innocent. She was confident. She was, you know, a little kooky. But she was gorgeous. She was, I thought, the most beautiful girl I'd ever seen. And she didn't know who I was, and I loved that." The two would eventually marry in 1985, the same year he was elected to the Pro Football Hall of Fame.

Simpson would continue a successful career in movies, product endorsements and as an analyst for "Monday Night Football." Unlike most athletes, Simpson was as recognizable after his playing days as he was during them. Unlike Jim Brown, who was considered a better actor and football player but had a rough and threatening public persona, Simpson's image had provided him with a relatively easy transition into retirement.

Murder and the Media

In 1989, Simpson was arrested for spousal battery after an incident on New Year's morning. Simpson's reputation, however, was unharmed and he received a relatively light sentence of probation, community service and fines. It marked the beginning, however, of an increasingly volatile period in his marriage that would culminate in 1994 when Nicole and friend Ronald Goldman were murdered outside her home, only a few miles away from Simpson's. His seemingly airtight alibi quickly began to unravel and after the LAPD announced their suspicions, Al Cowlings, Simpson's life long friend, led police on a 60-mile slow speed chase down the freeways of Los Angeles with a distraught Simpson in the backseat threatening suicide. The media obsession that followed the chase, viewed by 95 million Americans, was unprecedented and unstoppable. The trial that followed lasted until October 1995 and ended with Simpson's acquittal despite blood evidence that pointed to Simpson's guilt.

The country's obsession over his guilt or innocence became clearly divided along racial lines following the highly publicized acquittal. Simpson was seen as untouchable because of his celebrity and wealth. His "dream team" of defense lawyers were accused of playing to the country's racial prejudices and the LAPD was again painted as a racist police force that used Simpson as an opportunity to plant evidence on an extremely popular African-American. However, it became clear that Simpson's extremely lucrative career as a corporate pitchman was over. He had fallen out of the good graces of an increasingly divided and disbelieving American public. His many attempts to publicly declare his innocence fell largely on deaf ears. The civil trial that followed, in 1997, found Simpson liable and order him to pay $33.5 million in compensatory and punitive damages.

The details of Simpson's private life paint a picture of a man painfully out of touch with reality. Although he had remained an extremely popular figure after his retirement, his charisma and "good guy" persona could no longer carry him in the aftermath of the trial. Simpson's prospects are slim. His gridiron glory is a tarnished memory and his future forever clouded by the events of the mid-nineties.

FURTHER INFORMATION

Books

Contemporary Black Biography, Vol. 15 Detroit: Gale Research, 1997.

St. James Encyclopedia of Popular Culture. Detroit: St. James Press, 2000.

Periodicals

"Jury Acquits O.J. Simpson in Road Rage Trial." *Miami Herald*(October 24, 2001).

"A Look Back at the Glory Days." *Sports Illustrated* (June 27, 1994): 32.

"O.J. Simpson: A Cultural Icon." *Knight Ridder/Tribune News Service* (June 17, 1994).

"O.J. in S. Florida to Rebuild Career." *South Florida Business Journal* (March 2, 2001): 29.

"O.J. Gets Custody of his Kids." *Jet* (August 28, 2000): 48.

"O.J. Goes On the Record." *Newsweek* (June 23, 1997): 43.

"Race and the Simpson Verdict." *Commonwealth* (November 3, 1995): 19.

"Simpson Had Incredible Staying Power as a Star." Knight Ridder/Tribune News Service (June 18, 1994).

"The Man with Two Faces." *People* (July 4, 1994): 32.

"The Run: A long Goodbye To O.J. Simpson." *Los Angeles Magazine* (August, 1994): 8.

"The Sad Legacy of 1995." *U.S. News & World Report* (January 15, 1996): 68.

"Whistling in the Dark: You May Think O. J. Simpson Killed his Wife. But Does That Mean You Can't Be Friends?" *Esquire* (February, 1998): 54.

Sketch by Aric Karpinski

Lydia Skoblikova

Lydia Skoblikova
1939-

Russian speed skater

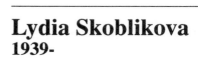efore American speed skaters **Eric Heiden** and **Bonnie Blair** raced to fame as Olympic champions, Soviet speed skater Lydia Skoblikova set a standard of excellence. She was the first athlete, man or woman, to win six gold medals in Olympic competition and remains the only woman to win four gold medals in a single Winter Olympic Games. Along the way, she debunked stereotypes about women athletes, Soviets in particular. Three decades later, despite the lack of widespread name recognition, her accomplishments still stand among the greatest in the sport.

A Natural Fit

Skoblikova was born March 8, 1939, into a large family in Zlatoust, a small mining town in the mountains of Siberia in the Soviet Union. Her father worked as a metallurgical engineer, a position that gave his daughter the chance to pursue skating and be educated in the Soviet system. With the area's long, cold winters and many rinks, skating was an obvious choice of recreation, and Skoblikova spent many hours on the ice. By the time she was twelve, her talent and fondness for speed skating took root, and she became serious about the sport.

In 1957, the 18-year old set the women's Soviet records in the 1,500 meter and 3,000 meter distances. That same year, she married her trainer, Alexander Skoblikova, who later placed her under the charge of a series of other trainers when he devoted himself to teaching at the Chelyabinsk Pedagogic Institute near Zlatoust. His wife supported the career change, explaining to Israel Shenker of *Sports Illustrated*, "I think it's better not to be married to a skater. You have more to talk about." This attitude reflected her broad base of interests, including music and literature. Soon, she too became a teacher at the Chelyabinsk Pedagogic Institute, concentrating on physiology.

Although Skoblikova was not single-minded in her pursuit of speed skating glory, she did want to be the best. Along with her teammates, she undertook a strenuous and innovative training regimen that included gymnastics, running, and an early form of in-line skating for times when ice was unavailable. She was driven to work harder than anyone, telling Shenker of *Sports Illustrated,* "If anyone else runs 20 times 200, I can do 40 times 200. And at faster speed."

Speed Skating's First Big Star

Skoblikova began her international skating career in 1959, winning an all-around bronze medal at the World Championships. At the 1960 Winter Olympics in Squaw Valley, California, the first to offer women's speed skat-

Chronology

1939	Born March 8 in Zlatoust in the Soviet Union
1952	Decides to pursue competitive speed skating
1957	Marries Alexander Skoblikova
1959	Begins her international speed skating career
1960	Wins two races in first women's speed skating events in Winter Olympics history
1962	Begins teaching physiology at the Chelyabinsk Pedagogic Institute
1963	Sweeps all four events at World Championships and is crowned world champion
1964	Competes in her second Winter Olympics and wins all four races
1974	Becomes head of the physical education department at a Moscow university

Awards and Accomplishments

1957	Sets women's Soviet records in the 1,500 meter and 3,000 meter distances
1959-61	Wins all-around bronze medal at USSR National Championships
1959-61	Wins all-around bronze medal at World Championships
1960	Wins two gold medals at Winter Olympics
1962	Wins all-around silver medal at World Championships
1962-64	Wins all-around silver medal at USSR National Championships
1963	Wins four gold medals at World Championships and is named world champion
1964	Wins three gold medals at World Championships and is named world champion
1964	Wins four gold medals at Winter Olympics
1964	First woman named Soviet Athlete of the Year
1967	Wins overall silver medal at USSR National Championships
1996	Inducted into the International Women's Sports Hall of Fame
1999	Named by *Associated Press* as one of top 10 female Winter Olympians of the 20th century
2002	Named to Bud Greenspan's list of 25 Greatest Winter Olympians

ing, she competed in three out of the four events. She placed fourth in the 1,000 meter but won a gold medal in the 1,500 meter (setting a world record) and the 3,000 meter, her favorite distance. She didn't race in the 500 meter, thought to be her only weakness.

Skoblikova cut back on her training during 1961 and 1962 to focus on teaching, but still won the all-around bronze medal at the 1961 World Championships and the all-around silver medal the following year. She returned in a big way in 1963. At the World Championships in Karuizawa, Japan, she swept all four races—the 500 meter, the 1,000 meter, the 1,500 meter, and the 3,000 meter. She was humble in victory, telling *Sports Illustrated*'s Shenker, "The others were just skating worse than I was."

Her greatest triumph, however, came at the 1964 Winter Olympics in Innsbruck, Austria, where the 24-year old duplicated her world championship success. The heavy favorite, she swept all four events: the 500, the 1,000, the 1,500, and the 3,000. She set world records in all but the 3,000. This last race took place as the ice was melting, so Skoblikova had to skate through some puddles, which slowed her pace. Yet instead of blaming host officials for the track's condition, writer Robert Condon quoted her in *Great Women Athletes of the 20th Century.* as saying, "The ice was perfect."

This feat—winning four gold medals in a single Olympics—has not been repeated by any other woman. Only two male athletes, American Eric Heiden and Norwegian biathlete **Ole Einar Bjoerndalen**, have since done so. Only one other woman, Russian cross-country skier Lyubov Egorova, managed to equal, almost thirty years later, her tally of six gold medals. As a reward for Skoblikova's singular success, Premier Nikita Khrushchev informed her that she was being made a member of the Communist Party.

Skoblikova added to her gold medal collection at the 1964 World Championships in Kristinehamn, Sweden, where she won the 1,000, the 1,500, and the 3,000 meter races. For the second year in a row, she was named the world champion.

Challenging Stereotypes

When Skoblikova entered the 1960 Winter Olympics, she encountered both gender and political preconceptions. As the first Games to feature women's speed skating, Skoblikova and the other female competitors were looked upon with suspicion. Speed skating requires quickness, strength, and endurance—attributes that many felt were unbecoming, if not absent, in females. Skoblikova offered a defense to Shenker of *Sports Illustrated*: "Skating makes us more feminine. . . . Cycling or skiing takes a lot of muscle, but skating does you no harm."

Skoblikova's appearance and personality played a role in disarming detractors. The 5-foot, 5-inch blue-eyed blonde weighed a slim 126 pounds and was typically described as attractive in press accounts. Her ready, warm smile and gracious manner charmed spectators. After winning a race, she played to the crowd, waving and smiling broadly. As she told *Sports Illustrated*'s Shenker, "At the theater you applaud a good actor who gives you pleasure. When I have won a race, giving people pleasure, I like to skate around the stadium wearing the laurel wreath of victory. People applaud and that gives me pleasure."

The dominance of the Soviet women at many of these Games' events also fueled rumors about the use of performance-enhancing drugs and even female impersonators. No one suggested Skoblikova, with her petite and shapely figure, was anything but a very talented skater.

The atmosphere at these Olympics, moreover, was thick with patriotic fervor. The Soviets seemed particularly unwilling to embrace the Games as a friendly competition. Instead, they viewed the Games as a way to prove Communist superiority and to instill pride among their people. Toward that end, the Soviets had supported and promoted their best athletes. Skoblikova benefited, receiving financial support and time off from her teaching duties to train. This led to charges, officially denied by the Soviets, that their athletes violated the Olympics' amateur-only requirement.

Despite the tension, Skoblikova won over many fans, including American figure skater Carol Heiss, who won a gold medal at the 1960 Games, where she met Skoblikova. Heiss later told Mechelle Voepel of *The Kansas City Star,* "The Russians always intrigued us, and she was so nice. But the ways things were, I didn't see her again until about 10 years ago. It was so much fun. It was like the years melted away."

An Enduring Legacy

Nearing thirty, Skoblikova competed in the 1968 Winter Games in Grenoble, France, but was not able to replicate her previous success. She raced in the 1,500 and 3,000 meters but failed to medal. Although her achievements had already earned her a celebrated place in sports history, her name remains relatively unknown outside her native country, mainly a result of the Cold War context in which she competed and the extent to which the sport has evolved. But her speed skating exploits have not been forgotten. Among her honors, she was inducted into the International Women's Sports Hall of Fame in 1996 and was named by Olympic historian and filmmaker **Bud Greenspan** in 2002 as one of the 25 Greatest Winter Olympians of All Time.

Nathan Aaseng, in his book *Women Olympic Champions,* wrote about Skoblikova's legacy: "First, she was a key member of a Soviet national women's team that pushed the limits of achievement far beyond those of the previous generation.... The Russians' success in turn pushed East Germany, the United States, and other countries into developing female athletes.... Second, Skoblikova stood out as an important contradiction to the stereotype of Soviet female athletes as cold, masculine machines. Her combination of incredible strength and endurance, grace under pressure, willingness to let her emotions show, and pride in her appearance, reinforced the idea that women could be warm and feminine and still enjoy and excel in sports."

FURTHER INFORMATION

Books

Aaseng, Nathan *Women Olympic Champions.* San Diego: Lucent Books, Inc., 2001.

Condon, Robert J. *Great Women Athletes of the 20th Century.* Jefferson, NC: McFarland & Company, Inc., 1991.

Greenspan, Bud. *Frozen in Time: The Greatest Moments at the Winter Olympics.* Santa Monica, CA: General Publishing Group, 1997.

Related Biography: Russian Skier Lyubov Egorova

At the 1994 Winter Olympics in Lillehammer, Norway, Russian cross-country skier Lyubov Egorova tied Skoblikova's record of six Olympic gold medals and was hailed as a sports hero. Her career and reputation, however, were derailed when she failed a drug test at the 1997 World Championships.

Egorova was born in Siberia in 1966 and moved to St. Petersburg as a teen to train on her country's best cross-country course. Described as a late bloomer, she didn't win her first international competition until she was 25. At the 1991 and 1993 World Championships, she won three gold medals. She also was the 1993 World Cup overall champion. Competing for the Unified Team at the 1992 Winter Olympics in Albertville, France, she medaled in all five nordic skiing events, winning three golds and two silvers. She matched Skoblikova's gold count at the 1994 Games, winning three more golds and a silver.

Egorova's downfall came in 1997, when she was caught taking a banned substance, Bromantan, which can enhance performance and mask other drugs. She was stripped of the gold medal she won days earlier and was barred from World Championship competition for two years. Egorova professed shock, insisting that she did not knowingly take Bromantan. Many did not believe her explanation that she accidentally consumed the substance by taking a medication.

Egorova lives in St. Petersburg with her husband and resumed competing at the end of her two-year ban. Although her Olympic record is unaffected, the scandal angered fans and competitors.

Tinovitsky, G., contributor. *How They Reached the Top: Stories of Soviet Sports Champions.* Moscow: Progress Publishers, 1966.

Periodicals

Bruno, Luca. "Norway Crowns Ole King." *Toronto Star* (February 21, 2002): D11.

Elliott, Helene. "Olympic Scene." *Los Angeles Times* (January 24, 2002): D7.

Shenker, Israel. "Curls and Cold Steel." *Sports Illustrated* (January 27, 1964): 40.

Voepel, Mechelle. "Three Previous Games Have Been American Beauties." *Kansas City Star* (February 3, 2002): I3.

Other

"34. Lyubov Egorova, Cross Country Skiing." *Sports Illustrated for Women.* http://sportsillustrated.cnn.com/siforwomen/top_100/34/ (November 29, 2002).

"Bud Greenspan's 10 Greatest Winter Olympians." http://media.gm.com/events/olympics/25_greatest.html(October 24, 2002).

"Championships of Russia and USSR. Ladies." www.speedskating.ru/en/stat/wrch1.html (November 22, 2002).

"Hall of Fame." Women's Sports Foundation. www.womenssportsfoundation.org/cg...iowa/about/awards/results.html?record=4 (October 24, 2002).

"History of Women in Sports Timeline." http://www.northnet.org/stlawrenceaauw/timelne8.htm (November 22, 2002).

"Lidia P. Skoblikova." International Journalists' Association ASMO-press. http://analytics.ex.ru/cgi-bin/

txtnscr.pl?node=589&=472⟨=2=1 (November 22, 2002).

"Lydia Skoblikova." Women's Sports Foundation. www.womenssportsfoundation.org/cgi-bin/iowa/ athletes/record.html?record=818 (October 24, 2002).

"Skoblikova, Lidiya Pavlovna." Chambers Biographical Dictionary 1997 http://vweb.hwwilsonweb.com/ cgi-bin/webspirs.cgi?sp.usernumbe (November 1, 2002).

Sketch by Carole Manny

Billy Smith
1950-

Canadian hockey player

Billy Smith was the National Hockey League's (NHL) dominant goalie of the early 1980s. A clutch performer who shone particularly bright in the post-season, Smith's goaltending led the New York Islanders to four consecutive Stanley Cup championships between 1979 and 1983, during which he set an NHL record for goalies, winning eighty-eight of 132 playoff games. Smith's playoff performance led Islander coach Al Arbour to call Smith "the greatest money goaltender of all time" in *Newsday*. But more than his dogged Stanley Cup play, "Battlin' Billy" was famous for his unrelenting aggression—some would have called it viciousness—in the goal crease. He used his stick like a battle axe on the bodies of opponents who came too close and he regularly led NHL goalies in penalty minutes. In 1979, Smith earned a place in NHL history, becoming the first goalie in NHL history to score a goal.

William John Smith was born in Perth, Ontario. Growing up with his brother Gord, who would later play with the NHL's Washington Capitals. Billy played junior hockey in the Perth area, first with the Smiths Falls Bears and then with the Cornwall Royals. The sixth round choice of the Los Angeles Kings in the 1970 amateur draft, Smith was sent to the Kings' Springfield farm club in the American Hockey League where he spent the 1970-71 and 1971-72 seasons. In 1971, with Smith in the net, Springfield won the Calder Cup.

Replacing the King's injured Rogie Vachon, Smith played five games with Los Angeles, winning one, with the Kings during the 1971-72 campaign. His violent style of play was already in evidence. The fights he was involved in those five games had repercussions for his future with the less aggressive Kings. "Rumor has it," he told Brian Biggane of the *Palm Beach Post,* "I was too violent for that team, so they left me unprotected in the 1972 expansion draft." The newborn New York Islanders grabbed him. In New York Smith continued his rough and tumble ways, fearlessly defending his goal crease against encroachment by opponents. He used whatever tactics were necessary—in one game against Buffalo he broke three of his sticks on the ankles of Sabres players—and along the way he set a season record for penalty minutes by a goalie.

Smith, though, was more than simply the brutal goalie the press would later make him out as. He trimmed a full goal from his goals against average in his second season, lowering it from 4.16 to 3.07. After sharing net-minding responsibilities with Gerry Dejardins for two years, Smith was made the Islanders number one goalie in 1974-75. He took the team to the Stanley Cup playoffs for the first time that season, attracting attention for his tenacious defense in a hard-fought overtime victory against the rival New York Rangers.

In 1975-76, Smith was platooned again, this time with Islander goalie Glenn "Chico" Resch, an arrangement Smith accepted graciously. On November 28, 1979, Smith made history in a game against the Colorado Rockies. When a delayed penalty against the Islanders was blown, the Rockies pulled their goalie. After an errant pass by a Rockies defenseman sailed into the team's undefended net, tape replays showed that Smith had been the last Islander to touch the puck, when it bounced off his chest. As a result he became the first goalie in NHL history to be credited with scoring a goal.

By the end of the 1970s, Smith had established himself as a goalie who refused to be intimidated. At the time, the NHL's smaller crease gave goalies less room to maneuver against opposing forwards who frequently threw violent body checks to get at the puck. Smith,

Career Statistics

Yr	Team	GP	W	L	T	GAA	TGA	SV	SV%	TSA	SHO
1971-72	LA	5	1	3	1	4.60	23	--	--	--	0
1972-73	NY	37	7	24	3	4.16	147	--	--	--	0
1973-74	NY	46	9	23	12	3.07	134	--	--	--	0
1974-75	NY	58	21	18	17	2.78	156	--	--	--	3
1975-76	NY	39	19	10	9	2.61	98	--	--	--	3
1976-77	NY	36	21	8	6	2.50	87	--	--	--	2
1977-78	NY	38	20	8	8	2.65	95	--	--	--	2
1978-79	NY	40	25	8	4	2.87	108	--	--	--	1
1979-80	NY	38	15	14	7	2.95	104	--	--	--	2
1980-81	NY	41	22	10	8	3.28	129	--	--	--	2
1981-82	NY	46	32	9	4	2.97	133	--	--	--	0
1982-83	NY	41	18	14	7	2.87	112	1083	.906	1195	1
1983-84	NY	42	23	13	2	3.42	130	1122	.896	1252	2
1984-85	NY	37	18	14	3	3.82	133	967	.879	1100	0
1985-86	NY	41	20	14	4	3.72	143	1061	.881	1204	1
1986-87	NY	40	14	18	5	3.52	132	875	.869	1007	1
1987-88	NY	38	17	14	5	3.22	113	949	.894	1062	2
1988-89	NY	17	3	11	0	4.44	54	310	.852	364	0
TOTAL		680	305	233	105	3.17	2031	--	--	--	22

LA: Los Angeles Kings; NY: New York Islanders.

concerned that such play could result in a career-shortening injury, fought for his ground. All was fair in the on-ice war. His chopping attacks at opponents' legs earned him the moniker "Hatchet Man." He jabbed opponents regularly with the butt end of this stick; however, after Smith hit Lindy Ruff in the eye, the NHL initiated a rule that required goalies to have a large knob on the end of their stick's handle. In 1987, largely as a consequence of Smith's aggressively violent play, the NHL enlarged the goal crease to a six-foot semicircle.

Smith was his own man in every way. After an Islander loss in a playoff round, Smith refused to take part in the traditional NHL handshakes, finding the ritual hypocritical. Even among his own teammates, Smith had a reputation as a loner. He avoided team meetings. He disliked practice and training camp, seeing them as likely opportunities for an unnecessary injury. He got into fights with teammates who shot too high in practice rounds, and he would whack his own defensemen on the leg with his stick if they got in his line of sight during a game.

The Islanders appreciated his play however. "Playing with Billy Smith you knew what was expected," teammate Denis Potvin told Brian Biggane. "He wouldn't overhandle the puck ever, and if he went out and handled it behind the net he always left it. So there was no guessing or hesitation on our part, and his whole game was like that, to us very predictable." Smith revolutionized the goalie's conditioning regimen, playing tennis to improve his footwork and video games to sharpen his hand-eye coordination.

Billy Smith came into his own in the 1979-80 season and when Resch left the team late in the year,

Smith was left to mind the net for Stanley Cup play. The Islanders won the Cup, a feat they repeated in the next three seasons as well. The playoffs brought out the best in Smith. His goal against average was consistently better in the playoffs than in the regular season. The high-point was his play in the hard-fought 1983 Stanley Cup finals, in which the Islanders swept the Vancouver Canucks and Smith allowed only six goals, holding **Wayne Gretzky** scoreless for the entire series. Smith's performance led to his being awarded the Conn Smythe Trophy as the most valuable player in the 1983 playoffs.

In 1985 the aging Islanders launched a youth movement that saw Smith share net-minding duties with new players. In the 1988-89 season, he played in a mere seventeen games. Seeing the writing on the wall, the 38-year-old Smith announced his retirement in June 1989. When he ended his playing career, his eighty-eight playoff victories and 489 penalty minutes were NHL records for goalies. Smith stayed on with the Islanders as an assistant coach through the end of the 1992-93 season. In 1993 he was signed as goaltending coach by the expansion Florida Panthers. He became the Panthers' assistant head coach in 1999. In 2001 Smith rejoined the New York Islanders as the team's goaltending coach.

With 305 regular season victories and his remarkable playoff record—eighty-eight victories and a 2.73 goal against average—Billy Smith proved himself one of the great goalies of the last three decades of the 20th century. In February 1993, his number was retired by the New York Islanders. That same year, Smith was elected to the Hockey Hall of Fame.

Awards and Accomplishments

1982	NHL All-Star, First Team
1982	Vezina Trophy
1983	Conn Smythe Trophy
1983	William Jennings Trophy
1993	Elected to NHL Hall of Fame
1993	Number retired by New York Islanders

FURTHER INFORMATION

Books

Diamond, Dan. *Total Hockey,* 2nd ed. New York: Total Sports Publishing, 2000.

Fishler, Stan, and Shirley Fishler. *Fishler's Ice Hockey Encyclopedia.* New York: Thomas Y. Crowell Company.

Hunter, Douglas. *Hockey's Greatest Stars.* New York: Benchmark Press, 1995.

McDowell, Chris. *Hockey All-Stars: The NHL Honor Roll.* Buffalo, NY: Firefly Books, 2000.

Periodicals

Beech, Mark. "Billy Smith, Islanders Goaltender." *Sports Illustrated* (May 10, 1999): 17.

Biggane, Brian. "Billy Smith, Coach." *Palm Beach Post* (September 11, 1998): 1C.

Calabria, Pat. "Last Fight for Isles' Battlin' Billy?" *Sporting News* (April 3, 1989): 35.

Finn, Robert. "Smith Retires, Will Coach Goalies." *New York Times* (June 6, 1989): A27.

LaPointe, Joe. "This Time, His Number Will Raise to the Roof." *New York Times* (February 20, 1993): A30.

Rosa, Francis. "Smith seeks an end to the cheap shots." *Boston Globe* (January 17, 1991): 64.

Vescey, George. "Smitty Gave Acupuncture On the Ice." *New York Times* (February 24, 1993): B 9.

Williams, Jeff. "From Volatile To Vaunted—Battlin' Billy Smith Enters Hall." *Newsday* (November 17, 1993): 172.

Williams, Jeff. "Isles to raise Smith's sweater to Coliseum rafters." *Newsday* (February 18, 1993): 150.

Other

"Billy Smith." http://www.legendsofhockey.net (January 18, 2003).

Sketch by Gerald E. Brennan

Emmitt Smith
1969-

American football player

Emmitt Smith

Running back Emmitt Smith has been playing with the Dallas Cowboys football team since 1990. He is the NFL's all-time rushing leader, and was the first player to rush for more than 1,400 yards in five straight NFL seasons (1991-1995); he won rushing titles in 1991, 1992, 1993, and 1995. He has led the Cowboys to three Super Bowl titles and was named MVP of Super Bowl XXVII in 1994. Smith has been to the Pro Bowl nine times and has established himself as one of the NFL's all-time greats.

Football Dreams Come True

Smith grew up as a fan of the Dallas Cowboys, and always dreamed of playing with them. His family didn't have much income, and sometimes relied on government programs providing cheese and milk. When his mother couldn't afford to buy him new clothes for middle school, he worked as a handyman, then at K-mart and at a television station in order to earn the money to buy the clothes himself. As a young man, he learned to cook so that he could help take care of his bedridden grandmother.

He attended the University of Florida, but in 1990, after his junior year, he left school and decided to play professional football. He is not tall—at five-foot nine he is shorter than most other players. When he was being assessed by scouts for the football draft, 16 teams passed him up, considering him too small and too slow.

Chronology	
1969	Born in Pensacola, Florida
1988-90	Attends University of Florida
1990	Drafted by Dallas Cowboys, leaves school to play pro football
1990- **present**	Plays with Dallas Cowboys
2000	Marries Patricia Southall

Awards and Accomplishments	
1990-95, **1998-2000**	Pro Bowl player
1991	Wins rushing title
1991-95	First player to rush more than 1,400 yards in five straight NFL seasons
1992	Wins rushing title
1992	NFL MVP
1993	Wins rushing title
1993	Cowboys win Super Bowl
1994	Cowboys win Super Bowl
1994	MVP, Super Bowl XXVIII
1995	Wins rushing title
1996	Cowboys win Super Bowl
2002	Becomes NFL all-time rushing leader

However, he is strong and has a low center of gravity. He uses this to his advantage to gain leverage on other players who are often bigger and heavier than he is. The Dallas Cowboys decided to take him on, and he was drafted in 1990.

Smith was happy not only because he was playing for the team that he had idolized as a child, but also because he would have the chance to improve his family's economic situation. He told a *Sports Illustrated for Kids* reporter, "I looked at my Mama, and I looked at where we were living. I said to her that we have a chance to move on up."

Smith was an instant success with the Cowboys. He gained 937 yards rushing in his rookie season (1990) and led the NFL the next season with 1,563 yards. Smith teamed up with quarterback **Troy Aikman** and wide receiver **Michael Irvin** to give Dallas the league's most potent offense.

It all came together for the Cowboys in 1992. Smith won the league's Most Valuable Player award after leading the league once again with 1,713 yards and 18 touchdowns. Dallas finished the season with a 13-3 record and went on to win Super Bowl XXVII 52-17 over the Buffalo Bills. Smith gained 101 yards in the game.

The Cowboys repeated as Super Bowl champions the next season, once again defeating the Bills, this time 30-13. Behind the scenes, Smith's journey to that Super Bowl was excruciatingly painful, as he suffered a separated right shoulder during the season-finale game against the Giants. Despite the injury, he continued to play. Teammate Darren Woodson told Paul Attner in the *Sporting News,* "No question, he has the biggest heart here. He expects to win games and he doesn't expect anyone else to do it for him. Because he cares."

Super Bowl MVP

After the game, Smith was in such severe pain that he thought he was having a heart attack. He spent a night in the hospital, but took part in three playoff games, including that year's Super Bowl; he was chosen as MVP of the Super Bowl after rushing for 132 yards and scoring two second-half touchdowns. Smith was also named *Sporting News* Sportsman of the Year in 1994. He told Attner that he played despite the injury because "You have players relying on you. I didn't want to let them down." When asked whether winning was worth the

pain, Smith replied, "It would be kind of hard to say I would do it again. . . . But we won. That felt great."

In 1996, the Cowboys won the Super Bowl for a third time, defeating the Pittsburgh Steelers 27-17. In that same year, Smith, who had dropped out of college after his junior year to play football, completed his degree in public recreation. He had attended classes during the off-season to complete his education, because he had once promised his mother that he would get a degree. "I've always been a man of my word," Smith explained to a reporter in *Time for Kids.* "It was super important to me."

Smith continued to play at a high level, earning Pro Bowl honors in 1997, 1998, and 1999. But the team's play began to suffer. When the Cowboys did poorly in 2000 and 2001, Smith wrote a letter to his teammates, whose morale was slumping. He asked them all to train harder during the off-season, saying that if they were tired of losing, they should be willing to make sacrifices and work hard in order to win. In 2000, Smith married Patricia Southall Lawrence, a former beauty queen. They would later have three children.

At the end of the 2001 season, Smith had under 1,000 yards to go in order to break the all-time rushing record, set by Hall-of-Famer **Walter Payton** of the Chicago Bears, with 16,726. Smith believed he could set a new record. In an interview in *Sports Illustrated* for Kids, Smith said, "One thing I have no control over is injuries. But I've done all I can to prepare myself on the football field." Smith said that when he broke the record, he would be "so emotional," and commented, "It is something that my heart has been set on since I became a professional athlete."

Smith told a *Sports Illustrated for Kids* reporter that he planned to dedicate the 2002 season to Walter Payton. "I love him like my own father and my own teammates. He is a part of me, and I'm a part of him. There is no way I could find myself on the football field without thinking of him." Smith had met Payton in 1995, and Payton had told him that he had a chance to break the record. The two men became friends, and supported each other during times when Smith was injured or

Career Statistics

		Rushing				Receiving				Fumbles	
Yr	Team	ATT	YDS	AVG	TD	REC	YDS	AVG	TD	FUM	LST
1990	DAL	241	937	3.9	11	24	228	9.5	0	7	0
1991	DAL	365	1563	4.3	12	49	258	5.3	1	8	0
1992	DAL	373	1713	4.6	18	59	335	5.7	1	4	0
1993	DAL	283	1486	5.3	9	57	414	7.3	1	4	0
1994	DAL	368	1484	4.0	21	50	341	6.8	1	1	0
1995	DAL	377	1773	4.7	25	62	375	6.0	0	7	6
1996	DAL	327	1204	3.7	12	47	249	5.3	3	5	2
1997	DAL	261	1074	4.1	4	40	234	5.8	0	1	1
1998	DAL	319	1332	4.2	13	27	175	6.5	2	3	2
1999	DAL	329	1397	4.2	11	27	119	4.4	2	5	3
2000	DAL	294	1203	4.1	9	11	79	7.2	0	6	5
2001	DAL	261	1021	3.9	3	17	116	6.8	0	1	1
2002	DAL	254	975	3.8	5	16	89	5.6	0	3	1
TOTAL		4052	17162	4.2	153	186	3012	6.2	11	55	21

DAL: Dallas Cowboys.

when Payton became terminally ill with liver disease. Payton died in 1999, and Smith became a mentor to Payton's son Jarrett, also a football player.

A New Rushing Record

On November 3, 2002, Smith broke the record in a game against the Seattle Seahawks. So far that season, he had averaged only 63.9 yards per game, and he needed 93 to break the record. According to S.L. Price in *Sports Illustrated,* Seahawks defensive lineman Chad Eaton said during the coin toss, "You're not going to get it today on us." Eaton was wrong—by the fourth quarter, Smith was just 13 yards short of the record. When he broke the record. Price wrote, "The game stopped, he saw his mother's face and wept, kissed his wife, Pat, and their three kids, hugged former teammate Daryl Johnston and wept again." The players took a five-minute break, and when the game resumed, Smith played hard, finishing the day with 109 yards on 24 carries. Payton's son Jarrett told Price that Smith was so similar to his father that if the record had to be broken, he was glad Smith was the one to do it.

Despite his record, Smith was battling assessments that said he was too old to keep playing and that he had lost his power, according to Price. However, Smith explained to Price, "Don't tell me I should quit because of my age. That's what makes this frustrating. You have to know who you are. I know who I am."

Smith's future in Dallas is uncertain. In an article posted on the Cowboys Web site, new Dallas coach **Bill Parcells** told Nick Eatman that Smith's $9.8 million salary was expensive for the team, and commented, "I am certainly aware of what Emmitt Smith has accomplished. This is a thing that we'll have to. . . discuss at a later time. I think we'll have to talk about that. . . . But, obviously, there will be changes, there's no doubt about that."

When Smith is not playing football, he frequently donates his time to helping sick children. He receives frequent requests from sick children who want to meet him. He told Attner, "You try to do the best you can and meet as many as time allows. You know they aren't physically able, and you aren't sure how long they are going to be on this earth." He expressed surprise that out of all the people they could see, they choose to meet him, and said he is glad he can make them happy. He told Attner, "I want them to touch me and feel me and let me cuddle them, so they know I am a person, not some kind of myth."

In the mid-1990s, Smith established Emmitt Smith Charities, Inc., which provides food and other necessities to poor families, and also provides toys to poor children. Dallas running backs coach Joe Brodsky told Attner, "I credit his upbringing for the way he conducts himself. When he talks about his feelings for others, he means it." Dallas safety James Washington said that Smith's loving relationship with his mother is probably part of this. "You can see Emmitt is truly loved. It is real neat to see."

Smith is proud that he has spent his entire football career with the Cowboys. He told the *Sports Illustrated for Kids* reporter that he wanted to be remembered as "a guy who came to work every day. A guy who didn't take a lot of days off. Dependable, durable, but also smart."

CONTACT INFORMATION

Address: c/o Dallas Cowboys, One Cowboy Way, Irving, TX 75063-4727; c/o Emmitt Smith Charities Inc., 880 N. Reus Street, Pensacola, FL 32501. Fax: 850-432-2414. Phone: 850-469-1544. Online: www.dallascowboys.com.

Emmitt's Domain

The line kept opening holes, and Emmitt Smith kept hitting them hard and gliding through, getting closer. Thirteen years ago he had vowed that he would get here, to this moment in football history. . . . He spun. He juked. He ground out yard after yard against the Seattle Seahawks, 55 in the first quarter alone, each step taking him closer to Walter Payton's NFL rushing record. . . .

On second down he took the ball. . . cut left, found a seam, stumbled over a defender's arm, placed his right hand on the turf, kept his balance and kept on chugging until he had caught Payton and passed him by.

Source: Price, S. L. *Sports Illustrated,* November 4, 2002: 42.

SELECTED WRITINGS BY SMITH:

Smith, Emmitt. "Run for the Record." *Sports Illustrated for Kids,* September 1, 2002, 29.

FURTHER INFORMATION

Periodicals

Attner, Paul. "Star Power." *Sporting News,* December 19, 1994, 10.
"Emmitt Smith Sets All-Time Touchdown Record." *Jet,* January 18, 1999: 47.
"Emmitt Smith Weds Patricia Lawrence in Dallas." *Jet,* May 8, 2000: 58.
"Emmitt's Promise." *Time for Kids,* May 10, 1996: 8.
King, Peter. "The Quest." *Sports Illustrated,* October 18, 1993: 79.
Price, S.L. "Emmitt's Domain." *Sports Illustrated,* November 4, 2002: 42.

Other

Armour, Nancy. "Walter Payton Dies at 45." November 9, 1999. Canoe. http://www.canoe.ca/ (January 5, 2003)
Eatman, Nick. "Coaching Staff, Emmitt and More." Dallas Cowboys Official Web site. http://www. dallascowboys.com/ (January 3, 2002).
"Player Profile: Emmitt Smith." Dallas Cowboys Official Web site. http://www.dallascowboys.com/ (January 2, 2003).
"#22 Emmitt Smith." ESPN.com. http://sports.espn.go. com/ (January 2, 2003).

Sketch by Kelly Winters

Tommie Smith
1944-

American track and field athlete

Tommie Smith

Sprinter Tommie Smith once held eleven world and American records at the same time, but is most noted for his silent civil rights protest at the Mexico City Olympics in 1968. Standing on the podium after accepting his gold medal for a world-record performance in the 200 meters, Smith raised one black-gloved fist in a salute to African-American power, inciting both controversy and praise.

A Hard-Working Childhood

Smith was the seventh of twelve children born to Richard and Dora Smith, migrant workers near Clarksville, Texas, a rural town close to the Oklahoma border. His family subsisted on what they could make by picking cotton, hunting, and fishing, but when Smith was six-years-old, his father decided they could make a better life in California, and piled the family into an old truck. Eventually, they made it to California, where, as Smith told John Maher in the *Austin-American Statesman,* the work was no better, but "there was more of it." Smith worked in the fields with the rest of his family.

Smith also attended school in the town of Lemoore, where during high school he was voted Most Valuable Athlete for three years in a row in basketball, football, and track and field. He particularly loved basketball, and eventually earned a scholarship to San Jose State University. The basketball court was too small for his long legs, though, and he kept crashing into the walls of the

Chronology	
1944	Born June 6, in Clarksville, Texas
1950	Moves to California with his family
1968	Wins gold medal at Mexico City Olympics, makes protest on medal stand
1968	Dropped from Olympic team as a result of his protest
1969-71	Plays with Cincinnati Bengals of National Football League (NFL)
1971	Coaches at Oberlin College
1971-present	Coaches at Santa Monica College

Awards and Achievements	
1966	World and American record in 200 meters, 20.0
1966	American record in 220 yards (straightaway), 19.5
1967	U.S. National Champion, 200 meters, 20.4
1967	American record, 200 meters, 20.26
1967	NCAA Champion, 200 meters, 20.2
1967	World and American record, 400 meters, 44.5
1968	U.S. National Champion, 200 meters, 20.3
1968	American record, 200 meters, 20.18
1968	World record in 200 meters, 19.83
1968	Olympic gold medal, 200 meters, 19.83
1993	Mt. Sac Relays Hall of Fame
1996	California Black Sports Hall of Fame
1999	California Black Sports Hall of Fame Sportsman of the Year
1999	Bay Area Hall of Fame
1999	Lemoore Union High School Hall of Fame
1999	San Jose University Sports Hall of Fame
2000-01	Commendation, Recognition, and Proclamation Awards, County of Los Angeles and State of Texas

school's tiny gym. He eventually switched to track and field, where he starred, breaking thirteen world records.

At college, Smith also became politically active. Filled with an awareness of the huge gap in civil rights between African Americans and white Americans, Smith, like some of the other students, was aware that as a young African American man, he had fewer opportunities than white students. If he was successful, he could use that success to make a point on behalf of African American equality. As he told David Steele in the *San Francisco Chronicle,* "I had nothing [to lose]. I had God-given ability, but no place in society."

Civil Rights Protests

American society at the time was filled with protest and strife. In 1968, for example, Robert Kennedy and civil rights leader Martin Luther King were both assassinated; the Democratic national convention led to riots in the streets; and activists for black power, such as Eldridge Cleaver and Huey Newton, were in the headlines. In Vietnam, U.S. troops launched the Tet Offensive, sparking violent antiwar protests at home.

Many American athletes were unsure whether the Olympic Games would even be held. Riots in Mexico City, where the Games would be held, led to the deaths of 200 protesters. In addition, some athletes were considering boycotting the Games in a protest against racial discrimination.

By the time Smith graduated from college in 1967, he was the best 200- and 400-meter runner in the world, and was a member of the first mile-relay team to run the distance in under three minutes. In October of 1968, Smith went to the Olympics in Mexico City. In the semifinals of the 200 meters, he injured his thigh, was carried out on a stretcher, and was unsure whether he would be able to run in the finals. When the finals came, however, he took off and beat the field so easily that he raised his arms in triumph ten yards before crossing the finish line. He had run the distance in 19.83 seconds, a world record.

As the American national anthem began, Smith and American teammate John Carlos, who won the bronze medal, stood on the podium at the award ceremony, heads down, and raised black-gloved fists in a silent protest against racism and the lack of civil rights given to African Americans. According to Maher, Smith said at the time, "White America will only give us credit for an Olympic victory. [If I win] they'll say I'm an American, but if I did something bad, they'd say [I'm] a Negro."

According to Mike Cassidy in the *Knight Ridder/Tribune News Service,* Smith later said that he expected to be shot dead for this action. "I kept waiting for the gunshot," he said. "I thought we were dead men. And when all was said and done, I knew this is what we'd be remembered for."

Of his action, Smith told Lynn Zinser in the *Knight Ridder/Tribune News Service,* "When you have a platform, use it. You're kind of dumb if you don't." And, he said, "What we did, that was something for pride. That wasn't for the money. That was for blood. That was for the dignity."

Kicked off the Olympic Team

As a result of his protest, Smith and Carlos were kicked off the U.S. Olympic team. The International Olympic Committee threw Smith and Carlos out of the Olympic village, and they were suspended from all further Olympic competition.

Responses to the protest were mixed, even among other African Americans. Some resented the fact that after the protest, reporters didn't want to talk about athletic events—they only wanted to know what the athletes thought of the protest. Some athletes made their own statements: long jumper Bob Beamon wore black socks on the victory stand, and the 400-meter relay team raised their fists on the medal stand, but not while the national anthem was playing.

After the Olympics, Smith played football with the Cincinnati Bengals in the National Football League (NFL) for three years, and then became an assistant professor of physical education at Oberlin College. He was then hired to coach track and teach physical education at Santa Monica College in California, where he has remained for over twenty-five years. At the college, Smith told Steele, he doesn't discuss what he views as trivial matters with students: how fast they are, what their relationships are like, how they dress or do their hair. Instead, he said, "I ask them what their goal is, what their future is, what they plan to do in life when they are through with athletics, do they have a plan. . . . Sometimes they walk right out. . . . I'm not there just to praise them and how they play. I make kids mad." Smith also told Steele that he is often annoyed by the shallowness of students' concerns, their emphasis on money and fame, and their lack of appreciation for the sacrifices made by those who came before them.

In recent years, Smith has been honored by those who see him as a civil rights hero. He was inducted into the California Black Sports Hall of Fame in 1996, and in 1999, he was honored as the California Black Sports Hall of Fame Sportsman of the Millennium. In that same year, he was also inducted into the Bay Area Hall of Fame, the Lemoore Union High School Hall of Fame, and the San Jose University Sports Hall of Fame. At the 2000 Olympic track and field trials, Smith was chosen to give the medals to the winners in the 200 meters. In 2000-2001, Smith was presented with Commendation, Recognition, and Proclamation Awards by the County of Los Angeles and the State of Texas.

Smith's Legacy

Smith and Carlos' act of rebellion made millions of television viewers aware of civil rights issues. Smith told Maher that his protest helped pave the way for other civil rights and social changes, including Title IX, a groundbreaking federal law that mandated that female athletes be given opportunity and funding equal to that given to males.

As Zinser noted, although racism is still present in American society, many African American athletes take the money they are offered and do not take the risk of making potentially controversial political or social statements. For example she wrote that golfer **Tiger Woods** "tolerates discriminatory country clubs." Basketball player **Michael Jordan**, who "had the biggest stage of any athlete ever . . . used it to advance nothing other than his legend and his bank account." Few athletes now take the risk of losing money, in favor of political or social action. Although Smith was reviled at the time for his action, now he is widely recognized for his integrity. As Zinser wrote, he and Carlos "took the risk because of what they believed. It took unimaginable courage."

CONTACT INFORMATION

Address: c/o Santa Monica College Athletic and Physical Education, 1900 Pico Blvd., Santa Monica, CA 90405-1628. Phone: (310) 434-4310. Online: www.tommiesmith.com.

FURTHER INFORMATION

Periodicals

Cassidy, Mike. "Auction of Tommie Smith's Medal Raises Questions." *Knight Ridder/Tribune News Service* (April 18, 2001): K7982.

Harris, Beth. "'68 Medalist Who Shocked World Joins Torch Relay." *Daily News* (Los Angeles, CA) (April 28, 1996): N8.

Maher, John. "Two Fists Jarred the World." *Austin-American Statesman* (July 13, 1996), p. D1.

Meacham, Jody. "U.S. Olympian Tommie Smith to be Honored for Records Overshadowed by Protest in Mexico City." *Knight Ridder/Tribune News Service* (May 26, 1994): 0526K4905.

Moore, Kenny. "The Eye of the Storm." *Sports Illustrated* (August 12, 1991): 60.

Steele, David. "Smith's Crusade is Still on Track." *San Francisco Chronicle* (November 12, 1999): E1.

Zinser, Lynn. "Tommie Smith Talks of Higher Goals for Athletes." *Knight Ridder/Tribune News Service* (July 22, 2000): K4945.

Other

"Black-Fist Display Gets Varied Reaction in Olympic Village." *Sporting News* (October 16, 1968), http://www.sportingnews.com/ (November 18, 2002).

"John Carlos." *New York Beacon* (August 7, 2002), http://www.newyorkbeacon.com (December 11, 2002).

Sports Stars USA Web site. http://www.sportsstarsusa.com/ (November 8, 2002).

"Tommie Smith." Mt. Sac College Web site. http://vm.mtsac.edu/relays/HallFame/Smith2.htm (November 18, 2002).

Tommie Smith's Web site. http://www.tommiesmith.com/ (November 11, 2002).

Sketch by Kelly Winters

Karen Smyers
1961-

American triathlete

Endurance athlete Karen Smyers, who has participated in triathlons since 1984, has a never-give-up attitude. A seven-time U.S.A. Triathlon Elite National Champion and winner of both the Hawaiian Ironman

Chronology

1961	Born September 1 in Corry, Pennsylvania
1983	Graduates from Princeton University with a degree in economics
1984	Enters her first triathlon, using bicycle she rides to work; enters Bud Light Series triathlon in Boston as an amateur and finishes second overall
1984-89	Works at computer consulting firm, training and competing in triathlons in spare time
1985	Begins entering triathlons as a professional
1989	Computer consulting firm closes; Smyers becomes full-time triathlete; places fourth in International Triathlon Union (ITU) World Championships at Avignon, France
1990	Places first at ITU World Championships in Orlando, Florida
1992	With prize money and product endorsement contracts, begins earning a six-figure income
1994	Enters first Hawaiian Ironman Triathlete after husband, Michael King, enters as an amateur; Smyers places fourth
1995	Wins Hawaiian Ironman after champion Paula Newby-Fraser collapses near finish line; wins ITU World Championship, making her the only woman to win both titles in the same year
1996	Wins Long Distance World Championship at Muncie, Indiana
1997	Storm window falls and shatters, cutting Smyers's left thigh and severing her hamstring
1998	Daughter, Jenna, is born by Caesarian section, in May; in August, Smyers is hit by 18-wheel truck while riding her bicycle and badly injured; resumes training four months later
1999	Finishes 38th at ITU World Championships, in spite of having bronchitis; in September, doctors diagnose probable thyroid cancer; finishes second in Hawaiian Ironman in October and postpones biopsies until after race in Ixtapa, Mexico, in November; at Ixtapa race, fallen cyclist causes Smyers to flip her bike, breaking her collarbone; cancerous thyroid is removed in December
2000	Places fourth among American women, 22nd overall, at 2000 Olympics trials in Sydney, Australia, but fails to make U.S. Olympic team due to seventh place finish in finals; begins radioactive iodine treatments for thyroid cancer
2001	Finishes fifth in Hawaiian Ironman in October; wins U.S. Elite National Championship; in December, first annual checkup shows no cancer
2002	Continues to compete in triathlons; although plagued by a bladder problem, finishes Hawaiian Ironman in October, placing 27th; sister Donna Smyers breaks Hawaiian Ironman record in her 45-49 age group

Awards and Accomplishments

1989	Fourth place, International Triathlon Union (ITU) Triathlon World Championships
1990	ITU Triathlon World Champion
1990-95	Won U.S.A. Triathlon Elite National Championships
1991, 1994-95	Named Triathlete of the Year by *Triathlete Magazine*
1992-94, 1997, 1999	Won St. Croix (Virgin Islands) International Half Ironman Triathlon
1993	Second place, ITU Triathlon World Championships; fourth place, Gatorade Ironman; voted #1 in Readers' Poll by *Triathlete Magazine*
1994	Second place, Gatorade Ironman; fourth place, Hawaiian Ironman
1994-96	USOC Athlete of the Year, Triathlon
1995	Hawaiian Ironman World Champion; ITU Triathlon World Champion; won gold medal at Pan Am Games; New England Leadership Award
1996	ITU Triathlon World Champion-Long Course; fifth place, ITU Triathlon World Championships
1998	Fifth place, ITU Triathlon World Championships-Long Course
2001	Won U.S.A. Elite National Championships; first place, Muskoka, Canada, Triathlon; first place, New York City Triathlon; fifth place, Hawaiian Ironman; fifth place Roth Ironman; won Trek Arete Comeback Athlete Award; voted Sports Mom of the Year by *Working Mother* Magazine

The Trek Arete Awards, sponsored by Trek Bicycles, is given to inspirational athletes who overcome tremendous obstacles in the pursuit of their goals.

World Championship and the International Triathlon Union (ITU) Triathlon World Championship in 1995, Smyers soon afterward became known for her brave battles against injury and cancer. In spite of daunting obstacles, which contributed to her failure to make the 2000 U.S. Olympic triathlon team, Smyers kept training, competing, and winning. In 2002, at age forty-one, she finished the Hawaiian Ironman—with its 2.4-mile ocean swim, 112-mile bike ride, and 26.2-mile run—for the seventh time. Smyers said she hopes to continue competing for years to come.

Young Swimmer

Karen Smyers was born September 1, 1961, in Corry, Pennsylvania. She grew up in Wethersfield, Connecticut, in an athletic family of eight children. She joined her older siblings on the town swim team at age eight. She swam competitively at Wethersfield High School and was named All-State. After graduation Smyers entered Princeton University and swam on the Princeton team, which won the Association of Intercollegiate Athletics for Women (AIAW) Conference Division I Eastern Championships three of the four years she was on the team. She has credited swimming with giving her the aerobic capacity and competitive drive that propelled her to success in the triathlon.

After graduating from Princeton in 1983 with a degree in economics, Smyers was looking for a sport in which she could nurture her drive to compete. Her former roommate was planning to enter a triathlon, so the two trained together. Smyers entered her first triathlon in 1984, although her only bicycle was the one she used to ride to work at a computer consulting firm.

From Amateur to Full-time Pro

Upgrading to a better bike, Smyers entered the Bud Light Series triathlon in Boston, also in 1984, as an amateur. She finished first in her division and second overall but missed out on the $500 prize money because of her amateur status. From then on, she entered triathlons as a professional, although still working at the computer firm until it closed in 1989. She then turned full-time pro and by the early 1990s began earning a six-figure income, including prize money and product endorsements for shoe, sportswear, and bicycle companies.

In 1989, Smyers placed fourth in the International Triathlon Union (ITU) Triathlon World Championships. Then in 1990 she began a six-year first-place winning streak in the U.S.A. Triathlon Elite National Championships. She also won the ITU World Championship in 1990.

In the early 1990s, Smyers had been entering the shorter triathlons—the World Championship consists of a .9-mile swim, a 24.8-mile bike ride, and a 6.2-mile run—but the longer and more grueling Ironman races began to intrigue her. First winning the St. Croix (Virgin Islands) International Half Ironman triathlon in 1992, 1993, and 1994, and placing in the top five in the Gatorade Ironman in 1993 and 1994, Smyers entered her first Hawaiian Ironman in 1994 and placed fourth. Her husband, film producer Michael King, also entered, as an amateur. Smyers's time in the 1994 Ironman was the fastest ever among women entering the race for the first time. She was hooked on the most challenging race in the sport.

Iron Woman

In 1995, Smyers returned to the lava fields of Kailua-Kona, Hawaii, for the Ironman Triathlon. Close on the heels of seven-time victor **Paula Newby-Fraser** in the final event, the run, Smyers won the Ironman after Fraser collapsed short of the finish line. Smyers's total time in the event was nine hours, sixteen minutes, and forty-six seconds. (The total time allowed to finish the Ironman is seventeen hours.) In the same year, Smyers again won the ITU Triathlon World Championship and also won a gold medal at the Pan American Games. She was the first woman ever to win both the Ironman and the ITU championship in the same year.

By 1997, Smyers was looking forward to the 2000 Olympics, in which the women's triathlon would become an event for the first time. She again won the St. Croix International Half Ironman in the spring of 1997, but then in June a streak of ill luck befell her. As she was changing a storm window at her home in Lincoln, Massachusetts, the window fell and shattered, sending a glass shard through her left thigh and severing her hamstring. During the months of healing and rehabilitation, she and Michael de-

cided it was time to start a family. Their daughter, Jenna, was born in May 1998, by Caesarian section. After a brief period of recovery, Smyers was training again in August, when another accident occurred. She was riding her bike on a narrow road with training partner Glenn Cunha when a passing 18-wheel truck hit her bike. The fall caused six broken ribs, a lung contusion, and a separated shoulder.

Four months later, at the end of 1998, Smyers resumed training. Racing again in 1999, she was proud to finish, albeit in 38th place, the ITU World Championships—she had bronchitis at the time. In September 1999, doctors told her she probably had thyroid cancer. Because this type of cancer is typically slow growing, she went on to finish second in the Hawaiian Ironman in October and to enter a race in Ixtapa, Mexico, in November, before having biopsies performed. At the Ixtapa triathlon, another cyclist overturned in front of Smyers, causing her to flip off her bike, breaking her collarbone. It was the first time in her career that she did not finish a race.

2000 Olympic Trials

Smyers's biopsies did show a cancerous thyroid, which she had removed in December 1999, just a few months before the Olympic trials began in Sydney, Australia. Back in training, she placed 22nd overall and fourth among American women in the Sydney competition to choose the first member of the U.S. team. She still had to compete in Dallas, where the other two members would be chosen. As the media began covering her Olympic hopes, in light of her bad luck over the preceding few years, *Sports Illustrated* called her "the Triathlete Most Likely to be Eaten by a Shark at the Sydney Olympics" (there had been nine shark sightings near the swim course). Always one with a sense of humor—she writes a column called "Laughter Is the Best Medicine" for a triathlon magazine—Smyers took it all in stride. But when it came time for the Dallas trials, she placed seventh instead of in the top two she needed to make the Olympic team.

Continuing Competition

In August, Smyers had another surgery to remove cancerous lymph nodes and then began radioactive-iodine therapy, joking, "I will be able to read in bed without a night light." After the surgery, her daughter, Jenna, wore Band-Aids on her neck just like her mother.

Smyers continued to train and compete throughout 2001, bringing home several wins, including her seventh U.S.A. Elite National Championship and first place in the 2001 U.S.A. Triathlon pro championships at the first New York City Triathlon. She also took fifth place at the Hawaiian Ironman. Trek Bicycles gave her the Trek Arete Comeback Athlete Award, given to athletes who have overcome tremendous obstacles while pursuing their goals.

In December 2001, Smyers's annual checkup showed no cancer, to her great relief. She told *Swim Magazine* that it was immensely helpful to her as she battled cancer to hear about others who have survived serious illnesses and are thriving and competing. She now participates in such events as the Against the Tide swim, which raises money to fight breast cancer.

At age forty-one and still competing in 2002, Smyers had a bladder problem during the final leg of the 2002 Hawaiian Ironman, although she did finish the tough race when many others could not; she placed 27th. Her older sister Donna, also a triathlete, set a record for the event in the women's 45-49 age group.

Karen Smyers is truly an Iron Woman, one who has proven her strength and endurance in both the triathlon and in her personal life. She told *Runner's World* Magazine, "If there's one thing I want to pass on to my daughter, it's the strength of perseverance." She also said, "I'd feel incomplete if I didn't have sports. I absolutely love competition. It's been my life."

CONTACT INFORMATION

Address: c/o USA Triathlon, 616 W. Monument St., Colorado Springs, CO 80905. Email: Karen.Smyers@ triathloncentral.com.

FURTHER INFORMATION

Books

Great Women in Sports. "Karen Smyers." Detroit: Visible Ink Press, 1996.

Periodicals

Cazeneuve, Brian. "A Few Bumps in the Road: Hit by a Truck, Flying Glass, and Cancer, Triathlete Karen Smyers Rides On." *Sports Illustrated* (May 1, 2000): 83.

Gordon, Devin. "The Iron Woman: The Triathlon Is a Bitterly Grueling Event, but Karen Smyers Is Used to Tribulation." *Newsweek* (May 22, 2000): 65.

McAlpine, Ken. "Tips from the top." *Runner's World* (June 1991): 46.

Volckening, Bill. "Amazing Journey" (interview with Karen Smyers). *Swim Magazine* (September-October 2002).

Wischnia, Bob. "Karen Smyers." *Runner's World* (October 2001): 56.

Other

Carlson, Timothy. "Karen Smyers, Hunter Kemper Win U.S. Titles at New York City Triathlon." *Inside Triathlon.com.* http://www.insidetri.com/ (August 12, 2001).

DMSE Sports.com. "Profile: Professional Triathlete Karen Smyers." http://www.dmsesports.com/ (January 14, 2003).

Facteau, Shane. "Smyers & Van Lierde Added to St. Croix Field." http://www.duathlon.com/ (April 22, 2002).

Facteau, Shane. "St. Croix Women's Preview." http://www.duathlon.com/ (May 1, 2002).

Fraiegari, Priscilla. "Ironman Hawaii on TV Saturday." http://www.duathlon.com/ (November 19, 2002).

Gandolfo, Christina. "New England Triathlete Donna Smyers Triumphs in Hawaii." From *Triathlete Magazine*. TransitionTimes.com. http://www.transition times.com/ (January 15, 2003).

OutsideOnline.com. "Karen Smyers." http://web.outside online.com/events/ironman/ (January 14, 2003).

TrekBikes.com. "Karen Smyers Captures Comeback Athlete Award." http://www.trekbikes.com/news/ (January 14, 2003).

TrekBikes.com. "Trek Triathlete Karen Smyers—Sports Mom of the Year." http://www.trekbikes.com/news/ (January 15, 2003).

TriathlonCentral.com. http://www.triathloncentral.com/ (January 14, 2003).

Triathlon.org. "Karen Smyers." http://www.triathlon.org/ profiles/ (January 14, 2003).

USA Triathlon.org. http://www.usatriathlon.org/ (January 14, 2003).

Sketch by Ann H. Shurgin

Annika Sorenstam
1970-

Swedish golfer

Swedish star Annika Sorenstam is one of the best players, male or female, in the history of golf. This hard-working young woman has shattered numerous records in the course of her career; in 2001 alone she tied or broke thirty of them. Yet even though her dominance in the sport of golf seems nearly unchallenged, she still continues to push herself to work harder and to further improve her game.

Early Influences

Sorenstam grew up in a golfing family-her mother and father are both good recreational players, and her younger sister Charlotta is also on the Ladies Professional Golf Association (LPGA) Tour-but Annika's first sports love was tennis. Swedish tennis star of the late 1970s and early 1980s **Bjorn Borg** was her hero, and for seven years, starting at age five, Sorenstam tried to learn how to emulate him. She only turned to golf as a potential career when she was 12, but by age 14 she had joined the Swedish junior golf program.

Annika Sorenstam

Sorenstam's father worked for IBM when she was a child, and from him she acquired another enduring love: computers. She combines this passion with her golf by keeping detailed statistics of her rounds, as she has done since she was 14. By examining the charts and graphs that she created from her statistics, Sorenstam can easily see where the flaws in her playing are and work to improve them.

Sorenstam joined the Swedish national golf team in 1987, when she was still a teenager. There she fell under the influence of the team's coach, Pia Nilsson. Nilsson taught her players to think about golf with "54-vision": golfers should think that it is possible to birdie (shoot a score of one less stroke than par on a hole) every hole of a golf course and then should visualize themselves doing just that. No one has ever actually scored a 54, of course, but still, it was the goal her team was to shoot for.

Becoming a Professional

Sorenstam played golf for the University of Arizona for two years, from 1990 until 1992. She was the National Collegiate Athletic Association (NCAA) champion in 1991, but after the 1992 college season she quit school to become a professional. Sorenstam joined the LPGA Tour in 1993, and by the end of the 1994 season she had finished in the top ten at LPGA events five times. She got her first victory ever on the tour in 1995, at the U.S. Women's Open, and after that she seemed to be unstoppable. By the end of the 1996 season Soren-

stam had won four more tournaments, two Vare Trophies, and one Player of the Year award.

Sorenstam's dominance, however, was slowly being challenged by a phenomenal young Australian named **Karrie Webb**. Although Sorenstam continued to improve, Webb had a better seasonal scoring average than Sorenstam did in three years, was named player of the year twice, and won seven tournaments to Sorenstam's five in 2000. But Webb's presence actually encouraged Sorenstam to be a better player. "If Karrie wins five tournaments, it makes for tougher expectations and makes me think, 'What else do I have to do?' I really want to reach my goals and I have the extra desire now to play. I wake up every morning wanting to practice," she told Tom Spousta of *Golf World* early in 2001. Sorenstam concentrated particularly on improving her putting, but she also worked to increase her strength. As a result she added 15 yards to her drives.

Two Historic Seasons

Sorenstam's hard work paid off in the 2001 and 2002 seasons, as she became a breathtakingly consistent golfing machine. In 2001 Sorenstam reclaimed the Vare Trophy with a 69.42 scoring average, only one one-hundredth of a point below Webb's record-breaking 1999 average, and then in 2002 Sorenstam shattered her own record with a 68.70. She hit the fairway from the tee and the green from the fairway 80 percent of the time, which made her the most accurate golfer, male or female, in the world.

Armed with her new strength and her consistency, Sorenstam shot the best single round of golf ever by a woman on the LPGA Tour at the Standard Register Ping in 2001. She scored a 59, something that only six male golfers have done. Had she not missed a 9-foot putt on the last hole, Sorenstam could have claimed the scoring record all for herself: No one on the Professional Golfers' Association or LPGA Tour has ever scored a 58 in competition. Nilsson was in the gallery at that event, watching her former pupil put the "54-vision" into practice.

In 2002 Sorenstam tied another longstanding record by winning 13 tournaments in a single season, something that had been done only once before, by **Mickey Wright**. Sorenstam's achievement was even more impres-

Awards and Accomplishments

1991	Becomes NCAA Champion
1991	Named NCAA Co-College Player of the Year
1991-92	Named an NCAA All-American
1992	Named World Amateur Champion
1992	Named PAC-10 Champion
1994	Named Rolex Rookie of the Year
1994, 1996, 1998, 2000, 2002	Wins Solheim Cup
1995	Wins Athlete of the Year Award in Sweden
1995-96	Wins U.S. Women's Open
1995, 1997-98, 2001-02	Named Rolex Player of the Year
1995-96, 1998, 2001-02	Wins Vare Trophy for lowest scoring average
2001	Standard Register Ping (LPGA record-low score of 59 in the second round)
2001	Wins Nabisco Championship
2001	Set or tied 30 different LPGA records
2002	Wins Kraft Nabisco Championship

Forty-two official and two unofficial total career victories.

sive because she compiled her 13 wins in only 25 tournaments, while Wright played in 33 in 1963. Sorenstam added two competitions to her schedule in October in order to give herself a better chance at reaching 13, but it still came down to her last tournament of the year, the ADT Championship, which Sorenstam won with a score of 13 under par.

Aiming for the Hall of Fame

Sorenstam long ago acquired all of the points she needed to be inducted into the LPGA Hall of Fame; she merely needed to complete ten seasons on the tour to be eligible. This means that, barring any disasters, Sorenstam would be inducted into the Hall of Fame after the 2003 season. She was not sure yet what she would do after that. "I want to play 2004 as a Hall of Famer," she told *Sports Illustrated*'s Michael Bamberger after the 2002 season, but "[a]fter that, I don't know. I want to be a mother. I don't think I can be a mother and devote myself to golf the way I need to. I'm too competitive." That competitiveness means that, even though she is already one of the best golfers in history, she continues to work on improving her strength. Her hard work should ensure at least two more phenomenal seasons from Sorenstam, and perhaps a few more records to remember her by when she is gone.

SELECTED WRITINGS BY SORENSTAM:

(With Cameron Morfit) "The Amazing Adventures of Annika." *Sports Illustrated Women* (October 1, 2001): 22.

FURTHER INFORMATION

Periodicals

Bamberger, Michael. "The Amazing Annika." *Sports Illustrated* (December 2, 2002): 46+.

Burnside, Elspeth. "It's Annika Again." *Golf World* (June 21, 2002): 84.

Burnside, Elspeth, and John Huggan. "Sorenstam Strikes First." *Golf World* (March 1, 2002): 56.

Esch, David. "Pro Husband." *Sports Illustrated* (August 31, 1998): G11.

Galvin, Terry. "Solo Act." *Golf World* (October 11, 2002): 18.

Garrity, John. "Peer Group." *Sports Illustrated* (May 12, 1997): 68-71.

Johnson, Sal. "The Week." *Sports Illustrated* (March 4, 2002): G25+.

Lipsey, Rick. "Numbers Game." *Sports Illustrated* (October 26, 1998): G10.

Mickey, Lisa D. "59! It's a Vision Thing." *Golf World* (March 23, 2001): 22.

Shipnuck, Alan. "Sweet 'n Low." *Sports Illustrated* (March 26, 2001): G9+.

Sirak, Ron. "The Ultimate Trophy Wife." *Golf World* (June 14, 2002): 22.

Spousta, Tom. "Cookie Monster." *Golf World* (March 16, 2001): 24.

Strege, John, and Annmarie Dodd. "Land of Opportunity." *Golf World* (April 5, 2002): 19.

Van Sickle, Gary. "Fighting for Five." *Sports Illustrated* (April 30, 2001).

Yen, Yi-Wyn. "Trumped." *Sports Illustrated* (November 26, 2001): G17+.

Other

"Annika Sorenstam." LPGA.com. http://www.lpga.com/players/playerpage.cfm?player_id=52 (January 16, 2002).

"The Vare Trophy." HickokSports.com. http://www/hickoksports.com/history/varetrop.shtml (January 19, 2002).

Sketch by Julia Bauder

Sammy Sosa
1968-

Dominican baseball player

Relatively unknown outside Chicago, Cubs outfielder Sammy Sosa burst upon the national scene with a vengeance during the summer of 1998, as he battled

Sammy Sosa

Mark McGwire of the St. Louis Cardinals for the single-season home run record. Although McGwire eventually won the competition, besting **Roger Maris**'s 1961 record of 61 homers by nine for a new record of 70 home runs in a single season, Sosa finished not far behind with 66 homers. In the process Sosa endeared himself to millions of baseball fans in the United States and abroad and proved himself one of the game's most productive power hitters. As if to prove that his headline-grabbing performance in 1998 was no mere fluke, Sosa knocked in 63 home runs in 1999 and 64 in 2001. Long after he leaves major league baseball, Sosa will be fondly remembered not only for his achievements on the field but for the classy and sportsmanlike way in which he and McGwire conducted their 1998 battle for the record.

Born in Dominican Republic

Sammy Sosa was born Samuel Sosa Peralta in San Pedro de Marcoris, Dominican Republic, on November 12, 1968. His father, Juan, a farmer, died when Sosa was only 7 years old, leaving his mother, Lucrecia, to raise him, his four brothers, and two sisters. To help support his family, Sosa shined shoes, sold oranges by the roadside, and later worked as a janitor in a local shoe factory. As a boy, he played a primitive form of baseball in the streets near his home, but it was not until he was 14 years old that he joined what he later described as "a real team." He quickly showed an aptitude for the game. Only a year later, at age 15, Sosa signed a contract with

Chronology

1968	Born in San Pedro de Marcoris, Dominican Republic, on November 12
1984	Signs contract with Philadelphia Phillies at the age of 15; contract later voided because of his age
1985	Signs contract with Texas Rangers at the age of 16
1986	Leaves Dominican Republic to play for Gulf Coast League's Sarasota (FL) team
1987	Plays Class A ball for Port Charlotte (FL) team
1988	Plays for Rangers' AA Tulsa club
1989	Makes major league debut for Rangers on June 16
1989	Traded by Rangers to Chicago White Sox on July 29
1992	Traded by White Sox to Chicago Cubs
1997	Signed by Cubs to four-year, $42.5 million contract

the Philadelphia Phillies; the contract, however, was later declared void because of Sosa's age.

When Sosa was 16, Omar Minaya, a scout for the Texas Rangers, invited the young Dominican to a tryout in the northern city of Puerto Plata, five hours by bus from his home. Malnourished and frail, Sosa nevertheless showed promise. Recalling his first impressions of Sosa, Minaya later said, "I saw athletic talent, and I saw courage. I saw a guy who was not afraid to air it out and to play. I saw bat speed. I saw a good arm." Convinced that Sosa was a worthwhile prospect, Minaya offered him a contract for a signing bonus of $3,000. Sosa asked for $4,000, and they eventually settled on a bonus of $3,500. Sosa took out only enough to buy himself a bike and turned the rest of the money over to his mother.

Makes Professional Debut in Florida

Just shy of his 18th birthday, Sosa in 1986 left the Dominican Republic and came to Sarasota, Florida, to make his professional debut with a minor league team in the Gulf Coast League. He spoke little or no English, but he had no trouble being understood on the diamond. In his first year, he led the league with 19 doubles and a total of 96 bases. In 1987 he moved to a Class A team in nearby Port Charlotte, where he led the Florida State League with 12 triples and 42 stolen bases. The following year, Sosa played for the Texas Rangers' Class AA club in Tulsa. At the age of 20, he made his major league debut with the Texas Rangers on June 16, 1989. Barely six weeks later, Sosa was traded by the Rangers to the Chicago White Sox. In 1990, his first year as a regular with the White Sox, he hit 15 home runs and stole 32 bases, posting a batting average of .233. He also became the only player in the American League to reach double digits in doubles, triples, home runs, and stolen bases.

Sosa's second season with the White Sox proved a bit of a comedown from 1990. His batting average slipped to .203, and his home run total slipped by a third to 10 in 1991. Sosa's RBI total also slipped significantly, down to 33 from 70 in 1990. He was traded by the White Sox to the Chicago Cubs on March 30, 1992, but his first

Career Statistics

Yr	Team	AVG	GP	AB	R	H	HR	RBI	BB	SO	SB
1989	TEX	.238	25	84	8	20	1	3	0	20	0
	CWS	.273	33	99	19	27	3	10	11	27	7
1990	CWS	.233	153	532	72	124	15	70	33	150	32
1991	CWS	.203	116	316	39	64	10	33	14	98	13
1992	CHC	.260	67	262	41	68	8	25	19	63	15
1993	CHC	.261	159	598	92	156	33	93	38	135	36
1994	CHC	.300	105	426	59	128	25	70	25	92	22
1995	CHC	.268	144	564	89	151	36	119	58	134	34
1996	CHC	.273	124	498	84	136	40	100	34	134	18
1997	CHC	.251	162	642	90	161	36	119	45	174	22
1998	CHC	.308	159	643	134	198	66	158	73	171	18
1999	CHC	.288	162	625	114	180	63	141	78	171	7
2000	CHC	.320	156	604	106	193	50	138	91	168	7
2001	CHC	.328	160	577	146	189	64	160	116	153	0
2002	CHC	.288	150	556	122	160	49	108	103	144	2
TOTAL		.278	1875	7026	1215	1955	499	1347	738	1834	233

CHC: Chicago Cubs; CWS: Chicago White Sox; TEX: Texas Rangers.

season with the Cubs was marred by a hand injury that kept him sidelined for nearly half of the season. In the 67 games he did take the field, however, he managed to compile a batting average of .260. He bounced back dramatically in 1993, hitting 33 home runs and stealing 36 bases, becoming the first player in Cubs history to hit 30 home runs and steal 30 bases in a single season.

Criticism of Sosa's Style Mounts

Over the next four years with the Cubs, Sosa continued to post some impressive statistics, but increasingly he came under fire for a seeming inability to focus his talents. Commentators criticized the Dominican for his "hot-dogging." His batting average increased to .300 in 1994, with a total of 25 home runs and 70 RBIs. The following year he walloped 36 home runs and 119 RBIs, although his batting average slipped to .267. *Sporting News* named Sosa to both its NL All-Star Team and Silver Slugger Team in 1995. His home run total soared to 40 in 1996 and almost certainly would have gone higher had his season not been cut short by a wrist injury. Despite boasts that he might hit the 60-home run mark in 1997, Sosa managed to post only 36 homers and 119 RBIs. On top of that, his batting average slipped to .250, and he logged more strikeouts than anyone else in the NL. Despite these weaknesses, Cubs general manager Ed Lynch seemed confident that Sosa soon would come into his own, and the team signed him to a four-year, $42.5 million contract.

Early in the 1998 season, it was clear from Sosa's performance that Lynch's faith had not been misplaced. In a four-week stretch from May 25 through June 21, Sosa hit 21 home runs in 22 games, one of the most remarkable achievements in major league history. He broke a 61-year-old major league record in a June game against the Detroit Tigers, hitting his 19th home run for

the month. He finished the month with a total of home runs and by the All-Star break had run that number to 33 for the season. Sosa suddenly found himself in a race with Mark McGwire of the St. Louis Cardinals for the single-season home run record. The standing record was 61 homers, set by Roger Maris in 1961. Sosa and McGwire became the only two hitters in NL history to hit 30 or more home runs by July 1. Sosa confessed to a reporter a deep admiration for his rival in the home run race. "Mark McGwire is the man. Mark McGwire is in a different world. He's my idol. He's the man."

Sosa's feelings for McGwire did nothing to inhibit his push for the record. The two stayed neck and neck for much of the season. McGwire was the first to reach Maris's 61-homer mark. The red-headed Cardinal also was the first to set a new record. McGwire's 62nd homer came during his team's final game of the season with the Cubs. As Sosa watched from right field, McGwire blasted number 62 into the left field stands. Sosa ran in from the outfield to congratulate the new record-holder. With a handful of games left in the season, however, the homer derby of 1998 was not yet over. Sosa blasted four homers in a three-game series with the Milwaukee Brewers, taking his total to 62 and tying McGwire. In the final three games of the season, Sosa pulled ahead of McGwire for the first time when he hit his 66th homer in a game against the Houston Astros. It was to be Sosa's last homer of the year. In the end, McGwire pushed his total for the year to 70. However, Sosa's overall statistics for the year—batting average of .308, 158 RBIs, and 132 runs scored—made him the runaway choice for the NL Most Valuable Player Award.

Although he has yet to equal or top his home run performance of 1998, Sosa has come close. In each of the three seasons immediately following 1998, Sosa man-

Related Biography: General Manager Ed Lynch

Even when others were vocal in their criticism of Sammy Sosa—some calling him "Sammy So-So"—charging that he was more interested in personal statistics than being a team player, one man remained steadfast in his faith that Sosa had the stuff to make an all-round baseball star. That man was Ed Lynch, general manager/vice president of the Chicago Cubs. It was Lynch who engineered Sosa's lucrative four-year, $42.5 million contract extension in 1997. He didn't have to wait long to be proved right. The following year, Sosa tallied an incredible 66 home runs, powering the Cubs into the playoffs for the first time since 1989.

On September 20, 1998, as the Cubs celebrated Sosa's accomplishments in Wrigley Field, Lynch presented the Dominican superstar with several gifts, including a purple Chrysler Prowler. To Sosa, Lynch said: "I am proud and honored to have you as my friend. I don't think there's any way that we can properly show the depths of our appreciation and respect for all that you've accomplished in 1998 and throughout your entire career."

Lynch, who pitched in the major leagues for eight seasons from 1980 through 1987, was born in Brooklyn, New York, February 25, 1956. After studying at the University of Miami, he made his professional debut as a pitcher for the New York Mets in 1980. He was traded to the Cubs in 1986 and pitched in Chicago for most of 1986 and all of the 1987 season. He was brought on as general manager of the Cubs in October 1994 and resigned in July 1999 after five seasons in which the Cubs finished above .500 only twice.

Awards and Accomplishments

1986	Leads Gulf Coast League with 96 total bases
1987	Ties for South Atlantic League lead in double plays by outfielder with four
1993	Collects six hits in a single game on July 2
1995	Ties for NL lead in double plays by outfielder with four
1995, 1998-99	Named outfielder on *Sporting News* NL All-Star Team and NL Silver Slugger Team
1996	Hits three home runs in a single game on June 5
1998	Hits 21 home runs in 22 games from May 25 through June 21
1998	Hits three home runs in a single game on June 15
1998	Collects 66 home runs for the year but trails Mark McGwire's 70
1998	Named Co-Sportsman of the Year by *Sporting News*
1998	Named NL's Most Valuable Player by Baseball Writers' Association of America
1999	Leads NL with 397 total bases for the year

aged to hit 50 or more home runs—64 in 1999, 50 in 2000, and 63 in 2001. In 2002, his homers total dropped just below the 50-mark to 49. During the baseball season, Sosa and his wife, Sonia, live in Chicago with their four children, Keysha, Kenia, Sammy Jr., and Michael. The Sosa family spends most of the rest of the year at a home they maintain in the Dominican Republic.

Sosa will long be remembered for what he accomplished in the summer of 1998, but he's not content to rest upon his laurels. He knows that he can't have a season like that every year, "but I believe in myself, I have a lot of ability, and if I've done it once I know I can come back and do it again. I know I'll never forget '98."

CONTACT INFORMATION

Address: Sammy Sosa, c/o Chicago Cubs, 1060 W. Addison St., Chicago, IL 60613.

SELECTED WRITINGS BY SOSA:

(With Marcos Breton) *Sosa: An Autobiography,* Warner Books, 2000.

FURTHER INFORMATION

Books

Christopher, Matt. *At the Plate with Sammy Sosa.* Boston: Little Brown, 1999.

Gutman, Bill, and Rob Meyer.*Sammy Sosa: A Biography.* Dimensions, 1998.

"Sammy Sosa." *Contemporary Black Biography,* Volume 21. Detroit, MI: Gale Group, 1999.

"Sammy Sosa."*Newsmakers 1999,* Issue 1. Detroit, MI: Gale Group, 1999.

"Sammy Sosa." *Sports Stars,* Series 5. U•X•L, 1999.

Periodicals

Johnson, Chuck. "Cubs, MLB Give Slugger Due on Sammy Sosa Day." *USA Today* (September 21, 1998): 6C.

"Lynch to Stay in Cubs' Office." *Sports Network* (November 10, 1998).

"Sosa Hits Home Run No. 63." *AP Online* (October 3, 1999).

Other

"Ed Lynch." *Baseball Almanac.* http://www.baseball-almanac.com/players/player.php?p=lynched01 (November 8, 2002).

"Sammy Sosa." *Sporting News.* http://www.sporting news.com/baseball/players/4344/index.html (November 7, 2002).

"Sammy Sosa." Baseball-Reference.com. http://www. baseball-reference.com/s/sosasa01.shtml (November 1, 2002).

Sketch by Don Amerman

Michael Spinks
1956-

American boxer

Michael Spinks was a virtual unknown, a tough young fighter from a rough part of St. Louis, when he and his older brother Leon rocketed to fame by

Michael Spinks

both winning gold medals in boxing at the 1976 Montreal Olympics. With his "Spinks Jinx," a mean cross-over right-handed punch, Spinks was unbeatable for over ten years. His one and only professional loss came at the hands of an undefeated, up-and-coming twenty-one-year-old named **Mike Tyson**.

Fighting for Survival

Spinks did not have an easy childhood. His family lived in the infamous northern St. Louis Pruitt-Igoe housing project, which was condemned and demolished in 1976. The area was rough, full of gangs and murders, and the Spinks children suffered from frequent bullying. Spinks's older brother Leon was often attacked on the streets, and in 1969 he started learning to box at a neighborhood gym, the Capri, to be able to defend himself. Soon, at Leon's urging, Spinks started boxing there, too.

From a young age, Spinks was the man of the house: his father abandoned the family when Spinks was four, and his older brother Leon was not as responsible as Spinks. Their mother, Kay, was by all accounts a remarkable woman, an ordained minister who did her best to provide for the family of eight (herself, six sons, and one daughter). Spinks helped as well, selling newspapers and getting positions as newsboys for two of his younger brothers. As a teenager, Spinks also brought in some money by boxing. Capri coach Jim Merrill sent some of his boxers, including Spinks, on trips to attend tournaments. The young boxers were given five dollars a day for their meals, but many of them saved up their money instead. The fact that they had to go home and stop receiving money if they lost was a powerful incentive for these young men to win.

Glory Days

By the beginning of 1976, the name of Spinks was becoming known in the boxing world. Michael lost a fight to the Soviet champion, Rufat Riskiev, that January, but still made it to the Montreal Olympics as a middleweight. Leon, now in the Marines, competed in Montreal as a light heavyweight. Both won gold, Michael by defeating Riskiev in only three rounds.

After the Olympics, Spinks returned to St. Louis and took a night shift job as a janitor at a Monsanto plant—a decent-paying, steady job which allowed him to provide for his mother—while Leon turned professional and signed a contract with the promoter Butch Lewis. However, Spinks fell asleep on the job one night and was fired, and early in 1977 he signed with Lewis, too. Both Spinks brothers moved to the Philadelphia area, the center of heavyweight boxing in the United States, living with Lewis in Wilmington, Delaware for a time before moving out on their own.

Leon shot to fame first, defeating **Muhammad Ali** in 1978 to become the world heavyweight champion in what was only Leon's eighth professional fight. However, a mere seven months later Leon faced Ali again and lost, becoming the shortest-reigning heavyweight champion in history. Soon Leon became the punchline of many jokes. He was missing all of his front teeth, and photographs of his wide, toothless grin upon his victory over Ali were widely distributed. He was notorious for his numerous traffic accidents, and he had many problems with his personal life and his finances. In 1986, he was forced to declare bankruptcy. For a time he was even homeless, living in a shelter and working as a day laborer.

Spinks achieved success more slowly, but he proved more durable. Spinks's record was 17-0 before he first challenged for a title, the World Boxing Association light heavyweight crown, on July 18, 1981. He defeated Eddie Mustafa Muhammad to win that title,

Awards and Accomplishments

1976	National Golden Glove Championships
1976	Olympic middleweight boxing Gold Medal
1981	World Boxing Association light-heavyweight champion
1983	World Boxing Council light-heavyweight champion
1985	International Boxing Federation heavyweight champion

and successfully defended it five times in the next fourteen months. Then, on March 18, 1983, he defeated Dwight Braxton (also known as Dwight Qawi) to win the World Boxing Council light-heavyweight crown as well.

Spinks's victory over Braxton was exceptional for the personal turmoil he had to overcome to be able to focus in the ring that day. His wife, a dancer named Sandra Massey, was killed in an automobile accident two months before the fight, leaving him to raise their two-year-old daughter, Michelle, alone. Spinks was extremely distraught over his loss, even breaking down and crying when asked about it at a press conference just days before the fight. Then, ten minutes before Spinks was to step into the ring, his sister-in-law brought Michelle backstage to see him. The first thing she said was, "Where's Mommy?," and Spinks fell apart. But he pulled himself back together, went out, and jabbed his way to victory in a fight that went for a full fifteen rounds.

In 1985, Spinks started a new training regimen, beefed up, and prepared to contest for the International Boxing Federation heavyweight title. He succeeded against all odds, beating the 22 pounds heavier, 48-0 Larry Holmes in fifteen rounds on September 21, 1985. Spinks defended the title three times in 1986 and 1987, going another fifteen rounds with Holmes and knocking out two other challengers. Then came Mike Tyson.

Spinks suffered his only loss in a professional fight to Tyson on June 27, 1988. The twenty-one-year-old Tyson was at the top of his form. "When he hit me I lost my temper and forgot my strategy," Spinks told *Sports Illustrated* reporter John O'Keefe in 1999. Instead of ducking and jabbing, Spinks tried to stand his ground and slug it out, but Tyson was the better slugger. The fight ended with a knockout for Tyson in a mere ninety-one seconds. Spinks tearfully announced his retirement a month later, returned to his home in Delaware, and settled down, out of the spotlight, living off of the wise investments he made with his winnings and concentrating on raising his daughter. Spinks continues to work out at his long-time training location, **Joe Frazier**'s gym in Philadelphia. He also for his old promoter, Butch Lewis, training up-and-coming boxers and speaks to children about following their dreams. His daughter, Michelle, is following in her mother's footsteps and studying to become a dancer.

The Next Generation

Leon Spinks had three sons, all of whom tried boxing. The oldest son, Darrell, boxed professionally for a time but has since retired. The middle son, Leon, was killed in a drive-by shooting in 1993 after winning one professional match, but the youngest son, Cory Spinks, who was born five days after Leon's victory over Ali, is a rising star. He won the Golden Gloves amateur championship in the welterweight category in 1997, and in 2002 he lost a closely contested championship fight on a controversial decision which denied him the IBF welterweight title. However, a rematch is expected in the near future, and there may soon be a third world champion boxer named Spinks.

FURTHER INFORMATION

Periodicals

Fussman, Calvin. "A Yawning Gap in His Life." *Sports Illustrated* (March 14, 1983): 34-38.

Gustkey, Earl. "Spinks Hung In There for About Half a Round." *Los Angeles Times* (June 27, 1999): 1.

"Michael Spinks Survives Ring, Stays Retired in Style." *Seattle Times* (August 16, 1998): D6.

Nack, William. "A Crowning Achievement." *Sports Illustrated* (March 28, 1983): 14-21.

Nack, William. "Say Good Night, Gerry." *Sports Illustrated* (June 22, 1987): 22-23.

O'Keefe, John. "Michael Spinks, Champion Boxer: March 28, 1983 ." *Sports Illustrated* (August 9, 1999): 21.

Outnam, Pat. "A Champ with Strange Ideas: Michael Spinks Beat Larry Holmes Thanks to a Training Regimen That Took the Light Out of Heavyweight." *Sports Illustrated* (October 7, 1985): 44-46.

Perez, Santos A. "Name Has a Ring to It: C. Spinks Proud of His Pedigree." *Miami Herald* (August 22, 2002).

Putnam, Pat. "Battle of the Ballot ." *Sports Illustrated* (April 28, 1986): 22-25.

Putnam, Pat. "The Big Showdown: After a Soap-Opera Prelude, Mike Tyson and Michael Spinks Meet at Last." *Sports Illustrated* (June 27, 1988): 42-45.

Other

Alvarez, Armando. "Spinks Bloodied But Victorious." Boxing News. http://www.maxboxing.com/Alvarez/alvarez082402.asp (August 24, 2002).

Boxing Press. http://www.boxingpress.de/ (October 7, 2002).

Cyber Boxing Zone. http://www.cyberboxingzone.com/ (October 7, 2002).

"Former Champ Michael Spinks Gets Year's Probation." Atlanta Journal-Constitution Sports Blotter. http://www.accessatlanta.com/ajc/sports/blotter (September 20, 2002).

International Boxing Hall of Fame. http://www.ibhof. com/ (October 7, 2002).

Kanew, Evan. "The Dream Team." Sports Illustrated Olympic Daily. http://sportsillustrated.cnn.com/ events/1996/olympics/daily/aug3/boxing.html (October 11, 2002).

"Michael Spinks v. Larry Holmes: A Look Back." East Side Boxing. http://www.eastsideboxing.com/news/ LarryHolmesvMichaelSpinks.php (October 7, 2002).

Robb, Sharon. "Looking for Redemption." International Brotherhood of Prizefighters. http://www.ibop.tv/ article2/article288a.htm (October 11, 2002).

Siuntres, John. "Lil' Spinks Takes USBA Belt." Sporting News Radio. http://radio.sportingnews.com/ profiles/john_siuntres/20010820.html (October 11, 2002).

"Spinks, Leon; and Spinks, Michael." Encyclopedia Britannica Online. http://www.eb.com/blackhistory/ micro/723/1.html (October 7, 2002).

Sketch by Julia Bauder

Mark Spitz

Mark Spitz
1950-

American swimmer

During the 1972 Olympic Games in Munich, West Germany, young American swimmer Mark Spitz won seven gold medals, the most by any individual in any Olympiad, and set as many world records. Spitz, a detailed strategist in and out of the water, was named 1972 World Swimmer of the Year. He overcame his share of disappointment and even tragedy, which may have made him an even stronger competitor. Three decades later, he continues to be a booster for his sport.

"Swimming Isn't Everything"

As soon as he began walking, Mark Spitz began to swim. At age two, his parents, Lenore and Arnold Spitz, moved to Honolulu, Hawaii, where Arnold Spitz, an executive with a steel company, had been transferred. He swam daily at Waikiki Beach. "You should have seen that little boy dash into the ocean," his mother later told a *Time* magazine reporter.

Soon, with strong encouragement from his family, Spitz was swimming competitively. Having returned to his native California at age six, he began his formal training at the Sacramento YMCA. Three years later, Arnold Spitz took his precocious son to the Arden Hills Swim Club to train with Sherm Chavoor, who would re-

main a mentor for many years. By age ten, Spitz had won 17 age-group events. That year, Spitz had a scheduling problem when his after-school swim workout conflicted with Hebrew school. His father intervened and told the rabbi, "Even God likes a winner." The family relocated to Santa Clara so that, despite an 80-mile commute for his father, Spitz could train with the celebrated George Haines at the Santa Clara Swim Club. "Swimming isn't everything," his father used to tell his son, "winning is." In 1965, the teenager entered his first international competition at the Olympic-style Maccabiah Games in Tel Aviv and won four gold medals. (Upon his return four years later, he won six more golds.)

In 1966, the high school student won the national Amateur Athletic Union (AAU) championships with the 100-meter butterfly. By age 17, Spitz broke his first world record with a time of 4 minutes, 10.6 seconds in the 400-meter freestyle. Full of confidence, Spitz qualified for the 1968 Summer Olympic Games in Mexico City and boasted he would win six medals. He faced bitter disappointment. Not only was he a target of anti-Semitism from some team members, he also failed to meet his own expectations. He won only two golds, both in relay events, though he did take the silver in the 100-meter butterfly and the bronze in the 100-meter freestyle. It was, he told a journalist, "the worst meet of my life." While many athletes would have reveled in medaling at all, for Spitz the event was a disaster. There was little the 18-year-old could do but to brace himself for a comeback, or quit.

Chronology

1950	Born February 10 in Modesto, California
1958	Begins swimming competitively
1961	Comes under guidance of coach Sherm Chavoor
1965	Competes in Maccabiah Games in Tel Aviv, his first international event
1966	Competes in National Amateur Athletic Union 100-meter butterfly
1967	Competes in Pan-American Games in Winnipeg, Canada
1968	Vows to win gold in all events at Mexico City Olympics but takes gold only in the 4x100-meter and 4x200-meter freestyle relays
1969	Graduates from Indiana University, where he swims for coach James "Doc" Counsilman
1972	Leaves Olympic Games early after winning gold medals and after killing of Israeli athletes in Olympic village
1973	Formally retires from swimming
1973	Signs with William Morris Agency, earning $5 million in endorsements
1973	Marries Suzy Weiner
1987	Autobiography *Seven Golds* published
1989	Attempts a comeback and begins training for the 1992 Barcelona Olympics
1992	Fails to qualify in the 100-meter butterfly and concedes defeat, beginning second retirement
1998	Proposes creating initiative to address problem of swimmers and performance-enhancing drugs

Awards and Accomplishments

1960	Wins seventeen national age-group titles
1966	Wins first of 24 national Amateur Athletic Union championships
1967	World records in 400-meter freestyle, 100-meter butterfly, and 200-meter butterfly events; five gold medals at Pan-American Games
1968	Individual bronze and silver medalist at Mexico City Olympics, gold in the 4x100-meter and 4x200-meter freestyle relays
1969	World Swimmer of the Year
1971	Amateur Athletic Union's James E. Sullivan Memorial Award; World Swimmer of the Year
1972	World records in all seven events at Munich Olympics, first athlete to win seven Olympic gold medals in one Olympiad; World Swimmer of the Year; Associated Press Male Athlete of the Year
1977	Inducted into International Swimming Hall of Fame in Ft. Lauderdale, Florida, as an honor swimmer
1983	Inducted into U.S. Olympic Hall of Fame, with first class of inductees

Glory Days

Spitz was no quitter. Knowing he had a long road ahead, he vowed to commit himself to training with the finest. Recruited by Indiana University in Bloomington, which had one of the nation's most outstanding aquatics program, Spitz enrolled in 1969. A pre-dental student, Spitz worked with working with James "Doc" Counsilman, former national swimming champion, coach, and kinetics researcher. By the time he graduated, Spitz, who had been captain of the Hoosiers, earned World Swimmer of the Year award from *Swimming World* magazine in 1967, 1971 and 1972. In 1971 he became the first Jewish recipient of the AAU's annual James E. Sullivan Memorial Award for athleticism, leadership, character, and sportsmanship.

Spitz won five gold medals at the 1967 Pan American Games in Winnipeg, thirty-one AAU titles, eight National Collegiate Athletic Association (NCAA) championships (four times in the 100-yard butterfly), and 33 world records. His contact with coaches Chavoor, Haines, and Counsilman, all members of the International Swimming Hall of Fame in Ft. Lauderdale, Florida, helped Spitz mature as a man and a swimmer. As the 1972 Olympics advanced, Spitz had established himself. Gone was the pretense of 1968 and in its place was a focused competitor—with a mustache.

It took four months to grow, but Spitz was proud of it. He had intended to shave his mustache for the Munich Olympics but since he did so well at the trials—he broke the world record in the 200-meter butterfly—he decided the mustache was a "good-luck piece." During a

practice swim, Spitz noticed the Soviets photographing him. Asked whether the mustache added unwanted drag to the swimmer. Spitz answered, "No, it actually deflects water from my mouth and allows me to keep my head in a lower position that helps my speed," he later told *Newsweek* magazine. His answer was pure invention, but the Soviets didn't know that. Suddenly, several Soviet swimmers began sporting mustaches in competition. Another Spitz tactic included changing his usual stroke to a highly inefficient one during practice, so that the spying Soviets might again be thrown off. When they inquired about his "unconventional" stroke, Spitz again spouted nonsense, this time about how the ungainly stroke actually builds muscle.

Prepares Seriously

Prior to the athletic events, Spitz spoke to the media and though he was brief, his remarks reflected his new-found seriousness. "I can't devote too much time to you guys," he told the press. "I need the time to psyche myself up."

That he did. The first event was the 200-meter butterfly. Spitz won it in a record-breaking 2:00.7. His pure joy launched him from the water and he stood by the poolside, arms raised in victory. That same day, he swam his leg in the 4x100-meter freestyle relay, and though his team took the gold, Spitz was a bit unnerved by teammate Jerry Heidenreich's time, which clocked .12 of a second faster than his.

Nevertheless, he won gold in his second solo event, the 200-meter freestyle in 1:52.78, though it ignited controversy from the Soviet contingent. The brouhaha began when Spitz stood barefoot on the medal stand, shoes in hand. During the national anthem, he dropped his shoes by his side, only to retrieve them and wave them to the applauding audience. The Soviets complained to the International Olympic Committee, charging Spitz with

Mark Spitz

promoting a commercial product. Spitz defended himself by saying the gesture was completely spontaneous, the shoes were old, and he was receiving no financial reward. Spitz was cleared and concentrated on the next event, the 100-meter butterfly, his favorite. He won it by a full body length in a record 54.27 seconds.

After the 4x200-meter freestyle relay, which brought yet another gold for the Americans, the swimmer got cold feet. Spitz had so far swum a perfect Olympics, winning gold in all five events. With two more events to go and a case of nerves, Spitz contacted his former coach, Sherm Chavoor, who was in Munich with the American women's team. Concerned about both saving his strength for the 4x100-meter medley relay, and haunted by Heidenreich's performance in the 400-meter relay, Spitz asked Chavoor whether he ought to duck out of the next event, the 100-meter freestyle. The coach urged Spitz to compete, and warned that sitting out the race would look as though he had lost his competitive edge. In a later interview, Spitz told journalists, "I just tried to keep my cool and continue with my race plan: to win."

Spitz proved unpredictable to his competitors in the 100-meter freestyle as he swam the first lap at full strength, being the first to touch the wall in 24.56 seconds. During the semifinal heat, he had stayed behind, finishing after Australia's defending champion Michael Wenden and Heidenreich. But during the final it was a completely different race. Though he lost his rhythm during the second lap, Spitz continued charging ahead to beat Heidenreich by half a stroke, winning the event in 51.22, shaving his own world record by .25 seconds. The final event was the 4 x 100-meter relay. For Spitz, as a member of the American team, this would be the final hurdle in a bid to make a clean, unprecedented sweep of Olympic gold. On September 4, 1972, Spitz, in the Munich Schwimhalle, won his seventh gold in his seventh event, all of which set world records.

Olympic Tragedy

The day after Spitz's heroics was even more memorable than the days that preceded it. Early on the morning of September 5, eight Palestinian terrorists invaded the Israeli team headquarters in the Olympic Village, killing two Israeli athletes. Nine Israeli athletes were taken hostage. The terrorists, known as Black September, demanded the release of political prisoners. As the world watched the

---

One Day in September

More than a quarter century after the Munich massacre, when Palestinian terrorists killed 11 Israeli athletes at the Munich Olympics, director Kevin Macdonald made an award-winning documentary on the subject. Narrated by veteran actor Michael Douglas, the film also featured Ankie Spitzer, widow of Israeli fencing coach Andre Spitzer, and the one surviving terrorist, Jamal Al Gashey. "Macdonald brings remarkable research to the film," wrote film critic Roger Ebert of the *Chicago Sun-Times.* "His reporting is extraordinary, as he relentlessly builds up a case against the way the Germans and the International Olympic Committee handled the crisis." The film exposed several unsettling facts, such as the utter incompetence of the German police, the participation of Yassir Arafat, and a covert plan by which the Germans released the three surviving terrorists to disown the whole affair. (The Israeli government later assassinated two of these survivors.) *One Day in September* won many prizes, including the Academy Award for Best Documentary Feature in 2000.

Where Is He Now?

Prior to the 1992 Olympics in Barcelona, Spain, Spitz attempted a comeback. But at age 39 and eight pounds heavier than in 1972, he failed to qualify. At the 1998 World Championships in Perth, Australia, Spitz addressed the problems of drug abuse and athletes, and he continues to make personal appearances at various competitions and sporting events. As a member of the World Sports Academy, he works to bring sports to less fortunate children of the world. Following his retirement, Spitz ventured into motivational speaking, real-estate investment, and swimming-pool design. He recently left real estate to focus on his entrepreneurial work. Spitz lives in Los Angeles with his wife and two sons, Matt and Justin. A veteran sailor, Spitz has often participated in the Trans Pacific Yacht Race from Los Angeles to Honolulu. He swims with the masters team at UCLA. "I squeak, rattle, and roll," Spitz said. "I'm swimming because I love it and because it's the best thing I can do to keep myself healthy. It's something I hope to do for the rest of my life."

---

standoff on live television, German authorities took the terrorists and their prisoners to an airfield for a flight out of the country. But later in the day, a German police rescue attempt failed, ending in the killing of all nine hostages.

By 11:30 that morning, a security detail surrounded Spitz, who, as an American Jew, was considered a potential terrorist target. The plans for him to attend various winners' ceremonies throughout Germany were suddenly and secretly changed. "I completely freaked out," he told Phillip Whitten of *SwimInfo.* "Here it was, twenty-seven years after the end of World War II, and there were still madmen killing Jews because they are Jews." Surrounded by six armed guards, Spitz was taken to London for a photo shoot to which he had committed with a German magazine, and then flown home to California, where he expected to begin dental school.

When he finally arrived home that Wednesday morning, he watched the Olympic memorial service on television with his two sisters. "The whole thing took on a surreal quality," he told Whitten. "I was in Sacramento, sitting in my living room like Johnny Lunchbucket, watching the Olympics on TV, as if I had never been there.... A few days later I was in temple for a Rosh Hashanah service, sitting next to Governor [Ronald] Reagan. That's when the significance of the whole sequence of events really hit me."

A New Identity

The Munich massacre overshadowed Spitz's achievements. The tragedy reverberates today, Spitz, told Whitten in 2002. "The Games have lost a sense of spontaneity. A sense of the whole world coming together in peaceful competition." On a deeply personal level, the events gave Spitz a sense of "responsibility" about publicly identifying himself as a Jew. "I felt an obligation to affirm my ties as a Jew," he added, "and to become educated on the issues so I could speak knowledgeably."

Spitz quickly became one of the most familiar faces in America, if not the world. His agent boasted that he was the greatest American hero since aviator Charles Lindbergh. He quit swimming, put his plans for dental school on ice, and sifted through the barrage of endorsement offers. In 1973 he signed a contract with the prestigious William Morris Agency, which was supposed to manage his career as a celebrity. That year, he also married Suzy Weiner, a model and theatre student at the University of California, Los Angeles. The latter move proved more successful than the former.

Spitz became the spokesman for the Schick Company, and his commercials promoting its razors were widely aired. He also represented Adidas, the California Milk Advisory Board, Speedo, and various other companies vending everything from swimming pool accessories to hairdryers and men's underwear. An image of the times, a poster of Spitz wearing his swimsuit and seven gold medals, appeared everywhere from college dorms to locker rooms and sporting goods stores. Spitz also had theatrical aspirations and appeared on television shows with luminaries that included Sonny and Cher, Bob Hope, and Johnny Carson. He made a guest appearance in the series *Emergency* and got a role as an announcer in the 1985 made-for-television movie *Challenge of a Lifetime,* starring Penny Marshall.

Producers and audiences found Spitz's on-screen persona lackluster. Gradually, advertisers also withdrew from Spitz, saying he was losing his appeal because he endorsed too many products. In addition, public relations executives and agents of the time weren't as savvy about successfully marketing athletes. As a result, Spitz lacked the guidance from his handlers that athletes today receive. In earning a reported $5 million, however, Spitz helped pioneer the lucrative game of athletic endorsements.

Self-confident and determined, Mark Spitz became the first swimmer to win seven medals in one Olympiad. That this victory followed the bitter disappointment and chastening during his first Olympic bid, and that it occurred during the most tragic Olympics of all time make Spitz's triumph that much more inspiring.

CONTACT INFORMATION

Address: c/o CMG Worldwide, 8560 Sunset Boulevard, 10th Floor Penthouse, West Hollywood, CA 90069. Fax: 317-570-5500. Phone: 310-854-1005. Online: www. cmgww.com/.

SELECTED WRITINGS BY SPITZ:

Spitz, Mark and Alan LeMond. *The Mark Spitz Complete Book of Swimming* New York: Crowell, 1976.

Seven Golds: Mark Spitz, My Own Story, New York: Doubleday, 1987.

FURTHER INFORMATION

Books

American Decades CD-ROM, Detroit: Gale Research, 1998.

St. James Encyclopedia of Popular Culture. CD-ROM, Detroit: Gale Group, 2002.

Periodicals

"Cold War at the Pool, Shaking a Leg, in Pantyhose." *Newsweek* (October 25, 1999): 63.

Ebert, Roger. "One Day in September." *Chicago Sun-Times* (March 9, 2001).

Lowitt, Bruce. "All He Touches Turns to Gold."*St. Petersburg Times* (November 8, 1999).

Meza, Ed. "World Sports Acad. Tees Up Award Noms."*Variety* (March 19, 2001): 25.

Noden, Merrell. "Catching Up with … Swimming Champion Mark Spitz." *Sports Illustrated* (August 4, 1997): 11.

"Olympic Legends Attend Launch of 'Unified Sports Day,"*Xinuha New Agency* (October 25, 1999).

"The Way We Were: A Look Back at the Year People Began: Week of July 5-11, 1974.*People Weekly* (July 5, 1999): 23.

Other

CMG Worldwide. www.cmgww.com/ (December 29, 2002).

Contemporary Authors Online. Gale Group, 2000.

Encarta. encarta.msn.com/ (December 29, 2002).

ESPN.com, msn.espn.go.com/ (December 29, 2002).

History Channel. www.historychannel.com/ (January 4, 2003).

Internet Movie Database. www.imdb.com (December 30, 2002).

Jewishpeople.net. www.jewishpeople.net/ (January 4, 2003).

Jewishsport.com. store.yahoo.net/jewishsport/ markspitz.html (January 4, 2003).

Jews in Sports. www.jewsinsports.org/ (January 4, 2003).

"Legend Mark Spitz." Swimsport.com, www.swimsprt. com/ (January 4, 2003).

"Munich Massacre Remembered." ABC Online. www. abc.net.au/ (September 5, 2002).

"Munich Olympic Victims Remembered." BBC News. news.bbc.co.uk/ (August 11, 2002).

Sacramento Bee, www.sacbee.com/ (December 29, 2002).

SwimInfo, www.swiminfo.com/ (December 29, 2002; January 4, 2003).

Trans Pacific Yacht Club, www.transpacificyc.org/ (January 9, 2003).

Sketch by Jane Summer

Latrell Sprewell
1970-

American basketball player

Latrell Sprewell, a gutsy floor leader, became an unexpected, and at times highly unpopular, star in the National Basketball Association (NBA). He did not play organized basketball until he was a senior in high school, and his college play, although outstanding, drew little recognition. Even after posting stellar numbers as a rookie playing for the Golden State Warriors in 1992, few people knew who he was. That all changed on December 1, 1997 when he twice attacked his coach, P.J. Carlesimo, during practice.

The Back Roads to the NBA

Latrell Sprewell was born on September 8, 1970 in Milwaukee, Wisconsin. As a young child Sprewell's parents, Pamela Sprewell and Latoska Field, moved the family to Flint, Michigan. When his parents separated during Sprewell's sophomore year in high school, he moved back to Milwaukee with his mother, where he attended Washington High School. Sprewell did not play organized basketball until his senior year, when he was approached by the basketball coach in the hallway and invited to try out for the team. Not only did Sprewell make the team, he scored an average of twenty-eight points per game.

With only one, albeit impressive, year of high school experience, Sprewell had little name recognition and was not highly recruited by colleges. As a result, he enrolled in Three Rivers Junior College, where he played junior college ball for the next two years. Earning a reputation as a hard worker and defensive specialist, Sprewell was invited to transfer to the University of Alabama, where he played his last two years of college eligibility. During his senior year he averaged 17.8 points, 5.2 rebounds,

Latrell Sprewell

Chronology

1970	Born September 8 in Milwaukee, Wisconsin
1987-88	First plays organized basketball as a senior at Washington High School in Milwaukee; averages 28 points per game
1988-90	Plays junior college ball at Three Rivers Junior College
1990-92	Plays basketball for the University of Alabama
1992	Selected as the 24th pick in the National Basketball Association draft by the Golden State Warriors
1997	Attacks coach P.J. Carlesimo during a practice; contract is terminated and suspension for one year is invoked by the NBA
1998	Arbitration leads to team reinstatement and a reduction in the NBA suspension; arrested for reckless driving
1999	Traded to the New York Knicks

and 1.8 steals per game. Despite being named to the All-Southeastern Conference team, Sprewell entered the 1992 NBA draft without much fanfare.

Selected by the Golden State Warriors as the twenty-fourth pick of the draft, Sprewell made an impressive start during his rookie season. He became the first rookie in Golden State's history to accumulate 1,000 points, 250 rebounds, 250 assists, 100 steals, and fifty blocks in a season. He also led his team in minutes played with 2,741. His efforts earned him a place on the second team of the 1993 NBA All-Rookie Team. In his second season with Golden State, Sprewell continued to excel, finishing the 1993-94 season with a per-game average of twenty-one points, 4.9 rebounds, 4.7 assists, and 2.2 steals. He was named to the 1994 All-NBA First Team.

A Tarnished Reputation

During the 1994-95 season, Sprewell, who was having trouble forgiving the Warriors' management for trading away friends **Chris Webber** and Billy Owens, was twice suspended during the season for conduct deemed detrimental to the team. Yet, because his play on the court remained impressive, the Warriors agreed to a four-year contract in 1996 worth $32 million. During the 1996-97 season, Sprewell averaged over twenty-four points per game and was the Western Conference's leading scorer in the 1996 NBA All-Star game, with nineteen points. Despite Sprewell's efforts, the Warriors were floundering badly at the beginning of the 1997-98

season, and Sprewell's frustration erupted into a career altering confrontation with his coach, P.J. Carlesimo.

Sprewell did not react positively to Carlesimo's in-your-face coaching style and made known openly his lack of respect for his coach. Carlesimo benched Sprewell during a blowout against the Los Angeles Lakers early in the season because Sprewell refused to stop laughing during a timeout. Two days after that incident, Sprewell was tossed out of practice for ignoring Carlesimo's instructions. Then in November, Sprewell was fined for missing the arrival deadline for a game. Two days later during practice, after being reprimanded for his lackluster effort, Sprewell physically attacked Carlesimo when the coach tried to approach him. Reportedly Sprewell grabbed Carlesimo by the throat, demanded to be traded, and threatened to kill him if he wasn't. Pulled off by other players, Sprewell removed himself to the locker room but returned to the court fifteen minutes later and once again lunged at Carlesimo, this time punching him in the neck, a charge the Sprewell later denied.

Initially the team responded to the incident by suspending Sprewell for ten games, but then decided to terminate his $32 million contract for failing to abide by the basic conduct clause of the player agreement. After losing the last three years of a contract valued at nearly $25 million, Sprewell was then suspended from basketball for one year by NBA Commissioner David Stern. Sprewell also lost an endorsement contract with Converse. After the NBA players' association filed a grievance on behalf of Sprewell, arguing that the punishment was too harsh, the matter went before an arbitrator who eventually ruled that the Warriors could not terminate Sprewell's contract and reduced the suspension to the remainder of the 1997-98.

Sprewell did not help redeem his image when he was arrested three days before the arbitration decision for reckless driving, after being in a car accident that injured two people. In an out-of-court settlement, Sprewell was fined $1,000 and sentenced to three months home detention and two years probation. Although he apologized publicly to fans and supporters for his behavior, Sprewell

Career Statistics

Yr	Team	GP	PTS	P/G	FG%	3P%	FT%	RPG	APG	SPG	TO
1993	GS	77	1182	15.4	.464	.369	.746	3.5	3.8	1.6	203
1994	GS	82	1720	21.0	.433	.361	.774	4.9	4.7	2.2	226
1995	GS	69	1420	20.6	.418	.276	.781	3.7	4.0	1.6	230
1996	GS	78	1473	18.9	.428	.323	.789	4.9	4.2	1.6	222
1997	GS	80	1938	24.2	.449	.354	.843	4.6	6.3	1.7	322
1998	GS	14	299	21.4	.397	.188	.745	3.6	4.9	1.4	44
1999	GS	37	606	16.4	.415	.273	.812	4.2	2.5	1.2	79
2000	NY	82	1524	18.6	.435	.346	.866	4.3	4.0	1.3	226
2001	NY	77	1364	17.7	.430	.304	.783	4.5	3.5	1.4	218
2002	NY	81	1575	19.4	.404	.360	.821	3.7	3.9	1.2	223
TOTAL		677	13101	19.4	.430	.333	.810	4.2	4.2	1.6	1993

GS: Golden State Warriors; NY: New York Knicks.

Awards and Accomplishments

1992	Named All Southeastern Conference; twenty-fourth overall pick in the National Basketball Association (NBA) draft by the Golden State Warriors
1993	Named NBA All Rookie Second Team
1994	Named All NBA First Team and All Defensive Second Team
1994-95, 1997	Named NBA All Star

did not allow the matter to drop. He filed suit against the NBA for anti-trust and civil rights violations, suing the league for $30 million; however, the suit was thrown out in July of 1998 by a federal judge.

A New Start in New York

Cleared to return to the court for the 1998-99 season, Sprewell remained sidelined by a players' strike that lasted until January 1999, at which time he was traded from the Warriors to the New York Knicks. Joining the Knicks gave Sprewell a much-needed chance to redeem himself and his career. In his first game in a Knicks uniform, Sprewell scored a game-high twenty-four points. As the Knicks continued to win, memories of Sprewell's past altercations began to fade from the public mind. He became a popular player in New York and the team's emotional leader, helping his team reach the 1999 NBA championship series, which the Knicks lost to the San Antonio Spurs.

During the next three seasons, Sprewell averaged 18.6 points per game for the Knicks, despite the team's downward spiral in the league standings. Although he continues to incur occasional fines for being late or absent from required team functions, Sprewell quietly pays his fines. The final chapter of his career has yet to be written. Whether history will judge him as a misunderstood nice guy who tries to mind his own business for the most part or yet one more overpaid egomaniacal professional athlete remains to be seen.

CONTACT INFORMATION

Address: New York Knicks, Two Pennsylvania Plaza, New York, New York 10121. Phone: (212)465-5867.

FURTHER INFORMATION

Books

Oblender, David G., and Shirelle Phelps, eds. *Contemporary Black Biography,* Volume 23. Detroit: Gale Group, 1999.

Who's Who Among African Americans, 14th ed. Detroit: Gale Group, 2001.

Periodicals

Ballantini, Brett. "The New York State of Mind: Sully Spree." *Basketball Digest* (December 2002): 6+.

Brennan, John. "The Real Sprewell." *Sporting News* (February 26, 2001): 22.

D'Alessandro, Dave. "Despite Choking His Coach, Sprewell will be in Demand." *Sporting News* (November 30, 1998): 92.

D'Alessandro, Dave. "Talk is Cheap, But Sprewell Ruling was on the Money." *Sporting News* (March 16, 1998): 63.

"His Daze in Court." *Sports Illustrated* (June 1, 1998): 22.

Kertes, Tom. "All's Well That Ends Well." *Basketball Digest* (April 2002): 20+.

Lavnick, Mitchell. "Why Can't I Have a Team Full of Sprees?" *Basketball Digest* (March 2001): 28.

McCallum, Jack. "Spree for All." *Sports Illustrated* (May 15, 2000): 62+

Starr, Mark, and Allison Samuels. "Hoop Nightmare." *Newsweek* (December 15, 1997): 26.

Stein, Joel. "Tall Men Behaving Badly." *Time* (December 15, 1997): 91-92.

Taylor, Phil. "Center of the Storm." *Sports Illustrated* (December 15, 1997): 60.

Other

Biography Resource Center Online. Gale Group, 1999. Reproduced in *Biography Resource Center.* Farmington Hills, Mich.: The Gale Group, 2002. http://www.galenet.com/servlet/BioRC/ (December 11, 2002).

"Latrell Sprewell." National Basketball Association. http://www.nba.com/ (December 11, 2002)

Sketch by Kari Bethel

Dawn Staley

Dawn Staley
1970-

American basketball player

From humble beginnings in a North Philadelphia housing project, Dawn Staley dedicated herself to being one of the best female basketball players. Among her numerous honors, are USA Basketball Female Athlete of the Year, National Player of the Year, and NCAA Region Most Outstanding Player. Staley was a member of the first women's Dream Team in the 1996 and 2000 Olympics, winning gold both times. While playing for the Charlotte Sting, she was hired as coach for the Temple Owls. In 1996, Staley created the Dawn Staley Foundation to offer girls in her old neighborhood of Philadelphia an After School Project that focused on academics and athletics.

Up from the Projects, Onto the Basketball Court

Growing up in a housing project in North Philadelphia, Dawn Staley played basketball at Dobbins Technical High School. In 1988, *USA Today* named the 5 foot 5 inch young woman national high school player of the year, the only player under 6 feet to win. She also managed to led Dobbins to three consecutive Philadelphia Public League championships.

Staley began her 1989-92 collegiate career when Temple associate head coach Shawn Campbell recruited her to play at the University of Virginia for the Cavaliers. As a freshman, she became a starter for the team, averaging 18.5 points per game, and helped the team to a 110-21 record. This propelled the Cavaliers to four appearances in the NCAA Tournament, which led to three consecutive Final Four. In her four years as a starter, she personally scored 2,135 points.

Staley earned an astonishing array of awards and honors during her college years, including 10 Player of the Year awards. Among her titles were ACC Rookie of the Year, then ACC Player of the Year for 1991 and 1992, National Player of the Year, Most Outstanding Player of the Final Four All-Tournament, and Kodak All-American for three consecutive years. In just the 1991-92 season alone, she received the Naismith Trophy for outstanding woman collegiate player, Sport Illustrated Player of the Year, Honda Broderick Cup for outstanding college athlete of the year, and USBWA Player of the Year.

Her basketball record reflects her honorary achievements. She holds the ACC mark for career assists with 729, and captured two ACC regular season and three ACC All-Tournament titles. She holds the NCAA record of 454 steals, which now ranks sixth all-time among NCAA Division I leaders, and was named outstanding player in the 1991 NCAA tournament, even though Virginia lost in the finals to Tennessee.

After college, Staley began her professional career in 1992 playing with a team in Spain, and continued to travel the world playing in France, Italy, and Brazil. After returning to the US in 1994, she competed for the US National Team in the Goodwill Games, earning MVP for averaging 9.3 points per game and a team high 5.8 assists per game. She also played in the 1994 World Championships.

Giving Back to the Community

With a desire to return her good fortune to her community back home in Philadelphia, Staley created the

Career Statistics

Yr	Team	GP	PTS	FG%	3P%	FT%	RPG	APG	SPG	BPG	TO	PF
1999	CHA	32	11.5	.415	.317	.934	2.3	5.5	1.19	.09	2.81	2.2
2000	CHA	32	8.8	.372	.330	.878	2.4	5.9	1.16	.03	2.84	2.5
2001	CHA	32	9.3	.381	.371	.895	2.2	5.6	1.63	.03	3.13	1.7
2002	CHA	32	8.7	.364	.398	.762	1.8	5.1	1.5	.00	2.50	2.1
TOTAL		128	9.6	.385	.352	.861	2.2	5.5	1.37	.04	2.82	2.1

CHA: Charlotte Sting.

Dawn Staley Foundation. The foundation offers under-privileged girls programs that develop leadership, team-work, and social skills. The organization also fosters civic pride, mentoring, and self-confidence. Staley's work for the foundation has earned her the 1998 American Red Cross Spectrum Award for her contributions to her community and the 1999 WNBA Entrepreneurial Spirit Award. The year she started the foundation, a seven-story mural of Staley was painted on the side of a building in Philadelphia overlooking her neighborhood.

For US professional teams, Staley began playing in the 1996-97 season with the American Basketball League's Richmond Rage and helped the team to a 1997 runner-up finish. In 1998, she became a member of the USA World Championship Team, which won a gold medal, finishing with a perfect 9-0 record and earning the team USA Basketball Team of the Year.

The following year, Staley switched to the WNBA and joined the Charlotte Sting. That year the team placed second in the WNBA Eastern Conference and went to the finals. Staley ranked third in the league with 190 assists, and set a franchise record 13 assists vs. Washington. Also in 1999, she played in the USA Basketball Women's Winter European Tour Team, which compiled a 4-1 record, and went on to help capture the 1999 US Olympic Cup and USA Basketball International Invitational titles. Her continuing achievements earned her the 1999 WNBA Sportsmanship Award.

Staley at the Olympics

Staley took pride in being a member of women's basketball team in the 1996 Olympic Games in Atlanta. The US team compiled a perfect 60-0 record to win the gold medal. During the game, she held the USA Olympic single-game record with 9 free throws. Before the games, she participated in the Olympic Torch Relay, running the torch up the steps of the Philadelphia Museum of Arts.

Repeating her team's Olympic success, now as a member of the first women's Dream Team of professional players representing the US, she helped earn another gold medal in the 2000 Olympics in Sydney. She

Chronology

1970	Born in Philadelphia May 4
1988	Played on Dobbins Technical High School basketball team
1989-92	All-ACC
1990-92	Final Four Tournament
1990-92	Member of ACC All-Tournament Team
1994	Member of gold medal-winning US National Team in the Goodwill Games
1994	Played in World Championships
1996	Began playing with ABL team Richmond Rage
1996	Created Dawn Staley Foundation
1996	Member of US women's basketball team for Atlanta Olympics, won gold
1998	Member of gold-winning USA World Championship Team
1999	WNBA's Charlotte Sting
2000	Member of Olympic team in Sydney
2000	Named women's coach for Temple Owls
2001	Named to the Eastern Conference All-Star Team
2001	First woman in US professional basketball to record 1,000 career assists
2002	Named to the USA Basketball World Championship Team
2002	Signed 5-year extension to coach Temple

hit a perfect 12-of-12 free throws to tie for first for US single-competition free throw percentage.

In addition to the Olympics, Staley played a full season in 2000 at point guard with the WNBA's Charlotte Sting. The team registered an 8-0 record, averaged 4.0 points per game and achieved a team high 3.6 assists per game.

Staley as Coach

Although never having coached a game, Staley agreed to become women's coach at Temple University for the Owls in April 2000. At first denying the offer, she was persuaded by Olympic teammate **Teresa Edwards**. At that point, Temple had not seen a winning season in more than 10 years. Staley managed to achieve an impressive 10-6 start the first season. Even the fans took notice. Previously averaging 518 fans per game, 1,754 people attended for Staley's regular-season coaching debut.

After Temple won the Philadelphia Big Five Championship and its first-ever Atlantic 10 Conference Championship and an NCAA Tournament berth, Staley was

Awards and Accomplishments

1988	Named USA Today National High School Player of the Year
1989	ACC Rookie of the Year
1990-92	Kodak All-American
1990-92	NCAA Regional Most Outstanding Player (East and Midwest region)
1991	World University Games gold medal
1991	Named National Player of the Year
1991	Named most outstanding player of the Final Four
1991	Sports Illustrated Player of the Year
1991	Honda Broderick Cup as the outstanding college athlete of the year
1991-92	State Player of the Year
1991-92	ACC Player of the Year
1991-92	ACC Mary Garber Award (Female Athlete of the Year)
1991-92	Naismith Trophy as the nation's outstanding woman collegiate player
1991-92	NCAA Final Four All-Tournament Team most outstanding player
1991-92	USBWA Player of the Year
1992	Named National Player of the Year
1992	R. William Jones Cup gold medal
1993	World Championship Qualifying Tournament gold medal
1994	Goodwill Games gold medal and MVP
1994	World Championship bronze medal
1994	Named USA Basketball Female Athlete of the Year
1996	Olympic gold medal in Atlanta
1998	World Championship gold medal, team named USA Basketball Team of the Year
1998	American Red Cross Spectrum Award
1999	US Olympic Cup gold medal
1999	WNBA Entrepreneurial Spirit Award
1999	WNBA Sportsmanship Award
1999	US Olympic Cup title
1999	USA Basketball International Invitational title
2000	Olympic Games gold medal
2001-02	Big Five Coach of the Year

named 2001-02 Big Five Coach of the Year. In October 2002, she signed a five-year contract extension to coach Temple. The agreement includes the NCAA tournament.

While she coached, Staley still played for the Charlotte Sting, which went to the WNBA Championship finals. There she averaged 9.3 points per game and a league third best 5.6 assists per game. She also played in the 2001 WNBA All-Star Games, racking up 4 points and 3 assists in 15 minutes for the East Team. In 2002, she was named to the USA Basketball World Championship Team.

Dawn Staley earned awards and recognition on the basketball court as well as in her community. She achieved Olympic gold, national championships, and numerous player of the year and MVP awards as a basketball star. The skilled player easily made the transition to coach to teach a new generation of young players. Assisting others to achieve their dreams, she founded the Dawn Staley Foundation, and an after school projects and scholarship programs that help economically underprivileged girls become self-confident young women. The foundation's mission is to create a future of hope for at-risk youth by providing opportunities which help them realize their dreams and become productive and responsible citizens. The creation and support of educational and sports programs which challenge minds, build character, and help youth to develop to their fullest potential academically, socially, and physically is the essence of the foundation. To achieve its mission, the foundation supports a variety of programs in North Philadelphia.

The Dawn Staley After School Project provides a multi-faceted program designed to empower young women with the necessary education and life skills to become responsible and proactive community leaders through academics, sport activity, and community outreach. Staley is noted for her work ethic, dedication, and commitment to both basketball and to young people.

FURTHER INFORMATION

Books

Hickok, Ralph. *Who's Who of Sports Champions.* Boston, MA; Houghton Mifflin, 1995.

Periodicals

Crothers, Tim. "Dawn of a New Era." *Sports Illustrated* 94 (January 29, 2001): 104.

Other

Dawn Staley Foundation, http://www.dawnstaley5.com/dsf.html (December 15, 2002).

Temple Times, http://www.temple.edu/news/Oct02/staleycontract.html (December 15, 2002).

USA Basketball, http://www.usabasketball.com/bios women/dawn_staley_bio.html (December 15, 2002).

Virginia Women's Basketball, http://virginiasports.ocsn.com/sports/w-baskbl/archive/va-w-baskbl-honors.html (December 15, 2002).

Women's National Basketball Association, http://www.wnba.com/playerfile/dawn_staley.html (December 15, 2002).

Sketch by Lorraine Savage

Bart Starr
1934-

American football player

Hall-of-Fame quarterback Bart Starr led the Green Bay Packers to six division championships, five NFL championships, and two Super Bowl titles; he was Most Valuable Player for Super Bowl I and Super Bowl

Bart Starr

Chronology

1934	Born January 9, in Montgomery, Alabama
1949-52	Attends Sidney Lanier High School in Montgomery
1951	Receives special coaching from Vito "Babe Parilli"
1952-56	Plays college football for University of Alabama
1954	Marries Cherry Louise Morton
1954-55	Benched because of back injuries
1955-56	Benched after spraining his ankle
1956	Drafted by Green Bay Packers, plays backup quarterback
1957	Called up to active duty in U.S. Air Force, but discharged because of back injury
1957	Resumes playing for Green Bay Packers
1959	Vince Lombardi becomes coach of the Packers
1960	Packers win Western Division title, lose NFL championship
1961	Becomes Packers' star quarterback; Packers win division title and NFL championship
1962	Leads NFL in passing; Packers win division title and NFL championship
1964	Leads NFL in passing
1965	Packers win division title and NFL championship
1966	Leads NFL in passing; Packers win division title and NFL championship
1966	Named NFL Player of the Year; Packers win division title and NFL championship
1967	Packers win division title and famed "Ice Bowl" NFL championship
1967	Packers win Super Bowl I
1967	Named Most Valuable Player of Super Bowl I
1968	Packers win Super Bowl II
1968	Named Most Valuable Player of Super Bowl II
1971	Undergoes shoulder surgery
1972	Retires from play, but remains on team as quarterback coach
1973	Officially retires from Packers, becomes sports analyst for CBS
1975-84	Head coach of the Packers
1976	Elected to Alabama Sports Hall of Fame
1977	Inducted into National Football Hall of Fame
1984	Starr and his wife Cherry move to Phoenix, Arizona
1988	Starr's son Bret dies; Starr and Cherry move to Birmingham, Alabama
1988-present	Becomes chair of a real-estate investment firm
1988-present	Devotes time to charitable and nonprofit organizations

II, and NFL Most Valuable Player in 1966. He later coached the Packers for nine seasons, from 1975 to 1984.

Determination Pays Off

Born Bryan Bartlett Starr in Montgomery, Alabama in 1934, Starr was one of two children of U.S. Air Force master sergeant Benjamin Bryan Starr and homemaker Lulu Inez Tucker. His father ran the household with the same discipline and insistence on responsibility that he demanded from his squadron, and at his father's insistence, Starr attended school at Hurt Military Academy.

Starr enjoyed playing baseball with friends in a vacant lot during the summers, but in the fall he played football, often imagining that he was playing in a championship game. His football hero during this period was Harry Gilmer, a star tailback at the University of Alabama, and he dreamed of throwing as well as Gilmer did.

At Baldwin Junior High in Montgomery, Alabama, Starr played wingback, as well as running back, blocker, and receiver. The school often used the "box formation," devised by famed Notre Dame coach **Knute Rockne**. By the time Starr entered Sidney Lanier High School in 1949, his coach, Bill Moseley, noted that Starr was not particularly talented for the game. His personality was a factor in this: Starr was notably modest and quiet, and his coach believed he was too shy to be a good quarterback. However, Moseley did praise Starr's focused concentration on football, as well as his determination to become a good player.

In 1951, Starr began receiving special coaching from Vito "Babe" Parilli, an All-American quarterback at the University of Kentucky. Parilli taught Starr basic skills and encouraged him to feel confident in himself. Under Parilli's tutelage, Starr began dreaming of becoming a star player for coach Paul "Bear" Bryant at the University of Kentucky.

Starr improved so much that at the end of his senior year of high school he was selected for the All-Star team. Every college in the Southeastern Conference except Tennessee tried to recruit him to play for their team. Starr was still interested in playing for Bryant at Kentucky and visited the school with some of his friends, but Starr's father urged him to stay closer to home and play for Alabama. In addition, Starr's girlfriend's school was close to the University of Alabama, and the issue was decided: he would accept a football scholarship from Alabama.

Bart Starr

During Starr's freshman year, in 1953, Alabama and Syracuse competed in the Orange Bowl; Alabama won 61-6. Starr, playing third quarterback, threw 29 passes in the game and completed 17 for 170 yards. Partly as a result of this performance, in the following year, Starr became the team's starting quarterback. His punting average was 41.4, the second-highest in the Southeastern Conference; only Zeke Bratkowski of Georgia beat him.

On May 8, 1954, Starr married Cherry Louise Morton; they would later have two children.

In the 1954-1955 season, Starr was out of play because of back injuries. Alabama scored 4-5-2 without his contribution. In 1955-1956, Starr was benched again after spraining his ankle; Alabama then lost ten games in a row, ending the year with 0-10.

Drafted by Green Bay Packers

The basketball coach at Alabama, Johnny Dee, convinced the personnel director of the Green Bay Packers to suggest Starr as a prospect, and in January of 1956, the Packers chose Starr in the seventeenth round of the National Football League (NFL) draft. He was the 200th player chosen overall. In early summer of that year, Starr graduated from Alabama with a bachelor's degree in history, and began his professional football career with rigorous training.

Awards and Accomplishments

1960	Packers win Western Division title, lose NFL championship
1961-62, 1965-66	Packers win division title and NFL championship
1962, 1964, 1966	Leads NFL in passing
1963-64	Throws 294 passes with no interceptions, setting NFL record
1966	Named NFL Player of the Year
1967	Packers win division title and famed "Ice Bowl" NFL championship
1967	Packers win Super Bowl I; named Super Bowl Most Valuable Player (MVP)
1968	Packers win Super Bowl II; named Super Bowl MVP
1976	Elected to Alabama Sports Hall of Fame
1977	Inducted into National Football Hall of Fame

Starr was backup quarterback to Tobin Rote for his first four years with the team. According to the *St. James Encyclopedia of Popular Culture,* observers repeated the old criticisms of him: his "arm was weak and he was too passive and nice to develop the presence necessary for a championship quarterback."

In his first season, 1956-1957, Starr made forty-four attempts and completed twenty-four, with two touchdowns and three interceptions. The Packers had a 4-8 record in that season.

After that season ended, Starr, who has been commissioned in the Reserve Officer Training Corps when he graduated from college, was called up to active duty in the U.S. Air Force. He was assigned to Eglin Air Force Base near Panama City in Florida. However, a physical exam soon revealed his back problems, and he was discharged. He returned to Green Bay and the Packers.

In 1957-1958, Starr and his mentor Babe Parilli, who had come to the Packers when Tobin Rote was traded to the Detroit Lions, took turns as quarterback. The Packers completed the season with a 3-9 record. Packers coach Lisle Blackburn was released and was briefly replaced by Ray "Scooter" McLean, but during McLean's tenure, the team only won one game.

On February 4, 1959, **Vince Lombardi** became coach of the Packers. He would later become the most famed coach in the team's history, largely because of his all-encompassing attitude toward the game as a microcosm of life, and his insistence on winning. During his first year, the Packers finished with a record of 7-5.

Lombardi initially agreed with earlier assessments of Starr's potential. Like Blackburn, he badgered Starr, telling him he would have to become more assertive. In time, however, according to the *St. James Encyclopedia,* "Lombardi recognized that Starr's future depended on quiet encouragement instead of public humiliation," and Lombardi changed his tactics for dealing with Starr. The quiet encouragement worked. Starr blossomed as a player, and wholeheartedly accepted Lombardi's famed drive to

Career Statistics

Yr	Team	Passing								Rushing			
		ATT	COM	YDS	COM%	TD	INT	RAT	ATT	YDS	AVG	TD
1956	GB	44	24	325	54.5	2	3	65.1	5	35	7.0	0
1957	GB	215	117	1489	54.4	8	10	69.3	31	98	3.2	3
1958	GB	157	78	875	49.7	3	12	41.2	25	113	4.5	1
1959	GB	134	70	972	52.2	6	7	69.0	16	83	5.2	0
1960	GB	172	98	1358	57.0	4	8	70.8	7	12	1.7	0
1961	GB	295	172	2418	58.3	16	16	80.3	12	56	4.7	1
1962	GB	285	178	2438	62.5	12	9	90.7	21	72	3.4	1
1963	GB	244	132	1855	54.1	15	10	82.3	13	116	8.9	0
1964	GB	272	163	2144	59.9	15	4	97.1	24	165	6.9	3
1965	GB	251	140	2055	55.8	16	9	89.0	18	169	9.4	1
1966	GB	251	156	2257	62.2	14	3	105.0	21	104	5.0	2
1967	GB	210	115	1823	54.8	9	17	64.4	21	90	4.3	0
1968	GB	171	109	1617	63.7	15	8	104.3	11	62	5.6	1
1969	GB	148	92	1161	62.2	9	6	89.9	7	0	8.6	0
1970	GB	255	140	1645	54.9	8	13	63.9	12	62	5.2	1
1971	GB	45	24	286	53.3	0	3	45.2	3	11	3.7	1
TOTAL		3149	1808	24718	57.4	152	138	66.0	247	1308	5.3	15

GB: Green Bay Packers.

win. In addition, because Lombardi was volatile and aggressive, Starr's quiet focus and firm but modest demeanor provided the perfect balance for the team. According to the *St. James Encyclopedia,* Starr later said, "Everything I am as a man and a football player I owe to Vince Lombardi. He is the man who taught me everything I know about football, about leadership, about life. He took a kid and made a man out of him, with his example, with his faith."

On December 17, 1960, Starr quarterbacked while the Packers beat the Los Angeles Rams 35-21 to win the Western Division title; they later lost the league title to the Philadelphia Eagles.

In 1961, Starr became the team's star quarterback. On December 31, 1961, Green Bay played a championship against the New York Giants at the Packers' stadium, Lambeau Field, winning with a score of 37-0.

Starr soon became known as one of the most efficient passers in football history. His constant study of player behavior in films of games allowed him to set NFL records for the lowest percentage of passes intercepted in a season (1.2 percent), fewest interceptions in a full season (3), and lifetime passing completion percentage (57.4 percent). In 1964 and 1965, he threw 294 passes without an interception, setting another NFL record.

In 1965, the American Football League was established, and many Green Bay players left the relatively remote Wisconsin town to play for other franchises. Starr, however, had become involved in various opportunities in Wisconsin, including television commercials and car dealerships, and he decided to stay in Green Bay.

Throughout the 1960s, Starr quarterbacked the team to win six Western Division title games, five league championships, and two Super Bowl wins.

Starr was named Most Valuable Player of Super Bowl I in 1967, and Super Bowl II in 1968. He led the NFL in passing in 1962, 1964, and 1966. In 1966 he was named NFL Player of the Year.

The Ice Bowl

Starr's most famous move occurred on December 31, 1967, in the final minutes of the 1967 NFL championship, against the Dallas Cowboys. This game, later famed as the "Ice Bowl" because it was played at fourteen degrees below zero with a wind chill of forty-nine below, tested both players and fans in the Packers' outdoor stadium. The testing began before the players arrived at the stadium: some of them couldn't start their cars and had to hitch rides to the stadium. At the Cowboys' hotel, the doors were frozen shut and had to be kicked open.

On the first play of the game, referee Norm Schachter's whistle froze to his lip. After that, plays were yelled instead of whistled. The halftime show was canceled when a band member's lip froze to his horn during the rehearsal.

Nevertheless, the game went on as scheduled. The Packers, who lived in the cold Wisconsin climate and who were used to playing at the team's frigid Lambeau Field, were ahead 14-0 early in the game. However, as the weather deteriorated, the Packers fumbled twice, allowing Dallas to score a touchdown and a field goal. In the fourth quarter, Dallas added another touchdown. With 4:50 left in the game, the Packers were losing, seventeen to fourteen. By this time, the temperature had dropped to eighteen below zero and the wind was forty miles per hour. Over 50,000 fans huddled in their parkas in the stands, waiting for the outcome.

Starr called a time out, his last. The playing field was now a sheet of ice. The team's only chance was to pass: an incomplete pass would stop the clock, allowing the Packers to set up a field goal, tying the game and sending it into overtime. A completed pass would allow them to win. Starr consulted with Lombardi. According to a writer for *ESPN SportsCenter,* Lombardi said, "Run it, and let's get the hell out of here." Starr returned to the huddle.

Starr took the snap from center Ken Bowman. Bowman, along with guard Jerry Kramer, stopped Dallas tackle Jethro Pugh. Starr sneaked behind Jerry Kramer, who was on the one-yard line, and dove into the end zone, scoring a touchdown with only 13 seconds to go and winning the championship.

"We were supremely confident," Starr reflected in the *ESPN SportsCenter* article. "We were never arrogant. I think there's a huge difference. I think arrogance can bury you, but confidence can put you right on the edge of invincibility."

In 1971, Starr underwent surgery on both shoulders and missed the first ten games of the season. In July of 1972, he decided to retire from play, although he remained on the team as quarterback coach for the rest of the year.

In 1973, Starr officially retired. He became a sports analyst for the CBS network. In 1975, Starr became head coach of the Packers, a position he held until 1984. In 1976 Starr was elected to the Alabama Sports Hall of Fame, and in 1977 he was inducted into the National Football Hall of Fame. In 1984, Starr and Cherry moved to Phoenix, Arizona, where they and others hoped to start a new NFL team.

In July of 1988, Starr and Cherry became uneasy because they had not heard from their younger son, Bret, who was then 24 years old. Bret was recovering from an addiction to cocaine, and called his parents daily. After three days passed with no contact from Bret, Starr flew to Tampa, where Bret lived, to check on him. "I just had a gut feeling that something was wrong," Starr told Loren Mooney in *Sports Illustrated.* Tragically, he found his son dead on the floor in his apartment. An investigation revealed that Bret had died from irregular heart rhythms, a complication of his addiction.

As a result of this loss, Starr's older son, Bart Jr., told his parents that he thought it would be a good idea for them to move to Birmingham, Alabama, where he lived and worked as an investment advisor. He wanted them to be together as a family. Starr and Cherry agreed, and moved to Birmingham nine months later.

Starr became chair of Starr Sanders Projects, a subsidiary of Healthcare Realty, a real estate investment firm, and director of Barry, Huey, Bulek, and Cook, an advertising firm. He and his wife frequently saw their son, and his family. Starr told Mooney, "They are really our family. We'll always be indebted to Bart Jr. for bringing us back."

Starr is still considered a hero both in Wisconsin and in his home state of Alabama. As a writer noted in the *St. James Encyclopedia,* "To many, he will always be the hard-working conscience behind the Packer dynasty."

CONTACT INFORMATION

Address: c/o Celebrity Speakers and Entertainers, 23852 Pacific Coast Highway, Suite 401, Malibu, CA 90265. Phone: 800-516-9090. Online: www.speakerbooking. com.

FURTHER INFORMATION

Books

"Bart Starr." *St. James Encyclopedia of Popular Culture.* Detroit: St. James Press, 2000.

Vinson, Betty B. "Bart Starr." in *Scribner Encyclopedia of American Lives: Sports Figures,* edited by Arnold Markoe. New York: Charles Scribner's Sons, 2002: 391.

Periodicals

Mooney, Loren. "Bart Starr, Green Bay Packers Legend: August 25, 1975." *Sports Illustrated* (October 12, 1998): 24.

Stapleton, Arnie. "Memories of Packers-Cowboys Ice Bowl Game Remain Frozen in Time." *Rocky Mountain News* (January 4, 1998): 9C.

Other

"Bart Starr." *Biography.com.* http://www.biography. com/ (November 20, 2002).

"Catch a Shining Starr in the Ice Bowl." *ESPN SportsCenter* (January 16, 1999), http://espn.go.com/ (November 20, 2002).

Green Bay Packers. http://www.packers.com/ (November 15, 2002).

Pro Football Hall of Fame. http://www.profootballhof. com/ (November 20, 2002).

Sketch by Kelly Winters

Peter Stastny
1956-

Czech hockey player

Peter Stastny was one of the dominant offensive players of the National Hockey League (NHL). In the 1980s he was second only to **Wayne Gretzky** in points scored; the 1,239 points Stastny scored during his sixteen-year career with Quebec, New Jersey and St. Louis rank him as the second-best European scorer in NHL history. Of equal significance, when Stastny and his brother Anton defected from their native Czechoslovakia in 1980 to play in the NHL, they unleashed a wave of Eastern European players that changed the face of the league.

Peter Stastny was one of four sons born to Stanislav and Franciska Stastny in Bratislava, a city in the Slovak region of Czechoslovakia. Growing up in an ice hockey-crazed nation, Peter and his brothers Marian and Anton grew up with hockey sticks in their hands. They played whenever they could, and all three developed into excellent players. Marian eventually joined the Bratislava team of the Czech league; Anton and Peter soon joined him there. They later played on the national team that represented Czechoslovakia in international competitions. In 1976 they were members of the Czech team in the Canada Cup. At the 1980 Lake Placid Olympic Games, the Stastny brothers combined to score sixteen goals for the Czech team in six Olympic matches.

With the memory of the 1968 Soviet invasion of Czechoslovakia to suppress democratization fresh in the country's memory, Stastny always played particularly hard in matches against USSR teams. Once on the Czech national team, his remarks criticizing political abuses in Czechoslovakia brought him into conflict with the Communist regime there. He was warned that if his public statements did not follow the government line, he would be banished from the Czech team. The threat shook Stastny to his core. "To hear this, it was like someone poured icy cold water on your naked body," Stastny told Eric Duhatschek of Toronto's *Globe and Mail.* "This is when I realized, because they had total control and could manipulate you anyway they wanted, there was no future for me [in Czechoslovakia] as a player or a person." After much soul-searching, Stastny made up his mind to leave the country.

Stastny, his pregnant wife Darina, and his brother Anton defected while the Czech National team was in Innsbruck, Austria playing a tournament. Their escape was like a story from a spy novel. They left under cover of night and made their way to the airport where they boarded a plane booked by executives of the Quebec Nordiques, an NHL club. The decision to leave his

Chronology

1956	Born September 18 in Bratislava, Czechoslovakia
1974-80	Plays for Slovan Bratislava in Slovakia
1976	Plays for Czechoslovakia in Canada Cup
1976-80	Plays for Czechoslovakia in World Championships
1980	Plays for Czechoslovakia in Lake Placid Olympics
1980	Defects from Czechoslovakia; joins Quebec Nordiques
1981	Wins Calder Memorial Trophy as best NHL rookie
1984	Plays for Canada in Canada Cup
1990	Returns to Czechoslovakia for first time in ten years
1990	Is traded to New Jersey Devils
1994	Coaches Slovakian National hockey team in Lillehammer Olympics
1995	Retires from National Hockey League
1998	Elected to Hockey Hall of Fame

homeland was a frightening one for Stastny. He was leaving behind everything he knew and knew he would probably never return. Most difficult, he was leaving his brother and parents to the caprices of the Communist government he hated. Stastny's fears were justified. After his defection, his parents were denied a new apartment for which they had been waiting for years. Marian, who was unable to defect at the same time, was suspended from the national hockey team and put under police surveillance. Small wonder that Peter Stastny deeply resented taunts from opposing NHL players that he was a "Commie." "I hated communism more than anybody," he told the *Denver Post*'s Terry Frei. "I never accepted that without coming back at the guy."

In October 1980, the Stastny brothers joined the Quebec Nordiques. Their hard, intelligent, wide open style of hockey was an instant hit in Quebec. Peter was a team leader from the day he arrived. "On the ice, Peter was the guy that made things go," teammate Jamie Hilsop told the *Globe and Mail*'s Duhatschek. "he sat me down in the stands before the game and diagrammed out exactly where he wanted me to be. Even back then, he wanted to use the full width of the ice."

Stastny's first season was a difficult one. He was not used to the constant travel or the large number of games played at NHL intensity. By Christmas 1980, he was exhausted. By the All-Star break he had caught his second wind, and his play in the second half of the season was phenomenal. In two consecutive games against Vancouver and Washington, he and Anton scored a combined twenty-eight points. The sixteen points they scored in the Washington match still stands as a road game record. Stastny had scored thirty-nine goals and 109 points in 1980; he was named the NHL's top rookie and awarded the Calder Trophy.

1981-82 was equally notable. He and Anton were able to ransom their brother from Czechoslovakia with $30,000 they saved during their first season with the Nordiques. For a while afterwards, the three brothers

Career Statistics

Yr	Team	GP	G	A	PTS	+/-	PIM
1980-81	QUE	77	39	70	109	+11	37
1981-82	QUE	80	46	93	139	-10	91
1982-83	QUE	75	47	77	124	+28	78
1983-84	QUE	80	46	73	119	+22	73
1984-85	QUE	75	32	68	100	+23	95
1985-86	QUE	76	41	81	122	+2	60
1986-87	QUE	64	24	53	77	-21	43
1987-88	QUE	76	46	65	111	+2	69
1988-89	QUE	72	35	50	85	-23	117
1989-90	QUE	62	24	38	62	-45	24
1989-90	NJ	12	5	6	11	-1	16
1990-91	NJ	77	18	42	60	0	53
1991-92	NJ	66	24	38	62	+6	42
1992-93	NJ	62	17	23	40	-5	22
1993-94	STL	17	5	11	16	-2	4
1994-95	STL	6	1	1	2	+1	0
TOTAL		977	450	789	1239	-10	824

NJ: New Jersey Devils; QUE: Quebec Nordiques; STL: St. Louis Blues.

Awards and Accomplishments

1976-77	World Championship Gold Medal
1980	Czechoslovakian Player of the Year
1981	Calder Memorial Trophy
1981-84, 1986, 1988	NHL All-Star
1995	World Championship Best Forward Award (Pool B)
1998	Hockey Hall of Fame
2000	IIHF Hall of Fame

With 1,239 career points, he is the second-highest scorer among Europeans to play NHL. In 1998 Stastny was inducted into the Hockey Hall of Fame. Of his success on the ice he told Eric Duhatschek, "I had a passion for the game of hockey. I believe, if you want to achieve something and you put your mind and all your skills into it, you just achieve it."

FURTHER INFORMATION

Periodicals

Allen, Kevin. "Stastnys scored despite duress." *USA Today* (February 16, 2001): C3.

Duhatschek, Eric. "New kid on the bloc altered it all." *Globe and Mail* (Toronto, Canada) (October 9, 2000).

Frei, Terry. "First Eastern Bloc players show great courage to reach dreams." *Denver Post* (February 2, 2001).

"Hall of Fame has new Nordiques' connection." Associated Press (September 16, 1998).

Luecking, Dave. "Reaching The Hall Of Fame Is Stastny's Dream Come True." *St. Louis Post-Dispatch* (November 15, 1998): F10.

"Peter Stastny Possible Candidate For Slovak President." Czech News Agency (May 9, 2002).

Strachan, Al. "Stastny's career undergoes revival with young, talented New Jersey." *Globe and Mail* (November 1, 1991).

Sullivan, Jerry. "Stastny Finally Competing In The Name Of Slovakia." *Buffalo News* (February 16, 1994): D1.

Other

"Peter Stastny." A-Z Encyclopedia of Ice Hockey. http://www.azhockey.com/St.htm (January 5, 2003).

Sketch by Gerald E. Brennan

skated on the same line for Quebec. His second season, with forty-six goals and ninety-three assists, was the most productive of Stastny's career. He would go on to score 110 points or more in five more seasons as well. During the 1984-85 season, Stastny played on the Canadian team in the Canada Cup tournament, scoring one goal and two assists. Quebec traded Peter Stastny to the New Jersey Devils toward the end of the 1989-90 season. Though older, Stastny was far from washed up as a player. He remained among the NHL's leading scorers with New Jersey, and in the early 1990s the Devils were regular Stanley Cup contenders.

Following the Velvet Revolution and the fall of Czechoslovak Communism in late 1989, Stastny was able to visit his homeland in 1990 for the first time in ten years. In 1993, Slovakia became an independent nation and Stastny returned again to prepare the Slovakian hockey team for the 1994 Olympics in Lillehammer Norway. With Stastny as player-coach, the Slovakian team proved unexpectedly strong against some heavily favored opponents despite not winning a medal. Stastny was jubilant despite the disappointing finish. After the Olympics, Stastny returned to the NHL and played twenty-three games for the St. Louis Blues before retiring in 1995. Peter Stastny lives in St. Louis Missouri with his wife Darina, his daughters Katarina and Kristina, and his sons, Yan and Paul. Stastny works as a scout for the St. Louis Blues organization. There was talk in spring 2002 of his running for the Slovakian presidency.

Peter Stastny scored 450 NHL career goals—if one added the approximately 120 he scored playing club hockey in Czechoslovakia in his early 20s, he would easily be among the top ten scorers in NHL history.

Roger Staubach
1942-

American football player

Roger Staubach

A star quarterback for the Dallas Cowboys for nearly a decade, Roger Staubach endeared himself to fans of "America's team" with his last-minute heroics that led Dallas to two Super Bowl victories and four National Football Conference (NFC) championships. As successful as he was on the gridiron, both in college and in the National Football League (NFL), Staubach realized early on that there was a life for him beyond football. During the off-season from 1970 to 1977, he worked as a salesman and assistant vice president for Henry S. Miller Realty in Dallas. In 1977, while still playing for the Cowboys, Staubach founded a Dallas-based commercial real estate firm that would form the basis for his successful post-football career. In addition to his responsibilities as chairman and chief executive officer of Staubach Company, he finds time to write occasionally and involve himself in community and charitable affairs.

Born in Cincinnati

He was born Roger Thomas Staubach in Cincinnati, Ohio, on February 5, 1942. The only child of Robert Joseph and Elizabeth (Smyth) Staubach, he attended Purcell High School, a parochial school in Cincinnati where he played baseball, basketball, and football. He showed particular promise in baseball and football. Staubach set his sights on playing football for Notre Dame, but when they passed on him he decided to enroll at Purdue. A recruiter for the U.S. Naval Academy, sent to Purcell to sign up the team's center, became interested in Staubach

after seeing the quarterback in action on some of the team's game films. At least initially, Staubach had no interest in attending a service academy, but he was persuaded by the recruiter, Rick Foranzo, to pay a visit to Annapolis. Staubach made the trip and liked what he saw of the school, being particularly impressed by the academy's strong moral environment. When scores on his initial college entrance exams revealed a weakness in English, Staubach decided to seek help to prepare him for the rigorous standards of the academy. He enrolled at New Mexico Military Institute (NMMI) in Roswell, New Mexico, where he not only boned up on his English, but honed his passing skills. He led the institute's football team to a 9-1 record.

Staubach entered the Naval Academy in 1961, kicking off a year of unparalleled misery for the Ohioan. Plagued by homesickness, he found it difficult to fit into the rigid lifestyle of a plebe. Even more depressing was his seeming inability to do anything without running afoul of the academy's rules. In his first four months, he collected 150 demerits; he knew if he collected 150 more during the remainder of the school year, he'd be on his way home from Annapolis. After some serious soul-searching during the Christmas break, Staubach returned to the academy with a new outlook and attitude. He managed to get through the rest of the school year with only 20 additional demerits, escaping the embarrassment of expulsion.

Shines in Game against Cornell

It was not until the fourth game of his sophomore year that Staubach truly came into his own as a quarterback. Although he'd previously seen little play and was ranked well down on Navy's quarterback ranks, the coach sent him into a scoreless game with Cornell. Staubach passed for one touchdown and ran for two others to lead Navy to a lopsided 41-0 victory. For the 1962 season, he led the NCAA in passing with a completion rate of 67.3 percent. Perhaps the most memorable mo-

Awards and Accomplishments

1962	Led NCAA with pass completion rate of 67.3 percent
1962-64	U.S. Naval Academy's Thompson Trophy Cup
1963	Heisman Trophy
1971, 1973, 1978-79	Leading NFL passer
1972	Super Bowl VI victory; Super Bowl MVP
1972, 1977-80	Selected to play in Pro Bowl
1978	Super Bowl XII victory
1981	Elected to National Football Hall of Fame
1985	Elected to Pro Football Hall of Fame
2000	Receives NCAA's Theodore Roosevelt Award

Related Biography: Football Player Craig Morton

Craig Morton, the Dallas Cowboys' starting quarterback unseated by Roger Staubach, eventually faced off against Staubach in 1978's Super Bowl XII. Morton was raised in Campbell, California. A stand-out football star at Campbell High School, winning Central Coast MVP honors, Morton received a flood of scholarship offers. He decided to play for the University of California, where he received All-American honors during his third year as the Golden Bears' starting quarterback. At the 1965 NFL draft, Morton was chosen by the Dallas Cowboys as the fifth pick overall in the first round of the draft. For his first few years with the Cowboys, Morton was a backup for legendary quarterback Don Meredith. In 1969, the season after Meredith's retirement, Morton took over as starting quarterback. During the Cowboys' 1970-1971 season, Morton led the team to the Super Bowl, where they lost to the Baltimore Colts by a score of 16-13.

In the 1971-1972 season following the Cowboys' loss in Super Bowl V, coach Tom Landry decided to let Morton and Staubach duel it out for starting quarterback honors. By mid-season, Staubach had won the job, and although Morton stayed on in Dallas for a couple of years after losing to Staubach, he saw only limited action. He next played with the New York Giants before joining the Denver Broncos in 1977. Morton helped lead the Broncos to their first Super Bowl in January 1978, only to lose, 27-10, to the Cowboys, led by Staubach. Morton continued to play for the Broncos until 1982, when he retired from professional football. In 1988, he was inducted into the Broncos Ring of Fame, and in 1992 was similarly honored by the College Football Hall of Fame and the Cal Athletic Hall of Fame. In November 2002, the Santa Clara County native was inducted into the San Jose Sports Hall of Fame. Morton currently is the proprietor of Mel Hollen's Restaurant in San Francisco.

ment of the 1962 season for Staubach was Navy's upset win over Army in the academies' traditional end-of-season game. Navy overpowered Army, 34-14, largely on the strength of four touchdowns credited to Staubach, two on the ground and two in the air.

Staubach led Navy to a 9-1 record in his junior year, compiling a total of fifteen touchdowns—seven passing and eight running—for the season. His impressive performance earned him the covers of Time and Sports Illustrated. In the post-season, Navy faced off against top-ranked Texas in the Cotton Bowl. Although Texas won the game, 28-6, Staubach performed admirably, completing twenty-one of thirty-one pass attempts for a total of 228 yards. In late November 1963, Staubach learned that he had won the coveted Heisman Trophy. Because he'd earned a year of college credit by attending NMMI, a junior college, Staubach became eligible for the NFL draft in the spring of 1964. However, his commitments to the Navy hardly made him an eagerly sought-after property. He was eventually drafted by the Cowboys in the 10th round of the draft. An injury at the start of Staubach's senior year significantly compromised his value to the team, and Navy finished the 1964 season with a record of 3-6-1.

Begins Service in the Navy

Staubach graduated from the Naval Academy in 1965 with an engineering degree. A few months later, he married longtime girlfriend, Marianne Hoobler, and prepared to begin his naval service. Over the next four years, he satisfied his active duty requirements, serving one year in Vietnam as a supply officer. Although he had at one time considered a career in the military, he found the urge to play professional football too strong to resist and in 1969 reported to the Dallas Cowboys training camp. With Craig Morton firmly entrenched as the team's starting quarterback, Staubach saw limited action his first few seasons. After the Cowboys, quarterbacked by Morton, narrowly lost Super Bowl V to Baltimore in January 1971, Cowboys coach **Tom Landry** decided to give Staubach a chance to compete for the quarterback's job during the 1971-1972 season. By mid-season,

Staubach had won the job, eventually leading the Cowboys to the NFC Championship and a chance to reverse its Super Bowl fortunes. At Super Bowl VI, Dallas blew away the Miami Dolphins, 24-3, earning Staubach the Super Bowl MVP Award.

For Staubach, much of the 1972-1973 season was marred by a shoulder injury he suffered in the pre-season. After surgery and a lengthy recuperation, he did return to the team late in the season. In a first-round playoff game against the San Francisco 49ers, the Cowboys were trailing when Staubach led the team to two touchdowns in the final two minutes of the game for a 30-28 victory over San Francisco. This come-from-behind victory earned Staubach the nickname "Captain Comeback." In the race for the NFC Championship, the Cowboys reached the finals but lost, 26-3, to the Washington Redskins. In the second half of the 1970s, Staubach led the Cowboys to the Super Bowl three times—1976, 1978, and 1979. In two of those Super Bowl appearances, Dallas was overpowered by the Pittsburgh Steelers, but in 1978 Staubach led the Cowboys to a lopsided victory, 27-10, over the Denver Broncos.

Retires from Football

By the end of the 1970s, Staubach's enthusiasm for the game was beginning to wane noticeably, as he yearned to spend more time with his family. In 1980, Staubach announced his retirement from the NFL. Since about 1970 Staubach had been heavily involved in the commercial real estate business in and around Dallas, working first for Henry S. Miller Realty until 1977

Career Statistics

| Yr | Team | GP | Passing | | | | | | Rushing | | | |
---	---	---	ATT	COM	YDS	COM%	Y/A	TD	INT	ATT	YDS	TD
1969	DAL	6	47	23	421	48.9	9.0	1	2	15	60	1
1970	DAL	8	82	44	542	53.7	6.6	2	8	27	221	0
1971	DAL	13	211	126	1882	59.7	8.9	15	4	41	343	2
1972	DAL	4	20	9	98	45.0	4.9	0	2	6	45	0
1973	DAL	14	286	179	2428	62.6	8.5	23	15	46	250	3
1974	DAL	14	360	190	2552	52.8	7.1	11	15	47	320	3
1975	DAL	13	348	198	2666	56.9	7.7	17	16	55	316	4
1976	DAL	14	369	208	2715	56.4	7.4	14	11	43	184	3
1977	DAL	14	361	210	2620	58.2	7.3	18	9	51	171	3
1978	DAL	15	413	231	3190	55.9	7.7	25	16	42	182	1
1979	DAL	16	461	267	3586	57.9	7.8	27	11	37	172	0
TOTAL		131	2958	1685	22700	57.0	7.7	153	109	410	2264	20

DAL: Dallas Cowboys.

when he co-founded Holloway-Staubach Corporation, which he served as chairman and CEO until 1981. By 1981, Holloway-Staubach had become Staubach Company, which Staubach continues to lead as chairman and CEO. The company, a full-service real estate strategy and services firm, works for clients around the world. Shortly after leaving pro football, Staubach worked briefly as a commentator for CBS Sports, but today he concentrates on running his real estate business. He and wife Marianne live in the Dallas area and have five children, Jennifer Anne, Michelle Elizabeth, Stephanie Marie, Jeffrey Roger, and Amy Lynn.

In the years since he left football, Staubach has been widely honored not only for his football prowess but for his accomplishments in business and civic affairs. He was inducted into the National Football Hall of Fame in 1981 and the Pro Football Hall of Fame in 1985. In January 2002, Staubach received the NCAA's Theodore Roosevelt Award, which is presented annually to a former college student-athlete "who has exemplified the ideals and purposes of college athletics by demonstrating a continuing interest and concern for physical fitness and sport." Staubach's other awards include the 1988 Henry Cohn Humanitarian Award, 1990 Dallas/Fort Worth Entrepreneur of the Year Award, 1992-1993 Oak Cliff Lions Club Humanitarian Award, and 1998 Mission Award from St. Edward's University.

Staubach, a successful businessman today, will be long remembered as one of football's most outstanding quarterbacks as well as a consummate team leader. The late Sid Luckman, a Hall of Fame quarterback with the Chicago Bears, said of Staubach: "He had an air about him. You knew someone special was on the field." In a profile of Staubach in *Time,* reporter Peter Ainslie wrote: "Staubach's greatest asset [was] his fierce competitiveness, fierce even by the standards of a league filled with men who brood for days after a defeat."

CONTACT INFORMATION

Address: Roger Staubach, c/o Staubach Company, 15601 Dallas Pkwy., Ste. 400, Addison, TX 75001. Phone: (800) 944-0012. Online: http://www.staubach.com.

SELECTED WRITINGS BY STAUBACH:

(With Sam Blair and Bob St. John) *First Down, Lifetime to Go,* Word, 1974.

(With Frank Luksa) *Time Enough to Win,* Word, 1980.

(With Jack Kinder Jr. and Garry D. Kinder) *Winning Strategies in Selling,* Prentice-Hall, 1981.

The Staubach Planner: A Tool for Success, Prentice-Hall, 1983.

(With Troy Aikman and Jeanne T. Warren) *Reaching for the Stars,* Taylor, 1993.

(With Richard Whittingham) *Rites of Autumn: The Story of College Football,* Simon & Schuster, 2001.

FURTHER INFORMATION

Books

Burchard, Marshall. *Sports Hero Roger Staubach.* New York: Putnam, 1973.

"Roger Staubach." *American Decades CD-ROM.* Detroit: Gale Group, 1998.

"Roger Staubach." *St. James Encyclopedia of Popular Culture,* five volumes. Detroit: St. James Press, 2000.

"Roger (Thomas) Staubach." *Contemporary Authors Online.* Detroit: Gale Group, 2002.

Sullivan, George. *Roger Staubach: A Special Kind of Quarterback.* New York: Putnam, 1974.

Towle, Mike (Editor). *Roger Staubach, Captain America.* Nashville, TN: Cumberland House, 2002.

Other

"1963: Roger Staubach, Navy Back." Heisman.com. http://heismanmemorialtrophy.com/years/1963.html (October 16, 2002).

"Craig Morton." Football-Reference.com. http://www. football-reference.com/players/MortCr00.htm (October 18, 2002).

"Craig Morton to Join San Jose Sports Hall of Fame." University of California. http://calbears.ocsn.com/ sports/m-footbl/spec-rel/080702aaa.html (October 18, 2002).

"Ring of Fame: Craig Morton." Denver Broncos. http://www. denverbroncos.com/history/ringoffame/ morton.php3 (October 18, 2002).

"Roger Staubach." Famous Texans. http://www.famous-texans.com/rogerstaubach.htm (October 16, 2002).

"Roger Staubach: Biography." Pro Football Hall of Fame. http://www.profootballhof.com/players/ enshrinees/rstaubach.cfm (October 16, 2002).

"Roger Staubach: Quarterback." Football-Reference. com. http://www.football-reference.com/players/ StauRo00.htm (October 16, 2002).

"Roger Staubach, Chairman of the Board and Chief Executive Officer." Staubach Company. http://www. staubach.com/staubach/home.nsf/main/people-stau bach (October 18, 2002).

"Staubach Recognized with NCAA's Highest Honor." NCAA. http://www.ncaa.org/releases/makepage. cgi/awards/1999120601aw.htm (October 18, 2002).

Sketch by Don Amerman

George Steinbrenner
1930-

American baseball executive

Called by the *Tampa Tribune* "Tampa's biggest icon," George Steinbrenner is best known today as the owner of the New York Yankees baseball team, arguably the best baseball team in the United States. Under Steinbrenner, the team won six World Series championships by 2002 (in 1977, 1978, 1996, 1998, 1999, and 2000). On the occasion of Steinbrenner's 72nd birthday in 2002, the *Tampa Tribune*'s Ira Kaufman summed up Steinbrenner's career by, "few individuals have changed the face of baseball or Tampa Bay more profoundly." And *Sporting News* has called Steinbrenner the second most influential person in sports, after Paul Tagliabue, the commissioner of the National Football League.

Chronology

1930	Born on July 4 in Rocky River, Ohio
1948	Attends Williams College in Massachusetts
1952	Earns B.A. from Williams College
1952	Serves in U.S. Air Force
1952	Pursues master's degree in physical education at Ohio State University
1955	Relocates to Evanston, Illinois to become assistant football coach at Northwestern University
1956	Joins football coaching staff at Purdue University
1956	Marries Joan Zieg
1958	Returns home to Ohio of work for Kinsman Marine Transit Company
1960	Purchases Cleveland Pipers basketball team
1962	Becomes president of Kinsman Marine Transit Company
1967	Merges Kinsman Marine Transit Company with American Ship Building Company
1973	Buys New York Yankees
1974	Pleads guilty to running an illegal scheme to raise money for Richard Nixon's 1972 presidential campaign
1976	Leads New York Yankees to its first World Series game since 1964
1989	Receives pardon from President Ronald Reagan
1999	Merges New York Yankees with New Jersey Nets into YankeeNets

Born on the Fourth of July

George Steinbrenner was born on July 4, 1930, in Rocky River, Ohio, to Rita and Henry Steinbrenner. He was the oldest of three children born to the couple. His father was the president of Kinsman Marine Transit Company, a shipping company based in Cleveland, Ohio. While a student at Massachusetts Institute of Technology (MIT), Henry Steinbrenner competed on the track team, and became a national low-hurdle champion. Steinbrenner later said of his father, wrote Carol Slezak in the *Chicago Sun-Times,* "My father was an outstanding man. I never worked as hard as him and I never was as smart as him."

Steinbrenner grew up on a farm near the Ohio town of Bay Village, on the banks of Lake Erie. He attended high school at the Culver Military Academy in Indiana beginning in 1944. At Culver, he excelled in athletics, playing both on the football team and on the track team. After graduating from high school in 1948, Steinbrenner went on to Williams College in Massachusetts, where he earned a B.A. Following in his father's footsteps, at Williams Steinbrenner ran on the school's track team. He also worked on the school newspaper, and became president of the school's glee club (men's chorus).

After his graduation from college in 1952, Steinbrenner served in the United States Air Force. Stationed in Columbus, Ohio, he served as a general's aid. He also coached his base's basketball and baseball teams, and set an Armed Forces low-hurdle record. While in the Air Force, Steinbrenner met his future wife, Joan Zieg, a civilian living in Columbus. (They were married in 1956, and they eventually had four children—Hank,

Hal, Jenny, and Jessica. By 2002, Steinbrenner had a total of 12 grandchildren.)

A Career in Athletics

After leaving the Air Force, Steinbrenner went on to Ohio State University to work toward a master's degree in physical education. Leaving graduate school, Steinbrenner took a stab at athletic coaching, becoming an assistant football coach at Chicago's Northwestern University. His first foray into coaching did not go well, however, and he and his entire staff were fired because his team made an extremely poor showing. Undaunted, Steinbrenner went on to become assistant coach at Purdue University in Indiana, where he achieved better results.

Success in Business

Two years into his tenure at Purdue, in 1957, Steinbrenner received a call from his father, who wanted to him to work for the family business, which was in danger of failing. "He told me to get home and get busy," he later told Slezak. "I wish I could have stayed in coaching. My father never asked that much, but when he did it was an order."

Working in the family business as treasurer, Steinbrenner proved himself as a businessman, becoming president of Kinsman after four years. He stayed involved in sports as a businessman, however, in 1960 establishing a partnership to purchase a semiprofessional basketball team called the Cleveland Pipers. This enterprise was ultimately not successful, but it gave him a taste for what was to come. In 1967, he completed a merger of Kinsman and the American Ship Building Company, a move that firmly established Steinbrenner as a wealthy man.

Also active in politics, Steinbrenner served as chairman of the Democratic Congressional Dinner (a political fundraising event) in 1969, and again in 1970. But he always stopped short of running for political office himself, in the early 1970s turning down a chance to run for the governorship of Ohio. A supporter of both Democratic and Republican candidates, Steinbrenner has told Kaufman, "I don't stay on one side of the aisle or the other. I go for the man."

Steinbrenner's success with the shipbuilding company gave him the clout he needed to purchase a major athletic team, and in 1972, he almost completed a deal for the Cleveland Indians. After the deal collapsed, he looked around for another, comparable venture, and that's when the New York Yankees baseball team came up for sale.

The Yankees' New Owner

In 1973, Steinbrenner entered into the business venture for which he was to become best known. That year, he became head of a group of 17 investors that bought the New York Yankees from the CBS television and radio network.

Related Biography: Television Executive William Paley

Called by Patricia Hluchy of *Maclean's* the "unrivalled godfather of American Broadcasting," William Paley is the CBS chairman from whom Steinbrenner bought the New York Yankees in 1973. Paley is credited with building CBS from what was a group of 22 struggling radio stations when he bought the company in 1929, into a vast empire that helped to usher in the era of television. He retained control of his company until his death in 1990 at the age of 89.

William Paley was born in Chicago in 1901. His father was a Russian Jewish immigrant and a prosperous cigar merchant. Paley became vice president of his father's company in 1922, and he became interested in broadcasting when his company purchased advertising time on a radio station. The station was part of the United Independent Broadcasters Network, and Paley later bought that company, later known as CBS, for $400,000.

Paley was among the first to recognize the potential of the medium of television, and his company first began regular television broadcasts in 1939, by 1950 becoming the leading American broadcaster.

CBS bought an 80 percent stake in the Yankees in 1964, and later bought the remaining 20 percent. The company paid $13.2 million for the Yankees—$3.2 million more than Steinbrenner was to later pay for the team.

At the time, the team was down on its luck, not having made it to a World Series game since 1964. The sale was reported at $10 million. By 2002, the team was said to be worth $730 million. Kaufman called the mere $10 million Steinbrenner paid for the Yankees "astonishing," especially considering that the City of New York foot the bill for a more than $1 million parking lot to go with it, making Steinbrenner's effective purchase price even lower.

Steinbrenner has admitted that he has been tempted to sell the team to realize the enormous profit. "But," he told Kaufman, "athletics are in my blood, and being a successful team owner gives you prestige you can't get anywhere else."

At the time of the Yankees deal, Steinbrenner was an unknown businessman from the Midwest, so nervous at meeting the legendary chairman of CBS, William Paley, that he could hardly eat breakfast that morning. The two met in Paley's office, and verbally agreed on the deal. Steinbrenner spoke at a press conference soon after and promised to end the Yankees' losing streak within four years.

A Controversial Figure

Steinbrenner's political activities put him in the public eye in 1974, when he was formally charged with running a scheme to illegally funnel funds through his shipping company's employees to contribute to the 1972 presidential campaign of Richard M. Nixon. He admitted guilt in the ensuing court proceedings, but he refused to turn over any of his associates who were also involved in the deal. As he later told Kaufman, "There are lots of things you wish you could do over. But you have to live with it. You make your mistakes and there's no reason to get anyone else involved." Steinbrenner was pardoned by President Ronald Reagan in 1989.

Awards and Accomplishments

1976	Led Yankees to their first World Series since 1964
1977-78, 1996, 1998-2000	Led New York Yankees to World Series victory
2002	Won top National Football Foundation honor, the Gold Medal Award

The Yankees allowed Steinbrenner to keep his promise that he would make them a winning team by the fourth team of his ownership. In 1976, Steinbrenner's fourth year as owner, the Yankees went to their first World Series in more than ten years, and the following year his team won the World Series.

As owner of the Yankees, Steinbrenner became known for his fiery disposition, and for impulsively firing managers, most notably former player **Billy Martin**, who was dismissed by Steinbrenner a total of five times. He also once fired an assistant after she brought him the wrong sandwich for lunch.

However, he is also known for his loyalty, for instance, sticking by **Darryl Strawberry** even when the star Yankee repeatedly ran afoul of the law for drug possession and other charges. "Straw has a bad sickness," Steinbrenner explained to Kaufman. "He needs to know there's someone out there for him if he turns things around."

Active in Many Ventures

Steinbrenner's many philanthropic activities include the founding of the Gold Shield Foundation in 1982. This is an organization of business executives in Tampa Bay, Florida dedicated to providing support to the families of police officers and firefighters who were killed on the job. "It's nice to have money because of what you can do with it," he later told Kaufman. "I live OK because I work hard, but when I see a need is there, I like to give."

In addition to the Yankees, Steinbrenner has remained involved in several other business ventures, including operating Kinsman Stud Farm, a sprawling thoroughbred horse farm in Ocala, Florida that has regularly bred and trained champion race horses. He has also invested in several Broadway theater productions; he is said to enjoy attending theater productions and other art events near his home in Tampa, Florida. To succeed him as Yankees owner, Steinbrenner has been grooming his two sons, Hal and Hank, and his son-in-law, Steve Swindal. All are general partners in the Yankees already.

FURTHER INFORMATION

Periodicals

Hluchy, Patricia. "Broadcast Visionary." *Maclean's* (November 5, 1990): 58.

Kaufman, Ira. "Yankee Doing Dandy." *Tampa Tribune* (July 4, 2002): Sports, 1.

Slezak, Carol. "Curious About George." *Chicago Sun-Times* (April 2, 2001): Baseball 2001, 1.

Other

"George Steinbrenner." Infoplease.com. http://www. infoplease.com/ipsa/A0109670.html (November 13, 2002).

"George M. Steinbrenner III, A Profile." Cleveland-magazine.com. http://www.clevelandmagazine.com/editorial/thismonth_features.asp?docid=278 (November 27, 2002).

"New York Yankees History." Official site of the New York Yankees. http://newyork.yankees.mlb.com/NASApp/mlb/nyy/history/nyy_history_timeline.jsp?period=3 (November 27, 2002).

"Paley, William S." Museum of Broadcast Communications. http://www.museum.tv/archives/etv/P/htmlP/paleywillia/paleywillia.htm (November 27, 2002).

Sketch by Michael Belfiore

Casey Stengel
1890-1975

American baseball manager

Charles Dillon "Casey" Stengel is a legendary figure in baseball, as well known for his comedic talent and long-winded, convoluted way of speaking, called "Stengelese," as for his gift for managing some of the best and worst baseball teams in U.S. history. He led the New York Yankees to ten American League pennants and seven World Series championships between 1949 and 1960, working with such superstars as **Joe DiMaggio**, **Mickey Mantle**, **Yogi Berra**, Whitey Ford, and **Roger Maris**. Stengel started the Yankees' "instructional school," a training camp that soon came to be emulated by other major league teams. He also developed an intricate system of "platooning" his players to get the most from his roster. At age 72, two years after the Yankees let him go, he took on the management of the newly created New York Mets. Although the team won only 194 games and lost 452 during Stengel's four years as manager, the bumbling new team drew many fans to the stadium, thanks to Stengel's sense of humor and ability to entertain a crowd. After a lifetime in baseball, "the Old Perfesser," as Stengel had come to be known, retired at age 75 after he suffered a broken hip. The Baseball Writers Association of America voted to waive the five-year waiting period and named Stengel to the Baseball Hall of Fame in 1966.

Casey Stengel

Young Athlete

Charles Dillon Stengel was born July 30, 1890, the son of Louis E. Stengel, an insurance salesman of German ancestry, and Jennie Jordan Stengel, of Irish family background. He had an older brother, Grant, and an older sister, Louise. The family was closely knit and happy, and their neighborhood in Kansas City, Missouri, was upper middle class. Charley Stengel was a three-sport athlete in high school and pitched for his state-championship-winning team in 1909. The following year, at age 20, he signed with the Kansas City Blues, a top minor league team.

In 1911, after a short time in dental school, he went to Aurora, Chicago, with the Blues and led the league in stolen bases, catching the eye of a scout for the Brooklyn Dodgers. In 1912 the Dodgers drafted him and sent him to Montgomery, Alabama, under the tutelage of 37-year-old shortstop Kid Elberfeld, who told Stengel: "If you're going to be a big leaguer, act like a big leaguer."

"Casey at the Bat"

Stengel was soon called up to Brooklyn to play. Because he talked so much about Kansas City, he earned the nickname "K.C.," which became "Casey" after Ernest Thayer's popular poem "Casey at the Bat." By 1914 the press had passed the nickname on to all the fans. During this period, Stengel also earned another nickname that would stick with him in later years. After helping coach the University of Mississippi team, Sten-

gel rejoined the Dodgers so full of campus stories that his teammates began calling him "Professor."

Wilbert Robinson became manager of the Dodgers in 1915, and they played at the newly built Ebbets Field, where Stengel became an expert on the caroms off the angled concrete wall at right field. Always a lover of practical jokes, Stengel was suspected in a prank at Daytona Beach in which aviator Ruth Law was supposed to fly over the field and drop a baseball for Robinson to catch. By some mix-up the ball became a grapefruit; Robinson thought he had been killed when the fruit hit his chest, splattering red pulp.

Stengel played fairly regularly for the Dodgers, sometimes finding himself subject to "platooning," a system of playing a roster to best advantage by shifting players' positions. He was a fast outfielder and a strong hitter, batting .364 for Brooklyn in the 1916 World Series. However, he was traded in 1918 to the Pittsburgh Pirates and sat on the bench for two seasons.

Clown and Hero

During a Pirates game against the Dodgers in 1919, Stengel entertained the fans with what became a famous stunt. While sitting in the dugout he acquired a sparrow and put it under his cap. At bat, he tipped his cap to the crowd, releasing the bird and delighting the fans. In 1920, after he was traded to the Philadelphia Phillies, he repeated the trick, among other antics, including popping up from a manhole to catch a fly ball. In 1921, Stengel was traded to the New York Giants, where he would play for John McGraw, his greatest teacher and the manager by whom Stengel would set his standards in the future.

In the 1923 World Series, played in New York's brand new Yankee Stadium, Stengel hit two game-winning home runs—the first World Series homers hit in the stadium. In Game One, he hit a home run in the ninth inning, winning the game for the Giants over the Yankees, 5-4. After he loped around the bases, he attracted numerous comments from sports writers about his gait. They speculated on everything from age-related stiffness to a broken leg. However, according to Stengel biographer Robert W. Creamer, what really happened was that a rubber pad placed in one of Stengel's shoes to ease a bruised heel had shifted, causing him to think his shoe was coming off. In the third game of the Series, Stengel hit the only home run of the game, slamming the ball into the bleachers.

Shifting Ball Clubs

Over the next twenty-five years, Stengel moved from team to team, first as a player and then as a coach and manager. At the end of the 1923 season he was traded to the Boston Braves, then called the Bees, and played right field throughout 1924. During that year he married Edna Lawson, an accountant from Glendale, California,

Chronology

1890	Born July 30 in Kansas City, Missouri, to Louis E. and Jennie Jordan Stengel	**1926**	Takes over as manager of Toledo Mud Hens; they win first championship in 1927
1908-09	Plays semipro baseball with the Kansas City Red Sox	**1931**	Mud Hens team goes bankrupt; Stengel is hired as coach for Brooklyn Dodgers
1910	Signs a contract to play with the Kansas City Blues	**1934**	Signs contract to manage Dodgers
1910-11	Tries dental school but drops out	**1936**	Is fired by Dodgers after three losing seasons
1912	Is drafted by the Brooklyn Dodgers and becomes the protégé of shortstop Kid Elberfeld	**1938**	Becomes manager of the Boston Bees (later Braves)
1913	Hits the first home run in Ebbets Field	**1943**	Is hit by a taxi, fracturing a leg, an injury that never properly heals
1913-14	Is given nickname "Casey" by Dodgers teammates	**1944**	Is fired as manager of Bees after team finishes no higher than fifth place
1915	Wilbert Robinson takes over as manager of Brooklyn Dodgers; the infamous "grapefruit drop" occurs at Daytona Beach	**1944**	Takes over as manager of Milwaukee Brewers and leads them to first place in the minor leagues
1916	Hits .364 in the World Series for Brooklyn	**1945**	Becomes manager at Kansas City
1918	Is traded to the Pittsburgh Pirates	**1946**	Takes over management of the Oakland Oaks, under general manager George Weiss
1919	In a game against former teammates the Brooklyn Dodgers, tips his hat when he comes up to bat and a sparrow flies out, to the delight of the crowd	**1949**	Takes managerial reins of New York Yankees on recommendation of Weiss, then Yankees general manager
1919	Is traded to the Philadelphia Phillies	**1951**	Establishes first "instructional school" for Yankees
1921	Is traded to the New York Giants	**1958**	Testifies before Senate Subcommittee on Antitrust and Monopoly, giving a forty-five minute monologue in Stengelese that leaves senators confused and laughing
1922	Plays with the Herb Hunter All-Americans on their tour of the Far East; first team of major leaguers to play a Chinese team and first to lose a game in Japan.	**1960**	Is let go by the Yankees, at age 70
1923	Becomes a hero for the Giants in the World Series, hitting two game-winning home runs, the first World Series home runs ever hit in Yankee Stadium	**1962**	Becomes manager of newly created New York Mets
1923	Is traded to the Boston Braves	**1965**	Retires after suffering broken hip
1924	Marries accountant Edna Lawson and sets up home in Glendale, California	**1966**	Is named to Baseball Hall of Fame
1925	Retires as a player and takes first managerial job, at Worcester	**1975**	Dies of lymphatic cancer on September 29, the day after baseball season ends, in Glendale, California

whom he had met at a baseball game. They made their home in Glendale and had no children. In 1925 Stengel retired as a player. In 1926 he began managing the Toledo Mud Hens, in the minor leagues. The team went bankrupt in 1931 and Stengel lost his job, but the Brooklyn Dodgers hired him as coach the same year. In 1934 he took over management of the Dodgers, but they fired Stengel during the World Series of 1936, with one year left on his contract. The blow was eased by a large farewell dinner given to him by the sportswriters, an indication of the broad popularity he had gained. According to Creamer, Giants coach Steve Owens remarked, "This must be the first time anyone was given a party for being fired."

In 1938 Stengel was named manager of the Boston Bees but was let go after six years, when the team never finished higher than fifth place. He became manager of the Milwaukee Brewers in 1944, but he left the team in 1945 and took over at Kansas City and then Oakland, California, from 1946 through 1948. At Oakland, Stengel had a chance to tutor the young **Billy Martin**, who would later play for him with the New York Yankees.

Managing the Yankees

When old friend and admirer George Weiss, who had taken over general management of the New York Yankees, called on Stengel to manage the team in 1949, he accepted, saying at a press conference, "This is a big job, fellows, and I barely have had time to study it. In fact, I scarcely know where I am at." Conservative Yankee business staffers winced when the press ran a photo of Stengel in a Yankee uniform holding a baseball and gazing at it as though it were a crystal ball. Stengel, taking on the biggest challenge of his life at age 59, led the Yankees to a World Series championship his first season as manager and followed that with four more consecutive world championships. Under Stengel, the Yankees had seven wins in ten World Series over a twelve-year period.

Stengel's instructional school, first held in 1951, soon became a Yankee institution that was copied by the other major league teams. The young Mickey Mantle was Stengel's protégé. Stengel is said to have built his team around the powerhouse hitter and lightning-fast runner, along with Berra and Ford. With such superstars as DiMaggio and Phil Rizzuto also on the team, Stengel developed the art of platooning to its highest form. In 1953 the Yankees won eighteen straight games, just one short of the American League record.

The Yankees renewed Stengel's contract in 1954, and he became a baseball legend when his team won pennants for the next four years and again took the World Series title in 1956 and 1958. Continually in the newspapers and on television, Stengel became as well known as his players, as the world chuckled and scratched its head over his "Stengelese." On July 9, 1958, Stengel, Mantle, and a few others were called to testify before the U.S. Senate Subcommittee on Antitrust and Monopoly in Washington, D.C. The Senate

Career Statistics

Yr	Team	AVG	GP	AB	R	H	HR	RBI	BB	SO	SB
1912	BRO	.316	17	57	9	18	1	13	15	9	5
1913	BRO	.272	124	438	60	119	7	43	56	58	19
1914	BRO	.316	126	412	55	130	4	60	56	55	19
1915	BRO	.237	132	459	52	109	3	50	34	46	5
1916	BRO	.279	127	462	66	129	8	53	33	51	11
1917	BRO	.257	150	549	69	141	6	73	60	62	18
1918	PIT	.246	39	122	18	30	1	12	16	14	11
1919	PIT	.293	89	321	38	94	4	43	35	35	12
1920	PHI	.292	129	445	53	130	9	50	38	35	7
1921	PHI	.305	24	59	7	18	0	4	6	7	1
1921	NYG	.227	18	22	4	5	0	2	1	5	0
1922	NYG	.368	84	250	48	92	7	48	21	17	4
1923	NYG	.339	75	218	39	74	5	43	20	18	6
1924	BSN	.280	131	461	57	129	5	39	45	39	13
1925	BSN	.077	12	13	0	1	0	2	1	2	0
TOTAL		.284	1277	4288	575	1219	60	535	437	453	131

BRO: Brooklyn Dodgers; BSN: Boston Braves (then Bees); NYG: New York Giants; PHI: Philadelphia Phillies; PIT: Pittsburgh Pirates.

was considering a popular bill that would exempt professional baseball and other sports from certain antitrust restrictions and wanted a hearing on the bill before taking a vote. Asked to briefly give his background and his views on the legislation, Stengel delivered a forty-five-minute monologue that repeatedly filled the room with laughter. When Stengel was finished, Mantle was asked for his opinion on the bill. He said, "My views are about the same as Casey's."

In 1960, Stengel suffered chest pains and spent some time in the hospital but soon returned to the Yankees. However, the team had finished third in 1959 and lost the World Series to Pittsburgh in 1960. The Yankees let Stengel go, with a $160,000 profit-sharing payoff. Stengel told a crowd of reporters, "Write anything you want. Quit, fired, whatever you please." He also quipped, "I'll never make the mistake of being seventy again."

Managing the Amazin' Mets

In 1962, at age 72, Stengel was called on to manage the new Metropolitan Baseball Club of New York, better known as the Mets. On accepting the position, Stengel said, "Most people my age are dead at the present time." Drumming up support for his new team, he announced, "Come see my amazin' Mets!" and the name stuck. The 1962 Mets became known as the worst baseball club in history. Stengel said, "I been in this game a hundred years but I see new ways to lose I never knew existed before." In spite of their losses, Stengel kept up the humor, and the Mets drew ever larger crowds to the rundown Polo Grounds, where they played. Near the end of the 1962 season, some 923,000 fans filled the park, a very respectable number when compared to the 1.5 million drawn by the Yankees. Before their final home game, the Mets carried placards onto the field spelling

out "We Love You Mets Fans Too," and Stengel ran to the end of the line with an exclamation point. Stengel stayed with the Mets until 1965, when he broke his hip and was forced to retire, at age 75. Four years later, the Mets won the pennant, after winning 100 games.

In 1966 the Baseball Writers Association of America met in secret and elected Stengel to the Baseball Hall of Fame. Thrilled with the honor, he said, "This Hall of Fame thing is bigger than anything I ever saw."

Baseball Legend

Stengel spent some of his retirement years at work in a Glendale bank, with a sign on his desk that read "Stengelese Spoken Here." In the fall of 1975, as he lay in a hospital bed watching baseball on television, he reportedly got to his feet one last time to stand at attention as they played the national anthem, with his right hand over his heart. He died of a form of lymphatic cancer on Monday, September 29, 1975, the day after the baseball season ended. He was 85. His funeral was delayed until the following Monday so that baseball people could travel to attend. According to Creamer, the best tribute was paid before the services began, as chuckles and giggles rose throughout the church: his friends and colleagues were telling stories about him.

Baseball was Casey Stengel's life. A talented player and manager and a delightful comic, he was loved by players, fans, and the press. His teams won 1,905 games and lost 1,842. He led the New York Yankees to some of their greatest victories and nurtured the New York Mets through their greatest defeats. He played for, managed, and taught many other legendary figures in baseball and set a number of records himself, including the most World Series games managed (63) and won (37). The Stengel legend has lived on through the work of his

---

Stengel: His Life and Times

On March 8 [1966], a few days after he had arrived in Florida, the Mets asked Casey to come out to the spring training field to take part in a ceremony. The sportswriters were giving a plaque to George Weiss, he was told, and they wanted Casey to make the presentation. They told him to bring Edna along, too. Stengel, wielding his cane, limped onto the field and walked with surprising quickness toward the clubhouse. He had on street clothes but wore a Mets baseball cap. As he reached the clubhouse he was surrounded by writers and photographers, and he saw TV cameras, and he began to suspect something. The Commissioner of Baseball, General William Eckert, was on the field, and so was Ford Frick, Eckert's predecessor and a member of the Hall of Fame committee.

The Met players stopped practicing and gathered around. The small crowd of spectators who had come to watch practice crowded closer to the chain-link fence that kept them off the field. Frick began to speak. He explained the eligibility rule and the fact that it had been waived and said a special vote had been held and Stengel had been elected to Cooperstown.

Casey, holding his cap in his hand, bowed his head quickly, then waved his cap, and everyone applauded. Edna kissed him. Casey was grinning, his wrinkled face beaming, looking, as Cannon wrote, very young. He stepped to the microphone.

That summer he and Edna went to Cooperstown for his formal induction to the Hall of Fame. . . . He said, "I want to thank everybody. I want to thank some of the owners who were amazing to me, and those big presidents of the leagues who were so kind to me when I was obnoxious." He thanked his parents and he thanked George Weiss, "who would find out whenever I was discharged and would reemploy me." Casting back over his half century in baseball, he encapsulated his career in one brief sentence: "I chased the balls that Babe Ruth hit."

Source: Creamer, Robert W. *Stengel: His Life and Times.* New York: Simon and Schuster, 1984, pp. 314-315.

Awards and Accomplishments

1949-53, 1956, 1958	Won World Series and American League pennant as manager of New York Yankees
1949-60	Set records, including most years as a championship manager in the American League (10); most consecutive first-place finishes (5); most World Series games managed (63); and most World Series games won (37)
1955, 1957, 1960	Won American League pennant as manager of New York Yankees
1966	Inducted into Baseball Hall of Fame

Noble, Marty. "NY Fell in Love with Casey's Born Losers." *Newsday* (March 26, 2002): E17.

Olson, Stan. "Baseball's All-time Worst Team? '62 Mets." *Knight Ridder/Tribune News Service* (September 15, 2001): K2642.

Rushin, Steve. "Bad beyond Belief." *Sports Illustrated* (May 25, 1992): 82.

Other

Arthurs, Al. "Casey Stengel," BaseballLibrary.com. http://www.baseballlibrary.com/ (September 19, 2002).

"Casey Stengel Statistics," Baseball-Reference.com. http:// www.baseball-reference.com/ (September 19, 2002).

Sketch by Ann H. Shurgin

many biographers and through the baseball institutions he helped to establish.

SELECTED WRITINGS BY STENGEL:

(With Harry Paxton) *Casey at the Bat: The Story of My Life in Baseball,* Random House, 1961.

FURTHER INFORMATION

Books

Creamer, Robert W. *Stengel: His Life and Times.* New York: Simon and Schuster, 1984.

Encyclopedia of World Biography Supplement, Vol. 19. Detroit: Gale Group, 1999.

Koppett, Leonard. *The Man in the Dugout: Baseball's Top Managers and How They Got That Way.* Philadelphia: Temple University Press, 2000.

Periodicals

"Dustbin." *Sporting News* (November 6, 2000): 8.

Frayne, Trent. "'The Lovable Old Perfesser.'" *Maclean's* (May 11, 1992): 50.

Herzog, Bob. "World Series 2001: Managing the Dynasty; The Stengel Era." *Newsday* (October 25, 2001): H11.

Ingemar Stenmark
1956-

Swedish skier

Ingemar Stenmark won a record 86 World Cup races during his 15-year career. He dominated the slalom and giant slalom courses, winning titles in both events for seven consecutive years, from 1975 to 1981. A three-time winner of the overall World Cup, Stenmark also has two Olympic and three World Championship gold medals. Known as the King of Slalom because of his unmatched technical skiing that took him through the gates with very little upper body movement, he was also known as the Silent Swede because of his famously stoic and taciturn personality.

Arctic Existence

Ingemar Stenmark was born on March 18, 1956, in Josesjo, Sweden, in the Swedish Lapland, near the Norwegian border. He was raised in the nearby small town of Tarnaby, just 60 miles south of the Arctic Circle. During the summer, the sun hardly set, and in the winter, hardly

Ingemar Stenmark

rose. Stenmark spent the first six years of his life with his grandparents on their farm outside of Tarnaby before moving into town. It was a lonely, isolated existence with few children. His father, Erik Stenmark, an avid skier who had placed as high as fifth in a national slalom event, was a road construction worker and bulldozer operator who also owned three ski lifts. Encouraged and trained by his father, Stenmark began to ski at the age of five, using simple toe-strap bindings. Painfully shy and reserved, he began to ski because it was something he could do alone. Also, skiing was one of the few available activities in the community with a population of just 700.

In a region known to produce top-notched cross country skiers, Stenmark was drawn to the nearby 600-foot hill called Laxtjallet, meaning Salmon Mountain, that provided 2,000-foot slope, making it good only for slalom skiing. Because the course was lighted, Stenmark could ski after school during the cold winter months, when daylight dwindled quickly. Stenmark won his first race when he was seven and the following year won his first national competition in the slalom. In 1965 he qualified for an annual international race held in Italy, where he placed fourteen in his first attempt at the giant slalom. Stoic in personality, Stenmark was a perfectionist who scorned defeat. As a child he would sob in anger if he lost a race. Stenmark began training with the Swiss junior national team when he was thirteen years old.

Stenmark was an indifferent student, who didn't particularly enjoy school. After completing the required nine years of basic schooling, Stenmark decided to forego secondary school, partly because the nearest gymnasium, or school, was 150 miles away and partly because he wanted to concentrate on his skiing. "School was a drag," he later told *Newsweek*. "I couldn't develop as a skier and be a good student at the same time. I decided to do one thing well." Stenmark was also acutely aware that the Swiss national team, which had been a consistent and abysmal failure, had disbanded to use its limited resources to help support a group of fourteen- to sixteen-year-old trainees, including Stenmark.

During his first year with the junior national team, Stenmark trained for the giant slalom on the steeper, more challenging courses in Italy. His best finishes during the 1972-73 Swedish junior national season were fourth and fifth place. During the 1973-74 season Stenmark made remarkable progress. He began to understand that he could win with more consistency if he did not take unnecessary daredevil risks that often resulted in a fall. Although he did not win any junior World Cup races, he place second twice in the slalom and earned a third and fourth place in the giant slalom. The crowning moment came during the European junior championships, where he won gold in the giant slalom.

King of Slalom

In 1974 Stenmark, at the age of seventeen, joined the European racing circuit. In his first World Cup event in March of 1974, Stenmark placed second in the slalom. On December 17, 1974 he earned his first World Cup victory on the slalom course at Madonna di Campiglio, Italy. He was soon challenging Italy's Gustavo Thoeni for the World Cup title but was edged out by Thoeni, 250 points to 245 points. The following season Stenmark surpassed Thoeni to win his first overall World Cup in 1976, thus beginning his decade-long reign of dominance in the slalom and giant slalom. He was heralded as a hero in

Related Biography: Skier Gustavo Thoeni

Gustavo Thoeni was a member of the Italian national ski team from 1968 to 1980. Like Stenmark, Thoeni won the overall World Cup three consecutive years, from 1971 to 1973. Finishing second in 1974, he edged by the younger Stenmark to take his fourth World Cup title in 1975. He ranked first or second in the slalom and giant slalom every year from 1970 to 1974, and remained one of Stenmark's top competitors up to 1977.

Thoeni won three Olympic medals, including a gold in the giant slalom in 1972 and silver medals in the slalom both in 1972 and 1976. He swept the 1974 World Championships, taking gold in both the slalom and giant slalom. After retiring from competition in 1980, he turned to coaching. From 1989 to 1996 he worked with Alberto Tomba. Currently he is the head coach of the Italian national men's team.

Awards and Accomplishments

1976	Wins Olympic bronze medal in the giant slalom
1976-78	Three time winner of overall World Cup
1978	Wins gold medals in both the slalom and giant slalom at the World Championships
1980	Wins Olympic gold medals in both slalom and giant slalom
1982	Wins gold medal in the slalom and silver medal in the giant slalom at World Championships

Stenmark won the individual event titles in slalom and giant slalom seven consecutive years, from 1975 to 1981. He won the slalom again in 1983 and the giant slalom again in 1984.

Sweden, and Sweden's King Carl XVI Gustaf received Stenmark in a private audience and awarded him with a special gold medal, the highest honor bestowed on a Swedish citizen. Stenmark's first appearance in the Olympics in 1976, however, proved rather disappointing. Going in as the favorite for the gold in at least one, if not both, slalom events, he fell in the slalom and only managed a bronze medal in the giant slalom.

In 1977 and 1978, Stenmark won two more World Cup titles. He also won gold medals in both the slalom and giant slalom at the 1978 World Championships in Garmisch. During the 1978-79 season he won a total of 13 slalom and giant slalom races, breaking the previous record of 12 set by renowned skier **Jean-Claude Killy**. In fact, Stenmark outscored the remainder of the field so badly during the 1978-79 season that he had the World Cup title locked up in January, two months before the season's end. In an effort to balance the playing field, the International Skiing Association altered its point system so that the overall World Cup ranking was based on points not only from the slalom and giant slalom, but also the downhill, an event in which Stenmark had never competed. As a result, even though he won both the slalom and giant slalom in 1979, he placed fifth in the overall World Cup standings due to his lack of points from downhill races.

Following the 1978-79 season, after fulfilling his mandatory three-month obligation to the Swedish army, Stenmark decided to prepare for the downhill so that he could once again be competitive for the World Cup title. During a training run on the Italian Alps in September 1979 he hit a compression at a high rate of speed, was buffeted by the wind, and flew wildly out of control. Rushed to a hospital via helicopter, Stenmark was diagnosed with a severe concussion and remained in the hospital three weeks. After he recuperated, he competed in a downhill race in January 1980, in which he finished thirty-four among thirty-nine finishers. Following that event, he decided to put away his downhill skis and focus on the slalom and giant slalom. At the 1980 Olympic Games in Lake Placid, New York, Stenmark took gold medals in both the slalom and giant slalom. During the 1979-80

World Cup competition, he won ten races and once again took both the slalom and giant slalom titles, but finished second in overall World Cup points.

Twilight of His Career

During the 1980s the reign of the King of Slalom drew slowly to a close. In 1981 Stenmark once again took the slalom and the giant slalom titles. Winning ten races, he lost out on the World Cup by six points to **Phil Mahre**. The following year Stenmark won gold in the slalom at the World Championship in Schladming and took silver in the giant slalom. Although he failed to retain both the slalom and giant slalom World Cup event titles, he still finished second in overall World Cup points. In 1983 he won his last slalom title and in 1984 he won his last giant slalom title. Both years he once again finished second in the World Cup standings. Stenmark's numerous endorsement contracts gave him professional status and made him ineligible for 1984 Olympic Games.

In 1984, for the first time since he was a small child, Stenmark's focus shifted from skiing. In April 1984 his daughter Nathalie was born, and in September 1984 Stenmark married his longtime live-in girlfriend Ann Ufhagen. Although he had lost some of his snap and speed in his dynamically precise skiing, Stenmark, who had achieved just about all there was to achieve, continued to ski because he still enjoyed it, but winning became a lesser priority. After rearranging his endorsement contracts, Stenmark was allowed to participate in the 1988 Olympics in Calgary, Alberta, Canada, but his best finish was fifth in the slalom.

On March 12, 1989, Stenmark retired from skiing with a record 86 World Cup victories, consisting of 46 giant slaloms and 40 slaloms. That the second-best win record—belonging to Pirmin Zurbriggen—is 31 World Cup wins is a testament to the Silent Swede's total domination. Stenmark, who divorced in 1988 and remains unmarried, stays out of the public eye. He splits his time between Monte Carlo and Sweden and works for a Japanese sports clothing company. Despite detesting his celebrity status and all but shunning media attention throughout his career, Stenmark became an international star and a nation hero. He is arguably the best skier of all time.

FURTHER INFORMATION

Periodicals

Chamberlain, Tony. "Stenmark Nears End of the Line." *The Boston Globe,* (February 11, 1989): 35.

"Giant in the Slalom." *Time,* (February 11, 1980): 84.

Johnson, William Oscar. "Silence Was Golden." *Sports Illustrated,* (March 3, 1980): 23-25.

Montgomery, Paul L. "Stenmark, at 31, is Proving He Still Can Tackle Slalom." *New York Times,* (January 10, 1988): S10.

Nasstrom, Stephan. "Ingemar Stenmark Dismisses Thought of Retiring." *Associated Press,* (November 21, 1987).

Pucin, Diane. "Winter Olympics: Where Are They Now? Stenmark Found Fame, Not Solitude." *Los Angeles Times,* (February 10, 2002): U5.

Verschoth, Anita. "Just Like a Three-Ring Circus." *Sports Illustrated,* (February 3, 1986): 44-48.

Other

"Ingemar Stenmark." Alpine World Cup Ski Database. http://www.ski-db.com/db/profiles/stnin.asp (January 22, 2003).

"Ingemar Stenmark." The Lincoln Library of Sports Champions, September 1, 2001. http://www.elibrary. com (January 22, 2003).

Lang, Patrick, and Serge Lang. "The History of the World Cup." Alpine Ski World Cup. http://www. skiworldcup.org (January 22, 2003).

Sketch by Kari Bethel

Jackie Stewart
1939-

Scottish race car driver

The name Jackie Stewart is synonymous in America with auto racing. The series he became a legend of, Formula One (F1), however, is virtually unknown in the States. Arguably the most watched sport internationally, F1 is the most advanced auto racing series in the world. From 1964-73, The "Wee Scot" established a race-win record in his trademark tartan helmet that remained unbroken in F1 for fourteen years. His driving style has been characterized as smooth, precise, persistent, consistent, and remarkably quick. Off the track, he is known to be good natured and humorous. Beyond his illustrious career, Stewart's greatest contribution to motorsports may be his relentless campaign for track and driver safety after surviving a crash in 1966. He became a house-

Jackie Stewart

hold name in the 1970s and 1980s as a commentator for ABC's Wide World of Sports, and maintained a partnership for Ford Motor Company for three decades. The F1 squad he launched with his son became Jaguar Racing.

Put Down Gun To Get Behind Wheel

Stewart was born June 11, 1939 in Dumbartonshire, Scotland. He began competitive shooting at age fourteen, and discovered something he was very good at. After frustrating experiences in school, he quit at age fifteen to work at Dumbuck's, his family's garage, and apprentice as a mechanic. It was not until later that he was diagnosed with dyslexia, which explained his difficulties with learning. Stewart's brother Jimmy was an accomplished semi-professional driver for the Scottish Ecurie Ecosse team by the time Stewart first drove an old race car on the snowy streets of Dumbartonshire. When Jimmy crashed soon after, the younger Stewart was warned away from motorsports, and encouraged to pursue his marksmanship talents.

The young Scot excelled in shooting, winning British, Scottish, Irish, Welsh, and English trap shooting championships between 1959-62. He began to find his way back to racecar driving against his parents' wishes after failing to make the 1960 British Olympic shooting team. He was twenty-three years old—a late bloomer in auto racing—when he drove his first race at the Scottish airfield circuit Charterhall in 1962. He also married his wife Helen that year. By 1963 Stewart was driving for

Related Biography: Driver Jim Clark

Fellow Scot Jim Clark was the greatest racing driver on the track when Jackie Stewart entered F1. Competition between the legend and the rookie promised to develop into a rich rivalry, but Clark died before Stewart had fully hit his stride. Born March 4, 1936 in Kilmany, Scotland, Clark, like Stewart, went into racing against his parents' wishes. He proved his mettle at first in friends' cars, but began to attract attention in the Jaguar D Type he drove for the Border Reivers team. After plans for an Aston Martin Grand Prix team collapsed, he signed with Lotus to drive in the Formula Two and Formula Junior series. His relationship with the manufacturer carried him into F1 with the team, which was running the fastest cars, though not always the most mechanically reliable. He first raced F1 in 1960, and was a leading contender until his death. He won the World Championship in 1963, and was challenged by newcomer Stewart for the 1965 title, which he also took home. Reserved and gentlemanly, Clark preferred his family and farm in Scotland to the cosmopolitan life of an F1 driver. He was just beginning to come into his own in the spotlight when he died. Still considered by many the greatest racing driver in history, Clark was killed April 7, 1968 in a crash at Hockenheim.

his brother's old team, Ecurie Ecosse, and was noticed by race team manager Ken Tyrell. Stewart out drove Bruce McLaren, already an experienced F1 driver, in a test for Tyrell. McLaren would later head the formidable McLaren racing team. Tyrell's offer to let Stewart drive for him in the British Formula Three series in 1964, and Stewart's subsequent domination of the series, pushed the young driver into the spotlight as an F1 hopeful.

Stewart made a calculated decision about his 1965 start in F1 racing. He turned down an offer from the legendary Team Lotus to drive alongside fellow Scot Jim Clark in lieu of a more competitive spot alongside Graham Hill on the BRM team. Clark's firm position as Lotus' number-one driver would have placed Stewart chronically in his shadow. At BRM, the hungry young driver would be able to shine. At the time of his death in 1968, Clark was the winningest F1 driver in history, with twenty-five career wins. Though he drove for BRM in 1965, Stewart made his F1 debut in a Lotus car. He guest drove the Lotus, qualifying in pole position in the non-title Rand Grand Prix in South Africa in December 1964.

Survived Near-Fatal Crash A Champion

Stewart placed in the top six spots, earning championship points in his first six Grand Prix races. He qualified in pole position for a non- championship race at Goodwood, and beat World Champion John Surtees into second place in the International Silverstone Trophy race. He beat teammate Graham Hill to the finish line at the 1965 Italian Grand Prix at Monza. He finished the season third overall for the World Championship, an amazing finish for a rookie driver. The 1966 season started promisingly with a win for Stewart at Monaco, but technical problems kept him out of the competition for the remainder of the season, and he finished sixth in the World Championship. He almost won the Indianapolis 500 that year, his first, but mechanical failure took him out of the race with only eight laps to go.

When he entered F1, the sport was "horrendously dangerous," he is quoted as saying in *Forbes*. "There were no seat belts worn, the medical care was pathetic, and there was no firefighting equipment to speak of." Stewart witnessed the deaths of many friends and rivals during his racing career, Jim Clark, Jochen Rindt, and Francois Cevert among them. Like all F1 drivers of the time, Stewart was driving without a seatbelt when he crashed during the Belgian Grand Prix at Spa-Francorchamps in 1966. He ran off the track while driving 165 mph in heavy rain, and proceeded to crash into a telephone pole and a shed before driving into a farmer's outbuilding. A ruptured fuel tank filled the cockpit with fuel, and could have ignited at the tiniest spark with Stewart trapped inside. He was extracted from what could easily have been a fatal crash, having suffered broken ribs and shoulder and rib injuries.

Stewart emerged from the experience a lifelong champion of safety reform who instituted countless changes in auto racing safety regulations. He was able to return to the driver's seat after a few weeks, and never again drove without a seatbelt, full-faced helmet, and fireproof racing suit. BRM head Louis Stanley backed Stewart's safety campaign to improve track and car standards and medical facilities. Track improvements in the name of safety that were unpopular with circuit owners have now be-

Jackie Stewart, sitting in car

come the norm. "If I have any legacy to leave the sport I hope it will be seen to be in an area of safety," Stewart is quoted as saying on the Grand Prix Hall of Fame Web site, "because when I arrived in Grand Prix racing, so-called precautions and safety measures were diabolical."

Went Out On Top

After a lackluster 1967 season with BRM, Stewart had outgrown the fading team, and signed on to drive once again for Ken Tyrell, who was heading up a new F1 team. The German Grand Prix at Nurburgring may be Stewart's greatest race, according to Formula One Art & Genius on-line. He drove the fourteen-mile, 187-corner track in torrential rain and with a broken wrist, and beat Graham Hill to the finish line. "I can't remember doing one more balls-out lap of the 'Ring than I needed to," he is quoted as saying online at Formula One Art & Genius. "It gave you amazing satisfaction, but anyone who says he loved it is either a liar or wasn't going fast enough." Stewart lost the World Championship to Hill that year, coming in second, but clinched his first World Championship title in Tyrell's Matra-Ford in 1969. He qualified at the front of the pack often during the 1970 season, but did not regain the World Championship until 1971. Stomach ulcers kept him off the track for many races of the 1972 season, but returned in 1973 to drive another World Championship season. Unknown to his fans, Stewart had decided early in the season that the year would be his last.

Just thirty-four years old, Stewart announced his retirement in 1973, after winning his third Grand Prix title. "The key in life," Stewart told *Sports Illustrated* in 2002, "is deciding when to go into something and when to get out of it." He broke Jim Clark's record with twenty-seven career Grands Prix out of 99 entered, a record that remained until **Alain Prost** broke it in 1987. He was named both *Sports Illustrated*'s Sportsman of the Year, and Wide World of Sport's Athlete of the Year, an honor he shared that year with football player **O.J. Simpson**. Stewart, who has admitted that he "got big-headed" during this time, according to ABC Sports online, is also quick to point out, humorously, that the race horse **Secretariat** was chosen third for the ABC honor. Secretariat apparently was not in contention for the World, British, and Scottish Sportsman of the Year awards, which Stewart also won in 1973. Stewart had managed to become a legendary racing driver while remaining alive and in one piece, which is in itself an accomplishment.

Retirement Was A Relative Term

He had managed to beat the odds in auto racing and had come out on top, but Stewart also was "just plain bored, burned out, restless," Duncan Christy wrote in *Forbes*. "Where was I going?" he recalled asking himself. "What else was there to do? It was the same old ground. I could have stayed on as a racing car driver. I mean, Mario [Andretti] is the same age as I am. **A.J. Foyt**

```
Awards and Accomplishments

1965        Wins Italian Grand Prix at Monza
1965        Third place, F1 World Championship
1966        Seventh place, F1 World Championship
1967        Ninth place, F1 World Championship
1968        Second place, F1 World Championship
1969, 1971, F1 World Championship
   1973
1970        Sixth place, F1 World Championship
1972        Second place, F1 World Championship
1973        World record for 27 career wins
1973        Named World Wide of Sports Athlete of the Year and
            Personality of the Year; named World, British, and Scottish
            Sportsman of the Year; and Sports Illustrated's Sportsman of
            the Year
2001        Knighted by Queen of England
2001        Named Scotsman and Woman of the Year with wife Helen
```

Where Is He Now?

Stewart founded a shooting school at Scotland's prestigious Gleneagle Hotel in the early 1980s. Nearly thirty years after joining forces with Ford, he signed on in February 2002 for another three years in research and development with the American auto company. He has served since 1995 as president of the Scottish Dyslexia Trust. He has also been on the boards of and a spokesman for Moet & Chandon champagne and Rolex watches. Stewart's wife Helen was diagnosed with breast cancer in 2001 just eighteen months after their son Paul was told he had colon cancer, which went into remission. "For years she stood waiting to see if I would survive a race; now it's me waiting," Stewart is quoted as saying by *Sports Illustrated* in 2002. "The past two years are probably the toughest thing I've had to deal with in my life." Stewart's younger son Mark, who runs a television production company, is making a four-part documentary of his father's life called *The Flying Scot.*

is a lot older. But I would never have developed; I would never have expanded as an individual."

Retirement meant nothing to Stewart; it kept him out of the cockpit but, career-wise, he remained very much in the driver's seat. He has worked as an advisor and ambassador for several international companies, including Ford and Goodyear Tire. "I knew it would be a good way to make money without the capital investment and risk necessary when you go into business yourself." He signed a five-year contract as an engineering consultant for Ford Motor Company, working with Ford engineers to improve handling. "American cars used to be like pregnant elephants," he told *U.S. News & World Report,* "Now, at least, Fords have become lean and clean in their response."

Stewart also joined ABC's *Wide World of Sports* as a commentator, which made him a household name in the 1970s and 1980s. "*Wide World of Sports* had a considerable impact on my life in general," Stewart is quoted as saying at ABC Sports online. "As a race driver it projected me in a way in the United States of America. I would otherwise never have been able to be put in the minds of sports fans in America. It helped my commercial life, my business life, and it helped my racing life. It was a good thing for me to have done." He was voted Wide World of Sports' Personality of the Year in 1973, which he was particularly honored by. "There's not country in the world that could give your sports people … more focus or more illumination," Stewart told ABC Sports online. In "such a galaxy" of American sports personalities, it was a "big thing" to be non-American and win the award. Stewart also has admitted that his title, "winningest driver in the history of Grand Prix," was like currency in his many lucrative business deals.

Stewart moved his family to Switzerland to avoid strict British tax laws early in his racing career, and he has long been known for his globetrotting lifestyle. Stewart travels upwards of 400,000 miles a year on the Concorde or in his private jet. Though his friend Prince

Charles did not knight him until 2001, Sir Stewart has always kept company with royalty and celebrities, who adore him. He has rubbed elbows with Sean Connery, Prince Edward, Steven Spielberg, and Jordan's King Hussein, to name a few. Beatle George Harrison taught his sons to play guitar. Helen Stewart is godmother to Princess Anne's daughter Zara.

All in all, Stewart's long-held record earns him status in motor-racing history, but his impact on the sport is much greater than statistics can show. Every driver on the track has Stewart to thank for the safety mandates he championed that have saved many lives. Because of his American media exposure, he is surely the most-known F1 driver in the States. But his reputation as a class-act sportsman and businessman are the result of a lifetime of integrity and good humor both on and off the track.

FURTHER INFORMATION

Books

Henry, Alan. *Grand Prix Champions: From Jackie Stewart to Michael Schumacher.* Osceola, WI: Motorbooks International, 1995.

Periodicals

Bechtel, Mark. "Catching up with … Jackie Stewart, Auto racer September 6, 1971." *Sports Illustrated* (February 25, 2002): 19.

Bronson, Gail. "As stars hawk their hidden talents—some have more than a famous face and name to sell." *U.S. News & World Report* (February 17, 1986): 44.

Christy, Duncan. "Jackie Stewart aims to please." *Forbes* (May 10, 1993): 118.

"The art of pit-stop management." *Economist* (August 10, 1996): 52.

Other

"Grand Prix drivers: Jackie Stewart." GrandPrix.com. http://www.grandprix.com (October 30, 2002).

"Grand Prix drivers: Jim Clark." GrandPrix.com. http://www.grandprix.com (October 30, 2002).

"Jackie Stewart." Formula One Art & Genius. http://f1-grandprix.com (October 30, 2002).

"Jackie Stewart." Formula One Database. http://f1db.com (October 30, 2002).

"Jackie Stewart." Grand Prix Hall of Fame. http://www.ddavid.com/formula1 (October 30, 2002).

"Jimmy Clark." Grand Prix Hall of Fame. http://www.ddavid.com/formula1 (October 30, 2002).

"Stewart: Monaco and Indy were special." ABC Sports. http://espn.go.com/abcsports (October 30, 2002).

Sketch by Brenna Sanchez

Kordell Stewart

Kordell Stewart
1972-

American football player

Star quarterback of the Pittsburgh Steelers, Kordell Stewart led his team to the Super Bowl his very first season in the National Football League (NFL). After seven seasons as a quarterback with the Steelers, Stewart boasted a pass-completion rate of 55.7 percent for a total of 12,173 yards and sixty-four touchdowns. Despite his obvious prowess as a quarterback, Stewart has also seen service as a wide receiver, running back, and punter, making him one of pro football's most versatile players and earning him the nickname "Slash" from head coach Bill Cowher. Of Stewart's importance to the Steelers, Cowher told *Sports Illustrated*: "No one can exemplify this team's unselfish attitude more than Kordell Stewart. I'm sure he'll never forget some of the things he's had to go through, and I wouldn't wish them upon anyone, but he's buried the hatchet and handled himself like the consummate pro."

Born in New Orleans

Stewart was born in New Orleans on October 16, 1972. The son of Robert (a barber, house painter, and carpenter) and Florence Stewart, he was raised in Marrero, a suburb of New Orleans. It was not an easy childhood for Stewart. As he told Reuters, "my mom passed away when I was eleven, and my dad's been there for me ever since. It's been a rough one for me, but when things like that happen to you, you can either be a person who goes astray or understand that things happen for a reason, and that's the approach that I have taken." As a boy, Stewart managed to stay out of trouble by spending his free time helping his father in the barber shop or various other endeavors

and handling the cooking and laundry chores on the home front.

Because of his responsibilities at home, Stewart didn't really get involved in football until he joined the varsity team at the beginning of his junior year at John Ehret High School in Marrero. Despite his late start, he quickly demonstrated his talents on the gridiron, passing for a total of 1,645 yards and nineteen touchdowns his first season. The following year, Stewart, now a senior, ran an option-attack, throwing for 942 yards and seventeen touchdowns and carrying the ball for a total of 923 yards and twenty-three touchdowns. Stewart's versatile performance powered Ehret to a record of 8-3 and the district championship. Stewart was named Louisiana's Most Valuable Player and New Orleans Player of the Year, making him one of the most sought-after high school option-quarterback prospects in the country.

Accepts Scholarship to Colorado

Heavily recruited by a number of top colleges, Stewart eventually accepted a football scholarship to the University of Colorado. Although he saw limited action on the football field his freshman year, he became Colorado's starting quarterback during his sophomore year. He quickly proved his worth by passing for a new school record of 2,109 yards and tying Colorado's record with twelve touchdown passes. As a junior, he

Career Statistics

Yr	Team	GP	ATT	COM	YDS	COM%	Y/A	TD	INT
1995	PIT	10	7	5	60	71.4	8.6	1	0
1996	PIT	16	30	11	100	36.7	3.3	0	2
1997	PIT	16	440	236	3020	53.6	6.9	21	17
1998	PIT	16	458	252	2560	55.0	5.6	11	18
1999	PIT	16	275	160	1464	58.2	5.3	6	10
2000	PIT	15	289	151	1860	52.2	6.4	11	8
2001	PIT	16	442	266	3109	60.2	7.0	14	11
TOTAL		105	1941	1081	12173	55.7	6.3	4	66

PIT: Pittsburgh Steelers.

Chronology

1972	Born October 16 in New Orleans
1984	Loses mother to liver cancer
1990	Graduates from John Ehret High School in Marrero, Louisiana
1990-94	Attends University of Colorado
1994	Picked by Pittsburgh Steelers in second round of NFL draft

broke his own passing record by throwing for 2,299 yards and starting every game of the season despite a fractured bone in his left hand.

Stewart credits Colorado coach Rich Neuheisel with helping him to improve his game as a quarterback. The summer before his senior season, Stewart worked closely with Neuheisel, as the coach had done with **Troy Aikman** when Neuheisel coached at UCLA. Stewart later told *Sports Illustrated*: "If I'd had [Neuheisel as a coach] since my freshman year, I would have gone in the first round [of the NFL draft]. He taught me about coverages and gave me confidence." Stewart's work with the coach paid off, for Colorado enjoyed one of its best seasons ever, finishing with a 11-1 record and going on to beat Notre Dame, 41-24, in the Fiesta Bowl. After the Fiesta Bowl victory, Stewart, who passed for 226 yards and rushed for another 143, was named the game's MVP. For his four years at Colorado, Stewart compiled a brilliant record of 6,481 yards passing for thirty-three touchdowns and 1,289 yards running for another fifteen touchdowns.

Declares for 1995 NFL Draft

Stewart declared for the 1995 NFL draft as a quarterback despite suggestions from pro scouts that he would probably enhance his chances for an early pick if he signaled a willingness to play other positions. Stewart refused to do so and was selected by the Steelers in the second round of the draft. Although he was hopeful of getting a shot as starting quarterback, Stewart was listed as fourth-string quarterback after the end of the exhibi-

tion season. After sitting out the first few games of the 1995 season, Stewart was put to work by coach Cowher at three different positions on offense—quarterback, running back, and wide receiver. Cowher's decision to utilize Stewart's versatility paid dividends for the Steelers, who finished the 1995 season with a record of 11-5 and faced off against the Dallas Cowboys in Super Bowl XXX. Despite an impressive performance by Stewart, the Steelers fell to the Cowboys, 27-17.

During his second season with the Steelers, Stewart still was used sparingly at quarterback, passing for only 100 yards. He rushed for 171 yards and five touchdowns and was selected as an alternate for the Pro Bowl. Before the 1997 season began, coach Cowher made it clear that Stewart would be starting as quarterback. Stewart proved himself equal to the task, passing for a total of 3,020 yards and 17 touchdowns to lead the Steelers to the AFC Central Division title. Pittsburgh went on to lose narrowly, 24-21, to the Denver Broncos in the AFC Championship game.

Steelers Fare Poorly in 1998, 1999

Despite creditable performances from Stewart in both 1998 and 1999, the Steelers ended those seasons with losing records of 7-9 and 6-10, respectively. Pittsburgh bounced back in 2000 with a season's record of 9-7. In 2001 the Steelers had its best season in several years, ending with a record of 13-3 and making it to the AFC Championship Game, which they lost, 24-17, to the New England Patriots.

With two weeks left in the 2002 regular season, the Steelers held first place in the AFC North Division, with a record of 8-5-1, but Stewart spent much of his time on the bench. After a disappointing start to the season, coach Cowher in early October benched Stewart as quarterback in favor of Tommy Maddox, former star of the Arena League and the XFL. Although the move cast his future with the Steelers into doubt, Stewart seemed confident he'd return to the game as a starting quarterback, if not in Pittsburgh than elsewhere in the NFL. "I can't control what other people do," Stewart told the As-

Awards and Accomplishments	
1990	Named Louisiana's Most Valuable Player in High School Football
1990	New Orleans Player of the Year
1990	Named to Louisiana All-State Football Team
1994	Named to All-American Second Team by Associated Press
1995	Named Most Valuable Rookie by Pittsburgh Steelers teammates
1995	Led Steelers to Super Bowl
1995	Joe Greene Great Performance Award
1996	Voted an alternate to Pro Bowl
1997	Selected as an alternate to Pro Bowl
1998	Led Steelers to AFC Championship Game
2001	Picked to play in the Pro Bowl

sociated Press. "I've proven myself time and time again, so to express myself and explain myself again, what would that benefit? ... If this is the direction they want to go, fine, so be it, but everybody else knows, and this organization knows, what I can do."

CONTACT INFORMATION

Address: Kordell Stewart, c/o Pittsburgh Steelers, 100 Art Rooney Ave., Pittsburgh, PA 15212-5721. Phone: (412) 697-7181.

FURTHER INFORMATION

Books

"Kordell Stewart." *Contemporary Black Biography,* Volume 21. Detroit: Gale Group, 1999.

"Kordell Stewart." *Sports Stars,* Series 1-4. U•X•L, 1994-1998.

Periodicals

Pompei, Dan. "Happily Ever After Returns to Slash's Tale." *Sporting News* (December 10, 2001): 24.

Silver, Michael. "In Control: Kordell Stewart Demanded His Coach's Support and Excelled When He Got It, But Can He Lead the Steelers to a Title?" *Sports Illustrated* (January 14, 2002): 40.

Other

"Bill Cowher." Steelref.com. http://www.steelref.com/cowher.html (December 19, 2002).

"Kordell Stewart: Bio." NFL. com. http://www.nfl.com/players/playerpage/1054/bios (December 17, 2002).

"Kordell Stewart: Career Highlights." Steelers.com. http://www.pittsburghsteelers.com/team/playerbio.cfm?player_id=4923 (December 17, 2002).

"Kordell Stewart, Career Stats." NFL. com. http://www.nfl.com/players/playerpage/1054 (December 17, 2002).

"Kordell Stewart, Quarterback."Pro-Football-Reference. com. http://www.football-reference.com/players/StewKo00.htm (December 17, 2002).

Sketch by Don Amerman

Lyn St. James
1947-

American race car driver

At age 45, when many athletes are retired or over the hill, Lyn St. James was blazing a trail. St. James, one of the few women in professional automobile racing, was a rookie of the year at that age, finishing 11th at the 1992 Indianapolis 500 among 33 competitors. She became the second woman to race at Indy and competed in that event a total of seven times.

St. James became the first woman to win a solo North American professional road race at Watkins Glen, New York, in 1985. In 1996 she acquired her own team, Lyn St. James racing. When she switched from road racers to Indy cars in 1988, she became the first woman to compete full-time on the Indy circuit.

St. James, whose career thrived despite occasional problems finding a sponsor and frequent crashes in races, retired in 2001 to write a book, *Ride of Your Life.* Auto racing, she says, can cross gender lines. She has worked as a columnist, motivational speaker and television commentator.

"Be a Nice Lady"

Maxine Cornwall had not intended to raise her daughter, Evelyn, in Willoughby, Ohio, for the gritty, male-oriented world of car racing. But, ironically, she instilled a love of cars in her daughter. Cornwall, a polio victim, found an automobile empowering. Mother and daughter would take long weekend drives.

Evelyn Cornwall, who later changed her name to Lyn St. James to make it more marketable, credited sports for helping make her more outgoing as an adolescent. She played basketball, volleyball, tennis, and field hockey, and attended the Andrews School for Girls, near Cleveland. She took an interest in drag racing through male friends. One night in 1964, while attending races with friends in Louisville, Kentucky, she made an off-hand remark to someone who had lost a heat and was told, "If you think you can do better, go ahead." She took up the offer and won the race. Attending the Indianapolis 500 in 1969 and getting star A. J. Foyt's autograph furthered her zeal.

Lyn St. James

Begins Racing Career

St. James began competing in local Sports Car Club of America events in 1973. She experienced a bad beginning in racing, having spun into a pond at Palm Beach International Raceway with a Ford Pinto that was her street car, and escaped from her car about eight seconds before it sank. She rebounded to win Florida regional championships in 1976 and 1977. In her first pro season, 1979, she finished eighth, and came in second in the Kellygirl Challenge series.

Having read about Ford Motor Company's attempts to market its products to women, St. James lobbied hard for the motor company to sponsor her career. Ford signed her in 1981 and, although she sometimes raced poorly, she traveled extensively to speak on the company's behalf. "For a good while she was far more successful at that than she was at driving," *Sports Illustrated* wrote in 1993. "Five years passed before she won her first race, at Elkhart Lake, Wis. (in 1985)" Then came the breakthrough victory at Watkins Glen that same year.

Wakeup Call, Then Indy

St. James's career received a jolt in 1991 when Ford sharply curtailed its road racing involvement and dropped her as a driver. "St. James had to shop around for rides," *Sports Illustrated* said. After attending self-awareness seminars, she declared she would drive in the Indianapolis 500. **Janet Guthrie**, the only other woman to race at

Indy to this point, first entered in 1977. Engine trouble forced her out that year, but Guthrie returned in 1978 to finish ninth. She pitched sponsors hard, and got such corporations as J. C. Penney, Agency Rent-a-Car, Goodyear, and Danskin, to sponsor her on the Indy car tour.

St. James finished ninth in her first Indy, her best finish among her seven there. She had her share of misfortunes at the Brickyard, including a drive-train problem and some crashes. One mishap, in 2000, involved 19-year-old Sarah Fisher in the first-ever two-woman field at the Brickyard. Apparent frostiness between the two women fueled headlines about the crash. "Despite teaming up to make Indy history, it was clear the two women were not close," the Associated Press wrote. "They had not talked since Fisher attended St. James' driving school four years ago. Fisher said she didn't learn much at the school and boasted that she would bring a new attitude to female drivers at the Brickyard, hinting that St. James and Janet Guthrie were merely satisfied to qualify and didn't race to win."

St. James also won a reputation as a spokesperson for women in sports and other male-dominated professions. She wrote auto-related columns for the *Detroit Free Press,* was president of the Women's Sports Foundation in the early 1990s and a guest at the White House five times. She wrote her first book, *Lyn St. James's Car Owner's Manual,* in 1984. She credits retailer J.C. Penney for having saved her program in 1993. J.C. Penney chief executive officer W.R. Howell found out about the driver through Carrie Rozelle, the wife of former National Football League Commissioner Alvin "Pete" Rozelle. When St. James, at Howell's invitation, made a marketing presentation at company headquarters in Dallas, St. James discovered three female Penney executives. In 1998 the women's television network Lifetime became one of her sponsors.

St. James found appreciation as an auto racing pioneer when she toured in 2002 to promote her latest book. "My entire career, it has always been, 'Who's going to work with the girl driver?'" St. James said an in

Awards and Accomplishments

1976-77	Wins Florida Regional championships
1979	Top woman driver, International Motor Sports Association Kelly American Challenge Series
1984	Rookie of the Year, IMSA Camel GT series
1985	First woman to average more than 200 miles per hour on an oval track, at Talladega, Alabama
1985	First woman to win a North American professional road race driving solo at Watkins Glen, New York
1987	Part of winning team in GTO Class at Daytona 24 Hours marathon
1988	Only driver to score championship points in every SCCA Trans Am event
1992	Indianapolis 500 Rookie of the Year
1995	Sets closed-course speed record for women for fifth time in Indy 500 qualifying

Where Is She Now?

St. James, who lives in Daytona Beach, Florida, wrote her second book, *Ride of your Life*, in 2001, upon retiring from Indy car racing. She is a frequent public speaker.

St. James offers a course for up-and-coming drivers that addresses business strategies and handling the media as much as it does driving skills. She says keeping its status non-profit makes it affordable for the most needy. She told the Elmira *Star-Gazette* that while she has retired from Indy, she has not retired from racing. "When drivers get old, they drive old cars," she said jokingly. She said she intends to drive in some endurance races in 2003. "We'll see what develops," she said.

interview with *Sports Illustrated* in 1993. "Many male drivers have told me, 'I couldn't do what you do.'"

St. James retired from the Indy circuit in 2001 at age 54, before the start of practice for the Indy 500. She took two ceremonial laps, then pulled into the pits. St. James has lectured and worked as a commentator for ESPN, ABC and Showtime, and has appeared as a guest on The David Letterman Show and Good Morning America. She also serves on the boards of many organizations.

SELECTED WRITINGS BY ST. JAMES:

Lyn St. James's Car Owner's Manual for Women. New York: Penguin, 1984.
Ride of Your Life: A Race Car Driver's Journey. New York: Hyperion, 2002.

FURTHER INFORMATION

Books

Olney, Ross R. *Lyn St. James: Driven to be First.* Minneapolis: Lerner, 1997.
Stewart, Mark. *Lyn St. James.* New York: Children's Press, 1996.

Periodicals

Sports Illustrated (May 3, 1993).

Other

"93. Lyn St. James, Auto Racing." Sports Illustrated for Women, 100 Greatest Female Athletes. http://sports illustrated.cnn.com/siforwomen/top_100/93/, (November 29, 1999).
"About Lyn." Lyn St. James Web site, http://www. lynstjames.com/about_lyn2.htm, (January 22, 2003).
Biography Resource Center. http://galenet.galegroup. com, (January 22, 2003).

"Book Review: *Ride of Your Life* by Lyn St. James." RacingPress, http://www.racingpress.com/publish/ printer_55.shtml, (July 7, 2002).
"Fisher, St. James Make Quick Exit at Indy." CNN-Sports Illustrated, http://sportsillustrated.cnn.com/ motorsports/2000/indy500/news/2000/05/28/fisher_ update/, (May 29, 2000).
"Love of the Sport Drives St. James." *(Elmira) Star-Gazette.* http://www.stargazettesports.com, (August 10, 2002).
"Lyn St. James: Business Principles Pay Off in Sponsorships." Indianapolis 500 Web site, http://www.indy 500.com/press/1998stjames-051098.html, (May 10, 1998).
"Turning the Key: St. James Announces Retirement from Indy."*CNN-Sports Illustrated.* http://sports illustrated.cnn.com/motorsports/news/2001/05/06/ stjames_retire_ap, (May 6, 2001).

Sketch by Paul Burton

John Stockton
1962-

American basketball player

The NBA all-time leader in assists and steals, John Stockton loves to play basketball. Holding the record for most NBA games with the same team, the Utah Jazz, Stockton became one of the best shooting point guards and helped the Jazz to 19 straight play-off appearances. Eagle-eyed on the court, he holds the record for most assists in a single game, most assists in a single season, and most career assists with an unsurmountable 15,177. He played nine consecutive All-Star Games, and played on the US Olympic Dream Team which won gold in both the 1992 Barcelona Games and 1996 Atlanta Games. Stockton is one of a few members of the NBA to play into his forties, and he is known as a gentleman off the court.

John Stockton

Underrated But Proved His Worth

John Stockton was born in Spokane, Washington, and attended the little-known Gonzaga University in his home town. A star player on the school's basketball team, Stockton averaged 20.9 points and 7.2 assists as a senior. He was the first player at his school to accumulate more than 1,000 points and 500 assists.

In 1984, the Utah Jazz selected Stockton with the 16th overall pick in the NBA Draft. Underrated at the start, Stockton soon proved his worth. He earned a reputation as being the best point guard in the league, and a reputation for longevity, when in 1984 he began what would become the record for most NBA games with the same team—1,271.

During his career with the Jazz, Stockton racked up a string of achievements. Named NBA Player of the Month in February 1988, he would eventually earn two-time All-NBA First Team selection (for 1993 and 1994), plus six-time All-NBA Second Team selection, five-time NBA All-Defensive Second Team selection, three-time All-NBA Third Team selection, and play nine consecutive All-Star Games, averaging 7.8 ppg and 8.2 apg.

Steals and Assist Champion

Showing that his skill lay in steals and assists, Stockton led the NBA in steals in 1988 (3.21 spg) and again in 1991 (2.98 spg). In 1989, he rolled in the highest single-season assists-per-game, an average 14.5. The following

season, he recorded most assists in a single season—1,164. Stockton accounted for seven of the nine seasons of 1,000 or more assists in league history.

He took a brief time out to help the 1992 US Olympic Dream Team win a gold medal at the Barcelona games, and served four years later with the team at the 1996 Atlanta Games. In 1993, the All-Star Game in Salt Lake City saw Stockton and teammate **Karl Malone** named co-MVPs. Stockton registered 15 assists, with 9 points and 6 rebounds.

Stockton became a free agent following the 1995-96 season and signed a three-year deal with the Jazz for $15 million. Continuing his astonishing performance that season, Stockton broke the NBA record of 9,921 career assists previous held by Los Angeles Lakers' **Magic Johnson**. Stockton now held the record for nine seasons leading the league in assists. That same season, he surpassed Maurice Cheeks' record of 2,310 steals during a 112-98 victory over the Boston Celtics. Not surprisingly, Stockton was named in 1996 one of the 50 greatest players in NBA History.

In game six of the 1997 Western Conference Finals, Stockton nailed the game-winning three-pointer at the buzzer in a 103-100 win over the Houston Rockets to propel the Jazz to their first trip to the NBA Finals.

Longevity and Durability

Although he missed the first 18 games of the 1997-98 campaign due to preseason knee surgery, Stockton is renowned for his near-perfect attendance. He played in

Career Statistics

Yr	Team	GP	PTS	FG%	3P%	FT%	RPG	APG	SPG	BPG	TO	PF
1984	UT	82	458	.471	.182	.736	105	415	109	11	1.8	2.5
1985	UT	82	630	.489	.133	.839	179	610	157	10	2.0	2.8
1986	UT	82	648	.499	.184	.782	151	670	177	14	2.0	2.7
1987	UT	82	1204	.574	.358	.840	237	1128	242	16	3.2	3.0
1988	UT	82	1400	.538	.242	.863	248	1118	263	14	3.8	2.9
1989	UT	78	1345	.514	.416	.819	206	1134	207	18	3.5	3.0
1990	UT	82	1413	.507	.345	.836	237	1164	234	16	3.6	2.8
1991	UT	82	1297	.482	.407	.842	270	1126	244	22	3.5	2.9
1992	UT	82	1239	.486	.385	.798	237	987	199	21	3.2	2.7
1993	UT	82	1236	.528	.322	.805	258	1031	199	22	3.2	2.9
1994	UT	82	1206	.542	.449	.804	251	1011	194	22	3.3	2.6
1995	UT	82	1209	.538	.422	.830	226	916	140	15	3.0	2.5
1996	UT	82	1183	.548	.422	.846	228	860	166	15	3.0	2.4
1997	UT	64	770	.528	.429	.827	166	543	89	10	2.5	2.2
1998	UT	50	553	.488	.320	.811	146	374	81	13	2.2	2.1
1999	UT	82	990	.501	.355	.860	215	703	143	15	2.2	2.3
2000	UT	82	944	.504	.462	.817	227	713	132	21	2.5	2.4
2001	UT	82	1102	.517	.321	.857	263	674	152	24	2.5	2.5
2002	UT	30	327	.466	.400	.785	69	219	50	2	2.3	2.3
TOTAL		1452	19154	.516	.385	.825	3919	15396	3178	301	2.8	2.6

UT: Utah Jazz.

Chronology

1962	Born March 26 in Spokane, Washington
1984	Is named to Utah Jazz
1992	US Olympic basketball Dream Team in Barcelona
1992	Competes in the Long-Distance Shootout during All-Star Weekend
1995-96	Signs a three-year deal with the Jazz for $15 million
1996	US Olympic basketball Dream Team in Atlanta
1997	Competes in the Long-Distance Shootout during All-Star Weekend
1999	Is named to All-NBA team
1999	Is re-signed by Utah for $22 million for two years
2001-02	Is re-signed by Utah for $18 million for two years

Awards and Accomplishments

1988	Named NBA Player of the Month in February
1988-89	Led the NBA in steals (3.21 spg)
1989-90	Highest single-season assists-per-game, average 14.5
1990-91	Record for most assists in a single season, 1,164
1992	Won Olympic gold in Barcelona
1993	Named co-MVP with teammate Karl Malone
1994	Selected to the All-NBA team First Team
1995	Selected to the All-NBA team First Team
1995	Set the NBA record for career assists
1996	Set the NBA record for career steals
1996	Record for most seasons leading league in assists
1996	Selected as one of the 50 Greatest Players in NBA History
1996	Won Olympic gold in Atlanta
1997	Played nine consecutive All-Star games, since 1988
2000	Broke John Havlicek's record of 1,270 games played with one team
2001-02	NBA career leader with 15,177 assists and 3,128 career steals

609 consecutive games from 1990 through 1997, the 8th longest streak in NBA history. He missed only four games in his first 13 profession seasons, and played in every game in 15 of his 17 seasons. In November 2000, he broke **John Havlicek**'s record of 1,270 games played with a single team.

Overall for his career, by the 2001-02 season, Stockton ranked third all-time in games played at 1,340, just behind Robert Parish's 1,611 and **Kareem Abdul-Jabbar**'s 1,560. He holds the NBA record for 15,177 assists and 3,128 steals. His career assists average is a record 11.1 apg. In all 17 of his seasons, he participated in the NBA Playoffs.

Continuing his streak with the Utah Jazz, in September 1999 he signed a two-year contract for $22 million. With no hint of retirement in the air, the nearly 40-year-old Stockton signed another two-year, $18 million contract during the 2000-01 season. He is one of only a handful of men who are still playing basketball into their forties.

Stockton and his wife, Nada, have six children and own homes in Salt Lake City and Spokane, Washington.

FURTHER INFORMATION

Books

Heeren, Dave. *The Basketball Abstract*. Edgewood Cliffs, NJ: Prentice Hall, 1988.

Hickok, Ralph. *Who's Who of Sports Champions*. Boston, MA; Houghton Mifflin, 1995.

Other

The John Stockton Pages. http://members.tripod.com/ johnstockton0/index.html (December 15, 2002).

The NBA. www.nba.com/playerfile/john_stockton (December 15, 2002).

Sports Illustrated. http://sportsillustrated.cnn.com/basketball/nba/players/John.Stockton (December 15, 2002).

The University of North Carolina at Chapel Hill. www.unc.edu/~lbrooks2/stockton1.html (December 15, 2002).

Utah Jazz. www.utjazz.com/team/stockton.shtml (December 15, 2002).

Sketch by Lorraine Savage

Elvis Stojko

Elvis Stojko
1972-

Canadian figure skater

During the 1990s Canadian skater Elvis Stojko (pronounced STOY-ko) revolutionized the field of men's figure skating with his athletic prowess. In 1991 he became the first figure skater to land a quadruple jump followed by a double jump at the world championships, and then in 1997 he surpassed himself by becoming the first person to land a quadruple-triple combination. Although Stojko was often hampered by judges who preferred dance-based, graceful programs to Stojko's athletic, often martial arts-inspired offerings, he still won the world championships three times, twice finished second at the Olympics, and earned the unofficial title "the King of Jumps" from sportswriters and fans.

Early Influences

As the family story goes, when Stojko was two he saw figure skating on the family television, pointed at the screen, and declared, "I do dat!" His mother, Irene, signed him up for skating lessons at age five, and within a few years he was jumping better than many adult skaters. At age 15 he became the Canadian junior champion; Canada's other male figure skating stars, Brian Orser and Kurt Browing, did not achieve that status at such an early age: Orser was 17 and Browing was 18.

Although Stojko's mother introduced him to skating, it was his father, Steve, who enrolled him in karate lessons at age nine. He earned his black belt a mere seven years later. Karate has long been nearly as much of a love for Stojko as figure skating, and the influence that martial arts have had upon him can be clearly seen in many of his programs. Over the years he has skated to sound tracks from martial-arts themed films and to the sounds of Japanese *taiko* drummers, and his choreography owes much more to Bruce Lee than it does to ballet.

Taking on the World

When Stojko graduated to the adult level of competition, he quickly established himself as a force to be reckoned with there as well, finishing ninth at the 1990 world championships. He moved up in 1991, but only to sixth, despite landing an unprecedented quadruple-double jump combination. Then he suffered a major disappointment at the 1992 Olympics. In sixth place after the short program, he finished seventh despite being the only competitor not to make any mistakes during the long program. The international judges, who were used to elegant costumes, classical music, and ballet-style dancing on ice, "ridiculed" Stojko's uncut hair and the punk-inspired costumes that his mother sewed for him, he said. "I was told to get in touch with my feminine side," Stojko later recalled to *Time* magazine's Robert Sullivan. "I said, 'Buddy, I don't have a feminine side.'"

Two years later, Stojko returned to the Olympics and skated such a clean and athletic program that the judges were forced to give him a silver, if only because he was the only one of the major competitors who did not make any mistakes. It was certainly not because he had become more classical in his style: He skated to music from the sound track of the film *Dragon: The Bruce Lee Story*. A month later, skating the same program at the world championships, Stojko won the gold.

Chronology

1972	Born March 22 in Newmarket, Ontario
1990	First finishes in the medals in adult competition
1990	Joins the Canadian national team
1991	Becomes the first person to land a quadruple jump in combination at the world championships
1992	Competes in his first Olympics; finishes seventh
2002	Retires from amateur competition after finishing eighth at the 2002 Olympics

Awards and Accomplishments

1988	Canadian Junior Championships
1991-92,	Skate Canada
1994,	
1996-98	
1993	Piruetten
1994	Nations Cup
1994-95,	World Championships
1997	
1994,	Canadian Championships
1996-99	
1994, 1998	Wins silver medal in Olympics
1995	Named Canadian Athlete of the Year
1995-96	NHK Trophy
1996	Awarded the Governor General's Meritorious Service Medal
1997	Champions Series Final
1997	Sparkassen Cup

Quest to Stay on Top

Stojko retained the title of world champion in 1995, despite suffering a partially torn ligament in his ankle a few weeks before that prevented him from practicing many of his jumps until ten days before the competition. He failed to nail the landing of his quadruple toe loop early in his long program, so to compensate he added an extra, unplanned jump combination, a triple toe loop-triple Lutz, four minutes into his already strenuous program.

Stojko was the favorite going into the 1996 world championships, since they were held on Canadian ice in Edmonton, Alberta, but a poor showing in the short program put him in seventh place going into the long program. He gave a fabulous performance in front of a crowd that was shouting, clapping, and on their feet through much of his long program, but it was not enough. He finished fourth.

Stojko came back in 1997, again doing things his way: His music that year was from the sound track of the film *Dragonheart*. Stojko also had a new jump in his program, a quadruple toe loop-triple toe loop combination. He was the only person ever to have landed this jump in competition, and even he had done it only once, a mere two weeks earlier. Still, he nailed the combination, and with a little help from the rest of the field-defending champion Todd Eldridge fell, and of the two Russian competitors one performed poorly and one withdrew because of an injury-Stojko reclaimed his world title for the third time in four years.

This would be Stojko's last major victory in an international competition. He competed in the 1998 Olympics, but he had a badly pulled muscle in his groin that prevented him from doing any quadruple jumps. He skated a clean program of all triple jumps, which earned him a silver medal. Stojko decided to remain an amateur and to take one more shot at winning an Olympic gold, but his career was slowly sliding, in large part because of a series of injuries. He managed a silver at the 2000 world championships, but he wobbled on several of his jumps at the 2002 Olympics, where he skated a reprise of his 1994 *Dragon: The Bruce Lee Story* program, and finished eighth. He retired at the end of that season.

Stojko did not appear in competition for the first time in over 20 years in the 2002-03 skating season. During some of that time, he was the star performer in a month-long professional skating tour called Canon SK8 with Elvis. Stojko said that he enjoyed having the opportunity to skate purely for fun, but that he had not ruled out skating in professional competitions in the future.

Doing His Own Thing

Throughout his career, Stojko remained faithful to his artistic vision, even though avoiding the typical, classical style of figure skating quite possibly cost him two Olympic gold medals. "If I skated like someone else because I was told to, that would be plagiarism," Stojko explained to Sullivan. When Stojko finally did win the world championships, skating in his own style, he was quite conscious of the prejudice that he had overcome and the rules that he had changed. In 1994 he declared to *Maclean's* Mary Nemeth, "I've opened the door for younger skaters to come up and do their own things."

FURTHER INFORMATION

Periodicals

Bellafante, Ginia. "Look Who's Standing." *Time* (February 23, 1998): 76-77.

Deacon, James. "Elvis Hasn't Quite Left the Building Yet." *Maclean's* (November 11, 2002): 89.

———. "Elvis Time!" *Maclean's* (February 16, 1998): 50-53.

———. "Leaps of Faith." *Maclean's* (February 9, 1998): 36-38.

———. "The Nagano Factor: Canadian Skating Slumps as the Olympics Approach." *Maclean's* (February 17, 1997): 64-65.

———. "Profile in Courage." *Maclean's* (February 23, 1998): 36-37.

———. "The Superstar Next Door: Elvis Stojko." *Maclean's* (December 18, 1995): 72-73.

————. "The World at His Feet." *Maclean's* (March 20, 1995): 45-46.

Jenish, D'Arcy. "Elvis Reigns Again." *Maclean's* (March 31, 1997): 52-53.

————. "Sharing the Podium: Browning and Stojko Win Silver and Bronze." *Maclean's* (April 6, 1992): 51.

————. "Talent under Pressure." *Maclean's* (February 3, 1992): 36-37.

Knisley, Michael. "Elvis Left the Building Unhappy." *Sporting News* (February 28, 1994): 12.

Lefton, Terry. "MasterCard Campaign Takes NHL Tack with Orr, Stojko on Ice." *Brandweek* (November 9, 1998): 16.

Martin, Sandra. "Elvis Thrills!" *Chatelaine* (September, 1994): 110-112.

Nemeth, Mary. "Hail to the King: Elvis Stojko Turns Innovation into Gold." *Maclean's* (April 4, 1994): 50.

————. "The High Price of Pressure at the Top." *Maclean's* (April 1, 1996): 62-63.

Starr, Mark. "The King of Jumps." *Newsweek* (February 16, 1998): 50-51.

Sullivan, Robert. "Is the King Going to Take the Crown?" *Time* (February 9, 1998): 90-91.

Swift, E. M. "They're the Tops." *Sports Illustrated* (March 31, 1997): 46-49.

Other

Canon SK8 with Elvis Stojko. http://www.skate withelvis.com (January 5, 2003).

"SLAM! Presents Elvis Stojko." Canoe.ca. http://www. canoe.ca/SlamElvisStojko/home.html (January 5, 2003).

"Stojko Finishes Eighth in Olympics, Says He'll Go to Worlds." Canoe.ca. http://www.canoe.ca/2002Games FigureSkatingArchive/feb14_king-cp.html (January 17, 2003).

Sketch by Julia Bauder

Darryl Strawberry

Darryl Strawberry
1962-

American baseball player

When Darryl Strawberry was sentenced to an eighteen-month prison term in April 2002 for violating the terms of his court-ordered drug treatment, it marked the lowest point in a decline that had stared two decades earlier. Signed to the New York Mets in 1980 right after he had finished high school, Strawberry's career as a baseball player got off to a promising start. He was named the Rookie of the Year in 1983 and helped the Mets win a World Series championship in 1986. Yet he had begun abusing amphetamines to enhance his performance in the majors and fell into the habit of easing his pressures through the consumption of alcohol.

The habits first derailed him in 1990 when he entered a treatment center for substance abuse. The next decade was marked by repeated brushes with the law for domestic violence, weapons charges, and drug abuse. Meanwhile, Strawberry moved to the Los Angeles Dodgers for three seasons, followed by a twenty-nine game stint with the San Francisco Giants that was curtailed when he tested positive for cocaine use. Going back to the minor leagues in 1995, Strawberry was signed by the New York Yankees and claimed to have turned his professional and personal lives around. A diagnosis of colon cancer in 1998 generated public sympathy for Strawberry's struggles, but he continued to abuse drugs during his recovery and ended up back in court on drug charges in 1999. After violating his parole in 2000, Strawberry was placed under house arrest to force him to complete another drug-treatment program. After violating his parole for a sixth time in April 2002, he was sentenced to an eighteen-month term in the Florida prison system.

Grew up in Compton

Darryl Strawberry was born on March 12, 1962, in Los Angeles, California to Ruby and Henry Strawberry. He had two older brothers, Michael and Ron, and two younger sisters, Regina and Michelle. The family resided in Compton, a neighborhood in south-central

Chronology

1962	Born March 12 in Los Angeles, California to Ruby and Henry Strawberry
1980	Drafted by New York Mets
1983	Named MLB Rookie of the Year
1985	Marries Lisa Andrews in January
1986	World Series Championship (with New York Mets)
1990	Undergoes treatment for alcoholism
1990	Arrested on weapons charge and convicted of tax evasion
1990	Loses paternity suit brought by Lisa Clayton
1991	Signs with Los Angeles Dodgers
1993	Divorces Lisa Andrews; marries Charisse Simons on December 3
1994	Undergoes treatment for alcoholism and drug dependency
1994	Signs with San Francisco Giants; released from contract after testing positive for drug use
1995	Suspended from major league baseball for cocaine use
1995	Signs with New York Yankees, but released from contract in December
1996	New York Yankees pick up Strawberry's contract; becomes active player the following year
1998	Undergoes surgery for colon cancer
1999	Arrested for solicitation and drug possession
1999	Placed on leave by baseball Commissioner Bud Selig
2000	Received one-year suspension from baseball after testing positive for drug use
2000	Arrested for parole violations; ordered into drug treatment for two years
2002	Sentenced to eighteen months in Florida prison for parole violations

Awards and Accomplishments

1982	Named Most Valuable Player in Texas League
1983	Named MLB Rookie of the Year
1986	World Series Championship (with New York Mets)

had a .268 batting average in forty-four games. In 1981 he advanced to the Lynchburg, Virginia Hillcats, where his batting average remained a steady .255. Strawberry spent part of the 1982 season with the Jackson, Mississippi Generals—where he was the leading home run hitter and earned Most Valuable Player (MVP) status in the Texas League—before returning to Virginia to play for the Tidewater Hurricanes in the playoffs. Often homesick and uncomfortable with the racism that he sometimes encountered in the South, Strawberry was eager to join the roster of the Mets in New York. He spent just a few games with Tidewater in the 1983 season before being brought up to the major league in May of that year.

When Strawberry joined the Mets, he was hailed as the team's best hope in restoring its fortunes after years of lackluster performance. Although the "Marvelous Mets" had won a surprising World Series championship in 1969, they were often derided by New York fans in favor of the Yankees, who were perennial title contenders. When pitcher Dwight Gooden—who would face his own substance-abuse problems in later years—joined the Mets' lineup in 1984, the team completed its turnaround. With a .257 batting average the prior year, Strawberry had already won MLB Rookie of the Year honors. Along with first baseman Keith Hernandez, Strawberry and Gooden powered the Mets to a World Series victory in seven games over the Boston Red Sox in 1986. By that time, however, Strawberry already faced the first of his legal troubles.

Substance Abuse Problems

In January 1987, just a few months after Strawberry's World Series appearance with the Mets, his wife, Lisa Andrews Strawberry, filed for legal separation. The couple had been married in January 1985, but in an October 1986 incident, Lisa Strawberry claimed that her husband had broken her nose. The couple reconciled, but Lisa Strawberry filed for divorce in May 1989, a few weeks after her husband was named in a paternity suit filed by Lisa Clayton. Blood tests eventually verified Clayton's claim that Strawberry had fathered their child. Strawberry also had two children by his wife: Darryl, Jr. and Diamond Nicole. In January 1990 Strawberry was arrested again for hitting his wife and threatening her with a handgun. After Strawberry agreed to enter a rehabilitation center to deal with his substance-abuse problems, the charges were dropped. The Strawberrys eventually separated and were divorced in 1993.

Los Angeles not far from Dodger Stadium. His father was an employee of the U.S. Postal Service and his mother worked for the phone company; the couple divorced in 1974, in part due to Henry Strawberry's heavy drinking, gambling, and sometimes explosive temper. Greatly affected by his father's departure, Darryl Strawberry looked up to his two older brothers as role models. He shared their love of basketball and baseball and immediately became a star player on the Crenshaw High School's baseball team.

Despite his obvious athletic talent, Strawberry ran into difficulties with authority figures from the start. Criticized by his coach for taking his time getting onto the baseball field one day in his sophomore year, Strawberry quit the team for the rest of the season. When he returned to the team as a six-foot, six-inch, 200 pound junior, Strawberry began attracting interest from baseball scouts from around the country. Despite his reputation as an undisciplined player who took his natural athletic abilities for granted, Strawberry ended up as the first pick in the first round of the Major League Baseball (MLB) draft in 1980. He was selected by the New York Mets, a team perennial dwarfed by their metropolitan rivals, the New York Yankees.

Drafted by New York Mets

Strawberry's first assignment was with the Kingsport, Pennsylvania Mets, where the right fielder

Career Statistics

Yr	Team	AVG	GP	AB	R	H	HR	RBI	BB	SO	SB	E
1983	NYM	.257	122	420	63	108	26	74	47	128	19	4
1984	NYM	.251	147	522	75	131	26	97	75	131	27	6
1985	NYM	.277	111	393	78	109	29	79	73	96	26	2
1986	NYM	.259	136	475	76	123	27	93	72	141	28	6
1987	NYM	.284	154	532	106	151	39	104	97	122	36	8
1988	NYM	.269	153	543	101	146	39	101	85	127	29	9
1989	NYM	.225	134	476	69	107	29	77	61	105	11	8
1990	NYM	.277	152	542	92	150	37	108	70	110	15	3
1991	LA	.265	139	505	86	134	28	99	75	125	10	5
1992	LA	.237	43	156	20	37	5	25	19	34	3	1
1993	LA	.140	32	100	12	14	5	12	16	19	1	4
1994	SF	.239	29	92	13	22	4	17	19	22	0	2
1995	NYY	.276	32	87	15	24	3	13	10	22	0	2
1996	NYY	.262	63	202	35	53	11	36	31	55	6	0
1997	NYY	.103	11	29	1	3	0	2	3	9	0	0
1998	NYY	.247	101	295	44	73	24	57	46	90	8	2
1999	NYY	.327	24	49	10	16	3	6	17	16	2	0
TOTAL		.259	1583	5418	896	1401	335	1000	816	1352	221	62

LA: Los Angeles Dodgers; NYM: New York Mets; NYY: New York Yankees;
SF: San Francisco Giants.

Although Strawberry publicly blamed his erratic behavior on his alcohol consumption, he had also been abusing amphetamines and cocaine. His addictions began during his second season with the Mets and continued after he signed with the Los Angeles Dodgers in 1991. In 1992 a serious back injury that required surgery limited Strawberry to just forty-three games with the Dodgers. His recovery also sent him back into drug dependency. In 1993 he played thirty-two games and his batting average dropped to .140. In September 1993 he was back in court after he was arrested for domestic abuse against his girlfriend, Charisse Simons. Simons dropped the charges and married Strawberry on December 3. The couple subsequently had three children.

After failing to show up for a Dodgers game in April 1994, Strawberry entered the Betty Ford Center for a twenty-eight day drug dependency treatment. Released from his contract by the Dodgers, Strawberry signed with the San Francisco Giants. He played just twenty-nine games for the team before being released after testing positive for cocaine use in February 1995; he also received a sixty-day suspension from baseball. Strawberry also faced an indictment for tax evasion; according to the IRS, Strawberry had failed to declare over $300,000 in earnings from selling memorabilia with his autograph. Despite his plea of not guilty, Strawberry was ordered in April 1995 to pay $350,000 in back taxes.

Signed with New York Yankees

Although the New York Yankees picked up Strawberry's contract in 1995, the team decided to waive the option at the end of the year. Joining the minor-league St. Paul Saints for the 1996 season, Strawberry attempted to

rebuild his career. In July 1996 the Yankees decided to sign Strawberry again and this time put him on the roster in August of that year. With the support of Yankees owner **George Steinbrenner**, Strawberry seemed to complete his career comeback with a .262 batting average in sixty-three games in 1996. Injuries curtailed his 1997 season, but Strawberry returned to play 101 games in 1998, attaining a .247 batting average.

In October 1998 Strawberry underwent surgery to remove a cancerous tumor in his colon. The surgery ended his season but generated enormous public sympathy for the embattled star, who seemed to have finally put his problems behind him. During his recovery, however, Strawberry was arrested in April 1999 for soliciting sex from an undercover police officer and was found to be in possession of cocaine. He later pleaded no contest to the charges and rejoined the Yankees in September 1999 after serving a four-month suspension from baseball. Strawberry ended up playing twenty-four games with the Yankees at the end of the 1999 season and compiled a .327 batting average.

Continuing Legal Problems

Despite his ongoing legal and drug-abuse problems, the Yankees signed Strawberry for the 2000 season at $750,000. Testing positive for cocaine use in January 2000, however, Strawberry was suspended from baseball again, this time for a year. Entering a clinic for drug treatment in March 2000, Strawberry left the program before completing the program. When a medical check-up revealed the presence of more cancer in his lymph nodes, Strawberry had surgery to remove a stomach tumor in August 2000. The following month he was in-

Darryl Strawberry

volved in a car accident and was later found to be driving under the influence of pain killers. Arrested in October 2000 for violating his parole requirements, another drug test showed that Strawberry was again using cocaine; in a subsequent trial he was ordered to a thirty-day jail term. Strawberry also was put under house arrest, which required him to live in a drug treatment center after his release from jail. In March 2001, after leaving the center without authorization, Strawberry was arrested again. Facing the possibility of another jail term, Strawberry was instead sentenced in May 2001 to a residential drug treatment center in Ocala, Florida.

Sent to Prison in 2002

In March 2001 Strawberry left his drug-treatment program for four days and tested positive for drug use upon his return. He was also found to have conducted a sexual relationship with another resident of the program, a violation of the center's rules. As both actions were in violation of his parole agreement, Strawberry returned to court in April 2002. Having racked up six parole violations, Strawberry received a prison sentence of eighteen months, which he began serving on April 29, 2002. Now forty years old, Strawberry's eighteen-month prison sentence indicated that any future in professional sports was over. Suffering from bipolar disorder, Strawberry's health had also suffered from cocaine use, which had possibly caused brain damage.

Sympathy for Strawberry's latest round of legal and personal problems in 2002 focused on the lost potential of a once-great athlete. Although Strawberry had achieved more in his seventeen years in the major leagues than most other players—and in fact still held the Mets' records for most hits and most runs batted in—he seemed to have wasted his natural abilities in favor of decades of alcohol and drug use. Once a Rookie of the Year and World Series champion, Strawberry's personal demons were so strong that they eventually ended his career and landed him in jail. Few could have imagined that the former first-round draft pick would have fallen so far. His fate stood in particularly stark contrast with the hopeful tone that Strawberry presented in the conclusion of his 1992 memoir *Darryl*. "Now my days of hanging back are over," he wrote, "I've made too many mistakes that way and let too many people down. You want to see a leader? Just watch us play next year. There's a long winter ahead of us, a long time to think about what's going to happen next season. But as someone once wrote, When winter comes, can spring training be far behind?"

SELECTED WRITINGS BY STRAWBERRY:

(With Art Rust, Jr.) *Darryl,* Bantam Books, 1992.

FURTHER INFORMATION

Books

Klapisch, Bob. *High and Tight: The Rise and Fall of Dwight Gooden and Darryl Strawberry.* New York: Villard, 1996.

Strawberry, Darryl, with Art Rust, Jr. *Darryl.* New York: Bantam Books, 1992.

Thorn, John, et al., eds. *Total Baseball: The Official Encyclopedia of Major League Baseball.* New York: Viking, 1995.

Periodicals

Burleigh, Nina. "For Better and Worse." *Redbook* (December 1999).

Kaplan, David A., and Karen Springen. "Are Two Chances Too Many?" *Newsweek* (August 21, 1995).

Kurkjian, Tim. "A New Straw Stirs" *Sports Illustrated* (July 29, 1996).

Lopresti, Mike. "Strawberry Reaches Critical Crossroads." *USA Today* (April 30, 2002).

O'Brien, Richard and Jack McCallum. "Strawberry's Jam." *Sports Illustrated* (June 6, 1994).

Tresiniowski, Alex et al. "Crunch Time." *People* (October 19, 1998).

Other

"Darryl Strawberry." Baseball Reference Web site. http://www.baseball-reference.com/s/strawda01.shtml (December 4, 2002).

"Darryl Strawberry." Darryl Strawberry Web site. http://www.darrylstrawberry.org/highlights.html (December 5, 2002).

"Darryl Strawberry." ESPN Web site. http://baseball.espn.go.com/mlb/players/stats?statsId=3216 (December 2, 2002).

"Darryl Strawberry Sentenced to 18 Months in State Prison." Florida Department of Corrections Web site. http://www.dc.state.fl.us/secretary/press/2002/Strawberry.html (April 29, 2002).

Puma, Mike. "Strawberry's Story One of Unfulfilled Potential." ESPN Web site. http://espn.go.com/classic/biography/s/strawberry_darryl.html (December 5, 2002).

Seybert, Adrien. "Strawberry Gets Treatment Instead of Prison for Drug Bings." Court TV Web site. http://www.courttv.com/people/2001/0517/straw_ap.html (May 17, 2001).

"Strawberry Gets Thirty Days in Jail." CBS News Web site. http://www.cbsnews.com/stories/2000/11/09/sports.main24864.shtml (November 9, 2001).

Wang, Karissa S. "Charisse Strawberry Joins Bay News 9." Darryl Strawberry Web site. http://www.darrylstrawberry.org/charisse_strawberry.html (March 21, 2001).

Sketch by Timothy Borden

Picabo Street
1971-

American skier

Picabo Street can be called many things, from a "skiing phenomenon" to a "Brat" to an "Amazing Super-G Downhill Force." Street, one of the greatest downhill skiers in U.S. downhill women's history, accumulated an

Picabo Street

incredible collection of World Championships and Olympic medals in her short career before choosing to retire in 2002. Her can-do attitude and willingness to speak her mind brought popularity to the women's downhill, and Street's good-natured outlook on life and girl-next-door face made her the hero of many young women who also want to do more than just succeed in life and, as Street has said of her own desires as a child, not only "be as good as the boys … [but] be *better.*"

Growing Up

Picabo Street was born on August 3, 1971, in Triumph, Idaho, located near Sun Valley, some of the best skiing in the state. Her parents are self-confessed hippies, and her father, Roland Wayne Street (who also goes by "Ron" or "Stubby")and mother Dee were liberal in their views about raising children, and gave their children the freedom to pick their own names. Picabo—who actually did enjoy playing the game peek-a-boo when she was a child—did not have a name for several years. Her birth certificate simply listed her as "Baby Girl." The name "Picabo" actually comes from a nearby Indian town and means "shining waters" or "silver creek," and was finally chosen when the Streets needed something to put on a passport when they traveled to Mexico.

Street began her career as a downhill racer at an early age, taking to the slopes when she was not yet in high

Chronology

1971	Born April 3 in Triumph, Idaho
1978	Started organized racing because she wanted to "race the boys"
1985	Lands a spot on the U.S. junior ski team—she's fifteen years old
1986	Moves up to work with the U.S. ski team for the 1987-88 season
1988	Wins the national junior downhill and Super G titles
1989	Joins U.S. Ski Team
1990	Suspended from the team for her attitude and her tendency to stay out past curfew and falling out of shape
1991	Returns to the U.S. ski team in better shape and with a better attitude
1992	Ranked eighth in the world, Picabo is the U.S. ski team's top racer
1993	Takes the World Championship silver medal in combined downhill and slalom in Morioka, Japan (also wins gold at U.S. Alpine Championships)
1994	Earns her first silver medal in the downhill at Winter Olympics
1994-95	Becomes the first American to win the World Cup women's downhill championship
1996	Captures the World Cup women's downhill for a second time
1996	Suffers a serious knee injury in December after crashing on a course
1998	Brings home gold medal for the super giant slalom (Super G) after slowly recovering from her injury and returning full strength in time for the games
1998	Breaks her left femur in March in final World Cup race of the season. Suffers several other injuries following her broken leg. She is out of action for 33 months
2001	Kicked off the slopes at Copper Mountain for skiing too fast on an intermediate run
2001-02	Leading downhill qualifier for U.S. Olympic ski team
2002	Retires from competetive skiing after finishing 16th in Women's Olympic downhill

Awards and Accomplishments

1991	U.S. Championships (3rd)
1993	U.S. Championships Super-G (1st); U.S. Championships Combined (2nd); U.S. Championships Downhill (3rd); World Championships Combined (2nd); World Championships Downhill (10th)
1994	U.S. Championships Downhill (1st); U.S. Championships Super-G (2nd); Olympics Downhill (2nd); Olympics Super-G (10th)
1996	U.S. Championships Downhill (1st); U.S. Championships Super-G (1st); World Championships Downhill (1st); World Championships Super-G (3rd)
1998	Olympics Super-G (1st); Olympics Downhill (6th)
2001	U.S. Championships Downhill (2nd)

school. Her father (a stonemason) and mother (a music teacher) were not able to afford the best and most up-to-date ski equipment, but this did not deter Picabo. She consistently beat kids who were much older and much wealthier than she was, learning to fight back early and developing her tough attitude in order to deal with their derisive comments. After all, Street was a young girl—with hippie parents and low-grade equipment—who showed up at competitions and easily beat *older kids*. They were not happy about it.

Not Amateur For Long

The regular rich kids on the slopes would not have to put up with Street for long. When she was 15 she joined the U.S. junior ski team, and soon won the National Junior downhill and Super Giant (Super G) slaloms. The coaches decided to move her up the next level, and she started training with the U.S. ski team in 1986.

No one could deny Street's natural ability, but for too long she had relied on that and only that, failing to heed authority. This often got her in trouble. Picabo stayed out late, spoke without thinking, and all too often ignored the coach's curfew. In 1990 she was suspended from the team for her attitude. That, and the fact that she showed up to training camp overweight and out of shape.

Rebuilding

Her father encouraged Picabo to head down to Hawaii with him to train, convincing her that she could easily get back up to where she was, or become even better. She agreed, and in what *Newsday* reporter Tim Layden referred to as a "boot camp," Street shaped up and came back ready to dominate once again.

In 1991 Street was fierce on the slopes. She became overall champion for the North American Championship series, earning a ranking of eighth in the world in 1992 after winning silver in the downhill combined at the world championships in Japan. She also earned second place at the World Cup downhill in Norway, and later won the gold medal at the U.S. Alpine Championships. Throughout the first half of the nineties, Street stair-stepped her way up in the rankings, moving from 65 place all the way into first (in spite of the fact that she was consistently in trouble with her coaches for her continued questioning of authority). At only 22, Street fulfilled one of her dreams by medaling in the 1994 Olympics and earning silver in the downhill. After the Olympics, she continued her stellar ways that season, becoming the first American to win the World Cup women's downhill, taking six out of the nine races she participated in that season.

Plagued by Injuries

Though she would continue to add some phenomenal victories to her accomplishments (she repeated at the World Cup the following year, and won a gold medal in the Super-G in the 1998 Winter Olympics), Picabo's career was soon hampered by a string of injuries. When she crashed in December of 1996, she tore the anterior cruciate and medial collateral ligaments of her left knee. She also pulled her calf muscle off the bone and broken her femur. Following a 1998 Olympic gold medal, she crashed yet again, in January, and though she did not sustain any major injuries, was bruised badly and was unconscious for several minutes.

In March of 1998, Street crashed yet again, this time breaking her leg in nine different places. The injury was

Picabo Street

severe enough to put her out of competition for over a year, as well as force her to endure several painful operations. She vowed to come back, however, and after another dedicated few years of training, qualified for the 2002 Olympic Games.

Olympic Disappointment

In February of 2002, after a disappointing 16th place finish in the Women's Olympic Downhill, Picabo Street put away her competitive skis at the age of thirty and opted instead for a more laid-back life, all things considered. "I'm not going to have to live without skiing," she told the BBC news. "I'm just going to have to live without trying to be perfect on my skis every day, which is wonderful."

Street is a role model for many young women. She told *Great Women in Sports* that "Sports are an avenue to be happy with myself. And that's why I do the media I do," she said, referring to her appearances not on Letterman and Leno but instead on Sesame Street and other children-oriented programs. "It's important," she continues, "for girls to see bigger women with strong opinions, who are also sensitive and vulnerable. I want to tell them, 'You can be a strong athlete and still be feminine.'"

CONTACT INFORMATION

Address: Office—c/o U.S. Olympic Committee, 1750 E. Boulder St., Colorado Springs, CO 80909-5724; c/o U.S. Ski Team, P.O. Box 100, Park City, UT 84060.

SELECTED WRITINGS BY STREET:

(With Dana White) *Picabo: Nothing to Hide.* McGraw-Hill, 2001.

FURTHER INFORMATION

Books

Dippold, Joel. *Picabo Street: Downhill Dynamo.* Minneapolis: Lerner Publications, 1998.

"Picabo Street." *Great Women in Sports.* Detroit: Visible Ink Press, 1996.

"Picabo Street." *Newsmakers 1999,* Issue 3. Farmington Hills, MI: Gale Group, 1999.

Street, Picabo and Dana White. *Picabo: Nothing to Hide.* New York: McGraw Hill, 2001.

Periodicals

Chicago Tribune (February 21, 1994; January 26, 1995).

Cooper, Christian. "Picabo Rules." *Skiing* (September 1995): 102-107.

Farber, Michael. "All World." *Sports Illustrated* (February 26, 1996).

Farber, Michael. "Playing Picabo." *Sports Illustrated* (December 18, 1995).

Layden, Tim. "Street Fighting." *Sports Illustrated* (February 23, 1998).

Los Angeles Times (March 14, 1998; January 8, 1999).

"Making a Rainbow." *Sports Illustrated* (March 27, 1995).

New York Times (February 24, 1999).

Redbook (November 1995).

Reece, Gabrielle. "Picabo." *Women's Sports and Fitness* (November/December 1998): 70-73.

Reibstein, Larry. "The Golden Girl." *Newsweek* (February 23, 1998): 46-48.

Skiing (September 1994; September 1995; September 1996; October 1992; December 1996; February 1997; Octover 1997; November 1997; November 1997; February 1998).

Time (February 1998).

Other

"Picabo Street." Athlete Bio on U.S. Olympic Ski Team Website. http://www.usolympicteam.com/athlete_profiles/p_street.html (January 23, 2003).

"Picabo Street." Washington Post Olympics Page on Street. http://www.washingtonpost.com/wp-srv/sports/longterm/olympics1998/sport/profiles/street.htm (January 23, 2003).

"Street Hangs Up Her Skis." News of Street's retirement. http://news.bbc.co.uk/winterolympics2002/hi/english/alpine_skiing/newsid_1817000/1817370.stm (January 23, 2003).

Sketch by Eric Lagergren

Kerri Strug
1977-

American gymnast

Most notable sports figures cannot—and would not want to—claim that their fame is derived from a single moment. This, however, is the case with Kerri Strug. Before the 1996 Olympics in Atlanta, Georgia, Strug had earned a reputation as a solid performer in the gymnastics world. The shy, reserved Strug, however, was never a household name like some of her other, flashier teammates, such as **Shannon Miller** and **Dominique Dawes**. In one moment on July 23, 1996, this all changed when Strug vaulted into the world's consciousness—literally. As the final performer during the final event of the women's team competition, Strug completed her second and final vault, in obvious pain on a sprained ankle, to secure the first ever Olympic gold medal for the United States women's gymnastics team. This courageous and heroic moment was captured in countless media images and broadcast around the world, and secured her own place in Olympic and sports history.

A Lifelong Passion

Kerri Allyson Strug was born on November 19, 1977, in Tucson, Arizona. Unlike many other gymnasts, who are pushed into the sport by their parents from an early age, Strug chose the hard life of a gymnast herself. When she was only a few years old, Strug asked her parents to enroll her in tumbling classes. Strug had attended the meets of her older sister, Lisa, and older brother, Kevin, and decided that she wanted to try it, too. Strug quickly proved that her interest stemmed from more than just a natural desire to emulate her older siblings— she also had natural talent. Strug's parents supported her ambition, and enrolled her in gymnastics classes at the age of four. By the age of six, Strug was taking private lessons from Jim Gault, a gymnastics coach at the University of Arizona.

When she was seven, Strug visited her sister at a gymnastics summer camp in Texas, run by the famous gymnastics coach, **Bela Karolyi**, who had trained such past gymnastics champions as **Nadia Comaneci**, and who was then training America's star gymnast, **Mary Lou Retton**. A member of Karolyi's coaching staff noticed Kerri's back flips and encouraged Strug's parents to enroll her in Karolyi's school full-time. Strug's parents refused, however. They had always stressed the importance of education to their children, and worried that gymnastics would take precedence over Kerri's education.

Strug continued to work hard in school, and even harder in her after-school gymnastics lessons. She also started to compete, entering her first gymnastics compe-

Kerri Strug

tition at the age of eight. She advanced quickly over the next several years, earning top finishes in local and regional events. At the age of twelve, however, Strug decided that she wanted more—she wanted to make it to the Olympics. In order to compete with the best, she knew she needed to train with the best: Karolyi. Strug's parents reluctantly agreed to send her to Karolyi's expensive school full-time, on the condition that she not neglect her education. In January 1991, at the age of thirteen, Strug moved to Houston to begin her new life.

Triumph and Heartbreak

From the moment Strug began training with Karolyi, all aspects of her life were monitored by the notoriously demanding coach and his wife, Martha. Karolyi pushed Strug to her physical and mental limits to prepare her for international competition. Strug worked hard, and her efforts paid off. In 1991, she won first place in the vault at the U.S. Gymnastics Championships, becoming the youngest female ever to win an event at this competition. The next year, she qualified for the 1992 Olympics in Barcelona, and helped the women's team win a bronze medal. Her Olympic performance was bittersweet, however, because she narrowly missed making the individual all-around finals.

After the Olympics, Karolyi announced his retirement and Strug was left without a coach. Over the next few years, Strug bounced from gym to gym, moving to Florida, Oklahoma, and Colorado, but she was unable

Chronology

1977	Born November 19 in Tucson, Arizona
1982	Begins gymnastics
1984	Noticed by a coach at Karolyi's summer camp, who encourages Strug's parents to have Kerri train full-time with Karolyi
1989	Begins training with Bela Karolyi
1989	Member of Junior Pacific Alliance Team
1990	Member of Junior Pan Am Games Team
1991	Member of World Gymnastics Championship Team
1992	Member of United States Olympic Team
1992	Karolyi announces retirement; Strug changes coaches repeatedly for next several years
1993	Member of Hilton Challenge Team
1994	Member of Team World Championship Team
1995	Graduates from high school a year ahead of schedule—with a perfect 4.0 GPA—and earns a scholarship to University of California, Los Angeles, but defers enrollment for a year so that she can train for the 1996 Olympics
1995	Resumes training with Karolyi, who had come out of retirement in 1994
1995	Member of World Champion Team
1996	Member of United States Olympic Team
1996	Performs historic vault on an injured ankle in final round of the women's gymnastics team competition to help United States women's gymnastics team win first ever gold medal
1996	Featured on the Wheaties cereal box with her Olympic teammates
1996	Appears on an episode of "Saturday Night Live," in which she makes fun of her infamous high-pitched voice
1997	Works as an intern on the sports staff of KNBC-TV in Los Angeles
1998	Works as an intern for *Entertainment Tonight*
1999	Competes in her first marathon
2001	Graduates from Stanford with a Communications degree
2001	Works as an intern for Republican Senator John McCain

to find a coach who could help her the way Karolyi had. Worse yet, Strug also experienced a number of debilitating injuries during this time period, including a torn stomach muscle that forced her to move back with her parents for six months to heal. In 1994, during a small competition, Strug fell off of the uneven bars and landed on her back, severely pulling her back muscles, which required another six-month break to heal. Despite these setbacks, Strug hoped to be competitive long enough to make it to the 1996 Olympics. Her ultimate dream was to compete in the Olympics' individual all-around finals that she had narrowly missed qualifying for in 1992.

Once again, she recognized that the key to trying to achieve her dreams was Bela Karolyi, who had come out of retirement in 1994. In 1995, she resumed training with Karolyi, who was coaching newcomer Dominique Moceanu—a young gymnast who had attracted attention when she won the all-around competition at the 1995 United States Gymnastics Championships. Most had high hopes for Moceanu, while Strug received little media attention. This trend remained true even after Strug won her first international competition at the McDonald's American Cup in March 1996. Likewise, when

Awards and Accomplishments

1989	First place all around at the American Classic, California and second place all around at the American Classic, Texas
1990	Second place for uneven bars and balance beam, Dutch Open
1991	First place for vault, United States Gymnastics Championships; becomes the youngest female ever to win an event at this competition
1991	First place for vault, United States vs. Romania
1991	Team silver medal in World Championships
1992	Finished first place for vault and balance beam, second place for all-around competition and floor exercises at the United States Gymnastics Championships
1992	Helped United States women's gymnastics team earn Olympic bronze medal; at fourteen, Strug is the team's youngest member
1993	First place all around, uneven bars, balance beam, and floor exercise, American Classic/World Championships Trials
1993	First place for uneven bars and second place for all around, balance beam, and floor exercise at the United States Olympic Festival
1993	Second place for uneven bars at the Coca-Cola National Championships
1993	First place for balance beam and second place all around at the McDonald's American Cup
1993	Second place all around at the Reebok International Mixed Pairs
1994	Second place all around at the NationsBank World Team Trials
1994	Silver medal in Team World Championships
1995	First place all around and for uneven bars at the United States Olympic Festival
1995	Team bronze medal in World Championships
1996	First place all around at the McDonald's American Cup; also first place for balance beam and floor exercise, and second place for vault and uneven bars
1996	Clinched United States women's gymnastics team's first ever Olympic gold medal
1996	Won Olympic Spirit Award for performing her famous vault on an injured ankle during the 1996 Olympics

Strug was a six-year member of the United States National Gymnastics Team.

Where Is She Now?

Strug's ankle injury in the Olympics got worse after she performed on it for various publicity tours and promotional stunts without giving it time to heal properly, which ultimately meant that her competition days were over. She turned her focus to education instead. After graduating from Stanford University with bachelor's and master's degrees, Strug began a career in elementary education. She currently lives in Palo Alto California, and works as a second-grade teacher in the San Francisco Bay area. Since the 1996 Olympics she has endorsed several charities, including DARE, Pediatric AIDS, Make-a-Wish Foundation, Childhelp, and NO-ADDiction. As part of these and other promotions, Strug has sometimes performed in gymnastics events, although she avoids high-impact gymnastics moves to minimize the strain on her ankle. Partially as an attempt to strengthen her weak ankle, Strug took up running. In 1999, she completed her first marathon.

she earned a spot on the 1996 Olympics women's gymnastics team—by finishing second in the all-around competition at the United States Olympic trials—the press still favored Strug's teammates.

This might have happened at the Atlanta Olympics, too. Normally, Karolyi, like many coaches, place the gymnasts who they think will perform the best in the coveted anchor position for each event. This time, however, Karolyi changed his coaching strategy, and decided to determine the individual positions based only on the gymnasts' performance at the Olympic trials. Since Strug had placed so high in the trials, she earned the anchor position on both the floor exercise and vault events. Throughout the team competition, the United States performed well, and by the end of the second night, they were in first place, ahead of the second-place Russian team. The race was still close, however, as the American team entered its final event, the vault.

The Historic Vault

Although Strug's teammates did well in the beginning of the competition, Moceanu fell on both of her vault attempts. Gymnasts are generally taught to focus on their performances, not their scores, so by the time Strug prepared to vault, the American team had not been averaging their posted scores and so did not know how close they were to the Russians. By Karolyi's calculations, Strug, the final competitor in the final team event, needed to earn at least a 9.6 on the vault to secure the gold medal for the American team. On the first of her two vaults, Strug also fell, landing wrong on her ankle and limping back to the starting line, visibly injured. When her 9.162 score was posted, Strug believed that she would have to complete the second vault for her team to win, and she was urged by Karolyi and her teammates to shake off her injury. Although Strug had heard something snap in her ankle on her first vault, and her leg was numb, she decided to complete her second vault. She sprinted down the runway, executed a clean vault, and landed solidly on both of her feet, the grimace on her face revealing the obvious pain that she was feeling standing on her injured ankle. After the few seconds necessary to stick her vault and give the customary acknowledgement to the judges, Strug collapsed to the mat and cried for help. Her courageous vault earned Strug a 9.712 score, more than enough to secure the gold medal for the American team.

Unfortunately, in the process, Strug sprained her ankle and tore two ligaments. As in the bittersweet 1992 Olympics, when she helped her team win a bronze medal but did not qualify to compete in the all-around singles event, Strug was prevented from achieving this ultimate Olympic dream once again. This time, she had earned a spot in the singles competition, but the severity of her ankle injury prevented her from competing.

Strug's heroic vault and the American team's gold medal created a media blitz that had several effects, both positive and negative. It was revealed that Karolyi's calculations were incorrect, and Strug did not even have to vault for the women's team to win the gold medal. While some chose not to focus on this fact, and instead catapulted Strug to instant fame as a symbol of Olympic bravery and strength, others used her vault to add fuel to the idea that the particular rigors associated with women's gymnastics were destructive to young girls. Strug herself was outspoken about this issue, giving her support to Karolyi and saying that it was her decision to vault. In highly publicized interviews she noted the double standard, where people try to protect female athletes from injuring themselves, while male athletes injure themselves just as much and are considered brave and tough for their efforts.

Strug's Legacy

In the end, despite the fact that Strug successfully competed in international gymnastics competitions for years, she will most likely always be remembered for her heroic sacrifice at the end of the 1996 Olympics. The fact that this sacrifice was unnecessary for the win is irrelevant, as many commentators noted. It is what Strug's vault symbolized that is important. Before the vault, Strug was passed over by the media because she was never considered to be as tough as her competitors. Few in the gymnastics world, including Karolyi, ever expected that Strug would be a hero. When she defied all expectations and proved to herself, her teammates, her coach, and the world that she could be gutsy, too, she became a symbol of quiet strength and unexpected bravery. Her sacrifice gave hope to others—athletes and non-athletes alike—that they, too, could defy the odds and achieve their dreams, regardless of what anybody said.

CONTACT INFORMATION

Address: Kerri Strug Fan Club, 2801 N. Camino Principal, Tucson, AZ 85715.

SELECTED WRITINGS BY STRUG:

(With Greg Brown) *Heart of Gold,* Taylor, 1996.
(With John P. Lopez) *Landing on My Feet: A Diary of Dreams,* Andrews McMeel, 1997.
Girls Know Best, MJF Books, 1999.

FURTHER INFORMATION

Books

Kleinbaum, Nancy H. *Magnificent Seven: The Authorized Story of American Gold.* New York: Bantam Doubleday Dell, 1996.
Layden, Joe. *Women In Sports: The Complete Book on the World's Greatest Female Athletes.* Los Angeles: General Publishing Group, 1997.
Newsmakers 1997 (Issue 4) Detroit: Gale Group, 1997.
Woolum, Janet. *Outstanding Women Athletes: Who They Are and How They Influenced Sports in America.* Phoenix: Oryx Press, 1998.

Periodicals

"A team torn apart." *Sports Illustrated* (September 9, 1996): p. 9.
Baldwin, Kristen. "Kerri Struggles." *Entertainment Weekly* (October 18, 1996): 12.
Cooper, Bob. "Happy Landing." *Runner's World* (May 1999): p. 76.
Hoffer, Richard. "Day 5: a most unlikely hero." *Sports Illustrated* (August, 1996, Special Issue): 40.
Leavy, Jane. "Happy Landing." *Sports Illustrated* (August 11, 1997): p. 54.
Starr, Mark. "Leap of faith—gymnastics: with one inspiring vault, the U.S. women's team won a gold medal—and an honored place in Olympic history." *Newsweek* (August 5, 1996): 40.
Swanson, Neil. "Gold Medal Detector." *National Journal* (August 18, 2001): 2635.
Swift, E.M. "Carried away with emotion." *Sports Illustrated* (August 12, 1996): 104.

Other

Contemporary Authors Online, Detroit: Gale Group, 2003. Reproduced in *Biography Resource Center,* Detroit: Gale Group. 2003. http://www.galenet.com/servlet/BioRC (January 24, 2003).
Kerri Strug's Home Page. http://www.strug.org. (January 25, 2003).
Sports Stars Series 1–4. U•X•L, 1994-98. Reproduced in *Biography Resource Center.* Detroit: Gale Group. 2003. http://www.galenet.com/servlet/BioRC (January 24, 2003).
USA Gymnastics Online. http://www.usa-gymnastics. org/athletes/bios/s/kstrug.html. (January 20, 2003).

Sketch by Ryan Poquette

Naim Suleymanoglu
1967-

Turkish weightlifter

Naim Suleymanoglu, known as the "Pocket Hercules" because he combined a very small stature with great strength, is the only weightlifter ever to win gold medals in three different Olympics. Born in Kircali, Bulgaria in 1967, Suleymanoglu was the son of very poor parents who were members of that country's oppressed ethnic Turkish minority. His father was a bus driver and zinc miner in the mountain town of Momchilgrad.

"A Back Wide Enough to Play Poker On"

At birth, Suleymanoglu had very short arms and legs, with a long torso. His odd proportions worried his mother. When he began lifting weights as a boy, she worried

Naim Suleymanoglu

that the weights would compress his body even more and make him stop growing. When he was ten years old, he was sent away from his family and to a sports school where he could be trained.

Suleymanoglu eventually grew to his adult height of 4'11" and a weight of 141 pounds, with what Paul Kent called in the Adelaide, Australia *Advertiser,* "a back wide enough to play poker on." These proportions allowed him to lift enormous amounts of weight, far more than many men who were much bigger than he was. In 1982, at the age of 15, he set his first world record. A year later, he became only the second person in history to lift three times his body weight. That year, when he was 16, Suleymanoglu missed the chance to participate in the 1984 Summer Olympics because of the Soviet Union's boycott of the games.

Escapes to Turkey

As part of a campaign to eliminate Turkish culture and identity within their borders, Bulgarian officials closed Turkish mosques and schools, passed laws prohibiting people from speaking Turkish, and ordered all of the country's 900,000 Turks to change their names to Bulgarian ones. Suleymanoglu was ordered to change his name to Naum Shalamanov. The last straw came one day when Communist officials showed up with a television crew and told him to say that he had always been Bulgar, and that the only reason he had a Turkish name was that his ancestors had been forced to adopt one by the Ottoman rulers. He refused, but the next day there was an article in the paper, claiming he had said this. He had never even spoken to the author of the article, much less denied his Turkish heritage.

In response, during a 1986 competition in Australia, he defected from Bulgaria and sought Turkish citizenship. Although athletes who changed citizenship were normally not allowed to compete for their new country until three years had passed, the Turkish government paid Bulgaria $1 million in order to have this ban waived so that Suleymanoglu could compete for Turkey in the 1988 Olympics. It was money well spent. At the Games in Seoul, Korea, Suleymanoglu set six world records, won a gold medal, and even out-lifted the winner of the weight class above his own.

As a Turkish athlete, Suleymanoglu became a national hero in his new country, receiving parades and over 20 houses as a reward for his achievements. According to Pat Forde in the Louisville, Kentucky *Courier-Journal,* one million fans showed up at the airport to welcome him home to Turkey after his gold medal. Also, because of the enormous publicity he received, the world became aware of Bulgaria's oppression of Turks. In response to world outcry, Bulgarian officials had to allow Suleymanoglu's parents to emigrate to Turkey, and they also let over 320,000 Turks leave their country and settle in Turkey.

Suleymanoglu quit his sport in 1990 but soon returned to competition. At the 1992 Olympics in Barcelona, Spain, Suleymanoglu won a second gold medal, making him the most famed athlete in Turkey. According to Alan Abrahamson in the *Los Angeles Times,* a Turkish television sports director said of Suleymanoglu, "If he comes to a roadblock when he is driving, it is removed for him. If he eats in a restaurant, no one will ask him to pay. If he drives beyond the speed limit, police wave him on ahead."

A Third Gold Medal

At the 1996 Olympics in Atlanta, Georgia, Suleymanoglu battled for the gold medal with Greek lifter Va-

Awards and Accomplishments

1983	World champion in the snatch
1985	World champion in the snatch
1985	World champion in the clean-and-jerk
1985	World champion in total
1986	World champion in the snatch
1986	World champion in the clean-and-jerk
1986	World champion in total
1988	Gold medal, Seoul Olympics
1989	World champion in the snatch
1989	World champion in the clean-and-jerk
1989	World champion in total
1991	World champion in the snatch
1991	World champion in the clean-and-jerk
1991	World champion in total
1992	Gold medal, Barcelona Olympics
1993	World champion in the snatch
1993	World champion in the clean-and-jerk
1993	World champion in total
1994	World champion in the snatch
1994	World champion in the clean-and-jerk
1994	World champion in total
1995	World champion in the snatch
1995	World champion in the clean-and-jerk
1995	World champion in total
1996	Gold medal, Atlanta Olympics

Related Biography: Discus Thrower Al Oerter

American discus thrower Al Oerter is one of only three people ever to win gold medals in four different Olympic Games. He won gold in the discus in 1956, 1960, 1964, and 1968.

Born in Astoria, New York, Oerter was a champion in high school; he set a national prep record of 184 feet, 2 inches. At the University of Kansas, he set an NCAA record. As a college sophomore, he went to the 1956 Olympics. Although he was ranked sixth in the world, he was not expected to win. He set a personal best and an Olympic record, and won gold. In 1960, after receiving advice from teammate Richard Babka, he threw a winning distance, winning gold, and Babka took the silver.

On May 18, 1962, Oerter set a world record by hurling the discus 200 feet five inches. He was the first person to throw it over 200 feet, and he soon bettered his record with a throw of 204-10. He would continue to beat his own record, eventually throwing 212-6.

In 1964 he battled a rib injury but still set an Olympic record of 200 1/2, winning a third gold medal. He won his fourth gold at the 1968 Olympics, despite more injuries, with an Olympic record throw of 121-6.

Oerter retired from competition in 1969, but in 1980 was still good enough to qualify as an alternate on the Olympic team. But because the United States boycotted the Olympics that year, he was unable to compete, and missed his chance for a fifth gold medal.

In the *Encyclopedia of World Biography Supplement*, Oerter explained why he liked the discus: "I like the beauty, the grace, and the movement. I can feel myself through the throw and can feel the discus in flight." Oerter is a member of the U.S Track and Field Hall of Fame and the Olympic Hall of Fame.

lerios Leonidas. Setting world records one after the other, they had a close competition. Suleymanoglu lifted a world-record 185 kg, and Leonidas beat him with 187.5 kg. Now the pressure was on Suleymanoglu to match Leonidas's lift for the gold.

And he did, tying Leonidas's world record just minutes after it was set. Announcer Lynn Jones said, "You have just witnessed the greatest weightlifting competition in history," according to Ken Jones in the London *Independent*. With this gold medal, Suleymanoglu became the first weightlifter in history to win gold medals at three different Olympics.

Suleymanoglu's Psychological Tactics

Suleymanoglu was known for his showmanship, as well as for his psychological strategy during competitions. According to a writer for the *Seattle Post-Intelligencer*, Suleymanoglu often sat quietly offstage, passing up his turn to lift, while competitors tried to lift huge amounts of weight in order to beat them. When they were exhausted, Suleymanoglu would stride out on stage, ask for more weight to be put on the bar, and then lift it easily, beating everyone.

After winning his third gold medal in Atlanta, Suleymanoglu retired from competition and enjoyed his fame and wealth for a few years; he frequently appeared in Turkish tabloid newspapers, which told scandalous stories about his wild lifestyle. However, in 1999, he decided to make a comeback and compete in the 2000 Olympic Games. He trained for just over a year before

the Games, hoping to win an unprecedented fourth gold medal. Only three other athletes had ever won medals in four different Olympics: Danish sailor Paul Elvstrom, American discus thrower Al Oerter, and American long jumper **Carl Lewis**.

According to Forde, Suleymanoglu said that he thought a gold-medal win at Sydney would be easier than winning gold in Atlanta. "Silver or bronze is nothing for me. I am only satisfied with gold." But in April of 2000, he came in third in the European championships; it was only his second defeat in 16 years.

"Everyone Tries to Be a Champion"

At the 2000 Olympics in Sydney, Australia, Suleymanoglu started the final competition with a very heavy weight—145 kg. If he could lift it, this would match his own Olympic record. As Phil Sheridan commented in the *Knight Ridder/Tribune News Service*, "That kind of gamesmanship is standard in weightlifting, as competitors try to psyche each other out." However, he tried to lift the weight three times, and failed all of them. Kent commented that perhaps Suleymanoglu "had bitten off too much for his first lift, not allowing him to settle into a rhythm before attacking the massive weights."

After his last attempt, Suleymanoglu said, "Thank you, goodnight, it's over," according to Jeff Dunne in the Adelaide *Advertiser*. Duncan noted that Croatian weightlifter Nikolay Pechalov, who beat Suleymanoglu and took the gold, said, "Naim is still the greatest weightlifter on the planet." Suleymanoglu said, according to Jones, "That's for others to decide. I am human. Everybody makes failure. Everyone tries to be a champion."

CONTACT INFORMATION

Address: c/o International Weightlifting Federation, H-1054-Budapest Hold.u.1. Hungary. Phone: +36-1-353-0530. Online: www.iwf.net.

FURTHER INFORMATION

Periodicals

Abrahamson, Ann, "Hercules Can't Pocket This One," *Los Angeles Times,* (September 18, 2000): U8.

Clarey, Christopher, "Naim Suleymanoglu," *International Herald Tribune,* (September 15, 2000): 31.

Dunne, Jeff, "Hercules Crashes," *Advertiser* (Adelaide, Australia), (September 18, 2000): L13.

Forde, Pat, "A Legend Crumbles Suddenly and Sadly," *Courier-Journal* (Louisville, KY), (September 18, 2000): 1C.

Jones, Ken, "Turkey's Flame Lit by 'The Greatest' Olympic Games," *Independent* (London, England), (July 24, 1996): SS12.

Kent, Paul, "Weight of Expectation Sinks Turk," *Advertiser* (Adelaide, Australia), (September 18, 2000): L13.

Neff, Craig, "Heavy Burdens," *Sports Illustrated,* (October 3, 1988): 68.

Neff, Craig, "Heroic and Herculean," *Sports Illustrated,* (May 9, 1988): 42.

Sheridan, Phil, "No Fourth Gold for Pocket Hercules," *Knight Ridder/Tribune News Service,* (September 17, 2000): K2353.

Smith, Jerry, "The Weight of the World," *Sports Illustrated,* (July 22, 1992): 130.

Sullivan, Jerry, "Tiny Turk Takes Record Third Gold," *Buffalo News,* (July 23, 1996): B5.

"Two Legends of Their Sport Retire," *Seattle Post-Intelligencer,* (January 3, 1997): E3.

"Weightlifter Diplomacy," *Economist,* (May 7, 1988): 49.

Other

"Suleymanoglu Offers Rezazadeh Turkish Citizenship," *Payvand.com,* http://www.payvand.com (January 27, 2003).

Sketch by Kelly Winters

John L. Sullivan
1858-1918

American boxer

John L. Sullivan was the last of the "bare-knuckle" boxing champions. Heavyweight champion of the world from 1882 to 1892, he lost his title to **Jim Corbett** in the first heavyweight boxing championship to be fought with gloves. Considered by many to be the first American sports star , Sullivan was undefeated in his twenty-seven-year career until his bout with Corbett. He was inducted into the International Boxing Hall of Fame in 1990.

The First Boxing Celebrity

John L. Sullivan was born in 1858 in the Roxbury section of Boston, Massachusetts to Irish immigrant parents. If his parents had had their way, their son would have become a Catholic priest. But he showed a propensity for fighting at an early age, and boxing was a natural career choice for him. He became champion of Massachusetts in 1879. In 1882, he challenged the reigning heavyweight champion, Paddy Ryan, and they fought in Mississippi City, Mississippi. Sullivan scored a knockout in nine rounds, becoming the new heavyweight champion of the world.

Reveling in his new role as heavyweight champion of the world, Sullivan toured around the United States fighting in matches and performing in theatres. He was knocked down for the first time in his career when he fought Charley Mitchell in 1883. Sullivan rallied, however, and gave Mitchell a thorough hammering in the third round before the fight was stopped by police. They fought again in 1888 in a bare knuckle contest that lasted more than three hours in a freezing drizzle on an estate in France. The fight was finally declared a draw.

An actor as well as a boxer, Sullivan depended on his standing as reining heavyweight champion of the world to draw crowds to the plays he appeared in. Therefore it was with some reluctance that he accepted Jim Corbett's challenge to the boxing crown in 1892. But accept it he must; to reject a legitimate challenge would spell the end of his career just as surely as to lose.

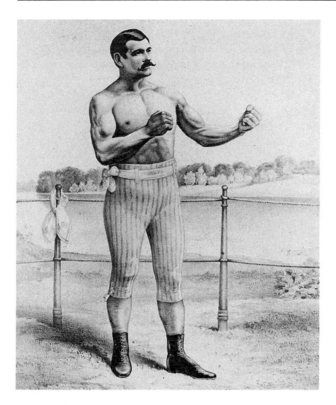

John L. Sullivan

It had been three years since Sullivan had last defended his title. That was when he defeated Jake Kilrain in a punishing three round bout. The fight, like all other heavyweight fights before it, had been fought with bare knuckles. After this match, Sullivan vowed never to fight with bare fists again; from then on, he would fight under the Marquis of Queensbury Rules, which required the use of gloves. This made the bout with Kilrain the last heavyweight championship to be fought with bare fists.

End of an Era

With public pressure growing for the champion to defend his title, Sullivan finally issued a challenge, which was published in the *New York World* in March, 1892. But he shrewdly insisted that the challenger put down a $10,000 bet that he would match. This effectively weeded out most challengers. But Jim Corbett and his manager raised the required amount from backers, and met the challenge.

Sullivan was said to intensely dislike Corbett, not just because he was a serious challenge to his jealously-guarded title, but because Corbett represented a new breed of fighter—socially refined, well-dressed and groomed, and a "scientific" fighter who relied more on finesse and speed than on the brute strength that was then the norm in the ring. Sullivan was also given to hard drinking and hard living, in contrast to Corbett who preferred a more discrete lifestyle.

Sullivan and Corbett squared off on September 7, 1892 at New Orleans's Olympic Club. The winner was to take away $25,000 in addition to the stake money of $10,000, with the loser to receive nothing. Betting odds were four to one in Sullivan's favor; the Boston Strong Boy, as Sullivan was then called, had never been defeated.

Boxing at the time was barely tolerated by law enforcement officials. Boxers, and even spectators, were often arrested for attending matches. Boxing with bare fists was particularly frowned upon, and it was partly for this reason that fighting with gloves eventually became the preferred method of fighting. The Marquis of Queensbury Rules brought other improvements to the game, for example, specifying time limits for rounds. The rules also forbade wrestling and head butting.

Thousands of spectators turned out to watch the match between Sullivan and Corbett, and reporters from most of the major newspapers in the country were present, along with many from around the world. Fifty Western Union telegraph operators sat ringside to send blow-by-blow accounts to pool halls and bars around the country.

The championship bout lasted an hour and twenty minutes, twenty-one rounds, and Sullivan was solidly beaten by the younger, faster man. Unable to land a punch in the first round, Sullivan got two strong shots in at Corbett's head in the second. Corbett came back in the third round, however, landing a solid left to Sullivan's nose, breaking it. Now seriously worried, Sullivan tried to rush Corbett, and get in the powerful punch that could end the match. But Corbett, a "scientific" boxing master, successfully avoided Sullivan's best punches, and darted in for quick, hard jabs that gradually wore Sullivan down. Puffing and bleeding, Sullivan was ripe for the final blow in the twenty-first round that sent him to the turf floor of the ring.

After Corbett was declared the new world heavyweight champion to an exultant crowd, Sullivan staggered to his feet and held up a hand for silence. "Gentlemen, all I have to say is that I came into the ring once too often, and if I had to get licked I'm glad it was by an American," he told the spectators, according the Patrick Myler in *Gentleman Jim Corbett*. "I remain your warm and personal friend, John L. Sullivan."

Last of the Bare-Knuckle Champions

Sullivan was reportedly devastated at losing his title, according to one account, sobbing in his dressing room afterwards, and drinking heavily through the night. To add insult to injury, Sullivan took home no money from the fight that cost him his title; he had insisted on "winner take all" rules. He did, however, recoup some of the money he lost betting on himself in the fight by sparring in an exhibition match with Corbett ten days later at New York's Madison Square Garden. The exhibition was organized as a benefit for the hard-up ex-champion, who earned $6,000 for it.

Sullivan stayed in the game for few more years sparring in exhibition matches before hanging up his gloves for good to become an advocate for the prohibition of alcohol. He died in 1818 of a heart attack and was buried in Boston. Jim Corbett served as an honorary pall bearer.

John L. Sullivan, the Boston Strong Boy, ended an era when he was defeated in the first heavyweight boxing championship in which the participants wore gloves. A heavy drinker and a barroom brawler, Sullivan also represented the end of boxing's street fighting days; with his defeat he helped to usher in the modern era of professional boxing, in which skill and strategy are as highly valued as strength.

FURTHER INFORMATION

Books

Encyclopedia of World Biography. Detroit: Gale Group, 1998.

Myler, Patrick. *Gentleman Jim Corbett: The Truth Behind a Boxing Legend*. London: Robson Books, 1998.

St. James Encyclopedia of Popular Culture. Detroit: St. James Press, 2000.

Other

"Bareknuckle Boxing in America." Hickok Sports.com. http://www.hickoksports.com/history/boxing02.shtml (October 30, 2002).

"John L. Sullivan (the 'Boston Strong Boy')." Cyber Boxing Zone. http://www.cyberboxingzone.com/boxing/sully.htm (October 15, 2002).

"John L. Sullivan." Infoplease.com. http://www.infoplease.com/ipsa/A0109684.html (October 15, 2002).

"Paddy Ryan." Cyber Boxing Zone. http://www.cyberboxingzone.com/boxing/ryan-p.htm (October 30, 2002).

Sketch by Michael Belfiore

Patricia Head Summitt
1952-

American college basketball coach

Patricia Head Summitt is one of college basketball's greatest coaches. In 2003, during her 29th season with the University of Tennessee Lady Volunteers, Summitt earned her 800th win. She is the first women's basketball coach and one of four Division I coaches to hit that mark. Summitt's six National Collegiate Athletic Association (NCAA) championships are surpassed only by UCLA men's coach **John Wooden**'s ten. Summitt is an inspiration in her childhood hometown of Henrietta, Tennessee, where the city limits sign proclaims: Welcome to Henrietta, home of Pat Head Summitt.

Learns Discipline on Farm

Summitt was born into the Henrietta farm family of Richard and Hazel Head. She grew up northwest of Nashville, in a part of the state dotted with tobacco barns, lean-tos, and one-lane blacktop roads.

Summitt, or Trish, as she was known back then, learned about the payoffs of hard work as she came of age on the family dairy and tobacco farm. From her father, Summit learned about disciplined guidance, about how to prod people beyond their potential. It's a lesson she learned well. Summit has often retold how at 12, her father dumped her off in the middle of an endless hayfield, gestured toward the tractor, and left. Completing the task was grueling, but Summit learned about her own potential, and also about expecting the maximum out of people. Consequently, she has become known as a demanding coach.

Plays on Barn-loft Court

Despite the endless chores, Summit and her three older brothers found time for play. They would climb to the top of the barn loft and play two-on-two basketball on the makeshift court, shooting jump shots among the rafters. Summit took her skills to Chatham

Patricia Head Summitt

County High School in Ashland City and played from 1967-70. Her senior year, she was an All-District 20 Tournament choice.

In the fall of 1970, the 5-foot-11Summitt began playing basketball at the University of Tennessee-Martin, where she established herself as a defensive ace and accurate shooter. Over four seasons, she led the team to a 64-29 record and graduated in 1974 as the school's all-time leading scorer with 1,045 points.

However, during Summitt's senior season, she tore her anterior cruciate ligament (ACL), and a surgeon told her to give up the sport. At the time, sports rehabilitation was in its infancy, and ACL tears forced most professional athletes into retirement. Summit, however, had her sights set on the 1976 Olympics. Women's basketball was new to the Games that year, and Summit yearned to make the inaugural team.

Builds Basketball Powerhouse

Over the next two decades, Summit modeled her basketball empire after her father's example of steady, disciplined guidance. She demands a lot—players must sit in the first three rows of the classroom, and if they skip a class, they're benched. On the court, she demands even more, and though playing for Summitt is tough, her players concede she changes their lives in positive ways.

"She makes you feel there's nothing to be afraid of in life," Michelle Marciniak, Most Valuable Player of the

Chronology

1952	Born June 14 in Henrietta, Tennessee
1970	High school All-District 20 Tournament selection
1970	Graduates from Chatham County High School in Ashland City, Tennessee, and enters the University of Tennessee-Martin
1974	Receives bachelor's degree in physical education from UT-Martin; becomes head coach of the University of Tennessee-Knoxville Lady Volunteers
1975	Receives master's degree in physical education from UT-Knoxville
1976	Plays for United States at Montreal Olympic Games
1980	Marries RB Summit
1990	Gives birth to Ross Tyler Summitt on September 21

1996 Final Four for the champion Lady Vols, told *Sports Illustrated*. "If you want something, you go after it as hard as you can, and you make no excuses."

Summitt's methods have worked. Her teams have won six NCAA titles (1987, 1989, 1991, 1996, 1997, 1998). Her 1997-98 squad had a perfect season of 39-0, and won the NCAA championship. Summitt has also produced 11 Olympians and 16 Kodak All-Americans. At the end of the 2001-2002 basketball season, Summitt had a phenomenal collegiate record of 788-158, a win percentage of .833. Win No. 800 came on January 14, 2003, a 76-57 victory over DePaul at home. Under her direction, the Vols have also captured 21 Southeastern Conference tournament and regular-season championships. She also coached the 1984 women's U.S. Olympic basketball team to its first gold.

Along the way, Summitt also found time for a family. She married banker R.B. Summitt in 1980. A decade later, she gave birth to Ross Tyler Summitt, a fixture alongside the Lady Vols' bench. Summitt's son, incidentally, was almost born in an airplane because even though Summitt was in labor, she insisted on making a recruiting visit to Pennsylvania because she feared losing an All-American to Notre Dame.

Record Hard to Beat

Still going strong, Summitt has raised the bar for women's coaches. As former UCLA coach Billie Moore told *USA Today*, "She's going to set a standard that I don't want to say will be impossible to beat but it will be very, very difficult to duplicate."

Years from now, *Sports Illustrated*'s Gary Smith writes, "her players will tell of this woman who never rased a placard or a peep for women's rights, who never filed a suit or overturned a statute or gave a flying hoot about isms or movements, this unconscious revolutionary who's tearing up the terrain of sexual stereotypes and seeding it with young women who have an altered vision of what a female can be."

Summitt is also active in many community endeavors. First Lady Hilary Rodham Clinton honored her at the

Awards and Accomplishments

1973	Captures silver medal as member of U.S. World Games team
1975	Earns gold medal as member of U.S. basketball team at Pan American Games
1976	Earns silver medal as member of U.S. basketball team at Olympics in Montreal
1979	Coaches U.S. women's basketball team to gold at the Pan American Games
1984	Coaches U.S. women's basketball team to its first Olympic gold
1987, 1989	Leads Lady Vols to NCAA championship; named Naismith College Coach of the Year
1990	Receives the Basketball Hall of Fame's John Bunn Award
1991	Leads Lady Vols to NCAA championship
1993	Named Southeastern Conference (SEC) Coach of the Year
1994	Named Naismith College Coach of the Year
1995	Named SEC Coach of the Year
1996-98	Leads Lady Vols to three consecutive NCAA championships
1997-98	Leads Lady Vols to a perfect 39-0 record
1998	Naismith College Coach of the Year and SEC Coach of the Year
2000	Inducted into the Women's Basketball Hall of Fame inaugural class
2000	Named Naismith Women's Collegiate Coach of the Century
2003	First women's college basketball coach and fourth overall to win 800 games

White House in 1997 as among *Working Woman* magazine's 25 Most Influential Working Mothers. Summitt's name was also in the news in the late 1990s as a possible candidate for U.S. Senate. She says her book, *Reach for the Summit: The Definite Dozen System for Succeeding at Whatever You Do,* is for everyone, not just coaches.

CONTACT INFORMATION

Address: 117 Stokely Athletics Center, University of Tennessee, Knoxville, TN, 37996. Phone: (865) 974-4275. Email: ath.utsports@gw.utk.edu. Online: http://ath.utk.edu/womens/info/volinfo.htm.

SELECTED WRITINGS BY SUMMITT:

(With Debby Jennings) *Basketball.* Dubuque, IA: William C. Brown, 1991.
(With Debby Jennings) *Basketball: Fundamentals and Team Play.* Madison, WI: Brown & Benchmark, 1996.
(With Sally Jenkins) *Raise the Roof: The Inspiring Inside Story of the Tennessee Lady Vols Undefeated 1997-98 Season.* New York: Broadway Books, 1998.
(With Sally Jenkins) *Reach for the Summit: The Definite Dozen System for Succeeding at Whatever You Do.* New York: Broadway Books, 1998.

FURTHER INFORMATION

Periodicals

Patrick, Dick. "800 Wins." *USA Today* (December 20, 2002).

Smith, Gary. "Eyes of the Storm." *Sports Illustrated* (March 2, 1998).
"Summit Wins No. 800." *The New York Times* (January 15, 2003).

Other

"Hall of Famers: Pat Head Summit." Basketball Hall of Fame. http://www.hoophall.com/halloffamers/PatheadSummitt.htm (January 13, 2003).
"Pat Summit." University of Tennessee Basketball. http://ath.utk.edu/womens/wbb/bios/summitt.htm (January 13, 2003).
"Pat Summit Profile." University of Tennessee Women's Collegiate Athletics. http://utladyvols.ocsn.com/sports/w-baskbl/mtt/summitt_pat00.html (January 13, 2003).

Sketch by Lisa Frick

Rell Sunn
1950-1998

American surfer

Surfing champion Rell Sunn fought almost single-handedly to grant women access to the sport at a time when it was still very much a male-dominated pursuit, and along the way emerged as one of the top female longboarders in the world. Often compared to **Duke Kahanamoku**, considered the founder of modern surfing, Sunn was "the modern archetype of the Hawaiian waterwoman," declared *Independent* writer Andy Martin.

Sunn was born in 1950 in Makaha, on the west side of the island of Oahu. Her family was of Chinese-Hawaiian heritage, and her middle name, "Kapolioka'ehukai" meant, prophetically, "heart of the sea." The beach near her Makaha home was famous among surfers for its waves, and she began surfing there at the age of four. At the time, women surfers were a rarity—"although women had surfed alongside men in Hawaii for centuries," noted Robert McG. Thomas Jr. of the *New York Times*. "Since the arrival of Western missionaries in the 19th century their participation had been discouraged. In the 1950's, boys rode the boards, and girls stayed on the beach, tanning their bodies and looking good in bikinis."

First Competed at Age 14

Sunn was devoted to the sport as a youngster, and entered her first competition in 1964, at the age of 14. As with many of the early contests she competed in, there were no "wahine" or women's categories, so she simply registered alongside the boys. As a young woman in the early 1970s, Sunn worked hard to establish a parallel women's circuit with other early women surfing champs like Joyce Hoffman and Linda Benson, and became one of the co-founders of the Women's Professional Surfing Association in 1975. When a ranking system was established, Sunn held the number one spot in the world for a time.

Not surprisingly, Sunn was a strong swimmer, and was Hawaii's first female lifeguard; at times she was treated rudely by men she had rescued. Proud of her Polynesian heritage, she was also a skilled spear fisher, and once wrote an article about capturing a prize, 45-pound ulua fish. She speared it, then followed it down with her snorkel on. "I sunk the fingers of one hand into his eye socket and gripped the spear shaft protruding from his head with the other, and began to guide him out and up toward the surface," she wrote in the *Honolulu Star-Bulletin*. Back on her board with it, she saw a tiger shark coming after her, and was forced to let the ulua go; the shark devoured it within seconds, and Sunn made it to shore safely. She observed that in the water, "under the deceptively placid surface, was a world blind to gender. Though I was taught by men, I was formed by and subjected to the rigid laws of a seemingly lawless realm that treated me and every grazing ulua or marauding shark with the same utter equanimity."

Inducted into Surfing Walk of Fame

Sunn also took part in Hokule'a crew events. These involved a double-hulled canoe similar to those used by Polynesians who came to Hawaii from the South Seas around 800 C.E. She was also a key figure in a project that gave underprivileged Hawaiian children the chance to make a sailing trip around the state's islands, giving them a deeper sense of their cultural heritage. A respected surfing instructor, she established the Menehune ("little people") Surfing Championships in 1976, which became the largest junior surf competition in the world. She was one of the first five women inducted into the Surfing Walk of Fame in Huntington Beach, California, in 1996. That year, she also received the Waterman Achievement Award from the Surf Industry Manufacturer's Association.

Sunn was a local celebrity on Oahu. "Hawaiians considered her a state treasure who used her fame to celebrate Hawaiian culture," Thomas wrote in the *New York Times,* and fellow lifeguard Brian Keaulana asserted that Sunn

"was the greatest in surfing, swimming, sailing, spearfishing—but more than that, she was the embodiment of the aloha spirit," he told Martin in the *Independent*. Diagnosed with breast cancer in 1983, she endured a mastectomy, and then a bone marrow transplant. After losing her hair because of chemotherapy, she went out surfing wearing a swim cap soon afterward; when her fellow surfers saw this, they arrived the next day wearing similar headgear in solidarity. Sunn often begged doctors to discharge her from the hospital, and they would do so only on the condition that she rest at home; instead, she returned as soon as possible to the waves with her board. She was fond of saying that surfing was, for her, the best therapy.

Succumbed to 15-Year Fight

On New Year's Day of 1998, Sunn's friends brought her on a stretcher to the beach so that she could taste ocean one more time; she died the next day at her home in Makaha. She dismissed the idea that with her death she would arrive in paradise. "There's no better place than Makaha," Sunn was quoted as saying by Martin in the *Independent*. "This is heaven on earth." Two weeks later in Makaha thousands attended her memorial service. Four years after her death, Sunn was the subject of a documentary film, *Heart of the Sea*. The Rell Sunn-Queen of Makaha award was established as part of the University of California at San Diego Luau and Longboard Invitational, and is bestowed annually on an individual for his or her cancer-fighting efforts.

Sunn was profiled in a 2001 book by Andrea Gabbard, *Girl in the Curl: A Century of Women Surfing*. *Honolulu Star-Bulletin* writer Greg Ambrose reviewed it and discussed the tremendous changes in the sport in Sunn's lifetime alone, exemplified by the 2002 film *Blue Crush*. Sunn was a rarity on the waves in her teen years, Ambrose noted, "but as the 21st century gathers momentum, more wahine young and old are reveling in the ocean's exhilarating embrace, and capturing a larger share of contest prize money, sponsorships, media attention and respect from their fellow wave riders.... Somewhere, you just know that Rell Sunn is smiling as wahine take their rightful place in the ocean."

SELECTED WRITINGS BY SUNN:

"A Young Woman and the Sea." *Honolulu Star-Bulletin* (January 12, 1998).

FURTHER INFORMATION

Periodicals

Altonn, Helen. "Aloha, Rell." *Honolulu Star-Bulletin* (January 17, 1998).

Ambrose, Greg. "'Girls' Make a Comeback in the Waves." *Honolulu Star-Bulletin* (June 24, 2001).

<table>
<tr><td colspan="2">Awards and Accomplishments</td></tr>
<tr><td>1982</td><td>Rated number one women surfer in International Surfing Association rankings</td></tr>
<tr><td>1996</td><td>Inducted into the Surfing Walk of Fame in Huntington Beach, California; received Waterman Achievement Award from the Surf Industry Manufacturer's Association</td></tr>
</table>

Ambrose, Greg. "Sunn Gets Her Chance to Shine." *Honolulu Star-Bulletin* (August, 8, 1996).

Martin, Andy. "Obituary: Rell Sunn." (London, England) *Independent* (January 16, 1998): 19.

Oda, Dennis. "In Memory of Rell Sunn." *Honolulu Star-Bulletin* (January 13, 1998).

Oldfield, Andy. "Book of the Week." (London, England) *Independent* (June 4, 2001): 6.

"Rell Sunn (Obituary)." *San Francisco Chronicle* (January 6, 1998): A17.

Thomas Jr., Robert McG. "Rell Sunn, 47, Hawaiian Surfing Champion." *New York Times* (January 26, 1998): A17.

Sketch by Carol Brennan

Ichiro Suzuki

Ichiro Suzuki
1973-

Japanese baseball player

Ichiro Suzuki—already a bona fide hero in his native Japan—made a sensational debut in American baseball in the opening years of the 21st century. Suzuki, adjudged the best-known person in Japan—even better known than Emperor Akihito, who came in second—in a popularity poll during the 1990s, ended his first two seasons in Major League Baseball with a total of 450 hits, more than any other player in major league history. In his first two seasons with the Seattle Mariners, the outfielder compiled a batting average of .336 and in 2002 collected more votes than any other American League (AL) player in balloting for the All-Star Game. Even his opponents are full of praise for Suzuki's batting power. "There's no secret way to get him out," Boston Red Sox manager Grady Little told *Sports Illustrated*. "All you can do is concentrate on the other eight guys." After more than two years in the United States, Suzuki still speaks very little English, but it seems to have done nothing to dampen the enthusiasm of either baseball fans or the media. He remains wildly popular in Japan, where early morning television broadcasts each of his games, and his face is forever present on T-shirts, subway ads, and in the newspapers.

Born in Kasugai, Japan

Suzuki was born in Kasugai in the Aichi prefecture of Japan on October 22, 1973. By the age of three, he was playing with a toddler-sized bat and ball outside his home. When he was only eight years old, Suzuki convinced his father to let him join a local baseball club. Since the local ball club played only on Sundays, Suzuki prevailed on his father to play catch and pitch to him whenever possible during the rest of the week. His father, Nobuyuki Suzuki, later became a coach for his son's baseball club. The younger Suzuki's talents as a ballplayer were already abundantly evident by the time he entered Nagoya Electric High School, also known as Aikodai Meiden. While in high school, Suzuki participated in Japan's National High School Baseball Tournament, or Koshien.

Fresh out of high school, Suzuki was drafted in the fourth round of 1991's Japanese free agent draft by the Orix Blue Wave of Kobe, a member of the Pacific League and one of the leading Japanese pro baseball teams. During his nine seasons with the Blue Wave, he collected seven consecutive Pacific League batting titles, was named Most Valuable Player three times, and in 1998 led his team to a Pacific League pennant. In 1992, his first year with the Wave, Suzuki split his time between one of the team's minor league ball clubs and the majors. He hit .366 in fifty-eight games with the minor league club before he was called up to the majors where he batted .253 in forty games. The following year, Suzuki started off again with the minors, hitting .371 in

Chronology

1973	Born October 22 in Kasugai, Aichi Prefecture, Japan
1982	Joins local baseball club at the age of 8
1992-2000	Plays nine seasons with Japan's Orix Blue Wave
1999	Marries television personality Yumiko Fukushima
2000	Signs three-year contract with Seattle Mariners
2001	Makes major league debut with Seattle Mariners

Related Biography: Manager Akira Ogi

Not until Akira Ogi was brought in as the new manager of Kobe's Orix Blue Wave in 1994 did Ikiro Suzuki truly come into his own as a player. Before Ogi arrived on the scene, tension between the previous manager, Shozo Doi, and Suzuki had kept the batter from performing at his best. Doi, frustrated by Suzuki's failure to follow his orders, kept the player in the minors for much of Suzuki's first two years. Among the first things Ogi did after joining the Blue Wave was to bring Suzuki back to the majors. Confident that the batter had what it took, he added him as starter and then just left him alone to do his own thing.

Suzuki did not disappoint, batting .385 and tallying a record 210 hits in the 1994 season. Suzuki's breakthrough, under the guidance of Ogi, helped to power the Blue Wave to Pacific League pennants in both 1995 and 1996. In 1995, Ogi's team faced off against the Yakult Swallows in the Japan Series, losing the series in five games to the Swallows. The Blue Wave went all the way in 1996, vanquishing the Yomiuri Giants in the fifth game of the Japan Series.

Before beginning his career as a manager, Ogi played second base for the Nishitetsu Lions from 1954 to 1967, compiling a batting average of .229 with seventy home runs in 1,328 games. Ogi coached the Kintetsu Buffalos from 1988 to 1992, winning a Pacific League pennant in 1989.

forty-eight games but only a disappointing .188 in 164 at-bats with the majors. He hit his first home run in the majors on June 12, 1993, off a pitch from **Hideo Nomo** of the Kinetsu Buffalos. His first exposure to baseball outside Japan came in 1993 when he played a season for the Hilo Stars in Hawaii Winter Baseball.

Comes Into His Own in 1994

Suzuki really came into his own during the 1994 season with the Blue Wave, batting .385 and setting a Japanese record with 210 hits in only 130 games. That same year, he scored in sixty-nine consecutive games between May 21 and August 26. In 1995 Suzuki led the Pacific League with forty-nine stolen bases and knocked home a career-high total of twenty-five home runs. Suzuki in 1996 led the Blue Wave to a Pacific League pennant and the Japanese championship with a win over the Yomiuri Giants. In 1997 with Akira Ogi as the new manager of the Blue Wave, Suzuki enjoyed a string of 216 consecutive at-bats without a strikeout. He won his fifth straight Pacific League batting title in 1998.

Suzuki's 1999 season was cut short when he was struck by a pitch in late August, breaking the ulna bone in his right hand. He nevertheless managed to lead the league for the sixth straight year with a batting average of .343. In 2000, his final year with the Blue Wave, Suzuki maintained a batting average of .387, a Japanese record. For the second year in a row, an injury in August cut short his season. Suzuki's magic on the ball field elevated him to super-celebrity status in Japan, where a poll in the 1990s showed him to be the country's best-known person, trailed closely by Japanese Emperor Akihito. So popular was Suzuki in his homeland that it became difficult for him to go anywhere in Japan without being overwhelmed by fans and the media. So intense was the media scrutiny that when Suzuki and television personality Yumiko Fukushima decided to marry, they flew to Los Angeles for the ceremony. In an interview with ESPN.com, Suzuki said the intrusiveness of the Japanese media had become intolerable. "They would even watch me go to the haircut place or the restaurant. Then they would interview the people at the haircutters."

Mariners Seek Out Suzuki's Services

Suzuki's outstanding performance on the baseball diamonds of Japan had not gone unnoticed on the other side of the Pacific. So excited were the Seattle Mariners about the possibility of landing Suzuki that the team paid the Blue Wave just over $13 million for the right to offer the dynamic batter a contract. On November 18, 2000, Suzuki signed a three-year deal with the Mariners. The contract was reportedly worth about $16 million. The ballplayer and his wife flew to Seattle and fell almost immediately in love with their new home. They were particularly pleased to find a city where they could go out in public without being mobbed by fans and the local paparazzi.

America's Suzuki fans were not disappointed when their hero finally made his debut in Major League Baseball in April 2001. The Japanese import kicked off his American baseball career with a 23-game hitting streak that fell only one game short of the club record set by Joey Cora. With two home runs and a total of eleven RBIs, Suzuki batted .336 in his first twenty-five games with the Mariners. But his statistics only seemed to get better with time. By season's end, he boasted a batting average of .350 with a total of 242 hits. Suzuki also became the first rookie ever to garner the most ballots for the All-Star Game. A big factor in his All-Star balloting popularity was the decision by Major League Baseball to distribute ballots in Japan. After the end of the regular season, Suzuki became the first rookie since Fred Lynn (in 1975) to win both the MVP and Rookie of the Year awards.

Compared to Rod Carew, Ralph Garr

To many seasoned baseball observers, Suzuki's incredible bat control evoked memories of Rod Carew, but Mariners manager **Lou Piniella** said that he found his new star's playing style more reminiscent of Ralph Garr. (Garr, who played thirteen seasons with the Atlanta Braves, Chicago White Sox, and California Angels between 1968 and 1980, had a career batting average of .306.) Piniella observed that the momentum from Suzu-

Career Statistics

Yr	Team	AVG	GP	AB	R	H	2B	3B	HR	RBI	BB
2001	SEA	.350	157	692	127	242	34	8	8	69	30
2002	SEA	.321	157	647	111	208	27	8	8	51	68
TOTAL		.336	314	1339	238	450	61	16	16	120	98

SEA: Seattle Mariners.

ki's left-handed swing propelled the batter toward first base even before he'd left the batter's box, forcing infielders to rush their throws—even on routine grounders.

Even in the Pacific Northwest of the United States, Suzuki could not escape the scrutiny of the Japanese media. In 2001 reports circulated that a Japanese Web site owner was willing to pay $2 million to anyone who could bring him a photograph of Suzuki in the nude. To preserve his privacy, Suzuki was forced to change clothes in a secluded area of the Mariners' locker room. Increasingly upset by the persistence of the Japanese media, Suzuki and Mariners teammate Kazuhiro Sasaki in July 2001 staged a brief boycott of members of the Japanese press.

Suzuki is the only player in Major League Baseball to be identified by his first name on the back of his jersey, a practice that originated in Japan under Blue Wave manager Akira Ogi. Although a few of Japanese baseball's better known pitchers came to Major League Baseball before him, Suzuki was the first position player to be signed by a MLB club. Despite the enormous sums the Mariners spent to land Suzuki, there were loads of skeptics in Seattle and elsewhere around the United States who doubted that the Japanese player would do well on this side of the Pacific. His spectacular performance during his debut major league season convinced all but the most diehard doubters.

Player Exodus May Hurt Japanese Baseball

Ironically, Suzuki's phenomenal success in Major League Baseball may well eventually help to undermine the pro game in Japan that gave him his start. Los Angeles Dodgers pitching coach Jim Colborn told *Sports Illustrated* that approximately three dozen of Japan's best players could end up playing in the major leagues. Colborn, a former Mariners director of Pacific Rim scouting who coached in Japan, said the likely loss of such top players as Seibu Lions shortstop Kazuo Matsui, Kintetsu Buffalos third baseman Norihiro Nakamura, and Yomiuri Giants centerfielder Hideki Matsui to the MLB threatens to turn Japanese baseball into a farm system for MLB. Even Japanese baseball fans are increasingly turning their attention to American baseball. Former Blue Wave general manager Steve Inow told *Sports Il-*

Awards and Accomplishments

1994	Named Pacific League's Most Valuable Player
1995-96	Named MVP of Pacific League
1998	Led Japan's Orix Blue Wave to Pacific League pennant
2000	Compiled batting average of .387 for the year, a Japanese record
2001	Named American League Rookie of the Year
2001	Named American League Most Valuable Player
2002	Voted to All-Star Game

lustrated: "Every day, people [in Japan] are watching major league baseball games, and short term, that's not so good for us. These are difficult times. Japanese baseball is at a turning point. Which way do we go?"

In his second season with the Mariners, Suzuki slipped slightly from the stellar performance of his debut year, but only slightly. His batting average fell to .321 from .350 in 2001. Suzuki's hits in 2002 totaled 208, down from 242 in 2001. Although the total number of Mariners selected to play in the 2002 All-Star Game was down sharply—from eight to three—from the previous year, Suzuki led the major leagues in the total number of votes received. More than 2.5 million votes were cast for the Seattle rightfielder. He was joined by fellow Mariners Freddy Garcia and Kazuhiro Sasaki, both pitchers. Interviewed by the Associated Press only days before the game on July 9, Suzuki said, "I'm a little bit excited knowing I'm going to be in that event again. I've been around a year and a half, and the votes I got this year are a different quality of votes."

Helps Lead MLB All-Stars to Victory in Japan

In November 2002 Suzuki went 4-for-4 to help lead the Major League Baseball All-Stars to victory over their Japanese counterparts in the seventh game of the annual exhibition series in Japan's Sapporo Dome. The Japanese team took the first three games of the series, but the MLB team bounced back to take the next four games and win the series. In the final game, Suzuki hit three singles and a double for the major leaguers.

At five feet, nine inches and 160 pounds, Suzuki is a little bit diminutive compared to most American ballplayers, but it's obviously done nothing to hamper

Ichiro Suzuki

his performance. In just two years, he's taken Major League Baseball by storm, amassing a total of 450 hits, more than any other player in history. As Ray Knight, bench coach for the Cincinnati Reds, told *Sports Illustrated,* Suzuki is "impossible to defend, but he's a joy to watch." Just how far he will go remains to be seen, but there's no doubt that Suzuki will remain a force to be reckoned with for several years.

CONTACT INFORMATION

Address: Ichiro Suzuki, c/o Seattle Mariners, SAFECO Field, 1250 1st Ave. S., Seattle, WA 98134.

FURTHER INFORMATION

Books

"Ichiro Suzuki." *Biography Resource Center.* Detroit: Gale Group, 2002.
"Ichiro Suzuki." *Newsmakers,* Issue 2. Detroit: Gale Group, 2002.

Periodicals

"10 Burning Questions for Ichiro Suzuki." *ESPN.com* (May 7, 2001).
Armstrong, Jim. "MLB All Stars Win Japan Series." Associated Press (November 17, 2002).

Eder, Steve. "Fans, Media Follow Ichiro." *Cincinnati Enquirer* (June 20, 2002).
"Fewer Mariners Picked; Ichiro Gets Most Votes." *Columbian* (July 1, 2002).
Price, S.L. "The Ichiro Paradox." *Sports Illustrated* (July 8, 2002): 50.
Schwarz, Alan. "Ichiro Steals the Show." *Sports Illustrated for Kids* (August 2001): 46.
"Suzuki Leads AL All-Star Voting." Associated Press (June 4, 2002).

Other

"#51, Ichiro Suzuki." ESPN.com. http://sports.espn.go.com/mlb/players/stats?statsId=6615 (November 1, 2002).
"History of the Orix BlueWave." Japanese Baseball. http://www.baywell.ne.jp/users/drlatham/baseball/yakyu/history/bluewav.htm (November 19, 2002).
"Ichiro Suzuki." BaseballLibrary.com. http://www.pubdim.net/baseballlibrary/ballplayers/S/Suzuki_Ichiro.stm (November 19, 2002).
"Orix BlueWave Manager Akira Ogi." Japanese Baseball. http://ww1.baywell.ne.jp/fpweb/drlatham/manager/blue.htm (November 19, 2002).
"Player Pages: Ichiro Suzuki." The Baseball Page. http://www.thebaseballpage.com/past/pp/suzukiichiro/default.htm (November 19, 2002).

"Players Choice: Ichiro Suzuki." Bigleaguers.com. http://bigleaguers.yahoo.com/mlbpa/players/6/6615 (October 14, 2002).

"Player Pages: Honus Wagner." The Baseball Page.com. http://www.thebaseballpage.com/past/pp/wagners honus/default.htm (November 19, 2002).

"Suzuki, Ichiro." Nippon Professional Baseball. http://www.inter.co.jp/Baseball/player/register/japan/01020904.html (November 19, 2002).

Sketch by Don Amerman

Lynn Swann
1952-

American football player

Blessed with incredible speed and an ability to catch the football with leaps almost ballet-like in gracefulness, wide receiver Lynn Swann also had an impeccable sense of timing. He joined the Pittsburgh Steelers just as the team embarked on its most spectacular winning streak in history. Swann, an All-American at USC, was the Steelers' No. 1 draft pick in the 1974 draft, and he wasted no time in proving that he had what it took to make it in the NFL. During his rookie season, he led the league in punt returns with 577 yards on 41 returns, which was, at that time, a club record and the fourth best in NFL history. The following season he became a regular at wide receiver, which was to be his home for the rest of his NFL career. And what a career it was. During his nine seasons with the Steelers, Swann amassed a total of 336 receptions for 5,462 yards and 51 touchdowns. With Swann's help, the Steelers chalked up four Super Bowl victories in the wide receiver's first six years with the team. At the time of his retirement after the 1982 season, Swann's combined total of 364 receiving yards in four games ranked first in Super Bowl history.

Born in Alcoa, Tennessee

He was born Lynn Curtis Swann in Alcoa, Tennessee, on March 7, 1952. The third of three boys, Swann first demonstrated his amazing physical ability by walking at the age of 7 months. His mother, disappointed at not having a daughter, persuaded Swann to take dance lessons, which he took to naturally and at which he excelled. Years later, he told *Runner's World*: "People think football and dancing are so different. They think it's contradictory for a boy to dance, but dancing is a sport." Those dancing lessons were to come in handy later in Swann's football career. The Swann family moved from eastern Tennessee to San Mateo, California,

Lynn Swann

where he attended Serra High School. A member of his high school's track team, Swann competed in both the pole vault and the long jump, in which event he won the California High School State Championship with a jump of 25 feet, 4 inches. His football career really began at the University of Southern California in Los Angeles, where Swann enrolled in the fall of 1970 to study public relations.

In his senior year at USC, Swann was a unanimous choice for the college All-American team, further enhancing his desirability to the pro teams. In the 1974 NFL draft, Swann was the Pittsburgh Steelers' first-round pick and the 21st player overall to be selected. During his rookie season with the Steelers, Swann led the league in punt returns with 577 yards on 41 returns, a club record and the fourth best in NFL history. Late in the season, he saw limited action as a wide receiver. However, his touchdown catch in the AFC championship game against the Oakland Raiders cinched the game for the Steelers and laid the groundwork for the rest of Swann's career in the NFL.

Having displayed his talents as a wide receiver late in his rookie year, Swann became a regular in that job his second year with the Steelers. For the 1975 season as a whole, he compiled an impressive record of 49 catches for a total of 781 yards and a league-high 11 touchdowns. Swann ended the Steelers' post-season in a blaze of glory, helping to power Pittsburgh to a 21-17 victory over the Dallas Cowboys in Super Bowl X. Swann's con-

Career Statistics

Yr	Team	GP	Rushing					Receiving			
			ATT	YDS	AVG	TD		REC	YDS	AVG	TD
1974	PIT	11	1	14	14.0	0		11	208	18.9	2
1975	PIT	14	3	13	4.3	0		49	781	15.9	11
1976	PIT	12	1	2	2.0	0		28	516	18.4	3
1977	PIT	14	2	6	3.0	0		50	789	15.8	7
1978	PIT	16	1	7	7.0	0		61	880	14.4	11
1979	PIT	13	1	9	9.0	1		41	808	19.7	5
1980	PIT	13	1	-4	-4.0	0		44	710	16.1	7
1981	PIT	13	0	0	0.0	0		34	505	14.9	5
1982	PIT	9	1	25	25.0	0		18	265	14.7	0
TOTAL		115	11	72	6.5	1		336	5462	16.3	51

PIT: Pittsburgh Steelers.

Chronology

1952	Born in Alcoa, Tennessee, on March 7
1970	Graduates from Serra High School in San Mateo, California
1970-74	Attends University of Southern California to study public relations
1974	Drafted by the Pittsburgh Steelers
1975, 1978-79	Leads Steelers to Super Bowl
1982	Retires from professional football
1983-85	Provides commentary for ABC Sports coverage of U.S. Football League
1984	Covers Summer Olympics in Los Angeles for ABC Sports
1988	Covers Winter Olympics in Calgary for ABC Sports
1988-91	Hosts ABC's coverage of Iditarod dog sled races in Alaska

tributions included four receptions for 161 yards (a Super Bowl record at the time), including an amazing 64-yard catch and run that produced the winning touchdown. He was named Most Valuable Player for Super Bowl X.

A major factor in the success of the Steelers during this period was the teaming of Swann with fellow wide receiver John Stallworth, also drafted in 1974. With the combination of Stallworth and Swann at wide receiver, quarterback **Terry Bradshaw** had a choice of targets, and opponents couldn't focus all their defensive attention on just one player. Wide receivers John Stallworth and Lynn Swann competed with one another to be quarterback Terry Bradshaw's number one target. In the process, they made each other better players but remained somewhat cool on a personal level. All that changed after both men had left pro football. When Swann was inducted into the Pro Football Hall of Fame in 2001, he asked that Stallworth present him. To boost his former teammate's candidacy for the Hall of Fame, Swann in his acceptance speech said: "I don't think I could be in the Hall of Fame unless there was a John Stallworth. The competition between John and me, the things that we made each other do in terms of working and getting ready, I knew I al-

ways had to be ready." Stallworth followed Swann into the Hall of Fame in 2002.

The high point of Swann's pro football career came during the regular season of 1978 when he caught 61 passes for a total of 880 yards and 11 touchdowns. In Super Bowl XIII in January 1979, Swann caught an 18-yard touchdown pass from Bradshaw that cinched the Steelers' 35-31 victory over the Dallas Cowboys. Swann's game-winning contribution was particularly impressive since he had not been expected to play at all because of a head injury suffered in the Steelers' AFC championship victory over the Oakland Raiders. In the 1979 season, Swann caught 41 passes for a total of 808 yards and five touchdowns, fueling the Steelers' drive to the playoffs. In Super Bowl XIV, as the Steelers faced off against the Los Angeles Rams, the wide receiver grabbed five passes for a total of 79 yards and a touchdown, powering Pittsburgh past the Rams by a score of 31-19.

During the 1980 regular season, Swann caught 44 passes for 710 yards and seven touchdowns. The following year he snared 34 passes for 505 yards and five touchdowns. His totals dropped significantly in the strike-shortened regular season of 1982, when Swann caught 18 passes for a total of 265 yards. Long before he retired from the Steelers, Swann had begun laying the groundwork for a life after professional football, beginning to work whenever possible as a commentator for ABC Sports. When he finally left the game after the 1982 season, he moved effortlessly into a full-time broadcasting career in a working atmosphere he already knew intimately. In one of his first big jobs for ABC after leaving football, Swann provided expert commentary in the network's coverage of the United States Football League from 1983 to 1985. During the summer of 1984 he covered the weightlifting coverage at the Summer Olympics in Los Angeles, and four years later, provided commentary for the bobsled competition at the

Awards and Accomplishments

1970	Wins California High School State Championship in long jump
1973	Named to All-American College Team
1974	Leads NFL in punt returns with 577 yards on 41 returns
1974	Named to NFL's All-Rookie Team
1975, 1977, 1979	Named to NFL's All-Pro Team
1976	Named Super Bowl's Most Valuable Player
1978	Named NFL Man of the Year
1993	Elected to College Football Hall of Fame
1997	Receives Walter Camp Football Foundation Man of the Year Award
2001	Inducted into the Pro Football Hall of Fame
2002	Inducted into the Bay Area Sports Hall of Fame

Other

"Inductees: Lynn Swann." Bay Area Sports Hall of Fame. http://www.bashof.org/Lswann.htm (November 6, 2002).

"Lynn Swann, Sideline Reporter." ABC Sports. http://espn.go.com/abcsports/columns/swann_lynn/bio.html (November 2, 2002).

"Lynn Swann: Wide Receiver." Football-Reference.com. http://www.football-reference.com/players/SwanLy00.htm (November 2, 2002).

"Lynn Swann, WR-1974-82." Pro Football Hall of Fame. http://www.profootballhof.com/players/mainpage.cfm?cont_id=45252 (November 6, 2002).

Sketch by Don Amerman

Winter Olympics in Calgary, Alberta. Swann has also appeared frequently on ABC's *Wide World of Sports* covering a wide variety of sporting events. Swann lives with wife Charena and two sons in the Pittsburgh area.

Although Swann has made a new life for himself away from professional football, his heart and mind are never far from the game. An avid Steelers fan, he follows the fortunes of his former team closely. Recalling the incomparable thrill of playing in the Super Bowl, he once told an interviewer for *Runner's World*: "Having 70,000 people in the stands cheering for you like demons for three hours during the Super Bowl, and knowing that millions are watching you on TV worldwide, is not an experience that can be simulated."

CONTACT INFORMATION

Address: Lynn Swann, c/o ABC Sports, 47 W. 66th St., New York, NY 10023.

FURTHER INFORMATION

Books

"John Lee Stallworth." *Who's Who Among African Americans,* 14th ed. Detroit, MI: Gale Group, 2001.

"John(ny) Lee Stallworth." *Almanac of Famous People,* 6th ed. Detroit: Gale Group, 1998.

"Lynn Curtis Swann." *Who's Who Among African Americans,* 14th ed. Detroit, MI: Gale Group, 2001.

"Lynn Swann." *Contemporary Black Biography,* Volume 28. Detroit, MI: Gale Group, 2002.

"Lynn Swann." *St. James Encyclopedia of Popular Culture,* five volumes. Detroit, MI: St. James Press, 2000.

Periodicals

Averbuch, Gloria. "Swann's Song." *Runner's World* (October 3, 1993): 44.

Robinson, Alan. "Teammates Together in Hall of Fame." *AP Online* (July 31, 2002).

Sheryl Swoopes
1971-

American basketball player

Sheryl Swoopes has played on college, professional and Olympic championship basketball teams. She has won all sorts of individual awards, owns countless records and even had a sneaker named after her. She has also played one-on-one against the redoubtable **Michael Jordan**. And, she has rebounded from serious knee injuries to earn league honors. But perhaps her most noteworthy achievement was playing, and staying on top of her game, shortly after having a baby.

Swoopes, a 6-foot shooting guard who once scored a record 47 points in the NCAA championship game while leading Texas Tech to the 1993 national title, led the Houston Comets of the Women's National Basketball Association to four consecutive titles from 1997-2000, and played on two gold-medal winning U.S. Olympic teams. In the midst of her competitive season the "Texas Tornado" gave birth to her son, Jordan, in July, 1997. "When she found out she was pregnant with Jordan at age 25, she committed herself to playing in basketball and staying in shape throughout the pregnancy," Elisa Ast All wrote in *Pregnancy Today.* "She had no morning sickness or any other symptoms that hindered her lifestyle."

Big Star in Texas

Shortly after Swoopes was born, on March 21, 1971, her father left home. Her mother, sometimes relying on welfare to meet family needs, raised Swoopes and her three brothers by herself. Swoopes began playing basketball at age seven. After earning national junior college Player of the Year honors at South Plains

Sheryl Swoopes

J.C. in Texas, Swoopes transferred to Texas Tech University. Despite playing only two seasons there, she ranked fourth among all-time Lady Raiders with 1,645 points and sixth for steals. She averaged 24.9 points per game.

Swoopes scored 47 points in the NCAA championship game as the Lady Raiders held off Ohio State with a score of 84-82. In that game she made 16 of 24 shots and all 11 of her free throws. She scored 53 points in the conference championship game, then totaled 130 points and 43 rebounds in the first four games of the NCAA tournament. During her two seasons of play, Texas Tech sported a 58-8 record. The school retired her jersey number (22) the following season. That winter she also played ten games for Basket Bari, a professional team in Italy. Swoopes was also a member of the gold medal-winning 1996 Olympic team. The championship culminated a 60-0 run over two years.

Sneaker Deal, WNBA and Baby

In a tribute to Swoopes's marketability, and the rising popularity of women's sports in general, the Nike shoe company in October, 1995 introduced the Air Swoopes women's basketball footwear. Nike paralleled the announcement with an extensive advertising campaign with Swoopes appearing in newspaper and television advertisements, and retail displays. Swoopes has also represented such companies as Kellogg, Wilson, Hasbro and Discover Car.

Chronology

1971	Born March 25 in Brownfield, Texas
1989	Named to U.S. Olympic Festival South Team but sidelined because of injury
1991	Transfers from South Plains Junior College (Texas) to Texas Tech University
1993-94	Plays ten games with Basket Bari of Italian professional league
1997	Signed by Women's National Basketball Association and assigned to Houston Comets
1997	Gives birth to son, Jordan, on June 25 and makes WNBA debut on August 7; plays nine games of season
2000	Divorces husband Eric Jackson
2001	Misses season after tearing anterior cruciate ligament and lateral meniscus in left knee

Swoopes was the first player chosen by the WNBA, which assigned her to the Houston Rockets as play began in June, 1997. Then along came the baby. She gave birth to Jordan, named after Michael Jordan, on June 27. About six weeks later, on August 7, Swoopes took the court in her WNBA debut, playing about five minutes in a 74-70 victory by the host Comets over the Phoenix Mercury. "I was very nervous for the first game after being out of competitive basketball for a year," the Associated Press quoted Swoopes. "There's a big difference in pickup ball and getting out here. It's going to take awhile to get the butterflies out."

Swoopes received a warm applause from the crowd. At courtside, some fans hovered around the baby, held by her husband, former football player Eric Jackson (the two divorced in 2000). "Upon learning she was unexpectedly pregnant, her biggest fear was telling her agent and other WNBA associates about her condition," All wrote in *Pregnancy Today*. "She kept her special secret throughout the first trimester 'in case something happened,' and then shared the news. 'I was nervous about what everyone would think, but they were all very supportive,' she says."

Swoopes played nine games that season (the WNBA, plays during the summer, and plays a much shorter season than the men's National Basketball Association) as the Comets won the inaugural league championship. Houston added three more, registering a rare four-peat in professional sports. Swoopes was voted the WNBA's Most Valuable Player and Best Defensive Player in 2000.

Swoopes missed the 2001 WNBA season after tearing the anterior cruciate ligament and lateral meniscus in her left knee. She recovered in 2002 to earn her second MVP award from the league, averaging 18.5 points per game. She scored 32 points in a game against Sacramento, one point shy of her career high. She was also named the league's top defensive player, securing a team-record 88 steals. The Comets became the only team to make the playoffs in all six WNBA seasons.

Career Statistics

Yr	Team	GP	Pts	FG%	FT%	RPG	APG	SPG	BPG	TO
1992	TXT	32	690	.503	.808	8.9	4.8	3.43	–	–
1993	TXT	34	955	.546	.868	9.2	4.1	3.41	–	–
1996	US	8	104	.547	.750	3.5	3.9	1.50	0.63	–
1997	HOU	9	64	.472	.714	1.70	.8	.78	.44	4
1998	HOU	29	453	.427	.826	5.10	2.1	2.48	.48	58
1999	HOU	32	585	.462	.820	6.30	4.0	2.38	1.44	83
2000	HOU	31	643	.506	.821	6.30	3.8	2.81	1.06	82
2000	US	8	107	.517	.692	4.6	3.0	1.00	1.00	–
2002	HOU	32	592	.434	.825	4.90	3.3	2.75	.72	87

HOU: Houston Comets (WNBA); TXT: Texas Tech University; US: United States Olympic Team.

Awards and Accomplishments

1991	Junior College Player of the Year while at South Plains J.C.
1992	Southwest Conference Newcomer of the Year and Postseason Classic MVP
1992	Named to Kodak All-America team.
1992-93	Southwest Conference player of the year in successive seasons
1993	Final Four MVP with record-setting 47 points in championship game as Texas Tech defeats Ohio State, 84-82
1993	Named national college basketball player of the year by nine organizations, including *USA Today* and *Sports Illustrated*
1994	Texas Tech jersey (No. 22) retired
1994	Member of bronze medalist U.S. team in World Championship
1996	Member of gold medalist U.S. Olympic team and women's national basketball teams that won a combined 60 straight games
1997-2000	Leads Houston Comets to four consecutive WNBA championships
1998	Named Sportswoman of the Year by Greater New York chapter of March of Dimes
1998-2000	WNBA First-Team selection
1999	Led U.S. in scoring on Winter European Tour team as Americans sport 4-1 record
1999	WNBA Player of the Week for July 18 and August 1
1999-2000	Leading vote-getter in WNBA All-Star balloting for two successive seasons
2000	Averaged 13.4 points per game for gold medalist Olympic team
2000	WNBA Most Valuable Player and best Defensive Player
2000	WNBA Player of the Week for June 12
2000	Posted 500th rebound, 300th assist and 200th steal
2001	Wins Espy award from cable network ESPN for Women's Pro Basketball Player of the Year
2002	Named WNBA Most Valuable Player and Best Defensive Player
2002	Invited to join President Bush for opening ceremonies of Winter Olympic Games in Sale Lake City
2002	Rang opening bell of American Stock Exchange in New York with USA Basketball teammate Dawn Staley

"Ultimate Star"

Swoopes, arguably, is the prototype of today's moden woman athlete, as marketable as she is athletic. "Swoopes," Hall of Famer and former WNBA coach Nancy Lieberman wrote on *ESPN*'s Web site, "is the definition of the ultimate star and you can't help but have an incredible respect for her game."

SELECTED WRITINGS BY SWOOPES:

(With Greg Brown) *Bounce Back,* Dallas: Taylor, 1996.

FURTHER INFORMATION

Books

Burby, Liza N. *Sheryl Swoopes: All-Star Basketball Player.* New York: Rosen, 1997.

Burgan, Michael. *Sheryl Swoopes.* Philadelphia: Chelsea House, 2001.

Kuklin, Susan. *Hoops with Swoopes.* New York: Jump at the Sun Hyperion Books for Children, 2001.

Rappoport, Ken. *Sheryl Swoopes, Star Forward.* Berkeley Heights, NJ: Enslow, 2002.

Sehnert, Chris W. *Sheryl Swoopes.* Edina, MN: Abdo & Daughters, 1998.

Torres, John Albert. *Sheryl Swoopes.* Bear, DE: Mitchell Lane, 2002.

Walker, Rosemary. *Sheryl Swoopes.* Mankato, MN: Capstone High-Interest Books, 2001.

Other

All, Elisa Ast. "Bouncing Back from Baby." *Pregnancy Today,* http://pregnancytoday.com/reference/articles/swoopes.htm, (January 6, 2003).

"Rockets Five Days of Giving Slated to Help Diverse Group of Houstonians in Need." Houston Rockets, http://www.nba.com/rockets/news/fivedays_001219.html, (December 19, 2002).

"Sheryl Swoopes." National Sports Agency, http://www.nationalsportsagency.com/sswoopes.html, (January 12, 2003).

Sweet, Jacinda. "For Former Texas Tech Star, Shoe Is 'a Dream Come True,' *Arizona Daily Wildcat,* http://wildcat.arizona.edu, (October 9, 1995).

USA Basketball, http://www.usabasketball.com/bioswomen/sheryl_swoopes_bio.html, (January 12, 2002).

Wiechmann, David. "A Decade-Old Dynasty," *University Daily,* http://www.universitydaily.net/vnews/

display.v/ART/2003/01/15/3e24dbc2409ab, (January 15, 2003).

WNBA.com, http://www.wnba.com/playerfile/sheryl_swoopes/index.html, (January 12, 2002).

Sketch by Paul Burton